# The Law of Higher Education

## Fifth Edition

## Student Version

*William A. Kaplin*

*Barbara A. Lee*

# The Law of Higher Education

## Fifth Edition

## Student Version

JB JOSSEY-BASS™

A Wiley Brand

Published by Jossey-Bass
A Wiley Brand
One Montgomery Street, Suite 1200, San Francisco, CA 94104-4594
www.josseybass.com

Jossey-Bass books and products are available through most bookstores. To contact Jossey-Bass directly call our Customer Care Department within the U.S. at 800-956-7739, outside the U.S. at 317-572-3986, or fax 317-572-4002

Wiley publishes in a variety of print and electronic formats and by print-on-demand. Some material included with standard print versions of this book may not be included in e-books or in print-on-demand. If this book refers to media such as a CD or DVD that is not included in the version you purchased, you may download this material at http://booksupport.wiley.com. For more information about Wiley products, visit www.wiley.com

*Library of Congress Cataloging-in-Publication Data*

Kaplin, William A.
     The law of higher education : a comprehensive guide to legal implications of administrative
  decision making / William A. Kaplin, Barbara A. Lee. — Fifth edition.
         volumes cm. — (The Jossey-Bass higher and adult education series)
     Includes bibliographical references and index.
     ISBN 978-1-118-03662-4 (paperback); ISBN 978-1-118-75596-9 (ebk.);
     ISBN 978-1-118-75586-0 (ebk.)
         1. Universities and colleges—Law and legislation—United States.  2. Universities and
  colleges—United States—Administration.  I. Lee, Barbara A.  II. Title.
  KF4225.K36  2013
  344.73'074—dc23                                                                      2013017886

Printed in the United States of America

FIFTH EDITION

*PB Printing*   10 9 8 7

The Jossey-Bass Higher and Adult Education Series

# Notice to Instructors

The authors have prepared a volume of teaching materials for classroom use (see below) that is available in electronic format free of charge for instructors who adopt this *Student Version* as a required text. In addition, we have a Web site supporting the *Student Version* (as well as the full fifth edition of *The Law of Higher Education*) that is accessible to both instructors and students; it includes new developments, clarifications, and errata that update and supplement the fifth edition and the *Student Version*. We have also prepared an *Instructor's Manual* that provides suggestions on using the *Student Version* as a course text and on organizing and teaching higher education law courses. It is available, only to instructors, on the Web site. This Web site is hosted by the National Association of College and University Attorneys (NACUA), and is available at http://www.nacua.org/publications/lohe/index.asp.

The teaching materials, *Cases, Problems, and Materials for Use with the Law of Higher Education, Fifth Edition: Student Version*, are for instructors and students in courses on higher education law or administration, as well as for leaders and participants in workshops that address higher education legal issues. These teaching materials include court opinions carefully edited by the authors and keyed to the *Student Version*, notes and questions about the cases, short problems designed to elicit discussion on particular issues, a series of "large-scale" problems suitable for role playing, and guidelines for analyzing and answering all the problems. *Cases, Problems, and Materials (Student Version)* is published by NACUA (which also hosts the Web site for the *Student Version* and the full fifth edition) and is available both in electronic format that can be downloaded from NACUA's Web site ((http://www.nacua.org/publications/lohe/index.asp) and in hard copies that may be purchased at cost from NACUA. Any instructor who has adopted the *Student Version* as a required course text may download a copy of *Cases, Problems, and Materials*, or selected portions of it, free of charge and reproduce the materials for distribution to the students in the course. No other reproduction, distribution, or transmission is permitted. For hard copies, direct inquiries and orders to:

Meetings and Office Services Assistant

National Association of College and University Attorneys

Suite 620, One Dupont Circle, NW

Washington, D.C. 20036

(202) 833-8390; Fax (202) 296-8379

Further instructions for downloading or purchasing *Cases, Problems, and Materials* are on the NACUA Web site (http://www.nacua.org/publications/lohe/index.asp).

# Notice of Web Site and Periodic Supplements for the *Student Version*

The authors, in cooperation with the publisher, have made arrangements for two types of periodic updates for the *Student Version* (and the full fifth edition) of *The Law of Higher Education*. First, the National Association of College and University Attorneys (NACUA) has generously agreed to host a Web site for the *Student Version* and the full fifth edition to provide periodic postings of new developments and clarifications that update and supplement both books. This Web site is available to all readers and may be accessed through the NACUA Web site (http://www.nacua.org/publications/lohe/index.asp). Second, the authors intend to prepare periodic supplements to the *Student Version* (and the full fifth edition) as feasible. Both of these updating services are intended as a response to the law's dynamism—to the rapid and frequent change that occurs as courts, legislatures, government agencies, and private organizations develop new requirements, revise or eliminate old requirements, and devise new ways to regulate and influence institutions of higher education.

# Contents

ı

## PART THREE  THE COLLEGE AND ITS FACULTY  211

## 5  Special Issues in Faculty Employment  213

## 6  Faculty Academic Freedom and Freedom of Expression  275

## PART FOUR  THE COLLEGE AND ITS STUDENTS  341

## 7  The Student-Institution Relationship  343

## 8   Student Academic Issues   507

## 9   Student Disciplinary Issues   569

## 12 The College and External Private Entities  816

## APPENDICES

# Crosswalk for the *Student Version* of *The Law of Higher Education, Fifth Edition*

The crosswalk below directs interested readers from particular sections of the *Student Version* to the parallel section or sections in *The Law of Higher Education, Fifth Edition.* Since *LHE 5th* is a larger work (two volumes), it contains more citations of resources and more case examples than the *Student Version.* This additional material in *LHE 5th* may be useful to instructors preparing classes and to students engaging in research or independent study. In addition, *LHE 5th* includes various sections covering topics—usually specialized topics of primary interest to practitioners—that are not treated in the *Student Version.* Although these additional sections in *LHE 5th* are not shown on this crosswalk, interested readers may view the entire Table of Contents of *LHE 5th* by going to the NACUA Web site that supports *LHE 5th* and the *Student Version* (see Notice of Web Site and Periodic Supplements, previously in the front matter).

*Much as it takes a village to raise a child (a saying of obscure origin), it takes an "academical village" (Thomas Jefferson's phrase) to raise a book—at least a book such as this that arises from, and whose purpose is to serve, a national (and now international) academic community. This Student Version of the fifth edition is dedicated to all those members of our academical village, especially the instructors and students, who in numerous and varied ways have helped raise this book from its origins through this fifth edition, and this Student Version, and to all those members who will face the great challenges of law and policy that will shape higher education's future.*

# Preface

Operating the colleges and universities of today presents a multitude of challenges for their leaders and personnel. Often the issues they face involve institutional policy, but with continually increasing frequency they have legal implications as well. For example:

- A staff member may decide to become a whistleblower and assert that another college employee is violating the law. If the complaining staff member's performance has been problematic, and just cause exists for dismissal, may the college discharge the whistleblowing staff member?

- A tenured faculty member may have been accused of sexually harassing a student by requiring the student to complete a project that the student finds offensive. What standards and processes should be used to determine whether the faculty member should be discharged, disciplined, or reprimanded?

- A student religious organization may approach the dean of students seeking recognition or an allocation from the fund for student activities. If membership is limited to students of a particular faith, or if the student organization does not admit gays or lesbians, how should the administration respond?

- A group of students petitions the administration to develop a hate speech code because they believe it will reduce the number of bias incidents on campus. Can a public institution enforce such a provision?

- A wealthy alumna may call the vice president for student affairs and offer to make a multimillion dollar donation for scholarships on the condition that they be awarded only to African American students from disadvantaged families. Can and should the vice president accept the donation and follow the potential donor's wishes?

To assist students and instructors who wish to study, research, or teach about issues such as these and innumerable others, we have prepared this *Student Version* of our two-volume work, *The Law of Higher Education, Fifth Edition* ("*LHE 5th*" or "full fifth edition"). The *Student Version* provides foundational information, in-depth analysis, and practical suggestions on a wide array of legal issues faced by public and private institutions. The discussions draw upon pertinent court opinions, constitutional provisions, statutes, administrative regulations, and related developments. In order to enhance readability and keep the *Student Version* of manageable size, we have only occasionally included text or footnote citations to resources for further study and research, such as selected journal articles, books, and Web sites. We have, however, included a bibliography of such resources at the end of this book. In addition, we have created a convenient crosswalk from the various sections of the *Student Version* to the corresponding sections of the full fifth edition, which are chock full of text citations, footnotes, and annotated bibliographies (at the end of each chapter) that will be highly useful for any student or instructor seeking such resources. The crosswalk appears in the front matter of this book.

## *How the Student Version Was Developed*

We have designed this special edition of *LHE 5th* for use in higher education law and higher education administration courses. Guided by our own experiences teaching courses and workshops in higher education law, and by the suggestions of teaching colleagues, we have selected the topics from the full fifth edition that we believe are of greatest importance and interest to students of higher education law and their instructors. We have given primary consideration to the significance of the topic for the development of higher education law and policy, the topic's currency or timelessness for administrators of colleges and universities, and its usefulness in illustrating particular legal problems or the application of particular legal principles. The issues we have emphasized for each topic are usually ones that administrators, faculty members, or students could encounter at virtually any institution of higher education in the country (or, sometimes, in the world). In developing these issues, we have focused not only on the applicable law, but also on pertinent policy considerations and on implications for practice.

We had to make difficult choices about which topics to omit or to treat much less expansively than they were treated in the full fifth edition. For example, we included most of the topics and discussion in the chapters from the full fifth edition involving institutional liability for tort claims, faculty employment issues, academic freedom, student affairs, and academic issues concerning students. On the other hand, we omitted many of the topics and discussions involving the employment of administrators and staff members. We also omitted most of the full fifth edition's discussion of government regulation of higher education—although we retained overviews of each level of government and illustrative examples of regulatory activities at each level. For the federal government, for example, we retained a discussion of federal copyright law and a discussion of federal civil rights laws (such as Title IX) prohibiting discrimination in programs that receive federal funding. Similarly, we omitted most of the material in the full fifth edition that discusses the various private educational associations, in particular the American Association of University Professors (AAUP), the accrediting agencies, and the intercollegiate athletics associations; and most of the material on college and university relationships with the business world. But we retained overviews and illustrative examples for each of these topics. (The material on the AAUP is in Section 6.1.3). Readers interested in further information on topics or issues that we have compressed are invited to consult the crosswalk to *LHE 5th* and to consult the Table of Contents of *LHE 5th* for topics we have omitted from the *Student Version*.

Besides re-editing and reorganizing the materials that we have adapted from *LHE 5th*, we have updated these materials to account for the most important developments occurring from the press deadline for *LHE 5th* to the press deadline for this *Student Version*; and we occasionally have made small insertions of new material to capture points of particular interest to students. In addition, we have prepared numerous study aids designed specifically for students and instructors and integrated them into this book. These enhancements are:

- Introductory materials, titled "General Introduction to the Study of Higher Education Law," that lay the foundation for, and facilitate the study of, the subject matter; and also provide guidance for students who do not have background or training in the law.

- An appendix (Appendix B) that provides an overview of the American system of courts and highlights key distinctions between federal and state courts, and between trial and appellate courts.

- An appendix (Appendix C) that provides practical guidelines for reading and analyzing judicial opinions.

- An appendix (Appendix D) that presents a glossary of legal terms used in this book.

- Overviews at the beginning of chapters (in italics) that introduce the topics and concepts to be addressed in each chapter.

- Figures throughout the book that illustrate particular legal concepts and distinctions.

- A crosswalk (in the front matter) connecting each section in the *Student Version* to the corresponding section in the full fifth edition and designed for readers who may seek additional discussion, cases, or bibliographical resources available in *LHE 5th*.

- In addition to these study aids that are incorporated into this *Student Version*, we have also prepared a separate volume of edited cases and practice problems, keyed to the *Student Version*, which is available to instructors for distribution to students. (See Notice to Instructors in the front matter of this book.)

## Developments in Higher Education Law since the Publication of the Fourth Edition

In the seven years since publication of the fourth edition, and subsequently its supplement, many new and newly complex legal concerns have arisen on America's campuses—from the implications of the explosion in social media on faculty and student conduct and rights, to the continuing challenges to affirmative action in admissions and financial aid, to the membership practices of student religious organizations in the context of institutions' nondiscrimination policies, to the clash between faculty and "institutional" academic freedom, to the rights of intercollegiate athletes. Indeed, it is difficult to identify any other entities—including large corporations and government agencies—that are subject to as great an array of legal requirements as colleges and universities are. To serve the needs occasioned by this continual growth of the law, this *Student Version* of *LHE 5th* retains the material of continuing legal currency from *LHE 4th*, and the 2009 supplement, that is within the parameters we have set out above. We reorganized and re-edited this material to accommodate the deletion of old and the addition of new developments, and to maximize clarity and accessibility. To this base, we added considerable new material: more than one-third of the material in the twelve chapters of the *Student Version* did not appear in earlier editions of *The Law of Higher Education* or the supplement. This new material integrates pertinent new developments and insights regarding topics in the earlier editions and introduces numerous new topics and issues not covered in earlier editions.

Like the full fifth edition, this *Student Version* covers all of *postsecondary* education—from the large state university to the small private liberal arts college, from the graduate and professional school to the community college and vocational and technical institution, and from the traditional campus-based program to the innovative off-campus or multistate program, and now to distance learning as well. The *Student Version* also reflects the same perspective as the full fifth edition and earlier editions on the intersection of law and education. As described in the preface to the first edition:

> The law has arrived on the campus. Sometimes it has been a beacon, at other times a blanket of ground fog. But even in its murkiness, the law has not come "on little cat feet," like Carl Sandburg's "Fog"; nor has it sat silently on its haunches; nor will it soon move on. It has come noisily and sometimes has stumbled. And even in its imperfections, the law has spoken forcefully and meaningfully to the higher education community and will continue to do so.

## Organization and Content of the Student Version

This *Student Version* is organized into five parts: (1) Perspectives and Foundations; (2) The College and Its Governing Board and Staff; (3) The College and Its Faculty; (4) The College and Its Students; and (5) The College and the Outside World. In turn, we have divided these five parts into twelve chapters. Each chapter is divided into numerous sections and subsections with their own titles. Chapter 1 provides a framework for understanding and integrating what is presented in subsequent chapters and a perspective for assimilating future legal developments. Chapter 2 addresses foundational concepts concerning legal liability, preventive law, and the processes of litigation and alternative dispute resolution. Chapters 3 through 10 develop the legal concepts and issues that define the *internal* relationships among the various members of the campus community, and address the law's impact on particular roles, functions, and responsibilities of students, faculty members, and trustees and administrators. Chapter 11 is concerned with the postsecondary institution's *external* relationships with government at the federal, state, and local levels. This chapter examines broad questions of governmental power and process that cut across all the *internal* relationships and administrative functions considered in Chapters 3 through 10. Chapter 12 also deals with the institution's *external* relationships, but the relationships are those with the private sector rather than with government. This chapter explores the various national and regional education associations with which postsecondary institutions interact, as well as the various research ventures that institutions engage in with private entities from the commercial world.

Prior to the first chapter, we have included a General Introduction with six sections. After the last chapter, we have included a bibliography of resources for research and independent study, as well as four appendices containing various study aids.

## *A Note on Nomenclature*

The *Student Version* uses the terms "higher education" and "postsecondary education" to refer to education that follows a high school (or K–12) education. Usually these terms are used interchangeably; but occasionally "postsecondary education" is used as the broader of the two terms, encompassing formal post–high school education programs whether or not they build on academic subjects studied in high school or are considered to be "advanced" studies of academic subjects. Similarly, this book uses the terms "higher education institution," "postsecondary institution," "college," and "university" to refer to the institutions and programs that provide post–high school (or post–K–12) education. These terms are also usually used interchangeably; but occasionally "postsecondary institution" is used in the broader sense suggested above, and occasionally "college" is used to connote an academic unit within a university or an independent institution that emphasizes two-year or four-year undergraduate programs. The context generally makes clear when we intend a more specific meaning and are not using the above terms interchangeably.

The term "public institution" generally means an educational institution operated under the auspices of a state, county, or occasionally, city government. The term "private institution" means a nongovernmental, nonprofit, or proprietary educational institution. The term "religious institution" encompasses a private educational institution that is operated by a church or other sectarian organization (a "sectarian institution"), or is otherwise formally affiliated with a church or sectarian organization (a "religiously affiliated institution"), as well as an institution that has no affiliation with an outside religious organization but nevertheless proclaims a religious mission and is guided by religious values.

### Recommendations for Using the Student Version and Keeping Up-to-Date

There are some precautions to keep in mind when using this book. The legal analyses throughout the book, and the practical suggestions, are not adapted to the law of any particular state or to the circumstances prevailing at any particular postsecondary institution. The book is not a substitute for the advice of legal counsel, nor a substitute for further research into the particular legal authorities and factual circumstances that pertain to any legal problem that an institution, administrator, student, or faculty member may face in real life.

Nor is the book necessarily the latest word on the law. There is a saying among lawyers that "the law must be stable and yet it cannot stand still" (Roscoe Pound, *Interpretations of Legal History*, p. 1 (1923)), and the law moves especially fast in its applications to postsecondary education. Thus, we suggest that instructors and students keep abreast of ongoing developments concerning the topics and issues in this book. Various aids (described below) are available for this purpose.

First, we maintain a Web site, hosted by the National Association of College and University Attorneys (NACUA), Washington, D.C. (http://www.nacua.org/publications/lohe/index.asp), on which we announce or post pertinent new developments, keying them to this *Student Version* as well as to the full ffith edition. Periodically we expect to organize and expand these postings into a supplement for the *Student Version* (as well as the full fifth edition), to be published by NACUA. For further information on the Web site and the supplements, see page vii in the front matter of this book.

Next, there is another, very helpful, Web site: the Campus Legal Information Clearinghouse (CLIC), http://counsel.cua.edu, operated by the General Counsel's Office at The Catholic University of America in conjunction with the American Council on Education, that includes information on recent developments, especially federal statutory and federal agency developments. In addition, there is a legal reporter that reprints new court opinions on higher education law and provides commentary on recent developments: *West's Education Law Reporter*, published biweekly by Thomson/West Publishing Company, St. Paul, Minnesota.

For news reporting of current events in higher education generally, but particularly for substantial coverage of legal developments, instructors or students may wish to consult the *Chronicle of Higher Education*, published weekly in hard copy and daily online (http://www.chronicle.com); or *Inside Higher Ed.*, published daily online (http://insidehighered.com).

Other resources will be helpful not only for keeping abreast of recent developments, but also for identifying pertinent research. *Higher Education Abstracts* provides information on conference papers, journal articles, and government and association reports; it is published quarterly by the Claremont Graduate School, Claremont, California (http://highereducationabstracts.org). The database of the Educational Resources Information Center (ERIC) (http://www.eric .ed.gov/), sponsored by the U.S. Department of Education, performs a similar service encompassing books, monographs, research reports, conference papers and proceedings, bibliographies, legislative materials, dissertations, and journal articles on higher education. In addition, the IHELG monograph series published each year by the Institute for Higher Education Law and Governance, University of Houston Law Center, provides papers on a wide variety of research projects and timely topics.

Two specialty journals provide extended legal analysis on recent developments as well as classical concerns: the *Journal of College and University Law*, published quarterly by the National Association of College and University Attorneys (NACUA) and focusing exclusively on postsecondary education; and the *Journal of Law and Education*, which covers elementary and secondary as well as postsecondary education, and is published quarterly by Jefferson Lawbook Company, Cincinnati, Ohio.

## *Endnote*

Although the specific goal of this *Student Version* is to support the effective teaching and learning of higher education law, its broader goal is much the same as the goal for the full fifth edition and its predecessor editions, as set out in their prefaces. This goal is to provide a base for the debate concerning law's role on campus; for effective relationships between administrators and their counsel; and for improved understanding between the academic and legal worlds. The challenge of our age is not to remove the law from the campus or to marginalize it. The law is here to stay, and it will continue to play a major role in campus affairs (both internal and external). The challenge of our age, rather, is to make law more a beacon and less a fog. The challenge is for law and higher education to accommodate one another, preserving the best values of each for the mutual benefit of both. Just as academia benefits from the understanding and respect of the legal community, so law benefits from the understanding and respect of academia.

September 2013
*William A. Kaplin*
Washington, D.C.
*Barbara A. Lee*
New Brunswick, N.J.

# Acknowledgments

Many persons graciously provided assistance to us in the preparation of *The Law of Higher Education, Fifth Edition*, and this *Student Version* that is adapted from the fifth edition. We are grateful for each person and each contribution listed below, and for all other support and encouragement that we received along the way.

For the fifth edition, we are particularly grateful that Jonathan Alger, now President of James Madison University, agreed to update and edit nine sections and subsections of that book. Jon made these contributions while serving as Senior Vice President for Legal Affairs and General Counsel of Rutgers University, as well as serving as President of the National Association of College and University Attorneys. We are also grateful to additional colleagues whom we invited to update and edit sections of the manuscript because of their special expertise. Madelyn Wessel, Associate General Counsel at the University of Virginia, revised the section on copyright law, and Madelyn and Jacob Rooksby, Assistant Professor of Law, Duquesne University, revised the section on patent law. Randolph M. Goodman and J. Barclay Collins, partners at Wilmer, Cutler, Pickering, Hale and Dorr, LLP, updated the main section and several other subsections on federal tax law. (Most of these sections do not appear in the *Student Version*. For those sections included in the *Student Version*, the work of the contributor is identified by a footnote reference at the beginning of each section that was revised and updated.)

Various colleagues reviewed sections of the fifth edition manuscript, providing helpful feedback on matters within their expertise and good wishes for the project: Steven J. McDonald, General Counsel, Rhode Island School of Design; Leigh Polk Cole, Partner in Dinse, Knapp & McAndrew, P.C.; Eileen Goldgeier, Vice Chancellor and General Counsel, North Carolina State University; Theresa

Colecchia, Associate General Counsel, University of Pittsburgh; Nina Lavoie, Senior Associate Counsel, University of Maine System; Andrew Newton, General Counsel, Georgia Health Sciences University; and Jeffrey Swope, Partner in Edwards Wildman Palmer, LLC.

Our student research assistants provided valuable help with manuscript preparation: Taylor Stevens, Andrew Garcia, Sarah Grimme, Jana Belflower, and Tom Lyden at Stetson University; and Scott Goldschmidt and Evan Hamme at Catholic University. Jon Alger was assisted in his research by attorneys Jennifer Frost Hellstern, Sarah Luke, and Rhea Gordon at Rutgers University.

A number of persons skillfully performed invaluable word processing and administrative services during the years in which this manuscript was in process—in particular Donna Snyder at Catholic University and Dianne Oeste at Stetson University. Emily Black, Research Librarian at Catholic University's school of law, provided valuable assistance with locating resource materials, checking bibliography, and selecting and using a cite-checking program.

We are also grateful for the excellent work of Cathy Mallon, who managed the copyediting process; Cathy Cambron, the copy editor; Sylvia Coates, who created the indexes; and Shana Harrington, the proofreader. Their attention to detail and their helpful suggestions played an important role in readying the manuscript for publication.

Dean Veryl Miles at Catholic University's school of law provided summer research grants to BK that helped greatly in moving this massive project along; and Dean Darby Dickerson at Stetson University College of Law also provided research remuneration that served the same purpose. The Dean's Offices at both schools also supplied BK with the student research assistants named above.

The National Association of College and University Attorneys (NACUA) published the 2009 Supplement to *The Law of Higher Education, Fourth Edition* and the 2009 Supplement to the *Student Version* of the fourth edition, as well as our supplementary teaching materials, *Cases, Problems and Materials for Use with The Law of Higher Education, Fourth Edition*. Linda Henderson, formerly Manager of Publications at NACUA, was primarily responsible for managing the smooth publication processes and designing the high-quality final products. Kathleen Curry Santora and Karl Brevitz at NACUA supported these publications and worked with Ms. Henderson to arrange for a Web site to support the fourth edition (and now the fifth edition and this *Student Version*). NACUA publications also provided us with important information and guidance in the development of several sections of the fifth edition.

Barbara Kaplin accurately assisted with proofreading for the entire length of this project and also typed manuscript inserts as needed.

Our spouses and families once again tolerated the years of intrusion that successive editions of "the book" have imposed on our personal lives. They encouraged us when the fifth edition, and this subsequent *Student Version*, seemed too overwhelming to ever end. And they looked forward (usually patiently) to the time when the fifth edition would finally be finished—and we would get a little breathing space before any of us dare mention the forbidden words "sixth edition."

# The Authors

**William A. Kaplin** is professor of law emeritus at the Columbus School of Law, Catholic University of America, in Washington, D.C., where he also served for many years as Special Counsel to the Office of General Counsel. He has been a visiting professor at Cornell Law School, at Wake Forest University School of Law, and at Stetson University College of Law; a distinguished visiting scholar at the Institute for Higher Education Law and Governance, University of Houston; and a visiting scholar at the Institute for Educational Leadership, George Washington University. He is a former member of the Education Appeal Board at the U.S. Department of Education and the former editor of the *Journal of College and University Law,* and has served on the *Journal*'s editorial board for many years. He is also a Senior Fellow at Stetson's Center for Excellence in Higher Education Law and Policy; a founding member of the U.S./U.K. Higher Education Law Roundtable that meets every three years at New College, Oxford University; and a mentor/leader for the biannual Higher Education Law Roundtable for emerging scholars at the University of Houston Law Center.

Professor Kaplin received the American Council on Education's Borden Award, in recognition of the first edition of *The Law of Higher Education;* and the Association for Student Judicial Affairs' D. Parker Young Award, in recognition of research contributions; and he has been named a Fellow of the National Association of College and University Attorneys. He has also been honored through the establishment, by the Center for Excellence in Higher Education Law and Policy at Stetson University, of the *William A. Kaplin Award for Excellence in Higher Education Law and Policy Scholarship*, a national award presented annually to a leading scholar in the field.

In addition to the various editions and updates of *The Law of Higher Education*, Professor Kaplin's books include *The Law of Higher Education,*

*Fourth Edition: Student Version* (with Barbara Lee) (Jossey-Bass, Inc., 2007); *Cases, Problems, and Materials for Use with The Law of Higher Education* (with Barbara Lee) (NACUA, 2006); and *A Legal Guide for Student Affairs Professionals, Second Edition* (with Barbara Lee) (Jossey-Bass, Inc., 2009). Among his other books is *Constitutional Law: An Overview, Analysis, and Integration* (Carolina Academic Press, 2004). He has also authored numerous articles, monographs, and reports on education law and policy and on constitutional law.

Bill Kaplin received his B.A. degree (1964) in political science from the University of Rochester and his J.D. degree *with distinction* (1967) from Cornell University, where he was editor-in-chief of the *Cornell Law Review*. He then worked with a Washington, D.C., law firm, served as a judicial clerk at the U.S. Court of Appeals for the District of Columbia Circuit, and was an attorney in the education division of the U.S. Department of Health, Education and Welfare, before joining the Catholic University law faculty.

**Barbara A. Lee** is professor of human resource management at the School of Management and Labor Relations, Rutgers University, in New Brunswick, New Jersey. She is also of counsel to the law firm of Edwards Wildman Palmer, LLP. She is a former dean of the School of Management and Labor Relations, and also served as associate provost, department chair, and director of the Center for Women and Work at Rutgers University. She chaired the editorial board of the *Journal of College and University Law*, served as a member of the Board of Directors of the National Association of College and University Attorneys, and was named a NACUA Fellow. She also serves on the Executive Committee of the New Jersey State Bar Association's Section on Labor and Employment Law, and formerly served on the executive committee of the Human Resource Management Division of the Academy of Management. She is also a founding member of the U.S./U.K. Higher Education Law Roundtable. She received a distinguished alumni award from the University of Vermont in 2003 and the Daniel Gorenstein award from Rutgers University in 2009.

In addition to coauthoring the third, fourth, and fifth editions of *The Law of Higher Education* and *The Law of Higher Education, Student Version*, supplements and updates to the main volume, as well as *A Legal Guide for Student Affairs Professionals* (1997, 2009), Professor Lee also coauthored *Academics in Court* (1987, with George LaNoue), as well as numerous articles, chapters, and monographs on legal aspects of academic employment. She serves as an expert witness in tenure, discharge, and discrimination cases, and is a frequent lecturer and trainer for academic and corporate audiences.

Barbara Lee received her B.A. degree, *summa cum laude* (1971), in English and French from the University of Vermont. She received an M.A. degree (1972) in English and a Ph.D. (1977) in higher education administration from The Ohio State University. She earned a J.D., *cum laude* (1982), from the Georgetown University Law Center. Prior to joining Rutgers University in 1982, she held professional positions with the U.S. Department of Education and the Carnegie Foundation for the Advancement of Teaching.

# The Law of Higher Education

## Fifth Edition

## Student Version

# General Introduction:
# The Study of Higher Education Law

In the study of higher education law, as with most learning, it is important to begin with a foundation on which to build. This General Introduction to the *Student Version*, combined with Chapter 1 that follows, provides this foundation. The materials in the General Introduction have two purposes: (1) to introduce, illustrate, and integrate particular foundational matters that are discussed in greater depth in Chapter 1; and (2) to help students develop a framework for organizing their thinking about, and integrating, the materials that are contained in the succeeding chapters of this book.

## A. *The Universe of Education Law*

Higher education law is part of a broader universe of education law. This universe encompasses not only the law regarding higher and other postsecondary education but also the law regarding "lower" education, that is, elementary and secondary (K–12) education and preschool education.[1] These "higher" and "lower" sectors can be further divided into public education and private education sectors, as indicated in Figure I.1, thus producing a universe of four quadrants: public higher education, private higher education, public elementary/secondary and preschool education, and private elementary/secondary and preschool education. Finally, the private education quadrants can be subdivided into private education provided by secular institutions and private education provided by religious institutions, as Figure I.1 also indicates. Each sector displayed in Figure I.1 is legally distinct from the other sectors. The boundary lines within the education law universe thus represent important legal

---

[1] For resources on elementary/secondary education, see Victoria Dodd, *Practical Education Law for the Twenty-First Century*, 2d ed. (Carolina Academic Press, 2010); Ronna Greff Schneider, *Education Law: First Amendment, Due Process and Discrimination Litigation* (Thomson/West, 2004, supplemented in 2012); and William Valente & Christina Valente, *Law in the Schools* (6th ed., Pearson, 2004).

|  | PUBLIC EDUCATION | PRIVATE EDUCATION | |
|---|---|---|---|
|  |  | Secular | Sectarian |
| HIGHER EDUCATION | Public Colleges, Universities, and Community Colleges | Private, Secular Colleges and Universities | Private, Religiously Affiliated Colleges and Universities |
| LOWER EDUCATION | Public Elementary Schools, Secondary Schools, and Preschools | Private, Secular Elem. Schools, Secondary Schools, and Preschools | Private, Religiously Affiliated Elem. Schools, Secondary Schools, and Preschools |

**Figure I.1**  The Education Law Universe

distinctions—distinctions undergirding legal analysis of education law cases and problems. (For an example, see State ex rel. *Gallwey v. Grimm*, 48 P.3d 274, 279–84 (Wash. S. Ct., 2002) (state constitution's restriction on state funding of "schools" does not apply to higher education).) Because the applicable sources of law (Section 1.4 of this book), the legal reasoning, and the results or conclusions reached may differ from one sector to another, it is important to begin analysis of each judicial opinion by determining the sector of the education law universe with which it deals. Similarly, when first approaching a new issue or problem, it is important to ascertain its location within this universe.

In a higher education law course, therefore, one would ask: Does this case or problem involve public higher education or, rather, private higher education? (See Section 1.5 of this book for discussion of this distinction.) If it is private higher education, then one would next ask: Does this case or problem involve secular higher education or, rather, religious higher education? (See Section 1.6 of this book for discussion of this distinction.) To further expand understanding, one could also ask whether the case or problem would be reasoned or resolved differently—and why—if it had involved private rather than public (or public rather than private) higher education, or had involved religious rather than secular (or secular rather than religious) higher education. Finally, for the broadest perspective, one might ask whether the case or problem would be reasoned or resolved differently if it had involved lower education rather than higher education.

These distinctions, and their significance in various contexts, are emphasized throughout the *Student Version*.

## B. The Governance of Higher Education

Early in the study of higher education law, attention should be given to the governance of higher education, that is, the structures and processes by which higher education institutions and systems are governed. As more fully explained in Section 1.3 of this book, the concept of governance can be divided into two categories: internal governance (that is, within the institution) and external governance (that is, external to the institution). External governance, in turn, may be further divided into two subcategories: public external governance (that is, by government) and private external governance (that is, by private associations).

A focus on governance is important to the study of higher education law because, as also explained in Section 1.3, "[g]overnance structures and processes provide the legal and administrative context within which issues and disputes arise" and "the framework within which parties seek to resolve problems and disputes." Since the structures and processes for higher education governance differ markedly from those for elementary and secondary education, the basic boundary line in the "education law universe" (Section A above) is equally applicable to matters of governance. Similarly, the boundary lines between public and private higher education institutions, and between private secular and private religious institutions, also indicate parallel distinctions in the governance of higher education. Thus, just as the law may vary from one sector to another of the education law universe, the governance structures and processes may vary as well. Whenever one is analyzing a legal problem or reading a judicial opinion, therefore, it is helpful to begin, not only by determining the sector of the universe within which the problem or case falls, but also by identifying the particular governance structure or process from which the problem or case arose and through which it might be (or might have been) resolved.

## C. Sources of Higher Education Law

As a keystone of their internal governance systems (see Section B above), higher education institutions create "internal law" that delineates authority and rights, and embodies the rules and procedures, by which the institutions govern themselves. There are three main sources of internal law: institutional rules and regulations (see Section 1.4.3.1 of this book), institutional contracts (see Section 1.4.3.2), and academic custom and usage (see Section 1.4.3.3). Circumscribing, and thus constraining, this internal law is the external law (here, public external law) created by the federal government and state and local governments through their own governance processes (see Section 1.4.2). These sources of law, and the interrelations among them, are another factor to consider—along with the education law universe sectors (Section A above) and the governance structures and processes (Section B above)—when reading judicial opinions or analyzing problems concerning higher education law. It will be helpful, therefore, to identify the pertinent source or sources of law

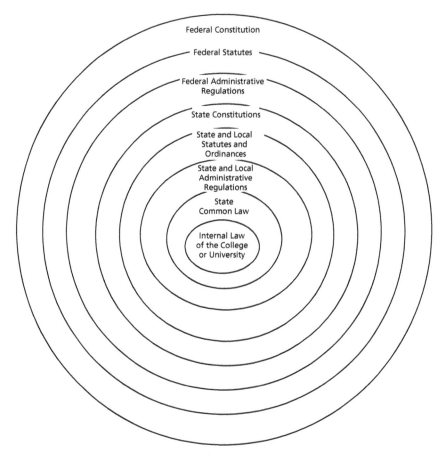

**Figure I.2** The External Law Circumscribing the Internal Law

that provide(s) the basis for the judicial opinion or that can be used to analyze the problem.

Figure I.2 depicts the various sources of law and the order in which each source "trumps" other sources. Each ring of law in the figure is superior to the other rings that are farther inside, and is inferior to the other rings of law that are farther outside. Thus, when there is inconsistency or conflict between two applicable sources of law, the law in the ring farthest from the center will prevail.

## D. The Legal Relationships Within Institutions of Higher Education

The internal governance of an institution of higher education (see Section B above) is generally the responsibility of a board of trustees or board of regents (see Section 3.1 of this book). The board, as the entity vested with the institution's legal authority, has legal relationships with the institution's officers, administrators, and staff members; with its faculty members; and with its

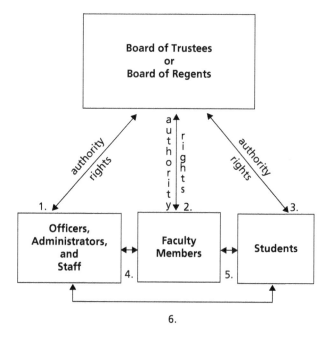

1,2,3: Primary Relationships
4,5,6: Secondary Relationships

**Figure I.3** Internal Legal Relationships in Higher Education Institutions

students. These three relationships are depicted as primary relationships in Figure I.3. Each relationship encompasses both questions of authority (usually the board's [or institution's] authority) and questions of rights (usually the rights of officers, administrators, and staff, of faculty members, or of students). In turn, there are legal relationships among the institution's officers, administrators, and staff; its faculty members; and its students. These are the three secondary relationships depicted in Figure I.3.[2] The secondary relationships also encompass both questions of authority and questions of rights. (For illustrative examples of such secondary relationships, see *Woodruff v. Ohman*, 2002 WL 193915, 162 *Ed. Law Rep.* 707 (6th Cir. 2002), and 2006 WL 305670 (6th Cir. 2006) (faculty member/staff member conflict); *Fiacco v. Sigma Alpha Epsilon*, 528 F.3d 94 (1st Cir. 2008) (administrator/student organization conflict).)

The three primary legal relationships depicted in Figure I.3 typically are the primary focus of higher education law. Chapters 3 and 4 of this *Student Version* focus on the legal relationships between the institution (board) and its officers,

---

[2] Faculty members may also have legal relationships with other faculty members, as students may with other students, and as officers, administrators, and staff members may with other officers, administrators, and staff. For an example of a faculty/faculty conflict, see *Slack v. Stream*, 988 So.2d 516 (Ala. 2008). For an example of a student/student conflict, see *Henri v. Curto*, 891 N.E.2d 135 (Ind. App. 2008), 908 N.E.2d 196 (Ind. S. Ct. 2009). For an extended discussion of student-to-student legal relationships, see Section 7.1.5 of this book.

administrators, and staff; Chapters 5 and 6 focus on the legal relationships between the institution (board) and its faculty; and Chapters 7 through 10 focus on the legal relationships between the institution (board) and its students. In addition, the institution has legal relationships with the outside world—for example, with government agencies, private education associations, and corporate research partners and other commercial entities. These external relationships are depicted in Figure I.4 and are addressed in Chapters 11 and 12. For external relationships, as for internal, there are also secondary relationships that may develop between external entities and the institution's officers, administrators, staff, faculty members, or students. For example, a government agency may award a student financial assistance, thus creating a legal relationship between the agency and the student with respect to the conditions for retaining the assistance. These secondary external relationships are not depicted in Figure I.4.

External relationships often intersect with and help define the internal relationships that are depicted in Figure I.3. The rights that faculty members may assert against their institutions (boards), for example, such as rights to nondiscrimination in employment, are created in part by federal law; and the federal government's obligation to enforce this external law (see Section 5.4.1 of this book) creates legal relationships between the federal government and postsecondary institutions.

In the study of higher education law, it is important to look for these various legal relationships and to sort them out as best one can. Thus, whenever analyzing a judicial opinion or addressing a legal problem, it will be helpful to determine not only what sector of the education law universe is implicated, what governance structure or process is involved, and what source(s) of law applies (see Sections A, B, and C above), but also what legal relationship(s) is at issue and how it helps to define the contours of the dispute.

**Figure I.4** External Legal Relationships in Higher Education Institutions

## E. The Law/Policy Distinction

In addition to the various distinctions addressed in Sections A–D above, there is another overarching distinction between legal issues and policy issues that students must take into account when studying higher education law. As explained in Section 1.7 of this book, legal issues are stated and analyzed using the norms and principles of the legal system, while policy issues are stated and analyzed using norms and principles of administration and management, ethics, the social sciences and physical sciences, and other relevant disciplines.

It is important to sort out these varying norms and principles when analyzing judicial opinions or addressing particular problems. Thus, in addition to considering the legal issues that are presented by the case or problem, one may also ask, "What are the educational policy or public policy issues presented?" and "How do the legal issues and policy issues relate to one another?" Law students and lawyers may, and do, think about and react to legal issues differently from education students, educators, and administrators; and the same may be said for policy issues. Among the most practical insights that may come from a higher education law course or workshop are these insights concerning respective norms and roles, and the ways in which administrators, educators, and attorneys may be guided by these norms and roles in working together on matters with legal ramifications.

## F. The U.S. Legal System as It Relates to Higher Education Law

The law applicable to higher education emerges from both the context of federalism (the division of powers between federal and state governments) and the context of separation of powers (the allocation of powers among the legislative, executive, and judicial branches of government). Legal issues concerning higher education may thus arise not only in the courts (state courts and federal courts) but also in Congress, state legislatures, and local government legislative bodies, and in a wide variety of federal, state, and local administrative agencies—all of which are important participants in the external governance of higher education (see Section B above). Similarly, legal disputes and problems may be resolved not only in judicial opinions but also in **statutes** and ordinances, and in **administrative** regulations and rulings. It is important, therefore, for students studying higher education law to have a basic understanding—in relation to higher education's concerns—of the U.S. legal system, the system of courts that is a constituent part of the legal system, the use of court cases as legal **precedents,** the roles of lawyers within the legal system, and the legal materials and research tools by which one accesses the law developed through the legal system.

Various sections of Chapters 1 and 2 of the *Student Version* include basic introductory background on these matters. Some of the legal concepts and descriptive material in these chapters may already be generally familiar to law students and lawyers, who may use this material for review and to sensitize themselves to the particular concerns of higher education. Students and educators without legal training or background, on the other hand, should find these materials to be particularly helpful: Sections 1.3.3, 1.5.1, and 1.6.1 provide basic information on the U.S. legal system; Sections 1.4.4, 2.1.4, and 2.2.1 provide basic information on the U.S. court system; Sections 1.7 and 2.1.7 provide basic information on the roles of attorneys; Sections 1.4.2, 1.4.4, and 1.4.5 provide basic information on case law and other legal materials and research tools; Sections 11.1.1, 11.2.1, and 11.3.1, taken together, describe the constitutional structure of federalism as it applies to higher education. In addition, Appendix A of this book, The Constitution of the United States: Provisions of Particular Interest to Postsecondary Education, provides an overview of the U.S. Constitution, which is the foundation and framework for the entire U.S. legal system; Appendix B, The Judicial System of the United States, provides an organizational overview of the federal and state courts; and Appendix C, Reading and Analyzing Judicial Opinions, provides an introduction to the study of case law.

For further information on these matters geared specifically to education students and educators, but also of use to law students and lawyers, see Sarah Redfield, *Thinking Like a Lawyer: An Educator's Guide to Legal Analysis and Research* (Carolina Academic Press, 2002), a resource that focuses directly on education students' and educators' interactions with law and lawyers; and Steve Permuth and Ralph Mawdsley, *Research Methods for Studying Legal Issues in Education* (Education Law Association, 2006), which addresses qualitative and quantitative methods as well as policy-oriented methods for research in education law. For other helpful resources, see the following publications:

1. Regarding an introduction to the American legal system, including the system of federal and state courts, see Margaret Johns and Rex Perschbacher, *The United States Legal System: An Introduction* (3d ed., Carolina Academic Press, 2012); E. Allan Farnsworth, *An Introduction to the Legal System of the United States* (4th ed., Oxford Univ. Press, 2010); Stephen Elias, *Legal Research: How to Find and Understand the Law* (16th ed., Nolo, 2012), Chapters 3 and 7; and Steven Burton, *An Introduction to Law and Legal Reasoning* (3d ed., Aspen Publishers, 2007), Chaps. 6–9.

2. Regarding the legal profession and the role of lawyers, see Johns and Perschbacher, above, Chapter 2.

3. Regarding the basics of legal research and analysis, see AALL Legal Information Service to the Public, *How to Research a Legal Problem: A Guide for Non-Lawyers* (American Association of Law Libraries), available at http://www.aallnet.org/main-menu/Publications/products/How-To -Research-A-Legal-Problem; and see also Burton, above, Introduction and Chaps. 1–5; Elias and Levinkind, above; and Christopher Wren and Jill Wren, *The Legal Research Manual* (2nd ed., Legal Educ. Pub., 1999).

4. For definitions and explanations of legal terms, see D. Mellinkoff, *Dictionary of American Legal Usage* (West, 1992); Elias and Levinkind, above, App. C; and Wren and Wren, above, Apps. L and M.

# PART ONE

# PERSPECTIVES
# AND FOUNDATIONS

# 1

# Overview of Higher Education Law

*Chapter 1 provides background information on the reach of law into virtually every aspect of higher education and develops the foundational principles and conceptual distinctions that have guided the law's ever-expanding reach. After brief overviews of how the law's impact on academia has expanded, and the body of higher education law has evolved, since the 1950s, the chapter explains how decisions concerning colleges and universities, and their personnel and students, are made (governance). The chapter then reviews the sources of higher education law, distinguishing between those from outside the institution (such as constitutions, statutes, and common law) and those from within the institution (such as policies and contracts). Differences in how the law treats public institutions versus private institutions are examined, as is the state action doctrine (which serves to require public institutions, but usually not private institutions, to comply with the individual rights guarantees of the U.S. Constitution). Differences in how the law treats private religious, versus private secular, institutions are also addressed. The chapter then concludes with an examination of the relationship between law and policy (institutional policy as well as public policy), and legal counsel's role in advising the institution on the development and implementation of policy.*

## Section 1.1. How Far the Law Reaches and How Loudly It Speaks

Law's presence on the campus and its impact on the daily affairs of postsecondary institutions are pervasive and inescapable. Litigation and government regulation expose colleges and universities to jury trials and large monetary damage awards, to court injunctions affecting institutions' internal affairs, to government agency compliance investigations and hearings, and even to criminal prosecutions against administrative officers, faculty members, and students.

Many factors have contributed over the years to the development of this legalistic and litigious environment. Students' and parents' expectations have increased, spurred in part by increases in tuition and fees and in part by society's consumer orientation. The greater availability of data that measures and compares institutions, and greater political savvy among students and faculty, has led to more sophisticated demands on institutions. Satellite campuses, off-campus programs, and distance learning have extended the reach of the "campus," bringing into higher education's fold a diverse array of persons whose interests may conflict with those of more traditional populations. And an increasingly adversarial mindset, a decrease in civility, and a diminishing level of trust in societal institutions have made it more acceptable to assert legal claims at the drop of a hat.

In addition, advocacy groups have used litigation against institutions as the means to assert faculty and student claims against institutions—and applicant claims as well, in suits concerning **affirmative action**[1] in admissions and employment. Contemporary examples of such groups include the Foundation for Individual Rights in Education (FIRE) (http://www.thefire.org); Students for Academic Freedom (see Section 7.1.4); the Center for Law and Religious Freedom (http://www.clsnet.org/clrfpages), a project of the Christian Legal Society; the Student Press Law Center (http://www.splc.org); and the Center for Individual Rights (http://www.cir-usa.org), which has been particularly active in the cases on affirmative action in admissions. More traditional examples of advocacy groups include the American Civil Liberties Union (ACLU) (www.aclu.org) and the NAACP Legal Defense and Educational Fund, Inc. (http://www.naacpldf.org). National higher education associations also sometimes involve themselves in advocacy (in court or in legislative forums) on behalf of their members. The American Council on Education, whose members are institutions, is one example (http://www.acenet.org); the American Association of University Professors (AAUP), whose members are individual faculty members, is another example (http://www.aaup.org; see Section 6.1.3 of this book).

In this environment, law is an indispensable consideration, whether one is responding to campus disputes, planning to avoid future disputes, or crafting an institution's policies and priorities. Institutions have responded by expanding their legal staffs and outside counsel relationships and by increasing the numbers of administrators in legally sensitive positions. As this trend has continued, more and more questions of educational policy have become converted into legal questions as well (see Section 1.7). Law and litigation have extended into every corner of campus activity.[2]

There are many striking examples of cutting-edge cases that have attracted considerable attention in higher education circles or have had a substantial

---

[1] Terms appearing in **bold face** type are included in the Glossary, which is found in Appendix D.

[2] Much of the introductory content of this section is adapted from Kathleen Curry Santora and William Kaplin, "Preventive Law: How Colleges Can Avoid Legal Problems," *Chron. Higher Educ.*, April 18, 2003, B20 (copyright © 2004 by Chronicle of Higher Education, Inc.).

impact on higher education. Students have sued their institutions for damages after being accused of plagiarism or cheating or after being penalized for improper use of a campus computer network; objecting students have sued over mandatory student fee allocations; victims of harassment have sued their institutions and professors alleged to be harassers; student athletes have sought injunctions ordering their institutions or athletic conferences to grant or reinstate eligibility for intercollegiate sports; disabled students have filed suits against their institutions or state rehabilitation agencies, seeking accommodations to support their education; students who have been victims of violence have sued their institutions for alleged failures of campus security; hazing victims have sued fraternities, fraternity members, and institutions; parents have sued administrators and institutions after students have committed suicide; and former students involved in bankruptcy proceedings have sought judicial discharge of student loan debts owed to institutions. Disappointed students have challenged their grades in court, such as the student who filed suit in 2007 claiming that being required to type led to his receiving a lower grade because he typed more slowly than other students, or the student who fell asleep during an exam and claimed that she was unfairly penalized on the basis of a disability. Students and others supporting animal rights have used lawsuits (and civil disobedience as well) to pressure research laboratories to reduce or eliminate the use of animals. And another student, injured in a Jell-O wrestling event at a college residence hall party that he himself had organized, attempted to pin liability on his university.

Faculty members have been similarly active. Professors have sought legal redress after their institutions changed the professors' laboratory or office space, their teaching assignments, or the size of their classes or after research data or curricular materials were discarded when a faculty member's office was relocated. A group of faculty challenged their institution's decision to terminate several women's studies courses, alleging sex discrimination and violation of free speech. Female coaches have sued over salaries and support for women's teams. Across the country, suits brought by faculty members who have been denied **tenure**—once one of the most closely guarded and sacrosanct of all institutional judgments—have become commonplace.

Outside parties also have been increasingly involved in postsecondary education litigation. Athletic conferences have been named as defendants in cases brought by student athletes. Fraternities are sometimes defendants in the hazing cases. Media organizations have brought suits and other complaints under open meetings and public records laws. Drug companies have sued and been sued in disputes over human subjects research and patent rights to discoveries. Community groups, environmental organizations, taxpayers, and other outsiders have also gotten into the act, suing institutions for a wide variety of reasons, from curriculum to land use. Recipients of university services have also resorted to the courts. In 2009, clients of a university's Center for Reproductive Health sued the university when the center gave fertilized embryos to unrelated couples without the consent of the parents of the embryos; another institution was sued for alleged mishandling of the cremated remains of a cadaver donated to the university's research program.

More recently, other societal developments have led to new types of lawsuits and new issues for legal planning. And, of course, myriad government agencies at federal, state, and local levels have frequently been involved in civil suits as well as criminal prosecutions concerning higher education. Drug abuse problems have spawned legal issues, especially those concerning mandatory drug testing of employees or student athletes and compliance with "drug-free campus" laws. Federal government regulation of Internet communications has led to new questions about liability for the spread of computer viruses, copyright infringement in cyberspace, transmission of sexually explicit materials, and defamation by cyberspeech. Outbreaks of racial, anti-Semitic, anti-Arab, homophobic, and political and ideological tensions on campuses have led to speech codes, academic bills of rights, and the eruption of a range of issues concerning student and faculty academic freedom. Initiatives to strengthen women's teams, prompted by alleged sex-based inequities in intercollegiate athletics, have led to suits by male athletes and coaches whose teams have been eliminated or downsized. Sexual harassment concerns have grown to include student peer harassment and harassment based on sexual orientation, as well as date rape and sexual assault. Hazing, alcohol use, and behavioral problems, implicating fraternities and men's athletic teams especially, have reemerged as major issues.

The development of more relationships between research universities and private industry has led to more legal issues concerning technology transfer. Heightened sensitivities to alleged sexual harassment and political bias in academia have prompted disputes between faculty and students over academic freedom, manifested especially in student complaints about faculty members' classroom comments and course assignments. Increased attention to student learning disabilities and to psychological and emotional conditions that may interfere with learning has led to new types of disability discrimination claims and issues concerning the modification of academic standards. Renewed attention to affirmative action policies for admissions and financial aid has resulted in lawsuits, state legislation, and state referenda and initiative drives among voters. Disputes persist on campus concerning student organizations that promote gay rights, student religious organizations that exclude gay and lesbian students from membership or leadership, and the rights and concerns of transgender students.

As the number and variety of disputes have increased, the use of administrative agencies as alternative forums for airing disputes has grown alongside litigation in court. Administrative agency regulations at federal, state, and local levels may now routinely be enforced through agency compliance proceedings and private complaints filed with administrative agencies. Thus, postsecondary institutions may find themselves before the federal Equal Employment Opportunity Commission or an analogous state agency; the National Labor Relations Board or a state's public employee relations board; the administrative law judges of the U.S. Department of Education; contract dispute boards of federal and state contracting agencies; state workers' compensation and unemployment insurance boards; state licensing boards; state civil service commissions; the boards or officers of federal, state, and local taxing authorities; local zoning boards; or mediators or arbitrators of various agencies at all levels of government.

Paralleling these administrative developments has been an increase in the internal forums created by postsecondary institutions for their own use in resolving disputes. Faculty and staff grievance committees, processes for appealing denials of promotion or tenure, student judiciaries, honor boards, and grade appeals panels are common examples. In recent years, **mediation** has assumed a major role in some of these processes. In addition to such internal forums, private organizations and associations involved in postsecondary governance have given increased attention to their own dispute resolution mechanisms. Thus, besides appearing before courts and administrative agencies, postsecondary institutions may become involved in grievance procedures of faculty and staff unions, hearings of accrediting agencies on the accreditation status of institutional programs, probation hearings of athletic conferences, and censure proceedings of the American Association of University Professors.

Of course, some counter-trends have emerged over time that have served to ameliorate the more negative aspects of the greater role of law and litigiousness in academia. The alternative dispute resolution (ADR) movement in society generally has led to the use of mediation and other constructive mechanisms for the internal resolution of campus disputes (see Section 2.3 of this book). Colleges and universities have increased their commitments to and capabilities for risk management and preventive legal planning. On a broader scale, not only institutions but also their officers have increasingly banded together in associations to maximize their influence on the development of legislation and agency regulations affecting postsecondary education. These associations also facilitate the sharing of strategies and resources for managing campus affairs in ways that minimize legal problems. Government agencies have developed processes for "notice" and "comment" prior to implementing regulations, for negotiated rule making, and for mediation of disputes. The trial courts have developed processes for pretrial mediation, and the appellate courts, including the U.S. Supreme Court, have developed a concept of "judicial deference" or "academic deference" that is used by both trial and appellate courts to limit judicial intrusion into the genuinely academic decisions of postsecondary institutions.

Administrators, counsel, public policy makers, and scholars have all reflected on the role of law on campus. While the influence of law is frequently criticized, this criticism is becoming more perceptive and more balanced. It is still often asserted that the law reaches too far and speaks too loudly. Especially because of the courts' and federal government's involvement, it is said that legal proceedings and compliance with legal requirements are too costly, not only in monetary terms but also in terms of the talents and energies expended; that they divert higher education from its primary mission of teaching and scholarship; and that they erode the integrity of campus decision making by bending it to real or perceived legal technicalities that are not always in the academic community's best interests. It is increasingly recognized, however, that such criticisms—although highlighting pressing issues for higher education's future—do not acknowledge all sides of these issues. We cannot evaluate the role of law on campus by looking only at dollars expended, hours of time logged, pages of compliance reports completed, or numbers of legal proceedings participated in. We must also consider a number of less quantifiable questions: Are legal claims made against institutions, faculty, or staff usually frivolous or unimportant, or are they sometimes justified? Are institutions providing effective mechanisms for dealing with claims and complaints internally, thus helping themselves avoid any negative effects of outside legal proceedings? Are the courts and counsel for colleges and universities doing an adequate job of sorting out frivolous from justifiable claims and of developing means for summary disposition of frivolous claims and settlement of justifiable ones? Have administrators and counsel ensured that their legal houses are in order by engaging in effective preventive planning? Are courts being sensitive to the mission of higher education when they apply legal rules to campuses and when they devise remedies in suits lost by institutions? Do government regulations for higher education implement worthy policy goals, and are they adequately sensitive to the mission of higher education? In situations where the message of the law has appeared to conflict with the best interests of academia, how has academia responded? Has the inclination been to kill the messenger or to develop more positive remedies—to hide behind rhetoric or to forthrightly document and defend the interests of higher education?

We still do not know all we should about these questions. But we know that they are clearly a critical counterpoint to questions about money, time, and energy expended. We must have insight into both sets of questions before we can fully judge law's impact on the campus—before we can know, in particular situations, whether law is more a beacon or a blanket of ground fog.

## Section 1.2. *Evolution of Higher Education Law*

Throughout the nineteenth and much of the twentieth centuries, the law's relationship to higher education was very different from what it is now. There were few legal requirements relating to the educational administrator's functions, and these requirements were not a major factor in most administrative decisions. Those in the higher education world, moreover, tended to think of themselves as removed from and perhaps above the world of law and lawyers. The roots of this traditional separation between academia and law are several.

Higher education (particularly private education) was often viewed as a unique enterprise that could regulate itself through reliance on tradition and consensual agreement. It was thought to operate best by operating autonomously, and it thrived on the privacy afforded by autonomy. Academia, in short, was like a Victorian gentlemen's club whose sacred precincts were not to be profaned by the involvement of outside agents in its internal governance.

The special higher education environment was also thought to support a special virtue and ability in its personnel. College faculty and administrators (often themselves respected scholars) had knowledge and training far beyond that of the general populace, and they were charged with the guardianship of knowledge for future generations. Theirs was a special mission pursued with special expertise and often at a considerable financial sacrifice. The combination spawned the perception that ill will and personal bias were strangers to academia and that outside monitoring of its affairs was therefore largely unnecessary.

The law to a remarkable extent reflected and reinforced such attitudes. Federal and state governments generally avoided any substantial regulation of higher education. Legislatures and administrative agencies imposed few legal obligations on institutions and provided few official channels through which their activities could be legally challenged. What legal oversight existed was generally centered in the courts. But the judiciary was also highly deferential to higher education. In matters concerning students, courts found refuge in the *in loco parentis* doctrine borrowed from early English **common law.** By placing the educational institution in the parents' shoes, the doctrine permitted the institution to exert almost untrammeled authority over students' lives.

Nor could students lay claim to constitutional rights in the higher education environment. In private education the U.S. Constitution had no application; and in the public realm, courts accepted the proposition that attendance at a public postsecondary institution was a privilege and not a right. Being a "privilege," attendance could constitutionally be extended and was subject to termination on whatever conditions the institution determined were in its and the students' best interests. Occasionally courts did hold that students had some **contract** rights under an express or implied contractual relationship with the institution. But—as in *Anthony v. Syracuse University*, 231 N.Y.S. 435 (N.Y. App. Div. 1928), where the court upheld the university's dismissal of a student without assigning any reason other than that she was not "a typical Syracuse girl"—contract law provided little meaningful recourse for students. The institution was given virtually unlimited power to dictate the contract terms; and the contract, once made, was construed heavily in the institution's favor.

As further support for these judicial hands-off attitudes, higher education institutions also enjoyed immunity from a broad range of lawsuits alleging **negligence** or other **torts.** For public institutions, this protection arose from the **governmental immunity** doctrine, which shielded state and local governments and their instrumentalities from legal liability for their sovereign acts. For private institutions, a comparable result was reached under the **charitable immunity** doctrine, which shielded charitable organizations from legal liability that would divert their funds from the purposes for which they were intended.

In the latter half of the twentieth century, however, events and changing circumstances worked a revolution in the relationship between academia and the law. Changes in the composition of student bodies and faculties, growth in the numbers and diversity of institutions and educational programs, advances in technology, greater dependence of both private and public institutions on federal financial assistance and research support, increases in study abroad programs and joint ventures between American institutions and those in other countries, and expanded relationships with private sector commercial entities dramatically altered the legal and policy landscape for colleges and universities. The civil rights and student rights movements contributed to the legal demands on institutions, as individuals and groups claimed new rights and brought new challenges. Demands for accountability by federal and state governments and private donors also spawned new challenges, including most recently issues concerning inadequate access to higher education for students from families of lower socioeconomic status.

As a result of these developments, the federal government and state governments became heavily involved in postsecondary education, creating many new legal requirements and new forums for raising legal challenges. Students, faculty, other employees, and outsiders became more willing and more able to sue postsecondary institutions and their officers (see Section 1.1). Courts became more willing to entertain such suits on their merits and to offer relief from certain institutional actions. New legal doctrines and requirements that developed outside of higher education increasingly were applied to colleges and universities. In short, by the end of the twentieth century, higher education no longer enjoyed much of the judicial and legislative deference it once knew. Virtually every area of the law now applies to institutions of higher education, and keeping up with this vast body of continually evolving law is a great challenge for administrators, faculty, students, and scholars of higher education.

As these developments continue into the twenty-first century, postsecondary education remains a dynamic enterprise, as societal developments and technological breakthroughs continue to be mirrored in the issues, conflicts, and litigation that colleges and universities face. The key trends that are now shaping the future, broadly speaking, are the *diversification* of higher education, the *technologization* of higher education, the *commercialization* of higher education, and the *globalization* of higher education. In this context, the challenge for the law is to keep pace with such trends by maintaining a dynamism of its own that is sensitive to institutions' evolving missions and the varying conflicts that institutions confront. And the challenge for higher education is to understand and respond constructively to change and growth in the law while maintaining focus on multiple purposes and constituencies.

### Section 1.3. The Governance of Higher Education

**1.3.1. Basic concepts and distinctions.** Governance refers to the structures and processes by which higher education institutions and systems are governed in their day-to-day operations as well as their longer-range policy making. Governance encompasses (1) the organizational structures of individual institutions and (in the public sector) of statewide systems of higher education; (2) the delineation and allocation of decision-making authority within these organizational structures and within the structures of other organizations with authority over higher education; (3) the processes by which decisions are made; and (4) the processes by which, and forums within which, decisions may be challenged.

Higher education governance can be divided into two categories: internal governance and external governance. "Internal governance" refers to the structures and processes by which an institution governs itself. "External governance" refers to the structures and processes by which outside entities (that is, entities external to the institution itself) play a role in the governance of institutional affairs. Internal governance usually involves "internal" sources of law (see Section 1.4.3 of this book); and external governance generally involves "external" sources of law (see Section 1.4.2). In turn, external governance can be further divided into two subcategories: public external governance and private external governance. "Public external governance" refers to the structures and processes by which the federal government (see Section 11.3), state governments (see Section 11.2), and local governments (see Section 11.1) participate in the governance of higher education. "Private external governance" refers to the structures and processes by which private associations and organizations participate in the governance of higher education. Major examples of such external private entities include accrediting agencies (see Section 12.1.2), athletic associations and conferences (see Section 12.1.3), the American Association of University Professors, and other higher education associations. Other examples include national employee unions with "locals" or chapters at individual institutions (see Sections 4.3 and 5.3); outside commercial, research, public service, or other entities with which institutions may affiliate; and public interest and lobbying organizations that support particular causes.

The governance structures and processes for higher education, both internal and external, differ markedly from those for elementary and secondary education. Similarly, the structures and processes for public higher education differ from those for private higher education. These variations between public and private institutions exist in part because they are created in different ways, have different missions, and draw their authority to operate from different sources (see generally Section 3.1), and in part because the federal Constitution's and state constitutions' rights clauses apply directly to public institutions and impose duties on them that these clauses do not impose on private institutions (see generally Section 1.5 below). Furthermore, the governance structures and processes for private secular institutions differ from those for private **religious institutions**. These variations exist in part because religious institutions have different origins and sponsorship, and different missions, than private secular institutions, and in part because the federal First Amendment and comparable state constitutional provisions afford religious institutions an extra measure of autonomy from government regulations, beyond that of private secular institutions, and also limit their eligibility to receive government support (see generally Section 1.6 below).

Governance structures and processes provide the legal and administrative framework within which higher education problems and disputes arise. They also provide the framework within which parties seek to resolve problems and disputes (see, for example, Section 2.3) and institutions seek to prevent or curtail problems and disputes by engaging in legal and policy planning (see Section 1.7). In some circumstances, governance structures and processes may themselves create problems or become the focus of disputes. Internal disputes (often turf battles) may erupt between various constituencies within the institution—for example, a dispute over administrators' authority to change student grades given by faculty members. External governance disputes may erupt between an institution and an outside entity—for example, a dispute over a state board of education's authority to approve or terminate certain academic programs at a state institution, or a dispute over an athletic association's charges of irregularities in an institution's intercollegiate basketball program. Such disputes may spawn major legal issues about governance structures and processes that are played out in the courts. (See Section 6.2.3 for examples concerning internal governance and Sections 11.2 and 12.1 for examples concerning external governance.) Whether a problem or dispute centers on governance, or governance simply provides the framework, a full appreciation of the problem or dispute and the institution's capacity for addressing it effectively requires a firm grasp of the pertinent governance structures and processes.

Typically, when internal governance is the context, an institution's governing board or officers are pitted against one or more faculty members, staff members, or students; or members of these constituencies are pitted against one another. Chapters 3 through 9 of this book focus primarily on such issues. When external governance is the context, typically a legislature, a government agency or board, a private association or other private organization, or sometimes an affiliated entity or outside contractor is pitted against a higher educational institution (or system) or against officers, faculty members, or students of an institution. Chapters 10 and 11 of this book focus primarily on such issues.

The two categories of internal and external governance often overlap, especially in public institutions, and a problem in one category may often cross over to the other. An internal dispute about sexual harassment of a student by an employee, for instance, may be governed not only by the institution's internal policies on harassment but also by the external nondiscrimination requirements in Title IX of the Education Amendments of 1972 (see Section 8.5 of this book). Similarly, such a sexual harassment dispute may be heard and resolved not only through the institution's internal processes (such as a grievance mechanism), but also externally through the state or federal courts, the U.S. Department of Education, or a state civil rights agency. There are many examples of such crossovers throughout this book.

***1.3.2. Internal governance.*** As a keystone of their internal governance systems, colleges and universities create "internal law" (see Section 1.4.3 below) that delineates the authority of the institution and delegates portions of it to various institutional officers, managers, and directors, to departmental and school faculties, to the student body, and sometimes to captive or affiliated organizations. Equally important, internal law establishes the rights and responsibilities of individual members of the campus community and the processes by which these rights and responsibilities are enforced. Circumscribing this internal law is the "external law" (see Section 1.4.2 below) created by the federal government, state governments, and local governments through their own governance processes. Since the external law takes precedence over internal law when the two are in conflict, institutions' internal law must be framed against the backdrop of applicable external law.

Internal governance structures and processes may differ among institutions depending on their status as public, private secular, or private religious (as indicated in Section 1.3.1), and also depending on their size and the degree programs that they offer. The internal governance of a large research university, for instance, may differ from that of a small liberal arts college, which in turn may differ from that of a community college. Regardless of the type of institution, however, there is substantial commonality among the internal structures of U.S. institutions of higher education. In general, every institution has, at its head, a governing board that is usually called a board of trustees or (for some public institutions) a board of regents. Below this board is a chief executive officer, usually called the president or (for some public institutions) the chancellor. Below the president or chancellor are various other executive officers— for example, a chief business officer, a chief information officer, and a general counsel. In addition, there are typically numerous academic officers, chief of whom is a provost or vice president for academic affairs. Below the provost or vice president are the deans of the various schools, the department chairs, and the academic program directors (for instance, a director of distance learning, a director of internship programs, or a director of academic support programs). There are also managers and compliance officers, such as risk managers, facilities managers, affirmative action officers, and environmental or health and safety officers; and directors of particular functions, such as admissions, financial aid, and alumni affairs. These managers, officers, and directors may serve the entire institution or may serve only a particular school within the institution. In addition to these officers and administrators, there is usually a campus-wide organization that represents the interests of faculty members (such as a faculty senate) and a campus-wide organization that represents the interests of students (such as a student government association).

In addition to their involvement in a faculty senate or similar organization, faculty members are usually directly involved in the governance of individual departments and schools. Nationwide, faculty participation in governance has long been sufficiently established that internal governance is often referred to as "shared governance" or "shared institutional governance." In recent times, as many institutions have been reconsidering their governance structures, usually under pressure to attain greater efficiency and cost-effectiveness, the concept and the actual operation of shared governance have become a subject of renewed attention.

### *1.3.3. External governance.* The states are generally considered to be the primary external "governors" of higher education, at least in terms of legal theory. State governments are governments of general powers that typically have express authority over education built into their state constitutions. They have plenary authority to create, organize, support, and dissolve public higher educational institutions (see Section 11.2.1 of this book); and they have general police powers under which they charter and license private higher educational

institutions and recognize their authority to grant degrees (see Section 11.2.3). The states also promulgate state administrative procedure acts, open meetings and open records laws, and ethics codes that guide the operations of most state institutions. In addition, states have fiscal powers (especially taxation powers) and police powers regarding health and safety (including the power to create and enforce criminal law) that they apply to private institutions and that substantially affect their operations. And more generally, state courts establish and enforce the common law of contracts and torts that forms the foundation of the legal relationships between institutions and their faculty members, students, administrators, and staffs. (See Section 1.4.2.4 regarding common law and Section 1.4.4 regarding the role of the courts.)

The federal government, in contrast to the state governments, is a government of limited powers, and its constitutional powers, as enumerated in the federal Constitution, do not include any express power over education (Section 11.3.1 of this book). Through other express powers, however, such as its spending power, and through its implied powers,[3] the federal government exercises substantial governance authority over both public and private higher education. Under its express powers to raise and spend money, for example, Congress provides various types of federal aid to most public and private institutions in the United States, and under its implied powers Congress establishes conditions on how institutions spend and account for these funds. Also under its implied powers, Congress provides for federal recognition of private accrediting agencies—among the primary external private "governors" of education— whose accreditation judgments federal agencies rely on in determining institutions' eligibility for federal funds (see Section 12.1.2). The federal government also uses its spending power in other ways that directly affect the governance processes of public and private higher educational institutions. Examples include the federally required processes for accommodating students with disabilities (see Section 8.4); for keeping student records (see Section 7.8.1); for achieving racial and ethnic diversity through admissions and financial aid programs (see Sections 7.2.5 and 7.3.4); and for preventing and remedying sex discrimination and sexual harassment (see, for example, Sections 8.5 and 11.5.3).

Under other powers, and pursuing other priorities, the federal government also establishes processes for copyrighting works and patenting inventions of faculty members and others (see, for example, Section 11.3.2.3); for enrolling and monitoring foreign students (see Section 7.7.3); for resolving employment disputes involving unionized workers in private institutions (see Sections 4.3 and 5.3); and for resolving other employment disputes concerning health and safety, wages and hours, leaves of absence, unemployment compensation, retirement benefits, and discrimination. In all these arenas, federal law is supreme over state and local law, and federal law will preempt state and local law that is incompatible with the federal law.

---

[3] For an overview of Congress's express powers, and an explanation of its implied powers, see William Kaplin, *American Constitutional Law: An Overview, Analysis, and Integration* (Carolina Academic Press, 2004), chapter 6, section B. A through F.

Furthermore, the federal courts are the primary forum for resolving disputes about the scope of federal powers over education, and for enforcing the federal constitutional rights of faculty members, students, and others (see, for example, Sections 6.1 and 9.4).Thus, federal court judgments upholding federal powers or individuals' constitutional rights serve to alter, channel, and check the governance activities of higher education institutions, especially public institutions, in many important ways.

Local governments, in general, have much less involvement in the governance of higher education than either state governments or the federal government. The most important and pertinent aspect of local governance is the authority to establish, or to exercise control over, community colleges. But this local authority does not exist in all states, since state legislatures and state boards may have primary governance authority in some states. Local governments may also have some effect on institutions' internal governance—and may superimpose their own structures and processes upon institutions—in certain areas such as law enforcement, public health, zoning, and local taxation. But local governments' authority in such areas is usually delegated to it by the states, and is thus dependent on, and subject to being preempted by, state law (see Section 11.1.1).

External public governance structures and processes are more varied than those for internal governance—especially with regard to public institutions whose governance depends on the particular law of the state in which the institution is located (see Section 11.2.2). The statewide structures for higher education, public and private, also differ from state to state (see Section 11.2.1). What is common to most states is a state board (such as a state board of higher education) or state officer (such as a commissioner) that is responsible for public higher education statewide. This board or officer may also be responsible for private higher education statewide, or some other board or officer may have that responsibility. If a state has more than one statewide system of higher education, there may also be separate boards for each system (for example, the University of California system and the California State University system). In all of these variations, states are typically much more involved in external governance for public institutions than they are for private institutions.

At the federal level, there are also a variety of structures pertinent to the external governance of higher education, but they tend to encompass all postsecondary institutions, public or private, in much the same way. The most obvious and well known part of the federal structure is the U.S. Department of Education. In addition, there are numerous other cabinet-level departments and administrative agencies that have either spending authority or regulatory authority over higher education. The Department of Homeland Security (DHS), for instance, monitors foreign students while they are in the country to study (see Section 7.7.4); the Department of Health and Human Services (HHS) administers the Medicare program, which is important to institutions with medical centers; the Department of Labor administers various laws concerning wages, hours, and working conditions; the Occupational Safety and Health Administration (OSHA) administers workplace health and safety laws; several agencies have authority over certain research conducted by colleges and universities; and various other agencies, such as the National Institutes of Health (NIH) and the Department of Defense (DOD), provide research grants to institutions of higher education and grants or fellowships to faculty members and students.

At the local level, there is less public external governance than at the state and federal levels. The primary local structures are community college districts that have the status of local governments and community college boards of trustees that are appointed by or have some particular relationship with a county or city government. In some states, issues may arise concerning the respective authority of the community college board and the county legislative body (see Section 11.1.1). Some local administrative agencies, such as a human relations commission or an agency that issues permits for new construction, will also have influence over certain aspects of governance, as will local police forces.

Private external governance, like public external governance, also varies from institution to institution. Most postsecondary institutions, for example, are within the jurisdiction of several, often many, accrediting agencies. The agencies to which an institution is subject will depend on the region of the country in which the institution is located and the types of academic and professional programs that the institution offers. There are also various athletic conferences to which institutions may belong, depending on the level of competition, the status of athletics within the institution, and the region of the country; and there are several different national athletic associations that may govern an institution's intercollegiate competitions, as well as several different divisions with the primary association, the National Collegiate Athletic Association (NCAA) (see Section 12.1.3). Whether there is an outside sponsoring entity (especially a religious sponsor) with some role in governance will also depend on the particular institution, as will the existence and identity of labor unions that have established bargaining units. The influence that affiliated entities or grant-making foundations may have on institutional governance will also depend on the institution. One relative constant is the American Association of University Professors, which is concerned with all types of degree-granting postsecondary institutions nationwide.

### Section 1.4. Sources of Higher Education Law

**1.4.1. Overview.** The modern law of postsecondary education is not simply a product of what the courts say, or refuse to say, about educational problems. The modern law comes from a variety of sources, some "external" to the postsecondary institution and some "internal." The internal law, as described in Section 1.4.3 below, is at the core of the institution's operations. It is the law the institution creates for itself in its own exercise of institutional governance. The external law, as described in Section 1.4.2 below, is created and enforced by bodies external to the institution. It circumscribes the internal law, thus limiting the institution's options in the creation of internal law. (See Figure 1.2, "The External Law Circumscribing the Internal Law," in the General Introduction to this book, Section C).

## *1.4.2. External sources of law.*

### *1.4.2.1. Federal and state constitutions.* Constitutions are the fundamental source for determining the nature and extent of governmental powers. Constitutions are also the fundamental source of guarantees of individual rights that limit government powers and protect citizens generally, including members of the academic community. The federal Constitution is by far the most prominent and important source of individual liberties. The First Amendment protections for speech, press, and religion are often litigated in major court cases involving postsecondary institutions, as are the Fourteenth Amendment guarantees of due process and equal protection. As explained in Section 1.5, these federal constitutional provisions apply differently to public and to private institutions.

The federal Constitution has no provision that specifically refers to education. State constitutions, however, often have specific provisions establishing state colleges and universities or state college and university systems, and occasionally community college systems. State constitutions may also have provisions establishing a state department of education or other governing authority with some responsibility for postsecondary education.

The federal Constitution is the highest legal authority that exists. No other law, either state or federal, may conflict with its provisions. Thus, although a state constitution is the highest state law authority, and all state statutes and other state laws must be consistent with it, any of its provisions that conflict with the federal Constitution will be subject to invalidation by the courts. It is not considered a conflict, however, if state constitutions establish more expansive individual rights than those guaranteed by parallel provisions of the federal Constitution (see the discussion of state constitutions in Section 1.5.3).

An abridged version of the federal Constitution, highlighting provisions of particular interest to higher education, is contained in Appendix A of this book.

### *1.4.2.2. Statutes.* Statutes are enacted both by states and by the federal government. Ordinances, which are in effect local statutes, are enacted by local legislative bodies, such as county and city councils. While laws at all three levels may refer specifically to postsecondary education or postsecondary institutions, the greatest amount of such specific legislation is written by the states. Examples include laws establishing and regulating state postsecondary institutions or systems, laws creating statewide coordinating councils for postsecondary education, and laws providing for the licensure of postsecondary institutions (see Section 11.2.3). At the federal level, the major examples of such specific legislation are the federal grant-in-aid statutes, such as the Higher Education Act of 1965 (see Section 11.4). At all three levels, there is also a considerable amount of legislation that applies to postsecondary institutions in common with other entities in the jurisdiction. Examples are the federal tax laws and civil rights laws (see Section 11.5), state unemployment compensation and workers' compensation laws, and local zoning and tax laws. All of these state and federal statutes and local ordinances are subject to the higher constitutional authorities.

Federal statutes, for the most part, are collected and codified in the *United States Code* (U.S.C.) or *United States Code Annotated* (U.S.C.A.). State statutes are similarly gathered in state codifications, such as the *Minnesota Statutes Annotated* (Minn. Stat. Ann.) or the *Annotated Code of Maryland* (Md. Code Ann.). Federal and state codifications are available in many law libraries or online. Local ordinances are usually collected in local ordinance books, but those may be difficult to find and may not be organized as systematically as state and federal codifications are. Moreover, local ordinance books—and state codes as well—may be considerably out of date. In order to be sure that the statutory law on a particular point is up to date, one must check what are called the "session" or "slip" laws of the jurisdiction for the current year or sometimes the preceding year. These laws are usually issued by a designated state or local office in the order in which the laws are passed; many law libraries maintain current session laws of individual states in loose-leaf volumes and may maintain similar collections of current local ordinances for area jurisdictions.

**1.4.2.3. *Administrative rules and regulations.*** The most rapidly expanding sources of postsecondary education law are the directives of state and federal administrative agencies. The number and size of these bodies are increasing, and the number and complexity of their directives are easily keeping pace. In recent years the rules applicable to postsecondary institutions, especially those issued at the federal level, have often generated controversy in the education world, which must negotiate a substantial regulatory maze in order to receive federal grants or contracts or to comply with federal employment laws and other requirements in areas of federal concern.

Administrative agency directives are often published as regulations that have the status of law and are as binding as a statute would be. But agency directives do not always have such status. Thus, in order to determine their exact status, administrators must check with legal counsel when problems arise.

Federal administrative agencies publish both *proposed regulations*, which are issued to elicit public comment, and *final regulations*, which have the status of law. These agencies also publish other types of documents, such as policy interpretations of statutes or regulations, notices of meetings, and invitations to submit grant proposals. Such regulations and documents appear upon issuance in the *Federal Register* (Fed. Reg.), a daily government publication. Final regulations appearing in the *Federal Register* are eventually republished—without the agency's explanatory commentary, which sometimes accompanies the *Federal Register* version—in the *Code of Federal Regulations* (C.F.R.).

State administrative agencies have various ways of publicizing their rules and regulations, sometimes in government publications comparable to the *Federal Register* or the *Code of Federal Regulations*. Generally speaking, however, administrative rules and regulations are harder to find and are less likely to be codified at the state level than at the federal level.

Besides promulgating rules and regulations (called "rule making"), administrative agencies often also have the authority to enforce their rules by applying them to particular parties and issuing decisions regarding these parties' compliance with the rules (called "adjudication"). The extent of an administrative agency's adjudicatory authority, as well as its rule-making powers, depends on the relevant statutes that establish and empower the agency. An agency's adjudicatory decisions must be consistent with its own rules and regulations and with any applicable statutory or constitutional provisions. Legal questions concerning the validity of an adjudicatory decision are usually reviewable in the courts. Examples of such decisions at the federal level include a National Labor Relations Board decision on an unfair labor practice charge or, in another area, a Department of Education decision on whether to terminate funds to a federal grantee for noncompliance with statutory or administrative requirements. Examples at the state level include the determination of a state human relations commission on a complaint charging violation of individual rights, or the decision of a state workers' compensation board in a case involving workers' compensation benefits. Administrative agencies may or may not officially publish compilations of their adjudicatory decisions.

***1.4.2.4. State common law.*** Sometimes courts issue opinions that interpret neither a statute, nor an administrative rule or regulation, nor a constitutional provision. In breach of contract disputes, for instance, the applicable precedents are typically those the courts have created themselves. These decisions create what is called American common law. Common law, in short, is judge-made law rather than law that originates from constitutions or from legislatures or administrative agencies. Contract law (see, for example, Sections 4.2 and 7.1.3) is a critical component of this common law. Tort law (Sections 3.2 and 4.4.2) and agency law (Sections 3.1 and 3.3) are comparably important. Such common law is developed primarily by the state courts and thus varies somewhat from state to state.

***1.4.2.5. Foreign and international law.*** In addition to all the U.S., or domestic, sources of law noted, the laws of other countries (**foreign law**) and international law have become increasingly important to postsecondary education. This source of law may come into play, for instance, when the institution sends faculty members or students on trips to foreign countries, or engages in business transactions with companies or institutions in foreign countries (see Section 12.2.1), or seeks to establish educational programs in other countries. (For a discussion of potential liability for **injuries** that may occur in study abroad programs, see Section 3.2.2.4.)

Just as business is now global, so, in many respects, is higher education. For example, U.S. institutions of higher education are entering business partnerships with for-profit or nonprofit entities in other countries. If the institution enters into contracts with local suppliers, other educational institutions, or financial institutions, the law of the country in which the services are provided will very likely control unless the parties specify otherwise. Such partnerships may raise choice-of-law issues if a dispute arises. If the contract between the U.S. institution and its foreign business partner does not specify that the contract will be interpreted under U.S. law, the institution may find itself subject to litigation in another country, under the requirements of laws that may be very different from those in the United States.

If the institution operates an academic program in another country and hires local nationals to manage the program, or to provide other services, the institution must comply with the employment and other relevant laws of that country (as well as, in many cases, U.S. employment law). Employment laws of other nations may differ in important respects from U.S. law. For example, some European countries sharply limit an employer's ability to use independent contractors, and terminating an employee may be far more complicated than in the United States. Pension and other social security taxes are higher in many nations than in the United States, and penalties for noncompliance may be substantial. Tax treaties between the United States and foreign nations may exempt some compensation paid to faculty, students, or others from taxation. Definitions of fellowships or scholarships may differ outside the borders of the United States, which could affect their taxability. And international agreements and treaties, such as the World Trade Organization's Agreement on Trade-Related Aspects of Intellectual Property Rights, have important implications for colleges and universities.

### *1.4.3. Internal sources of law.*

***1.4.3.1. Institutional rules and regulations.*** The rules and regulations promulgated by individual institutions are also a source of postsecondary education law. These rules and regulations are subject to all the external sources of law listed in Section 1.4.2 and must be consistent with all the legal requirements of those sources that apply to the particular institution and to the subject matter of the internal rule or regulation. Courts may consider some institutional rules and regulations to be part of the faculty-institution contract or the student-institution contract (see Section 1.4.3.2), in which case these rules and regulations are enforceable by contract actions in the courts. Some rules and regulations of public institutions may also be legally enforceable as administrative regulations of a government agency (see Section 1.4.2.3). Even where such rules are not legally enforceable by courts or outside agencies, a postsecondary institution will likely want to follow and enforce them internally, to achieve fairness and consistency in its dealings with the campus community.

Institutions may establish adjudicatory bodies with authority to interpret and enforce institutional rules and regulations (see, for example, Section 9.1). When such decision-making bodies operate within the scope of their authority under institutional rules and regulations, their decisions also become part of the governing law in the institution; and courts may regard these decisions as part of the faculty-institution or student-institution contract, at least in the sense that they become part of the applicable custom and usage (see Section 1.4.3.3) in the institution.

***1.4.3.2. Institutional contracts.*** Postsecondary institutions have contractual relationships of various kinds with faculties (see Section 5.2), staff (see Section

4.2), students (see Section 7.1.3), government agencies (see Section 11.4.1), and outside parties such as construction firms, suppliers, research sponsors from private industry, and other institutions. These contracts create binding legal arrangements between the contracting parties, enforceable by either party in case of the other's breach. In this sense a contract is a source of law governing a particular subject matter and relationship. When a question arises concerning a subject matter or relationship covered by a contract, the first legal source to consult is usually the contract's terms.

Contracts, especially with faculty members and students, may incorporate some institutional rules and regulations (see Section 1.4.3.1), so that these become part of the contract terms. Contracts are interpreted and enforced according to the common law of contracts (Section 1.4.2.4) and any applicable statute or administrative rule or regulation (Sections 1.4.2.2 and 1.4.2.3). Contracts may also be interpreted with reference to academic custom and usage.

**1.4.3.3. Academic custom and usage.** By far the most amorphous source of postsecondary education law, academic custom and usage comprises the particular established practices and understandings within particular institutions. Academic custom and usage differs from institutional rules and regulations (Section 1.4.3.1) in that custom and usage is not necessarily a written source of law and, even if written, is far more informal; custom and usage may be found, for instance, in policy statements from speeches, internal memoranda, and other such documentation within the institution.

This source of postsecondary education law, sometimes called "campus common law," is important in particular institutions because it helps define what the various members of the academic community expect of one another as well as of the institution itself. Whenever the institution has internal decision-making processes, such as a faculty grievance process or a student disciplinary procedure, campus common law can be an important guide for decision making. In this sense, campus common law does not displace formal institutional rules and regulations but supplements them, helping the decision maker and the parties in situations where rules and regulations are ambiguous or do not exist for the particular point at issue.

Academic custom and usage is also important in another, and broader, sense: it can supplement contractual understandings between the institution and its faculty and between the institution and its students. Whenever the terms of such a contractual relationship are unclear, courts may look to academic custom and usage in order to interpret the terms of the contract. In *Perry v. Sindermann*, 408 U.S. 593 (1972), the U.S. Supreme Court placed its imprimatur on this concept of academic custom and usage when it analyzed a professor's claim that he was entitled to tenure at Odessa College:

> The law of contracts in most, if not all, jurisdictions long has employed a
> process by which agreements, though not formalized in writing, may be
> "implied" (3 *Corbin on Contracts*, §§ 561–672A). Explicit contractual provisions

may be supplemented by other agreements implied from "the promisor's words and conduct in the light of the surrounding circumstances" (§ 562). And "the meaning of [the promisor's] words and acts is found by relating them to the usage of the past" (§ 562).

A teacher, like the respondent, who has held his position for a number of years might be able to show from the circumstances of this service—and from other relevant facts—that he has a legitimate claim of entitlement to job tenure. Just as this Court has found there to be a "common law of a particular industry or of a particular plant" that may supplement a collective bargaining agreement (*United Steelworkers v. Warrior & Gulf Nav. Co.*, 363 U.S. 574, 579 . . . (1960)), so there may be an unwritten "common law" in a particular university that certain employees shall have the equivalent of tenure [408 U.S. at 602].

*Sindermann* was a constitutional due process case, and academic custom and usage was relevant to determining whether the professor had a **property interest** in continued employment that would entitle him to a hearing prior to nonrenewal (see Section 5.7.2). Academic custom and usage is also important in contract cases in which courts, arbitrators, or grievance committees must interpret provisions of the faculty-institution contract (see Sections 5.2 and 5.3) or the student-institution contract (see Section 7.1.3). In *Strank v. Mercy Hospital of Johnstown*, 117 A.2d 697 (Pa. 1955), a student nurse who had been dismissed from nursing school sought to require the school to award her transfer credits for the two years' work she had successfully completed. The student alleged that she had "oral arrangements with the school at the time she entered, later confirmed in part by writing and carried out by both parties for a period of two years, . . . [and] that these arrangements and understandings imposed upon defendant the legal duty to give her proper credits for work completed." When the school argued that the court had no jurisdiction over such a claim, the court responded: "[Courts] have jurisdiction . . . for the enforcement of obligations whether arising under **express contracts**, written or oral, or **implied contracts**, including those in which a duty may have resulted from long recognized and established customs and usages, as in this case, perhaps, between an educational institution and its students" (117 A.2d at 698). Similarly, in *Krotkoff v. Goucher College*, 585 F.2d 675 (4th Cir. 1978), the court rejected another professor's claim that "national" academic custom and usage protected her from termination of tenure due to financial exigency.

Asserting that academic custom and usage is relevant to a faculty member's contract claim may help the faculty member survive a motion for **summary judgment**. In *Bason v. American University*, 414 A.2d 522 (D.C. 1980), a law professor denied tenure asserted that he had a contractual right to be informed of his progress toward tenure, which had not occurred. The court reversed a trial court's summary judgment ruling for the employer, stating that "resolution of the matter involves not only a consideration of the *Faculty Manual*, but of the University's 'customs and practices.' . . . The existence of an issue of custom and practice also precludes summary judgment" (414 A.2d at 525). The same court stated, in *Howard University v. Best*, 547 A.2d 144 (D.C. 1988), "[i]n order for a custom and practice to be binding on the parties to a transaction, it must be proved that the custom is definite, uniform, and well known, and it must be established by 'clear and satisfactory evidence.'" **Plaintiffs** are rarely successful, however, in attempting to argue that academic custom and usage supplants written institutional rules or a reasonable or consistent interpretation of such rules (see, for example, *Brown v. George Washington University*, 802 A.2d 382 (D.C. App. 2002)).

Custom and usage may also sometimes apply to outsiders who are not members of the campus community. In *Gilles v. Blanchard*, 477 F.3d 466 (7th Cir. 2007), for example, a federal appellate court cited a university's unwritten custom of barring all "uninvited" individuals from speaking on the "library lawn." An itinerant preacher, Gilles, had attempted to preach on the library lawn of the Vincennes University, a public university. The university cited its policy of requiring that anyone speaking on campus property be invited by a faculty member or student; Gilles had not been invited to speak. Rejecting Gilles's First Amendment claim, the court noted that the university's custom and practice was content-neutral and thus not a violation of Gilles's right to free speech.

**1.4.4. The role of case law.** Every year, the state and federal courts reach decisions in hundreds of cases involving postsecondary education. Opinions are issued and published for many of these decisions. Many more decisions are reached and opinions rendered each year in cases that do not involve postsecondary education but do elucidate important established legal principles with potential application to postsecondary education. Judicial opinions (case law) may interpret federal, state, or local statutes. They may also interpret the rules and regulations of administrative agencies. Therefore, in order to understand the meaning of statutes, rules, and regulations, one must understand the case law that has construed them. Judicial opinions may also interpret federal or state constitutional provisions and may sometimes determine the constitutionality of particular statutes or rules and regulations. A statute, rule, or regulation that is found to be unconstitutional because it conflicts with a particular provision of the federal or a state constitution is void and no longer enforceable by the courts. In addition to these functions, judicial opinions also frequently develop and apply the common law of the jurisdiction in which the court sits. And judicial opinions may interpret postsecondary institutions' "internal law" (Section 1.4.3) and measure its validity against the backdrop of the constitutional provisions, statutes, and regulations (the "external law"; Section 1.4.2) that binds institutions.

Besides their opinions in postsecondary education cases, courts issue numerous opinions each year in cases concerning elementary and secondary education (see, for example, the *Wood v. Strickland* case in Section 4.4.4 and the *Goss v. Lopez* case in Section 9.3.2). Insights and principles from these cases are often transferable to postsecondary education. But elementary or secondary precedents cannot be applied routinely or uncritically to postsecondary education. Differences in the structures, missions, and clienteles of these levels of education may make precedents from one level inapplicable to the other or may require that the precedent's application be modified to account for the differences. (For an example of a court's application of precedent developed in the secondary education context to a higher education issue, see the discussion of *Hosty v. Carter* in Section 10.3.3.)

A court's decision has the effect of binding precedent only within its own jurisdiction. Thus, at the state level, a particular decision may be binding either on the entire state or only on a subdivision of the state, depending on the court's jurisdiction. At the federal level, decisions by district courts and appellate courts are binding within a particular district or region of the country, while decisions of the U.S. Supreme Court are binding precedent throughout the country. Since the Supreme Court's decisions are the supreme law of the land, they bind all lower federal courts as well as all state courts, even the highest court of the state.

***1.4.5. Researching case law.*** The important opinions of state and federal courts are published periodically and collected in bound volumes that are available in most law libraries. For state court decisions, besides each state's official reports, there is the National Reporter System, a series of regional case reports comprising the (1) *Atlantic Reporter* (cited A., A.2d, or A.3d), (2) *North Eastern Reporter* (N.E. or N.E.2d), (3) *North Western Reporter* (N.W. or N.W.2d), (4) *Pacific Reporter* (P., P.2d, or P.3d), (5) *South Eastern Reporter* (S.E. or S.E.2d), (6) *South Western Reporter* (S.W., S.W.2d, or S.W.3d), and (7) *Southern Reporter* (So., So.2d, or So.3d). Each regional reporter publishes opinions of the courts in that particular region. There are also special reporters in the National Reporter System for the states of New York (*New York Supplement*, cited N.Y.S.) and California (*California Reporter*, cited Cal. Rptr.).

In the federal system, U.S. Supreme Court opinions are published in the *United States Supreme Court Reports* (U.S.), the official reporter, as well as in two unofficial reporters, the *Supreme Court Reporter* (S. Ct.) and the *United States Supreme Court Reports—Lawyers' Edition* (L. Ed. or L. Ed. 2d). Supreme Court opinions are also available, shortly after issuance, in the loose-leaf format of *United States Law Week* (U.S.L.W.), which also contains digests of other recent selected opinions from federal and state courts. Opinions of the U.S. Courts of Appeals are published in the *Federal Reporter* (F., F.2d, or F.3d). U.S. District Court opinions are published in the *Federal Supplement* (F. Supp. or F. Supp. 2d) or, for decisions regarding federal rules of judicial procedure, in *Federal Rules Decisions* (F.R.D.). All of these sources, as well as those for state court decisions, are online in both the Westlaw and LexisNexis legal research databases. Opinions are also available online, in most cases, from the courts themselves. For example, opinions of the U.S. Supreme Court are available from the Court's Web site at http://www.supremecourtus.gov/opinions/opinions.html. The Federal Judicial Center's Web site (http://www.uscourts.gov/links.html) provides links to the Web sites of the U.S. Courts of Appeals and the U.S. District Courts. There are also other free Web sites that provide access to court opinions. Two good examples are FindLaw (http://www.findlaw.com) and Cornell Law School's Legal Information Institute (http://www.law.cornell.edu).

## Section 1.5. The Public-Private Dichotomy

***1.5.1. Overview.*** Historically, higher education has roots in both the public and the private sectors, although the strength of each one's influence has varied over time. Sometimes following and sometimes leading this historical development, the law has tended to support and reflect the fundamental dichotomy between public and private education.

A forerunner of the present university was the Christian seminary. Yale was an early example. Dartmouth began as a school to teach Christianity to the Indians. Similar schools sprang up throughout the American colonies. Though often established through private charitable trusts, they were also chartered by the colony, received some financial support from the colony, and were subject to its regulation. Thus, colonial colleges were often a mixture of public and private activity. The nineteenth century witnessed a gradual decline in governmental involvement with sectarian schools. As states began to establish their own institutions, the public-private dichotomy emerged. In recent years this dichotomy has again faded, as state and federal governments have provided larger amounts of financial support to private institutions, many of which are now secular.

Although **private institutions** have always been more expensive to attend than **public institutions,** private higher education has been a vital and influential force in American intellectual history. The private school can cater to special interests that a public one often cannot serve because of legal or political constraints. Private education thus draws strength from "the very possibility of doing something different than government can do, of creating an institution free to make choices government cannot—even seemingly arbitrary ones— without having to provide a justification that will be examined in a court of law" (H. Friendly, *The Dartmouth College Case and the Public-Private Penumbra* (Humanities Research Center, University of Texas, 1969), 30).

Though modern-day private institutions are not always free from examination "in a court of law," the law often does treat public and private institutions differently. These differences underlie much of the discussion in this book. They are critically important in assessing the law's impact on the roles of particular institutions and the duties of their administrators.

Whereas public institutions are usually subject to the plenary authority of the government that creates them, the law protects private institutions from such extensive governmental control. Government can usually alter, enlarge, or completely abolish its public institutions (see Section 11.2.2 of this book); private institutions, however, can obtain their own perpetual charters of incorporation, and, since the famous *Dartmouth College* case (*Trustees of Dartmouth College v. Woodward*, 17 U.S. 518 (1819)), government has been prohibited from impairing such charters. In that case, the U.S. Supreme Court turned back New Hampshire's attempt to assume control of Dartmouth by finding that such action would violate the Constitution's contracts clause. Subsequently, in three other landmark cases—*Meyer v. Nebraska*, 262 U.S. 390 (1923); *Pierce v. Society of Sisters*, 268 U.S. 510 (1925); and *Farrington v. Tokushige*, 273 U.S. 284 (1927)—the

Supreme Court used the **due process clause** to strike down unreasonable governmental interference with teaching and learning in private schools.

Nonetheless, government does retain substantial authority to regulate private education. But—whether for legal, political, or policy reasons—state governments usually regulate private institutions less than they regulate public institutions. The federal government, on the other hand, has tended to apply its regulations comparably to both public and private institutions, or, bowing to considerations of **federalism**, has regulated private institutions while leaving public institutions to the states.

In addition to these differences in regulatory patterns, the law makes a second and more pervasive distinction between public and private institutions: public institutions and their officers are fully subject to the constraints of the federal Constitution, whereas private institutions and their officers are not. Because the Constitution was designed to limit only the exercise of government power, it does not prohibit private individuals or corporations from impinging on such freedoms as free speech, equal protection, and due process. Thus, *insofar as the federal Constitution is concerned*, a private university can engage in private acts of discrimination, prohibit student protests, or expel a student without affording the procedural safeguards that a public university is constitutionally required to provide.

### 1.5.2. The state action doctrine.

**1.5.2.1. When private postsecondary institutions may be engaged in state action.** Before a court will require that a postsecondary institution comply with the individual rights requirements in the federal Constitution, it must first determine that the institution's challenged action is **state action.**[4] When suit is filed under 42 U.S.C. § 1983 **(Section 1983)** (see Sections 3.4 and 4.4.4 of this book), the question is rephrased as whether the challenged action was taken "under color of" state law, an inquiry that is the functional equivalent of the state action inquiry (see, for example, *West v. Atkins*, 487 U.S. 42 (1988)). Although the state action (or color of law) determination is essentially a matter of distinguishing public institutions from private institutions, and the public parts of an institution from the private parts—or more generally, distinguishing public "actors" from private "actors"—these distinctions do not necessarily depend on traditional notions of public or private. Due to varying patterns of government assistance and involvement, a continuum exists, ranging from the obvious public institution (such as a tax-supported state university) to the obvious private institution (such as a religious seminary). The gray area between these poles is a subject of continuing debate about how much the government must be involved in the affairs of a "private" institution or one of its programs before it will be considered "public" for purposes of the state action doctrine.

---

[4]Although this inquiry has arisen mainly with regard to the federal Constitution, it may also arise in applying state constitutional guarantees. See, for example, *Stone by Stone v. Cornell University*, 510 N.Y.S.2d 313 (N.Y. 1987) (no state action).

As the U.S. Supreme Court noted in the landmark case of *Burton v. Wilmington Parking Authority*, 365 U.S. 715, 722 (1961), "Only by sifting facts and weighing circumstances can the non-obvious involvement of the State in private conduct be attributed its true significance."

Since the early 1970s, the trend of the U.S. Supreme Court's opinions has been to trim back the state action concept, making it less likely that courts will find state action to exist in particular cases. The leading education case in this line of cases is *Rendell-Baker v. Kohn*, 457 U.S. 830 (1982). Another leading case, *Blum v. Yaretsky*, 457 U.S. 991 (1982), was decided the same day as *Rendell-Baker* and reinforces its narrowing effect on the law.

*Rendell-Baker* was a suit brought by teachers at a private high school who had been discharged as a result of their opposition to school policies. They sued the school and its director, Kohn, alleging that the discharges violated their federal constitutional rights to free speech and due process. The issue before the Court was whether the private school's discharge of the teachers was "state action" and thus subject to the federal Constitution's individual rights requirements.

The defendant school specialized in education for students who had drug, alcohol, or behavioral problems or other special needs. Nearly all students were referred by local public schools or by the drug rehabilitation division of the state's department of health. The school received funds for student tuition from the local public school systems from which the students came and were reimbursed by the state department of health for services provided to students referred by the department. The school also received funds from other state and federal agencies. Virtually all the school's income, therefore, was derived from government funding. The school was also subject to state regulations on various matters, such as record keeping and student-teacher ratios, and requirements concerning services provided under its contracts with the local school boards and the state health department. Few of these regulations and requirements, however, related to personnel policy.

The teachers argued that the school had sufficient contacts with the state and local governments so that the school's discharge decision should be considered state action. The Court disagreed, holding that neither the government funding nor the government regulation was sufficient to make the school's discharge of the teachers state action. As to the funding, the Court analogized the school's situation to that of a private corporation whose business depends heavily on government contracts to build "roads, bridges, dams, ships, or submarines" for the government, but is not considered to be engaged in state action. And as to the regulation, it did not address personnel matters. Therefore, said the court, state regulation was insufficient to transform a private personnel decision into state action.

The Court also rejected two other arguments of the teachers: that the school was engaged in state action because it performed a "public function" and that the school had a "symbiotic relationship" with—that is, was engaged in a "joint venture" with—government, which constitutes state action under the Court's earlier case of *Burton v. Wilmington Parking Authority*, 365 U.S. 715 (1961).

As to the former argument, the Court reasoned in *Rendall-Baker* that the appropriate inquiry was whether the function performed has been "traditionally the *exclusive* prerogative of the state" (quoting *Jackson v. Metropolitan Edison Co.*, 419 U.S. at 353). The court explained that the state never had exclusive jurisdiction over the education of students with special needs and had only recently assumed the responsibility to educate them.

As to the teachers' second argument, the Court concluded simply that "the school's fiscal relationship with the state is not different from that of many contractors performing services for the government. No symbiotic relationship such as existed in *Burton* exists here."

Having rejected all the teachers' arguments, the Court, by a 7-to-2 vote, concluded that the school's discharge decisions did not constitute state action. It therefore affirmed the lower court's dismissal of the teachers' lawsuit.

In the years preceding *Rendell-Baker*, courts and commentators had dissected the state action concept in various ways. At the core, however, three main approaches to making state action determinations had emerged: the "nexus" approach, the "symbiotic relationship" approach, and the "public function" approach. The Court in *Rendall-Baker* evaluated each of these approaches. The first approach, *nexus*, focuses on the state's involvement in the particular action being challenged and whether there is a sufficient "nexus" between that action and the state. According to the foundational case for this approach, *Jackson v. Metropolitan Edison Co.*, 419 U.S. 345 (1974), "the inquiry must be whether there is a sufficiently close nexus between the State and the challenged action of the [private] entity so that the action of the latter may be fairly treated as that of the State itself" (419 U.S. at 351 (1974)). Generally, courts will find such a nexus only when the state has compelled or directed, or fostered or encouraged, the challenged action.

The second approach, usually called the "symbiotic relationship" or "joint venturer" approach, has a broader focus than the nexus approach, encompassing the full range of contacts between the state and the private entity. According to the foundational case for this approach, *Burton v. Wilmington Parking Authority*, 365 U.S. 715 (1961), the inquiry is whether "the State has so far insinuated itself into a position of interdependence with [the institution] that it must be recognized as a joint participant in the challenged activity" (365 U.S. at 725). When the state is so substantially involved in the whole of the private entity's activities, it is not necessary to prove that the state was specifically involved in (or had a "nexus" with) the particular activity challenged in the lawsuit.

The third approach, "public function," focuses on the particular function being performed by the private entity. The Court has very narrowly defined the type of function that will give rise to a state action finding. It is not sufficient that the private entity provide services to the public, or that the services are considered essential, or that government also provides such services. Rather, according to the *Jackson* case (above), the function must be one that is "traditionally exclusively reserved to the State . . . [and] traditionally associated with sovereignty" (419 U.S. at 352–53) in order to support a state action finding.

In *Rendell-Baker*, the Court considered all three of these approaches, specifically finding that the high school's termination of the teachers did not constitute state action under any of the approaches. In its analysis, as set out above, the Court first rejected a nexus argument; then rejected a public function argument; and finally rejected a symbiotic relationship argument. The Court narrowly defined all three approaches, consistent with other cases it had decided since the early 1970s. Lower courts following *Rendell-Baker* and other cases in this line have continued to recognize the same three approaches, but only two of them—the nexus approach and the symbiotic relationship approach—have had meaningful application to postsecondary education. The other approach, public function, has essentially dropped out of the picture in light of the Court's sweeping declaration that education programs cannot meet the restrictive definition of public function in the *Jackson* case.[5] Various lower court cases subsequent to *Rendell-Baker* illustrate the application of the nexus and symbiotic relationship approaches to higher education, and also illustrate how *Rendell-Baker, Blum v. Yaretsky* (*Rendell-Baker*'s companion case (see above)), and other Supreme Court cases such as *Jackson v. Metropolitan Edison* (see above) have served to insulate postsecondary institutions from state action findings and the resultant application of federal constitutional constraints to their activities. The following cases are instructive examples.

In *Albert v. Carovano*, 824 F.2d 1333, *modified on rehearing*, 839 F.2d 871 (2d Cir. 1987), *panel opinion vacated*, 851 F.2d 561 (2d Cir. 1988) (*en banc*), a federal appellate court, after protracted litigation, refused to extend the state action doctrine to the disciplinary actions of Hamilton College, a private institution. The suit was brought by students whom the college had disciplined under authority of its policy guide on freedom of expression and maintenance of public order. The college had promulgated this guide in compliance with the New York Education Law, Section 6450 (the Henderson Act), which requires colleges to adopt rules for maintaining public order on campus and file them with the state. The trial court dismissed the students' complaint on the grounds that they could not prove that the college's disciplinary action was state action. After an appellate court panel reversed, the full appellate court affirmed the pertinent part of the trial court's dismissal. The court (*en banc*) concluded:

> [A]ppellants' theory of state action suffers from a fatal flaw. That theory assumes that either Section 6450 or the rules Hamilton filed pursuant to that statute constitute "a rule of conduct imposed by the state" [citing *Lugar v. Edmondson Oil Co.*, 457 U.S. 922, 937–39 (1982)]. Yet nothing in either the legislation or those rules required that these appellants be suspended for

---

[5]This recognition that education, having a history of strong roots in the private sector, does not fit within the public function category, was evident well before *Rendell-Baker*; see, for example, *Greenya v. George Washington University*, 512 F.2d 556, 561 (D.C. Cir. 1975). For the most extensive work-up of this issue in the case law, see *State v. Schmid*, 423 A.2d 615, 622–24 (majority opinion), 633–36 (Pashman, J., concurring and dissenting), 639–40 (Schreiber, J., concurring in result) (N.J. 1980). For another substantial and more recent work-up, see *Mentavlos v. Anderson*, 249 F.3d 301, 314–18 (4th Cir. 2001), discussed below in this subsection.

occupying Buttrick Hall. Moreover, it is undisputed that the state's role under the Henderson Act has been merely to keep on file rules submitted by colleges and universities. The state has never sought to compel schools to enforce these rules and has never even inquired about such enforcement [851 F.2d at 568].

Finding that the state had not undertaken to regulate the disciplinary policies of private colleges in the state, and that the administrators of Hamilton College did not believe that the Henderson Act required them to take particular disciplinary actions, the court refused to find state action.

In *Smith v. Duquesne University*, 612 F. Supp. 72 (W.D. Pa. 1985), *affirmed without opinion*, 787 F.2d 583 (3d Cir. 1986), a graduate student challenged his expulsion on due process and equal protection grounds, asserting that Duquesne's action constituted state action. The court used both the symbiotic relationship and the nexus approaches to determine that Duquesne was not a state actor. Regarding the former, the court distinguished Duquesne's relationship with the state of Pennsylvania from that of Temple University and the University of Pittsburgh, which were determined to be state actors in *Krynicky v. University of Pittsburgh* and *Schier v. Temple University*, 742 F.2d 94 (3d Cir. 1984). There was no statutory relationship between the state and the university, the state did not review the university's expenditures, and the university was not required to submit the types of financial reports to the state that state-related institutions, such as Temple and Pitt, were required to submit. Thus the state's relationship with Duquesne was "so tenuous as to lead to no other conclusion but that Duquesne is a private institution and not a state actor" (612 F. Supp. at 77–78).

Regarding the latter approach (the nexus test), the court determined that the state could not "be deemed responsible for the specific act" complained of by the plaintiff. The court characterized the expulsion decision as "an academic judgment made by a purely private institution according to its official university policy" (612 F. Supp. at 78), a decision in which the government had played no part.

*Rendell-Baker* and later cases, however, do not create an impenetrable protective barrier for ostensibly private postsecondary institutions. In particular, there may be situations in which government is directly involved in some challenged activity—in contrast to the absence of government involvement in the actions challenged in *Rendell-Baker* and the lower court cases above. Such involvement may supply the "nexus" that was missing in these cases. In *Doe v. Gonzaga University*, 24 P.3d 390 (Wash. 2001), for example, the court upheld a jury verdict that a private university and its teacher certification specialist were engaged in action "under color of state law" (that is, state action) when completing state certification forms for students applying to be certified as teachers. The private institution and the state certification office, said the court, were cooperating in "joint action" regarding the certification process.[6] Moreover, there may be situations, unlike *Rendell-Baker* and the cases above, in which government officials by virtue of their offices sit on, or nominate others for, an institution's board of trustees. Such involvement, perhaps in combination with other "contacts" between the state and the institution, may create a "symbiotic relationship" that constitutes state action, as the court held in *Krynicky v. University of Pittsburgh* and *Schier v. Temple University*, above.

*Craft v. Vanderbilt University*, 940 F. Supp. 1185 (M.D. Tenn. 1996), provides another instructive example of how the symbiotic relationship approach might still be used to find state action. A federal district court ruled that Vanderbilt University's participation with the state government in experiments using radiation in the 1940s might constitute state action for purposes of a civil rights action against the university. The plaintiffs were individuals who, without their knowledge or consent, were involved in these experiments, which were conducted at a Vanderbilt clinic in conjunction with the Rockefeller Foundation and the Tennessee Department of Public Health. The plaintiffs alleged that the university and its codefendants infringed their due process liberty interests by withholding information regarding the experiment from them. Using the symbiotic relationship approach, the court determined that the project was funded by the state and that state officials were closely involved in approving research projects and making day-to-day management decisions. Since a jury could find on these facts that the university's participation with the state in these experiments created a symbiotic relationship, summary judgment for the university was inappropriate. Further proceedings were required to determine whether Vanderbilt and the state were sufficiently "intertwined" with respect to the research project to hold Vanderbilt to constitutional standards under the state action doctrine.

Over the years since *Rendell-Baker*, the U.S. Supreme Court has, of course, also considered various other state action cases. One of its major decisions was in another education case, *Brentwood Academy v. Tennessee Secondary School Athletic Association*, 531 U.S. 288 (2001). *Brentwood* is particularly important because the Court advanced a new test—a fourth approach—for determining when a private entity may be found to be a state actor. The defendant Association, a private nonprofit membership organization composed of public and private high schools, regulated interscholastic sports throughout the state. Brentwood Academy, a private parochial high school and a member of the Association, had mailed athletic information to the homes of prospective student athletes. The Association's board of control, composed primarily of public school district officials and Tennessee State Board of Education officials, determined that the mailing violated the Association's recruitment rules; it therefore placed Brentwood on probation. Brentwood claimed that this action violated its equal protection and free speech rights under the federal Constitution. As a predicate to its constitutional claims, Brentwood argued that, because of the significant involvement of state officials and public school officials in the Association's operations, the Association was engaged in state action when it enforced its rules.

By a 5-to-4 vote, the U.S. Supreme Court agreed that the Association was engaged in state action. But the Court did not rely on *Rendell-Baker* or on

---

[6]The Washington Supreme Court's decision was reversed, on other grounds, by the U.S. Supreme Court in *Gonzaga University v. Doe*, 536 U.S. 273 (2002). The Supreme Court's decision is discussed in Section 8.7.1 of this book.

any of the three analytical approaches sketched above. Instead, Justice Souter, writing for the majority, articulated a "pervasive entwinement" test under which a private entity will be found to be engaged in state action when "the relevant facts show pervasive entwinement to the point of largely overlapping identity" between the state and the private entity (531 U.S. at 303). The majority grounded this entwinement theory in *Evans v. Newton*, 382 U.S. 296 (1966), where the Court had "treated a nominally private entity as a state actor . . . when it is 'entwined with governmental policies,' or when government is 'entwined in [its] management or control'" (531 U.S. at 296, quoting *Evans*, 382 U.S. at 299, 301). Following this approach, the Court held that "[t]he nominally private character of the Association is overborne by the pervasive entwinement of public institutions and public officials in its composition and workings . . ." (531 U.S. at 298).

The entwinement identified by the Court was of two types: "entwinement . . . from the bottom up" and "entwinement from the top down" (531 U.S. at 300). The former focused on the relationship between the public school members of the Association (the bottom) and the Association itself; the latter focused on the relationship between the State Board of Education (the top) and the Association. As for "entwinement . . . up," 84 percent of the Association's members are public schools, and the Association is "overwhelmingly composed of public school officials who select representatives . . ., who in turn adopt and enforce the rules that make the system work" (531 U.S. at 299). "There would be no recognizable Association, legal or tangible, without the public school officials, who do not merely control but overwhelmingly perform all but the purely ministerial acts by which the Association exists and functions in practical terms" (531 U.S. at 300). As for "entwinement . . . down," Tennessee State Board of Education members "are assigned ex officio to serve as members" of the Association's two governing boards (531 U.S. at 300). In addition, the Association's paid employees "are treated as state employees to the extent of being eligible for membership in the state retirement system" (531 U.S. at 300). The Court concluded that "[t]he entwinement down from the State Board is . . . unmistakable, just as the entwinement up from the member public schools is overwhelming." Entwinement "to the degree shown here" required that the Association be "charged with a public character" as a state actor, and that its adoption and enforcement of athletics rules be "judged by constitutional standards" (531 U.S. at 302).

The most obvious application of *Brentwood* is to situations where state action issues arise with respect to an association of postsecondary institutions rather than an individual institution. But the *Brentwood* entwinement approach would also be pertinent in situations in which a state system of higher education is bringing a formerly private institution into the system, and an "entwinement up" analysis might be used to determine whether the private institution would become a state actor for purposes of the federal Constitution. Similarly, the entwinement approach might be useful in circumstances in which a postsecondary institution has created a captive organization (such as an athletics booster club), or affiliated with another organization outside the university (such as a hospital or health clinic), and the question is whether the captive or the affiliate would be considered a state actor.

### 1.5.2.2. When students, employees, and others may be engaged in state action.

In addition to all the cases above, in which the question is whether a postsecondary institution was engaged in state action, there have also been cases on whether a particular student, employee, student organization, or affiliated entity—at a private or a public institution—was engaged in state action; as well as cases on whether a private individual or organization that cooperates with a public institution for some particular purpose was engaged in state action. While the cases focusing on the institution, as discussed in Section 1.5.2.1 above, are primarily of interest to ostensibly private institutions, the state action cases focusing on individuals and organizations can be pertinent to public institutions as well as private.

In a case involving both students and an employee (a dean), *Leeds v. Meltz*, 898 F. Supp. 146 (E.D.N.Y. 1995), *affirmed*, 85 F.3d 51 (2d Cir. 1996), Leeds, a graduate of the City University of New York (CUNY) School of Law (a public law school) submitted an advertisement for printing in the law school's newspaper. The student editors rejected the advertisement because they believed it could subject them to a defamation lawsuit. Leeds sued the student editors and the acting dean of the law school, asserting that the rejection of his advertisement violated his free speech rights. The federal district court, relying on *Rendell-Baker v. Kohn*, held that neither the student editors nor the dean were engaged in state action. Law school employees exercised little or no control over the publications or activities of the editors. Although the student paper was funded in part with mandatory student activity fees, this did not make the student editors' actions attributable to the CUNY administration or to the state. (For other student newspaper cases on this point, see Section 10.3.3 of this book.) The court granted the defendants' motion to dismiss, stating that the plaintiff's allegations failed to support any plausible inference of state action. The appellate court affirmed the district court's dismissal of the case, emphasizing that the CUNY administration had issued a memo prior to the litigation disclaiming any right to control student publications, even those financed through student activity fees.

In another case involving students, *Mentavlos v. Anderson*, 249 F.3d 301 (4th Cir. 2001), the court considered whether two cadets at the Citadel, a state military college, were engaged in state action when they disciplined a first-year (or "fourth-class") cadet. The first-year cadet, a female who subsequently withdrew from the college, alleged that the two male, upper-class cadets had sexually harassed, insulted, and assaulted her using their authority under the "Fourth-Class System," as described in the school's Cadet Regulations (the Blue Book), and thereby violated her right to equal protection under the Fourteenth Amendment. The regulations granted upper-class students limited authority to correct and report violations of school rules by first-year students. While hazing and discrimination based on gender as means of punishment for rules violations were expressly prohibited, punishments meted out by upper-class cadets might include mild verbal abuse or assignment to complete undesirable maintenance tasks. Ultimately, authority for observing the Citadel's rules rested with the college administration, not the upper-class cadets.

The appellate court affirmed the federal district court's decision that the upper-class students were not state actors and were not engaged in state action. Using the nexus approach,[7] the court emphasized that the upperclassmen enjoyed only limited disciplinary authority over students, authority that was not analogous to the broad discretionary powers of law enforcement officers. Moreover, the upperclassmen's actions were not authorized by the school and were in violation of the Blue Book rules, violations for which the cadets were disciplined. "Because the cadets' decision to engage in unauthorized harassment of [the plaintiff] was not coerced, compelled, or encouraged by any law, regulation or custom" of the state or the college, there was no "close nexus" between the cadets' action and the state, and the cadets were not state actors when they disciplined the plaintiff.[8]

Although the facts of the *Mentavlos* case are somewhat unique, involving a military-style discipline system at a military college, the court made clear that its analysis could have some application to honor code systems and other disciplinary systems at other public colleges.

*Husain v. Springer,* 494 F.3d 108 (2d. Cir. 2007), provides another example of state action issues concerning students. A Student Government Publications Commissioner at a public university impounded copies of an issue of the student newspaper, and certain members of the student senate had supported this action. These students were among the defendants in a First Amendment suit brought by the newspaper editors and other students. (For analysis of the First Amendment issues in *Husain,* see Section 10.3.3.) The student defendants argued that they had not engaged in state action and therefore should be dismissed from the case. The district court and the appellate court agreed. The college did not compel or require the student defendants to impound the newspaper, nor did the college encourage this action. To the contrary, the college president had overruled the student government's action. Moreover, even if it could be said that college regulations and policies provided authorization for the students to act, "state authorization was insufficient to establish that the student government defendants were state actors in the circumstances presented here." (For a contrary case, in which a court held student government members to be engaged in state action, see *Amidon v. Student Association of the State University of New York at Albany,* 399 F. Supp.2d 136 (N.D.N.Y. 2005).)

---

[7] The court also used public function analysis (see 249 F.3d at 314–18), rejecting the plaintiff's arguments based on this approach because the Citadel was not analogous to the federal military academies, and the institution and the cadets therefore were not performing the traditional sovereign function of training men and women for service in the U.S. Armed Forces.

[8] As *Mentavlos* suggests, if the harassers had been employees of a public institution rather than students, the employees would likely have been found to be engaged in state action. For a case reaching this result, see *Hayut v. State University of New York,* 352 F.3d 733, 743–45 (2d Cir. 2003).

The case of *Limpuangthip v. United States*, 932 A.2d 1137 (D.C. Ct. App. 2007), provides another example of state action issues concerning employees. A private university's search of a student's room had led to the student's conviction on drug charges, and the student argued that the search was state action violating the Fourth Amendment. The search had been conducted by a university administrator accompanied by two university police officers. The administrator was concededly a private actor, not subject to the Fourth Amendment, but the police officers, although employees of the university, were Special Police Officers (SPOs) under District of Columbia law, "authorized to exercise arrest powers broader than that of ordinary citizens and security guards." The student claimed that this governmental authority of the SPOs present at the search made the search state action. The appellate court agreed that SPOs do become state actors when they invoke their state authority "through manner, word, or deed"—that is, when they act "like . . . regular police officer[s]" rather than employees of a private entity. But the two SPOs, according to the court, did not act in this manner at the search. The administrator had initiated and conducted the search herself; the SPOs had not influenced the administrator's actions; and their "involvement in the search was peripheral." Their conduct therefore "does not amount to state action." (For a contrary case, in which university police officers were found to be state actors, see *Boyle v. Torres*, 756 F. Supp. 2d 983 (N. Dist. Ill. 2010).)

In contrast, *Shapiro v. Columbia Union National Bank & Trust Co.*, 576 S.W.2d 310 (Mo. 1978), considers when a private entity's relationship with a public institution may subject the private entity to a state action finding. The specific question was whether the public institution, the University of Missouri at Kansas City, was so entwined with the administration of a private scholarship trust fund that the fund's activities became state action. The plaintiff, a female student, sued the university and the bank that was the fund's trustee. The fund had been established as a trust by a private individual, who had stipulated that all scholarship recipients be male. The student alleged that, although the Columbia Union National Bank was named as trustee, the university in fact administered the scholarship fund; that she was ineligible for the scholarship solely because of her sex; and that the university's conduct in administering the trust therefore was unconstitutional. She further claimed that the trust constituted three-fourths of the scholarship money available at the university and that the school's entire scholarship program was thereby discriminatory.

The trial court twice dismissed the complaint for failure to state a **cause of action**, reasoning that the trust was private and the plaintiff had not stated facts sufficient to demonstrate state action. On appeal, the Supreme Court of Missouri affirmed the dismissal:

> [We] cannot conclude that by sifting all the facts and circumstances there was state action involved here. Mr. Victor Wilson established a private trust for the benefit of deserving Kansas City "boys." He was a private individual; he established a trust with his private funds; he appointed a bank as trustee; he

established in his will a procedure by which recipients of the trust fund would be selected. The trustee was to approve the selections. Under the terms of the will, no public agency or state action is involved. Discrimination on the basis of sex results from Mr. Wilson's personal predilection. That is clearly not unlawful. . . The dissemination of information by the university in a catalogue and by other means, the accepting and processing of applications by the financial aid office, the determining of academic standards and financial needs, the making of a tentative award or nomination and forwarding the names of qualified male students to the private trustee . . . does not in our opinion rise to the level of state action [576 S.W.2d at 320].

Disagreeing with this conclusion, one member of the appellate court wrote a strong dissent:

The University accepts the applications, makes a tentative award, and in effect "selects" the male applicants who are to receive the benefits of the scholarship fund. The acts of the University are more than ministerial. The trust as it has been administered by the University has shed its purely private character and has become a public one. The involvement of the public University is . . . of such a prevailing nature that there is governmental entwinement constituting state action [576 S.W.2d at 323].

(For a discussion of the treatment of sex-restricted scholarships under the federal Title IX statute, see Section 7.3.3 of this book.)

### 1.5.3. Other bases for legal rights in private institutions.

The inapplicability of the federal Constitution to private schools does not necessarily mean that students, faculty members, and other members of the private school community have no legal rights assertable against the school. There are other sources for individual rights, and these sources may sometimes resemble those found in the Constitution.

The federal government and, to a lesser extent, state governments have increasingly created statutory rights enforceable against private institutions, particularly in the discrimination area. The federal Title VII prohibition on employment discrimination (42 U.S.C. §§ 2000e et seq., discussed in Section 4.5.2.1), applicable generally to public and private employment relationships, is a prominent example. Other major examples are the Title VI race discrimination law (42 U.S.C. §§ 2000d et seq.) and the Title IX sex discrimination law (20 U.S.C. §§ 1681 et seq.) (see Sections 11.5.2 and 11.5.3 of this book), applicable to institutions receiving federal aid. Such sources provide a large body of nondiscrimination law, which parallels and in some ways is more protective than the equal protection principles derived from the Fourteenth Amendment.

Beyond such statutory rights, several common law theories for protecting individual rights in private postsecondary institutions have been advanced. Most prominent by far is the contract theory, under which students and faculty members are said to have a contractual relationship with the private school. A related claim of breach of **fiduciary duty** has also been gaining traction in recent years, in particular for student claims (see Section 7.1.3). Under the contract theory, implied contract terms as well as express terms may establish legal rights enforceable in court if the contract is breached. Although the theory is a useful one that is often referred to in the cases (see Sections 5.2.1 and 7.1.3), most courts agree that the contract law of the commercial world cannot be imported wholesale into the academic environment. The theory must thus be applied with sensitivity to academic customs and usages. Moreover, the theory's usefulness is somewhat limited. The "terms" of the "contract" may be difficult to identify, particularly in the case of students. (To what extent, for instance, is the college catalog a source of contract terms?) Some of the terms, once identified, may be too vague or ambiguous to enforce. Or the contract may be so barren of content or so one-sided in favor of the institution that it is an insignificant source of individual rights.

Despite its shortcomings, the contract theory has gained in importance. As it has become clear that most private institutions can escape the tentacles of the state action doctrine, students, faculty, and staff have increasingly had to rely on alternative theories for protecting individual rights. Since the lowering of the age of majority, postsecondary students have had a capacity to contract under state law—a capacity that many previously did not have. In what has become the age of the consumer, students have been encouraged to import consumer rights into postsecondary education. And, in an age of collective negotiation, faculties and staff have often sought to rely on a contract model for ordering employment relationships on campus (see Section 4.3).

State constitutions have also assumed critical importance as a source of legal rights for individuals to assert against private institutions. The key case is *Robins v. PruneYard Shopping Center*, 592 P.2d 341 (Cal. 1979), *affirmed*, *PruneYard Shopping Center v. Robins*, 447 U.S. 74 (1980). In this case a group of high school students who were distributing political material and soliciting petition signatures had been excluded from a private shopping center. The students sought an injunction in state court to prevent further exclusions. The California Supreme Court sided with the students, holding that they had a state constitutional right of access to the shopping center to engage in expressive activity. In the U.S. Supreme Court, the shopping center argued that the California court's ruling was inconsistent with an earlier U.S. Supreme Court precedent, *Lloyd v. Tanner*, 407 U.S. 551 (1972), which held that the First Amendment of the federal Constitution does not guarantee individuals a right to free expression on the premises of a private shopping center. The Court rejected the argument, emphasizing that the state had a "sovereign right to adopt in its own constitution individual liberties more expansive than those conferred by the federal Constitution." The shopping center also argued that the California court's decision, in denying it the right to exclude others from its premises, violated its **property rights** under the Fifth and Fourteenth Amendments of the federal Constitution. The Supreme Court rejected this argument as well.

*PruneYard* has gained significance in educational settings with the New Jersey Supreme Court's decision in *State v. Schmid*, 423 A.2d 615 (N.J. 1980) (see Section 11.1.2 of this book). The defendant, who was not a student, had been charged with criminal trespass for distributing political material on the

Princeton University campus in violation of Princeton regulations. The New Jersey court declined to rely on the federal First Amendment, instead deciding the case on state constitutional grounds. It held that, even without a finding of state action (a prerequisite to applying the federal First Amendment), Princeton had a state constitutional obligation to protect Schmid's expressional rights (N.J. Const. art. I, paras. 6, 18). In justifying its authority to construe the state constitution in this expansive manner, the court relied on *PruneYard*. A subsequent case involving Muhlenberg College, *Pennsylvania v. Tate*, 432 A.2d 1382 (Pa. 1981), follows the *Schmid* reasoning in holding that the Pennsylvania state constitution protected the defendant's rights.

In contrast, a New York court refused to permit a student to rely on the state constitution in a challenge to her expulsion from a summer program for high school students at Cornell. In *Stone v. Cornell University*, 510 N.Y.S.2d 313 (N.Y. App. Div. 1987), the sixteen-year-old student was expelled after she admitted smoking marijuana and drinking alcohol while enrolled in the program and living on campus. No hearing was held. The student argued that the lack of a hearing violated her rights under New York's constitution (art. I, § 6). Disagreeing, the court invoked a "state action" doctrine similar to that used for the federal Constitution (see Section 1.5.2 of this book) and concluded that there was insufficient state involvement in Cornell's summer program to warrant constitutional due process protections.

Additional problems may arise when rights are asserted against a private *religious* (rather than a private *secular*) institution (see generally Sections 1.6.1 and 1.6.2 below). Federal and state statutes may provide exemptions for certain actions of religious institutions (see, for example, Section 4.7). Furthermore, courts may refuse to assert jurisdiction over certain statutory and common law claims against religious institutions, or may refuse to grant certain **discovery** requests of plaintiffs or to order certain remedies proposed by plaintiffs, out of concern for the institution's establishment and free exercise rights under the First Amendment or parallel state constitutional provisions (see, for example, Section 5.2.4). These types of defenses by religious institutions will not always succeed, however, even when the institution is a seminary. In *McKelvey v. Pierce*, 800 A.2d 840 (2002), for instance, the New Jersey Supreme Court reversed the lower court's dismissal of various contract and tort claims brought by a former student and seminarian against his diocese and several priests, emphasizing that "[t]he First Amendment does not immunize every legal claim against a religious institution and its members."

## Section 1.6. Religion and the Public-Private Dichotomy

**1.6.1. Overview.** Under the **establishment clause** of the First Amendment, public institutions must maintain a neutral stance regarding religious beliefs and activities; they must, in other words, maintain religious neutrality. Public institutions cannot favor or support one religion over another, and they cannot favor or support religion over nonreligion. Thus, for instance, public schools have been prohibited from using an official nondenominational prayer (*Engel v.*

*Vitale*, 370 U.S. 421 (1962)) and from prescribing the reading of verses from the Bible at the opening of each school day (*School District of Abington Township v. Schempp*, 374 U.S. 203 (1963)).

The First Amendment contains two "religion" clauses. The first prohibits government from "establishing" religion; the second protects individuals' "free exercise" of religion from governmental interference. Although the two clauses have a common objective of ensuring governmental "neutrality," they pursue it in different ways. As the U.S. Supreme Court explained in *School District of Abington Township v. Schempp*:

> The wholesome "neutrality" of which this Court's cases speak thus stems from a recognition of the teaching of history that powerful sects or groups might bring about a fusion of governmental and religious functions or a concert or dependency of one upon the other to the end that official support of the state or federal government would be placed behind the tenets of one or of all orthodoxies. This the establishment clause prohibits. And a further reason for neutrality is found in the free exercise clause, which recognizes the value of religious training, teaching, and observance and, more particularly, the right of every person to freely choose his own course with reference thereto, free of any compulsion from the state. This the free exercise clause guarantees. . . The distinction between the two clauses is apparent—a violation of the free exercise clause is predicated on coercion, whereas the establishment clause violation need not be so attended [374 U.S. at 222–23].

Neutrality, however, does not necessarily require a public institution to prohibit all religious activity on its campus or at off-campus events it sponsors. In some circumstances the institution may have discretion to permit noncoercive religious activities (see *Lee v. Weisman*, 505 U.S. 577 (1992) (finding indirect coercion in context of religious invocation at high school graduation)). Moreover, if a rigidly observed policy of neutrality would discriminate against campus organizations with religious purposes or impinge on an individual's right to freedom of speech or free exercise of religion, the institution may be required to allow some religion on campus.

In a case that has now become a landmark decision, *Widmar v. Vincent*, 454 U.S. 263 (1981) (see Section 10.1.5 of this book), the U.S. Supreme Court determined that student religious activities on public campuses are protected by the First Amendment's free speech clause. The Court indicated a preference for using this clause, rather than the free exercise of religion clause, whenever the institution has created a **public forum** generally open for student use. The Court also concluded that the First Amendment's establishment clause would not be violated by an "open-forum" or "equal-access" policy permitting student use of campus facilities for both nonreligious and religious purposes.

### 1.6.2. Religious autonomy rights of religious institutions and their personnel.

A private institution's position under the establishment and free exercise clauses differs markedly from that of a public institution. Private institutions have no obligation of neutrality under these clauses. Moreover, these clauses affirmatively protect the religious beliefs and practices of private religious institutions from government interference. For example, establishment and free exercise considerations may restrict the judiciary's capacity to entertain lawsuits against religious institutions. Such litigation may involve the court in the interpretation of religious doctrine or in the process of church governance, thus creating a danger that the court—an arm of government—would entangle itself in religious affairs in violation of the establishment clause.

Such litigation may also invite the court to enforce discovery requests (such as subpoenas) or award injunctive relief that would interfere with the religious practices of the institution or its sponsoring body, thus creating dangers that the court's orders would violate the institution's rights under the free exercise clause. Sometimes such litigation may present both types of federal constitutional problems or, alternatively, may present parallel problems under the state constitution. When the judicial involvement requested by the plaintiff(s) would cause the court to intrude upon establishment or free exercise values, the court must decline to enforce certain discovery requests, or must modify the terms of any remedy or relief it orders, or must decline to exercise any jurisdiction over the dispute, thus protecting the institution against governmental incursions into its religious beliefs and practices. These issues are addressed with respect to suits by faculty members in Sections 4.7 and 6.4 of this book; for a parallel example regarding a suit by a student, see *McKelvey v. Pierce*, discussed in Section 1.5.3.

A private institution's constitutional protection under the establishment and free exercise clauses is by no means absolute. Its limits are illustrated by *Bob Jones University v. United States*, 461 U.S. 574 (1983). Because the university maintained racially restrictive policies on dating and marriage, the Internal Revenue Service had denied it tax-exempt status under federal tax laws. The university argued that its racial practices were religiously based and that the denial abridged its right to free exercise of religion. The U.S. Supreme Court, rejecting this argument, emphasized that the federal government has a "compelling" interest in "eradicating racial discrimination in education" and that interest "substantially outweighs whatever burden denial of tax benefits places on [the university's] exercise of . . . religious beliefs" (461 U.S. at 575).

Although the institution did not prevail in *Bob Jones*, the "compelling interest" test that the Court used to evaluate free exercise claims does provide substantial protection for religiously affiliated institutions. The Court severely restricted the use of this **strict scrutiny** test, however, in *Employment Division v. Smith*, 494 U.S. 872 (1990), and thus severely limited the protection against governmental burdens on religious practice that is available under the free exercise clause. Congress sought to legislatively overrule *Employment Division v. Smith* and restore broad use of the compelling interest test in the Religious Freedom Restoration Act of 1993 (RFRA), 42 U.S.C. §§ 2000bb et seq., but the U.S. Supreme Court invalidated this legislation.

Congress had passed RFRA pursuant to its power under section 5 of the Fourteenth Amendment to enforce that amendment and the Bill of Rights against the states and their political subdivisions. In *City of Boerne v. Flores*, 521 U.S. 507 (1997), the Court held that RFRA is beyond the scope of Congress's section 5 enforcement power. Although the Court addressed only RFRA's validity as it applies to the states, the statute by its express terms also applies to the federal government (§§ 2000bb-2(1), 2000bb-3(a)). As to these applications, the Court has apparently conceded that RFRA remains constitutional (*Gonzales v. O Centro Espirita Beneficente Unias Do Vegetal*, 126 S. Ct. 1211 (2006)).

The invalidation of RFRA's application to the states has serious consequences for the free exercise rights of both religious institutions and the members of their academic communities. The earlier case of *Employment Division v. Smith* (above) is reinstituted as the controlling authority on the right to free exercise of religion. Whereas RFRA provided protection against generally applicable, religiously neutral laws that substantially burden religious practice, *Smith* provides no such protection. Thus, religiously affiliated institutions no longer have federal religious freedom rights that guard them from general and neutral regulations of state and local governments that interfere with the institutions' religious mission. Moreover, individual students, faculty, and staff—whether at religious institutions, private secular institutions, or public institutions—no longer have federal religious freedom rights to guard them from general and neutral regulations of state and local governments that interfere with these individuals' personal religious practices. And individuals at public institutions no longer have federal religious freedom rights to guard them from general and neutral institutional regulations that interfere with personal religious practices.

There are at least three avenues that an individual religious adherent or a religiously affiliated institution might now pursue to reclaim some of the protection taken away first by *Smith* and then by *Boerne*. The first avenue is to seek maximum advantage from an important post-*Smith* case, *Church of the Lukumi Babalu Aye v. City of Hialeah*, 508 U.S. 520 (1993), that limits the impact of *Smith*. Under *Lukumi Babalu Aye*, challengers may look beyond the face of a regulation to discern its "object" from the background and context of its passage and enforcement. If this investigation reveals an object of "animosity" to religion or a particular religious practice, then the court will not view the regulation as religiously neutral and will, instead, subject the regulation to a strict "compelling interest" test. (For an example of a case addressing a student's First Amendment free exercise claim and utilizing *Lukumi Babalu Aye*, see *Axson-Flynn v. Johnson*, 356 F.3d 1277 (10th Cir. 2004), discussed in Section 7.1.4 of this book.)

The second avenue is to seek protection under some other clause of the federal Constitution. The best bet is probably to look to the free speech and press clauses of the First Amendment, which cover religious activity that is expressive (communicative). The U.S. Supreme Court's decisions in *Widmar v. Vincent* (see Section 10.1.5) and *Rosenberger v. Rectors and Visitors of the University of Virginia* (see Sections 10.1.5 and 10.3.2) provide good examples of protecting religious activity under these clauses. Another possibility is to rely on the due process clauses of the Fifth and Fourteenth Amendments, which protect certain privacy interests regarding personal, intimate matters. The *Smith* case itself includes a discussion of this due process privacy protection for religious activity (494 U.S. at 881–82). Yet another possibility is to invoke the freedom of association that is implicit in the First Amendment and that the courts usually call the "freedom of expressive association" to distinguish it from a "freedom of intimate association" protected by the Fifth and Fourteenth Amendment due process clauses (see *Roberts v. United States Jaycees*, 468 U.S. 609, 617–18, 622–23 (1984)). The leading case is *Boy Scouts of America v. Dale*, 530 U.S. 640 (2000), in which the Court, by a 5-to-4 vote, upheld the Boy Scouts' action revoking the membership of a homosexual scoutmaster. In its reasoning, the Court indicated that the "freedom of expressive association" protects private organizations from government action that "affects in a significant way the [organization's] ability to advocate public or private viewpoints" (530 U.S. at 648).

The third avenue is to look beyond the U.S. Constitution for some other source of law (see Section 1.4 of this book) that protects religious freedom. Some state constitutions, for instance, may have protections that are stronger than what is now provided by the federal free exercise clause (see Section 1.6.3 below). Similarly, federal and state statutes will sometimes protect religious freedom. The federal Title VII statute on employment discrimination, for example, protects religious institutions from federal government intrusions into some religiously based employment policies (see Section 4.7 of this book) and protects employees from intrusions by employers into some religious practices. And some states have their own RFRA-type statutes that protect religious exercise (see, e.g., Fla. Stat. Ann. § 761.01).

***1.6.3. Government support for religious institutions.*** Although the establishment clause itself imposes no neutrality obligation on private institutions, this clause does have another kind of importance for private institutions that are religious. When government—federal, state, or local—undertakes to provide financial or other support for private postsecondary education, the question arises whether this support, insofar as it benefits religious institutions, constitutes government support for religion. If it does, such support would violate the establishment clause because government would have departed from its position of neutrality.

Two 1971 cases decided by the Supreme Court provide the foundation for the modern law on government support for church-related schools. *Lemon v. Kurtzman*, 403 U.S. 602 (1971), invalidated two state programs providing aid for church-related elementary and secondary schools. *Tilton v. Richardson*, 403 U.S. 672 (1971), held constitutional a federal aid program providing construction grants to higher education institutions, including those that are church related. In deciding the cases, the Court developed a three-pronged test for determining when a government support program passes muster under the establishment clause:

> First, the statute must have a secular legislative purpose; second, its principal or primary effect must be one that neither advances nor inhibits religion . . .; finally, the statute must not foster "an excessive government entanglement with religion" [403 U.S. at 612–13, quoting *Walz v. Tax Commission*, 397 U.S. 664, 674 (1970)].

All three prongs have proved to be very difficult to apply in particular cases. The Court has provided guidance in *Lemon* and in later cases, however, that has been of some help. In *Lemon*, for instance, the Court explained the entanglement prong as follows:

> In order to determine whether the government entanglement with religion is excessive, we must examine (1) the character and purposes of the institutions which are benefitted, (2) the nature of the aid that the state provides, and (3) the resulting relationship between the government and the religious authority [403 U.S. at 615].

In *Hunt v. McNair*, 413 U.S. 734 (1973), the Court gave this explanation of the effect prong:

> Aid normally may be thought to have a primary effect of advancing religion when it flows to an institution in which religion is so pervasive that a substantial portion of its functions are subsumed in the religious mission or when it funds a specifically religious activity in an otherwise substantially secular setting [413 U.S. at 743].

But in *Agostini v. Felton*, 521 U.S. 203 (1997), the U.S. Supreme Court refined the three-prong *Lemon* test, specifically affirming that the first prong (purpose) has become a significant part of the test and determining that the second prong (effect) and third prong (entanglement) have, in essence, become combined into a single broad inquiry into effect. (See 521 U.S. at 222, 232–33.) And in *Mitchell v. Helms*, 530 U.S. 793 (2000), four Justices in a **plurality opinion** and two Justices in a **concurring opinion** criticized the "pervasively sectarian" test that had been developed in *Hunt v. McNair* (above) as part of the effect prong of *Lemon*, and overruled two earlier U.S. Supreme Court cases on elementary and secondary education that had relied on this test. These Justices also gave much stronger emphasis to the neutrality principle that is a foundation of establishment clause analysis.

Four U.S. Supreme Court cases have applied the complex *Lemon* test to religious postsecondary institutions. In each case the aid program passed the test. In *Tilton v. Richardson* (above), the Court approved the federal construction grant program, and the grants to the particular colleges involved in that case, by a narrow 5-to-4 vote. In *Hunt v. McNair* (above), the Court, by a 6-to-3 vote, sustained the issuance of revenue bonds on behalf of a religious college, under a South Carolina program designed to help private nonprofit colleges finance construction projects. Applying the "primary effect" test defined in the quotation above, the court determined that the college receiving the bond proceeds was not "pervasively sectarian" (413 U.S. at 743) and would not use the financial facilities for specifically religious activities. In *Roemer v. Board of Public Works*, 426 U.S. 736 (1976), by a 5-to-4 vote, the Court upheld the award of annual support grants to four Catholic colleges under a Maryland grant program for private postsecondary institutions. As in *Hunt*, the Court majority (in a plurality opinion and a concurring opinion) determined that the colleges at issue were not "pervasively sectarian" (426 U.S. at 752, 755) and that, had they been so, the establishment clause might have prohibited the state from awarding the grants. And in the fourth case, *Witters v. Washington Department of Services for the Blind*, 474 U.S. 481 (1986), the Court rejected an establishment clause challenge to a state vocational rehabilitation program for the blind that provided assistance directly to a student enrolled in a religious ministry program at a private Christian college. Distinguishing between institution-based aid and student-based aid, the unanimous Court concluded that the aid plan did not violate the second prong of the *Lemon* test, since any state payments that were ultimately channeled to the educational institution were based solely on the "genuinely independent and private choices of the aid recipients." Taken together, these U.S. Supreme Court cases suggest that a wide range of postsecondary support programs can be devised compatibly with the establishment clause and that a wide range of church-related institutions can be eligible to receive government support.

Of the four Supreme Court cases, only *Witters* focuses on student-based aid. Its distinction between institutional-based aid (as in the other three Supreme Court cases) and student-based aid has become a critical component of establishment clause analysis. In a later case, *Zelman v. Simmons-Harris*, 536 U.S. 639 (2002) (an elementary/secondary education case), the Court broadly affirmed the vitality of this distinction and its role in upholding government aid programs that benefit religious schools. Of the other three Supreme Court cases—*Tilton, Hunt,* and *Roemer—Roemer* is the most revealing. There the Court refused to find that the grants given a group of Catholic colleges constituted support for religion—even though the funds were granted annually and could be put to a wide range of uses, and even though the schools had church representatives on their governing boards, employed Roman Catholic chaplains, held Roman Catholic religious exercises, required students to take religion or theology classes taught primarily by Roman Catholic clerics, made some hiring decisions for theology departments partly on the basis of religious considerations, and began some classes with prayers.

The current status of the U.S. Supreme Court's 1976 decision in *Roemer v. Board of Public Works* was the focus of extensive litigation in the Fourth Circuit involving Columbia Union College, a small Seventh-Day Adventist college in Maryland. *Columbia Union College v. Clarke*, 159 F.3d 151 (4th Cir. 1998) (hereafter, *Columbia Union College I*), involved the same Maryland grant program that was at issue in *Roemer*. The questions for the court were whether, under then-current U.S. Supreme Court law on the establishment clause, a "pervasively sectarian" institution could ever be eligible for direct government funding of its core educational functions; and whether the institution seeking the funds here (Columbia Union College) was "pervasively sectarian." In a 2-to-1 decision, the court answered no to the first question, asserting that *Roemer* has not been implicitly overruled by subsequent Supreme Court cases (such as *Agostini*, above), and **remanded** the second question to the district court for further fact findings. The debate between the majority and dissent illustrates the two contending perspectives on the continuing validity of *Roemer* and that case's criteria for determining whether an institution is "pervasively sectarian." In addition, the court in *Columbia Union College I* considered a new issue that was not evident in *Roemer* but was interjected into this area of law by the U.S. Supreme Court's 1995 decision in *Rosenberger v. Rector & Visitors of the University of Virginia* (see Section 10.1.5 of this book). The issue was whether a decision to deny funds to Columbia Union would violate its free speech rights under the First Amendment. The court answered yes to this question because Maryland had denied the funding "solely because of [Columbia Union's] alleged pervasively partisan religious viewpoint" (159 F.3d at 156). That ruling did not dispose of the case, however, because the court determined that the need to avoid an establishment clause violation would provide a justification for this infringement of free speech.

On remand, and after extensive discovery and a lengthy trial, the federal district court ruled that Columbia Union was not pervasively sectarian and was therefore entitled to participate in the state grant program. Maryland then appealed, and the U.S. Fourth Circuit Court of Appeals reviewed the case for a second time in *Columbia Union College v. Oliver*, 254 F.3d 496 (4th Cir. 2001) (hereafter, *Columbia Union College II*). In its opinion in *Columbia Union College II*, the appellate court emphasized that, since its decision in *Columbia Union College I*, the U.S. Supreme Court had "significantly altered the Establishment Clause landscape" (254 F.3d at 501) by its decision in *Mitchell v. Helms*, 530 U.S. 793 (2000). In *Mitchell*, as the Fourth Circuit explained, the Supreme Court upheld an aid program for elementary and secondary schools in which the federal government distributed funds to local school districts, which then purchased educational materials and equipment, a portion of which were loaned to private, including religious, schools. In the school district whose lending program was challenged, "approximately 30% of the funds" went to forty-six private schools, forty-one of which were religiously affiliated (254 F.3d at 501).

Applying *Mitchell*, the Fourth Circuit noted that Justice O'Connor's concurring opinion, "which is the controlling opinion in *Mitchell*," replaced the "pervasively sectarian" test with a "neutrality-plus" test (254 F.3d at 504). The Fourth Circuit summarized this "neutrality-plus" test and its "three fundamental guideposts for Establishment Clause cases" as follows:

> First, the neutrality of aid criteria is an important factor, even if it is not the only factor, in assessing a public assistance program. Second, the actual diversion of government aid to religious purposes is prohibited. Third, and relatedly, "presumptions of religious indoctrination" inherent in the pervasively sectarian analysis "are normally inappropriate when evaluating neutral school-aid programs under the Establishment Clause" [254 F.3d at 505, citations omitted].

Using this "neutrality-plus" analysis derived from *Mitchell*, instead of *Roemer*'s "pervasively sectarian" analysis, the Fourth Circuit found that Maryland's grant program had a secular purpose and used neutral criteria to dispense aid, that there was no evidence "of actual diversion of government aid for religious purposes," and that safeguards were in place to protect against future diversion of funds for sectarian purposes. The appellate court therefore affirmed the district court's ruling that the state's funding of Columbia Union College would not violate the establishment clause. Since a grant of funds would not violate the establishment clause, "the State cannot advance a compelling interest for refusing the college its [grant] funds." Such a refusal would therefore, as the appellate court had already held in *Columbia Union I*, violate the college's free speech rights.

Alternatively, the Fourth Circuit concluded that the college would prevail even if the "pervasively sectarian" test were still the controlling law. Reviewing the district court's findings and the factors set out in the U.S. Supreme Court's decision in *Roemer*, the appellate court also affirmed the district court's ruling that the college is not pervasively sectarian and, on that ground as well, is eligible to receive the state grant funds.

When issues arise concerning governmental support for religious institutions, or their students or faculty members, the federal Constitution (as in the cases above) is not the only source of law that may apply. In some states, for instance, the state constitution will also play an important role independent of the federal Constitution. A line of cases concerning various student aid programs of the state of Washington provides an instructive example of the role of state constitutions and the complex interrelationships between the federal establishment and **free exercise clauses** and parallel provisions in state constitutions. The first case in the line is the U.S. Supreme Court's decision in *Witters v. Washington Department of Services for the Blind* (hereinafter, *Witters I*), discussed earlier in this subsection, in which the Court remanded the case to the Supreme Court of Washington (whose decision the U.S. Supreme Court had reversed), observing that the state court was free to consider the "far stricter" church-state provision of the state constitution. On remand, the state court concluded that the state constitutional provision—prohibiting use of public moneys to pay for any religious instruction—precluded the grant of state funds to the student enrolled in the religious ministry program (*Witters v. State Commission for the Blind*, 771 P.2d 1119 (Wash. 1989) (hereinafter, *Witters II*)). First the court held that providing vocational rehabilitation funds to the student would violate the state constitution because the funds would pay for "a religious course of study at a religious school, with a religious career as [the student's] goal" (771 P.2d at 1121). Distinguishing the establishment clause of the U.S. Constitution from the state constitution's provision, the court noted that the latter provision "prohibits not only the appropriation of public money for religious instruction, but also the application of public funds to religious instruction" (771 P.2d at 1122). Then the court held that the student's federal constitutional right to free exercise of religion was not infringed by denial of the funds, because he is "not being asked to violate any tenet of his religious beliefs nor is he being denied benefits 'because of conduct mandated by religious belief'" (771 P.2d at 1123). Third, the court held that denial of the funds did not violate the student's equal protection rights under the Fourteenth Amendment, because the state has a "compelling interest in maintaining the strict separation of church and state set forth" in its constitution, and the student's "individual interest in receiving a religious education must . . . give way to the state's greater need to uphold its constitution" (771 P.2d at 1123).

Almost twenty years after *Witters I* and *II*, establishment clause issues arose again in the context of another state of Washington student aid program. This time, in *State ex rel. Mary Gallwey v. Grimm*, 48 P.3d 274 (Wash. 2002), the Supreme Court of Washington declared that the state program did not violate the state constitution's establishment clause, nor did it violate the federal establishment clause. At issue was the Educational Opportunity Grant (EOG) Program, which provided aid to "place-bound" students who lived in disadvantaged counties and were unable to travel to distant state universities and colleges. Qualifying students were awarded vouchers that they could use at a select number of participating public and private institutions in the state. Some of the private institutions were religiously affiliated, and a state taxpayer challenged their inclusion in the program as a violation of article I, section 11 of the state constitution (the same provision that was at issue in *Witters II*, above, and *Locke v. Davey*, below), as well as the federal Constitution's establishment clause.

The Washington Supreme Court rejected the challenges, determining that it was permissible for the state to include religious colleges in the program. The court relied on a provision in the statute creating the EOG Program requiring that "no student will be enrolled in any program that includes religious worship, exercise, or instruction" (48 P.3d at 285, citing Wash. Rev. Code § 28B.101.040). Under this provision, according to the court, a student could use an EOG voucher to pay educational costs at a "religious [college] with a religious mission," so long as the student is pursuing a "general, nonreligious, four-year college degree." Such use of the vouchers, the court concluded, would not violate article I, section 11.

Similarly, applying the three-pronged *Lemon* test (see above, this Section), the Washington court determined that such inclusion of religiously affiliated schools in the EOG program did not violate the federal establishment clause. It was important, in this regard, that the EOG funds were awarded to the student directly, rather than to the school itself—a factor that the U.S. Supreme Court had emphasized in *Witters I*. The EOG Program was a "neutrally administered" program, said the Washington court, that represented an even more distant relationship between government and religion than the program upheld in *Witters I*.

The federal free exercise clause, which had been considered in the *Witters II* litigation, was not at issue in *Gallwey*. Had the state of Washington prohibited students from using EOG vouchers at religiously affiliated schools, even to pursue "non-religious" studies, then the prohibition could have been challenged as a violation of the excluded students' free exercise rights—much as the student in *Witters II* had challenged his exclusion from using state vocational rehabilitation funds. The specific issue would be different from that in *Witters II*, however, since *Witters II* concerned only a prohibition on using student aid funds for religious studies preparing the student for a religious vocation, and not a more general prohibition on using state funds for any studies at a religiously affiliated school. Students' challenges to such prohibitions, broad or narrow, in

Washington and other states, are now governed by a 2004 decision of the U.S. Supreme Court in *Locke v. Davey*, discussed below. In addition, challenges to such prohibitions may be brought by the religiously affiliated institutions that are excluded from the student aid program. An institution's challenge could also be based on *Locke v. Davey* (below), at least if the institution offered "nonreligious" studies; but could just as likely be based on an equal protection claim of discrimination against religious organizations or an establishment clause claim of hostility toward religion (see Section 1.6.2 above).

*Locke v. Davey*, 540 U.S. 712 (2004), involved a free exercise clause challenge to yet another student financial aid program of the state of Washington. In its opinion rejecting the challenge, the U.S. Supreme Court probed the relationship between the federal Constitution's two religion clauses and the relationship between these clauses and the religion clauses in state constitutions.

At issue was the state of Washington's Promise Scholarship Program, which provided scholarships to academically gifted students for use at either public or private institutions—including religiously affiliated institutions—in the state. Consistent with article I, section 11 of the state constitution as interpreted by the Washington Supreme Court in *Witters II* (see above), however, the state stipulated that aid may not be awarded to "any student who is pursuing a degree in theology" (see Wash. Rev. Code § 28B.10.814). The plaintiff, Joshua Davey, had been awarded a Promise Scholarship and decided to attend a Christian college in the state to pursue a double major in pastoral ministries and business administration. When he subsequently learned that the pastoral ministries degree would be considered a degree in theology and that he could not use his Promise Scholarship for this purpose, Davey declined the scholarship. He then sued the state, alleging violations of his First Amendment speech, establishment, and free exercise rights as well as a violation of his equal protection rights under the Fourteenth Amendment.

In the federal district court, Davey lost on all counts. On appeal, however, the U.S. Court of Appeals for the Ninth Circuit upheld Davey's free exercise claim. Applying strict scrutiny and relying on the U.S. Supreme Court's decision in *Church of Lukumi Babalu Aye, Inc. v. Hialeah*, 508 U.S. 520 (1993), the appellate court invalidated the state's exclusion of Davey from the scholarship program "based on his being a theology major." By a 7-to-2 vote, the U.S. Supreme Court reversed the Ninth Circuit and upheld the state's exclusion of theology degrees from the Promise Scholarship Program. In the majority opinion by Chief Justice Rehnquist, the Court declined to apply the strict scrutiny analysis of *Lukumi Babalu Aye*. Characterizing the dispute as one that implicated both the free exercise clause and the establishment clause of the federal Constitution, the Court recognized that "these two clauses . . . are frequently in tension" but that there is "play in the joints" (540 U.S. at 718, quoting *Walz v. Tax Comm'n of City of New York*, 397 U.S. 664, 669 (1970)) that provides states some discretion to work out the tensions between the two clauses. In particular, a state may sometimes give precedence to the antiestablishment values embedded in its own state constitution rather than the federal free exercise interests of particular individuals. To implement this "play-in-the-joints" principle, the Court applied a standard of review that was less strict than the standard it had usually applied to cases of religious discrimination.

Under the Court's prior decision in *Witters I* (above), "the State could . . . permit Promise Scholars to pursue a degree in devotional theology" (emphasis added). It did not necessarily follow, however, that the federal free exercise clause would require the state to cover students pursuing theology degrees. The question therefore was "whether Washington, pursuant to its own constitution, which has been authoritatively interpreted [by the state courts] as prohibiting even indirectly funding religious instruction that will prepare students for the ministry, . . . can deny them such funding without violating the [federal] Free Exercise Clause" (540 U.S. at 719).

The Court found that "[t]he State has merely chosen not to fund a distinct category of instruction"—an action that "places a relatively minor burden on Promise Scholars" (540 U.S. at 721, 725). Moreover, the state's different treatment of theology majors was not based on "hostility toward religion," nor did the "history or text of Article I, § 11 of the Washington Constitution . . . [suggest] animus towards religion." The difference instead reflects the state's "historic and substantial state interest," reflected in article I, section 11, in declining to support religion by funding the religious training of the clergy. Based on these considerations, and applying its lesser scrutiny standard, the Court held that the state of Washington's exclusion of theology majors from the Promise Scholarship program did not violate the free exercise clause.

The Court has thus created, in *Locke v. Davey*, a kind of balancing test for certain free exercise cases in which a state's different treatment of religion does not evince "hostility" or "animus." Under the balancing test, the extent of the burden the state has placed on religious practice is weighed against the substantiality of the state's interest in promoting antiestablishment values. The lesser scrutiny, or intermediate scrutiny, that this balancing test produces stands in marked contrast to both the strict scrutiny required in cases like *Lukumi Babalu Aye* and the minimal scrutiny used in cases, like *Employment Division v. Smith* (Section 1.6.2 above), that involve religiously neutral statutes of general applicability. Some of the Court's reasoning supporting this balancing test and its application to the Promise Scholarships seems questionable, as Justice Scalia pointed out in a dissent (540 U.S. at 731–32). Moreover, the circumstances in which the balancing test should be used—beyond the specific circumstance of a government aid program such as that in *Locke*—are unclear. But the 7-to-2 vote upholding Washington's action nevertheless indicates strong support for a flexible and somewhat deferential approach to free exercise issues arising in programs of government support for higher education and, more specifically, strong support for the exclusion (if the state so chooses) of theological and ministerial education from state student aid programs—at least when the applicable state constitution has a strong antiestablishment clause.

Taken together, the *Locke v. Davey* case and the earlier *Witters I* case serve to accord a substantial range of discretion to the states (and presumably the federal government as well) to determine whether or not to include students pursuing religious studies in their student aid programs. The range of discretion may be less when a state is determining whether to include students studying secular subjects at a religiously affiliated institution, since the free exercise clause may have greater force in this context. And when a state determines whether to provide aid directly to religiously affiliated institutions rather than to students, the range of discretion will be slim because the federal establishment clause and many state constitutional clauses would apply with added force, as discussed earlier in this Section.

Though the federal cases have been quite hospitable to the inclusion of church-related institutions in government support programs for postsecondary education, religious institutions should still be most sensitive to establishment clause issues. As *Witters* indicates, state constitutions may contain clauses that restrict government support for church-related institutions more vigorously than the federal establishment clause does. The statutes creating funding programs may also contain provisions that restrict the programs' application to religious institutions or activities. Moreover, even the federal establishment clause cases have historically been decided by close votes, with considerable disagreement among the Justices and continuing questions about the current status of the *Lemon* test and spin-off tests such as the "pervasively sectarian" test. Thus, religious institutions should exercise great care in using government funds and should keep in mind that, at some point, religious influences within the institution can still jeopardize government funding, especially institution-based funding.

### 1.6.4. Religious autonomy rights of individuals in public post-secondary institutions.
Whereas Sections 1.6.2 and 1.6.3 focused on church-state problems involving private institutions, this section focuses on church-state problems in public institutions. As explained in Section 1.6.1, public institutions are subject to the strictures of the First Amendment's establishment and free exercise clauses and parallel clauses in state constitutions, which are the source of rights that faculty members, students, and staff members may assert against their institutions. The most visible and contentious of these disputes involve situations in which a public institution has incorporated prayer or some other religious activity into an institutional activity or event.

In *Tanford v. Brand*, 104 F.3d 982 (7th Cir. 1997), for example, the U.S. Court of Appeals for the Seventh Circuit addressed the issue of prayer as part of the commencement exercises at a state university. A law school professor, law students, and an undergraduate student brought suit, challenging Indiana University's 155-year-old tradition of nonsectarian invocations and benedictions during commencement. The court rejected the plaintiffs' First Amendment establishment clause claims, holding that the prayer tradition "'is simply a tolerable acknowledgement of beliefs widely held among the people of this country.' *Marsh v. Chambers*, 463 U.S. 783, 792 (1983)." Moreover, according to the Court, the prayers at the commencements were voluntary and not coercive. Nearly 2,500 of the 7,400 graduating students had elected not to attend the previous commencement; those that did attend were free to exit before both the invocation and benediction and return after each was completed; and those choosing not to exit were free to sit, as did most in attendance, during both ceremonies.

In *Chaudhuri v. Tennessee*, 130 F.3d 232 (6th Cir. 1997), the court endorsed and extended the **holding** in *Tanford*. The plaintiff, a practicing Hindu originally from India and a tenured professor at Tennessee State University (TSU), claimed that the use of prayers at university functions violated the First Amendment's establishment clause. The functions at issue were not only graduation ceremonies as in *Tanford*, but also "faculty meetings, dedication ceremonies, and guest lectures." After the suit was filed, TSU discontinued the prayers and instead adopted a "moment-of-silence" policy. The professor then challenged the moment of silence as well, alleging that the policy had been adopted in order to allow continued use of prayers. The appellate court determined that neither the prayers nor the moments of silence violated the establishment clause.

The *Chaudhuri* court used the three-part test from *Lemon v. Kurtzman*, 403 U.S. 602 (1971) (Section 1.6.3), to resolve both the prayer claim and the moment-of-silence claim. Under the first prong of the *Lemon* test, the court found, as in *Tanford*, that a prayer may "serve to dignify or to memorialize a public occasion" and therefore has a legitimate secular purpose. Moreover, "if the verbal prayers had a legitimate secular purpose . . . it follows almost a fortiori that the moments of silence have such a purpose." Under the second prong, the court found that the principal or primary effect of the nonsectarian prayers was not "to indoctrinate the audience," but rather "to solemnize the events and to encourage reflection." As to the moment of silence, it was "even clearer" that the practice did not significantly advance or inhibit religion because individuals could use the moment of silence for any purpose—religious or not. And, under the final prong of the *Lemon* test, the court found that "any entanglement resulting from the inclusion of nonsectarian prayers at public university functions is, at most, *de minimis*" and that the "entanglement created by a moment of silence is nil."

As in *Tanford*, the *Chaudhuri* court also concluded that the "coercion" test established in *Lee v. Weisman*, 505 U.S. 577 (1992), was not controlling. At Tennessee State University (TSU) (in contrast to the secondary school in *Lee*), according to the court, there was no coercion to participate in the prayers. It was not mandatory for Professor Chaudhuri or any other faculty member to attend the TSU functions at issue, and there was no penalty for nonattendance. Moreover, there was no "peer pressure" to attend the functions or to participate in the prayers (as there had been in *Lee*), and there was "absolutely no risk" that any adult member present at a TSU function would be indoctrinated by the prayers.

Although both courts resolved the establishment clause issues in the same way, these issues may have been more difficult in *Chaudhuri* than in *Tanford*; and the *Chaudhuri* court may have given inadequate consideration to some pertinent factors that were present in that case but apparently not in *Tanford*. As a dissenting opinion in *Chaudhuri* points out, the court may have discounted "the strength of the prayer tradition" at TSU, the strength of the "community expectations" regarding prayer, and the significant Christian elements in the prayers that had been used. Moreover, the court lumped the graduation exercises together with other university functions as if the relevant facts and considerations were the same for all functions. Instead, each type of function deserves its own distinct analysis, because the context of a graduation ceremony, for instance, may be quite different from the context of a faculty meeting or a guest lecture.

The reasoning and the result in *Tanford* and *Chaudhuri* may be further subject to question in the wake of the U.S. Supreme Court's ruling in *Santa Fe Independent School District v. Doe*, 530 U.S. 290 (2000). In considering the validity, under the establishment clause, of a school district policy providing for student-led invocations before high school football games, the Court placed little reliance on factors emphasized by the *Tanford* and *Chaudhuri* courts, and instead focused on factors to which these courts gave little attention—for example, the "perceived" endorsement of religion implicit in the policy itself, the "history" of prayer practices in the district and the intention to "preserve" them, and the possible "sham secular purposes" underlying the student-led invocation policy. In effect, the arguments that worked in *Tanford* and *Chaudhuri* did not work in *Santa Fe*, and factors touched upon only lightly in *Tanford* and *Chaudhuri* were considered in depth in *Santa Fe*, thus leading to the Court's invalidation of the Santa Fe School District's invocation policy.

A 2005 case provides an instructive example of institutional activities other than group prayer that may raise establishment clause issues. The case, *O'Connor v. Washburn University*, 416 F.3d 1216 (10th Cir. 2005), also illustrates the type of establishment claim premised on institutional *disapproval* of or *hostility* to religion rather than institutional *endorsement* of or *support* for religion.

In *O'Connor*, a professor and a student claimed that the university (a public university) had installed a statue on campus that negatively and offensively portrayed Roman Catholicism, thus violating their establishment clause rights. According to the appellate court, the statue, "entitled 'Holier Than Thou,' depicts a Roman Catholic Bishop with a contorted facial expression and a miter that some have interpreted as a stylized representation of a phallus." The statue had been selected, along with four others, in an annual competition, "for displaying in a temporary outdoor sculpture exhibition [that] supplements the university's collection of twenty-five [permanent] outdoor statues." Selection of the five temporary statues was made by a three-person jury of art professionals chosen by the university's Campus Beautification Committee, and both the committee and the university president had approved the selections. Once the statue was installed along a "high traffic sidewalk," the university began receiving numerous complaints from within and outside the university. The university considered the complaints but declined to remove the statue.

In ruling on the establishment clause claim, the appellate court applied the *Lemon* test, as modified by the "endorsement or disapproval" test (see 416 F.3d at 1223–24), placing more emphasis on the latter test (often called just the "endorsement test") than did the courts in the cases discussed above. The endorsement test focuses on whether the governmental activity at issue "has either (1) the purpose or (2) the effect of conveying a message that religion or a particular religious belief is favored or preferred," on the one hand, or disapproved or disparaged on the other. Under the first prong of the test, "purpose," the question is "whether 'the government's actual purpose is to endorse or disapprove of religion.'" Under the second prong, "effect," the question is "whether a reasonable observer aware of the history and context of the [activity at issue] would find the [activity] had the effect of favoring or disfavoring a certain religion [or religious belief]." (See 415 F.3d at 1227–31, quoting *Bauchman ex rel. Bauchman v. W. High School*, 132 F.3d at 551–52.) Applying this test, the court focused on whether, in the context of all the pertinent facts, the university's selection or placement of the statue, or its refusal to remove it after receiving complaints, had "either (1) the purpose or (2) the effect of conveying a message" that the university disapproved of or disparaged Roman Catholicism or a particular Catholic belief. Regarding "purpose," the court determined that the plaintiffs had not produced any evidence that the university's actions were motivated by a disapproval of Catholicism and that the university had other aesthetic and educational "reasons" for its decisions. Regarding "effect," the court determined that, even if the effect of the statue was to convey "an anti-Catholic message" (a point on which the court did not rule), a "reasonable observer viewing [the statue] in context would understand that the university had not approved or agreed with that message."

It was important to the court's reasoning that the "Holier Than Thou" statue was displayed on a university campus rather than, say, in a city park or on the grounds of a county office building. The court emphasized that a campus is "peculiarly the marketplace of ideas" (citing *Healy v. James*, 408 U.S. at 180), a place where government "acts against a background and tradition" of **academic freedom** (citing *Rosenberger v. Rector & Visitors of Univ. of Va.*, 515 U.S. at 835)). Moreover, the placement and retention of the statue, in context, had implicated the university's educational mission and its curriculum. Even though the statue was not created as part of a course, it was nevertheless "part of [the University's] educational curriculum"; the president and the vice-president of academic affairs had both "testified that they strove to extend the educational environment . . . beyond the classroom to encompass various stimuli including art, theatre, music, debate, athletics, and other activities."

Apparently, in such academic, higher education contexts, courts may accord public colleges and universities more leeway than other governmental entities to establish religiously neutral educational reasons for engaging in activities that involve religion in some way. Similarly, in this context, courts may find it less likely that a reasonable observer "would associate" a particular, allegedly religious message with the college or university itself (416 F.3d at 1229–1230). More broadly, these attributes of higher education serve to support the assertion, made by the U.S. Supreme Court and repeated by lower courts, "that religious themes 'may constitutionally be used in an appropriate study of history, civilization, ethics, comparative religion, or the like'" (416 F.3d at 1230, quoting *Stone v. Graham*, 449 U.S. 39, 42 (1980)).

A recent U.S. Supreme Court case, *Pleasant Grove City v. Summum*, 555 U.S. 460 (2009), introduces an additional dimension to cases like *O'Connor v. Washburn University*. In particular, *Pleasant Grove* illustrates how there could be not only an establishment challenge but also a free speech clause challenge to a governmental entity's placement of religious monuments or statues on public property. Faced with such a challenge, according to the Court, the governmental entity may often prevail by characterizing the placement of the monument or statue as "governmental speech" rather than "private speech." Success with this argument, however, would not insulate the governmental entity from an establishment clause challenge, which requires a separate analysis as illustrated by *O'Connor*.

## Section 1.7. The Relationship Between Law and Policy

There is an overarching distinction between law and policy, and thus between legal issues and policy issues, that informs the work of administrators and policy makers in higher education, as well as the work of lawyers.[9] In brief, legal issues are stated and analyzed using the norms and principles of the legal system, resulting in conclusions and advice on what the law requires or permits in a given circumstance. Policy issues, in comparison, are stated and analyzed using norms and principles of administration and management, the social sciences (including the psychology of teaching and learning), the physical sciences (especially the health sciences), ethics, and other relevant disciplines; the resulting conclusions and advice focus on the best policy options available in a particular circumstance. Or, to put it another way, law focuses primarily on the legality of a particular course of action, while policy focuses primarily on the efficacy of a particular course of action. Legality is determined using the various sources of law set out in Section 1.4 of this book; efficacy is determined by using sources drawn from the various disciplines just mentioned. The work of ascertaining legality is primarily for the attorneys, while the work of ascertaining efficacy is primarily for the policy makers and administrators.

Just as legal issues may arise from sources both internal and external to the institution (see Section 1.4), policy issues may arise, and policy may be made, both within and outside the institution. Internally, the educators and administrators, including the trustees or regents, make policy decisions that create what we may think of as "institutional policy" or "internal policy." Externally,

---

[9] The discussion in this section—especially the middle portions that differentiate particular policy makers' functions from those of attorneys, identify alternative policy-making processes, set out the steps of the policy-making process and the characteristics of good policy, and review structural arrangements for facilitating policy making—draws substantially upon these very helpful materials: Stephen Dunham, "Preventive Lawyering: Drafting and Administering Policies to Avoid Litigation" (February 2001), a conference paper delivered at the 22nd Annual Law and Higher Education Conference sponsored by Stetson University College of Law; Linda Langford & Miriam McKendall, "Assessing Legal Initiatives" (February 2004), a conference paper delivered at the 25th Annual Law and Higher Education Conference sponsored by Stetson University College of Law; Kathryn Bender, "Making and Modifying Policy on Campus: The 'When and Why' of Policymaking" (June 2004), a conference paper delivered at the 2004 Annual Conference of the National Association of College and University Attorneys; Tracy Smith, "Making and Modifying Policy on Campus" (June 2004), a conference paper delivered at the 2004 Annual Conference of the National Association of College and University Attorneys; and "Policy Development Process with Best Practices," a document of the Association of College and University Policy Administrators, available (along with additional resources on developing and implementing policy) on the association's Web site at http://www.acupa.org/.

legislatures, executive branch officials, and administrative agencies make policy decisions that create what we may think of as "public policy" or "external policy." In either case, policy must be made and policy issues must be resolved within the constraints of the law.

It is critically important for institutional administrators and counsel to focus on this vital interrelationship between law and policy whenever they are addressing particular problems, reviewing existing institutional policies, or creating new policies. In these settings, with most problems and policies, the two foundational questions to ask are, "What are the institutional policy or public policy issues presented?" and "What are the legal issues presented?" The two sets of issues often overlap and intertwine. Administrators and counsel may study both sets of issues; neither area is reserved exclusively for the cognitive processes of one profession to the exclusion of the other. Yet lawyers may appropriately think about and react to legal issues differently than administrators do; and administrators may appropriately think about and react to policy issues differently than do attorneys. These matters of role and expertise are central to the process of problem solving as well as the process of policy making, in particular for internal policy. While policy aspects of a task are more the bailiwick of the administrator and the legal aspects more the bailiwick of the lawyer, the professional expertise of each comes together in the policy-making process. In this sense, policy making is a joint project, a team effort. The policy choices suggested by the administrators may implicate legal issues, and different policy choices may implicate different legal issues; legal requirements, in turn, will affect the viability of various policy choices.[10]

The administrators' and attorneys' roles in policy making can be described and differentiated in the following way. Administrators identify actual and potential problems that are interfering or may interfere with the furtherance of institutional goals or the accomplishment of the institutional mission, or that are creating or may create threats to the health or safety of the campus community; they identify the causes of these problems; they identify other contributing factors pertinent to understanding each problem and its scope; they assess the likelihood and gravity of the risks that these problems create for the institution; they generate options for resolving the identified problems; and they accommodate, balance, and prioritize the interests of the various constituencies that would be affected by the various options proposed. In addition, administrators identify opportunities and challenges that may entail new policy-making initiatives; assess compliance with current institutional policies and identify needs for change; and assess the efficacy of existing policies (How well do

---

[10]The focus on administrators and counsel, here and elsewhere in this section, does not mean that faculty (the educators) are, or should be, cut out of the policy-making process. This section is based on the assumptions that administrators are sometimes faculty members or educators themselves; that administrators will regularly provide for faculty participation in policy-making committees and task forces; that administrators who oversee academic functions will regularly consult with pertinent faculties of the institution, directly and/or through their deans; and that administrators will respect whatever policy-making and decision-making roles are assigned to faculty under the institution's internal governance documents.

they work?) and of proposed policies (How well will they work?). Attorneys, in contrast:

- Identify existing and potential problems that create, or may create, exposure to legal risk for the institution or that may raise legal compliance issues
- Analyze the legal aspects of these problems using the applicable sources of law (Section 1.4)
- Generate legally sound options for resolving these problems and present them to the responsible administrators
- Assess the legal risk (if any) to which the institution would be exposed (see Section 2.4) under policy options that the policy makers have proposed either in response to the attorneys' advice or on their own initiative
- Participate in—and often take the lead in—drafting new policies and revising existing policies
- Suggest legally sound procedures for implementing and enforcing the policy choices of the policy makers
- Review existing institutional policies to ascertain whether they are in compliance with applicable legal requirements and whether there are any conflicts between or among existing policies
- Make suggestions for enhancing the legal soundness of existing policies and reducing or eliminating any risk of legal liability that they may pose
- Identify other legal consequences or by-products of particular policy choices (for example, that a choice may invite a governmental investigation, subject the institution to some new governmental regulatory regime, expose institutional employees to potential liability, or necessitate changes in the institution's relationships with its contractors).

Still other connections between law and policy are important for administrators and attorneys, as well as faculty and student leaders, to understand. One of the most important points about the relationship between the two, concerning which there is a growing consensus, is that policy should transcend law. This does not mean that policy should trump law but rather that policy is more than legal compliance, and the law leaves considerable room for policy making that is not dictated by legal considerations. Legal considerations, therefore, generally should not drive policy making, and policy making generally should not be confined to that which is necessary to fulfill legal requirements. Regarding internal policy, institutions that are serious about their institutional missions and goals will often choose to do more than the law requires. As an example, under Title IX of the Education Amendments of 1972, the courts have created lenient liability standards for institutions with regard to faculty members' harassment of students (see Section 8.5 of this book). An institution will be liable to the victim for money damages only when it had "actual notice" of the faculty harassment and only when its response is so insufficient that it amounts to "deliberate indifference." It is usually easy to avoid monetary liability under these standards, but doing so would not come close to ensuring the safety and health of students or ensuring that there is no hostile learning environment on campus. Institutions, therefore, would be unwise to limit their policy making regarding sexual harassment to only what the courts require under Title IX.

Policy, moreover, can become law—a particularly important interrelationship between the two. In the external realm of public policy, legislatures customarily write their policy choices into law, as do administrative agencies responsible for implementing legislation. There are also instances where courts have leeway to analyze public policy and make policy choices in the course of deciding cases. Courts may do so, for instance, when considering duties of care under negligence law, when determining whether certain contracts or contract provisions are contrary to public policy, and when making decisions, in various fields of law, based on a general standard of "reasonableness." In the internal realm of institutional policy, institutions also sometimes write their policy choices into law. They do so primarily by incorporating these choices into the institution's contracts with faculty members; students, administrators, and staff; and agents of the institution. This incorporation may be accomplished either by creating contract language that parallels the language in a particular policy or by "incorporating by reference," that is, by identifying particular policies by name in the contract and indicating that the policy's terms are to be considered terms of the contract. In such situations, the policy choices become law because they then may be enforced under the common law of contract whenever it can be shown that the institution has breached one or more of the policy's terms.

Finally, regarding the interrelationship between law and policy, it is important to emphasize that good policy should encourage **judicial deference** or **academic deference** by the courts in situations when the policy, or a particular application of it, is challenged in court. For internal policy, such deference would be given to the higher educational institution; for external policy, it would be given to the legislature or administrative agency whose policy is being challenged. Courts often defer to particular decisions or judgments of the institution, for example, when they are genuinely based upon the academic expertise of the institution and its faculty (see Section 2.2.2). It is therefore both good policy and good law for institutions to follow suggestions such as those outlined here, relying to the fullest extent feasible upon the academic expertise of administrators and faculty members, so as to maximize the likelihood that institutional policies, on their face and in their application, will be upheld by the courts if these policies are challenged.

# 2

# Legal Planning
# and Dispute Resolution

*Chapter 2 provides foundational information on the sources of legal liability for colleges and universities and how legal disputes are initiated and resolved. It discusses litigation, that is, the process of resolving a dispute in a court or government agency proceeding, and provides suggestions for how institutions can work to avoid litigation and ensuing legal liability. The concept of risk management is introduced; the role of counsel is explored, particularly with respect to the differences between treatment law (responding to litigation, threatened litigation, and government compliance investigations) and preventive law (developing policies and practices that minimize or forestall legal disputes); and the concept of preventive legal planning is explained. Finally, several models of alternative dispute resolution, which avoids agency or court litigation, are discussed and evaluated.*

## Section 2.1. Legal Liability

***2.1.1. Overview.*** Postsecondary institutions and their agents—the officers, administrators, faculty members, staff members, and others through whom the institution acts—may encounter various forms of **legal liability**. The type and extent of liability depends on the source of the legal responsibility that the institution or its agents have failed to meet, and also on the power of the tribunal that determines whether the institution or its agents have violated some legal responsibility.

The three sources of law that typically create legal liabilities are the federal Constitution and state constitutions, statutes and regulations (at federal, state, and local levels), and state common law (see Section 1.4.2.4). Constitutions typically govern actions by public institutions and their agents, although state constitutions may also be applied, under certain circumstances, to the conduct of private institutions and individuals. Statutes typically address who is subject to the law, the conduct prohibited or required by the law, and the consequences of failing to comply with the law. For example, employment discrimination laws specify what entities (employers, labor unions, employment agencies) are subject to the law's requirements, specify the types of discrimination that are prohibited by the law (race discrimination, disability discrimination, and so on), and address the penalties for violating the law (back pay, injunctions, and so on). For many statutes, administrative agency regulations elaborate on the actions required or prohibited by the statute, the criteria for determining that an institution or individual has violated the statute or regulation, and the methods of enforcement. Finally, the common law, particularly contract and tort law, has developed standards of conduct (for example, tort law's concept of legal duty and its various "reasonable person" standards) that, if violated, lead to legal liability.

***2.1.2. Types of liability.*** Liability may be institutional (corporate) liability on the one hand, or personal (individual) liability on the other. Depending on who is sued, both types of liability may be involved in the same case. Constitutional claims brought by faculty, students, or others against public institutions may create institutional liability (unless the institution enjoys sovereign immunity, as discussed in Section 3.4) as well as individual liability, if individuals are also sued and their acts constitute "state action" or action under "color of law" (see Section 4.4.4). Statutory claims often (especially under federal nondiscrimination statutes) create only institutional liability, but sometimes also provide for individual liability. Contract claims usually involve institutional liability, but occasionally may involve individual liability as well. Tort claims frequently involve both institutional and individual liability, except for situations in which the institution enjoys sovereign or charitable immunity. Institutional liability for tort, contract, and constitutional claims is discussed in Sections 3.2, 3.3, and 3.4; personal liability for these claims is discussed in Section 4.4.

***2.1.3. Agency law.*** Since postsecondary institutions act through their officers, employees, and other agents, the law of agency plays an important role in assessing liability, particularly in the area of tort law. Agency law provides that the employer (called the "principal" or the "master") must assume legal responsibility for the actions of its employees (called "agents" or "servants") and other "agents" under certain circumstances. Under the general rules of the law of agency, as applied to tort claims, the master may be liable for torts committed by its employees while they are acting in the scope of their employment. But the employer will not be liable for its employees' torts if they are acting outside the scope of their employment, unless one of four exceptions can be proven: for example, (1) if the employer intended that the tort or its consequences be committed; (2) if the master was negligent or reckless; (3) if the master had delegated a duty to the employee that was not delegable and the tort was committed as a result; or (4) if the employee relied on "apparent authority" by purporting to act or speak on behalf of the master (American Law Institute, Restatement (Third) of Agency §§ 7.03–7.08 (2006)). Generally speaking, it is difficult for an employer to avoid liability for the unlawful acts of an employee unless the allegedly unlawful act is taken to further a personal interest of the employee or is so distant from the employee's work-related responsibilities as to suggest that holding the employer legally responsible for the act would be unjust.

Students may on occasion be regarded as agents of the institution, even if they are not employees. See, for example, *Fils-Aime v. Ryder TRS, Inc. and Cornell University*, 837 N.Y.S.2d 199 (N.Y. App. Div. 2007). The institution's liability for the acts of its agents is discussed in Section 3.1 of this book and in various places in Sections 3.2 through 3.4. Sections 4.5 and 8.5 discuss institutional liability for agents' acts under federal civil rights statutes.

### 2.1.4. *Enforcement mechanisms.*

Postsecondary institutions may incur legal liability in a variety of proceedings. Students, employees, or others who believe that the institution has wronged them may often be able to sue the institution in court. Cases are usually (but not always) tried before a jury when the plaintiff claims monetary damages, but are tried before a judge when the plaintiff seeks only equitable remedies such as an injunction.

Some federal statutes permit an individual to sue for alleged statutory violations in federal court, but if the statute does not contain explicit language authorizing a private cause of action, an individual may be limited to seeking enforcement by a federal agency. (See, for example, Section 7.8.1 for a discussion of private lawsuits under the Family Educational Rights and Privacy Act (FERPA).)

Various federal laws are enforced through administrative mechanisms established by the administrative agency (or agencies) responsible for that law. For example, the U.S. Education Department enforces nondiscrimination requirements under federal spending statutes such as Title VI of the Civil Rights Act of 1964, Title IX of the Education Amendments of 1972, and Section 504 of the Rehabilitation Act of 1973 (see Sections 11.5.2–11.5.4 of this book). Similarly, the federal Occupational Safety and Health Administration (OSHA) enforces the Occupational Safety and Health Act, and the U.S. Department of Labor enforces the Fair Labor Standards Act and the Family and Medical Leave Act. Administrative enforcement may involve a compliance review of institutional programs, facilities, and records; negotiations and conciliation agreements; hearings before an administrative law judge; and appeals through the agency prior to resort to the courts. Many states have their own counterparts to the federal administrative agency enforcement system for similar state laws.

Several federal statutes provide for lawsuits to be brought by either an individual or a federal agency. In other cases, a federal agency may bring constitutional claims on behalf of one plaintiff or a class of plaintiffs. The U.S. Department of Justice, on occasion, acts as a plaintiff in civil cases against postsecondary institutions. For example, the Department of Justice sued Virginia Military Institute (VMI) under the U.S. Constitution's Fourteenth Amendment for VMI's refusal to admit women (see Section 7.2.4.2). It also sued the state of Mississippi under Title VI of the Civil Rights Act of 1964 and the Fourteenth Amendment, seeking to desegregate the state's dual system of higher education (see *United States v. Fordice*, discussed in Section 7.2.4.1). The Justice Department acts as a plaintiff in antitrust cases as well (see, for example, *United States v. Brown University*, 5 F.3d 658 (3d Cir. 1993)). The Justice Department also plays a role in cases brought under the False Claims Act. Other federal or state agencies may also sue postsecondary institutions in court. Such litigation may follow years of enforcement actions by the agency, and may result in fines or court orders to comply with the law.

Some institutions are turning to alternative methods of resolving disputes in order to avoid the time, expense, and public nature of litigation. Section 2.3 discusses the use of mediation, **arbitration,** and other methods of resolving disputes on campus.

**2.1.5. Remedies for legal violations.** The source of legal responsibility determines the type of remedy that may be ordered if an institution or its agent is judged liable. For example, violations of statutes and administrative agency regulations may lead to the termination of federal or state funding for institutional programs, debarment from future contracts or grants from the government agency, audit exceptions, or fines. Violations of statutes (and sometimes regulations) may also lead to an order that money damages be paid to the prevailing party. Equitable remedies may also be ordered, such as reinstatement of a terminated employee, cessation of the practice judged to be unlawful, or an injunction requiring the institution to perform particular acts (such as abating an environmental violation). Occasionally, criminal penalties may be imposed. For example, the Occupational Safety and Health Act provides for imprisonment for individuals who willfully violate the act. Criminal penalties may also be imposed for violations of certain computer fraud and crime statutes.

**2.1.6. Avoiding legal liability.** Legal compliance should be thought of as the minimum that the institution must do and not as the maximum that it should do. Policy considerations may often lead institutional decision makers to do more than the law actually requires (see Section 1.7). The culture of the institution, its mission, the prevailing academic norms and customs, and particular institutional priorities, as well as the law, may help shape the institution's legal and policy responses to potential legal liability. To capture this dynamic, discussions of legal liability throughout this book are interwoven with discussions of policy concerns; administrators and counsel are often encouraged (explicitly and implicitly) to base decisions on this law/policy dynamic. Section 2.4 discusses various strategies for managing the risk of legal liability.

**2.1.7. Treatment law and preventive law.** Institutions should give serious consideration to the particular functions that counsel will perform and to the relationships that will be fostered between counsel and administrators. Broadly stated, counsel's role is to identify and define actual or potential legal problems and provide options for resolving or preventing them. There are two basic, and different, ways to fulfill this role: through treatment law and through preventive law. To analogize to another profession, the goal of treatment law is to cure legal diseases, while the goal of preventive law is to maintain legal health. Under either approach, counsel will be guided not only by legal considerations and institutional goals and policies, but also by the ethical standards of the legal profession that shape the responsibilities of individual practitioners to their clients and the public.

Treatment law is the more traditional of the two practice approaches. It focuses on actual challenges to institutional practices and on affirmative legal steps by the institution to protect its interests when they are threatened. When suit is filed against the institution or litigation is threatened, when a government agency cites the institution for noncompliance with its regulations, when the institution needs formal permission of a government agency to undertake a proposed course of action, when the institution wishes to sue some other party—then treatment law operates. Counsel seeks to resolve the specific legal problem at hand. Treatment law today is indispensable to the functioning of a postsecondary institution, and virtually all institutions have such legal service.

Preventive law, in contrast, focuses on initiatives that the institution can take before actual legal disputes arise. Preventive law involves administrators and counsel in a continual cooperative process of setting the legal and policy parameters within which the institution will operate to forestall or minimize legal disputes. Counsel identifies the legal consequences of proposed actions; pinpoints the range of alternatives for avoiding problems and the legal risks of each alternative; sensitizes administrators and the campus community to legal issues and the importance of recognizing them early; determines the impact of new or proposed laws and regulations, and new court decisions, on institutional operations; and helps devise internal processes that support constructive relationships among members of the campus community. Administrators (and trustees) work with counsel in all of these respects. They also take the lead in choosing which policy options the institution will pursue (in light of counsel's advice concerning the risks of each option) and in making other policy decisions concerning institutional operations.

Prior to the 1980s, preventive law was not a general practice of postsecondary institutions. But this approach became increasingly valuable as the presence of law on the campus increased, and acceptance of preventive law within postsecondary education grew substantially. Today preventive law is as indispensable as treatment law and provides the more constructive overall posture from which to conduct institutional legal affairs.

Institutions using or considering the use of preventive law will need to determine what working arrangements will best ensure that administrators are alert to incipient legal problems and that counsel is involved in institutional decision making at an early stage. In addition, institutions will also need to delineate carefully the respective roles of administrators and counsel in the decision-making process. Once an institution has worked through these considerations, it should be positioned to engage in a continuing course of preventive legal planning. Legal planning is the process by which an institution identifies and assesses legal risks, determines the extent of legal risk exposure it is willing to assume in particular situations, and implements strategies for avoiding or resolving legal risks it is not willing to assume. In addition to legal considerations, legal planning encompasses ethical, administrative, and financial considerations, as well as the institution's policy preferences and priorities. Sometimes the law may be in tension with institutional policy; legal planners then may seek to devise alternative means for achieving a particular policy objective consistent with the law. Often, however, the law will be consistent with institutional policy; legal planners then may use the law to support and strengthen the institution's policy choices and may, indeed, implement initiatives more extensive than the law would require. Successful legal planning thus depends on a careful sorting out and interrelating of legal and policy issues, which in turn depends upon a teamwork relationship between administrators and counsel.

### Section 2.2. Litigation in the Courts

**2.2.1. Overview.** Of all the forums available for the resolution of higher education disputes (see Sections 1.1 and 2.3), administrators are usually most concerned about court litigation. There is good reason for the concern. Courts are the most public and thus most visible of the various dispute resolution forums. Courts are also the most formal, involving numerous technical matters that require extensive involvement of attorneys. In addition, courts may order the strongest and the widest range of remedies, including both compensatory and punitive money damages and both prohibitive and mandatory (affirmative) injunctive relief. Court decrees and opinions also have the highest level of authoritativeness; not only do a court's judgments and orders bind the parties for the future regarding the issues litigated, subject to enforcement through judicial contempt powers and other mechanisms, but a court's written opinions may also create precedents binding other litigants in future disputes as well (see Section 1.4.4).

For these reasons and others, court litigation is the costliest means of dispute resolution that institutions engage in—costly in time and emotional effort as well as in money—and the most risky. Thus, although lawsuits have become a regular occurrence in the lives of postsecondary institutions, involving a broad array of parties and situations (see Section 1.1), administrators should never trivialize the prospect of litigation. Involvement in a lawsuit is a serious and often complex business that can create internal campus friction, drain institutional resources, and affect an institution's public image, even if the institution eventually emerges as the "winner."

Even a "simple" lawsuit can become complex and lengthy. It can involve extensive formal pretrial activities, such as depositions, interrogatories, subpoenas, pretrial conferences, and motion hearings, as well as various informal pretrial activities such as attorney-administrator conferences, witness interviews, document searches and document reviews, and negotiation sessions with opposing parties. If the case proceeds to trial, there are all the difficulties associated with presenting a case before a judge or jury: further preparatory meetings with the attorneys; preparation of trial exhibits; scheduling, travel, and preparation of witnesses; the actual trial time; and the possibility of appeals. In order for the institution to present its best case, administrators will need to be intimately involved with most stages of the process. Litigation is also monetarily expensive, since a large amount of employee time must be committed to it and various fees must be paid for outside attorneys, court reporters, perhaps expert witnesses, and so forth. Fortunately, lawsuits proceed to trial and judgment less often than most laypeople believe. The vast majority of disputes are resolved through settlement negotiations. Although administrators must also be involved in such negotiations, the process is less protracted, more informal, and more private than a trial.

Despite the potential costs and complexities, administrators should avoid overreacting to the threat of litigation and, instead, develop a balanced view of the litigation process. Lawsuits can usually be made manageable with careful litigation planning, resulting from good working relationships between the institution's lawyers and its administrators. Often lawsuits can be avoided entirely with careful preventive planning. And preventive planning, even when it does not deflect the lawsuit, will likely strengthen the institution's litigation position, narrow the range of viable issues in the case, and help ensure that the institution retains control of its institutional resources and maintains focus on its institutional mission. Particularly for administrators, sound understanding of the litigation process is prerequisite to both constructive litigation planning and constructive preventive planning.

### 2.2.2. Judicial (academic) deference.

**2.2.2. Judicial (academic) deference.** Another consideration that should play a role in the management of litigation, and in an institution's presentation of its case, is "judicial deference" or "academic deference." At trial as well as on appeal, issues may arise concerning the extent to which the court should defer to, or give "deference" to, the institution whose decision or other action is at issue. As one commentator has explained:

> [A] concept of academic deference justifies treating many university processes and decisions differently from off-campus matters. This formulation is hardly novel. In fact, . . . many university cases recognize in this way the distinctive nature of the academic environment. Illustrations come from many areas. [Examples] that seem especially apt [include] university based research, personnel decisions, admissions of students, evaluation of student performance, and use of university facilities [Robert O'Neil, "Academic Freedom and the Constitution," 11 J.C. & U.L. 275, 283 (1984)].

This concept of academic deference is part of a more general concept of judicial deference that encompasses a variety of circumstances and reasons that indicate when a court should defer to the expertise of some decision maker other than itself.[1] Issues regarding academic deference can play a vital, sometimes even dispositive, role in litigation involving higher educational institutions. Institutions may therefore seek to claim deference at various points in the litigation process. (See generally O'Neil, *supra*, at 283–89.) Deference issues may arise, for example, with regard to whether a court should recognize an **implied private cause of action** (see, for example, *Cannon v. University of Chicago*, 441 U.S. 677, 709–10 (1979); with regard to the issuance of subpoenas and other aspects of the discovery process (see, for example, *University of Pennsylvania v. EEOC*, 493 U.S. 182 (1990); with regard to standards of review and burdens of proof; and with regard to the remedies to be imposed against a losing defendant (see, for example, *Kunda v. Muhlenberg College*, 621 F.2d 532, 547–51 (3d Cir. 1980)), discussed in Section 5.4.2). Sometimes requests for deference are framed as claims to institutional autonomy; sometimes as "institutional academic freedom" claims (see Section 6.1.7) or faculty academic freedom claims (see Section 6.2); and sometimes as "relative institutional competence" claims, asserting that the institution's or the faculty's competence concerning the matter at issue overshadows that of the court. Sometimes institutions may contend that their claim to deference is constitutionally based—especially when they rely on the academic freedom rationale for deference and seek to ground academic freedom in the First Amendment. At other times, in statutory cases, the deference claim may be based on statutory interpretation; in effect, the institution contends that, under the statute that is at issue, Congress was deferential to higher educational institutions and intended that courts should be deferential as well. And in yet other situations, especially in common law contract or tort cases, the deference claim may be based on public policy or legal policy considerations—for instance, that any court intervention would unduly interfere with the institution's internal affairs, or that vigorous enforcement of legal principles against higher education institutions would not be an effective use of the court's limited resources (see, for example, the discussions of deference in Sections 6.1.3 and 8.1 of this book).

When plaintiffs assert constitutional claims against an institution of higher education, deference issues may work out differently than when statutory claims are asserted. In a statutory case—for example, a case asserting that an institution has violated a federal civil rights law—the court will first be concerned with interpreting and applying the law consistent with Congress's intentions and in this regard will generally defer to Congress's own judgments about the law's application (see, for example, *Eldred v. Ashcroft*, 537 U.S. 186 (2003)). Thus the court will take its cue on deference from Congress rather than developing its own independent judgment on the matter. In *Cannon v.*

---

[1] Another branch of judicial deference that is highly important to higher education arises when an institution, or an association of institutions, challenges a rule or decision of a federal or state administrative agency in court. Questions may then arise concerning the extent to which the court should defer to the expertise or authority of the administrative agency.

*University of Chicago*, 441 U.S. 677 (1979), for example, the plaintiff sought to subject admissions decisions to the nondiscrimination requirements of Title IX of the Education Amendments of 1972. The defendant argued that it would be "unwise to subject admissions decisions of universities to judicial scrutiny at the behest of disappointed applicants" because "this kind of litigation is burdensome and inevitably will have an adverse effect on the independence of members of university committees." Responding, the Court asserted that "[t]his argument is not new to this litigation. It was forcefully advanced in both 1964 and 1972 by congressional opponents of Title VI and Title IX, and squarely rejected by the congressional majorities that passed the two statutes." The Court followed suit, rejecting the defendant's claim to deference. In other cases, involving other statutes, however, courts may discern that Congress intended to be deferential to postsecondary institutions in some circumstances and that courts should do the same.

In contrast, when plaintiffs assert constitutional claims and institutions ask the court for deference, the court is on its own; its response is shaped by consideration of applicable prior precedents and the applicable standard of judicial review. *Grutter v. Bollinger* (discussed in Section 7.2.5), a constitutional challenge to the University of Michigan Law School's race-conscious admission policy, is a leading example of this type of case. The plaintiffs, rejected applicants, sought a rigorous, nondeferential application of the federal Constitution's equal protection clause; the university sought deference for the academic judgments it had made in designing and implementing its diversity plan for admissions. The Court applied strict scrutiny review, requiring the university to show that maintaining the diversity of its student body was a compelling state interest. In applying this standard, however, the Court emphasized:

> The Law School's educational judgment that such diversity is essential to its educational mission is one to which we defer. . . Our scrutiny of the interest asserted by the Law School is no less strict for taking into account complex educational judgments in an area that lies primarily within the expertise of the university. Our holding today is in keeping with our tradition of giving a degree of deference to a university's academic decisions, within constitutionally prescribed limits [539 U.S. at 328].

This deference was a critical aspect of the Court's reasoning that led it, in a landmark decision, to uphold the law school's admissions policy. A more recent example of judicial deference occurs in *Christian Legal Society v. Martinez*, 130 S. Ct. 2971 (2010), discussed in Section 10.1.4 of this book. Both the majority opinion and Justice Stevens's concurrence note that judges should leave policy making to the educators.

In other constitutional cases, courts may reach the opposite result. In the Virginia Military Institute (VMI) case, *United States v. Virginia*, 518 U.S. 515 (1996) (discussed in Section 7.2.4.2), for instance, the U.S. Supreme Court bypassed the defendant institution's expert evidence and declined to defer to its judgment that maintaining VMI as an all-male institution was essential to the institution's educational mission. The Court's apparent reason for refusing to defer, and the apparent distinction between *Grutter* and *United States v. Virginia*, is that the Court did not view the state's judgments over the years about VMI's all-male character to be genuinely academic judgments, but rather viewed them as judgments based on other factors and later dressed up with educational research for purposes of the litigation. The state's proffered educational reasons for the all-male policy were "rationalizations for actions in fact differently grounded," said the Court, and were based on "overbroad generalizations" about the abilities and interests of the sexes.

The paradigmatic setting for institutions' invoking **academic deference,** and courts' granting it, is the setting of faculty tenure, promotion, and termination decisions. The deference issues arising in this setting and the key cases are discussed in Section 5.4.2, as is the evolving tendency of courts to subject these decisions to thorough scrutiny for fairness while deferring to the academic standards used to evaluate a candidate for promotion or tenure.

When faculty members challenge adverse personnel decisions, they may assert statutory claims (such as a Title VII sex discrimination claim), or constitutional claims (such as a First Amendment free speech or academic freedom claim), or sometimes common law claims (such as a breach of contract claim). In response, institutions typically argue that courts should not involve themselves in institutional personnel judgments concerning faculty members, since these are expert and evaluative (often subjective) academic judgments to which courts should defer.[2] Institutions have had considerable success with such arguments in this setting. They have also achieved similar success in cases concerning their academic evaluations of students; indeed, a student case, *Regents of the University of Michigan v. Ewing*, 474 U.S. 214 (1985) (discussed below), is one of the primary authorities on academic deference.

In a constitutional case, *Feldman v. Ho*, 171 F.3d 494 (7th Cir. 1999), for example, a professor claimed that Southern Illinois University did not renew his contract because he had accused a colleague of academic misconduct. The court rejected his First Amendment free speech claim by emphasizing the university's own academic freedom to make its own personnel decisions:

> A university seeks to accumulate and disseminate knowledge; for a university to function well, it must be able to decide which members of its faculty are productive scholars and which are not (or, worse, are distracting those who are)...
>
> If the University erred in telling [Professor] Feldman to seek employment elsewhere that is unfortunate, but the only way to preserve academic freedom is to keep claims of academic error out of the legal maw [171 F.3d at 495–97].

---

[2] Some personnel disputes will have gone to arbitration before landing in court. When an institution prevails in arbitration and the faculty member then files suit in court, the institution has an additional argument for deference: that the court should accord deference not only to the institution's judgment but also to the arbitrator's decision. See, for example, *Samoan v. Trustees of California State University and Colleges*, 197 Cal. Rptr. 856 (Cal. 1983).

At the same time, the court in *Feldman* issued a strong statement on the need for courts to defer to the academic judgments of colleges and universities:

> [A]n unsubstantiated charge of academic misconduct not only squanders the time of other faculty members (who must analyze the charge, or defend against it) but also reflects poorly on the judgment of the accuser. A university is entitled to decide for itself whether the charge is sound; transferring that decision to the jury in the name of the first amendment would undermine the university's mission—not only by committing an academic decision to amateurs (is a jury really the best institution to determine who should receive credit for a paper in mathematics?) but also by creating the possibility of substantial damages when jurors disagree with the faculty's resolution, a possibility that could discourage universities from acting to improve their faculty ... If the kind of decision Southern Illinois University made about Feldman is mete for litigation, then we might as well commit all tenure decisions to juries, for all are equally based on speech [171 F.3d at 497].

Like the *Feldman* court, most contemporary courts will recognize that they should accord deference to the academic decisions of academic institutions with regard to faculty personnel matters. But seldom are courts as outspoken on this point as was the court in *Feldman*. Other courts, moreover, may (and should) give more attention than the *Feldman* court to whether the decision being challenged was a *genuinely academic decision*, based on expert review of professional qualifications and performance.

There are also many statutory employment discrimination cases in which courts defer substantially to the faculty personnel judgments of colleges and universities (see generally Section 5.4 of this book), sometimes with language as striking as that in the *Feldman* opinion (see, for example, *Kyriakopoulos v. George Washington University*, 657 F. Supp. 1525, 1529 (1987)). But this does not mean that courts will, or should, defer broadly in all or most cases challenging faculty personnel decisions. There have been and will continue to be cases where countervailing considerations counsel against deference—for example, cases where there is evidence that an institution has relied on race, ethnicity, or gender in making an adverse personnel judgment; or where an institution has relied on personal animosity or bias, internal politics, or other nonacademic factors; or where an institution has declined to afford the faculty member procedural safeguards; or where a decision for the plaintiff would not significantly intrude on university decision makers' ability to apply their expertise and discretion in making personnel decisions. The court in *Kunda v. Muhlenberg College*, above, strikes the right note about such situations:

> The fact that the discrimination in this case took place in an academic rather than commercial setting does not permit the court to abdicate its responsibility ... Congress did not intend that those institutions which employ persons who work primarily with their mental faculties should enjoy a different status under Title VII than those which employ persons who work primarily with their hands [621 F.2d at 550].

As the preceding discussion suggests, several interrelated factors are key in determining when a court should defer to the judgments of a postsecondary institution. First and foremost, the judgment must be a genuine academic judgment. In *Regents of the University of Michigan v. Ewing*, 474 U.S. 214 (1985), the Court stated this requirement well: "When judges are asked to review the substance of a *genuinely academic decision* . . ., they should show great respect for the faculty's professional judgment" (474 U.S. at 225 (emphasis added)). The demonstrated exercise of "professional judgment" is a hallmark of an academic decision. Generally, as *Ewing* indicates, such judgments must be made in large part by faculty members based on their expertise as scholars and teachers. Such judgments usually require "an expert evaluation of cumulative information" and, for that reason, are not readily amenable to being reviewed using "the procedural tools of judicial or administrative decisionmaking" (*Board of Curators, University of Missouri v. Horowitz*, 435 U.S. 78, 90 (1978)). Such judgments are also usually "discretionary" and "subjective," and thus even less amenable to reasoned review on their merits by the courts.

A second key factor, related to the first, concerns relative institutional competence. Courts are more likely to defer when the judgment or decision being reviewed, even if not academic in character, involves considerations regarding which the postsecondary institution's competence is superior to that of the courts. The *Kunda* court, for instance, spoke of inquiries whose substance is "beyond the competence of individual judges" (621 F.2d at 548). Another court has advised that "courts must be ever-mindful of relative institutional competencies" (*Powell v. Syracuse University*, 580 F.2d 1150, 1153 (2d Cir. 1978)).

Third, courts are more likely to defer to the institution when a judicial decision against it would create undue burdens that would unduly interfere with its ability to perform its educational functions—or when similar judgments to follow, against other institutions, would subject them to similar burdens. The *Kunda* court (above), for instance, suggested that deference may be appropriate when a court decision would "necessarily intrude upon the nature of the educational process itself" (621 F.2d at 547). The U.S. Supreme Court in the *Cannon* case (above) suggested that deference may be appropriate if litigating issues of the type before the court would be "so costly or voluminous that . . . the academic community [would be] unduly burdened" (441 U.S. at 710). And the court in *Feldman* warned of judicial decisions that would interfere with the institution's ability to fulfill its educational mission.

And fourth, occasionally a court may assert that the plaintiff's claim is not significant enough to warrant judicial intervention. For example, a Georgia state appellate court ruled broadly that "disputes concerning academic decisions made by public institutions of learning present no justiciable controversy" and that a trial court's injunction requiring a university to reinstate a student was erroneously awarded. In *Board of Regents of University System of Georgia v. Houston*, 638 S.E. 2d 750 (Ga. Ct. App. 2006), a student who was suspended for two semesters after he was arrested for attempting to arrange a marijuana sale sought a temporary restraining order to reinstate him at Georgia Institute of Technology (Georgia Tech) and on the football team. Despite the fact that the discipline was for social (and criminal) misconduct rather than for academic misconduct, the court, quoting earlier decisions by the Georgia Supreme Court, applied the academic abstention doctrine to the case. Said the court, "[a]bsent plain necessity impelled by a deprivation of major proportion, the hand of the judicial branch alike must be withheld," citing *McDaniel v. Thomas*, 285 S.E.2d 156 (Ga. 1981). The court explained that the student had not raised an equal protection claim of disparate treatment in punishment and that "there is no right to participate in extracurricular sports, including football." Therefore, the trial court lacked jurisdiction over the controversy.

By developing the converse of the reasons for according deference, one can discern various reasons why a court would or should *not* defer to a college or university. Again, there are three overlapping categories of reasons. First, if the judgment to be reviewed by the court is not a "genuinely academic decision," courts are less likely to defer. As the Court in *Ewing* noted, if "the person or committee responsible did not actually exercise professional judgment" (474 U.S. at 225), there is little reason to defer. This is particularly so if the nonacademic reason for the decision may be an illegitimate reason, such as racial or gender bias (see *Gray v. Board of Higher Education*, 692 F.2d 901, 909 (2d Cir. 1982), and *Williams v. Lindenwood*, 288 F.3d 349, 356 (8th Cir. 2002)). Second, if the judgment being reviewed is a disciplinary rather than an academic judgment, the court's competence is relatively greater and the university's is relatively less; the factor of relative institutional competence may therefore become a wash or weigh more heavily in the court's (and thus the challenger's) favor. Similarly, when the challenge to the institution's decision concerns the procedures it used rather than the substance or merits of the decision itself, the court's competence is greater than the institution's, and there is usually little or no room for deference. The case of *Board of Curators v. Horowitz*, above, explores these two distinctions at length. Third, when reviewing and overturning an institutional decision would not intrude upon the institution's core functions, or would not likely burden other institutions with a flood of litigation, these reasons for deference diminish as well. The U.S. Supreme Court used this point in *University of Pennsylvania v. EEOC*, above, when it declined to defer to the university because upholding the plaintiff's request would have only an "extremely attenuated" effect on academic freedom. And fourth, if the plaintiff alleges significant constitutional deprivations, it is unlikely that the court will withhold review.

### 2.2.3. *Managing litigation and the threat of litigation.*

Managing, settling, and conducting litigation, like planning to avoid it, requires at all stages the in-depth involvement of attorneys.[3] Institutions should place heavy

---

[3] The suggestions in this section apply not only to litigation against the institution but also to suits against officers or employees of the institution when the institution is providing them, or considering providing them, with legal representation or related assistance. In suits in which both the institution and one or more named institutional officers or employees are defendants, questions may arise concerning possible conflicts of interest that could preclude the institution's legal staff from representing all or some of the officers or employees.

emphasis on this aspect of institutional operations. Both administrators and counsel should cultivate conditions in which they can work together as a team in a treatment law mode (see Section 2.1.7). The administrator's basic understanding of the tactical and technical matters concerning jurisdiction, procedure, evidence, and remedies, and counsel's mastery of these technicalities and the tactical options and difficulties they present, will greatly enhance the institution's capacity to engage in treatment law that successfully protects the institution's mission as well as its reputation and financial resources. Counsel's understanding of judicial deference (see Section 2.2.2 above) and its tactical role in litigation is also of critical importance.

Litigation management is a two-way street. It may be employed either in a defensive posture, when the institution or its employees are sued or threatened with suit, or in an offensive posture, when the institution seeks access to the courts as the best means of protecting its interests with respect to a particular dispute. Administrators, like counsel, will thus do well to consider treatment law from both perspectives and to view courts and litigation as offering, in some circumstances, a potential benefit, rather than only as presenting a hindrance.

Although administrators and counsel must accord great attention and energy to lawsuits when they arise and thus must emphasize the expert practice of treatment law, their primary and broader objective should be to avoid lawsuits or limit their scope whenever that can be accomplished consistently with the institutional mission. Once a lawsuit has been filed, administrators and counsel sometimes can achieve this objective by using summary judgment motions or (if the institution is a defendant) motions to dismiss, or by encouraging pretrial negotiation and settlement. Moreover, by agreement of the parties, the dispute may be diverted from the courts to a mediator or an arbitrator. Even better, administrators and counsel may be able to derail disputes from the litigation track before any suit is filed by providing for a suitable alternative mechanism for resolving the dispute. Mediation and arbitration are common and increasingly important examples of such alternative dispute resolution (ADR) mechanisms (see Section 2.3 below), which are usable whether the institution is a defendant or a plaintiff and whether the dispute is an internal campus dispute or an external dispute with a commercial vendor, construction contractor, or other outside entity. For internal campus disputes, internal grievance processes and hearing panels (see, for example, Section 9.1) are also important ADR mechanisms and may frequently constitute remedies that, under the "exhaustion-of-remedies" doctrine (see, for example, *Florida Board of Regents v. Armesto*, 563 So. 2d 1080 (Fla. Sup. Ct. 1990)), disputants must utilize before resorting to court.

Even before disputes arise, administrators and counsel should be actively engaging in preventive law (Section 2.1.7) as the most comprehensive and forward-looking means of avoiding and limiting lawsuits. Preventive law also has a useful role to play in the wake of a lawsuit, especially a major one in which the institution is sued and loses. In such a circumstance, administrators may engage in a "post-litigation audit" of the institutional offices and functions involved in the lawsuit—using the audit as a lens through which to view institutional shortcomings of the type that led to the judgment against the institution and to rectify such shortcomings in a way that serves to avoid future lawsuits in that area of concern.

## Section 2.3.  Alternative Dispute Resolution

***2.3.1.  Overview.***  The substantial cost of litigation, in terms of both time and money, and the law's limited capacity to fully resolve some types of disputes, have encouraged businesses, other organizations, and even courts to turn to alternative dispute resolution (ADR). ADR encompasses a variety of approaches to resolving disputes, from informal consultation with an ombudsperson who is vested with the authority to resolve some disputes and to seek resolution of others, to more formal processes such as grievance procedures, mediation, or arbitration. Commercial disputes and disputes in the financial services industry have been resolved through arbitration for decades. Academe has been slow to accept ADR, but it is becoming more common for certain kinds of disputes, and more institutions are turning to ADR in an attempt to reduce litigation costs and to resolve disputes, if possible, in a less adversarial manner.

Many employers embrace ADR because of its promise of quicker, less expensive resolution of disputes, and this promise is often realized. Some for-profit colleges have also begun to include arbitration clauses in their enrollment agreements with students for the same reasons. Discovery is not used in mediation and is limited in arbitration as well. Arbitrators typically do not use judicial rules of evidence, may admit evidence that a court would not (such as hearsay evidence), and generally issue a ruling (called an "award") a month or two after the hearing, unless they issue an oral award on the spot. The parties select the mediator or arbitrator jointly, rather than being assigned a judge, which may give them more confidence in the process. Indeed, the parties design the process in order to meet their needs, and can change the process if it needs improvement.

ADR has some disadvantages, however. ADR is a private process, and there is typically no public record made of the outcome. This characteristic of ADR tends to benefit the college or university, which would prefer to avoid public inquiry into personnel or student academic performance decisions, and may make it difficult for an employee or student who must help to select a mediator or arbitrator to evaluate that individual's record or previous rulings. The lack of public accountability is viewed as problematic because many of these claims have a statutory basis, yet they are resolved without judicial or regulatory agency scrutiny. As discussed below, the decisions of arbitrators are difficult to appeal and are usually considered final. Furthermore, there may be a substantial difference in skill and knowledge between the employee or student who is challenging an institution's decision and the individual who is representing the institution before the mediator or arbitrator. Many ADR systems prohibit attorneys for either party, and even if attorneys are permitted, the employee or student may not be able to afford to retain one.

***2.3.2. Types of ADR.*** ADR may use internal processes, external third parties, or both. Internal processes include grievance procedures, in which a student or employee may challenge a decision by invoking a right, usually created by the employee's contract, state law, or a student code of conduct, to have the decision reviewed by an individual or small group who were not involved in the challenged decision. Mediation and arbitration involve a third party neutral, who may be a noninvolved student or employee, or a professional trained in dispute resolution. Some ADR processes use all of these mechanisms to resolve disputes.

Grievance procedures, particularly those included in collective bargaining agreements, may have multiple steps, and may culminate either in a final decision by a high-level administrator or a neutral individual who is not an employee of the institution. Depending upon the language of any contracts with employees or relevant state law, the fact finding of a grievance panel may be viewed by a reviewing court as binding on the institution and the grievant. For example, in *Murphy v. Duquesne University of the Holy Ghost*, 777 A.2d 418 (Pa. 2001), a tenure revocation case discussed in Section 5.7.3 of this book, the court ruled that a faculty panel's fact finding was binding on the plaintiff, who could not relitigate the issue of whether the institution had demonstrated that his misconduct satisfied the contractual grounds for termination. However, if a faculty grievance panel recommends a resolution to a dispute that involves compromise or other ADR mechanisms, a court may not allow the plaintiff to argue that this finding has **preclusive effect** in a breach of contract claim, as in *Breiner-Sanders v. Georgetown University*, 118 F. Supp. 2d 1 (D.D.C. 1999). In that case, the court ruled that the grievance panel had not applied contract law principles in its hearing of a faculty member's grievance and thus the panel's decision, which was favorable to the faculty member, did not have preclusive effect and did not support a motion for summary judgment on behalf of the faculty member.

The inclusion of a grievance procedure in a faculty or staff employee handbook may convince a court that a plaintiff who has not exhausted internal remedies may not pursue contractual remedies in court. For example, in *Brennan v. King*, 139 F.3d 258 (1st Cir. 1998), an assistant professor who was denied tenure by Northeastern University brought breach of contract and discrimination claims against the university. With respect to the professor's contract claims, the court ruled that Massachusetts law required him to exhaust his contractual remedies before bringing suit. However, the court allowed his discrimination claims to go forward because the faculty handbook did not provide a remedy for the denial of tenure.

Even if there is no formal grievance process, in situations where faculty are challenging negative employment decisions (such as discipline or termination), a panel of peers may be convened to consider whether there are sufficient grounds for a challenged employment decision. The outcome of the peer panel's deliberations is usually considered a recommendation, which the administration may accept, modify, or reject. In addition, student judicial boards are a form of peer review of student charges of misconduct, although appeals are usually ultimately decided by a high-level administrator. Finally, ombudspersons, or neutral employees of the institution who have the responsibility to try to resolve disputes informally and confidentially, are appearing with more frequency on campus.[4]

ADR processes involving individuals external to the institution include mediation, in which a neutral third party is engaged to work with the parties to a dispute in an effort to resolve the conflict. The mediator may meet with the parties together to attempt to resolve the dispute or may meet with each party separately, hearing their concerns and helping to craft a resolution. The mediator has no authority to decide the outcome but may provide suggestions to the parties after listening to each party's concerns. All parties to the dispute must agree with the outcome in order for the process to be final.

Although mediation can be very successful in resolving disputes between employees or even between students (such as roommate disputes), there is one area in which mediation may not be used. The Office for Civil Rights (OCR), in its Title IX enforcement guidance for the sexual harassment of students, states that Title IX regulations require schools and colleges to adopt grievance procedures. The guidance, however, goes on to state the following:

> Grievance procedures may include informal mechanisms for resolving sexual harassment complaints to be used if the parties agree to do so. OCR has frequently advised schools, however, that it is not appropriate for a student who is complaining of harassment to be required to work out the problem directly with the individual alleged to be harassing him or her, and certainly not without appropriate involvement by the school (e.g., participation by a counselor, trained mediator, or, if appropriate, a teacher or administrator). In addition, the complainant must be notified of the right to end the informal process at any time and begin the formal stage of the complaint process. In some cases, such as alleged sexual assaults, mediation will not be appropriate even on a voluntary basis . . . [*Revised Sexual Harassment Guidance: Harassment of Students by School Employees, Other Students, or Third Parties* (2001), available at http://www2.ed.gov/about/offices/list/ocr/docs/shguide.html#IX].

In addition to concerns about an alleged victim's right to pursue a more formal grievance process, mediation of harassment or assault claims may mean that no formal record is made of the harassment or assault claim or its resolution, which could pose a problem if the alleged victim subsequently filed a lawsuit against the college or university or its staff.

Another form of ADR, used frequently on campuses where employees are represented by unions, is arbitration. An arbitrator, a third-party neutral with experience in employment issues, is brought in to act as a "private judge."

---

[4]Information about ombudspersons may be found on the Web site of the International Ombudsman Association (www.ombudsassociation.org). For basic information on the role of ombudspersons at colleges and universities, see "Nuts and Bolts: Establishing and Operating a College or University Ombuds Office," available at http://www.ombudsassociation.org/sites/default/files/NutsandBolts102308.pdf.

The parties present their concerns to the arbitrator at a hearing at which the employer has the burden of proving that the termination or discipline was justified. Arbitration is also used to resolve disputes over the meaning of contract language; in that case, the party disputing the application of the contract language to a problem (usually, but not always, the union) has the burden of demonstrating that the contract has been breached. Under a trio of U.S. Supreme Court cases called the "Steelworkers Trilogy,"[5] arbitration decisions are not reviewable by courts unless the arbitrator has exceeded the authority given to him or her by the contract, the arbitrator has engaged in misconduct, or the outcome of the arbitration violates some important principle of public policy.

ADR systems in collective bargaining agreements are subject to the negotiation process and typically state that all claims arising under the contract will be subject to a grievance procedure that culminates in arbitration. Arbitration may be advisory to the parties, or they may agree to be bound by the decision of the arbitrator (in which case the arbitration is called "binding arbitration"). At some colleges and universities, nonunionized employees may be asked to sign agreements to arbitrate all employment-related disputes, rather than filing lawsuits. These "mandatory arbitration agreements" have sustained vigorous court challenges, particularly by plaintiffs attempting to litigate employment discrimination claims. The legal standards for enforcing an arbitration agreement when employment discrimination claims are brought by unionized employees are discussed in Section 4.3.3 of this book.

If the employees are not unionized, however, the standards for enforcing arbitration clauses are somewhat less strict. Beginning with a decision by the U.S. Supreme Court in *Gilmer v. Interstate-Johnson Lane*, 500 U.S. 20 (1991), courts have agreed to enforce arbitration clauses in individual employment contracts. Gilmer, a registered securities representative, had signed a contract that required him to submit all employment disputes to compulsory arbitration. When he challenged his discharge by filing an age discrimination claim, his employer filed a motion to compel arbitration, which the trial court upheld. The appellate court reversed, but the U.S. Supreme Court sided with the trial court, ruling that the language of the contract must be enforced.

In several cases decided after *Gilmer*, trial courts have enforced arbitration clauses in situations where plaintiffs have filed employment discrimination claims with an administrative agency or in court. The Supreme Court in *Gilmer* noted that the Federal Arbitration Act (9 U.S.C. §§ 1 et seq.) favors arbitration agreements and that they should be upheld whenever appropriate. Since *Gilmer*, most lower federal courts, as well as the U.S. Supreme Court, have upheld most arbitration agreements; these cases are discussed in Section 4.3.3.

Courts typically use contract law principles to determine whether an employee's agreement to use arbitration rather than to litigate is binding. In *Futrelle v.*

---

[5] *Steelworkers v. American Manufacturing Co.*, 363 U.S. 564 (1960); *Steelworkers v. Enterprise Wheel and Car Corp.*, 363 U.S. 593 (1960); and *Steelworkers v. Warrior and Gulf Navigation*, 363 U.S. 574 (1960).

*Duke University*, 488 S.E.2d 635 (N.C. Ct. App. 1997), a state appellate court dismissed a medical librarian's breach of contract, wrongful discharge, and defamation claims because she had used Duke University's internal grievance procedure, which culminated in arbitration. The plaintiff had prevailed at arbitration and Duke gave her a check for the damages the university had been ordered to pay by the arbitrator. The court ruled that, because the plaintiff had cashed the check, which was in satisfaction of the arbitration award, she was precluded from initiating litigation about the same issues that had been determined through arbitration.

### 2.3.3. Applications to colleges and universities.

Litigation involving ADR in colleges and universities has focused primarily on arbitration and on these issues: Are arbitration clauses lawful in student enrollment agreements, what issues may an arbitrator decide, and under what circumstances may an arbitration award be overturned by a court?

With respect to the second issue, because ADR mechanisms are created by the parties in contracts, an arbitrator's authority to resolve a particular issue and the authority to impose a sanction are creatures of the arbitration agreement. Although faculty at a number of unionized colleges and universities are covered by collective bargaining agreements that provide for arbitral review of most employment decisions, many agreements do not permit the arbitrator to grant or deny tenure, although they may allow the arbitrator to determine the procedural compliance or fairness of the tenure decision. In *Board of Trustees of the California State University v. Public Employment Relations Board*, 66 Cal. Rptr. 3d 389 (Cal. Ct. App., 2d Dist. 2007), the state's Public Employment Relations Board, interpreting the state's enabling legislation for collective bargaining at the state university system, had ruled that a collective bargaining agreement between the faculty union and the California State University system could not include a provision that limited the power of an arbitrator to reverse a campus president's decision on appointment, reappointment, tenure, or promotion. A state appellate court reversed the board's ruling, stating that the board had misinterpreted the statute, and allowed the limitation on the arbitrator's authority to stand.

Grievants challenging a tenure denial may attempt to state claims of procedural noncompliance that actually attack the substance of the tenure decision. For example, in *AAUP, University of Toledo Chapter v. University of Toledo*, 797 N.E.2d 583 (Oh. Ct. C.P. 2003), an assistant professor denied tenure challenged the negative decision as a procedural violation, stating that the determinations of the department chair and the dean that the professor had produced an insufficient number of publications violated the contract's procedural requirements. The arbitrator ruled that the agreement had not been violated and found for the university, and the plaintiff appealed the award to a state trial court. The court upheld the arbitrator's award, stating that the contract's procedural requirements afforded the chair and the dean the latitude to determine what weight to give a tenure candidate's publications compared with teaching and service, and that the arbitrator did not exceed his authority by interpreting the contract in the university's favor.

The decision of an institution to limit arbitration of employment decisions to procedural issues rather than to the merits of the decision may persuade a court to allow a plaintiff to litigate the merits of the decision in court—at least when discrimination is alleged. In *Brennan v. King*, cited above, a faculty handbook provided for arbitration of procedural issues in tenure disputes but specifically provided that the arbitrator was without the power to grant or deny tenure. Because the arbitration procedure did not provide "a forum for the entire resolution" of the candidate's tenure dispute, said the court, the plaintiff did not have to exhaust his arbitral remedies prior to bringing a lawsuit alleging discrimination.

Although arbitration awards are usually final and binding (unless the agreement provides for some other arrangement, such as "advisory arbitration"), courts are reluctant to overturn an arbitrator's award because its finality was intended by the parties to the agreement. Nevertheless, courts will overturn arbitration awards that go beyond the power of the arbitrator, that are viewed as harmful to public policy, or that are a result of arbitrator misconduct (such as a conflict of interest or dishonesty). Generally speaking, a court will examine whether the issues as defined by the parties and the arbitrator are within the terms of the agreement. Second, the authority for the arbitrator's award must be rationally derived from the agreement (*State System of Higher Education v. State College and University Professional Association*, 743 A.2d 405 (Pa. 1999)). (See *Luzerne County Community College Association of Higher Education v. Luzerne County Community College*, 916 A.2d 731 (Pa. Commw. Ct. 2007), upholding the arbitrator's award of promotion because the agreement included such authority; but see *Massachusetts Board of Higher Education v. Massachusetts Teachers Association*, 943 N.E. 2d 485 (Mass. App. Ct. 2011), holding that an arbitrator had exceeded his authority by ordering a college to hire a grievant.)

If an arbitration award is challenged on public policy grounds, the party seeking to overturn the award must demonstrate that the award is contrary to law or some recognized source of public policy. For example, in *Illinois Nurses Association v. Board of Trustees of the University of Illinois*, 741 N.E.2d 1014 (Ill. App. Ct. 2000), a nurse had been fired for actions that endangered patient safety. An arbitrator reinstated her, ruling that the hospital had not proved one of the charges and that the nurse's long seniority and otherwise good work record mitigated the severity of her misconduct. The court refused to enforce the arbitrator's award, ruling that the nurse's actions had threatened patient safety and thus her reinstatement violated public policy with respect to patient care.

Arbitration clauses are appearing in student enrollment agreements, particularly those used by for-profit proprietary schools. To date, most students who have signed such agreements, but who have then attempted to avoid arbitration and pursue class action claims for fraud, breach of contract, and other state law claims, have been unsuccessful. The decision of the U.S. Supreme Court in *AT&T Mobility v. Conception*, 131 S. Ct. 1740 (2011), which ruled that arbitration clauses containing waivers of class action claims, both in court and in arbitration, were not preempted by the Federal Arbitration Act, is in large part responsible for this lack of success.

Faculty and administrators should carefully weigh the benefits and challenges of ADR systems when considering whether to implement such innovations as mediation, arbitration, or the creation of a campus ombudsperson. Although these systems are useful in channeling disputes away from the courts, they require extensive internal processes, additional staff, and careful adherence to procedural requirements in order to be effective.

### Section 2.4. *Institutional Management of Liability Risk*[6]

**2.4.1. *Overview and suggestions.*** The risk of financial liability for injury to another party remains a major concern for postsecondary institutions as well as their officers, faculties, and other personnel. This section examines various methods for managing such risk exposure and thus minimizing the detrimental effects of liability on the institution and members of the campus community. Risk management may be advisable not only because it helps stabilize the institution's financial condition over time but also because it can improve the morale and performance of institutional personnel by alleviating their concerns about potential personal liability. In addition, risk management can implement the institution's humanistic concern for minimizing the potential for injuries to innocent third parties resulting from its operations, and for compensating any such injuries that do occur.

The major methods of risk management may be called risk avoidance, risk control, risk transfer, and risk retention. For risk transfer, there are three subcategories of methods: liability insurance, indemnity (or "hold-harmless") agreements, and releases (or waivers).

Institutions should find it helpful to develop these various methods of risk management, and strategies for their implementation, into a campus risk management plan. A key component of any such plan is a professional risk manager or an office of risk management that provides a focal point for the institution's risk management efforts. The institution's legal counsel should also be involved in all phases of risk management. Another helpful organizational device would be an institution-wide risk management team or committee, which may also include school-level or division-level coordinators or teams. Risk assessment should be an essential aspect of any risk management plan. For some institutions, external consultants may be an important source of assistance in undertaking a comprehensive assessment of institutional risks or periodically updating this assessment. Risk assessment teams from within various sectors of the institution may also be helpful. (For additional guidance and resources, see the Web site of the University Risk Management and Insurance Association, at http://www.URMIA.org.)

**2.4.2. *Risk management strategies.*** The most certain method for managing a known exposure to liability is *risk avoidance*—the elimination of conditions, activities, or programs that are the sources of the risks. This

---

[6]This section was updated by Jonathan R. Alger, former senior vice president and general counsel at Rutgers University and currently president of James Madison University.

method is often not realistic, however, since it could require institutions to forgo activities important to their educational missions. It might also require greater knowledge of the details of myriad campus activities than administrators typically can acquire and greater certainty about the legal principles of liability (see Sections 3.2–3.4 and 4.4) than the law typically affords.

*Risk control* is less drastic than risk avoidance. The goal is to reduce, rather than eliminate entirely, the frequency or severity of potential exposures to liability—mainly by improving the physical environment or by modifying hazardous behavior or activities in ways that reduce the recognized risks. Although this method may have less impact on an institution's educational mission than would risk avoidance, it may similarly require considerable detailed knowledge of campus facilities and functions and of legal liability principles.

Risk assessments (see Section 2.4.1 above) are critical to the implementation of risk avoidance and control strategies. Risk assessment teams would therefore be an important organizational device to use with these methods of risk management. Another important organizational device is a crisis management team to manage institution-wide crises, along with other smaller teams to deal with particular crises affecting an individual or a small number of individuals (for example, a mental health crisis).

Purchasing commercial liability insurance is the first way in which institutions can *transfer the risk of liability* to others. An institution can insure against liability for its own acts, as well as liability transferred to it by a "hold-harmless" agreement (discussed below) with its personnel. With the advice of insurance experts, the institution can determine the kinds and amounts of liability protection it needs and provide for the necessary premium expenditures in its budgeting process.

There are two basic types of insurance policies important to higher education institutions. The first and primary type is general liability insurance; it provides broad coverage of bodily injury and property damage claims, such as would arise in the case of a negligently caused injury to a student or staff member. The second type is directors and officers insurance ("D & O" coverage, or sometimes "errors and omissions" coverage). It typically covers claims for wrongful acts without bodily injury, such as employment claims, student discipline, and due process violations.

General liability insurance policies usually exclude from their coverage both intentionally or maliciously caused damage and damage caused by acts that violate penal laws. Liability arising from the violation of an individual's constitutional or civil rights is also commonly excluded from general liability insurance coverage—an exclusion that can pose considerable problems for administrators and institutions, whose exposure to such liability has escalated greatly since the 1960s. In specific cases, questions about this exclusion may become entwined with questions concerning intent or malice.

Exclusions from coverage may exist either because state law requires the exclusion or because the insurer has made its own business decision to exclude certain actions from its standard coverages. When the exclusion is of the latter type, institutions may nevertheless be able to cover such risks by combining a

standard policy with one or more specialty endorsements or companion policies, such as a directors and officers policy. If this arrangement still does not
provide all the coverage the institution desires, and if the institution can afford
the substantial expense, it may request a "manuscript" policy tailored to its
specific needs.

A second method of risk transfer is a "hold-harmless" or **indemnification**
agreement, by which institutions can transfer their liability risks to other parties
or transfer to themselves the liability risks of their officers or employees or other
parties. In a broad sense, the term "indemnification" refers to any compensation
for loss or damage. Insurance is thus one method of indemnifying someone.
But in the narrower sense used here, indemnification refers to an arrangement
whereby one party (for example, the institution) agrees to hold another party
(for example, an individual officer or employee) harmless from financial liability for certain acts or omissions of that party that cause damage to another.
Institutions may also hold, or be asked to hold, outside parties harmless from
liability in certain circumstances. This matter is most likely to arise with parties
that have some kind of professional affiliation (for example, for internship placements) or ongoing business relationship with the institution.

Like insurance policies, indemnification agreements often do not cover liability resulting from intentional or malicious action or from action violating the
state's penal laws. Just as public policy may limit the types of acts or omissions
that may be insured against, it may also limit those for which indemnification
may be received.

Both public and private institutions may enter indemnification agreements.
A public institution, however, may need specific authorizing legislation (see,
for example, Mich. Comp. Laws § 691.1408), while private institutions usually
can rely on the general laws of their states for sufficient authority. Some states
also provide for indemnification of state employees for injuries caused by their
acts or omissions on behalf of the state (see, for example, Cal. Gov't Code
§§ 995 et seq.) or for torts committed within the scope of their employment
(see, for example, Ill. Code, 5 Ill. Comp. Stat. 350(2)(d)).

State laws on defense and indemnification are often general, and may vary
considerably from state to state. To have a sound and clear institutional policy,
adapted to the academic environment, public institutions may need to expand
upon applicable state law.

A third method of risk transfer is the release or waiver agreement. This
type of arrangement releases one party from liability to another for injuries
arising from some particular undertaking in which both parties are involved.
In postsecondary education, this mechanism is most likely to be used for student activities and services, such as intercollegiate athletics, provision of medical services, study abroad programs, and student field trips, which involve
acknowledged risks. In such circumstances, the institution may require the
student to execute a release or waiver as a precondition to participation in
the activity or receipt of the service.

Postsecondary institutions may also use "consent forms" for certain activities or services—for example, a form securing a consent to a particular medical

treatment, or consent for the institution to authorize medical treatment on the participant's or recipient's behalf. Consent forms are not the same as releases and will not have the legal effect of a release unless clear exculpatory language, like that used in releases, is added to the consent form. Absent such exculpatory clauses, use of a consent form may actually increase, rather than decrease, an institution's potential liability. In *Fay v. Thiel College*, 2001 WL 1910037 (Pa. 2001), for example, a college had had students sign medical consent forms before participating in a study abroad trip. The form authorized the college's representatives to secure medical treatment in case of emergency. The plaintiff, a student who became ill on the trip and was left behind for medical treatment at a medical clinic, alleged that she had received unnecessary surgery and been sexually assaulted at the clinic. The court held that the consent form created a "special relationship" between the college and the student and that, due to this relationship, the college owed the student a "special duty of care" regarding medical treatment while she was on the trip. The court therefore denied the college's motion for summary judgment and ordered a jury trial on whether the college had breached this duty.

The most practical option for the institution in some circumstances may be to retain the risk of financial liability. *Risk retention* may be appropriate, for instance, in situations where commercial insurance is unavailable or too costly, the expected losses are so small that they can be considered normal operating expenses, or the probability of loss is so remote that it does not justify any insurance expense. Both insurance policy deductibles and methods of self-insurance are examples of risk retention. The deductible amounts in an insurance policy allocate the first dollar coverage of liability, up to the amount of the deductible, to the institution. The institution becomes a self-insurer by maintaining a separate bank account to pay appropriate claims. The institution's risk managers must determine the amount to be available in the account and the frequency and amount of regular payments to the account. This approach is distinguished from simple noninsurance by the planning and actuarial calculations that it involves.

### 2.4.3. Enterprise risk management.
In recent years, universities have been considering and implementing more comprehensive programs for risk assessment, management and prevention, which can be grouped under the category of "enterprise risk management" (ERM). ERM focuses on various risk areas within an institution, such as strategic, competitive, operational, and financial risks, among others. The goal of ERM is to manage risk across the university in a holistic way, which requires buy-in from all levels in the university. In 2007, the National Association of College and University Business Officers (NACUBO) and the Association of Governing Boards of Universities and Colleges (AGB) convened a summit on ERM and later published their findings in a user-friendly white paper called "Meeting the Challenges of Enterprise Risk Management in Higher Education," available at http://www .ucop.edu/riskmgt/erm/documents/agb_nacubo_hied.pdf. This white paper was followed in 2009 by "The State of Enterprise Risk Management at Colleges

and Universities Today," published by AGB and available at http://agb.org/ sites/agb.org/files/u3/AGBUE_FINAL.pdf. The same year, Arthur J. Gallagher & Co., a private insurance brokerage and risk management services firm, published a white paper entitled "Road to Implementation: Enterprise Risk Management for College and Universities," available at http://www.ajgrms .com/portal/server.pt/gateway/PTARGS_0_28406_570311_0_0_18/ERM%20 TT%20Report%20Final%209-23-09.pdf. Each of these publications provides a useful framework for reviewing risk in higher education institutions and implementing a comprehensive strategy for managing and preventing risk.

# PART TWO

# THE COLLEGE AND ITS GOVERNING BOARD AND STAFF

# 3

# The College's Authority
# and Liability

*Chapter 3 addresses the concept of authority—specifically, the college or university's authority to take particular actions and its potential legal liability for exercising authority in certain ways. Explanations are given for three types of authority (express, implied, and apparent authority) and three types of liability (tort law [especially negligence], contract law, and civil rights law liability). More specifically, the institution's potential premises liability (for allegedly unsafe buildings or grounds) is discussed, followed by liability for injuries related to on- and off-campus courses, co-curricular or outreach activities (such as social events or summer programs on campus), and liability related to self-destructive conduct of students. Institutional contract liability is then addressed, including the question of an institution's (or individual's) authority to enter a contract that will bind the institution. Finally, the institution's potential liability for civil rights violations under Section 1983 of the Civil Rights Act is examined, along with the defense of sovereign immunity.*

## Section 3.1. The Question of Authority

***3.1.1. Overview.*** Trustees, officers, and administrators of postsecondary institutions—public or private—may take only those actions and make only those decisions that they have **authority** to take or make. Acting or deciding without authority to do so can have legal consequences, both for the responsible individual and for the institution. It is thus critical, from a legal standpoint, for trustees, officers, and other administrators to understand and adhere to the scope and limits of their authority and that of other institutional functionaries with whom they deal. Such sensitivity to questions of authority will also normally be good administrative practice, since it can contribute order and structure to institutional governance and make the internal governance system more understandable, accessible, and accountable to those who deal with it (see Section 1.3.2).

Authority generally originates from some fundamental legal source that establishes the institution as a legal entity. For public institutions, the source is usually a state constitution or state authorizing legislation (see Section 11.2); for private institutions, it is usually articles of incorporation, sometimes in combination with some form of state license (see Section 11.2.3). These sources, though fundamental, are only the starting point for legal analysis of authority questions. To be fully understood and utilized, an institution's authority must be construed and implemented in light of all the sources of law described in Section 1.4. For public institutions, state administrative law (**administrative procedure acts** and similar statutes, plus court decisions) and agency law (court decisions) provide the backdrop against which authority is construed and implemented; for private institutions, state corporation law or trust law (statutes and court decisions) plus agency law (court decisions) are the bases. Authority is particularized and dispersed (delegated) to institutional officers, employees, committees and boards, and internal organizations such as a faculty senate or a student government. The vehicles for such delegations are usually the governing board bylaws, institutional rules and regulations, the institution's employment contracts, and, for public institutions, the administrative regulations of state education boards or agencies. Authority may also be delegated to outside entities such as an athletic booster club, a university research foundation, or a private business performing services for the institution. Vehicles for such delegations include separate corporate charters for **captive organizations**, memoranda of understanding with affiliated entities, and service contracts (for contracting out of services). Gaps in internal delegations may be filled by resort to the institution's customs and usages (see Section 1.4.3.3), and vagueness or ambiguity may be clarified in the same way. For some external delegations, the custom and usage of the business or trade involved may be used in such circumstances rather than that of the institution.

There are several generic types of authority. As explained in *Brown v. Wichita State University* (Section 3.3), authority may be express, implied, or apparent. "Express authority" is that which is found within the plain meaning of a written grant of authority. "Implied authority" is that which is necessary or appropriate for exercising express authority and can therefore be inferred from the express authority. "Apparent authority" is not actual authority at all; the term is used to describe the situation where someone acting for the institution induces a belief in other persons that authority exists when in fact it does not. Administrators should avoid this appearance of authority and should not rely on apparent authority as a basis for acting, because the institution may be held liable, under the doctrine of **estoppel**, for resultant harm to persons who rely to their detriment on an appearance of authority (see Section 3.3). When an institutional officer or employee does mistakenly act without authority, the action can sometimes be corrected through ratification by the board of trustees or other officer or employee who does have authority to undertake the act in question (Section 3.3).

One other type of authority is occasionally referred to in the postsecondary context: inherent authority. In *Morris v. Nowotny*, 323 S.W.2d 301 (Tex. 1959), for instance, the court remarked that the statutes establishing the University of Texas "imply the power, and, if they do not so imply, then that power is inherent in University officials to maintain proper order and decorum on the premises of the University." In *Esteban v. Central Missouri State College*, 415 F.2d 1077 (8th Cir. 1969), the court held that the college had "inherent authority to maintain order and to discipline students." And in *Waliga v. Board of Trustees of Kent State University*, 488 N.E.2d 850 (Ohio 1986), the court found inherent authority in the university's trustees to revoke an academic degree that had been obtained by fraud. Inherent authority is sometimes confused with implied authority, and courts do not always clearly distinguish the two; overall, inherent authority is an elusive concept and a slender reed to rely on to justify particular institutional actions and decisions.

The law is not clear on how broadly or narrowly authority should be construed in the postsecondary context. To some extent, the answer will vary from state to state and, within a state, may depend on whether the institution is established by the state constitution, by state statutes, or by articles of incorporation (see Sections 11.2.2 and 11.2.3). Although authority issues have been addressed in judicial opinions, the analysis is sometimes cursory. There has been debate among courts and commentators on whether postsecondary institutions should be subject to traditional legal principles for construing authority or whether such principles should be applied in a more flexible, less demanding way that takes into account the unique characteristics of postsecondary education. Given the uncertainty, administrators should rely when possible on express rather than implied or inherent authority and should seek clarity in statements of express authority, in order to avoid leaving authority questions to the vagaries of judicial interpretation.

Miscalculations of the institution's authority, or the authority of particular officers or employees, can have various adverse legal consequences. For public institutions, unauthorized acts may be invalidated by courts or administrative agencies under the *ultra vires* doctrine in the state's administrative law (a doctrine applied to acts that are beyond the delegated authority of a public body or official). For private institutions, a similar result occasionally can be reached under state corporation law.

When the unauthorized act is a failure to follow institutional regulations and the institution is public (see Section 1.5.2), courts will sometimes hold that the act violated procedural due process. In *Escobar v. State University of New York/ College at Old Westbury*, 427 F. Supp. 850 (E.D.N.Y. 1977), a student sought to enjoin the college from suspending him or taking any further disciplinary action against him. The student had been disciplined by the judicial review committee, acting under the college's Code of Community Conduct. After the college president learned of the disciplinary action, he rejected it and imposed more severe penalties on the student. The president purported to act under the

Rules of Public Order adopted by the Board of Trustees of the State University of New York rather than under the college Code. The court found that the president had violated the Rules, and it enjoined enforcement of his decision:

> [N]ot every deviation from a university's regulations constitutes a deprivation of due process . . . But where, as here, an offending student has been formally charged under the college's disciplinary code, has been subjected to a hearing, has been officially sentenced, and has commenced compliance with that sentence, it is a denial of due process of law for the chief administrative officer to step in, conduct his own in camera review of the student's record, and impose a different punishment without complying with any of the procedures which have been formally established for the college. Here the President simply brushed aside the college's formal regulations and procedures and, without specific authority, imposed a punishment of greater severity than determined by the hearing panel, a result directly contrary to the Code's appeal provisions [427 F. Supp. at 858].

For both public and private institutions, an unauthorized act violating institutional regulations may also be invalidated as a breach of an express or implied contract with students or the faculty. *Lyons v. Salve Regina College*, 422 F. Supp. 1354 (D.R.I. 1976), *reversed*, 565 F.2d 200 (1st Cir. 1977), involved a student who had received an F grade in a required nursing course because she had been absent from several classes and clinical sessions. After the student appealed the grade under the college's published Grade Appeal Process, the grade appeal committee voted that the student receive an Incomplete rather than an F. Characterizing the committee's action as a recommendation rather than a final decision, the associate dean overruled the committee, and the student was dismissed from the nursing program.

The parties agreed that the Grade Appeal Process was part of the terms of a contract between them. Though the grade appeal committee's determination was termed a "recommendation" in the college's publications, the lower court found that, as the parties understood the process, the recommendation was to be binding on the associate dean. The associate dean's overruling of the committee was therefore unauthorized and constituted a breach of contract. The lower court ordered the college to change the student's grade to an Incomplete and reinstate her in the nursing program. The appellate court reversed but did not disavow the contract theory of authority. Instead, it found that the committee's determination was not intended to be binding on the associate dean and that the dean therefore had not exceeded his authority in overruling the committee.

Authority questions are also central to a determination of various questions concerning liability for harm to third parties. The institution's tort liability may depend on whether the officer or employee committing the tort was acting within the scope of his or her authority (see Section 3.2). The institution's contract liability may depend on whether the officer or employee entering the contract was authorized to do so (Section 3.3). And, under the estoppel doctrine, both the institution and the individual may be liable where the institution or individual had apparent authority to act.

**_3.1.2. Trustee authority._** The law regarding the authority of boards of trustees may vary from state to state and, within each state, will vary depending on whether the college is public or private. In public institutions, the authority of trustees (or in some states, regents or visitors or curators) is defined and limited by the state statutes, and sometimes constitutional provisions, that create trustee boards for individual institutions. Such laws generally confer power on the board itself as an entity separate from its individual members. Individual trustees generally have authority to act only on behalf of the board, pursuant to some board bylaw, resolution, or other delegation of authority from the board. Other state laws, such as conflict-of-interest laws or ethics codes, may place obligations on individual board members as well as on the board itself. In private colleges, trustee authority typically emanates from the college's charter or articles of incorporation, but state regulatory or licensing laws may limit or dictate trustee action under certain circumstances.

## Section 3.2. Institutional Tort Liability

**_3.2.1. Overview._** Several common law doctrines provide remedies to individuals who are injured through the action (or, on occasion, the inaction) of others. Colleges and universities are subject to common law liability as well as to statutory liability. (See Section 2.1 for a general discussion of the sources of liability for colleges and universities.) Although the college is usually named as a defendant when common law claims are brought, claims may also be brought against faculty and staff in their personal capacities; these theories of liability are discussed in Section 4.4.

The most frequent source of potential common law liability is tort law, which requires a college or university and its agents to refrain from injuring any individual to which the college owes a duty. Negligence or defamation claims may be brought against the institution itself or against faculty or staff (or, occasionally, against students). And contract law (discussed in Section 3.3) is increasingly being used by employees, students, and others to seek redress from the institution for alleged wrongdoing.

A tort is broadly defined as a civil wrong, other than a breach of contract, for which the courts will allow a remedy. A tort claim involves a claim that the institution, or its agents, owed a duty to one or more individuals to behave according to a defined standard of care, that the duty was breached, and that the breach of that duty was the cause of the injury.

While there is a broad range of actions that may expose an institution to tort liability, and any act fitting this definition may be considered a tort, there are certain classic torts for which the essential elements of the plaintiff's prima facie case and the defendant's acceptable defenses are already established. The two classic torts that most frequently arise in the setting of postsecondary education are negligence and defamation, both of which are discussed in this section; but other tort theories, such as common law fraud, are also appearing in lawsuits against colleges and universities.

A college or university is not subject to liability for every tortious act of its trustees, employees, or other agents. But the institution will generally be liable, lacking immunity or some other recognized defense, for tortious acts committed within the scope of the actor's employment or otherwise authorized by the institution or subject to its control. For example, if a student, employee, or other invitee (an individual who is entitled or permitted to be on college property) is injured as a result of a careless or wrongful act of a college employee, the college may be liable for that injury, just as any landlord or business owner would be under similar circumstances (see, for example, *Lombard v. Fireman's Fund Insurance Co.*, 302 So. 2d 394 (La. Ct. App. 1974)) (university was liable to student injured when she fell in hallway of classroom building because janitors had applied excessive oil to floor, rendering it slippery; the duty to keep the premises in a safe condition was breached). A similar duty may exist in classroom, residence hall, athletics, or other settings—even, on occasion, if the activity is performed off-campus or abroad.

Whether or not a college or university may be held liable for torts committed by student organizations may depend upon whether a supervisory relationship exists between the institution and the organization. Although dated, the case of *Mazart v. State*, 441 N.Y.S.2d 600 (N.Y. Ct. Cl. 1981), contains a valuable analysis of an institution's liability for the tortious acts of its student organizations. The case concerned a libelous letter to the editor, published by the student newspaper at SUNY Binghamton. The court's opinion noted two possible theories for holding postsecondary institutions liable: (1) that the student organization was acting as an agent of the institution, and this institution, its principal, is vicariously liable for its agents' torts (the ***respondeat superior*** doctrine); and (2) that the institution had a legal duty to supervise the student organization, even if it was not acting as the institution's agent, because the institution supported or provided the environment for the organization's operation. In a lengthy analysis, the court refused to apply either theory against the institution, holding that (1) the institution did not exercise sufficient control over the newspaper to establish an agency relationship; and (2) given the relative maturity of college students and the rudimentary need and generally understood procedure for verifying information, the institution had no legal duty to supervise the newspaper's editorial process.

Colleges may be able to escape tort liability under various immunity theories. Public colleges may assert sovereign or governmental immunity, while in some states the charitable immunity doctrine protects nonprofit educational organizations. Each theory is discussed below.

**Sovereign immunity** is a common law doctrine that protects the state as an entity and its agencies from litigation concerning common law or certain statutory claims. (Immunity of a state and its agencies from suit in federal courts is also guaranteed by the Eleventh Amendment to the U.S. Constitution, and is discussed in Section 3.4 of this book.) The availability of the sovereign immunity defense varies greatly from state to state. While the doctrine was generally recognized in early American common law, it has been abrogated or modified in many states by judicial decisions, state legislation, or a combination of the two.

When a public institution raises a defense of sovereign immunity, the court must first determine whether the institution is an arm of the state. Because the doctrine does not protect the state's political subdivisions, entities that are separate and distinct from the state are not protected by sovereign immunity. If the court finds that the institution is a state entity, then the court must determine whether the state has taken some action that would divest the institution of sovereign immunity, at least for purposes of the lawsuit. Some states, for example, have passed tort claims acts, which define the types of lawsuits that may be brought against the state and the procedures that must be followed (see, for example, Florida's Tort Claims Act, Fla. Stat. § 768.28 (2011)). Other exceptions have been created by decisions of state supreme courts.

A case decided by a Texas appellate court illustrates the substantial protection afforded a public university—but not one of its employees—by a state tort claims act. In *Prairie View A&M University of Texas v. Mitchell*, 27 S.W.3d 323 (Tex. App., 1st Dist. 2000), a former student sued the university when it would not provide verification of his engineering degree. Despite the fact that the student produced a valid transcript and a diploma issued to him earlier by the university, the university registrar's office would not confirm that he had earned a degree, and the former student's employer required him to take a leave of absence without pay because his degree could not be confirmed by the university. The university defended the negligence lawsuit by claiming that it was protected by sovereign immunity under the Texas Tort Claims Act (Tex. Civ. Prac. & Rem. Code Ann. § 101.021(2) (West 1997)).

Although the trial court rejected the university's defense, the appellate court sided with the university. The student cited an exception in the state's Tort Claims Act that abrogated immunity if a "personal injury" had resulted from "a condition or use of tangible personal or real property." Arguing that it was the university's misuse of its computers or other equipment that caused his injury, the student asserted that the university's actions should fall within this exception to immunity. The court disagreed. It was actions of university employees, rather than the "defective property," that caused the alleged injury to the plaintiff, according to the court. Although the university was immune from liability in this case, the court noted that the registrar, who had been sued individually, was not.

A college may not be able to take advantage of the sovereign immunity defense in a situation where the action complained of is not a governmental function, but one that a private entity could perform. For example, in *Brown v. Florida State Board of Regents*, 513 So. 2d 184 (Fla. Dist. Ct. App. 1987), a student at the University of Florida drowned in a lake owned and maintained by the university. In response to the university's defense of sovereign immunity in the ensuing wrongful death claim, the appellate court ruled that since the type of activity was not a governmental one, the university could not assert the immunity defense; once the university decided to operate a lake, it then assumed the common law duty of care to those who used it.

But the definition of a governmental function is inconsistent across states. A New York appellate court determined that when a state university provides security at a university-sponsored concert, it is performing a governmental function and is thus immune from tort liability. In *Rashed v. State of New York*, 648 N.Y.S.2d 131 (Sup. Ct., App. Div. 1996), the plaintiff had been stabbed by another individual in the audience at a rap concert sponsored by City University. The plaintiff claimed that the university failed to provide adequate security, despite the fact that audience members were screened with a metal detector and a pat-down search. The court ruled that, unless the plaintiff could show that the university had assumed a "special duty of protection," a showing that the plaintiff had not made, no liability could arise for this government function.

Although private institutions can make no claim to sovereign immunity, nonprofit schools may sometimes be able to assert a limited "charitable" immunity defense to certain tort actions. The availability of this defense varies from state to state. For example, a federal appellate court roundly criticized the charitable immunity doctrine in *President and Directors of Georgetown College v. Hughes*, 130 F.2d 810 (D.C. Cir. 1942), refusing to apply it to a tort suit brought by a special nurse injured on the premises of the college's hospital. And in *Mullins v. Pine Manor College*, 449 N.E.2d 331 (Mass. 1983), the Supreme Court of Massachusetts, noting that the state legislature had abrogated charitable immunity for torts committed in the course of activity that was primarily commercial (Mass. Gen. Laws ch. 231, § 85K (2010)), rejected the college's charitable immunity defense. The court also refused the college president's request to apply a good-faith standard, rather than a negligence standard, to his actions. (A good-faith standard would absolve the president of liability even if he were found negligent, as long as he had acted in good faith.) The *Mullins* case is discussed further in Section 7.6.2 of this book.

Despite these attacks on the charitable immunity doctrine in other states, the New Jersey Supreme Court has upheld the doctrine and has applied it to public as well as private colleges. In *O'Connell v. State of New Jersey*, 795 A.2d 857 (N.J. 2002), the court interpreted the state's Charitable Immunity Act (N.J. Stat. Ann. § 2A:53A-7-11), which applies to any "nonprofit corporation, society or association organized exclusively for religious, charitable or educational purposes." The plaintiff, injured when he fell down a stairway on campus, had claimed that, as a recipient of public funds, Montclair State University should not be protected under this doctrine from its alleged negligence. The court disagreed, stating that the public university was a nonprofit entity organized exclusively for educational purposes, and the court found no legislative intent to exclude public colleges from the protections of the Charitable Immunity Act. Because the student was a beneficiary of the university's educational purposes, said the court, the plain meaning of the statute gave the university immunity from liability. An institution's charitable immunity may also protect it from liability if one of its students is injured as a result of a school-sponsored event in another state (*Gilbert v. Seton Hall University*, 332 F.3d 105 (2d Cir. 2003)). Similarly, a New Jersey appellate court ruled that charitable immunity precluded an award of damages by a jury against the university when the parents of a student who fell out of a residence hall window and died sued the university for negligence (*Orzech v. Fairleigh Dickinson University*, 985 A.2d 189 (N.J. Super. Ct. App. Div. 2009)).

Charitable immunity may not protect an institution, however, in cases where willful, wanton, or grossly negligent conduct or intentional acts are alleged. In *Hardwicke v. American Boychoir School*, 902 A.2d 900 (N.J. 2006), the New Jersey Supreme Court rejected the defendant boarding school's claim that the plaintiff's negligence lawsuit, alleging sexual abuse when he was a twelve-year-old residential student, was barred by charitable immunity. The court also held that the defendant could be held vicariously liable for acts of its employees if they were found to have engaged in child abuse.

Because these are common law claims, state law governs the legal analysis and the outcome. The cases discussed in this section provide a representative selection of issues and resolutions. Administrators and faculty should use caution, however, in assuming that the analysis or the outcome of any particular case in another state would be replicated in the state in which the college is located. As always, there is no substitute for experienced legal counsel in responding to actual or threatened litigation involving common law liability issues.

The remainder of this section discusses the most frequently occurring subjects of tort litigation faced by colleges. Although negligence claims outnumber other types of tort claims, defamation claims (discussed in Section 3.2.4 below) are increasing, as are claims of educational malpractice (a hybrid of tort and contract claims, discussed in Section 3.2.3 below). The complexity and variety of a college's activities are matched by the complexity and variety of the legal claims brought by individuals who claim to have been injured by the actions—or inaction—of a college or its agents.

### 3.2.2. Negligence.

*3.2.2.1. Overview.* Higher education institutions are facing a growing array of negligence lawsuits, often related to students or others injured on campus or at off-campus functions. Although most college students have reached the age of majority and, theoretically, are responsible for their own behavior, injured students and their parents are increasingly asserting that the institution has a duty of supervision or a duty based on its "special relationship" with the student that goes beyond the institution's ordinary duty to invitees, tenants, or trespassers. Courts have rejected this special relationship argument for most tort claims, but they have imposed on colleges and universities a duty to protect students from foreseeable harm, such as in cases of hazing or the presence of dangerous persons on campus.

When a postsecondary institution is not immune from negligence suits under either sovereign or charitable immunity, liability depends, first, on whether the institution's actions fit the legal definition of the tort with which it is charged; and, second, on whether the institution's actions are covered by one of the recognized defenses that protect against liability for the tort with which it is charged. For the tort of negligence, the legal definition will be met if the institution owed a duty to the injured party, the institution failed to exercise due care to avoid the injury, and that failure was the proximate cause of the injury. Whether or not a duty exists is a matter of state common law. Typical defenses to tort claims include the claim that there was no duty (because the injury was not foreseeable), the plaintiff's own negligence, or the assumption of risk doctrine.

Negligence claims against colleges and universities are typically a result of injury to a student or other invitee (an individual who is lawfully on campus or participating in a college or university activity) as a result of allegedly defective buildings or grounds (premises liability); accidents or other events occurring either on or off campus as a result of instructional activities, cocurricular activities, or outreach activities; or alleged educational malpractice. Cases involving claims in each of these areas are discussed below.

Although courts were historically reluctant to hold colleges to the same standard of care applied to business organizations, landlords, and other noneducational organizations, that attitude has changed markedly in the last decade. Whereas courts in the early and mid-twentieth century applied the doctrine of *in loco parentis* to shield colleges and universities from liability in tort claims brought by students or their parents, that doctrine fell out of favor when the age of majority for students was lowered to eighteen, making virtually all college students "adults" in the eyes of the law. Following the demise of *in loco parentis*, a few courts issued influential rulings that characterized colleges and universities as "bystanders" with respect to the activities of "adult" students.

The seminal case involving a college as bystander is *Bradshaw v. Rawlings*, 612 F.2d 135 (3d Cir. 1979), *cert. denied*, 446 U.S. 909 (1980), in which the court refused to impose liability on a college for injuries suffered by a student. The student, a sophomore at Delaware Valley College in Doylestown, Pennsylvania, was seriously injured in an automobile accident following the annual sophomore class picnic, which had been held off campus. The injured student was a passenger in a car driven by another student, who had become intoxicated at the picnic. Flyers announcing the picnic were mimeographed by the college duplicating facility. They featured drawings of beer mugs and were prominently displayed across the campus. The sophomore class's faculty advisor, who did not attend the picnic, cosigned the check that was used to purchase beer. The injured student brought his action against the college, as well as the beer distributor and the municipality, alleging that the college owed him a duty of care to protect him from harm resulting from the beer drinking at the picnic. The jury in the trial court awarded the student, who was rendered quadriplegic, damages in the amount of $1,108,067 against all defendants, and each appealed on separate grounds.

The college argued on appeal that the plaintiff had failed to establish that the college owed him a legal duty of care. The appellate court agreed with this argument. The court's opinion began with a discussion of the changes that have taken place on college campuses in recent decades that lessen the duty of protection that institutions once owed to their students. Assertions by students of their legal rights as adults reduced the colleges' duty to protect them, according to the court.

The student had the burden of proving the existence of a legal duty by identifying specific interests that arose from his relationship with the college. Concentrating on the college's regulation prohibiting the possession or consumption of alcoholic beverages on campus or at off-campus college-sponsored functions, he argued that this regulation created a custodial relationship between the college and its students. A basic principle of law holds that one who voluntarily takes custody of another is under a duty to protect that person. The plaintiff reasoned that he was entitled to the protection voluntarily assumed by the college when it promulgated the regulation. The court dismissed this argument on the ground that the college regulation merely tracked state law, which prohibited persons under the age of twenty-one from drinking intoxicants.[1] By promulgating the regulation, then, the college did not voluntarily assume a custodial relationship but only reaffirmed the necessity of student compliance with Pennsylvania law.

*Bradshaw* influenced the rulings of other courts throughout the 1980s, the most frequently cited of which are *Beach v. University of Utah*, 726 P.2d 413 (Utah 1986), and *Rabel v. Illinois Wesleyan University*, 514 N.E.2d 552 (Ill. App. Ct. 1987). The student in *Beach* was injured after falling off a cliff while participating in a university-sponsored field trip. The student, who was under the legal age for drinking alcohol, had consumed alcohol in full view of the faculty advisor shortly before wandering off and falling. Despite the fact that the university had promulgated regulations against drinking, and the faculty member had failed to enforce those regulations, the court refused to impose liability on the university. The student in *Rabel* was abducted from her residence hall by a fellow student engaged in a fraternity initiation; the court found no duty, even with respect to the university's role as landlord of the residence hall.

This bystander approach appears to be falling out of favor with courts, which, in cases decided over the past decade, are now imposing the same duty on colleges and universities that has traditionally been required of business organizations, landlords, and other nonacademic entities. Institutions may be liable for the negligence of their employees and, under certain circumstances, may even be found liable for the negligence of nonemployees. For example, in *Foster v. Board of Trustees of Butler County Community College*, 771 F. Supp. 1122 (D. Kan. 1991), a basketball coach had asked a student to pick up a potential recruit at the airport and drive him to a nearby motel. On his return from the airport, the student ran a red light and hit a truck, resulting in his death and injuries to the recruit and the truck driver. Both injured parties sued the college.

---

[1] In actuality the regulation went beyond the statute because it applied to every student regardless of age—a point that could have favored the plaintiff had the court been sensitive to it. Lawyers will thus want to exercise caution in relying on the court's analysis of this particular issue.

A jury awarded the injured recruit $2.26 million against the college and the estate of the driver. On appeal, the college argued that it was not responsible for the actions of the student driver. The court, noting that the student's car was uninsured and unregistered and that the student had no valid driver's license, ruled that "the Butler Community College defendants could have discovered [the driver's] unfitness for the task had any investigation been conducted" (771 F. Supp. at 1128). The college had policies requiring students driving on the college's behalf to be licensed; the college's failure to follow its policies and its failure to ascertain whether the student was qualified to undertake the responsibility it assigned him resulted in the court's determination that, for purposes of *respondeat superior* liability, the student was a "gratuitous employee" of the college.

An emerging area of potential negligence liability for colleges, and their staffs, is computer security. For example, in addition to potential liability for computer usages that violate federal statutes or the First Amendment (see Section 7.5.1), institutions may become liable for negligent loss or disclosure of confidential electronic records, negligent supervision of employees who use electronic information for unlawful purposes, negligent failures to keep networks secure from outsiders who gain access for unlawful purposes, or negligent transmission of data that intrudes upon privacy interests of students, faculty, staff, or outsiders. (For discussion of federal law immunity from some negligence liability related to campus computer systems, see Section 7.5.3.)

**3.2.2.2. Premises liability.** These claims involve injuries to students or other invitees who allege that a college or university breached its duty as a landlord or landowner to maintain reasonably safe buildings (classrooms, residence halls, sports facilities, performing arts centers) and land (parking lots, athletics field, pathway, sidewalks). If a dangerous condition is obvious, there is no duty to warn an invitee of potential danger. For example, in *Shimer v. Bowling Green State University*, 708 N.E.2d 305 (Ohio Ct. Cl. 1999), a student who fell into an open orchestra pit sued the college for the injuries she sustained. The court found for the college, stating that the plaintiff, who had been working on a theater production and was familiar with the stage and the orchestra pit's location, was negligent in not using care to avoid falling into the pit. But see *Almarante v. Art Institute of Fort Lauderdale, Inc.*, 921 So. 2d 703 (Fla. Dist. Ct. App. 2006), where the court ruled that a student injured while crossing a highway that divided the college's campus stated a negligence claim against the college.

The majority rule that landowners are liable only for those injuries on their property that are foreseeable remains intact, but courts are differing sharply on what injuries they view as foreseeable. For example, in *Pitre v. Louisiana Tech University*, 655 So. 2d 659 (La. Ct. App. 1995), *reversed*, 673 So. 2d 585 (La. 1996), the intermediate appellate court had found the university liable for injuries to a student who was paralyzed during a sledding accident. When a rare snowstorm blanketed the university's campus, the administration issued a written warning to its students, placing it on each student's bed, urging them to use good judgment and to avoid sledding in dangerous areas. Pitre and two classmates used a trash can lid as a sled and rode it down a hill; Pitre struck the base of a light pole in a university parking lot. The appellate court ruled that the university had a duty to prevent unreasonably unsafe student activities and viewed the written warning as an encouragement to engage in sledding. Although the court acknowledged that Pitre's own behavior contributed to his injuries, it found the university 25 percent liable.

The Supreme Court of Louisiana reversed, reasoning that the danger encountered by Pitre and his friends was obvious to a reasonably careful invitee. The court stated that, since sledding is not inherently dangerous, the university could not foresee that Pitre would select a location unsuitable for sledding; furthermore, said the court, it was reasonable for the university to install light poles as a safety mechanism. The court ruled that the university bore no liability for the plaintiff's injuries.

Premises liability claims may also arise when an invitee misuses a college or university building or other property of an institution, but that misuse is claimed to be foreseeable. For example, in *Robertson v. State of Louisiana*, 747 So. 2d 1276 (La. Ct. App. 1999), the parents sued Louisiana Tech University for negligence after their son died from falling from the roof of a campus building. The university had built a roof over its swimming pool; the roof, whose apex was 56 feet high, extended to within several feet of the ground. The son, a twenty-three-year-old senior, had climbed onto the roof after spending the evening drinking with friends. There had been several earlier incidents of students climbing on the roof; in all cases the students were intoxicated, and in two cases the students had been seriously injured. The parents of the student who died claimed that, because of these earlier climbing incidents, the injury to their son was foreseeable, and the university should have erected some form of barrier to prevent students from climbing onto the roof. Despite the university's knowledge of the earlier climbing incidents, and testimony that a modest investment in shrubbery would likely have prevented future climbing expeditions, the court ruled that the roof was not unreasonably dangerous, that the danger of falling off the roof was obvious, and therefore that the university owed no duty to prevent the student from climbing onto the roof. For a case involving a trespasser's death after climbing a cliff on college property, in which the court entered summary judgment for the college, see *Blust v. Berea College*, 431 F. Supp. 2d 703 (E.D. Ky. 2006). And for an application of the assumption of risk doctrine in a case in which a student sued New York University when he was injured during a Jell-O wrestling event in a residence hall courtyard, see *Wisnia v. New York University*, 2008 N.Y. Misc. LEXIS 718 (N.Y. Sup. Ct. January 23, 2008).

Colleges and universities in Florida have gained some protection from liability in cases such as *Nicholson*. The legislature of Florida has enacted a law creating a potential bar to recovery in a negligence lawsuit if the plaintiff is voluntarily intoxicated by drugs or alcohol and the court determines that the plaintiff is the primary cause of his or her injuries (Fla. Stat. Ann. § 768.075 (West 2011)). The statute also exempts property owners and their agents from liability for injuries to trespassers.

Invitees have attempted to impose tort liability on a college when some form of criminal activity on campus results in injury. Again, the majority rule is that the criminal activity must have been foreseeable. For example, in *Nero v. Kansas State University*, 861 P.2d 768 (Kan. 1993) (discussed in Section 7.6.2), the Kansas Supreme Court reversed a summary judgment award for the university and ordered the case to be tried, ruling that a jury would need to decide whether the alleged sexual assault of a student by a fellow student in a residence hall was foreseeable because the student had been accused of an earlier sexual assault on campus and university officials were aware of that fact when they assigned him to live during summer session in a coed residence hall. But in *L.W. v. Western Golf Association*, 712 N.E.2d 983 (Ind. 1999), the Indiana Supreme Court ruled that the owners of a "scholarship house" at Purdue University were not liable to a student who became intoxicated and later was raped in her room by a fellow scholarship house resident. Finding that there was no record of similar incidents that would have made such a criminal act foreseeable, the court refused to impose liability.

Premises liability claims may also be brought in conjunction with athletics events on campus. In *Hayden v. University of Notre Dame*, 716 N.E.2d 603 (Ind. Ct. App. 1999), a state appellate court reversed a summary judgment award for the university. A football fan with season tickets was injured when a football was kicked into the stands and spectators lunged for it. The plaintiff argued that the university should have protected its spectators from being injured and that lunging fans were common at Notre Dame football games. The court ruled that, because there were many prior incidents of fans lunging for footballs, Notre Dame should have foreseen the type of injury sustained by the plaintiff. Given the foreseeability of this behavior, the court ruled that Notre Dame owed the plaintiff a duty to protect her from injury.

Even if a college is not the owner of the premises alleged to be dangerous, if it has some control over that property, or if students have access to the property, the college could be liable for injuries related to that property. For example, in *Ginsburg v. City of Ithaca, Cornell University et al.*, 839 F. Supp.2d 537 (N.D.N.Y. 2012), the father of a Cornell student who had committed suicide by jumping from a bridge on the Cornell University campus in 2009 sued Ithaca (which owned the bridge) and Cornell for negligence. The father claimed that, because twenty-nine individuals had jumped from several bridges on or near Cornell's campus since 1990, Cornell and Ithaca had a duty to "implement appropriate suicide prevention measures on the bridge" when it was redesigned and reconstructed two years earlier. The trial court ruled that "it was clearly foreseeable that someone may commit suicide" by jumping from the bridge used by the son and rejected Cornell's motion for summary judgment. The court explained that, "given the history of suicides and suicide attempts, defendants' public acknowledgement of the phenomenon, and the bridge's accessibility to a student population—fifteen percent of which regularly considers suicide—shows defendants had actual, or at least constructive, knowledge that a suicide attempt from the bridge was foreseeable" [839 F. Supp2d. at 541]. Landowners and landlords also have a duty to provide accurate information about potentially dangerous conditions to independent contractors working on their property. For a discussion of this duty, see *Bennett v. Trevecca Nazarene University*, 216 S.W.3d 293 (Tenn. 2007).

***3.2.2.3. Liability for injuries related to on-campus instruction.*** Students or other invitees injured while involved in on-campus instructional activities may file negligence claims against the institution, the instructor, or both. For example, in *McDonald v. University of West Virginia Board of Trustees*, 444 S.E.2d 57 (W. Va. 1994), a student enrolled in a theater course sued the university for negligence, seeking damages for a broken leg and ankle. The professor was teaching a class in stage movement and had taken the class outdoors, where the students were asked to run across a lawn simulating fear. Several students performed the exercise before the plaintiff took her turn. As she was running, she encountered a small depression in the lawn, stumbled and fell, and was injured.

Although the jury had found for the plaintiff, the trial judge had entered judgment for the university, which the Supreme Court of West Virginia affirmed. The student had sought to demonstrate that the professor's supervision of the class was negligent, but the court disagreed. The professor had inspected the lawn area before the class and had not noticed the small depression. Furthermore, evidence showed that theater students at the university were given safety instructions and that the professor had discussed safety issues in that class. The syllabus included information on safety, including what clothing to wear, layering of clothing, and body positioning. The faculty member required students to wear high-top tennis shoes as a further safety precaution. The faculty member was present at the time of the student's injury, and the court found that no amount of supervision or scrutiny would have discovered the "small depression" that caused the student to fall. Therefore, said the court, the faculty member's actions were not a proximate cause of the injury, and the university itself was not required to maintain a lawn completely free of small depressions.

This case is notable because of the relatively high level of caution apparently displayed by the faculty member. Clearly, the safety instructions (which, since they were on the course syllabus, were easily proven) and the faculty member's statement that she inspected the lawn area prior to the class were important to the defense of this lawsuit. A similar degree of care could not be demonstrated in another case in New York, and this difference appears to have caused a very different result. In *Loder v. State of New York*, 607 N.Y.S.2d 151 (N.Y. App. Div. 1994), Alda Loder was enrolled in an equine studies course at the State University of New York at Cobleskill. It was her first such course. Each student was required to perform two weeks of "barn duty," which included grooming a horse assigned to the student. When Ms. Loder approached the stall of the mare to which she was assigned and attempted to enter the stall, the mare kicked her in the face, causing serious injuries. The student sued, alleging that the university was negligent both in the way that the horse was tethered in the stall and in its failure to properly instruct the student with respect to how to enter the stall of a fractious horse.

The trial court had found the university 60 percent liable for the student's injury. The university appealed, but the appellate court sided with the student. First, said the appellate court, there was sufficient evidence of the horse's propensity to kick to suggest that the university was negligent in its method of tethering the horse. Furthermore, there were no written instructions on how to enter the horse's stall. The university employee who had shown the student how to enter the stall had used the incorrect procedure, according to an expert witness called by the university. Therefore, the court concluded, although the owner of a domestic animal normally is not responsible for injuries caused by that animal unless the animal is known to be abnormally dangerous, in these circumstances, the university was negligent both in failing to instruct the student regarding safety and in the method used to secure the horse.

The student in *Loder* was a beginning student, and her lack of familiarity or experience with horses was a significant factor. If a student is experienced, however, a court may be less sympathetic. In *Niles v. Board of Regents of the University System of Georgia*, 473 S.E.2d 173 (Ga. Ct. App. 1996), the plaintiff, a doctoral student in physics at Georgia Tech, was injured in a laboratory accident. The student had been working in the laboratory on a project related to a course in superconducting crystals and had been cleaning some equipment with a mixture of acetone, ethanol, and nitric acid, a highly explosive combination. A more senior doctoral student had suggested that recipe as a cleaning solution. Following the accident, the student asserted that the university, through his professor, was negligent in its failure to instruct him that this combination of substances was volatile.

The court was not sympathetic to the student's claim that he needed instruction. He had graduated summa cum laude with a major in chemistry and had obtained a master's degree in physics with a 4.0 average. He had spent "hundreds of hours" in laboratories, according to the court, and had previously worked with all three of the substances. Therefore, said the court, the professor had the right to assume that the student either would know of the dangers of these substances or would "perform the research necessary to determine those dangers and take the necessary precautions" (473 S.E.2d at 175). Therefore, the faculty member had no duty to warn the student about the dangers of mixing "common chemicals," said the court.

The defense of "assumption of risk" is routinely used against negligence claims, as a defendant argues that a plaintiff was fully aware of the risks of a particular course of action so that the defendant had no duty to warn the plaintiff of those dangers. In cases involving classroom instruction, however, this defense may have limited success. For example, in *Drogaris v. Trustees of Columbia University*, 743 N.Y.S.2d 115 (N.Y. App. Div., 2d Dept. 2002), the court denied a university's motion for summary judgment in a case in which a student enrolled in a graduate course in kinesiology (the study of movement) was injured after the course instructor used her for a physical demonstration of a clinical test. The student alleged that the instructor hyperextended her leg, resulting in a muscle tear. The court rejected the university's argument that the student assumed the risk of injury by participating in the class.

If the equipment that a college or university provides for a student's use is defective or incorrectly assembled and the student is injured as a result of an otherwise proper use of the equipment, it is likely that a court will find the school liable for negligence, even if it is in a state with a tort claims act. See, for example, *Texas State Technical College v. Beavers*, 218 S.W.3d 258 (Tex. App. 2007). And if an instructor allows a student to engage in potentially dangerous activities (here, welding metal with a torch) without supervision or proper protective clothing, the university may be held responsible for the student's injuries (*Lei v. City University of New York*, 823 N.Y.S.2d 129 (N.Y. App. Div. 2006)).

In physical injury claims related to classroom activities, courts seemingly will consider a student's knowledge level. If the student is a novice, as in *Loder, Lei, Beavers*, and *Drogaris*, there is likely to be a duty to instruct and supervise. If the student is experienced, however, and has knowledge that is similar to the knowledge of the professor, then the court may not find a duty to supervise or instruct. And, of course, the more an institution can demonstrate that safety precautions and safety training were carried out, the more likely the institution is to prevail.

### 3.2.2.4. Liability for injuries in off-campus instruction.

An increasing number of lawsuits seek to impose liability on colleges, universities, and their staff for injuries occurring during off-campus courses. Many graduate programs and an increasing number of undergraduate programs require some form of off-campus internship experience for students. Student teaching is required for students seeking degrees or licenses in education; social work students are typically required to complete a practicum in a social service agency; and students enrolled in health care–related programs may also have off-campus educational requirements. These experiences provide valuable opportunities for student learning but may create liability for a college or university, even if it has no real control over what the student encounters in the off-campus placement.

Liability for activities at an off-campus site can occur in several ways. For example, an institution may be responsible for maintaining the safety of premises it does not own if it schedules a course there. In *Delbridge v. Maricopa County Community College District*, 893 P.2d 55 (Ariz. Ct. App. 1994), a college offered a course in plant mechanics to employees of the Salt River Project (SRP) on the site of that organization. Although SRP employees performed the instruction, they were considered adjunct faculty of the college, and they were paid by the college. Individuals participating in the course were considered students of the college. As part of the course, the students were required to learn to climb a utility pole. The plaintiff, a student in the class, climbed the pole, lost his grip, fell, and was seriously injured. His lawsuit alleged negligence on the part of the college in not providing him with a safe environment.

The trial court awarded summary judgment to the college, but the appellate court reversed, ruling that there was a special relationship between the college and the student. Despite the fact that the premises were also under the control of SRP, said the court, the college also had a duty not to expose its students to an unreasonable risk of harm. Furthermore, the student was acting under the supervision of a college instructor. The case was remanded for a trial court's determination as to whether the college breached its duty to the plaintiff.

Institutions may also have liability for injuries to students that occur at an off-campus internship site. In *Gross v. Family Services Agency and Nova Southeastern University, Inc.*, 716 So. 2d 337 (Fla. Dist. Ct. App. 1998), the plaintiff had enrolled in the doctoral program in psychology at Nova Southeastern University. The program required her to complete an eleven-month practicum at an off-campus organization. Nova gave each student a list of preapproved practicum sites, and students selected six possible sites. Nova controlled the placement of students at the sites. Gross was placed at Family Services Agency, approximately 15 miles from the university. One evening, while leaving the agency, Gross was assaulted by a man in the agency's parking lot and was injured. Previous assaults had occurred in the parking lot, a fact of which the university was aware but the student was not. The student sued the university for negligence in assigning her to an unreasonably dangerous internship site without adequate warning. She also sued the agency, which settled her claim.

Although the trial court awarded summary judgment to the university, stating that it had no duty to control the agency's parking lot, the appellate court reversed. The court rejected the trial court's determination that this was a premises liability case, characterizing the college's duty as one of exercising "reasonable care in assigning [the student] to an internship site, including the duty to warn her of foreseeable and unreasonable risks of injury" (716 So. 2d at 337). The court characterized the relationship between the student and the university as "an adult who pays a fee for services [the student] and the provider of those services [the university]." Therefore, said the court, the university had a duty to use ordinary care in providing educational services and programs. If the student was injured by the acts of a third party, then the university would be liable only if a special relationship existed. The court ruled that a special relationship did exist in this situation, relying upon a case involving litigation by a British tourist who sued a car rental company for failure to warn customers about the risk of crime in certain areas of Miami. The car agency's knowledge of the risk of crime, and the fact that the tourist was not from the United States, created a special duty, said that court, to warn the foreign tourist of "foreseeable criminal conduct" (*Shurben v. Dollar Rent-A-Car*, 676 So. 2d 467 (Fla. Dist. Ct. App. 1996)). So, too, the university had a duty to warn the student of the risk of assault, given its knowledge that previous assaults had occurred in the vicinity.

The Supreme Court of Florida affirmed the appellate court's ruling on the issue of the university's duty to warn the student (*Nova Southeastern University v. Gross*, 758 So. 2d 86 (Fla. 2000)). In addition to agreeing with the appellate court's reasoning that the university had assumed a duty of "acting reasonably in making [those] assignments" to a specific location, the court declared: "There is no reason why a university may act without regard to the consequences of its actions while every other legal entity is charged with acting as a reasonably prudent person would in like or similar circumstances" (758 So. 2d at 90). The court stated that the college's duty was one of reasonableness in assigning students to practicum locations, a duty that required the university to warn students of potential dangers posed by that location.

Universities and their employees may also face negligence liability claims for actions by third parties at off-campus locations. In *Rinsky v. Trustees of Boston University*, 2010 U.S. Dist. LEXIS 136876 (D. Mass. December 27, 2010), a social work student was required to complete an internship at a social service agency as part of her academic program. The student notified both the faculty supervisors and the on-site supervisor that a client was physically touching and stalking her. She alleged that neither the on-site supervisor nor the faculty members took action either to stop the offensive touching or to assign her to a different internship. She sued both the agency and the university for sexual harassment, negligence, and several other tort claims. The court rejected the university's motion to dismiss the student's negligence and sexual harassment claims.

For negligence liability purposes, then, whether the location at which a student or staff member is injured is on or off campus is not the controlling issue. What is more important, according to these cases, is whether the college took adequate precautions to ensure the safety of its students, even if it did not have total physical control of the site.

Study abroad programs may present liability issues for colleges as well. Since the mid-1990s, several colleges have been sued by students, or their families, for injuries or deaths to students participating in study abroad programs. Although the courts have rejected claims that a college that sponsors a study abroad program is the insurer of students' safety, the courts are imposing a duty of reasonable care on colleges and universities that requires them to take steps to protect students, faculty, and staff from reasonably foreseeable harm. Particularly if the program takes place in a country, or in a portion of a country, that is deemed unsafe or prone to criminal activity, considerable precautions will need to be taken by the college.

For example, St. Mary's College (a public college in Maryland) settled a lawsuit filed by three students who were injured during a study abroad trip to Guatemala. While a group of thirteen students, two faculty members, and the study abroad director were returning by bus to Guatemala City from a trip to a rural area, the bus was stopped by armed bandits and robbed. Five of the students were raped. Three of the students sued the college, arguing that insufficient precautions were taken for their safety and that additional precautions, such as an armed guard, a convoy of several vehicles, and the selection of a safer route would have prevented the injuries. The college argued that sufficient precautions had been taken and that, because previous study abroad trips to Guatemala had been uneventful, the injuries were not foreseeable. However, the college settled with the plaintiffs in order to avoid prolonging the dispute (Beth McMurtrie, "College Settles Suit by 3 Students Over '98 Attack in Guatemala," *Chron. Higher Educ.*, July 5, 2002, available at http://chronicle .com/daily/2002/07/2002070502n.htm).

A student was unsuccessful in persuading a Minnesota court to impose liability on the University of Minnesota for an assault by a taxi driver in Cuernavaca, Mexico, where the student was participating in a study abroad program. In *Bloss v. University of Minnesota*, 590 N.W.2d 661 (Minn. Ct. App. 1999), the student asserted that the university was negligent in not obtaining housing closer to the location of the classes, in not providing safe transportation to and from campus, and in not warning the students about the possibility of assault. The court ruled that governmental immunity protected the university from liability for its decision to use host families to house the students. But with respect to the student's allegations concerning safety issues, immunity would not protect the university if it had breached its duty in that regard. In this case, however, the court ruled that the university had behaved reasonably. There was no history of assaults on students or tourists in the eighteen years that the program had operated in Cuernavaca. Students had been given a mandatory orientation session on safety and had been told not to hail a taxi on the street (which the student had done), but to call a taxi company. The assault occurred when the student took a taxi to meet friends—not to attend class. Given the university's efforts to warn students and the lack of foreseeability of the assault, the court refused to impose liability on the university. For a case with similar facts and the same outcome, although based upon sovereign immunity, see *Mattingly v. University of Louisville*, 2006 U.S. Dist. LEXIS 53259 (W.D. Ky. July 28, 2006).

***3.2.2.5. Liability for cocurricular and social activities.*** In addition to potential premises liability claims, discussed in Section 3.2.2.2 above, an individual injured as the result of a college- or university-sponsored event, or as a result of activity that is allegedly related to school activities, may attempt to hold the college or university liable for negligence.

For example, in *Bishop v. Texas A&M University*, 35 S.W.3d 605 (Tex. 2000), a student participating in a university-sponsored play was stabbed accidentally during a performance of *Dracula*. The play was directed by a nonemployee, but two faculty members served as advisors to the student production. The Texas Supreme Court said that, although the faculty advisors were volunteers, their participation as advisors was considered when salary increase decisions were made, the drama club was required to have a faculty advisor as a condition of receiving university recognition, and university policies required the faculty advisors to enforce its rules and regulations. The high court ruled that a jury could potentially find that the faculty advisors were negligent and thus that the university was liable to the injured student.

If an institution sponsors an activity such as intercollegiate sports, a court may find that a special relationship exists beyond that owed to invitees or to the general public. For example, in *Kleinknecht v. Gettysburg College*, 989 F.2d 1360 (3d Cir. 1993) (discussed in Section 10.4.9 of this book), a federal appellate court applying Pennsylvania law held that a special relationship existed between a college and a student who collapsed as a result of cardiac arrest and died during lacrosse practice, and that because of this special relationship the college had a duty to provide treatment to the student in the event of such a medical emergency.

In determining whether a duty exists, a court will consider whether the harm that befell the individual was foreseeable. In *Kleinknecht*, the court noted that the specific event need not be foreseeable, but the risk of harm must be both foreseeable and unreasonable. In analyzing the standard of care required, the court noted that the potential for life-threatening injuries occurring during practice or an athletic event was clearly foreseeable and thus the college's failure to provide facilities for emergency medical attention was unreasonable.

But if a cocurricular activity is not sponsored or supervised by the institution, it is unlikely that a court will find that the institution has a duty to protect the student from injury. Or if the student is pursuing private social activities that the institution has not undertaken to supervise or control, a court may find that no duty exists. In *University of Denver v. Whitlock*, 744 P.2d 54 (Colo. 1987), for example, the Supreme Court of Colorado reversed a $5.26 million judgment against the University of Denver for a student rendered a quadriplegic in a trampoline accident.

The accident in *Whitlock* occurred in the front yard of a fraternity house on the university campus. The university had leased the land to the fraternity. Whitlock asserted that the university had a duty, based on a special relationship, to make sure that the fraternity's trampoline was used only under supervised conditions. The special relationship, Whitlock asserted, arose either from his status as a student or the university's status as landowner and lessor to the fraternity. But the court held that the university's power to regulate student conduct on campus did not give rise to a duty to regulate student conduct or to monitor the conduct of every student on campus. Citing earlier cases in which no duty to supervise social activity was found (including *Bradshaw v. Rawlings*, discussed in Section 3.2.2.1 above), the court concluded that the university did not have a special relationship based merely on the fact that Whitlock was a student. Inspection of the lease between the university and the fraternity disclosed no right to direct or control the activities of the fraternity members, and the fire inspections and drills conducted by the university did not create a special relationship.

Similarly, in *Guest v. Hansen*, 603 F.3d 15 (2d Cir. 2010), a federal appellate court ruled that staff of Paul Smith College (a private college) did not have a duty to protect a student from injuries sustained in a snowmobile accident. The college was located on a lake, which the college did not own. Students had a practice of building bonfires on the frozen lake and using it as a location for consuming alcohol. A student and his guest had consumed a considerable amount of alcohol and went for a snowmobile ride around the lake. The snowmobile crashed and the two were killed. The guest was twenty years old.

The guest's father sued Paul Smith College and its director of residence life for negligence, stating that college administrators knew that students were consuming alcohol and partying on the frozen lake and neither attempted to stop the partying nor enforced the college's alcohol policy. The court affirmed the trial court's ruling that neither the college nor the director of residence life owed the decedents a duty of care because they were not on property controlled by the College. Even if the college had the ability to control the off-campus activities of its students and their guests, said the court, it had no obligation to do so.

But when an institution attempts to prohibit or to control inherently dangerous activities in which its students participate, a court may find that it has a duty to those students. In *Furek v. University of Delaware*, 594 A.2d 506 (Del. 1991), the Supreme Court of Delaware ruled that the university's pervasive regulation of hazing during fraternity rush created a duty to protect students from injuries suffered as a result of that hazing. Furek, who had pledged the local chapter of Sigma Phi Epsilon, was seriously burned and permanently scarred when a fraternity member poured a lye-based liquid oven cleaner over his back and neck as part of a hazing ritual. After he withdrew from the university and lost his football scholarship, he sued the university and was awarded $30,000 by a jury, 93 percent of which was to be paid by the university and the remainder by the student who poured the liquid on Furek.[2]

The university asserted on appeal that it had no duty to Furek. While agreeing that "the university's duty is a limited one," the court was "not persuaded that none exists" (594 A.2d at 517). Rejecting the rationales of *Bradshaw* (discussed in Section 3.2.2.1 above) and its progeny, the court used a public policy argument to find that the university did have a duty:

> It seems . . . reasonable to conclude that university supervision of potentially dangerous student activities is not fundamentally at odds with the nature of the parties' relationship, particularly if such supervision advances the health and safety of at least some students [594 A.2d at 518].

Although it refused to find a special duty based on the dangerous activities of fraternities and their members, the court held that:

> Certain established principles of tort law provide a sufficient basis for the imposition of a duty on the [u]niversity to use reasonable care to protect resident students against the dangerous acts of third parties . . . [W]here there is direct university involvement in, and knowledge of, certain dangerous practices of its students, the university cannot abandon its residual duty of control [594 A.2d at 519–20].

---

[2] Subsequent to the ruling of the trial court, the university moved for judgment notwithstanding the verdict, which the trial court awarded. While that ruling was on appeal, the student who had poured the substance on Furek agreed to pay all but $100 of the $30,000 compensatory damages award. Although the Delaware Supreme Court subsequently overturned the judgment for the university, and ordered a new trial on the apportionment of liability between the student and the university, it does not appear that Furek availed himself of the opportunity for a new trial, leaving the university responsible for only $100 of the damage award.

The court determined that the university's own policy against hazing, and its repeated warnings to students against the hazards of hazing, "constituted an assumed duty" (594 A.2d at 520). Relying on section 314A of the Restatement (Second) of Torts, the court determined that the "pervasive" regulation of hazing by the university amounted to an undertaking by the university to protect students from the dangers related to hazing and created a duty to do so.

Because the outcomes in cases involving injuries related to cocurricular or social events are particularly fact sensitive, it is difficult to formulate concrete suggestions for avoiding or limiting legal liability. The cases seem to turn on whether the court believes that the injury was foreseeable. For example, in *Knoll v. Board of Regents of the University of Nebraska* (discussed in Section 10.2.3 of this book), the court refused to award summary judgment to a university when a student attempted to hold the university responsible for the injuries he sustained during hazing in a fraternity house, which, under university policy, was considered student housing controlled by the university. The court ruled that the kidnapping and hazing of a student by a fraternity known to have engaged in prior acts of hazing could have been foreseen by the university.

A case decided by the U.S. Court of Appeals for the Eighth Circuit illustrates the continuing influence of *Bradshaw* and *Beach* (see Section 3.2.2.1) and some courts' continuing reluctance to find a special relationship that would create a duty on the college's part to protect students from their own risky behavior. In *Freeman v. Busch*, 349 F.3d 582 (8th Cir. 2003), a female student was sexually assaulted after consuming alcohol at a private party in a college dorm room. She sought to hold the college and the resident advisor liable for negligence because the resident advisor, who had been told that she was intoxicated and unconscious, did nothing to assist her. The court refused to find that a college has a "custodial duty" to protect an adult college student, and affirmed the trial court's summary judgment ruling for the college and the resident advisor.

Additional sources of liability may arise in states where case or statutory law establishes civil liability for private hosts who furnish intoxicating beverages (see *Kelly v. Gwinnell*, 476 A.2d 1219 (N.J. 1984), and *Bauer v. Dann*, 428 N.W.2d 658 (Iowa 1988)) or for retail establishments that sell alcohol to minors. Sponsors of parties at which intoxicants are served, particularly to minors, could be found negligent under the social host doctrine. A court in such a jurisdiction could rely on this law to impose a legal duty on the institution when alcohol is served at college-sponsored activities. Many states also have Dram Shop Acts, which strictly regulate licensed establishments engaged in the sale of intoxicants and impose civil liability for dispensing intoxicants to an intoxicated patron. A college or university that holds a liquor license, or contracts with a concessionaire who holds one, may wish to enlist the aid of legal counsel to assess its legal obligations as a license holder.

***3.2.2.6. Student suicide.*** According to the National Center for Health Statistics, suicide is the third-leading cause of death among individuals between the ages of fifteen and twenty-four,[3] and it is the second leading cause of death for college students.[4] A survey of college students in 2010 found that one third had sought mental health services and that 7 percent had seriously considered suicide.[5]

Several high-profile lawsuits, some of which have been resolved against institutions of higher education, make it clear that faculty and administrators must take this issue very seriously, become educated about the warning signs of a potential suicide, and ensure that proper actions are taken if a student exhibits those signs. Although courts in the past refused to create a duty to prevent suicide, holding that it was the act of the suicide victim that was the proximate cause of the death, more recently courts are beginning to find, under certain circumstances, a duty to prevent the suicide or a duty to warn appropriate individuals that a student is a suicide risk.

In a series of lawsuits concerning the potential liability of a college or university for the suicide of a student, plaintiffs have attempted to persuade courts to find a "duty to warn" parents or others of potential dangers to students or a special relationship that requires the college to prevent the harm. In *Jain v. State of Iowa*, 617 N.W.2d 293 (Iowa 2000), the state supreme court rejected the claims of the parents of a student who committed suicide that a special relationship between the university and the student required the university to notify the parents of a student's destructive behavior. Unlike the outcome of the *Tarasoff* case (discussed in Section 4.4.2.2), the Iowa court ruled that the failure of university staff to warn the student's parents did not increase the risk of his committing suicide; university staff had encouraged him to seek counseling and had asked him for permission to contact his parents, which he had refused.

More recently, however, courts have found that, under certain circumstances, there may be a duty to take affirmative action to prevent a student from harming himself. In *Schieszler v. Ferrum College*, 236 F. Supp. 2d 602 (W.D. Va. 2002), the aunt of a college student, Michael Frentzel, sued the college, the dean of student affairs, and a resident assistant for wrongful death after the student committed suicide by hanging himself. Frentzel had a history of disciplinary problems during his freshman year, and the college had required him to enroll in anger management counseling. After completing the counseling, Frentzel had an argument with his girlfriend, and the campus police and Frentzel's resident assistant were called. At the same time, Frentzel sent the girlfriend a note indicating that he planned to hang himself. The campus police and resident assistant were shown the note. Frentzel wrote several notes over

---

[3] Melonie Heron, *Deaths: Leading Causes for 2006* (National Center for Health Statistics, Centers for Disease Control, 2010), available at http://www.cdc.gov/nchs/data/nvsr/nvsr58/nvsr58_14 .pdf.

[4] See http://www.suicide.org/college-student-suicide.html.

[5] Lauren Sieben, "Nearly a Third of College Students Have Had Mental Health Counseling, Study Finds," *Chron. Higher Educ.*, March 14, 2011, available at http://chronicle.com/article/Nearly-a -Third-of-College/126726/.

the next few days, but the police and residence hall advisor took no action, except to forbid the girlfriend to see Frentzel. Frentzel hanged himself three days after the initial altercation.

The plaintiff claimed that a special relationship existed between Frentzel and the college that created a duty to protect him from harm about which the college had knowledge. The defendants asked the court to dismiss the claim, stating that there was no duty to prevent Frentzel from harming himself. The court concluded that, because college employees knew of Frentzel's threats to kill himself, the self-inflicted injuries, and his history of emotional problems, the plaintiff had alleged sufficient facts to support a claim that a special relationship existed, which created a duty to protect Frentzel from "the foreseeable danger that he would hurt himself." The court also ruled that the plaintiff had alleged sufficient facts to support her claim that the defendants breached their duty to Frentzel. Although the court dismissed the claim against the resident assistant, it ruled that a wrongful death action could be maintained against the college and the dean. The college later settled the case (Eric Hoover, "Ferrum College Concedes 'Shared Responsibility' in a Student's Suicide," *Chron. Higher Educ.*, July 29, 2003, available at http://chronicle.com/daily/2003/07/2003072902n.htm).

The outcome in the *Ferrum College* case may have influenced a preliminary ruling in another case, *Shin v. Massachusetts Institute of Technology*. A student's parents asserted breach of contract and negligence claims against the Massachusetts Institute of Technology (MIT) alleging ineffective psychiatric care for their daughter, who committed suicide in an MIT residence hall. A state trial judge dismissed the claims of the parents against MIT itself, but allowed some of the claims against administrators and staff to go forward (see Marcella Bombardieri, "Lawsuit Allowed in MIT Suicide," *Boston Globe*, July 30, 2005, available at http://www.boston.com/news/education/higher/articles/2005/07/30/lawsuit_allowed_in_mit-suicide/). The judge cited the *Ferrum College* case and its finding that administrators and staff had a special relationship with the student that created a duty to protect her from reasonably foreseeable harm to herself. In April of 2006, the parties settled the case, agreeing that the student's death was probably accidental and not a suicide.

If college staff members do not know that a student is suicidal or engaging in risky behavior, it is less likely that the institution, or its employees, will be found liable for negligence (see, for example, *Ginsburg v. City of Ithaca and Cornell University*, 839 F. Supp.2d 537 (N.D.N.Y. 2012), dismissing negligence claims against a university's mental health staff because the student who committed suicide had shown no signs of depression or suicidal ideation and had not sought or received counseling). In *Bash v. Clark University*, 2006 Mass. Super. LEXIS 657 (Mass. Super. Ct., Worcester, November 20, 2006), a state trial court rejected the claim of parents of a student who died of a heroin overdose that the college was negligent and fraudulently misrepresented its efforts to maintain a safe environment for its students. The father of the deceased student sued the university, eight administrators, and the individual who had supplied the heroin to his daughter. He claimed that the university and its administrators had been negligent because they did not take steps to prevent his daughter from obtaining and using heroin, and that he had relied on statements made in university documents and by a university administrator that the university would provide a safe environment for its students.

Citing *Baldwin* and *Bradshaw* (Section 3.2.2.1 of this book) for the proposition that the doctrine of *in loco parentis* no longer applied, the trial court ruled that the university did not have a duty to prevent the student from taking heroin because it was not reasonably foreseeable that she would do so. Because of this lack of foreseeability, no special relationship existed between the university and Michele. The court distinguished the outcome in *Mullins v. Pine Manor College* (Section 7.6.2) because that case involved the physical safety of students in residence halls rather than the "burden associated with maintaining the moral well being of students." The court distinguished *Schieszler v. Ferrum College* and *Shin v. Massachusetts Institute of Technology*, saying that the suicides in those cases were foreseeable because administrators had specific information indicating that the students were suicidal. And finally, the court said that recognizing a legal duty for university officials to prevent voluntary use of illegal drugs would "conflict with the expanded right of privacy that society has come to regard as the norm in connection with the activities of college students."

With respect to the misrepresentation claim, the court stated that "generalized statements in promotional materials or brochures are too vague and indefinite to give rise to a cause of action." In addition, the promise of an administrator that she would "get rid of heroin on the Clark campus" was not sufficiently strong to induce a parent to send a child only to that particular institution.

Students who behave in ways that are risky to themselves or to other students may violate a college's code of student conduct or may violate housing policies or academic policies. The limitations on a college's ability to require a student to involuntarily withdraw from the institution because the student is or may be a "direct threat," along with regulations issued by the U.S. Department of Justice that complicate the determination of the direct threat status, are discussed in Section 9.2.4 of this book.

A misconception among some college administrators is that the Family Educational Rights and Privacy Act (FERPA, discussed in Section 7.8.1) prevents college administrators from contacting parents or other relatives, or other college staff, if a student is threatening suicide. FERPA contains an exception for emergencies, including those involving health and safety. Furthermore, there is no private right of action under FERPA since the decision of the U.S. Supreme Court in *Doe v. Gonzaga University* (discussed in Section 7.8.1). Therefore, a proactive stance could both save the lives of students and protect the institution against legal liability.

***3.2.2.7. Liability for injuries related to outreach programs.*** Programs open to the community or to certain nonstudent groups may involve litigation over the college's supervision of its own students or of invitees to the campus (such as children or high school students enrolled in precollege programs). Children may be on campus for at least three reasons: they are enrolled in campus educational, athletic, or social programs (such as summer camps); they are attending an event or using a campus facility, such as a library or day care center; or they are trespassers. Potential claims may involve liability for injuries sustained in sporting events, assault or other crimes, vehicular accidents, or allegedly defective premises. The fact that children are below the age of majority makes it difficult for a college defendant to argue that a particular danger was "open and obvious," or that the child assumed the risk of the danger.

A case illustrative of the college's potential liability when minors are involved in campus programs is *Dismuke v. Quaynor*, 637 So. 2d 555 (La. App. 1994). Dismuke, a fifteen-year-old, was a participant in a summer camp sponsored by Grambling State University. The university hired college students as counselors. Dismuke alleged that Quaynor, a Grambling student and counselor, had sexually assaulted her in the student union building after the campers had been dismissed early because of inclement weather. She sued both Quaynor and the university. Quaynor did not respond, and the court entered a default judgment against him. In ruling against the university, the trial court found that Quaynor was acting within the scope of his employment when the alleged assault took place because he had gone to the student union to supervise boys attending the summer camp. This finding provided the basis for the court's ruling that the university was vicariously liable for the injury.

Failure to supervise the activities of minors in campus programs can lead to liability. In *Glover v. Jackson State University*, 968 So. 2d 1267 (Miss. 2007), the parents of a fourteen-year-old girl who was enrolled in an on-campus sports program sued the university. They alleged that she had been raped in an on-campus men's room by two fifteen-year-old boys who were also attending the program. A bus driver who was employed by the university had dropped the teenagers off on campus and left them unsupervised. Although a trial court had awarded summary judgment to the university, the state's highest court reversed and remanded the case for trial. The court explained that the university hired the program director and that the boys involved in the rape had a history of violence, both in program activities and on the bus, both that year and in previous years. This knowledge, said the court, suggested that a reasonable fact finder could conclude that the rape was foreseeable, and thus a trial was required.

### 3.2.3. *Educational malpractice and related claims.*  Another potential source of negligence liability, albeit a generally unsuccessful one for plaintiffs, is the doctrine of "educational malpractice." The claim (which may also be based on contract law, as discussed in Sections 3.3 and 7.1.3 of this book) arises from the duty assumed by a professional not to harm the individuals relying on the professional's expertise.

Although courts often sympathize with students who claim that they have not learned what they should have learned or that their professors were negligent in teaching or supervising them, courts have been reluctant to create a cause of action for educational malpractice. In *Ross v. Creighton University*, 740 F. Supp. 1319 (N.D. Ill. 1990), discussed in Section 10.4.5 of this book, a trial judge dismissed the claim by a former athlete that the university had negligently failed to educate him, although it did allow a contract claim to survive dismissal. Asserting that the university's curriculum was too difficult for him, the former basketball player argued that Creighton had a duty to educate him and not simply allow him to attend while maintaining his athletic eligibility. The judge disagreed, ruling that the student was ultimately responsible for his academic success. The appellate court affirmed (957 F.2d 410 (7th Cir. 1992)).

Individuals claiming to have been harmed by students whose instruction was inadequate have also failed in their claims of educational malpractice. In *Moore v. Vanderloo*, 386 N.W.2d 108 (Iowa 1986), the plaintiff was a patient injured by a chiropractor trained at Palmer College of Chiropractic. The patient sued the college, claiming that the injuries were a result of the chiropractor's inadequate training. After reviewing cases from other jurisdictions, the Iowa Supreme Court decided against permitting a cause of action for educational malpractice.

The court gave four reasons for its decision:

1. There is no satisfactory standard of care by which to measure an educator's conduct.
2. The cause of the student's failure to learn is inherently uncertain, as is the nature of damages.
3. Permitting such claims would flood the courts with litigation and would thus place a substantial burden on educational institutions.
4. The courts are not equipped to oversee the day-to-day operation of educational institutions.

Citing *Moore*, a Missouri appellate court awarded summary judgment to a flight school that was sued for negligence after a plane, piloted by a student trained at the school, crashed, killing him and four passengers. The court in *Dallas Airmotive v. Flightsafety International, Inc.*, 277 S.W.3d 696 (Mo. Ct. App. 2008), characterized the lawsuit, brought by the relatives of the individuals killed in the crash, as a claim for educational malpractice and stated that there was no duty on the school's part to protect students from harm related to negligent instruction. An Ohio appellate court refused to consider educational malpractice claims as well (*Trutschel v. Kettering Medical Center*, 2009 Ohio App. LEXIS 2862 (Ohio Ct. App. July 2, 2009)).

In addition to attempting to state claims of educational malpractice, students have turned to other theories in an attempt to recover for injuries allegedly incurred by relying on incorrect advice of academic advisors. In *Hendricks v. Clemson University*, 578 S.E. 2d 711 (S.C. 2003), the South Carolina Supreme Court reversed the ruling of a state appellate court that would have allowed the plaintiff, a student-athlete who lost eligibility to play baseball because of the incorrect advice he received from an academic advisor, to state claims of negligence, breach of contract, and breach of fiduciary duty. The court rejected the student's argument that the university had affirmatively assumed a duty of care when it undertook to advise him on the courses necessary for National Collegiate Athletic Association eligibility, finding no state law precedents that recognized such a duty. The court also refused to recognize a fiduciary relationship between the student and the advisor, and similarly rejected the breach of contract claim, finding no written promise by the university to ensure the student's athletic eligibility.

Another case, however, demonstrates a court's willingness to entertain student negligence claims for specific acts of alleged misfeasance or nonfeasance. In *Johnson v. Schmitz*, 119 F. Supp. 2d 90 (D. Conn. 2000), a doctoral student sued Yale University and several faculty members, alleging that the chair of his dissertation committee had misappropriated the student's idea for his dissertation research and took credit for it himself. The student filed claims of negligence, breach of contract, breach of a **fiduciary duty**, and defamation. The breach of contract claim was premised on the argument that Yale had made both express and implied promises to "safeguard students from academic misconduct" (119 F. Supp. 2d at 96), and is discussed in Section 7.1.3 of this book. The court refused to dismiss the negligence claim, stating that because the student was alleging intentional misconduct by the faculty members, it was not an educational malpractice claim. The court ruled that the student should be given an opportunity to demonstrate that Yale had a duty to protect him against faculty misconduct and that such misconduct was foreseeable. Similarly, the court refused to dismiss the claim that Yale had a fiduciary duty to the student, stating: "Given the collaborative nature of the relationship between a graduate student and a dissertation advisor who necessarily shares the same academic interests, the Court can envision a situation in which a graduate school, knowing the nature of this relationship, may assume a fiduciary duty to the student" (119 F. Supp. 2d at 97–98).

Another student claim related to educational malpractice is negligent misrepresentation or fraud. A New York appellate court allowed students to proceed with a negligent misrepresentation claim against a college of chiropractic. The students alleged that the college's promotional materials had promised them that, upon graduation, they would be "eligible for licensure examination in all states," a claim that was false. In *Enzinna v. D'Youville College*, 2011 WL 1733907 (N.Y. App. Div., 4th Jud. Dep't 2011), the court also allowed the students to proceed with claims brought under state laws regarding deceptive business practices and false advertising.

The Alabama Supreme Court refused to dismiss a claim of promissory fraud against a dean and vice president of academic affairs brought by a student who alleged that he had been fraudulently advised about the music media curriculum at Alabama State University. In *Byrd v. Lamar*, 846 So. 2d 334 (Ala. 2003), the plaintiff alleged that, despite descriptions of such a program in institutional publications and the representations of the dean that he could complete the program within four years, no such program existed at the university. Finding that the student had sufficiently alleged facts to preclude summary judgment, the court ordered that the promissory fraud claim be tried.

***3.2.4. Defamation.***   Another tort asserted against postsecondary institutions, defamation, is committed by the oral or written publication of information that tends to injure a person's reputation. The information must have been communicated to some third person and must have been capable of defamatory meaning, and understood as referring to the plaintiff in a defamatory sense. (See Sections 10.3.6 and 10.3.7 for a further discussion of defamation.) Defamation claims are also asserted against officials of the institution, such as deans or department chairs, and even occasionally against students. These claims are discussed in Section 4.4.2.3.

Defamation claims may be brought against faculty who write letters of reference for students or in the context of giving a (negative) evaluation of a student or subordinate. In such cases, the alleged defamer may be protected by the "opinion privilege" if the communication provides an opinion rather than reciting facts. Defamation claims may also arise when an individual testifies in an internal grievance or appeal hearing. In most cases, courts have rejected defamation claims against institutions, although in some cases they have been more sympathetic to plaintiffs who sue individuals for defamation (see Section 4.4.2.3).

One of the most important defenses against a defamation action is the conditional or qualified privilege of fair comment and criticism. An application of this privilege occurred in *Olsson v. Indiana University Board of Trustees*, 571 N.E.2d 585 (Ind. Ct. App. 1991). A prospective teacher, who had graduated from the university and had performed her student teaching under the supervision of one of its faculty, sued the university, claiming that a letter of reference written by a faculty member was libelous. The faculty member had described both the plaintiff's strengths and weaknesses with apparent candor.

The court ruled that the faculty member and the university were protected by a qualified privilege that may be asserted "if a need exists for full and unrestricted communication regarding matters on which the parties have a common interest or duty" (571 N.E.2d at 587). Such a privilege would cover any communication "if made in good faith on any subject matter in which the party making the communication has an interest or in reference to which he has a duty, either public or private, whether legal or moral, or social, if made to a person having a corresponding interest or duty" (571 N.E.2d at 587). Noting that the university had a responsibility to prepare teachers, the court ruled that this letter of recommendation was an appropriate occasion for the use of the qualified privilege.

The scope of the qualified privilege is a matter of state law and may differ by state. A case decided by a federal trial court, applying District of Columbia law, examined that jurisdiction's case law regarding the qualified privilege in a defamation claim. In *Tacka v. Georgetown University*, 193 F. Supp. 2d 43 (D.D.C. 2001), a faculty member, Tacka, sued Georgetown University for breach of contract and defamation. His defamation claim was based on the use of an allegedly defamatory evaluation of his scholarly work by a faculty rank and tenure committee that was considering whether to recommend that Tacka receive tenure. The evaluation, written by an untenured professor at a university in another state, accused Tacka of plagiarizing portions of a journal article. Without determining whether the plagiarism claim was true, the rank and tenure committee recommended against tenure for Professor Tacka. Later, the University's Research Integrity Committee exonerated Tacka of plagiarism, and he was granted tenure the following year.

In its motion for summary judgment, the university claimed that the department chair's "publication" of the allegedly defamatory external evaluation to the rank and tenure committee was protected by a qualified privilege. The trial court ruled that the qualified privilege could be lost if the plaintiff could demonstrate that the publisher acted with malice or published the evaluation beyond those who had a business reason for receiving the information. Tacka had alleged that the department chair's decision to solicit the sole external evaluation of his work from an individual who held a personal bias against him, and who was allegedly unqualified to perform the evaluation, demonstrated that the chair had acted with malice. The court ruled that Tacka should have the opportunity to have a jury decide whether the privilege was lost.

Although an individual who testifies in court is protected from defamation liability by an absolute privilege, a court determined that statements made in an internal grievance hearing are not protected by such a privilege. In *Overall v. University of Pennsylvania*, 412 F.3d 492 (3d Cir. 2005), the plaintiff sued the University and a department chair for defamation and sex discrimination when she was not hired for a tenure track position. Although the trial court ruled that the allegedly defamatory statements made by the department chair during a grievance hearing involving the University's decision not to hire her were privileged, the appellate court disagreed. Because the University was private, the appellate court ruled that the grievance hearing was not a "quasi-judicial" proceeding and thus the privilege did not apply. The court remanded the plaintiff's defamation claim to the trial court.

Another conditional privilege that is important for administrators in state institutions is the privilege afforded to executive and administrative officers of government. In *Shearer v. Lambert*, 547 P.2d 98 (Or. 1976), an assistant professor at Oregon State University brought a libel action against the head of her department. While admitting that the statement was defamatory, the defendant argued that the privilege of government officers should be extended to lesser executive or administrative officers, such as the head of a department. The court agreed, reasoning that, since "the privilege is designed to free public officials from intimidation in the discharge of their duties, we are unable to explain why this policy would not apply equally to inferior as well as to high-ranking officers." This qualified privilege is available, however, only where the defendant "publishes the defamatory matter in the performance of his official duties."

If a defamation lawsuit is brought against an institution by a prominent administrator, trustee, or faculty member, a constitutional privilege may come into play. If the plaintiff is a public figure, he or she must prove that the defendant acted with "actual malice," and the privilege to defame is thus broader than it would be if the plaintiff were a private figure. If a person is a public figure, another person may not be held liable for defaming him unless that other person's comment "was made with knowledge of its falsity or in reckless disregard of whether it was false or true" (*Garrison v. Louisiana*, 379 U.S. 64, 74 (1964)). Thus, to the extent that members of the academic community can be characterized as public figures, the institution's potential liability for defamation is reduced. It is unlikely on any given campus at any particular time, however, that many administrators, staff, or faculty would be considered public figures.

Charges of sexual misconduct against students have provided multiple opportunities for defamation litigation against colleges. One of the more famous cases is *Doe v. Gonzaga University*, 24 P.3d 390 (Wash. 2001), *reversed on other grounds, Gonzaga University v. Doe*, 536 U.S. 273 (2002). In *Doe*, a university administrator overheard a student office assistant tell another student that John Doe, an education student in his senior year, had raped a female student. The alleged victim had not reported any assault and refused to meet with the administrators to discuss the alleged incident. Despite the fact that the alleged victim would not provide information or corroborate the assault claim, the administrators decided not to recommend Doe for teacher certification because of these allegations. They gave Doe a letter to that effect; when Doe and his parents asked about his appeal rights, they were told there were none.

John Doe sued Gonzaga and several administrators for defamation, negligence, and breach of contract. At trial, Doe testified that his sexual relationship with the female student was consensual; in a videotaped deposition, the alleged student victim denied that Doe had assaulted her and denied that she had made any accusatory statements to university staff. A jury awarded Doe $500,000 for defamation and an additional $655,000 in compensatory and punitive damages for other claims.

Although the appellate court reversed the jury's defamation verdict, the Washington Supreme Court reinstated that verdict but affirmed the appellate court's dismissal of the negligence claim, stating that the university had no duty to the education licensing authority to investigate the allegations of sexual assault; when there was no duty, said the court, there was no claim for negligence. With respect to the defamation claim, the court ruled that the administrators were not protected by a qualified privilege because they were not acting "in the ordinary course of their work" when they involved themselves in the allegations of the student whose conversation the administrators secretly overheard.

Institutions that publish allegedly defamatory material in official publications or operate computer networks may be sued for transmitted libelous statements. See, for example, *Rudloe v. Karl*, 899 So. 2d 1161 (Fla. Dist. Ct. App. 2005), in which the court ruled that sovereign immunity did not protect Florida State University from being sued by an alumnus for printing an allegedly libelous article in an alumni newsletter. Computer service providers will often be immune from such liability, however, under 47 U.S.C. § 230 (see Section 7.5.3 of this book).

## Section 3.3.  Institutional Contract Liability

Institutions of higher education face potential breach of contract claims from employees (see Sections 4.2 and 5.2), students (see Sections 7.1.3, 7.2.3, and 9.3.3), and vendors, purchasers, or business partners (see Section 12.2.2). In this section, an institution's potential liability for contracts entered into by its employees or other agents is discussed.

The institution may be characterized as a principal and its trustees, administrators, and other employees as agents for purposes of discussing the potential liability of each on contracts transacted by an agent for, or on behalf of, the institution. The fact that an agent acts with the principal in mind does not necessarily excuse the agent from personal liability (see Section 4.4.3), nor does it automatically make the principal liable. The key to the institution's liability is authorization—that is, the institution may be held liable if it authorized the agent's action before it occurred or if it subsequently ratified the action. However, even when an agent's acts were properly authorized, an institution may be able to escape liability by raising a legally recognized defense, such as sovereign immunity. As mentioned in Section 3.2, this defense is available in some states to public institutions but not to private institutions.

The issue of authorization can become very complex. In *Brown v. Wichita State University*, 540 P.2d 66 (Kan. 1975),[6] the court discussed the issue at length:

> To determine whether the record establishes an agency by agreement, it must be examined to ascertain if the party sought to be charged as principal had delegated authority to the alleged agent by words which expressly authorize the agent to do the delegated act. If there is evidence of that character, the authority of the agent is express. If no express authorization is found, then the evidence must be considered to determine whether the alleged agent possesses implied powers. The test utilized by this court to determine if the alleged agent possesses implied powers is whether, from the facts and circumstances of the particular case, it appears there was an implied intention to create an agency, in which event the relation may be held to exist, notwithstanding either a denial by the alleged principal, or whether the parties understood it to be an agency.
>
> "On the question of implied agency, it is the manifestation of the alleged principal and agent as between themselves that is decisive, and not the appearance to a third party or what the third party should have known. An agency will not be inferred because a third person assumed that it existed, or because the alleged agent assumed to act as such, or because the conditions and circumstances were such as to make such an agency seem natural and probable and to the advantage of the supposed principal, or from facts which show that the alleged agent was a mere instrumentality" [quoting *Corpus Juris Secundum*,

---

[6]This decision reverses and remands a summary judgment in favor of the university by the trial court. In a second opinion in this case, 547 P.2d 1015 (1976), the court reaffirmed (without discussion) the portion of its first opinion dealing with authorization.

a leading legal encyclopedia]. . . . The doctrine of apparent or ostensible authority is predicated upon the theory of estoppel. An ostensible or apparent agent is one whom the principal has intentionally or by want of ordinary care induced and permitted third persons to believe to be his agent even though no authority, either express or implied, has been conferred upon him.

Ratification is the adoption or confirmation by a principal of an act performed on his behalf by an agent, which act was performed without authority. The doctrine of ratification is based upon the assumption there has been no prior authority, and ratification by the principal of the agent's unauthorized act is equivalent to an original grant of authority. Upon acquiring knowledge of his agent's unauthorized act, the principal should promptly repudiate the act; otherwise it will be presumed he has ratified and affirmed the act [540 P.2d at 74–75].

The existence and scope of sovereign immunity from contract liability vary from state to state. The Texas Court of Appeals, in considering a coach's breach of contract claim against Texas Tech University, explained the genesis of sovereign immunity:

[S]overeign immunity . . . found its genesis in old England. Then, as most will admit, the king (or queen as the case may be) was omnipotent . . . [A]ny rights or privileges [their subjects] enjoyed were no greater than those the monarch deigned to bestow on them. Moreover, the judiciary that he created not only recognized this relationship between the king and his people but also deduced from it that since the former was sovereign over all, the latter could not be [*sic*] sue him without his approval . . .

With the discovery and population of the New World, our forefathers were called upon to establish their own system of government. Having rebelled against the tyranny of British rule, one would think that they would instill a government of limited powers . . . Nonetheless, not all things British were rejected for our own courts adopted much of the common law developed overseas. And, included in that body of law was the doctrine of sovereign immunity . . . So, though we have no king . . ., the government (e.g., State, county, and municipalities) and those working for it in their official capacities came to enjoy that created to protect monarchs so many years ago [*Leach v. Texas Tech University*, 2011 Tex. App. LEXIS 445 at *3–4 (Tex. App. January 20, 2011)].

The court ruled that the university had not waived sovereign immunity and thus could not be sued for breach of contract.

Regarding contract liability, there is little distinction to be made among trustees, administrators, employees, and other agents of the institution. Whether the actor is a member of the board of trustees or its equivalent—the president, the director of athletics, the dean of arts and sciences, or some other functionary—the critical question is whether the action was authorized by the institution.

For a more contemporary example of a case in which a court ruled that the individual signing a contract on behalf of the Arizona Board of Regents lacked the authority to modify a contract, making the contract modification unenforceable, see *Kaman Aerospace Corp. v. Arizona Board of Regents*, 171 P.3d 599 (Ariz. Ct. App. August 23, 2007).

In a case involving both apparent authority and ratification doctrines, the Supreme Court of Massachusetts ruled that Boston University had to pay a technical training company more than $5.7 million for its "willful and knowing" breach of contract (*Linkage Corporation v. Trustees of Boston University*, 679 N.E.2d 191 (Mass. 1997), *cert. denied*, 522 U.S. 1015 (1997)). One important issue in the case was whether an earlier contract between Boston University and Linkage for the provision of educational services by Linkage had been renewed; Linkage asserted that it had, but the university stated that the contract had not been renewed but had been lawfully terminated. A jury had found that the university's vice president for external programs had apparent authority to enter a renewal contract with Linkage and also found that the university had ratified that agreement.

With respect to the apparent authority issue, the court noted that the vice president had "virtual autonomy" in supervising the relationship between Linkage and the university. He had been the university's representative in the negotiation of the earlier contract and was named in the contractual documents as the university's primary representative for all legal notices. Boston University argued that the vice president lacked authority to enter the agreement because, at the same time that negotiations for the contract renewal were taking place, the university had issued a directive that required all payments greater than $5,000 to be authorized by the senior vice president. The court, however, ruled that, because the vice president for external programs had direct access to the president and because the contractual relationship predated the directive, it was reasonable for Linkage's president to conclude that the directive would not be enforced with respect to its contract with the university.

With respect to the ratification issue, the court agreed with the jury that the conduct of university officials subsequent to the execution of the renewal contract supported the ratification argument. The vice president had asked his superiors, in writing, if additional review was necessary after he executed the renewal contract. Neither the senior vice president nor the president advised Linkage's president or their own vice president that they did not approve of the renewal contract. Characterizing the conduct of university officials as "informed acquiescence," the court endorsed the jury's finding that the university had ratified the agreement. Although the behavior of university officials was sufficient to establish ratification, the court added that, because the university benefited financially from the execution of the renewal contract, this benefit was additional evidence of its ratification of the agreement.

Colleges and universities are increasingly being sued for breach of contract by current or former employees. These issues are discussed in Section 4.2 of this book. Even colleges controlled by religious organizations may be subject to breach of contract claims. For example, the Supreme Court of New Jersey ruled, in *McKelvy v. Diocese of Camden*, 800 A.2d 840 (N.J. 2002), that a former seminarian could sue the Diocese of Camden, New Jersey, for breach of contract. The plaintiff alleged that he had been sexually harassed while a student at the seminary; he sued for reimbursement of his tuition and loans, and for compensatory damages. Despite the argument by the diocese that such a lawsuit violated the First Amendment's free exercise clause, the state court ruled unanimously that the case could proceed. Jurisprudence on the liability of religiously affiliated colleges for discrimination lawsuits is discussed in Section 4.7 of this book.

Although students attempting to assert claims for educational malpractice are finding their tort claims dismissed (discussed in Section 3.2.3), their contract claims sometimes survive summary judgment or dismissal, as long as the contract claim is not an attempt to state a claim for educational malpractice. In *Swartley v. Hoffner*, 734 A.2d 915 (Pa. Super. Ct. 1999), *appeal denied*, 747 A.2d 902 (Pa. 1999), a doctoral student who was denied a degree brought a breach of contract claim against Lehigh University and her dissertation committee members, claiming that they had failed to carry out their duties as required by university policies. The court ruled that "the relationship between a private educational institution and an enrolled student is contractual in nature; therefore, a student can bring a cause of action against said institution for breach of contract where the institution ignores or violates portions of the written contract" (734 A.2d at 919). But the court nevertheless affirmed the trial court's award of summary judgment to the defendants, finding no evidence that university policies required dissertation committee members to give the student a passing grade once her dissertation defense had been scheduled. But not all courts will allow breach of contract claims to proceed in these circumstances. In *Gally v. Columbia University*, 22 F. Supp. 2d 199 (S.D.N.Y. 1998), a trial judge dismissed the student's contract claim, ruling that it was a disguised attempt to state a claim for educational malpractice.

Although most claims involving injury to students or other invitees are brought under negligence theories, one court allowed a contract claim to be brought against a public university as a result of injuries to a camper at a university-based program. In *Quinn v. Mississippi State University*, 720 So. 2d 843 (Miss. 1998), parents of a child injured at a baseball camp sponsored by the university filed both tort and contract claims against the university. The Supreme Court of Mississippi determined that their tort claim was barred by the university's sovereign immunity but found that an implied contract existed between the plaintiffs and the defendants to provide baseball instruction safely at the baseball camp. The university argued that the plaintiffs had signed a waiver that released the university from liability. Because it was not clear from the language of the waiver whether the plaintiffs had waived liability for acts committed by the coach, the court remanded the matter for a jury's determination.

An institution sued for breach of contract can raise defenses arising from the contract itself or from some circumstance unique to the institution. Defenses that arise from the contract include the other party's fraud, the other party's breach of the contract, and the absence of one of the requisite elements (offer, acceptance, consideration) in the formation of a contract. Defenses unique to the institution may include a counterclaim against the other party, the other party's previous collection of damages from the agent, or, for public institutions, the sovereign immunity defense discussed earlier. Even if one of these defenses—for instance, that the agent or institution lacked authority or that a contract element was absent—is successfully asserted, a private institution may be held liable for any benefit it received as a result of the other party's performance. But public institutions sometimes may not even be required to pay for benefits received under such circumstances.

## Section 3.4. Institutional Liability for Violating Federal Constitutional Rights (Section 1983 Liability)

**3.4.1. Overview.**  The tort and contract liabilities of postsecondary institutions (discussed in Sections 3.2 and 3.3) are based in state law and, for the most part, are relatively well settled. The institution's federal constitutional rights liability, in contrast, is primarily a matter of federal law, which has undergone a complex evolutionary development. The key statute governing the enforcement of constitutional rights,[7] commonly known as Section 1983 and codified at 42 U.S.C. § 1983, reads in pertinent part:

> Every person who, under color of any statute, ordinance, regulation, custom, or usage, of any State or Territory or the District of Columbia, subjects, or causes to be subjected, any citizen of the United States or other person within the jurisdiction thereof to the deprivation of any rights, privileges, or immunities secured by the Constitution and laws, shall be liable to the party injured in an action at law, suit in equity, or other proper proceeding for redress.

Section 1983's coverage is limited in two major ways. First, it imposes liability only for actions carried out "under color of" state law, custom, or usage. Under this language the statute applies only to actions attributable to the state, in much the same way that, under the state action doctrine (see Section 1.5.2 of this book), the U.S. Constitution applies only to actions attributable to the state. While public institutions clearly meet this statutory test, private postsecondary institutions cannot be subjected to Section 1983 liability unless the action complained of was so connected with the state that it can be said to have been done under color of state law, custom, or usage.

Second, Section 1983 imposes liability only on a "person"—a term not defined in the statute. Thus, Section 1983's application to postsecondary education also depends on whether the particular institution or system being sued

---

[7]In addition to federal constitutional rights, there are numerous federal statutes that create statutory civil rights, violation of which will also subject institutions to liability. (See, for example, Sections 4.5.2.1.1–4.5.2.6 and 11.5.2–11.5.5 of this book.) These statutory rights are enforced under the statutes that create them, rather than under Section 1983. Institutions may also be liable for violations of state constitutional rights, which are enforced under state law rather than Section 1983.

is considered to be a person, as the courts construe that term. Although private institutions would usually meet this test because they are corporations, which are considered to be legal persons under state law, most private institutions would be excluded from Section 1983 anyway under the "color of law" test. Thus, the crucial coverage issue under Section 1983 is one that primarily concerns public institutions: whether a public postsecondary institution is a person for purposes of Section 1983 and thus subject to civil rights liability under that statute.

A related issue, which also helps shape a public institution's liability for violations of federal constitutional rights, is the extent to which Article III and the Eleventh Amendment of the U.S. Constitution immunize public institutions from suit. While the person issue is a matter of statutory interpretation, the immunity issue is a matter of constitutional interpretation. In general, if a lawsuit is against the state itself or against a state official or employee sued in his or her official capacity, and the plaintiff seeks money damages that would come from the state treasury,[8] Eleventh Amendment immunity from federal court suit will apply. As discussed below, in Section 1983 litigation, the immunity issue usually parallels the person issue, and the courts have used Eleventh Amendment immunity law as a backdrop against which to fashion and apply a definition of person under Section 1983.

In a series of cases beginning in 1978, the U.S. Supreme Court dramatically expanded the potential Section 1983 liability of various government entities. As a result of these cases, it became clear that any political subdivision of a state may be sued under this statute; that such political subdivisions may not assert a **qualified immunity** from liability based on the reasonableness or good faith of their actions; that the officers and employees of political subdivisions, as well as officers and employees of state agencies, may sometimes be sued under Section 1983; and that Section 1983 plaintiffs may not be required to resort to state administrative forums before seeking redress in court.

The first, and key, case in this series is the U.S. Supreme Court's decision in *Monell v. Department of Social Services of the City of New York*, 436 U.S. 658 (1978). Overruling prior precedents that had held the contrary, the Court decided that local government units, such as school boards and municipal corporations, are persons under Section 1983 and thus subject to liability for violating constitutional rights protected by that statute. Since the definition of person is central to Section 1983's applicability, the question is whether the Court's definition in *Monell* is broad enough to encompass postsecondary institutions: Are some public postsecondary institutions sufficiently like local government units that they will be considered persons subject to Section 1983 liability?

---

[8]State employees and officials may be sued in either their "official" capacities or their "personal" (or "individual") capacities under Section 1983. For the distinction between the two capacities, see *Hafer v. Melo*, 502 U.S. 21, 25–31 (1991). Since lawsuits seeking money damages against employees or officers in their official capacities are generally considered to be covered by a state's Eleventh Amendment immunity, such suits are discussed in this section of the book. Suits against employees or officials in their personal capacities are discussed in Section 4.4.4.1.

The answer depends not only on a close analysis of *Monell* but also on an analysis of the particular institution's organization and structure under state law. Locally based institutions, such as community colleges established as an arm of the county or as a community college district, are the most likely candidates for person status. At the other end of the spectrum, state universities established and operated by the state itself are apparently the least likely candidates. This distinction between local entities and state entities is appropriate because the Eleventh Amendment immunizes the states, but not local governments, from federal court suits on federal constitutional claims. Consequently, the Court in *Monell* limited its person definition "to local government units which are not considered part of the state for Eleventh Amendment purposes." And in a subsequent case, *Quern v. Jordan*, 440 U.S. 332 (1979), the Court emphasized this limitation in *Monell* and asserted that neither the language nor the history of Section 1983 evidences any congressional intention to abrogate the states' Eleventh Amendment immunity (440 U.S. at 341–45).

The clear implication, reading *Monell* and *Quern* together, is that local governments—such as school boards, cities, and counties—are persons suable under Section 1983 and are not immune from suit under the Eleventh Amendment, whereas state governments and state agencies controlled by the state are not persons under Section 1983 and are immune under the Eleventh Amendment. The issue in any particular case, then, as phrased by the Court in another case decided the same day as *Quern*, is whether the entity in question "is to be regarded as a political subdivision" of the state (and thus not immune) or as "an arm of the state subject to its control" (and thus immune) (*Lake County Estates v. Tahoe Regional Planning Agency*, 440 U.S. 391, 401–2 (1979)).

***3.4.2. Eleventh Amendment immunity.*** The case law in Section 3.4.1 above added clarity to what had been the confusing and uncertain status of postsecondary institutions under Section 1983 and the Eleventh Amendment. In subsequent cases, the courts have frequently equated the Eleventh Amendment immunity analysis with the person analysis under Section 1983. In determining whether to place particular institutions on the person (not immune) or nonperson (immune) side of the liability line, the courts have generally given separate consideration to each state and each type of institution within the state. Nevertheless, various courts have affirmed the proposition that the Eleventh Amendment and Section 1983 shield most state universities from damages liability in federal constitutional rights cases.[9]

The courts have applied a variety of factors in resolving Eleventh Amendment sovereign immunity issues. In *Kashani v. Purdue University*, 813 F.2d 843 (7th Cir. 1987), for example, in determining whether Purdue

---

[9] For one example to the contrary, see the *Kovats* case concerning Rutgers University, discussed below in this section. For another such example, see *Honadle v. University of Vermont & State Agricultural College*, 115 F. Supp. 2d 468 (D. Vt. 2000).

University was entitled to Eleventh Amendment immunity, the court placed primary importance on the "extent of the entity's financial autonomy from the state." The relevant considerations were "the extent of state funding, the state's oversight and control of the university's fiscal affairs, the university's ability independently to raise funds, whether the state taxes the university, and whether a judgment against the university would result in the state increasing its appropriations to the university." Applying these considerations, the court dismissed the plaintiff's Section 1983 claim, concluding that Purdue was entitled to immunity because it "is dependent upon and functionally integrated with the state treasury." The court also suggested that, although the states have structured their educational systems in many ways and courts review each case on its facts, "it would be an unusual state university that would not receive immunity" (813 F.2d at 845).

In contrast, the court in *Kovats v. Rutgers, The State University*, 822 F.2d 1303 (3d Cir. 1987), determined that Rutgers is not an arm of the state of New Jersey and thus is not entitled to Eleventh Amendment immunity. The case involved Section 1983 claims of faculty members who had been dismissed. The court considered whether a judgment against Rutgers would be paid by Rutgers or by the state and determined that Rutgers in its discretion could pay the judgment either with segregated non-state funds or with non-state funds that were commingled with state funds. Rutgers argued that, if it paid the judgment, the state would have to increase its appropriations to the university, thus affecting the state treasury. The court held that such an appropriations increase following a judgment would be in the legislature's discretion and that "[i]f the state structures an entity in such a way that the other relevant criteria indicate it to be an arm of the state, then immunity may be retained even where damage awards are funded by the state at the state's discretion." Then, the court determined that, although Rutgers "is now, at least in part, a state-created entity which serves a state purpose with a large degree of state financing, it remains under state law an independent entity able to direct its own actions and responsible on its own for judgments resulting from those actions."

More recent cases on the Eleventh Amendment immunity of state universities have generally upheld the universities' immunity claims, continuing to rely on a variety of factors to reach this result. In *Sherman v. Curators of the University of Missouri*, 16 F.3d 860 (8th Cir. 1994), *on remand*, 871 F. Supp. 344 (W.D. Mo. 1994), for instance, the appellate court focused on two factors: the university's degree of autonomy from the state and the university's fiscal dependence on state funds as the source for payments of damage awards against the university. Applying these factors on remand, the district court ruled that the university was immune from suit under the Eleventh Amendment. In *Rounds v. Oregon State Board of Higher Education*, 166 F.3d 1032 (9th Cir. 1999), the court focused on two primary factors in granting immunity to the University of Oregon, looking, first, to the university's "nature as created by state law," especially the extent to which the university is subject to the supervision of state officials or a state board of higher education; and, second, to the university functions, particularly whether the university "performs central governmental functions." And in *Bowers v. National Collegiate Athletic Association*, 475 F. 3d 524 (3d Cir. 2007), a case involving the University of Iowa, a court applied what it now called the *"Fitchik* factors," after the case that catalogued these factors. The factors constitute a "three-part test" that "examines [these] three elements: (1) whether the payment of the judgment would come from the state; (2) what status the [university] has under state law; and (3) what degree of autonomy the [university] has" (475 F. 3d at 546). Each factor is to be given equal weight. Applying the factors in "a fact-intensive review that calls for individualized determination," the court concluded that "the first *Fitchik* factor weighed slightly against immunity, while the second and third factors weighed heavily in favor of immunity." Accordingly, the court ruled that the University of Iowa came within the scope of Eleventh Amendment immunity.

When the Eleventh Amendment immunity of a community college, technical college, or junior college, rather than a state university, is at issue, courts have been more reluctant to grant immunity, since the various factors that courts use may indicate that community and junior colleges have greater institutional autonomy from the state government. In *Board of Regents of Stephen F. Austin State University*, 665 F.2d 553 (5th Cir. 1982), for example, the court distinguished Texas junior colleges from the Texas state universities. Reaffirming its earlier decisions in *Hander v. San Jacinto Junior College*, 519 F.2d 273 (5th Cir. 1975), and *Goss v. San Jacinto Junior College*, 588 F.2d 96 (5th Cir. 1979), the court concluded that Texas junior colleges are not arms of the state and are thus suable under Section 1983:

> Junior colleges, rather than being established by the legislature, are created by local initiative. Tex. Educ. Code Ann. § 130.031. Their governing bodies are elected by local voters rather than being appointed by the Governor with the advice and consent of the Senate. Id. § 130.083(e). Most telling is the power of junior colleges to levy *ad valorem* taxes, id. § 130.122, a power which the Board of SFA lacks. Under Texas law, political subdivisions are sometimes defined as entities authorized to levy taxes. Tex. Rev. Civ. Stat. Ann. art. 2351b-3 [665 F.2d at 558].

Similarly, in *Leach v. New Mexico Jr. College*, 45 P.3d 46 (N.M. 2002), the court denied immunity to a New Mexico junior college relying especially on the facts that the college had its own powers to levy taxes and to issue bonds and that its board members were not appointed by the governor.

In contrast, in *Hadley v. North Arkansas Community Technical College*, 76 F.3d 1437 (8th Cir. 1996), the court, by a 2-to-1 split vote, upheld the Eleventh Amendment immunity claim of a community college. The case also flags some unresolved issues concerning Eleventh Amendment immunity for community colleges (and for state institutions as well) and reemphasizes the important role that fiscal factors play in determining an institution's Eleventh Amendment status.

In *Hadley*, a vocational instructor filed a Section 1983 claim in federal court, alleging that the defendant's decision to terminate him violated his due process rights. The issue before the court was whether North Arkansas Community

Technical College (NACTC) should be classified as an arm of the state, entitled to Eleventh Amendment immunity from damages claims, or instead as a state political subdivision or municipal corporation that is not immune. According to the court,

> State universities and colleges almost always enjoy Eleventh Amendment immunity. On the other hand, community and technical colleges often have deep roots in a local community. When those roots include local political and financial involvement, the resulting Eleventh Amendment immunity questions tend to be difficult and very fact specific [citing cases] [76 F.3d at 1438–39].

Examining the structure and authority of NACTC under state law, the court determined "that NACTC is, both financially and institutionally, an arm of the State, and that any damage award to Hadley [the instructor] would inevitably be paid from the state treasury." Weighed against these factors, however, was the contrasting consideration that "Arkansas community colleges also have elements of local funding and control" suggestive of a political subdivision. The court considered the former factors to prevail over the latter because "exposure of the state treasury is a more important factor than whether the State controls the entity in question" (citing *Hess v. Port Authority Trans-Hudson Corp.*, 513 U.S. 30 (1994)). Thus, despite the fact that NACTC's daily operations were largely controlled by locally elected officials of a community college district, the district had residual authority to supplement NACTC's operating budget with local tax revenues, and it had the responsibility for funding capital improvements from local tax revenues, NACTC nevertheless remained financially dependent upon the state for its daily operations and, therefore, should be afforded immunity.

In other more recent cases, courts have also begun to make clear that a state university's Eleventh Amendment immunity may sometimes extend to other entities that the university has recognized or with which it is otherwise affiliated. In the *Rounds* case (above), for example, the plaintiffs also sued the student government, the Associated Students of the University of Oregon. The court held that "[t]o the extent that the [plaintiffs] assert a Section 1983 claim against the Associated Students, this claim also is barred, as the Associated Students' status as the recognized student government at the University allows it to claim the same Eleventh Amendment immunity that shields the University itself" (166 F.3d at 1035–36).

Since the Eleventh Amendment provides states and "arms of the state" with immunity only from *federal* court suits, it does not directly apply to Section 1983 suits in *state* courts. The definition of person may thus be the primary focus of the analysis in state court Section 1983 suits. In *Will v. Michigan Department of State Police*, 491 U.S. 58 (1989), the U.S. Supreme Court ruled that Section 1983 suits may be brought in state courts, but that neither the state nor state officials sued in their official capacities would be considered persons for purposes of such suits. In *Howlett v. Rose*, 496 U.S. 356 (1990), the Court reaffirmed that Section 1983 suits may be brought in state courts against other government entities (or against individuals) that are considered "persons" under Section 1983. In such cases, state law protections of sovereign immunity and other state procedural limitations on suits against the sovereign (see *Felder v. Casey*, 487 U.S. 131 (1988)) will not generally be available to the governmental (or individual) defendants.

In *Alden v. Maine*, 527 U.S. 706 (1999), however, the Court determined that, even though the Eleventh Amendment does not apply in state courts, the states do have an implied constitutional immunity from suits in state court. Thus states sued in state court under Section 1983 may now invoke an implied sovereign immunity from state court suits that would protect them much as the Eleventh Amendment immunity protects them in federal court. States may assert this immunity defense in lieu of arguing, under *Will* and *Howlett*, that they are not "persons"; or may argue that, if they fall within the protection of *Alden*'s implied sovereign immunity, they cannot be "persons" under Section 1983.

Given these substantial and complex legal developments, various public postsecondary institutions are now subject to Section 1983 liability, in both federal courts and state courts, for violations of federal constitutional rights—either because they have no Eleventh Amendment immunity and thus are "persons" under Section 1983, or because they or the state have waived immunity. Those that are subject to suit may be exposed to extensive judicial remedies, which they are unlikely to escape by asserting procedural technicalities. Moreover, institutions and systems that can escape Section 1983 liability, because they are not "persons," and are protected by sovereign immunity will find that they are subject in other ways to liability for violations of civil rights. They may be reachable under Section 1983 through "official capacity" suits against institutional officers that seek only injunctive relief (*Power v. Summers*, 226 F.3d 815, 819 (7th Cir. 2000))—relief that is directed to the particular officer or officers being sued but that effectively would bind the institution. Institutions may be reachable through "personal capacity" suits against the institution's officers or employees and seeking money damages from them individually, rather than from the institution or the state (see Section 4.4.1 of this book). Institutions are suable under other federal civil rights laws establishing statutory rights that parallel those protected by the Constitution and that serve to abrogate or waive state sovereign immunity. (For examples, see the statutes discussed in Sections 4.5.2.1 to 4.5.2.3 and 4.5.2.5 to 4.5.2.6.) Institutions may also be subject to suit under similar state civil rights laws or under state statutes similar to Section 1983 that authorize state court suits for the vindication of state or federal constitutional rights.

In such a legal environment, administrators and counsel should foster full and fair enjoyment of federal civil rights on their campuses. Even when it is clear that a particular public institution is not subject to Section 1983 damages liability, administrators should seek to comply with the spirit of Section 1983, which urges that where officials "may harbor doubt about the lawfulness of their intended actions . . . [they should] err on the side of protecting citizens' . . . rights" (*Owen v. City of Independence*, 445 U.S. 622, 652 (1980)).

# 4

# The College and Its Employees

*Chapter 4 addresses basic legal issues regarding employment, with numerous examples regarding colleges and universities. Both individual employment contracts and collective bargaining contracts are discussed. Sources of personal liability for employees are examined, including negligence liability, liability for entering a contract, and liability for deprivation of federal constitutional rights. The chapter then reviews the major federal civil rights laws that require nondiscrimination in every facet of employment. Federal constitutional protections against employment discrimination, federal executive orders requiring nondiscrimination by recipients of federal contracts, and state law prohibitions on sexual orientation discrimination in employment are also addressed. The chapter then discusses affirmative action in employment, distinguishing between mandatory and voluntary plans, and examining the validity of such plans under two sources of law: Title VII of the Civil Rights Act of 1964, and the U.S. Constitution's equal protection clause. Finally, the chapter examines differences in how nondiscrimination laws apply to religious colleges and universities compared with secular institutions.*

## Section 4.1. Overview of Employment Relationships

Employment laws and regulations pose some of the most complex legal issues faced by colleges and universities. Employees may be executive officers of the institution, administrators and staff members, or faculty members—some of whom may be in a dual appointment status as administrators and faculty members and others of whom may be in a dual employee-student status.

The discussion in this chapter applies to all individuals employed by a college or university, whether they are officers, faculty, or staff. Particular applications of employment law to faculty members, and concepts unique to faculty employment (such as academic freedom and tenure), are the subject of Chapters 5 and 6.

136

The institution's relationships with its employees are governed by a complex web of state and federal (and sometimes local) law. Contract law principles, based in state common law, provide the basic legal foundation for employment relationships (see Section 4.2 below). For employees who are covered by a **collective bargaining agreement**, however, federal or state statutory law and labor board rulings supplement, and to a substantial extent replace, common law contract principles (see Section 4.3 below). And for employees located in a foreign country, the civil law of that country will sometimes replace or supplement the contract law principles of a college or university's home state.

In addition to contract law and collective bargaining laws, public institutions' employment relationships are also governed by other federal and state statutes, federal and state agency regulations (including state civil service regulations), constitutional law (both federal and state), administrative law (both federal and state), and sometimes local civil rights and health and safety ordinances of cities and counties. For private institutions, the web of employment law includes (in addition to contract and collective bargaining law) various federal and state statutes and regulations, local ordinances, state constitutional provisions (in some states), and federal and state administrative law (in some circumstances). Whenever a public or private institution employs workers under a government procurement contract or grant, any contract or grant terms covering employment will also come into play, as will federal or state statutes and regulations on government contracts and grants; these sources of law may serve to modify common law contract principles. Moreover, for both public and private institutions, state tort law affects employment relationships because institutions and employees are both subject to a duty of care arising from common law tort principles (see Sections 3.2 and 4.4.2). Like common law contract principles, however, common law tort principles are sometimes modified by statute as, for example, is the case with workers' compensation laws.

Among the most complex of the federal and state laws on particular aspects of employment are the nondiscrimination statutes and regulations—the subject of Chapter 5. Other examples of complex and specialized laws include collective bargaining laws (Section 4.3 below), immigration laws, tax laws, and employee benefits laws.

A fundamental issue that each college or university must resolve for itself is whether all individuals working for the institution are its employees or whether some are independent contractors. Similar issues may also arise concerning whether a particular worker is an employee or is working only in a student status. Colleges and universities also need to address the issue of where their employees are working and what effect the location has on the applicable law. Other legal concerns that may arise for colleges as employers include the free expression rights of employees, particularly in public colleges (see generally Section 6.1), privacy in the workplace (including "snail mail" and e-mail privacy), background checks on applicants for employment, drug and alcohol use by employers, and potential workplace violence.

The college may also face a variety of particularized legal issues, or particular risks of legal liability, regarding specific groups of employees. Security personnel, particularly those who are "sworn officers" and carry firearms, may involve their institutions in claims regarding the use of force or off-campus law enforcement activities (see Section 7.6.1). Security personnel may also become the focus of negligence claims if crimes of violence occur on campus (see Section 7.6.1). Arrests and searches conducted by security personnel at public (and sometimes private) institutions may raise issues under the Fourth Amendment or comparable state constitutional provisions (see Sections 7.4.3 and 7.6.1). And the records kept by security personnel may raise special issues under the federal Campus Security Act (see Section 7.6.3) and under the Family Educational Rights and Privacy Act (FERPA) (see Section 7.8.1).

Student judicial officers may involve their institutions in due process claims that arise when students contest penalties imposed upon them for infractions of the college's code of conduct (see Sections 9.1, 9.2, and 9.3). Student judicial officers may also become involved in various issues concerning the confidentiality of their investigations and deliberations, including issues regarding a "mediation privilege."

Health care personnel, including physicians and mental health counselors, may involve their institutions in negligence claims when students under their care injure or kill themselves or others (see Sections 3.2.2.6 and 4.4.2), or in malpractice claims when something else goes wrong in the diagnosis or treatment process. Physicians and counselors who serve members of the campus community may also confront issues concerning the doctor-patient privilege and other confidentiality privileges.

Coaches of sports teams may file claims of sex discrimination against their institutions, either because they believe they have been discriminated against or because of a perceived inequity in resources allocated to women's teams. Or coaches may have lucrative contracts and fringe benefits that (in public institutions) prompt requests under open records laws. Coaches may also become involved in disputes regarding NCAA rules.

The management of the institution's numerous and varying employment relationships requires the regular attention of professionally trained and experienced staff. In addition to human resource managers, the institution will need compliance officers to handle legal requirements in specialized areas such as nondiscrimination and affirmative action, immigration status, employee benefits, and health and safety; and a risk manager to handle liability matters concerning employees. The institution's legal counsel will also need to be involved in many compliance and risk management issues, as well as in the preparation of standard contracts and other employment forms, the preparation and modification of employee manuals and other written policies, the establishment and operation of employee grievance processes, and the preparation of negotiated (individual or collective) employment contracts.

## Section 4.2. Employment Contracts

***4.2.1. Defining the contract.*** The basic relationship between an employee and a college or university is governed by contract. Contracts may be either written or oral; and even when there is no express contract, common law principles may allow the courts to imply a contract between the parties. Contracts may be very basic; for example, an offer letter from the college stating a position title and a wage or salary may, upon acceptance, be construed to be a contract. In *Small v. Juniata College*, 682 A.2d 350 (Pa. Super. Ct. 1996), for example, the court ruled that an offer letter to a college's football coach created a one-year contract and thus the employee handbook's provisions regarding grounds for termination did not apply. Absent any writing, oral promises by a manager or supervisor may nevertheless be binding on a college through the application of agency law (see Section 3.1 of this book). A court may also look to the written policies of an institution, or to its consistent past practices, to imply a contract with certain employment guarantees. For these reasons, it is important that administrators and counsel ensure that communications to employees and applicants, whether written or oral, and the provisions in employee manuals or policies clearly represent the institution's actual intent regarding the binding nature of its statements.

Sometimes a state statute will supersede common law contract principles as to a particular issue. This is the case, for instance, with state workers' compensation laws, which substitute for any contractual provisions the parties might otherwise have used to cover employee injuries on the job.

### 4.2.2. The at-will doctrine.

**4.2.2. *The at-will doctrine.*** Until the late 1970s, the common law doctrine of "employment at will" shielded employers from most common law contract claims unless an individual had a written contract spelling out job security protections. Employers had the right to discharge an individual for any reason, or no reason, unless the termination violated some state or federal statute. The at-will doctrine may apply to employees at both private and public colleges and universities for those employees who are not otherwise protected by a state statute, civil service regulations, or contractual provisions according some right to continued employment. Even if an institution and an employee have entered an employment agreement, if the agreement does not specify the length of employment, the employee may be viewed by the court as terminable at the employer's will. In fact, at-will employment at public colleges may defeat an employee's assertion of due process protections because no property interest is created in at-will employment.

Although the at-will doctrine is still the prevailing view in many states, judges have developed exceptions to the doctrine in order to avoid its harsher consequences when individuals with long service and good work records were terminated without cause. Because these exceptions are created by state court rulings, the status of the at-will doctrine varies by state. The two primary approaches to creating exceptions have been through the use of contract law and tort law. In some states, employee handbooks or other policy documents have been found to have contractual status, although courts in a minority of states have rejected this interpretation of contract law. In other cases, courts have allowed employees asserting that they were terminated for improper reasons to state tort claims for wrongful discharge. In *Wounaris v. West Virginia*

*State College*, 588 S.E.2d 406 (W. Va. 2003), for example, the court held that it was against public policy for a college to terminate a staff member for defending himself against an allegedly unfair termination.

### Section 4.3. Collective Bargaining

**4.3.1. Overview.** Collective bargaining has existed on many college campuses since the late 1960s, yet some institutions have recently faced the prospect of bargaining with their faculty or staff for the first time. Whether a union is a fixture or a recent arrival, it presents administrators with a complex mixture of the familiar and the foreign. Many demands, such as for shorter staff work weeks, lighter teaching loads. smaller class sizes, and larger salaries, may be familiar on many campuses, but other demands sometimes voiced, such as for standardized pay scales rather than individualized "merit" salary determinations, may present unfamiliar situations. Legal, policy, and political issues may arise concerning the extent to which collective bargaining and the bargained agreement preempt or circumscribe not merely traditional administrative "elbow room" but also the customary forms of shared governance.

Although the number of unionized faculty and staff has increased only slightly in the past few years, most union organizing has occurred among graduate students and adjunct or part-time faculty. Graduate teaching and research assistants won and then lost the right to bargain at several elite private and public research universities (*Brown University and International Union, United Automobile, Aerospace and Agricultural Implement Workers of America*, 342 N.L.R.B. No. 42 (July 13, 2004)). And bargaining is not limited to full-time employees of the college; adjunct and part-time faculty have won the right to bargain at institutions throughout the country (see Section 5.2.3).

Although state law regulates bargaining at public colleges and universities, and federal law regulates bargaining at private universities, many of these rights are similar. Employees typically have the right to organize and to select a representative to negotiate on their behalf with the employer over terms and conditions of employment. Once a representative is selected by a majority of the employees in a particular bargaining unit, the employer has a statutory duty to bargain with the employees' representative, and employees may not negotiate individually with the employer over issues that are mandatory subjects of bargaining. Either the union or the employer may file an "unfair labor practice" charge with a government agency alleging that the other party committed infractions of the bargaining laws. In the private sector, the National Labor Relations Board hears these claims, and in the public sector a state public employment relations board provides recourse for aggrieved unions or employers. Hearings before these agencies take the place of a civil trial; the rulings of these agencies are typically appealed to state or federal appellate courts. In addition to claims of failure to bargain, one party may claim that the other has engaged in activity that breaches an existing collective bargaining agreement.

### 4.3.2. The public-private dichotomy in collective bargaining.

Theoretically, the legal aspects of collective bargaining divide into two distinct categories: public and private. However, these categories are not necessarily defined in the same way as they are for constitutional state action purposes (see Section 1.5.2). In relation to collective bargaining, "public" and "private" are defined by the collective bargaining legislation and interpretive precedents. Private institutions are subject to the federal law controlling collective bargaining, the National Labor Relations Act of 1935 (the Wagner Act) as amended by the Labor-Management Relations Act of 1947 (the Taft-Hartley Act), 29 U.S.C. § 141 et seq. Collective bargaining in public institutions is regulated by state law.

### 4.3.3. Collective bargaining and antidiscrimination laws.

A body of case law is developing on the applicability of federal and state laws prohibiting discrimination in employment (see Section 4.5) to the collective bargaining process. Courts have interpreted federal labor relations law (Section 4.3.2) to impose on unions a duty to represent each employee fairly—without arbitrariness, discrimination, or bad faith (see *Vaca v. Sipes*, 386 U.S. 171 (1967)). In addition, some antidiscrimination statutes, such as Title VII of the Civil Rights Act of 1964 (see Section 5.2.1) and the Age Discrimination in Employment Act (ADEA) (see Section 5.2.6), apply directly to unions as well as employers. But these laws have left open several questions concerning the relationships between collective bargaining and antidiscrimination statutes. For instance, when employment discrimination problems are covered in the bargaining contract, can such coverage be construed to preclude employees from seeking other remedies under antidiscrimination statutes? If an employee resorts to a negotiated grievance procedure to resolve a discrimination dispute, can that employee then be precluded from using remedies provided under antidiscrimination statutes?

Most cases presenting such issues have arisen under Title VII of the Civil Rights Act of 1964 (see Section 4.5.2.1 of this book). The leading case is *Alexander v. Gardner-Denver Co.*, 415 U.S. 36 (1974). A discharged employee claimed that the discharge was motivated by racial discrimination, and he contested his discharge in a grievance proceeding provided under a collective bargaining contract. Having lost before an arbitrator in the grievance proceeding, and having had a complaint to the federal Equal Employment Opportunity Commission dismissed, the employee filed a Title VII action in federal district court. The district court, citing earlier Supreme Court precedent regarding the finality of arbitration awards, had held that the employee was bound by the arbitration decision and thus had no right to sue under Title VII. The U.S. Supreme Court reversed. The Court held that the employee could still sue under Title VII, which creates statutory rights "distinctly separate" from the contractual right to arbitration under the collective bargaining agreement. Such independent rights "are not waived either by inclusion of discrimination disputes within the collective bargaining agreement or by submitting the nondiscrimination claim to arbitration."

The fact that the grievance system was part of a collectively negotiated agreement, and not an individual employment contract, is important to the reasoning of *Gardner-Denver*. The Court noted in *Gardner-Denver* that it may be possible to waive a Title VII cause of action (and presumably actions under other statutes) "as part of a voluntary settlement" of a discrimination claim. The employee's consent to such a settlement would have to be "voluntary and knowing," however, and "mere resort to the arbitral forum to enforce contractual rights" could not constitute such a waiver (see 415 U.S. at 52).

In 2009 the U.S. Supreme Court issued a 5-to-4 ruling that narrows its ruling in *Gardner-Denver*. In *14 Penn Plaza LLC, et al. v. Pyett*, 556 U.S. 247 (2009), the court ruled that a detailed grievance and arbitration provision in a collective bargaining agreement that specifically included discrimination claims was binding on the individual bargaining unit members, despite its earlier ruling in *Gardner-Denver*. The Court distinguished *Gardner-Denver* from the situation in the *14 Penn Plaza* case. In *14 Penn Plaza*, the grievance and arbitration provision specifically included discrimination claims and had been "freely negotiated" between the union and the multiemployer association, while in *Gardner-Denver*, the issue was whether contract-based discrimination claims were limited to an arbitration forum. Furthermore, said Justice Thomas, writing for the majority, the Court had upheld the lawfulness of arbitration clauses agreed to by employees who were not represented by unions that require that discrimination claims be arbitrated. The result in *14 Penn Plaza* removes the "advantage" that unionized employees previously enjoyed of being able to process their discrimination claims both through a grievance and arbitration process and through a lawsuit.

The U.S. Supreme Court addressed the waiver issue in a case involving the waiver of the right to a judicial forum in an *individual* employment contract rather than in a collective bargaining agreement. In *Gilmer v. Interstate-Johnson Lane*, 500 U.S. 20 (1991), the Court ruled that an express waiver in an individual employment contract was lawful. The U.S. Supreme Court revisited the issue of waivers in the collective bargaining context in *Wright v. Universal Maritime Service Corp.*, 525 U.S. 70 (1998). In *Wright*, the question was whether an arbitration clause in a collective bargaining agreement limited a bargaining unit member to an arbitral forum in seeking a remedy for an alleged violation of the Americans with Disabilities Act. In a unanimous opinion written by Justice Scalia, the Court determined that the arbitration clause in the agreement was too broad to constitute a "clear and unmistakable waiver" of the plaintiff's right to pursue a civil rights claim in court. Because the waiver was neither clear nor unmistakable with respect to the waiver of statutory rights, the Court found it unnecessary to reconcile *Gardner-Denver* and *Gilmer*. *Wright* was applied to the higher education context in *Rogers v. New York University*, 220 F.3d 73 (2d Cir. 2000), in which the court ruled that the union did not waive plaintiff's right to bring an action for ADA and Family and Medical Leave Act (FMLA) discrimination in federal court.

Given the holding of *Gardner-Denver*, some institutions have negotiated collective bargaining agreements with their faculty that contain a choice-of-forum provision that requires the employee to use either the campus grievance system or the external judicial system, but not both. This requirement has been found to violate federal nondiscrimination laws. In *EEOC v. Board of Governors of State Colleges and Universities*, 957 F.2d 424 (7th Cir. 1992), the court, citing *Gardner-Denver*, reaffirmed the right of employees to overlapping contractual and statutory remedies and called the contractual provision "discriminatory on its face" (957 F.2d at 431).

But in a more recent case, a federal appellate court ruled that a union contract provision that required an employee to choose between arbitrating a grievance and pursing a discrimination charge with the EEOC or in the courts did not violate the law. In *Richardson v. Commission on Human Rights and Opportunities*, 532 F.3d 114 (2d Cir. 2008), the plaintiff had been terminated, and filed a grievance with her union. She also filed a claim of race discrimination against her employer with the state Commission on Human Rights and Opportunities. The collective bargaining agreement stated that "disputes over claimed unlawful discrimination shall be subject to the grievance procedure but shall not be arbitrable if a complaint is filed with the Commission on Human Rights and Opportunities arising from the same common nucleus of operative fact." Relying on that contract language, the union refused to take the grievance to arbitration. The plaintiff then filed a retaliation claim against the union with the state Commission on Human Rights and Opportunities as well as with the EEOC.

The court awarded summary judgment to the employer on both the discrimination and retaliation claims, finding that the collective bargaining agreement language allowed the plaintiff to file an EEOC charge and to sue her employer in court; the lack of access to arbitration under the contract did not diminish any of the plaintiff's rights, according to the court. The court distinguished *Gardner-Denver* because the contract in that case had required a plaintiff pursuing a grievance under a collective bargaining agreement to waive his or her right to file an EEOC charge or a lawsuit. The provision in question in this case, said the court, was the opposite in that it allowed a plaintiff to select an administrative or judicial forum for resolution of the dispute rather than arbitration.

Title VII protections may also conflict with the rights of the union as exclusive bargaining agent in situations where Title VII's prohibition against religious discrimination clashes with the union's right to collect an **agency fee** from nonmembers. Robert Roesser, an associate professor of electrical engineering at the University of Detroit, refused to pay his agency fee to the local union because, as a Catholic, he objected to the pro-choice position on abortion taken by the state union and the national union (the National Education Association). According to the university's contract with the union, nonpayment of the agency fee was grounds for termination, and Roesser was discharged.

Roesser filed a complaint with the EEOC, which sued both the union and the university on his behalf. The EEOC claimed that, under Title VII, the union was required to make a reasonable accommodation to Roesser's religious objections unless the accommodation posed an undue hardship. Roesser had offered to donate to a charity either the entire agency fee or the portion of the fee that was sent to the state and national unions. The union refused, but countered with the suggestion that the amount of the agency fee used for all social and political issues generally, including pro-choice and other issues, be deducted. Roesser refused because he did not want to be associated in any way with the state or national union (adding a First Amendment issue to the Title VII litigation).

The federal district court granted summary judgment to the union and the university, ruling that the union's accommodation was reasonable and that Roesser's proposal imposed undue hardship on the union. That ruling was overturned by the U.S. Court of Appeals for the Sixth Circuit (*EEOC v. University of Detroit*, 904 F.2d 331 (6th Cir. 1990)). The appellate court stated that Roesser's objection to the agency fee had two prongs, only one of which the district court had recognized. Roesser had objected to both the contribution to and the association with the state and national unions because of their position on abortion; the district court had ruled only on the contribution issue and had not addressed the association issue.

Thus, collective bargaining does not provide an occasion for postsecondary administrators to lessen their attention to the institution's Title VII responsibilities or its responsibilities under other antidiscrimination and civil rights laws. In many instances, faculty members can avail themselves of rights and remedies both under the bargaining agreement and under civil rights statutes.

### Section 4.4. Personal Liability of Employees

**4.4.1. Overview.** Although most individuals seeking redress for alleged wrongs in academe sue their institutions, they may choose to add individuals as defendants, or they may sue only the person or persons who allegedly harmed them. Most colleges have indemnification policies that provide for defending a faculty or staff member who is sued for acts that occurred while performing his or her job.

Individuals may face personal liability under various common law claims, such as negligence, defamation, intentional or negligent infliction of emotional distress, or fraud. In *Minger v. Green*, 239 F.3d 793 (6th Cir. 2001), a federal appellate court applying Kentucky law ruled that the associate director of the housing office at Murray State University was not immune from personal liability in a wrongful death and intentional misrepresentation lawsuit brought by the deceased student's mother. The associate director was accused of intentionally misrepresenting the seriousness of an earlier fire in the student's residence hall to his mother; the mother claimed that had she known that the first fire had been set by an arsonist, she would have removed her son from the residence hall, thus preventing his death when the arsonist returned and set a subsequent fire five days later.

Although courts have ruled that individuals typically are not liable for violations of federal nondiscrimination laws such as Title VII of the Civil Rights Act of 1964 or the Age Discrimination in Employment Act, since these laws impose obligations on the "employer," not on managers or individuals, some state courts have imposed individual liability under state nondiscrimination laws (see, for example, *Matthews v. Superior Court*, 40 Cal. Rptr. 2d 350 (Cal. Ct. App., 2d Dist. 1995), holding supervisors who participated in sexual harassment individually liable under California's Fair Employment and Housing Act). Other federal laws, such as 42 U.S.C. § 1981 and 42 U.S.C. §1983 (see Sections 3.4 and 4.4.4 of this book) do provide for individual liability. In addition, whistleblower laws in some states provide for individual liability of managers or supervisors.

Individuals may also face liability for intentional torts, and they may face liability as well when they enter contracts on behalf of the college or university. Personal contract liability is discussed in Section 4.4.3 below.

### 4.4.2. Tort liability.

**4.4.2.1. Overview.** An employee of a postsecondary institution who commits a tort may be liable even if the tort was committed while he or she was conducting the institution's affairs. The individual must have actually committed the tortious act, directed it, or otherwise participated in its commission, however, before personal liability will attach. The individual will not be personally liable for torts of other institutional agents merely because he or she represents the institution for whom the other agents were acting. The elements of a tort and the defenses against a tort claim (see Section 3.2.2.1 of this book) in suits against the individual personally are generally the same as those in suits against the institution. An individual sued in his or her personal capacity, however, is usually not shielded by the sovereign immunity and charitable immunity defenses that sometimes protect the institution, although the laws of some states may provide for sovereign immunity for individuals if they were acting within the scope of their employment.

If an employee commits a tort while acting on behalf of the institution and within the scope of the authority delegated to him or her, both the individual and the institution may be liable for the harm caused by the tort. But the institution's potential liability does not relieve the individual of any measure of liability; the injured party could choose to collect a judgment solely from the individual, and the individual would have no claim against the institution for any part of the judgment he or she was required to pay. However, where individual and institution are both potentially liable, the individual may receive practical relief from liability if the injured party squeezes the entire judgment from the institution or the institution chooses to pay the entire amount.

If an employee commits a tort while acting outside the scope of delegated authority, he or she may be personally liable, but the institution would not be liable (see Section 3.2.1). Thus, the injured party could obtain a judgment only against the individual, and only the individual would be responsible for satisfying the judgment. The institution, however, may affirm the individual's unauthorized action ("affirmance" is similar to the "ratification" discussed in connection with contract liability in Section 3.3), in which case the individual will be deemed to have acted within his or her authority, and both institution and individual will be potentially liable.

Employees of public institutions can sometimes escape tort liability by proving the defense of **official immunity**. For this defense to apply, the individual's act must have been within the scope of his or her authority and must have been a discretionary act involving policy judgment, as opposed to a "ministerial duty" (involving little or no discretion with regard to the choices to be made). Because of this element of discretion and policy judgment, official immunity is more likely to apply to a particular individual the higher he or she is in the hierarchy of authority.

State tort claims acts may also define the degree to which public employees will be protected from individual liability. For example, the Georgia Tort Claims Act has been interpreted by that state's courts in two cases as extending immunity to a department chair and an academic vice president at Gordon College who recommended that one professor be denied tenure (*Hardin v. Phillips*, 547 S.E.2d 565 (Ga. Ct. App. 2001)) and that an untenured professor be fired for neglect of duty and insubordination (*Wang v. Moore*, 544 S.E.2d 486 (Ga. Ct. App. 2001)).

**4.4.2.2. Negligence.** Although typically the defendant of choice in a negligence claim involving a college or university is the institution, faculty and staff are occasionally found liable for negligence if their failure to act, or their negligent act, contributed to the plaintiff's injury. The elements of a tort claim (discussed in Section 3.2.1 of this book) are the same for suits against institutions and suits against individuals. But employees of public institutions may enjoy immunity from liability, whereas employees of private institutions may not (unless they are shielded by charitable immunity, also discussed in Section 3.2.1). For example, in *Defoor v. Evesque*, 694 So. 2d 1302 (Ala. 1997), the Supreme Court of Alabama ruled that an employee of a public college was not immune from personal tort liability in relation to a slip-and-fall claim. The college had entered a contract with USX Corporation to provide testing services for individuals applying for certain jobs at USX. A college administrator hired Evesque to administer the tests. Although Evesque usually made certain that there was no spilled hydraulic fluid in the testing area, on the day that Defoor took his test, fluid was spilled on the floor, and Defoor fell, sustaining injuries. Although the college and USX were absolved from potential liability, Evesque was not, because the court characterized his duty to clean up the spill as "ministerial" rather than "discretionary."

As discussed in Section 3.2.2.4 of this book, liability related to off-campus internships may occur when students are injured. Although most litigation has targeted colleges as defendants, a federal trial court allowed several claims related to a student's internship to go forward against individual faculty members as well as the university. In *Rinsky v. Trustees of Boston University*, 2010 U.S. Dist. LEXIS 136876 (D. Mass. 2010), a social work student had been assigned to an internship at a nearby town's senior center. While performing her required internship, the student was physically assaulted and stalked by a client. The student, Rinsky, told both the senior center supervisor and her faculty supervisors about the client's misconduct, but the center supervisor refused to reassign her and required her to work alone with the client, who continued the misconduct. According to Rinsky, when she told her faculty supervisors about the client's behavior, they told her that she could file a complaint with the state human rights agency, but that "if she brought up her sexual harassment at problem resolution meetings, she would be demonstrating a 'lack of commitment to the social work profession.'" They did not transfer Rinsky to a different internship. Rinsky's center supervisor gave her negative performance reviews and she was dismissed from the graduate program.

Rinsky sued the supervisors individually and the university for negligence, assault and battery, and invasion of privacy, and sued the university under Title IX of the Education Amendments of 1972 (see Section 11.5.3 of this book). The defendants filed a motion to dismiss. The trial court dismissed some of the claims, but allowed Rinsky's negligence claims against all the supervisors and the university to proceed to trial, as well as her Title IX claim and state law sex discrimination claim against the university.

Medical professionals and counselors may face individual liability for alleged negligence in treating student patients. In a widely reported case, *Tarasoff v. Regents of the University of California*, 551 P.2d 334 (Cal. 1976), the parents of a girl murdered by a psychiatric patient at the university hospital sued the university regents, four psychotherapists employed by the hospital, and the campus police. The patient had confided his intention to kill the daughter to a staff psychotherapist. Though the patient was briefly detained by the campus police at the psychotherapist's request, no further action was taken to protect the daughter. The parents alleged that the defendants should be held liable for a tortious failure to confine a dangerous patient and a tortious failure to warn them or their daughter of a dangerous patient. The psychotherapists and campus police claimed official immunity under a California statute freeing "public employee(s)" from liability for acts or omissions resulting from "the exercise of discretion vested in [them]" (Cal. Gov't Code § 820.2). The court accepted the official immunity defense in relation to the failure to confine, because that failure involved a "basic policy decision" sufficient to constitute discretion under the statute. But regarding the failure to warn, the court refused to accept the psychotherapists' official immunity claim, because the decision whether to warn was not a basic policy decision. The campus police needed no official immunity from their failure to warn, because, the court held, they had no legal duty to warn in light of the facts in the complaint.

The Supreme Court of Rhode Island, addressing a similar issue, ruled that a jury must determine whether a psychologist was individually liable for a student's suicide. In *Klein v. Solomon*, 713 A.2d 764 (R.I. 1998), the mother of a Brown University student who had committed suicide filed a negligence suit against the university, the psychologist who had diagnosed her son as having suicidal tendencies, and another counselor to whom the psychologist had referred the son. She alleged that the psychologist was negligent in referring her son to a list of four therapists, none of whom specialized in suicide prevention, and none of whom could prescribe medication. The court affirmed a summary judgment for the university with respect to its own liability, but reversed the lower court's summary judgment award to the psychologist. The court stated that a jury could have concluded that the psychologist was negligent in failing to refer the student to someone who was qualified to treat him for suicidal tendencies.

Because immunity from suit on negligence claims is a matter of state law, the application and interpretation of this doctrine differ among the states. For example, a federal appellate court found several members of the athletics staff protected by a qualified immunity against liability for negligence in the death of a student. In *Sorey v. Kellett*, 849 F.2d 960 (5th Cir. 1988), a football player at the University of Southern Mississippi collapsed during practice and died shortly thereafter. The court applied Mississippi's qualified immunity for public officials performing discretionary, rather than ministerial, acts to the trainer, the team physician, and the football coach, finding that the first two were performing a discretionary act in administering medical treatment to the student. The coach was entitled to qualified immunity because of his general authority over the football program. Noting that "a public official charged only with general authority over a program or institution naturally is exercising discretionary functions" (849 F.2d at 964), the court denied recovery to the plaintiff.

Other potential sources of individual liability for alleged negligence include claims of negligent hiring, supervision, and retention. Both employers and individuals may be found liable under these theories.

**4.4.2.3. Defamation.** As discussed in Section 3.2.4, claims that an oral or written communication resulted in injury to an individual are a rapidly increasing area of litigation for colleges. College employees may face individual liability for defamation as well. Administrators and faculty have been sued for defamation by both faculty and students who allege that oral or written statements made by college employees have derailed academic careers or have interfered with employment opportunities.

Defamation claims brought by faculty and staff against college officials who have been critical of their work performance or their behavior have proliferated over the past few years, but few have been successful. Plaintiffs must meet a four-part test (discussed in Section 3.2.4) in order to make a claim of defamation. In some cases, courts have found that a communication was not defamatory either because it did not harm the individual's reputation; because the statement was an opinion, which is not actionable; because the information in the communication was too general to cause harm to the plaintiff; or because the allegedly defamatory information was true. For example, in *Constantino v. University of Pittsburgh*, 766 A.2d 1265 (Pa. Super. Ct. 2001), a department chair who wrote a letter stating that there were "problems" with a faculty member's teaching was found not to have defamed the faculty member because the letter was sent to officials who were responsible for evaluating the plaintiff's performance, and the statements were general in nature.

However, if a plaintiff can demonstrate that the defendant acted with malice or knowingly communicated false information, the plaintiff may prevail. For example, in *Woodruff v. Ohman*, 166 F. App'x 212 (6th Cir. 2006), an employee claimed that the principal investigator for the grant on which she was working at the University of Tennessee had sent letters to a research council and to immigration authorities criticizing her performance and falsely stating that she was unproductive. The trial court found that many of the statements in these letters were not only knowingly false but also damaged the plaintiff's reputation and awarded her both compensatory and punitive damages, which the appellate court upheld. And in *Slack v. Stream*, 988 So.2d 516 (Ala. 2008), the state's highest court affirmed a judgment for a professor who sued his former department chair for defamation after the chair publicized allegations of plagiarism against the plaintiff and violated university policy in investigating the allegations. In particular, said the court, the chair's decision to send copies of a letter of reprimand to individuals at universities across the country, including a university that had recently hired the plaintiff, defeated his claim of state-agent immunity and justified the award of punitive damages.

Defendants who are employed by public colleges or universities may be shielded by state law official immunity. *Staheli v. Smith*, 548 So. 2d 1299 (Miss. 1989), provides an example of the application of state law official immunity. The Supreme Court of Mississippi was asked to determine whether the dean of the School of Engineering at the University of Mississippi was a public official for purposes of governmental immunity against a defamation lawsuit. A faculty member had sued the dean, stating that a letter from the dean recommending against tenure for the plaintiff was libelous. The court found that the dean was, indeed, a public official, had not exceeded the scope of his authority, and thus was protected by qualified government immunity. Since the faculty handbook authorized administrators to make "appropriate" comments, and since making a subjective evaluation of a faculty member's performance is a discretionary, rather than a ministerial, duty, the court found that the dean had acted within the scope of his authority and had not lost the immunity by exceeding his authority.

Employees acting within the scope of their authority may also be protected by a common law privilege for communications between persons sharing a common duty or interest, such as communications between individuals within a business or an academic organization. In *Kraft v. William Alanson White Psychiatric Foundation*, 498 A.2d 1145 (D.C. 1985), the court applied an "absolute privilege" to communications among faculty members about the plaintiff's inadequate academic performance in a postgraduate certificate program. The court stated: "A person who seeks an academic credential and who is on notice that satisfactory performance is a prerequisite to his receipt of that credential consents to frank evaluation by those charged with the responsibility to supervise him" (498 A.2d at 1149). Despite the court's application of an "absolute" privilege in *Kraft*, the more typical approach is for a court to consider whether the communication should be protected by a "qualified" or "conditional" privilege, which may be lost if the confidential information is shared with one or more individuals who do not have a business-related reason to receive the information.

*Dean v. Wissmann*, 996 S.W.2d 631 (Mo. Ct. App. 1999), provides an example of the successful use of the qualified privilege because the communication at issue was limited to individuals with a business need for the information. In this case, the professor had written a letter accusing the plaintiff, a nursing student, of stealing a test. The letter was read by the head of the nursing department, the college dean, and the vice president of student affairs. The court held that the professor had reported the alleged dishonesty to the appropriate people, and thus, the letter was not "published," an essential element of a defamation claim. Because the professor had communicated the allegedly defamatory information only to individuals within the organization with a legitimate organizational reason to be informed about the situation, the court ruled that internal communication of this information did not meet the "publication" element of the defamation claim. And in *Chandok v. Klessig*, 632 F.3d 803 (2d Cir. 2011), the court applied a "conditional [privilege] for statements on matters as to which the speaker has a legal or moral obligation to speak or for statements among communicants who share a common interest" in affirming summary judgment for the defendant, Klessig. Klessig, a professor who supervised Chandok, a postdoctoral associate, accused her of falsifying research results when his team of scientists could not reproduce the results she had obtained. Because the research was federally funded, said the court, Klessig had a legal obligation to disclose possible research fraud; he had a moral obligation, according to the court, to notify journals in which the research had been published, and colleagues who were attempting to replicate the research results, without success.

The privilege may be lost if an employee acts with malice or otherwise unprofessionally. In *Smith v. Atkins*, 622 So. 2d 795 (La. Ct. App. 1993), Theresa Smith, a first-year law student at Southern University, filed claims of defamation, invasion of privacy, and intentional infliction of emotional distress against one of her law professors, Atkins. Professor Atkins routinely discussed his social life in class and directed many sexually explicit comments to Smith and another female student. He called Smith a "slut" in front of the entire class on two occasions and, also in front of the entire class, related a humiliating event experienced by Smith at a local bar. The trial court ruled in the plaintiff's favor on the defamation claim, but rejected her emotional distress claim. The appellate court affirmed the defamation ruling, but reversed the emotional distress ruling, and held in the student's favor, finding that "calling a female law student a 'slut' is defamatory *per se*" (622 So. 2d 799) and, thus, she had sustained an intentional injury.

If a court rules that an allegedly defamatory statement was opinion, rather than a purported fact, liability for defamation will typically not ensue. Characterizing statements as opinion, however, may not provide complete protection against liability for defamation. A ruling by the U.S. Supreme Court in *Milkovich v. Lorain Journal Co.*, 497 U.S. 1 (1990), suggests that this "opinion privilege" to defamation liability may not be legally sound when applied to a "public figure" (see Section 3.2.4 of this book). The scope of the "opinion privilege" was at issue in *Mehta v. Ohio University*, 958 N.E.2d 598 (Ohio Ct. App. 2011). Mehta, a professor whose contract was not renewed after an investigation uncovered alleged plagiarism by several of his graduate students, sued the university, claiming that statements made by a dean and the university's general counsel to the press regarding his alleged failure to properly supervise his advisees were defamatory. A trial court concluded that these statements were opinion and thus not actionable, but the appellate court disagreed. Reviewing what was written in the investigative report and what was said to the press by university representatives, the appellate court determined that the written and oral communications were statements of fact and thus actionable.

Defendants in certain defamation cases may be protected by the concept of "invited libel" and thus found not to have been responsible for the "publication" element of a defamation claim. In *Sophianopoulous v. McCormick*, 385 S.E.2d 682 (Ga. Ct. App. 1989), for example, a state appellate court rejected a faculty member's defamation claim against his department chair. The professor had complained to the American Association of University Professors (AAUP) that his chair had mistreated him. When the AAUP contacted the chair to inquire about the professor's performance, the chair sent the AAUP copies of memoranda critical of the professor's performance. The judges ruled that, by involving the AAUP in the dispute with his chair, the plaintiff consented to having the offending information published to the AAUP.

On occasion, faculty members have sued students for defamation. These claims tend to occur when sexual harassment is alleged by a student. For example, in *Chiavarelli v. Williams*, 681 N.Y.S.2d 276 (N.Y. App. Div. 1998), the chair of the division of cardiothoracic surgery at the SUNY Health Science Center in Brooklyn sued the chief resident for defamation. The plaintiff claimed that the defendant wrote a libelous letter concerning sexual advances the plaintiff had allegedly made toward the defendant, and then circulated the letter to the plaintiff's supervisors. The letter claimed that the plaintiff had given the defendant negative evaluations because the defendant had spurned the plaintiff's sexual advances. Although the defendant sought to have the complaint dismissed because the plaintiff had not alleged or proven special damages, the court agreed that the claim should be characterized as a claim of libel per se, which does not require a plaintiff to allege special damages. Allegations suggesting that a professional is unfit for his or her professional role reflect adversely on that individual's integrity, and even if no claims are made that the professional is incompetent in his or her profession, defamation per se may be established without evidence of special damages.

### 4.4.3. Contract liability.

An employee who signs a contract on behalf of an institution may be personally liable for its performance if the institution breaches the contract. The extent of personal liability depends on whether the agent's participation on behalf of the institution was authorized—either by a grant of express authority or by an implied authority, an apparent authority, or a subsequent ratification by the institution. (See the discussion of authority in Sections 3.1 and 3.3.) If the individual's participation was properly authorized and if that individual signed the contract only in the capacity of an institutional agent, he or she will not be personally liable for performance of the contract. If, however, the participation was not properly authorized or if the individual signed in an individual capacity rather than as an institutional agent, he or she may be personally liable.

In some cases the other contracting party may be able to sue both the institution and the agent or to choose between them. This option is presented when the contracting party did not know at the time of contracting that the individual participated in an agency capacity, but later learned that was the case. The option is also presented when the contracting party knew that the individual was acting as an institutional agent, but the individual also gave a personal promise that the contract would be performed. In such situations, if the contracting party obtains a judgment against both the institution and the agent, the judgment may be satisfied against either or against both, but the contracting party may receive no more than the total amount of the judgment. Where the contracting party receives payment from only one of the two liable parties, the paying party may have a claim against the nonpayer for part of the judgment amount.

An agent who is a party to the contract in a personal capacity, and thus potentially liable on it, can assert the same defenses that are available to any contracting party. These defenses may arise from the contract (for instance, the absence of some formality necessary to complete the contract, or fraud, or inadequate performance by the other party), or they may be personal to the agent (for instance, a particular counterclaim against the other party).

Even if a contract does not exist, the doctrine of promissory estoppel may be used by a candidate for a position who is given an offer of employment that is subsequently withdrawn. This claim allows an individual to seek a remedy for detrimental reliance on a promise of employment, even where no contract existed. In *Bicknese v. Sutula*, 635 N.W.2d 905 (Wis. Ct. App. 2001), *reversed*, 660 N.W.2d 289 (Wis. 2003), the plaintiff had applied for a faculty position at the University of Wisconsin. The plaintiff claimed that the department chair, Sutula, had offered her the position, promising her a five-year probationary period instead of three years, and that she resigned her faculty position at Stony Brook University–SUNY and rejected a job offer from SUNY at Buffalo in reliance on Sutula's promises. A university committee rejected Sutula's recommendation that Bicknese be hired. She sued Sutula individually, and a jury ruled in her favor on her claim of promissory estoppel. Sutula appealed, claiming that he had been performing discretionary acts within the scope of his employment, and thus was protected from liability under "public officer immunity." The intermediate appellate court agreed, rejecting the plaintiff's contentions that Sutula had acted maliciously or with the intent to deceive and finding that his acts were discretionary rather than ministerial.

But the Supreme Court of Wisconsin reversed the appellate court and reinstated the jury verdict for Bicknese. Although the high court agreed that Sutula's actions had not been malicious or deceptive, it ruled that his dealings with Bicknese were ministerial, not discretionary, since he did not have the discretion to depart from the university's policies and procedures. And because he deviated from those policies and procedures, his conduct was not immunized from liability.

### 4.4.4. *Constitutional liability (personal liability under Section 1983).*

**4.4.4.1. *Qualified immunity.*** The liability of administrators and other employees of public postsecondary institutions (and also individual trustees) for constitutional rights violations is determined under the same body of law that determines the liability of the institutions themselves (see Section 3.4) and presents many of the same legal issues. As with institutional liability, an individual's action must usually be taken "under color of" state law or must be characterizable as "state action" before personal liability will attach. But, as with tort and contract liability, the liability of individual administrators and other employees (and trustees) is not coterminous with that of the institution itself. Defenses that may be available to the institution (such as the sovereign immunity defense) may not be available to individuals sued in their personal capacities; conversely, defenses that may be available to individuals (such as the qualified immunity defense discussed later in this subsection) may not be available to the institution.

The federal statute referred to as Section 1983 (42 U.S.C. § 1983), quoted in Section 3.4 of this book, is again the key statute. Unlike the states themselves, state government officials and employees sued in their personal capacities are clearly "persons" under Section 1983 and thus subject to its provisions whenever they are acting under color of state law. The same is true for local government officials and employees. State and local officials and employees sued in their personal capacities are not protected from suit by the constitutional sovereign immunity that protects state governments. But courts have recognized a qualified immunity for public officials and employees that protects them from liability for monetary damages under Section 1983. This immunity applies to officials and employees sued in their *personal* (or *individual*) capacities rather than their official (or representational) capacities. *Mangaroo v. Nelson*, 864 F.2d 1202 (5th Cir. 1989), illustrates the distinction. The plaintiff had been demoted from a deanship to a tenured faculty position. She sued both Nelson, the acting president who demoted her, and Pierre, Nelson's successor, alleging that their actions violated her procedural due process rights. She sued the former in his personal (or individual) capacity, seeking monetary damages, and the latter in his official (or representational) capacity, seeking injunctive relief. The court held that Nelson was entitled to claim qualified immunity, since the plaintiff sought money damages from him in his personal capacity for the harm he had caused. In contrast, the court held that Pierre was not eligible for qualified immunity, because the plaintiff sued him only in his official capacity, seeking only an injunctive order compelling him, as president, to take action to remedy the violation of her due process rights.

In *Harlow v. Fitzgerald*, 457 U.S. 800 (1982), the Court modified and clarified the qualified immunity analysis it had established in an earlier case, *Wood v. Strickland*, 420 U.S. 308 (1975). The immunity test developed in *Wood* had two parts. The first part was objective, focusing on whether the defendant "knew or reasonably should have known that the action he took . . . would violate the constitutional rights" of the plaintiff (420 U.S. at 322). The second part was subjective, focusing on the defendant's "malicious intention to cause a deprivation of constitutional rights." The Court in *Harlow* deleted the subjective part of the test because it had inhibited courts from dismissing insubstantial lawsuits prior to trial:

> [W]e conclude today that bare allegations of malice should not suffice to subject government officials either to the costs of trial or to the burdens of broad-reaching discovery. We therefore hold that government officials performing discretionary functions generally are shielded from liability for civil damages insofar as their conduct does not violate clearly established statutory or constitutional rights of which a reasonable person would have known (see *Procunier v. Navarette*, 434 U.S. 555, 565 (1978); *Wood v. Strickland*, 420 U.S. at 321).
>
> Reliance on the objective reasonableness of an official's conduct, as measured by reference to clearly established law, should avoid excessive disruption of government and permit the resolution of many insubstantial claims on summary judgment . . . If the law at that time was not clearly established, an official could not reasonably be expected to anticipate subsequent legal developments, nor could he fairly be said to "know" that the law forbade conduct not previously identified as unlawful . . . If the law was clearly established, the immunity defense ordinarily should fail, since a reasonably competent public official should know the law governing his conduct. Nevertheless, if the official pleading the defense claims extraordinary circumstances and can prove that he neither knew nor should have known of the relevant legal standard, the defense should be sustained [457 U.S. at 817–19].

In Section 1983 litigation, qualified immunity is an affirmative defense to be pleaded by the individual seeking to assert the immunity claim (see *Gomez v. Toledo*, 446 U.S. 635 (1980)). Once the defendant has asserted the claim, the court must determine (1) whether the plaintiff's complaint alleges the violation of a right protected by Section 1983; and (2), if so, whether this right "was clearly established at the time of [the defendant's] actions" (*Siegert v. Gilley*, 500 U.S. 226, 232–33 (1991). In *Saucier v. Katz*, 533 U.S. 194 (2001), the U.S. Supreme Court had mandated that courts take up these two immunity inquiries in the order specified. In *Pearson v. Callahan*, 129 S.Ct. 808 (2009), however, the Court determined that "while the sequence set forth [in *Saucier*] is often appropriate, it should no longer be regarded as mandatory. The judges of the district courts and the courts of appeals should be permitted to exercise their sound discretion in deciding which of the two prongs of the qualified immunity analysis should be addressed first in light of the circumstances in the particular case at hand" (129 S. Ct. at 818).

If the court answers both of these *Saucier/Pearson* inquiries affirmatively, it will reject the immunity claim unless the defendant can prove that, because of "extraordinary circumstances," he "neither knew nor should have known" the clearly established law applicable to the case (see *Harlow*, above). The burden of proof here is clearly on the defendant, and it would be a rare case in which the defendant would sustain this burden.

As a result of this line of cases, personnel of public colleges and universities are charged with responsibility for knowing "clearly established law." Unless "extraordinary circumstances" prevent an individual from gaining such knowledge, the disregard of clearly established law is considered unreasonable and thus unprotected by the cloak of immunity. "The relevant, dispositive inquiry in determining whether a right is clearly established is whether it would be clear to a reasonable [person] that his conduct was unlawful in the situation he confronted" (*Saucier v. Katz*, 533 U.S. 194, 202 (2001)). This is a test of "objective legal reasonableness" (*Behrens v. Pelletier*, 516 U.S. 299, 306 (1996)), that is, a test that focuses on what an objective reasonable person would know rather than on what the actual defendant subjectively thought. Thus, a determination of qualified immunity "turns on the 'objective legal reasonableness' of the [challenged] action . . . assessed in light of the legal rules that were 'clearly established' at the time [the action] was taken" (*Anderson v. Creighton*, 483 U.S. 635, 639 (1987), quoting *Harlow*, 457 U.S. at 818–19).

The state of the law under Section 1983 and the Eleventh Amendment, taken together, gives administrators of public postsecondary institutions no cause to feel confident that either they or other institutional officers or employees are insulated from liability for possible violations of personal constitutional rights. Since it is extremely difficult to predict what unlawful actions would fall within the scope of qualified immunity, administrative efforts will be far better spent taking preventive measures to ensure that Section 1983 violations do not occur than in trusting that immunity will usually protect university officers and employees if violations do occur. To minimize the liability risk in this critical area of law and social responsibility, administrators should make legal counsel available to institutional personnel for consultation, encourage review by counsel of institutional policies that may affect constitutional rights, and provide personnel with information on and training in basic constitutional law. To absolve personnel of the emotional drain of potential liability, and the financial drain of any liability that actually does occur, administrators should consider the purchase of special insurance coverage or the development of indemnity plans if state law permits use of these techniques to cover intentional constitutional rights violations.

***4.4.4.2. Issues on the merits: State-created dangers.*** In Section 1983 suits against individuals, difficult issues also arise concerning the merits of the plaintiffs' claims. (Such issues on the merits arise much less frequently in suits against institutions, since public institutions may usually assert sovereign immunity as a basis for dismissing the suit before reaching the merits (see Section 3.4 of this book).) Since Section 1983 provides remedies for "the deprivation of . . . rights . . . secured by the Constitution," analysis of the merits of a Section 1983 claim depends on the particular constitutional clause involved and the particular constitutional right asserted.

One particularly difficult and contentious set of issues on the merits has arisen concerning the "substantive" (as opposed to the procedural) content of the Fourteenth Amendment's due process clause. In *DeShaney v. Winnebago*

*County Dept. of Social Services*, 489 U.S. 189 (1989), the U.S. Supreme Court held that the due process clause does not impose any general "affirmative obligation" on state officials to protect private individuals from danger. The Court did acknowledge, however, that such a duty may exist in "certain limited circumstances" where the state has a "special relationship" with the endangered person. As an example, the Court noted situations in which a state agency has an individual in its custody and "so restrains [the] individual's liberty that it renders him unable to care for himself" (489 U.S. at 200). In later cases, lower courts expanded this state duty to situations in which state officers or employers have themselves created the danger. (See, for example, *Kniepp v. Tedder*, 95 F.3d 1199, 1208–9 (3d Cir. 1996), and *Bright v. Westmoreland County*, 443 F.3d 276, 281–82 (3d Cir. 2006), which explicate four factors to apply in determining liability.) This approach to substantive due process liability under Section 1983 is now called "the state-created danger theory" (95 F.3d at 1205). While lower courts differ on the particulars of this state duty and on the extent of their support for the theory, a state-created danger claim usually requires proof that "a state actor affirmatively used his or her authority in a way that created a danger [to the plaintiff] or that rendered [the plaintiff] more vulnerable to danger than had the state not acted at all" (443 F.3d at 281)—thus depriving the plaintiff of a "liberty interest in personal security" (95 F.3d at 1203). In addition, a plaintiff generally must show that, in acting as they did or failing to act, the state actors were deliberately indifferent to the plaintiff's safety.

The leading example of state-created danger claims in higher education is the litigation concerning the 1999 Texas A&M University Bonfire collapse in which twelve students were killed and twenty-seven others were injured. In the aftermath, six civil suits were filed in federal court on behalf of eleven of the victims, alleging state claims as well as federal Section 1983 claims against the university and various university officials. The court dismissed the Section 1983 claims against the university because it had sovereign immunity (see Section 3.4 of this book), and the focus of the litigation became the plaintiff's substantive due process claims against university officials, based on the state-created danger theory.

The tradition of the Texas A&M Bonfire began in 1909. Over the years it became a symbol "not only of one school deeply rooted in tradition, but . . . representative of the entire Nation's passionate fascination with the most venerated aspects of collegiate football" (*Self v. Texas A&M University, et al.*, 2002 WL 32113753 (S.D. Tex. 2002)). Prior to the tragedy, the building of the bonfire had "occupied over five thousand students for an estimated 125,000 hours each fall." The students had developed a complex "wedding cake design" for the bonfire, weighing in at "over two million pounds" and standing "sixty to eighty feet tall" (*Self v. Texas A&M University*, 2002 WL 32113753). The tower of logs collapsed on November 18, 1999, resulting in the twelve deaths and twenty-seven injuries. The university quickly appointed a special commission to investigate the bonfire collapse, which issued a final report in May 2000 (Special Commission on the 1999 Texas A&M Bonfire, *Final Report*, May 2, 2000, available at http://archive.theeagle.com/bonfire/storyarchive/may2000/Final.pdf).

In the preliminary stages of the ensuing litigation, the parties accepted the commission's *Final Report* as an authoritative account of the bonfire collapse.

In *Self v. Texas A&M University*, above, the district court combined the six lawsuits for a common ruling on the Section 1983 claims asserted in each case. As the court summarized these claims, the plaintiffs alleged that university officials "deprived the bonfire victims of their Fourteenth Amendment right to substantive due process by acting with deliberate indifference to the state-created danger that killed or injured them." In considering these claims the court acknowledged that an affirmative state duty arises in two situations: "when the state has a special relationship with the person or when the state exposes a person to a danger of its own creation" (2002 WL 32113753, at *6, citing *McClendon v. City of Columbia*, 258 F.3d 432, 436 (5th Cir. 2001)). Under the second approach, a plaintiff must prove that "(1) the state actors increased the danger to him or her; and (2) the state actors acted with deliberate indifference" (2002 WL 32113753, at *6, citing *Piotrowski v. City of Houston*, 51 F.3d 512 (5th Cir. 1995)). Applying these principles, the district court determined that "[t]he facts . . . clearly tend to suggest that the conduct of the University Officials may have contributed, at least in part, to the 1999 Bonfire collapse," but "it is quite clear that they did not do so with 'deliberate indifference'—the requisite culpability to make out a constitutional violation." Deliberate indifference, said the court, is "'a lesser form of intent' rather than a 'heightened form of negligence'" (2002 WL 32113753, at *7, quoting *Leffall v. Dallas Independent School District*, 28 F.2d 521, 531 (5th Cir. 1994)). To establish deliberate indifference, "the environment created by the state actors must be dangerous; they must know it is dangerous; and . . . they must have used their authority to create an opportunity that would not have otherwise existed for the injury to occur" (2002 WL 32113753, at *7, quoting *Johnson v. Dallas Independent School District*, 38 F.3d 198, 201 (5th Cir. 1994)). The "key . . . lies in the state actors' culpable knowledge and conduct in affirmatively placing an individual in a position of danger, effectively stripping a person of her ability to defend herself, or cutting off potential sources of private aid" (2002 WL 32113753, at *7, quoting *Johnson*, 38 F.3d at 201).

In resolving the plaintiffs' state-created danger claims, the district court adopted the Special Commission's *Final Report*, above, as the "definitive narrative of the relevant facts" and cited the report's conclusion that the "absence of a proactive risk management model; the University community's cultural bias impeding risk identification; the lack of student leadership, knowledge and skills pertaining to structural integrity; and the lack of formal, written . . . design plans or construction methodology" were "the overarching factors that brought about the physical collapse." Thus, said the court, the "bonfire collapse was not caused by a specific event, error or omission in 1999, but, rather, by decisions and actions taken by both students and University officials over many, many years" (2002 WL 32113753, at *4). Relying on findings from the *Final Report*, the court reasoned that, although university officials "may have contributed" to the danger, they lacked the "requisite culpability" to meet the deliberate indifference prong. They "were aware of the dangers posed" and failed "to pro-actively avert or reduce those risks," but they "were unaware of the precise risk at hand—the risk that the entire bonfire would come tumbling down." Such ignorance "might appear naive," but "it cannot support a finding of deliberate indifference" in light of measures that were taken with respect to bonfire safety. The court then concluded that, because the officials' conduct was not sufficiently culpable to meet the deliberate indifference prong of the state-created danger test, plaintiffs' Section 1983 claims failed on the merits, and the defendants were therefore entitled to summary judgment.

On appeal, the U.S. Court of Appeals for the Fifth Circuit generally agreed with the legal principles stated by the district court, in particular that "plaintiff must show the defendants used their authority to create a dangerous environment for the plaintiff and that the defendants acted with deliberate indifference to the plight of the plaintiff" (*Scanlan v. Texas A&M University, et al.*, 343 F.3d 533, 537–38 (5th Cir. 2003), citing *Johnson v. Dallas Independent School District*, 38 F.3d 198, 201 (5th Cir. 1994)). But the appellate court held that the district court had erred in adopting the report of "a defendant-created commission rather than presenting the questions of material fact to a trier of fact" (*Scanlan v. Texas A&M University, et al.*, 343 F.3d at 539). Instead, construing allegations in the complaints in the light most favorable to the plaintiffs, the district court "should have determined the plaintiffs had pleaded sufficient factual allegations to show the bonfire construction environment was dangerous, the University Officials knew it was dangerous, and the University Officials used their authority to create an opportunity for the resulting harm to occur." The Fifth Circuit therefore reversed the district court's judgment for the university officials and remanded the case to the district court for further proceedings.

On remand, the district court again dismissed the plaintiffs' Section 1983 claims, this time on "qualified immunity" grounds (see Section 4.4.4.1 above) that had not been addressed in the district court's prior opinion. In its new opinion, in a case renamed *Davis v. Southerland*, 2004 WL 1230278 (S.D. Tex. 2004), the district court asserted that the Fifth Circuit had been noncommittal about the state-created danger theory in the decade preceding the bonfire collapse, and that the "validity of the state-created danger theory is uncertain in the Fifth Circuit." Thus the theory "was not clearly established at the time of Defendants' bonfire-related activities," and "a reasonable school official would not have been aware that the Fourteenth Amendment's Due Process Clause provided a constitutional right to be free from state-created danger, much less that an injury caused by a school administrator's failure to exercise control over an activity such as [the] bonfire would violate that right."

In addition, deferring to the circuit court's determination in *Scanlan* that the district court "should have concluded that the plaintiffs stated a Section 1983 claim under the state-created danger theory," the district court analyzed the merits of the plaintiffs' claims "as if the theory is a valid one" and "the violations Plaintiffs claim are indeed constitutional ones." The court's conclusion was that resolution of the plaintiffs' rights "requires examination of literally hundreds of contested facts," and that the persistence of "multiple questions of fact . . . prevents the Court from deciding whether Defendants did or did not act with deliberate indifference as a matter of law."

Other contexts in which issues of state-created danger may arise include stalking, sexual assaults, and other crimes of violence that take place on campus and of which a student or employee is the victim. The institution, to be subject to suit, must be a public institution or otherwise be acting "under color of law" when it creates the alleged danger. It will be very difficult for plaintiffs to prevail in such suits, as the Texas A&M litigation suggests. It is not necessarily enough that institutional employees were aware of the stalking or impending violence, or that they were negligent in their response or lack thereof. In *Thomas v. City of Mount Vernon*, 215 F. Supp. 2d 329 (S.D.N.Y. 2002), for example, neither a professor who witnessed a student being confronted by her former boyfriend in the hallway of a classroom building, nor office personnel who declined to offer the student assistance when she ran into their office, were liable under Section 1983 for the severe injuries the student received when the boyfriend shot her shortly thereafter. The professor and staff members had not deprived the student of liberty or property "by virtue of their own actions"; and under *DeShaney* (above), "'a state's failure to protect an individual against private violence does not constitute a violation of the due process clause'" (215 F. Supp. 2d at 334, quoting 489 U.S. at 197).

### Section 4.5. Employment Discrimination

***4.5.1. Overview: The interplay of statutes, regulations, and constitutional protections.*** Both federal and state law prohibit employment discrimination, which occurs when an employer uses some "protected" characteristic to make an employment decision, rather than evaluating the individual solely on the basis of his or her qualifications. Several federal statutes and one major executive order prohibit discrimination by employers, including postsecondary institutions, and each has its own comprehensive set of administrative regulations or guidelines. Several of these laws also prohibit retaliation for the exercise of rights provided by these laws—also a form of discrimination. Forty-eight states and the District of Columbia also have fair employment practices statutes, some of which provide greater protections to employees than federal nondiscrimination statutes.

Race discrimination in employment is prohibited by Title VII of the Civil Rights Act of 1964 as amended, by 42 U.S.C. § 1981, and by Executive Order 11246 as amended. Sex discrimination is prohibited by Title VII, by Title IX of the Education Amendments of 1972, by the Equal Pay Act, and by Executive Order 11246. Age discrimination is outlawed by the Age Discrimination in Employment Act (ADEA). Discrimination against employees with disabilities is prohibited by both the Americans with Disabilities Act (ADA) and the Rehabilitation Act of 1973. Discrimination on the basis of religion is outlawed by Title VII and Executive Order 11246. Discrimination on the basis of national origin is prohibited by Title VII and by Executive Order 11246. Discrimination against aliens is prohibited indirectly under Title VII and directly under the Immigration Reform and Control Act of 1986 (IRCA). Discrimination against veterans is covered in part by 38 U.S.C. § 4301. Some courts have ruled that discrimination against transgendered individuals is sex discrimination and thus violates Title VII (see, for example, *Smith v. City of Salem*, 378 F.3d 566 (6th Cir. 2004)). Other forms of discrimination, such as marital status discrimination or discrimination on the basis of sexual orientation, are prohibited by the laws of some states.

The nondiscrimination aspects of the statutes and Executive Order 11246 are discussed in this section, and they are contrasted with the requirements of the federal Constitution, as interpreted by the courts in the context of discrimination claims. The affirmative action aspects of the statutes and Executive Order 11246 are discussed in Section 4.6 (as applied to staff) and Section 5.5 (as applied to faculty).

The rationale for laws prohibiting discrimination in employment decisions is that characteristics such as race, sex, religion, or age (among others) are irrelevant for employment decisions. In debates prior to the passage of the Civil Rights Act of 1964, the first comprehensive federal law prohibiting employment discrimination, congressional leaders stressed the financial cost to both business and members of minority groups of employment decisions based not on individual qualifications or merit, but on "immutable" characteristics such as sex or race.

In cases where discrimination is alleged, the parties must follow a prescribed order of proof, which is described later in Section 4.5. In cases of intentional discrimination, for example, the plaintiff must present sufficient evidence to raise an inference of discrimination; the defense then is allowed to rebut that inference by presenting evidence of a legitimate, nondiscriminatory reason for the action the plaintiff alleges was discriminatory. The plaintiff then has an opportunity to demonstrate that the defendant's "legitimate nondiscriminatory reason" is a pretext, that it is unworthy of belief.

Beginning in the late 1990s, the U.S. Supreme Court handed down a series of rulings limiting congressional authority to abrogate the sovereign immunity of states with respect to their liability for violations of federal nondiscrimination laws. These rulings apply to claims asserted against state colleges and universities by their employees in federal court but by extension may now also apply to such claims brought in state court (see *Alden v. Maine*, 527 U.S. 706 (1999)). These cases have addressed some, but not all, of the federal nondiscrimination laws discussed in this section. Application of the sovereign immunity doctrine to discrimination claims against state colleges is discussed for each law so affected.

Several of the federal nondiscrimination laws have extraterritorial application. This is significant for colleges that employ U.S. citizens outside the United States to staff study abroad programs or other college programs that occur outside of the United States. The Civil Rights Act of 1991, discussed in Section 4.5.2.1, amended Title VII and the Americans with Disabilities Act to provide for extraterritorial application, thus legislatively overruling a U.S. Supreme Court decision, in *EEOC v. Arabian American Oil Co.*, 498 U.S. 808 (1990), that Title VII did not have extraterritorial application. The Age Discrimination in Employment Act was amended in 1984 to extend extraterritorial jurisdiction to U.S. citizens working abroad for U.S. employers or for a foreign company that is owned or controlled by a U.S. company (29 U.S.C. § 623(h)). The Equal Pay Act also provides for extraterritorial application; a 1984 amendment changed the definition of "employee" in the Fair Labor Standards Act (of which the Equal Pay Act is a part) to include "any individual who is a citizen of the United States employed by an employer in a workplace in a foreign country" (29 U.S.C. § 630(f)).

Another issue of increasing importance is the number of retaliation claims now being filed by employees who allege discrimination. The nondiscrimination laws contain language that makes it unlawful to take an adverse employment action against an individual who opposes or otherwise complains about alleged employment discrimination. Retaliation claims have more than doubled since the mid-1990s; 37 percent of all claims filed with the EEOC in 2011 included a claim of retaliation.

## 4.5.2. Sources of Law.

***4.5.2.1. Title VII.*** Title VII of the Civil Rights Act of 1964, 42 U.S.C. §§ 2000e et seq., is the most comprehensive and most frequently utilized of the federal employment discrimination laws. It was extended in 1972 to cover educational institutions both public and private. According to the statute's basic prohibition, 42 U.S.C. § 2000e-2(a):

> It shall be an unlawful employment practice for an employer—
> (1) to fail or refuse to hire or to discharge any individual, or otherwise to discriminate against any individual with respect to his compensation, terms, conditions, or privileges of employment, because of such individual's race, color, religion, sex, or national origin; or
> (2) to limit, segregate, or classify his employees or applicants for employment in any way which would deprive or tend to deprive any individual of employment opportunities or otherwise adversely affect his status as an employee, because of such individual's race, color, religion, sex, or national origin.

The law covers not only employers but labor unions and employment agencies as well. Liability under Title VII is corporate; supervisors cannot be held individually liable under Title VII, although they may under other legal theories (*Miller v. Maxwell's International*, 991 F.2d 583 (9th Cir. 1993)).

Students who are employees may be protected under Title VII, but whether a student is also an employee is a factual issue (see, for example, *Cuddeback v. Florida Board of Education*, 381 F.3d 1230 (11th Cir. 2004), ruling that a graduate student research assistant was an employee for Title VII purposes under the "economic realities test"). Fellowships may be considered wages, or they may be characterized as financial aid.

The major exception to the general prohibition against discrimination is the "BFOQ" exception, which permits hiring and employing based on "religion, sex, or national origin" when such a characteristic is a "bona fide occupational qualification necessary to the normal operation of that particular business or enterprise" (42 U.S.C. § 2000e-2(e)(1)). Religion as a BFOQ is examined in Section 4.7 of this book in the context of employment decisions at religious institutions of higher education. Sex could be a permissible BFOQ for a locker room attendant or, perhaps, for certain staff of a single-sex residence hall. National origin is not a permissible BFOQ for positions at colleges and universities because the "normal operation of the business" of higher education does not require an employee to be of a particular national origin.

Title VII is enforced by the Equal Employment Opportunity Commission, which has issued a series of regulations and guidelines published at 29 C.F.R. Parts 1600 through 1610. The EEOC may receive, investigate, and conciliate complaints of unlawful employment discrimination, and may initiate lawsuits against violators in court or issue right-to-sue letters to complainants (29 C.F.R. Part 1601). After the EEOC has issued a right-to-sue letter, an individual may file a Title VII claim in federal court.

Although Title VII broadly prohibits employment discrimination, it does not limit the right of postsecondary institutions to hire employees on the basis of job-related qualifications or to distinguish among employees on the basis of seniority or merit in pay, promotion, and tenure policies. Institutions retain the discretion to hire, promote, reward, and terminate employees, as long as the institutions do not make distinctions based on race, color, religion, sex, or national origin. If, however, an institution does distinguish among employees on one of these bases, courts have broad powers to remedy the Title VII violation by "making persons whole for injuries suffered through past discrimination" (*Albemarle Paper Co. v. Moody*, 422 U.S. 405 (1975)). Remedies may include back pay awards (*Albemarle*), awards of retroactive seniority (*Franks v. Bowman Transportation Co.*, 424 U.S. 747 (1976)), reinstatement, and various affirmative action measures to benefit the group whose members were the subject of the discrimination (see Section 4.6), as well as the right, in disparate treatment cases, to compensatory and punitive damages.[1]

There are two basic types of Title VII claims: the "disparate treatment" claim and the "disparate impact" or "adverse impact" claim. In the former type of suit, an individual denied a job, promotion, or tenure, or subjected to a detrimental employment condition, claims to have been treated less favorably than other applicants or employees because of his or her race, sex, national origin, or religion (see, for example, *Lynn v. Regents of the University of California*, 656 F.2d 1337 (9th Cir. 1981) (alleged sex discrimination in denial of tenure)). In the "disparate impact" or "adverse impact" type of suit, the claim is that some ostensibly neutral policy of the employer has a discriminatory impact on the claimants or the class of persons they represent (see, for example, *Scott v. University of Delaware*, 455 F. Supp. 1102, 1123–32 (D. Del. 1978), *affirmed on other grounds*, 601 F.2d 76 (3d Cir. 1979) (alleging that requirement of Ph.D. for faculty positions discriminated against racial minorities)). Of the two types

---

[1] Compensatory and punitive damages are capped on the basis of the size of the employer: organizations with 15–100 employees may be assessed up to $50,000; 101–201 employees, $100,000; 201–500 employees, $200,000; and more than 500 employees, $300,000. These damages may be assessed in addition to the "make-whole" remedies of back pay and attorney's fees. With the exception of the Americans with Disabilities Act, other nondiscrimination statutes do not have these caps. Awards of "front pay" are not considered to be compensatory damages and thus are not subject to the statutory cap (*Pollard v. E. I. duPont de Nemours & Co.*, 532 U.S. 843 (2001)).

of suits, disparate treatment is the more common for postsecondary education. The disparate treatment and disparate impact theories are also sometimes used when claims are litigated under other nondiscrimination laws, such as the Equal Pay Act and the Age Discrimination in Employment Act.

Although the disparate treatment claim may involve either direct or circumstantial evidence of discrimination, most plaintiffs are unable to present direct evidence of discrimination (such as written statements that the institution will not hire or promote them because of their race, sex, and so on, or corroborated oral statements that provide direct evidence of discrimination). An example of direct evidence of discrimination occurred in *Clark v. Claremont University*, 6 Cal. App. 4th 639 (Cal. Ct. App. 1992), a case brought under California's Fair Housing and Employment Act (Cal. Gov't Code §§ 12900 et seq.) but analyzed under the Title VII disparate treatment theory. The plaintiff, an assistant professor who was denied tenure, introduced evidence of numerous racist remarks made by faculty members involved in the tenure review process, and a jury found that racial discrimination had motivated the tenure denial. The appellate court upheld the jury verdict, finding that the number and the nature of the racist remarks made by the faculty members provided substantial evidence of race discrimination.

Most plaintiffs, however, must use circumstantial evidence to attempt to demonstrate that discrimination motivated some negative employment action. The U.S. Supreme Court developed a burden-shifting paradigm that allows the plaintiff to demonstrate his or her qualifications for the position, promotion, or other employment action, and then requires the employer to introduce evidence of the reason for the negative decision (*McDonnell Douglas Corp. v. Green*, 411 U.S. 792 (1973)). Under that decision,

> [t]he complainant in a Title VII trial must carry the initial burden under the statute of establishing a prima facie case of racial discrimination. This may be done by showing (i) that he belongs to a [category protected by Title VII]; (ii) that he applied and was qualified for a job for which the employer was seeking applicants; (iii) that, despite his qualifications, he was rejected; and (iv) that, after his rejection, the position remained open and the employer continued to seek applicants from persons of complainant's qualifications . . .
>
> The burden then must shift to the employer to articulate some legitimate, nondiscriminatory reason for the employee's rejection [411 U.S. at 802].

This burden-shifting approach requires the employer to provide a reasonable, job- or performance-related reason for the negative decision. It does not require the employer to prove that it did not discriminate. In a later case, *Texas Department of Community Affairs v. Burdine*, 450 U.S. 248 (1981), the Supreme Court emphasized that the employer's burden was merely to rebut that presumption established by the plaintiff, not to persuade the factfinder that the employer did not discriminate. The burden of persuasion, said the Court, always remained with the plaintiff.[2]

---

[2]See *LHE 5th*, pp. 437–440, for a fuller discussion of burdens of persuasion and proof in Title VII cases.

The *McDonnell Douglas* methodology has been applied to other types of discriminatory treatment prohibited by Title VII; likewise, though that case concerned only job applications, courts have adapted its methodology to hiring, termination, discipline, salary decisions, promotion, and tenure situations. This paradigm is used for the litigation of discrimination claims under other nondiscrimination laws as well.

Although most Title VII litigation in academe involves allegations of disparate treatment, several class action complaints have been brought against colleges and universities using the disparate impact theory. For example, in *Scott v. University of Delaware*, 455 F. Supp. 1102 (D. Del. 1987), *affirmed on other grounds*, 601 F.2d 76 (3d Cir. 1979), an African-American professor alleged, on behalf of himself and other African-American faculty, that requiring applicants for faculty positions to hold a Ph.D. had a disparate impact on African-Americans because they are underrepresented among holders of Ph.D. degrees. The court agreed with the university's argument that training in research, symbolized by the doctoral degree, was necessary for universities because of their research mission.[3]

Remedies available to prevailing parties in Title VII litigation include reinstatement, back pay, compensatory and punitive damages (for disparate treatment discrimination), and attorney's fees. Front pay is also available to plaintiffs who can demonstrate that the discrimination diminished their future ability to earn an income at the level they would have enjoyed absent the discrimination. For example, in *Thornton v. Kaplan*, 958 F. Supp. 502 (D. Colo. 1996), a jury had found that the university had discriminated against the plaintiff when it denied him tenure; the jury awarded him $250,000 in compensatory damages, plus attorney's fees and court costs. The university argued that the award was excessive and moved for remittitur (a request that the judge reduce the damage award) to $50,000. The judge refused, citing evidence that the denial of tenure resulted in a "loss of enjoyment" that the plaintiff derived from teaching, a loss of income, diminished prospects for future employment, humiliation, stress, depression, and feelings of exclusion from the academic community, which the judge characterized as "significant" losses.

Punitive damage awards are unusual in employment discrimination cases (except for sexual harassment complaints), but plaintiffs often demand punitive as well as compensatory damages in discrimination lawsuits. The U.S. Supreme Court established the standard for awarding punitive damages in Title VII cases in *Kolstad v. American Dental Association*, 527 U.S. 526 (1999). The plaintiff must demonstrate that the individual found to have engaged in the discrimination is an agent of the employer, employed in a managerial capacity, acting within the scope of employment, and acting with malice or reckless indifference toward the plaintiff's federally protected rights (527 U.S. at 535–45). A finding that an employer has made a good-faith effort to comply with Title

---

[3] The paradigm for disparate impact suits is *Griggs v. Duke Power Co.*, 401 U.S. 424 (1971), discussed in *LHE 5th* on pp. 440–441.

VII, despite the unlawful actions of one particular manager or supervisor, will prevent the award of punitive damages. (For a discussion of the *Kolstad* standard and its application to a sexual harassment lawsuit against Tulane University, see *Green v. Administrators of the Tulane Educational Fund*, 284 F.3d 642 (5th Cir. 2002) (*overruled in part on other grounds*).) As long as the plaintiff can establish the required "malice" or "reckless indifference" of the employer, she may receive punitive damages even if no compensatory damages are awarded (*Cush-Crawford v. Adchem Corp.*, 271 F.3d 352 (2d Cir. 2001)).

Although Title VII remains an important source of protection for faculty alleging discrimination, an increasing number of discrimination claims are being brought under state nondiscrimination laws. Unlike Title VII, many state laws have no caps on damages, and thus allow more generous damage awards. Other states may have laws that make it easier for a plaintiff to establish a prima facie case of discrimination than is the case under Title VII. (For an example of the use of state law to challenge an allegedly discriminatory tenure decision in a case against Trinity College, see Section 5.4.)

Much attention has been given to the issue of sexual harassment in recent years, and it continues to be a problem on college and university campuses. Sexual harassment of staff and faculty is addressed in this section; harassment of students is discussed in Sections 7.1.5 and 8.5.

Sexual harassment is a violation of Title VII of the Civil Rights Act of 1964 because it is workplace conduct experienced by an individual on the basis of his or her sex. It is also a violation of Title IX of the Education Amendments of 1972, and there are various advantages and disadvantages to using Title IX rather than Title VII. The laws of every state also prohibit sex discrimination and recognize sexual harassment as a form of unlawful discrimination. Sexual harassment victims may be male or female, and harassers may be of either gender as well. Furthermore, same-sex sexual harassment is also a violation of Title VII and Title IX.

The EEOC's guidelines prohibiting sexual harassment expansively define sexual harassment and establish standards under which an employer can be liable for harassment occasioned by its own acts as well as the acts of its agents and supervisory employees. The guidelines define sexual harassment as follows:

> Unwelcome sexual advances, requests for sexual favors, and other verbal or physical conduct of a sexual nature constitute sexual harassment when (1) submission to such conduct is made either explicitly or implicitly a term or condition of an individual's employment, (2) submission to or rejection of such conduct by an individual is used as the basis for employment decisions affecting such individual, or (3) such conduct has the purpose or effect of unreasonably interfering with an individual's work performance or creating an intimidating, hostile, or offensive working environment [29 C.F.R. § 1604.11(a)].

Whether or not the alleged harasser is an employee, if the target of the harassment is an employee, the employer may be liable for the unlawful behavior. Because the EEOC guidelines focus on both speech and conduct, the question of the interplay between sexual harassment and academic freedom arises, particularly in the classroom context. This interplay is discussed in Sections 6.2.2 and 8.5.

Two forms of sexual harassment have been considered by the courts, and each has a different consequence with regard to employer liability and potential remedies. Harassment that involves the exchange of sexual favors for employment benefits, or the threat of negative action if sexual favors are not granted, is known as "quid pro quo harassment." The U.S. Supreme Court addressed this form of sexual harassment for the first time in *Meritor Savings Bank v. Vinson*, 477 U.S. 57 (1986), ruling that, if quid pro quo harassment were proven, employer liability under Title VII would ensue even if the victim had not reported the harassment. Using principles of agency law, the Court asserted that harassment involving an actual or threatened change in terms and conditions of employment would result in a form of strict liability for the employer, whether or not the employer knew, or should have known, about the harassment.

The other form of harassment, the creation of a hostile or offensive work environment, may involve virtually anyone whom the target employee encounters because of the employment relationship. Supervisors, coworkers, clients, customers, and vendors have been accused of sexual harassment. (For an example of potential university liability for harassment of an employee by a homeless individual who frequented the law school library, see *Martin v. Howard University*, 1999 U.S. Dist. LEXIS 19516 (D.D.C. 1999).) If the allegations are proven, and if the employer cannot demonstrate that it responded appropriately when it learned of the harassment, the employer may be found to have violated Title VII or state law.

Although the standard for quid pro quo harassment is clear in that the accused harasser must have the power to affect the target's terms and conditions of employment, the standard for establishing hostile or offensive environment is less clear and is particularly fact sensitive. Name-calling, sexual jokes, sexual touching, sexually explicit cartoons, and other sexual behavior by supervisors or coworkers have been found to constitute sexual harassment (see, for example, *Alston v. North Carolina A&T State University*, 304 F. Supp. 2d 774 (M.D.N.C. 2004)). Furthermore, vandalism or harassing conduct of a nonsexual nature directed at a target because of his or her gender has also been found to violate Title VII, sometimes as sexual harassment and sometimes as sex discrimination (see, for example, *Hall v. Gus Construction Co.*, 842 F.2d 1010 (8th Cir. 1988)).

Words alone may be sufficient to constitute sexual harassment. In a case involving a female faculty member, *Jew v. University of Iowa*, 749 F. Supp. 946 (S.D. Iowa 1990), false rumors that the plaintiff had engaged in a sexual relationship with her department chair in order to obtain favorable treatment were found to constitute actionable sexual harassment, and the institution was ordered to promote the plaintiff and to give her back pay and attorney's fees. But a single remark, even if "crude," will probably not be sufficient to establish a claim of sexual harassment, according to the U.S. Supreme Court (*Clark County School District v. Breeden*, 532 U.S. 268 (2001)).

The U.S. Court of Appeals for the Ninth Circuit, in *Jordan v. Clark*, 847 F.2d 1368 (9th Cir. 1988), described the showing that the plaintiff must make in order to demonstrate a hostile environment. The plaintiff must prove:

(1) that he or she was subjected to demands for sexual favors, or other verbal or physical conduct of a sexual nature;

(2) that this conduct was unwelcome;

(3) that the conduct was sufficiently severe or pervasive to alter the conditions of the victim's employment and create an abusive working environment [847 F.2d at 1373].

But the definition of an "abusive working environment" has not been uniformly interpreted. Establishing whether the conduct is sufficiently severe or pervasive, and whether the plaintiff's claim that the behavior was offensive meets the standard for liability, has been a problem for the courts.

As sexual harassment jurisprudence developed in the federal courts, there was disagreement as to whether an employer could escape liability for harassment if it were unaware of the harassment or if no negative employment action had been taken. In 1998, the U.S. Supreme Court issued opinions in two cases that crafted guidelines for employer responses to harassment complaints and also created an affirmative defense for employers who had acted in good faith. In *Faragher v. City of Boca Raton*, 524 U.S. 775 (1998), and in *Burlington Industries v. Ellerth*, 524 U.S. 742 (1998), the Court addressed the issue of an employer's liability for a supervisor's verbal sexual harassment when no negative employment action had been taken against the target of the harassment. In both cases, supervisors had made numerous offensive remarks based on the targets' gender and had threatened to deny them job benefits. Neither of the plaintiffs had filed an internal complaint with the employer; both had resigned and filed a sexual harassment claim under Title VII. The employers in both cases had argued that, because no negative employment actions were taken against the plaintiffs, and because the plaintiffs had not notified the employer of the alleged misconduct, the employers should not be liable under Title VII.

The Supreme Court rejected this argument, ruling that an employer can be vicariously liable for actionable discrimination caused by a supervisor. The employer, however, may assert an affirmative defense that examines the reasonableness of the employer's and the target's conduct. If the employer had not circulated a policy against sexual harassment, had not trained its employees concerning harassment, and had not communicated to employees how to file a harassment complaint, then the target's failure to use an internal complaint process might be completely reasonable, according to the Court. But if the employer had been proactive in preventing and responding to sexual harassment, then a plaintiff's failure to use an internal complaint process might not be reasonable.

The Court explained that the employer can establish an affirmative defense to a sexual harassment claim if it can demonstrate

(a) that the employer exercised reasonable care to prevent and correct promptly any sexually harassing behavior and

(b) that the plaintiff employee unreasonably failed to take advantage of any preventive or corrective opportunities provided by the employer or to avoid harm otherwise [524 U.S. at 807].

The Court's rulings in *Ellerth* and *Faragher* blur the previous distinction between liability for quid pro quo harassment and liability for hostile environment harassment. But the cases also recognize an important defense for those "good employers" who have developed clear policies, advised employees of the complaint process, and conducted training about avoiding harassment. The approach taken by the Court has subsequently been applied to litigation concerning harassment on the basis of race (*Wright-Simmons v. The City of Oklahoma City*, 155 F.3d 1264 (10th Cir. 1998)).

An example of a university's successful use of the affirmative defense is *Gawley v. Indiana University*, 276 F.3d 301 (7th Cir. 2001). A female police officer alleged that she had endured verbal and physical sexual harassment by a supervisor for a period of seven months. At that point, the plaintiff filed a formal complaint under the university's harassment complaint process. The university investigated promptly and issued a report finding that harassment had occurred, and the harassment stopped as soon as the report was issued. The court ruled that the plaintiff's delay in reporting the harassment was unreasonable, and that, given the university's response when it learned of the harassment, filing a complaint promptly would have ended the harassment at a much earlier point in time. The appellate court affirmed the trial court's award of summary judgment to the university.

In order to take advantage of the *Faragher/Ellerth* affirmative defense, the employer must demonstrate that its policy effectively communicates to supervisors how they should handle harassment complaints and provides an effective mechanism for bypassing the supervisor should that individual be the alleged harasser. In *Wilson v. Tulsa Junior College*, 164 F.3d 534 (10th Cir. 1998), the Court ruled that the college had not established an affirmative defense because its complaint procedure was inadequate and it did not take timely and effective remedial action. The court criticized the college's harassment policy because it did not discuss the responsibilities of a supervisor who learned of alleged harassment through informal means. Furthermore, said the court, the unavailability of individuals to receive harassment complaints during the evening or on weekends, when the college was open and students and employees were present, was additional evidence of an ineffective harassment policy.

Consensual relationships that turn sour may result in sexual harassment claims and liability for the college. For example, in *Green v. Administrators of the Tulane Education Fund*, 284 F.3d 642 (5th Cir. 2002), a former office manager for a department chair alleged that the chair harassed her because their sexual relationship had ended and because the chair's new love interest insisted that the plaintiff be fired. Although the university provided evidence that it had attempted to transfer the plaintiff to another position and had attempted to ensure that the chair did not retaliate against her, a jury reached a verdict for the plaintiff and awarded her $300,000 in compensatory damages, in addition to back pay and front pay awards, and more than $300,000 in attorney's fees. The trial court had not allowed the jury to address the plaintiff's claim for punitive damages. The appellate court upheld the jury award, as well as the trial judge's determination that the institution's conduct had not met the "malice" or "reckless indifference" standard necessary for the award of punitive damages.

Offensive behavior of a sexual nature does not necessarily have to be directed at an employee for liability under Title VII to attach. In *Patane v. Clark*, 508 F.3d 106 (2d Cir. 2007), Patane, a department secretary, sued Fordham University, claiming that her supervisor, the department chair, regularly viewed pornographic videos in his office and required her to open such videotapes that were delivered to his office. He also used her computer to view pornographic Web sites. When Patane complained about the chair's actions, she alleged that he retaliated against her, as did his successor, by giving her a negative performance evaluation, removing responsibilities, and imposing "unwarranted" discipline. Although the trial court dismissed her claim, the appellate court reversed, stating that these allegations were sufficient to state a claim under Title VII.

Although Title VII does not forbid harassment on the basis of sexual orientation, it does permit claims of same-sex sexual harassment if the target can demonstrate that the harassment was based on the sex of the target. The U.S. Supreme Court addressed this issue for the first time in *Oncale v. Sundowner Offshore Services*, 523 U.S. 75 (1997). The Court ruled that a claim of male-to-male harassment was cognizable under Title VII if the plaintiff could demonstrate that the offensive conduct occurred "because of" his gender. In a unanimous opinion, the Court, through Justice Scalia, stated that "[Title VII] does not reach genuine but innocuous differences in the ways men and women routinely interact with members of the same sex and of the opposite sex. [The law] forbids only behavior so objectively offensive as to alter the 'conditions' of the victim's employment" (523 U.S. at 81).

Same-sex sexual harassment claims have increased substantially since the Court's ruling in *Oncale*. Courts have allowed plaintiffs to state claims of same-sex sexual harassment if the alleged harasser is homosexual. For example, in *Mota v. University of Texas Houston Health Science Center*, 261 F.3d 512 (5th Cir. 2001), the appellate court affirmed an award of back pay, front pay, and compensatory damages and attorney's fees to a male professor harassed and retaliated against by a male superior whose sexual advances he had rejected. The trial judge had given the plaintiff a substantial award of front pay because, after the jury returned a verdict of retaliation against the plaintiff by the university, the university president sent an e-mail message to 8,000 university employees stating that the plaintiff had not been terminated but had failed to return from a leave of absence. Because of those comments, the trial judge added five years of front pay to the plaintiff's original front pay award, reasoning that such negative remarks would make it difficult for the plaintiff to find another position. In other cases, plaintiffs who can demonstrate that they are harassed because of hatred or hostility toward them because of their gender may be allowed to state same-sex harassment claims.

Subsection (f) of the EEOC guidelines (29 C.F.R. § 1604.11(f)) emphasizes the advisability of implementing clear internal guidelines and sensitive grievance procedures for resolving sexual harassment complaints. The EEOC guidelines' emphasis on prevention suggests that the use of such internal processes may alleviate the postsecondary institution's liability under subsections (d) and (e) and diminish the likelihood of occurrences occasioning liability under subsections (c) and (g). Title IX requires grievance procedures as well.

In light of the social and legal developments, postsecondary institutions should give serious attention and sensitive treatment to sexual harassment issues. Sexual harassment on campus may be not only an employment issue but, for affected faculty and students, an academic freedom issue as well. Advance preventive planning is the key to successful management of these issues, as the EEOC guidelines indicate. Institutions should involve the academic community in developing specific written policies and information on what the community will consider to be sexual harassment. Training of faculty and staff on how to recognize and respond to sexual harassment is also an important litigation prevention strategy. In fact, three states—California, Connecticut, and Maine—require employers of a certain size to train either supervisors or all employees. See, for example, Cal. Gov't Code §12950.1, which requires employers with fifty or more employees to provide supervisors at least two hours of sexual harassment training every two years and to all new supervisors within six months of their assuming that role.

*4.5.2.2. Equal Pay Act.* Both the Equal Pay Act (part of the Fair Labor Standards Act (FSLA), 29 U.S.C. § 206(d)) and Title VII prohibit sex discrimination in compensation. Because of the similarity of the issues, pay discrimination claims under both laws are discussed in this subsection.

The Equal Pay Act provides that:

> no employer [subject to the Fair Labor Standards Act] shall discriminate . . .
> between employees on the basis of sex . . . on jobs the performance of which
> requires equal skill, effort, and responsibility, and which are performed under
> similar working conditions, except where such payment is made pursuant to
> (i) a seniority system; (ii) a merit system; (iii) a system which measures
> earnings by quantity or quality of production; or (iv) a differential based on any
> other factor other than sex [29 U.S.C. § 206(d)(1)].

Thus, the determination of whether jobs are equal, and the judgment as to whether one of the four exceptions applies to a particular claim, is the essence of an equal pay claim under this law.

The plaintiff in an Equal Pay Act lawsuit must find an employee of a different gender who holds the same job and is paid more. Even if the titles and job descriptions are the same, the court examines the actual responsibilities of the plaintiff and the comparator. For example, in *Gustin v. West Virginia University*, 63 F. App'x 695 (4th Cir. 2003), the court ruled that the job responsibilities of a female assistant dean for student affairs were not equal to the responsibilities of a male assistant dean who had responsibilities for physical facilities and budget, and thus her Equal Pay Act claim failed.

Replacing a staff member with one who is paid substantially more for performing the same job could expose the institution to liability under the Equal Pay Act. In *Dixon v. University of Toledo*, 638 F. Supp. 2d 847 (N.D. Ohio 2009), a federal trial court concluded that a salary difference of more than $40,000 paid to the male replacement for a female associate vice president could provide sufficient evidence of a sex-based motive for the salary difference such that the female plaintiff could establish a prima facie case of sex discrimination.

Nonwage benefits may also be subject to the provisions of the Equal Pay Act. For example, in *Stewart v. SUNY Maritime College*, 83 Fair Empl. Prac. Cas. (BNA) 1610 (S.D.N.Y. 2000), a female public safety officer at a college was denied on-campus housing, although all male public safety officers doing the same work as the plaintiff were provided free on-campus housing. The trial court denied the college's motion for summary judgment, ruling that whether the on-campus housing provided to male public safety officers constituted "wages" for purposes of the Equal Pay Act was a question of fact that must be determined at trial.

As part of the FLSA, the Equal Pay Act provides for double back pay damages in cases of willful violations of the Act. A plaintiff must demonstrate an employer's knowing or reckless disregard for its responsibilities under this law to establish a willful violation. (For an example of a successful plaintiff in this regard, see *Pollis v. The New School for Social Research*, 132 F.3d 115 (2d Cir. 1997).)

Although several public colleges have attempted to argue that they are shielded from liability for Equal Pay Act violations by Eleventh Amendment immunity, the courts have disagreed. Because the Equal Pay Act prohibits discrimination on the basis of sex, courts have ruled that it was promulgated under the authority of the Fourteenth Amendment. (See, for example, *Cherry v. University of Wisconsin System Board of Regents*, 265 F.3d 541 (7th Cir. 2001); see also *Varner v. Illinois State University*, 226 F.3d 927 (7th Cir. 2000).)

Equal Pay Act claims may be brought by an individual or by a class of individuals who allege that a college underpaid them relative to members of the opposite sex who were doing equal work. Most class action Equal Pay Act cases against colleges have been brought by women faculty. The Equal Pay Act is enforced by the Equal Employment Opportunity Commission. The EEOC's procedural regulations for the act are codified in 29 C.F.R. Parts 1620–21.

A U.S. Supreme Court ruling involving the timeliness of a pay discrimination complaint brought under Title VII was later overturned by Congress. *In Ledbetter v. Goodyear Tire and Rubber*, 550 U.S. 618 (2007), the court ruled

5 to 4, in an opinion by Justice Alito, that employees claiming pay discrimination under Title VII must file their claims within the 180- or 300-day limitations period after the pay decision had been made. The plaintiff had argued that the regular issuance of paychecks that were less than those of men doing the same job was a continuing violation and should toll the statute of limitations. The majority explained that, in order to apply Title VII's requirement that the discrimination be intentional, the specific date on which an allegedly discriminatory pay decision was made must be the date of reference for the beginning of the limitations period. The dissent, written by Justice Ginsburg, argued that pay discrimination decisions are more difficult to detect than decisions such as failure to hire or promote, or termination decisions. She noted that pay discrimination decisions have a cumulative effect and thus should be treated as continuing violations rather than a single decision at a particular point in time.

Congress responded by passing the Lilly Ledbetter Fair Pay Act, Pub. L. No. 111-2, 123 Stat. 5, in 2009. The law amends Section 706(e) of Title VII (42 U.S.C. 2000e-5(e)), as well as Section 7(d) of the Age Discrimination in Employment Act of 1967 (29 U.S.C. 626(d)), Title I, Section 503 of the Americans with Disabilities Act, and Sections 501 and 504 of the Rehabilitation Act of 1973, to provide that a violation occurs each time compensation resulting from a discriminatory decision is paid.

A particularly troubling issue in salary discrimination claims is the determination of whether pay differentials are, in fact, caused by sex or race discrimination or by legitimate factors such as performance differences, market factors, or educational background. These issues have been debated fiercely in the courts and in the literature.

**4.5.2.3. *Title IX*.** Title IX of the Education Amendments of 1972, 20 U.S.C. §§ 1681 et seq., prohibits sex discrimination by public and private educational institutions receiving federal funds (see Section 11.5.3 of this book). The statute is administered by the Office for Civil Rights (OCR) of the Department of Education. The department's regulations, found at 34 C.F.R. Part 106, contain provisions on employment (34 C.F.R. §§ 106.51–106.61) that are similar in many respects to the EEOC's sex discrimination guidelines under Title VII. Like Title VII, the Title IX regulations contain a provision permitting sex-based distinctions in employment where sex is a "bona fide occupational qualification" (34 C.F.R. § 106.61). Title IX also contains a provision exempting any "educational institution which is controlled by a religious organization" if Title IX's requirements "would not be consistent with the religious tenets of such organization" (20 U.S.C. § 1681(a)(3); 34 C.F.R. § 106.12).

The applicability of Title IX to employment discrimination was hotly contested in a series of cases beginning in the mid-1970s. The U.S. Supreme Court resolved the dispute, holding that Title IX does apply to and prohibit sex discrimination in employment (see *North Haven Board of Education v. Bell*, 456 U.S. 512 (1982)).

The decision of the U.S. Supreme Court in *Franklin v. Gwinnett County Public Schools*, 503 U.S. 60 (1992) (discussed in Section 11.5.3), that plaintiffs alleging discrimination under Title IX may be awarded compensatory damages, has stimulated discrimination claims under Title IX that might otherwise have been brought under Title VII, given Title VII's cap on damages (see Section 4.5.2.1). Title IX does not require the exhaustion of administrative remedies, and it borrows its statute of limitations from state law, which may be more generous than the relatively short period under Title VII. Plaintiffs with dual status as employees and students (for example, graduate teaching assistants, work-study students, and residence hall counselors) may find Title IX appealing because they need not prove they are "employees" rather than students in order to seek relief.

Some courts have held, however, that plaintiffs are barred from filing employment discrimination claims seeking money damages under Title IX (rather than the fund termination remedies provided under Title IX by the U.S. Department of Education), and must, instead, use Title VII to redress alleged discrimination. The federal appellate courts are split on this issue.

The U.S. Supreme Court resolved the issue of whether a plaintiff may state a Title IX claim for retaliation even if he does not claim sex discrimination. The male coach of a high school girls' basketball team claimed that he was terminated in retaliation for complaining about allegedly unequal facilities for boys' and girls' teams. In *Jackson v. Birmingham Board of Education*, 309 F.3d 1333 (11th Cir. 2002), *reversed*, 544 U.S. 167 (2005), the appellate court had dismissed the case, stating that the plaintiff was not himself a victim of sex discrimination and thus could not sue under Title IX. The U.S. Supreme Court reversed, stating that retaliating against an individual for complaining about unlawful sex discrimination against others was itself intentional sex discrimination, a violation of Title IX.

***4.5.2.4. Section 1981.*** A post–Civil War civil rights statute, 42 U.S.C. § 1981, commonly known as "Section 1981," states:

> All persons within the jurisdiction of the United States shall have the same right in every state and territory to make and enforce contracts, to sue, be parties, give evidence, and to the full and equal benefit of all laws and proceedings for the security of persons and property as is enjoyed by white citizens, and shall be subject to like punishment, pains, penalties, taxes, licenses, and exactions of every kind, and to no other.

Section 1981 is enforced through court litigation by persons denied the equality that the statute guarantees. The statute prohibits discrimination in both public and private employment, as the U.S. Supreme Court affirmed in *Johnson v. Railway Express Agency*, 421 U.S. 454 (1975).

Section 1981 covers racially based employment discrimination against white persons as well as racial minorities (*McDonald v. Santa Fe Trail Transportation Co.*, 427 U.S. 273 (1976)). Although in earlier cases Section 1981 had been held to apply to employment discrimination against aliens (*Guerra v. Manchester Terminal Corp.*, 498 F.2d 641 (5th Cir. 1974)), later federal appellate court rulings suggest that this broad reading of the law is inappropriate. In *Bhandari v. First National Bank of Commerce*, 887 F.2d 609 (5th Cir. 1989) (*en banc*), a federal appellate court overturned *Guerra* and, after a lengthy review of the 1866 Civil Rights Act, determined that Congress had not intended Section 1981 to cover private discrimination against aliens, although the court did not address the issue of such discrimination by a public entity.

Although Section 1981 does not specifically prohibit discrimination on the basis of national origin (*Ohemeng v. Delaware State College*, 676 F. Supp. 65 (D. Del. 1988), *affirmed*, 862 F.2d 309 (3d Cir. 1988)), some courts have permitted plaintiffs to pursue national origin discrimination claims under Section 1981 in cases where race and national origin were intertwined. In two special cases, moreover, the U.S. Supreme Court has interpreted Section 1981 to apply to certain types of national origin and ethnicity discrimination. In *St. Francis College v. Al-Khazraji*, 481 U.S. 604 (1987), the Court permitted a professor of Arabian descent to challenge his tenure denial under Section 1981. And in *Shaare Tefila Congregation v. Cobb*, 481 U.S. 615 (1987), the Court extended similar protections to Jews. In both cases the Court looked to the dictionary definition of "race" in the 1860s, when Section 1981 was enacted by Congress; the definition included both Arabs and Jews as examples of races.

While Section 1981 overlaps Title VII (see Section 4.5.2.1 of this book) in its coverage of racial discrimination in employment, a back pay award is not restricted to two years of back pay under Section 1981, as it is under Title VII (see *Johnson v. Railway Express Agency*, 421 U.S. 454 (1975)). Furthermore, Section 1981 does not have the short statute of limitations that Title VII imposes. In *Jones v. R. R. Donnelley & Sons Co.*, 541 U.S. 369 (2004), the U.S. Supreme Court ruled that a four-year statute of limitations should apply to claims brought under the Civil Rights Act of 1866, of which Section 1981 is a part. Therefore, individuals alleging race discrimination in employment are likely to file claims under both Section 1981 and Title VII.

In *General Building Contractors Association. v. Pennsylvania*, 458 U.S. 375 (1982), the U.S. Supreme Court engrafted an intent requirement onto the Section 1981 statute. To prevail in a Section 1981 claim, therefore, a plaintiff must prove that the defendant intentionally or purposefully engaged in discriminatory acts. This requirement is the same as the Court previously applied to discrimination claims brought under the equal protection clause (see Section 4.5.2.7 of this book).

Section 1981 does not have extraterritorial application because the language of the statute limits its protections to persons "within the jurisdiction of the United States" (*Ofori-Tenkorang v. American International Group Inc.*, 460 F.3d 296 (2d Cir. 2006)). Although Section 1981 has been found to cover employment decisions of both private and public employers, institutions that are arms of the state are immune from Section 1981 damages liability under the Eleventh Amendment of the U.S. Constitution. (For an illustrative case holding that a federal trial court lacked jurisdiction to hear an employee's suit against the City University of New York, see *Bunch v. The City University of New York Queens College*, 2000 U.S. Dist. LEXIS 14227 (S.D.N.Y. 2000).)

***4.5.2.5. Americans with Disabilities Act and Rehabilitation Act of 1973.*** Two
federal laws forbid employment discrimination against individuals with disabilities. The Americans with Disabilities Act (ADA), 42 U.S.C. §§ 12101 et
seq., prohibits employment discrimination by employers with fifteen or more
employees, and also applies to labor unions, and employment agencies. Section
504 of the Rehabilitation Act, 29 U.S.C. § 794, also prohibits discrimination
against individuals with disabilities, but unlike the ADA, there is no threshold
number of employees required for coverage by Section 504 (*Schrader v. Fred
A. Ray M.D.*, 296 F.3d 968 (10th Cir. 2002)). Section 504 is patterned after
Title VI and Title IX (see Sections 11.5.2 and 11.5.3 of this book), which prohibit, respectively, race and sex discrimination in federally funded programs
and activities. Each federal funding agency enforces the Rehabilitation Act with
respect to its own funding programs.

Title I of the Americans with Disabilities Act of 1990 prohibits employment
discrimination against "qualified" individuals who are disabled. The prohibition of discrimination in the ADA uses language very similar to that of Title VII:

(a) No covered entity shall discriminate against a qualified individual with
a disability because of the disability of such individual in regard to job
application procedures, the hiring, advancement, or discharge of employees,
employee compensation, job training, and other terms, conditions, and
privileges of employment [42 U.S.C. §12102(a)].

The law defines a "qualified individual with a disability" as "an individual
with a disability who, with or without reasonable accommodation, can perform
the essential functions of the employment position that such individual holds
or desires" (42 U.S.C. § 12111(8)). This definition, which would apply to an
individual with a disability who could perform the job only if accommodated,
rejects the U.S. Supreme Court's interpretation of the Rehabilitation Act's definition of "otherwise qualified" in *Southeastern Community College v. Davis*, 442
U.S. 397 (1979) (see below, this section).

The law requires that, if an applicant or a current employee meets the definition of "qualified individual with a disability," the employer must provide
a reasonable accommodation unless the accommodation presents an "undue
hardship" for the employer. The terms are defined thus in the statute:

The term "reasonable accommodation" may include—
(A)  making existing facilities used by employees readily accessible to and
usable by individuals with disabilities; and
(B)  job restructuring, part-time or modified work schedules, reassignment to
a vacant position, acquisition or modification of equipment or devices,
appropriate adjustment or modifications of examinations, training materials
or policies, the provision of qualified readers or interpreters, and other
similar accommodations for individuals with disabilities [42 U.S.C.
§12111(9)].

(10) (A) The term "undue hardship" means an action requiring significant difficulty or expense, when considered in light of the factors set forth in subparagraph (B).

(B) In determining whether an accommodation would impose an undue hardship on a covered entity, factors to be considered include—

(i) the nature and cost of the accommodation needed under this chapter;

(ii) the overall financial resources of the facility or facilities involved in the provision of the reasonable accommodation; the number of persons employed at such facility; the effect on expenses and resources, or the impact otherwise of such accommodation upon the operation of the facility;

(iii) the overall financial resources of the covered entity; the overall size of the business of a covered entity with respect to the number of its employees, the number, type, and location of its facilities; and

(iv) the type of operation or operations of the covered entity, including the composition, structure, and functions of the workforce of such entity; the geographic separateness, administrative, or fiscal relationship of the facility or facilities in question to the covered entity [42 U.S.C. § 12111(10)].

The ADA also contains provisions regarding the use of preemployment medical examinations, the confidentiality of an individual's medical records, and the individuals who may have access to information about the individual's disability.

The law specifically excludes current abusers of controlled substances from coverage, but it does protect recovering abusers, individuals who are incorrectly perceived to be abusers of controlled substances, and individuals who have completed or are participating in a supervised rehabilitation program and are no longer using controlled substances. Since the law does not exclude persons with alcoholism, they are protected by the ADA, even if their abuse is current. However, the law permits employers to prohibit the use of alcohol or drugs at the workplace, to outlaw intoxication on the job, and to conform with the Drug-Free Workplace Act of 1988 (41 U.S.C. §§ 701 et seq.). Employers may also hold users of drugs or alcohol to the same performance standards as other employees, and the law neither requires nor prohibits drug testing.

The Americans with Disabilities Act was amended by the ADA Amendments Act, Pub. L. No. 110-325, which took effect on January 1, 2009. The amendments retain the original definition of a "disability," but include language instructing courts to construe the definition of disability broadly. The amendments specifically overturn four controversial decisions of the U.S. Supreme Court that had narrowed the definition of "disability" to the extent that few plaintiffs were able to meet it. The amendments state that courts must not consider the effect of "mitigating measures" (such as medication or prosthetic devices) in determining whether an individual's impairment meets the law's definition of "disability." The amendments also include an illustrative list of "major life activities": caring for oneself, performing manual tasks, seeing, hearing, eating, sleeping, walking, standing, lifting, bending, speaking, breathing, learning, reading, concentrating, thinking, communicating, and working. Working had on occasion been rejected by courts as a major life activity.

The amendments also broaden the definition of "major life activity" to include "major bodily functions" such as functions of the immune system, normal cell growth, digestive, bowel, bladder, neurological, brain, respiratory, circulatory, endocrine, and reproductive functions. And the amendments note that an employee need not prove that he or she has a disability in order to state a claim that the employer regarded the employee as disabled.

Given the broadening of the definition of disability, it is likely that courts will focus less on that issue and more directly on whether the individual was qualified for the position, with or without reasonable accommodation, and whether the accommodation the employee sought or was offered met the law's definition of "reasonable."

The ADA's employment discrimination remedies are identical to those of Title VII, and the act is enforced by the EEOC, as is Title VII. The same limitation on damages found in Title VII applies to actions brought under the ADA, except that language applicable to the ADA provides that if an employer makes a good-faith attempt at reasonable accommodation but is still found to have violated the ADA, neither compensatory nor punitive damages will be available to the plaintiff (42 U.S.C. § 1981A). This provision also applies to the Rehabilitation Act.

Furthermore, plaintiffs claiming retaliation may not receive compensatory or punitive damages for such claims under the ADA, although these damages are available for plaintiffs who prevail in their underlying disability discrimination claims. See, for example, *Alvarado v. Cajun Operating Co.*, 588 F.3d 1261 (9th Cir. 2009).

Regulations interpreting the ADA are published at 29 C.F.R. § 1630, and have been amended to reflect the changes occasioned by the ADA Amendments Act. In addition to expanding on the concepts of "qualified," "reasonable accommodation," and "undue hardship," these regulations include guidelines for determining whether hiring or retaining an employee with a disability would pose a safety hazard to coworkers or to the employee (29 C.F.R. § 1630.2(r)). The EEOC has also issued several enforcement guidance documents that state the agency's position on and interpretation of the ADA. These documents are available on the agency's Web site at http://www.eeoc.gov.

Title II of the ADA prohibits discrimination on the basis of disability by "public entities," which includes public colleges and universities. The language of Title II mirrors the language of Title VI and Section 504 of the Rehabilitation Act:

> [N]o qualified individual with a disability shall, by reason of such disability, be excluded from participation in or be denied the benefits of the services, programs, or activities of a public entity, or be subjected to discrimination by any such entity [42 U.S.C. § 12132].

The regulations interpreting Title II prohibit employment discrimination by a public entity (28 C.F.R. § 35.140). Title II adopts the remedies, rights, and procedures of Section 505 of the Rehabilitation Act, which has been interpreted to provide a private right of action for individuals alleging discrimination under the Rehabilitation Act (see Section 11.5.4 of this book). No exhaustion of administrative remedies is explicitly required by either Title II or Section 505.

As is the case with Title VII, individuals may not be sued for disability discrimination under the ADA (see, for example, *Walsh v. Nevada Department of Human Resources*, 471 F.3d 1033 (9th Cir. 2006)). In addition, individuals may not be sued for retaliation under Title I of the ADA (see, for example, *Albra v. Advan Inc.*, 490 F.3d 826 (11th Cir. 2007)), although some federal courts have ruled that individuals may be sued for retaliation when they bring claims under Title II of the ADA (see, for example, *Shotz v. Plantation, Florida*, 344 F.3d 1161 (11th Cir. 2003)).

Colleges and universities have been subject to the Rehabilitation Act since 1973, and a body of judicial precedent has developed interpreting that act's requirements. The law was amended by the Rehabilitation Act Amendments of 1992 (Pub. L. No. 102-569, 106 Stat. 4344) to replace the word "handicap" with the word "disability" and to conform the language of the Rehabilitation Act in other ways with that of the ADA (see Section 11.5.4 of this book). Regulations interpreting the Rehabilitation Act's prohibitions against disability discrimination by federal contractors have been revised to conform to ADA provisions, and are found at 34 C.F.R. § 104.11 and 29 C.F.R. Part 1641.

The regulations implementing Section 504 of the Rehabilitation Act prohibit discrimination against qualified disabled persons with regard to any term or condition of employment, including selection for training or conference attendance and employers' social or recreational programs. Furthermore, the regulations state that the employer's obligations under the statute are not affected by any inconsistent term of any collective bargaining agreement to which the employer is a party (34 C.F.R. § 104.11).

In language similar to that of the ADA, the Section 504 regulations define a qualified person with a disability as one who "with reasonable accommodation can perform the essential functions" of the job in question (34 C.F.R. § 104.3(k)(1)). The regulations impose an affirmative obligation on the recipient to make "reasonable accommodation to the known physical or mental limitations of an otherwise qualified handicapped applicant or employee unless the recipient can demonstrate that the accommodation would impose an undue hardship on the operation of its program" (34 C.F.R. § 104.12(a)). Reasonable accommodations can take the form of modification of the job site, of equipment, or of a position itself. What hardship would relieve a recipient of the obligation to make reasonable accommodation depends on the facts of each case. As a related affirmative requirement, the recipient must adapt its employment tests to accommodate an applicant's sensory, manual, or speaking disability unless the tests are intended to measure those types of skills (34 C.F.R. § 104.13(b)).

The regulations include explicit prohibitions regarding employee selection procedures and pre-employment questioning. As a general rule, the fund recipient cannot make any pre-employment inquiry or require a pre-employment medical examination to determine whether an applicant is disabled or to determine the nature or severity of a disability (34 C.F.R. § 104.14(a)). Nor can a recipient use any employment criterion, such as a test, that has the effect of eliminating qualified applicants with disabilities, unless the criterion is job related and there is no alternative job-related criterion that does not have the same effect (34 C.F.R. § 104.13(a)). These prohibitions are also found in the ADA and its regulations.

In *Southeastern Community College v. Davis,* 442 U.S. 397 (1979), discussed in Sections 7.2.4.3 and 11.5.4 of this book, the U.S. Supreme Court addressed for the first time the extent of the obligation that Section 504 of the Rehabilitation Act imposes on colleges and universities. The case involved the admission of a disabled applicant to a clinical nursing program, but the Court's opinion also sheds light on the Rehabilitation Act's application to employment of disabled persons.

In *Davis,* the Court determined that an "otherwise qualified handicapped individual" protected by Section 504 is one who is qualified in spite of his or her disability, and thus ruled that the institution need not make major program modifications to accommodate the individual. Because the definition of "otherwise qualified" appears only in the Department of Education's regulations implementing Section 504, not in the statute, the Court did not consider itself bound by the language of the regulations, which defined a "qualified handicapped individual" for employment purposes as one who, "with reasonable accommodation," can perform the job's essential functions. However, statutory language in the ADA virtually repeats the language of Section 504's regulations; thus, the Court's opinion in *Davis* has limited relevance for employment challenges under the ADA.

The U.S. Supreme Court again interpreted the Rehabilitation Act in *School Board of Nassau County v. Arline,* 480 U.S. 273 (1987), in which the Court determined that persons suffering from a contagious disease (in this case, tuberculosis) were protected by the act. The Court listed four factors that employers must take into consideration when determining whether an employee with a potentially contagious disease poses a danger to other employees or to clients, customers, or students:

(1) the nature of the risk (how the disease is transmitted);

(2) the duration of the risk (how long is the carrier infectious);

(3) the severity of the risk (what is the potential harm to third parties); and

(4) the probabilities the disease will be transmitted and will cause varying degrees of harm [480 U.S. at 288].

Congress adopted the Court's position in this case in an amendment to the Rehabilitation Act tacked onto the Civil Rights Restoration Act of 1987 (Pub. L. No. 100-259, 102 Stat. 28, § 9).

Section 503 of the Rehabilitation Act requires all institutions holding contracts with the federal government in excess of $10,000 to "take affirmative action to employ and advance in employment qualified handicapped individuals." While the Court in *Davis* emphatically rejected an affirmative action obligation under Section 504, its decision in no way affects the express obligation imposed on federal contractors by Section 503 of the act (see Section 4.6 of this book).

The U.S. Supreme Court has added Title I of the ADA to the list of federal nondiscrimination laws that are unenforceable against state entities in federal court. In *Board of Trustees of the University of Alabama v. Garrett*, 531 U.S. 356 (2001), the Court ruled that Congress had not validly abrogated the states' Eleventh Amendment immunity when it enacted the ADA. Although the Court agreed that the statutory language makes it clear that Congress intended the ADA to apply to states as employers, the Court found that Congress was primarily concerned with disability-based employment discrimination by private employers and that Congress had not identified a history and pattern of disability-based discrimination by states sufficient to provide a constitutional foundation for outlawing such discrimination. Comparing the amount of state-created discrimination that engendered the Voting Rights Act to the legislative history of the ADA, the majority found insufficient justification to provide a rationale for abrogating the states' immunity to suit in federal courts. On remand, the U.S. Court of Appeals for the Eleventh Circuit ruled that the state had waived sovereign immunity by accepting federal funds, so it could be sued in federal court under Section 504 of the Rehabilitation Act (*Garrett v. University of Alabama at Birmingham Board of Trustees*, 344 F.3d 1288 (11th Cir. 1288)). The U.S. Court of Appeals for the Third Circuit reached a similar conclusion *in Koslow v. Pennsylvania*, 302 F.3d 161 (3d Cir. 2002).

***4.5.2.6. Age Discrimination in Employment Act.*** The Age Discrimination in Employment Act (ADEA), 29 U.S.C. §§ 621 et seq., prohibits age discrimination only with respect to persons who are at least forty years of age. It is contained within the Fair Labor Standards Act (29 U.S.C. §§ 201–19) and is subject to the requirements of that act.

Prior to the act's amendment in 1978, the protection ended at age sixty-five (29 U.S.C. § 631). The 1978 amendments raised the end of protection to age seventy, effective January 1, 1979; and amendments added in 1986 removed the limit completely, except for persons in certain professions. Individuals in public safety positions (police officers, firefighters), "high-level policy makers,"[4] and tenured college faculty could be required to retire at certain ages (seventy for tenured faculty). The amendment provided that the exemption for individuals in public safety positions and tenured faculty would expire on December 31, 1993. Thus, as of January 1, 1994, mandatory retirement for most employees, whether tenured or not, became unlawful.

---

[4] "High-level policy makers" are considered to be those few individuals who are senior executives of the organization. For an example of a university that applied this exemption to a wide array of administrators and ran afoul of the ADEA as a result, see Alex P. Kellogg, "Under Federal Pressure, Indiana U. Will Scale Back Mandatory-Retirement Policy," *Chron. Higher Educ.*, January 30, 2002, at http://chronicle.com/daily/2002/01/2002013004n.htm.

The ADEA, which is applicable to both public and private institutions, makes it unlawful for an employer

(1) to fail or refuse to hire or to discharge any individual with respect to his compensation, terms, conditions, or privileges of employment, because of such individual's age;

(2) to limit, segregate, or classify his employees in any way which would deprive or tend to deprive any individual of employment opportunities or otherwise adversely affect his status as an employee, because of such individual's age; or

(3) to reduce the wage rate of any employee in order to comply with this chapter [29 U.S.C. § 623].

The ADEA is enforced by the Equal Employment Opportunity Commission (EEOC), and implementing regulations appear at 29 C.F.R. Parts 1625–27. The law, regulations, and enforcement guidance may be found on the EEOC Web site at http://www.eeoc.gov. Among other matters, the interpretations specify the criteria an employer must meet to establish age as a bona fide occupational qualification (BFOQ).

As under other statutes, the burden of proof has been an issue in litigation. Generally, the plaintiff must make a prima facie showing of age discrimination, at which point the burden shifts to the employer to show that "age is a bona fide occupational qualification reasonably necessary to the normal operation of the particular business" at issue (29 U.S.C. § 623(f)(1)); or that distinctions among employees or applicants were "based on reasonable factors other than age" (29 U.S.C. § 623(f)(1)); or that, in the case of discipline or discharge, the action was taken "for good cause" (29 U.S.C. § 623(f)(3)). (See *Laugeson v. Anaconda Co.*, 510 F.2d 307 (6th Cir. 1975); and *Hodgson v. First Federal Savings and Loan*, 455 F.2d 818 (5th Cir. 1972).) Employment decisions that appear neutral on their face, but that use criteria that are closely linked with age (such as length of service) and that tend to disadvantage over-forty employees disproportionately, may run afoul of the ADEA. Litigation is particularly likely when colleges are merged or when there is a reduction in force of faculty and/or staff.

For more than a decade it has been unclear whether plaintiffs may use the "disparate impact" theory (see Section 4.5.2.1 of this book) to attack alleged discrimination that is unintentional under the ADEA. In *Smith v. City of Jackson*, 544 U.S. 228 (2005), the U.S. Supreme Court ruled 8–0 that plaintiffs challenging alleged discrimination under the ADEA may use the disparate impact theory.

Individuals claiming age discrimination under the ADEA must first file a claim either with the federal EEOC (within 180 days) or with the appropriate state civil rights agency. Sixty days after such a claim is filed, the individual may bring a civil action in federal court (29 U.S.C. § 626(d)). A jury trial is provided for by the statute, and remedies include two years of back pay, liquidated damages (double back pay), front pay, and other make-whole remedies.

The ADEA was amended in 1990 by the Older Workers Benefit Protection Act (OWBPA), 104 Stat. 981, in part as a reaction to a decision by the U.S. Supreme Court in *Public Employees Retirement System of Ohio v. Betts*, 492 U.S. 158 (1989). In that opinion, the Court had ruled that only employee benefit plans that could be shown to be a subterfuge for discrimination violated the ADEA, even if their terms had the effect of discriminating against older workers. OWBPA prohibited discriminatory employee benefit plans (29 U.S.C. § 623(k)) and codified the "equal benefits or equal cost" principle articulated in *Karlen v. City Colleges of Chicago*, 837 F.2d 314 (7th Cir. 1988). In *Karlen*, the appellate court had found discriminatory two provisions of a retirement plan that gave more generous benefits to faculty who were sixty-five years old and under. The court ruled that employers could provide benefits of equal cost to the employer, even if older workers received benefits of less value because of the higher cost of benefits to older workers. An employer, however, could not vary benefits (such as sick leave or severance pay) in ways that favored younger employees.

The law requires employers to give older workers benefits that are equal to or better than those given younger workers, unless the employer can demonstrate that benefits (such as term life insurance) carry a higher cost for older workers. The legislation also defines requirements for early retirement plans and regulates the conditions under which severance benefits may be offset by other benefits included in early retirement plans (29 U.S.C. § 623(1)). Furthermore, the law specifies how releases or waivers of an employee's right to sue under the ADEA must be formulated and requires a twenty-one-day waiting period and a seven-day revocation period for releases (29 U.S.C. § 626(f)(1)). Employees who sign such waivers and then institute litigation, claiming that the waivers were not knowing or voluntary, are not required to return the additional payment they were given as an inducement to sign the waiver (29 C.F.R. § 1625.23).

Congress included language in the Higher Education Amendments of 1998 (Pub. L. No. 105-244, October 7, 1998) that amends the Age Discrimination in Employment Act only for institutions of higher education. The amendments allow colleges and universities to offer tenured faculty retirement incentive packages that include supplementary benefits that are reduced or eliminated on the basis of age, as long as there is compliance with certain provisions.

The U.S. Supreme Court has ruled that states and their agencies cannot be sued under the ADEA in federal court by private individuals (*Kimel v. Florida Board of Regents*, 528 U.S. 62 (2000)). Relying on its earlier decision in *Seminole Tribe of Florida v. Florida*, 517 U.S. 44 (1996), the Court stated that, although Congress had made its intent to abrogate states' Eleventh Amendment immunity "unmistakably clear," the ADEA had been enacted under the authority of the commerce clause. And because age is not a **suspect classification** under the equal protection clause, said the Court, states could discriminate on the basis of age without violating the Fourteenth Amendment if the use of age was rationally related to a legitimate state interest.

### 4.5.2.7. Constitutional prohibitions against employment discrimination.
The Fourteenth Amendment's equal protection clause applies to all employment discrimination by public institutions (see Section 1.5.2). The standards of review, or standards of "scrutiny," used by the courts vary, however, depending on the type of discrimination being challenged. As Figure 4.1 depicts, there are three levels or tiers of scrutiny. For the upper, strict scrutiny tier (which includes race discrimination, for example), and the middle, intermediate scrutiny tier (which includes sex discrimination, for example), the standards are similar to those for the federal statutes covering such discrimination. For the bottom tier, however, the equal protection standards are more lenient than those for federal statutes; the standards for disability discrimination provide the primary example of such a discrepancy.

Even where constitutional standards are very strong, as for race discrimination, the courts usually strike down only discrimination found to be intentional;

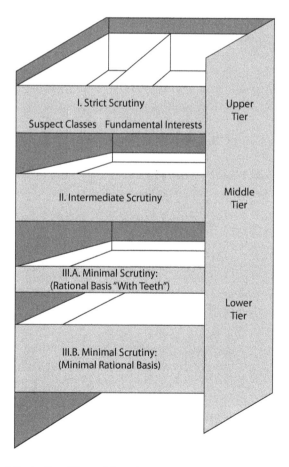

**Figure 4.1** Equal Protection Tiers of Scrutiny

*Source:* From W. Kaplin, *The Concepts and Methods of Constitutional Law* (Carolina Academic Press, 1992). Copyright © by W. A. Kaplin; all rights reserved.

the federal statutes, on the other hand, do not always require a showing of discriminatory intent. In *Washington v. Davis*, 426 U.S. 229 (1976), for instance, the U.S. Supreme Court distinguished between disparate impact cases brought under Title VII (see Section 4.5.2.1) and those brought under the equal protection clause, noting that the equal protection cases "have not embraced the proposition that a law or other official act, without regard to whether it reflects a racially discriminatory purpose, is unconstitutional solely because it has a racially disproportionate impact." Under Title VII, in contrast, "discriminatory purpose need not be proved." Title VII thus "involves a more probing judicial review of, and less deference to, the seemingly reasonable acts of administrators and executives than is appropriate under the Constitution where special racial impact, without discriminatory purpose, is claimed."

In *Personnel Administrator of Massachusetts v. Feeney*, 442 U.S. 256 (1979), the Court elaborated on the requirement of discriminatory intent, which must be met to establish a violation of the equal protection clause. *Feeney* concerned a female civil servant who challenged the constitutionality of a state law providing that all veterans who qualify for civil service positions must be considered ahead of any qualified nonveteran. The statute's language was gender neutral—its benefits extended to "any person" who had served in official U.S. military units or unofficial auxiliary units during wartime. The veterans' preference law had a disproportionate impact on women, however, because 98 percent of the veterans in Massachusetts were men. Consequently, nonveteran women who received high scores on competitive examinations were repeatedly displaced by lower-scoring male veterans. Feeney claimed that the preference law discriminated against women in violation of the Fourteenth Amendment.

The Court summarized the general approach it would take in ruling on such constitutional challenges of state statutes:

> In assessing an equal protection challenge, a court is called upon only
> to measure the basic validity of the . . . classification. When some other
> independent right is not at stake . . . and when there is no "reason to infer
> antipathy," it is presumed that "even improvident decisions will eventually be
> rectified by the democratic process" (*Vance v. Bradley*, 440 U.S. 93) [442 U.S. at
> 272; citations omitted].

The Supreme Court agreed with the district court's finding that the law was enacted not for the purpose of preferring males but, rather, to give a competitive advantage to veterans. Since the classification "nonveterans" includes both men and women, both sexes could be disadvantaged by the laws. The Court concluded that too many men were disadvantaged to permit the inference that the classification was a pretext for discrimination against women. Since neither the statute's language nor the facts concerning its passage demonstrated that the preference was designed to deny women opportunity for employment or advancement in the Massachusetts civil service, the Court, with two Justices dissenting, upheld the statute.

*Feeney* extends the reasoning in *Washington v. Davis* by stating unequivocally that a statute that has a disproportionate impact on a particular group will withstand an equal protection challenge unless the plaintiff can show that it was enacted in order to affect that group adversely. Thus, a statute neutral on its face will be upheld unless the disparate impact of the law "could not plausibly be explained on neutral grounds," in which case "impact itself would signal that the classification made by the law was in fact not neutral." The effect of this reasoning—controversial especially among civil rights advocates—is to increase the difficulty of proving equal protection violations.

Besides its less vigorous standards, the equal protection clause also lacks the administrative implementation and enforcement mechanisms that exist for most federal nondiscrimination statutes. Consequently, postsecondary institutions will be subject to a narrower range of remedies for ensuring compliance under the Constitution, compared with the statutes, and also will not have the benefit of administrative agency guidance via regulations and interpretive bulletins.

In employment discrimination, the Constitution assumes its greatest importance in areas not covered by any federal statute. Age discrimination against persons less than forty years old is one such area, since the Age Discrimination in Employment Act does not cover individuals under age forty (although the laws of some states do). A second example is discrimination against aliens, which is no longer covered by 42 U.S.C. § 1981. Another important uncovered area is discrimination on the basis of sexual orientation, which is discussed in Section 4.5.2.9. Discrimination on the basis of residence is a fourth important example.

**4.5.2.8. *Executive Orders 11246 and 11375.*** Executive Order 11246, 30 Fed. Reg. 12319, as amended by Executive Order 11375, 32 Fed. Reg. 14303 (adding sex to the list of prohibited discriminations), prohibits discrimination "because of race, color, religion, sex, or national origin," thus paralleling Title VII (see Section 4.5.2.1 of this book). Unlike Title VII, the executive orders apply only to contractors and subcontractors who received $10,000 or more in federal government contracts and federally assisted construction contracts (41 C.F.R. § 60-1.5). Agreements with each such contractor must include an equal opportunity clause (41 C.F.R. § 60-1.4), and contractors must file compliance reports after receiving the award and annual compliance reports thereafter (41 C.F.R. § 60-1.7(a)) with the federal contracting agency. In addition to their equal opportunity provisions, the executive orders and regulations place heavy emphasis on affirmative action by federal contractors, as discussed in Section 4.6 of this book.

The regulations implementing these executive orders exempt various contracts and contractors (41 C.F.R. § 60-1.5), including church-related educational institutions defined in Title VII (41 C.F.R. § 60-1.5(a)(5)). While the regulations contain a partial exemption for state and local government contractors, "educational institutions and medical facilities" are specifically excluded from this exemption (41 C.F.R. § 60-1.5(a)(4)). The enforcing agency may hold compliance reviews (41 C.F.R. § 60-1.20), receive and investigate complaints from employees and applicants (41 C.F.R. §§ 60-1.21 to 60-1.24), and initiate administrative or judicial enforcement proceedings (41 C.F.R. § 60-1.26(a)(1)). It may seek orders enjoining violations and providing other relief, as well as orders terminating, canceling, or suspending contracts (41 C.F.R. § 60-1.26(b)(2)). The enforcing agency may also seek to debar contractors from further contract awards (41 C.F.R. § 60-1.27(b)).

The requirements of the executive orders are enforced by the Office of Federal Contract Compliance Programs (OFCCP), located within the U.S. Department of Labor. The regulations require each federal contractor subject to the executive orders to develop a written affirmative action program (AAP) for each of its establishments. In 2000, a provision was added at 41 C.F.R. § 60-2.1(d)(4) that permits federal contractors to develop AAPs organized by business or functional unit rather than by geographical location.

The regulations interpreting the executive orders and explaining the enforcement process were revised, and a final rule was published at 165 Fed. Reg. 68022-47 (November 13, 2000). The final rule can be accessed from the OFFCP Web site. Other regulations elaborate on how contractors must define who is considered an "applicant" and how demographic information should be collected, particularly with respect to online applications. These regulations were published at 70 Fed. Reg. 58946–58963 and are found at 41 C.F.R. Part 60-1.

The primary remedy for violation of the executive orders is cutoff of federal funds, debarment from future contracts, or both. Individuals alleging employment discrimination by federal contractors have sought to file discrimination claims in court but have been rebuffed. For example, in *Weise v. Syracuse University*, 522 F.2d 397 (2d Cir. 1975), two women faculty members filed sex discrimination claims against the university under authority of the executive orders. Their claims were dismissed; the court found no private right of action in the executive orders. Similar outcomes occurred in *Braden v. University of Pittsburgh*, 343 F. Supp. 836 (W.D. Pa. 1972), *vacated on other grounds*, 477 F.2d 1 (3d Cir. 1973), and *Cap v. Lehigh University*, 433 F. Supp. 1275 (E.D. Pa. 1977).

**4.5.2.9. *Laws prohibiting sexual orientation discrimination*.** Discrimination on the basis of sexual orientation is not prohibited by Title VII, nor is there any other federal law directed at such discrimination. However, twenty states and the District of Columbia prohibit employment discrimination on the basis of sexual orientation in both the public and private sectors,[5] and numerous municipalities have enacted similar local laws prohibiting such discrimination.

---

[5] As of early 2013, the following states prohibited discrimination on the basis of sexual orientation in both private and public sector employment: California, Colorado, Connecticut, Hawaii, Illinois, Iowa, Maine, Maryland, Massachusetts, Minnesota, Nevada, New Hampshire, New Jersey, New Mexico, New York, Oregon, Rhode Island, Vermont, Washington, and Wisconsin. The District of Columbia also prohibits such discrimination in both private and public employment. See http://www.nolo.com/legal-encyclopedia/sexual-orientation-discrimination-rights-29541.html. In several other states, governors have issued executive orders (or rescinded earlier such orders) prohibiting discrimination on the basis of sexual orientation for the state's public employees.

Employment issues related to sexual orientation go beyond the issues—such as discipline, discharge, or salary discrimination—faced by other protected class members. Access to benefits for unmarried same-sex partners and access to campus housing reserved for heterosexual couples add to the complexity of dealing with this issue.

The U.S. Supreme Court has not yet ruled in a case directly involving alleged employment discrimination on the basis of sexual orientation. The Court's opinion in *Oncale*, discussed in Section 4.5.2.1 of this book, involved same-sex sexual harassment, rather than sexual orientation discrimination, and was brought under Title VII. In 2003, the Court overruled its earlier holding in *Bowers v. Hardwick*, 478 U.S. 186 (1986), that had upheld a Georgia law criminalizing sodomy. In *Lawrence v. Texas*, 539 U.S. 558 (2003), the Court struck down a Texas law that made sodomy a criminal offense on due process clause grounds. The Court stated that the individuals' "right to liberty under the Due Process Clause gives them the full right to engage in private conduct without government intervention . . . The Texas statute furthers no legitimate state interest which can justify its intrusion into the individual's personal and private life."

In contrast, the Court upheld the right of the Boy Scouts of America to exclude homosexuals from positions as volunteer leaders, ruling that the First Amendment's freedom of association protections prohibited New Jersey from using its nondiscrimination law, which includes sexual orientation as a protected class, to require that the Boy Scouts accept leaders who are homosexual (*Boy Scouts of America v. Dale*, 530 U.S. 640 (2000)).

Although the EEOC's enforcement responsibility does not extend to sexual orientation discrimination, state and federal courts have been more responsive to sexual orientation discrimination claims brought under 42 U.S.C. § 1983 (see Section 3.4 of this book), alleging violations of the Fourteenth Amendment's equal protection clause. For example, in *Miguel v. Guess*, 51 P.3d 89 (Wash. Ct. App. 2002), a state appellate court rejected the employer's motion to dismiss a claim brought by a hospital employee under Section 1983 that her dismissal was a result of her sexual orientation and that the dismissal violated the equal protection clause. Although the employee was allowed to proceed on her Section 1983 claim, the court rejected her claim that a dismissal based on one's sexual orientation violated the public policy of the State of Washington because at the time of the litigation, the state legislature had not enacted a law prohibiting discrimination on the basis of sexual orientation (although it later did so). Similarly, in *Lovell v. Comsewogue School District*, 214 F. Supp. 2d 319 (E.D.N.Y. 2002), a federal trial court denied the school district's motion to dismiss a teacher's claims that the school principal was less responsive to claims of sexual orientation harassment than he was to other types of harassment claims. The court stated that treating harassment complaints on the basis of sexual orientation differently than other types of harassment claims was, if proven, an equal protection clause violation, actionable under Section 1983. In contrast, a college that responded promptly to a staff member's complaints of sexual orientation harassment was successful in obtaining a summary judgment when the staff member resigned and then sued under Section 1983, asserting an equal protection clause violation (*Cracolice v. Metropolitan Community College*, 2002 U.S. Dist. LEXIS 22283 (D. Neb., November 15, 2002)).

Although not all same-sex harassment claims involve claims of sexual orientation discrimination, there is considerable overlap between the two. Same-sex harassment claims are potentially actionable under Title VII, while claims of sexual orientation discrimination or harassment are much more difficult to maintain. (The following discussion is adapted from Mary Ann Connell and Donna Euben, "Evolving Law in Same-Sex Sexual Harassment and Sexual Orientation Discrimination," 31 *J.Coll. & Univ. Law* 193 (2004).)

The U.S. Supreme Court recognized a cause of action for same-sex sexual harassment in *Oncale v. Sundowner Offshore Services*, 523 U.S. 75 (1997), discussed in Section 4.5.2.1 of this book. Connell and Euben divide post-*Oncale* claims of same-sex harassment into three categories: (1) "desire" cases, in which there is evidence that the harasser sexually desires the target; (2) "hatred" cases, in which there is evidence that the harasser is hostile to the presence of a particular sex in the workplace; and (3) cases in which the court examines the alleged harasser's treatment of both sexes in the workplace.

An illustrative "desire" case is *Mota v. University of Texas Houston Health Science Center*, 261 F.3d 512 (5th Cir. 2001). The plaintiff claimed that he was harassed repeatedly by his male supervisor and department chair, who made unwanted and offensive sexual advances toward the plaintiff on several occasions at out-of-town conferences. The jury found for the plaintiff against the university (the alleged harasser had settled with the plaintiff prior to trial); the appellate court upheld the jury verdict, ruling that the university had failed to respond properly and to correct the harassment.

"Hatred" cases involve claims that the plaintiff was harassed either because he or she did not conform to gender stereotypes or because the alleged harasser was motivated by contempt for the individual's sexual orientation. Plaintiffs bringing hatred cases based on sex stereotyping have been successful in a limited number of cases, but plaintiffs attempting to attack alleged harassment based on sexual orientation have usually been unsuccessful under Title VII. For example, the U.S. Court of Appeals for the Ninth Circuit found for a plaintiff who claimed that he was harassed because his behavior did not conform to the male stereotype. In *Nichols v. Azteca Restaurant Enterprises*, 256 F.3d 864 (9th Cir. 2001), the court ruled that a four-year pattern of verbal abuse by coworkers based on the plaintiff's effeminate behavior violated Title VII. But those courts that have characterized a same-sex harassment claim as grounded in sexual orientation discrimination rather than stereotyping have rejected plaintiffs' Title VII claims (see, for example, *Dandan v. Radisson Hotel Lisle*, 2000 U.S. Dist. LEXIS 5876 (N.D. Ill. March 28, 2000)), even if the harassment was instigated by individuals who disliked the plaintiff's nonconforming behavior.

An *en banc* ruling by the U.S. Court of Appeals for the Ninth Circuit, if followed by other circuits, may enable plaintiffs to establish sexual orientation harassment claims under Title VII. In *Rene v. MGM Grand Hotel, Inc.*, 243 F.3d 1206 (9th Cir. 2001), *reversed and remanded*, 305 F.3d 1061 (9th Cir. 2002) (*en banc*), the plaintiff asserted that he had endured severe and pervasive offensive physical conduct of a sexual nature, including numerous assaults, because of his perceived homosexuality. The trial court had granted the employer's motion for summary judgment, ruling that the plaintiff had not stated a claim under Title VII because the law did not prohibit discrimination on the basis of sexual orientation. A split three-judge panel of the Ninth Circuit agreed. That ruling was vacated, and the eleven-judge *en banc* court reversed. With four dissenting votes, the judges ruled that

> an employee's sexual orientation is irrelevant for purposes of Title VII. It neither provides nor precludes a cause of action for sexual harassment. That the harasser is, or may be, motivated by hostility based on sexual orientation is similarly irrelevant, and neither provides nor precludes a cause of action. It is enough that the harasser have [*sic*] engaged in severe or pervasive unwelcome physical conduct of a sexual nature. We therefore would hold that the plaintiff in this case has stated a cause of action under Title VII [305 F.3d at 1063–64].

The *en banc* court justified its reasoning by explaining that the conduct in *Rene* was similar to the offensive conduct in *Oncale*, which occurred in an all-male work environment, as did the harassment in *Rene*. But the ruling in this case appears to be a departure from the language of *Oncale*, which states that the offensive conduct must be directed at the target because of his or her sex; *Rene* appears to base its ruling on the sexual nature of the conduct, not the sex of the target. Two judges wrote opinions concurring in the result, but stating that they believed the proper theory of the case was sexual stereotyping, citing the Ninth Circuit's opinion in *Nichols*, discussed above. The dissenters disagreed with the majority's assertion that the sex or motive of the harasser was irrelevant as long as the conduct was sexual in nature.

The third category of post-*Oncale* cases involves claims that both men and women were subject to offensive sexualized treatment at work. In these cases, if the employer can demonstrate that both sexes were equally subject to the same type of offensive behavior, there is no Title VII violation (see, for example, *Holman v. Indiana*, 211 F.3d 399 (7th Cir. 2000)). But in some cases, the courts have ruled that the motives for the sexualized treatment of men were different than the motives of the offensive behavior toward women and have allowed the claims to go forward (see, for example, *Steiner v. Showboat Operating Company*, 25 F.3d 1459 (9th Cir. 1994)).

Title IX prohibits discrimination on the basis of sex at colleges and universities receiving federal funds, and its enforcement guidelines specifically address the possibility of claims involving same-sex discrimination or harassment (Office of Civil Rights, "Revised Sexual Harassment Guidance: Harassment of Students by School Employees, Other Students, or Third Parties" (available at http://www2.ed.gov/offices/OCR/archives/pdf/shguide.pdf)). Most federal courts, however, have ruled that claims of employment discrimination cannot be brought under Title IX because Title VII provides the federal remedy for sex discrimination.

In addition to employment discrimination or harassment claims, some colleges have faced litigation concerning the availability of medical and other benefits for the partners of gay employees. Access to employment benefits for the partners of homosexual employees is a matter generally governed by state or local law. Several states have enacted laws permitting same-sex marriages or establishing civil unions, both of which would entitle partners of employees to seek benefits for their spouses or domestic partners. Unless state law forbids it, a college may offer benefits to unmarried domestic partners and may choose to limit this benefit to same-sex domestic partners on the ground that they are not allowed to marry in the majority of states where same-sex marriage is not yet legal.

Unmarried heterosexual individuals have been unsuccessful in claiming that providing benefits to unmarried same-sex couples, but not to unmarried opposite-sex couples, violates a state's nondiscrimination law on the basis of sex or sexual orientation. See, for example, *Miller v. University of Vermont*, 24 VLRB 1 (2001), in which an unmarried faculty member claimed that the university's refusal to provide medical and dental benefits to his female domestic partner violated the university's own policies against discrimination on the basis of sexual orientation. Shortly after the Vermont civil union law was passed, the university notified all of its employees that dependents (whose definition includes spouses or "same-sex spousal equivalents") would be entitled to medical and dental benefits only if the employee was either married to the spouse or had entered a civil union with a "same-sex spousal equivalent." The labor board reasoned that there was no disparate impact on unmarried heterosexual employees with domestic partners because there was no legal impediment to their marrying. Now that employees could qualify for health benefits for spouses by either marrying or entering a civil union, there was no disparate impact on the ground of sexual orientation. The labor board denied Miller's claim. For additional cases reaching the same conclusion, see *Irizarry v. Board of Education of Chicago*, 83 FEP Cases 808 (N.D. Ill. 2000), *affirmed*, 251 F.3d 604 (7th Cir. 2001) (denying that the employer had violated the Fourteenth Amendment's equal protection clause), and *Foray v. Bell Atlantic*, 56 F. Supp. 2d 327 (S.D.N.Y. 1999) (finding no sex discrimination).

As this book was going to press, the U.S. Supreme Court ruled, in *United States v. Windsor*, 133 S. Ct. 2675 (2013), that the Defense of Marriage Act, which effectively denied federal benefits to spouses of same-sex married couples, violated the Constitution's Fifth Amendment equal liberty protections. Thus, federal benefits, such as Social Security survivor benefits, must be available to the spouses of same-sex married couples.

***4.5.2.10. Laws prohibiting transgender discrimination.*** Although at the time this book went to press no federal law prohibited employment discrimination on the basis of transgender status (typically referred to as "gender identity or expression"), the laws of sixteen states and the District of Columbia did.[6] An additional

---

[6] As of early 2013, the following states prohibited employment discrimination on the basis of gender identity or expression: California, Colorado, Connecticut, Illinois, Iowa, Maine, Massachusetts, Minnesota, Nevada, New Jersey, New Mexico, Oregon, Rhode Island, Vermont, and Washington. The District of Columbia also prohibits such discrimination.

five states prohibit such discrimination in public employment.[7] And the federal EEOC has ruled that discrimination based on gender identity or transgender status is a form of sex discrimination and thus violates Title VII (*Macy v. Holder*, EEOC Appeal No. 0120120821 (April 20, 2012)).

The "category" of transgendered individuals is fluid and resistant to labels. Individuals who are transgendered may identify with a different biological sex than that with which they were born, they may identify with neither biological sex, or they may identify with both. There is a rich literature about this issue, and many points of view. Most agree, however, that the term "sex" is biologically determined, while "gender" is culturally determined. (For a brief review of gender identity from a medical perspective, see http://emedicine. medscape.com/article/917990-overview.) The purpose of this section is to sketch out developments in the law that provide some protection for individuals who are denied employment or harassed because of their gender identity or expression.

Although Title VII does not include specific protections for individuals discriminated against on the basis of gender identity or expression, some plaintiffs have had success challenging such discrimination under the *Price Waterhouse* theory of sex stereotyping, a theory developed by the U.S. Supreme Court in *Price Waterhouse v. Hopkins*, 490 U.S. 228 (1989). For example, the court in *Smith v. City of Salem, Ohio*, 378 F.3d 566 (6th Cir. 2004), permitted the plaintiff, a biologically male firefighter who was disciplined after beginning the process of sexual reassignment, to state a claim under the *Price Waterhouse* theory, and in *Barnes v. Cincinnati*, 401 F.3d 729 (6th Cir. 2005), a federal appellate court affirmed a jury verdict for a police officer who alleged that his demotion was a result of transgender discrimination. A federal trial court ruled that the plain language of Title VII permits claims of discrimination by transgendered individuals. Plaintiffs have also had some success stating claims for transgender employment discrimination under the equal protection clause. For example, in *Glenn v. Brumby*, 632 F. Supp. 2d 1308 (N.D. Ga. 2009), the plaintiff's case survived the employer's motion to dismiss her Section 1983 claim, based on the equal protection clause.

Transgendered individuals have also been permitted to state claims of harassment on the basis of gender identity or expression under both Title VII and state law. See, for example, *Mitchell v. Axcan Scandipharm, Inc.*, 2006 U.S. Dist. LEXIS 6521 (W.D. Pa. Feb. 21. 2006) (stating that *Price Waterhouse* precludes dismissal of plaintiff's claims of sexual harassment and discriminatory discharge under Title VII), and *Del Piano v. Atlantic County*, 2005 U.S. Dist. LEXIS 20250 (D.N.J. Sept. 2, 2005) (stating that a cause of action exists under the New Jersey Law Against Discrimination for a corrections officer who alleged harassment and discrimination for cross-dressing while not at work).

---

[7] Indiana, Kansas, Kentucky, Michigan, and Pennsylvania.

## Section 4.6. Affirmative Action[8]

**4.6.1. Overview.** Affirmative action has been an intensely controversial concept in many areas of American life. While the ongoing debate on affirmative action in student admissions (see Section 7.2.5 of this book) parallels in its intensity the affirmative action debate on employment, the latter has been even more controversial because it is more crowded with federal regulations and requirements. In addition, beneficiaries of affirmative action in employment may be more visible because they compete for often-scarce openings, particularly for faculty or other professional positions.

Affirmative action in employment is governed by federal Executive Orders 11246 and 11375 (Section 4.5.2.8 of this book) and related federal contracting statutes, by Title VII of the Civil Rights Act of 1964 (Section 4.5.2.1 of this book), and by the equal protection clause of the Constitution's Fourteenth Amendment (Section 4.5.2.7 of this book). The affirmative action requirements of the executive orders apply to contractors with fifty or more employees who receive federal contracts of at least $50,000 (which covers most colleges and universities), while the equal protection clause applies only to public colleges and universities. Title VII applies to both private and public colleges. Each of these authorities poses somewhat different obligations for employers and involves different legal analyses.

Affirmative action became a major issue because the federal government's initiatives regarding discrimination have a dual aim: to "bar like discrimination in the future" and to "eliminate the discriminatory effects of the past" (*Albemarle Paper Co. v. Moody*, 422 U.S. 405 (1975)). Addressing this latter objective under Title VII, courts may "'order such affirmative action as may be appropriate'" (*Franks v. Bowman Transportation Co.*, 424 U.S. 747 (1976), quoting *Albemarle*). Affirmative action can be appropriate under *Franks* even though it may adversely affect other employees, since "a sharing of the burden of the past discrimination is presumptively necessary." Under statutes other than Title VII, and under Executive Orders 11246 and 11375, courts or administrative agencies may similarly require employers, including public and private postsecondary institutions, to engage in affirmative action to eliminate the effects of past discrimination.

Executive Orders 11246 and 11375 have been the major focus of federal affirmative action initiatives. Aside from their basic prohibition of race, color, religion, sex, and national origin discrimination, these executive orders require federal contractors and subcontractors employing fifty or more employees and receiving at least $50,000 in federal contracts to develop affirmative action plans. The implementing regulations were revised in 2000 (65 Fed. Reg. 68022–47, November 13, 2000) and are codified at 41 C.F.R. Parts 60-1 and 60-2. Section 60-1.40 of the regulations requires that a contractor have an affirmative action program. Section 60-2.10 of the regulations lists the required elements of an affirmative action program. One requirement is "placement goals" (41 C.F.R. § 60-2.16), which the contractor must establish in light of the availability of women and minorities for each job group. The regulation states that "placement goals may not be rigid and inflexible quotas which must be met, nor

---

[8] This section was revised and updated by Jonathan R. Alger, former senior vice president and general counsel at Rutgers University and currently president of James Madison University.

are they to be considered as either a ceiling or a floor for the employment of particular groups. Quotas are expressly forbidden" (41 C.F.R. § 60-2.16 (e)(1)).

An institution's compliance with affirmative action requirements is monitored and enforced by the Office of Federal Contract Compliance Programs (OFCCP), located in the U.S. Department of Labor. The OFCCP may also conduct an investigation of an institution's employment practices before a federal contract is awarded.

Postsecondary institutions contracting with the federal government are also subject to federal affirmative action requirements regarding persons with disabilities and veterans. "Qualified" persons with disabilities are covered by Section 503 of the Rehabilitation Act of 1973 (29 U.S.C. § 793), which requires affirmative action "to employ and advance in employment qualified individuals with disabilities" on contracts of $10,000 or more.

A variety of laws regarding the employment and training of veterans are codified at 38 U.S.C. § 4212. The law specifies that organizations that enter a contract with the U.S. government worth $100,000 or more must "take affirmative action to employ and advance in employment qualified covered veterans" (38 U.S.C. § 4212(a)(1)). Covered veterans include both disabled and nondisabled veterans who served on active duty "during a war or in a campaign or expedition for which a campaign badge has been authorized." The law regarding veterans thus has a broader scope than Section 503.

Under the various affirmative action provisions in federal law, the most sensitive nerves are hit when affirmative action creates "reverse discrimination"—that is, when the employer responds to a statistical "underrepresentation" of women or minorities by granting employment preferences to members of the underrepresented or previously victimized group, thus discriminating "in reverse" against other employees or applicants. Besides creating policy issues of the highest order, such affirmative action measures create two sets of complex legal questions: (1) To what extent does the applicable statute, executive order, or implementing regulation require or permit the employer to utilize such employment preferences? (2) What limitations does the Constitution place on the federal government's authority to require or permit, or the employer's authority to utilize, such employment preferences, particularly in the absence of direct evidence of discrimination by the employer?

The response to the first question depends on a close analysis of the particular legal authority involved. The answer is not necessarily the same under each authority. In general, however, federal law is more likely to require or permit hiring preferences when necessary to overcome the effects of the employer's own past discrimination than it is when no such past discrimination is shown or when preferences are not necessary to eliminate its effects. Section 703(j) of Title VII, for instance, relieves employers of any obligation to give "preferential treatment" to an individual or group merely because of an "imbalance" in the number or percentage of employed persons from that group compared with the number or percentage of persons from that group in the "community, state, section, or other area" (42 U.S.C. § 2000e-2(j)). But where an imbalance does not arise innocently but, rather, arises because of the employer's discriminatory practices, courts in Title VII suits have sometimes required the use of hiring preferences or goals to remedy the effects of such discrimination (see, for example, *Local 28 of the Sheet Metal Workers' International Ass'n. v. EEOC*, 478 U.S. 421 (1986)).

Constitutional limitations on the use of employment preferences by public employers stem from the Fourteenth Amendment's equal protection clause. (See the discussion of that clause's application to admissions preferences in Section 7.2.5 of this book.) Even if the applicable statute, executive order, or regulation is construed to require or permit employment preferences, such preferences may still be invalid under the federal Constitution unless a court or an agency has found that the employer has discriminated in the past. Courts have usually held hiring preferences to be constitutional where necessary to eradicate the effects of the employer's past discrimination, as in *Carter v. Gallagher*, 452 F.2d 315 (8th Cir. 1971). Where there is no such showing of past discrimination, the constitutionality of employment preferences is more in doubt.

The U.S. Supreme Court has analyzed the legality of voluntary affirmative action plans and race- or gender-conscious employment decisions made under the authority of these plans. The cases have involved sharp divisions among the Justices and are inconsistent in several ways. Furthermore, the Court's decision in *Grutter v. Bollinger*, 539 U.S. 306 (2003), discussed in Section 7.2.5 of this book, arose in the context of student admissions rather than employment, and its implications for employment are not clear. Moreover, changes in the composition of the Court may alter its stance on the legality of voluntary affirmative action in employment. Therefore, the analysis of Supreme Court jurisprudence in the area of affirmative action is difficult, and predictions about future directions of the Court in this volatile area are nearly impossible.

### 4.6.2. Affirmative action under Title VII.

The U.S. Supreme Court has addressed challenges to employment decisions in cases of both voluntary and court-ordered affirmative action plans. The Court has issued a few rulings involving voluntary affirmative action plans in employment that were challenged under Title VII under a "reverse discrimination" theory. In its first examination of a voluntary affirmative action plan involving a private employer, the Court strongly endorsed the concept.

In *Weber v. Kaiser Aluminum Co.*, 443 U.S. 193 (1979), the Court considered a white steelworker's challenge to an affirmative action plan negotiated by his union and employer. The plan provided for a new craft-training program, with admission to be on the basis of one black worker for every white worker selected. The race-conscious admission practice was to cease when the proportion of black skilled craft workers at the plant reflected the proportion of black workers in the local labor force. During the first year the plan was in effect, the most junior black worker selected for the training program was less senior than several white workers whose requests to enter the training program were denied. One of those denied admission to the program filed a class action claim, alleging "reverse discrimination."

The federal district court ruled that the plan unlawfully discriminated against white employees and therefore violated Title VII of the Civil Rights Act (415 F. Supp. 761 (E.D. La. 1976)), and the appellate court affirmed (563 F.2d 216 (5th Cir. 1978)). In a 5-to-2 decision written by Justice Brennan, the Supreme Court reversed, ruling that employers and unions in the private sector may take race-conscious steps to eliminate "manifest racial imbalance" in "traditionally segregated job categories." Such action, the Court said, does not run afoul of Title VII's prohibition on racial discrimination (see Section 4.5.2.1 of this book).

The Court considered Weber's claim that, by giving preference to junior black employees over more senior white employees, the training program discriminated against white employees in violation of the 1964 Civil Rights Act. Because the employment action did not involve state action, no constitutional issues were involved. The Court framed the issue as an inquiry into whether private parties could voluntarily agree to give racial preferences such as those in the collective bargaining agreement.

After reviewing the legislative history describing the concerns that led Congress to pass Title VII, the Court stated that, given Title VII's intent, voluntary efforts to achieve greater racial balance in the workforce did not violate the law. Thus concluding that the use of racial preferences in hiring is sometimes permissible, the Court went on to uphold the Kaiser plan in particular. In doing so, the Court found it unnecessary to set forth detailed guidelines for employers and unions. Instead, it identified several factors that courts in subsequent cases have used to measure the lawfulness of affirmative action programs.

First, there was a "manifest racial imbalance" in the job categories for which Kaiser had established the special training program. While the percentage of blacks in the area workforce was approximately 39 percent, fewer than 2 percent of the craft jobs at Kaiser were filled by black workers. Second, as the Court noted in a footnote to its opinion, these crafts had been "traditionally segregated"; rampant discrimination in the past had contributed to the present imbalance at Kaiser. Third, the Court emphasized that the plan in *Weber* did not "unnecessarily trammel" the interests of white employees; it did not operate as a total bar to whites, and it was temporary, designed to bring minority representation up to that of the area's workforce rather than to maintain racial balance permanently.

These factors cited by the Court left several questions open: How great a racial imbalance must there be before it will be considered "manifest"? What kind of showing must be made before a job category will be considered "traditionally segregated"? At what point will the effects of a plan on white workers be so great as to be considered "unnecessary trammeling"? These questions were raised in a subsequent challenge to a gender-conscious employment decision made under the authority of an affirmative action plan, this time by a public employer. To date, it is the only Supreme Court analysis of gender preferences in employment.

In *Johnson v. Transportation Agency, Santa Clara County*, 480 U.S. 616 (1987), Paul Johnson, who had applied for a promotion, alleged that the agency had promoted a less qualified woman, Diane Joyce, because of her gender, in violation of Title VII. In a 6-to-3 opinion, the Supreme Court, relying on its *Weber* precedent, held that neither the affirmative action plan nor Joyce's promotion violated Title VII.

As is the practice in many public agencies, the agency's promotion policies permitted the decision maker to select one of several individuals who were certified to be minimally qualified for the position in question—in this case, a road maintenance dispatcher. Both Joyce and Johnson, as well as several other men, had been rated "qualified," although Johnson's total score (based on experience, an interview, and other factors) was slightly higher than Joyce's.

The agency had developed an affirmative action plan that attempted to increase the number of women and racial minorities in jobs in which they were traditionally underrepresented. The agency had not submitted evidence of any prior discrimination on its part, but noted the statistical disparities between the proportion of potentially qualified women and their low representation in certain occupations.

The majority opinion, written by Justice Brennan, first addressed the burden-of-proof issue. It is up to the plaintiff, wrote Brennan, to establish that the affirmative action plan is invalid. In assessing the plan's validity, the Court applied the tests from *Weber*. First, the plan had to address a "manifest imbalance" that reflected underrepresentation of women in traditionally segregated job categories. Statistical comparisons between the proportion of qualified women in the labor market and those in segregated job categories would demonstrate the imbalance. Regarding the employer's responsibility for that imbalance, the majority rejected the notion that the employer must demonstrate prior discrimination, a requirement that would be imposed if the case had been brought under the equal protection clause of the Fourteenth Amendment.

Having determined that the affirmative action plan satisfied the first part of the *Weber* test, the majority then examined whether the plan "unnecessarily trammeled" the rights of male employees or created an absolute bar to their advancement. Finding that Johnson had no absolute entitlement to the promotion, and that he retained his position, salary, and seniority, the majority found that the plan met the second *Weber* test.

The majority then assessed whether the plan was a temporary measure, the third requirement of *Weber*. Although the plan was silent with regard to its duration, the Court found that the plan was intended to attain, rather than to maintain, a balanced workforce, thus satisfying the third *Weber* test. Justice Brennan wrote that "substantial evidence shows that the Agency has sought to take a moderate, gradual approach to eliminating the imbalance in its work force, one which establishes realistic guidance for employment decisions, and which visits minimal intrusion on the legitimate expectations of other employees" (480 U.S. at 640).

Both the *Weber* and the *Johnson* cases involved voluntary affirmative action plans that were challenged under Title VII. A year before *Johnson*, the Supreme Court had addressed the legality, under Title VII, of race-conscious hiring and promotion as part of court-ordered remedies after intentional discrimination had been proved. One issue in both cases centered on whether individuals who had not been actual victims of discrimination could benefit from race-conscious remedies applied to hiring and promotion. In both cases, the Supreme Court upheld those remedies in situations where lower courts had found the discrimination to be egregious (*Local 93, International Association of Firefighters v. City of Cleveland*, 478 U.S. 501 (1986), and *Local 28 of the Sheet Metal Workers' International Ass'n. v. EEOC*, 478 U.S. 421 (1986)).

In *Ricci v. DeStefano*, 557 U.S. 557 (2009), the Supreme Court decided a case requiring the balancing of Title VII's prohibition on policies or practices that are not intended to discriminate but in fact have a disproportionately adverse impact on minorities, 42 U.S.C. §200e-2(k)(1)(A)(i) (disparate impact), with the prohibition on intentional acts of employment discrimination based on race, color, religion, sex, and national origin, §200e-2(a)(1) (disparate treatment). The City of New Haven, Connecticut, had refused to certify promotion test results after learning that those results showed that white candidates outperformed candidates from racial groups that were traditionally underrepresented in higher-level positions within the fire department. The city argued that it could have faced Title VII liability for adopting a practice that would have had a disparate impact on minority firefighters, while the (mostly white) plaintiffs argued that the city's decision amounted to deliberate "reverse discrimination" against their interests.

In a 5-to-4 decision, a sharply divided Supreme Court held as follows:

> Under Title VII, before an employer can engage in intentional discrimination for the asserted purpose of avoiding or remedying an unintentional, disparate impact, the employer must have a strong basis in evidence to believe that it will be subject to disparate-impact liability if it fails to take the race-conscious, discriminatory action [129 S. Ct. at 2661].

The Court's decision suggests that institutions should choose selection criteria with care in the context of hiring and promotions. Much of the Court's analysis focused on the expectations that were created by the system that the city had put in place using the tests. Institutions of higher education may be unlikely to use easily quantifiable, "objective" criteria as the sole basis on which to hire or promote candidates—especially when it comes to faculty (although institutions may find that they are using more quantifiable measures with at least some other types of staff positions). Nevertheless, the decision in *Ricci* should lead institutions to think carefully before setting specific numerical criteria (such as publication of a specific number of articles) from which they might subsequently decide to deviate. If institutional practices make clear that a variety of factors will be considered in a holistic manner (much like the admissions analysis under *Grutter*) in hiring and promotions—consistent with their educational mission—they can help to manage expectations of all parties involved and avoid the difficult position in which the City of New Haven found itself.

A challenge to an affirmative action hiring program at Illinois State University resulted in a ruling against the university. In *United States v. Board of Trustees of Illinois State University*, 944 F. Supp. 714 (C.D. Ill. 1996), the U.S. Department of Justice filed a Title VII lawsuit against the university, asserting that a program designed to circumvent veterans' preferences by filling custodial positions through a "learner's program" violated the statute. White males were not selected for the learner's program, as it was limited to women and to nonwhite males. The court ruled that the program failed all of the *Weber* tests in that it did not remedy a manifest imbalance, its purpose was to circumvent the veterans' preference rather than to remedy prior discrimination, and it trammeled the rights of white males who wished to be employed in these jobs.

Despite the difficulty of translating the outcome in *Grutter* to the employment context, it appears that employers who can demonstrate a "manifest imbalance" and whose voluntary affirmative action plans—and actions taken under their guidance—can pass the *Weber* test, may be able to practice affirmative action in hiring and promotion decisions. But the lessons of *Grutter* and its companion case, *Gratz*, discussed in Section 7.2.5 of this book, should be heeded, so that these programs are not practicing racial balancing or using quotas to accomplish the goal of diversity.

**4.6.3. Affirmative action under the equal protection clause.** The U.S. Supreme Court has also addressed the validity of affirmative action plans—both voluntary and involuntary—under the equal protection clause. In these cases, courts subject the plan to a "**strict scrutiny**" standard of review, requiring proof that remedying the targeted discrimination is a "compelling government interest" and that the plan's race- or gender-conscious employment criteria are "narrowly tailored" to accomplish the goal of remedying the targeted discrimination.

In *United States v. Paradise*, 480 U.S. 149 (1987), an involuntary (or mandatory) affirmative action case, federal courts had ordered that 50 percent of the promotions to corporal for Alabama state troopers be awarded to qualified black candidates. The lower courts found that the state police department had systematically excluded black candidates for more than four decades, and for another decade had resisted following court orders to increase the proportion of black troopers. The Supreme Court, in a 5-to-4 decision, found ample justification to uphold the one-black-for-one-white promotion requirement imposed by the lower federal courts.

The United States, acting as plaintiff in this case, argued that the remedy imposed by the court violated the equal protection clause. Justice Brennan, writing for the majority, noted that the Court had yet to agree on the appropriate standard of review for affirmative action cases brought under the equal protection clause. He refused to do so in *Paradise* because "we conclude that the relief ordered survives even strict scrutiny analysis: it is 'narrowly tailored' to serve a 'compelling [governmental] purpose'" (480 U.S. at 167). In reaching this conclusion, the majority determined that "the pervasive, systematic, and obstinate discriminatory conduct of the Department created a profound need and firm justification for the race-conscious relief ordered by the District Court" (480 U.S. at 167). The Court left for another day the delineation of more specific equal protection guidelines for remedial affirmative action plans.

The Supreme Court's opinion in *Paradise*, like its opinions in *Weber, Sheet Metal Workers, Cleveland Firefighters*, and *Johnson* (all Title VII cases analyzed in Section 4.6.2 above), involved promotions or other advancement opportunities that did not result in job loss for majority individuals. When affirmative action plans are used to justify racial preferences in layoffs, however, the response of the Supreme Court has been quite different. In *Firefighters v. Stotts,*

467 U.S. 561 (1984), for example, the Court invalidated a remedial consent decree that approved race-conscious layoff decisions in order to preserve the jobs of more recently hired minorities under the city's affirmative action plan.

In another case, *Wygant v. Jackson Board of Education*, 476 U.S. 267 (1986), the Supreme Court addressed the issue of voluntary racial preferences in reductions-in-force. The school board and the teachers' union had responded to a pending race discrimination claim by black teachers and applicants for teaching positions by adopting a race-conscious layoff provision in their collective bargaining agreement. The agreement specified that, if a layoff occurred, those teachers with the most seniority would be retained, except that at no time would there be a greater percentage of minority personnel laid off than the percentage of minority personnel employed at the time of the layoff. A layoff occurred, and the board, following the bargaining agreement, laid off some white teachers with more seniority than minority teachers who were retained in order to meet the proportionality requirement. The more senior white teachers challenged the constitutionality of the contractual provision. Both the federal district court and the U.S. Court of Appeals for the Sixth Circuit upheld the provision as permissible action taken to remedy prior societal discrimination and to provide role models for minority children. In a 5-to-4 decision, the Court reversed the lower courts, concluding that the race-conscious layoff provision violated the equal protection clause. In a plurality opinion by Justice Powell, four Justices agreed that the bargaining agreement provision should be subjected to the "strict scrutiny" test used for other racial classifications challenged under the equal protection clause (476 U.S. at 274, citing *Fullilove v. Klutznick*, 448 U.S. 448, 480). The fifth Justice concurring in the judgment, Justice White, did not address the strict scrutiny issue.

Rejecting the school board's argument that remedying societal discrimination provided a sufficient justification for the race-conscious layoffs, the plurality opinion stated:

> This Court never has held that societal discrimination alone is sufficient to justify a racial classification. Rather, the Court has insisted upon some showing of prior discrimination by the governmental unit involved before allowing limited use of racial classifications in order to remedy such discrimination [476 U.S. at 274].

The plurality then discussed the Court's ruling in *Hazelwood School District v. United States*, 433 U.S. 299 (1977), which established a method for demonstrating the employer's prior discrimination by comparing qualified minorities in the relevant labor market with their representation in the employer's workforce. The correct comparison was of teachers to qualified blacks in the labor market, not of minority teachers to minority children. Moreover, said the plurality:

> [B]ecause the role model theory does not necessarily bear a relationship to the harm caused by prior discriminatory hiring practices, it actually could be used to

escape the obligation to remedy such practices by justifying the small percentage
of black teachers by reference to the small percentage of black students [476
U.S. at 275–76].

Having rejected the "societal discrimination" and "role model" arguments,
and having found no history of prior discrimination by the school board, the
plurality concluded that the school board had not made the showing of a compelling interest required by the strict scrutiny test.

In a concurring opinion, Justice O'Connor considered whether it was necessary for a public employer to make specific findings of prior discrimination at
the time it adopted an affirmative action plan. She concluded that requiring
such a finding would be a powerful disincentive for a public employer to initiate a voluntary affirmative action plan and stated that "a contemporaneous or
antecedent finding of past discrimination by a court or other competent body
is not a constitutional prerequisite to a public employer's voluntary agreement
to an affirmative action plan" (476 U.S. at 289). But the employer should "act
on the basis of information which gives [the public employer] a sufficient basis
for concluding that remedial action is necessary" (476 U.S. at 291), so that findings by a court or an enforcement agency would be unnecessary. As long as the
public employer had a "firm basis for believing that remedial action is required"
(476 U.S. at 286), presumably through evidence demonstrating statistical disparity between the proportion of minorities in the qualified labor market and
those in the workforce, a state's interest in affirmative action could be found
to be "compelling." In addition, in a comment with potential significance for
proponents of affirmative action as a tool to promote racial diversity, O'Connor
noted: "Although its precise contours are uncertain, a state interest in the promotion of racial diversity has been found sufficiently 'compelling,' at least in the
context of higher education, to support the use of racial considerations in furthering that interest" (476 U.S. at 286; citing *Bakke*, discussed in Section 7.2.5).

Justice Marshall, in a dissent joined by Justices Brennan and Blackmun,
characterized the case quite differently from the plurality:

> The sole question posed by this case is whether the Constitution prohibits
> a union and a local school board from developing a collective-bargaining
> agreement that apportions layoffs between two racially determined groups
> as a means of preserving the effects of an affirmative hiring policy, the
> constitutionality of which is unchallenged [476 U.S. at 300].

Justice Marshall found that the school board's goal of preserving minority representation of teachers was a compelling interest under the factual record presented to the court. He concluded that the contractual provision was narrowly
tailored because it neither burdened nor benefited one race but, instead, substituted a criterion other than absolute seniority for layoff decisions.

Two later Supreme Court cases, *Croson* and *Adarand* (below), confirm
the applicability of the strict scrutiny test to affirmative action programs and
provide additional guidance on use of the narrow tailoring test. In addition,

although these cases did not involve employment, they suggest that public employers may need to demonstrate a history of race or sex discrimination in employment, rather than simply a statistical disparity between minority representation in the workforce and the labor market. In *City of Richmond v. J. A. Croson Co.*, 488 U.S. 469 (1989), the Court, again sharply divided, ruled 6 to 3 that a set-aside program of public construction contract funds for minority subcontractors violated the Constitution's equal protection clause. Applying the strict scrutiny test, a plurality of Justices (plus Justice Scalia, using different reasoning) ruled that the city's requirement that prime contractors awarded city construction contracts must subcontract at least 30 percent of the amount of each contract to minority-owned businesses was not justified by a compelling governmental interest and that the set-aside requirement was not narrowly tailored to accomplish the purpose of remedying prior discrimination.

The Supreme Court extended its analysis of *Croson* in *Adarand Constructors v. Pena*, 515 U.S. 200 (1995), a case involving contracts awarded by the U.S. Department of Transportation (DOT). Adarand, the low bidder on a subcontract for guard rails for a highway project, mounted an equal protection challenge under the Fifth Amendment to the DOT's regulations concerning preferences for minority subcontractors. The regulations provided the prime contractor with a financial incentive to award subcontracts to small businesses certified as controlled by "socially and economically disadvantaged" individuals. Adarand was not so certified, and the contract was awarded to a certified subcontractor whose bid was higher than Adarand's.

In a 5-to-4 ruling, the Court held that "all racial classifications, imposed by whatever federal, state, or local governmental actor, must be analyzed by a reviewing court under strict scrutiny." The Court then remanded the case for a trial on the issue of whether the federal contracting program's subcontracting regulations met the strict scrutiny test.

Since *Croson* and *Adarand*, litigation challenging race- or gender-conscious employment decisions, most of which involves challenges by white male police officers or firefighters to race- or gender-conscious hiring and promotion decisions, has often focused squarely on the employer's ability to demonstrate its own prior discrimination. Affirmative action plans were invalidated in *Middleton v. City of Flint*, 92 F.3d 396 (6th Cir. 1996), *cert. denied*, 520 U.S. 1196 (1997); *Dallas Fire Fighters Association v. City of Dallas*, 150 F.3d 438 (5th Cir. 1998), *cert. denied*, 526 U.S. 1046 (1999); and *Alexander v. Estepp*, 95 F.3d 312 (4th Cir. 1996), *cert. denied*, 520 U.S. 1165 (1997). The courts in these cases determined either that there was insufficient data indicating the employer's discrimination or that the race-conscious provisions were not sufficiently narrowly tailored. However, in three other cases—*Majeske v. City of Chicago*, 218 F.3d 816 (7th Cir. 2000); *Danskine v. Miami Dade Fire Department*, 253 F.3d 1288 (11th Cir. 2001); and *Boston Police Superior Officers Federation*, 147 F.3d 13 (1st Cir. 1998)—affirmative action plans were upheld. The respective appellate courts cited substantial evidence of prior discrimination, and determined that the employers' race- or gender-conscious hiring and promotion criteria were narrowly tailored remedies for that discrimination.

The U.S. Supreme Court's decisions in *Gratz v. Bollinger* and *Grutter v. Bollinger*, both discussed in Section 7.2.5 of this book, concerned the diversity rationale for affirmative action rather than the remedying prior discrimination rationale, and neither case directly concerned employment. These cases therefore do not add to or change the analysis in *Croson* and *Adarand* or the lower court cases applying this analysis. But *Gratz* and *Grutter* do indirectly raise the important question of whether the diversity rationale, recognized in those cases for affirmative action in admissions, may have some applicability to employment affirmative action.

### 4.6.4. State regulation of affirmative action. In 1996, California voters approved Proposition 209, a state constitutional provision that prohibits public organizations from having affirmative action employment programs. The provision also applies to college admissions. This constitutional provision was used to invalidate a California state law (Cal. Educ. Code §§ 87100–107) that required each community college district to have an affirmative action plan. The purpose of the plans was to "hire and promote persons who are underrepresented in the work force compared to their number in the population," including disabled individuals, women, and racial and ethnic minorities (Cal. Educ. Code § 87101(d)).

In *Connerly v. State Personnel Board*, 92 Cal. App. 4th 16 (Ct. Ct. App., 3d Dist. 2001), a group of plaintiffs challenged this law, and others involving affirmative action in the sale of state bonds, in the state lottery, and in the state civil service system. Although a state trial court had upheld the law, ruling that the community college law did not require the colleges to grant preferential treatment to any particular group, a state appellate court reversed, ruling that the law was incompatible with Proposition 209.

Voters in the states of Washington, Michigan, Nebraska, and Arizona have also approved ballot questions that outlawed the use of affirmative action in employment or admissions decisions (see Section 7.2.5 of this book). In July 2011 a federal appeals court held that those portions of a Michigan voter referendum (Proposal 2) that affected Michigan's public institutions of higher education violated the equal protection clause because the ban had a racial focus and had reordered the political process so as to place special burdens on racial minorities (*Coalition to Defend Affirmative Action v. Regents of the University of Michigan et al.*, 652 F.3d 607 (6th Cir. 2011)). The full Sixth Circuit vacated this opinion, however, and agreed to rehear the case *en banc* (2011 U.S. App. LEXIS 18875 (6th Cir. Sept. 9, 2011)). The *en banc* court agreed with the earlier panel decision that the amendment violated the equal protection clause because the amendment reordered the political process by placing a special burden on racial minorities (701 F.3d 466 (2012)). The plaintiffs appealed to the U.S. Supreme Court, and the Court agreed to hear the case in its 2013–14 term (*Schuette v. Coalition to Defend Affirmative Action*, 133 S. Ct. 1633 (2013)).

If the U.S. Supreme Court affirms the *en banc* opinion, it could encourage subsequent challenges to similar ballot initiatives in other states.

***4.6.5. Conclusions.*** The collective implications of the complex decisions discussed in Sections 4.6.1 to 4.6.4 above, and especially the sharp differences of opinion among the Supreme Court Justices regarding the lawfulness of race- or gender-conscious employment decisions, mean that employment decisions linked to affirmative action should be made with caution. It appears that private institutions that can meet the tests of *Weber* and *Johnson* by documenting "manifest" underrepresentation of women or minority faculty or staff in certain positions in that there is a substantial gap between the proportion of qualified women and minorities in the relevant labor market and their representation in the institution's faculty workforce, may be able to act in conformance with a carefully developed affirmative action plan.

Public colleges and universities located in states subject to *Adams* agreements (see Section 11.5.2) will very likely have an easier time meeting the standards of the equal protection clause for voluntary affirmative action plans. Furthermore, for public institutions operating under the dictates of a judicially supervised consent decree regarding remedies for prior discrimination, the Civil Rights Act of 1991 has removed the threat of challenges to remedial employment decisions made under the aegis of the consent decree. In *Martin v. Wilks*, 490 U.S. 755 (1989), the Supreme Court had ruled that any nonparty to the litigation culminating in a consent decree could later challenge both the decree and employment decisions made in conformance with that decree. Congress overturned the result in *Martin v. Wilks* by adding a new subsection to Section 703 of Title VII of the Civil Rights Act of 1964 (42 U.S.C. § 2000e-2). The law now provides that a litigated or consent judgment may not be challenged by a person who had actual notice of the proposed judgment or order prior to its entry and an opportunity to object or by a person whose interests were adequately represented by another person who had challenged the judgment or order.

For public colleges and universities that do not have a clearly documented history of prior discrimination, or that are unwilling to rely on such a rationale, it will apparently be necessary to rely on a diversity rationale in any attempt to justify the use of race or gender preferences in employment. In such a situation, to maximize its chance of success, the institution would need to demonstrate clearly how affirmative action–related hiring or promotion will promote the benefits of educational diversity that the Court found to be a compelling state interest in *Grutter* and *Gratz*. This showing may depend upon the specifics of each job or position covered by the affirmative action plan. For example, the race, gender, or national origin of a residence hall counselor or a teaching assistant might be linked to educational diversity, whereas it might be more difficult to demonstrate this linkage for a dining service worker, custodian, or groundskeeper.

## Section 4.7. Application of Nondiscrimination Laws to Religious Institutions

A major coverage issue under federal and state employment discrimination statutes is their applicability to religious institutions, including religiously affiliated colleges and universities. The issue parallels those that have arisen under federal collective bargaining law (see *NLRB v. Catholic Bishop of Chicago*, 440 U.S. 490 (1979), unemployment compensation law (see *St. Martin Evangelical Lutheran Church v. South Dakota*, 451 U.S. 772 (1981)), and federal tax law (see *Bob Jones University v. United States*, 461 U.S. 574(1983)). Title VII (see Section 4.5.2.1 of this book), the primary federal employment discrimination statute, has been the focus of most litigation on religious institutions.

Section 702(a) of Title VII, 42 U.S.C. § 2000e-1(a), specifically exempts "a religious corporation, association, educational institution, or society" from the statute's prohibition against religious discrimination "with respect to the employment of individuals of a particular religion" if they are hired to "perform work connected with the carrying on by such corporation, association, educational institution, or society of its activities."[9] The phrase "its activities" is not addressed in the statute, and it was unclear whether the organization's "activities" had to be closely related to its religious mission to be included within the exemption or whether all of the organization's activities would be exempt. The U.S. Supreme Court addressed this issue in *Corporation of the Presiding Bishop of the Church of Jesus Christ of Latter-day Saints v. Amos*, 483 U.S. 327 (1987), a case concerning a challenge to the Mormon Church's decision that all employees working for a gymnasium owned by the church but open to the public must be members of the Mormon Church. The plaintiffs argued that, although Section 702(a) could properly be applied to the religious activities of a religious organization, the First Amendment's establishment clause did not permit the government to extend the exemption to jobs that had no relationship to religion. The Supreme Court held that Section 702 does not distinguish between secular and religious job activities, and that the Section 702 exemption could apply to all job positions of a religious organization without violating the establishment clause. The Court reasoned that Section 702's purpose is to minimize governmental interference with the decisions of religious organizations, and it would be "a significant burden on a religious organization to require it, on pain of substantial liability, to predict which of its activities a secular court will consider religious" (483 U.S. at 336).

Section 702(a) was also at issue in *Killinger v. Samford University*, 917 F. Supp. 773 (N.D. Ala. 1996), *affirmed*, 113 F.3d 196 (11th Cir. 1997)—as was Section 703(e)(2) (42 U.S.C. § 2000e-2(e)(2)), another Title VII provision providing a similar exemption for some religiously affiliated schools. Section 703(e)(2) applies to any "school, college, university, or other educational institution" that is "owned, supported, controlled, or managed by a particular

---

[9] A college need not be affiliated with a particular denomination in order to receive the protection of the Section 702(a) exemption. In *Wirth v. College of the Ozarks*, 26 F. Supp. 2d 1185 (W.D. Mo. 1998), for example, a federal district court ruled that the College of the Ozarks was a religious organization that qualified for the exemption despite the fact that the college is a nondenominational Christian organization. Significant indicators of its religious nature were that the college's mission is to provide a "Christian education," that it belongs to the Coalition for Christian Colleges, and that it is a member of the Association of Presbyterian Colleges and Universities. The appellate court affirmed the trial court's ruling in an unpublished *per curiam* opinion (2000 U.S. App. LEXIS 3549 (8th Cir. 2000)).

religion or religious corporation, association, or society." Institutions fitting this characterization are exempted from Title VII with respect to "hir[ing] and employ[ing] employees of a particular religion." In *Killinger*, the plaintiff was a faculty member at Samford University, a private institution affiliated with the Baptist faith. He alleged that administrators at Samford would not permit him to teach certain religion courses at its Beeson Divinity School because of the theological and philosophical positions that Killinger had taken. In defense, the university invoked the Section 702(a) and Section 703(e)(2) exemptions. The major issue was whether the university was a "religious" institution or was supported or controlled by a "religious" entity for purposes of the exemptions. The federal district court, and then the appellate court, determined that the university is religious and is supported by a religious entity, and therefore applied both exemptions. The courts reasoned that the university was controlled by the Baptists, since all of its trustees were required to be practicing Baptists; that its students were required to attend religious convocations; and that university publications emphasized the religious nature of the education provided. Moreover, Samford received a substantial proportion of its budget (7 percent) from the Alabama Baptist State Convention, and the university required all faculty to subscribe to the Baptist Statement of Faith and Message. Both the Internal Revenue Service and the U.S. Department of Education recognized Samford as a religious institution. The appellate court noted that the substantial contribution from the Baptist Convention was sufficient, standing alone, to bring the university within the reach of Section 703(e)(2), since the university was "supported" in "substantial part" by a religious corporation.

In *Pime v. Loyola University of Chicago*, 803 F.2d 351 (7th Cir. 1986), the court used a different provision of Title VII to protect a religious institution's autonomy to engage in preferential hiring. Affirming a lower court ruling (585 F. Supp. 435 (N.D. Ill. 1984)), the appellate court held that membership in a religious order can be a "bona fide occupational qualification" (BFOQ) within the meaning of Section 703(e)(1) (42 U.S.C. §2000e-2(e)(1)) of Title VII. The plaintiff, who was Jewish, had been a part-time lecturer in the university's philosophy department when it adopted a resolution requiring that seven of the department's thirty-one tenure-track positions be reserved for Jesuit priests. The court, finding a historical relationship between members of the religious order and the university, concluded that the Jesuit "presence" was a significant aspect of the university's educational traditions and character, and important to its successful operation.

But in *EEOC v. Kamehameha Schools*, 990 F.2d 458 (9th Cir. 1993), the court distinguished *Pime* and ruled that two private schools could not restrict their hiring to Protestant Christians, even though the will that established the schools so required. The court examined the schools' ownership and affiliation, their purpose, the religious affiliations of the students, and the degree to which the education provided by the schools was religious in character, concluding that the schools did not fit within the Section 702(a) exemption. The court then also ruled that being Protestant was not a bona fide occupational qualification for employment at the schools.

The cases above provide substantial clarification of Title VII's application to religious preferences in employment used by religious colleges and universities. What emerges is a balanced interpretation of the Section 702(a) and 703(e)(2) exemptions, and the BFOQ exception, against the backdrop of First Amendment law. It is clear that these statutory exemptions protect only employment decisions based on the religion of the applicant or employee. In most circumstances, the First Amendment does not appear to provide any additional protection for religious colleges' use of religious preferences in employment decisions. The two exemptions and the BFOQ exception provide the full extent of protection that the First Amendment requires.

Although Title VII, as construed in *Amos, Killinger, Pime,* and *Kamehameha Schools,* sanctions religious preferences in employment for religious institutions that qualify for the pertinent exemptions, the statute does not exempt religious institutions from its other prohibitions on race, national origin, and gender discrimination. If an institution seeks to escape these prohibitions, it must rely on the religion clauses of the First Amendment. (See, for example, *EEOC v. Mississippi College,* 626 F.2d 477 (5th Cir. 1980); and see generally Section 1.6.2 of this book.)

The most prominent First Amendment exception to the applicability of Title VII's race, sex, and national origin prohibitions is the "ministerial exception." In the context of religious seminaries, this exception was recognized in *EEOC v. Southwestern Baptist Theological Seminary,* 651 F.2d 277 (5th Cir. 1981), in which the court exempted the seminary from Title VII nondiscrimination requirements when making employment decisions regarding its faculty and administrators "who equate to or supervise faculty."

Later cases have extended the ministerial exception beyond the context of seminaries. In *EEOC v. Catholic University,* 83 F.3d 455 (D.C. Cir. 1996), for example, Sister McDonough, a Catholic nun in the Dominican Order, challenged a negative tenure decision at Catholic University. She had been hired as an assistant professor in the department of canon law, the first woman to hold a tenure-track position in the department. Five years later, she was promoted to associate professor and shortly afterward submitted an application for tenure. After a series of split votes and revotes at various levels of review, McDonough was ultimately denied tenure after a negative vote of the Academic Senate's Committee on Appointments and Promotions. McDonough, joined by the EEOC, filed a Title VII sex discrimination claim against the university. The district court determined that it could not review the university's tenure decision because McDonough's role in the department of canon law was the "functional equivalent of the task of a minister," and judicial review would therefore violate both the free exercise and the establishment clauses of the First Amendment (856 F. Supp. 1 (D.D.C. 1994)). In affirming, the U.S. Court of Appeals for the D.C. Circuit rejected the plaintiffs' argument that the "ministerial" exception should not apply to McDonough because she was neither an ordained priest nor did she perform religious duties. The appellate court determined, first, that ordination was irrelevant; the ministerial exception applies to individuals who perform religious duties, whether or not they have been ordained. Second, the court determined that McDonough's duties were indeed religious because the department's mission was to instruct students in "the fundamental body of ecclesiastical laws" and, as the only department in the United States empowered by the Vatican to confer ecclesiastical degrees in canon law, the mission of its faculty, including McDonough, was "to foster and teach sacred doctrine and the disciplines related to it" (quoting from the university's Canonical Statutes). Furthermore, said the court, it was irrelevant that the tenure denial had not been on religious grounds. The act of reviewing the employment decision of a religious body concerning someone with "ministerial" duties was offensive to the U.S. Constitution, regardless of the basis for the decision.

Subsequent to, and consistent with, the *Catholic University* case, other U.S. courts of appeals have agreed that the "ministerial exception" defense is not limited to claims of persons who have been ordained as ministers. In *Hollins v. Methodist Healthcare Inc.*, 474 F.3d 223 (6th Cir. 2007), for example, the court applied the exception to "a resident in [a] hospital's clinical pastoral education program," reasoning that the exception depends on "the function of the plaintiff's employment position rather than the fact of ordination." And in *Petruska v. Gannon University*, 462 F.3d 294 (3d Cir. 2006), the court applied the exception to a vice president for mission and ministry and, by extension, to other administrators whose "primary duties" include supervising employees who perform "spiritual functions." In addition, the court in *Petruska* extended the ministerial exception defense to any decisions of the religious institution, and its officers and administrators, that concern "spiritual functions"—specifically, decisions "about who would perform spiritual functions and about how those functions would be divided" or otherwise structured.

In 2012, the U.S. Supreme Court spoke, for the first time, on the existence and breadth of the ministerial exception. In *Hosanna-Tabor Evangelical Lutheran Church and School v. EEOC*, 132 S. Ct. 694 (2012), the Court ruled unanimously that allowing an employee with religious duties to sue a religious organization for employment discrimination contravened both the free exercise and establishment clauses of the First Amendment. The plaintiff taught at an elementary school operated by the Lutheran Church. In addition to teaching nonreligious subjects, she taught religion, occasionally led school-sponsored religious services, and led her students in daily prayer. She had completed a program of theological study leading to commissioning by the Lutheran Church as a minister, although she had not been ordained. Commissioned ministers, who were known as "called teachers," served open-ended terms and could be dismissed only for cause and after a "supermajority" vote of the church congregation. Lay teachers, in contrast, were hired on annual contracts.

After two years of teaching, the plaintiff, Cheryl Perich, became ill and was diagnosed with narcolepsy, causing her to suddenly fall into a deep sleep from which she could not be roused. The school gave her a medical leave at the beginning of the school year and hired a lay teacher to replace her for that year. When Perich sought to return to work in the middle of the school year, the administration refused, saying that she was not ready and that they had replaced her for the rest of the year. When Perich continued to insist that she could work and threatened to sue the school, the congregation voted to rescind her "calling" and Perich was dismissed. She then filed a charge with the Equal Employment Opportunity Commission (EEOC) under the Americans with Disabilities Act (ADA) (see Section 4.5.2.5 of this book), claiming both disability discrimination and retaliation. The EEOC filed suit on Perich's behalf, in which she intervened. The school claimed that the First Amendment's religion clauses prohibited the court from addressing Perich's claims and that Perich's threat to sue the school was contrary to the church's religious belief that "Christians should resolve their disputes internally," justifying her dismissal.

The case eventually reached the U.S. Supreme Court, which, in an opinion by Chief Justice Roberts, examined the background and rationale for the First Amendment's establishment and free exercise clauses, concluding that the ministerial exception was necessary to effectuate their intent. Turning to the application of the exemption to the case at hand, the Court refused to craft a "rigid formula" for determining which employees would qualify as ministers; instead, the appropriate approach for a court faced with such a claim was to examine "all the circumstances" of each individual's employment. The Court noted Perich's religious training, her certification as a minister, her title as a "called" teacher, the religious nature of many of her job responsibilities, the fact that she called herself a minister, and the tax breaks she received because of her ministerial duties. It also noted that, despite the fact that Perich's religious duties occupied only 45 minutes of her time each week, the amount of time spent was only one of several factors to be considered. (The Court also noted that its ruling applied to state nondiscrimination laws as well as federal nondiscrimination laws.)

In response to the EEOC's claims that a ruling for the school would seriously affect its ability to combat discrimination, the Court replied:

> The case before us is an employment discrimination suit brought on behalf of a minister, challenging her church's decision to fire her. Today we hold only that the ministerial exception bars such a suit. We express no view on whether the exception bars other types of suits, including actions by employees alleging breach of contract or tortious conduct by their religious employers . . .
>
> The interest of society in the enforcement of employment discrimination statutes is undoubtedly important. But so too is the interest of religious groups in choosing who will preach their beliefs, teach their faith, and carry out their mission. When a minister who has been fired sues her church alleging that her termination was discriminatory, the First Amendment has struck the balance for us. The church must be free to choose those who will guide it on its way [132 S. Ct. at 710].

Although all the Justices joined Chief Justice Roberts' opinion as to the outcome of the case, there were two separate concurrences. Justice Thomas did not think that a court should evaluate on a case-by-case basis whether any particular individual is a "minister," but should accept the religious organization's "good faith understanding" of which employees qualify for the ministerial exception. And Justices Alito and Kagan objected to the term "minister," since that term is used by Protestants, but not by other religious groups. In their view, the exception "should apply to any 'employee' who leads a religious organization, conducts worship services or important religious ceremonies or rituals, or serves as a messenger or teacher of its faith" (132 S. Ct. at 669).

Another type of exception for religious institutions was recognized in a 2006 case, *Curay-Cramer v. Ursaline Academy*, 450 F.3d 130 (3d Cir. 2006). This exception, like the ministerial exception, provides some protection for religious institutions against employees' claims of sex, race, or national origin discrimination. Also, like the ministerial exception, the *Curay-Cramer* exemption is not in the statute as such but rather is based on the First Amendment religion clauses. In this case, a dismissed female instructor argued that her dismissal constituted sex discrimination because the defendant academy had treated her more harshly than the male employees who had committed similar offenses—in this case, supporting women's abortion rights, an act directly contrary to the teachings of her employer, a Catholic institution. The court determined that an analysis of the plaintiff's claim would implicate the academy's religious mission and its religious reasons for the dismissal. "We [the court] would have to measure the degree of severity of various violations of church doctrine." "[W]e would be meddling in matters related to a religious organization's ability to define the parameters of what constitutes orthodoxy." It would be "impossible to avoid inquiry into a religious employer's religious mission or the plausibility of its religious justification for an employment decision."

The court thus concluded that, when a religious employer's religious mission would be jeopardized in this way by a court's review of a gender discrimination claim (or other discrimination claim based on 42 U.S.C. § 2000e-2a of Title VII), the court may not proceed. Court review under such circumstances would raise "serious constitutional questions" under the religion clauses. Moreover, in the legislative history of Title VII, "Congress has not manifested an affirmative intention to apply the statute to a religious employer in the face of such constitutional difficulties." The court made it clear, however, that this exception is a limited one and that many gender (and presumably race and national origin) discrimination claims would not raise serious constitutional issues under the religion clauses.

The *Hosanna-Tabor* case and the other "ministerial exception" cases discussed above, along with the exception recognized in *Curay-Cramer*, serve to make substantial inroads into the general understanding that Title VII's prohibitions on race, sex, and national origin discrimination apply to religious higher education institutions. The *Hosanna-Tabor* and *Curay-Cramer* exceptions clarify the extent to which religiously affiliated organizations may be free from the obligation to comply with the Title VII nondiscrimination requirements—and apparently also from similar requirements under other employment discrimination statutes, such as the ADA that was at issue in *Hosanna-Tabor*. Unlike the exceptions for religious discrimination discussed above in this section, which are based on express statutory provisions, the *Hosanna-Tabor* (ministerial) exception and the *Curay-Cramer* (religious mission) exception derive from the First Amendment religion clauses, and their future development will depend upon judicial interpretation of these clauses.

PART THREE

# THE COLLEGE AND ITS FACULTY

# 5

# Special Issues in Faculty Employment

*Chapter 5 focuses on legal issues specifically related to faculty employment. The sources of faculty members' contracts and the rights that they afford faculty members are discussed, as well as the application of "academic custom and usage," a concept that helps courts interpret contract terms that are unclear or that do not address the question raised in the case. After a brief review of faculty collective bargaining under both federal and state law, the chapter examines the application of nondiscrimination law to faculty employment decisions such as hiring, promotion, tenure, and the termination of tenure. It also provides examples of judicial deference to academic judgments that undergird faculty employment decisions and examples of judicial remedies for tenure denials that have been found to be discriminatory. The chapter then examines how courts review an institution's application of its standards and criteria for faculty employment decisions, particularly denial of promotion or tenure; and how courts review institutional compliance (or noncompliance) with the procedural requirements for employment decisions, in both the public and the private sector.*

## Section 5.1. Overview

The legal relationship between a college or university and its **faculty** members is defined by an increasingly complex web of principles and authorities. In general, this relationship is governed by the common law doctrines, statutes, and constitutional provisions discussed in Chapter 4. The particular applications of this law to faculty may differ from its applications to other employees, however, because courts and administrative agencies often take account of the unique characteristics of institutional customs and practices regarding faculty (such as tenure) and of academic freedom principles that protect faculty members but not all other employees. Therefore, special protections for faculty may emanate from contract law (see especially Section 5.2), labor relations law (Section 5.3), employment discrimination law (Sections 5.4 and 5.5), and, in public institutions, constitutional law (see especially Sections 5.6 and 5.7) and public employment statutes and regulations. Federal regulations also affect the faculty employment relationship.

## Section 5.2. Faculty Contracts

**5.2.1. Overview.** The special nature of a college's relationship with its faculty complicates the development and interpretation of faculty contracts. The college may enter formal written contracts with individual faculty members, or it may simply send an annual letter stating the faculty member's teaching and other obligations for the year. The college may have a faculty handbook that discusses faculty governance rights and responsibilities, or it may have a detailed, collectively negotiated agreement with an agent of the faculty (or both). Particularly for faculty at private colleges, contracts are a very important source of faculty and institutional rights and responsibilities. Faculty at public colleges may enjoy rights created by statute, but public colleges are making increasing use of contracts to define and delimit faculty—and institutional— rights and responsibilities.

Contracts are governed by common law, which may vary considerably by state. As is the case for non-faculty employees (see Section 4.2.1), faculty handbooks and oral promises to faculty have been ruled to create binding contracts in some states, whereas other state courts have rejected this theory. For example, in *Sola v. Lafayette College*, 804 F.2d 40 (3d Cir. 1986), a faculty member sought to maintain a cause of action for tenure denial by relying on the faculty handbook's language concerning affirmative action. The court ruled that such language had contractual status and provided the faculty member with a cause of action. Similarly, in *Arneson v. Board of Trustees, McKendree College*, 569 N.E.2d 252 (Ill. App. Ct. 1991), the court ruled that the faculty manual was a contract; however, a state appellate court in Louisiana reached the opposite result in *Stanton v. Tulane Univ. of La.*, 777 So. 2d 1242 (La. Ct. App. 2001). In *Yates v. Board of Regents of Lamar University System*, 654 F. Supp. 979 (E.D. Tex. 1987), an untenured faculty member who had no written contract challenged a midyear dismissal, asserting that oral representations made by the institution's officials constituted a contract not to be dismissed prior to the end of the academic year. The court, in denying summary judgment for the university, agreed that oral promises and policies could create an implied contract, citing *Perry v. Sindermann* (see Section 5.7.2.1). However, if an institution has a written tenure policy, a faculty member's claim that he gained tenure through an unwritten, informal "understanding" will not succeed (*Jones v. University of Central Oklahoma*, 910 P.2d 987 (Okla. 1995)).

Unless a faculty handbook, individual contract, or other written policy document promises tenure, courts may be hesitant to infer that a tenure system exists. In *Tuomala v. Regent University*, 477 S.E.2d 501 (Va. 1996), for example, the Supreme Court of Virginia ruled that faculty at Regent University did not have tenure. Three professors at Regent had filed declaratory judgment suits asking the court to declare that they had tenure and could be dismissed only if they were in breach of their contracts or their academic unit were disbanded. The university defended the suits by stating that the individual contracts that the faculty had signed indicated that they were "three-year continuing contracts" that, under the terms of the faculty handbook, could be renewed annually. Determining that the language of both the contracts and the faculty handbook was ambiguous, the court reviewed testimony by members of the board of trustees concerning their intent vis-à-vis tenure. The board members denied that the university had a tenure system, stating that the three-year "continuing contracts" were a mechanism for cushioning the economic blow of job loss for a faculty member by ensuring two years of income after the faculty member's services were no longer desired. Although the university president had stated, during an accreditation team visit by the American Bar Association, that the law school faculty members were tenured, the court ruled that the president did not have the discretion to modify the trustees' determination that there would be no tenure system at Regent University.

A lawsuit brought against Cornell University shows the importance of careful drafting of offer letters to faculty. In *Weston v. Cornell University*, 868 N.Y.S.2d 364 (N.Y. App. Div. 2008), a professor who was terminated sued for breach of contract. The professor had left a tenured position at another university on the strength of a written letter that offered her "an appointment as Associate Professor with tenure," according to the court. Another section of the letter described the process for approving and conferring tenure. A later sentence stated that the university did not anticipate problems with the approval of tenure for the plaintiff. Because these three statements appeared to the court to be potentially contradictory, the appellate court reversed the trial court's partial granting of the university's motion to dismiss the breach of contract claim, saying that the matter had to be tried.

Even if written institutional policies are clear, administrators may make oral representations to faculty members or candidates for faculty positions that either contradict the written policies or that seem to create additional employment security that the institution may not have intended to provide. For example, in The *Johns Hopkins University v. Ritter* (discussed in Section 5.7.1), two faculty members with "visiting professor" titles failed to convince a state appellate court that they had tenured status on the basis of the department chair's assurances to that effect. The court rejected that argument, stating that the chair lacked both actual and apparent authority to abrogate the university's written tenure policies, which provided that only the board of trustees could grant tenure.

Some contracts clearly state that another document has been incorporated into the terms of employment. For a postsecondary institution, such documents as the faculty handbook, institutional bylaws, or guidelines of the American Association of University Professors (AAUP) may be referred to in the contract. The extent to which the terms of such outside writings become part of the faculty employment contract is discussed in *Brady v. Board of Trustees of Nebraska State Colleges*, 242 N.W.2d 616 (Neb. 1976), where the contract of a tenured professor at Wayne State College incorporated "the college bylaws, policies, and practices relating to academic tenure and faculty dismissal procedures." When the institution dismissed the professor, using procedures that violated a section of the bylaws, the court held that the termination was ineffective.

A case litigated under New York law demonstrates the significance of an institution's decision to adopt certain AAUP policy statements and not to adopt others. Fordham University had adopted the AAUP's "1940 Statement of Principles on Academic Freedom and Tenure" but not its 1973 statement "On the Imposition of Tenure Quotas," in which the AAUP opposed tenure quotas. (Both statements can be found at http://aaup.org.) Fordham denied tenure to faculty whose departments would exceed 60 percent tenured faculty if they were awarded tenure. A professor of social service who had been denied tenure because of the quota policy sued the university, claiming that the tenure quota policy violated both of the AAUP statements. In *Waring v. Fordham University*, 640 F. Supp. 42 (S.D.N.Y. 1986), the court, noting that the university had not adopted the 1973 AAUP statement, ruled that the university's action was appropriate and not a breach of contract.

On occasion a court is asked to fill in the "gaps" in a written or unwritten contract by determining what the intent of the parties was, even if that intent was not directly or indirectly expressed. The parties' intent may sometimes be ascertained from oral statements made at the time a hiring decision is made. In *Lewis v. Loyola University of Chicago*, 500 N.E.2d 47 (Ill. App. Ct. 1986), the plaintiff, a professor of medicine and chair of the pathology department at the university's medical school, argued that two letters from the dean of the medical school, in which the dean promised to recommend Dr. Lewis for early tenure consideration as soon as he obtained a license to practice medicine in Illinois, constituted a contract and that the institution's failure to grant him tenure breached that contract.

Lewis accepted the university's offer, and his official appointment letter incorporated by reference the provisions of the faculty handbook. Lewis served as chair for three years on one-year contracts; just before the expiration of the third one-year contract, he received notice relieving him of his duties as department chair and advising him that his next one-year contract would be a terminal contract.

The dean did not submit Lewis's tenure candidacy at the time he had promised to, and several months later he resigned as dean and became a full-time faculty member. Before his resignation, the dean told Lewis orally that he had forgotten to submit his name for tenure and that he would do it the following year. The dean assured Lewis that the oversight would not be harmful.

Although the university argued that the letters and the dean's oral promises should not be considered part of Lewis's employment contract, the court disagreed. Noting that "the record discloses conversations, meetings and correspondence over a period of a year," the court asserted that "[it] cannot seriously be argued that a form contract for a teaching position . . . embodied the complete agreement and understanding of the parties" (500 N.E.2d at 50). Furthermore, said the court, objective—rather than subjective—criteria were used to make the tenure decision at the medical school, and Lewis was able to demonstrate that deans' tenure recommendations were rarely reversed. The court agreed with the trial judge's finding of "ample evidence" to indicate that Lewis would have been tenured absent the dean's oversight.

Challenges to tenure denials brought by faculty against private colleges are usually framed as breach of contract claims. Many of these cases involved alleged failure by the college or its faculty and administrators to follow written policies and procedures, such as in *Berkowitz v. President and Fellows of Harvard College*, 2001 Mass. Super. LEXIS 4 (Mass. Super. Ct. January 4, 2001). In *Berkowitz*, a professor denied tenure by Harvard brought a breach of contract claim, alleging that Harvard had failed to follow its written grievance procedures as set forth in the faculty handbook. The court denied the college's motion to dismiss the claim, stating that it was reasonable for the plaintiff to rely on the procedures in the handbook.

Although judicial review is often deferential in cases involving subjective judgments about faculty performance (see the discussions of judicial deference in Sections 2.2.2 and 5.4.2), the courts will apply standard tools of contractual interpretation if the terms of the contract are unambiguous. For example, in *Ferrer v. Trustees of the University of Pennsylvania*, 825 A.2d 591 (Pa. 2002), a jury found that the university had breached the plaintiff's employment contract by punishing him for alleged research misconduct when he had been found innocent by a faculty investigative committee. Under the university's policies, the finding of the committee was binding on the institution, but the dean and provost imposed sanctions on the plaintiff despite the finding of the committee. The jury awarded Ferrer $5 million in damages. The appellate court reversed, ruling that the standard of review for decisions by the leadership of a private university was deferential and that the punishment was reasonable. The Supreme Court of Pennsylvania reversed, rejecting the deferential standard of review. The high court reinstated the jury verdict, but reduced the damage award to $2.9 million. The court emphasized that ordinary principles of contract interpretation applied to its review of the institution's compliance with its own rules and procedures. Although the court noted that it was not appropriate to review the correctness of the decision, review of the institution's procedural compliance was within the competence of the court.

Although tenured faculty are typically protected from termination from their faculty positions without reasonable cause, most faculty who also hold administrative positions do not have tenure in those administrative roles. Unless some written document provides for tenure in an administrative role, or unless a contract states that the individual will serve a specific length of time in office, courts will reject breach of contract claims brought by tenured faculty who are ousted from administrative positions, as in *Murtaugh v. Emory University*, 152 F. Supp. 2d 1356 (N.D. Ga. 2001). Contracts not only may specify faculty's duties and rights but also may have additional requirements, such as acceptance of the tenets of a particular religion (if the institution is affiliated with a religious organization) or a code of conduct. For example, several colleges and universities have promulgated policies that forbid faculty from entering into sexual relationships with students who are in their classes or under their supervision.

Given the rapid changes in state common law of contract and the interest of state legislators in the conditions of faculty employment, administrators and faculty should continually be sensitive to what institutional documents or practices are or should be part of the faculty contract. And both faculty and administrators need to understand how the law of their state interprets handbooks, policy manuals, and oral promises.

### 5.2.2. *Academic custom and usage.* As a method of contractual interpretation, a court may look beyond the policies of the institution to the manner in which faculty employment terms are shaped in higher education generally. In these cases the court may use "academic custom and usage" to determine what the parties would have agreed to had they addressed a particular issue. This interpretive device is only used, however, when the contract is ambiguous or when a court believes that a significant element of the contract is missing. If the intent of the parties is clear, the court will not look beyond the words of the contract. (See, for example, *Kashif v. Central State University*, 729 N.E.2d 787 (Ohio Ct. App. 1999). For a general discussion of academic custom and usage as an "internal" source of law, see Section 1.4.3.3.)

If a contract's wording is alleged to be unclear, a court may be persuaded to look to external writings or statements for help in interpreting the parties' intent. For example, in *Katz v. Georgetown University*, 246 F.3d 685 (D.C. Cir. 2001), the appellate court referred to writings of experts and to policy statements of the American Association of University Professors to define the meaning of "tenure" in the university's faculty handbook. And in *Greene v. Howard University*, 412 F.2d 1128 (D.C. Cir. 1969), the court looked to outside writings to determine the customs and usual practices of the institution and interpret the contract in light of such custom and usage.

The plaintiffs in *Greene* were five nontenured professors who had been fired after a university investigation purported to find that they had been involved in disorders on campus. When the university terminated the professors as of the close of the academic year, the professors asserted that the university had breached a contractual obligation to give appropriate advance notice of nonrenewal or to provide a hearing prior to nonrenewal. The court concluded: "The contractual relationship existing here, when viewed against the regulations provided for, and the practices customarily followed in, their administration, required the university in the special circumstances here involved to afford the teachers an opportunity to be heard" (412 F.2d at 1131).

The court derived the institution's customary practices from the faculty handbook, buttressed by testimony in court, even though the handbook was not specifically incorporated by reference and even though it stated that the university did not have a contractual obligation to follow the procedures for notice of nonreappointment. The professors were found to be relying "not only on personal assurances from university officials and on their recognition of the common practice of the university, but also on the written statements of university policy contained in the faculty handbook under whose terms they were employed." The court reasoned:

> Contracts are written, and are to be read, by reference to the norms of conduct and expectations founded upon them. This is especially true of contracts in and among a community of scholars, which is what a university is. The readings of the marketplace are not invariably apt in this noncommercial context . . . The employment contracts of [the professors] here comprehend as essential parts of themselves the hiring policies and practices of the university as embodied in its employment regulations and customs [412 F.2d at 1135].

Courts may also look to an institution's customary practice for assistance in understanding the reasonable expectations of the parties to the contract. For example, in *Brown v. George Washington University*, 802 A.2d 382 (D.C. 2002), a faculty member denied tenure and promotion asserted that the university had breached her employment contract because the department's written policy provided that the candidate(s) for promotion would be invited to appear before the promotion committee "to provide additional information as may appear relevant." Departmental members testified that the department had a past practice of interpreting this language as discretionary and had, in fact, excluded other candidates for promotion from the same meeting. The court ruled that the department faculty's interpretation of this policy was reasonable and not a breach of contract.

Another possible source of contractual protection for faculty could be the code of student conduct. In *McConnell v. Howard University*, 818 F.2d 58 (D.C. Cir. 1987), a professor refused to meet his class because the administration would not remove a disruptive student from the class. When the professor was discharged for failure to perform his professional duties, he sued for breach of contract, claiming that both the faculty handbook and the code of student conduct created a duty on the part of the university to protect his professional authority. The court ruled that he should have the opportunity to demonstrate that the university owed him this duty.

Although academic custom and usage can fill in gaps in the employment contract, it cannot be used to contradict the contract's express terms. An attempt to convince a court to consider academic custom and usage in determining whether tenure survived the affiliation or merger of two colleges failed because the court found that the terms of the faculty handbook were clear (*Gray v. Mundelein College*, 695 N.E.2d 1379, *appeal denied*, 705 N.E.2d 436 (Ill. 1998)).

Selective incorporation of AAUP policies into handbooks or other policy documents will bind a college (and the faculty) only with respect to those policies that are clearly incorporated (*Jacobs v. Mundelein College*, 628 N.E.2d 201 (Ill. App. Ct. 1993)). Furthermore, the college may decide to incorporate AAUP policies that regulate faculty conduct (such as its "Statement on Professional

Ethics"), but not those that protect the faculty member's rights under other AAUP policy statements (*Barham v. University of Northern Colorado*, 964 P.2d 545 (Colo. App. 1997)).

While academic custom and usage as a device for interpreting contracts is useful under some circumstances, both the faculty and the college are better served by contracts that are specific and clear with respect to their protections for each party. If the parties wish AAUP statements or other recognized sources of academic custom and usage to be used as interpretation devices, incorporating these into faculty handbooks, policy documents, or other sources of contractual rights (see Section 5.2.1) will provide more predictability in their later interpretation by courts.

### 5.2.3. Part-time faculty.

Facing ever-increasing financial constraints, many colleges and universities have increasingly turned to part-time faculty to provide instruction at considerably lower cost than hiring a full-time faculty member. Part-time faculty often are paid on a per-course basis and generally are not entitled to employee benefits such as medical insurance or pensions.

The questions being raised about part-time faculty involve such matters as pay scales, eligibility for fringe benefits (life insurance, health insurance, sick leave, sabbaticals, retirement contributions, unemployment benefits), access to tenure, rights upon dismissal or nonrenewal, and status for collective bargaining purposes. Each of these questions may be affected by two more general questions: (1) How is the distinction between a part-time and a full-time faculty member defined? (2) Are distinctions made among categories of part-time faculty members? The initial and primary source for answering these questions is the faculty contract (see Section 5.2.1). Also important are state and federal statutes and administrative rulings on such matters as defining bargaining units for collective bargaining (see *University of San Francisco and University of San Francisco Faculty Association*, 265 N.L.R.B. 1221 (1982) (approving part-time faculty unit), retirement plans, civil service classifications, faculty tenure, wage-and-hour requirements, and unemployment compensation. These statutes and rulings may substantially affect what can and cannot be provided for in faculty contracts.

Two lawsuits brought by part-time faculty in the state of Washington highlight the difficult financial and policy issues related to the heavy reliance of colleges on part-time faculty. In the first, *Mader v. Health Care Authority*, 37 P.3d 1244 (Wash. Super. Ct. 2002), a group of part-time faculty members appealed the denial of their claim for paid health care coverage during the summer. The faculty plaintiffs acknowledged that they did not teach during the summer, but based their claim on language in state regulations that provided for paid health care during the summer to "seasonal" employees. The court rejected that argument because the language of the regulation explicitly excluded employees such as the plaintiffs. The plaintiffs' second claim was equally unsuccessful. A state regulation provides that employees who teach for two consecutive academic terms are entitled to paid health care benefits; it provides that the intervening summer between the spring and fall terms does not break the consecutive nature of the teaching. The court rejected the plaintiffs' claim that this language entitled them to paid health benefits during the summer if they had taught during the spring term.

The state supreme court reversed both rulings of the superior court, stating that the state's Health Care Authority was required to make an individualized determination, based upon the employee's actual work circumstances, as to whether the employee was eligible for employer contributions to their health care coverage (70 P.3d 931 (Wash. 2003)).

The same group of plaintiffs brought a second lawsuit against the state, this time claiming that the state had miscalculated the number of hours they had taught and thus had not contributed the appropriate amount to their retirement plans. They sought adjusted contributions back to 1977, and a ruling that future contributions would be made correctly. The parties settled this case for $12 million; $8.3 million for the underpayment of retirement benefits, and $3.6 million in attorney's fees (*Mader v. State of Washington*, King Co. Cause No. 98-2-30850 SEA settlement agreement, discussed in Daniel Underwood, "Adjunct Faculty and Emerging Legal Trends," presentation to the 24th Annual National Conference on Law and Higher Education, Stetson University College of Law (February 16–18, 2003)).

Another issue relevant to the status of part-time faculty is whether full-time faculty at a community college engaged in a reduction in force can "bump" part-time faculty from courses that faculty to be laid off are qualified to teach. In *Biggiam v. Board of Trustees of Community College District No. 516*, 506 N.E.2d 1011 (Ill. App. Ct. 1987), the court was required to determine whether the Illinois Community College Tenure Act, the collective bargaining agreement between the faculty and the board, or both afforded tenured faculty the right to bump any instructor or just full-time faculty members. The court agreed with the board's argument that full-time faculty could bump nontenured or less senior faculty from "positions," but that part-time instructors were not "faculty"; they did not have "positions" but only taught courses. Thus, faculty could not bump part-time instructors from courses. Although this case rested on interpretation of a state law, it may have relevance to institutions in other states that need to reduce the number of full-time faculty.

As the proportion of part-time faculty continues to increase in relation to the proportion of full-time, tenure-track faculty, the scholarly debate continues about the propriety of using part-timers to avoid the long-term financial commitment of tenure. The AAUP has developed statements and guidelines regarding the use of part-time faculty, such as "Contingent Appointments and the Academic Profession," available at http://www.aaup.org/AAUP/pubsres/policydocs/contents/conting-stmt.htm, which contains a discussion of the status of part-time and non-tenure-track faculty and offers recommendations for their employment. The American Federation of Teachers has also issued standards for the treatment of part-time faculty members, entitled "Standards of Good Practice in the Employment of Part-Time/Adjunct Faculty" (2006). The statement can be found at http://www.aft.org/pdfs/highered/standards profstaff0106.pdf.

To respond effectively to issues involving part-time faculty, administrators should understand the differences in legal status of part-time and full-time faculty members at their institutions. In consultation with counsel, they should make sure that the existing differences in status and any future changes are adequately expressed in faculty contracts and institutional rules and regulations. Administrators should also consider the extent and clarity of their institution's legal authority to maintain the existing differences if they are challenged or to change the legal status of part-timers if changes are advisable to effectuate new educational policy.

### 5.2.4. Contracts in religious institutions.

In religious institutions, employment issues involving the interplay between religious doctrine and civil law have been litigated primarily in cases construing state and federal employment discrimination laws (see Section 4.7); however, when the faculty member is a member of a religious order or when the institution makes employment decisions on religious grounds, complex questions of contract law may also arise.

The contract made between a faculty member and a religious institution would normally be governed by state contract law unless the parties explicitly or implicitly intended that additional sources of law be used to interpret the contract. Some religiously affiliated institutions require their faculty to observe the code of conduct dictated by the doctrine of the religious sponsor; others incorporate church law or canon law into their contracts. Judicial interpretation of contracts is limited by the religion clauses of the First Amendment (see Section 1.6.2).

Conflicts between faculty and religious institutions may also arise when the faculty member's lifestyle or personal decisions do not comport with the college's religious doctrine. For example, one religious institution, Oklahoma Christian University, considered developing a policy stating that employees who obtain a divorce may lose their jobs, then decided not to have a policy but to consider whether to take action against an employee who "exhibit[s] a non-Christian marriage model" on a case-by-case basis (Scott Jaschik, "Oklahoma Christian Withdraws Divorce Policy (Sort of)," *Inside HigherEd*, January 13, 2006, available at http://insidehighered.com/news/2006/01/13/divorce). A professor who converted from Protestant to the Catholic faith was dismissed by Wheaton College (Illinois) (see "Tests of Faith," *Chron. Higher Educ.* January 12, 2006, available at http://www.insidehighered.com/news/2006/01/12/faith). And when an African-American professor at Calvin College, which requires its faculty to join a Christian Reformed Church, asked to join a black Baptist church, he was denied an exemption and his appointment was converted from a tenure track to a term appointment (see Elizabeth Redden, "When Identity Trumps Diversity," *Inside Higher Ed*, January 4, 2008, available at http://www.insidehighered.com/news/2008/01/04/calvin).

Several cases have addressed the nature of the contract between a religious institution and a faculty member. The religious institution typically argues that the U.S. Constitution's First Amendment prevents the court from reviewing the substance of the employment dispute. Both the free exercise and the establishment clauses have been invoked by religious colleges seeking to avoid judicial review of these employment disputes. In some of these cases, the courts have determined that the issues involved religious matters and that judicial intervention would be unconstitutional; in others, the court determined that only secular issues were involved and no constitutional violation was present.

In *Curran v. Catholic University of America*, Civ. No. 1562–87, 117 *Daily Wash. L.R.* 656 (D.C. Super. Ct. February 28, 1987), a tenured professor of Catholic theology filed a breach of contract claim when the university prohibited him from teaching courses involving Catholic theology. Curran had taken a public stand against several of the Catholic Church's teachings, and the Holy See had ruled him ineligible to teach Catholic theology. The university's board of trustees then withdrew Curran's ecclesiastical license, which is required of all faculty who teach in departments that confer ecclesiastical degrees. Although the university attempted to place Curran in another, nontheological teaching assignment, Curran argued that the university had constructively discharged him without a finding that he was not competent to teach Catholic theology. He also argued that the university had incorporated protections for academic freedom into his contract and that the treatment afforded him because of his scholarly beliefs constituted a violation of those protections.

The court was faced with three potential sources of contract law: District of Columbia common law, canon law, and explicit or implied contractual promises of academic freedom that were judicially enforceable (see Section 5.2.2). The court saw its duty as not to interpret canon law, which it was forbidden to do by establishment clause principles, but to determine whether the parties had intended to be bound by canon law, a question of fact. The court found that, even though his contract did not explicitly mention canon law or its requirements, Curran knew that ecclesiastical faculties were different from nonecclesiastical faculties, that the Holy See could change the requirements for ecclesiastical faculties, and that the university was obligated to accede to those changes.

The court ruled that the university had the right to require faculty who taught theology to meet the requirements of the Holy See, since that body could withdraw the university's authority to award ecclesiastical degrees if the university failed to comply with its requirements. Because the university had a special relationship with the Holy See, the court found implied in Curran's contract with the university an obligation to abide by the Holy See's requirements. The court also found that, whatever academic freedom Curran was due, his academic freedom could not limit the Holy See's authority to determine which ecclesiastical faculty were qualified to teach theology. (For a discussion of academic freedom in religious institutions, see Section 6.4.)

The New Jersey Supreme Court was faced with two cases involving the interplay between religious doctrine and civil contract law. In *Alicea v. New Brunswick Theological Seminary*, 608 A.2d 218 (N.J. 1992), an untenured assistant professor of theology who was an ordained minister claimed that the seminary's president offered him a non-tenure-track position with the promise of an eventual tenured position. When that promise was not acted upon, Alicea resigned, claiming constructive discharge and breach of contract. The ecclesiastical body that governed the seminary, the Reformed Church's Board of Theological Education (BTE), had reserved to itself all final decision-making power regarding the hiring and retention of faculty. Alicea claimed that the BTE had impliedly ratified the promise made to him by the president and that the president had the apparent authority to make such promises. The court ruled that it could not determine whether the seminary had breached an implied contract with an untenured professor because such an inquiry would constitute an inquiry into ecclesiastical polity or doctrine. Although the court refused to adopt a per se rule that courts may not hear employees' lawsuits against religious institutions, the court noted that "governmental interference with the polity, i.e., church governance, of a religious institution could also violate the First Amendment by impermissibly limiting the institution's options in choosing those employees whose role is instrumental in charting the course for the faithful" (608 A.2d at 222).

The court noted that because Alicea taught theology and counseled prospective ministers, he performed a ministerial function. Therefore, although the case involved issues of church governance (rather than doctrine, as in the *Curran* case), the court was similarly required to abstain from exercising jurisdiction.

The court outlined the analysis to be applied to such cases:

> [A] court should first ascertain whether, because of the ministerial role played by the employee, the doctrinal nature of the controversy, or the practical effect of applying neutral principles of law, the court should abstain from entertaining jurisdiction . . . In assessing the extent to which the dispute implicates issues of doctrine or polity, factors such as the function of the employee under the relationship sought to be enforced, the clarity of contractual provisions relating to the employee's function, and the defendant's plausible justifications for its actions should influence the resolution of that threshold question . . . If neither the threat of regulatory entanglement, the employee's ministerial function, nor the primarily-doctrinal nature of the underlying dispute mandates abstention, courts should effectuate the intent of the parties to the contract [608 A.2d at 223–224].

The court explained that, if compliance with the contract could be determined through the application of "neutral principles of law," then courts could enforce promises to comply with religious doctrine or waivers of rights to act in compliance with religious beliefs. Examination of the text of the contract or handbook, the type of employees supervised by the individual seeking judicial review, and the parties' positions as church officials would be relevant, as well as the apparent intent of the parties to seek judicial review of disputes arising under the contract.

The same court decided a case with similar issues on the same day as *Alicea*. In *Welter v. Seton Hall University*, 608 A.2d 206 (1992), two Ursuline nuns who had taught for three years at Seton Hall, a Catholic university, filed breach of contract claims when their contracts were not renewed. The university claimed that the sisters' order, the Ursuline Convent of the Sacred Heart, had refused permission for the sisters to continue teaching at the university and that the court lacked jurisdiction to entertain the breach of contract claims.

The New Jersey Supreme Court ruled against the university on several grounds. First, the sisters did not perform a ministerial (pastoral) function—they taught computer science. Second, the dispute did not implicate either doctrinal issues or matters of church polity; the university simply refused to honor its contractual obligation to give the untenured sisters twelve months' notice (a one-year terminal contract) before discharging them. The contract included no mention of canon law, nor did it require the sisters to obtain the permission of their religious superiors before accepting employment. It was the same contract that the university used for lay faculty. Furthermore, when the Ursuline convent requested that the university forward the sisters' paychecks directly to it, the university refused and advised the sisters to open a checking account and deposit their paychecks.

There was substantial evidence that the university desired to terminate the sisters' employment because of dissatisfaction with their performance. Instead of issuing the terminal contracts, university administrators contacted the sisters' religious superiors and asked that they be recalled. The university then terminated the sisters' employment without the required notice. The university admitted that the issue would be a completely secular one if the sisters were not members of a religious order. In deciding this case, the court applied a two-part test. First, the court analyzed whether the sisters performed any ministerial functions for the university, and found that they did not. Second, the court assessed whether the sisters could have contemplated that canon law would have superseded the procedural safeguards of the contract, and found no such evidence.

Courts have also been asked to construe the authority of religiously affiliated colleges to require lay faculty to adhere to religious doctrine in their teaching. In *McEnroy v. St. Meinrad School of Theology*, 713 N.E.2d 334 (Ind. Ct. App. 1999) (also discussed in Section 6.4), a professor of Catholic theology and doctrine at a seminary that trains candidates for the priesthood signed a statement opposing the pope's teachings on the ordination of women as priests. After learning that Professor McEnroy had signed this statement, the head of the seminary removed her as a professor. McEnroy sued for breach of contract and several related tort claims. The seminary sought dismissal of the case on First Amendment grounds, arguing that judicial review of the complaint would require the court to "decide religious issues regarding the Church's good faith motivation and doctrinal basis for removing [the plaintiff] under canon law" (713 N.E.2d at 336). The trial court agreed with the seminary's argument, and a state appellate court affirmed. Two years later, the U.S. Conference of Catholic Bishops issued "Guidelines Concerning the Academic Mandatum in Catholic Universities" (June 15, 2001), which specifies that all faculty who teach "theological disciplines" in a Catholic college or university must receive a mandatum (an acknowledgment by church authority that a Catholic professor of a theological discipline is teaching "within the full communion of the Catholic Church").

In another case, a lay faculty member was discharged by a Baptist seminary for failing to adhere to the "lifestyle and behavior" expected of a faculty member at the seminary. In *Patterson v. Southwestern Baptist Theological Seminary*, 858 S.W.2d 602 (Tex. App. 1993), a faculty member filed a wrongful discharge claim, alleging that his contractual rights had been violated. The faculty handbook required each faculty member to be an "active and faithful member of a Baptist church" and to "subscribe in writing to the Articles of Faith" of the Southern Baptist Convention. The court ruled that the explicit inclusion of these requirements in the faculty handbook made it evident that the seminary "makes employment decisions regarding faculty members largely upon religious criteria" (858 S.W.2d at 1199), rendering judicial review of the discharge decision a violation of the Constitution's First and Fourteenth Amendments.

The cases are consistent in deferring to religious institutions on matters that involve the interpretation of church doctrine (*Curran, Hartwig*) or matters of church governance. The decisions have clear implications for academic freedom disputes at religious institutions (Section 6.4), especially where issues of adherence to religious doctrine are intertwined with free speech issues. Counsel acting for religiously affiliated institutions whose leaders intend their faculty employment contracts to be interpreted under church law as well as civil contract law should specify in written contracts and other institutional documents that church law or religious doctrine will be binding on the parties to the contract and that church law will prevail in any conflict between church and civil law.

### Section 5.3. Faculty Collective Bargaining

Although the laws, cases, and doctrines discussed in Section 4.3 apply to faculty as well as to staff (and, in some cases, to students), the special nature of the faculty role has required labor boards and courts to interpret labor law in sometimes unique ways. Federal law, which regulates collective bargaining in the private sector, contains no special provisions (or exceptions) for college faculty. State law, which regulates collective bargaining in the public sector, may deal specifically with higher education (as in California), or may include college faculty with public school teachers or public employees in general (as in many other states). For this reason, faculty and administrators at public colleges need to pay special attention to their state's regulation of public sector bargaining, while the interpretation of federal labor relations law is somewhat more uniform across the country.

The National Labor Relations Board (NLRB) asserted jurisdiction over higher education in 1970 and determined in 1971 that college faculty in private institutions could organize under the protections of the National Labor Relations Act (NLRA) (see Section 4.3.2). Between 1971 and 1980, the NLRB routinely ruled that faculty were "employees" and thus were eligible to form unions under the NLRA, even if they participated in hiring, promotion, and tenure decisions and controlled the curriculum and their course content. The routine inclusion of faculty under the NLRA came to an abrupt halt, however, in 1980.

In *NLRB v. Yeshiva University*, 444 U.S. 672 (1980), the U.S. Supreme Court considered, for the first time, how federal collective bargaining principles developed to deal with industrial labor-management relations apply to private academic institutions. Adopting a view of academic employment relationships very different from that of the dissenting Justices, a bare majority of the Court denied enforcement of an NLRB order requiring Yeshiva University to bargain collectively with a union certified as the representative of its faculty. The Court held that Yeshiva's full-time faculty members were "managerial" personnel and thus excluded from the coverage of the NLRA.

In 1975 a three-member panel of the NLRB had reviewed the Yeshiva University Faculty Association's petition seeking certification as bargaining agent for the full-time faculty members of certain of Yeshiva's schools. The university opposed the petition on the ground that its faculty members were managerial or supervisory personnel and hence not covered by the NLRA. The NLRB certified the faculty association as the exclusive bargaining representative, but the university refused to bargain, maintaining that its faculty members' extensive involvement in university governance excluded them from the NLRA. When the faculty association charged that the refusal was an unfair labor practice, the NLRB ordered the university to bargain and sought enforcement of its order in federal court. The U.S. Court of Appeals for the Second Circuit denied enforcement, holding that Yeshiva's faculty were endowed with "managerial status" sufficient to remove them from the coverage of the NLRA (*NLRB v. Yeshiva University*, 582 F.2d 686 (2d Cir. 1978)).

Applying this standard to the Yeshiva faculty, the Court concluded that the faculty exercised "managerial" authority because of their "absolute" authority over academic matters, such as which courses would be offered and when; the determination of teaching methods, grading policies, and admission standards; and admissions, retention, and graduation decisions. Said the court:

> When one considers the function of a university, it is difficult to imagine
> decisions more managerial than these. To the extent the industrial analogy
> applies, the faculty determines within each school the product to be produced,
> the terms upon which it will be offered, and the customers who will be served
> [444 U.S. at 686].

The NLRB had acknowledged this decision-making function of the Yeshiva faculty but argued that "alignment with management" was the proper criterion for assessing management status. Because the faculty were not evaluated on their compliance with university policy, nor on their effectiveness in carrying out university policy, according to the NLRB, their independence would not be compromised by allowing them to unionize and negotiate with the administration. Rather than being aligned with management, said the NLRB, the faculty pursued their own professional interests and should be allowed to organize as other professional employees do.

The Court explicitly rejected the NLRB's approach, noting that "the Board routinely has applied the managerial and supervisory exclusions to professionals in executive positions without inquiring whether their decisions were based on management policy rather than professional expertise." And furthermore, said the Court, the NLRB's determination that the "professional interests of the faculty and the interests of the institution are distinct, separable entities with which a faculty member could not simultaneously be aligned" was incorrect. According to the Court, "the faculty's professional interests—as applied to governance at a university like Yeshiva—cannot be separated from those of the institution" (444 U.S. at 686–88).

Four members of the Court dissented. On behalf of these dissenters, Justice Brennan argued that the NLRB's decision should be upheld. He argued that "mature" universities had dual authority systems: a hierarchical system of authority culminating in a governing board, and a professional network that enabled professional expertise to inform and advise the formal authority system. According to Brennan, the faculty has an independent interest that underlies its recommendations, but the university retains "the ultimate decision-making authority" and defers to faculty judgment, or not, as it "deems consistent with its own perception of the institution's needs and objectives." Brennan also argued that the faculty were not accountable to the administration for their governance functions, nor did the faculty act as "representatives of management" in performing their governance roles.

Just as the Yeshiva case sparked sharp debate within the Court, it generated much dialogue and disagreement among commentators. The debate has developed on two levels. The first is whether the Court majority's view of academic governance and its adaptation of labor law principles to that context are justifiable—an issue well framed by Justice Brennan's dissenting opinion. The second level concerns the extent to which the "management exclusion" fashioned by the Court should be applied to university settings and faculty governance systems different from Yeshiva's.

The Yeshiva decision appears to create a managerial exclusion only for faculty at "Yeshiva-like," or what the Court called "mature," private universities. Even at such institutions, it is unlikely that all faculty would be excluded from bargaining under federal law. Most part-time faculty, for instance, would not be considered managers and would thus remain eligible to bargain. Legitimate questions also exist concerning faculty with "soft money" research appointments, instructors and lecturers not on a tenure track, visiting professors, and even nontenured faculty generally, at mature universities.

At private institutions that are not "Yeshiva-like," the NLRB and reviewing appellate courts have refused to apply the managerial exclusion to faculty. For example, NLRB v. Stephens Institute, 620 F.2d 720 (9th Cir. 1980), concerned the faculty of an art academy on the opposite end of the spectrum from Yeshiva. The academy was a corporation whose principal shareholder was also chief executive officer. Faculty members, except department heads, were paid according to the number of courses they taught each semester. According to the court: "The instructors at the academy . . . have no input into policy decisions and do not engage in management-level decision making. They are simply employees. Also, the academy bears little resemblance to the nonprofit 'mature' university discussed in Yeshiva."

Another case, in which the court reached a similar conclusion, concerned the faculty of a liberal arts college that was closer to Yeshiva on the spectrum than was the art academy. In *Loretto Heights College v. NLRB*, 742 F.2d 1245 (10th Cir. 1984), the court determined that "faculty participation in college governance occurs largely through committees and other such groups" and that, outside such committees, faculty members' governance roles were limited to participation in decision making "within or concerning particular program areas" in matters such as hiring and curriculum development. Concluding that the faculty's authority in institutional governance was "severely circumscribed," the court concluded that they did not meet the "managerial employee" test and thus were permitted to organize.

Attempts have been made to apply *Yeshiva* by analogy to public sector institutions, but without success. The most notable example involved the University of Pittsburgh. Although a hearing examiner for the Pennsylvania Labor Relations Board ruled that the faculty were managerial, the full board reversed that finding and allowed an election to proceed (*University of Pittsburgh*, 21 Pa. Pub. Empl. Rep. 203 (1990)). The faculty elected "no agent," rejecting union representation.

At institutions that are not "Yeshiva-like," the managerial exclusion could apply to individual faculty members who have special governing responsibilities. Department heads, members of academic senates, or members of grievance committees or other institutional bodies with governance functions could be excluded as managerial employees and have been excluded at institutions where they have supervisory authority over faculty. But the numbers involved are not likely to be so large as to preclude formation and recognition of a substantial bargaining unit.

The NLRB and state employment relations agencies make decisions about which employees should be included in the same bargaining unit on the basis of the "community of interest" of the employees. Generally, several factors have traditionally been used to determine a "community of interest," including the history of past bargaining (if any), the extent of organization, the skills and duties of the employees, and common supervision. But these factors are difficult to apply in postsecondary education's complex world of collegially shared decision making. To define the proposed unit as "all faculty members" does not resolve the issue. For example, does the unit include all faculty of the institution, or only the faculty of a particular school, such as the law school? Part-time as well as full-time faculty members? Researchers and librarians as well as teachers? Graduate teaching assistants? Chairs of small departments whose administrative duties are incidental to their primary teaching and research functions? The problems are compounded in multicampus institutions, especially if the programs offered by the individual campuses vary significantly from one another.

The question of whether department chairs or coordinators are "employees" (who are protected by the NLRA) or "supervisors" (who are not) was addressed by the NLRB in *Detroit College of Business and Detroit College of Business Faculty Association*, 296 N.L.R.B. 318 (1989). Prior to this case, the board had used the "50 percent" rule developed in *Adelphi University*, 195

N.L.R.B. 639 (1972), which stated that, unless an individual spent at least half of his or her time in supervisory functions, the supervisory exclusion did not apply. In *Detroit College of Business*, the NLRB rejected the "50 percent" rule, stating that even though the department coordinators spent the majority of their time teaching, their responsibilities to evaluate and hire part-time faculty brought them within the definition of "supervisor" and thus excluded them from the NLRA's protection. Given the breadth of this definition of supervisor, it is possible that faculty members who supervise graduate student research or teaching assistants (who are employees also) could theoretically be excluded from the protections of the NLRA.

Part-time faculty have won the right to bargain, although they may be required to form a separate bargaining unit, rather than being included with full-time faculty, if a state labor board or NLRB panel finds that they do not share a "community of interest" with full-time faculty. In most cases, part-time faculty are found not to share a community of interest with full-time faculty.

The nature of the employment relationship between part-time or adjunct faculty and their institutions has posed complex issues for labor relations agencies. For example, in *Appeal of the University System of New Hampshire Board of Trustees*, 795 A.2d 840 (N.H. 2002), the New Hampshire Supreme Court upheld the state labor board's decision to certifying a bargaining unit of adjunct faculty who had taught for the state university system, but remanded to the labor board the question of how to determine which adjuncts were "not temporary" and thus eligible for the unit. Furthermore, adjunct faculty at "mature" private universities have been given the right to unionize that has been denied to full-time faculty at those same universities under the *Yeshiva* doctrine.

Given the many possible variations from the circumstances in *Yeshiva*, faculty, administrators, and counsel can estimate the case's application to their campus only by comprehensively analyzing the institution's governance structure, the faculty's governance role in this structure, and the resulting decision-making experience.

On campuses with faculty members who would be considered "managers," bargaining does not become unlawful as a result of *Yeshiva*. The remaining faculty members not subject to exclusion may still form bargaining units under the protection of federal law. And even faculty members subject to the managerial exclusion may still agree among themselves to organize, and the institution may still voluntarily choose to bargain with them. But the administration may block the protection of federal law. Thus, for instance, faculty managers would have no federally enforceable right to be included in a certified bargaining unit or to demand good-faith bargaining over mandatory bargaining subjects. Conversely, the institution would have no federally enforceable right to file an unfair labor practice charge against a union representing only faculty managers for engaging in recognitional picketing, secondary boycotts, or other activity that would violate Section 8(b) of the NLRA (29 U.S.C. § 158(b)) if the federal law applied. A collective bargaining agreement entered through such a voluntary process could, however, be enforced in state court under the common law of contract.

## Section 5.4. Application of Nondiscrimination Laws to Faculty Employment Decisions

***5.4.1. Overview.*** Discrimination claims are particularly complex for faculty to prove and for colleges to defend against because of the subjective nature of employment decisions in academe. A successful discrimination claim generally depends on a plaintiff's ability to demonstrate unequal treatment of otherwise similar individuals. But identifying "similar" faculty members or demonstrating unequal treatment can be difficult. Particularly at institutions where faculty peers play a significant role in recommending candidates for hiring, promotion, or tenure, the locus of decision-making responsibility and the effect on upper levels of administration of potentially tainted recommendations at lower levels can be difficult to trace and to prove. Furthermore, opinions about what is "excellent" research or teaching may differ, even within the same academic department; and a plaintiff who attempts to compare herself or himself to colleagues in order to demonstrate unequal treatment may have difficulty doing so, especially in a small department.

Other issues facing academic institutions involve shifting performance standards, which may result in greater demands on recently hired faculty than those conducting the evaluation were required to meet—an outcome that can appear discriminatory whether or not there was a discriminatory intent. Comparisons of faculty productivity or quality across disciplines pose difficulties as well. And the practice at many colleges and universities of shielding the deliberations of committees or individuals from the scrutiny of the candidate or, in some cases, the courts adds to the complexity of academic discrimination cases.

Discrimination claims have been brought by faculty challenging negative hiring, promotion, or tenure decisions or objecting to work assignments or other types of decisions (salary increases, office or lab space, and so on). A few cases, discussed in the next section, illustrate the range of issues and the judicial reaction to these discrimination claims.

***5.4.2. Judicial deference and remedies for tenure denial.*** Faculty challenging negative promotion or tenure decisions typically claim that the decision-making process was flawed or that the denial was a result of unlawful bias rather than some performance-related reason. Cases involving allegations of flawed decision-making processes are discussed in Section 5.7. Cases involving the rationale for the negative decision are discussed in this section.

Despite the relatively large number of discrimination claims brought by faculty denied tenure or promotion, very few faculty members have prevailed on the merits. A study of discrimination lawsuits brought between 1972 and 1986 by faculty denied tenure found that plaintiffs won on the merits only about 20 percent of the time (George R. LaNoue & Barbara A. Lee, *Academics in Court: The Consequences of Faculty Discrimination Litigation* (University of Michigan Press, 1987)). Litigation results in subsequent years have been similar. In addition to the fact that the subjective nature of these decisions makes it difficult for a judge or jury to second-guess the determination of a university with regard to the quality of a faculty member's work, many courts have deferred to the judgment of faculty peers or other experts in these cases, finding for plaintiffs only if significant procedural errors had been made or if there was strong evidence that discrimination motivated the negative decision.

Early cases in which courts were asked to review denials of tenure or promotion made clear judges' discomfort with the request. In situations where peer review committees had determined that a plaintiff's scholarship, teaching, or both did not meet the proper standards, judges were reluctant to impose either their own judgment or their own performance standards on peer review committees, external evaluators, or college administrators. In an early case, *Faro v. New York University*, 502 F.2d 1229 (2d Cir. 1974), the U.S. Court of Appeals for the Second Circuit stated:

> [O]f all fields which the federal courts should hesitate to invade and take over, education and faculty appointments at a university level are probably the least suited for federal court supervision. Dr. Faro would remove any subjective judgments by her faculty colleagues in the decisionmaking process [502 F.2d at 1231–32].

The Fourth Circuit, echoing *Faro*, stated that "[c]ourts are not qualified to review and substitute their judgment for the subjective, discretionary judgments of professional experts on faculty promotions" (*Clark v. Whiting*, 607 F.2d 634, 640 (1979)).

Federal appellate courts in subsequent academic discrimination cases were more willing to review academic judgments. In *Powell v. Syracuse University*, 580 F.2d 1150 (2d Cir. 1978), the court rejected its earlier deference, stating that the courts' "anti-interventionist policy has rendered colleges and universities virtually immune to charges of employment bias" and that the court would not "rely on any such policy of self-abnegation where colleges are concerned" (580 F.2d at 1153). Despite this apparent rejection of the *Faro* deferential standard, courts have generally refused to overturn tenure decisions where there has been an internal determination that the candidate's performance does not meet the institution's standard for tenure. One state court declared flatly that the "arbitrary and capricious" standard should be used to evaluate tenured faculty's recommendation against granting tenure, because such a recommendation is a professional judgment, not an employment decision (*Daley v. Wesleyan University*, 772 A.2d 725 (Conn. App. Ct. 2000), *appeal denied*, 776 A.2d 1145 (Conn. 2001)). In most cases, however, the courts do examine a college or university's justification for denying tenure to determine the credibility of the nondiscriminatory reason for the negative decision.

Such was the case in *Ohio University v. Ohio Civil Rights Commission*, 887 N.E. 2d 403 (Ohio Ct. App. 2008). Lipset, a professor of industrial and manufacturing systems engineering, was denied tenure by Ohio University, primarily on the ground that he had applied for and received very few external grants, although his teaching and service were regarded very positively. The state civil rights commission agreed with Lipset that the tenure denial was based on his age (51), not his performance. The university appealed, and a trial court reversed the commission's finding. A state appellate court agreed, evidencing strong deference to the professional judgments of Lipset's peers:

> Although many may argue that the promotion and tenure committee's focus was misguided and that Ohio University should have been primarily concerned about a candidate's teaching ability, neither this appellate court, nor . . . the commission is vested with the authority to make this policy determination . . . We do not sit as a promotion and tenure committee with the duty to resolve promotion and tenure issues. A court's role (and the commission's role) in this arena must be limited to a determination whether discrimination occurred . . . not whether a candidate, in the court's view, may deserve tenure. Courts and commissions are ill-suited to evaluate various academic criteria used for promotion and tenure decisions, and courts should not generally invade the faculty employment decision process . . . [887 N.E. 2d at 435].

In *Shepard v. Temple University*, 948 A.2d 852 (Pa. Super. Ct. 2008), a professor of nursing was denied tenure by the university's president, who disagreed with the positive recommendations of the individuals and groups at previous stages of the decision-making process. Professor Shepard filed a breach of contract claim, stating that the president's negative decision violated the collective bargaining agreement. The court noted that Shepard had not identified procedural violations and characterized her lawsuit as a claim that the president's decision "altered the substantive manner in which her dossier was reviewed" and changed the requirements for tenure. The court rejected her claim as a challenge to the weights that the president gave to various criteria for tenure and the reasons he provided to support his negative recommendation. The court quoted the trial court with approval:

> With respect to a decision to not renew an employment contract, the evaluation of the philosophies of a particular institution necessarily involves many subjective, nonquantifiable factors. The assessment of these factors is best performed by those closely involved in the life of the institution, not by judges. As a matter of sound public policy, an institution of higher learning should be free to make such decisions. Engrafting a right to judicial second-guessing of the soundness of personnel decisions made under employment contracts would hamper this decision-making freedom. It would require courts to inquire into the truth or falsity of matters which are not amenable to such determination (948 A.2d at 858, citing *Baker v. Lafayette College*, 532 A.2d 399 (Pa. 1987)).

Another illustrative case is *Fisher v. Vassar College*, 114 F.3d 1332 (2d Cir. 1997) (*en banc*), a case involving claims of age, marital status, and sex discrimination. The college had stated that Cynthia Fisher, a professor of biology, had been denied tenure in part because she "had been away from science" for too long. Fisher had interrupted her academic career for nine years to raise her children. The trial court had ruled in Fisher's favor, citing Fisher's strong publication record (finding it superior to that of several male faculty who were tenured just before and just after Fisher was denied tenure), her success at obtaining research grants, and the fact that no married woman had received tenure in the hard sciences at Vassar for the thirty years prior to Fisher's tenure review, as evidence that the college had engaged in age and "sex plus marital status" discrimination (852 F. Supp. 1193 (S.D.N.Y. 1994)). The court did not find that the college had engaged in sex discrimination, as such, because another female faculty member in that department had received tenure the same year that Fisher's tenure bid was denied. Instead, the trial court relied on a ruling by the U.S. Supreme Court in *Phillips v. Martin Marietta*, 400 U.S. 542 (1971), that a Title VII claim may arise if an employer discriminates against an employee because of sex plus another characteristic, such as marital status. The trial court also found that Fisher's salary was depressed as a result of sex discrimination, an Equal Pay Act violation.

On appeal, a panel of the U.S. Court of Appeals for the Second Circuit reversed. Although the panel upheld the trial court's rulings for the plaintiff in both the prima facie and pretext portions of the case (see Section 4.5.2.1), the panel reversed the trial court's ultimate finding that the college intentionally discriminated against Fisher, stating that there was insufficient direct evidence of such discrimination. That opinion was withdrawn when the full court determined to hear oral arguments *en banc*. The *en banc* court confined its review to whether it was permissible for an appellate court to affirm rulings for the plaintiff on the prima facie case and pretext issues, and yet reverse the ultimate finding of discrimination. The *en banc* majority insisted that some evidence of bias was needed; proving that the college was untruthful in the reasons it gave was insufficient to justify a verdict for Fisher. The minority argued that if the plaintiff prevailed at the pretext stage, the plaintiff should prevail in the lawsuit. Six judges joined the majority, one judge concurred in part and dissented in part, and four judges dissented from the majority opinion.

Simply because the plaintiff might have been able to demonstrate that the college's reason for the tenure denial was pretextual, said the majority, did not mean that a finding of discrimination was warranted. Showing some understanding of academic politics, the judge writing for the majority commented:

> In some cases, an employer's proffered reason is a mask for unlawful discrimination. But discrimination does not lurk behind every inaccurate statement. Individual decision-makers may intentionally dissemble in order to hide a reason that is non-discriminatory but unbecoming or small-minded, such as back-scratching, log-rolling, horse-trading, institutional politics, envy, nepotism, spite, or personal hostility. For example, a member of a tenure selection committee may support a protégé who will be eligible for tenure the following year. If only one tenure line is available, that committee member might be inclined to vote against tenure . . . thereby ensuring that the tenure line remains open. Any reason given by the committee member, other than the preference for his protégé, will be false . . . [T]he fact that the proffered reason was false does not necessarily mean that the true motive was the illegal one argued by the plaintiff [114 F.3d at 1337].

The *en banc* majority left undisturbed the ruling by the appellate panel that, although Fisher had established a prima facie case of age and marital status discrimination, the college had supplied sufficient neutral reasons for the tenure denial (inability to meet the standards for tenure and qualifications inferior to those of other tenure candidates). Despite the trial court's finding that some of the college's reasons were inaccurate, the panel had held that the trial court's findings were insufficient to support a finding of actual discrimination against Fisher. The *en banc* majority fully concurred with this reasoning and outcome of the panel discussion.

Faculty plaintiffs seeking to avoid the problems encountered in *Fisher* may not fare any better under state nondiscrimination laws. In a widely reported decision, a Connecticut jury had awarded more than $12.6 million to a female chemistry professor who claimed sex discrimination in her tenure denial. In *Craine v. Trinity College*, 791 A.2d 518 (Conn. 2002), the state's high court affirmed the jury's finding that the college had breached Craine's employment contract and had negligently misrepresented the tenure criteria but ruled that the plaintiff had not demonstrated a discriminatory motive on the part of the college and thus the jury award had to be reduced. Because the plaintiff could not identify males with similar qualifications who had been granted tenure the same year she was denied tenure, she had to rely on procedural violations in order to make out a prima facie case of sex discrimination. The high court found that the breach of contract (the college's failure to advise Craine that she was not making adequate progress toward tenure) provided a rebuttable inference of discrimination. However, the court ruled that the procedural inconsistency and a single reference to a male tenure candidate as "old boy Jack" were insufficient to permit a reasonable jury to find that sex discrimination was the motive for the tenure denial. The college's defense that the plaintiff's scholarly productivity was too low was a legitimate nondiscriminatory reason for the tenure denial, according to the court, and it ruled that the plaintiff had not demonstrated that the college's reason was a pretext for discrimination.

Although the plaintiff claimed that two successful male candidates for tenure were no better qualified than she, the court refused to perform a comparative analysis of the qualifications. First, said the court, the comparator faculty were in different departments (history and math). But more important, said the court:

> The first amendment guarantees that the defendant may pass its own judgment on the plaintiff's scholarship and accept or reject other evaluations in the process ... To compare these publication records would require [the court to make] an inadmissible substantive comparison between the candidates and an improper intrusion into the right of the defendant to decide for itself which candidates satisfied its publication requirements. In the absence of any independent evidence of discrimination, evidence that an academic institution appears to have been more critical of one candidate than of another is not sufficient to raise an inference of discrimination [791 A.2d at 537, 538].

An issue that has troubled courts analyzing academic Title VII cases is the appropriate remedy for a denial of tenure or promotion that is found to have been discriminatory. In nonacademic settings, reinstatement to the position along with retroactive promotion is a routine remedy. But the courts, citing their lack of expertise in evaluating the scholarly or teaching ability of college faculty, sometimes have been reluctant to award "make-whole" remedies to college faculty seeking tenure.

The issue of a remedy for a discriminatory denial of tenure was addressed squarely in *Kunda v. Muhlenberg College*, 621 F.2d 532 (3d Cir. 1980). The decision, written by Judge Dolores Sloviter, a former law professor, takes into account the need for academic freedom and the significance of peer evaluation while also recognizing that individuals who make academic judgments are still subject to Title VII's prohibitions on discrimination.

Connie Kunda, a physical education instructor, brought suit after the college had denied her applications for promotion and tenure. The trial court (463 F. Supp. 294 (E.D. Pa. 1978)), holding that the college had intentionally discriminated against Kunda because of her sex, awarded her (1) reinstatement to her position; (2) back pay from the date her employment terminated, less amounts earned in the interim; (3) promotion to the rank of assistant professor, back-dated to the time her application was denied; and (4) the opportunity to complete the requirements for a master's degree within two full school years from the date of the court's decree, in which case she would be granted tenure.

In affirming the trial court's award of relief, the appellate court carefully analyzed the particular facts of the case. These facts, as set out below, played a vital role in supporting and limiting the precedent set by this opinion.

When Kunda was appointed an instructor in the Muhlenberg College physical education department in September 1966, she held a bachelor of arts degree in physical education. Although the department's terminal degree requirement, for tenure purposes, was the master's, Kunda was never informed that a master's was needed for advancement, although male faculty in her department had been so advised. Kunda was first recommended for promotion in the academic year 1971–72. Although her department supported the promotion, the Faculty Personnel and Policies Committee (FPPC) of the college rejected the recommendation after the dean of the college, who seldom attended FPPC deliberations on promotions, spoke against the recommendation. Subsequently, to determine the reasons for the denial, Kunda met individually with her department chairman, the dean, and the college's president. The court found that none of these persons told her that she had been denied promotion because she lacked a master's degree.

In the two subsequent years, Kunda's department colleagues and all relevant faculty committees recommended that she be promoted and, in the last year, granted tenure. Both times, the dean recommended against promotion and tenure, citing various institutional concerns rather than Kunda's lack of a master's degree. Both years, the president recommended against promotion and tenure, and Kunda was given a terminal contract.

Kunda appealed the tenure denial to the Faculty Board of Appeals (FBA). The FBA recommended that Kunda be promoted and awarded tenure because (1) Kunda displayed the "scholarly equivalent" of a master's degree, (2) the policy of granting promotions only to faculty possessing the terminal degree had been bypassed frequently for the physical education department, and (3) no significant financial considerations mandated a denial of tenure. The board of trustees voted to deny tenure.

After reviewing these facts, the court of appeals compared Kunda's treatment by the college with that of similarly situated males at Muhlenberg. With respect to promotion, three male members of the physical education department had been promoted during the period of Kunda's employment, notwithstanding their lack of master's degrees. There was also a difference between the counseling offered Kunda and that offered similarly situated males; while Kunda was not told that the master's would be a prerequisite for a grant of tenure, male faculty had been so advised.

The appellate court agreed that Kunda had been discriminated against in both the denial of promotion and the denial of tenure. Concerning promotion, the appellate court affirmed the finding that the defendant's reason for denial articulated at trial, lack of the terminal degree, was a pretext for discrimination. Concerning tenure, the appellate court affirmed the trial court's determination that the articulated reason (lack of terminal degree) was not pretextual but that Kunda had been subjected to intentional disparate treatment with respect to counseling on the need for the degree.

Having held the college in violation of Title VII, the court turned to what it considered the most provocative issue raised on appeal: the propriety of the remedy fashioned by the trial court. Awards of back pay and reinstatement are not unusual in academic employment discrimination litigation; awards of promotion or conditional tenure are. The appellate court therefore treated the latter remedies extensively, emphasizing the special academic freedom context in which they arose.

The court discussed the tension between the freedom of a college to make employment decisions based upon institutional considerations and the academic judgment that is necessary to review a faculty member's qualifications for promotion or tenure. It also acknowledged the need for academics, rather than judges, to evaluate faculty performance. Said the court:

> Wherever the responsibility [for evaluating faculty performance] lies within the institution, it is clear that courts must be vigilant not to intrude into that determination, and should not substitute their judgment for that of the college with respect to the qualifications of faculty members for promotion and tenure. Determinations about such matters as teaching ability, research scholarship, and professional stature are subjective, and unless they can be shown to have been used as the mechanism to obscure discrimination, they must be left for evaluation by the professionals, particularly since they often involve inquiry into aspects of arcane scholarship beyond the competence of individual judges [621 F.2d at 547–48].

The court noted that all faculty committees had judged Kunda to be qualified for promotion and tenure, and that the dean had recommended extending her a non-tenure-track appointment. Since the tenure denial was premised on the lack of a master's degree rather than upon the quality of her performance, the court found that its decision to award promotion and conditional tenure was consistent with the academic judgments made about Kunda.

The appellate court stated that the trial judge's award of "conditional tenure" placed Kunda in the position she would have been in had the dean and president informed her of the requirement of a master's degree. This ruling was consistent with remedies for discrimination in nonacademic settings, according to the court.

> The fact that the discrimination in this case took place in an academic rather than commercial setting does not permit the court to abdicate its responsibility to insure the award of a meaningful remedy. Congress did not intend that those institutions which employ persons who work primarily with their mental faculties should enjoy a different status under Title VII than those which employ persons who work primarily with their hands [621 F.2d at 550].

*Kunda* was a groundbreaking case because the court in effect awarded a promotion and conditional tenure as the remedy for the discrimination against the plaintiff. The case was also controversial because the remedy is subject to the charge that it interferes with institutional autonomy in areas (promotion and tenure) where autonomy is most important to postsecondary education. Yet, as a careful reading of the opinion indicates, the court's holding is actually narrow and its reasoning sensitive to the academic community's needs and the relative competencies of college and court. The court emphasizes that the case was unusual in that Kunda's performance had been found by all involved to be acceptable. Thus, the case's significance is tied tightly to its facts.

The first time a federal appellate court examined and approved the outright award of tenure occurred in *Brown v. Trustees of Boston University*, 891 F.2d 337 (1st Cir. 1989). Julia Brown, an assistant professor of English, had received the unanimous recommendation of her department and positive recommendations from outside evaluators but was denied tenure by the university's president. After a jury trial, the university was found to have discriminated in its denial of tenure to Brown. The court, in reinstating Brown with tenure, noted that her peers had judged her to be qualified and that the president's sexist remarks about the English department showed evidence of gender bias. The university had raised an academic freedom challenge to a court award of tenure, stating that it infringed upon its First Amendment right to determine "who may teach" (see *Sweezy v. New Hampshire*, discussed in Section 6.1). The appellate court rejected that argument, noting that the First Amendment could not insulate the university against civil rights

The court also rejected the university's argument that the appropriate remedy be another three-year probationary period or a nondiscriminatory tenure review. The court said these remedies would not make the plaintiff whole. The court engaged in an extensive review of Brown's publications and teaching record, an unusual level of scrutiny for academic employment discrimination claims. Thus, the appellate court reviewed the substance of the decision as well as its procedural fairness, rather than the deferential review used by courts in previous cases.

Recent court opinions in academic discrimination cases make it clear that postsecondary institutions have no special dispensation from the requirements of federal antidiscrimination legislation. Courts will defer to institutions' expert judgments concerning scholarship, teaching, and other educational qualifications if they believe that those judgments are fairly reached, but courts will not subject institutions to a more deferential standard of review or a lesser obligation to repair the adverse effects of discrimination. And despite the fact that tenure is an unusual remedy in that it has the potential to give lifetime job security to a faculty member, the federal courts appear to have lost their reluctance to order tenure as a remedy when they believe that discrimination has occurred.

## Section 5.5. *Affirmative Action in Faculty Employment Decisions*

As discussed in Section 4.6, affirmative action in employment has had a volatile history, and that history is still being written. The principles of affirmative action, the legal justifications and criticisms, and judicial reaction to affirmative action in employment are discussed in Section 4.6. The rulings of the U.S. Supreme Court in two college admissions cases involving affirmative action, *Gratz v. Bollinger* and *Grutter v. Bollinger*, are discussed in Section 7.2.5.

Race- or gender-conscious faculty hiring or promotion decisions are equally controversial, if not more so, because of the relative scarcity of faculty positions and the intense competition for them. Challenges to such hiring or promotion decisions tend to be brought under federal or state employment discrimination laws by a white plaintiff who alleges "reverse discrimination," a claim that the college improperly used race, gender, or some other protected characteristic to make the employment decision.

Affirmative action for remedial purposes requires the college to prove a history of racial segregation or other racial discrimination. Even for those colleges in states where segregation was practiced prior to the Civil Rights Act of 1964, showing the present effects of past discrimination may be difficult (see, for example, the *Podberesky* case, discussed in Section 7.3.4). For public institutions in states where a history of *de jure* segregation of public higher education has not been documented or addressed, however, establishing prior discrimination in the employment of faculty may be even more difficult. Similar difficulties may arise in attempting to ascertain the present effects of prior gender discrimination.

Given the outcomes in *Weber, Wygant,* and related cases (discussed in Section 4.6), both public and private institutions should analyze carefully the effect of their affirmative action plans on existing and prospective nonminority faculty members to ensure that racial or gender preferences are not implemented in a way that would "unnecessarily trammel" their interests (under Title VII) or fail the strict scrutiny test (under the federal equal protection clause). Two of the factors relied on in *Weber*—that the plan did not require the discharge of any white workers and that the plan was temporary—appear to be easily transferable to and easily met in the context of postsecondary faculty hiring. But the third factor—that the plan did not "create an absolute bar to the advancement of white employees"—bears careful watching in postsecondary education. The special training programs at issue in *Weber* benefited both black and white employees. Thirteen workers were selected, seven black and six white. At postsecondary institutions, however, faculty vacancies or special opportunities such as department chairmanships generally occur one at a time and on an irregular basis. A decision that a particular opening will be filled by a minority (or a woman) may, in effect, serve as a complete bar to whites (or men), especially in a small department where there is little turnover and where the date of the next opening cannot be predicted. Institutions that use race or gender only as a "plus" factor, rather than targeting specific positions for a particular race or gender, may be able to satisfy the *Weber* test more successfully (see the *Johnson* case in Section 4.6.2). Public institutions, however, must still satisfy the requirements of the equal protection clause. The rulings of the U.S Supreme Court in *Gratz v. Bollinger* and *Grutter v. Bollinger* (2003) suggest that using race or gender as one nondecisive criterion among others used to make a hiring or promotion decision may pass equal protection clause scrutiny (and Title VII scrutiny as well). The success of such arguments will depend on whether the courts accept a diversity rationale as a basis for affirmative action in employment (see Section 4.6.3).

Once findings of the institution's historical discrimination and its present effects are made, a public college or university apparently has much the same authority as a private institution to implement a remedial affirmative action plan. One difference is that *Weber* allows private employers to use explicit quotas under Title VII, whereas the equal protection clause, applicable to public employers, prohibits the use of explicit quotas (see *Bakke*, *Croson*, *Adarand*, *Grutter*, and *Gratz*).

Three "reverse discrimination" cases demonstrate the continuing struggles of courts to reconcile the equal opportunity laws with universities' concern for diversity. The most thoughtful discussion of the issue occurs in *Hill v. Ross*, 183 F.3d 586 (7th Cir. 1999). In *Hill*, the psychology department at the University of Wisconsin at Whitewater had selected a male candidate for a tenure-track position. The dean rejected the department's recommendation, stating that the department was required to hire a woman because there were fewer women faculty in the department than their proportion among holders of doctoral degrees in psychology. Hill, the male candidate who was not hired, filed a sex discrimination claim against the dean and the university under both Title VII and the equal protection clause. The university defended its actions on the basis of its affirmative action plan, and the trial court awarded summary judgment to the university. The appellate court reversed.

The appellate court reviewed U.S. Supreme Court affirmative action cases, including *Wygant* and *Johnson*. Those cases, the court said, concluded that race or gender could be used "only as factors in a more complex calculus, not as independently dispositive criteria" (183 F.3d at 588). The dean had used gender as the "sole basis" for the hiring decision and did not discuss Hill's qualifications nor the department's recommendation in his memo rejecting Hill's candidacy. Nor did the dean use the department's apparent failure to follow the recruitment process required by the university's affirmative action plan as justification for rejecting Hill. A jury could conclude, said the court, that the dean had created a quota system for hiring in the psychology department.

In *Stern v. Trustees of Columbia University*, 131 F.3d 305 (2d Cir. 1997), the court vacated the trial court's grant of summary judgment for the university in a "reverse" national origin discrimination case. Professor Stern, a white male, had served as acting director of the Spanish language program. The university decided to appoint a full-time director. Following the requirements of its affirmative action plan, and despite the department's strong preference that Stern be given the full-time position, the university initiated a national search for applicants. The vice president for arts and sciences appointed an interdepartmental search committee, most of whom did not speak, read, or write Spanish. Stern was among three finalists for the position. The other candidates were a white woman and a Latino male, Augustus Puelo. After conducting interviews and observing each of the candidates teaching a "model" class, the search committee recommended that Puelo be given the position on the strength of his superior teaching. Stern was the only candidate who held a doctorate, the only candidate who had extensive publications and teaching experience, and the only candidate who could teach Portuguese, a language that the department needed additional faculty to teach. Stern then sued the university for national origin discrimination under Title VII.

The trial court granted the university's motion for summary judgment, stating that Stern had not provided sufficient evidence to rebut the university's contention that Puelo had administrative and teaching skills that were superior to Stern's. The appellate court vacated that judgment, ruling that the trial court had given insufficient weight to Stern's assertions that the vice president had predetermined the outcome of the search and that members of the search committee had stated that Stern would not be given serious consideration for the job. Stern had also offered evidence of the preference of several search committee members for a Latino director. The court ruled that Stern's case should go to trial.

In contrast to *Stern* and *Hill*, the Nevada Supreme Court was more deferential to the judgment of a university with respect to an allegation of "reverse discrimination." The reasoning used by that court was closer to the reasoning of *Grutter*, particularly in its reliance on *Bakke*, than the decisions discussed above. In *University and Community College System of Nevada v. Farmer*, 930 P.2d 730 (Nev. 1997), the state's highest court reversed a state trial court's ruling that the University of Nevada, Reno, impermissibly used racial criteria to hire a black male for a faculty position in the sociology department. The university had instituted a "minority bonus policy" because of its concern that only 1 percent of its faculty were black and 25 percent were women. The policy allowed a department to hire an additional faculty member if it first hired a candidate from a racial minority group.

The department of sociology had a vacant faculty position in 1990 and instituted a national search. Farmer, a white female, and Makoba, a black male, were two of the three finalists. The department sought permission to interview only Makoba, the candidate ranked most qualified by the department. The university agreed, and Makoba was hired at a salary of $35,000, which would increase to $40,000 when he completed his dissertation. This salary exceeded the published salary range in the position description. One year later, Farmer was hired by the same department at a starting salary of $31,000, and a $2,000 increase upon completion of her dissertation.

Farmer subsequently sued the university, challenging its affirmative action plan and its "minority bonus policy" as both unconstitutional and as contrary to Title VII's proscription of race and gender discrimination. The trial court entered judgment for Farmer in the amount of $40,000. On appeal, the Nevada Supreme Court reversed the trial court. Citing *Bakke* (see Section 7.2.5), the court noted that Makoba had been selected not only because of his race, but because he was well qualified for the position by virtue of his publications, his teaching experience, and his area of specialization. The court said: "We also view the desirability of a racially diverse faculty as sufficiently analogous to the constitutionally permissible attainment of a racially diverse student body countenanced by the *Bakke* Court" (930 P.2d at 735). The university's affirmative action plan complied with the *Weber* factors, said the court, and even passed the strict scrutiny test:

> The University demonstrated that it has a compelling interest in fostering a culturally and ethnically diverse faculty. A failure to attract minority faculty perpetuates the University's white enclave and further limits student exposure to multicultural diversity. Moreover, the minority bonus policy is narrowly tailored to accelerate racial and gender diversity [930 P.2d at 735].

Thus, the plan passed constitutional muster, and, since the court determined the qualifications of the candidates to be equivalent (although the university had concluded that Makoba was slightly better qualified), "the University must be given the latitude to make its own employment decisions provided that they are not discriminatory" (930 P.2d at 735).

The Supreme Court's ruling in *Grutter* established that student body diversity is a compelling interest for public colleges and universities. Although it remains to be seen how directly subsequent courts will apply *Grutter* to affirmative action in employment (rather than in admissions), it appears that colleges could make the argument that diversity of faculty is as important to "educational diversity" as the diversity of the student body. The opinion in *Farmer* suggests that such an argument could comply with *Grutter* if the protected characteristic (race, gender) were not the sole reason for the hiring or promotion decision, but only one factor among others used after determining that the individual was well qualified for the position and that there was a "manifest imbalance" that needed to be addressed. Although the Court in *Grutter* did not explicitly apply the *Weber* test to the admissions decisions at the University of Michigan Law School, it stated that narrow tailoring (a required element of strict scrutiny under the equal protection clause) requires that there be no "undue harm" to nonminorities and that the affirmative action plan be limited in time—two of the *Weber* criteria. *Grutter* also exhibits deference to the decisions of academic institutions, citing *Sweezy* (see Section 6.1.5) regarding the academic freedom of institutions to select their own students. That case also discusses the selection of "who may teach" as an element of an institution's academic freedom, suggesting that the rationale of *Grutter* could also be applied to academic employment decisions.

Although *Grutter* did not address employment at all, its declaration that diversity in an educational institution is a compelling state interest, as well as its reaffirmation of the vitality of Justice Powell's opinion in *Bakke*, provides some guidance for colleges and universities with respect to academic employment. For private colleges, *Grutter* does not limit the colleges' ability to implement carefully developed voluntary affirmative action programs for faculty hiring that meet the *Weber* test and that involve hiring and promotions rather than dismissals or layoffs. For public colleges, *Grutter* suggests that affirmative action plans that are closely linked to the institution's educational mission, and that can demonstrate a strong relationship between the institution's educational mission and the diversity of its faculty, may survive constitutional challenge. Of course, the plan would need to use goals rather than quotas, and would need to ensure that the protected characteristic (race, gender) was not the sole criterion, but one of a constellation of relevant factors, in the hiring decision.

## Section 5.6.  Standards and Criteria for Faculty Employment Decisions

### 5.6.1. General principles. Postsecondary institutions commonly have written and published standards or criteria to guide decisions regarding faculty appointments, contract renewals, promotions, and the granting and termination of tenure. Since they will often constitute part of the contract between the institution and the faculty member (see Section 5.2) and thus bind the institution, such evaluative standards and criteria should receive the careful attention of administrators and faculty members alike.

While courts will enforce standards or criteria found to be part of the faculty contract, they accord postsecondary institutions wide discretion in determining the content and specificity of those standards and criteria. And although the traditional criteria of teaching, scholarship (or creative activity), and service have been applied for decades to faculty employment decisions, additional criteria (and challenges to the use of those criteria) have developed more recently. Additional performance criteria addressing the interpersonal relationships of the tenure or promotion candidate ("collegiality") have been applied—and challenged—on many campuses. Cases alleging that the interpretation of tenure criteria has changed between a faculty member's hiring and eventual tenure review have also been brought—and generally rejected by courts. And criteria unrelated to a faculty member's performance, such as the proportion of tenured faculty already present in a department, have been used, and challenged, as well.

Courts are less likely to become involved in disputes concerning the substance of standards and criteria than in disputes over procedures for applying standards and criteria. (Courts draw the same distinction in cases concerning students; see the discussion in Sections 8.6, 9.2, and 9.3.) In *Riggin v. Board of Trustees of Ball State University*, 489 N.E.2d 616 (Ind. Ct. App. 1986), the court indicated that it "must give deference to [the board of trustees'] expertise" and that it "may not reweigh the evidence or determine the credibility of witnesses," since "peer groups make the judgment on the performance of a faculty member." And in *Dorsett v. Board of Trustees for State Colleges and Universities*, 940 F.2d 121, 123 (5th Cir. 1991) (quoting earlier cases), the court warned that "[o]f all fields that the federal courts 'should hesitate to invade and take over, education and faculty appointments at the university level are probably the least suited for federal court supervision.'"

Despite this generally deferential judicial attitude, there are several bases on which an institution's standards and criteria may be legally scrutinized. For both public and private institutions, questions regarding consistency with AAUP policies may be raised in AAUP investigations or in court (Section 5.2.2). When standards or criteria are part of the faculty contract, both public and private institutions' disputes over interpretation may wind up in court or in the institution's internal grievance process. Cases on attaining tenure and on dismissal from tenured positions for "just cause" are prominent examples. For public institutions, standards or criteria may also be embodied in state statutes or administrative regulations that are subject to interpretation by courts, state administrative agencies (such as boards of regents or civil service commissions), or decision makers within the institution's internal grievance process. The tenure denial and termination cases are again excellent examples. And under the various federal nondiscrimination statutes discussed in Section 4.5, courts or federal administrative agencies may scrutinize the standards and criteria of public and private institutions for their potential discriminatory applications; these standards and criteria also may be examined in the course of an internal grievance process.

In public institutions, standards and criteria may also be subjected to constitutional scrutiny under the First and Fourteenth Amendments. Under the First Amendment, a standard or criterion can be challenged as "overbroad" if it is so broadly worded that it can be used to penalize faculty members for having exercised constitutionally protected rights of free expression. Under the Fourteenth Amendment, a standard or criterion can be challenged as "vague" if it is so unclear that institutional personnel cannot understand its meaning in concrete circumstances. (The **overbreadth** and **vagueness** doctrines are discussed further in Sections 9.1.3, 9.2.2, and 9.5.2.) The leading U.S. Supreme Court case on overbreadth and vagueness in public employment standards is *Arnett v. Kennedy*, 416 U.S. 134 (1974). A federal civil servant had been dismissed under a statute authorizing dismissal "for such cause as will promote the efficiency of the service." A majority of the Court held that this standard, as applied in the federal service, was neither overbroad nor vague.

While the result in *Arnett* suggests that the overbreadth and vagueness doctrines do not substantially restrict the standard-setting process, it does not necessarily mean that public postsecondary institutions can use the same "cause" standard approved in *Arnett*. Employment standards should be adapted to the characteristics and functions of the group to which the standards apply. Courts may thus be somewhat stricter with a postsecondary institution's standards than with the federal government's—particularly when the standards are applied to what is arguably expressive activity, in which case the overbreadth and vagueness doctrines would combine with academic freedom principles (see Section 6.1) to create important limits on institutional discretion in devising employment standards.

Under the Fourteenth Amendment, a public institution's standards and criteria for personnel decisions may also be challenged using **substantive due process** principles. Such challenges are only occasionally successful. In *Harrington v. Harris*, 118 F.3d 359 (5th Cir. 1997), for instance, a federal appellate court affirmed a jury's verdict that the manner in which merit pay decisions were made at the Thurgood Marshall School of Law of Texas Southern University was arbitrary and capricious, and constituted a violation of professors' substantive due process rights. The parties had agreed that the professors had a property interest in a "rational application" of the university's merit pay policy. The court assumed, without deciding, that such a **property interest** existed, and held that the jury could reasonably conclude, based on the evidence, that the dean and associate dean had "acted in an arbitrary and capricious manner" in making their recommendations for merit pay increases. The most important evidence, apparently, concerned the possible manipulation of the evaluation system so that black faculty members would receive higher increases than white faculty members with similar records of scholarship and teaching achievements. Other courts will not be as hospitable to substantive due process claims as the *Harrington* court. (See, for example, *Boyett v. Troy State University at Montgomery*, 971 F. Supp. 1403, 1414 (M.D. Ala. 1997), *affirmed without opinion*, 142 F.3d 1284 (11th Cir. 1998).)

**5.6.2. Terminations of tenure for cause.** Perhaps the most sensitive issues concerning standards arise in situations where institutions attempt to dismiss a tenured faculty member for cause (see T. Lovain, "Grounds for Dismissing Tenured Postsecondary Faculty for Cause," 10 *J. Coll. & Univ. Law* 419 (1983–84)). Such dismissals should be distinguished from dismissals due to financial exigency or program discontinuance. For-cause dismissals— being more personal, potentially more subjective, and more debilitating to the individual concerned—may be even more troublesome and agonizing for the parties than dismissals for reasons of financial exigency or program discontinuance. Similarly, they may give rise to even more complex legal issues concerning adequate procedures for effecting dismissal (see Section 5.7); the adequacy of standards for defining and determining "cause"; and the types and amount of evidence needed to sustain a termination decision under a particular standard of cause.

The American Association of University Professors' 1976 "Recommended Institutional Regulations on Academic Freedom and Tenure" (available at http://www.aaup.org/AAUP/pubsres/policydocs/contents/RIR.htm) acknowledges "adequate cause" as an appropriate standard for dismissal of tenured faculty. These guidelines caution, however, that "adequate cause for a dismissal will be related, directly and substantially, to the fitness of faculty members in their professional capacities as teachers or researchers." Since the guidelines do not further define the concept, institutions are left to devise cause standards on their own or, occasionally for public institutions, to find standards in state statutes or agency regulations.

A straightforward example of a dismissal for cause—incompetence—occurred in *Weist v. State of Kansas*, Docket No. 00 C 3 09 (Kan. Dist. Ct., Riley Co. October 17, 2002). The university had adopted a post-tenure review program that provided that if a tenured faculty member's performance had been found to be unsatisfactory for two consecutive years, the faculty member could be terminated after a hearing before a faculty committee. The university's procedure provided that there must be clear and convincing evidence that the faculty member was performing below the "minimum level of productivity." Furthermore, the department had provided the faculty member with an "improvement plan" that he failed to follow. The court upheld the termination.

Performance failures may also be characterized as "neglect of duty," as in *In re Bigler v. Cornell University*, 698 N.Y.S.2d 472 (N.Y. App. Div. 1999), *Gutkin v. University of Southern California*, 125 Cal. Rptr. 2d 115 (Cal. Ct. App., 2d Dist. 2002), and *Peterson v. North Dakota University System*, 678 N.W.2d 163 (N.D. 2004); or as misconduct, as in *Wells v. Tennessee Board of Regents*, 9 S.W.3d 779 (Tenn. 1999) (alleged sexual harassment of student by tenured professor), and *Holm v. Ithaca College*, 682 N.Y.S.2d 295 (N.Y. App. Div. 1998) (sexual harassment of multiple students by tenured professor). Dishonesty as a justification for dismissal of a tenured faculty member has also been sanctioned by the courts (see, for example, *Lamvermeyer v. Denison University*, 2000 Ohio App. LEXIS 861 (Ohio Ct. App., 5th Dist. 2000) ("moral delinquency"—falsification of expense vouchers)). And serious violation of collegiality expectations has also served as the basis for dismissal of a tenured faculty member, as in *Davenport v. Board of Trustees of State Center Community College Dist.*, 654 F. Supp. 2d 1073 (E.D. Cal. 2009) (harsh and inappropriate treatment of faculty, students, and staff), *Bernold v. Board of Governors of University of North Carolina*, 683 S.E. 2d 428 (N.C. Ct. App. 2009) (disruptiveness by professor that substantially interfered with department's ability to function), and *Boises v. New York Univ.*, 2005 U.S. Dist. LEXIS 26378 (S.D.N.Y. Nov. 3, 2005), *affirmed*, 201 F. App'x 796 (2d Cir. 2006) (faculty member used improper grading practices, tampered with faculty mail, and harassed faculty and staff).

For-cause dismissals may raise numerous questions about contract interpretation. In *McConnell v. Howard University*, 818 F.2d 58 (D.C. Cir. 1987), for example, a mathematics professor had been verbally abused during class by a student and refused to resume teaching his course until "the proper teaching atmosphere was restored" (818 F.2d at 61). The university did not take any disciplinary action against the student, did not take other initiatives to resolve the situation, and rejected a grievance committee's recommendation in favor of the professor. It then dismissed the professor for "neglect of professional responsibilities"—an enumerated "cause" stated in the faculty handbook. The professor sued the institution for breach of contract. Construing the pertinent contract provisions in light of custom and usage (see Section 1.4.3.3), the court held that the institution, in a for-cause dismissal, must consider not only the literal meaning of the term "cause" but also all surrounding and mitigating circumstances; in addition, the institution must evaluate the professor's actions "according to the standards of the profession." Since the institution had not done so, the court remanded the case to the district court for further proceedings.

Courts also might question the clarity or specificity of an institution's dismissal standards. In *San Filippo v. Bongiovanni*, 961 F.2d 1125 (3d Cir. 1992), Rutgers University had adopted the AAUP's "Statement on Professional Ethics" (University Regulation 3.91). In separate regulations, however, it had also adopted an adequate-cause standard to govern dismissals of tenured faculty (University Regulation 3.93) and had defined "adequate cause" as "failure to maintain standards of sound scholarship and competent teaching, or gross neglect of established University obligations appropriate to the appointment, or incompetence, or incapacitation, or conviction of a crime of moral turpitude" (University Regulation 3.94). Relying on both the AAUP Statement and the adequate-cause regulations, the university dismissed the plaintiff, a tenured chemistry professor. The charges stemmed from the professor's "conduct towards visiting Chinese scholars brought to the University to work with him on research projects." A university hearing panel found that the professor had "'exploited, threatened and been abusive'" to these student scholars and had "'demonstrated a serious lack of integrity in his professional dealings'" (961 F.2d at 1132, quoting the panel report).

The professor challenged his dismissal in federal court, arguing (among other things) that the university's dismissal regulations were unconstitutionally vague because they did not give him fair notice that he could be dismissed for the conduct with which he was charged. The university argued that the adequate-cause regulations (Regulations 3.93 and 3.94) "incorporated" the AAUP "Statement on Professional Ethics" (3.91), which applied to the professor's conduct and gave him sufficient notice. The appellate court (like the district court) rejected the university's "incorporation" argument and determined that the grounds for dismissal must be found in the adequate-cause regulations themselves, apart from the AAUP statement. But the appellate court (unlike the district court) nevertheless rejected the professor's vagueness argument because the portion of the adequate-cause regulation on "failure to maintain standards of sound scholarship and competent teaching" (3.94) was itself sufficient to provide fair notice:

> A reasonable, ordinary person using his common sense and general knowledge
> of employer-employee relationships would have fair notice that the conduct
> the University charged Dr. San Filippo with put him at risk of dismissal under
> a regulation stating he could be dismissed for "failure to maintain standards of
> sound scholarship and competent teaching." Regulation 3.94. He would know
> that the standard did not encompass only actual teaching or research skills . . . It
> is not unfair or unforeseeable for a tenured professor to be expected to behave
> decently towards students and coworkers, to comply with a superior's directive,
> and to be truthful and forthcoming in dealing with payroll, federal research funds
> or applications for academic positions. Such behavior is required for the purpose
> of maintaining sound scholarship and competent teaching [961 F.2d at 1137].

Freedom-of-expression issues may also become implicated in the institution's application of its dismissal standards. In *Adamian v. Jacobson*, 523 F.2d 929 (9th Cir. 1975), a professor from the University of Nevada at Reno had allegedly led a disruptive demonstration on campus. Charges were brought against him under a university code provision requiring faculty members "to exercise appropriate restraint [and] to show respect for the opinions of others," and the board of regents determined that violation of this provision was adequate cause for dismissal. In court the professor argued that this standard was not only unconstitutionally vague but also unconstitutionally "overbroad" in violation of the First Amendment (see Sections 9.1.3, 9.2.2, and 9.4.3 regarding overbreadth). The appellate court held that the standard would violate the First Amendment if interpreted broadly but could be constitutional if interpreted narrowly, as prescribed by AAUP academic freedom guidelines, so as not to refer to the content of the professor's remarks. The court therefore remanded the case to the trial court for further findings on how the university interpreted its code provision. On a second appeal, the court confined itself to the narrow issue of the construction of the code provision. Determining that the university's construction was consistent with the AAUP guidelines and reflected a limitation on the manner, rather than the content, of expression, the court held that the code provision was sufficiently narrow to avoid an overbreadth (as well as a vagueness) challenge (608 F.2d 1224 (9th Cir. 1979)).

Institutions should not comfortably settle for a bald adequate-cause standard. Good policy and (especially for public institutions) good law should demand more. Since incompetence, insubordination, immorality, lack of collegiality, and unethical conduct are the most commonly asserted grounds for dismissals for cause, institutions may wish to specifically include them in their dismissal policies.[1] If unethical conduct is a stated ground for dismissal, the

---

[1] Another ground for dismissal or other discipline is the ground of research misconduct. The ground refers to particular types of ethical problems that arise in the context of scientific research.

institution should consider adopting the AAUP "Statement on Professional Ethics." If it adopts the AAUP statement or its own version of ethical standards, the institution should make clear how and when violations of the statement or standards may be considered grounds for dismissal—thus avoiding the problem facing the university in *San Filippo*.

For each ground (or "cause") included in its dismissal policy, the institution should also include a definition of that ground, along with the criteria or standards for applying the definition to particular cases. (The AAUP "Statement on Professional Ethics" may serve this purpose for the "unethical conduct" ground.) Since such definitions and criteria may become part of the institution's contract with faculty members, they should be drafted clearly and specifically enough, and applied sensitively enough, to avoid contract interpretation problems such as those faced by the institution in the *McConnell* case. Such definitions and criteria should also be sufficiently clear to guide the decision makers who will apply them and to forewarn the faculty members who will be subject to them, thus avoiding vagueness problems; and they should be sufficiently specific to preclude dismissal of faculty members because of the content of their expression. In addition, such definitions and criteria should conform to the AAUP's caution that cause standards must have a direct and substantial relationship to the faculty member's professional fitness. Along with such standards, if the institution chooses to adopt them, the institution will want to develop record-keeping policies and perhaps periodic faculty review policies that will provide the facts necessary to make reliable termination decisions.

Administrators will also want to keep in mind that involuntary terminations of tenured faculty, because of their coercive and stigmatizing effect on the individuals involved, usually create a far greater number of legal problems than voluntary means for dissolving a tenured faculty member's employment relationship with the institution. Thus, another way to minimize legal vulnerability is to rely on voluntary alternatives to dismissals for cause. For example, the institution might provide increased incentives for retirement, opportunities for phased or partial retirement, or retraining for midcareer shifts to underserved areas of teaching or research. Or it might maintain flexibility in faculty development by increased use of fixed-term contracts, visiting professorships, part-time appointments, and other non-tenure-track appointments. All these alternatives have one thing in common with involuntary termination: their success depends on thorough review of personnel policies, coordinated planning for future contingencies, and careful articulation into written institutional policies.

*5.6.3. Denial of tenure.* Although the typical criteria for evaluating a faculty member for tenure are the quality of the individual's performance in teaching, scholarship (at research-oriented institutions), and service, additional criteria are sometimes used. Religiously affiliated colleges and universities may require faculty members to adhere to the religion's tenets or the institution's religious mission, or may even require that the faculty member be a member of that particular religion. At research institutions, tenure candidates in certain disciplines may be evaluated on the basis of their ability to obtain external funding for research or other activities. Collegiality, or institutional "citizenship," is increasingly being used, either openly or covertly, to make tenure decisions. And considerations of student enrollment trends or institutional or departmental financial health may also figure (either openly or covertly) into tenure decisions.

A line of cases has examined whether departments are permitted to interpret criteria for promotion or tenure more strictly than the way they were interpreted for previous tenure decisions. For example, plaintiffs denied tenure have argued that requirements for numbers or quality of publications had risen between the time they were hired and the time they were evaluated for tenure. The courts have been unsympathetic to these claims. In *Lim v. Trustees of Indiana University*, 297 F.3d 575 (7th Cir. 2002), for example, a federal appellate court affirmed a trial court's award of summary judgment to the university. Professor Lim, who was denied tenure at Indiana University, alleged that she had been discriminated against on the basis of sex. The same year that Lim was hired as an assistant professor, the department chair, who recruited and hired Lim, instituted higher standards for research and publication for untenured faculty than had been expected in the past. Lim was denied tenure, in large part for her failure to meet these higher standards.

The court noted that Lim had been warned on a regular basis during her six-year probationary period that she was not meeting the department's publication standards. The court rejected Lim's attempt to compare her publication record to that of male faculty who were tenured prior to the implementation of the new standards. The court ruled that these faculty were not similarly situated and could not serve as comparators for purposes of Lim's sex discrimination claim.

Disputes over the propriety of using collegiality as a criterion for tenure decisions have flared for more than two decades. In an early case, *Mayberry v. Dees*, 663 F.2d 502 (4th Cir. 1981), a federal appellate court ruled that collegiality was an appropriate criterion for evaluating faculty members for tenure. Federal trial courts have also upheld tenure denials on the grounds of poor relationships between the candidate and faculty colleagues (*Stein v. Kent State University Board of Trustees*, 994 F. Supp. 898 (N.D. Ohio 1998); *Bresnick v. Manhattanville College*, 864 F. Supp. 327 (S.D.N.Y. 1994)), and *University of Baltimore v. Peri Iz*, 716 A.2d 1107 (Md. Ct. Spec. App. 1998). The plaintiffs in these cases argued that college documents did not list collegiality as a criterion for tenure and that it was therefore improper to judge them on this basis. The courts replied that, even if institutional documents do not specifically mention collegiality, this criterion is implicit in the other express criteria or otherwise appropriate for consideration.

In *Ward v. Midwestern State University*, 217 F. App'x 325 (5th Cir. 2007), Ward, an associate professor of public administration, was denied tenure by the university because he "lacked the interpersonal skills necessary to serve . . . as an associate professor." Ward, an African-American, sued the university, alleging race discrimination and a variety of constitutional claims. The university provided evidence that Ward had shouted at faculty colleagues during meetings, had sent chastising emails to fellow faculty members, and failed to attend mandatory college and program faculty meetings. The lack of collegiality appeared to be the university's primary defense; the court did not discuss the quality of Ward's teaching, scholarship, or service. The appellate court affirmed the trial court's award of summary judgment. (For another case upholding a university's decision to deny tenure to a professor on the grounds of noncollegiality, which also included claims of difficult interpersonal relationships with students, see *Sawicki v. Morgan State University*, 2005 U.S. Dist. LEXIS 41174, *affirmed*, 170 F. App'x 271 (4th Cir. March 1, 2006).)

Another controversial criterion for tenure that has been reviewed in court is "academic politics," which is closely related to "collegiality." In *Kumbhojkar v. University of Miami*, 727 So. 2d 275 (Fla. Dist. Ct. App. 1999), a state appellate court rejected the plaintiff's claim that his tenure denial was inappropriately based on personal animosity between himself and his department head because the department head was not the ultimate decision maker in the case. The plaintiff had also claimed that the negative decision was inappropriately based on "prior internal disputes within his department." Characterizing these disputes as "academic politics," the court rejected the plaintiff's claim that "academic politics" was an inappropriate ground for tenure denial, noting that academic politics was a fact of life on campus.

A similar result was reached in *Slatkin v. University of Redlands*, 88 Cal. App. 4th 1147 (Cal. Ct. App., 4th Dist. 2001), in which the court ruled that academic politics could be viewed as a legitimate nondiscriminatory reason for denying a professor tenure. The professor had made negative comments about a departmental colleague; the court ruled that the "inability of colleagues to forgive her" for making these comments was the motive for the negative tenure recommendation, and that such a motive was not discriminatory. (See also the discussion of the *Fisher* case in Section 5.4.2 for another example of judicial understanding of "academic politics.")

Over the past several years, a number of faculty members denied tenure on the basis of inadequate evidence of strong teaching have challenged the institution's reliance on student course evaluations in making such negative tenure decisions. In virtually all of these cases, the institution has prevailed.

In *Sawicki v. Morgan State University*, 2006 U.S. App. LEXIS 5206 (4th Cir. 2006), for example, a woman hired as a nontenured full professor was denied tenure, in large part because of student complaints about her teaching. She was seen as "pedantic" and "condescending" to the students, although a few students praised her teaching. The court awarded summary judgment to the university on her sex discrimination claim. Similarly, in *Byerly v. Ithaca College*, 290 F. Supp. 2d 301 (N.D.N.Y. 2003), a faculty member characterized as "condescending" and "intimidating" to students was denied tenure and lost her sex discrimination claim, and in *Kautt v. University of Texas San Antonio*, 2003 U.S. Dist. LEXIS 16392 (W.D. Tex. 2003), a female faculty member's contract was not renewed on the basis of poor student evaluations and her tendency to impose discipline on students for "minor infractions." The court rejected her sex discrimination claim.

In reviewing these claims, the courts have resoundingly agreed with institutions that student complaints and course evaluation results are legitimate reasons to deny tenure or to decline to reappoint individuals, and several have expressed frustration that plaintiffs attempt to use the courts to second-guess institutions' tenure decisions. See, for example, *Murungi v. Xavier University*, 2008 U.S. App. LEXIS 8114 (5th Cir. April 15, 2008); see also *Doucet v. University of Cincinnati*, 2007 U.S App. LEXIS 21570 (6th Cir., August 28, 2007). Courts have also rejected claims by faculty members that using student, rather than peer, evaluations of teaching is a violation of their rights (see, for example, *Yarcheski v. Reiner et al.*, 669 N.W.2d 487 (S.D. 2003)).

Other colleges have faced challenges to tenure denials made on the basis of declining enrollments or concerns about the financial health of the institution. There is strong judicial support for the removal of tenured faculty due to documented financial difficulties of the institution, and unless an institution has somehow limited its authority to use financial reasons or enrollment declines as a criterion for denying tenure, courts usually will affirm its discretion to do so. (See, for example, *Hudson v. Wesley College*, 1998 Del. Ch. LEXIS 235 (Del. Ch. December 23, 1998) (unpublished); see also *Roklina v. Skidmore College*, 702 N.Y.S.2d 161 (N.Y. App. Div. 2000), *appeal denied*, 95 N.Y.2d 758 (N.Y. 2000) (unpublished).) In *Spuler v. Pickar*, 958 F.2d 103 (5th Cir. 1992), a federal appellate court upheld the authority of the University of Houston to deny tenure to a faculty member for financial reasons, even though the university hired a new faculty member in the same department shortly after Spuler was denied tenure. The court found that Spuler was not qualified to teach upper-level courses that the department needed and that legitimate financial considerations motivated the tenure denial.

But if the institution has promised not to use enrollment stability as a criterion for determining tenure, it cannot do so, even in a time of enrollment downturn, without first changing its written policy. In *In Re Bennett v. Wells College*, 641 N.Y.S.2d 929 (N.Y. App. Div. 1996), the college's faculty manual stated that if the college determined that a tenure-track position was necessary at the time of hiring a faculty member, the status of enrollment would not be used at the time of the tenure decision. Bennett was denied tenure because of declining enrollments in her department. Because the dean and president used a criterion that the college's own policies forbade them to use, the court ruled that the tenure decision had to be repeated without consideration of enrollment issues.

Some institutions have implemented "tenure caps" that limit the proportion of tenured faculty in a particular department. In *Roufaiel v. Ithaca College*, 660 N.Y.S.2d 595 (N.Y. App. Div. 1997), Ithaca College had a tenure cap of 75 percent, a figure that was included in offer letters to faculty and in the faculty handbook. When Professor Roufaiel was hired as an accounting instructor, she was advised of the tenure cap in writing. But at the time that Roufaiel was evaluated for tenure, the provost told the dean of the business school that the tenure cap would not be applied to the accounting department, assuming that enrollment remained stable. Roufaiel was recommended for tenure, but the provost rejected the recommendation, stating that enrollment considerations precluded a favorable decision. Roufaiel filed breach of contract, estoppel, and fraudulent misrepresentation claims.

The court denied the college's summary judgment motion because the parties disagreed about the enrollment numbers, an issue that was central to the college's defense. But the court dismissed the estoppel and fraudulent misrepresentation claims because the plaintiff could not provide evidence that she had been promised tenure.

These cases suggest that, if an institution can articulate a reasonable justification for a particular tenure criterion, and if it has not explicitly prevented itself from using that criterion, the courts will typically defer to the institution even if it has not expressly stated the criterion in its tenure policies. Of course, the institution will still have to demonstrate that it applies the criterion evenhandedly and reasonably, and that the criterion furthers the institutional interest in providing high-quality teaching, research, or service to its students or the wider community. The better practice, however, will be to expressly and clearly articulate each tenure criterion in the institution's written policies, and to maintain mechanisms for systematically evaluating tenure candidates against these criteria. To the extent the institution does so, litigation should be either reduced or, at a minimum, more easily defended against.

### Section 5.7. Procedures for Faculty Employment Decisions

**5.7.1. General principles.** Postsecondary educational institutions have established varying procedural requirements for making and internally reviewing faculty personnel decisions. Administrators should look first at these requirements when they are attempting to resolve procedural issues concerning appointment, retention, promotion, and tenure. Whenever such requirements can reasonably be construed as part of the faculty member's contract with the institution (see Section 5.2), the law will usually expect both public and private institutions to comply with them. In *Skehan v. Board of Trustees of Bloomsburg State College*, 501 F.2d 31 (3d Cir. 1976), for instance, a nonrenewed professor alleged that the institution had not complied with a college policy statement providing for hearings in academic freedom cases. The appellate court held that the college would have to follow the policy statement if, on remand, the lower court found that the statement granted a contractual right under state law and that the professor's case involved academic freedom within the meaning of the statement. Upon remand and a second appeal, the court held that the professor did have a contractual right to the procedures specified in the statement and that the college had violated this right (590 F.2d 470 (3d Cir. 1978)). Similarly, in *Zuelsdorf v. University of Alaska, Fairbanks*, 794 P.2d 932 (Alaska 1990), the court held that a notice requirement in the university's personnel regulations was part of the faculty contract and that the university had breached the contract by not giving the plaintiffs timely notice of nonrenewal.

Public institutions will also often be subject to state statutes or administrative regulations that establish procedures applicable to faculty personnel decisions. In *Brouillette v. Board of Directors of Merged Area IX*, 519 F.2d 126 (8th Cir. 1975), for example, the court determined that a state statute requiring a public pretermination hearing for public school teachers applied to the termination of a community college faculty member as well. The institution had, however, complied with the statutory requirements. In a "turnabout" case, *Rutcosky v. Board of Trustees of Community College District No. 18*, 545 P.2d 567 (1976), the court found that the plaintiff faculty member had not complied with a state procedural requirement applicable to termination-of-employment hearings and therefore refused to grant him any relief.

Institutional procedures, state laws, or both also control the conditions under which a faculty member acquires tenured status. Many institutions have adopted policies that state that only the trustees can grant tenure, and courts have denied an award of **de facto tenure** in those cases. For example, in *Hill v. Talladega College*, 502 So. 2d 735 (Ala. 1987), the court refused to award de facto tenure to a faculty member employed at the college for ten years because the faculty handbook specifically stated that only the trustees could grant tenure and that tenure could not be acquired automatically at the college. And in *Gray v. Board of Regents of University System of Georgia*, 150 F.3d 1347 (11th Cir. 1999), the court ruled that, absent evidence of either a custom of awarding de facto tenure or some established institutional understanding that de facto tenure existed, an assistant professor employed under annual contracts for nine years did not acquire tenure simply by being so employed for more than the seven-year probationary period.

The procedures used by a state institution or other institution whose personnel decision is considered state action (see Section 1.5.2) are also subject to constitutional requirements of procedural due process. These requirements are discussed in Section 5.7.2.

Since private institutions are not subject to these constitutional requirements, or to state procedural statutes and regulations, contract law may be the primary or sole basis for establishing and testing the scope of their procedural obligation to faculty members. In *Johnson v. Christian Brothers College*, 565 S.W.2d 872 (Tenn. 1978), for example, an associate professor instituted suit for breach of his employment contract when the college did not grant him tenure. The college, a religiously affiliated institution in Memphis, had a formal tenure program detailed in its faculty handbook. The program included a seven-year probationary period, during which the faculty member worked under a series of one-year contracts. After seven years, on the prior recommendation of the tenure committee and approval of the president, the faculty member either received tenure along with the award of the eighth contract or was dismissed. The plaintiff claimed that, once he had reached the final probationary year and was being considered for tenure, he was entitled to the formal notice and hearing procedures utilized by the college in terminating tenured faculty. The Supreme Court of Tennessee held that nothing in the terms of the one-year contracts, the published tenure program, or the commonly used procedure of the college evidenced an agreement or practice of treating teachers in their final probationary year as equivalent to tenured faculty. The college therefore had no express or implied contractual obligation to afford the professor notice and an opportunity to be heard.

A Maryland appellate court rejected the claims of two professors that Johns Hopkins University hired them with tenure in *The Johns Hopkins University v. Ritter*, 689 A.2d 91 (Md. Ct. Spec. App. 1996). Professors Ritter and Snider were recruited from tenured positions at Cornell and Duke Universities, respectively, to join the department of pediatrics at Johns Hopkins. The department chair, Professor Oski, assured them that they would be hired at the full professor rank; consequently, both resigned tenured professorships at their respective institutions and joined the faculty at Johns Hopkins. Oski had told them, both orally and in writing, that their rank and salary had to be formally approved by a faculty committee and by the dean. The professors began work at Johns Hopkins in January 1994 as visiting professors without tenure, but their rank and tenure review had not been completed by the end of spring semester and, thus, was held over until the fall of 1994. During the spring and summer of 1994, according to the court, Ritter and Snider had many disagreements with their new colleagues, and many faculty and staff complained about the new professors to the dean of the medical school. The dean decided to terminate the appointments of the pair before the medical school's advisory board or the university's board of trustees had acted on their appointments.

Ritter and Snider brought a breach of contract claim against the university, asserting that Oski had promised them tenure and that they had resigned their tenured positions at other institutions in reliance on his representations in letters and oral communications to the pair. A jury found for the plaintiffs, but the appellate court overturned those verdicts.

The appellate court addressed the nature of the contract and Oski's authority to alter the university's written tenure procedures. Although the court agreed with the plaintiffs that both the letters and the conversations with Oski were included in the contract, it found that Oski had no authority to abrogate the university's written tenure procedures. He did not have actual authority to do so because there was no evidence that the board of trustees or the advisory board of the medical school (both of which had to approve a faculty personnel decision) had authorized Oski to make a commitment on their behalf. Nor did Oski have apparent authority to bind the university, for no one at a higher level than Oski met with or told the plaintiffs that Oski was authorized to promise tenure. The court also rejected the plaintiffs' estoppel claim, noting that no one, including Oski, had ever represented that he had the authority to bypass the written tenure procedure.

This case is important for private institutions that are subject primarily to common law contract challenges, particularly in de facto tenure claims such as that against Johns Hopkins. It also suggests that deans or other officials should oversee contractual negotiations and be the ones to offer letters in order to avoid the misunderstandings that led to this litigation.

### 5.7.2. The public faculty member's right to constitutional due process.

In two landmark cases, *Board of Regents v. Roth*, 408 U.S. 564 (1972), and *Perry v. Sindermann*, 408 U.S. 593 (1972), the U.S. Supreme Court established that faculty members have a right to a fair hearing whenever a personnel decision deprives them of a "property interest" or a "liberty interest" under the Fourteenth Amendment's due process clause. The "property" and "liberty" terminology is derived from the wording of the Fourteenth Amendment itself, which provides that states shall not "deprive any person of life, liberty, or property, without due process of law." (The identification of property and liberty interests is also important to many procedural due process questions concerning students; see Sections 7.3.1, 7.6.1, 9.4.2, and 10.4.2.)

In identifying these property and liberty interests, one must make the critical distinction between faculty members who are under continuing contracts and those whose contracts have expired. It is clear, as *Roth* notes, that "a public college professor dismissed from an office held under tenure provisions . . . and college professors and staff members dismissed during the terms of their contracts . . . have interests in continued employment that are safeguarded by due process" (408 U.S. at 576–77). But the situation is less clear with respect to faculty members whose contracts are expiring and are up for renewal or a tenure review. Moreover, when a personnel decision would infringe a property or liberty interest, as in tenure termination, other questions then arise concerning the particular procedures that the institution must follow.

#### 5.7.2.1. Nonrenewal of contracts.

*Roth* and *Perry* (above) are the leading cases on the nonrenewal of faculty contracts. The respondent in *Roth* had been hired as an assistant professor at Wisconsin State University for a fixed term of one year. A state statute provided that all state university teachers would be employed for one-year terms and would be eligible for tenure only after four years of continuous service. The professor was notified before February 1 that he would not be rehired. No reason for the decision was given, nor was there an opportunity for a hearing or an appeal.

The question considered by the Supreme Court was "whether the [professor] had a constitutional right to a statement of reasons and a hearing on the university's decision not to rehire him for another year." The Court ruled that he had no such right because neither a "liberty" nor a "property" interest had been violated by the nonrenewal. Concerning liberty interests, the Court reasoned:

> The state, in declining to rehire the respondent, did not make any charge against him that might seriously damage his standing and associations in his community. It did not base the nonrenewal of his contract on a charge, for example, that he had been guilty of dishonesty or immorality. Had it done so, this would be a different case . . . In such a case, due process would accord an opportunity to refute the charge before university officials. In the present case, however, there is no suggestion whatever that the respondent's "good name, reputation, honor, or integrity" is at stake.

Similarly, there is no suggestion that the state, in declining to reemploy the respondent, imposed on him a stigma or other disability that foreclosed his freedom to take advantage of other employment opportunities. The state, for example, did not invoke any regulations to bar the respondent from all other public employment in state universities. Had it done so, this, again, would be a different case . . .

Hence, on the record before us, all that clearly appears is that the respondent was not rehired for one year at one university. It stretches the concept too far to suggest that a person is deprived of "liberty" when he simply is not rehired in one job but remains as free as before to seek another [408 U.S. at 573–74, 575].

The Court also held that the respondent had not been deprived of any property interest in future employment:

To have a property interest in a benefit, a person clearly must have more than an abstract need or desire for it. He must have more than a unilateral expectation of it. He must, instead, have a legitimate claim of entitlement to it . . . Property interests, of course, are not created by the Constitution. Rather, they are created and their dimensions are defined by existing rules or understandings that stem from an independent source such as state law—rules or understandings that secure certain benefits and that support claims of entitlement to those benefits . . . Respondent's "property" interest in employment at Wisconsin State University-Oshkosh was created and defined by the terms of his appointment, [which] specifically provided that the respondent's employment was to terminate on June 30. They did not provide for contract renewal absent "sufficient cause." Indeed, they made no provision for renewal whatsoever . . . In these circumstances, the respondent surely had an abstract concern in being rehired, but he did not have a property interest sufficient to require the university authorities to give him a hearing when they declined to renew his contract of employment [408 U.S. at 578].

Since the professor had no protected liberty or property interest, his Fourteenth Amendment rights had not been violated, and the university was not required to provide a reason for its nonrenewal of the contract or to afford the professor a hearing on the nonrenewal.

In the *Perry* case, the respondent had been employed as a professor by the Texas state college system for ten consecutive years. While employed, he was actively involved in public disagreements with the board of regents. He was employed on a series of one-year contracts, and at the end of his tenth year the board elected not to rehire him. The professor was given neither an official reason nor the opportunity for a hearing. Like Roth, Perry argued that the board's action violated his Fourteenth Amendment right to procedural due process.

But in the *Perry* case, unlike the *Roth* case, the Supreme Court ruled that the professor had raised a genuine claim to de facto tenure, which would create a constitutionally protected property interest in continued employment. The professor relied on tenure guidelines promulgated by the coordinating board of the Texas College and University System and on an official faculty guide's statement that

> Odessa College has no tenure system. The administration of the college wishes the faculty member to feel that he has permanent tenure as long as his teaching services are satisfactory and as long as he displays a cooperative attitude toward his coworkers and his superiors, and as long as he is happy in his work [408 U.S. at 600].

According to the Court:

> We have made clear in *Roth* . . . that "property" interests subject to procedural due process protection are not limited by a few rigid technical forms. Rather, "property" denotes a broad range of interests that are secured by "existing rules or understandings." A person's interest in a benefit is a "property" interest for due process purposes if there are such rules or mutually explicit understandings that support his claim of entitlement to the benefit and that he may invoke at a hearing . . . In this case, the respondent has alleged the existence of rules and understandings, promulgated and fostered by state officials, that may justify his legitimate claim of entitlement to continued employment absent "sufficient cause." . . . [W]e agree that the respondent must be given an opportunity to prove the legitimacy of his claim of such entitlement in light of "the policies and practices of the institution." . . . [S]uch proof would obligate officials to grant a hearing at his request, where he could be informed of the grounds for his nonretention and challenge their sufficiency [408 U.S. at 603].

One other Supreme Court case should be read together with *Roth* and *Perry* for a fuller understanding of the Court's due process analysis. *Bishop v. Wood*, 426 U.S. 341 (1976), concerned a policeman who had been discharged, allegedly on the basis of incorrect information, and orally informed of the reasons in a private conference. With four Justices strongly dissenting, the Court held that the discharge infringed neither property nor liberty interests of the policeman. Regarding property, the Court, adopting a stilted lower-court interpretation of the ordinance governing employment of policemen, held that the ordinance created no expectation of continued employment but only required the employer to provide certain procedural protections, all of which had been provided in this case. Regarding liberty, the Court held that the charges against an employee cannot form the basis for a deprivation of liberty claim if they are privately communicated to the employee and not made public. The Court also held that the truth or falsity of the charges is irrelevant to the question of whether a liberty interest has been infringed.

Under *Roth*, *Perry*, and *Bishop*, there are three basic situations in which courts will require that a nonrenewal decision be accompanied by appropriate procedural safeguards:

1. The existing rules, policies, or practices of the institution, or "mutually explicit understandings" between the faculty member and the institution,

support the faculty member's claim of entitlement to continued employment. Such circumstances would create a property interest. In *Soni v. Board of Trustees of University of Tennessee*, 513 F.2d 347 (6th Cir. 1975), for example, the court held that a nonrenewed, nontenured mathematics professor had such a property interest because voting and retirement plan privileges had been extended to him and he had been told that he could expect his contract to be renewed. But if the contract is silent on renewal, and no promises have been made as to the likelihood of renewal, then no property right exists. See, for example, *Embury v. King*, 179 F. App'x 409 (9th Cir. 2006).

2. The institution, in the course of nonrenewal, makes charges against the faculty member that could seriously damage his or her reputation, standing, or associations in the community. Such circumstances would create a liberty interest.[2] *Roth*, for instance, suggests that charges of dishonesty or immorality accompanying nonrenewal could infringe a faculty member's liberty interest. And in *Wellner v. Minnesota State Junior College Board*, 487 F.2d 153 (8th Cir. 1973), the court held that charges of racism deprived the faculty member of a liberty interest. The *Bishop* case makes clear that charges or accusations against a faculty member must in some way be made public before they can form the basis of a liberty claim.

3. The nonrenewal imposes a "stigma or other disability" on the faculty member that "foreclose[s] his freedom to take advantage of other employment opportunities." Such circumstances would create a liberty interest. *Roth*, for instance, suggests that a nonrenewal that bars the faculty member from other employment in the state higher education system would infringe a liberty interest. Presumably, charges impugning the faculty member's professional competence or integrity could also infringe a liberty interest if the institution keeps records of the charges and if the contents of these records could be divulged to potential future employers of the faculty member. But if the faculty member's contract is merely not renewed, the fact that it may be difficult for an individual to locate another teaching position does not mean that the nonrenewal creates a liberty interest. In *Putnam v. Keller*, 332 F.3d 541 (8th Cir. 2003), the court ruled that a nonrenewed faculty member accused of misappropriating funds and planning musical events with "inappropriate sexual overtones" had a liberty interest and was entitled to a hearing on his nonrenewal decision. The court determined that these charges stigmatized the plaintiff, and had been made known to other faculty and staff members at the college, thus entitling him to a hearing to clear his name.

---

[2] In *Paul v. Davis*, 424 U.S. 693 (1976), the U.S. Supreme Court held that "defamation, standing alone" does not infringe a liberty interest. But defamation can still create a liberty infringement when combined with some "alteration of legal status" under state law, and termination or nonrenewal of public employment is such a change in status. Defamation "in the course of declining to rehire" would therefore infringe a faculty member's liberty interest even under *Paul v. Davis*.

A liberty or property interest might also be infringed when the nonrenewal is based on, and thus would penalize, the faculty member's exercise of freedom of expression. The Supreme Court dealt with this issue briefly in a footnote in the *Roth* case (408 U.S. at 575 n.14), appearing to suggest that a hearing may be required in some circumstances where the nonrenewal "would directly impinge upon interests in free speech or free press." In the *Putnam* case, discussed above, the college had banned Professor Putnam from the campus, an act that resulted in a free speech and freedom of association claim by the plaintiff in addition to his liberty interest claim. Again, the court ruled in Putnam's favor, stating that the campus is a public forum, thus giving Putnam the same right of access to the campus as any other citizen enjoys. Another federal appellate court ruled that a multistep grievance process used by a nonreappointed faculty member who challenged his nonrenewal was sufficient to protect his liberty interest (*Feterle v. Chowdhury*, 148 F. App'x 524 (6th Cir. 2005)).

Whenever a nonrenewed faculty member has a basis for making a liberty or property interest claim, administrators should consider providing a hearing. Properly conducted, a hearing may not only vitiate any subsequent procedural due process litigation by the faculty member but may also resolve or defuse First Amendment claims that otherwise might be taken to court. The hearing may be informal, as long as the institution follows its own procedures and provides the accused faculty member with notice of the charges and an opportunity to respond to them. And, as seen in *Feterle*, the institution's grievance process, if available to a faculty member whose appointment was not renewed, would generally provide sufficient due process to protect a liberty interest.

In 1971, the American Association of University Professors adopted a "Statement on Procedural Standards in the Renewal or Nonrenewal of Faculty Appointments" (available at http://www.aaup.org/AAUP/pubsres/policydocs/contents/nonreapp-stmt.htm). The procedures include notice of criteria for reappointment, periodic review of the performance of probationary faculty, notice of reasons for nonreappointment, and an appeal process for decisions that allegedly involved academic freedom violations or gave inadequate consideration to the department's recommendation.

**5.7.2.2. Denial of tenure.** Denials of tenure, like contract nonrenewals, must be distinguished analytically from terminations of tenure. Whereas a tenure termination always infringes the faculty member's property interests, a tenure denial may or may not infringe a property or liberty interest, triggering due process protections. The answer in any particular case will depend on application of the teachings from *Roth* and *Perry* (Section 5.7.2.1) and their progeny. Denials of promotions, for due process purposes, are generally analogous to denials of tenure and thus are subject to the general principles developed in the tenure denial cases below. For a leading illustration, see *Clark v. Whiting*, 607 F.2d 634 (4th Cir. 1979), where the court held that an associate professor had no right to an evidentiary hearing upon denial of promotion to full professor.

In 1978, a West Virginia court determined that a faculty member denied tenure had been deprived of a property interest (*McLendon v. Morton*, 249

S.E.2d 919 (W. Va. 1978)). Parkersburg Community College published eligibility criteria for tenure, which included six years as a teaching member of the full-time faculty and attainment of the rank of assistant professor. Having fulfilled both requirements, McLendon applied for tenure. After her tenure application was rejected on grounds of incompetence, McLendon filed suit, claiming that the institution's failure to provide her a hearing abridged her due process rights. The court held that (1) satisfying "objective eligibility standards gave McLendon a sufficient entitlement, so that she could not be denied tenure on the basis of her competence without some procedural due process"; and (2) minimal due process necessitates notice of the reasons for denial and a hearing before an unbiased tribunal, at which the professor can refute the issues raised in the notice. This decision thus extends the *Roth* doctrine to include, among persons who have a property interest in continued employment, faculty members who teach at public institutions and have met specified objective criteria for tenure eligibility (assuming that the institution uses objective criteria). In West Virginia and any other jurisdiction that may accept the *McLendon* reasoning, institutions must give such faculty members notice and an opportunity for a hearing before any final decision to deny tenure. Most institutions, however, use subjective criteria, or a combination of objective and subjective criteria, for making tenure decisions, and thus would not be bound by *McLendon*.

In contrast to *McLendon*, the court in *Beitzel v. Jeffrey*, 643 F.2d 870 (1st Cir. 1981), held that a professor hired as a "probationary employee" did not have a sufficient property interest at stake under *Roth* to challenge his denial of tenure on due process grounds. The standards for the granting or denial of tenure were outlined in the university handbook; but, unlike those in *McLendon*, these standards were subjective. The court determined that the professor had no basis for the expectation that he would be granted tenure automatically.

Institutional procedures for making a tenure decision do not themselves create a property interest, according to *Siu v. Johnson*, 748 F.2d 238 (4th Cir. 1984). Siu was denied tenure by George Mason University, a public institution, despite the positive recommendation of her departmental colleagues. Citing language in the faculty handbook that "the faculty is primarily responsible for recommendations involving appointments, reappointments, promotions, [and] the granting of tenure" (748 F.2d at 241) (although the final decision was explicitly afforded to the board or president), Siu asserted that the university's written procedures for making tenure decisions created a constitutionally protected property interest and that the institution's failure to defer to the peer evaluation violated that property interest. The court stated that most untenured faculty were at-will employees and thus had no legitimate expectation of reemployment.

The court then turned to Siu's contention that detailed procedures for making tenure decisions created a property interest in having those procedures followed. The court responded:

> Put this way the claim is a circular one: the state's detailed procedures provide the due process guarantees which create the very property interest protected by

those guarantees. This is conceptually unacceptable. Its logical effect would be to "constitutionalize" all state contractual provisions respecting the continuation of public employment [748 F.2d at 244].

The court then provided guidance regarding the analysis of whether a property interest exists, noting that the decision-making procedures used are not coextensive with the property right, which, in this case, was created by state law.

> The special relevance of the procedures to this limited inquiry is their indication of the general nature of the decisional process by which it is contemplated that the "interest" may be terminated. In particular, the procedures will likely indicate whether the decisional process is intended to be essentially an objective one designed to find facts establishing fault, or cause, or justification or the like, or instead to be essentially a subjective, evaluative one committed by the sources to the professional judgment of persons presumed to possess special competence in making the evaluation [748 F.2d at 244].

Concluding that the process in tenure decisions was subjective rather than objective, the court held that:

> the process due one subject to this highly subjective evaluative decision can only be the exercise of professional judgment by those empowered to make the final decision in a way not so manifestly arbitrary and capricious that a reviewing court could confidently say of it that it did not in the end involve the exercise of professional judgment [748 F.2d at 245].

The court then turned to Siu's claim that the institution's refusal to defer to the faculty's judgment violated its tenure procedures, an alleged violation of substantive, rather than procedural, due process:

> Required deference to "working" faculty judgments in evaluating the professional qualifications of their peers may . . . be a proper subject for vigorous faculty associational efforts, for negotiated contractual ordering, or for voluntary conferral by sufficiently enlightened and secure academic institutions. But we are not prepared to hold that it is an essential element of constitutionally guaranteed due process, whether or not it is contractually ordered or otherwise observed as a matter of custom in a particular institution [748 F.2d at 245].

The court in *Kilcoyne v. Morgan*, 664 F.2d 940 (4th Cir. 1981), rejected yet another argument for procedural protections prior to denial of tenure. The plaintiff, a nontenured faculty member at East Carolina University, argued that his employment contract incorporated a provision of the faculty manual requiring department chairmen to apprise nontenured faculty—both by personal conference and written evaluation—of their progress toward tenure. Although Kilcoyne received a letter from the department chairman and had a follow-up conference toward the end of each of his first two years at the university, he argued that these procedures did not conform to the faculty manual. University guidelines also mandated a tenure decision following a three-year probationary period. At the beginning of his third year, Kilcoyne was notified that he would be rehired for a fourth year; later in the third year, however, he was informed that he would not be granted tenure or employed beyond the fourth year. Kilcoyne argued that the alleged failure of the university to conform precisely to the faculty manual procedures incorporated into his contract deprived him of procedural due process. The court held that Kilcoyne lacked any *Roth* property interest in further employment at the university; denial of tenure would thus have been constitutionally permissible even if accompanied by no procedural safeguards. According to the court, if a state university gratuitously provides procedural safeguards that are not constitutionally mandated, deviations from such procedures will not violate due process even if the procedures are enumerated in the faculty contract. Although the contract may provide a basis for a breach of contract action, the mere fact that the state is a contracting party does not raise the contract problem to the status of a constitutional issue.

A few courts have ordered a college to grant tenure to a faculty member who has prevailed in a constitutional or civil rights challenge to a tenure denial (see the discussion in Section 5.4.2), but it is much more common for a court to remand the decision to the university for a new tenure review that avoids the procedural violations found by the court to have prejudiced the review process. For example, in *Sugano v. University of Washington*, 2000 Wash. App. LEXIS 504 (Wash. Ct. App. March 27, 2000) (unpublished), a state appellate court determined that an untenured professor of romance languages had not been properly mentored and also ruled that the university had not followed the appropriate process in the plaintiff's tenure review. Although the plaintiff was subsequently denied tenure after a second review, the court awarded her back pay and ordered the university to pay her attorney's fees.

In *Skorin-Kapov v. State University of New York at Stony Brook*, 722 N.Y.S.2d 576 (N.Y. App. Div. 2001), *appeal denied*, 96 N.Y.2d 720 (N.Y. 2001), a state appellate court reversed the order of a trial court to grant the plaintiff tenure after a finding that the tenure denial was arbitrary, capricious, and "without a sound basis in reason." Although the appellate court agreed with the trial court's findings of fact, it rejected its remedy and remanded the matter to the university to conduct a new tenure evaluation.

Procedural protections for public college faculty may also be found in faculty handbooks or other college policies that have contractual significance. For example, the faculty handbook at Washington State University requires that tenured faculty members conduct annual evaluations of untenured faculty. In *Trimble v. Washington State University*, 993 P.2d 259 (Wash. 2000), a faculty member denied tenure filed a breach of contract claim, stating that the failure of the mentoring process caused his tenure denial. The state's Supreme Court affirmed a summary judgment ruling for the university, stating that the tenured faculty members' failure to provide written evaluations of an untenured faculty member during his probationary period did not constitute a breach of contract. One justice dissented, stating that the failure to provide feedback to the untenured faculty member from tenured faculty in his department prevented him from making the kind of changes in his research program that could have led to a positive tenure decision.

Carefully drafted contract language can help colleges deflect contractual claims to tenure as a result of defective procedures. For example, in *University of Nevada v. Stacey*, 997 P.2d 812 (Nev. 2000), the state's highest court rejected a breach of contract claim brought by a professor who had received excellent evaluations during his employment at the university. He argued that the positive evaluations that, under the university's handbook, allowed him to be evaluated for tenure actually required the university to *grant* him tenure. The court reviewed all of the university's policies related to tenure and found no procedural violation. With respect to the alleged breach of contract, the court ruled that a decision to grant tenure was discretionary, and therefore denial of tenure was not a breach of contract.

With the exception of *McLendon*, which addressed issues not usually present in challenges to tenure denials, the courts have clearly stated that denial of tenure is not a "termination" per se and affords no constitutional due process guarantees (although state statutes or regulations may provide procedural guarantees, which, if violated, could form the basis for a claim under state law). As is the case with nonreappointment, however, if the faculty member alleges that the tenure denial was grounded in unconstitutional reasons (retaliation for constitutionally protected speech, for example), then liberty interests would arguably have been infringed and procedural due process protections would therefore apply.

### 5.7.2.3. *Termination of tenure.*

Whenever a public institution's personnel decision would infringe a property or liberty interest, constitutional due process requires that the institution offer the faculty member procedural safeguards before the decision becomes final. The crux of these safeguards is notice and opportunity for a hearing. In other words, the institution must notify the faculty member of the reasons for the decision and provide a fair opportunity for him or her to challenge these reasons in a hearing before an impartial body.

Decisions to terminate tenured faculty members at public institutions must always be accompanied by notice and opportunity for a hearing, since such decisions always infringe property interests. The cases in this section provide specific illustrations of the procedural due process requirements applicable to tenure termination cases. Decisions to terminate a nontenured faculty member during the contract term are generally analogous to tenure terminations and thus are subject to principles similar to those in the cases below; the same is true for nonrenewal and denial-of-tenure decisions when they would infringe property or liberty interests.

Because of the significance of the property interest, a pretermination hearing is required before the termination decision is final. The standards for the pretermination hearing that must be provided to a discharged faculty member were developed by the U.S. Supreme Court in *Cleveland Board of Education v. Loudermill*, 470 U.S. 532 (1985). According to the *Loudermill* opinion, "The tenured public employee is entitled to oral or written notice of the charges against him, an explanation of the employer's evidence, and an opportunity to present his side of the story" (470 U.S. at 546). If the pretermination hearing is as informal as the *Loudermill* criteria suggest is permissible, then a post-termination hearing is necessary to permit the individual to challenge the decision in a manner designed to protect his or her rights to due process. The nature of the hearing and the degree of formality of the procedures have been the subjects of much litigation by tenured faculty who were discharged.

Although there is no requirement that the termination hearing have all the elements of a judicial hearing (*Toney v. Reagan*, 467 F.2d 953 (9th Cir. 1972)), such hearings must meet minimal constitutional standards. A federal appeals court set forth such standards in *Levitt v. University of Texas*, 759 F.2d 1224 (5th Cir. 1985):

1. The employee must be given notice of the cause for dismissal.
2. The employee must be given notice of the names of witnesses and told what each will testify to.
3. The employee must be given a meaningful opportunity to be heard.
4. The hearing must be held within a reasonable time.
5. The hearing must be conducted before an impartial panel with appropriate academic expertise.

Many institutions, however, have adopted the procedures recommended by the American Association of University Professors. Formal adoption of the AAUP's 1958 "Statement on Procedural Standards in Faculty Dismissal Proceedings" (available at http://www.aaup.org/AAUP/pubsres/policydocs/contents/statementon + proceduralstandardsinfaculty + dismissal + proceedings.htm) will require the institution to follow them.

A federal trial court developed a set of carefully reasoned and articulated due process standards in *Potemra v. Ping*, 462 F. Supp. 328 (E.D. Ohio 1978). In that case, a tenured member of the economics department at Ohio University claimed that he was denied due process when the university dismissed him for failure to perform his faculty duties and inability to communicate with students. The court ruled that the teacher's minimum due process safeguards included (1) a written statement of the reasons for the proposed termination prior to final action, (2) adequate notice of a hearing, (3) a hearing at which the teacher has an opportunity to submit evidence to controvert the grounds for dismissal, (4) a final statement of the grounds for dismissal if it does occur. The court held that the university had complied with these requirements and had not infringed the faculty member's due process rights.

In another case, *King v. University of Minnesota*, 774 F.2d 224 (8th Cir. 1985), the court upheld the university's dismissal of a tenured faculty member for neglect of his teaching responsibilities and lack of scholarship. The university had provided the following due process protections:

1. Frequent communications with King concerning his poor teaching, his unexcused absences, and his refusal to cooperate with the department.
2. A departmental vote, with King present, to remove him from the department because of his history of poor performance.

3. Notice to King of the charges against him and the university's intent to initiate removal proceedings.

4. A hearing panel of tenured faculty and the right to object to any of the individual members (a right that King used to object to one member, who was replaced).

5. Representation by counsel and substantial documentary discovery, including depositions of administrators.

6. A prehearing conference in which the parties exchanged issue lists, witness lists, and exhibit lists.

7. A hearing occurring over a two-week period, during which King was represented by counsel, who cross-examined witnesses, presented witnesses and documentary evidence, and made oral and written arguments.

8. Review of the entire record by the university president.

9. Review by the regents of the panel's findings, the president's recommendation, and briefs from each of the parties.

10. An opportunity for King to appear before the regents before they made the termination decision.

The appellate court characterized the procedural protections that King received as "exhaustive" and determined that they satisfied constitutional requirements (774 F.2d at 228).

In *Frumkin v. Board of Trustees, Kent State*, 626 F.2d 19 (6th Cir. 1980), the court focused particularly on the type of hearing an institution must provide prior to a decision to terminate tenure. The university had slated the professor for dismissal after federal funding for his position was cut. In support of the recommendation for dismissal, the university charged the professor with "unsatisfactory performance as grant director, recurring unproven charges against faculty members, unprofessional conduct, false charges against the department, and violation of university policy." When the professor chose to contest his dismissal, the university scheduled a hearing. The professor was permitted to have a lawyer present at the hearing, but the lawyer's role was limited. He was permitted to consult and advise his client and to make closing arguments in his client's behalf. But he was prohibited from conducting any cross-examination or direct examination of witnesses or from raising objections.

Reasoning that this limited hearing was well suited to the type of decision to be made, the court held that the university had not violated the professor's due process rights. The court examined the ruling in *Mathews v. Eldridge*, 424 U.S. 319 (1976), in which the U.S. Supreme Court had established guidelines for procedural due process. In *Mathews*, the Court had identified three factors which must be considered:

> [F]irst, the private interest that will be affected by the official action; second, the risk of an erroneous deprivation of such interest through the procedures

used, and the probable value, if any, of additional or substitute procedural safeguards; and finally, the government's interest, including the function involved and the fiscal and administrative burdens that the additional or substitute procedural requirement would entail [626 F.2d at 21].

Using these criteria, the court rejected Frumkin's contention that his counsel's inability to cross-examine witnesses was a violation of procedural due process. Despite the fact that the administrative burden on the university would have been "comparatively slight" should Frumkin's attorney have been permitted to examine witnesses, said the court, the institution's interest in avoiding a "full-fledged adversary trial" was reasonable and there was no showing that Frumkin had been prejudiced by the limited role played by his attorney.

*Clarke v. West Virginia Board of Regents*, 279 S.E.2d 169 (W. Va. 1981), provides particularly useful guidance to administrators and counsel in developing a written decision based on the record upon which a reviewing court may rely. In this case, the court considered the reasons and evidence an institution must provide to support a decision terminating tenure. Clarke, a tenured professor at Fairmont State College, had been dismissed following a hearing before a hearing examiner. The hearing examiner made a written report, which merely cited the testimony of witnesses who supported dismissal and did not state any specific reasons or factual basis for affirming the dismissal. The professor argued in court that this report did not comply with due process requirements. Although the court's analysis is based on the state constitution, the opinion relied on federal constitutional precedents and is indicative of federal constitutional analysis as well.

As a starting point for determining what a hearing examiner's report must contain, the court consulted a policy bulletin of the West Virginia Board of Regents. The policy bulletin did not require the hearing examiner to make findings of fact and conclusions of law, but did require the hearing examiner to "enter such recommendations as the facts justify and the circumstances may require" and to "state the reasons for his determination and indicate the evidence he relied on" (279 S.E.2d at 177). The court stressed the importance of an adequate report to give a reviewing court a basis for review and to give the affected individual a basis for identifying grounds for review:

> The need for an adequate statement of the hearing examiner's reasons for his determination and the evidence supporting them is obvious. Our function as a reviewing court is to review the record to determine if the evidence adduced at the hearing supports the findings of the hearing examiner and whether his conclusions follow from those findings. We must rely on the facts and logic upon which the hearing examiner ruled . . . and determine whether he erroneously applied them in reaching his final determination. If the record of the administrative proceeding does not reveal those facts which were determinative of the ruling or the logic behind the ruling, we are powerless to review the administrative action. We are thrust into the position of a trier of fact and are asked to substitute our judgment for that of the hearing examiner. That we cannot do [279 S.E.2d at 178].

The court also noted that the party appealing a hearing examiner's ruling needed a statement of findings and the evidence which the examiner relied upon in making those findings in order to develop an appropriate appeal.

On the basis of its review of the regents' bulletin and applicable constitutional principles, the court held that the hearing examiner's report did not meet due process standards:

> In the report of findings and recommendations, a hearing examiner should list the specific charges found to be supported by the evidence adduced at the hearing and provide some reference to the evidence supporting those findings. In view of our discussion above, we conclude that the failure of the hearing examiner to state on the record the charges against Dr. Clarke which were found to be supported by the evidence constitutes reversible error [279 S.E.2d at 178].

Substantial procedural compliance, rather than full compliance, with an institution's de-tenuring procedures may be sufficient to pass constitutional muster. In *de Llano v. Berglund*, 282 F.3d 1031 (8th Cir. 2002), an appellate court upheld a trial court's award of summary judgment to North Dakota State University (NDSU). De Llano, a tenured professor of physics, had a troubled history at the university. He had been hired to chair the department, but was removed five years later at the request of the departmental faculty to improve departmental morale. After being removed as chair, de Llano began a letter-writing campaign, critical of faculty colleagues and discussing various intradepartmental conflicts. Some of these letters were sent to the press. Students disliked de Llano as well—one semester more than 90 percent of the students in his introductory physics class requested a transfer to a different section. The university decided to terminate de Llano on six grounds: (1) lack of collegiality, (2) harassment of departmental staff, (3) refusal to process complaints through proper channels, (4) making false accusations about the department chair and dean, (5) failure to correct problem behavior after several reprimands, and (6) excessive filing of frivolous grievances.

A faculty review committee concluded that the charges were insufficient to support his termination. After the president rejected the findings of that committee, at de Llano's request a second faculty committee held a hearing and concluded that there was adequate cause for his dismissal. The president accepted the findings of this committee and dismissed de Llano; he then appealed to the state board of higher education, which upheld the dismissal. The lawsuit followed, claiming due process violations (for not following university procedures) and First Amendment violations (for punishing him for his oral and written statements of criticism).

The court looked to *Loudermill*, cited above, for the type of due process protections to which an individual with a property interest in his job is entitled. The court concluded that the university had afforded de Llano notice of the charges against him (the multiple reprimands as well as the final notice of charges), an explanation of those charges, and an opportunity to respond to those charges (two hearings). Despite the fact that de Llano claimed that there were several violations of university procedure, the court concluded that "federal law, not state law or NDSU policy, determines what constitutes adequate procedural due process" (282 F.3d at 1035).

In addition to claims of procedural due process violations, a faculty member whose tenure has been terminated may bring a substantive due process claim. At a minimum, the faculty member must prove that the termination decision was arbitrary, capricious, or irrational—an extremely difficult showing to make. To have a better chance of prevailing, the plaintiff must demonstrate that the interest at stake is "fundamental" under the U.S. Constitution. But federal courts have been reluctant to create a substantive due process right in continued public employment, following the reasoning of Justice Powell's concurring opinion in *Regents of University of Michigan v. Ewing*, 474 U.S. 214 (1985) (discussed in Section 8.2). See, for example, *Nicholas v. Pennsylvania State University*, 227 F.3d 133 (3d Cir. 2000), in which a federal appellate court upheld a jury finding of procedural due process violations but rejected the plaintiff's substantive due process claims, stating that a property right in public employment was not a fundamental constitutional right.

In *Dismissal Proceedings Against Huang*, 431 S.E.2d 541 (N.C. Ct. App. 1993), a tenured faculty member was dismissed after committing several assaults against colleagues and a graduate student. Because the assaults had occurred as long as fifteen years earlier, the professor claimed that the use of "old" misconduct violated his substantive due process rights. Although the appellate court agreed, characterizing the university's actions as arbitrary and capricious, the state's supreme court reversed (441 S.E.2d 696 (1994)), finding ample evidence that the professor had engaged in conduct that constituted just cause for dismissal. Although the university ultimately prevailed, the case underscores the importance of prompt administrative response to faculty misconduct.

If a long-tenured professor is dismissed for a single incident, the failure to use progressive discipline may be construed as an unconstitutional procedural violation. In *Trimble v. West Virginia Board of Directors, Southern West Virginia Community & Technical College*, 549 S.E.2d 294 (W. Va. 2001), the court reversed the termination of a tenured assistant professor of English on the grounds of alleged insubordination. Trimble had claimed that the termination violated his First Amendment rights, and that his property right to continued employment required the college administration to provide progressive discipline before terminating him.

Trimble's performance had been acceptable for nearly twenty years. When a new president took office at the college, Trimble helped organize a faculty labor union and became its president. Trimble and several faculty colleagues objected to the new president's insistence that all faculty use a particular type of software to generate course syllabi and to evaluate student achievement. Trimble refused to attend four "mandatory" meetings about the software and was terminated for insubordination.

The court found that, given Trimble's nineteen years of satisfactory service to the college and the lack of any criticism of his teaching or relationships with students, dismissal was too harsh a penalty, particularly given what the court characterized as a property right in his faculty position. "Because of Mr. Trimble's property interest in continued employment with the College and his previously unblemished record, due process required the College to utilize progressive disciplinary measures against Mr. Trimble" (549 S.E.2d at 305). The court ordered Trimble reinstated with back pay and retroactive benefits. One judge dissented, commenting that the majority was "micro managing" the college's employment decisions and applying its "own subjective notions of justice." An alternative interpretation of the outcome in *Trimble* could be that refusing to attend "mandatory" meetings was not a sufficient ground for terminating a tenured faculty member.

Procedural due process may also be required for a faculty member whose employment contract has been rescinded. In *Garner v. Michigan State University*, 462 N.W.2d 832 (Mich. Ct. App. 1990), the university, without holding a hearing, rescinded the contract of a tenured professor who allegedly lied to the dean about allegations of unprofessional conduct in his prior faculty position. When the dean discovered that serious charges had been made against the professor at his former place of employment, the university rescinded the professor's tenured contract of employment. The professor denied that he had lied about the charges. Although the university asserted its right to rescind an employment contract because of the employee's misrepresentations, citing *Morgan v. American University*, 534 A.2d 323 (D.C. 1987), the court disagreed, distinguishing *Morgan* on two grounds. First, the plaintiff in *Morgan* had admitted the misrepresentation, meaning that there was no factual dispute. Second, *Morgan* involved a private institution. The court noted that the plaintiff, as a tenured professor, had a property interest in continued employment and must be afforded the same due process protections that he would be entitled to if the university had terminated him.

Taken together, these cases provide a helpful picture of how courts will craft procedural requirements for tenure termination decisions. When reviewing such decisions, courts will generally look for compliance with basic elements of due process, as set out in *Potemra*. When an institution fails to accord the faculty member one or more of these basic elements, *Clarke*, *Garner*, and *Trimble* indicate that courts will invalidate the institution's decision. But *Frumkin* illustrates judicial reluctance to provide more specific checklists of procedures mandated by due process. Beyond the minimum requirements, such as those in *Potemra*, courts will usually defer to institutional procedures that appear suited to the needs and expectations of the faculty member and the institution.

### 5.7.3. The private faculty member's procedural rights.

The rights of faculty employed by private colleges and universities are governed primarily by state contract law and occasionally by state constitutions or statutes. Although the lack of federal (and usually state) constitutional protections for faculty at private institutions gives the institution more flexibility in fashioning its decision-making procedures and in determining what procedural protections it will afford faculty, written policies, faculty handbooks, and other policy documents are interpreted as binding contracts in many states (see Section 5.2), and "academic custom and usage" (see Section 1.4.3.3) may also be used by judges to evaluate whether a private institution afforded a faculty member the appropriate protections. Because challenges to negative employment decisions brought by faculty against private institutions are interpreted under state law, the outcomes and reasoning of any particular case must be applied with care to institutions in states other than the state in which the litigation occurred.

Many private institutions have adopted, either in whole or in part, policy statements promulgated by the American Association of University Professors with regard to reappointment and dismissal of tenured faculty. Formal adoption of these policy statements, or consistent adherence to their terms (which could create an implied contract, as discussed in Section 5.2.1), will require the private institution to follow them. Failure to follow these policies can result in breach of contract claims.

The term of the contract, the conditions under which it may be renewed, and the individual's right to certain procedures in the renewal decision are all matters of contract law. If the contract states a specific term (one year, three years), then language to the contrary in other documents may not afford the faculty member greater protection. For example, in *Upadhya v. Langenburg*, 834 F.2d 661 (7th Cir. 1987), a faculty member was employed under several one-year contracts, which stated that the tenure evaluation would take place during the fifth year of employment. The faculty member was notified that he would not be given a fourth one-year contract. Asserting that language in the contracts guaranteed him five years of employment, the faculty member sued for breach of contract. The court disagreed with the plaintiff's interpretation, stating that the language regarding a fifth-year tenure review was not contractually binding on the college and that the contract was clearly intended to be issued for only a one-year period. Furthermore, the faculty handbook stated that there was no guaranteed right to renewal for probationary faculty members.

The written terms of the contract will generally prevail, even if the faculty member can demonstrate that oral representations were made that modified the written contract. In *Baker v. Lafayette College*, 504 A.2d 247 (Pa. Super. Ct. 1986), the plaintiff argued that the head of his department had promised him a full four-year probationary period. When Baker's two-year contract was not renewed, he sued for breach of contract. Pointing to language in the faculty handbook that gave the faculty member a right to consideration for reappointment, rather than an absolute right to reappointment, the court denied the claim.

Even handbook language that appears to afford probationary faculty members rights to reappointment may not bind the institution. In *Brumbach v. Rensselaer Polytechnic Institute*, 510 N.Y.S.2d 762 (N.Y. App. Div. 1987), the plaintiff, an assistant professor of public archaeology, was given a three-year contract. Her work was evaluated formally each year and was found to be satisfactory. Just before the contract's expiration, the department faculty decided to change the plaintiff's position to one in computer archaeology, a position for which the plaintiff was not qualified. The department offered the plaintiff a one-year terminal contract. At its expiration, the plaintiff instituted an action for breach of contract, asserting that the faculty handbook's statement, "If the result of the evaluation is satisfactory, it is normal for an assistant professor to be re-employed for a second three-year period," obligated the institution to reappoint her.

The court disagreed, stating that, upon expiration of the contract, the plaintiff became an employee at will. The handbook's language regarding evaluation did not amount to a promise to dismiss a probationary faculty member only for just cause, and there was no showing that the decision to modify the plaintiff's position was arbitrary or capricious. For those reasons, the trial court's grant of summary judgment to the institution was affirmed.

Faculty contesting denial of tenure at private colleges have asserted that procedural violations materially altered the outcome of the tenure decision. In most cases, courts have ruled that substantial compliance with the college's policies is sufficient to defend against such claims. For example, a state supreme court ruled that, although the dean violated the faculty handbook provisions by not providing a formal written annual evaluation of an untenured faculty member prior to the tenure evaluation, the informal annual evaluation provided the faculty member gave her notice that her performance did not meet the requirements for tenure and thus there was no procedural violation (*Karle v. Board of Trustees/Marshall University*, 575 S.E. 2d 267 (W. Va. 2002)). Another state court ruled that, despite the fact that the plaintiff did not receive the annual evaluations to which he was entitled under the faculty handbook, he admitted that he knew he needed to publish in order to obtain tenure, and evaluations would not have given him any additional information on that score (*Rafalko v. University of New Haven*, 19 A.3d 215 (Conn. App. Ct. 2011)). But in a case against Howard University, a jury found that the failure to conduct biennial evaluations of an untenured faculty member, as required by the faculty handbook, was a "substantial factor" in her denial of tenure and that this failure breached her contract with the university. An appellate court affirmed that finding (*Howard University v. Roberts-Williams*, 2012 D.C. App. LEXIS 79 (D.C. February 23, 2012)).

Similarly, informal means of complying with the procedures may be sufficient. For example, a state appellate court ruled that, although the university did not follow its written procedures that required notification of the plaintiff in writing that he was being considered for tenure, the professor knew about the meetings at which his tenure candidacy was discussed, he was invited to several meetings to respond to questions about his performance, and he was informed in writing about the department's concerns. The court ruled that the lack of procedural compliance did not prejudice his application for tenure (*Galiatsatos v. University of Akron*, 2001 Ohio App. LEXIS 4051 (Ohio Ct. App., 10th Dist. September 13, 2001), *appeal denied*, 761 N.E.2d 47 (Ohio 2002)).

A state appellate court ruled that New York University substantially complied with its rules and procedures in a remanded tenure review of the plaintiff. The dean's failure to include the department chair on the ad hoc review committee and the university's determination not to follow the advice of the grievance committee concerning the conduct of the remanded evaluation did not render the dean's or the university's actions arbitrary or capricious. Simply because some faculty disagreed with the dean's conclusions and recommendations did not make them arbitrary, according to the court (*In re Loebl v. New York University*, 680 N.Y.S.2d 495 (N.Y. App. Div. 1998)).

On the other hand, providing misleading information to an untenured faculty member concerning his or her progress toward tenure has been found to be a major procedural violation that will sustain a breach of contract claim. For example, a state supreme court ruled that a college's deviation from its tenure standards was a breach of contract, and the misleading assurances of the candidate's department chair that she was performing adequately supported her claim for negligent misrepresentation, although she did not prevail in her discrimination claims (*Craine v. Trinity College*, 791 A.2d 518 (Conn. 2002), discussed in Section 5.4.2).

In addition to procedural claims, faculty denied tenure may assert that the criteria used, or the basis for the decision, were arbitrary and capricious (a substantive rather than a procedural violation of the contract). Courts are most reluctant to entertain these claims, as they require the court to substitute its judgment for the decisions of faculty and administrators. For example, in *Daley v. Wesleyan University*, 772 A.2d 725 (Conn. App. Ct. 2001), *appeal denied*, 776 A.2d 1145 (Conn. 2001), a professor denied tenure claimed that the department's report to the vice president mischaracterized the evaluations of his scholarly work by external evaluators. The court rejected the breach of contract claim, ruling that the plaintiff was required to prove by a preponderance of the evidence that the tenure denial decision was made arbitrarily, capriciously, or in bad faith, and upheld the jury's verdict for the college. And in *Allworth v. Howard University*, 890 A.2d 194 (D.C. 2006), an appellate court affirmed an award of summary judgment to the university, ruling that even though the university might have been negligent in providing laboratory facilities to an assistant professor of medicine that she needed for her research, its conduct did not violate the duty of good faith and fair dealing, and did not breach its contract with the professor.

The importance of carefully drafting tenure revocation policies is highlighted in cases involving breach of contract claims. The case *of Murphy v. Duquesne University of the Holy Ghost*, 777 A.2d 418 (Pa. 2001), is instructive. Murphy, a tenured professor of law, was terminated after the university determined that he had violated its sexual harassment policy. Murphy challenged his dismissal, asserting, among other claims, that his conduct did not meet the standard for "serious misconduct" as articulated in the faculty handbook, and that the university had not followed its tenure revocation processes, also contained in the faculty handbook.

The state supreme court upheld the judgment of the state appellate court that the university had not breached the terms of the faculty handbook, but chastised the appellate court for using a "substantial evidence" standard rather than traditional principles of contract interpretation. The court then explained the extent of its role when reviewing the decisions of private parties under contract law.

> [P]rivate parties, including religious or educational institutions, may draft employment contracts which restrict review of professional employees' qualifications to an internal process that, if conducted in good faith, is final within the institution and precludes or prohibits review in a court of law . . . When a contract so specifies, generally applicable principles of contract law will suffice to insulate the institution's internal, private decisions from judicial review [777 A.2d at 428].

The court then turned to the language of the faculty handbook, and determined that it reserved to the faculty and the university the determination of whether a faculty member's conduct met the definition of "serious misconduct" such that it justified a decision to dismiss a tenured faculty member. The handbook required the university to demonstrate to the faculty hearing body by clear and convincing evidence that the individual had engaged in serious misconduct. It provided that the president could disagree with the faculty hearing body and that, if such a disagreement occurred, the individual could appeal that decision to the board of trustees. Given the specificity of the process and the clear allocation of the decision-making authority to the president and the trustees, the court ruled, Murphy was not entitled to have a jury "re-consider the merits of his termination."

Another state appellate court concurred with an institution's argument that a court may not review the merits of a tenure denial decision in a breach of contract claim. In *Halper v. University of the Incarnate Word*, 90 S.W.3d 842 (Tex. App. 2002), the court agreed with the institution's assertion that "so long as UIW properly followed its procedures in making its decision not to grant tenure, UIW's professional decision that Halper did not qualify for tenure is not subject to judicial review" (90 S.W.3d at 845), citing *Siu v. Johnson* (discussed in Section 5.7.2.3) for the proposition that "the judicial inquiry is properly only whether the decision was made, wisely or not, by a specific exercise of professional judgment and on the basis of factors clearly bearing on the appropriateness of conferring academic tenure" (748 F.2d at 245).

Faculty and administrators can help ensure that judges and juries do not second-guess the judgments of academics by ensuring that written policies are clear, that the criteria applicable to faculty employment decisions are stated clearly, that the procedures for making these decisions are followed carefully, and that written justifications are given for recommendations or decisions made under the faculty handbook or other policies. Because these documents are the source of employment rights at private colleges, they should reflect the consensus of the academic community with respect to both the criteria and procedures that will be used to make these critical employment decisions.

# 6

# Faculty Academic Freedom and Freedom of Expression

*Chapter 6 focuses on a unique dimension of faculty employment status—faculty academic freedom. The chapter distinguishes between legal and professional concepts of academic freedom; between First Amendment free expression rights and First Amendment academic freedom rights, which may overlap but are not necessarily the same; and between First Amendment rights and other legal bases for academic freedom. The faculties of public institutions are protected by the Constitution's First Amendment and may also be protected under contractual theories supplemented by reference to academic custom and usage. The faculties of private institutions enjoy only the latter set of legal protections for their academic freedom. Having elucidated all the fundamental distinctions, the chapter analyzes faculty academic freedom issues regarding teaching and then regarding research, and concludes with an examination of academic freedom in religious institutions.*

## Section 6.1. General Concepts and Principles

***6.1.1. Faculty freedom of expression in general.*** Whether they are employed by public or private institutions of higher education, faculty members as citizens are protected by the First Amendment from governmental censorship and other governmental actions that infringe citizens' freedoms of speech, press, and association. When the restraint on such freedoms originates from a governmental body external to an institution (see Section 6.1.6), the First Amendment protects faculty members in both public and private institutions. When the restraint is internal, however (for example, when a provost or dean allegedly infringes a faculty member's free speech), the First Amendment generally protects faculty members only in public institutions. Absent a finding of state action (see Section 1.5.2), an internal restraint in a private institution does not implicate government, and the First Amendment therefore does not apply. The protection accorded to faculty expression and association in private institutions is thus usually a matter of contract law (see Section 1.5.3).

While faculty contracts may distinguish between tenured and nontenured faculty, as may state statutes and regulations applicable to public institutions, tenure is immaterial to most freedom of expression claims. Other aspects of job status, such as whether employment is tenure track or non–tenure track and whether it is full time or part time, are also generally immaterial to freedom of expression claims. In *Perry v. Sindermann*, 408 U.S. 593 (1972), discussed in Section 5.7.2, the U.S. Supreme Court held that a nonrenewed faculty member's "lack of a contractual or tenure right to reemployment . . . is immaterial to his free speech claim" and that "regardless of the . . . [teacher's] contractual or other claim to a job," government cannot "deny a benefit to a person because of his constitutionally protected speech or associations."

When faculty members at public institutions assert First Amendment free speech claims, these claims are usually subject to a line of U.S. Supreme Court cases applicable to all public employees: the *Pickering-Connick* line. (As we shall see below, this line is now usually called the *Pickering-Connick-Garcetti* line to account for an influential new case, *Garcetti v. Ceballos*, that the Court decided in 2006.) The foundational case in this line, *Pickering v. Board of Education*, 391 U.S. 563 (1968), concerned a public high school teacher who had been dismissed for writing the local newspaper a letter in which he criticized the board of education's financial plans for the high schools. Pickering brought suit, alleging that the dismissal violated his First Amendment freedom of speech. The school board argued that the dismissal was justified because the letter "damaged the professional reputations of . . . [the school board] members and of the school administrators, would be disruptive of faculty discipline, and would tend to foment 'controversy, conflict, and dissension' among teachers, administrators, the board of education, and the residents of the district."

The U.S. Supreme Court determined that the teacher's letter addressed "a matter of legitimate public concern," thus implicating his free speech rights as a citizen. The Court then balanced the teacher's free speech interests against the state's interest, as employer, in maintaining an efficient educational system. In gauging the state's interest as an employer, these considerations were particularly important: whether the teacher's speech was "directed towards any person with whom [the teacher] would normally be in contact in the course of his daily work as a teacher"; if so, whether the teacher's speech could create difficulties "of maintaining either discipline by immediate supervisors or harmony among co-workers"; whether the teacher's speech had "in any way either impeded the teacher's proper performance of his daily duties in the classroom"; and whether the teacher's speech in any way "interfered with the regular operation of the schools generally." The Court found that Pickering had no working relationship with the board of education, that his letter had no detrimental effect on the schools, and that his performance as a teacher was not hindered by the letter. Based on these considerations and the pertinent facts, the Court concluded that the school administration's interest in limiting Pickering's opportunities to contribute to public debate was not significantly greater than its interest in limiting a similar contribution by any member of the general public and that, "in a case such as this, absent proof of false statements knowingly or recklessly made by him, a teacher's exercise of his right to speak on issues of public importance may not furnish the basis for his dismissal from public employment."

The *Pickering* analysis was further explicated in later Supreme Court cases. The most important of these cases are *Givhan v. Western Line Consolidated School District*, 439 U.S. 410 (1979); *Connick v. Myers*, 461 U.S. 138 (1983); *Waters v. Churchill*, 511 U.S. 661 (1994); and more recently, *Garcetti v. Ceballos*, 547 U.S. 410 (2006). They are discussed seriatim below.

In *Givhan*, the issue was whether *Pickering* protects public school teachers who communicate their views in private rather than in public. In a series of private meetings with her school principal, the plaintiff teacher in *Givhan* had made complaints and expressed opinions about school employment practices that she considered racially discriminatory. When the school district did not renew her contract, the teacher filed suit, claiming an infringement of her First Amendment rights. The trial court found that the school district had not renewed the teacher's contract primarily because of her criticisms of school employment practices, and it held that such action violated the First Amendment. The U.S. Court of Appeals reversed, reasoning that the teacher's expression was not protected by the First Amendment because she had expressed her views privately. The U.S. Supreme Court, in a unanimous opinion, disagreed with the appeals court and remanded the case to the trial court for further proceedings. According to the Supreme Court, "[N]either the [First] Amendment itself nor our decisions indicate that . . . freedom [of speech] is lost to the public employee who arranges to communicate privately with his employer rather than to spread his views before the public" (439 U.S. at 415–16). Rather, private expression, like public expression, is subject to the same balancing of factors that the Court utilized in *Pickering*. The Court did suggest in a footnote, however, that private expression may involve some different considerations:

> Although the First Amendment's protection of government employees extends to private as well as public expression, striking the *Pickering* balance in each context may involve different considerations. When a teacher speaks publicly, it is generally the content of his statements that must be assessed to determine whether they "in any way either impeded the teacher's proper performance of his daily duties in the classroom or . . . interfered with the regular operation of the schools generally" (*Pickering v. Board of Education*, 391 U.S. at 572–73). Private expression, however, may in some situations bring additional factors to the *Pickering* calculus. When a government employee personally confronts his immediate superior, the employing agency's institutional efficiency may be threatened not only by the content of the employee's message but also by the manner, time, and place in which it is delivered [439 U.S. at 415 n.4].

In *Connick v. Myers*, the issue was whether *Pickering* protects public employees who communicate views to office staff about office personnel matters. The plaintiff, Myers, was an assistant district attorney who had been scheduled for transfer to another division of the office. In opposing the transfer, she circulated a questionnaire on office operations to other assistant district attorneys. Later on the same day, she was discharged. In a 5-to-4 decision, the Court declined to apply *Givhan*, arguing that *Givhan*'s statements about employment practices had "involved a matter of public concern." In contrast, the various questions in Myers's questionnaire about office transfer policy and other office practices, with one exception, "[did] not fall under the rubric of matters of 'public concern.'" The exception, a question on whether office personnel ever felt pressured to work in political campaigns, did "touch upon a matter of public concern." In the overall context of the questionnaire, which otherwise concerned only internal office matters, this one question provided only a "limited First Amendment interest" for Myers. Therefore, applying *Pickering* factors, the Court determined that Myers had spoken "not as a citizen upon matters of public concern, but instead as an employee upon matters only of personal interest"; and that circulation of the questionnaire interfered with "close working relationships" within the office. The discharge thus did not violate the plaintiff's freedom of speech.

*Givhan* and *Connick* emphasize the need to distinguish between communications on matters of public concern and communications on matters of private or personal concern—a distinction that, under *Givhan*, does not depend on whether the communication is itself made in public or in private. The dispute between the majority and dissenters in *Connick* reveals how slippery this distinction can be. The majority did, however, provide a helpful methodological guideline for drawing the distinction. "Whether an employee's speech addresses a matter of public concern," said the Court, "must be determined by the content, form, and context of a given statement, as revealed by the whole record" (461 U.S. at 147–48; emphasis added). Because the "content, form, and context" will depend on the specific circumstances of each case, courts must remain attentive to the "enormous variety of fact situations" that these cases may present. In a more recent case, *City of San Diego v. Roe*, 543 U.S. 77 (2004), the Court reiterated this aspect of *Connick* and added that "public concern is something that is a subject of legitimate news interest; that is, a subject of general interest and of value and concern to the public at the time of publication" (543 U.S. at 83–84).

In *Waters v. Churchill*, 511 U.S. 661 (1994), the third key case explicating *Pickering*, a public hospital had terminated a nurse because of statements concerning the hospital that she had made to a coworker. In remanding the case to the trial court for further proceedings, the Justices filed four opinions displaying different perspectives on the First Amendment issues. Although there was no majority opinion, the plurality opinion by Justice O'Connor and two concurring opinions (by Justice Souter and Justice Scalia) stressed the need for courts to be deferential to employers when applying the *Pickering-Connick* factors. In particular, according to these Justices, it appears that (1) in evaluating the impact of the employee's speech, the public employer may rely on its own reasonable belief regarding the content of the speech, even if that belief later proves to be inaccurate; and (2) in evaluating the disruptiveness of the employee's speech, a public employer does not need to determine that the speech actually disrupted operations, but only that the speech was potentially disruptive.

Under the first of these points from *Waters*—the "reasonable belief" requirement—the employer's belief concerning the content of the employee's speech apparently must be an actual or real belief arrived at in good faith. Justice O'Connor's plurality opinion, for instance, indicates that the employer must "really . . . believe" (511 U.S. at 679) the version of the facts on which the employer relies. In addition, the belief must also be objectively reasonable in the sense that it is based on "an objectively reasonable investigation" of the facts (511 U.S. at 683; opinion of Souter, J.) or based on a standard of care that "a reasonable manager" would use under the circumstances (511 U.S. at 678; plurality opinion of O'Connor, J.).

Under the second point from *Waters*—the potential disruption requirement—the employer may prevail by showing that it made a "reasonable prediction of disruption, to the effect" that "the [employee's] speech is, in fact, likely to be disruptive" (511 U.S. at 674; opinion of O'Connor, J.). The reasonableness of the prediction would likely be evaluated under an objective standard much like that which Justice O'Connor would use to determine the reasonableness of the employer's belief about the facts. Even if the predicted harm "is mostly speculative," the Court apparently will be deferential to the employer's interests and give the employer's finding substantial weight (511 U.S. at 673; opinion of O'Connor, J.). In *Waters* itself, for instance, "the potential disruptiveness of the [nurse's] speech as reported was enough to outweigh whatever First Amendment value it might have had" (511 U.S. at 680; opinion of O'Connor, J.).

The fourth key case in the *Pickering-Connick* line, *Garcetti v. Ceballos*, 547 U.S. 410 (2006), involved a free speech claim of a deputy district attorney. The Court held by a 5-to-4 vote that the First Amendment does not protect public employees whose statements are made as part of their official employment responsibilities. The Court majority emphasized and relied on the distinction between speaking as a "public employee" and speaking as a "private citizen": "when public employees make statements pursuant to their official duties, the employees are not speaking as citizens for First Amendment purposes, and the Constitution does not insulate their communications from employer discipline." As the Court explained, "[r]estricting speech that owes its existence to a public employee's professional responsibilities does not infringe any liberties the employee might have enjoyed as a private citizen. It simply reflects the exercise of employer control over what the employer itself has commissioned or created."

In the analysis set out in *Garcetti*, examining the dichotomy between employee speech and citizen speech becomes the critical first step in analyzing whether the public employee's speech is protected. If the employee is speaking as an employee as defined by the Court, the speech is not protected; one need never reach the question of whether the employee was speaking on a matter of public concern. In this sense, the *Garcetti* employee/citizen speech dichotomy apparently replaces the public concern/private concern dichotomy that had been the predominant (and often dispositive) starting point for the *Pickering-Connick* line. In the lower court cases that further developed that line, the employee speech concept appeared to merge with the private concern concept, and the private citizen speech concept with the public concern concept. Speaking as an employee usually meant speaking on matters of personal interest, whereas speaking as a private citizen usually meant speaking on matters of public interest or concern. This approach left room for the possibility that employees could speak as part of their official duties yet still be speaking on a matter of public concern and thus be protected. It appears that the leeway to make such arguments is no longer available under *Garcetti*, and the likelihood that courts will protect the speech is consequently reduced.

In various cases, courts have questioned whether there are circumstances in which they should not apply the *Pickering-Connick* (and now *Pickering-Connick-Garcetti*) analysis to public employees' free speech claims. Most important, at least for higher education, is the question raised in *Garcetti* itself: whether the employee speech doctrine and official duty test should not apply to public college and university professors when they are engaged in scholarship or teaching. Justice Kennedy, speaking for the majority in *Garcetti*, noted at the end of his opinion:

> There is some argument that expression related to academic scholarship or classroom instruction implicates additional constitutional interests that are not fully accounted for by this Court's customary employee-speech jurisprudence. We need not, and for that reason do not, decide whether the analysis we conduct today would apply in the same manner to a case involving speech related to scholarship or teaching [547 U.S. at 425].

Justice Kennedy was reacting to Justice Souter's concern expressed in his *Garcetti* dissenting opinion:

> [The] ostensible domain [of cases that the majority puts] beyond the pale of the First Amendment is spacious enough to include even the teaching of a public university professor, and I have to hope that today's majority does not mean to imperil First Amendment protection of academic freedom in public colleges and universities, whose teachers necessarily speak and write "pursuant to official duties" [547 U.S. at 438–39, Souter, J., dissenting].

Since *Garcetti* was decided, faculty litigants in numerous cases have asked lower courts to consider these comments of Justice Kennedy and Justice Souter. The issue, in effect, is whether there is to be an exception from *Garcetti* for speech related to classroom instruction, speech in the form of academic scholarship, or both, that will protect faculty members even if they are speaking as employees. As the cases indicate, if the courts do recognize a faculty exception to *Garcetti*, a further issue then arises concerning the scope of the exception— that is, when is faculty speech sufficiently "related to scholarship or teaching" (in the words of Justice Kennedy) to receive the protection of the exception? In the opposite situation, if the courts do not recognize an exception, or the exception does not apply to a particular case of faculty speech, then there is the further issue of delineating the scope of faculty members' "employee speech" and distinguishing it from private citizen speech.

Other cases have addressed other potential limits on application of the *Pickering-Connick* line. One question is whether there must be an "adverse employment action" by the employer before the *Pickering-Connick* line will apply. In *Harrington v. Harris*, 118 F.3d 359 (5th Cir. 1997), for instance, the plaintiffs were tenured law school professors at Texas Southern University who challenged the amount of the salary increases the dean had awarded them. The professors did not claim censorship, but rather retaliation—that the dean had lowered the amount of their salary increases in retaliation for critical statements they had made concerning the dean. The appellate court declined to apply the *Pickering-Connick* public concern analysis and rejected the professors' free speech retaliation claim because they had "failed to show that they suffered an adverse employment action."

The professors in *Harrington* had alleged two possible adverse actions: first, that the dean had evaluated one of the plaintiffs as "counterproductive"; and second, that the dean had perennially discriminated against the plaintiffs in awarding salary increases. As to the first, the court held that "an employer's criticism of an employee, without more, [does not constitute] an actionable adverse employment action . . . [M]ere criticisms do not give rise to a constitutional deprivation for purposes of the First Amendment." As to the second alleged adverse action, the court emphasized that each of the professors had received salary increases each year and that the professors' complaint "amounted to nothing more than a dispute over the quantum of pay increases." The court then limited its holding to these facts: "If Plaintiffs had received no merit pay increase at all or if the amount of such increase were so small as to be simply a token increase which was out of proportion to the merit pay increases granted to others, we might reach a different conclusion."

The appellate court in *Power v. Summers*, 226 F.3d 815 (7th Cir. 2000), however, disagreed with the *Harrington* analysis and ruled that proof of an adverse employment action is not a prerequisite for a faculty member's free speech claim against the institution. The case concerned a claim by three professors that they had received reduced bonuses in retaliation for their criticisms of institutional policies. The district court dismissed the case on the ground that the award of smaller bonuses was not an adverse employment action; the appellate court, in an opinion by Judge Posner, reversed. The court's opinion explained that proof of an adverse employment action is an appropriate component of a Title VII employment discrimination claim but not of a First Amendment free speech claim; employees asserting free speech claims need only show that some institutional action had inhibited their exercise of free expression: "Any deprivation under color of law that is likely to deter the exercise of free speech, whether by an employee or anyone else, is actionable . . . if the circumstances are such as to make a refusal an effective deterrent to the exercise of a fragile liberty"(226 F.3d at 820). This "deterrence" test is apparently objective in that it depends on whether, in the particular circumstances of the case, the average reasonable person would be deterred by the challenged action—not on whether the person asserting First Amendment rights was or would have been deterred in the particular circumstances (see, for example, *Davis v. Goord*, 320 F.3d 346, 352–54 (2d Cir. 2003)).

In *United States v. National Treasury Employees Union*, 513 U.S. 454 (1995) (the *NTEU* case), the U.S. Supreme Court considered another potential limit on application of the *Pickering-Connick* line and carved out a category of public employee speech cases to which *Pickering-Connick* does not apply. In the course of invalidating a federal statute that prohibited federal employees from receiving honoraria for writing and speaking activities undertaken on their own time, the Court developed an important distinction between (1) cases involving "a *post hoc* analysis of one employee's speech and its impact on that employee's professional responsibilities" and (2) cases involving a "sweeping statutory impediment to speech that potentially involves many employees." In the first type of case the employee challenges an employer's "adverse action taken in response to actual speech," whereas in the second type of case the employee challenges a statute or administrative regulation that "chills potential speech before it happens" (513 U.S. at 459–60). The *Pickering-Connick* analysis applies to the first type of case but not to the second. The reason is that the second type of case "gives rise to far more serious concerns" than does the first. Thus, "the Government's burden is greater with respect to [a] statutory restriction on expression" (the second type of case) than it is "with respect to an isolated disciplinary action" (the first type of case). To meet this greater burden of justification, the government must take into account the interests of "present and future employees in a broad range of present and future expression," as well as the interests of "potential audiences" that have a "right to read and hear what the employees would otherwise have written and said" (513 U.S. at 468, 470); and must demonstrate that those interests "are outweighed by that expression's 'necessary impact on the actual operation' of the Government" (513 U.S. at 468, quoting *Pickering*, 391 U.S. at 571).

The critical distinction that the Court made in the *NTEU* case—the distinction between a "single supervisory decision" and a "statutory impediment to speech"—seems compatible with the Court's earlier analysis in *Keyishian v. Board of Regents*, 385 U.S. 589 (1967) (discussed in Section 6.1.5). Both *NTEU* and *Keyishian* are concerned with statutes or administrative regulations that limit the speech of a broad range of government employees, rather than with a particular disciplinary decision of a particular administrator. Both cases also focus on the meaning and application of the statute or regulation itself, rather than on the motives and concerns of a particular employer at a particular workplace. And both cases focus on the special problems that arise under the First Amendment when a statute or regulation "chills potential speech before it happens" (513 U.S. at 468). Given these clear parallels, the *NTEU* case has apparently laid the foundation for a merger of that case with *Keyishian* as they apply to large-scale faculty free expression disputes, particularly **academic freedom**

disputes. The two cases, in tandem, would apply particularly to external conflicts arising under a state or federal statute or administrative regulation that
is alleged to impinge upon the free expression, or academic freedom, of many
faculty members at various institutions (see Section 6.1.6 below). But they
would also appear to apply to internal conflicts involving a college or university's written policy that applies broadly to all or most faculty members of the
institution.

The case of *Crue v. Aiken*, 370 F.3d 668 (7th Cir. 2004), provides an example
of the latter type of application of *NTEU*. There, the court majority applied
*NTEU* analysis to invalidate a chancellor's "preclearance directive" applicable
to all faculty and staff of the institution (370 F.3d at 678–80). A dissenting
judge argued that the *Pickering-Connick* line, and not *NTEU*, provided the applicable test (370 F.3d at 682–88). (For discussion of *Crue v. Aiken*, see Section
10.4.3 of this book.)

In addition to the *Pickering-Connick* line of cases, as well as *NTEU* and
*Keyishian*, the cases on the "public forum" doctrine might also be invoked as a
basis for some faculty free speech claims. Although the public forum doctrine is
often applied to free speech problems concerning students (see Section 9.4.2),
it will only occasionally apply to the analysis of faculty free speech rights on
campus. The mere fact that campus facilities are open to employees as work
space does not make the space a designated public forum or limited designated
forum. In *Tucker v. State of California Department of Education*, 97 F.3d 1204,
1209, 1214–15 (9th Cir. 1996), the court held that employer offices and work
spaces are not public forums. Similarly, in *Bishop v. Aronov*, 926 F.2d 1066,
1071 (11th Cir. 1991), and *Linnemeir v. Board of Trustees, Indiana University–
Purdue University*, 260 F.3d 757, 759–60 (7th Cir. 2001), the courts declined to
consider classrooms to be public forums during class time; and in *Piarowski
v. Illinois Community College District*, 759 F.2d 625 (7th Cir. 1985), the court
declined to apply public forum analysis to a campus art gallery used for displaying the works of faculty members. If, however, an institution opens certain
other types of property to use by faculty members, the academic community,
or the general public for their own personal expressive purposes, the institution will have created a designated forum, and faculty members will have the
same First Amendment rights of access as other persons to whom the property
is open. In *Giebel v. Sylvester*, 244 F.3d 1182 (9th Cir. 2001), for example, the
court considered certain bulletin boards on a state university's campus to be
designated public forums open to the public.

### 6.1.2. Other constitutional rights supporting faculty freedom of expression.
In addition to free expression rights under the First Amendment
(see Section 6.1.1), public employees, including faculty members, also have other
constitutional rights that in particular circumstances may provide additional
support for their freedom of expression. Public employees, for example, have a
right to freedom of association under the First Amendment. They are free to join
(or not join) a political party and to adopt whatever political views and beliefs
they choose (*Branti v. Finkel*, 445 U.S. 507 (1980)). Public employees cannot

be denied employment, terminated, or denied a promotion or raise due to their political affiliations or beliefs (*Rutan v. Republican Party of Illinois*, 497 U.S. 62 (1990)). Nor are these associational rights limited to political organizations and viewpoints; public employees may also join (or not join), subscribe to the beliefs of, and participate in social, economic, and other organizations (see *NAACP v. Button*, 371 U.S. 415 (1963)). Since these rights extend fully to faculty members (see *Jirau-Bernal v. Agrait*, 37 F.3d 1 (1st Cir. 1994)), they may—like other public employees—join organizations of their choice and participate as private citizens in their activities. Moreover, public employers, including institutions of higher education, may not require employees to affirm by oath that they will not join or participate in the activities of particular organizations. In *Cole v. Richardson*, 405 U.S. 676 (1972), however, the U.S. Supreme Court did uphold an oath that included a general commitment to "uphold and defend" the U.S. Constitution and a commitment to "oppose the overthrow of the government . . . by force, violence, or by any illegal or unconstitutional method." The Court upheld the second commitment's constitutionality only by reading it narrowly as merely "a commitment not to use illegal and constitutionally unprotected force to change the constitutional system." So interpreted, the second commitment "does not expand the obligation of the first [commitment]."

Public employees and faculty members also have other constitutional rights that are related to and supportive of their free expression and free association rights under the First Amendment. The petition clause of the First Amendment,[1] for example, may protect faculty members from retaliation for having filed grievances or lawsuits against an institution or its administrators (see, for example, *San Filippo v. Bongiovanni*, 30 F.3d 424 (3rd Cir. 1994)). For such a claim to succeed, however, the subject of the grievance or lawsuit must be a matter of public concern (see *Borough of Duryea v. Guarnieri*, 131 S. Ct. 2488 (2011)). And the Fourth Amendment search and seizure clause provides faculty members some protection for teaching and research materials, and other files that they keep in their offices. In *O'Connor v. Ortega*, 480 U.S. 709 (1987), for example, the Court used the Fourth Amendment to protect an employee who was in charge of training physicians in the psychiatric residency program at a state hospital. Hospital officials had searched his office. The Court determined that public employees may have reasonable expectations of privacy in their offices, desks, and files; and that these expectations may, in certain circumstances, be protected by the Fourth Amendment. A plurality of the Justices, however, asserted that an employer's warrantless search of such property would nevertheless be permissible if it is done for "noninvestigatory, work-related purposes" or for "investigations of work-related misconduct," and if it meets "the standard of reasonableness under all the circumstances."

The application of *O'Connor v. Ortega* and the Fourth Amendment to faculty members' computer files is illustrated by *Soderstrand v. Oklahoma, ex rel.*

---

[1] The petition clause prohibits government from "abridging . . . the right of the people . . . to petition the Government for a redress of grievances."

*Board of Regents of Oklahoma Agricultural and Mechanical Colleges*, 463 F. Supp. 2d 1308 (2006). A university employee had found pictures and images that appeared to be child pornography on CDs in a lock box kept in a storage room that was part of a faculty office complex. After attributing ownership of the box to Dr. Soderstrand, who was a university department head, two members of the OSU computing security office entered Dr. Soderstrand's office and seized the hard drive from his desktop computer as well as his *personal* laptop computer. The laptop computer screen displayed the university-supported e-mail client and showed various spreadsheets that appeared to contain office records. The desktop hard drive and personal laptop computer were taken without a warrant and without the consent of Dr. Soderstrand, who was not in the office. University police retained the laptop after reviewing its contents.

Dr. Soderstrand eventually filed an action under 42 U.S.C. § 1983 claiming that university personnel had unreasonably searched and seized his laptop in violation of the Fourth Amendment. In analyzing the claim, the court considered the university's warrantless search and seizure to have been undertaken while investigating the faculty member's alleged work-related misconduct, and determined that the standard to apply to this action was *O'Connor's* "reasonableness under all the circumstances." Two factors were to be considered in applying this standard: "whether the action was justified at its inception and whether the search as actually conducted was reasonably related in scope to the circumstances which justified the interference in the first place."

Applying these factors, the court determined that the seizure of the laptop was "reasonable" under *O'Connor*:

> Here, as in *O'Connor*, the office being searched was the office of a professional working for a public institution, and the search was to investigate work-related misconduct. In this case, the suspected misconduct involved possible child pornography stored on computers located in Dr. Soderstrand's office on campus. It is undisputed that OSU security officers entered plaintiff's OSU office and seized the hard drive of the desk top computer and plaintiff's laptop computer, and that the laptop computer was open, on and running at the time, with an OSU supported email program on the screen and with various spreadsheets that appeared to contain office records.
>
> Applying the standards of *O'Connor*, and construing all facts and allegations in plaintiff's favor, the court finds and concludes that the search was justified at its inception and that its scope was reasonably related to the circumstances which justified it [463 F. Supp. 2d at 1314].

The search and seizure therefore did not violate the Fourth Amendment privacy rights of Dr. Soderstrand, and the defendants were entitled to summary judgment.

Fourth Amendment issues concerning electronic and digital records, as in *Soderstrand*, have been increasingly arising on college campuses. If faculty members' academic writings, research results, or other research materials are stored in their offices or laboratories on their own computer disks or on the hard drive of a computer they own, there may be an expectation of privacy, and thus a level of Fourth Amendment protection, similar to that recognized in *O'Connor v. Ortega*. But if the writings or materials are stored on the hard drive of a computer that the institution (or the state) owns, or stored on the institution's network, the expectation of privacy and the Fourth Amendment protection will likely be less. In either case, the extent of protection afforded the digital materials would likely depend in part on the terms of the institution's computer use policies.

### 6.1.3. *Academic freedom: Basic concepts and distinctions.* Faculty academic freedom claims are often First Amendment freedom of expression claims; they thus may draw upon the same free expression principles as are set out in Section 6.1.1 above. Academic freedom claims may also be based, however, on unique applications of First Amendment free expression principles, on constitutional rights other than freedom of expression, or on principles of contract law. The distinction between public and private institutions applicable to free expression claims (Section 6.1.1 above) applies equally to academic freedom claims. Similarly, as is also the case for First Amendment freedom of expression claims, neither tenure, nor a particular faculty rank, nor even full-time status, is a legal prerequisite for faculty academic freedom claims.

Academic freedom traditionally has been considered to be an essential aspect of higher education in the United States. It has been a major determinant of the missions of higher educational institutions, both public and private, and a major factor in shaping the roles of faculty members as well as students. Yet the concept of academic freedom eludes precise definition. The concept draws meaning from both the world of education and the world of law. In the professional version of academic freedom familiar to the world of education, educators usually use the term with reference to the customs and practices by which, and the aspirations with which, faculties may best flourish in their work as teachers and researchers (see, for example, the "1940 Statement of Principles on Academic Freedom and Tenure" of the American Association of University Professors (AAUP), discussed later in this section and found in *AAUP Policy Documents and Reports* (10th ed., 2006), 3–11). In the legal version, lawyers and judges usually use "academic freedom" as a catchall term to describe the legal rights and responsibilities of the teaching profession, and courts usually attempt to define these rights by reconciling basic constitutional law or contract law principles with prevailing views of academic freedom's intellectual and social role in American life.

More broadly, academic freedom refers not only to the prerogatives and rights of faculty members but also to the prerogatives and rights of students. Student academic freedom is explored in Section 7.1.4 of this book.[2] In addition, especially for the legal version of academic freedom, the term increasingly is used to refer to the rights and interests of institutions themselves, as in

---

[2] For students, as for faculty members, there is both a professional version of academic freedom and a legal version.

"institutional academic freedom" or "institutional autonomy." This third facet of academic freedom is explored in Section 6.1.7 below.

In the realm of law and courts (the primary focus of this chapter), yet another distinction regarding academic freedom must be made: the distinction between constitutional law and contract law. Though courts usually discuss academic freedom in cases concerning the constitutional rights of faculty members, the legal boundaries of academic freedom are initially defined by contract law. Faculty members possess whatever academic freedom is guaranteed them under the faculty contract (see Section 5.2)—either an individual contract or (in some cases) a collective bargaining agreement. The "1940 Statement of Principles on Academic Freedom and Tenure," AAUP's 1970 "Interpretive Comments" on that statement, and AAUP's 1982 "Recommended Institutional Regulations on Academic Freedom and Tenure" (all included in *AAUP Policy Documents and Reports*, 3–11, 22–31) are sometimes incorporated by reference into faculty contracts, and it is crucial for administrators to determine whether this has been done—or should be done—with respect to all or any of these documents. For any document that has been incorporated, courts will interpret and enforce its terms by reference to contract law principles. Even when these documents have not been incorporated into the contract, they may be an important source of the "academic custom and usage" that courts will consider in interpreting unclear contract terms (see generally Section 5.2.2).

Contract law limits both public and private institutions' authority over their faculty members. Public institutions' authority is also limited by constitutional concepts of academic freedom, as discussed below, and sometimes also by state statutes or administrative regulations on academic freedom. But in private institutions, the faculty contract, perhaps supplemented by academic custom and usage, may be the only legal restriction on administrators' authority to limit faculty academic freedom. In private religious institutions, the institution's special religious mission may add additional complexities to contract law's application to academic freedom problems (see, for example, the *McEnroy* case discussed in Section 6.4 below). For instance, the establishment and free exercise clauses of the First Amendment may limit the capacity of the courts to entertain lawsuits against religious institutions brought by faculty members alleging breach of contract.

Constitutional principles of academic freedom have developed in two stages, each occupying a distinct time period and including distinct types of cases. The earlier stage, in the 1950s and 1960s, included the cases on faculty and institutional freedom from interference by external (extramural) governmental bodies. These earlier cases pitted faculties and their institutions against a state legislature or state agency—the external conflict paradigm of academic freedom (see Section 6.1.6 below). In the later stage, covering the 1970s and 1980s, the cases focused primarily on faculty freedom from institutional intrusion—the internal conflict paradigm. These later cases pitted faculty members against their institutions—thus illustrating the clash between faculty academic freedom and institutional prerogatives often referred to as "institutional academic freedom" or "institutional autonomy." Both lines of cases have continued to the present, and both retain high importance, but the more recent academic freedom cases based on the second stage of developments (internal conflicts) have been much more numerous than those based on the first stage of developments (external conflicts). Developments in the early years of the twenty-first century suggest, however, that cases involving external conflicts are becoming more numerous and are attracting much more attention than they have since the 1950s and 1960s (see Section 6.1.6 below).

### *6.1.4. Professional versus legal concepts of academic freedom.* The professional version of academic freedom common in the world of education is based on "professional" concepts, as distinguished from the "legal" concepts discussed later in this section. The professional concept of academic freedom finds its expression in the professional norms of the academy, which are in turn grounded in academic custom and usage. The most recognized and most generally applicable professional norms are those promulgated by the American Association of University Professors. Most of these norms appear in AAUP standards, statements, and reports that are collected in *AAUP Policy Documents and Reports* (2006). This publication, called "The Redbook," is available in a print version and also online on the AAUP's Web site, at http://www.aaup.org/statements/Redbook/.

The national academic community's commitment to academic freedom as a core value was formally documented in the "1915 Declaration of Principles on Academic Freedom and Academic Tenure," promulgated by the AAUP and currently reprinted in *AAUP Policy Documents and Reports* (at 291–301). The 1915 Declaration emphasized the importance of academic freedom to higher education and recognized two components of academic freedom: the teachers' freedom to teach and the students' freedom to learn. Twenty-five years later, the concept of academic freedom was further explicated, and its critical importance reaffirmed, in the "1940 Statement of Principles on Academic Freedom and Tenure" (*AAUP Policy Documents and Reports*, 3–11), developed by the AAUP in conjunction with the Association of American Colleges and Universities and subsequently endorsed by more than 185 educational and professional associations. The 1940 Statement emphasizes that "[i]nstitutions of higher education are conducted for the common good . . . The common good depends upon the free search for the truth and its free exposition. Academic freedom is essential to these purposes" (*AAUP Policy Documents and Reports*, 3).

The 1940 Statement then identifies three key aspects of faculty academic freedom: the teacher's "freedom in research and in the publication of the results"; the teacher's "freedom in the classroom in discussing [the subject matter of the course]"; and the teacher's freedom to speak or write "as a citizen," as "a member of a learned profession," and as "an officer of an educational institution." These freedoms are subject to various "duties correlative with rights" and "special obligations" imposed on the faculty member (*AAUP Policy Documents and Reports*, 3, 4).

In 1970, following extensive debate within the American higher education community, the AAUP reaffirmed the 1940 Statement and augmented it with a series of interpretive comments ("1970 Interpretive Comments," *AAUP Policy Documents and Reports*, 5–7). In addition, in 1957 the AAUP promulgated and adopted the first version of its "Recommended Institutional Regulations on Academic Freedom and Tenure," subsequently revised at various times, most recently in 2006 (*AAUP Policy Documents and Reports*, 22–31). Regulation 9, on academic freedom, provides that "[a]ll members of the faculty, whether tenured or not, are entitled to academic freedom as set forth in the 1940 Statement of Principles on Academic Freedom and Tenure" (*AAUP Policy Documents and Reports*, 28).

The 2006 revisions of the Recommended Institutional Regulations included a new Regulation 13 that set forth a new policy on part-time faculty appointments. (See http://www.aaup.org/AAUP/pubsres/policydocs/contents/RIR .htm.) The primary function of this policy is to accord greater academic freedom to part-time faculty and in particular to ensure that they enjoy the procedural safeguards of academic due process. Notably, the recommended regulation provides that a part-time faculty member who has been reappointed at least once, but subsequently is not reappointed, shall have the right to a statement of reasons and a right to review of the nonreappointment by a faculty committee. If the part-time faculty member can establish a "prima facie case" that his or her nonreappointment was due to considerations that violate academic freedom, the burden shifts to the administration that issued the nonreappointment to present credible evidence supporting its decision. The regulations further recognize the importance of seniority for part-time faculty who have served multiple appointments by providing them with additional due process protections beyond those offered to less senior faculty members.

The AAUP documents discussed above articulate national academic norms that evidence national custom and usage on academic freedom. Professional norms, however, are also embodied in the regulations, policies, and custom and usage of individual institutions. These institutional norms may overlap or coincide with national norms, especially if they incorporate or track AAUP statements. But institutional norms may also be local norms adapted to the particular institution's character and mission or that of some particular organization with which the institution is affiliated. Whether national or local, professional academic freedom norms are enforced through the internal procedures of individual institutions. In more egregious or intractable cases, or cases of broad professional interest that implicate national norms, AAUP investigations and censure actions may also become part of the enforcement process.

The legal version of academic freedom, in contrast to the professional version, is based on legal concepts that find their expression in legal norms enunciated by the courts. These legal norms, by definition, have the force of law and thus are binding on institutions and faculty members in a way that professional norms are not. In this sense, the distinction between legal norms of academic freedom and professional norms is similar to the broader distinction between law and policy (see Section 1.7). The primary source of legal norms of academic freedom is the decisions of the federal and state courts. These decisions are based primarily on federal constitutional law and on the common law of contract of the various states. (The foundational constitutional law principles are outlined in Section 6.1.5 below.) Legal norms are enforced through litigation and court orders, as well as through negotiations that the parties undertake to avoid the filing of a lawsuit or to settle a lawsuit before the court has rendered any decision.

Trends from the 1970s to the present suggest that, overall, there has been relatively too little emphasis on the professional norms of academic freedom within individual institutions and relatively too much emphasis on the legal norms. The time may be ripe for faculty members and their institutions to reclaim the classical heritage of professional academic freedom and recommit themselves to elucidating and supporting the professional norms within their campus communities. Such developments would increase the likelihood that litigation could be reserved for more extreme cases of recalcitrance and adamant refusals to respect academic custom and usage, national or institutional, and for cases where there is deep conflict between faculty academic freedom and "institutional" academic freedom, or between faculty academic freedom and student academic freedom. The law and the courts could then draw the outer boundaries of academic freedom, providing correctives in extreme cases (see, for example, Section 6.1.6 below), while institutions and the professoriate would do the day-by-day and year-by-year work of creating and maintaining an environment supportive of academic freedom on their own campuses.

**6.1.5. The foundational constitutional law cases.** In a series of cases in the 1950s and 1960s, the U.S. Supreme Court gave academic freedom constitutional status under the First Amendment freedoms of speech and association and to a lesser extent under the Fourteenth Amendment guarantee of procedural due process. The opinions in these cases include a number of ringing declarations on the importance of academic freedom. In *Sweezy v. New Hampshire*, 354 U.S. 234 (1957), both Chief Justice Warren's plurality opinion and Justice Frankfurter's concurring opinion lauded academic freedom in the course of reversing a contempt judgment against a professor who had refused to answer the state attorney general's questions concerning a lecture delivered at the state university. The Chief Justice, writing for a plurality of four Justices, stated that

> to summon a witness and compel him, against his will, to disclose the nature of his past expressions and associations is a measure of governmental interference in these matters. These are rights which are safeguarded by the Bill of Rights and the Fourteenth Amendment. We believe that there unquestionably was an invasion of petitioner's liberties in the area of academic freedom and political expression—areas in which the government should be extremely reticent to tread.
>
> The essentiality of freedom in the community of American universities is almost self-evident . . . Teachers and students must always remain free to inquire, to study and to evaluate, to gain new maturity and understanding; otherwise our civilization will stagnate and die [354 U.S. at 250].

Justice Frankfurter, writing for himself and Justice Harlan, made what has now become the classical statement on "the four essential freedoms" of the university:

It is the business of a university to provide that atmosphere which is most conducive to speculation, experiment and creation. It is an atmosphere in which there prevail "the four essential freedoms" of a university—to determine for itself on academic grounds who may teach, what may be taught, how it shall be taught, and who may be admitted to study [354 U.S. at 263, quoting a conference statement issued by scholars from the Union of South Africa].

In *Shelton v. Tucker*, 364 U.S. 479 (1960), the Court invalidated a state statute that compelled public school and college teachers to reveal all organizational affiliations or contributions for the previous five years. In its reasoning, the Court emphasized:

The vigilant protection of constitutional freedoms is nowhere more vital than in the community of American schools. "By limiting the power of the states to interfere with freedom of speech and freedom of inquiry and freedom of association, the Fourteenth Amendment protects all persons, no matter what their calling. But, in view of the nature of the teacher's relation to the effective exercise of the rights which are safeguarded by the Bill of Rights and by the Fourteenth Amendment, inhibition of freedom of thought, and of action upon thought, in the case of teachers brings the safeguards of those amendments vividly into operation. Such unwarranted inhibition upon the free spirit of teachers . . . has an unmistakable tendency to chill that free play of the spirit which all teachers ought especially to cultivate and practice; it makes for caution and timidity in their associations by potential teachers" [364 U.S. at 487, quoting *Wieman v. Updegraff*, 344 U.S. 183, 195 (1952) (Frankfurter, J., concurring)].

In *Griswold v. Connecticut*, 381 U.S. 479 (1965), the Court majority, in an opinion by Justice Douglas, stated that

the State may not, consistently with the spirit of the First Amendment, contract the spectrum of available knowledge. The right of freedom of speech and press includes not only the right to utter or to print, but the right to distribute, the right to receive, the right to read and freedom of inquiry, freedom of thought, and freedom to teach—indeed the freedom of the entire university community. Without those peripheral rights the specific rights would be less secure [381 U.S. at 482–83; emphasis added].

This statement is particularly important, not only for its comprehensiveness, but also because it focuses on "peripheral rights" under the First Amendment. These rights—better termed "correlative rights" or "ancillary rights"—are based on the principle that the express or core rights in the First Amendment are also the source of other included rights that correlate with or are ancillary to the express or core rights, and without which the core rights could not be fully protected. This principle is an important theoretical underpinning for the concept of academic freedom under the First Amendment. Academic freedom correlates to the express rights of free speech and press in the specific context of academia. The rights of speech and press, in other words, cannot be effectively protected in the college and university environment unless academic freedom, as a corollary of free speech and press, is also recognized. This correlative rights argument is closely related to the argument for implied rights under the First Amendment and other constitutional guarantees. Since it is generally accepted that the First Amendment is the source of an implied right of freedom of association (see, for example, *NAACP v. Alabama ex rel. Patterson*, 357 U.S. 449 (1958)), and since implied rights are recognized under other constitutional guarantees (see, for example, *Zablocki v. Redhail*, 434 U.S. 374 (1978), recognizing the right to marry as an implied right under the due process clause), there is considerable support, beyond *Griswold*, for a correlative or implied right to academic freedom under the First Amendment.

And in *Keyishian v. Board of Regents*, 385 U.S. 589 (1967), the Court quoted both *Sweezy* and *Shelton*, and added:

> Our nation is deeply committed to safeguarding academic freedom, which is of transcendent value to all of us and not merely to the teachers concerned. That freedom is therefore a special concern of the First Amendment, which does not tolerate laws that cast a pall of orthodoxy over the classroom . . . The classroom is peculiarly the "marketplace of ideas." The Nation's future depends upon leaders trained through wide exposure to that robust exchange of ideas which discovers truth "out of a multitude of tongues, [rather] than through any kind of authoritative selection" [385 U.S. at 603; emphasis added].

*Keyishian* is the centerpiece of the formative 1950s and 1960s cases. The appellants were State University of New York faculty members who refused to sign a certificate (the "Feinberg Certificate") stating that they were not and never had been Communists. This certificate was required under a set of laws and regulations designed to prevent "subversives" from obtaining employment in the state's educational system. The faculty members brought a First Amendment challenge against the certificate requirements and the underlying law barring employment to members of subversive organizations, as well as other provisions authorizing dismissal for the "utterance of any treasonable or seditious word or words or the doing of any treasonable or seditious act," and for "by word of mouth or writing willfully and deliberately advocating, advising, or teaching the doctrine of forceful overthrow of the government."

The Court held that the faculty members' First Amendment freedom of association had been violated by the existence and application of this series of laws and rules that were both vague and overbroad (see Sections 9.2.2 and 9.5.2 regarding the vagueness and overbreadth doctrines). The word "seditious" was held to be unconstitutionally vague, even when defined as advocacy of criminal anarchy:

> [T]he possible scope of "seditious utterances or acts" has virtually no limit. For under Penal Law § 161, one commits the felony of advocating criminal anarchy if he "publicly displays any book . . . containing or advocating, advising or teaching the doctrine that organized government should be overthrown by force, violence, or other unlawful means." Does the teacher who carries a copy of the Communist Manifesto on a public street thereby advocate criminal anarchy? . . . The teacher cannot know the extent, if any, to which a "seditious" utterance must transcend mere statement about abstract doctrine, the extent to which

it must be intended to and tend to indoctrinate or incite to action in furtherance of the defined doctrine. The crucial consideration is that no teacher can know just where the line is drawn between "seditious" and nonseditious utterances and acts [385 U.S. at 598–99].

The Court also found that the state's entire system of "intricate administrative machinery" was

a highly efficient *in terrorem* mechanism. . . It would be a bold teacher who would not stay as far as possible from utterances or acts which might jeopardize his living by enmeshing him in this intricate machinery . . . The result may be to stifle "that free play of the spirit which all teachers ought especially to cultivate and practice" [385 U.S. at 601, quoting *Wieman v. Updegraff*, 344 U.S. 183, 195 (Frankfurter, J., concurring)].

Noting that "the stifling effect on the academic mind from curtailing freedom of association in such a manner is manifest," the Court rejected the older case of *Adler v. Board of Education*, 342 U.S. 485 (1951), which permitted New York to bar employment to teachers who were members of listed subversive organizations. In its place, the Court adopted this rule:

Mere knowing membership without a specific intent to further the unlawful aims of an organization is not a constitutionally adequate basis for exclusion from such positions as those held by appellants . . . Legislation which sanctions membership unaccompanied by specific intent to further the unlawful goals of the organization or which is not active membership violates constitutional limitations [385 U.S. at 606, 608].

One year after *Keyishian*, the Supreme Court decided *Pickering v. Board of Education*, 391 U.S. 563 (1968), and thus stepped gingerly into a new line of cases that would become the basis for the second stage of academic freedom's development in the courts. This line of cases, now called "the *Pickering-Connick* line," or sometimes the *Pickering-Connick-Garcetti* line, centers on the free speech rights of all public employees, not merely faculty members, and is therefore addressed in Section 6.1.1.

In addition to its reliance on freedom of speech and of the press and procedural due process, the U.S. Supreme Court has also tapped into the First Amendment's religion clauses to develop supplementary protection for academic freedom. In *Epperson v. Arkansas*, 393 U.S. 97 (1968), and again in *Edwards v. Aguillard*, 482 U.S. 578 (1987), the Court used the establishment clause (see Section 1.6 of this book) to strike down state statutes that interfered with public school teachers' teaching of evolution. And in *O'Connor v. Ortega*, 480 U.S. 709 (1987), the U.S. Supreme Court used the Fourth Amendment's search and seizure clause in protecting an academic employee's office and his papers from a warrantless search. The *O'Connor* case and related Fourth Amendment issues are discussed in Section 6.1.2.

The lower federal and state courts have had many occasions to apply U.S. Supreme Court precedents to a variety of academic freedom disputes pitting faculty members against their institutions. The source of law most frequently invoked in these cases is the First Amendment's free speech clause, as interpreted in the *Pickering-Connick* line of cases. Some cases have also relied on *Keyishian* and its forerunners, either in lieu of or as a supplement to the *Pickering-Connick* line. The legal principles that the lower courts have developed based on these two lines of cases, however, are not as protective of faculty academic freedom as the Supreme Court's declarations in the 1950s and 1960s cases might have suggested. As could be expected, the courts have focused on the specific facts of each case and have reached varying conclusions based on the facts, the particular court's disposition on narrow versus broad construction of First Amendment protections, and the court's sensitivity to the nuances of academic freedom.

**6.1.6. *External versus internal restraints on academic freedom.*** As indicated in Section 6.1.3, there are two paradigms for academic freedom conflicts: they may be either external ("extramural") or internal ("intramural"). The first type of conflict occurs when a government body external to the institution has allegedly impinged upon the institution's academic freedom or that of its faculty or students. The second type of conflict occurs when the institution or its administrators have allegedly impinged upon the academic freedom of one or more of the institution's faculty members or students. The means of infringement, the competing interests, and, to some extent, the applicable law may differ from one type of conflict to the other. The first type is usually controlled by the *Keyishian* line of cases (see Section 6.1.5) or by the *NTEU* case that is an offshoot of *Pickering-Connick* analysis (see Section 6.1.1); the second type of conflict is usually controlled by the *Pickering-Connick* line of cases.

The primary source of law involved in external conflicts is likely to be the First Amendment—not only free speech and free press, but also freedom of association and freedom of religion. If the conflict were between a government body and a private institution, the institution would have its own First Amendment rights to assert against the government, as would its faculty members (and its students, as the case may be). If the conflict were between a government body and a public institution, the institution's faculty members (and students, as the case may be) could assert their First Amendment rights against the government; but the public institution itself would not have its own constitutional rights to assert, since it is an arm of government. (It could, however, assert and support the rights of its faculty members or students.) The government body that allegedly interferes with academic freedom could be a state legislature, a state legislative committee, a state attorney general, a grant-making agency, a regulatory agency, a grand jury, a police department, or a court.

External or extramural academic freedom conflicts may also involve *private* bodies external to the institution that allegedly interfere with the academic freedom of the institution or its faculty members (or students). The external private body may be a foundation or other funding organization, a political interest group, a religious organization or informal group of religious persons, or a group of taxpayers as in the *Linnemeir* case and the *Yacovelli* case discussed below. If it is a private body that infringes upon academic freedom, neither the institution nor its faculty members may assert constitutional claims against that body, except in a case where the private body is engaged in state action (see Section 1.5.2).

From the 1970s through the end of the twentieth century, internal academic freedom conflicts arose much more frequently than did external conflicts, at least in terms of litigation that resulted in published opinions of the courts. This ascendance of internal conflicts, at least in public institutions, was probably fueled by the U.S. Supreme Court's decision in the *Pickering* case (see Section 6.1.1), which provided a conceptual base upon which faculty members could assert free expression claims against their institutions. In the early years of the twenty-first century, however, external conflicts became more frequent and more visible, commanding considerably more attention from practitioners, scholars, courts, and the media. The impetus for this reemergence apparently came primarily from two developments. One was the escalating terrorism and national security concerns marked by the disasters of September 11, 2001. The other development was a resurgence of the "political correctness" phenomenon, particularly in situations involving allegations of political or intellectual bias as well as ethnic and religious bias on U.S. campuses.

Regarding the first development, the USA PATRIOT Act, 115 Stat 272 (2001), has been a focal point of concern. The act permits federal investigators to access various private communications, including those of faculty members, undertaken by way of telephones or computer networks; and permits access into certain library records kept by libraries, including those on U.S. campuses. The act also places certain restrictions on foreign students wishing to study at U.S. colleges and universities and foreign scholars seeking to visit U.S. colleges and universities. It has frequently been argued that some uses of these federal powers on American campuses would, by interfering with the privacy of academic communications, interfere with faculty academic freedom and institutional autonomy.

Concerns have also arisen after 9/11 regarding various federal government initiatives that restrict or potentially restrict scientific research undertaken at American colleges and universities. Some of these restrictions are in the PATRIOT Act itself; others are in regulations promulgated by various government agencies. It has frequently been argued that several of these restrictions on university research, including restrictions imposed upon the granting of federal research funds, can limit research and publication in ways that interfere with faculty academic freedom and institutional autonomy.

Regarding the second development mentioned above, there have been various challenges to college programs, events, or decisions that are said to reflect ethnic or religious bias. In *Linnemeir v. Board of Trustees, Indiana University-Purdue University, Fort Wayne*, 260 F.3d 757 (7th Cir. 2001), for example, state taxpayers and individual state legislators challenged the planned performance of a play that a student had selected for his senior thesis and his departmental faculty had approved. The plaintiffs argued that the play, which presented a critique of Christianity, would violate the First Amendment's establishment clause and would be offensive to many Christians. The federal district court denied the plaintiffs' motion for a preliminary injunction (155 F. Supp. 2d 1034 (N.D. Ind. 2001)), and the appellate court affirmed the denial (260 F.3d 757 (7th Cir. 2001)). Similarly, in *Yacovelli v. Moeser*, taxpayers and students challenged an orientation reading program planned for incoming students at the University of North Carolina at Chapel Hill. The plaintiffs claimed that use of the assigned book, which concerned the early history of the Islamic faith, would violate the federal establishment clause and free exercise clause, and would be an exercise in "political correctness." At around the same time, a legislative appropriations committee of the North Carolina legislature sought to block the use of public funds for the planned orientation program. (See Donna Euben, "Curriculum Matters," *Academe*, November–December 2002, 86.) Ultimately, the federal district court rejected the plaintiffs' claims on the merits.

There have also been various challenges to professors' or departmental faculties' decisions regarding courses, course materials, classroom discussions, and grades. The challengers typically cite particular decisions that they claim foster indoctrination or otherwise reflect a political (usually liberal) bias. The challengers often claim that such decisions violate student academic freedom, thus adding an additional dimension of conflict to the situation—a dimension that is illustrated by the *Yacovelli* case above. For additional examples of student academic freedom claims and challenges to faculty academic freedom, in the context of political or intellectual bias disputes, see the discussion of the proposed "Academic Bill of Rights" and the proposed "Intellectual Diversity in Higher Education Act" in Section 7.1.4 of this book.

### 6.1.7. *"Institutional" academic freedom.*

As academic freedom developed, originally in Europe and then later in the United States, it had two branches: faculty academic freedom and student academic freedom. But in modern parlance, articulated primarily in court decisions beginning in the early 1980s, a third type of academic freedom has joined the first two: that of the colleges and universities themselves, or "institutional academic freedom." (See, for example, *Edwards v. California University of Pennsylvania* in Section 6.2.2 and *Urofsky v. Gilmore* in Section 6.3.) Consequently, there are now three sets of beneficiaries of academic freedom protections: faculty members, students, and individual higher educational institutions. Obviously the interests of these three groups are not always compatible with one another, thereby ensuring that conflicts will arise among the various claimants of academic freedom.

Institutional academic freedom (or institutional autonomy) entails the freedom to determine who may teach, the freedom to determine what may be taught, the freedom to determine how the subject matter will be taught, and the freedom to determine who may be admitted to study. In American law and custom, these four freedoms are usually traced to Justice Felix Frankfurter's concurring opinion in *Sweezy v. New Hampshire*, 354 U.S. 234, 263 (1957) (discussed in Section 6.1.5 above). But it was not until the case of *Regents of University of Michigan v. Ewing*, 474 U.S. 214 (1985) (further discussed in

Section 8.2), that the U.S. Supreme Court explicitly distinguished between an institution's academic freedom and that of its faculty and students. "Academic freedom," said the Court, "thrives not only on the independent and uninhibited exchange of ideas among teachers and students . . . but also, and somewhat inconsistently, on autonomous decisionmaking by the academy itself" (474 U.S. at 226 n.12). This statement on institutional academic freedom, however, is not free from ambiguity. Although the Court did recognize the "academic freedom" of "state and local educational institutions," in the very same paragraph it also focused on "the multitude of academic decisions that are made daily by faculty members of public educational institutions" (474 U.S. at 226). Thus the Court may not have intended to juxtapose the interests of the institution against those of its faculty and was apparently assuming that the defendant university was either acting through its faculty members or acting in their interest.[3] The Court's distinction between institutional academic freedom and faculty (or student) academic freedom thus does not entail a separation of the institution's interests from those of its faculty members, nor does it suggest that institutional interests must prevail over faculty interests if the two are in conflict.

The same might be said of the Court's later statement on institutional academic freedom in *Grutter v. Bollinger*, 539 U.S. 306 (2003), the University of Michigan affirmative action case (see Section 7.2.5). As in *Ewing*, the Court in *Grutter* spoke of the academic freedom or autonomy interests of the institution (539 U.S. at 324, 329). But, as in *Ewing*, the Court did not separate those interests from the interests of the faculty, or pit the two sets of interests against one another, or suggest that the institutional academic freedom claims would necessarily prevail over faculty academic freedom claims.

Had the Court in *Ewing* or *Grutter* recognized institutional academic freedom as a First Amendment right separate from that of faculty members, additional conceptual difficulties would have arisen. The institution in these cases is a public institution that, like many other public colleges and universities, is an arm of the state government. States and state governmental entities do not have federal constitutional rights (see, for example, *Native American Heritage Commission v. Board of Trustees of the California State University*, 59 Cal. Rptr. 2d 402 (1996)). According to constitutional theory, persons (that is, private individuals and private corporations)—not governments—have rights; and rights are limits on governmental power to be asserted against government, rather than extensions of government power to be asserted on the government's own behalf. Public institutions' claims of institutional academic freedom therefore cannot be federal constitutional rights claims as such. These claims are better understood as claims based on interests—"governmental interests"—

---

[3] Indeed, in academic matters, institutions do not operate separately from their faculties. It is "the traditional role of deans, provosts, department heads, and faculty [to make] academic decisions," and they make "discretionary choices . . . in the contexts of hiring, tenure, curriculum selection, grants, and salaries" (*Urofsky v. Gilmore*, 216 F.3d 401, 432–33 (Wilkinson, Ch. J., concurring in result).

that can be asserted by public institutions to defend themselves against faculty members' or students' claims that the institution has violated their individual constitutional rights. This is the actual setting in which institutional academic freedom is discussed in both *Ewing* and *Grutter*. In this context, "institutional autonomy" is a more apt descriptor of the institution's interests than is "institutional academic freedom," since the former does not have the "rights" connotation that the latter phrase has.

Public colleges and universities may assert these institutional autonomy interests not only in internal or intramural academic freedom disputes with their faculties (or students) but also in external or extramural disputes with other governmental bodies or private entities that seek to interfere with the institution's internal affairs. In the context of an external dispute, there may be no conflict between the institution's interests and those of its faculty (or its students), in which case the institution may assert its faculty's (or student body's) academic interests as well as its own autonomy interests. If the institution is a private institution, however, and it is in conflict with an agency of government, it may also assert its own First Amendment constitutional right to academic freedom. A rights claim fits this context because a private college or university is a corporate person within the meaning of the federal Constitution and therefore may assert the same constitutional rights as a private individual may assert. This is the only context in which institutional academic freedom may be considered to be a constitutional rights claim.

### 6.1.8. "International" academic freedom.

**6.1.8. "International" academic freedom.** The continuing trend toward the globalization of higher education has spawned various new types of challenges for academic freedom. These challenges, like their more traditional predecessors, may implicate both the professional and the legal concepts of academic freedom (see Section 6.1.4) and both external and internal constraints on academic freedom (see Section 6.1.6). Moreover, these challenges may implicate the institution's own interests in academic freedom (or institutional autonomy) as well as the separate and sometimes inconsistent academic freedom interests of faculty members and students (see Section 6.1.7).

There are, however, important differences between "international" and "domestic" academic freedom issues. International academic freedom issues may arise in countries other than the United States and, even when arising in the U.S., will have implications for other countries as well. The federal government, a state government, an educational association, or an individual institution in the United States, for example, may take action that limits the freedom of faculty members or students from foreign countries to teach, study, or do research in the United States; or may take action that limits the freedom of U.S. faculty members or students to teach, study, or do research in other countries. Conversely, a government, educational association, or individual institution in a foreign country may take action that limits the freedom of U.S. faculty members or students to teach, study, or do research in that country; or may take action that limits the freedom of that country's faculty members or students to teach, study, or do research in the United States.

To address the emerging issues in these international contexts, one cannot rely only on the professional and legal concepts of academic freedom that are operative in the United States. The professional and legal concepts that are operative in other countries must often also be considered—including concepts that are inhospitable to academic freedom as it is understood in the United States. The disputes that have arisen thus far in this broader context suggest a need to consider the laws of foreign countries, international agreements, diplomatic relationships, the statements and practices of foreign and international academic (and academic labor) organizations, and the customs and practices of individual institutions, in developing a more global perspective on academic freedom. Moreover, such disputes suggest a need to examine whether there are, or can be, *international norms* of academic freedom that supplement the more traditional national and institutional norms of academic freedom.

The leading attempt by governments to develop such international norms is the *Recommendation Concerning the Status of Higher Education Teaching Personnel*, United Nations Educational, Scientific, and Cultural Organization (UNESCO), adopted November 11, 1997 (available at http://portal.unesco.org/en/ev.php-URL_ID = 13144&URL_DO = DO_TOPIC&URL_SECTION = 201.html). Private educational or academic labor associations may also devise statements of cross-country or international norms regarding academic freedom. One example of such a statement is "On Conditions of Employment at Overseas Campuses" (www.aaup.org/aaup/comm/rep/a/overseas.htm), jointly adopted in 2009 by the AAUP and the Canadian Association of University Teachers, which expressly incorporates the UNESCO statement. In addition, university presidents and rectors may also cooperate in developing statements of principles on academic freedom and institutional autonomy; see, for example, the Academic Freedom Statement of the first Global Colloquium of University Presidents, issued by the presidents' colloquium in 2005 and initially signed by sixteen presidents from the United States and seven foreign countries (see http://chronicle.com/article/Leading-Presidents-Issue-St/25635/). And academics, as well as other researchers and analysts, may develop model statements of academic freedom norms for consideration by policymakers; see, for example, Terence Karran, "Academic Freedom in Europe: Time for a Magna Charta?" 22 *Higher Education Policy* 163 (2009).

Recent controversies in the United States that implicate international academic freedom have often involved bans on travel for academic purposes. Three such controversies are analyzed below. As will be seen, such controversies may involve U.S. academics seeking to leave the United States for teaching or research purposes, or foreign academics seeking to enter the United States for teaching or research purposes.[4] The resulting issues, under U.S. law,

---

[4]Similar controversies may also involve U.S. students seeking to study or do research in foreign countries, or foreign students seeking to study or do research in the United States. Such student academic freedom issues may sometimes overlap with faculty academic freedom claims—as, for instance, when a faculty member's assertion of a right to teach may serve to protect students as well, and students' assertions of a right to learn (or right to hear) may serve also to protect faculty members.

may implicate the First Amendment freedom of speech, a Fifth and Fourteenth Amendment liberty interest in travel, and various administrative law and federal "supremacy" principles.

*Faculty Senate of Florida International University v. Roberts*, 574 F. Supp. 2d 1331 (S.D. Fla. 2008), *affirmed in part and reversed in part*, *Faculty Senate of Florida International University v. Winn*, 616 F. 3d 1206 (11th Cir. 2010), illustrates a ban imposed by a state on certain U.S. scholars seeking to travel abroad. The pertinent legislation is the Florida "Travel Act" (Fla. Stat. Ann. §§ 1011.90(6), 112.061(3)(e)), which, as described by the federal district court, "restricts state universities from spending both state and 'non-state' funds on activities related to travel to a 'terrorist state,'" as designated by the U.S. Department of State. The plaintiffs claimed that this act violated their academic freedom as researchers and teachers. They provided various examples, such as this one:

> Professor Lisandro Perez is a professor in the Sociology and Anthropology Department at Florida International University ("FIU"), a state university in Miami, Florida, and the founder and director of the Cuban Research Institute (the "CRI") at FIU, which fosters academic exchanges and collaborations with Cuba. Professor Perez is authorized by the United States to travel to Cuba in furtherance of his ongoing research relating to Cuba. Since its 1991 founding, the CRI has agreed with the FIU administration that it would not use state funds to pay for travel to and from Cuba, but rather it would raise funds from external sources to support its programs in Cuba. Funds from the foundations are received by FIU and placed into accounts and, while the CRI Director has the signature over the accounts, the FIU grants-administrator oversees all expenditures to make sure they are within the grant's guidelines. Professor Perez asserts that it is "not currently possible for the CRI to receive private grant funds without having the funds administered by FIU."
>
> Professor Perez testified that for purposes of researching a book on the Cuban community in New York City in the 19th century, he had planned to go to Cuba in December 2006, but was unable to take the trip as a result of the Travel Act. Moreover, Professor Perez stated that he is unable to continue with the subject in the future as a result of his inability to travel to Cuba and also that his teaching has suffered because he cannot do first-hand research. Professor Perez also represented that he is evaluated on his research, teaching and service to the community, and represented that his evaluation on [these] criteria would be harmed due to the Act. Finally, Professor Perez testified that his community service consists of offering commentary on current events involving Cuba through essays published in newspapers, interviews on television, or speaking at local events, and the inability to travel to Cuba affects these activities [574 F. Supp. 2d at 1339–40 (footnotes and transcript references omitted)].

The plaintiffs challenged the Travel Act on its face as a violation of their First Amendment freedom of speech. Working through the Travel Act's tortured legislative history, the court determined that "the Act only limits funding for activities related to, or involving, travel to a terrorist state." As narrowly construed, the court (with very little supportive analysis) held the act to be constitutional on its face. In dicta, however, the court did warn that, had "the Act preclude[d] funding for a broad scope of activities, such as lectures, dissertations, etc., relating to the designated countries, the Act would likely be a content-based restriction [on speech] in violation of the First Amendment" (574 F. Supp. 2d at 1354). Moreover, in another part of the opinion dealing with the act's interference with federal foreign affairs powers, the court invalidated the act's application to "non-state" funds, and "nominal state" funds necessary for the administration of "non-state" funds, leaving the act valid only in its application to state funding.

Although the plaintiffs had secured a partial victory for academic freedom, they nevertheless appealed, seeking complete invalidation of the statute on this same theory, that the act interfered with federal foreign affairs powers. The plaintiffs actually lost ground, however, when the U.S. Court of Appeals reversed the judgment regarding the "non-state" funds and vacated the injunction barring enforcement of the Travel Act as applied to such funds. The court, in a footnote, asserted that there was no meaningful difference between state-contributed funds and funds from outside grantors that were administered by the State, since both resulted in expense to Florida. Relying on the traditional grant of control to states over their spending for education, the court determined that concern for student and faculty safety and the avoidance of entanglement with "foreign espionage" were legitimate considerations when determining how to allocate limited education resources. Additionally, the court found that invalidation of the statute was not required because any conflict between federal law and Florida's statute was "too indirect, minor, incidental, and peripheral to trigger" application of the supremacy clause (616 F.3d at 1208). The plaintiffs attempted to prove a significant conflict did exist by offering evidence of a definitive federal policy favoring academic freedom, noting, for example, that general travel bans imposed by the federal government usually still allow for academic travel and that Title VI of the Higher Education Act of 1965 emphasizes the importance of "American experts in and citizens knowledgeable about world regions, foreign languages, and international affairs, as well as upon a strong research base in these areas." The court of appeals, however, found that there was nothing on record to show a "definite substantive foreign policy position . . . in favor of academic travel—much less in favor of travel to countries that sponsor terrorism—that could be undermined by Florida's act." The court further determined that even if there were "some indistinct desire on the part of the Executive Branch or Congress to encourage generally academic travel," the "traditional state interest" in managing the scope of and resource allocations for academic programs overcomes the conflict between federal policy and state law, "given the lack of the conflict's clarity and severity."

Another wrinkle in determining the validity of Florida's Travel Act could unfold as a result of a 2011 presidential directive regarding U.S. relations with Cuba, as implemented by amendment of the Office of Foreign Assets Control (OFAC) regulations that govern the Cuba Trade Embargo (31 C.F.R. Part 515) and are authorized by the Trading with the Enemy Act (50 U.S.C. app. § 5(b)).

302 Faculty Academic Freedom and Freedom of Expression

The newly amended regulations could become the "definite substantive foreign policy position . . . in favor of academic travel" that the U.S. Court of Appeals spoke of as requisite to invalidating the Travel Act. Both the directive and the regulations may at least give more "clarity" to the conflict between federal policy and Florida's law; the directive aims to "facilitate educational exchanges" with Cuba, and the OFAC regulations serve to "allow for greater licensing of travel to Cuba for educational . . . activities." While these purposes for the amended policy are part of the greater purpose of "reaching out to the Cuban people," it seems feasible that a court could construe them as more than "some indistinct desire on the part of the Executive Branch . . . to generally encourage academic travel." Then the question, in any case challenging Florida's Travel Act or similar legislation that other states could pass, would be whether the directive and amended regulations add sufficient weight to the federal policy supporting academic travel to create an actual conflict between state and federal law. If a court were to answer that question affirmatively, there then could be a second question: whether a ban on using non-state funds would be invalid only as to Cuba and not as to other terrorist states.

In contrast to the *Florida Senate of Florida International University* case, *American Academy of Religion, et al. v. Chertoff*, 463 F. Supp. 2d 400 (S.D.N.Y. 2006), and 2007 WL 4527504 (S.D.N.Y. 2007), illustrates a travel ban imposed by the federal government (rather than a state government) on a foreign scholar (rather than domestic scholar). The scholar, Dr. Tariq Ramadan, sought a nonimmigrant visa (a B visa) that would allow him to enter the United States to participate in various academic conferences as he had frequently done in the past. He applied for the B visa shortly after the Department of Homeland Security (DHS) revoked an H-1B visa that he had sought in order to accept a faculty position at the University of Notre Dame.

When DHS delayed any action on the B visa application, three U.S. nonprofit organizations brought suit, claiming that DHS was seeking to exclude Dr. Ramadan from the United States on the basis of his political views, in violation of the First Amendment. The plaintiffs asserted their own rights to hear (or receive information and ideas from) Ramadan. They sought a preliminary injunction allowing Ramadan to enter the United States temporarily to attend the organizations' annual conventions or, alternatively, to require DHS to promptly reach a final decision on Ramadan's pending B visa application. At the time the lawsuit was filed, and during its pendency, DHS had not "provided any explanation as to why it revoked Ramadan's H-1B visa in July 2004 or why it is unable to render a decision on Ramadan's pending B-visa application" (463 F. Supp. 2d at 408).

In its opinion, the court relied and built upon principles developed by the U.S. Supreme Court in *Kleindienst v. Mandel*, 408 U.S. 753, 762–66, 769–70 (1972). Based on these principles, the court affirmed that "the First Amendment rights of American citizens are implicated when the Government excludes an alien from the United States on the basis of his political views, even though the non-resident alien has no constitutionally or statutorily protected right to enter the United States to speak." Congress's power over immigration is of the highest order however, and the executive branch "has broad discretion over the admission and exclusion of aliens." Thus the "power of a court to override the Government's decision to exclude an alien is severely limited." The court in *American Academy of Religion* accommodated these contending principles in this helpful way:

> [W]hile the Executive may exclude an alien for almost any reason, it cannot do so solely because the Executive disagrees with the content of the alien's speech and therefore wants to prevent the alien from sharing this speech with a willing American audience.
>
> \* \* \* \* \*
>
> Only where the Government is unable to provide a facially legitimate and bona fide reason for excluding the alien, thereby revealing that the true reason for exclusion was the content of the alien's speech, may a court remedy the constitutional infirmity by enjoining the Government from excluding the alien in contravention to the First Amendment [463 F. Supp. 2d at 415, citing *Mandel*, 480 U.S. at 769–70].

In this litigation, the court noted, the government had not provided "any explanation at all" for excluding Ramadan from the United States or any explanation for the delay in ruling on his application (other than a few "totally inadequate," "bare assertions"), thus "making it impossible for the court to determine" whether, under the above guidelines, the government had violated the plaintiffs' First Amendment rights. The court therefore entered a preliminary injunction ordering the government "to issue a formal decision on Ramadan's pending nonimmigrant visa application" within ninety days.

A few days before expiration of the ninety-day deadline, the government denied Ramadan's visa request. The stated reason was that "Professor Ramadan had contributed money to an organization which provided material support to Hamas, a terrorist group," in violation of the Immigration and Nationality Act, 8 U.S.C. § 1182(a)(3)(B)(iv)(VI). The plaintiffs thereafter returned to court (2007 WL 45527504), claiming that the government's reason was not "facially legitimate and bona fide," as the court had required (see the language quoted above), and that the visa denial therefore infringed their First Amendment rights.

After methodically reviewing the statutory provision relied on by the government, and considering the limited judicial review of First Amendment claims asserted in visa cases, the district court rejected the plaintiffs' argument. The court concluded that the statute applied to Ramadan (even though the organization to which he contributed a thousand dollars was not designated an organization supporting terrorism until a year after his last contribution), that the government had provided a reason based on the statute, and that the government's reason for denying the visa "is unrelated to Professor Ramadan's speech."

The plaintiffs appealed, challenging the district court's acceptance of the government's application of the Immigration and Nationality Act to Ramadan (*American Academy of Religion v. Napolitano*, 573 F.3d 115 (2d Cir. 2009)). One of the main issues the appellate court addressed was "what will render the government's reason [for visa denial] 'facially legitimate and bona fide.'" In particular the court considered the provision of the Immigration and Nationality Act that made an alien ineligible for a visa if he has supplied "material support, including . . . funds . . . to a terrorist organization . . . or to any member of such an organization, *unless* the actor can demonstrate by clear and convincing evidence that the actor did not know, and should not reasonably have known, that the organization was a terrorist organization" (emphasis added). The court found that this provision implicitly required procedural protections allowing the alien "reasonable opportunity" to counter the government's determination under this statutory provision. Since there was no showing that the government had provided Ramadan this opportunity, the court could not ascertain whether the government's reason for the visa denial was "facially legitimate and bona fide." The court therefore remanded this issue to the district court so that the government could either show that Ramadan was confronted with the allegations and afforded the opportunity to counter them, or conduct a new visa hearing in which Ramadan would have the opportunity to confront and counter the allegations.

The third travel case is *Emergency Coalition to Defend Educational Travel v. United States Department of the Treasury*, 545 F.3d 4 (D.C. Cir. 2008). This case, like *Faculty Senate of Florida International University*, involved governmental restrictions on academics seeking to leave the country for academic purposes; but unlike *Faculty Senate* (and like *American Academy of Religion*), the *Emergency Coalition* case involved federal government rather than state government restrictions. At issue were 2004 amendments to the Office of Foreign Assets Control (OFAC) regulations (discussed earlier in this section) that govern the Cuba Trade Embargo (31 C.F.R. Part 515) and are authorized by the Trading with the Enemy Act (50 U.S.C. app. § 5(b)). The 2004 amendments (in contrast to the 2011 amendments discussed above in relation to the Faculty Senate case that loosened travel restrictions) had tightened the conditions under which U.S. colleges and universities could obtain licenses to conduct study programs in Cuba: the program had to be at least ten weeks' duration; only students from the licensed institution could enroll, not students from other institutions; and only permanent full-time faculty members of the licensed institution could teach in the program. The plaintiffs claimed that these restrictions violated faculty and student academic freedom. They argued, for example, that the first restriction ruled out all of the inter-session study programs that had been conducted prior to the amendments; that the second restriction banned "the prior practice of aggregating students from a variety of universities" into one university's course and thus "made it economically infeasible for most universities to offer courses in Cuba;" and that the third restriction had "drastically reduced the pool of professors eligible to teach such courses." These restrictions, the plaintiffs argued, affected "who may teach and what may be taught" (and presumably who may be admitted to study) without sufficient justification, and thus violated their academic freedom as protected under the First and Fifth Amendments.

In both the federal district court and the appellate court, however, the plaintiffs were tripped up by issues concerning the applicable standard of review for their claims. The court determined that "strict scrutiny" review of the plaintiffs' First Amendment claims did not apply because the government had not interfered with the content of professors' academic lectures or "academic speech." Rather, the government regulations at issue were "content neutral" because their purpose was to "curtail tourism" in Cuba and thus restrict the profits from tourism that Cuba relied on. The more lenient "intermediate scrutiny" test therefore applied—a test that the government was able to meet.

The plaintiffs fared no better with their Fifth Amendment claim—that the government regulation infringed upon their "right to travel" as a protected liberty interest under the Fifth Amendment due process clause. Although acknowledging that the U.S. Supreme Court, in *Kent v. Dulles*, 357 U.S. 116, 127 (1958), had "recognize[d] the right to international travel as part of a liberty interest," the court determined that "subsequent cases have distinguished [Kent]" and "disapproved of [its] broad protection of international travel." Under these cases, federal government regulations of international travel are valid under the Fifth Amendment so long as they "apply equally to all citizens and [are] rooted in foreign policy concerns." The 2004 amendments easily met this test, according to the court, especially since the Supreme Court had made it clear that "the federal judiciary was obliged to defer to the political branches" on questions concerning the importance of federal foreign policy objectives.

A concurring judge, Judge Edwards, issued a separate opinion specifically to address the academic freedom dimensions of the case—a matter given short shrift in the court's opinion written by Judge Silberman. Judge Edwards, however, ultimately reached essentially the same conclusion as the majority—that "in this case, the First Amendment rights implicated by appellants' claims are coterminous with any applicable rights to academic freedom," and that in this case, under the First Amendment, only intermediate scrutiny applied. Although Judge Edwards's more nuanced opinion does hold out hope to faculty members that the First Amendment can sometimes provide meaningful protections in international academic freedom cases, he spoke only for himself. In response to Judge Edwards, Judge Silberman issued a second opinion, a concurring opinion for himself alone, in which he cast doubt on the existence of any First Amendment academic freedom right and argued that, even if there were such a right, it would belong only to institutions of higher education and not to their faculties or students (see Section 7.1.7 above). This reasoning apparently explains why Judge Silberman's opinion for the court gave scant attention to the plaintiff's academic freedom arguments.

Although the *Emergency Coalition* case still stands as good law on all points, the travel restrictions that the plaintiffs challenged were eliminated or revised by the 2011 amendments to the OFAC regulations (76 Fed. Reg. 5072 (Jan. 28, 2011), 31 C.F.R. § 515.565). (The 2011 amendments are discussed above in relation to Faculty Senate of Florida International University.) Under the new regulations, for example, the old requirement that study programs at a Cuban institution be no shorter than ten weeks is eliminated, and instead the regulation mandates only that "the study in Cuba be accepted for credit toward the student's degree"; students are now permitted to participate in academic activities through any "sponsoring U.S. academic institution" rather than, as the old regulations prescribed, only through the "accredited U.S. academic institution at which the student is pursuing a degree"; and the ability to conduct study programs in Cuba has been extended to include all faculty and staff (including adjunct and part-time staff) of a sponsoring U.S. academic institution, rather than, as the old regulations required, only "full-time permanent employee[s] of the institution."

These amendments apparently resolved the issues the plaintiffs had raised in relation to the old regulations in the *Emergency Coalition* case. The new amended regulations clearly provide greater support for inter-country or international academic freedom and may indicate an important shift in federal policy. Viewed as just one of several changes regarding relations with Cuba, however, the greater academic freedom protection may just be a side effect of the overriding goal of increasing U.S. contact with Cuba and the Cuban people. So although the plaintiffs in *Emergency Coalition* may now in effect have the relief sought, the broader impact of this relief as related to international academic freedom remains to be seen.

Taken together, the three international travel cases provide little protection for international academic freedom. The court opinions evidence substantial deference to the federal government when it is exercising its foreign affairs powers, and the *Faculty Senate* case also evidences deference to the state government when it is exercising its spending powers regarding education. And all the courts' opinions (except Judge Edwards's concurrence in *Emergency Coalition*) suggest a reluctance to probe the academic freedom issues raised by the cases.

The cases do reveal two types of arguments, however, that may yield some judicial protection for international academic freedom in limited circumstances. First, the opinions in the *American Academy of Religion* case apparently accept the proposition that the U.S. may not exclude a foreign scholar from the country solely on the basis of his or her political beliefs. If plaintiffs could show that this kind of exclusion had occurred, they then would have a First Amendment free speech argument for challenging the government's action. The *Emergency Coalition* case also appears to support this type of argument, but the case qualifies the reach of the argument by emphasizing that governmental travel restrictions that implicate free speech are usually "content-neutral" restrictions and thus would not receive the "strict scrutiny" review that content-based restrictions (such as an exclusion based on political beliefs) would receive.

Second, the district court opinion in the *Faculty Senate* case accepted an argument based on the "supremacy" of federal foreign affairs powers over state law. This type of argument (unlike the free speech argument) applies only to state law restrictions on international academic travel. The supremacy argument was qualified on appeal in *Faculty Senate*, however, when the court applied a very strict guideline for determining when a state law actually conflicts with federal foreign affairs powers.

Although the three travel cases cover only a part of the much wider range of possible international academic freedom issues and do not provide a sufficient basis for drawing any firm conclusions, it is nevertheless important to note the tentative conclusions that one might draw from these opinions and the tentative advice that one might find in them. In short, at this time, courts may not be the best source for protection of international academic freedom. Rather, it appears that developments in U.S. foreign policy (and that of other countries) may provide a better way to establish protections, as suggested by the directive and regulations on Cuba and the State Department's intervention in the visa disputes involving foreign scholars discussed earlier in this section. Other sources where protections for international academic freedom may be found or developed are international treaties, other bilateral and multilateral agreements between the United States and other countries, agreements between U.S. institutions of higher education and government agencies in other countries, and agreements between U.S. institutions and collaborating institutions in other countries. In addition, as may also be seen regarding domestic academic freedom, it will be important to pay renewed attention to professional concepts of academic freedom as sources of protection and thus to engage in the difficult and slow work of developing international professional understandings and norms of academic freedom that are attentive to the continuing globalization of higher education.

## Section 6.2. Academic Freedom in Teaching

**6.2.1. In general.** Courts are generally reluctant to become involved in academic freedom disputes concerning course content, teaching methods, grading practices, classroom demeanor, and the assignment of instructors to particular courses, viewing these matters as best left to the competence of the educators themselves and the administrators who have primary responsibility over academic affairs. Academic custom also frequently leaves such matters primarily to faculty members and their deans and department chairs (see "1940 Statement of Principles on Academic Freedom and Tenure," in *AAUP Policy Documents and Reports* (9th ed., 2001), 3–11; and "Statement on Government of Colleges and Universities," in *AAUP Policy Documents and Reports*, 135). Sections 6.2.2 and 6.2.3 explore the circumstances in which courts may intervene in such disputes, particularly in public institutions. The concluding section (Section 6.2.4) considers the sources and extent of protections for the freedom to teach in private institutions.

The First Amendment issues analyzed in Sections 6.2.2 through 6.2.4, while always difficult, are now subject to additional complexity due to the U.S. Supreme Court's decision in *Garcetti v. Ceballos* (Section 6.1.1 of this book). The key question, yet to be resolved, is whether the courts will (a) analyze the protections for faculty teaching and grading at public institutions by using the dichotomy between "employee speech" and "private citizen speech" emphasized in *Garcetti*, or (b) create an exception from *Garcetti* for faculty speech related to teaching. If it is the former, much of the protection now afforded faculty classroom speech and grading under cases such as *Hardy* (see Section 6.2.2) and *Parate* (see Section 6.2.3) would apparently be lost. Moreover, if the *Garcetti* employee speech doctrine is to apply to faculty members' teaching activities, its application would not be limited to classroom speech. It would apply as well to teaching functions outside the classroom. The following case illustrates how courts might apply *Garcetti* to faculty teaching, including teaching outside the classroom, and how application of *Garcetti* would affect the analysis of faculty speech rights and diminish the protection of faculty speech.

In *Renken v. Gregory*, 541 F.3d 769 (7th Cir. 2008), a tenured professor at the University of Wisconsin–Milwaukee had applied for a federal grant from the National Science Foundation (NSF) "'to develop a mechanism for enhancing the education of engineering undergraduates . . . through the addition of laboratory components'" to courses that had no "hands-on laboratory content." The dean of the university's engineering school sent the professor a proposal about the conditions attached to the university's matching funds that it was required to provide under the grant. Renken, the professor, disagreed with the dean's proposal for handling matching funds. He complained to the dean and to other university officials regarding the grant project. As principal investigator (PI)/project director for the grant, he wrote a letter to the dean "cataloguing a list of criticisms regarding the project" and filed a complaint against the dean with the chair of the University Committee. Renken thereafter exchanged letters with the dean and wrote other university officials, including a member of the university's board of regents, continuing his complaints about the university's handling of the grant. After Renken rejected a final compromise proposal prepared by the dean of the graduate school, the university decided to return the grant money to NSF.

Renken filed suit, alleging that his criticisms were protected speech under the First Amendment and that the university had terminated the grant and reduced his pay in retaliation for those criticisms. The district court granted the university's motion for summary judgment because, under *Garcetti*, Renken had spoken as an employee and not as a private citizen. The appellate court affirmed. In its opinion, the court did not address a possible teaching or scholarship exception to *Garcetti*, focusing only on whether Renken had spoken as an employee.

Renken argued "that the tasks that he conducted in relation to the grant were implemented at his discretion '*while* in the course of his job and not as a *requirement* of his job'"; that "his job duties did not extend to making formal complaints"; and that "it was '[s]olely by the terms of the Grant, *not* his job,' [that he] was required to complain" of fiscal improprieties. The appellate court responded that these distinctions were not relevant to the *Garcetti* concept of employee speech. Either way, Renken was acting within his scope of his employment:

> In fulfillment of his acknowledged teaching and service responsibilities, Renken acted as a PI, applying for the NSF grant. This grant aided in the fulfillment of his teaching responsibilities because, as Renken notes in his reply brief, the

grant was an education grant for the benefit of students as "undergraduate education development . . ." In his capacity as PI, Renken . . . complained to several levels of University officials about the various difficulties he encountered in the course of administering the grant as a PI. Thereby, Renken called attention to fund misuse relating to a project that he was in charge of administering as a University faculty member. In so doing, Renken was speaking as a faculty employee, and not as a private citizen, because administering the grant as a PI fell within the teaching and service duties that he was employed to perform . . . Here, by Renken's own admission, his employment status as full professor depended on the administration of grants, such as the NSF grant. It was in the course of that administration, that Renken made his statements about funding improprieties within the confines of the University system and as the principal PI [541 F. 3d at 773–74].

Thus, even though the court consistently categorized the professor's work on the grant as part of his "teaching duties," the court gave no consideration to whether an exception for teaching activities would apply and provided no protection for the professor.

### 6.2.2. The classroom.
When First Amendment cases about classroom teaching began to arise in significant numbers (generally in the early 1970s), the courts assumed a posture of judicial deference to the decisions of higher education administrators and their institutions. Usually, the complaining faculty member received no protection from the courts. (See, for example, *Clark v. Holmes*, 474 F.2d 928 (7th Cir. 1972); *Hetrick v. Martin*, 480 F.2d 705 (6th Cir. 1973).) Later cases in the 1980s and 1990s tended to continue the same approach, while the problems and the analysis became more nuanced. The following two cases are illustrative.

In *Martin v. Parrish*, 805 F.2d 583 (5th Cir. 1986), the court upheld the dismissal of an economics instructor at Midland College in Texas, ruling that the instructor's use of profane language in a college classroom did not fall within the scope of First Amendment protection. Applying *Connick v. Myers* (see Section 6.1.1), the court held that the instructor's language did not constitute speech on "matters of public concern." The court also acknowledged the professor's claim that, apart from *Connick*, he had "a first amendment right to 'academic freedom' that permits use of the language in question," but the court summarily rejected this claim because "such language was not germane to the subject matter in his class and had no educational function" (805 F.2d at 584 n.2). In addition, the court used an alternative basis for upholding the dismissal. Applying elementary and secondary education precedents (see *Bethel School District v. Fraser*, 478 U.S. 675 (1986)), the court held that the instructor's use of the language was unprotected because "it was a deliberate, superfluous attack on a 'captive audience' with no academic purpose or justification."

In a separate opinion, a concurring judge, like the majority, acknowledged the possibility of a First Amendment academic freedom argument independent of the *Pickering-Connick* line of cases but rejected the notion that the professor's language was within the bounds of academic freedom. According to the concurring judge: "While some of [the professor's] comments arguably bear on economics and could be viewed as relevant to Martin's role as a teacher in motivating the interest of his students, his remarks as a whole are unrelated to economics and devoid of any educational function" (p. 587).

*Bishop v. Aronov*, 926 F.2d 1066 (11th Cir. 1991), continued the trend toward upholding institutional authority over faculty members' classroom conduct, while raising new issues concerning religion and religious speech in the classroom. An exercise physiology professor, as the court explained, "occasionally referred to his religious beliefs during instructional time." He also organized an optional after-class meeting, held shortly before the final examination, to discuss "Evidences of God in Human Physiology." But "[h]e never engaged in prayer, read passages from the Bible, handed out religious tracts, or arranged for guest speakers to lecture on a religious topic during instructional time." Some students nevertheless complained about the in-class comments and the optional meeting. The university responded by sending the professor a memo requiring that he discontinue "(1) the interjection of religious beliefs and/or preferences during instructional time periods and (2) the optional classes where a 'Christian Perspective' of an academic topic is delivered." The professor challenged the university's action as violating both his freedom of speech and his freedom of religion (see generally Section 1.6.2) under the First Amendment. The district court emphasized that "the university has created a forum for students and their professors to engage in a free interchange of ideas" and granted summary judgment for the professor (732 F. Supp. 1562 (N.D. Ala. 1990)). The U.S. Court of Appeals disagreed and upheld the university's actions.

With respect to the professor's free speech claims, the appellate court, like the majority in *Martin* (above), applied recent elementary and secondary education precedents that display considerable deference to educators—relying especially on *Hazelwood School District v. Kuhlmeier*, 484 U.S. 260 (1988), a secondary education case involving student rights. Without satisfactorily justifying *Hazelwood*'s extension either to higher education in general or to faculty members, the court asserted that "educators do not offend the First Amendment by exercising editorial control over the style and content of student [or professor] speech in school-sponsored expressive activities so long as their actions are reasonably related to legitimate pedagogical concerns" (926 F.2d at 1074, citing *Hazelwood*, 484 U.S. at 272–73). Addressing the academic freedom implications of its position, the court concluded:

> Though we are mindful of the invaluable role academic freedom plays in our public schools, particularly at the post-secondary level, we do not find support to conclude that academic freedom is an independent First Amendment right. And, in any event, we cannot supplant our discretion for that of the University. Federal judges should not be ersatz deans or educators. In this regard, we trust that the University will serve its own interests as well as those of its professors in pursuit of academic freedom [926 F.2d at 1075].

In upholding the university's authority in matters of course content as superior to that of the professor, the court accepted the validity and applicability of two particular institutional concerns underlying the university's decision to limit the professor's instructional activities. First was the university's "concern . . . that its courses be taught without personal religious bias unnecessarily infecting the teacher or the students." Second was the concern that optional classes not be conducted under circumstances that give "the impression of official sanction, which might [unduly pressure] students into attending and, at least for purposes of examination, into adopting the beliefs expressed" by the professor. Relying on these two concerns, against the backdrop of its general deference to the institution in curricular matters, the court concluded:

> In short, Dr. Bishop and the University disagree about a matter of content in the course he teaches. The University must have the final say in such a dispute. Though Dr. Bishop's sincerity cannot be doubted, his educational judgment can be questioned and redirected by the University when he is acting under its auspices as a course instructor, but not when he acts as an independent educator or researcher . . . We have simply concluded that the University as an employer and educator can direct Dr. Bishop to refrain from expression of religious viewpoints in the classroom and like settings [926 F.2d at 1076–77].

Though the appellate court's opinion may seem overly deferential to the institution's prerogatives as employer and insufficiently sensitive to the particular role of faculty academic freedom in higher education, the court did nevertheless demarcate limits on its holding. These limits are very important. Regarding the professor's classroom activities, the court clearly stated that the university's authority applies only "to the classroom speech of [the professor]—wherever he purports to conduct a class for the University." Even in that context, the court conceded that "[o]f course, if a student asks about [the professor's] religious views, he may fairly answer the question." Moreover, the court emphasized that "the university has not suggested that Dr. Bishop cannot hold his particular views; express them, on his own time, far and wide and to whomever will listen; or write and publish, no doubt authoritatively, on them; nor could it so prohibit him." Similarly, regarding the optional meetings, the court noted that "[t]he University has not suggested that [the professor] cannot organize such meetings, make notice of them on campus, or request University space to conduct them; nor could it so prohibit him." As long as the professor "makes it plain to his students that such meetings are not mandatory, not considered part of the coursework, and not related to grading, the university cannot prevent him from conducting such meetings."

With respect to the professor's freedom of religion claims, the court's analysis was much briefer than its free speech analysis but just as favorable for the university. The professor had claimed that the university's restrictions on his expression of religious views violated his rights under the free exercise clause and also violated the establishment clause, because only Christian viewpoints, but not other religious viewpoints, were restricted. The court rejected the professor's free exercise claim, characterizing the university's actions as directed at the professor's teaching practices, not his religious practices. In similar summary fashion, the court rejected the establishment clause claim because "the

University has simply attempted to maintain a neutral, secular classroom by its restrictions on Dr. Bishop's expressions."

More recent cases have served to enhance institutional authority to determine the content of particular courses and assign instructors to particular courses. For example, in *Webb v. Board of Trustees of Ball State University*, 167 F.3d 1146 (7th Cir. 1999), the court relied on the distinction between institutional academic freedom and faculty academic freedom (see Section 6.1.7) to reject a professor's claimed right to teach certain classes. Quoting from Justice Frankfurter's concurrence in *Sweezy* (see Section 6.1.5), the court asserted that recognizing such a claim would "impose costs . . . on the University, whose ability to set a curriculum is as much an element of academic freedom as any scholar's right to express a point of view" (167 F.3d at 1149). Moreover, said the court, "when deciding who to appoint as a leader or teacher of a particular class, every university considers speech (that's what teaching and scholarship consists in) without violating the Constitution."

Similarly, in *Edwards v. California University of Pennsylvania*, 156 F.3d 488 (3d Cir. 1998), perhaps the most far-reaching and deferential case to date, the court rejected the free speech claims of a tenured professor who was disciplined for failing to conform his course content to the syllabus provided by the departmental chair and faculty. The court held flatly that "the First Amendment does not place restrictions on a public university's ability to control its curriculum," and therefore "a public university professor does not have a First Amendment right to decide what will be taught in the classroom" (156 F.3d at 491). In its result, and in its complete reliance on the university's own academic freedom to decide what shall be taught, the *Edwards* court introduced new and potentially far-reaching reasoning that it based on the U.S. Supreme Court decision in *Rosenberger v. Rector & Visitors of University of Virginia* (Sections 10.1.4 and 10.3.2 of this book). Relying on the *Rosenberger* concept of the public university or the state as a "speaker," the *Edwards* court concluded that a university acts as a "speaker" when it enlists faculty members to convey the university's own message or preferred course content to its students and that the university was thus "entitled to make content-based choices in restricting Edwards' syllabus." (For criticism of *Edwards*, see the discussion of *Brown v. Armenti* in Section 6.2.3 below.)

A third case in which the court used the institutional academic freedom concept is *Johnson-Kurek v. Abu-Absi*, 423 F.3d 590 (6th Cir. 2005). In that case, the plaintiff faculty member challenged a directive from her departmental supervisor that she provide specific individual statements to students on what they must do to change their "incompletes" to final grades. In rejecting the faculty member's claim, the appellate court cited and quoted the *Urofsky* case (discussed in Section 6.3)—a case decided after *Webb* and *Edwards* that has become the leading case on institutional academic freedom. It is important, however, that, unlike the *Edwards* case (and the *Urofsky* case), *Johnson-Kurek* did not construe institutional academic freedom so broadly as to virtually eliminate the possibility of viable faculty academic freedom claims. Rather, after relying on institutional academic freedom reasoning, the court cautioned:

This is not to say that professors must leave their First Amendment rights at the campus gates. That a teacher does have First Amendment protection under certain circumstances cannot be denied. [Citations omitted.] . . . [T]he term academic freedom is used to denote both the freedom of the academy to pursue its ends without interference from the government . . . and the freedom of the individual teacher . . . to pursue his ends without inference from the academy [423 F.3d at 594].

As an example of such academic freedom protections for faculty, the *Johnson-Kurek* court addressed and confirmed its own prior decision in the *Parate* case on grading (Section 6.2.3). The court could also have cited its own prior decision in *Hardy v. Jefferson Community College* (discussed later in this section) on classroom teaching methods.

Other courts have relied on the *Pickering-Connick* distinction between matters of public concern and matters of private concern (Section 6.1.1) to analyze professors' free speech claims to academic freedom in teaching. In *Scallet v. Rosenblum*, 911 F. Supp. 999 (W.D. Va. 1996), *affirmed on other grounds*, 106 F.3d 391 (4th Cir. 1997) (unpublished), for example, the district court determined that an instructor's choices of course content could be considered speech on matters of public concern. The issue was whether a business school instructor's classroom materials and discussions on increasing racial and gender diversity in the business community were protected speech. Using the *Pickering-Connick* analysis, the court first determined that this speech did involve matters of public concern:

[I]t appears unassailable that [the instructor's] advocacy of diversity, through the materials he taught in class, relate to matters of public concern. Debate is incessant over the role of diversity in higher education, employment and government contracting, just to name a few spheres. Indeed, political debate over issues such as affirmative action is inescapable [911 F. Supp. at 1014].

In reaching this conclusion, the court rejected the university's argument that the instructor "was simply discharging his duties as an employee [of the business school] when he made his classroom remarks." Rather, said the court, a classroom instructor "routinely and necessarily discusses issues of public concern when speaking as an employee. Indeed, it is part of his educational mandate" (911 F. Supp. at 1013).

Nevertheless, the court ultimately sided with the university by concluding that the instructor's free speech interest was overridden by the business school's "powerful interest in the content of the [departmental] curriculum and its coordination with the content of other required courses." The school could restrict the classroom materials and discussions of its instructors when this speech "disrupt[ed], or sufficiently threaten[ed] to disrupt, [the school's] educational mandate in a significant way." The instructor's speech did so in this case because it "hamper[ed] the school's ability effectively to deliver the [required writing and speech] course to its students . . .; created divisions within the [departmental] faculty"; and raised concerns among faculty members outside the department about the instructor's class "trenching upon their own." (Interestingly, the instructor had raised diversity issues in faculty meetings that were comparable to the issues he had addressed in class. In that different context, the court held that the speech was protected "because the defendants offer no competing interest served by stifling that speech" (p. 1016).)

Another later case, *Bonnell v. Lorenzo*, 241 F.3d 800 (6th Cir. 2001), like *Martin* (above), arose from student complaints about a professor's vulgar and profane classroom speech. The appellate court sought to pattern its decision after *Martin v. Parrish* and, like *Martin*, the *Bonnell* case resulted in a victory for the college. After a female student in Professor Bonnell's English class had filed a sexual harassment complaint against him, the college disciplined him for using language in class that created a "hostile learning environment." The language, according to the court, included profanity such as "shit," "damn," and "fuck," and various sexual allusions such as "blow job," used to describe the relationship between a U.S. president and an intern. The college determined that these statements were "vulgar and obscene," were "not germane to course content," and were used "without reference to assigned readings." The professor disagreed and claimed that.

The appellate court accepted the college's characterization of the professor's statements and rejected the professor's free speech claims:

> Plaintiff may have a constitutional right to use words such as . . . "fuck," but he does not have a constitutional right to use them in a classroom setting where they are not germane to the subject matter, in contravention of the College's sexual harassment policy . . . This is particularly so when one considers the unique context in which the speech is conveyed—a classroom where a college professor is speaking to a captive audience of students (see *Martin* [*v. Parrish*], 805 F.2d at 586) who cannot "effectively avoid further bombardment of their sensibilities simply by averting their [ears]" [241 F.3d at 820–821, quoting *Hill v. Colorado*, 530 U.S. 703, 753 n.3 (2000)].

The court's result seems correct, and its "germaneness" and captive audience rationales seem relevant to the analysis, but in other respects the court's reasoning is shaky in ways that other courts and advocates should avoid. *First*, although the court grounded its analysis on the crucial characterization of the professor's speech as "not germane to course content," the court neither made its own findings on this issue nor reviewed (or even described) whether and how the college made and supported its findings. *Second*, the court relied on the college's sexual harassment policy without quoting it or considering whether it provided fair warning to the professor and a comprehensible guideline by which to gauge his classroom speech (see the *Cohen* and *Silva* cases below). *Third*, the court relied heavily on the captive audience rationale for restricting speech without asking the questions pertinent to making a well-founded captive audience determination. Such questions would include whether the course was a required or an elective course; whether there were multiple sections with different instructors that the students could choose from; whether the students could withdraw from the course or transfer to another section without penalty;

and whether the professor had given full and fair advance notice of the content and style of his class sessions. Fourth, the court began its discussion with lengthy references to the distinction between matters of public concern and matters of private concern drawn in the *Pickering-Connick* line of cases but did not apply this distinction specifically to the classroom speech. It is therefore unclear whether the court assumed that the professor's speech was not on a matter of public concern or whether the court assumed that the distinction between matters of public and private concern was not relevant to its analysis. And *fifth*, the court asserted that the college's case was strengthened because "it was not the content of Plaintiff's speech itself which led to the disciplinary action." This statement apparently ignores the U.S. Supreme Court's opinion in *Cohen v. California*, 403 U.S. 15 (1971), in which the Court determined that a punishment for using profanity was based on the content of the speech and also made clear that courts must protect the "emotive" as well as the "cognitive" content of speech (see Section 9.5 of this book).

Although the above cases generally support institutional authority over professors' instructional activities, it does not follow that institutions invariably prevail in instructional disputes. The courts in *Martin, Bishop, Scallet,* and *Bonnell*, in limiting their holdings, all suggest situations in which faculty members could prevail. Other cases also include strong language supportive of faculty rights. In *Dube v. State University of New York*, 900 F.2d 587 (2d Cir. 1990), for instance, the court acknowledged the legal sufficiency, under the First Amendment, of a former assistant professor's allegations that the university had denied him tenure due to a public controversy that had arisen concerning his course on the politics of race and the views on Zionism that he had expressed in the course. Relying on the *Sweezy, Shelton v. Tucker*, and *Keyishian* cases and quoting key academic freedom language from these opinions (see Section 6.1.5), the court emphasized that "for decades it has been [clear] that the First Amendment tolerates neither laws nor other means of coercion, persuasion or intimidation 'that cast a pall of orthodoxy' over the free exchange of ideas in the classroom"; and "that, assuming the defendants retaliated against [the professor] based on the content of his classroom discourse," such facts would support a claim that the defendants had violated the professor's free speech rights.

Moreover, in other cases, faculty members—and thus faculty academic freedom—have prevailed over institutional authority. In *DiBona v. Matthews*, 269 Cal. Rptr. 882 (Cal. Ct. App. 1990), for example, the court provided a measure of protection for a professor's artistic and literary expression as it relates to the choice of class content and materials. Specifically, the court held that San Diego Community College District administrators violated a teacher's free speech rights when they canceled a controversial play production and a drama class in which the play was to have been performed. The play that the instructor had selected, entitled *Split Second*, was about a black police officer who, in the course of an arrest, shot a white suspect after the suspect had subjected him to racial slurs and epithets. The play's theme closely paralleled the facts of a criminal case that was then being tried in San Diego. The court determined that the college administrators had canceled the class because of the content of the play. While the First Amendment free speech clause did not completely prevent the college from considering the play's content in deciding to cancel the drama class, the court held that the college's particular reasons—that the religious community opposed the play and that the subject was controversial and sensitive—were not valid reasons under the First Amendment. Moreover, distinguishing the present case from those involving minors in elementary and secondary schools, the court held that the college could not cancel the drama class solely because of the vulgar language included in the play.

In two other cases later in the 1990s, *Cohen v. San Bernardino Valley College* and *Silva v. University of New Hampshire,* courts also sided with the faculty member rather than the institution in disputes regarding teaching methods and classroom demeanor. Both cases, like *Bonnell,* above, arose in the context of alleged sexual harassment in the classroom, thus presenting potential clashes among faculty's interest in academic freedom, the institution's interest in enforcing sexual harassment policies, and students' interest in being protected against harassment.

In the *Cohen* case, 92 F.3d 968 (9th Cir. 1996), *reversing* 883 F. Supp. 1407 (C.D. Cal. 1995), the appellate court used the constitutional "void for vagueness" doctrine to invalidate a college's attempt to discipline a teacher for classroom speech. The plaintiff, Cohen, was a tenured professor at San Bernardino Valley College who was the subject of a sexual harassment complaint made by a student in his remedial English class. The student was uncomfortable with Cohen's frequent use of profanity and vulgarities, his sexual comments, and his use of topics of a sexual nature for class writing assignments. Over a period of many years, Cohen had assigned essays and led class discussions on "provocative" subjects such as pornography, cannibalism, and consensual sex with children. When Cohen directed the class to write essays defining pornography, the student asked for a different assignment; Cohen declined to accommodate her. The student stopped attending the class and failed the course.

The student filed a grievance against Cohen, alleging that his behavior violated the college's new sexual harassment policy, which provided that:

[s]exual harassment is defined as unwelcome sexual advances, requests for sexual favors, and other verbal, written, or physical conduct of a sexual nature. It includes, but is not limited to, circumstances in which:* * * *
(2) Such conduct has the purpose or effect of unreasonably interfering with an individual's academic performance or creating an intimidating, hostile, or offensive learning environment [92 F.3d at 971].

After a hearing and appeal, the college found that Cohen had violated the second part of the policy and ordered him, among other things, to "attend a sexual harassment seminar" and "[b]ecome sensitive to the particular needs and backgrounds of his students."

The district court rejected Cohen's claim that application of the sexual harassment policy violated his right to academic freedom because, "despite eloquent [judicial] rhetoric on 'academic freedom,' the courts have declined to cede all classroom control to teachers." The court also rejected Cohen's claim that, under *Connick v. Myers*, the college had violated his free speech rights as a public employee. The court divided Cohen's speech into two categories: (1) vulgarities and obscenities, and (2) comments related to the curriculum and focusing on pornography and other sexual topics. It concluded that the speech in the first category was not on matters of public concern but that the speech in the second category was, because Cohen did not speak merely to advance some purely private interest. Thus, under *Connick*, the college could regulate the first type of speech but could regulate the second only if it could justify a restriction in terms of the professor's job duties and the efficient operation of the college. The court agreed that the college had demonstrated sufficient justification, stating that Cohen had created a hostile learning environment for some of his students. In an important qualification, however, the district court addressed the problem of the "thin-skinned" student:

> In applying a "hostile environment" prohibition, there is the danger that the most sensitive and the most easily offended students will be given veto power over class content and methodology. Good teaching should challenge students and at times may intimidate students or make them uncomfortable . . . Colleges and universities . . . must avoid a tyranny of mediocrity, in which all discourse is made bland enough to suit the tastes of all the students. However, colleges and universities must have the power to require professors to effectively educate all segments of the student population, including those students unused to the rough and tumble of intellectual discussion. If colleges and universities lack this power, each classroom becomes a separate fiefdom in which the educational process is subject to professorial whim. Universities must be able to ensure that the more vulnerable as well as the more sophisticated students receive a suitable education . . . Within the educational context, the university's mission is to effectively educate students, keeping in mind students' varying backgrounds and sensitivities. Furthermore, the university has the right to preclude disruption of this educational mission through the creation of a hostile learning environment . . . The college's substantial interest in educating all students, not just the thick-skinned ones, warrants . . . requiring Cohen to put potential students on notice of his teaching methods [883 F. Supp. at 1419–21].

Thus, although the court ruled in the college's favor, at the same time it sought to uphold the proposition that the college "must avoid restricting creative and engaging teaching, even if some over-sensitive students object to it" (883 F. Supp. at 1422). Moreover, the court cautioned that "this ruling goes only to the narrow and reasonable discipline which the College seeks to impose. A case in which a professor is terminated or directly censored presents a far different balancing question."

On appeal, the U.S. Court of Appeals for the Ninth Circuit unanimously overruled the district court's decision, but did so on different grounds from those explored by the lower court. The appellate court emphasized that neither it nor the U.S. Supreme Court had yet determined the scope of First

Amendment protection for a professor's classroom speech. Rather than engage in this analysis, the court focused its opinion and analysis on the vagueness of the college's sexual harassment policy and held that "the Policy's terms [are] unconstitutionally vague as applied to Cohen in this case." The court did not address whether or not the "College could punish speech of this nature if the policy were more precisely construed by authoritative interpretive guidelines or if the College were to adopt a clearer and more precise policy."

In its analysis, the appellate court noted three objections to vague college policies:

> First, they trap the innocent by not providing fair warning. Second, they impermissibly delegate basic policy matters to low level officials for resolution on an ad hoc and subjective basis, with the attendant dangers of arbitrary and discriminatory application. Third, a vague policy discourages the exercise of first amendment freedoms [92 F.3d at 972].

Guided by these concerns, the court reasoned:

> Cohen's speech did not fall within the core region of sexual harassment as defined by the Policy. Instead, officials of the College, on an entirely ad hoc basis, applied the Policy's nebulous outer reaches to punish teaching methods that Cohen had used for many years. Regardless of what the intentions of the officials of the College may have been, the consequences of their actions can best be described as a legalistic ambush. Cohen was simply without any notice that the Policy would be applied in such a way as to punish his longstanding teaching style—a style which, until the College imposed punishment upon Cohen under the Policy, had apparently been considered pedagogically sound and within the bounds of teaching methodology permitted at the College [92 F.3d at 972].

Since the appellate court's reasoning was different from the district court's, and since the appellate court did not disagree with or address the issues that were dispositive for the district court, the district court's analysis remains a useful illustration of how other courts may handle such issues when they arise under policies that are not unconstitutionally vague.

In the second case, *Silva v. University of New Hampshire*, 888 F. Supp. 293 (D.N.H. 1994), a tenured faculty member at the University of New Hampshire (UNH) challenged the university's determination that he had created a hostile or offensive academic environment in his classroom and therefore violated the university's sexual harassment policy. Seven women students had filed formal complaints against Silva. These complaints alleged that, in a technical writing class, he had compared the concept of focus to sexual intercourse: "Focus is like sex. You seek a target. You zero in on your subject. You move from side to side. You close in on the subject. You bracket the subject and center on it. Focus connects the experience and language. You and the subject become one" (888 F. Supp. at 299). The complaints also alleged that two days later in the same class, Silva made the statement "[b]elly dancing is like jello on a plate with a vibrator under the plate" to illustrate the use of metaphor. In addition, several female students alleged that Silva had made sexually suggestive remarks to them, both in and out of the classroom. For example, there were allegations that Silva told a female student, whom he saw in the library kneeling down to look through a card catalog, that "it looks like you've had a lot of experience down there"; that he gave a spelling test to another student in which every third word had a "sexual slant"; that he had asked two of his female students how long they had been together, implying a lesbian relationship; that he had asked another female student, "How would you like to get an A?"; and that he had physically blockaded a student from exiting a vending machine room and complained to her about students' actions against him (888 F. Supp. at 310–11).

These complaints were presented to Silva in two "informal" meetings with university administrators, after which he was formally reprimanded. Silva then challenged the reprimand through the university's "formal" grievance process, culminating in hearings before a hearing panel and an appeals board. (The court reviewed these procedures and some potential flaws in them in its opinion (888 F. Supp. at 319–26).) Finding that Silva's language and innuendos violated the university's sexual harassment policy, the hearing panel emphasized that a reasonable female student would find Silva's comments and behavior to be offensive; that this was the second time in a two-year period that Silva had been formally notified "about his use of inappropriate and sexually explicit remarks in the classroom"; and that Silva had given the panel "no reason to believe that he understood the seriousness of his behavior" or its impact on the students he taught. The university thereupon suspended Silva without pay for at least one year, required him to undergo counseling at his own expense, and prohibited him from attempting to contact or retaliate against the complainants.

In court, prior to trial, Silva argued that the university's actions violated his First Amendment free speech rights. The court agreed that he was "likely to succeed on the merits of his First Amendment claims" and entered a preliminary injunction against the university. In its opinion, the court pursued three lines of analysis to support its ruling. First, relying on the U.S. Supreme Court's decision in the *Keyishian* case (Section 6.1.5), the court reasoned that the belly dancing comment was "not of a sexual nature," and the sexual harassment policy therefore did not give Silva adequate notice that this statement was prohibited—thus violating the First Amendment requirement that teachers be "clearly inform[ed]" of the proscribed conduct in order to guard against a "chilling effect" on their exercise of free speech rights. Second, relying in part on *Hazelwood v. Kuhlmeier* (see above), the court determined that the sexual harassment policy was invalid under the First Amendment, as applied to Silva's speech, because it "fails to take into account the nation's interest in academic freedom" and therefore is not "reasonably related to the legitimate pedagogical purpose of providing a congenial academic environment" (888 F. Supp. at 314). In reaching this conclusion, the court reasoned that (1) the students were "exclusively adult college students . . . presumed to have possessed the sophistication of adults"; (2) "Silva's classroom statements advanced his valid educational objective of conveying certain principles related to the subject matter of his course"; and (3) "Silva's classroom statements were made in a professionally appropriate manner" (888 F. Supp. at 313).

For its third line of analysis, the court resorted to the *Pickering* and *Connick* cases. Purporting to apply the public concern/private concern dichotomy, the court determined that "Silva's classroom statements . . . were made for the legitimate pedagogical, public purpose of conveying certain principles related to the subject matter of his course." Thus, these statements "were related to matters of public concern" and, on balance, "Silva's First Amendment interest in the speech at issue is overwhelmingly superior to UNH's interest in proscribing [the] speech" (888 F. Supp. at 316).

Yet another, more recent case in which a faculty member (and faculty academic freedom) prevailed over institutional authority is the important case of *Hardy v. Jefferson Community College*, 260 F.3d 671 (6th Cir. 2001). In this case, the U.S. Court of Appeals for the Sixth Circuit held that an adjunct instructor's classroom speech was protected because it was on a matter of public concern and was germane to the subject matter of the course. The instructor had claimed that the community college's refusal to rehire him violated his "rights of free speech and academic freedom," and the appellate court agreed.

The instructor, Hardy, was teaching a summer course, Introduction to Interpersonal Communication, when the incident prompting his nonrenewal occurred. He gave a lecture on "how language is used to marginalize minorities." Along with his lecture, he conducted a group exercise in which he asked students to suggest examples of words that had "historically served the interests of the dominant culture." Their suggestions included "the words 'girl,' 'lady,' 'faggot,' 'nigger,' and 'bitch.'" A student in the class who was offended by the latter two words raised her concerns with the instructor and college administrators, and the instructor apologized to the student. But the student took her complaint to a vocal religious leader in the community, who subsequently met with college administrators to discuss the incident. The administrators then met with the instructor to discuss the classroom exercise and, in the course of the discussion, informed him "that a 'prominent citizen' representing the interests of the African-American community had . . . threatened to affect the school's already declining enrollment if corrective action was not taken." After this meeting, Hardy completed his summer course without further incident and received positive student evaluations from all students except the one who had complained about the class exercise. Nevertheless, Hardy was informed that he would not be teaching the following semester; he then filed suit against the college, the president, the former acting dean, and the state community college system.

The appellate court used a *Pickering-Connick* analysis to determine whether the instructor's speech was on a matter of public concern and, if so, whether the employee's interest in speaking outweighed the college's interest in serving the public. Applying the first prong of the *Pickering-Connick* test, the court found that the instructor's speech "was germane to the subject matter of his lecture on the power and effect of language" and "was limited to an academic discussion of the words in question." The court also distinguished Hardy's speech from the unprotected speech at issue in its previous ruling in *Bonnell v. Lorenzo* (above); Bonnell's speech, unlike Hardy's, was "gratuitous" and "not germane to the subject matter of his course." Thus, in considering "the content, form, and context" of Hardy's speech, as the *Connick* case requires, the court emphasized the academic "content" and "form" of the speech and its higher education classroom "context." This same emphasis was apparent in the court's conclusion that Hardy's speech was on a matter of public concern:

> Because the essence of a teacher's role is to prepare students for their place in society as responsible citizens, classroom instruction will often fall within the Supreme Court's broad conception of "public concern." . . . Hardy's lecture on social deconstructivism and language, which explored the social and political impact of certain words, clearly meets this criterion. Although Hardy's in-class speech does not itself constitute pure public debate, it does relate to matters of overwhelming public concern—race, gender, and power conflicts in our society . . .
>
> Hardy has thus satisfied the first prong of the two-part test set forth in *Pickering* [260 F.3d at 679].

A similar emphasis on the academic context of the dispute also marked the court's application of the second prong of the *Pickering-Connick* test, in which it balanced Hardy's interest in speaking on a matter of public concern against the college's interest in efficiently providing services to its students and the community. Citing *Keyishian* and *Sweezy*, the court in *Hardy* asserted that "[i]n balancing the competing interests involved, we must take into account the robust tradition of academic freedom in our nation's post-secondary schools" (260 F.3d at 680). The college had presented no evidence that Hardy's speech had "undermined [his] working relationship within his department, interfered with his duties, or impaired discipline"[260 F.3d at 681]. In fact, Hardy had successfully completed his summer course and received favorable student course evaluations. Nor did the concerns about the religious leader's threat to affect the college's enrollment weigh in the college's favor. Such concerns represented no more than the college administrators' "undifferentiated fear of disturbance," which under the *Tinker* case (see Section 9.4.1) cannot "overcome the right to freedom of expression." The instructor's interests, supported by the tradition of academic freedom, therefore outweighed the interests of the college.

The court's analysis in *Hardy* draws upon both the *Pickering-Connick* line of cases and the germaneness approach to faculty academic freedom. The germaneness analysis follows the pathway that the court had previously sketched in *Bonnell*. *Hardy*, however, unlike *Bonnell*, places the germaneness analysis within the *Pickering-Connick* analysis, using it as a crucial component of its consideration of the content, form, and context of the speech, rather than as a separate analysis providing an alternative to *Pickering-Connick*. In doing so, the Sixth Circuit seems to have corrected much of the weakness of its reasoning in *Bonnell* and to have crafted an approach to faculty academic freedom claims that merges the better aspects of *Pickering-Connick* with the better aspects of the germaneness test.

Further development of the *Hardy* approach or other approaches that rely at least in part on the *Pickering-Connick* line, however, may be delayed by the uncertainties concerning the U.S. Supreme Court's ruling in *Garcetti v. Ceballos* (see Section 6.1.1), and could be shut down if the courts determine that there will be no exception from *Garcetti* for speech related to teaching. In the post-*Garcetti* era, some lower federal courts have declined to recognize any such exception (see, for example, *Renken v. Gregory*, discussed in Section 6.2.1). Other courts have evinced some sympathy for creating an exception. In *Gorum v. Sessoms*, 561 F.3d 179, 186 (3d Cir. 2009), the court suggested that *Garcetti's* "employee speech" doctrine should not apply to "expression related to academic scholarship or classroom instruction." This court also warned that, should an exception from *Garcetti* be developed for higher education faculty members, that would then lead to various issues regarding when professorial "employee" speech is "related to academic scholarship or classroom instruction" and thus eligible for the exception.

At least one lower court has recognized an exception from *Garcetti* for faculty classroom speech. In a medical school case, *Kerr v. Hurd*, 694 F. Supp. 2d 817 (S.D. Ohio 2010), the district court determined that the issue of a scholarship and teaching exception was left unresolved in *Garcetti* and that the district court would therefore follow precedent in its own district and circuit, which supported a classroom speech exception from *Garcetti's* employee speech doctrine. The court then made this statement:

> Even without the binding precedent, this Court would find an academic exception to *Garcetti*. Recognizing an academic freedom exception to *Garcetti* analysis is important to protecting First Amendment values. Universities should be the active trading floors in the marketplace of ideas. Public universities should be no different from private universities in that respect. At least where, as here, the expressed views are well within the range of accepted medical opinion, they should certainly receive First Amendment protection, particularly at the university level. See Justice Souter's dissent in *Garcetti*, citing *Keyishian v. Bd. of Regents*, 385 U.S. 589 (1967) [694 F. Supp. 2d at 843–44].

Most of the cases discussed in this section concern the "classroom" as a physical, on-campus location where a faculty member instructs students. In contemporary settings, however, instruction may often take place in varying locations that are not as fixed and not as tied to the campus as the traditional classroom, and some instructional activities may be optional rather than required. Such new settings may create new academic freedom issues. In the case of *Bishop v. Aranov* (discussed earlier in this section), for example, the court addressed the extent to which faculty members are free to have optional instructional meetings with students that they are currently teaching in a formal course. In *DiBona v. Matthews* (also cited earlier in this section), the court considered an issue involving a drama course that centered on the public performance of a play. A more recent case, *Hudson v. Craven*, 403 F.3d 691 (9th Cir. 2005), considered the scope of a faculty member's right to arrange optional field trips for her students. The court found that such activities implicate both freedom of association and freedom of speech but ruled, applying the *Pickering* balancing test (see Section 6.1.1), that the institution's interests prevailed over the instructor's on the particular facts of the case.

*Piggee v. Carl Sandburg College*, 464 F.3d 667 (7th Cir. 2006), also provides an example of an academic freedom claim arising in a nontraditional instructional setting. The setting was a "clinical beauty salon," and the instructor whose speech was at issue was a cosmetology instructor who supervised the students working in the salon. The instructor argued that the salon was not an instructional setting furthering the college's curricular interests but merely a "store." The court "[had] little trouble" rejecting this argument:

> [T]he beauty salon was, in fact, one of the places where cosmetology instruction was taking place. It is undisputed that students enrolled in this program must participate in two different kinds of instruction: classroom, and hands-on clinical work. This type of program is exceedingly common, especially for those learning some type of service. Law students almost universally have the opportunity to work in instructional clinics, which typically are open to the public and offer legal services to indigent clients; medical students begin supervised work with real patients in university-affiliated hospitals and clinics while they are still in medical school, even before they complete their formal education with a residency. The beauty clinic operated by Carl Sandburg College served exactly the same function: students were able to learn their trade by serving customers under the supervision of trained instructors [464 F.3d at 671–72].

Since the speech at issue thus occurred in an instructional setting, academic freedom concerns were implicated in the dispute. In this case, these concerns weighed in the college's favor; it had institutional interests in limiting an instructor's discussion of matters that are unrelated to the course's subject matter, and it "was entitled it insist" that instructors maintain "a professional relationship" with their students.

Increasingly, it seems, higher education institutions and courts will need to deal with faculty academic freedom issues in nontraditional instructional settings. Besides the examples immediately above, these settings might include law school legal services clinics (see *Wishnatsky v. Rovner*, 433 F. 3d 608, 612–13 (8th Cir. 2006)); medical or other health clinics in which students serve under faculty supervision; foreign travel locales; and most pervasively, cyberspace and distance learning.

### 6.2.3. Grading.

Grading is an extension of the teaching methods that faculty members use in the classroom and is an essential component of faculty members' evaluative functions. Just as courts are reluctant to intervene in disputes regarding the classroom (see Section 6.2.2), courts are hesitant to intervene in grading disputes among professors, students, and the administration. While the administration (representing the institution) usually prevails when a court rules on such disputes, there are circumstances in which faculty members may occasionally prevail.

In a case concerning grading policies in general, *Lovelace v. Southeastern Massachusetts University*, 793 F.2d 419 (1st Cir. 1986), the court upheld institutional authority over grading in much the same way that other courts had done in classroom cases. The university had declined to renew a faculty member's contract after he had rejected administration requests to lower the academic standards he used in grading his students. The faculty member claimed that the university's action violated his free speech rights. The court rejected the professor's claim because the university itself had the freedom to set its own grading standards, and "the first amendment does not require that each nontenured professor be made a sovereign unto himself."

When a dispute concerns an individual grade rather than general grading policies, however, different considerations are involved that may lead some courts to provide limited protection for the faculty member who has assigned the grade. The case of *Parate v. Isibor*, 868 F.2d 821 (6th Cir. 1989), provides an example. The defendant, dean of the school in which the plaintiff was a nontenured professor, ordered the plaintiff, over his objections, to execute a grade-change form raising the final grade of one of his students. The plaintiff argued that this incident, and several later incidents alleged to be in retaliation for his lack of cooperation regarding the grade change, violated his First Amendment academic freedom. Relying on the free speech clause, the court agreed that "[b]ecause the assignment of a letter grade is symbolic communication intended to send a specific message to the student, the individual professor's communicative act is entitled to some measure of First Amendment protection" (868 F.2d at 827). The court reasoned (without reliance on the *Pickering-Connick* methodology) that

> the professor's evaluation of her students and assignment of their grades is central to the professor's teaching method . . . Although the individual professor does not escape the reasonable review of university officials in the assignment of grades, she should remain free to decide, according to her own professional judgment, what grades to assign and what grades not to assign . . . Thus, the individual professor may not be compelled, by university officials, to change a grade that the professor previously assigned to her student. Because the individual professor's assignment of a letter grade is protected speech, the university officials' action to compel the professor to alter that grade would severely burden a protected activity [868 F.2d at 828].

Thus, the defendant's act of ordering the plaintiff to change the grade, contrary to the plaintiff's professional judgment, violated the First Amendment. The court indicated, however, that had university administrators changed the student's grade themselves, this action would not have violated the plaintiff's First Amendment rights. The protection that *Parate* accords to faculty grading and teaching methods is therefore quite narrow—more symbolic than real, perhaps, but nonetheless an important step away from the deference normally paid institutions in these matters.

The narrow protection accorded faculty members in *Parate* does not necessarily mean that administrators in public institutions can never direct a faculty member to change a grade or that faculty members can always refuse to do so. As in other free speech cases, the right is not absolute and must be balanced against the interests of the institution. The professor's free speech rights in *Parate* prevailed, apparently, because the subsequent administrative change could fulfill whatever interests the administration had in the professor's grading of the student whose grade was at issue. If, however, the administration or a faculty or faculty-student hearing panel were to find a professor's grade to be discriminatory or arbitrary, the institution's interests would be stronger, and perhaps a directive that the professor change the grade would not violate the professor's free speech rights. In *Keen v. Penson*, 970 F.2d 252 (7th Cir. 1992), for example, the court upheld the demotion of a professor due to unprofessional conduct regarding his grading of a student. The professor had argued that "the grade he gave [the student is] protected by the First Amendment under the concept of academic freedom." In rejecting the argument, the court explained that, even assuming that the First Amendment applied to grading, it would be necessary to "balance Keen's First Amendment right against the University's interest in ensuring that its students receive a fair grade and are not subject to demeaning, insulting, and inappropriate comments" [970 F.2d at 257–58].

Once a court accepts the propriety of balancing interests in grading cases, however, it is also possible that some post hoc administrative changes of grades could violate a faculty member's academic freedom rights. Such might be the case, for instance, if the faculty member could show that an administrator's change of a grade was itself discriminatory or arbitrary (see generally Section 8.2 of this book).

Some courts will avoid such a balancing of interests, and refuse to engage in reasoning such as that in the Sixth Circuit's *Parate* opinion, by emphasizing institutional academic freedom in grading (see the *Lovelace* case cited earlier in this section) or by positing that the faculty member acts as an "agent" of and thus a "speaker" for the institution when grading students. *Brown v. Armenti*, 247 F.3d 69 (3rd Cir. 2001), is the leading example of this judicial viewpoint. The professor (Brown) alleged that he had assigned an F to a student who had attended only three of the fifteen class sessions for his practicum course; that the university president (Armenti) had instructed him to change this student's grade from an F to an Incomplete; that he had refused to comply; and that he was therefore suspended from teaching the course. The professor claimed that the university had retaliated against him for refusing to change the student's grade, thus violating his right to "academic free expression." In an appeal from the district court's denial of the defendant's motion for summary judgment, the U.S. Court of Appeals for the Third Circuit sought to determine whether the facts alleged amounted to a violation of the professor's First Amendment rights.

The *Armenti* court declined to follow *Parate* and instead applied its own prior case of *Edwards v. California University of Pennsylvania*, 156 F.3d 488 (3d Cir. 1998), discussed in Section 6.2.2. The court drew from *Edwards* the proposition that "in the classroom, the university was the speaker and the professor was the agent of the university for First Amendment purposes" (*Armenti*, 247

F.3d at 74). Using this "university-as-speaker" theory, the *Edwards* court had asserted that, as the university's agent or "proxy," the professor in the classroom fulfills one of the university's "four essential freedoms" set out in Justice Frankfurter's concurring opinion in *Sweezy v. New Hampshire*, 354 U.S. at 263 (see Section 6.1.5 of this book). Thus, relying on *Edwards*, the court in *Armenti* reasoned that "[b]ecause grading is pedagogic, the assignment of the grade is subsumed under [one of the four essential freedoms], the university's freedom to determine how a course is to be taught." Since this freedom is the university's and not the professor's, the professor "does not have a First Amendment right to expression via the school's grade assignment procedures." The change of a grade from an F to an Incomplete, according to the court, is thus not a matter that warrants "'intrusive oversight by the judiciary in the name of the First Amendment'" (247 F.3d at 75, quoting *Connick v. Myers*, 461 U.S. 138, 146 (1983)).

Even though its opinion is in direct conflict with the Sixth Circuit's earlier opinion in *Parate*, the court in *Brown v. Armenti* does not explain or document why its reasoning based on *Edwards* is superior to the *Parate* reasoning. It makes the conclusory statement that the "*Edwards* framework . . . offers a more realistic view of the university-professor relationship" but provides neither empirical data nor expert opinion to support this conclusion. Nor does the *Armenti* court consider the broader implications of its global reasoning and conclusion. If the professor in the classroom—or its technological extensions— were merely the university's agent subject to the university's micromanagement, there would be no room at all for faculty academic freedom, and the full range of professors' academic judgment and professional discretion would be subject to check at the mere whim of university officials. These potential broader implications of *Armenti* (and the earlier *Edwards* case) seem discordant with the past seventy-five years' development of academic freedom in the United States, as well as with the spirit of the *Sweezy* and *Rosenberger* cases on which the *Armenti* court (and the *Edwards* court) relies.

The U.S. Supreme Court's decision in *Garcetti v. Ceballos* (see Section 6.1.1) may affect the scope of faculty First Amendment rights in grading, much as it may affect rights regarding classroom speech (see Section 6.2.2). In particular, should the courts decline to exempt faculty from the *Garcetti* employee speech doctrine, public institutions and administrators could then argue that grading is employee speech, not private citizen speech, and thus has no First Amendment protection. Future developments in grading cases should eventually reveal the extent to which the courts will accept such arguments.

### 6.2.4. *Private institutions.*

*6.2.4. Private institutions.* Since First Amendment rights and other federal constitutional rights generally do not apply to or limit private institutions, as explained in Section 1.5.2 of this book, legal arguments concerning the freedom to teach in private institutions are usually based on contract law. The sources, scope, and terms of faculty contracts are discussed in Section 5.2 of this book, and the contractual academic freedom rights of faculty members are discussed more specifically in Section 6.1.3. When the "1940 Statement of

Principles on Academic Freedom" is incorporated into the faculty contract or relied upon as a source of custom and usage (see Section 6.1.3), it will usually provide the starting point for analyzing the faculty member's freedom in teaching. The 1940 Statement provides that "[t]eachers are entitled to freedom in the classroom in discussing their subject," but also contains this limitation: "[Teachers] should be careful not to introduce into their teaching controversial matter which has no relationship to their subject" (*AAUP Policy Documents and Reports*, 10th ed., 2006, 3).

The case of *McConnell v. Howard University*, 818 F.2d 58 (D.C. Cir. 1987) (discussed further in Section 5.6.2), is an instructive example of a dispute in a private institution about contractual protections for the freedom to teach. In *McConnell*, a professor had been discharged after challenging his university's handling of an in-class conflict that arose between him and one of his students. The professor brought a breach of contract action, and the appellate court was sympathetic to the professor's argument that the university's actions breached the contract between the professor and the university. In reversing a summary judgment for the university, and remanding the case for a trial *de novo*, the appellate court declined to adopt traditional contract principles so as to accord deference to the judgments of the university's administrators. The court's reasoning indicates that, in some circumstances, contract law will protect the teaching freedom of faculty members in private institutions and that contract claims may sometimes be more promising vehicles for faculty members than federal constitutional claims.

Contractual freedom to teach issues may arise in private religious institutions as well as private secular institutions (as in *McConnell*), in which case additional complexities may be present (see Section 6.4). The unusual case of *Curran v. Catholic University of America* (discussed in Section 5.2.4) is an instructive example of this type of case.

### Section 6.3. *Academic Freedom in Research and Publication*

As a matter of policy, academic freedom protections clearly extend to the research and publication activities of faculty members. Such activities are apparently the most ardently protected of all faculty activities. In the 1940 "Statement of Principles on Academic Freedom and Tenure" (see Section 6.1.4 of this book), "full freedom in research and in the publication of the results" is presented as the first of three essential aspects of faculty academic freedom, and this "full freedom" does not include any limitation regarding subject matter, as does the freedom in the classroom that is listed second (*AAUP Policy Documents and Reports* (10th ed., 2006), 3). As a matter of law, moreover, courts tend to distinguish between research and teaching and to provide stronger protection for the former. In *Bishop v. Aronov*, 926 F.2d 1066 (11th Cir. 1991) (discussed in Section 6.2.2), for example, the court upheld university limitations on the content of a professor's classroom speech. At the same time, however, the court emphasized that "[t]he University has not suggested that [the professor] cannot hold his particular views; express them, on his own time, far and wide and to whomever will listen; or write and publish, no doubt authoritatively, on them, nor could it so prohibit him"; and that the professor's "educational judgment can be questioned and redirected by the University when he is acting under its auspices as a course instructor, but not when he acts as an independent . . . researcher" (926 F.2d at 1076–77, emphasis added). The case of *Levin v. Harleston*, discussed immediately below, illustrates this broad protection for faculty research and publication.

*Levin v. Harleston*, 770 F. Supp. 895 (S.D.N.Y. 1991), *affirmed in part and vacated in part*, 966 F.2d 895 (2d Cir. 1992), involves a faculty member's publication of controversial views and features the application of classical First Amendment and academic freedom principles. A philosophy professor at City College of the City University of New York had opined in certain writings and publications that blacks are less intelligent on average than whites. In addition, he had opposed all use of affirmative action quotas. As a result of these writings, he became controversial on campus. Student groups staged demonstrations; documents affixed to his door were burned; and students distributed pamphlets outside his classroom. The college took two affirmative steps to deal with the controversy regarding the professor. First, the college dean (one defendant) created "shadow sections" (alternative sections) for the professor's required introductory philosophy course. Second, the college president (another defendant) appointed an ad hoc faculty committee "to review the question of when speech both in and outside the classroom may go beyond the protection of academic freedom or become conduct unbecoming a member of the faculty."

To implement the shadow sections, the college dean sent letters to the professor's students, informing them of the option to enroll in these sections. The dean stated in the letter, however, that he was "aware of no evidence suggesting that Professor Levin's views on controversial matters have compromised his performance as an able teacher of Philosophy who is fair in his treatment of students." After implementation of the shadow sections, enrollment in the professor's classes decreased by one-half. The college had never before used such sections to allow students to avoid a particular professor because of his views.

To implement the ad hoc committee, the president charged the members "to specifically review information concerning Professor Michael Levin . . . and to include in its report its recommendations concerning what the response of the College should be." The language of the charge tracked certain language in college bylaws and professional contracts concerning the discipline of faculty members and the revocation of tenure. Three of the seven committee members had previously signed a faculty petition condemning the professor. Moreover, although the committee met more than ten times, it never extended the professor an opportunity to address it. The committee report, as summarized by the district court, stated "that Professor Levin's writings constitute unprofessional and inappropriate conduct that harms the educational process at the college, and that the college has properly intervened to protect his students from his views by creating the shadow sections" (770 F. Supp. at 914).

The professor sought declaratory and injunctive relief, claiming that the creation of the shadow sections and the operation of the ad hoc committee violated his rights under the federal Constitution's free speech and due process clauses. After trial, the district court issued a lengthy opinion agreeing with the professor. Relying on *Keyishian* (see Section 6.1.5), the court noted the chilling and stigmatizing effect of the ad hoc committee's activities, as demonstrated by the fact that, during the time the committee was meeting, the professor had declined more than twenty invitations to speak or write about his controversial views. The court held that the professor had "objectively reasonable bases" to fear losing his position, and that the effects on him were "exactly that predicted in *Keyishian* . . . Professor Levin was forced to 'stay as far away as possible from utterances or acts which might jeopardize his living.'" To determine whether this infringement on the professor's speech was nonetheless legitimate, the court then undertook a *Pickering-Connick* analysis. It held that there was "no question" that the professor's speech was "protected expression," since his writings and statements addressed matters that were "quintessentially 'issues of public importance.'" The only justification advanced by the defendants for the ad hoc committee and shadow sections was the need to protect the professor's students from harm that could accrue "if they thought, because of the expression of his views, that he might expect less of them or grade them unfairly." The court, however, rejected this justification because City College had presented no evidence at trial to support it. Consequently, the trial court granted injunctive relief, prohibiting the defendants from any further use of the shadow sections or the ad hoc committee.

The appellate court generally agreed with the district court's reasoning regarding the shadow sections and the ad hoc committee. The court noted that the "formation of the alternative sections would not be unlawful if done to further a legitimate educational purpose that outweighed the infringement on Professor Levin's First Amendment rights." But the defendants had presented no evidence to support their contention that the professor's expression of his ideas outside the classroom harmed the educational process within the classroom. In fact, "none of Professor Levin's students had ever complained of unfair treatment on the basis of race." The court concluded that the defendants' "encouragement of the continued erosion in the size of Professor Levin's class if he does not mend his extracurricular ways is the antithesis of freedom of expression." The appellate court also agreed that the operation of the ad hoc committee had a "chilling effect" on the professor's speech and thus violated his First Amendment rights. Affirming that "governmental action which falls short of direct prohibition on speech may violate the First Amendment by chilling the free exercise of speech," the court determined that, when the president "deliberately formed the committee's inquiry into Levin's conduct to mirror the contractual standard for disciplinary action, he conveyed the threat that Levin would be dismissed if he continued voicing his racial theories" (966 F.2d at 89).

To implement its conclusions, the appellate court affirmed the portion of the trial court's injunction prohibiting the defendants from using the shadow sections. Regarding the ad hoc committee, the appellate court modified the relief ordered by the trial court. Since the ad hoc committee had recommended no disciplinary action and had no further investigations or disciplinary proceedings pending, the injunction was unnecessary. It was sufficient to issue an order that merely declared the unconstitutionality of the defendants' use of the committee, since such declaratory relief would make clear that "disciplinary proceedings, or the threat thereof, predicated solely upon Levin's continued expression of his views outside of the classroom" would violate his free speech rights.

*Levin* is an important case for several reasons. It painstakingly chronicles a major academic freedom dispute centering on faculty publication activities; it demonstrates a relationship between academic freedom and the phenomenon of "political correctness"; and it strongly supports faculty academic freedom in research by using the federal Constitution as a basic source of protection. The courts' opinions do not break new legal ground, however, since they use established principles and precedents, in particular *Keyishian* and the *Pickering-Connick* line. But these opinions do provide a very useful response to the particular facts before the court. The case dealt with traditionally protected faculty speech—writing and outside publication expressing opinions on matters of public concern—and not with opinions expressed in classroom lectures or in course materials. Not only is such publication given the highest protection, but the defendants produced no evidence that the professor's writings and views had any adverse impact on his classroom performance or his treatment of students. The college had never before created shadow sections and had demonstrated no "legitimate educational interest" in using them in this circumstance. Finally, the numerous procedural flaws in the establishment and operation of the ad hoc committee strongly supported, if only circumstantially, the professor's claims that his constitutional rights were being chilled.

As colleges and universities have moved further into the age of information technology—and faculty members employ new means of researching, storing research, and disseminating their views—new questions have arisen about the freedom of research and publication. One example concerns institutions' attempts to access research or communications that faculty members have stored in their offices. Another example concerns faculty members' use of the institution's Web page and server to display research or communicate personal viewpoints, and the extent to which the institution might impose limits on such use. Issues might arise, for instance, if an institution orders a faculty member to remove controversial or offensive content from a Web log that he or she maintains on the university's Web site. A third example concerns research that faculty members do using computer equipment supplied by the institution and the extent to which the institution or (in the case of public institutions) the state might impose limitations on faculty members' research using such equipment. The case of *Urofsky v. Gilmore*, discussed in the next paragraph, illustrates the questions that may arise if the state or a public institution restricts the content of the materials that faculty members may access or store on state-owned computers. In most such situations—though they are tinged with new technological implications—the issues can nevertheless be resolved by careful application of traditional legal principles and sensitive consideration of the traditional attributes of the college and university environment, as addressed in the discussion below.

In *Urofsky v. Gilmore*, 216 F.3d 401 (4th Cir. 2000) (*en banc*), the full twelve-member bench of the Fourth Circuit issued a ruling that contrasts starkly with *Levin* and is deeply inhospitable to faculty academic freedom in research. The case concerns a Virginia statute, "Restrictions on State Employee Access to Information Infrastructure," then codified Va. Code Ann. §§ 2.2-804 to -806, and subsequently recodified as Va. Code Ann. §§ 2.2-2827 (B)(2001). This statute restricts the Internet-based research of state employees, including faculty members at the state's higher educational institutions, by prohibiting them from using state-owned or –leased "computer equipment" to access "sexually explicit" material without prior approval from the head of the agency for which the employee works.

The plaintiffs, who were professors at various Virginia state colleges and universities, argued that this statute interfered with their ability to do research concerning sexuality and the human body in various fields such as art, literature, psychology, history, and medicine. Specifically, the professors made two claims: (1) that the statute was unconstitutional on its face, since it restricted the content of the speech of public employees speaking on matters of public concern; and (2) that the statute was unconstitutional as applied to "academic employees," since it burdened their First Amendment "right to academic freedom" in research. The state responded that the statute restricted only employee speech, not the speech of citizens addressing matters of public concern, and that this restriction served state interests in "maintain[ing] operational efficiency in the workplace" and "prevent[ing] the creation of a sexually hostile work environment" (995 F. Supp. at 639).

The district court, using the *Pickering-Connick* standards (see Section 6.1.1 of this book), invalidated the statute as an impermissible restriction on speech on matters of public concern (*Urofsky v. Allen*, 995 F. Supp. 634 (E.D. Va. 1998)). In applying *Pickering-Connick*, the court emphasized various factors regarding the statute that served to increase the state's burden of justifying the statute's restrictions on speech. *First*, the statute is broad in scope, deterring a large number of potential speakers and covering a broad category of speech. *Second*, the statute has a substantial capacity to "chill" speakers in advance because of their concern that their speech activities may violate the statute. *Third*, the statute has a substantial adverse impact on the general public's right to receive information, an impact exacerbated by the fact that the information suppressed is that of state employees who have special expertise of particular benefit to the public. *Fourth*, the statutory restriction on speech is explicitly content based, targeting sexual speech, but not any other speech that could impinge on state interests in the workplace. *Fifth*, the statute restricts the use of the Internet, "arguably the most powerful tool for sharing information ever developed," thus enhancing the burden on speech.

On appeal, a three-judge panel of the Fourth Circuit reversed the district court, reasoning that the professors were speaking (and were restricted by the statute) only in their capacities as state employees, not as citizens commenting upon matters of public interest, and therefore had no First Amendment protection (*Urofsky v. Gilmore*, 167 F.3d 191 (4th Cir. 1999)). The full appellate court (all twelve judges) then reviewed the case *en banc*. The majority upheld the panel's decision, ruling that the Virginia statute did not violate the First Amendment. The majority opinion, however, is much more expansive than the panel's and even more inhospitable to faculty academic freedom. Seven judges joined in the majority opinion (two of whom also wrote concurring opinions); one judge (Chief Justice Wilkinson) wrote an opinion concurring only in the judgment, and four judges joined in a dissenting opinion.

The *en banc* majority relied on an abbreviated *Pickering-Connick* analysis based on the reasoning of the three-judge panel to conclude that the statute did not violate the free speech rights of public employees (that is, it was facially constitutional). The majority then undertook a lengthy review of the theory and practice of academic freedom to conclude that the statute did not violate faculty members' First Amendment rights regarding their research projects (that is, the statute was constitutional as applied to the plaintiffs). Under the majority's reasoning, therefore, faculty members, like all public employees, do have free speech rights, and these rights protect them in the same way and to the same extent as other public employees; but they do not have any additional or different free speech rights, beyond those of other public employees, that accrue to them because they work in academia.

In the *Pickering-Connick* part of its analysis (addressing the statute's facial constitutionality), the *en banc* court in *Urofsky* first reviewed the scope and application of the Virginia statute. The critical threshold question, according to the court, is whether the statute regulates employees "primarily in [their] role as citizen[s] or primarily in [their] role as employee[s]." Only in the former circumstance, according to the majority, do public employees enjoy the First Amendment protections articulated in the *Pickering-Connick* line of cases. The *Urofsky* court therefore focused only on the status or "role" of the person speaking—whether he or she is speaking as a citizen or as an employee— and did not consider the type of speech being regulated—whether the speech addresses a matter of public concern or a matter of private concern.

Having declared its preference for using the role or status of the speaker as the litmus test for employee speech protections, the court then determined that the professors were speaking only as employees and not as citizens. As a result, the court did not analyze whether the speech at issue—access to and dissemination of sexually explicit materials for particular professional research projects—could rise to the level of public concern speech. Nor did the majority balance the professors' free speech interests against the state's interest in maintaining an efficient and nonhostile workplace. Instead, the majority simply determined that the law did not abridge the faculty member's First Amendment rights as private citizens, but only regulated their speech as employees, and thus was not unconstitutional.

By adopting this strained view of the public concern test and thereby avoiding the *Pickering-Connick* balancing test, the *en banc* court also conveniently avoided the impact of *United States v. National Treasury Employees Union*, 513 U.S. 454 (1995) (discussed in Section 6.1.1 of this book). This case requires a different and stronger showing of government interest when the speech of a large group of employees is limited by statute or administrative regulation. The case also warns of the burdens placed on employee speech by a "ban" that "deters an enormous quantity of speech before it is uttered, based only on speculation that the speech might threaten the Government's interests" (513 U.S. at 467 n.11). The dissenting opinion in *Urofsky* provides an example of how the NTEU case's balancing analysis would apply to the Virginia statute (216 F.3d at 439–41 (Murnaghan, J., dissenting)). In addition, by taking the position it did on the public concern test, the court majority avoided the "overbreadth" and "vagueness" analysis often applied to statutes regulating speech and thus also avoided any application of the *Keyishian* case (see Section 6.1.5), which employed such analysis and warned against statutes that exert a "chilling effect" on free speech.

In his concurring opinion, Chief Judge Wilkinson criticized the *en banc* majority's use of the *Pickering-Connick* line of cases because

> by placing exclusive emphasis on the fact that the statute covers speech of "state employees in their capacity as employees . . ." the majority rests its conclusions solely on the "form" of the speech. The public concern inquiry, however, does not cease with form. The majority fails to examine the "content" of the speech, which surely touches on matters of political and social importance. It also fails to examine the "context" of the speech, which can occur in a variety of settings, including the public university. As this case was brought by public university professors, I consider the statute's application to academic inquiry as a useful illustration of how the statute restricts material of public concern [216 F.3d at 426–27].

Regarding "context," for instance, Chief Judge Wilkinson made these points that, in his view, are central to the first prong of the *Pickering-Connick* analysis but are ignored by the majority:

> [T]he context of the affected speech is unique. In the university setting "the State acts against a background and tradition of thought and experiment that is at the center of our intellectual and philosophic tradition." *Rosenberger v. Rector & Visitors of Univ. of Va.*, 515 U.S. 819, 835 (1995). Internet research, novel though it be, lies at the core of that tradition. These plaintiffs are state employees, it is true. But these particular employees are hired for the very purpose of inquiring into, reflecting upon, and speaking out on matters of public concern. A faculty is employed professionally to test ideas and to propose solutions, to deepen knowledge and refresh perspectives. See William W. Van Alstyne, "Academic Freedom and the First Amendment in the Supreme Court of the United States: An Unhurried Historical Review," 53 *Law & Contemp. Probs.* 79, 87 (1990). Provocative comment is endemic to the work of a university faculty whose "function is primarily one of critical review." Id.
>
> Furthermore, state university professors work in the context of considerable academic independence. The statute limits professors' ability to use the Internet to research and to write. But in their research and writing university professors are not state mouthpieces—they speak mainly for themselves. See generally David M. Rabban, "Functional Analysis of 'Individual' and 'Institutional'

Academic Freedom Under the First Amendment," 53 *Law & Contemp. Probs.* 227, 242–44 (1990). It is not enough to declare, as the majority does, "The speech at issue here . . . is clearly made in the employee's role as employee." No one assumes when reading a professor's work that it bears the imprimatur of the government or that it carries the approval of his or her academic institution [216 F.3d at 428–29].

By failing to consider the "content" and "context" of the prohibited speech, the Chief Judge said, the majority has reached a result under which

even the grossest statutory restrictions on public employee speech will be evaluated by a simple calculus: if speech involves one's position as a public employee, it will enjoy no First Amendment protection whatsoever. My colleagues in the majority would thus permit any statutory restriction on academic speech and research, even one that baldly discriminated on the basis of social perspective or political point of view [216 F.3d at 434].

The dissenting opinion (joined by four judges) also criticizes the majority's use of *Pickering-Connick,* arguing that "the majority has adopted an unduly restrictive interpretation of the 'public concern' doctrine" and that its "formalistic focus on the 'role of the speaker' in employee speech cases . . . runs directly contrary to Supreme Court precedent" (216 F.3d at 435–39). Even one of the judges joining in the majority opinion wrote a separate concurrence indicating that he had joined the majority because he felt bound by a prior Fourth Circuit case in which he had dissented, and that were he "left to [his] own devices," he "would hold that the [professors'] speech in this case is entitled to some measure of First Amendment protection, thus triggering application of the *Connick/Pickering* balancing test" (216 F.3d at 425–26 (Hamilton, J., concurring)).

In the academic freedom part of its analysis (addressing the Virginia statute's application to "academic employees' right to academic freedom"), the *Urofsky* majority acknowledged that the U.S. Supreme Court, in various cases, has addressed and supported a constitutional concept of academic freedom. The Supreme Court's focus, however—according to the *Urofsky* majority—was always on the institution's own academic freedom, and not on the academic freedom of individual faculty members: "[T]he Supreme Court, to the extent it has constitutionalized a right of academic freedom at all, appears to have recognized only an institutional right to self-governance in academic affairs" (216 F.3d at 412). (See Section 6.1.7 of this chapter for discussion of "institutional academic freedom.") The *Urofsky* majority then determined that faculty members do not have any constitutional right to academic freedom under the First Amendment, whether in regard to research or to other faculty functions. The majority therefore rejected the professors' academic freedom claim because its "review of the law" led it "to conclude that to the extent the Constitution recognizes any right of 'academic freedom' above and beyond the First Amendment rights to which every citizen is entitled, the right inheres in the University, not in individual professors" (216 F.3d at 410).

Although it rejected the professors' free speech and academic freedom claims, the *Urofksy* majority did acknowledge that other claims might validly arise when the Virginia statute's provision on prior approval for research with sexually explicit content (Va. Code Ann. § 2.2–2827(B)) is applied to individual cases: "[A] denial of an application under the Act based upon a refusal to approve a particular research project might raise genuine questions—perhaps even constitutional ones—concerning the extent of the authority of a university to control the work of its faculty." But, said the majority, "such questions are not presented here" (216 F.3d at 415 n.17). Thus the majority did recognize that other legal issues may arise if a faculty member who seeks prior approval is refused permission; but at the same time the majority determined that this possibility of future violations was not sufficient to invalidate the statute either on its face or as applied to the plaintiffs (who had not sought prior approvals).

The dissenters, in contrast, echoed the district court's opinion in arguing that the Virginia statute was unconstitutional because it gave institutions broad, virtually unfettered, discretion as the sole arbiters for approving prior requests for accessing and disseminating sexually explicit materials used for professional purposes. In rejecting the statute as both overinclusive and underinclusive in restricting broad categories of speech used for beneficial public purposes, the *Urofsky* dissent determined that the statute's prior approval requirement could lead to arbitrary decisions that could "chill" faculty members' speech:

> The danger of arbitrary censorship is particularly relevant in the instant case, given the differing views on the merits of research and discussion into sexually-related topics . . . [T]he mere existence of the licensor's unfettered discretion, coupled with the power of prior restraint, intimidates parties into censoring their own speech, even if the discretion and power are never actually abused [216 F.3d at 441].

Faculty members subject to the Virginia statute, or a similar statute or regulation in another state, apparently have two options for avoiding such strictures on computer-based research. First, a faculty member may conduct the research using personally owned computer equipment; and second, the faculty member may seek the institution's prior approval for a professional research project that will utilize the restricted materials. The first option is available because the statute addresses only a professor's use of "agency-owned or agency-leased computer equipment"; thus, as the majority acknowledged, "state employees remain free to access sexually explicit materials from their personal or other computers not owned or leased by the state." Presumably, faculty members could use personal computers in their faculty offices to access or store sexually explicit research material. But the statute may prohibit the use of personal computers to access the university's Internet connections or search engines, or to store sexually explicit materials on the university's network, since they may be considered to be "computer equipment" within the meaning of Va. Code Ann. § 2–2.2827.

The second option, prior approval, requires that faculty members be aware of how their institutions have interpreted and implemented this part of the statute. The option will be more meaningful if faculty members, collectively and individually, become involved in their institution's policy making and decision making on prior approvals. The institution could, apparently, adopt a blanket approval policy or an "advance permission" policy for faculty members in particular disciplines or departments—or perhaps all faculty members—thus minimizing the statute's constraint on faculty research. (See the district court's discussion of this point (*Urofsky v. Allen*, 995 F. Supp. 634, 642–43).) If an institution establishes more rigorous criteria for gaining prior approval to access the restricted materials, then it would be important to ensure that the criteria are clear, that there is a tight time frame for making decisions on approval requests, and that any faculty member whose request is denied will receive a full statement of the reasons for the denial. In the case of a denial, the decision may apparently be challenged in court, the *Urofsky* court having left the door open for such challenges (216 F.3d at 415 n.17; see also 216 F.3d at 441 (Murnaghan, J., dissenting)).

When the *en banc* majority opinion in *Urofsky* is viewed together with the concurrences and dissents, and with the district court's opinion, the case provides a highly instructive debate on faculty academic freedom, especially (but not only) with respect to academic research. While the majority opinion is the controlling law in the Fourth Circuit, there is good reason to question whether its abrupt rejection of public employee speech rights and faculty academic freedom rights will or should become the prevailing legal view. The seven judges in the *Urofsky* majority were strongly criticized by the remaining five judges: Chief Judge Wilkinson concurring in the result (216 F.3d at 426–35) and Judge Murnaghan and the other three judges joining in his dissenting opinion (216 F.3d at 435–41). The Wilkinson opinion and the dissent both make important points worth serious consideration, as does the district court's opinion in the same case (995 F. Supp. 634).

Subsequent to *Urofsky* and the uncertainties it added to the law, the U.S. Supreme Court created additional uncertainty concerning the First Amendment's application to faculty research and publication. The pertinent case is *Garcetti v. Ceballos* (discussed in Sections 6.1.1 and 6.2.1). The key questions emerging from *Garcetti* are these: (1) Will the courts now analyze First Amendment protections for faculty research and publication by using the *Garcetti* employee speech/private citizen speech dichotomy, or instead will the courts recognize an exception from *Garcetti* for research and publication? (2) If courts do apply the employee speech doctrine, what guidelines will they develop for determining when faculty research and publication is on the employee speech side of the line and thus unprotected? (3) If courts create a research and publication exception from *Garcetti*, how extensive will the exception be and how will courts determine what research and publication activities fall within it? The *Urofsky* case, which preceded the Supreme Court's decision in *Garcetti*, already provides an example of how protection for faculty research could be diminished (or emasculated) by courts emphasizing the distinction between employee speech and private citizen speech.

*Adams v. University of North Carolina at Wilmington*, 640 F.3d 550 (4th Cir. 2011), provides an example of a post-*Garcetti* case testing *Garcetti's* application to faculty publications. *Adams* also provides a new set of issues to contrast with those in *Levin* and *Urofsky*. The plaintiff faculty member had published "columns," "commentaries," and "books," and had delivered speeches, on a variety of subjects (for example, sex, feminism, homosexuality, and religion) that, according to the court were "unrelated to any of [the professor's] assigned teaching duties . . . or any other terms of his employment." These works did, however, have an "aspect of scholarship," and the defendants themselves agreed that the works "involve[d] scholarship and teaching."

When applying for promotion, the professor included various of these works in his application, even though (as the court indicated) they "were not primarily devoted to purely academic subjects in his field." (The professor also included a number of academic, refereed publications in his application.) When the professor's application for promotion to full professor was denied, he claimed that the rejection was due to disagreement with the views he expressed in the various works that were more commentaries on social and political issues than analysis of academic subjects in his field. The defendants argued that the professor had prepared these works in the capacity of an employee, or that they became the works of an employee when submitted as part of the promotion application, and they therefore were not protected under *Garcetti*.

The appellate court disagreed with the university:

> The scholarship and teaching in this case . . . was intended for and directed at a national or international audience on issues of public importance unrelated to any of [the professor's] assigned teaching duties at UNCW or any other terms of his employment found in the record . . . [N]one of [the professor's] speech was undertaken at the direction of UNCW, paid for by UNCW, or had any direct application to his UNCW duties [640 F.3d at 563–564].

Moreover:

> Applying *Garcetti* to the academic work of a public university faculty member under the facts of this case could place beyond the reach of First Amendment protection many forms of public speech or service a professor engaged in during his employment. That would not appear to be what *Garcetti* intended, nor is it consistent with our long-standing recognition that no individual loses his ability to speak as a private citizen by virtue of public employment [640 F.3d at 564].

Due to these factors, the court concluded, the professor's speech at issue was not undertaken "pursuant to [his] official duties' as intended by *Garcetti*," and "we will not apply *Garcetti* to the circumstances of this case."

In lieu of *Garcetti*, the court applied the *Pickering-Connick* analysis as it existed prior to *Garcetti* (see Section 6.1.1 above, and see the various examples in Section 6.2.1). The court concluded that the professor's "speech" at issue "was clearly that of a citizen speaking on [matters] of public concern"—the very kind of speech protected by the *Pickering-Connick* line of cases.

This result in *Adams* does not produce any clear holding on how the court would engraft a faculty "scholarship and teaching" exception onto the *Garcetti* case; and it is thus uncertain how the case would have come out if the publications and speeches at issue were on matters of public concern (as the court did hold; see 640 F.3d at 564–65) but also were undertaken pursuant to the professor's official duties as an employee. In general, however, the court's opinion does appear to be sensitive to and supportive of a scholarship and teaching exception to *Garcetti*. Similarly, the opinion acknowledges the special circumstances that can arise in faculty cases and suggests that courts should be willing to consider them in ways that limit the applicability of *Garcetti* to the scholarship of faculty members.

## Section 6.4. Academic Freedom in Religious Colleges and Universities

In general, academic freedom disputes in religious institutions[5] are governed by the same contract law principles that govern such disputes in other private institutions (see Section 6.1.3). (These principles, as applied to academic freedom in teaching, are discussed in Section 6.2.4.) But the religious missions of religious institutions, and their affiliations with churches or religious denominations, may give rise to contract law issues that are unique to religious institutions. In addition, religious institutions may have First Amendment defenses to litigation that secular institutions do not have. Both of these matters are discussed in Section 5.2.4, and a more general discussion of First Amendment defenses is in Section 1.6.2. The *McEnroy* case below, and the case of *Curran v. Catholic University of America*, discussed in Section 5.2.4, illustrates how these matters may play out in academic freedom disputes between faculty members and religious institutions.

Academic freedom customs or professional norms in religious institutions may also vary from those in secular private institutions—particularly in situations where a faculty member takes positions or engages in activities that are contrary to the institution's religious mission or the religious principles of a sponsoring religious denomination. This type of problem, and the potential for clashes between faculty academic freedom and institutional academic freedom, are illustrated by the debate concerning *Ex Corde Ecclesiae*, issued by Pope John Paul II in 1990, and *Ex Corde Ecclesiae: The Application to the United States* (http://www.nccbuscc.org/bishops/excorde.htm), subsequently adopted by the U.S. Conference of Catholic Bishops. (For commentary on this debate, see James Gordon III, "Individual and Institutional Academic Freedom at Religious Colleges and Universities," 30 *J. Coll. & Univ. Law* 1, 20–25 (2003).)

To account for possible differences in academic freedom norms at religious institutions, the "1940 Statement of Principles on Academic Freedom and Tenure" includes a "limitations clause" specifying that "[l]imitations on

---

[5] "Religious," when used in this section to refer to a college or university, covers institutions that are sponsored by or otherwise related to a particular church or denomination, as well as institutions that are nondenominational and independent of any particular church body.

academic freedom because of religious or other aims of the institution should be clearly stated in writing at the time of [a faculty member's] appointment" (*AAUP Policy Documents and Reports* (10th ed., 2006), 3). The meaning of this clause, its implementation, and its wisdom have been debated over the years (see, for example, the "1970 Interpretive Comments," comment 3, in *AAUP Policy Documents and Reports*, 6; and see generally the article by Gordon cited in the previous paragraph, at 16–20). In 1999, the AAUP issued "operating guidelines" for applying the clause ("The 'Limitations' Clause in the 1940 Statement of Principles on Academic Freedom and Tenure: Some Operating Guidelines," in *AAUP Policy Documents and Reports*, 41).

When a religious institution invokes the limitations clause and imposes limits on the scope of academic freedom, contract law issues may arise concerning the interpretation of these limits as expressed in faculty appointment documents, the faculty handbook, or other institutional regulations; in addition, issues may arise concerning the extent of the religious institution's prerogative, under AAUP policies, to limit its faculty's academic freedom. When a religious institution adopts AAUP policies but does not invoke the limitations clause, issues may still arise concerning whether religious law governing the institution can justify limits on academic freedom or affect the analysis of contract law issues. In either situation, if an institution's personnel action appears to conflict with AAUP policy or to breach a faculty member's contract, the aggrieved faculty member may seek the protection of the AAUP in lieu of or in addition to resorting to the courts. The case of Carmel McEnroy, then a professor at the Saint Meinrad School of Theology in Saint Meinrad, Indiana, is illustrative.

The school's administration dismissed Professor McEnroy after it learned, and she admitted, that she had "signed an open letter to Pope John Paul II asking that continued discussion be permitted concerning the question of ordaining women to the priesthood." McEnroy, a "member of the Congregation of Sisters of Mercy of Ireland and South Africa," signed the letter "without citing her academic or religious affiliations." She was one of more than fifteen hundred signatories. At the time of the dismissal, the "1940 Statement of Principles on Academic Freedom and Tenure was adopted as institutional policy [and] printed in full in the Faculty Handbook, without specification of any limitations on academic freedom." McEnroy contended that, in signing the letter, "she was exercising her right as a citizen as outlined in the 1940 Statement of Principles." Church and school officials, in contrast, contended "that she had publicly dissented from the teaching of the church and was therefore disqualified from continuing in her faculty position"—thus, in effect, asserting that McEnroy was dismissed on "ecclesial grounds" rather than "academic grounds," and that the 1940 Statement therefore did not apply. The AAUP's investigating committee concluded that the 1940 Statement did apply and that Saint Meinrad's administration "failed to meet its obligation to demonstrate that [Professor McEnroy's] signing of the letter to Pope John Paul II rendered her unfit to retain her faculty position," as required by the 1940 Statement, thereby "violat[ing] her academic freedom." (The committee also concluded that Saint Meinrad's administration violated the due process principles of the 1940 Statement when dismissing

McEnroy.) (See "Report: Academic Freedom and Tenure: Saint Meinrad School of Theology (Indiana)," in *Academe*, July–August 1996, 51–60.)

The AAUP's Committee A on Academic Freedom and Tenure accepted the investigating committee's report and recommended that the university be placed on the AAUP's list of censured administrations. At the AAUP's eighty-third annual meeting, the membership approved Committee A's recommendation (available at http://www.aaup.org/com-a/devcen.htm).

McEnroy subsequently filed suit against Saint Meinrad's and two of its administrators, claiming breach of contract. The trial court dismissed the case, and the Indiana appellate court affirmed (*McEnroy v. Saint Meinrad School of Theology*, 713 N.E.2d 334 (Ind. 1997)). Resolving an ambiguity in the professor's contract, the appellate court reasoned that, in addition to its academic freedom and due process terms, the contract also included terms regarding the Roman Catholic Church's jurisdiction over the school. Thus "resolution of Dr. McEnroy's claims would require the trial court to interpret and apply religious doctrine and ecclesiastical law," which would "clearly and excessively" entangle the trial court "in religious affairs in violation of the First Amendment."

A different type of academic freedom problem arises when a government agency seeks to investigate or penalize a religious college or university or one of its faculty members. Such disputes are "extramural" rather than "intramural" (see Section 6.1.6). The institution may claim in defense that the government's planned action would violate its institutional academic freedom, or the faculty member may claim in defense that the action would violate faculty academic freedom. Since the dispute concerns government action, both the religious institution and the faculty member may assert constitutional rights against the government. Sometimes these rights will be the same as secular private institutions and their faculty members would assert free speech and press rights. At other times these rights will belong only to religious institutions and their faculty members; these are the rights protected by the establishment and free exercise clauses of the First Amendment (see generally Section 1.6.2).[6] Examples would include cases in which an institution argues that federal or state court review of its religious practices would violate the establishment clause (see the *McEnroy* case above, and see also Section 5.2.4 of this book), and cases in which the institution challenges the authority of a government agency, such as the EEOC, to investigate or regulate its religiously based practices (see Section 4.7).

---

[6] Faculty members at private secular institutions could also invoke free exercise and establishment clause rights if the challenged government action interfered with their personal religious beliefs or practices. A private secular institution itself could also invoke these clauses if government were to require that the institution involve itself in religious matters or were to prohibit it from doing so.

PART FOUR

# THE COLLEGE AND ITS STUDENTS

# 7

# The Student-Institution Relationship

*Chapter 7 discusses a variety of institutional functions and services related to students, including services for students living on campus. The chapter begins with the age-of-majority concept and the state laws that establish the legal capacity of students to enter binding legal contracts (usually at age eighteen) and bestow other privileges and obligations on them. It then addresses the emergence of students' constitutional rights; analyzes the academic freedom rights of students (as compared to those of the faculty); and examines students' legal relationships with other students, with particular emphasis on peer sexual harassment. Legal aspects of admissions and financial aid are examined, with particular emphasis on nondiscrimination and affirmative action issues. The chapter then discusses the provision of various services for students—in particular, student housing, campus security, campus computer networks (with particular emphasis on free speech issues), services for international students, services for students with disabilities, and student privacy protections (FERPA)—and the differing legal issues that arise in each of these areas.*

## Section 7.1. The Legal Status of Students

**7.1.1. Overview.** The legal status of students in postsecondary institutions changed dramatically in the 1960s, changed further near the end of the twentieth century, and is still evolving. For most purposes, students are no longer second-class citizens under the law. They are recognized under the federal Constitution as "persons" with their own enforceable constitutional rights. They are recognized as adults, with the rights and responsibilities of adults, under many state laws. And they are accorded their own legal rights under various federal statutes. The background of this evolution is traced in

Section 1.2; the legal status that emerges from these developments, and its impact on postsecondary administration, is explored throughout this chapter.

Perhaps the key case in forging this shift in student status was *Dixon v. Alabama State Board of Education* (1961), discussed further in Section 9.3.2. The court in this case rejected the notion that education in state schools is a "privilege" to be dispensed on whatever conditions the state in its sole discretion deems advisable; it also implicitly rejected the *in loco parentis* concept, under which the law had bestowed on schools all the powers over students that parents had over minor children. The *Dixon* approach became a part of U.S. Supreme Court jurisprudence in cases such as *Tinker v. Des Moines School District* (see Section 9.4.1), *Healy v. James* (Sections 9.4.1 and 10.1.1), and *Goss v. Lopez* (Section 9.3.2). The impact of these public institution cases spilled over to private institutions, as courts increasingly viewed students as contracting parties having rights under express and implied contractual relationships with their institutions. Thus, at both public and private institutions, the failure to follow institutional policies, rules, and regulations has led to successful litigation by students who claimed that their rights were violated by this noncompliance (see Sections 7.1.3, 9.2, and 9.3).

Congress gave students at both public and private schools rights under various civil rights acts and, in the Family Educational Rights and Privacy Act (FERPA, discussed in Section 7.8.1 of this chapter), gave postsecondary students certain rights that were expressly independent of and in lieu of parental rights. State statutes lowering the age of majority also enhanced the independence of students from their parents and brought the bulk of postsecondary students, even undergraduates, into the category of adults.

Now another stage in the evolution of students' legal status has been emerging. Developments at this new stage suggest a renewed emphasis on the academic freedom of students. In classical thought on academic freedom, the student's freedom to learn is clearly recognized and considered to be at least as important as the faculty member's freedom to teach. In more modern legal developments, courts have occasionally recognized the concept of student academic freedom; in *Piarowski v. Illinois Community College*, 759 F.2d 625, 629 (7th Cir. 1985), for instance, the court noted that the term "academic freedom" is "used to denote" not only "the freedom of the individual teacher" but also "the [freedom of] the student." But most academic freedom cases have been brought by faculty members, and most academic freedom rights that courts have protected have belonged to faculty members (see especially Section 6.2). Student academic freedom issues are discussed in Section 7.1.4.

**7.1.2. The age of majority.** The age of majority is established by state law in all states. There may be a general statute prescribing an age of majority for all or most business and personal dealings in the state, or there may be specific statutes or regulations establishing varying ages of majority for specific purposes. Until the 1970s, the age of majority in most states was typically 21. But since the 1971 ratification of the Twenty-Sixth Amendment, lowering the voting age to 18, most states have lowered the age of majority to 18 or 19 for many other purposes as well. Some statutes, such as those in Michigan (Mich. Comp. Laws Ann. § 722.52), set age 18 as the age of majority for all purposes; other states have adopted more limited or more piecemeal legislation, sometimes using different minimum ages for different purposes. Given the lack of uniformity, administrators and counsel should carefully check state law in their own states.

Laws setting the age of majority can affect many postsecondary regulations and policies. For example, students at age 18 may be permitted to enter binding contracts without the need for a cosigner, give consent to medical treatment, declare financial independence, or establish a legal residence apart from the parents. But although students' legal capacity enables institutions to deal with them as adults at age 18, it does not necessarily require that institutions do so. Particularly in private institutions, administrators may still be able as a policy matter to require a cosigner on contracts with students, for instance, or to consider the resources of parents in awarding financial aid, even though the parents have no legal obligations to support the student. An institution's legal capacity to adopt such policy positions depends on the interpretation of the applicable age-of-majority law and the possible existence of special state law provisions for postsecondary institutions. A state loan program, for instance, may have special definitions of dependency or residency that may not conform to general age-of-majority laws.

### 7.1.3. The contractual rights of students. 
Both public and private institutions often have express contractual relationships with students. The most common examples are probably the housing contract or lease, the food service contract, and the loan agreement. In addition, courts are increasingly inclined to view the student handbook or college catalog as a contract, either express or implied. When problems arise in these areas, the written document (or Web site), including institutional regulations incorporated by reference, is usually the first source of legal guidance.

Courts have differed over the past few decades as to whether, and in what form, a contract exists between a college and its students. Variations in contract law between states also complicate the analysis of whether, and which, documents or policies are contractually binding. The following discussion examines a variety of approaches taken by courts, and addresses the inconsistencies among states in how their courts analyze student contract claims.

Early cases involving student contract claims looked beyond written documents and found a more amorphous contractual relationship, such as that recognized in *Carr v. St. John's University, New York*, 187 N.E.2d 18 (N.Y. 1962), the modern root of the contract theory of student status. In reviewing the institution's dismissal of students for having participated in a civil marriage ceremony, the court based its reasoning on the principle that "when a student is duly admitted by a private university, secular or religious, there is an implied contract between the student and the university that, if he complies with the terms prescribed by the university, he will obtain the degree which he sought." Construing a harsh and vague regulation in the university's favor, the court upheld the dismissal because the students had failed to comply with the university's prescribed terms. Although *Carr* dealt only with a private institution, a subsequent New York case, *Healy v. Larsson*, 323 N.Y.S.2d 625, *affirmed*, 318 N.E.2d 608 (N.Y. 1974), indicated that "there is no reason why . . . the *Carr* principle should not apply to a public university or community college."

Other courts have increasingly utilized the contract theory for both public and private institutions, as well as for both academic and disciplinary disputes. The theory, however, does not necessarily apply identically to all such situations. A public institution may have more defenses against a contract action. *Eden v. Board of Trustees of State University*, 374 N.Y.S.2d 686 (N.Y. App. Div. 1975), for instance, recognizes both an *ultra vires* defense and the state's power to terminate a contract when necessary in the public interest. ("Ultra vires" means "beyond authority"; the defense essentially says, "You can't enforce this contract against us because we didn't have authority to make it in the first place.") And courts may accord both public and private institutions more flexibility in drafting and interpreting contract terms involving academics than they do contract terms involving discipline. In holding that Georgia State University had not breached its contract with a student by withholding a master's degree, for example, the court in *Mahavongsanan v. Hall*, 529 F.2d 448 (5th Cir. 1976), recognized the "wide latitude and discretion afforded by the courts to educational institutions in framing their academic requirements." For a more recent case using a similar analysis, see *Seitz-Partridge v. Loyola University of Chicago*, 948 N.E.2d 219 (Ill. App. Ct. 2011).

In general, courts have applied the contract theory to postsecondary institutions in a deferential manner. Courts have accorded institutions considerable latitude to select and interpret their own contract terms and to change the terms to which students are subjected as they progress through the institution. In *Mahavongsanan*, for instance, the court rejected the plaintiff student's contract claim in part because an institution "clearly is entitled to modify [its regulations] so as to properly exercise its educational responsibility" (529 F.2d at 450). Nor have institutions been subjected to the rigors of contract law as it applies in the commercial world (see, for example, *Slaughter v. Brigham Young University*, discussed in Section 9.2.3).

In some instances, courts have preferred to use quasi-contract theory to examine the relationship between an institution and its students, and may hold the institution to a good-faith standard. In *Beukas v. Fairleigh Dickinson University*, 605 A.2d 776 (N.J. Super. Ct. Law Div. 1991), *affirmed*, 605 A.2d 708 (N.J. Super. Ct. App. Div. 1992), former dental students sued the university for closing its dental school when the state withdrew its subsidy. The university pointed to language in the catalog reserving the right to eliminate programs and schools, arguing that the language was binding on the students. But instead of applying a contract theory, the trial court preferred to analyze the issue using quasi-contract theory, and applied an arbitrariness standard:

> [T]his court rejects classic contract doctrine to resolve this dispute . . . [T]he "true" university-student "contract" is one of mutual obligations implied, not in

fact, but by law; it is a quasi-contract which is "created by law, for reasons of justice without regard to expressions of assent by either words or acts" [citation omitted] . . . The inquiry should be: "did the university act in good faith and, if so, did it deal fairly with its students?" [605 A.2d at 783, 784].

The state's appellate court upheld the result and the reasoning, but stated that if the catalog was a contract (a question that the court did not attempt to answer), the reservation of rights language would have permitted the university to close the dental school.

Similarly, another New Jersey appellate court refused to characterize the student-institution relationship as contractual in a student's challenge to his dismissal on academic (as opposed to disciplinary) grounds. In *Mittra v. University of Medicine and Dentistry of New Jersey*, 719 A.2d 693 (N.J. Super. Ct. App. Div. 1998), the court stated that when the institution's action was taken for academic reasons,

> [t]he relationship between the university and its students should not be analyzed in purely contractual terms. As long as the student is afforded reasonable notice and a fair hearing in general conformity with the institution's rules and regulations, we defer to the university's broad discretion in its evaluation of academic performance . . . Rigid application of contract principles to controversies concerning student academic performance would tend to intrude upon academic freedom and to generate precisely the kind of disputes that the courts should be hesitant to resolve [719 A.2d at 695, 697].

Since the student had not identified any specific rule or regulation alleged to have been violated, the appellate court affirmed the trial court's award of summary judgment to the university.

Students have also asserted breach of contract claims when challenging dismissals or other sanctions. Traditionally, courts have typically been more deferential to institutional decisions in dismissals for academic rather than for disciplinary reasons. For example, in a misconduct case, *Fellheimer v. Middlebury College*, 869 F. Supp. 238 (D. Vt. 1994), a federal court ruled that the student handbook of a private institution was contractually binding on the college and provided the basis for a breach of contract claim. In *Fellheimer*, a student challenged the fairness of the college's disciplinary process because he was not informed of all of the charges against him. (This case is discussed more fully in Section 9.3.3 of this book.) The court rejected the college's claim that the handbook was not a contract: "While [prior cases caution courts to] keep the unique educational setting in mind when interpreting university-student contracts, they do not alter the general proposition that a College is nonetheless contractually bound to provide students with the procedural safeguards that it has promised" (869 F. Supp. at 243). The court ruled that Middlebury had breached its contract with the student because the disciplinary hearing had been flawed.

Although various courts have applied contract law principles when an institution's written materials make certain representations, they may be more hesitant to do so if the promise relied upon is oral. In *Ottgen v. Clover Park Technical College*, 928 P.2d 1119 (Wash. Ct. App. 1996), a state appellate court affirmed the trial court's dismissal of contract and state consumer fraud claims against the college. Five students who had enrolled in the college's professional residential real estate appraiser program sued the college when a promise made by a course instructor, who was subsequently dismissed by the college, did not materialize. Although the instructor had promised the students that they would receive appraisal experience as well as classroom instruction, the opportunity for on-the-job experience did not occur. The court ruled that there was no contract between the college and the students to offer students anything but classroom education. College documents discussed only the classroom component and made no representations about the eligibility for licensure of individuals who had completed the program.

The contract theory has become a source of meaningful rights for students as well as for institutions, particularly when faculty or administrators either fail to follow institutional policies or apply those policies in an arbitrary way. Students have claimed, and courts have agreed, that student handbooks, college catalogs, and other policy documents are implied-in-fact contracts and that an institution's failure to follow these guidelines is a breach of an implied-in-fact contract (see, for example, *Zumbrun v. University of Southern California*, 101 Cal. Rptr. 499, 502 (Cal. Ct. App. 1972)). Other cases have involved student claims that the totality of the institution's policies and oral representations by faculty and administrators created an implied contract that, if the student paid tuition and demonstrated satisfactory academic performance, he or she would receive a degree. And although some public institutions have escaped liability in contract claims under the sovereign immunity doctrine (see Section 3.3 of this book), not all states apply this doctrine to public colleges (see, for example, *Stratton v. Kent State University*, 2003 Ohio App. LEXIS 1206 (Ohio Ct. App. March 18, 2003) (unpublished)).

The U.S. Court of Appeals for the First Circuit, applying Rhode Island law, provided an explicit recognition of the contractual relationship between a student and a college. In *Mangla v. Brown University*, 135 F.3d 80 (1st Cir. 1998), the court stated:

> The student-college relationship is essentially contractual in nature. The terms of the contract may include statements provided in student manuals and registration materials. The proper standard for interpreting the contractual terms is that of "reasonable expectation—what meaning the party making the manifestation, the university, should reasonably expect the other party to give it" [135 F.3d at 83].

Students seeking academic accommodations may combine breach of contract claims with civil rights claims. In *Coddington v. Adelphi University*, 45 F. Supp. 2d 211 (E.D.N.Y. 1999), a student claimed that the private university and several individual administrators had violated the Americans with Disabilities Act (ADA; see Section 8.4 of this book) and breached his contract with the university by failing to accommodate his learning disabilities. Although the court dismissed the student's ADA claim and the contract claims against individual administrators, the court rejected the university's motion to dismiss the contract claim against the university itself. Noting that the student had paid the required tuition and claimed to have relied upon "admission bulletins and other materials regarding Adelphi's programs and policies regarding students with learning disabilities" and the representations of certain administrators of his right to untimed tests and note takers, the court ruled that the student had sufficiently pleaded "the existence of a contractual agreement" with the university (but not with the individual administrators).

Although it is usually a student who relies on contractual provisions, the case of *Harwood v. Johns Hopkins*, 747 A.2d 205 (Md. Ct. Spec. App. 2000), provides an interesting example of an institution's successful use of a contract theory as a defense to a student lawsuit. Harwood, a student at Johns Hopkins University, had completed all of his degree requirements, but the degree had not yet been conferred when Harwood murdered a fellow student on the university's campus. The university notified Harwood that it would withhold his diploma pending the resolution of the criminal charges. Harwood pleaded guilty to the murder and was incarcerated. He then brought a declaratory judgment action against the university, seeking the conferral of his degree. The university argued that its written policies required students not only to complete the requirements for their degree but also to adhere to the university's code of conduct. The court ruled that, because the murder violated the university's code of conduct, the university had a contractual right to withhold the diploma.

The nature of damages in a successful breach of contract claim was addressed in a case brought under Florida law. In *Sharick v. Southeastern University of the Health Sciences, Inc.*, 780 So. 2d 136 (Fla. Dist. Ct. App. 2000), a fourth-year medical student was dismissed for failing his last course in medical school. He sued the university for breach of contract, and a jury found that the university's decision to dismiss Sharick was arbitrary, capricious, and "lacking any discernible rational basis." Sharick had sought damages for future lost earning capacity as well as reimbursement of the tuition he had paid, but the trial judge would allow the jury only to consider damages related to the tuition payments. Sharick appealed the trial court's ruling on the issue of future lost earnings. The university did not appeal the jury verdict.

The appellate court reversed the trial court's limitation of damages to tuition reimbursement. Since previous cases had established that other contractual remedies, such as specific performance and mandamus to grant a degree, were unavailable to plaintiffs suing colleges, the court stated that damages could properly include the value of the lost degree with respect to Sharick's future earnings. The Supreme Court of Florida first agreed to review the appellate court's ruling then changed its mind, leaving the appellate decision in force (*Southeastern University of the Health Sciences, Inc. v. Sharick*, 822 So. 2d 1290 (Fla. 2002)).

The contract theory of the relationship between students and institutions is still developing. Debate continues on issues such as the means for identifying the terms and conditions of a student-institution contract, the extent to which a school catalog constitutes part of the contract, and the extent to which an institution retains implied or inherent authority (see Section 3.1) not expressed in any written regulation or policy. Also still debatable is the extent to which courts will rely on certain contract law concepts, such as the doctrines of "unconscionable" contracts and "contracts of adhesion." An unconscionable contract is one that is so harsh and unfair to one of the parties that a reasonable person would not freely and knowingly agree to it. Unconscionable contracts are not enforceable in the courts. In *Albert Merrill School v. Godoy*, 357 N.Y.S.2d 378 (N.Y. Civ. Ct. 1974), the school sought to recover money due on a contract to provide data-processing training. Finding that the student did not speak English well and that the bargaining power of the parties was uneven, the court held the contract unconscionable and refused to enforce it.

A "contract of adhesion" is one offered by one party (usually the party in the stronger bargaining position) to the other party on a "take it or leave it" basis, with no opportunity to negotiate the terms. Ambiguities in contracts of adhesion will be construed against the drafting party (in these cases, the institution) because there was no opportunity for the parties to bargain over the terms of the contract (see, for example, *Corso v. Creighton University*, 731 F.2d 529 (8th Cir. 1984)). See also *K.D. v. Educational Testing Service*, 386 N.Y.S.2d 747 (N.Y. Sup. Ct. 1976), in which the court viewed the plaintiff's agreement with Educational Testing Service to take the Law School Admissions Test (LSAT) as a contract of adhesion, but ruled it valid because it was not "so unfair and unreasonable" that it should be disregarded by use of the available "pretexts," such as a declaration that it violated public policy.

The case of *Kyriazis v. University of West Virginia*, 450 S.E.2d 649 (W. Va. 1994), is an example of a contract of adhesion that a court invalidated as contrary to public policy. In particular, the court's opinion suggests factors relevant to determining whether the bargaining powers of the parties are substantially uneven. In *Kyriazis*, the court found that the university had a "decisive bargaining advantage" over the student because (1) the student had to sign the release as a condition of sports participation and thus had no real choice; (2) the release was prepared by counsel for the university, but the student had no benefit of counsel when he signed the release; and (3) the university's student code required students to follow the directions of university representatives.

Since these contract principles depend on the weak position of one of the parties and on determinations of overall "fairness," courts are unlikely to apply these principles against institutions that deal openly with their students—for instance, by following a good-practice code, operating grievance mechanisms for student complaints (see Sections 9.1.2–9.1.4), and affording students significant opportunity to participate in institutional governance.

Although a promise to treat the other party to a contract fairly and in good faith is part of every contract (Restatement (Second) of Contracts 205 (1981)), most claims by students using this theory have been unsuccessful. For example, in *Napolitano v. Trustees of Princeton University* (discussed in Section 8.6.2 of this book), the court rejected a student's claim that withholding her degree for one year as punishment for plagiarism was a breach of the covenant of good faith and fair dealing. Said the court: "To upset Princeton's decision here, this court would have to find that Princeton could not in good faith have assessed the penalties it did against the plaintiff" (453 A.2d at 284). Other examples of judicial rejection of these claims are *Coveney v. President and Trustees of the College of the Holy Cross*, 445 N.E.2d 136 (Mass. 1983), and *Seare v. University of Utah School of Medicine*, 882 P.2d 673 (Utah Ct. App. 1994). But if the facts demonstrate what a court may view as arbitrary or unreasonable behavior by faculty or administrators, the court may, in fact, rule that the covenant of good faith was breached (see, for example, *University of Southern Mississippi v. Williams*, 891 So.2d 160 (Miss. 2005)).

Students enrolled in programs that are terminated or changed prior to the students' graduation have found some state courts to be receptive to their claims that promotional materials, catalogs, and policy statements are contractually binding on the institution. An illustrative case is *Craig v. Forest Institute of Professional Psychology*, 713 So. 2d 967 (Ala. Civ. App. 1997), in which four students filed state law breach of contract and fraud claims against Forest. Forest, whose main campus was located in Wheeling, Illinois, opened a satellite campus in Huntsville, Alabama, and offered a doctoral degree program in psychology. Although the Huntsville campus was not accredited by the American Psychological Association, a regional accrediting association, or the state, Forest's written materials allegedly implied that its graduates were eligible to sit for licensing examinations and to be licensed in Alabama. The Alabama Board of Examiners would not allow Forest graduates to sit for a licensing examination because its regulations provided that only graduates of accredited institutions were eligible to take the examination.

The Alabama campus proved to be a financial drain on Forest, and it closed the campus before the students had completed their doctorates. Because the college was not accredited, the students were unable to transfer credits earned at Forest to other doctoral programs.

The students' claims were based on the college's alleged promises that they could obtain a doctorate at the Huntsville campus and be eligible for licensure in Alabama. The trial court granted summary judgment to the college, but the appellate court reversed. Disagreeing with a ruling by the South Dakota Supreme Court in an earlier case, *Aase v. State*, 400 N.W.2d 269 (S.D. 1987), the court ruled that "it is not clear that Forest fulfilled all of its contractual obligations to the students merely by providing them with instruction for which they had paid tuition on a semester-by-semester basis" (713 So. 2d at 973). The scope of the contract could not be determined without a trial, said the court; although Forest had pointed to language in one publication that reserved its right to modify or discontinue programs, the court stated that this language was not "dispositive" and that all relevant documents needed to be considered. The court also ruled that a trial was necessary on the plaintiffs' fraud claims.

The concept of fiduciary duty, once applied primarily in the higher education context to members of an institution's board of trustees and senior administrators, is now being discussed as a potential duty assumed by academic advisors, particularly with respect to the relationship between a graduate student and his or her thesis advisor. *Black's Law Dictionary* defines "fiduciary" as a relationship "founded on trust or confidence reposed by one person in the integrity and fidelity of another." It does not arise from contract, and typically requires a higher standard of conduct than the contractual concept of "good faith and fair dealing." Students have attempted to use this theory to argue that a graduate student depends upon the thesis advisor for assistance and support, and that the advisor must behave with complete integrity in carrying out his or her duties and always act in the best interest of the student.

Although one trial court found that there could be a fiduciary relationship between a graduate student and his advisor (*Johnson v. Schmitz*, discussed in Section 3.3), a state appellate court has rejected that theory. In *Swenson v. Bender*, 764 N.W.2d 596 (Minn. Ct. App. 2009), a doctoral student who was enrolled at Cappella University, an all-online university, sued her former advisor for breach of a fiduciary duty. The student, Swenson, accused the advisor, Bender, an adjunct instructor at the university, of "stealing" her dissertation idea and falsely accusing the student of plagiarism. Although Bender was not the chair of Swenson's dissertation committee, Bender worked closely with Swenson and shared many ideas with her. The two had discussed collaborating on a coauthored book and article. At some point disagreement arose about how to attribute credit for theoretical constructs the two had discussed while Bender was advising Swenson on her dissertation. Swenson accused Bender of "sabotaging" Swenson's efforts to obtain the doctoral degree and of "stealing" her ideas for use on Bender's academic Web site. Bender accused Swenson of plagiarism in her dissertation. The university's academic standards committee investigated but took no position on the plagiarism accusations. The committee did conclude, however, that Bender acted unethically by developing a personal relationship with Swenson; but the committee could not determine which material in Swenson's dissertation was her own and which should be attributed to Bender. The committee, which now no longer included Bender, required Swenson to rewrite her dissertation.

Swenson sued for conversion and breach of fiduciary duty. Although the trial court ruled for Swenson on the fiduciary duty claim, it rejected her conversion claim. Bender appealed. The appellate court reversed the trial court's ruling on the fiduciary duty claim. The trial court had based its ruling on three factors underpinning the relationship between a dissertation advisor and a doctoral student: (1) the relationship of trust and deference by the student, (2) the advisor's sole duty to assist the student with the dissertation, and (3) the student's reliance on the advisor in refining the dissertation and conducting the research and writing.

The appellate court stated that a dissertation committee member, even the chair, has an "independent obligation" to the university and does not just act on behalf of the student. Furthermore, the court noted that a faculty member has an obligation to report plagiarism. Because Bender's obligations were in some respects contrary to Swenson's interests (Bender's duty to be critical of the research and writing, her obligation to report academic misconduct), the court concluded that there could be no fiduciary duty between Swenson and Bender, and thus there was no breach.

In the context of a sexual harassment claim, however, a state's highest court approved of the use of fiduciary duty theory. See *Schneider v. Plymouth State College*, 744 A.2d 101 (N.H. 1999), discussed in Section 9.5. The court pointed to the power differential between the student and the professor, and the student's dependence upon the professor for grades, letters of reference, and other matters important to the student's academic career.

Contract law has become an important source of legal rights for students. Postsecondary administrators should be sensitive to the language used in all institutional rules and policies affecting students. Language suggestive of a commitment (or promise) to students should be used only when the institution is prepared to live up to the commitment. Limitations on the institution's commitments should be clearly noted where possible, and reservation of rights language should be used wherever appropriate. Administrators should consider the adoption of an official policy, perhaps even a "code of good practice," on fair dealing with students, and provide avenues for internal appeal of both academic and disciplinary decisions.

**7.1.4. Student academic freedom.**  Student academic freedom is not as well developed as faculty academic freedom (the focus of Chapter 6), either in terms of custom or in terms of law. Nevertheless, like faculty academic freedom, student academic freedom has important historical antecedents and is widely recognized in the academic community. Moreover, since the early 1990s, developments in academia and in the courts have focused attention on the academic freedom of students and raised new questions about its status and role.

The concept of student academic freedom was imported into the United States from Europe, where, in German universities, it was known as *Lernfreiheit*, the freedom to learn. In 1915, in its foundational "General Declaration of Principles," the American Association of University Professors (AAUP) recognized *Lernfreiheit*, the student's freedom to learn, as one of the two components of academic freedom—the other being *Lehrfreiheit*, the teacher's freedom to teach (*AAUP Policy Documents and Reports* (the "Redbook") (10th ed., 2006, 291–301). In the classic "1940 Statement of Principles on Academic Freedom and Tenure," the AAUP and the Association of American Colleges and Universities, eventually joined by more than 150 other higher education and professional associations as endorsers, specifically acknowledged "the rights of the . . . student to freedom in learning" (*AAUP Policy Documents and Reports*, 3). Subsequently, in its "Statement on Professional Ethics" (promulgated in 1966 and revised in 1987), the AAUP emphasized professors' responsibility to "encourage the free pursuit of learning in their students" and to "protect their academic freedom" (*AAUP Policy Documents and Reports*, 171).

In 1967, representatives of the AAUP, the Association of American Colleges and Universities, the U.S. Student Association, the National Association of

Student Personnel Administrators, and the National Association for Women in Education promulgated a "Statement on Rights and Freedoms of Students" that was endorsed by all five organizations and various other higher education and professional associations. The Joint Statement recognizes the "freedom to learn" and the freedom to teach as "inseparable facets of academic freedom" and emphasizes that "students should be encouraged to develop the capacity for critical judgment and to engage in a sustained and independent search for truth" (*AAUP Policy Documents and Reports*, 273). The statement then elucidates "the minimal standards of academic freedom of students" that apply "in the classroom, on the campus, and in the larger community." This very helpful listing and exposition includes the freedom of "discussion, inquiry, and expression" in the classroom and in conferences with the instructor; the freedom "to organize and join associations" of students, "to examine and discuss" issues and "express opinions publicly and privately" on campus, and "to invite and to hear" guest speakers; the freedom "individually and collectively [to] . . . express views on issues of institutional policy" and "to participate in the formulation and application of institutional policy affecting academic and student affairs"; the "editorial freedom of student publications," that is, "sufficient editorial freedom and financial autonomy . . . to maintain their integrity of purpose as vehicles for free inquiry . . . in an academic community"; and the freedom, "[a]s citizens," to "exercise the rights of citizenship," such as "freedom of speech, peaceful assembly, and right of petition," both on and off campus (*id.* at 273–76). In 1992, the Joint Statement was reviewed, updated (with interpretive footnotes), and reaffirmed by an interassociation task force.

Beginning in the 1950s, the U.S. Supreme Court has gradually, but increasingly, recognized student academic freedom. In one of the earliest and most influential academic freedom cases, *Sweezy v. New Hampshire*, Chief Justice Warren's plurality opinion declared that "[t]eachers *and students* must always remain free to inquire, to study and to evaluate, to gain new maturity and understanding; otherwise our civilization will stagnate and die" (354 U.S. 234, 250 (1957) (emphasis added)). In subsequent years, the Court decided various cases in which it protected students' rights to freedom of speech, press, and association on campus (see, for example, *Widmar v. Vincent*, 454 U.S. 263 (1981), discussed in Section 10.1.5, and *Papish v. Board of Curators of the University of Missouri*, 410 U.S. 667 (1973), discussed in Section 10.3.5). These cases typically were based on generic First Amendment principles that apply both outside and within the context of academia (for example, the "public forum" principles used in *Widmar*) and did not specifically rely on or develop the concept of student academic freedom. In one of these cases, however, *Healy v. James*, 408 U.S. 169 (1972) (Sections 9.4.1 and 10.1.1 of this book), the Court did emphasize that, in upholding the students' right to freedom of association, it was "reaffirming this Nation's dedication to safe-guarding academic freedom" (408 U.S. at 180–81, citing *Sweezy*). Then, in *Rosenberger v. Rector and Visitors of the University of Virginia*, 515 U.S. 819 (1995), the Court, citing both *Sweezy* and *Healy*, further linked student free expression rights with student academic freedom and provided historical context for the linkage.

*Rosenberger* involved a university's refusal to provide student activities funds to a student organization that published a Christian magazine. The Court determined that the refusal was "viewpoint discrimination" that violated the students' right to freedom of expression. (For discussion of this aspect of *Rosenberger*, see Section 10.3.2.) In supporting its conclusion, the Court reasoned:

> The danger [of chilling expression] is especially real in the University setting, where the State acts against a background and tradition of thought and experiment that is at the center of our intellectual and philosophic tradition. See *Healy v. James*, 408 U.S. 169, 180–181 (1972); *Keyishian v. Board of Regents of Univ. of State of N.Y.*, 385 U.S. 589, 603 (1967); *Sweezy v. New Hampshire*, 354 U.S. 234, 250 (1957). In ancient Athens, and, as Europe entered into a new period of intellectual awakening, in places like Bologna, Oxford, and Paris, universities began as voluntary and spontaneous assemblages or concourses for *students to speak and to write and to learn*. See generally R. Palmer & J. Colton, *A History of the Modern World* 39 (7th ed. 1992). The quality and creative power of *student intellectual life* to this day remains a vital measure of a school's influence and attainment. For the University, by regulation, to cast disapproval on particular viewpoints of its students risks the suppression of free speech and *creative inquiry* in one of the vital centers for the Nation's *intellectual life*, its college and university campuses [515 U.S. at 835–36 (emphasis added)].

Thus, although *Rosenberger* is based on free speech and press principles like those the Court used in the earlier students' rights cases, it goes further than these cases in stressing the academic freedom context of the dispute and in emphasizing the student's freedom to learn as well as the student's more generic right to speak.

The case of *Board of Regents of University of Wisconsin System v. Southworth*, 529 U.S. 217 (2000), a mandatory student fees case coming five years after *Rosenberger*, can also be seen as a student academic freedom case. (*Southworth* is discussed in Section 10.1.3 of this book.) Justice Kennedy's majority opinion in *Southworth* did not specifically invoke academic freedom, as his previous majority opinion did in *Rosenberger*, and the students did not prevail in *Southworth* to the extent that they had in *Rosenberger*. Nevertheless, the Court made clear that the justification for subsidizing student organizations through mandatory fee allocations is to provide students "the means to engage in dynamic discussions of philosophical, religious, scientific, social, and political subjects in their extracurricular campus life outside the lecture hall" (529 U.S. at 233). A university that subsidizes student speech for this purpose, however, has a "corresponding duty" to avoid infringing "the speech and beliefs" of students who object to this use of their student fees—a duty that may be fulfilled by assuring that the mandatory fee system is "viewpoint-neutral" (*id.* at 231–33). Thus, the overall justification for the viewpoint-neutral mandatory fee system is, in effect, the promotion of student academic freedom; the university's "duty" to protect objecting students is, in effect, a duty to protect their academic freedom; and the students' right to insist on such protection is, in effect, a First Amendment academic freedom right.

The three concurring Justices in *Southworth*, unlike the majority, did specifically invoke First Amendment academic freedom (*id.* at 236–39). In an opinion by Justice Souter, these three Justices argued that the Court's prior opinions on academic freedom (see generally Section 6.1.5 of this book) provide the legal principles that the Court should have considered in resolving the case, even though these prior precedents would not "control the result in this [case]." While the concurring Justices emphasized the "academic freedom and . . . autonomy" of the institution more than student academic freedom, they did make clear that institutional academic freedom or autonomy does not obliterate student academic freedom. From the concurring Justices' perspective, then, the objecting students' claims could be cast as student academic freedom claims, and the university's defense could be considered an institutional academic freedom or autonomy defense. (Institutional academic freedom is discussed in Section 6.1.7 of this book.)

Before *Rosenberger* and *Southworth*, as suggested above, most student academic freedom claims were based on generic free expression principles. If academic freedom was mentioned by advocates or by the courts, it was as an add-on that gave nuance and additional weight to the traditional free expression claim. *Rosenberger* itself is perhaps the best example of this use of academic freedom arguments. The interests at stake in the earlier cases (and in *Rosenberger* itself), moreover, were traditional First Amendment interests in the right to speak rather than specific interests in the freedom to learn. Some of the cases after *Rosenberger* and *Southworth*, however, can be viewed differently; they are cast as (or are subject to being recast as) freedom to learn cases, that is, true student academic freedom cases. The *Southworth* case, as explained above, provides a kind of transitional example, combining elements of traditional free speech claims and elements of contemporary freedom to learn arguments.

Two post-*Southworth* cases, *Brown v. Li* in 2002 and the *Axson-Flynn* case in 2004, provide instructive examples of the "newer" type of student academic freedom claim. Each of these novel U.S. Court of Appeals cases is discussed immediately below. In *Brown v. Li*, 308 F.3d 939 (9th Cir. 2002), a master's degree candidate at the University of California at Santa Barbara added a "Disacknowledgments" section in his master's thesis in which he crudely criticized the graduate school's dean, university library personnel, a former governor of the state, and others. Because the thesis contained this section, the student's thesis committee did not approve it, resulting in the student exceeding the time limit for completing his degree requirements and being placed on academic probation. Although the university did award the degree several months later, it declined to place the thesis in the university library's thesis archive. When the student (now a graduate) sued the dean, the chancellor, the professors on his thesis committee, and the library director in federal court, claiming that their actions violated his First Amendment free speech rights, both the trial court and the appellate court rejected his claim. The appellate court resolved the case by identifying and considering the academic and curricular interests at stake, taking into account the "university's interest in academic freedom," the "First Amendment rights" of the faculty members, and the "First Amendment rights" of the student. To guide its decision making, the court relied on *Hazelwood School District v. Kuhlmeier*, 484 U.S. 260 (1988), a U.S. Supreme Court precedent granting elementary and secondary school teachers and administrators extensive discretion to make curricular decisions, and expressly adopted the case's reasoning for use in higher education. (See 308 F.3d at 947–52; and see Section 1.4.3 of this book for discussion of transferring lower education precedents to higher education.) Under *Hazelwood*, the appellate court explained, the defendants would prevail if their rejection of the plaintiff's thesis "was reasonably related to a legitimate pedagogical objective" (as the court ruled it was); and in applying this standard, the court would generally "defer[ ] to the university's expertise in defining academic standards and teaching students to meet them" (which the court did).

To supplement this mode of analysis, the court also briefly considered the relationship between the faculty members' academic freedom under the First Amendment and that of the student. Describing a faculty member's right as "a right to . . . evaluate students as determined by his or her independent professional judgment" (see generally Section 6.2.3), the court determined that "the committee members had an affirmative First Amendment right not to approve Plaintiff's thesis." "The presence of [the faculty members'] affirmative right," the court emphasized, "underscores [the student's] lack of a First Amendment right to have his nonconforming thesis approved" (308 F.3d at 952).

Although one may question the court's willingness to apply *Hazelwood* with full force to higher education, as well as the court's stark manner of according faculty academic rights supremacy over student academic rights, *Brown v. Li* nevertheless provides a good description of basic limits on student academic freedom. As a general rule, said the court, faculty members and institutions, consistent with the First Amendment, may "require that a student comply with the terms of an academic assignment"; may refuse to "approve the work of a student that, in [the educator's] judgment, fails to meet a legitimate academic standard"; may limit a "student's speech to that which is germane to a particular academic assignment"; and may "require a student to write a paper from a particular viewpoint, even if it is a viewpoint with which the student disagrees, so long as the requirement serves a legitimate pedagogical purpose" (308 F.3d at 949, 951, 953).

*Axson-Flynn v. Johnson*, 356 F.3d 1277 (10th Cir. 2004), concerned a former student in the University of Utah's Actor in Training Program (ATP) who had objected to reciting certain language that appeared in the scripts she was assigned to perform in her classes. The student's involvement with the ATP had begun with an audition for acceptance into the program. At the audition, she stated that "she would not remove her clothing, 'take the name of God in vain,' 'take the name of Christ in vain,' or 'say the four-letter expletive beginning with the letter F.'" Despite her stipulations, she was admitted to the ATP and began attending classes. The student maintained that she informed her instructors that her stipulations were grounded in her Mormon faith.

When the student performed her first monologue, she omitted two instances of the word "goddamn" but still received an A for her performance. Later in the fall semester, she again sought to omit words that were offensive to her, but her instructor, Barbara Smith, advised her that she "would have to 'get over' her language concerns" and that she could "'still be a good Mormon and say these words.'" Smith delivered an ultimatum that either the student perform the scene as written or receive a zero on the assignment. The instructor eventually relented, however, and the student omitted the offensive words and received a high grade on the assignment. For the rest of the semester, the student continued to omit language that she found offensive from the scripts that she performed.

At the student's end-of-semester review, Smith and two other instructors addressed her omission of profane language from her performances. They advised her that "her request for an accommodation was 'unacceptable behavior'" and "recommended that she 'talk to some other Mormon girls who are good Mormons, who don't have a problem with this.'" The instructors then left the student with this choice: "'You can choose to continue in the program if you modify your values. If you don't, you can leave.'" When the student appealed to the ATP coordinator, he supported the instructors' position. Soon thereafter, the student withdrew from the program (and from the university) because she believed that she would be asked to leave.

Subsequently, the student filed suit against the ATP instructors and the ATP coordinator, alleging violations of her First Amendment rights. She claimed that (1) "forcing her to say the offensive words constitutes an effort to compel her to speak in violation of the First Amendment's free speech clause," and (2) "forcing her to say the offensive words, the utterance of which she considers a sin, violates the First Amendment's free exercise clause." Although the student did not explicitly base her claims on academic freedom principles, it is clear that she considered the defendants' actions to be a restriction on her freedom to learn. The defendants, in contrast, did rely on academic freedom principles, and claimed that "requiring students to perform offensive scripts advances the school's pedagogical interest in teaching acting" (356 F.3d at 1291). In response to the defendants' academic freedom arguments, the appellate court applied the "principle of judicial restraint in reviewing academic decisions" but explained that it did not "view [academic freedom] as constituting a separate right apart from the operation of the First Amendment within the university setting" (356 F.3d at 1293, n.14).

For her free speech claim, the student relied both on the public forum doctrine (see Section 9.4.2 of this book) and on U.S. Supreme Court precedents on "compelled speech" (see *Wooley v. Maynard*, 430 U.S. 705 (1977), and *West Virginia State Board of Education v. Barnette*, 319 U.S. 624 (1943)). The appellate court considered her argument to be that the ATP classrooms were a "public forum" in which the student had a right to be free from content restrictions on her speech, and that the state defendants had compelled her to speak (that is, to recite the profane words in the scripts), which government may not do. The public forum argument could not itself carry the day for the plaintiff, according to the court, since "[n]othing in the record leads us to conclude that . . . the ATP's classrooms could reasonably be considered a traditional public forum [or a] designated public forum" (356 F.3d at 1284–85).

The classrooms were therefore a "nonpublic forum" in which instructors and administrators can regulate student speech "in any reasonable manner." Neither could the compelled speech argument necessarily carry the day for the plaintiff because students' First Amendment rights, in the school environment, "'are not automatically coextensive with the rights of adults in other settings,'" especially "in the context of a school's right to determine what to teach and how to teach it in its classrooms" (356 F.3d at 1284, quoting *Hazelwood v. Kuhlmeier*, above in this section). In establishing these baselines for the analysis, the appellate court, like the court in the earlier *Brown v. Li* case, relied expressly on the U.S. Supreme Court's decision in *Hazelwood School District v. Kuhlmeier*, the elementary/secondary education case.

The *Axson-Flynn* court's analysis did not end there, however, nor should it have. Following *Hazelwood*, the court determined that the student's speech was "school-sponsored speech." This is speech that a school "affirmatively promote[s]" as opposed to speech that it merely "tolerate[s]" and that may fairly be characterized as a part of the school curriculum (whether or not it occurs in a traditional classroom setting) because the speech activities are supervised by faculty members and "designed to impart particular knowledge or skills to student participants and audiences" (356 F.3d at 1286, quoting *Hazelwood* at 271). Regarding such speech, the "school may exercise editorial control 'so long as its actions are reasonably related to legitimate pedagogical concerns'" (*id.* at 1286, quoting *Hazelwood* at 273). Under this standard, the school's restriction of student speech need not be "necessary to the achievement of its [pedagogical] goals," or "the most effective means" or "the most reasonable" means for fulfilling its goals; it need only be a reasonable means (or one among a range of reasonable means) for accomplishing a pedagogical objective.

In determining whether the defendants' compulsion of the student's classroom speech was "reasonably related to legitimate pedagogical concerns," the court gave "substantial deference to [the defendants'] stated pedagogical concern" (356 F.3d at 1290) and declined to "second-guess the pedagogical wisdom or efficacy of [their] goal." In extending this deference, the court noted the generally accepted propositions that "schools must be empowered at times to restrict the speech of their students for pedagogical purposes" and that "schools also routinely require students to express a viewpoint that is not their own in order to teach the students to think critically." As support for these propositions, the court cited *Brown v. Li* and the example from that case quoted earlier in this section.

The *Axson-Flynn* court emphasized, however, that the judicial deference accorded to educators' pedagogical choices is not limitless. In particular, courts may and must inquire "whether the educational goal or pedagogical concern was *pretextual*" (emphasis added). The court may "override an educator's judgment where the proffered goal or methodology was a sham pretext for an impermissible ulterior motive" (356 F.3d at 1292). Thus courts will not interfere "[s]o long as the teacher limits speech or grades speech in the classroom in the name of learning," but they may intervene when the limitation on speech is "a pretext for punishing the student for her race, gender, economic class, religion or political persuasion" (356 F.3d at 1287, quoting *Settle v. Dickson County School Bd.*, 53 F.3d 152, 155–56 (6th Cir. 1995)). Using these principles, the student argued that her instructors' insistence that she speak the words of the script exactly as written was motivated by an "anti-Mormon sentiment" and that their pedagogical justification for their action was merely a pretext. The court was sympathetic to this argument, pointing to the instructors' statements that the student should "speak with other 'good Mormon girls'" who would not omit words from the script, and indicating that these statements "raise[ ] concern that hostility to her faith rather than a pedagogical interest in her growth as an actress was at stake in Defendants' behavior." The appellate court therefore remanded the free speech claim to the district court for further examination of the pretext issue.

On the student's second claim, based on the free exercise of religion, the appellate court framed the issue as whether adherence to the script was a "neutral rule of general applicability" and therefore would not raise "free exercise concerns," or whether it was a "rule that is discriminatorily motivated and applied" and therefore would raise free exercise concerns (see generally Section 1.6.2 of this book). The possibility of pretext based on anti-Mormon sentiment, which the court relied on in remanding the free speech claim, also led it to remand the free exercise issue to the district court for a determination of "whether the script adherence requirement was discriminatorily applied" to the student based on her religion.

Alternatively, regarding free exercise, the student argued and the court considered whether the ATP had a system of "individual exemptions" from the script adherence requirement. If so, the ATP "may not refuse to extend that system to cases of religious hardship without compelling reason" (356 F.3d at 1297, quoting *Employment Division v. Smith*, 494 U.S. 872, 884 (1990)). According to the court, if the ATP instructors or the coordinator could make exceptions to class assignment requirements "on a case-by-case basis" by examining the "specific, personal circumstances" of individual students, this would be "a system of individualized exemptions." Furthermore, if ATP personnel granted exemptions for nonreligious but not for religious hardships, or discriminated among religions in granting or refusing exceptions, substantial free exercise issues would arise even if the class assignment requirements themselves were neutral and nondiscriminatory as to religion. Since there was evidence that one other ATP student, a Jewish student, had received an exception for a religious holiday, and there was no other clarifying information in the record concerning individualized exemptions, the appellate court remanded the free exercise claim to the district court as well.

The *Axson-Flynn* case therefore provides no definitive dispositions of the various issues raised, but it does provide an extended and instructive look at a contemporary "freedom to learn" problem. The court's analysis, once parsed as suggested above, contains numerous legal guidelines regarding the freedom to learn. These guidelines, combined with the more general guidelines found in the *Brown v. Li* case discussed earlier, will provide substantial assistance for administrators and counsel, and for future courts.

More recently, two similar cases from two different federal circuits provided yet other examples of the newer type of student academic freedom problem— although the courts did not explicitly present the cases in this way. In *Keeton v. Anderson-Wiley*, 664 F.3d 865 (11th Cir. 2011), *affirming* 733 F. Supp. 2d 1368 (S.D. Ga. 2010), and *Ward v. Polite*, 667 F.3d 727 (6th Cir. 2012), *reversing Ward v. Wilbanks*, 2010 WL 3026428 (E.D. Mich. 2010), the plaintiff students were enrolled in master's degree programs in counseling at, respectively, Augusta State University (ASU) and Eastern Michigan University. Both students asserted personal objections to program requirements concerning their counseling of homosexual clients. In *Keeton*, the student sought a preliminary injunction preventing her dismissal from the program; in *Ward*, the student was dismissed from the program and filed suit seeking to invalidate the dismissal. Both students asserted violations of their free speech rights and free exercise of religion rights, in particular regarding their expressed beliefs on homosexuality. The appellate courts ruled in the university's favor in the first case and in the student's favor in the other. Both appellate courts relied on the U.S. Supreme Court's opinion in *Hazelwood v. Kuhlmeier*, 484 U.S. 260 (1980), as had the courts in both *Brown v. Li* and *Axson-Flynn v Johnson*.

In *Keeton v. Anderson-Wiley*, the student plaintiff had voiced her intention to inform homosexual clients that their behavior was morally wrong, and to seek conversion therapy for such clients (733 F. Supp. 2d at 1374). The faculty "became concerned that [the student] may not be able to separate her personal, religious-based views . . . from her professional counseling duties, in violation of the ACA [American Counseling Association] Code of Ethics" to which the program adhered. The faculty therefore prescribed a remediation plan for the student. In order to complete this plan and not be dismissed, the student had to be "willing to refrain, in the counseling setting, consistent with professional counseling ethical rules, from imposing her personal views on a counselee's homosexual conduct" (733 F. Supp. 2d at 1375). After refusing to complete the plan, the student sued and sought a preliminary injunction.

Denying the student a preliminary injunction on her free speech claim, the district court found that "requiring students to adhere to the Code as a curricular requirement, appears at this time to be 'reasonably related to legitimate pedagogical concerns'" (733 F. Supp. 2d at 1379, quoting *Hazelwood*, 484 U.S. at 273). In addition, denying a preliminary injunction on the student's free exercise claim, the court found that the defendant's curricular requirement incorporating the ACA Code of Ethics "applies equally to all students enrolled in the program, regardless of religion" (733 F. Supp. 2d at 1380).

On appeal, a three-judge panel of the Eleventh Circuit unanimously affirmed the district court's decision. As a preliminary matter, the court found that ASU's counseling program constituted a nonpublic forum. "As such, school officials 'may impose restrictions on speech that are reasonable and viewpoint neutral'" (664 F.3d at 871, quoting *Pleasant Grove City v. Summum*, 555 U.S. 460, 470 (2009)). With regard to the student's claim that ASU's restrictions represented viewpoint discrimination against her speech, the appellate court acknowledged that "if ASU's officials imposed the remediation plan because of Keeton's personal religious views on homosexuality, it is presumed that they violated her constitutional rights" (664 F.3d at 872). The court determined, however, that

> the evidence in this record does not support [the plaintiff's] claim that ASU's officials imposed the remediation plan because of her views on homosexuality. Rather, as the district court found, the evidence shows that the remediation plan was imposed because she expressed an intent to impose her personal religious views on her clients, in violation of the ACA Code of Ethics, and that the objective of the remediation plan was to teach her how to effectively counsel GLBTQ clients in accordance with the ACA Code of Ethics [664 F.3d at 872].

Then, following the U. S. Supreme Court's *Hazelwood* analysis, the court concluded that the remediation plan "was reasonably related to ASU's legitimate pedagogical concerns in promoting compliance with the ACA Code of Ethics and teaching [the student] to become an effective counselor. Accordingly, the imposition of the remediation plan was a reasonable restriction on Keeton's speech" (644 F.3d at 876).

Concerning whether the university sought to unconstitutionally compel the student to express beliefs with which she disagreed, the court said that ASU was not forcing her to profess a belief contrary to her own personal beliefs. Rather, it was "compelling her to comply with the ACA Code of Ethics, which requires those who wish to be counselors to separate their personal beliefs from their work" (644 F.3d at 878). "If a client determines for himself that his conduct is moral, the ACA Code of Ethics requires the counselor to affirm the client, which means that the counselor must respect the dignity of the client by accepting the client's response without judgment, not that the counselor must say that she personally believes that the client is correct" (644 F.3d at 879).

In denying the student a preliminary injunction on her free exercise claim, the court again focused on the ACA Code of Ethics and the program's incorporation of the code into its curriculum. It concluded that "[n]othing in the record indicates that the object of [this] curricular requirement is to infringe upon or restrict practices because of their religious motivation" (644 F.3d at 880). The appellate court thus affirmed the ruling of the district court—that the student failed to satisfy the requirements for a preliminary injunction.

In *Ward v. Polite*, the student was enrolled in a practicum involving the actual counseling of real clients. She encountered a prospective client who had previously been counseled about his homosexual relationship. On account of her religious beliefs, the student requested that the client be referred to another counselor. Program officials then became concerned that the student was unable to "set aside [her] personal values or belief systems and work with the value system of the client," and that this inability was inconsistent with university policy and the ACA Code of Ethics, which was incorporated into the student handbook. After an informal and then a formal hearing on these charges, the student was dismissed from the program.

Rejecting the student's free speech arguments, the district court determined that the student's "refusal to counsel the client in question constitutes a refusal to complete a curriculum requirement," and that the officials' reasons for dismissing the student were supported by the ACA Code of Ethics and were not "a mere pretext to retaliate against her for expressing her religious beliefs." Referencing *Brown v. Li*, the district court further explained that the "plaintiff does not have a constitutional right to interfere with [the university's] curriculum by demanding that she be allowed to set her own standards for counseling clients under the faculty's State Licensure in the University's clinic." Also rejecting the student's free exercise arguments, based in part on the principles in *Axon-Flynn* above, the district court found that the ACA Code of Ethics applied equally to all students enrolled in the program and that the university did not target the student based on her religious beliefs. Accordingly, the defendants prevailed on a motion for summary judgment.

On appeal, the Sixth Circuit U.S. Court of Appeals reversed and remanded the case (*Ward v. Polite*, 667 F.2d 727 (6th Cir. 2012)). Since the student had appealed from the district court's granting of the defendant's summary judgment motion, the appellate court had to construe the facts in the student's favor. Considering the facts in that way, the court found that a reasonable jury could conclude that the student's professors ejected her from the program because of hostility toward her speech and faith.

Analyzing the student's free speech claim, the appellate court quoted from the U.S. Supreme Court's decision in *Hazelwood School District v. Kuhlmeier*, 484 U.S. at 271, 273, as had the courts in *Keeton* and in *Brown v. Li* and *Axson-Flynn*. According to the appellate court in *Ward*: "Public educators may limit 'student speech in school-sponsored expressive activities so long as their actions are reasonably related to legitimate pedagogical concerns.'" The court explained further, citing *Axson-Flynn*, 356 F.3d at 1289–93, that "the neutral enforcement of a legitimate school curriculum generally will satisfy this requirement; the selective enforcement of such a curriculum or the singling out of one student for discipline based on hostility to her speech will not."

Although the university argued that it dismissed the student from the program because her request for a referral violated the ACA Code of Ethics, the appellate court determined that "a reasonable jury could find . . . that the code of ethics contains no such bar and that the university deployed it as a pretext for punishing [the student's] religious views and speech."

The defendants further argued that, regardless of how the code of ethics has been interpreted, the school had a different policy, an unwritten "blanket rule" that practicum students could not refer any clients. The court held, however, that a reasonable jury could find that this was an after-the-fact invention. "The epitome of a pretextual explanation," the court said, "is a reason never expressed or invoked before."

Regarding the student's free exercise claim, the appellate court determined that the statements made by the program's decision makers at the student's hearing permitted the inference that their actions were motivated by the student's religious beliefs. The court described the hearing as "not a model of dispassion" and noted that many of the comments focused on the student's beliefs and her religious objection to affirming same-sex relationships. The court compared the facts to *Axson-Flynn*, in which the faculty members' statements "created a genuine issue of material fact as to whether [their] justification for [their actions] was truly pedagogical or whether it was a pretext for religious discrimination" (quoting *Axson-Flynn*, 356 F.3d at 1293) (667 F.3d at 735–36).

Since there were factual issues regarding the interpretation of the ACA Code of Ethics, the program's unwritten no-referral rule, and the possible pretext for religious discrimination, the appellate court remanded the case to the district court for further proceedings. The case was settled in late 2012.

Although the *Ward* case and the *Keeton* case have different outcomes, the difference is due more to different facts and different procedural postures of the cases than to judicial disagreements about legal principles. In *Ward*, for instance, the Sixth Circuit reconciled its decision with the Eleventh Circuit's decision in *Keeton* as follows:

> [T]here is less tension, or for that matter even disagreement, between the two cases than initially meets the eye. The procedural settings of the two cases differ. In *Keeton*, the district court made preliminary fact findings after holding a hearing in which both sides introduced evidence in support of their claims. Not only are there no trial-level fact findings here, but Ward also gets the benefit of all reasonable factual inferences in challenging the summary-judgment decision entered against her.
>
> The two claimants' theories of constitutional protection also are miles apart. Keeton insisted on a constitutional right to engage in conversion therapy—that is, if a "client discloses that he is gay, it was her intention to tell the client that this behavior is morally wrong and then try to change the client's behavior." That approach, all agree, violates the ACA Code of Ethics by imposing a counselor's values on a client, a form of conduct the university is free to prohibit as part of its curriculum. Instead of insisting on changing her clients, Ward asked only that the university not change her—that it permit her to refer some clients in some settings, an approach the code of ethics appears to permit and that no written school policy prohibits. Nothing in *Keeton* indicates that Augusta State applied the prohibition on imposing a counselor's values on the client in anything but an even-handed manner. Not so here, as the code of ethics, counseling norms, even the university's own practices, seem to permit the one thing Ward sought: a referral [667 F. 3d at 741].

The court in *Ward* also emphasized how the two decisions share the same legal framework and reasoning:

> They both apply *Hazelwood* to curricular speech at the university level, and they both show that the even-handed enforcement of a neutral policy is likely to steer clear of the First Amendment's free-speech and free-exercise protections. Both decisions also are consistent with *Christian Legal Society* [*v. Martinez*, 130 S. Ct. 2971 (2010), discussed in Section 10.1.4 of this book], which considered whether a Christian organization at a law school could insist that its members adhere to certain faith-based codes of conduct. 130 S. Ct. at 2978. The Court held that the law school's antidiscrimination policy, requiring registered student organizations to accept all comers, did not violate the First Amendment on its face, yet it

remanded the case to determine whether the school selectively enforced the policy against some organizations but not others. *Id*. at 2994–95. While *Keeton* involved Augusta State's across-the-board application of an ethical rule that prohibits counselors from imposing their values on clients, today's case reveals evidence that Eastern Michigan University selectively enforced a no-referral policy against Ward [667 F. 3d at 741–42].

In addition to the judicial developments in the cases above, there have been various other developments in academia that have reflected or stimulated greater emphasis on student academic freedom and what it entails. One major example is the concern about "hostile (learning) environments" (see Section 8.5). Most of the cases thus far have been brought by faculty members asserting violations of their own academic freedom. These cases have made clear that, although faculty members' academic freedom may be "paramount in the academic setting," the faculty members' rights "are not absolute to the point of compromising a student's right to learn in a hostile-free environment" (*Bonnell v. Lorenzo*, 241 F.3d 800, 823–24 (6th Cir. 2001)). Thus the faculty cases have had an important impact on the academic freedom of students, and students have had an increasingly important stake in the disputes between faculty members and their institutions. Indeed, students have lodged some of the complaints that have precipitated such disputes. (See, for example, the *Cohen* case, the *Silva* case, the *Bonnell* case, and the *Hardy* case in Section 6.2.2.) A faculty member's actions may have hindered the students' freedom to learn, for instance, by demeaning certain groups of students, ridiculing certain students' answers, or using the classroom to indoctrinate or proselytize. If the faculty member prevails in such a dispute, student academic freedom may be diminished, and if the institution prevails it may be enhanced (see, for example, the *Bonnell* case and the *Bishop* case in Section 6.2.2). Or a faculty member may have used methods or materials that intrude upon other student interests in learning—for example, their interests in fair grading practices or in freedom from harassment. If the faculty member prevails, such student interests may receive less protection, and if the institution prevails they may receive more (see, for example, the *Bonnell* case in Section 6.2.2). Conversely, a faculty member may have acted in a way that guarded the students' freedom to learn or promoted related student interests; if the faculty member prevails in this situation, the students win too, and if the institution prevails they lose (see, for example, the *Hardy* case in Section 6.2.2). Such faculty cases thus have the potential to focus attention on student academic freedom and to influence the protection of student academic freedom through judicial acceptance or rejection of particular claims of faculty members.

Another contemporary development implicating the freedom to learn is the continuing concern about "speech codes" and their effects on students (see Section 9.5), along with related concerns about the "political correctness" phenomenon on campus. An example of this type of student academic freedom case is *DeJohn v. Temple University*, 537 F.3d 301 (3d Cir. 2008). The plaintiff was "a graduate student pursuing a master's degree in Military and American

History." He was also a member of the Pennsylvania Army National Guard who had been called to active duty in Bosnia while in graduate school. He claimed that Temple's sexual harassment policy inhibited him from "expressing his opinions in class concerning women in combat and women in the military." Because he believed that such discussions could become subject to the Temple policy, he was "concerned that discussing his social, cultural, political, and/or religious views regarding these issues" could subject him to sanctions under the policy. Challenging the policy in court, he invoked the overbreadth doctrine (see generally Section 9.5.2 of this book) and claimed that the policy violated his First Amendment free speech rights because it was so broadly worded that it created a "chilling effect" on his willingness to express his opinions in class.

The federal appellate court, affirming the federal district court, determined that the overbreadth doctrine applies with full force "on public university campuses throughout this country, where free speech is of critical importance *because it is the lifeblood of academic freedom*" (537 F.3d at 314; emphasis added). The Temple policy explicitly applied to "expressive . . . conduct"; and it did not require any showing that the expression caused or would cause "actual, material disruption" (as required by the *Tinker* case; see Section 9.4.1 of this book). Moreover, the policy used words such as "hostile," "offensive," and "gender-motivated" that, on their face,

> [are] sufficiently broad and subjective that they "could conceivably be applied to cover any speech" of a "gender-motivated" nature "the content of which offends someone." This could include "core" political and religious speech, such as gender politics and sexual morality. Absent any requirement akin to a showing of severity or pervasiveness—that is, a requirement that the conduct objectively and subjectively creates a hostile environment or substantially interferes with an individual's work—the policy provides no shelter for core protected speech [537 F.3d at 317–18, citing and quoting *Saxe v. State College Area School District*, 240 F.3d 200 (3d Cir. 2001)].

Determining that the policy was therefore overbroad and that it was not "susceptible to a reasonable limiting construction" that would cure the overbreadth, the court held that the Temple sexual harassment policy was unconstitutional on its face.

Required readings and exercises for student orientation programs have also raised concerns. Diversity training programs for students have raised concerns as well. In *Yacovelli v. Moeser*, 2004 U.S. Dist. LEXIS 9152 (M.D. N.C. 2004), various students and state taxpayers challenged an orientation program at the University of North Carolina at Chapel Hill that involved reading and discussion of an abridged version of the Koran. In a judgment on the pleadings, the court rejected the plaintiffs' claim that the orientation program violated the First Amendment establishment clause. Using the *Lemon v. Kurtzman* three-pronged test (see Section 1.6.4 of this book), the court held that the program met all three prongs. In particular, the court emphasized that "UNC's orientation program does not require participation in a religious activity. The assignment is not to participate in prayer or any other act of worship. Instead, the orientation program is an experience in literary, artistic, and cultural understanding. The orientation program therefore satisfies the second prong of the *Lemon* test, regardless of whether attendance is mandatory." Moreover, the program "was scholarly discourse, not a proselytizing mission" (at *43). In a subsequent ruling in the same case, 324 F.Supp.2d 760 (M.D.N.C. 2004), the court in *Yacovelli* dismissed the plaintiffs' claims that the orientation program violated the free exercise clause. According to the court, the plaintiffs' complaint

> failed to provide sufficient allegations to show that UNC compelled students to perform acts which burdened their religious beliefs, or otherwise punished students on the basis of their religion. To the contrary, UNC implemented a program asking students to discuss a religion thrust into recent controversy, and to do so from an academic perspective. Part of the purpose of this program was to introduce students to the type of higher-level thinking that is required in a university setting. Students who were not members of the Islamic faith, probably the great majority of students, were neither asked nor forced to give up their own beliefs or to compromise their own beliefs in order to discuss the patterns, language, history, and cultural significance of the Qu'ran [324 F. Supp. 2d at 764].

Another example, this time involving training for a single student, arose in the *Keeton* case (discussed earlier in this section). Program officials had required the plaintiff student to complete a remediation plan akin to sensitivity training and focusing particularly on counseling clients who are gay, lesbian, bisexual, transgender, or queer/questioning. The student claimed that this requirement violated her free speech rights. As explained above, both the district and appellate courts denied the student's motion for a preliminary injunction.

In addition, there have been various claims (from within and outside the campus) about politicization and liberal bias in faculty hiring, selection of outside speakers for campus events, development of curriculum, selection of course materials, and the teaching methods, classroom remarks, and grading practices of instructors. In the first years of the twenty-first century, such allegations and concerns led interested parties to draft and sponsor an "Academic Bill of Rights" for consideration by colleges, universities, and state boards and legislatures. The text of the Academic Bill of Rights (ABOR), commentary on the document, and background information on the matters addressed in the document can all be found on the Web site of Students for Academic Freedom, a primary sponsor of ABOR (http://www. studentsforacademicfreedom.org). (For information on this organization, see Sara Hebel, "Students for Academic Freedom: A New Campus Movement," *Chron. Higher Educ.*, February 9, 2004, A18.)

Bills or resolutions supporting ABOR principles were introduced in a number of state legislatures, including those of California, Colorado, Florida, Georgia, Indiana, Ohio, and Pennsylvania. Two resolutions were adopted, one in Georgia and one in Pennsylvania. (See General Assembly of Pennsylvania, House Resolution No. 177, Session of 2005, which established a "select committee" to investigate "academic freedom and intellectual diversity" in Pennsylvania state colleges and universities and community colleges.) A resolution supporting ABOR was also introduced in Congress (House Concurrent Resolution 318, October 2003), and a similar provision was added to a House bill (H.R. 4283, May 2004).

Higher education associations and commentators in and out of academia also vigorously debated the Academic Bill of Rights and its underlying ideas. The debate has focused on the empirical basis for some of the expressed concerns, the nature and extent of the problems that such concerns may present, the extent to which student academic freedom (or faculty academic freedom) may be endangered by the alleged developments addressed by ABOR, and the extent to which ABOR and other suggested solutions for the perceived problems may themselves endanger student, faculty, or "institutional" academic freedom. In June 2005, the American Council on Education and other higher educational organizations released a statement titled "Academic Rights and Responsibilities" that served as a response to much of the debate surrounding the Academic Bill of Rights. The statement, containing "five central or overarching principles" concerning "intellectual pluralism and academic freedom" on campus, is available at http://www.acenet.edu/AM/Template .cfm?Section = HENA&template = /CM/ContentDisplay.cfm&ContentID = 10672.

Since these developments, however, the campaign to adopt ABOR has slowed down. Some of the momentum shifted to alternative proposals concerning "intellectual diversity." These proposals, sometimes in the form of a bill called the "Intellectual Diversity in Higher Education Act" (IDHEA), purport to support intellectual diversity and free exchange of ideas on campus, and to prohibit instructors from indoctrinating students with their own views. Although bills have been introduced in various states, none have become law. A coalition of organizations opposed to ABOR and to intellectual diversity initiatives emerged, called "Free Exchange on Campus." For information on coalition members and the principles and mission of the coalition, see the coalition's Web site, www.freeexchangeoncampus.org. To track these continuing developments, see that Web site, especially under "Legislation Tracker"; the Web site of Students for Academic Freedom, http://www. studentsforacademicfreedom .org; and the AAUP Web site, http://www.aaup.org, especially under "Issues in Higher Education."

### 7.1.5. Students' legal relationships with other students.

Students have a legal relationship not only with the institution, as discussed in many sections of this book, but also with other students, with faculty members, and with staff members. These legal relationships are framed both by external law (see Section 1.4.2), especially tort law and criminal law (which impose duties on all individuals in their relationships with other individuals), and by the internal law of the campus (see Section 1.4.3). For students' peer relationships, the most pertinent internal law is likely to be found in student conduct codes, housing rules, and rules regarding student organizations. Since such rules are created and enforced by and in the name of the institution, colleges and universities (as legal entities) are also typically implicated in student-student relationships and in the resolution of disputes between and among students. In addition, institutions may become implicated in student-student relationships because aggrieved students may sometimes claim that their institution is liable for particular acts of other students. Although students generally do not act as agents of their institutions in their relationships with other students (see generally Section 2.1.3), there are nevertheless various circumstances in which institutions may become liable for acts of students that injure other students.

In *Foster v. Board of Trustees of Butler County Community College*, 771 F. Supp. 1122 (D. Kan. 1991), for example, the institution was held liable for the acts of a student whom the court considered to be a "gratuitous employee" of the institution. In *Morse v. Regents of the University of Colorado*, 154 F.3d 1124 (10th Cir. 1998), the court ruled that the institution would be responsible, under Title IX (see Section 11.5.3 of this book), for the acts of a Reserve Officer Training Corps (ROTC) cadet who allegedly sexually harassed another cadet if the first cadet was "acting with authority bestowed by" the university's ROTC program. And in *Brueckner v. Norwich University*, 730 A.2d 1086 (Vt. 1999), the institution was held liable in tort for certain hazing actions of its upper-class cadets because the university had authorized the cadets to orient and indoctrinate the first-year students and was thus vicariously liable under the doctrine of respondeat superior for the damage the cadets caused by the hazing, even though written university policy forbade hazing activity.

Students themselves can also become liable for harm caused to other students. In some of the fraternity hazing cases, for instance, fraternity members have been held negligent and thus liable for harm to fraternity pledges. In defamation cases, students—especially student newspaper editors—could become liable for defamation of other students. *Mazart v. State* (discussed in Section 10.3.6) illustrates the type of dispute that could give rise to such liability. In other cases, relationships between students may occasion criminal liability. In *State v. Allen*, 905 S.W.2d 874 (Mo. 1995), for example, a student was prosecuted for hazing activities resulting in the death of a fraternity pledge, and the highest court of Missouri upheld the constitutionality of the state's anti-hazing criminal statute. Another possibility for student liability could arise under 42 U.S.C. § 1983, which creates individual liability for violation of persons' constitutional rights (see Section 4.4.4 of this book). This possibility is more theoretical than practical, however, since students, unlike faculty members, usually do not act under "color of law" or engage themselves in state action, as Section 1983 requires.

One of the most serious contemporary problems concerning student relationships is the problem of peer harassment—that is, one student's (or a group of students') harassment of another student (or group of students). The harassment may be on grounds of race, national origin, ethnicity, sex, sexual orientation, religion, disability, or other factors that happen to catch the attention of students at particular times on particular campuses. Such behavior may create disciplinary problems that result in student code of conduct proceedings, and more generally peer harassment may compromise the sense of community to which most institutions aspire.

In addition, peer harassment may sometimes result in legal liabilities: the harasser may become liable to the victim of the harassment, or the institution may become liable to the victim. Tort law—for instance, assault, battery, and intentional infliction of emotional distress—usually forms the basis for such liability. In more severe cases, the student perpetrator may also become subject to criminal liability—for instance, under a stalking law, a sexual assault law, a rape law, a hate crime law, or a criminal anti-hazing law. Some laws, especially federal and state civil rights laws, may also make the institution liable to the student victim in some circumstances in which the institution has supported, condoned, or ignored the harassment. Under the federal Title VI statute (see Section 11.5.2), for example, the Tenth Circuit held that a victim of peer racial harassment would have a private cause of action against a school if the school "intentionally allowed and nurtured a racially hostile educational environment" by being deliberately indifferent to incidents of peer harassment of which it was aware (*Bryant v. Independent School District No. I-38 of Gavin County*, 334 F.3d 928 (10th Cir. 2003)). And under the federal Title IX statute (see Section 11.5.3 of this book), another court held that a student alleging peer sexual harassment would have a cause of action against an institution if she had been sexually assaulted by another student and was "vulnerable" to possible future harassment by the alleged perpetrator due to the institution's unwillingness to provide her "accommodations, either academic or residential," pending completion of the alleged perpetrator's disciplinary hearing (*Kelly v. Yale University*, 2003 WL 1563424, 2003 U.S. Dist. LEXIS 4543 (D. Conn. 2003)).

Most of the rest of this section focuses on peer sexual harassment under Title IX of the Education Amendments of 1972, the statute under which most of the litigation regarding peer harassment has occurred. This material should be read in conjunction with the material in Section 8.5 of this book on faculty harassment of students. The definitions, examples, legal standards, and types of challenges addressed in that section apply, for the most part, to peer harassment as well. As Section 8.5 indicates, *Franklin v. Gwinnett County Public Schools*, 503 U.S. 60 (1992), was the U.S. Supreme Court's first look at student sexual harassment claims under Title IX. But since *Franklin* concerned a faculty member's harassment of a student, it did not address or resolve issues concerning peer sexual harassment or an educational institution's liability to victims of such harassment. These questions were extensively discussed in the lower courts after *Franklin*, however; and as with questions about an institution's liability for faculty harassment, the courts took varying approaches to the problem, ranging from no liability at all (see *Davis v. Monroe County Board of Education*, 120 F.3d 1390 (11th Cir. 1997) (*en banc*)) to liability whenever the institution "knew or should have known" of the harassment (see *Doe v. Petaluma City School District*, 949 F. Supp. 1415 (N.D. Cal. 1996)). The U.S. Department of Education also addressed peer harassment and related liability issues in its document *Sexual Harassment Guidance: Harassment of Students by School Employees, Other Students, or Third Parties*, 62 Fed. Reg. 12034 (March 13, 1997). Regarding peer sexual harassment, this guidance stated that an institution would be liable under Title IX for a student's sexual harassment of another student if "(i) a hostile environment exists in the school's programs or activities, (ii) the school knows or should have known of the harassment, and (iii) the school fails to take immediate and appropriate corrective action" (62 Fed. Reg. at 12039). The guidance also addressed how a school or college may avoid Title IX liability for peer harassment:

> [I]f, upon notice of hostile environment harassment, a school takes immediate and appropriate steps to remedy the hostile environment, the school has avoided violating Title IX . . . Title IX does not make a school responsible for the actions of harassing students, but rather for its own discrimination in failing to remedy it once the school has notice [62 Fed. Reg. at 12039–40].

In *Gebser v. Lago Vista Independent School District*, 524 U.S. 274 (1998), in a hotly contested 5-to-4 decision, the U.S. Supreme Court established an "actual knowledge" and "deliberate indifference" standard of liability for faculty harassment of a student. (For further discussion of this case, see Section 8.5.) It was not clear whether this standard would also apply to an institution's liability for peer harassment. One year later, in *Davis v. Monroe County Board of Education*, 526 U.S. 629 (1999), the Court relieved the uncertainty. In another 5-to-4 decision, the Court majority held that an educational institution's Title IX damages liability for peer harassment is based upon the same standard that the Court had established in *Gebser* to govern liability for faculty harassment:

> We consider here whether the misconduct identified in *Gebser*—deliberate indifference to known acts of harassment—amounts to an intentional violation of Title IX, capable of supporting a private damages action, when the harasser is a student rather than a teacher. We conclude that, in certain limited circumstances, it does [526 U.S. at 643].

The Court took considerable pains to develop the "limited circumstances" that must exist before a school will be liable for peer sexual harassment. First, the school must have "substantial control over both the harasser and the context in which the known harassment occurs" (526 U.S. at 645). Second, the sexual harassment must be "severe, pervasive, and objectively offensive":

> [A] plaintiff must establish sexual harassment of students that is so severe, pervasive, and objectively offensive, and that so undermines and detracts from the victims' educational experience, that the victim-students are effectively denied equal access to an institution's resources and opportunities. Cf. *Meritor Savings Bank, FSB v. Vinson*, 477 U.S. at 57, 67 (1986).
>
> \* \* \* \*
>
> Moreover, the [Title IX requirement] that the discrimination occur "under any education program or activity" suggests that the behavior be serious enough to have the systemic effect of denying the victim equal access to an educational program or activity. Although, in theory, a single instance of sufficiently severe one-on-one peer harassment could be said to have such an effect, we think it unlikely that Congress would have thought such behavior sufficient to rise to this level in light of the inevitability of student misconduct and the amount of litigation that would be invited by entertaining claims of official indifference to a single instance of one-on-one peer harassment. By limiting private damages

actions to cases having a systemic effect on educational programs or activities, we reconcile the general principle that Title IX prohibits official indifference to known peer sexual harassment with the practical realities of responding to student behavior, realities that Congress could not have meant to be ignored [526 U.S. at 651, 652–53].

Speaking for the four dissenters, Justice Kennedy issued a sharply worded and lengthy dissent. In somewhat overblown language, he asserted:

I can conceive of few interventions more intrusive upon the delicate and vital relations between teacher and student, between student and student, and between the State and its citizens than the one the Court creates today by its own hand. Trusted principles of federalism are superseded by a more contemporary imperative. . .

Today's decision mandates to teachers instructing and supervising their students the dubious assistance of federal court plaintiffs and their lawyers and makes the federal courts the final arbiters of school policy and of almost every disagreement between students [526 U.S. at 685, 686 (Kennedy, J., dissenting)].

By highlighting the "limiting circumstances" that confine a school's liability, and adding them to those already articulated in *Gebser*, the Court in *Davis* appears to create a four-part standard for determining when an educational institution would be liable in damages for peer sexual harassment, as follows:

1. The institution must have "actual knowledge" of the harassment;
2. The institution must have responded (or failed to respond) to the harassment with "deliberate indifference," which the *Davis* Court defines as a response that is "clearly unreasonable in light of the known circumstances" (526 U.S. at 648);
3. The institution must have had "substantial control" over the student harasser and the context of the harassment; and
4. The harassment must have been "severe, pervasive, and objectively offensive" to an extent that the victim of the harassment was in effect deprived of educational opportunities or services.

The Court in *Davis* did not address the question of who within the institution must have received notice of the harassment or whether this individual must have authority to initiate corrective action—both factors emphasized in *Gebser*. Presumably, however, these factors would transfer over from *Gebser* to the peer harassment context and become part of the actual knowledge element—the first part of the four-part *Davis* standard.

The *Davis* standard of liability, therefore, is based upon but is not identical to the *Gebser* standard. The Court added additional considerations to the *Davis* analysis that tend to make it even more difficult for a victim to establish a claim of peer harassment than to establish a claim of faculty harassment. As the Court noted near the end of its opinion in *Davis*:

The fact that it was a teacher who engaged in harassment in . . . *Gebser* is relevant. The relationship between the harasser and the victim necessarily affects the extent to which the misconduct can be said to breach Title IX's guarantee of equal access to educational benefits and to have a systemic effect on a program or activity. Peer harassment, in particular, is less likely to satisfy these requirements than is teacher-student harassment [526 U.S. at 653].

The *Davis* Court's emphasis on *control* also suggests that it is more difficult for victims to establish peer harassment claims in higher education litigation than in elementary/secondary litigation. The majority opinion indicates that institutional control over the harasser and the context of the harassment is a key to liability, that the control element of the liability standard "is sufficiently flexible to account . . . for the level of disciplinary authority available to the school," and that "[a] university [would not] . . . be expected to exercise the same degree of control over its students" as would elementary schools (526 U.S. at 649). It should follow that colleges and universities, in general, have less risk of money damages liability under Title IX for peer harassment than do elementary and secondary schools, because colleges and universities exert less control over students and over the educational environment.

Several cases subsequent to *Davis* have considered peer sexual harassment claims that arise in the context of intercollegiate athletics. In a leading case, *Williams v. Board of Regents of the University System of Georgia*, 477 F.3d 1282 (11th Cir. 2007), a female student alleged that she was sexually assaulted and raped by three student athletes, one of whom ("athlete no. 1") had invited her to his campus dormitory room, where the assault took place. The female student claimed that the university's actions with respect to this occurrence, and particularly with respect to athlete no. 1, violated Title IX. Overruling the district court, which had rejected the Title IX claim, the appellate court followed the elements of proof set out in the *Davis* case and concluded that the plaintiff's (female student's) allegations were sufficient to state a valid Title IX claim for damages.

The appellate court emphasized, however, that "this case presents a factually distinct scenario" from prior precedents such as the Supreme Court's decisions in *Gebser* and *Davis*. In those cases, "the defendant did not learn about the alleged harasser's proclivities until the alleged harasser became a teacher or a student at the defendant's school." In this case, in contrast, the plaintiff alleged that university officials "knew about [athlete no. 1's] past sexual conduct when they recruited him and gained his admission to [the university]." This "factual distinctiveness" of the case was "most relevant" to the issue of whether the university was "deliberately indifferent to the alleged discrimination." A concurring judge helpfully characterized the court's distinction as one between "after-the-fact" deliberate indifference and "before-the-fact" deliberate indifference:

> *Gebser* and *Davis* each involved what I would call alleged "after-the-fact" deliberate indifference. The funding recipients in *Gebser* and *Davis* had no knowledge prior to the first acts of discrimination or harassment by, respectively, the teacher and the student. There was no allegation in *Gebser* that the school district hired the offending teacher knowing that he had sexually harassed or

abused students in the past. Likewise, there was no allegation in *Davis* that the school district knew, prior to admitting the offending student, or placing him in a classroom with the plaintiff, that the student had a proclivity for sexual harassment. In both cases, therefore, it made sense to require the plaintiff to show that, after receiving actual notice of the discrimination or harassment, the funding recipient did nothing (or close to nothing) to correct the problem, and that this failure led to further discrimination or harassment against the plaintiff . . . This case is different, and significantly different, than the typical *Gebser/Davis* paradigm in which the funding recipient is oblivious to the threat of discrimination or harassment until some misconduct is committed. [The plaintiff] has alleged that the [university] knew, before recruiting and admitting [athlete no. 1]: (1) that he had sexually attacked two female school employees at his community college's athletic department by groping them and putting his hands down their pants, and (2) that he had made lewd suggestions to a store clerk while attending another college. Ms. Williams has also alleged that the [university], with knowledge of these facts, nevertheless admitted [the athlete] with a full scholarship, under a special admissions program, because it was believed that he could help the basketball program. Reading the complaint in the light most favorable to Ms. Williams, the [university] allegedly did nothing to monitor or counsel [the athlete] after his admission. In short, Ms. Williams has claimed that the deliberate indifference in this case preceded, and proximately caused, her sexual assault and rape. In other words, Ms. Williams has alleged "before-the-fact" deliberate indifference [477 F.3d at 1304–5].

The court determined that Title IX did extend to the "before-the-fact" type of harassment claim and that the plaintiff's allegations concerning the university's "before-the-fact" deliberate indifference (and actual notice) were sufficient to support the plaintiff's "before-the-fact" claim. The crux of these allegations, the court asserted, was that university officials had known of athlete no. 1's "past sexual misconduct" at the time they had him admitted to the university; that these officials had previously received suggestions from student athletes that coaches inform team members of the applicable sexual harassment policy; that these university officials nevertheless had placed athlete no. 1 in a student dormitory room and "failed to adequately supervise" him; and that the university officials' actions and inactions had caused the plaintiff to become the victim of the sexual attack by the three student athletes.

A second case, *Simpson v. University of Colorado Boulder*, 500 F.3d 1170 (10th Cir. 2007), provides another instructive example of peer sexual harassment claims involving student athletes. This case also supports the concept of the "before-the-fact" type of claim and the notion that inadequate training or supervision of student athletes may in some circumstances constitute deliberate indifference. Reversing the district court's grant of summary judgment to the university, and remanding the case for further proceedings, the appellate court in *Simpson* determined:

> In our view, the evidence presented to the district court on CU's motion for summary judgment is sufficient to support findings (1) that CU had an official policy of showing high-school football recruits a "good time" on their visits

to the CU campus, (2) that the alleged sexual assaults were caused by CU's failure to provide adequate supervision and guidance to player-hosts chosen to show the football recruits a "good time," and (3) that the likelihood of such misconduct was so obvious that CU's failure was the result of deliberate indifference. We therefore hold that CU was not entitled to summary judgment [500 F.3d at 1173].

*Davis* and the lower court litigation that has followed is not the last or only word for institutions regarding peer sexual harassment under Title IX. Subsequent to *Davis* (and *Gebser*), the U.S. Department of Education reconsidered and reaffirmed the Title IX guidelines on sexual harassment that it had originally promulgated in 1997. (See "Revised Sexual Harassment Guidance: Harassment of Students by School Employers, Other Students, or Third Parties," 66 Fed. Reg. 5512 (January 19, 2001), also available at http://www2.ed.gov/about/offices/list/ocr/docs/shguide.html.) This revised guidance, which applies to all the department's Title IX enforcement activities involving sexual harassment, was accompanied by substantial commentary (including commentary on the case law) prepared by the department. The guidance and commentary provide colleges and universities with a detailed blueprint for complying with their Title IX responsibilities regarding peer sexual harassment.

Subsequent to the revised guidance, the U.S. Department of Education issued two other sets of related guidelines. The first, a "guidance letter" of October 26, 2010, focuses on the problem of "bullying" that has been escalating in both higher education and K–12 education in recent years. The Education Department acknowledged in the letter that it "focuses on the elementary and secondary school context" but that "the legal principles also apply to postsecondary institutions." The letter frames bullying as conduct that may constitute "discriminatory harassment" by peers under federal civil rights laws enforced by the Education Department's Office for Civil Rights (OCR). Bullying a gay student, for example, may be covered by Title IX because "it can be sex discrimination if students are harassed either for exhibiting what is perceived as a stereotypical characteristic for their sex, or for failing to conform to stereotypical notions of masculinity and femininity"; and such coverage may apply "regardless of the actual or perceived sexual orientation or gender identity of the harasser or target." (See generally pp. 7–8 of the letter, discussing sexual orientation harassment.) The letter also explains and clarifies schools' and colleges' responsibilities to combat bullying under the laws enforced by OCR, and suggests various good practices and various resources for K–12 schools and higher educational institutions. The letter may be found at http://www2.ed.gov/about/offices/list/ocr/letters/colleague-201010.pdf.

The second related guidance is an April 4, 2011, "Dear Colleague" letter on sexual violence. This letter emphasizes that "[s]exual violence is a form of sexual harassment under Title IX," addresses colleges' and universities' responsibilities under Title IX when students report that they have been sexually assaulted, and outlines suggested procedures for institutions to take when fulfilling these responsibilities or seeking to avoid such situations. This Dear

Colleague letter may be found at http://www2.ed.gov/about/offices/list/ocr/letters/colleague-201104.html.

## Section 7.2. Admissions

### 7.2.1. Basic legal requirements.

Postsecondary institutions have traditionally been accorded wide discretion in formulating admissions standards. The law's deference to institutional decision making stems from the notion that tampering with admissions criteria is tampering with the expertise of educators. In the latter part of the twentieth century, however, some doorways were opened in the wall of deference, as dissatisfied applicants successfully pressed the courts for relief and legislatures and administrative agencies sought to regulate certain aspects of the admissions process.

Institutions are subject to three main constraints in formulating and applying admissions policies: (1) the selection process must not be arbitrary or capricious; (2) the institution may be bound, under a contract theory, to adhere to its published admissions standards and to honor its admissions decisions; and (3) the institution may not have admissions policies that unjustifiably discriminate on the basis of characteristics such as race, sex, disability, age, residence, or citizenship. These constraints are discussed in Sections 7.2.2 to 7.2.4.

Although institutions are also constrained in the admissions process by the Family Education and Privacy Rights Act (FERPA) regulations on education records (Section 7.8.1), these regulations have only limited applicability to admissions records. The regulations do not apply to the records of persons who are not or have not been students at the institution; thus, admissions records are not covered until the applicant has been accepted and is in attendance at the institution (34 C.F.R. §§ 99.1(d), 99.3 ("student")). The institution may also maintain the confidentiality of letters of recommendation if the student has waived the right of access; such a waiver may be sought by the letter writer during the application process (34 C.F.R. § 99.12). Moreover, when a student from one component unit of an institution applies for admission to another unit of the same institution, the student is treated as an applicant rather than as a student with respect to the second unit's admissions records; those records are therefore not subject to FERPA until the student is in attendance in the second unit (34 C.F.R. § 99.5).

Students applying to public institutions may also assert constitutional claims based on the due process clause of the Fourteenth Amendment. In *Phelps v. Washburn University of Topeka*, 634 F. Supp. 556 (D. Kan. 1986), for example, the plaintiffs asserted procedural due process claims regarding a grievance process available to rejected applicants. The court ruled that the plaintiffs had no property interest in being admitted to the university, thus defeating their due process claims. And in *Martin v. Helstad*, 578 F. Supp. 1473 (W.D. Wis. 1983), the plaintiff sued a law school that revoked its acceptance of his application when it learned that he had neglected to include on his application that he had been convicted of a felony and incarcerated. The court held that, although the applicant was entitled to minimal procedural due process to respond to the school's charge that he had falsified information on his application, the school had provided him sufficient due process in allowing him to explain his nondisclosure.

Falsification of information on an application may also be grounds for later discipline or expulsion. In *North v. West Virginia Board of Regents*, 332 S.E.2d 141 (W. Va. 1985), a medical student provided false information on his application concerning his grade point average, courses taken, degrees, birth date, and marital status. The court upheld the expulsion on two theories: that the student had breached the university's disciplinary code (even though he was not a student at the time) and that the student had committed fraud.

The University of California has a policy that requires admissions staff to review and approve high school courses involving religion or ethics taken by applicants in order to determine if these courses may be counted toward the required number of high school courses presented by applicants for admission. In *Association of Christian Schools International v. Stearns*, 362 F. App'x 640 (9th Cir. 2010), a federal appellate court rejected the claims of an association of Christian schools that the University of California's review policy violated the free speech, free expression, free exercise, and equal protection clauses of the U.S. Constitution. According to the court, the challenged policy "provides that in order to receive UC approval, religion and ethics courses should 'treat the study of religion or ethics from the standpoint of scholarly inquiry, rather than in a manner limited to one denomination or viewpoint.'"

The court rejected all of the plaintiffs' constitutional challenges to the policy, both facial and as applied. The admissions staff used consistent guidelines to evaluate the courses, said the court, and their review did not favor or disfavor any particular religion. Nor did the policy encourage viewpoint discrimination, because the staff had approved a variety of religion courses that included religious texts and religious doctrine. The issue, said the court, was whether the course treated religion in a scholarly fashion or was limited to one denomination or viewpoint. The policy did not suppress speech or punish schools for teaching these courses or students for taking them, said the court. The intent of the policy was to ensure that students were prepared for "the rigors of academic study at UC." Furthermore, said the court, the policy did not violate the equal protection clause; whether a course is rigorous enough to be considered "college preparatory" is not a suspect classification, and the policy easily met the rational basis test.

### 7.2.2. Arbitrariness.
The "arbitrariness" standard of review is the one most protective of the institution's prerogatives. The cases reflect a judicial hands-off attitude toward any admissions decision arguably based on academic qualifications. Under the arbitrariness standard, the court will overturn an institution's decision only if there is no reasonable explanation for the institution's actions. *Lesser v. Board of Education of New York*, 239 N.Y.S.2d 776 (N.Y. App. Div. 1963), provides a classic example. Lesser sued Brooklyn College after being rejected because his grade point average was below the cutoff. He argued that the college acted arbitrarily and unreasonably in not considering

that he had been enrolled in a demanding high school honors program. The court declined to overturn the judgment of the college, stating that discretionary decisions of educational institutions, particularly those related to determining the eligibility of applicants, should be left to the institutions.

Another court, in considering whether a public university's refusal to admit a student to veterinary school involved constitutional protections, rejected arbitrariness claims based on the due process and equal protection clauses. In *Grove v. Ohio State University*, 424 F. Supp. 377 (S.D. Ohio 1976), the plaintiff, denied admission to veterinary school three times, first argued that the use of a score from a personal interview introduced subjective factors into the admissions decision process that were arbitrary and capricious, thus depriving him of due process. Second, he claimed that the admission of students less well qualified than he deprived him of equal protection. And third, he claimed that a professor had told him he would be admitted if he took additional courses.

Citing *Roth* (see Section 5.7.2 of this book), the court determined that the plaintiff had a liberty interest in pursuing veterinary medicine. The court then examined the admissions procedure and concluded that, despite its subjective element, it provided sufficient due process protections. The court deferred to the academic judgment of the admissions committee with regard to the weight that should be given to the interview score. The court also found no property interest, since the plaintiff had no legitimate entitlement to a space in a class of 130 when more than 900 individuals had applied.

The court rejected the plaintiff's second and third claims as well. The plaintiff had not raised discrimination claims, but had asserted that the admission of students with lower grades was a denial of equal protection. The court stated: "This Court is reluctant to find that failure to adhere exactly to an admissions formula constitutes a denial of equal protection" (424 F. Supp. at 387), citing *Bakke* (see Section 7.2.5 of this book). Nor did the professor's statement that the plaintiff would be reconsidered for admission if he took additional courses constitute a promise to admit him once he completed the courses.

A convicted felon who was denied admission to a social work program at the University of Alaska at Anchorage was unsuccessful in his attempt to persuade a court that the university's decision was arbitrary. In *Purcell v. University of Alaska Anchorage*, Case No. 3AN-05-09374 CI (Alaska Ct. App. 2006), the judge ruled that the university had followed its policies for considering applicants with a history of felonies. Purcell had killed a man and had served twenty years in prison; the judge ruled that the university's "detailed deliberations" concerning his application defeated his claim that the decision was arbitrary (Peter Monaghan, "Judge Upholds U. of Alaska's Right to Deny Felon Admission to Social-Work Program," *Chron. Higher Educ.*, November 3, 2006, available at http://chronicle.com/article/Judge-Upholds-U-of-Alaskas/31715/).

The review standards in these cases establish a formidable barrier for disappointed applicants to cross. But occasionally someone succeeds. *State ex rel. Bartlett v. Pantzer*, 489 P.2d 375 (Mont. 1971), arose after the admissions committee of the University of Montana Law School had advised an applicant that he would be accepted if he completed a course in financial accounting. He took such a course and received a D. The law school refused to admit him, claiming that a D was an "acceptable" but not a "satisfactory" grade. The student argued that it was unreasonable for the law school to inject a requirement of receiving a "satisfactory grade" after he had completed the course. The court agreed, saying that the applicant was otherwise qualified for admission and that to make a distinction between "acceptable" and "satisfactory" was an abuse of institutional discretion.

All these cases involve public institutions; whether their principles would apply to private institutions is unclear. The "arbitrary and capricious" standard apparently arises from concepts of due process and administrative law that are applicable only to public institutions. Courts may be even less receptive to arbitrariness arguments lodged against private schools, although common law may provide some relief even here. In *Levine v. George Washington University* (discussed in Section 7.2.6), for example, common law principles protected students at private institutions against arbitrary interpretation of institutional policy.

The cases discussed in this section demonstrate that, if the individuals and groups who make admissions decisions adhere carefully to their published (or unwritten) criteria, give individual consideration to every applicant, and provide reasonable explanations for the criteria used in making decisions, judicial review will be deferential.

### 7.2.3. The contract theory.

Students who are accepted for admission, but whose admission is reversed by the institution through no fault of the student, have met with some success in stating breach of contract claims. For example, the plaintiffs in *Eden v. Board of Trustees of the State University*, 374 N.Y.S.2d 686 (N.Y. App. Div. 1975), had been accepted for admission to a new school of podiatry being established at the State University of New York (SUNY) at Stony Brook. Shortly before the scheduled opening, the state suspended its plans for the school, citing fiscal pressures in state government. The students argued that they had a contract with SUNY entitling them to instruction in the podiatry school. The court agreed that SUNY's "acceptance of the petitioners' applications satisfies the classic requirements of a contract." Though the state could legally abrogate its contracts when necessary in the public interest to alleviate a fiscal crisis, and though "the judicial branch . . . must exercise restraint in questioning executive prerogative," the court nevertheless ordered the state to enroll the students for the ensuing academic year. The court found that a large federal grant as well as tuition money would be lost if the school did not open, that the school's personnel were already under contract and would have to be paid anyway, and that postponement of the opening therefore would not save money. Since the fiscal crisis would not be alleviated, the state's decision was deemed "arbitrary and capricious" and a breach of contract.

An Illinois appellate court ruled that a combination of oral promises, past practice, written promises, and a lack of notice about a change in admission standards constituted an implied promise to admit ten students to the Chicago Medical School. In *Brody v. Finch University of Health Sciences/Chicago Medical*

*School*, 698 N.E.2d 257 (Ill. App. Ct. 1998), the plaintiffs enrolled in a master's degree program in applied physiology because they had been promised, both orally and in the college's written documents, that they would be admitted to the medical school if they earned a 3.0 average or better. They had also been told that the college had followed this practice for several years. The year that the plaintiffs applied to the medical school, however, the school changed its practice of accepting all qualified graduates from the applied physiology program and instead admitted only the top fifty. Six of the plaintiffs had received letters stating that they had been admitted, while the remaining plaintiffs had been told orally that they would be admitted. But the plaintiffs were not admitted and were not advised of this until shortly before the program was to begin. Some of the plaintiffs had resigned from their jobs and moved to Chicago; many had signed housing leases; and several had given up opportunities for study at other medical colleges.

The trial court ruled that the combination of the written statements, the oral promises, and the college's past practice created an implied contract, and that the college's determination two weeks prior to the beginning of the program to admit only fifty students from the applied physiology program was arbitrary and capricious. The college had made no effort to contact the students who were not admitted, and the applicants had reasonably relied on the representations of college employees, written documents from previous years, and the college's past practice of admitting all applicants with a 3.0 or better grade point average. The appellate court affirmed, endorsing the trial court's analysis. (The applicants' state law consumer fraud cause of action had been rejected by the trial court because they had not addressed consumer protection issues in their complaint; the appellate court affirmed on this claim as well.)

The contract theory clearly applies to both public and private schools, although, as *Eden* suggests, public institutions may have defenses not available to private schools. While the contract theory does not require administrators to adopt or to forgo any particular admissions standard, it does require that administrators honor their acceptance decisions once made and honor their published policies in deciding whom to accept and to reject. Administrators should thus carefully review their published admissions policies and any new policies to be published. The institution may wish to omit standards and criteria from its policies in order to avoid being pinned down under the contract theory. Conversely, the institution may decide that full disclosure is the best policy. In either case, administrators should make sure that published admissions policies state only what the institution is willing to abide by. If the institution needs to reserve the right to depart from or supplement its published policies, such reservation should be clearly inserted, with counsel's assistance, into all such policies.

### 7.2.4. *The principle of nondiscrimination*

***7.2.4.1. Race.*** It is clear under the Fourteenth Amendment's equal protection clause that, in the absence of a "compelling state interest" (see Section 7.2.5 of this book), no public institution may discriminate in admissions on the basis of race. The leading case is *Brown v. Board of Education*, 347 U.S. 483 (1954), which, although it concerned elementary and secondary schools, clearly applies to postsecondary education as well. The Supreme Court affirmed its relevance to higher education in *Florida ex rel. Hawkins v. Board of Control*, 350 U.S. 413 (1956). Cases involving postsecondary education have generally considered racial segregation within a state postsecondary system rather than within a single institution, and suits have been brought under Title VI of the Civil Rights Act of 1964 as well as the U.S. Constitution. These cases are discussed in Section 11.5.2.

Although most of the racial segregation cases focus on a broad array of issues, a decision by the U.S. Supreme Court addressed admissions issues, among others. In *United States v. Fordice*, 505 U.S. 717 (1992), private plaintiffs and the U.S. Department of Justice asserted that the Mississippi public higher education system was segregated, in violation of both the U.S. Constitution and Title VI of the Civil Rights Act of 1964. Although a federal trial judge had found the state system to be in compliance with both Title VI and the Constitution, a federal appellate court and the U.S. Supreme Court disagreed. (This case is also discussed in Section 11.5.2.)

Justice White, writing for a unanimous Court, found that the state's higher education system retained vestiges of its prior *de jure* segregation. With regard to admissions, Justice White cited the state's practice (initiated in 1963, just prior to Title VI's taking effect) of requiring all applicants for admission to the three flagship universities (which were predominantly white) to have a minimum composite score of 15 on the American College Testing (ACT) Program. Testimony had demonstrated that the average ACT score for white students was 18, and the average ACT score for African American students was 7. Justice White wrote: "Without doubt, these requirements restrict the range of choices of entering students as to which institution they may attend in a way that perpetuates segregation" (505 U.S. at 734).

These admissions standards were particularly revealing of continued segregation, according to Justice White, when one considered that institutions given the same mission within the state (regional universities) had different admissions standards, depending on the race of the predominant student group. For example, predominantly white regional universities had ACT requirements of 18 or 15, compared to minimum requirements of 13 at the predominantly black universities. Because the differential admissions standards were "remnants of the dual system with a continuing discriminatory effect" (505 U.S. at 736), the state was required to articulate an educational reason for those disparities, and it had not done so.

Furthermore, the institutions looked only at ACT scores and did not consider high school grades as a mitigating factor for applicants who could not meet the minimum ACT score. The gap between the grades of African American and white applicants was narrower than the gap between their ACT scores, "suggesting that an admissions formula which included grades would increase the number of black students eligible for automatic admission to all of Mississippi's public universities" (505 U.S. at 737). Although the state had argued that grade inflation and the lack of comparability among high schools' course offerings and grading practices made grades an unreliable indicator, the Court dismissed that argument:

> In our view, such justification is inadequate because the ACT was originally adopted for discriminatory purposes, the current requirement is traceable to that decision and seemingly continues to have segregative effects, and the State has so far failed to show that the "ACT-only" admission standard is not susceptible to elimination without eroding sound educational policy [505 U.S. at 737–38].

The use of high school grades as well as scores on standardized tests is common in higher education admissions decisions, and the state's attempt to rely solely on ACT scores was an important element of the Court's finding of continued segregation.

Although most challenges to allegedly discriminatory admissions requirements have come from African-American students, Asian and Latino students have filed challenges as well. In *United States v. League of United Latin American Citizens*, 793 F.2d 636 (5th Cir. 1986), African-American and Latino college students raised Title VI and constitutional challenges to Texas's requirement that college students pass a reading and mathematics skills test before enrolling in more than six hours of courses preparing students to be teachers at Texas public institutions. Passing rates on these tests were substantially lower for minority students than for white, non-Latino students.

Although the trial court had enjoined the practice, the appellate court vacated the injunction, noting that the state had validated the tests and that they were appropriate: "The State's duty . . . to eliminate the vestiges of past discrimination would indeed be violated were it to thrust upon minority students, both as role models and as pedagogues, teachers whose basic knowledge and skills were inferior to those required of majority race teachers" (793 F.2d at 643).

In response to the students' equal protection claim, the court found that the state had demonstrated a compelling interest in teacher competency and that the test was a valid predictor of success in the courses. Because the students could retake the test until they passed it, their admission was only delayed, not denied. In response to the students' liberty interest claim, the court found a valid liberty interest in pursuing a chosen profession, but also found that the state could require a reasonable examination for entry into that profession.

In another case, Latino students and civil rights groups challenged Texas's funding for public colleges and universities located near the Mexican border, arguing that they received fewer funds because of their high proportion of Latino students. A jury, applying the state constitution's requirement of equal access to education, found that the state higher education system did not provide equal access to citizens in southern Texas, although it also found that state officials had not discriminated against these persons. A state court judge later ordered the state to eliminate the funding inequities among state institutions.

But in *Richards v. League of United Latin American Citizens*, 868 S.W.2d 306 (Tex. 1993), the Texas Supreme Court ruled later that year that allegedly inequitable resource allocation to predominantly Hispanic public colleges did not violate students' equal protection rights.

Asian students have challenged the admissions practices of several institutions, alleging that the institutions either have "quotas" limiting the number of Asians who may be admitted or that they exclude Asians from minority admissions programs. Complaints filed with the Education Department's Office for Civil Rights (OCR), which enforces Title VI (see Section 11.5.2 of this book), have resulted in changes in admissions practices at both public and private colleges and universities.

In addition to the Constitution's equal protection clause and the desegregation criteria developed under Title VI, there are two other major legal bases for attacking racial discrimination in higher education. The first is the civil rights statute 42 U.S.C. § 1981 (discussed in Section 4.5.2.4 of this book). A post–Civil War statute guaranteeing the freedom to contract, Section 1981 has particular significance because (like Title VI) it applies to private as well as public institutions. In the leading case of *Runyon v. McCrary*, 427 U.S. 160 (1976), the U.S. Supreme Court used Section 1981 to prohibit two private, white elementary schools from discriminating against blacks in their admissions policies. Since the Court has applied Section 1981 to discrimination against white persons as well as blacks (*McDonald v. Santa Fe Trail Transportation Co.*, 427 U.S. 273 (1976)), this statute would also apparently prohibit predominantly minority private institutions from discriminating in admissions against white students. (For an example of a challenge to a denial of admission to graduate school brought under both Title VI and Section 1981, see *Woods v. The Wright Institute*, 1998 U.S. App. LEXIS 6012 (9th Cir. March 24, 1998) (using subjective judgments as one of several criteria for admissions is not racially discriminatory).)

Section 1981 was used in a challenge to the racially exclusive admissions policy of the Kamehameha Schools in Hawaii. The schools had been established under the will of Princess Bernice Pauahi Bishop, the last direct descendant of King Kamehameha I. Her will directed that private, nonsectarian schools be established, and three such schools now exist, none of which receives federal funds. Although the will did not direct that applicants of Hawaiian descent be preferred, the trustees of the trust created by her will directed that Native Hawaiians be preferred, which meant that, unless there were space available, only individuals of Hawaiian descent would be admitted to the schools. In *Doe v. Kamehameha Schools*, 416 F.3d 1025 (9th Cir. 2005), a white student challenged the admissions policy of the schools under Section 1981, suing the schools, the estate, and the trustees. The appellate court ruled that the schools' policy acted as an absolute bar to admission on the basis of race and thus violated Section 1981. Because the will had not specified racial criteria for admissions, the court upheld the lower court's award of summary judgment for the estate and the trustees.

The schools requested that the full Ninth Circuit review the ruling of the three-judge panel. In an *en banc* opinion, the court reversed, thus upholding the schools' racially exclusive admissions criteria favoring Native Hawaiian students. The *en banc* opinion, found at 470 F.3d 827 (9th Cir. 2006), first had to resolve what standard of review to use in assessing whether the admissions policy violated 42 U.S.C. § 1981. The majority determined that the *Weber* test (see Section 4.6.2 of this book), created in response to a Title VII challenge to affirmative action in employment, provided an appropriate standard for reviewing claims brought under Section 1981. Determining that the preferential admissions policy met all three prongs of the *Weber* test, the *en banc* majority ruled that the policy did not violate Section 1981.

Another mechanism for attacking race discrimination in admissions is federal income tax law. In Revenue Ruling 71447, 1971-2 C.B. 230 (*Cumulative Bulletin*, an annual multivolume compilation of various tax documents published by the Internal Revenue Service (IRS)), the IRS revised its former policy and ruled that schools practicing racial discrimination were violating public policy and should be denied tax-exempt status. Other IRS rulings enlarged on this basic rule. Revenue Procedure 72-54, 1972-2 C.B. 834, requires schools to publicize their nondiscrimination policies. Revenue Procedure 75-50, 1975-2 C.B. 587, requires that a school carry the burden of "show[ing] affirmatively . . . that it has adopted a racially nondiscriminatory policy as to students"; the ruling also establishes record-keeping and other guidelines through which a school can demonstrate its compliance. And Revenue Ruling 75-231, 1975-1 C.B. 158, furnishes a series of hypothetical cases to illustrate when a church-affiliated school would be considered to be discriminating and in danger of losing tax-exempt status. The U.S. Supreme Court upheld the basic policy of Revenue Ruling 71-447 in *Bob Jones University v. United States*, 461 U.S. 574 (1983). A private institution must certify that it has adopted and is following a policy of nondiscrimination in order for contributions to that institution to be tax deductible. However, the Internal Revenue Service has exempted organizations that provide instruction in a skilled trade to American Indians from the nondiscrimination requirement, ruling that limiting access to the training to American Indians was not the type of discrimination that federal law intended to prevent (Revenue Ruling 77-272, 1977-2 C.B. 191).

The combined impact of these various legal sources—the equal protection clause, Title VI, Section 1981, and IRS tax rulings—is clear: neither public nor private postsecondary institutions may maintain admissions policies (with a possible exception for affirmative action policies, as discussed in Section 7.2.5 of this book) that discriminate against students on the basis of race, nor may states maintain plans or practices that perpetuate racial segregation in a statewide system of postsecondary education.

**7.2.4.2. Sex.** Title IX of the Education Amendments of 1972 (20 U.S.C. §§ 1681 et seq.) (see Section 11.5.3 of this book) is the primary law governing sex discrimination in admissions policies. Although Title IX and its implementing regulations, 34 C.F.R. Part 106, apply nondiscrimination principles to both public and private institutions receiving federal funds, there are special exemptions concerning admissions. For the purposes of applying these admissions exemptions, each "administratively separate unit" of an institution is considered a separate institution (34 C.F.R. § 106.15(b)). An "administratively separate unit" is "a school, department, or college . . . admission to which is independent of admission to any other component of such institution" (34 C.F.R. § 106.2(p)). Private undergraduate institutions are not prohibited from discriminating in admissions on the basis of sex (20 U.S.C. § 1681(a)(1); 34 C.F.R. § 106.15(d)). Nor are public undergraduate institutions that have always been single-sex institutions (20 U.S.C. § 1681(a)(5); 34 C.F.R. § 106.15(e)); but compare the *Hogan* case, discussed later in this section). In addition, religious institutions, including all or any of their administratively separate units, may be exempted from nondiscrimination. The remaining institutions, which are prohibited from discriminating in admissions, are (1) graduate schools; (2) professional schools, unless they are part of an undergraduate institution exempted from Title IX's admissions requirements (see 34 C.F.R. § 106.2(n)); (3) vocational schools, unless they are part of an undergraduate institution exempted from Title IX's admissions requirements (see 34 C.F.R. § 106.2(o)); and (4) public undergraduate institutions that are not, or have not always been, single-sex schools.

Institutions subject to Title IX admissions requirements are prohibited from treating persons differently on the basis of sex in any phase of admissions and recruitment (34 C.F.R. §§ 106.21–106.23). Specifically, 34 C.F.R. § 106.21(b) provides that a covered institution, in its admissions process, shall not

(i)   Give preference to one person over another on the basis of sex, by ranking applicants separately on such basis, or otherwise;

(ii)  Apply numerical limitations upon the number or proportion of persons of either sex who may be admitted; or

(iii) Otherwise treat one individual differently from another on the basis of sex.

Section 106.21(c) prohibits covered institutions from treating the sexes differently in regard to "actual or potential parental, family, or marital status"; from discriminating against applicants because of pregnancy or conditions relating to childbirth; and from making preadmission inquiries concerning marital status. Sections 106.22 and 106.23(b) prohibit institutions from favoring single-sex or predominantly single-sex schools in their admissions or recruitment practices if such practices have "the effect of discriminating on the basis of sex."

Institutions that are exempt from Title IX admissions requirements are not necessarily free to discriminate at will on the basis of sex. Some will be caught in the net of other statutes or of constitutional equal protection principles. A state statute such as the Massachusetts statute prohibiting sex discrimination in vocational training institutions may catch other exempted undergraduate programs (Mass. Gen. Laws Ann. ch. 151C, § 2A(a)). More important, the Fourteenth Amendment's equal protection clause places restrictions on public undergraduate schools even if they are single-sex schools exempt from Title IX.

After a period of uncertainty concerning the extent to which equal protection principles would restrict a public institution's admissions policies, the U.S.

Supreme Court considered the question in *Mississippi University for Women v. Hogan*, 458 U.S. 718 (1982). In this case, the plaintiff challenged an admissions policy that excluded males from a professional nursing school. Ignoring the dissenting Justices' protestations that Mississippi provided baccalaureate nursing programs at other state coeducational institutions, the majority of five struck down the institution's policy as unconstitutional sex discrimination. In the process, the Court developed an important synthesis of constitutional principles applicable to sex discrimination claims. These principles would apply not only to admissions but also to all other aspects of a public institution's operations:

> Because the challenged policy expressly discriminates among applicants on the basis of gender, it is subject to scrutiny under the equal protection clause of the Fourteenth Amendment . . . That this statute discriminates against males rather than against females does not exempt it from scrutiny or reduce the standard of review . . . Our decisions also establish that the party seeking to uphold a statute that classifies individuals on the basis of their gender must carry the burden of showing an "exceedingly persuasive justification" for the classification . . . The burden is met only by showing at least that the classification serves "important governmental objectives and that the discriminatory means employed" are "substantially related to the achievement of those objectives" [citations omitted] . . . [458 U.S. at 723–24].

Applying the principles regarding the legitimacy and importance of the state's objective, the Court noted that the state's justification for prohibiting men from enrolling in the nursing program was to compensate for discrimination against women. On the contrary, the Court pointed out, women had never been denied entry to the nursing profession, and limiting admission to women actually perpetuated the stereotype that nursing is "women's work." The state had made no showing that women needed preferential treatment in being admitted to nursing programs, and the Court did not believe that that was the state's purpose in discriminating against men. And even if the state had a valid compensatory objective, said the Court, the university's practice of allowing men to audit the classes and to take part in continuing education courses offered by the school contradicted its position that its degree programs should be available only to women.

The Court's opinion on its face invalidated single-sex admissions policies only at the School of Nursing at Mississippi University for Women (MUW) and, by extension, other public postsecondary nursing schools. It is likely, however, that this reasoning would also invalidate single-sex policies in programs other than nursing and in entire institutions. The most arguable exception to this broad reading would be a single-sex policy that redresses the effects of past discrimination on a professional program in which one sex is substantially underrepresented. But even such a compensatory policy would be a form of explicit sexual quota, which could be questioned by analogy to the racial affirmative action cases (see this book, Section 7.2.5).

Whatever the remaining ambiguity about the scope of the *Hogan* decision, it will not be resolved by further litigation at the Mississippi University for

Women. After the Supreme Court decision, MUW's board of trustees—perhaps anticipating a broad application of the Court's reasoning—voted to admit men to all divisions of the university.

The *Hogan* opinion provided important guidance in a challenge to the lawfulness of male-only public military colleges. In *United States v. Commonwealth of Virginia*, 766 F. Supp. 1407, *vacated*, 976 F.2d 890 (4th Cir. 1992), the U.S. Department of Justice challenged the admissions policies of the Virginia Military Institute (VMI), which admitted only men. The government claimed that those policies violated the equal protection clause (it did not include a Title IX claim, since military academies and historically single-sex institutions are exempt from Title IX). Equal protection challenges to sex discrimination require the state to demonstrate "an exceedingly persuasive justification" for the classification (*Hogan*, 458 U.S. at 739). In this case the state argued that enhancing diversity by offering a distinctive single-sex military education to men was an important state interest. The district court found that the single-sex policy was justified because of the benefits of a single-sex education, and that requiring VMI to admit women would "fundamentally alter" the "distinctive ends" of the educational system (766 F. Supp. at 1411).

The appellate court vacated the district court's opinion, stating that Virginia had not articulated an important objective sufficient to overcome the burden on equal protection. While the appellate court agreed with the trial court's finding that the admission of women would materially affect several key elements of VMI's program—physical training, lack of privacy, and the adversative approach to character development—it was homogeneity of gender, not maleness, that justified the program (976 F.2d at 897). The appellate court also accepted the trial court's findings that single-sex education has important benefits. But these findings did not support the trial court's conclusion that VMI's male-only policy passed constitutional muster. Although VMI's single-gender education and "citizen-soldier" philosophy were permissible, the state's exclusion of women from such a program was not, and no other public postsecondary education institution in Virginia was devoted to educating only one gender.

The appellate court did not order VMI to admit women, but remanded the case to the district court to give Virginia the option to (1) admit women to VMI, (2) establish parallel institutions or programs for women, or (3) terminate state support for VMI. On appeal, the U.S. Supreme Court refused to hear the case (508 U.S. 946 (1993)). Following that action, the trustees of VMI voted to underwrite a military program at a neighboring private women's college, Mary Baldwin College.

The U.S. Department of Justice challenged the plan, saying that it was "based on gender stereotypes," and asked the trial court to order VMI to admit women and to integrate them into its full program. After the trial judge approved the parallel program at Mary Baldwin College, a divided panel of the U.S. Court of Appeals for the Fourth Circuit affirmed, finding that providing single-gender education was a legitimate objective of the state and that the leadership program at Mary Baldwin College was "sufficiently comparable" to the VMI program to satisfy the demands of the equal protection clause (44 F.3d 1229 (4th Cir. 1995)).

The United States again asked the Supreme Court to review the appellate court's ruling, and this time the Court agreed. In a 7-to-1 decision (Justice Thomas did not participate), the Court ruled that VMI's exclusion of women violated the equal protection clause (518 U.S. 515 (1996)). Since strict scrutiny is reserved for classifications based on race or national origin, the Court used intermediate scrutiny—which Justice Ginsburg, the author of the majority opinion, termed "skeptical scrutiny"—to analyze Virginia's claim that single-sex education provides important educational benefits. Reviewing the state's history of providing higher education for women, the Court concluded that women had first been excluded from public higher education, and then admitted to once all-male public universities, but that no public single-sex institution had been established for women, and thus the state had not provided equal benefits for women. With regard to the state's argument that VMI's adversative training method provided important educational benefits that could not be made available to women and thus their admission would "destroy" VMI's unique approach to education, the Court noted that both parties had agreed that some women could meet all of the physical standards imposed upon VMI cadets. Moreover, the experience with women cadets in the military academies suggested that the state's fear that the presence of women would force change upon VMI was based on overbroad generalizations about women as a group, rather than on an analysis of how individual women could perform.

The Court then turned to the issue of the remedy for VMI's constitutional violation. Characterizing the women's leadership program at Mary Baldwin College as "unequal in tangible and intangible facilities" and offering no opportunity for the type of military training for which VMI is famous, the Court stressed the differences between the two programs and institutions in terms of the quality of the faculty, the range of degrees offered, athletic and sports facilities, endowments, and the status of the degree earned by students. Criticizing the Fourth Circuit for applying an overly deferential standard of review that the Court characterized as one "of its own invention," the Court reversed the Fourth Circuit's decision and held that the separate program did not cure the constitutional violation.

Chief Justice Rehnquist voted with the majority but wrote a separate concurring opinion because he disagreed with Justice Ginsburg's analysis of the remedy. The "parallel program" at Mary Baldwin College was "distinctly inferior" to VMI, said Justice Rehnquist, but the state could cure the constitutional violation by providing a public institution for women that offered the "same quality of education and [was] of the same overall calibre" as VMI. Justice Rehnquist's opinion thus differs sharply from that of Justice Ginsburg, who characterized the exclusion of women as the constitutional violation, while Justice Rehnquist characterized the violation as the maintenance of an all-male institution without providing a comparable institution for women.

Justice Scalia, the sole dissenter, attacked the Court's interpretation of equal protection jurisprudence, saying that the Court had used a higher standard than the intermediate scrutiny that is typically used to analyze categories based on gender. Furthermore, stated Justice Scalia, since the Constitution does not specifically forbid distinctions based upon gender, the political process, not the courts, should be used to change state behavior. Finding that the maintenance of single-sex education is an important educational objective, Justice Scalia would have upheld the continued exclusion of women from VMI.

The only other all-male public college, the Citadel, was ordered by a panel of the U.S. Court of Appeals for the Fourth Circuit to admit a female applicant whom that college had admitted on the mistaken belief that she was male (*Faulkner v. Jones*, 10 F.3d 226 (4th Cir. 1993)). The court ordered that she be admitted as a day student and remanded to the district court the issue of whether she could become a full member of the college's corps of cadets. On remand the trial judge ordered that she become a member of the corps of cadets. The college appealed this ruling.

The U.S. Court of Appeals for the Fourth Circuit ruled that the Citadel's refusal to admit women violated the equal protection clause, and despite the state's promise to create a military-type college for women students, the court ordered the Citadel to admit women as students (51 F.3d 440 (4th Cir. 1995), affirming the order of the trial court in 858 F. Supp. 552 (D.S.C. 1994)).

Important as *Hogan* and the *VMI* cases may be to the law regarding sex discrimination in admissions, they are only part of the bigger picture, which already includes Title IX. Thus, to view the law in its current state, one must look both to *Hogan/U.S. v. Virginia* and to Title IX. *Hogan, U.S. v. Virginia*, and their progeny have at least limited, and apparently also undermined, the Title IX exemption for public undergraduate institutions that have always had single-sex admissions policies (20 U.S.C. § 1681(a)(5); 34 C.F.R. § 106.15(e)). Thus, the only programs and institutions that are still legally free to have single-sex admissions policies are (1) private undergraduate institutions and their constituent programs and (2) religious institutions, including their graduate, professional, and vocational programs, if the institution has obtained a waiver of Title IX admission requirements on religious grounds (20 U.S.C. § 1681(a)(3); 34 C.F.R. § 106.12).

Recent trends in student enrollment demonstrate that rates of undergraduate enrollment for women have bypassed those of men. Data collected by the U.S. Department of Education indicate that, in 2010, women comprised 57 percent of all undergraduates and 61 percent of all graduate students, and 59 percent of students enrolled that year who were attending part-time were women.

### 7.2.4.3. Disability. 

Two federal laws—Section 504 of the Rehabilitation Act of 1973 (29 U.S.C. § 794) and the Americans with Disabilities Act (ADA) (42 U.S.C. §§ 12101 et seq.)—prohibit discrimination against individuals with disabilities (see Sections 11.5.4 and 8.4 of this book). Before those laws were passed, these individuals had been the subject of a few scattered federal provisions (such as 20 U.S.C. § 1684, which prohibits discrimination against blind persons by institutions receiving federal funds) and a few constitutional equal protection cases (such as *PARC v. Pennsylvania*, 334 F. Supp. 1257 (E.D. Pa.

1971), which challenged discrimination against disabled students by public elementary and secondary schools). But none of these developments have had nearly the impact on postsecondary admissions that Section 504 and the ADA have.

As applied to postsecondary education, Section 504 generally prohibits discrimination on the basis of disability in federally funded programs and activities (see this book, Section 11.5.4). Section 104.42 of the implementing regulations, 34 C.F.R. Part 104, prohibits discrimination on the basis of disability in admissions and recruitment. This section contains several specific provisions similar to those prohibiting sex discrimination in admissions under Title IX (see this book, Section 7.2.4.2). These provisions prohibit (1) the imposition of limitations on "the number or proportion of individuals with disabilities who may be admitted" (34 C.F.R. § 104.42(b)(1)); (2) the use of any admissions criterion or test "that has a disproportionate, adverse effect" on individuals with disabilities, unless the criterion or test, as used, is shown to predict success validly and no alternative, nondiscriminatory criterion or test is available (34 C.F.R. § 104.42(b)(2)); and (3) any preadmission inquiry about whether the applicant has a disability, unless the recipient needs the information in order to correct the effects of past discrimination or to overcome past conditions that resulted in limited participation by people with disabilities (34 C.F.R. §§ 104.42(b)(4), 104.42(c)).

These prohibitions apply to discrimination directed against "qualified" individuals with disabilities. A disabled person is qualified, with respect to postsecondary and vocational services, if he or she "meets the academic and technical standards requisite to admission or participation in the recipient's education program or activity" (34 C.F.R. § 104.3(l)(3)). Thus, while the regulations do not prohibit an institution from denying admission to a person with a disability who does not meet the institution's "academic and technical" admissions standards, they do prohibit an institution from denying admission on the basis of the disability as such. (After a student is admitted, however, the institution can make confidential inquiry concerning the disability (34 C.F.R. § 104.42(b)(4)); in this way the institution can obtain advance information about disabilities that may require accommodation.)

In addition to these prohibitions, the institution has an affirmative duty to ascertain that its admissions tests are structured to accommodate applicants with disabilities that impair sensory, manual, or speaking skills, unless the test is intended to measure these skills. Such adapted tests must be offered as often and in as timely a way as other admissions tests and must be "administered in facilities that, on the whole, are accessible" to people with disabilities (34 C.F.R. § 104.42(b)(3)).

In *Southeastern Community College v. Davis*, 442 U.S. 397 (1979), the U.S. Supreme Court issued its first interpretation of Section 504. The case concerned a nursing school applicant who had been denied admission because she was deaf. The Supreme Court ruled that an "otherwise qualified handicapped individual" is one who is qualified in spite of (rather than except for) his disability. Since an applicant's disability is therefore relevant to his or her qualification for a specific program, Section 504 does not preclude a college or university from imposing "reasonable physical qualifications" on applicants for admission, where such qualifications are necessary for participation in the school's program. The Department of Education's regulations implementing Section 504 provide that a disabled applicant is "qualified" if he or she meets "the academic and technical standards" for admission; the Supreme Court has made it clear, however, that "technical standards" may sometimes encompass reasonable physical requirements. Under *Davis*, an applicant's failure to meet such requirements can be a legitimate ground for rejection.

The impact of *Davis* is limited, however, by the rather narrow and specific factual context in which the case arose. The plaintiff, who was severely hearing impaired, sought admission to a nursing program. It is important to emphasize that *Davis* involved admission to a professional, clinical training program. The demands of such a program, designed to train students in the practice of a profession, raise far different considerations from those involved in admission to an undergraduate or a graduate academic program, or even a nonclinically oriented professional school. The college denied her admission, believing that she would not be able to perform nursing duties in a safe manner and could not participate fully in the clinical portion of the program.

While the Court approved the imposition of "reasonable physical qualifications," it did so only for requirements that the institution can justify as necessary to the applicant's successful participation in the particular program involved. In *Davis*, the college had shown that an applicant's ability to understand speech without reliance on lip reading was necessary to ensure patient safety and to enable the student to realize the full benefit of its nursing program. For programs without clinical components, or without professional training goals, it would be much more difficult for the institution to justify such physical requirements. Even for other professional programs, the justification might be much more difficult than in *Davis*. In a law school program, for example, the safety factor would be lacking. Moreover, in most law schools, clinical training is offered as an elective rather than a required course. By enrolling only in the nonclinical courses, a deaf student would be able to complete the required program with the help of an interpreter.

Furthermore, the Court did not say that affirmative action is never required to accommodate the needs of disabled applicants. Although the Court asserted that Section 504 does not require institutions "to lower or to effect substantial modifications of standards" or to make "fundamental alteration[s] in the nature of a program," the Court did suggest that less substantial and burdensome program adjustments may sometimes be required. The Court also discussed, and did not question, the regulation requiring institutions to provide certain "auxiliary aids," such as interpreters for students with hearing impairments, to qualified students with disabilities (see Sections 7.7.2 and 11.5.4 of this book). This issue was addressed in *United States v. Board of Trustees for the University of Alabama*, 908 F.2d 740 (11th Cir. 1990), in which the court ordered the university to provide additional transportation for students with disabilities. Moreover, the Court said nothing that in any way precludes institutions from voluntarily making major program modifications for applicants who are disabled.

Several appellate court cases have applied the teachings of *Davis* to other admissions problems. The courts in these cases have refined the *Davis* analysis, especially in clarifying the burdens of proof in a discrimination suit under Section 504. In *Pushkin v. Regents of the University of Colorado*, 658 F.2d 1372 (10th Cir. 1981), the court affirmed the district court's decision that the plaintiff, a medical doctor suffering from multiple sclerosis, had been wrongfully denied admission to the university's psychiatric residency program. Agreeing that *Davis* permitted consideration of disabilities in determining whether an applicant is "otherwise qualified" for admission, the court outlined what the plaintiff had to prove in order to establish his case of discrimination:

1. The plaintiff must establish a prima facie case by showing that he was an otherwise qualified handicapped person apart from his handicap, and was rejected under circumstances which gave rise to the inference that his rejection was based solely on his handicap.

2. Once plaintiff establishes his prima facie case, defendants have the burden of going forward and proving that plaintiff was not an otherwise qualified handicapped person—that is, one who is able to meet all of the program's requirements in spite of his handicap—or that his rejection from the program was for reasons other than his handicap.

3. The plaintiff then has the burden of going forward with rebuttal evidence showing that the defendants' reasons for rejecting the plaintiff are based on misconceptions or unfounded factual conclusions, and that reasons articulated for the rejection other than the handicap encompass unjustified consideration of the handicap itself [658 F.2d at 1387].

In *Doherty v. Southern College of Optometry*, 862 F.2d 570 (6th Cir. 1988), a federal appellate court considered the relationship between Section 504's "otherwise qualified" requirement and the institution's duty to provide a "reasonable accommodation" for a student with a disability. The plaintiff—a student with retinitis pigmentosa (RP), which restricted his field of vision, and a neurological condition that affected his motor skills—asserted that the college should exempt him from recently introduced proficiency requirements related to the operation of optometric instruments. The student could not meet these requirements and claimed that they were a pretext for discrimination on the basis of disability, since he was "otherwise qualified" and therefore had the right to be accommodated.

In ruling for the school, the district court considered the "reasonable accommodation" inquiry to be separate from the "otherwise qualified" requirement; thus, in its view, the institution was obligated to accommodate only a student with a disability who has already been determined to be "otherwise qualified." The appeals court disagreed, indicating that the "inquiry into reasonable accommodation is one aspect of the 'otherwise qualified' analysis" (862 F.2d at 577). (This interpretation is consistent with the definition of "otherwise qualified" in the ADA.) The appellate court's interpretation did not change the result in the case; since the proficiency requirements were reasonably necessary to the practice of optometry, waiver of these requirements would not have been a "reasonable accommodation." But the court's emphasis on the proper relationship between the "otherwise qualified" and "reasonable accommodation" inquiries does serve to clarify and strengthen the institution's obligation to accommodate the particular needs of students with disabilities.

Students alleging discrimination on the basis of disability may file a complaint with the Education Department's Office for Civil Rights, or they may file a private lawsuit and receive compensatory damages (*Tanberg v. Weld County Sheriff*, 787 F. Supp. 970 (D. Colo. 1992)). Section 504 does not, however, provide a **private right of action** against the Secretary of Education, who enforces Section 504 (*Salvador v. Bennett*, 800 F.2d 97 (7th Cir. 1986)).

The provisions of the ADA are similar in many respects to those of Section 504, upon which, in large part, the ADA was based. In addition to prohibiting discrimination in employment (see this book, Section 4.5.2.5), Title II of the ADA prohibits discrimination in access to services or programs of a public entity (such as a public college or university), and Title III prohibits discrimination in access to places of public accommodation (including private colleges and universities).The ADA specifies ten areas in which colleges and universities may not discriminate against a qualified individual with a disability: eligibility criteria; modifications of policies, practices, and procedures; auxiliary aids and services; examinations and courses; removal of barriers in existing facilities; alternatives to barriers in existing facilities; personal devices and services; assistive technology; seating in assembly areas; and transportation services (28 C.F.R. §§ 36.301–10). The law also addresses accessibility issues for new construction or renovation of existing facilities (28 C.F.R. §§ 36.401–6).

The law's language regarding "eligibility criteria" means that in admissions or placement tests or other admission-related activities, colleges and universities must accommodate the needs of applicants or students with disabilities. For example, one court held that, under Section 504, the defendant medical school had to provide a dyslexic student with alternative exams unless it could demonstrate that its rejection of all other testing methods was based on rational reasons (*Wynne v. Tufts University School of Medicine*, 932 F.2d 19 (1st Cir. 1991), discussed in Section 8.4.2.1 of this book).

State courts have looked to ADA jurisprudence in interpreting state law prohibitions against disability discrimination. An illustrative case is *Ohio Civil Rights Commission v. Case Western Reserve University*, 666 N.E.2d 1376 (Ohio 1996). The plaintiff, Cheryl Fischer, an applicant to the Case Western Reserve (CWR) medical school, had become totally blind during her junior year at CWR. CWR had provided Fischer with several accommodations as an undergraduate, including lab assistants and readers, oral examinations instead of written ones, extended exam periods, and books on tape. Fischer graduated cum laude from CWR.

All U.S. medical schools belong to the Association of American Medical Colleges (AAMC), which requires candidates for a medical degree to be able to "observe" both laboratory demonstrations and patient appearance and behavior. Despite Fischer's excellent academic record, CWR's medical school admissions committee determined that she did not meet the AAMC requirements because she was unable to see and that she would be unable to complete the requirements of the medical school curriculum. Fischer reapplied the following year and again was denied admission. She filed a complaint under the Ohio nondiscrimination law with the Ohio Civil Rights Commission (OCRC), which found probable cause to believe that CWR had discriminated against Fischer. A county court affirmed the OCRC, but a state appellate court reversed, holding that CWR would be required to modify its program in order to accommodate Fischer's disability, which the law did not require. The Supreme Court of Ohio affirmed.

Because applicants must, under both Section 504 and the ADA, be able to meet admission standards, the issue of whether an applicant with a disability is "qualified" is central when students challenge admissions denials. And when a student asserts that the failure to admit is because of a disability, the student must demonstrate that the disorder "substantially limits" a major life activity. In *Ellenberg v. New Mexico Military Academy*, 572 F.3d 815 (10th Cir. 2009), the plaintiff applied for admission to a military high school. She was rejected on the basis of documented prior behavioral problems, prior drug use, and the need for continued medication and counseling. The plaintiff had been classified as disabled under the Individuals with Disabilities Education Act, 20 U.S.C. §§1400 et seq. (IDEA), a federal law that protects students with disabilities in elementary and secondary education. The plaintiff argued that this classification under the IDEA automatically gave her protection under Section 504 and the ADA. Although the court was willing to believe that the student had a disability, she had not articulated how the alleged disability "substantially limited" her ability to learn, as required by both Section 504 and the ADA. Therefore, the court ruled that simply because an individual qualifies for accommodations under the IDEA, she does not necessarily meet the requirements of the ADA or Section 504, and the court awarded summary judgment to the defendant school.

In sum, postsecondary administrators should still proceed very sensitively in making admission decisions concerning applicants with disabilities. *Davis* can be expected to have the greatest impact on professional and paraprofessional health care programs; beyond that, the circumstances in which physical requirements for admission may be used are less clear. Furthermore, while *Davis* relieves colleges and universities of any obligation to make substantial modifications in their program requirements, a refusal to make lesser modifications may in some instances constitute discrimination. Furthermore, interpretation of Section 504's requirements has evolved since *Davis*, as evidenced by the *Doherty* case; and in some cases the ADA provides additional protections for students.

A federal appellate court has ruled that "flagging" scores on standardized tests that have been taken with accommodations does not violate the ADA. In *Doe v. National Board of Medical Examiners*, 199 F.3d 146 (3d Cir. 1999), a medical student with multiple sclerosis requested, and obtained, additional time to take the U.S. Medical Licensing Examination, a standardized examination developed and administered by the National Board of Medical Examiners (NBME). The NBME's practice when reporting scores was to indicate that the examination had been taken with accommodations. The student asked the NBME to omit the "flagging" from his score report, but the organization refused. The student then sought a preliminary injunction, claiming that the practice of flagging test scores violated Title III of the ADA.

Although the trial court granted Doe a preliminary injunction, the appellate panel reversed. The NBME flagged scores only when the test taker had been granted an accommodation that the board's psychometric experts believed could affect the validity of the test score. Additional time, which was the accommodation that Doe received, could affect the validity of his score; the score of another test taker who only received a large-print version of the exam would not be flagged because this accommodation would not affect the validity of the score. The court ruled that, in order to be entitled to an injunction, Doe would have to demonstrate that the validity of his test score as a predictor of success in further medical training was comparable to the validity of the scores of test takers who had not been accommodated. Because the ADA does not bar the flagging of test scores, and because Doe had not demonstrated that the additional time had no effect on the validity of his score, the court vacated the preliminary injunction. To Doe's claim that he would be discriminated against by residency and internship programs to which he would apply, the court responded that such potential discrimination could not be attributed to the NBME and that his claim was speculative.

Subsequent to the ruling in *Doe*, the College Board announced that, effective October 2003, it would no longer "flag" the test scores for individuals who were given extra time or other accommodations when taking the SAT. The Educational Testing Service has also halted the practice of flagging scores on the Graduate Management Admission Test (GMAT) and the Graduate Record Examination (GRE). The ACT testing program ended its practice of flagging test scores as well.

**7.2.4.4. Immigration status.** The eligibility of aliens for admission to U.S. colleges and universities has received heightened attention since the terrorist attacks of September 11, 2001. Although the Supreme Court ruled on equal protection grounds in 1982 that states could not deny free public education to undocumented alien children (*Plyler v. Doe*, 457 U.S. 202 (1982)), litigation related to alien postsecondary students has more often involved their eligibility for in-state tuition in state institutions than their eligibility for admission as such.[1]

As discussed in *Nyquist v. Jean-Marie Mauclet*, 432 U.S. 1 (1977), alienage is a suspect classification for purposes of postsecondary education benefits. A public institution's refusal to admit permanent resident aliens would therefore likely violate the federal equal protection clause. Private institutions are

---

[1] For a discussion of in-state tuition issues regarding alien students, see *LHE 5th*, Section 8.3.6.

not bound by the equal protection clause, but could face liability for refusing to admit qualified resident aliens if the institution were engaged in some cooperative education program with the federal or state government that would be considered "state action" (see Section 1.5.2).

Temporary or nonimmigrant aliens have less protection under the federal Constitution. For example, in *Ahmed v. University of Toledo*, 664 F. Supp. 282 (N.D. Ohio 1986), the court distinguished between permanent resident aliens and temporary nonresident (nonimmigrant) aliens, refusing to subject a university policy that affected only nonresident aliens to strict scrutiny review under the equal protection clause. Under the lower "rational relationship" standard used by the court in *Ahmed*, a university policy that singled out nonresident aliens in order to meet a reasonable goal of the university would be constitutionally permissible. If a public institution were to deny admission only to aliens from a particular country, however, courts could view such a policy as national origin discrimination subject to strict scrutiny (see *Tayyari v. New Mexico State University*, 495 F. Supp. 1365 (D.N.M. 1980)).

More complicated are the legal issues that arise with respect to undocumented aliens. In 1996, Congress enacted the Illegal Immigration Reform and Immigrant Responsibility Act (IIRIRA, Pub. L. No. 104-208, 110 Stat. 3009, codified in scattered sections of 8 and 18 U.S.C.). One IIRIRA provision (8 U.S.C. § 1621(c)) declares that aliens who are not "qualified aliens" are ineligible for certain public benefits, including payments to individuals pursuing public postsecondary education. However, the same section of the law also allows a state, after August 22, 1996, to enact laws that specifically confer a "public benefit" on aliens.

It is not yet clear whether the IIRIRA applies to admissions policies at public colleges and universities. Although the court in the *Merten* case, discussed below, concluded that the IIRIRA was not intended to apply to college admissions, there have been no definitive rulings on whether college admission is a "benefit," and the views of commentators differ.

In 2002, the Attorney General of Virginia sent a memo to all public postsecondary institutions in the state stating that they should not admit undocumented aliens. The memo also encouraged officials of the institutions to report the presence of any undocumented students on campus to the federal authorities. When the public colleges and universities in Virginia followed the dictates of the memorandum with respect to admissions policies, an association that advocates for undocumented workers, as well as several undocumented individuals, filed a lawsuit against the boards of visitors of these colleges and universities, asserting that their refusal to admit undocumented alien applicants violated the U.S. Constitution's **supremacy, foreign commerce**, and due process clauses. The supremacy clause claim was based on the plaintiffs' assertion that the restrictive admissions policies of the institutions regulated immigration and thus interfered with federal immigration law. The plaintiffs' foreign commerce clause claim was based on the assertion that state policies denying admission to undocumented aliens burdened interstate commerce by precluding potential applicants from earning higher wages and sending funds to relatives living outside the United States. The due process claim was based on the plaintiffs' assertion that the policy of denying admission to undocumented aliens deprived them of a property interest in receiving a public education in Virginia community colleges, as well as a property interest in receiving fair and impartial admissions decisions based on review of their applications. The defendants moved for dismissal of all claims.

In *Equal Access Education v. Merten*, 305 F. Supp. 2d 585 (E.D. Va. 2004) (*Merten I*), the court first addressed the issue of **standing**. Several of the named plaintiffs were high school students whose academic achievement would have made them competitive for admission to Virginia universities, except for the fact that they were not citizens or lawful permanent residents. One plaintiff was a high school student who had temporary legal status, but who had been denied admission to a public university; he alleged that the denial was based on an inaccurate assumption that he did not have a lawful immigration status. The court found that the individual plaintiffs had standing to bring the suit, as did the association that had been formed to further the interests of undocumented high school students in attending public colleges and universities in Virginia.

In addressing the plaintiffs' supremacy clause claim, the court looked to *DeCanas v. Bica*, 424 U.S. 351 (1976), in which the U.S. Supreme Court upheld a California statute forbidding employers to hire undocumented aliens if such employment would have an adverse effect on lawful resident workers. The Supreme Court rejected a claim that the state law was preempted by federal law and set forth a three-part test for determining whether a state statute, action, or policy related to immigration was preempted by federal law. Under this test, federal law will preempt the state when (1) the state statute, action, or policy is an attempt to regulate immigration; (2) the subject matter of the state law, action, or policy is one that Congress intended to prevent states from regulating, even if the state law does not conflict with federal law; or (3) the state statute, action, or policy poses an obstacle to the execution of congressional objectives, or conflicts with federal law, making compliance with both federal and state law impossible.

Applying the *DeCanas* tests, the court determined, with one exception noted below, that the Virginia policy to deny admission to undocumented applicants did not meet any of the conditions under which federal law would preempt the policy. Specifically, the court determined that, in passing the IIRIRA, Congress did not intend to regulate the admission of undocumented aliens to college, leaving that issue to the states. The IIRIRA merely dictated that, if undocumented aliens were admitted to public colleges and universities, they would have to be charged the same out-of-state tuition paid by U.S. citizens (8 U.S.C. § 1623(a)). As long as the college officials used "federal immigration status standards" rather than creating different state standards for determining whether an applicant was undocumented or not a lawful resident, there was no violation of the supremacy clause. But because no trial had been held to determine whether the colleges had created an alternative set of "state standards" to evaluate applicants' citizenship status, the court declined to dismiss that part of the plaintiffs' supremacy clause claim.

The court then turned to the plaintiffs' foreign commerce clause claim, which asserted that the admissions policies relegated the plaintiffs to low-wage jobs by denying them access to postsecondary education, thus limiting their ability to send funds to relatives living outside the United States. The court rejected this claim, noting that there was no allegation that the plaintiffs made or intended to make such payments and that, since undocumented aliens are not eligible under federal law to work in the United States, it was unlikely that they would be able to earn the type of salaries that would result in significant payments to foreign nationals.

The court rejected the plaintiffs' due process claim, stating that they did not have a property right in admission to Virginia community colleges because admission was discretionary on the part of the colleges. And because public colleges and universities may deny admission to any applicant for any constitutionally permissible reason, said the court, there is no entitlement to any particular procedures or criteria for admission. In *Merten I*, therefore, the court dismissed all of the plaintiffs' claims except for the one portion of the supremacy clause claim.

In *Equal Access Education v. Merten*, 325 F. Supp. 2d 655 (E.D. Va. 2004) (*Merten II*), the court granted the defendant universities' motion for summary judgment on that claim. The court did not rule on the merits of the claim, however; instead it reconsidered the plaintiffs' standing in light of its rulings in *Merten I* and determined that the plaintiffs no longer had standing to continue the action.

Bills were introduced in both houses of Congress between 2000 and 2011 that would allow certain undocumented students to attend college in the United States and to begin the process of legalization of the students' immigration status. The most recent version of the bill, S. 3992 (the DREAM Act) in the 111th Congress, was passed by the House of Representatives in the fall of 2010 but with an insufficient number of votes to allow it to be acted upon by the Senate. In 2012, the Obama Administration promulgated the Deferred Action for Childhood Arrivals (DACA) program, which allows undocumented youth brought to the United States as children to avoid deportation and move toward legal status if they can meet certain criteria. (For information on DACA, see http://www.dhs.gov/deferred-action-childhood-arrivals.) As this book went to press, Congress was preparing legislation on immigration reform.

### 7.2.5. Affirmative action programs.[2] Designed to increase the number of persons from historically underrepresented groups admitted to academic programs, affirmative action policies pose delicate social, pedagogical, and legal questions. Educators and public policy makers have agonized over the extent to which race and gender (among other diversity-related factors) can be taken into account in admissions. Courts have grappled with the complaints of qualified but rejected nonminority applicants who claim to be victims

---

[2] This section was revised and updated by Jonathan R. Alger, former senior vice president and general counsel at Rutgers University and currently president of James Madison University.

of "reverse discrimination" because minority applicants were admitted in preference to them. Five cases have reached the U.S. Supreme Court: *DeFunis* in 1973, *Bakke* in 1978, *Grutter* and *Gratz* in 2003, and *Fisher* in 2013. The first four are discussed at some length in this section. *Fisher* was decided as this book went to press and is discussed briefly near the end of this section.

There are two types of affirmative action plans: "remedial" or "mandatory" plans and "voluntary" plans. The former are ordered by a court or government agency. There is only one justification that the courts have accepted for this type of affirmative action plan: remedying or dismantling the present effects of past discrimination that the institution has engaged in or supported. "Voluntary" affirmative action plans, in contrast, are adopted by the conscious choice of the institution. As the law has developed, there are two justifications for this type of plan. The first parallels the justification for remedial or mandatory affirmative action: alleviating the present effects of the institution's own past discrimination. The second justification is achieving and maintaining the diversity of the student body to foster educational benefits for the entire student body.

Just as there is a basic dichotomy between remedial and voluntary plans, there is also a basic distinction—developed in cases concerning race and ethnicity—between "race-conscious" or "race preferential" voluntary affirmative action plans and "race-neutral" or uniform voluntary affirmative action plans. The former take race into account in decision making by providing some type of preference or advantage for members of identified minority groups. Race-neutral plans, in contrast, do not use race as a factor in making decisions about particular individuals. Some allegedly race-neutral plans may have the foreseeable *effect* of benefiting certain racial or ethnic minorities, but this characteristic alone does not convert the neutral plan into a race-conscious plan, so long as the race of particular individuals is not itself considered in making decisions about them. Genuinely race-neutral plans raise fewer legal issues than race-conscious plans and are less amenable to challenge. If the plan is adopted for the purpose of benefiting some minorities over some nonminorities, however, and does have this intended effect, the plan could be subject to challenge as reverse discrimination and could be treated as a race-conscious plan.

The legal issues concerning affirmative action can be cast in both constitutional and statutory terms and apply to both public and private institutions. The constitutional issues arise under the Fourteenth Amendment's equal protection clause, which generally prohibits discriminatory treatment on the basis of race, ethnicity, or sex, including "reverse discrimination," but applies only to public institutions (see Section 1.5.2 of this book). The statutory issues arise under Title VI of the Civil Rights Act of 1964 (prohibiting race, color, and national origin discrimination), and Title IX of the Education Amendments of 1972 (prohibiting sex discrimination), which apply to discrimination by both public and private institutions receiving federal financial assistance (see generally Sections 11.5.2 and 11.5.3 of this book); and under 42 U.S.C. § 1981, which has been construed to prohibit race discrimination in admissions by private schools whether or not they receive federal assistance (see Section 7.2.4.1 of this book).[3] In the *Bakke* case, a majority of the Justices agreed that Title VI uses constitutional equal protection standards for determining the validity of affirmative action programs (438 U.S. 265 at 284–87 (Powell, J.), 328–41 (Brennan, J., concurring in judgment), 412–18 (Stevens, J., concurring in judgment). For Title IX affirmative action issues, equal protection standards would also apply; but it is not clear whether it would be the "intermediate scrutiny" standard that courts use when reviewing equal protection claims of sex discrimination (see *United States v. Commonwealth of Virginia*, 518 U.S. 515 (1996), discussed in Section 7.2.4.2) or the "strict scrutiny" standard applicable to race claims under Title VI. (See *Jeldness v. Pearce*, 30 F.3d 1220 (9th Cir. 1994); *Johnson v. University System. of Ga.*, 106 F. Supp. 2d 1362 (S.D. Ga. 2000).) Thus, *Bakke*, *Grutter*, and *Gratz*, taken together, establish a core of comparable legal parameters for affirmative action, applicable to public and private institutions alike.

Both the Title VI and the Title IX administrative regulations also address the subject of affirmative action. These regulations preceded *Bakke* and are brief and somewhat ambiguous. After *Bakke*, the U.S. Department of Health, Education, and Welfare (HEW, now the U.S. Department of Education) issued a "policy interpretation" of Title VI, indicating that the department had reviewed its regulations in light of *Bakke* and "concluded that no changes . . . are required or desirable" (44 Fed. Reg. 58509, at 58510 (October 10, 1979)). This policy interpretation, however, did set forth guidelines for applying the Title VI affirmative action regulations consistent with *Bakke*.

When an institution has discriminated in the past, the Title VI and Title IX regulations require it to implement affirmative action programs to overcome the effects of that discrimination—a kind of remedial or mandatory affirmative action (34 C.F.R. §§ 100.3(b)(6)(i), 100.5(i); 34 C.F.R. § 106.3(a)). When the institution has not discriminated, the regulations nevertheless permit affirmative action to overcome the present effects of past societal discrimination—a type of voluntary affirmative action (34 C.F.R. §§ 100.3(b)(6)(ii), 100.5(i); 34 C.F.R. § 106.3(b)). Under more recent judicial interpretations, however, these regulations and the 1979 policy interpretation could not validly extend to voluntary race-conscious or gender-conscious plans designed to remedy societal discrimination apart from the institution's own prior discrimination. (See the discussion in guideline 1 later in this section.)

---

[3] The cases discussed below, and all of the major cases on affirmative action in admissions, involved race or ethnicity discrimination. Sex discrimination claims, however, are also a realistic possibility. A Georgia case provides a concrete example. Several rejected female applicants filed a lawsuit against the University of Georgia, challenging its practice of using gender preferences to make admission decisions in borderline cases. The U.S. district court ruled in the plaintiffs' favor. See *Johnson v. University System of Georgia*, 106 F. Supp. 2d 1362, 1375–76 (S.D. Ga. 2000). Because far more female than male students would have been admitted if gender had not been considered, the university had applied a lower standard to male applicants in an attempt to narrow the gap between the proportions of female and male students. The university then eliminated consideration of gender in making admissions decisions.

The first case to confront the constitutionality of affirmative action admissions programs in postsecondary education was *DeFunis v. Odegaard*, 507 P.2d 1169 (Wash. 1973), *dismissed as moot*, 416 U.S. 312 (1974), *on remand*, 529 P.2d 438 (Wash. 1974). After DeFunis, a white male, was denied admission to the University of Washington's law school, he filed suit alleging that less-qualified minority applicants had been accepted and that, but for the affirmative action program, he would have been admitted. The law school admissions committee had calculated each applicant's predicted first-year average (PFYA) through a formula that considered the applicant's LSAT scores and junior-senior undergraduate average. The committee had attached less importance to a minority applicant's PFYA and had considered minority applications separately from other applications. DeFunis's PFYA was higher than those of all but one of the minority applicants admitted in the year he was rejected.

The state trial court ordered that DeFunis be admitted, and he entered the law school. The Washington State Supreme Court reversed the lower court and upheld the law school's affirmative action program under the equal protection clause as a constitutionally acceptable admissions tool justified by several "compelling" state interests. Among them were the "interest in promoting integration in public education," the "educational interest . . . in producing a racially balanced student body at the law school," and the interest in alleviating "the shortage of minority attorneys—and, consequently, minority prosecutors, judges, and public officials." When DeFunis sought review in the U.S. Supreme Court, he was permitted to remain in school pending the Court's final disposition of the case. Subsequently, in a *per curiam* opinion with four Justices dissenting, the Court declared the case moot because, by then, DeFunis was in his final quarter of law school, and the university had asserted that his registration would remain effective regardless of the case's final outcome. The Court vacated the Washington State Supreme Court's judgment and remanded the case to that court for appropriate disposition.

Five years after it had avoided the issue in *DeFunis*, the U.S. Supreme Court considered the legality of affirmative action in *Regents of the University of California v. Bakke*, 438 U.S. 265 (1978). The plaintiff, a white male twice rejected from the medical school of the University of California at Davis, challenged the school's affirmative action plan, under which it had set aside sixteen places out of one hundred for minority applicants whose applications were considered separately from other applicants. According to Justice Powell's description of the plan, with which a majority of the Justices agreed:

> [T]he faculty devised a special admissions program to increase the representation of "disadvantaged" students in each medical school class. The special program consisted of a separate admissions system operating in coordination with the regular admissions process . . .
>
> [C]andidates were asked to indicate whether they wished to be considered as . . . members of a "minority group," which the Medical School apparently viewed as "Blacks," "Chicanos," "Asians," and "American Indians." [If so], the application was forwarded to the special admissions committee . . . [T]he

applications then were rated by the special committee in a fashion similar to that used by the general admissions committee, except that special candidates did not have to meet the 2.5 grade point average cutoff applied to regular applicants . . .

From [1971] through 1974, the special program resulted in the admission of twenty-one black students, thirty Mexican-Americans, and twelve Asians, for a total of sixty-three minority students. Over the same period, the regular admissions program produced one black, six Mexican-Americans, and thirty-seven Asians, for a total of forty-four minority students. Although disadvantaged whites applied to the special program in large numbers, none received an offer of admission through that process [438 U.S. at 272–76].

The university sought to justify its program by citing the great need for doctors to work in underserved minority communities, the need to compensate for the effects of societal discrimination against minorities, the need to reduce the historical deficit of minorities in the medical profession, and the need to diversify the student body. In analyzing these justifications, the California Supreme Court applied a "compelling state interest" test, such as that used by the state court in *DeFunis*, along with a "less objectionable alternative test." Although it assumed that the university's interests were compelling, this court determined that the university had not demonstrated that the program was the least burdensome alternative available for achieving its goals. (This analysis of possible alternatives is comparable to the "narrow tailoring" test that appeared in later litigation and was used by the Court in *Grutter* and *Gratz*.) The California court therefore held that the program operated unconstitutionally to exclude Bakke on account of his race and ordered that Bakke be admitted to medical school. It further held that the Constitution prohibited the university from giving any consideration to race in its admissions process and enjoined the university from doing so (*Bakke v. Regents of the University of California*, 553 P.2d 1152 (Cal. 1976)).

The U.S. Supreme Court affirmed the first part of this decision and reversed the second part. The Justices wrote six opinions (totaling 157 pages), none of which commanded a majority of the Court. Three of these opinions deserve particular consideration: (1) Justice Powell's opinion—in some parts of which various of the other Justices joined; (2) Justice Brennan's opinion—in which three other Justices joined (referred to below as the "Brennan group"); and (3) Justice Stevens's opinion—in which three other Justices joined (referred to below as the "Stevens group").

A bare majority of the Justices—four (the "Stevens group") relying on Title VI and one (Justice Powell) relying on the Fourteenth Amendment's equal protection clause—agreed that the University of California at Davis program unlawfully discriminated against Bakke, thus affirming the first part of the California court's judgment (ordering Bakke's admission). A different majority of five Justices—Justice Powell and the "Brennan group"—agreed that "the state has a substantial interest that legitimately may be served by a properly devised admissions program involving the competitive consideration of race and ethnic origin" (438 U.S. 265, 320 (1978)), thus reversing the second part of the California court's judgment (prohibiting the consideration of race in admissions). In summary, then, the Court invalidated the medical school's affirmative action plan by a 5-to-4 vote; but by a different 5-to-4 vote, the Court ruled that some consideration of race is nevertheless permissible in affirmative action admissions plans. Justice Powell was the only Justice in the majority for both votes.

In their various opinions in *Bakke*, the Justices debated the issues of which standard of review applies under the equal protection clause, what are the valid justifications for affirmative action programs, and the extent to which such programs can be race conscious, as well as whether the Title VI requirements for affirmative action are the same as those under the equal protection clause. No majority agreed fully on any of these issues, and they continued to be debated in the years following *Bakke*. Nevertheless, a review and comparison of opinions reveals three basic principles established by *Bakke* that were followed by later courts.

First, racial preferences that partake of quotas—rigid numerical or percentage goals defined specifically by race—are impermissible. Second, separate systems for reviewing minority applications—with procedures and criteria different from those used for nonminority applications—are impermissible. Third, Title VI embodies Fourteenth Amendment principles of equal protection and applies to race discrimination in the same way as the equal protection clause.

In addition to these principles that a majority of the Court adhered to in their various opinions, the Powell opinion in *Bakke* also includes important additional guidance for affirmative action plans. This guidance focuses primarily on the concept of student body diversity and on the importance of individualized comparisons of all applicants. In addition, the Powell opinion addresses the concept of differential or compensatory affirmative action plans.

The core of Justice Powell's guidance on student body diversity is that

> the state interest that would justify consideration of race or ethnic background . . . is not an interest in simple ethnic diversity, in which a specified percentage of the student body is in effect guaranteed to be members of selected ethnic groups, with the remaining percentage an undifferentiated aggregation of students. The diversity that furthers a compelling state interest encompasses a far broader array of qualifications and characteristics of which racial or ethnic origin is but a single though important element [438 U.S. at 315 (Powell, J.)].

The crux of Justice Powell's guidance on individualized comparisons of applicants is that

> race or ethnic background may be deemed a "plus" in a particular applicant's file, yet it [may] not insulate the individual from comparison with all other candidates for the available seats. The file of a particular black applicant may be examined for his potential contribution to diversity without the factor of race being decisive when compared, for example, with that of an applicant identified as an Italian-American if the latter is thought to exhibit qualities more likely to promote beneficial education pluralism . . . In short, an admissions program operated in this way is flexible enough to consider all pertinent elements of

diversity in light of the particular qualifications of each applicant, and to place them on the same footing for consideration, although not necessarily according to them the same weight. Indeed, the weight attributed to a particular quality may vary from year to year depending upon the "mix" both of the student body and the applicants for the incoming class [438 U.S. at 317–18 (Powell, J.) (emphasis added)].

And regarding differential admissions plans, Powell stated:

Racial classifications in admissions conceivably could serve a . . . purpose . . . which petitioner does not articulate: fair appraisal of each individual's academic promise in light of some bias in grading or testing procedures. To the extent that race and ethnic background were considered only to the extent of curing established inaccuracies in predicting academic performance, it might be argued that there is no "preference" at all [438 U.S. at 306 (Powell, J.)].

In completing his analysis in *Bakke*, Justice Powell used a "strict scrutiny" standard of review. The Brennan group, in contrast, used an "intermediate scrutiny" standard; and the Stevens group, relying on Title VI, did not directly confront the standard-of-review issue. Cases after *Bakke* but before *Grutter* and *Gratz* did resolve this issue, however—in particular *City of Richmond v. J. A. Croson Co.*, 488 U.S. 469 (1989), and *Adarand Constructors, Inc., v. Pena*, 515 U.S. 200, 220–21 (1995), both discussed in Section 4.6.3 of this book. Under these cases, a race-conscious affirmative action plan will be constitutional only if the institution can prove that its use of race is (1) "narrowly tailored" to (2) further a "compelling governmental interest." This "strict scrutiny" standard of review had previously been used in equal protection race discrimination cases that did not involve reverse discrimination; it is also the standard that was used by Justice Powell in *Bakke* (see 438 U.S. at 290–91) and by the state supreme courts in *DeFunis* and *Bakke*.

After the *Bakke* case, absent any consensus on the Court, most colleges and universities with affirmative action admissions plans followed the Powell guidelines. As the Court later explained in *Grutter*: "Since this Court's splintered decision in *Bakke*, Justice Powell's opinion . . . has served as the touchstone for constitutional analysis of race-conscious admissions policies. Public and private universities across the Nation have modeled their own admissions programs on Justice Powell's views" (539 U.S. at 307). In early challenges to the Powell type of race-conscious plan, the institutions usually prevailed.

After a period of relative quiet, however, a new round of court challenges to race-conscious admissions plans began in the 1990s, with several leading cases using reasoning and reaching results different from the earlier post-*Bakke* cases. In *Hopwood v. Texas*, 78 F.3d 932 (5th Cir. 1996), for instance, four rejected applicants sued the state and the University of Texas (UT) under the equal protection clause and Title VI, claiming that they were denied admission to the UT law school on the basis of their race. The plaintiffs challenged the continuing vitality of Justice Powell's opinion in the *Bakke* case and more generally challenged the authority of colleges and universities to use "diversity" as a rationale for considering race, gender, or other such characteristics as a "plus" factor in admissions. The law school's affirmative action admissions program gave preferences to African-American and Mexican-American applicants only and used a separate committee to evaluate their applications. "Cutoff scores" used to allocate applicants to various categories in the admissions process were lower for blacks and Mexican-Americans than for other applicants, resulting in the admission of students in the "minority" category whose college grades and LSAT scores were lower than those of some white applicants who had been rejected.

The trial and appellate courts used the strict scrutiny standard of review, requiring the defendant to establish that it had a "compelling interest" in using racial preferences and that its use of racial preferences was "narrowly tailored" to achieve its compelling interest. The law school had presented five justifications for its affirmative action admissions program, each of which, it argued, met the compelling state interest test: (1) to achieve the law school's mission of providing a first-class legal education to members of the two largest minority groups in Texas; (2) to achieve a diverse student body; (3) to remedy the present effects of past discrimination in the Texas public school system; (4) to comply with the 1983 consent decree with the Office of Civil Rights, U.S. Department of Education, regarding recruitment of African-American and Mexican-American students; and (5) to comply with the standards of the American Bar Association and American Association of Law Schools regarding diversity. The federal district court ruled that the portions of the law school's admissions program that gave "minority" applicants a separate review process violated the Fourteenth Amendment—following Justice Powell's reasoning on this point in his *Bakke* opinion. The district court also held, however, that the affirmative action plan furthered the compelling interest of attaining diversity in the student body (the law school's second justification) and that it served to remedy prior discrimination by the State of Texas in its entire public school system, including elementary and secondary schools (the law school's third justification).

A three-judge panel of the appellate court rejected these justifications and invalidated the law school's program. Addressing the diversity rationale first, the Fifth Circuit panel specifically rejected Justice Powell's reasoning about diversity and ruled that "achieving a diverse student body is not a compelling interest under the Fourteenth Amendment" (78 F.3d at 944). The appellate court then addressed the rationale of remedying prior discrimination. Although the court recognized that the state of Texas had discriminated on the basis of race and ethnicity in its public education system, the law school's admission program was not designed to remedy that prior unlawful conduct because the program gave preferences to minorities from outside Texas and to minorities who had attended private schools. Furthermore, said the court, in order for the admissions program to comply with constitutional requirements, the law school would have had to present evidence of a history of its own prior unlawful segregation. "A broad program that sweeps in all minorities with a remedy that is in no way related to past harms cannot survive constitutional scrutiny" (78 F.3d at 951). Once prior discrimination had been established, the law school would then have to trace present effects from the prior discrimination, to establish the size of those effects, and to develop a limited plan to remedy the harm. The "present effects" cited by both the law school and the district court—a bad reputation in the minority community and a perceived hostile environment in the law school for minority students—were insufficient, said the court, citing the Fourth Circuit's earlier opinion in *Podberesky v. Kirwan*, 38 F.3d at 147 (4th Cir. 1994) (discussed in Section 7.3.4 of this book). One appellate judge, although concurring in the result reached by the panel, disagreed with the majority's statement that diversity could never be a compelling state interest and—foreshadowing *Grutter*—asserted that it was an open question whether diversity could provide a compelling interest for a public graduate school's use of racial preferences in its admissions program.

After *Hopwood*, but before *Grutter* and *Gratz*, various important developments took place outside the courts. In Texas, the state legislature passed a statute providing alternative means by which to foster diversity in the undergraduate programs of public colleges and universities in the state. The statute reads:

> (a) Each general academic teaching institution shall admit an applicant for admission to the institution as an undergraduate student if the applicant graduated with a grade point average in the top 10 percent of the student's high school graduating class in one of the two school years preceding the academic year for which the applicant is applying for admission and the applicant graduated from a public or private high school in this state accredited by a generally recognized accrediting organization or from a high school operated by the United States Department of Defense . . .
>
> (b) After admitting an applicant under this section, the institution shall review the applicant's record, and any other factor the institution considers appropriate, to determine whether the applicant may require additional preparation for college-level work or would benefit from inclusion in a retention program [Tex. Educ. Code title 3, ch. 51, § 51.803].

Florida and California also adopted "percentage plans."

In the state of Washington, voters passed Initiative Measure 200 (I-200) (codified as Wash. Rev. Code § 49.60.400(1)), which prohibited discrimination or preferential treatment on the basis of race (and other suspect classes) in the state's "operation of public employment, public education or public contracting." Similarly, the voters of California approved Proposition 209, an amendment to their state constitution that outlawed voluntary affirmative action. The California measure, passed in 1996, provides that "the state shall not discriminate against, or grant preferential treatment to, any individual or group on the basis of race, sex, color, ethnicity, or national origin in the operation of public employment, public education, or public contracting" (Cal. Const. art. I, § 31(a)). Several civil rights groups challenged the measure on constitutional grounds, arguing that the provision violated the equal protection clause of the Fourteenth Amendment. The trial court entered a preliminary injunction and temporary restraining order to stop the state from enforcing the law. In *Coalition for Economic Equity v. Wilson*, 122 F.3d 692 (9th Cir. 1997), the U.S. Court of Appeals overturned the ruling of the trial court. According to the appellate court, Proposition 209 imposed no burden on racial or gender minorities, since it forbade discrimination against them. Since there is no constitutional right to preferential treatment, said the court, forbidding preferential treatment on the basis of race or gender did not injure these groups. Characterizing the law as "neutral," and concluding that the plaintiffs had "no likelihood of success on the merits," the court vacated the preliminary injunction and remanded the case to the trial court.

In 2003, the U.S. Supreme Court heard and decided the two University of Michigan cases together as "companion cases." In *Grutter v. Bollinger*, 539 U.S. 306 (2003), rejected white applicants challenged the law school's plan for affirmative action in admissions; in *Gratz v. Bollinger*, 539 U.S. 244 (2003), rejected white applicants challenged a plan of the university's undergraduate College of Literature, Science, and the Arts (LSA). Both plans were voluntary, race-conscious plans, but they were quite different in their particulars, as explained below. In each case, the plaintiffs alleged that the affirmative action plan violated not only the equal protection clause but also Title VI (42 U.S.C. § 2000d) and Section 1981 (42 U.S.C. § 1981). In *Grutter*, the Court upheld the law school plan by a 5-to-4 vote; in *Gratz*, the Court invalidated the undergraduate plan by a 6-to-3 vote. Justice O'Connor, who authored the majority opinion in *Grutter*, was the only Justice in the majority in both cases. All together, the Justices issued thirteen opinions in the two cases.

The *Grutter* majority reaffirmed the two basic points upon which a majority of the Justices in *Bakke* agreed: that rigid racial quotas are impermissible and that other, more flexible forms of racial preferences are permissible. Further, the *Grutter* majority explicitly approved and adopted Justice Powell's reasoning in the *Bakke* case (539 U.S. at 323–25), and for the most part the *Gratz* majority did so as well (539 U.S. at 270–74). Justice Powell's principles regarding affirmative action in admissions, adhered to only by Justice Powell in *Bakke*, thus have now become the principles of the Court.

Like Justice Powell, both the *Grutter* and *Gratz* majorities applied a strict scrutiny standard of review. As explained by the *Gratz* majority, "strict scrutiny" review means that "'any person, of whatever race, has the right to demand that any governmental actor subject to the Constitution justify any racial classification subjecting that person to unequal treatment under the strictest of judicial scrutiny'" (*Gratz*, 539 U.S. at 270, quoting *Adarand*, 515 U.S. at 224). The *Grutter* majority used the same strict scrutiny standard but tempered its application to race-conscious admissions policies by emphasizing that courts should defer to the institution's own judgments about its educational mission. Both the law school policy (*Grutter*) and the undergraduate college policy (*Gratz*) met the "compelling interest" component of strict scrutiny (see below), but only the law school plan met the second, "narrow tailoring" component.[4] Analytically, that is the difference between the two cases and the reason for the differing results.

---

[4] The term "narrow tailoring" applies to the particular race-conscious means by which an institution seeks to achieve a "compelling interest" (here, the educational benefits of student body diversity).

In *Grutter*, the lead plaintiff, a white Michigan resident, sued university president Lee Bollinger and others, seeking damages, an order requiring her admission to the law school, and an injunction prohibiting continued racial discrimination by the law school. The plaintiff alleged that the law school used race "as a 'predominant' factor, giving applicants who belong to certain minority groups 'a significantly greater chance of admission than students with similar credentials from disfavored racial groups'" (539 U.S. at 306). The law school's admissions policy, drafted and adopted by a faculty committee in 1992, expresses the law school's interest in "achiev[ing] that diversity which has the potential to enrich everyone's education." The policy recognizes possible bases for diversity admissions and provides that all such "diversity contributions are eligible for 'substantial weight' in the admissions process." While diversity therefore is not defined "solely in terms of racial and ethnic status," the policy does reaffirm a commitment to "racial and ethnic diversity with special reference to the inclusion of students from groups that have been historically discriminated against, like African-Americans, Hispanics and Native Americans." (See 539 U.S. at 315–16, quoting from the trial court record.) The significance of race in admissions decisions "varies from one applicant to another"; although race may play no role in the decision to admit some students, for others "it may be a 'determinative' factor." The law school's goal is to include a "critical mass of under-represented minority students" in each class. "Meaningful numbers" rising to the level of a "critical mass" do not indicate a particular "number, percentage, or range of numbers or percentages," but only "numbers such that the under-represented minority students do not feel isolated or like spokespersons for their race." (See 539 U.S. at 314–16, quoting and paraphrasing testimony of the university's witnesses.)

The Court majority in *Grutter* (Justice O'Connor, joined by Justices Stevens, Souter, Ginsburg, and Breyer), adopting the reasoning of Justice Powell's *Bakke* opinion, rejected the plaintiffs' arguments. First, the *Grutter* majority held that "student body diversity is a compelling state interest that can justify the use of race in University admissions" (539 U.S. at 325). This is because "it is necessary that the path to leadership be visibly open to talented and qualified individuals of every race and ethnicity. All members of our heterogeneous society must have confidence in the openness and integrity of the educational institutions that provide . . . the training and education necessary to succeed in America" (539 U.S. at 332–33). Race and ethnicity, however, are not the only factors pertinent to student body diversity. Rather, student body diversity, as a compelling interest, entails a "broad range of qualities and experiences that may be considered valuable contributions" and "a wide variety of characteristics besides race and ethnicity" (*Grutter*, 539 U.S. at 338–39). Moreover, the majority indicated that courts should "defer" to universities' judgments about "the educational benefits that diversity is designed to produce." "The institution's educational judgment that [student body] diversity is essential to its educational mission," said the Court, "is one to which we defer" (539 U.S. at 328).

Next, the majority in *Grutter* held that the law school's admissions policy was "narrowly tailored" to the interest in student body diversity. The policy's stated goal of "attaining a critical mass of underrepresented minority students" did not constitute a prohibited quota (539 U.S. at 335–36). Instead, the admissions process was "flexible enough" to ensure individual treatment for each applicant without "race or ethnicity" becoming "the defining feature" of the application (539 U.S. at 337). It was particularly important to the Court, regarding narrow tailoring, that "the Law School engages in a highly individualized, holistic review of each applicant's file, giving serious consideration to all the ways an applicant might contribute to a diverse educational environment"; that "the Law School awards no mechanical, predetermined diversity 'bonuses' based on race or ethnicity" (as had occurred in the program at issue in *Gratz*); that the law school "adequately ensures that all factors that may contribute to student body diversity are meaningfully considered alongside race in admissions decisions" (as the Harvard plan approved by Justice Powell in *Bakke* had done); that the "Law School does not . . . limit in any way the broad range of qualities and experiences that may be considered valuable contributions to student body diversity" and "seriously considers each 'applicant's promise of making a notable contribution to the class by way of a particular strength, attainment, or characteristic'"; that all "applicants have the opportunity to highlight their own potential diversity contributions through the submission of a personal statement, letters of recommendation, and an essay describing the ways in which the applicant will contribute to the life and diversity of the Law School"; and that, in practice, "the Law School actually gives substantial weight to diversity factors besides race, . . . frequently accept[ing] nonminority applicants with grades and test scores lower than underrepresented minority applicants (and other nonminority applicants) who are rejected" (539 U.S. at 337–39).

Completing its narrow tailoring analysis, the Court in *Grutter* determined that the "holistic," individualized review provided for by the policy does not "unduly" burden individuals who are not members of the favored racial and ethnic groups. The law school, moreover, had "sufficiently considered workable race-neutral alternatives" before adopting any racial preferences. Since the law school's policy therefore met both components of strict scrutiny review, the Court upheld the policy.

In *Gratz v. Bollinger*, the case involving the University of Michigan's undergraduate College of Literature, Science, and the Arts, the plaintiffs sought damages, declaratory relief, and an injunction prohibiting continued discrimination by the university. They argued that "'diversity as a basis for employing racial preferences is simply too open-ended, ill-defined, and indefinite to constitute a compelling interest capable of supporting narrowly tailored means'" (539 U.S. at 268, quoting Brief for Petitioners) and, further, that the university's admissions policy was not narrowly tailored to achieve the end of student body diversity.

According to the Court, the university's "Office of Undergraduate Admissions [oversaw] the . . . admissions process" and promulgated "written guidelines for each academic year." Under its admissions policy, the undergraduate college considered African-Americans, Hispanics, and Native Americans to be "under-represented minorities." The admissions policy employed a "selection index" under which each applicant could score up to a maximum of 150 points.

Applicants received points in consideration of their "high school grade point average, standardized test scores, academic quality and curriculum strength of applicant's high school, in-state residency, alumni relationship, personal essay, and personal achievement or leadership" (539 U.S. at 254–55). Under an additional "miscellaneous" category, "an applicant was entitled to 20 points based upon . . . membership in an under-represented racial or ethnic minority group." An Admissions Review Committee provided an additional level of review for certain applicants flagged by admissions counselors. To be flagged, the applicant must have achieved "a minimum selection index score" and "possess a quality or characteristic important to the University's composition of its freshman class," examples of which included "socioeconomic disadvantage" and "under-represented race, ethnicity or geography." Although the evidence did not reveal "precisely how many applications [were] flagged for this individualized consideration . . ., it [was] undisputed that such consideration [was] the exception and not the rule" (539 U.S. at 274).

The *Gratz* majority (Chief Justice Rehnquist, joined by Justices Scalia, O'Connor, Kennedy, and Thomas) held that "the admissions policy violate[d] the Equal Protection Clause of the Fourteenth Amendment" (as well as Title VI and Section 1981) because it failed to provide "individualized consideration" of each applicant and therefore was not "narrowly tailored" to achieve the compelling interest in student body diversity. Specifically:

> The LSA's policy automatically distributes 20 points to every single applicant from an "underrepresented minority" group, as defined by the University. The only consideration that accompanies this distribution of points is a factual review of an application to determine whether an individual is a member of one of these minority groups. Moreover, unlike Justice Powell's example, where the race of a "particular black applicant" could be considered without being decisive, see *Bakke*, 438 U.S., at 317, 98 S. Ct. 2733, the LSA's automatic distribution of 20 points has the effect of making "the factor of race . . . decisive" for virtually every minimally qualified underrepresented minority applicant [539 U.S. at 271–72].

The undergraduate plan, therefore, was "not narrowly tailored to achieve the LSA's compelling interest in student body diversity" and therefore failed strict scrutiny review.

Because Title VI and the equal protection clause embody the same legal standards, the *Grutter* and *Gratz* principles are applicable to both public institutions and private institutions that receive federal financial assistance. These principles are also likely to apply, in general, to institutions' race-conscious decision making in areas beyond admissions (for example, financial aid (as discussed in Section 7.3.4), student orientation programs, or student housing). The principles of Justice Powell's opinion in *Bakke* also apply, since the Court approved and adopted them in *Grutter* and *Gratz*. These various principles, according to the Court, must be followed "in practice as well as in theory" (*Grutter*, 539 U.S. at 338).

The U.S. Supreme Court revisited and reviewed the *Grutter* and *Gratz* cases in *Parents Involved in Community Schools v. Seattle School District No. 1*, 551 U.S. 701 (2007). In this case, the Supreme Court struck down voluntary, race-conscious integration plans of school districts in Seattle, Washington, and Louisville, Kentucky. The school districts had voluntarily adopted student assignment plans that relied on race to determine which schools certain students could attend. There were five opinions in all; each in its own way and to varying degrees recognized the continuing authority of *Grutter* and *Gratz* in higher education (although the Court refused to apply the *Grutter* analysis on the educational benefits of diversity to the K–12 context). Chief Justice Roberts wrote an opinion that spoke for a majority of five Justices only in part; Justice Kennedy wrote a concurring opinion that provided the fifth vote for the parts of the Roberts opinion that spoke for a majority and declined to support other parts of the Roberts opinion and therefore spoke only for a plurality. The Court majority held that correcting a "racial imbalance" in K–12 schools was not a compelling governmental interest. The majority also reemphasized that, to survive strict scrutiny review, racial classifications must be calibrated so as to be effective in helping to achieve a compelling governmental interest, while not making race a predominant factor in decision making. In addition, the Court reiterated that institutions must be able to demonstrate that they have given serious consideration to race-neutral alternatives before using racial classifications.

Justice Kennedy's separate opinion is consistent with the Roberts opinion in insisting on a vigorous enforcement of strict scrutiny review for voluntary admissions plans that employ racial classifications (127 S. Ct. at 2789–910). But within this strict scrutiny framework, Justice Kennedy, unlike Chief Justice Roberts, took pains to carve out some room for the permissible use of race-conscious measures (127 S. Ct. at 2791–92). Of broader significance, Justice Kennedy's opinion in *Parents Involved* emphasizes that, in his view, there are other "race conscious measures," beyond the specific type of admissions plans permitted by *Grutter and Gratz*, that educational institutions may use to "pursue the goal of bringing together students of diverse backgrounds and races" (127 S. Ct. at 2792). Examples that Justice Kennedy used include: "allocating resources for special programs; recruiting students and faculty in a targeted fashion; and tracking enrollments, performance, and other statistics by race" (127 S. Ct. at 2792). According to the Kennedy opinion: "These mechanisms are race conscious but do not lead to different treatment based on a classification that tells each student he or she is to be defined by race, so it is unlikely any of them would demand strict scrutiny to be found permissible." The Roberts opinion makes a similar point that may be supportive of at least part of Justice Kennedy's position (see 127 S. Ct. at 2766; Roberts, C.J. for a plurality). Since Justice Kennedy cast the deciding fifth vote on these and other issues, his concurring opinion should be reviewed carefully by institutions considering race-conscious programs of any sort.

Since the U.S. Supreme Court's decision in the *Parents Involved* case, there have been further important developments in the lower federal courts and in the U.S. Department of Education. Four of these developments are discussed immediately below.

Prior to *Parents Involved*, and *Grutter* and *Gratz*, the Texas legislature passed legislation under which the top 10 percent of each high school class was guaranteed admission to a Texas state university—a facially "race-neutral" law that nevertheless was intended in large part to increase minority enrollment. (See discussion above in this section.) The University of Texas at Austin (UT-Austin) adopted a 10% plan based on this legislation; and subsequently it also reintroduced race as one of a number of factors in admissions to consider as part of a holistic assessment of applicants. Two white female Texas residents alleged that the university's admissions policy discriminated against them on the basis of race. The central question in the case was whether it was necessary for race to be a factor in admissions decisions in order for the university to achieve its educational goals regarding student body diversity. *Fisher v. University of Texas at Austin*, 631 F.3d 213 (5th Cir. 2011), *rehearing en banc denied*, 644 F.3d 301 (5th Cir. 2011), *cert. granted*, 80 U.S.L.W. 347 (Feb. 21, 2012).

Judge Higginbotham's opinion for a three-judge panel of the court concluded that the university had sought to achieve educational benefits that were "essential to its mission"—including those associated with promoting cross-racial understanding, preparing students to function in a multicultural workforce, and cultivating leadership—rather than mere racial balancing based on the state's demographics (*id.*). Applying Justice O'Connor's majority opinion in *Grutter*, the court identified at least three distinct educational objectives served by diversity: increased perspectives (contributing to the greatest possible variety of backgrounds), professionalism (preparing students for work and citizenship), and civic engagement (encouraging future leaders from previously underrepresented backgrounds) (*id.* at 219–220). Following *Grutter*'s lead, the court upheld the university's pursuit of a "critical mass" of students from various groups that were underrepresented on campus in order to achieve the educational benefits of diversity. The court also found that the state's percentage plan was not an adequate race-neutral alternative—in part because it was a "blunt tool" that essentially constituted a proxy for race while ignoring the full range of diversity contributions that would be captured in a broad individualized assessment, and in part because it relied on segregated communities to produce racial diversity (*id.* at 242). (In a concurring opinion, Judge King declined to endorse this critique of the percent plan because the issue had not been briefed for the court (*id.* at 247).) Echoing Justice O'Connor's admonition in *Grutter* that race-conscious plans must be of limited duration, the court also cautioned that "we cannot bless the university's race-conscious admissions program in perpetuity" (*id.* at 246). In an unusual and lengthy concurrence that reads more like a dissent, Judge Garza indicated that while the panel opinion was consistent with *Grutter*, he thought that *Grutter* had been incorrectly decided and called on the U.S. Supreme Court to overrule it (*id.* at 247–266).

The plaintiffs moved for a rehearing before the full court. Although the full court denied a rehearing, five judges dissented, arguing that the decision by the three-judge panel had failed to adhere rigidly to the narrow-tailoring requirements of *Grutter* (644 F.3d 301). The plaintiffs then asked the U.S. Supreme Court to review the Fifth Circuit panel decision, and it agreed in February of 2012. Justice Kagan recused herself; she had participated in developing a brief in support of the university prior to her appointment to the Supreme Court.

Just before this book went to press, the U.S. Supreme Court announced its opinion in *Fisher* (133 S. Ct. 2411 (2013)). The Court did not rule on whether or not UT-Austin had violated the equal protection clause, nor whether its admissions program complied with *Grutter*. Furthermore, it did not overrule *Grutter*, nor did the Court state that race could not be used as a factor in admissions decisions. Instead, the Court, in a 7-1 opinion (with Justice Ginsburg dissenting) vacated the appellate court opinion and remanded the case to that court for further analysis of whether the university had provided sufficient evidence of "narrow tailoring" under the strict scrutiny theory.

The Court did say, importantly, that a college must exhaust every race-neutral alternative to obtain a diverse student body before it may use race (or some other protected characteristic) as an explicit criterion in making admissions decisions. In examining a college's use of race, said the Court, a reviewing court must be satisfied that "no workable race-neutral alternatives would produce the educational benefits of diversity." This is a very high standard, one that may be impossible for many, if not most, colleges and universities to meet.

The Court criticized the panel of Fifth Circuit judges who, said the majority, were too deferential to the university's insistence that it had acted in "good faith," and explained that courts reviewing affirmative action plans must apply "strict scrutiny" to the program. The Court said: "Strict scrutiny does not permit a court to accept a school's assertion that its admissions process uses race in a permissible way without closely examining how the process works in practice," saying that the college must first have demonstrated that diversity is a compelling government interest (which the Court said it had done), and must then have "offered sufficient evidence to prove that its admissions program is narrowly tailored to obtain the educational benefits of diversity."

Justices Scalia and Thomas joined the majority opinion, but also wrote concurring opinions, stating that they believed any use of race to make admissions decisions was unlawful. Justice Ginsburg dissented, stating that the University of Texas had followed *Grutter*'s guidance in crafting its admissions program, that its evidence satisfied the strict scrutiny test, and thus its admissions program was lawful.

A second judicial development concerned a group of California high school and college students who challenged section 31 of article I of the California constitution, arguing that the result in *Grutter* required a finding that section 31 violated the equal protection clause. *Coalition to Defend Affirmative Action v. Brown*, 2012 U.S. App. LEXIS 6574 (9th Cir. April 2, 2012). (See discussion above of an earlier challenge to this same section of the California constitution.) A federal district court dismissed the lawsuit, and a panel of the U.S. Court of Appeals for the Ninth Circuit affirmed, stating that *Grutter* permitted but did not require affirmative action, and reiterating its support for its previous ruling in *Coalition for Economic Equity v. Wilson* (*Wilson II*) (see above).

Subsequently, the U.S. Court of Appeals for the Sixth Circuit considered a similar voter-initiated amendment to the Michigan Constitution that prohibited Michigan's public colleges and universities from granting "preferential treatment to any individual or group on the basis of race, sex, color, ethnicity, or national origin" (*BAMN v. Regents of the University of Michigan et al.*, 701 F.3d 466 (6th Cir., Nov. 2012) (*en banc*)). The Sixth Circuit reached a different result, however; in an *en banc* decision it held that the voter initiative violated the equal protection clause because it altered the state's political structure by impermissibly burdening racial minorities. The U.S. Supreme Court agreed to hear the case during its 2013–14 term (*Schuette v. Coalition to Defend Affirmative Action*, 133 S. Ct. 1633 (2013)).

In a fourth development subsequent to *Grutter* and *Gratz*, the U.S. Department of Education's Office for Civil Rights (OCR) issued a "Dear Colleague" letter reiterating the principles enunciated in *Grutter* and *Gratz* and discussing the ways in which postsecondary institutions can voluntarily consider race to further the compelling interest of achieving diversity (see http://www2.ed.gov/about/offices/list/ocr/letters/colleague-201111.html). This guidance, issued in December 2011, did not break new legal ground, but it did provide examples of approaches to affirmative action that the Department of Education considers to be consistent with case law under Title IV, Title VI, and the equal protection clause. An additional "Dear Colleague" letter, issued on September 27, 2013, supplements the 2011 letter and advises colleges that race-based admissions are still permissible in light of *Fisher*.

Although the fundamental principles enunciated in the *Grutter* case have been reaffirmed by the U.S. Supreme Court in *Parents Involved* and apparently accepted by the Court in *Fisher*, the sharply contrasting opinions in these cases are a reminder that the legal and policy issues remain sensitive and highly charged. Lower court opinions that are sure to follow will present further issues about affirmative action and eventually will give the Supreme Court another opportunity to reconsider and modify its analysis in *Grutter*, *Gratz* and *Fisher*. Thus, administrators should involve legal counsel fully when considering the adoption or revision of any affirmative action admissions policy. The following seventeen guidelines—the last twelve of which apply specifically to race-conscious plans—can assist institutions in their deliberations.[5]

1. As a threshold matter, an institution may wish to consider whether it has ever discriminated against minorities or women in its admissions policies. If any such unlawful discrimination has occurred in the past, and its existence can be demonstrated with evidence sufficient to support a judicial finding of unlawful discrimination, the law requires that the institution use affirmative action to the extent necessary to overcome any present effects of the past discrimination. (See the discussion in the *Bakke* opinions, 438 U.S. at 284, 328, 414; see also the *Hopwood* case (discussed earlier in this section); and

---

[5] As for the other parts of this book that set out guidelines or suggestions for institutions or others, the seventeen guidelines here are not intended as legal advice. For legal advice on the matters covered in these guidelines or elsewhere in this section, institutional administrators should consult their institution's legal counsel.

*Podberesky v. Kirwan*, discussed in Section 7.3.4 of this book.) The limits that *Grutter*, *Gratz*, and *Bakke* place on the voluntary use of racial preferences for diversity purposes do not apply to situations in which the institution itself has engaged in prior unlawful discrimination whose effects continue to the present. At least since *Bakke*, it has been clear that, when "an institution has been found, by a court, legislature, or administrative agency, to have discriminated on the basis of race, color, or national origin[,] [r]ace-conscious procedures that are impermissible in voluntary affirmative action programs may be required [in order] to correct specific acts of past discrimination committed by an institution or other entity to which the institution is directly related" (U.S. Department of Health, Education, and Welfare, "Policy Interpretation of Title VI," 44 Fed. Reg. 58509, 58510 (October 10, 1979)). (For an example of a case applying this principle, see *Geier v. Alexander*, 801 F.2d 799 (6th Cir. 1986).) If a court or administrative agency makes such a finding and orders the institution to remedy the present effects of the past discrimination, the institution's plan will be a *mandatory* (or remedial) affirmative action plan (see discussion at the beginning of this section). Absent any such finding and order by a government body, the institution may nevertheless implement a *voluntary* affirmative action plan designed to remedy the present effects of past discrimination, if it makes its own findings on past discrimination and its present effects, and if these findings are supportable with evidence of discrimination of the type and extent used by courts in affirmative action cases.

With respect to voluntary affirmative action, it is clear that institutions have a "compelling interest in remedying past and present discrimination" (*United States v. Paradise*, 480 U.S. 149, 167 (1987)). But this rationale may be used only when the institution seeks to remedy its own prior discrimination or that of other entities whose discrimination the institution has supported (or perhaps, for a public institution, the discrimination of the higher education system of which it is a constituent part). Remedying prior societal discrimination does not provide justification for the use of racial preferences—at least not unless the institution has been a participant or "passive participant" in such discrimination (see *City of Richmond v. Croson Co.*, 488 U.S. 469, 485–86, 492 (1989)). *Croson* and *Adarand Constructors, Inc., v. Pena*, 515 U.S. 200 (1995), taken together, make this point in cases that are not about education but whose reasoning would extend to education admissions. (For an education case that makes the same point, see *Wygant v. Jackson*, 476 U.S. 267, 274 (1986) (plurality opinion of Powell, J.).)

2. In considering whether to adopt or revise an affirmative action policy for admissions, an institution should rely demonstrably on the educational expertise of its faculty and academic administrators and involve policy makers at the highest levels of authority within the institution. These planners and decision makers should exercise special care in determining the institution's purposes and objectives in light of its educational mission, making their decisions in the context of these purposes and objectives. A lower court made these points clearly in a case decided two years before *Bakke* and more than twenty-five years before *Grutter* and *Gratz*. In this case, *Hupart v. Board of*

*Higher Education of the City of New York*, 420 F. Supp. 1087 (S.D.N.Y. 1976), the court warned:

> [E]very distinction made on a racial basis . . . must be justified . . . It cannot be accomplished thoughtlessly or covertly, then justified after the fact. The defendants cannot sustain their burden of justification by coming to court with an array of hypothetical and post facto justifications for discrimination that has occurred either without their approval or without their conscious and formal choice to discriminate as a matter of official policy. It is not for the court to supply a . . . compelling basis . . . to sustain the questioned state action [420 F. Supp. at 1106].

3. An institution may consider one or a combination of two basic approaches to voluntary affirmative action: the *race-neutral* or *uniform* approach, and the *race-conscious* or *preferential* approach (see guidelines 4 and 6 below). An institution might also consider a third possible approach, falling between the other two, which may be called a *differential*, or *compensatory*, approach (see guideline 5 below). While all three approaches can be implemented lawfully, the potential for legal challenge increases as the institution proceeds from a race-neutral to a differential to a race-conscious approach. The potential for substantially increasing minority enrollment also increases, however, so that an institution that is deterred by the possibility of legal action may also be forsaking part of the means to achieve its educational and societal goals.

4. A *race-neutral* or *uniform* affirmative action policy involves revising or supplementing the institution's general admissions standards or procedures so that they are more sensitively attuned to the varying qualifications and potential contributions of all applicants, including minority and disadvantaged applicants. These changes are then applied uniformly to all applicants. For example, all applicants might be eligible for credit for working to help put themselves through school, for demonstrated commitment to living and working in a blighted geographical area, for being the first in one's family to attend college, for residing in an inner-city area from which the institution typically draws very few students, or for overcoming handicaps or disadvantages. Or institutions might cease using preferences for "legacies," or for members of a particular religious denomination whose membership includes relatively few minorities. Or institutions may use test scores from additional tests that supplement traditional standardized tests and test abilities beyond what the standardized test measures. Such changes would allow all candidates—regardless of race, ethnicity, or sex—to demonstrate particular pertinent qualities that may not be reflected in grades or scores on traditional tests.

In the *Parents Involved* case, above in this section, the U.S. Supreme Court provided the beginnings of a conceptual basis for justifying some consideration of race in devising uniform plans that do not employ explicit race classifications. Justice Kennedy's concurring opinion, in particular, supports the use of "general policies" that are designed "to encourage a diverse study body, one aspect of which is its racial composition" (127 S. Ct. at 2792). Such policies may be "race-conscious" in the sense that the persons devising the policy may take account of the impact that it would have on racial diversity. This would likely occur with most of the examples of changes in admissions policies that are set out at the beginning of this guideline. Though race-conscious in this sense, such policies would apparently still be considered race-neutral because they do not use race as a criterion in making admission decisions about particular individuals. And being race-neutral, such policies apparently would not be subject to strict scrutiny review.

5. A *differential* or *compensatory* affirmative action policy would be based on the concept that equal treatment of differently situated individuals may itself create inequality. Different or supplementary standards for such individuals would become appropriate when use of uniform standards would in effect discriminate against them. In *Bakke*, Justice Powell referred to a differential system by noting:

> Racial classifications in admissions conceivably could serve a . . . purpose . . . which petitioner does not articulate: fair appraisal of each individual's academic promise in light of some bias in grading or testing procedures. To the extent that race and ethnic background were considered only to the extent of curing established inaccuracies in predicting academic performance, it might be argued that there is no "preference" at all [438 U.S. at 306 n.43].

Using such a rationale, the institution might, for example, apply psychometric measures to determine whether a standardized admissions test that it uses is less valid or reliable as applied to its minority or disadvantaged applicants. If it is, the institution might consider using another supplementary test or some other criterion in lieu of or in addition to the standardized test. Or if an institution provides preferences for "legacies," or for adherents of a particular religion or graduates of schools affiliated with a particular denomination, the institution may consider whether such a criterion discriminates in effect against applicants from particular minority groups; if it does, the institution may consider using other compensating criteria for the minority applicants who are disadvantaged by the institution's use of the discriminatory criterion. Since the institution would be revising its policies in order to advantage minority applicants, having determined that they are disadvantaged by the current policy, it is unlikely that such a revision would be considered race neutral, as a uniform system would be.

To remain true to the theory of a differential system, an institution can modify standards or procedures only to the extent necessary to counteract the discriminatory effect of applying a particular uniform standard or standards; and the substituted or supplementary standards or procedures must be designed to select only candidates whose qualifications and potential contributions are comparable to those of other candidates who are selected for admission. The goal, in other words, would be to avoid a disadvantage to minority applicants rather than to create a preference for them.[6] Furthermore, it may be problematic to modify standards or procedures in any particular admissions cycle in light of the need to set clear and consistent expectations for all applicants. See *Ricci v. DeStefano*, 129 S.Ct. 2658 (2009), discussed in Section 4.6.2 of this book.

6. A *race-conscious* or *race-preferential* affirmative action policy explicitly provides some form of advantage or preference that is available only to applicants of particular racial or ethnic backgrounds. The admissions policies at issue in the cases discussed above, for the most part, fit within this category. It is the advantage available only to minorities that creates the reverse discrimination claim. For some institutions, especially highly selective institutions and large institutions with graduate and professional programs, some form of racial preference may indeed be necessary for the institution (or a particular school within the institution) to achieve its educational and societal objectives. In *Bakke*, the four Justices in the Brennan group agreed that

> [t]here are no practical means by which . . . [the university] could achieve its
> ends in the foreseeable future without the use of race-conscious measures.
> With respect to any factor (such as poverty or family educational background)
> that may be used as a substitute for race as an indicator of past discrimination,
> whites greatly outnumber racial minorities simply because whites make up a far
> larger percentage of the total population and therefore far outnumber minorities
> in absolute terms at every socioeconomic level . . . Moreover, while race is
> positively correlated with differences in . . . [grades and standardized test]
> scores, economic disadvantage is not [438 U.S. at 376–77].

Race-conscious policies may thus fulfill objectives broader than those of differential policies, namely alleviating the effects of past institutional discrimination (see guideline 1 above) and diversifying the student body (see guidelines 11 and 12 below).

7. An institution opting for a voluntary, race-conscious policy must assure that its racial preferences do not constitute a "quota." In *Bakke*, the Court ruled, by a 5-to-4 vote, that explicit racial or ethnic quotas constitute unlawful reverse discrimination. The Court in *Grutter* and *Gratz* affirmed this basic point. As the majority in *Grutter* explained, a quota "is a program in which a certain fixed number or proportion of opportunities are 'reserved exclusively for certain minority groups'" (539 U.S. at 335, quoting *Croson*, 488 U.S. at 496). Quotas "'impose a fixed number or percentage, which must be attained, or which cannot be exceeded'" and thus "'insulate the individual from comparison with all other candidates for the available seats'" (539 U.S. at 335,

---

[6]Separate standards or procedures for minority applicants are generally impermissible when used in a way that provides a preference for such applicants (see guideline 8). Since a true differential plan does not provide any preference, it should follow that some separate treatment would be permissible when it serves the purposes of such a plan.

quoting *Sheet Metal Workers v. EEOC*, 478 U.S. 421, 495 (1986) (O'Connor, J., concurring and dissenting), and *Bakke*, 438 U.S. at 317 (Powell, J.)). Such a policy would violate the equal protection clause as well as Title VI. A goal, on the other hand, "'require[s] only a good-faith effort . . . to come within a range demarcated by the goal itself,' and permits consideration of race as a 'plus' factor in any given case while still ensuring that each candidate 'compete[s] with all other qualified applicants'" (539 U.S. at 335, citing and quoting *Sheet Metal Workers v. EEOC*, 478 U.S. at 495, and *Johnson v. Transportation Agency*, 480 U.S. 616, 638 (1987)). "[A] court would not assume that a university [employing such a policy] would operate it as a cover for the functional equivalent of a quota system" (*Bakke*, 438 U.S. at 317–18) (Powell, J.).

8. An institution using race-conscious policies should avoid using separate admissions committees, criteria, or cutoff scores for minority applicants. Such mechanisms are vulnerable to legal challenge, as the Court suggested in *Bakke* and directly held in *Grutter*. "[U]niversities cannot . . . put members of [certain racial] groups on separate admissions tracks . . . Nor can universities insulate applicants who belong to certain racial or ethnic groups from the competition for admission" (*Grutter*, 539 U.S. at 334, citing *Bakke*, 438 U.S. at 315–16) (Powell, J.). The district court in *Hopwood* (discussed earlier in this section) invalidated part of the University of Texas law school's plan on this basis (861 F. Supp. at 577–79). This does not necessarily mean, however, that any difference in treatment is always impermissible. In *Smith v. University of Washington*, 392 F.3d 367 (9th Cir. 2004), for instance, the court upheld a law school's use of a letter of inquiry that went only to some minority applicants, as well as a procedure for expedited review of certain minority applications done for recruitment purposes (392 F.3d at 376–78, 380–81).

9. Institutions should clarify exactly why and how they use racial and ethnic preferences, distinguishing between the "remedying past discrimination" rationale and the "student body diversity" rationale. If employing the remedial rationale, the institution should identify and document the particular present effects of past institutional discrimination that the institution seeks to remedy. For the diversity rationale, the institution should define its diversity objectives and identify the particular values of diversity for its academic environment (see guideline 11). The institution may also wish to justify its choices of which minority groups it covers. (For discussion of the use of preferences for Asian-American applicants, see *Smith v. University of Washington* in guideline 8, 392 F.3d at 378–79 (upholding a "slight plus" for Asian-American applicants.

10. An institution that has, or is considering, a voluntary, race-conscious admissions plan should be familiar with *state* law in its state regarding such plans. Some states have amended their state statutes or state constitutions to prohibit state institutions from using such plans. California, Washington, Michigan, Nebraska, Arizona, and New Hampshire are all examples. Other states may reach the same result through administrative regulations or through state court interpretations of the state constitution. Florida is a leading example (Fla. Admin. Code Ann. r. 6C-6.002(7)).

11. An institution relying on student body diversity as the justification for a voluntary, race-conscious admissions plan should consider clearly elucidating the importance of such diversity to the institution or to particular schools within the institutions and connecting student body diversity to the institution's or school's educational mission. The institution will likely want to make these judgments at a high level of authority and with substantial faculty participation (see guideline 2).

12. A race-conscious admissions policy should broadly define student body diversity to include numerous factors beyond race and ethnicity, and the policy in operation should result in substantial weight being given to such additional factors. "[A]n admissions program must be flexible enough to consider all pertinent elements of diversity in light of the particular qualifications of each applicant" (*Grutter*, 539 U.S. at 334). The policy must take into account "a wide variety of characteristics besides race and ethnicity that contribute to a diverse student body" (*Grutter*, 539 U.S. at 339) and must "ensure that all factors that may contribute to student body diversity are . . . fully considered alongside race in admissions decisions" (*Grutter*, 539 U.S. at 337). The admissions staff and committee must "giv[e] serious consideration to all the ways an applicant might contribute to a diverse educational environment" (*Grutter*, 539 U.S. at 337), so that these factors are taken into account and weighted appropriately "in practice as well as in theory" (*Grutter*, 539 U.S. at 338).

13. Race-conscious admissions policies must provide for "individualized consideration" of applicants. According to Justice Powell, the key to a permissible racial preference is "a policy of individual comparisons" that "assures a measure of competition among all applicants" (438 U.S. at 319, n.53) and that uses "race or ethnic background only as a 'plus' in a particular applicant's file" (438 U.S. at 317). Following Justice Powell, the *Grutter* majority specified that "race [must] be used in a flexible, nonmechanical way . . . as a 'plus' factor in the context of individualized consideration of each . . . applicant" (539 U.S. at 334, citing *Bakke*, 438 U.S. at 315–18) (Powell, J.). The institution's policy must "ensure that each applicant is evaluated as an individual and not in a way that makes an applicant's race or ethnicity the defining feature of his or her application. The importance of this individualized consideration in the context of a race-conscious admissions program is paramount" (*Grutter*, 539 U.S. at 337).

14. Consistent with guideline 13, an institution should avoid using "automatic" points or bonuses that are awarded to all applicants from specified minority groups. There may be no "mechanical, predetermined diversity 'bonuses' based on race or ethnicity" (*Grutter*, 539 U.S. at 337). Such mechanisms are prohibited whenever the "automatic distribution of . . . points has the effect of making 'the factor of race . . . decisive' for . . . qualified minority applicants" (*Gratz*, 539 U.S. at 272, citing *Bakke*, 438 U.S. at 317) (Powell, J.).

15. When devising, revising, or reviewing a race-conscious affirmative action policy, an institution should give serious, good faith consideration to

"race-neutral alternatives" for attaining racial diversity. Race-conscious provisions may be utilized only if no "workable" race-neutral alternatives are available. Institutions have no obligation, however, to exhaust "every conceivable race-neutral alternative," or to adopt race-neutral alternatives that "would require a dramatic sacrifice of [other types of] diversity, the academic quality of all admitted students, or both" (*Grutter*, 539 U.S. at 340).

16. An institution with a race-conscious affirmative action policy should monitor the results it obtains under its policy. In particular, the institution should determine whether its policy in practice is in fact achieving the goal of student body diversity, broadly defined. In addition, the institution should periodically determine whether consideration of race and ethnicity remains necessary to the achievement of racial and ethnic diversity. In doing so, institutions should monitor new developments regarding race-neutral alternatives and seriously consider any new alternatives that could prove "workable." Universities "can and should draw on the most promising aspects of . . . race-neutral alternatives as they develop" in other institutions and other states (*Grutter*, 539 U.S. at 342).

17. Institutions may not use race-conscious admissions policies as a permanent means for achieving racial and ethnic diversity. The Court in *Grutter* stated its belief that, in time (perhaps in twenty-five years, the Court predicted), societal conditions will progress to the point where such policies will no longer be needed. Thus, "race-conscious admissions policies must be limited in time" and must provide for "a logical end point" for the use of such policies. This limitation may be implemented "by sunset provisions . . . and periodic reviews to determine whether racial preferences are still necessary to achieve student body diversity" (*Grutter*, 539 U.S. at 342; see also guideline 16).

These seventeen guidelines can help postsecondary institutions, working with the active involvement of legal counsel, to expand the legal space they have to make their own policy choices about affirmative action in admissions. By carefully considering, justifying, documenting, and periodically reviewing their choices, especially choices involving racial and ethnic preferences, as suggested in these guidelines, institutions may increase the likelihood that their policies will meet constitutional and statutory requirements.

**7.2.6. Readmission.** The readmission of previously excluded students can pose additional legal problems for postsecondary institutions. Although the legal principles in Section 7.2 apply generally to readmissions, the contract theory (Section 7.2.3) may assume added prominence, because the student-institution contract (see Section 7.1.3) may include provisions concerning exclusion and readmission. The principles in Sections 8.6, 9.2, and 9.3 may also apply generally to readmissions where the student challenges the validity of the original exclusion. The nondiscrimination laws provide additional theories for challenges to institutional refusals to readmit students, and students seeking readmission to public institutions may attempt to state due process claims under the Fourteenth Amendment.

Institutions should have an explicit policy on readmission, even if that policy is simply that excluded students will never be considered for readmission. An explicit readmission policy can give students advance notice of their rights, or lack of rights, concerning readmission and, where readmission is permitted, can provide standards and procedures to promote fair and evenhanded decision making. If the institution has an explicit readmissions policy, administrators should take pains to follow it, especially since its violation could be considered a breach of contract. Similarly, if administrators make an agreement with a student concerning readmission, they should firmly adhere to it. *Levine v. George Washington University*, C.A. (Civil Action) 8230–76 (D.C. Super. Ct. 1976), for instance, concerned a medical student who had done poorly in his first year but was allowed to repeat the year, with the stipulation that he would be excluded for a "repeated performance of marginal quality." On the second try, he passed all his courses but ranked low in each. The school excluded him. The court used contract principles to overturn the exclusion, finding that the school's subjective and arbitrary interpretation of "marginal quality," without prior notice to the student, breached the agreement between student and school. In contrast, the court in *Giles v. Howard University*, 428 F. Supp. 603 (D.D.C. 1977), held that the university's refusal to readmit a former medical student was not a breach of contract, because the refusal was consistent with the "reasonable expectations" of the parties.

Although institutions must follow their written readmission policies, the burden of demonstrating that readmission is warranted is on the student. In *Organiscak v. Cleveland State University*, 762 N.E.2d 1078 (Ohio 2001), a student dismissed from a master's program in speech-language pathology sued the university after it rejected her petition for readmission. The court rejected the student's claim that it was the university's responsibility to collect evidence of an improvement in her clinical skills; the burden was on the student to convince the university that her prior academic performance was an inappropriate indicator of her present ability to complete the program.

Because readmission decisions are discretionary, students do not have a property right in readmission. Despite that fact, providing a form of due process can help a public institution defend itself against claims that a denial of readmission violated either substantive or procedural due process protections (or both). In *Ricci v. Rutgers, the State University of New Jersey School of Law-Camden*, 2011 U.S. Dist. LEXIS 21580 (D.N.J. March 3, 2011), the plaintiff, a student who sought and was denied readmission four times, was given a hearing each time she reapplied. The court found that, although she had no property right in readmission, she had received sufficient procedural due process, and the court rejected her substantive due process claim, saying that there was no evidence that Rutgers had "arbitrarily and capriciously deprived her" of the right to be readmitted.

Although private institutions would not be subject to the Fourteenth Amendment due process requirements, they should nevertheless note that readmission decisions encompass different considerations and consequences than original admission decisions. Even private institutions may therefore choose to clothe readmission decisions with greater procedural safeguards than they apply to admission decisions. Moreover, private institutions, like public institutions, should clearly state their readmission policies in writing and coordinate them with their policies on exclusion and leaves of absence. Once such policies are stated in writing, or if the institution has a relatively consistent practice of readmitting former students, contract claims may ensue if the institution does not follow its policies.

Students may also allege that denials of readmission are grounded in discrimination. In *Anderson v. University of Wisconsin*, 841 F.2d 737 (7th Cir. 1988), a black former law student sued the university when it refused to readmit him for a third time because of his low grade point average. To the student's race discrimination claim, the court replied that the law school had consistently readmitted black students with lower grades than those of whites it had readmitted; thus, no systemic race discrimination could be shown against black students. With regard to the plaintiff's claim that the law school had refused to readmit him, in part, because of his alcoholism, the court determined that Section 504 of the Rehabilitation Act of 1973 requires a plaintiff to demonstrate that he is "otherwise qualified" before relief can be granted. Given the plaintiff's inability to maintain the minimum grade point average required for retention, the court determined that the plaintiff was not "otherwise qualified" and ruled that "[l]aw schools may consider academic prospects and sobriety when deciding whether an applicant is entitled to a scarce opportunity for education" (841 F.2d at 742).

A federal appellate court allowed a challenge to a denial of readmission to go to trial on a gender discrimination theory. In *Gossett v. State of Oklahoma ex rel. Board of Regents*, 245 F.3d 1172 (10th Cir. 2001), a male nursing student was required to withdraw from the program after receiving a D grade in a course. The student had presented evidence to the trial court that female students were treated more leniently than their male counterparts when they encountered academic difficulty. Although the trial court had rejected the evidence and entered a summary judgment in favor of the university, the appellate court reversed, ruling that the student's evidence had raised material issues of fact that needed to be resolved at trial.

In *Carlin v. Trustees of Boston University*, 907 F. Supp. 509 (D. Mass. 1995), a student enrolled in a graduate program in pastoral psychology had requested a one-year leave of absence (later extended to two years) so that she could obtain treatment for a psychiatric disorder. Her academic performance prior to the leave had been satisfactory. The university denied her application for readmission, stating that she lacked the "psychodynamic orientation" for pastoral psychology. The student filed a Section 504 (Rehabilitation Act) claim against the university. Determining that the student was academically qualified and possessed the required clinical skills, and that the university's action was closely related to its knowledge that the student had been hospitalized, the court denied the university's summary judgment motion.

At the time an institution suspends or expels a student either for problematic academic performance or behavior, the institution may specify conditions that a student must meet in order to be considered for readmission. In *Rosenthal v. Webster University*, 2000 U.S. App. LEXIS 23733 (8th Cir. 2000) (unpublished), a federal appellate court backed a private university's refusal to readmit a former student with bipolar disorder after it expelled him for carrying a gun and threatening to use it. A condition of Rosenthal's readmission was that he conduct himself appropriately during the period of suspension. Because the plaintiff had been charged with harassment after his suspension, he had failed to meet the conditions of his readmission, and the court ruled that the university was justified in refusing to readmit him.

Administrators should be careful, however, when stating conditions for readmission of a student who has withdrawn, either voluntarily or involuntarily, because of a mental disorder. The U.S. Department of Justice has issued a regulation, 28 C.F.R. § 35.104, stating that only students who pose a risk of harm to *others* (rather than either to themselves or others) may have conditions placed on readmission or continuation of their enrollment; the U.S. Department of Education's Office for Civil Rights appears to be enforcing this approach as well. See "Education Dept. Seems to Shift Policy on Readmission of Students with Mental Disabilities," *Chron. Higher Educ.*, November 1, 2011, available at http://chronicle.com/blogs/ticker/education-dept-seems-to-shift-policy-on -readmission-of-students-with-mental-disabilities/37654.

Since the U.S. Supreme Court's *Garrett* decision (see Section 4.5.2.5 of this book), federal courts have struggled with the question of whether public universities can be sued under Title II of the ADA for money damages (*Garrett* involved Title I of the ADA). The U.S. Supreme Court has provided a partial answer. In *United States v. Georgia*, 546 U.S. 151 (2006), the Court ruled that Congress had validly abrogated sovereign immunity for claims which alleged conduct that would violate the Fourteenth Amendment. The ruling in *Georgia* suggests that students seeking readmission under disability discrimination theories can maintain claims against public institutions if they allege that their due process or equal protection rights, or both, have been violated.

Students may also raise tort claims in challenging denials of readmission. For example, in *Mason v. State of Oklahoma*, 23 P.3d 964 (Okla. Civ. App. 2000), a law student, Perry Mason, was expelled for dishonesty in applying for financial aid. Mason claimed negligent and intentional infliction of emotional distress, denial of due process, violation of public policy, and breach of an implied contract. The court rejected all of the claims, affirming the trial court's dismissal of Mason's lawsuit.

The readmission cases demonstrate that colleges that specify the procedures for readmission (and follow them), use reasonable and relevant criteria for making readmission decisions, and can link those criteria to programmatic needs should prevail in challenges to negative readmission decisions.

## Section 7.3. Financial Aid

*7.3.1. General principles.* The legal principles affecting financial aid have a wide variety of sources. Some principles apply generally to all financial aid, whether awarded as scholarships, assistantships, loans, fellowships, preferential tuition rates, or in some other form. Other principles depend on the particular source of funds being used and thus may vary with the aid program or the type of award. Sections 7.3.2 through 7.3.5 discuss the principles that present the most difficult problems for financial aid administrators, and specific legal requirements resulting from these principles. This section discusses more general principles affecting financial aid.

The principles of contract law may apply to financial aid awards, since an award once made may create a contract between the institution and the aid recipient. Typically, the institution's obligation is to provide a particular type of aid at certain times and in certain amounts. The student recipient's obligation depends on the type of aid. With loans, the typical obligation is to repay the principal and a prescribed rate of interest at certain times and in certain amounts. With other aid, the obligation may be only to spend the funds for specified academic expenses or to achieve a specified level of academic performance in order to maintain aid eligibility. Sometimes, however, the student recipient may have more extensive obligations—for instance, to perform instructional or laboratory duties, play on a varsity athletic team, or provide particular services after graduation. The defendant student in *State of New York v. Coury*, 359 N.Y.S.2d 486 (N.Y. Sup. Ct. 1974), for instance, had accepted a scholarship and agreed, as a condition of the award, to perform internship duties in a welfare agency for one year after graduation. When the student did not perform the duties, the state sought a refund of the scholarship money. The court held for the state because the student had "agreed to accept the terms of the contract" and had not performed as the contract required.

Students may also rely on contract law to challenge the withdrawal or reduction in amount of a scholarship. For example, in *Aronson v. University of Mississippi*, 828 So. 2d 752 (Miss. 2002), a student sued the university when it reduced the amount of a scholarship awarded to the student from $4,000 to $2,000. The university defended its decision by saying that the catalog, in which the scholarship amount had been listed as $4,000, was incorrect. Aronson filed a breach of contract claim against the university. The trial court dismissed the claim at the conclusion of the plaintiff's case, and the appellate court reversed, ruling for the student. The state supreme court reversed and remanded the case, saying that the university was entitled to present a defense. The university had argued that disclaimers in its student catalog and other information should have put the student on notice that the scholarship amount had been changed.

The law regarding gifts, grants, wills, and trusts may also apply to financial aid awards. These legal principles would generally require aid administrators to adhere to any conditions that the donor, grantor, testator, or settlor placed on use of the funds. But the conditions must be explicit at the time of the gift. For example, in *Hawes v. Emory University*, 374 S.E.2d 328 (Ga. Ct. App. 1988), a scholarship donor demanded that the university return the gift, asserting that the funds had not been disbursed as agreed upon. The court found the contribution to be a valid gift without any indication that its use was restricted in the way the donor later alleged. And the son of a donor who challenged the institution's awarding of scholarships could not convince the court that the donor's intent had not been met. In *Pearson v. Garrett-Evangelical Theological Seminary, Inc.*, 2011 U.S. Dist. LEXIS 51342 (N.D. Ill. May 13, 2011), the court analyzed the donation agreement and found that the seminary had complied with its provisions; thus there was no breach of contract.

Funds provided by government agencies or private foundations must be used in accordance with conditions in the program regulations, grant instrument, or other legal document formalizing the transaction. Section 7.3.2 illustrates such conditions in the context of federal aid programs. With respect to funds from a private donor, a widely reported lawsuit between the descendants of a donor and Princeton University resulted in a settlement after several years of litigation. In *Robertson v. Princeton University*, Dkt. No. C-99-02 (N. J. Super. Ct. App. Div.), the family members had alleged that Princeton had not used the donated funds for the purposes established by the donor; Princeton asserted that its expenditures of the funds had complied with the donor's intent. After several years of litigation and an expenditure of "tens of millions of dollars in legal fees," according to a statement released by the university, the university and the plaintiffs settled. Information about the lawsuit and the settlement can be found at www.princeton.edu/robertson.

Similarly, funds made available to an institution under wills or trusts must be used in accordance with conditions in the will or trust instrument, unless those conditions are themselves illegal. Conditions that discriminate by race, sex, or religion have posed the greatest problems in this respect. If a public agency or entity has compelled or affirmatively supported the imposition of such conditions, they will usually be considered to violate the federal Constitution's equal protection clause (see, for example, *In Re Certain Scholarship Funds*, 575 A.2d 1325 (N.H. 1990)). But if such conditions appear in a privately established and administered trust, they will usually be considered constitutional, because no state action is present. In *Shapiro v. Columbia Union National Bank and Trust Co.* (discussed in Section 1.5.2 of this book), for instance, the Supreme Court of Missouri refused to find state action to support a claim of sex discrimination lodged against a university's involvement in a private trust established to provide scholarships exclusively for male students. Even in the absence of state action, however, a discriminatory condition in a private trust may still be declared invalid if it violates one of the federal nondiscrimination requirements applicable to federal fund recipients (see Sections 7.3.3 and 7.3.4).

A third relevant body of legal principles is that of constitutional due process. These principles apply generally to public institutions; they also apply to private institutions when those institutions make awards from public funds (see Section 1.5.2). Since termination of aid may affect both "property" and "liberty" interests (see Section 5.7.2.1) of the student recipients, courts may sometimes require that termination be accompanied by some form of procedural safeguard. *Corr v. Mattheis*, 407 F. Supp. 847 (D.R.I. 1976), for instance, involved students who had their federal aid terminated in midyear, under a federal "student unrest" statute, after they participated in a campus protest against the Vietnam War. The court found that the students had been denied a property interest in continued receipt of funds awarded to them, as well as a liberty interest in being free from stigmas foreclosing further educational or employment opportunities. Termination thus had to be preceded by notice and a meaningful opportunity to contest the decision. In other cases, if the harm or stigma to students is less, the required procedural safeguards may be less stringent. Moreover, if aid is terminated for academic rather than disciplinary reasons, procedural safeguards may be almost nonexistent, as courts follow the distinction between academic deficiency problems and misconduct problems drawn in Section 8.1.

In *Conard v. University of Washington*, 834 P.2d 17 (Wash. 1992), the Washington Supreme Court ruled that student athletes do not have a constitutionally protected property interest in the renewal of their athletic scholarships. The court reversed a lower court's finding that the students, who had been dropped from the football team after several instances of misconduct, had a property interest in renewal of their scholarships. The financial aid agreements that the students had signed were for one academic year only and did not contain promises of renewal. The court interpreted the financial aid agreements as contracts that afforded the students the right to consideration for scholarship renewal and—citing *Board of Regents v. Roth* (see Sections 5.7.2.1 and 5.7.2.2)—refused to find a "common understanding" that athletic scholarships were given for a four-year period. Furthermore, the court said, the fact that both the university and the National Collegiate Athletic Association (NCAA) provided minimal due process guarantees did not create a property interest. Special considerations involving athletic scholarships and NCAA rules are discussed in Section 10.4.5.

Federal and state laws regulating lending and extensions of credit provide a fourth body of applicable legal constraints. At the federal level, for example, the Truth-in-Lending Act (15 U.S.C. §§ 1601 et seq.) establishes various disclosure requirements for loans and credit sales. Such provisions are of concern not only to institutions with typical loan programs but also to institutions with credit plans allowing students or parents to defer payment of tuition for extended periods of time. The federal Truth-in-Lending Act, however, exempts National Direct Student Loans (NDSLs; now Perkins Loans), Federal Stafford Loans, and Federal Family Education Loans (see Section 7.3.2) from its coverage (15 U.S.C. § 1603(7)).

The Higher Education Opportunity Act, Pub. L. No. 110-35 (August 14, 2008), amended the Truth in Lending Act by requiring that creditors obtain a self-certification form signed by the consumer before finalizing the loan and also by requiring creditors that have a preferred lender arrangement with colleges and universities to provide certain information to those institutions. The Federal Reserve Board has published a final rule amending Regulation Z, which implements the Truth in Lending Act. The final rule may be found at 74 Fed. Reg. 41194 (August 14, 2009).

As a result of congressional action in 1996 to amend the Internal Revenue Code, all states have adopted college savings plans. Congress added Section 529 to the Internal Revenue Code (26 U.S.C. § 529), which allows a "state agency or instrumentality" to establish a program under which a person "may purchase tuition credits or certificates on behalf of a designated beneficiary which entitle the beneficiary to the waiver or payment of qualified higher education expenses of the beneficiary" (26 U.S.C. § 529(b)(1)). States may establish either prepaid tuition plans or savings plans; educational institutions may establish only prepaid tuition plans. Contributions to the plans are excluded from the contributor's gross income for federal income tax purposes. An amendment to Section 529 in 2002 allows a beneficiary to make a "qualified withdrawal" from a 529 plan that is free of federal income tax. There are penalties for withdrawals from the fund for noneducational purposes, and prepaid tuition plans differ from savings plans in significant ways. Basic information on these plans is available at http://www.savingforcollege.com.

### 7.3.2. Federal programs.

The federal government provides or guarantees many millions of dollars per year in student aid for postsecondary education through a multitude of programs. To protect its investment and ensure the fulfillment of national priorities and goals, the federal government imposes many requirements on the way institutions manage and spend funds under federal programs. Some are general requirements applicable to student aid and all other federal assistance programs. Others are specific programmatic requirements applicable to one student aid program or to a related group of such programs. These requirements constitute the most prominent—and, critics would add, most prolific and burdensome—source of specific restrictions on an institution's administration of financial aid.

The most prominent general requirements are the nondiscrimination requirements discussed in Section 7.3.3, which apply to all financial aid, whether or not it is provided under federal programs. In addition, the Family Educational Rights and Privacy Act (FERPA) (discussed in Section 7.8.1) imposes various requirements on the institution's record-keeping practices for all the financial aid that it disburses. The FERPA regulations, however, do partly exempt financial aid records from nondisclosure requirements. They provide that an institution may disclose personally identifiable information from a student's records, without the student's consent, to the extent "necessary for such purposes as" determining the student's eligibility for financial aid, determining the amount of aid and the conditions that will be imposed regarding it, or enforcing the terms or conditions of the aid (34 C.F.R. § 99.31(a)(4)).

The Student Assistance General Provisions (34 C.F.R. Part 668) lay out eligibility criteria for institutions wishing to participate in federal student assistance programs, and for students wishing to obtain aid under these programs. Institutional eligibility criteria are addressed at 34 C.F.R. § 668.8. Generally, an educational program at a nonprofit institution of higher education that provides at least an associate's degree or the equivalent may participate in these programs if it meets federal requirements for program length, leads to at least an associate's degree or is "at least a one-academic-year training program that leads to a certificate, or other nondegree recognized credential, and prepares students for gainful employment in a recognized occupation" (the "gainful employment" rule), and meets other regulatory criteria. For-profit institutions may also participate in federal student aid programs if they provide at least fifteen weeks of instruction that prepares students for "gainful employment in a recognized occupation," and meet other regulatory criteria. For-profit institutions must also meet specific student completion rates and placement rates (34 C.F.R. § 668.8(e)). Final rules on "gainful employment" were released in June of 2011 (76 Fed. Reg. 34386–34539 (June 13, 2011)). Before the rules took effect, for-profit institutions challenged several aspects of the "gainful employment" rule, particularly with respect to the disclosure requirements for those institutions with vocational programs. In June 2012, a federal trial court struck the portions of the "gainful employment rules" involving debt measure and program approval, but upheld the requirement that schools disclose the occupation that the program prepares students to enter, the on-time graduation rate for students completing the program, the tuition and fees charged, and the placement rate and median loan debt for students completing the program (*Association of Private Colleges and Universities v. Duncan*, 2012 U.S. Dist. LEXIS 90434 (D.D.C. June 30, 2012)).

The Student Assistance General Provisions require institutions to enter into a written "program participation agreement" with the Secretary of Education. The program participation agreement applies to all of the branch campuses and other locations of the institution. The institution must agree to a variety of requirements, including a promise that it will comply with all provisions of Title IV of the Higher Education Act (HEA) (the portion of the HEA that authorizes the federal student assistance programs), all regulations promulgated under the authority of the HEA, and all special provisions allowed by the statute. The institution must also certify that it will not charge students a fee for processing applications for federal student aid and that it will maintain records and procedures that will allow it to report regularly to state and federal agencies. The institution must also certify that it complies with a variety of laws requiring the disclosure of information, including the Student Right-to-Know and Campus Security Act (discussed in Section 7.6.3 of this book). Specific requirements of program participation agreements are found at 20 U.S.C. § 1094; regulations concerning these agreements are codified at 34 C.F.R. § 668.14.

In 2009–2010, the Education Department promulgated new regulations, which they called "program integrity" rules. The new regulations changed some definitions and imposed additional requirements on institutions that participate in the federal student aid program. Some of these rules and requirements are discussed below. The changes to these rules have a particularly significant impact on for-profit, proprietary schools; those schools challenged several of the rules in court (see discussion later in this section). The entire package of program integrity rules is discussed in a question-and-answer format on a Web site maintained by the Education Department. It may be found at http://www2.ed.gov/policy/highered/reg/hearulemaking/2009/integrity-qa.html.

Students convicted of drug offenses are excluded from eligibility for federal student financial aid (20 U.S.C. § 1091(r)). The same section of the law provides that students who have satisfactorily completed a drug rehabilitation program that complies with criteria in federal regulations, and who have either had the conviction reversed or expunged or have passed two unannounced drug tests, may be restored to eligibility for federal student financial aid. Regulations for this provision are found at 34 C.F.R. § 668.40.

Most of the federal student aid programs were created by the Higher Education Act of 1965 (20 U.S.C. §§ 1070 et seq.), which has been reauthorized and amended regularly since that year. The most recent reauthorization is the Higher Education Opportunity Act (HEOA) (Pub. L. No. 110-315, 122 Stat. 3079), which was enacted on August 14, 2008. Most, but not all, of the HEOA's provisions involve federal financial aid programs. For a summary of the provisions of the HEOA, see the "Dear Colleague" letter available at http://ifap.ed.gov/dpcletters/GEN0812FP0810.html.

The specific programmatic restrictions on federal student aid depend on the particular program. There are various types of programs, with different structures, by which the government makes funds available:

1. Programs in which the federal government provides funds to institutions to establish revolving loan funds—as in the Perkins Loan program (20 U.S.C. §§ 1087aa–1087ii; 34 C.F.R. Parts 673, 674).

2. Programs in which the government grants funds to institutions, which in turn provide grants to students—as in the Federal Supplemental Educational Opportunity Grant (SEOG) program (20 U.S.C. §§ 1070b et seq.; 34 C.F.R. Parts 673, 676) and the Federal Work-Study (FWS) program (42 U.S.C. §§ 2751 et seq.; 34 C.F.R. Parts 673, 675).

3. Programs in which students receive grants directly from the federal government—as in the "New GI Bill" program (38 U.S.C. §§ 3001 et seq.; 38 C.F.R. Part 21) and the Pell Grant program (20 U.S.C. §§ 1070a et seq.; 34 C.F.R. Part 690).

4. Programs in which students receive funds from the federal government through the states—as in the Leveraging Educational Assistance Partnership Program (20 U.S.C. §§ 1070c et seq.; 34 C.F.R. Part 692) and the Robert C. Byrd Honors Scholarship Program (20 U.S.C. §§ 1070d-31, 1070d-33; 34 C.F.R. § 654.1).

5. Programs in which students and parents borrow directly from the federal government at participating schools. The William D. Ford Direct Loan Program (20 U.S.C. §§ 1087a et seq.; 34 C.F.R. Part 685) includes Direct Stafford Loans, Direct PLUS Loans, and Direct Consolidation Loans. These programs allow institutions authorized by the Department of Education to lend money directly to students through loan capital provided by the federal government.

In order to receive aid, students required to register with Selective Service must file statements with the institutions they attend, certifying that they have complied with the Selective Service law and regulations. The validity of this requirement was upheld by the U.S. Supreme Court in *Selective Service System v. Minnesota Public Interest Research Group*, 468 U.S. 841 (1984). Regulations implementing the certification requirement are published in 34 C.F.R. § 668.37.

The U.S. Department of Education has created a Web site that provides information on applying for federal grants, loans, and work-study assistance. It is available at http://www.studentaid.ed.gov. The Education Department also has a Web site entitled "Information for Financial Assistance Professionals" (IFAP), available at http://ifap.ed.gov, that provides information on the requirements for the various financial aid programs, lists available publications, and provides updates on recent changes in laws and regulations governing these programs. The Education Department publishes annually the *Federal Student Aid Handbook*, which may be downloaded free from the IFAP Web site.

Much of the controversy surrounding the federal student aid programs has concerned the sizable default rates on student loans, particularly at institutions that enroll large proportions of low-income students. Several reports issued by the U.S. Government Accountability Office (GAO) have been sharply critical of the practices of colleges, loan guarantee agencies, and the Department of Education in implementing the federally guaranteed student loan programs. As a result, substantial changes have been made in the laws and regulations related to eligibility, repayment, and collection practices.

A few courts, however, have permitted students to use state common law fraud or statutory consumer protection theories against the Education Department, colleges, or lenders when the college either ceased operations or provided a poor-quality education (see, for example, *Tipton v. Alexander*, 768 F. Supp. 540 (S.D. W. Va. 1991)). One court has permitted students to file a Racketeer Influenced and Corrupt Organizations (RICO) Act claim against a trade school, alleging mail fraud. In *Gonzalez v. North American College of Louisiana*, 700 F. Supp. 362 (S.D. Tex. 1988), the students charged that the school induced them to enroll and to obtain federal student loans, which they were required to repay. The school was unaccredited; and, after it had obtained the federal funds in the students' name, it closed and did not refund the loan proceeds.

Federal student aid programs bring substantial benefits to students and the colleges they attend. Their administrative and legal requirements, however, are complex and change constantly. It is imperative that administrators and counsel become conversant with these requirements and monitor legislative, regulatory, and judicial developments closely.

### 7.3.3. Nondiscrimination.

***7.3.3. Nondiscrimination.*** The legal principles of nondiscrimination apply to the financial aid process in much the same way they apply to the admissions process (see Sections 7.2.4 and 7.2.5). The same constitutional principles of equal protection apply to financial aid. The relevant statutes and regulations on nondiscrimination—Title VI, Title IX, Section 504, the Americans with Disabilities Act, and the Age Discrimination Act—all apply to financial aid, although Title IX's and Section 504's coverage and specific requirements for financial aid are different from those for admissions. And affirmative action poses difficulties for financial aid programs similar to those it poses for admissions programs. Challenges brought under Title VI and the equal protection clause against institutions that reserve certain scholarships for minority students are discussed in Section 7.3.4.

Of the federal statutes, Title IX has the most substantial impact on the financial aid programs and policies of postsecondary institutions. The regulations (34 C.F.R. § 106.37), with four important exceptions, prohibit the use of sex-restricted scholarships and virtually every other sex-based distinction in the financial aid program. Section 106.37(a)(1) prohibits the institution from providing "different amount[s] or types" of aid, "limit[ing] eligibility" for "any particular type or source" of aid, apply[ing] different criteria," or otherwise discriminating "on the basis of sex" in awarding financial aid. Section 106.37(a)(2) prohibits the institution from giving any assistance, "through solicitation, listing, approval, provision of facilities, or other services," to any "foundation, trust, agency, organization, or person" that discriminates on the basis of sex in providing financial aid to the institution's students. Section 106.37(a)(3) also prohibits aid eligibility rules that treat the sexes differently "with regard to marital or parental status."

The four exceptions to this broad nondiscrimination policy permit sex-restricted financial aid under certain circumstances. Section 106.37(b) permits an institution to "administer or assist in the administration of" sex-restricted financial assistance that is "established pursuant to domestic or foreign wills, trusts, bequests, or similar legal instruments or by acts of a foreign government." Institutions must administer such awards, however, in such a way that their "overall effect" is "nondiscriminatory" according to standards set out in 34 C.F.R. § 106.37(b)(2). Section 106.31(c) creates the same kind of exception for sex-restricted foreign-study scholarships awarded to the institution's students or graduates. Such awards must be established through the same legal channels specified for the first exception, and the institution must make available "reasonable opportunities for similar [foreign] studies for members of the other sex." The third exception, for athletic scholarships, is discussed in Section 10.4.6 of this book. A fourth exception was added by an amendment to Title IX included in the Education Amendments of 1976. Section 412(a)(4) of the amendments (20 U.S.C. § 1681(a)(9)) permits institutions to award financial assistance to winners of pageants based on "personal appearance, poise, and talent," even though the pageant is restricted to members of one sex.

Section 504 of the Rehabilitation Act of 1973 (see Section 11.5.4 of this book), as implemented by the Department of Education's regulations, restricts postsecondary institutions' financial aid processes as they relate to disabled persons. Section 104.46(a) of the regulations (34 C.F.R. Part 104) prohibits the institution from providing "less assistance" to qualified disabled students, from placing a "limit [on] eligibility for assistance," and from otherwise discriminating or assisting any other entity to discriminate on the basis of disability in providing financial aid. The major exception to this nondiscrimination requirement is that the institution may still administer financial assistance provided under a particular discriminatory will or trust, as long as "the overall effect of the award of scholarships, fellowships, and other forms of financial assistance is not discriminatory on the basis of handicap" (34 C.F.R. § 104.46(a)(2)).

The Americans with Disabilities Act also prohibits discrimination on the basis of disability in allocating financial aid. Title II, which covers state and local government agencies, applies to public colleges and universities that meet the definition of a state or local government agency. The regulations prohibit institutions from providing a benefit (here, financial aid) "that is not as effective in affording equal opportunity . . . to reach the same level of achievement as that provided to others" (28 C.F.R. § 35.130(b)(1)(iii)). Private colleges and universities are covered by Title III as "places of public accommodation" (28 C.F.R. § 36.104) and are prohibited from limiting the access of individuals with disabilities to the benefits enjoyed by other individuals (28 C.F.R. § 36.202(b)).

Regulations interpreting the Age Discrimination Act of 1975 (42 U.S.C. §§ 6101–6103) include the general regulations applicable to all government agencies dispensing federal aid as well as regulations governing the federal financial assistance programs for education. These regulations are found at 34 C.F.R. Part 110.

The regulations set forth a general prohibition against age discrimination in "any program or activity receiving Federal financial assistance" (34 C.F.R. § 110.10(a)), but permit funding recipients to use age as a criterion if the recipient "reasonably takes into account age as a factor necessary to the normal operation or the achievement of any statutory objective of a program or activity" (34 C.F.R. § 110.12) or if the action is based on "reasonable factors other than age," even though the action may have a disproportionate effect on a particular age group (34 C.F.R. § 110.13). With respect to the administration of federal financial aid, the regulations would generally prohibit age criteria for the receipt of student financial assistance.

Criteria used to make scholarship awards may have discriminatory effects even if they appear facially neutral. For example, research conducted in the 1980s demonstrated that women students tended to score approximately sixty points lower on the Scholastic Aptitude Test (SAT) than male students did, although women's high school and college grades tended to be higher than men's. In *Sharif by Salahuddin v. New York State Education Department*, 709 F. Supp. 345 (S.D.N.Y. 1989), a class of female high school students filed an equal protection claim, seeking to halt New York's practice of awarding Regents and Empire State Scholarships exclusively on the basis of SAT scores. The plaintiffs alleged that the practice discriminated against female students. The judge issued a preliminary injunction, ruling that the state should not use SAT scores as the sole criterion for awarding scholarships.

### *7.3.4. Affirmative action in financial aid programs.*[7] Just as colleges and universities may adopt voluntary affirmative action policies for

---

[7]This section was revised and updated by Jonathan R. Alger, former senior vice president and general counsel at Rutgers University and currently president of James Madison University.

admissions in certain circumstances (see Section 7.2.5), they may do so for their financial aid programs. As with admissions, when the institution takes race, ethnicity, or gender into account in allocating financial aid among its aid programs or in awarding aid to particular applicants, issues may arise under the equal protection clause (for public institutions), Title VI, Title IX, or 42 U.S.C. § 1981. When the issues arise under Title VI, the "1994 Policy Guidance" on financial aid issued by the U.S. Department of Education, 59 Fed. Reg. 8756–64 (February 23, 1994), provides an important supplement to the statute and regulations.

The case of *Flanagan v. President and Directors of Georgetown College*, 417 F. Supp. 377 (D.D.C. 1976), provides an early example of affirmative action issues regarding financial aid. The law school at Georgetown had allocated 60 percent of its financial aid for the first-year class to minority students, who constituted 11 percent of the class. The remaining 40 percent of the aid was reserved for nonminorities, the other 89 percent of the class. Within each category, funds were allocated on the basis of need; but, because of Georgetown's allocation policy, the plaintiff, a white law student, received less financial aid than some minority students, even though his financial need was greater. The school's threshold argument was that this program did not discriminate by race because disadvantaged white students were also included within the definition of minority. The court quickly rejected this argument because white students had to make a special showing of "disadvantage" in order to be included in the "minority" category, while minority students did not.

The school then defended its policy as part of an affirmative action program to increase minority enrollment. The student argued that the policy discriminated against nonminorities in violation of Title VI of the Civil Rights Act (see this volume, Section 11.5.2). The court sided with the student, determining that racial preferences for financial aid that favor minorities over nonminority students with equivalent financial need is impermissible reverse discrimination.

Although *Flanagan* broadly concludes that allotment of financial aid on an explicit racial basis is impermissible, at least for need-based aid, the U.S. Supreme Court's subsequent decision in *Bakke* (see Section 7.2.5) appeared to leave some room for the explicit consideration of race in financial aid programs. The Department of Education's 1994 Policy Guidance, cited earlier in this section, confirmed the view that race-conscious financial aid policies are permissible in some circumstances. And more recently, the Supreme Court's 2003 decisions in *Grutter v. Bollinger*, 539 U.S. 306 (2003), and *Gratz v. Bollinger*, 539 U.S. 244 (2003) (see Section 7.2.5), although concerned with admissions rather than financial aid, have given further support for the position that some consideration of race in allocating and awarding financial aid is permissible.

Since the U.S. Supreme Court has not yet decided a case on affirmative action in financial aid programs, the admissions cases, *Grutter* and *Gratz*, are therefore the precedents most nearly on point. It is likely that the general principles from these cases will apply to financial aid programs as well, and that courts will use these principles to resolve equal protection, Title VI, and Section 1981 challenges to financial aid policies of public institutions and Title VI and

Section 1981 challenges to financial aid policies of private institutions. This assessment does not necessarily mean, however, that race-conscious financial aid policies will always be valid or invalid under the law in the same circumstances and to the same extent as race-conscious admissions policies. The Court made clear in *Grutter* and *Gratz* that "[n]ot every decision influenced by race is equally objectionable" and that courts therefore must carefully consider the "context" in which a racial or ethnic preference is used. Since the "context" for financial aid policies typically has some differences from the "context" for admissions, as discussed below, these differences may lead to some differences in legal reasoning, and perhaps results, in cases challenging affirmative action in financial aid.

The basic principles guiding a court's analysis, however, probably would not change from one context to the other. The threshold questions would likely still include whether the policy on its face or in its operation takes race into account in allocating or awarding financial aid and, if so, whether the policy uses racial quotas for either the dollar amount of aid available to minority applicants or the number of scholarships, loans, or other aid awards for minority applicants. There would still most probably be a need to determine the institution's justification for taking race into account and to examine the documentation supporting this justification. The permissible justifications for financial aid policies are likely to be the same as for admissions policies—student body diversity and remedying the present effects of the institution's past discrimination; and just as these interests are "compelling interests" for purposes of admissions, they will likely be considered compelling for financial aid as well. The "narrow tailoring" test will also likely continue to apply as the basis for judging whether the consideration of race is designed, and carefully limited, to accomplish whichever compelling interest the institution has attributed to its race-conscious financial aid policies. Thus the strict scrutiny standard of review, as articulated and applied to admissions in *Grutter* and *Gratz*, also can guide analysis of race-conscious financial aid and "provide a framework for carefully examining the importance and the sincerity of the reasons advanced by the governmental decision-maker for the use of race *in that particular context*" (539 U.S. at 327; emphasis added).

There appear to be three particularly pertinent ways in which the context of financial aid differs from the context of admissions. First, institutions dispense financial aid through a variety of scholarship, loan, and work-study programs that may have differing eligibility requirements and types of aid packages. It may therefore be questionable, in particular cases, whether each "part" of the aid program that takes race into account may be analyzed independent of the other parts of the institution's overall aid program, or whether courts may or must consider how other parts of the program may work together with the challenged part in accomplishing the institution's interest in student body diversity or remedying past discrimination. Second, some of the institution's financial aid resources may come from private donors who have established their own eligibility requirements for the aid, and the institution may have various degrees of involvement in and control over the award of this aid from private sources. (The U.S. Department of Education's 1994 Policy Guidance, for example, distinguishes between private donors' awards of race-conscious aid directly to students, which aid is not covered by Title VI, and private donors' provision of funds to a college or university that in turn administers or provides significant assistance to the privately funded program, in which case the funds are covered by Title VI (see 59 Fed. Reg. at 8757–58, Principle 5); see also Jonathan Alger, *Race-Conscious Financial Aid After the University of Michigan Decisions* (National Association of College and University Attorneys, 2004)). Questions may therefore arise concerning whether and when such financial aid is fully subject to the requirements of the equal protection clause, or Title VI or Title IX, and whether such aid may or must be considered to be part of the institution's overall aid program if a court considers how all the parts work together to accomplish the institution's interests (see first point made earlier in this paragraph). Third, "the use of race in financial aid programs may have less impact on individuals who are not members of the favored group than the use of race in admissions. If individuals are not admitted to an institution, then they cannot attend it," but "individuals who do not receive a particular race-conscious scholarship may still be able to obtain loans, work-study funds, or other scholarships in order to attend" (Elizabeth Meers & William Thro, *Race Conscious Admissions and Financial Aid Programs* (National Association of College and University Attorneys, 2004) at 28).

The most vulnerable type of race-conscious aid in most circumstances is "race-exclusive" scholarships available only to persons of a particular race or ethnicity. Under the 1994 Policy Guidance, the Department of Education permits the use of race-exclusive scholarships in certain narrow circumstances (59 Fed. Reg. at 8757–58 (Principles 3, 4, 5)). But under the *Grutter* and *Gratz* principles, as applied to financial aid policies, such scholarships may be viewed as employing racial quotas as well as a separate process or separate consideration for minority aid applicants—both of which are prohibited for admission policies.

In a major case decided prior to *Grutter* and *Gratz*, *Podberesky v. Kirwan*, 38 F.3d 147 (4th Cir. 1994), the U.S. Court of Appeals for the Fourth Circuit invalidated a race-exclusive scholarship program of the University of Maryland. In *Podberesky*, a Hispanic student claimed that the university's Banneker Scholarship program violated Title VI and the equal protection clause. The district court and the appellate court applied strict scrutiny analysis. Defending its program, the university argued that it served the compelling state interest of remedying prior *de jure* discrimination, given the fact that the state was then still under order of the Office for Civil Rights, U.S. Department of Education, to remedy its formerly segregated system of public higher education. The university also argued that the goal of student body diversity was served by the scholarship program.

The district court found that the university had provided "overwhelming" evidence of the present effects of prior discrimination and upheld the program without considering the university's diversity argument (764 F. Supp. 364 (D. Md. 1991)). The federal appeals court, however, reversed the district court

(956 F.2d 52 (4th Cir. 1992)). Although the appellate court agreed that the university had provided sufficient evidence of prior discrimination, the court found the Office for Civil Rights' observations about the present effects of that discrimination unconvincing because they had been made too long ago (between 1969 and 1985); and the appellate court ordered the district court to make new findings on the present effects of prior discrimination. The appellate court also noted that race-exclusive scholarship programs violate the *Bakke* case (see Section 7.2.5) if their purpose is to increase student body diversity rather than to remedy prior discrimination.

On remand to the district court, the university presented voluminous evidence of the present effects of prior discrimination, including surveys of black high school students and their parents, information on the racial climate at the university, research on the economic status of black citizens in Maryland and the effects of unequal educational opportunity, and other studies. The district court found that the university had demonstrated a "strong basis in evidence" for four present effects of past discrimination: the university's poor reputation in the black community, underrepresentation of blacks in the student body, the low retention and graduation rates of black students at the university, and a racially hostile campus climate (838 F. Supp. 1075 (D. Md. 1993)).

With regard to the university's evidence of the present effects of past discrimination, the court also commented: "It is worthy of note that the University is (to put it mildly) in a somewhat unusual situation. It is not often that a litigant is required to engage in extended self-criticism in order to justify its pursuit of a goal that it deems worthy" (838 F. Supp. at 1082, n.47). The court also held that the Banneker Scholarship program was narrowly tailored to remedy the present effects of past discrimination because it demonstrated the university's commitment to black students, increased the number of peer mentors and role models available to black students, increased the enrollment of high-achieving black students, and improved the recipients' academic performance and persistence. Less restrictive alternatives did not produce these results. The court did not address the university's diversity argument.

On appeal, the U.S. Court of Appeals for the Fourth Circuit again overruled the district court (38 F.3d 147 (4th Cir. 1994)). Despite the university's voluminous evidence of present effects of prior racial discrimination, the appellate court held that there was insufficient proof of present effects to establish a compelling interest for the race-exclusive scholarships. Furthermore, said the court, the scholarship program was not narrowly tailored to accomplishing the university's interest. The program thus failed both prongs of the strict scrutiny test.

The appellate court also rejected the district court's finding that the program provided role models and mentors to other black students, noting that the "Supreme Court has expressly rejected the role-model theory as a basis for implementing a race-conscious remedy" (38 F.3d at 159, citing *Wygant v. Jackson Board of Education*, 476 U.S. 267, 276 (1986) (plurality opinion)). In addition, the appellate court also criticized the university for asserting that its program was narrowly tailored to increase the number of black Maryland residents at the university, since the Banneker program was open to out-of-state students. Thus, the court concluded: "[T]he program more resembles outright racial balancing than a tailored remedial program" (38 F.3d at 160).

Although the university had originally used two rationales for its race-conscious scholarship program—remediation of its own prior discrimination and enhancement of student diversity—the district court had addressed only the remediation rationale in its first decision. In the appellate court's first reversal of the district court, it rejected diversity as a rationale for race-exclusive programs. The university therefore did not argue that rationale in the second round of litigation, not did the district or appellate courts address it.

*Podberesky* illustrates how difficult it may be for an institution on its own to justify a race-based scholarship program using the "remedying prior discrimination" rationale. The other, less developed, part of *Podberesky*, rejecting the student diversity rationale, is inconsistent with the Supreme Court's later decisions in *Grutter* and *Gratz*, and *Podberesky* therefore cannot be used to foreclose diversity rationales for race-conscious student aid programs. Some room is apparently left open, by *Grutter* and *Gratz*, for an institution to argue that there are no race-neutral alternatives, or alternatives that do not involve exclusivity, for accomplishing the diversity objectives that it accomplishes with race-exclusive aid; or to argue that nonminority students are not unduly burdened by the race-exclusive program because their financial aid needs are met in other comparable ways with other funds under other programs. The Department of Education's 1994 Policy Guidance (cited earlier in this section) appears to adopt a similar position (59 Fed. Reg. at 8757) and thus provides further support for the validity of some race-exclusive scholarships, at least under Title VI.[8]

Both public and private institutions that have race-conscious or gender-conscious financial aid programs may wish to review them in light of these various considerations, and institutions considering the adoption or modification of any such program will want to do the same. In addition, careful monitoring of further developments in the courts, in the Department of Education, and in the states (including proposed amendments to the state constitution) is obviously warranted.

### 7.3.5. Discrimination against aliens.

**7.3.5.1. Documented (immigrant and nonimmigrant) aliens.** Two issues are significant in an analysis of the rights of aliens with respect to financial aid. First is the question of whether aliens are eligible for certain forms of financial aid, whether it is provided by public funds or by funds from other sources. And secondly, the question of an alien's eligibility for in-state tuition (a form of tuition discounting rather than direct financial aid) is also significant, as well as controversial.

---

[8] Similar issues could arise with sex-restricted scholarships, and similar arguments would be available to institutions. In addition, institutions may sometimes rely on a Title IX regulation that expressly permits sex-restricted scholarships awarded under wills, trusts, and other legal instruments if the "overall effect" of such awards is not discriminatory (34 C.F.R § 106.37 (b); see subsection 7.3.3 of this book).

In *Nyquist v. Jean-Marie Mauclet*, 432 U.S. 1 (1977), the U.S. Supreme Court set forth constitutional principles applicable to discrimination against resident aliens in student financial aid programs. The case involved a New York State statute that barred permanent resident aliens from eligibility for Regents' college scholarships, tuition assistance awards, and state-guaranteed student loans. Resident aliens denied financial aid argued that the New York law unconstitutionally discriminated against them in violation of the equal protection clause of the Fourteenth Amendment. The Supreme Court agreed.

The Court's opinion makes clear that alienage, somewhat like race, can be a "suspect classification." Discrimination against resident aliens in awarding financial aid can thus be justified only if the discrimination is necessary in order to achieve some compelling governmental interest. The *Nyquist* opinion indicates that the state's interests in offering an incentive for aliens to become naturalized, and in enhancing the educational level of the electorate, are not sufficiently strong to justify discrimination against resident aliens with regard to financial aid.

Since the case was brought against the state rather than against individual postsecondary institutions, *Nyquist*'s most direct effect is to prohibit states from discriminating against resident aliens in state financial aid programs. It does not matter whether the state programs are for students in public institutions, in private institutions, or both, since in any case the state would have created the discrimination. In addition, the case clearly would prohibit public institutions from discriminating against resident aliens in operating their own separate financial aid programs. Private institutions are affected by these constitutional principles only to the extent that they are participating in government-sponsored financial aid programs or are otherwise engaging in "state action" (see Section 1.5.2) in their aid programs.

It does not necessarily follow from *Nyquist* that all aliens must be considered eligible for financial aid. *Nyquist* concerned permanent resident aliens and determined that such aliens as a class do not differ sufficiently from U.S. citizens to permit different treatment. Courts might not reach the same conclusion about nonresident aliens whose permission to be in the United States is temporary. In *Ahmed v. University of Toledo*, 664 F. Supp. 282 (N.D. Ohio 1986), for example, the court considered a challenge to the University of Toledo's requirement that all international students purchase health insurance. Those students not able to show proof of coverage were deregistered, and their financial aid was discontinued. The trial court ruled that the affected international students were not a suspect class for equal protection purposes, because only nonresident aliens were required to purchase the insurance; resident aliens were not. Since the situation was thus unlike *Nyquist*, where the challenged policy had affected resident rather than nonresident aliens, the court used the more relaxed "rational relationship" standard of review for equal protection claims rather than *Nyquist*'s strict scrutiny standard (see generally, regarding strict scrutiny, Section 7.2.5 of this book), holding that the university's policy was rational and therefore constitutional. The U.S. Court of Appeals dismissed the students' appeal as moot (822 F.2d 26 (6th Cir. 1987)). In *Tayyari v. New*

*Mexico State University*, 495 F. Supp. 1365 (D.N.M. 1980), however, the court did invalidate a university policy denying reenrollment (during the Iranian hostage crisis) to Iranian students who were nonimmigrant aliens in this country on student visas. The court considered the Iranian students to be members of a suspect class and determined that the university's reasons for treating them differently could not pass strict scrutiny.

Despite the *Tayyari* reasoning, public colleges and universities subject to the *Nyquist* principles can probably comply by making sure that they do not require students to be U.S. citizens or to show evidence of intent to become citizens in order to be eligible for financial aid administered by the institution. (The U.S. Department of Education has similar eligibility requirements for its student aid programs; see "Student Aid Eligibility" on the Web site of the Education Department at http://studentaid.ed.gov/PORTALSWebApp/students/english/aideligibility.jsp?tab=funding.) Institutions thus may decline to provide institutional aid to aliens who have F, M, or J visas (see Section 7.7.3 of this book) and other temporary nonresident aliens. Such a distinction between permanent resident and temporary nonresident aliens may be justifiable on grounds that institutions (and states) need not spend their financial aid resources on individuals who have no intention to remain in and contribute to the state or the United States. Whether institutions may also make undocumented resident aliens ineligible for financial assistance is a separate question not controlled by *Nyquist* and is discussed in Section 7.3.5.2.

Moreover, since *Nyquist* does not affect state residency requirements, institutions may deny financial aid or in-state tuition status to aliens who are not state residents under certain circumstances. Aid thus would not be denied because the students are aliens but because they are nonresidents of the state. Although state residency for aliens may be determined in part by their particular status under federal immigration law (see especially 8 U.S.C. § 1101(a)(15)), it is well to be cautious in relying on federal law. In *Elkins v. Moreno*, 435 U.S. 647 (1978), the University of Maryland had denied "in-state" status, for purposes of tuition and fees, to aliens holding federal G-4 nonimmigrant visas (for employees of international treaty organizations and their immediate families). The university argued the G-4 aliens' federal status precluded them from demonstrating an intent to become permanent Maryland residents. The U.S. Supreme Court rejected this argument, holding that G-4 aliens (unlike some other categories of nonimmigrant aliens) are not incapable under federal law of becoming permanent residents and thus are not precluded from forming an intent to reside permanently in Maryland. The Court then certified to the Maryland Court of Appeals the question whether G-4 aliens or their dependents are incapable of establishing Maryland residency under the state's common law.

In "Act 2" of this litigation drama, *Toll v. Moreno*, 397 A.2d 1009 (Md. 1979), *judgment vacated*, 441 U.S. 458 (1979), the Maryland court answered no to the Supreme Court's question. In the interim, however, the university had adopted a new in-state policy, which no longer used state residency as the paramount factor in determining in-state status for tuition and fees. Because the changed policy raised new constitutional issues, the Supreme Court ended Act 2 by vacating the Maryland court's judgment and remanding the case to the federal district court where the *Elkins* case had begun.

After the district court invalidated Maryland's new policy and the U.S. Court of Appeals affirmed, the case returned to the U.S. Supreme Court (*Toll v. Moreno*, 458 U.S. 1 (1982)) for Act 3. The Court held that the university's new policy, insofar as it barred G-4 aliens and their dependents from acquiring in-state status, violated the supremacy clause of the U.S. Constitution (U.S. Const. art. VI, para. 2). The supremacy clause recognizes the primacy of federal regulatory authority over subjects within the scope of federal constitutional power and prevents state law from interfering with federal law regarding such subjects. Since the federal government's broad constitutional authority over immigration has long been recognized, federal law on immigration preempts any state or local law inconsistent with the federal law. Applying these principles in *Toll*, the Court reasoned:

> The Immigration and Nationality Act of 1952, 66 Stat. 163, as amended, 8 U.S.C. § 1101 et seq., . . . recognizes two basic classes of aliens, immigrant and nonimmigrant. With respect to the nonimmigrant class, the Act establishes various categories, the G-4 category among them. For many of these nonimmigrant categories, Congress has precluded the covered alien from establishing domicile in the United States . . . But significantly, Congress has allowed G-4 aliens—employees of various international organizations, and their immediate families—to enter the country on terms permitting the establishment of domicile in the United States . . . In light of Congress' explicit decision not to bar G-4 aliens from acquiring domicile, the State's decision to deny "in-state" status to G-4 aliens, solely on account of the G-4 alien's federal immigration status, surely amounts to an ancillary "burden not contemplated by Congress" in admitting these aliens to the United States [458 U.S. at 12–14; citations and footnotes omitted].

As a result of the *Elkins-Toll* litigation, it is now clear that postsecondary institutions may not use G-4 aliens' nonimmigrant status as a basis for denying in-state status for tuition and fees purposes. It does not follow, however, that institutions are similarly limited with respect to other categories of nonimmigrant aliens. The nonimmigrant categories comprise aliens who enter the United States temporarily for a specific purpose and who usually must maintain their domicile in a foreign country (see, for example, 8 U.S.C. § 1101(a)(15)(B) (temporary visitors for pleasure or business); § 1101(a)(15)(F) (temporary academic students); § 1101(a)(15)(M) (temporary vocational students). Such restrictions preclude most nonimmigrant aliens from forming an intent to establish permanent residency (or domicile), which is required under the residency laws of most states. Thus, federal and state law would apparently still allow public institutions to deny in-state status to nonimmigrant aliens, other than G-4s and other narrow categories that are not required to maintain domicile in their home countries.

It also remains important, after *Elkins-Toll*, to distinguish between nonimmigrant (nonresident) and immigrant (resident) aliens. Because immigrant aliens are permitted under federal law to establish U.S. and state residency, denial of in-state status because of their alienage would violate the federal supremacy principles relied on in *Toll* (Act 3). Moreover, such discrimination against immigrant aliens would violate the equal protection clause of the Fourteenth Amendment, as established in *Nyquist v. Mauclet*, discussed earlier in this section.

**7.3.5.2. Undocumented aliens.** Since the *Elkins-Toll* litigation, yet another critical distinction has emerged: the distinction between aliens with federal immigrant or nonimmigrant status on the one hand and undocumented aliens on the other. In some circumstances, the equal protection clause will also protect undocumented aliens from state discrimination in the delivery of educational services. In *Plyler v. Doe*, 457 U.S. 202 (1982), for instance, the U.S. Supreme Court used equal protection principles to invalidate a Texas statute that "den[ied] to undocumented school-age children the free public education that [the state] provides to children who are citizens of the United States or legally admitted aliens." Reasoning that the Texas law was "directed against children [who] . . . can have little control" over their undocumented status and that the law "den[ied] these children a basic education," thereby saddling them with the "enduring disability" of illiteracy, the Court held that the state's interests in protecting its education system and resources could not justify this discriminatory burden on the affected children. *Plyler* dealt with elementary education; the key question, then, is whether the case's reasoning and the equal protection principles that support it would apply to higher education as well—in particular to state policies that deny to undocumented aliens financial aid or in-state tuition status that is available to U.S. citizens and documented aliens.

This question attracted a great deal of attention in California, where courts wrestled with it in a complex chain of litigation. In 1983, the California legislature passed a statute providing that "[a]n alien, including an unmarried minor alien, may establish his or her residence, unless precluded by the Immigration and Nationality Act (8 U.S.C. § 1101 *et seq.*) from establishing domicile in the United States" (Cal. Educ. Code § 68062(h)). It was not clear how this statute would apply to undocumented aliens who had been living in California and sought to establish residency for in-state tuition purposes. At the request of the chancellor of the California State University, the Attorney General of California issued an interpretation of the statute, indicating that an undocumented alien's incapacity to establish residence in the United States under federal immigration law precluded that same alien from establishing residency in California for in-state tuition purposes (67 Opinions of Cal. Attorney General 241 (Opinion No. 84-101 (1984)). Subsequently, the University of California and the California state university and college system formulated identical policies charging all undocumented aliens out-of-state tuition.

In *Leticia A. v. Regents of the University of California*, No. 588-982-4 (Cal. Super. Ct., Alameda County, orders of April 3, 1985, May 7, 1985, and May 30, 1985 ("Statement of Decision")), four undocumented alien students challenged the constitutionality of these policies on equal protection grounds. The plaintiffs had been brought into this country during their minority and had graduated from California high schools. Relying on the Supreme Court's reasoning in *Plyler*, and on the equal protection clause of the state constitution, the *Leticia A.* court determined that "higher education is an 'important' interest in California" and that the defendants' policies can survive equal protection scrutiny only if "there is a 'substantial' state interest served by the [blanket] classification" of undocumented aliens as nonresidents. The court then compared the rationales supporting this classification and those supporting the federal immigration laws:

> The policies underlying the immigration laws and regulations are vastly different from those relating to residency for student fee purposes. The two systems are totally unrelated for purposes of administration, enforcement and legal analysis. The use of unrelated policies, statutes, regulations or case law from one system to govern portions of the other is irrational. The incorporation of policies governing adjustment of status for undocumented aliens into regulations and administration of a system for determining residence for student fee purposes is neither logical nor rational [*Leticia A.* at 9–10].

The court therefore declared the defendants' policies unconstitutional (without rendering any judgment on the validity of Cal. Educ. Code § 68062(h), on which the policies were based) and ordered the defendants to determine the state residence status of undocumented students and applicants for purposes of in-state tuition in the same way as it would make that determination for U.S. citizens.

Neither defendant appealed the *Leticia A.* decision. In 1990, however, a former employee of the University of California sued that institution to require it to reinstate its pre-*Leticia* policy. The employee, Bradford, had been terminated by the University of California for his "unwillingness to comply with the ruling of the [*Leticia A.*] court." The trial court granted summary judgment in favor of the employee. On appeal, in *Regents of the University of California v. Superior Court*, 276 Cal. Rptr. 197 (Cal. Ct. App., 2d Dist. 1990) (known as the *Bradford* case), the court reviewed the purpose and constitutionality of the defendant's pre-*Leticia A.* residency policy, as well as of Cal. Educ. Code § 68062(h) itself. The court held that, as originally argued by the defendants in the *Leticia A.* litigation, section 68062(h) "precludes undocumented alien students from qualifying as residents of California for tuition purposes." Then the court examined whether such an interpretation denied undocumented alien students the equal protection of the laws. Reasoning that undocumented aliens are commonly and legitimately denied basic rights and privileges under both state and federal law, that the university also denies the lower tuition rate to residents of other states and to aliens holding student visas, and that the state had "manifest and important" interests in extending this denial to undocumented aliens, the appellate court upheld the trial court's ruling.

Unlike the *Leticia A.* court, the appellate court in the *Bradford* case did not rely on the Supreme Court's *Plyler* decision but distinguished it on the basis of the "significant difference between an elementary education and a university education." Thus, the *Bradford* court's decision was in direct conflict with *Leticia A.* and served to uphold the constitutionality of Cal. Educ. Code § 68062(h) as well as the University of California's pre-*Leticia A.* policy. After *Bradford*, litigation continued in the California superior courts to work out the implementation of that decision and its application to the California state university and college system, which was not a defendant in *Bradford*. Then, in a taxpayer action, *American Association of Women v. Board of Trustees of the California State University*, 38 Cal. Rptr. 2d 15 (Ct. App. 2d Dist. 1995), the court expressly disagreed with the reasoning of *Leticia A.*, affirmed that the *Bradford* decision "was correctly decided," and held that *Bradford* is "binding upon the California State University System."

The practical significance of the California cases has been diminished, however, by later developments in California and nationwide. In late 1994, the California electorate approved Proposition 187, which, among other things, denied public services to undocumented aliens. Section 8 of the proposition, which was codified as Cal. Educ. Code § 66010.8, included public postsecondary education among the public services denied to undocumented aliens. In *League of United Latin American Citizens v. Wilson*, 908 F. Supp. 755 (C.D. Cal. 1995), the court invalidated most of the provisions of Proposition 187 and the implementing statutes on federal preemption grounds (see Section 11.3.1 of this book), but left intact the provision on denial of postsecondary education benefits in Cal. Educ. Code § 66010.8(a). Then, in 1996, Congress passed two new laws, the Personal Responsibility and Work Opportunity Reconciliation Act (PRWORA) and the Illegal Immigration Reform and Immigrant Responsibility Act (IIRIRA), to create uniform national rules regulating and restricting aliens' eligibility for public benefits. One provision of the IIRIRA, codified as 8 U.S.C. § 1621, makes undocumented aliens ineligible for "any state or local public benefit" (8 U.S.C. § 1621(a)) and defines such benefits to include "any . . . postsecondary education . . . benefit . . . for which payments or assistance are provided to an individual . . . by an agency of a state or local government" (8 U.S.C. § 1621(c)(1)(B)). Relying on this provision, the district court that had issued the 1995 opinion reconsidered and revised its earlier disposition, concluding that the IIRIRA preempted Cal. Educ. Code § 66010.8(a) and rendered it inoperative (*League of United Latin American Citizens v. Wilson*, 997 F. Supp. 1244 (C.D. Cal. 1997); see also *League of United Latin American Citizens v. Wilson*, 1998 WL 141325 (C.D. Cal. 1998)).

The end result appears to be that denial of state postsecondary education benefits to undocumented aliens—in California and in other states—is now governed primarily by federal law (the IIRIRA) rather than state law.[9] (Other provisions in 8 U.S.C. § 1611 govern undocumented aliens' eligibility for "Federal public benefit(s)," including "any . . . postsecondary education . . . benefit,"

---

[9] There is dispute, however, concerning whether the IIRIRA does, or should, apply in this way to benefits that are a function of state residency determinations, such as the in-state tuition rate; see Michael A. Olivas, "IIRIRA, The Dream Act, and Undocumented College Student Residency," 30 *J. Coll. & Univ. Law* 435, 449–57 (2004).

and impose restrictions similar to those for state and local benefits in 8 U.S.C. § 1621.) The IIRIRA does, however, permit states to make undocumented aliens eligible for postsecondary benefits (and other state and local benefits) for which they are otherwise ineligible under 8 U.S.C. § 1621(a), but only if states do so "through the enactment of a state law after August 22, 1996, which affirmatively provides for such eligibility" (8 U.S.C. § 1621(d)). Another provision of the IIRIRA limits this state authority, specifically with respect to "postsecondary education benefit(s)," by providing that states may not provide greater benefits to undocumented aliens than it provides to United States citizens who are not residents of the state (8 U.S.C. § 1623).

In the leading case to date, *Martinez v. Regents of the University of California*, 241 P.3d 855 (Cal. 2010), the Supreme Court of California upheld a state law that provides in-state tuition rates for some undocumented students. The case illustrates the potential conflicts between such laws and federal immigration laws and demonstrates one way in which courts may resolve such potential conflicts. The California law at issue exempts undocumented aliens (and others) from paying nonresident tuition if they had attended California high schools for at least three years and meet certain other requirements (Cal. Educ. Code § 68130.5). Federal law, however, prohibits states from making undocumented aliens eligible for postsecondary education benefits on the basis of state residency unless U.S. citizens and permanent residents are also eligible for these benefits (8 U.S.C. § 1623). The plaintiffs in *Martinez* argued (primarily) that the California statute violated the federal statute and was therefore invalid. The state Supreme Court determined otherwise.

> If Congress had intended to prohibit states entirely from making unlawful aliens eligible for in-state tuition, it could easily have done so. It could simply have provided, for example, that "an alien who is not lawfully present in the United States shall not be eligible" for a postsecondary education benefit. But it did not do so; instead, it provided that "an alien who is not lawfully present in the United States shall not be eligible *on the basis of residence within a State*" for a postsecondary education benefit. (§ 1623(a), italics added.) The reference to the benefit being on the basis of residence must have some meaning. It can only qualify, and thus limit, the prohibition's reach. Section 1623 does not govern this case [241 P.3d 864].

Higher education residency and immigration cases continue to proliferate. Two such cases involved U.S. citizen children with undocumented parents being precluded from receiving in-state tuition (*Ruiz v. Robinson*, 892 F. Supp. 2d 1321 (S.D. Fla. 2012)) and financial aid (*A.Z. v. Higher Educ. Student Assistance Auth.*, 48 A.3d 1151 (N.J. Super. Ct. App. Div. 2012)). In both instances, the state lost. As noted in Section 7.2.4.4 of this book, the Department of Homeland Security in 2012 began to provide Deferred Action for Childhood Arrivals (DACA) to certain undocumented college students; several legal challenges to DACA have ensued, with varying results. No state statute based upon federal law (such as IIRRIRA) has been successfully overturned by anti-immigrant challenges; this is true in federal and state courts, and in substantive rulings on the merits (see *Martinez v. Regents*, discussed above). As this book went to press, Congress was considering comprehensive immigration reform, signaling that this will remain a very fluid and complicated field.

IIRIRA is not likely to be the last word on these sensitive issues concerning financial aid for undocumented alien applicants and students. Some states are passing laws allowing undocumented students to qualify for in-state tuition rates or state financial aid (see, for example, Kan. Stat. Ann. §76-731(a) 2004) (litigated in *Day v. Bond*, 500 F. 3d 1127, but without any ruling on the merits), and a 2011 California law providing that undocumented students who graduated from California high schools are eligible for state-provided financial aid (2011 Cal. Legis. Serv. 2113 (West) and 2011 Cal. Legis. Serv. Ch. 604 (A.B. 131) (Westlaw)). In other states, such as Rhode Island, the state higher education board has extended in-state tuition rates to undocumented aliens (see E. Niedowski, "R.I. Education Board OK's In-State Tuition for Undocumented Students," September 27, 2011, available at http://articles.boston.com/2011 –09–27/news/30209209_1_illegal-immigrants-tuition-rates-reward-illegal-behavior). Other states, however, are passing laws that prohibit undocumented aliens from qualifying, on the basis of residency, for financial aid or in-state tuition rates. (See, for example, S.C. Code Ann. § 59-101-430(B).) Both types of laws are being challenged in court. And in some other states, state universities have allowed certain undocumented aliens to qualify for in-state tuition without the support of post-IIRIRA state legislation.

For information and citations on recent developments in state legislatures, Congress, and the courts, from 2005 to the present, go to http://www.law.uh.edu/ihelg, and click on "Downloadable Materials" in the upper right-hand corner (Web site of the Institute for Higher Education Law and Governance; recent developments compiled by Michael Olivas).

### Section 7.4. Student Housing

**7.4.1. Overview.** Postsecondary institutions with residential campuses usually have policies specifying which students may, and which students must, live in campus housing. Such regulations sometimes apply only to certain groups of students, using classifications based on the student's age, sex, class, or marital status. Institutions also typically have policies regulating living conditions in campus housing. Students in public institutions have sought to use the federal Constitution to challenge such housing policies, while students at both public and private colleges have used landlord-tenant law or nondiscrimination law to challenge housing regulations.

Challenges to housing regulations typically fall into two categories: challenges by students required to live on campus who do not wish to, and challenges by students (or, occasionally, nonstudents) who wish to live in campus housing (or housing affiliated with a college), but who are ineligible under the college's regulations. Besides these two types of challenges to student housing policies, there are also constitutional challenges to the authority of personnel of public institutions to enter student rooms without permission (see Section 7.4.3 of this book). In addition, there are cases concerning the potential tort liability of residential colleges and universities for foreseeable harm that occurs in a residence unit to students who live there. (See generally Section 7.6.2 of this book; and for an example in the same section, see *Knoll v. Board of Regents of the University of Nebraska*, which discusses institutional liability for an off-campus injury that occurred in a fraternity house subject to the college's student housing policies.)

An example of the first type of challenge is *Prostrollo v. University of South Dakota*, 507 F.2d 775 (8th Cir. 1974). In *Prostrollo*, students claimed that the university's regulation requiring all single freshmen and sophomores to live in university housing was unconstitutional because it denied them equal protection under the Fourteenth Amendment and infringed their constitutional rights of privacy and freedom of association. The university admitted that one purpose of the regulation was to maintain a certain level of dormitory occupancy to secure revenue to repay dormitory construction costs. But the university also offered testimony that the regulation was instituted to ensure that younger students would educationally benefit from the experience in self-government, community living, and group discipline and the opportunities for relationships with staff members that dormitory life provides. In addition, university officials contended that the dormitories provided easy access to study facilities and to films and discussion groups.

Although the lower court ruled that the regulation violated the equal protection clause, the appellate court reversed the lower court's decision. The appellate court reasoned that, even if the regulation's primary purpose was financial, there was no denial of equal protection because there was another rational basis for differentiating freshmen and sophomores from upper-division students: the university officials' belief that the regulation contributed to the younger students' adjustment to college life. The appellate court also rejected the students' challenges based on right to privacy and freedom of association. The court gave deference to school authorities' traditionally broad powers in formulating educational policy.

Conflicts about residence hall policies may also arise if there are Greek organizations with houses in which their student members wish to live. In *Illinois Beta Chapter of Sigma Phi Epsilon Fraternity Alumni Board v. Illinois State Institute of Technology*, 946 N.E.2d 1118 (Ill. App. Ct. 2011), a fraternity sought to enjoin the Institute from enforcing residence hall contracts for students who had signed housing contracts but subsequently moved into fraternity houses during their first semester on campus. (Students who moved to a fraternity house during the second semester were released from their housing contract.) The fraternity noted that a 1964 agreement with the Institute promised that the Institute would not "unreasonably refuse" to assign students to fraternity houses, and that the Institute's insistence on retaining the first-semester housing fee would have serious financial implications for the fraternity. Although the trial court granted the preliminary injunction, the appellate court reversed, stating that the dispute was not yet ripe for litigation and a breach of contract lawsuit would provide an adequate remedy for any losses incurred.

### 7.4.2. Discrimination claims.

Campus housing policies also may result in discrimination claims, either from students who wish to live in campus housing or from those who do not. Although early cases involved age and sex discrimination claims, conflict more recently has involved students with disabilities and gay or transgendered students and campus housing policies.

A housing regulation that used an age classification to prohibit certain students from living off campus was at issue in *Cooper v. Nix*, 496 F.2d 1285 (5th Cir. 1974). The regulation required all unmarried full-time undergraduate students, regardless of age and whether or not emancipated, to live on campus. The regulation contained an exemption for certain older students, which in practice the school enforced by simply exempting all undergraduates 23 years old and over. Neither the lower court nor the appeals court found any justification in the record for a distinction between 21-year-old students and 23-year-old students. Though the lower court had enjoined the school from requiring students 21 and older to live on campus, the appeals court narrowed the remedy to require only that the school not automatically exempt all 23-year-olds. Thus, the school could continue to enforce the regulation if it exempted students over 23 only on a case-by-case basis.

A regulation that allowed male students but not female students to live off campus was challenged in *Texas Woman's University v. Chayklintaste*, 521 S.W.2d 949 (Tex. Civ. App. 1975), and found unconstitutional. Though the university convinced the court that it did not have the space or the money to provide on-campus male housing, the court held that mere financial reasons could not justify the discrimination. The court concluded that the university was unconstitutionally discriminating against its male students by not providing them with any housing facilities and also was unconstitutionally discriminating against its female students by not permitting them to live off campus.

The university subsequently made housing available to males and changed its regulations to require both male and female undergraduates under twenty-three to live on campus. Although the regulation was now like the one found unconstitutional in *Cooper*, above, the Texas Supreme Court upheld its constitutionality in a later appeal of *Texas Woman's University v. Chayklintaste*, 530 S.W.2d 927 (Tex. 1975). In this case the university justified the age classification with reasons similar to those used in *Prostrollo* (discussed in Section 7.4.2). The university argued that on-campus dormitory life added to the intellectual and emotional development of its students and supported this argument with evidence from published research and experts in student affairs.

In *Bynes v. Toll*, 512 F.2d 252 (2d Cir. 1975), another university housing regulation was challenged—in this case a regulation that permitted married students to live on campus but barred their children from living on campus. The court found that there was no denial of equal protection, since the university had several very sound safety reasons for not allowing children to reside in the dormitories. The court also found that the regulation did not interfere with the marital privacy of the students or their natural right to bring up their children.

Housing regulations limiting residence hall visitors have also been constitutionally challenged. In *Futrell v. Ahrens*, 540 P.2d 214 (N.M. 1975), students claimed that a regulation prohibiting visits by members of the opposite sex in dormitory bedrooms violated their rights of privacy and free association. The regulation did not apply to the lounges or lobbies of the dorms. The court held for the institution, reasoning that even if the regulation affected rights of privacy and association, it was a reasonable time-and-place restriction on exercise of those rights, since it served legitimate educational interests and conformed with accepted standards of conduct.

A federal court's analysis of a student's religious discrimination challenge to mandatory on-campus residency is instructive. In *Rader v. Johnston*, 924 F. Supp. 1540 (D. Neb. 1996), an eighteen-year-old first-year student at the University of Nebraska at Kearney brought a First Amendment challenge to the university's policy requiring first-year students to live on campus. Students who were nineteen, married, or living with their parents or legal guardians were expressly exempted from the policy. The rationale for the policy, according to the university, was that it "fosters diversity, promotes tolerance, increases the level of academic achievement, and improves the graduation rate of its students, [while] ensur[ing] full occupancy of . . . residence halls" (924 F. Supp. at 1543). The student contended that living in the campus residence halls would hinder the free exercise of his religion. Since he did not qualify for exemption under any of the enumerated exceptions to the residency policy, he petitioned the university for an ad hoc exemption "on the ground that his religious convictions exhort him to live in an environment that encourages moral excellence during [his] college career," and, to this end, he requested that the university "allow him to live with other students of similar faith in the Christian Student Fellowship facility, across the street from the . . . campus." The university denied the student's request, citing its rationale for the residency requirement and finding that nothing in the residence hall environment would hinder the student's practice of religion.

The court, relying on a U.S. Supreme Court decision in *Church of the Lukumi Babalu Aye v. City of Hialeah*, 508 U.S. 520 (1993) (Section 1.6.2 of this book), found in favor of the student. It noted that more than one-third of first-year students had been granted exemptions from the residency requirement under both enumerated and ad hoc exemptions for nonreligious reasons, but not for religious reasons. Under *Lukumi Babalu Aye*, therefore, the university's on-campus residency policy for first-year students was not "generally applicable" or "neutrally applied" to all students and could withstand judicial scrutiny, as applied to Rader, only if the denial of his request for an exception "serves a compelling state interest." Conceding that the university's interests could be legitimate and important, the numerous exemptions undercut the university's argument that its interest was compelling. These interests therefore could not justify the resulting infringement on Rader's free exercise rights.

Students lodged a claim against Yale University that was similar to the *Rader* claim. This suit was dismissed by a federal district court in *Hack v. The President and Fellows of Yale College*, 16 F. Supp. 2d 183 (D. Conn. 1998), *affirmed*, 237 F.3d 81 (2d Cir. 2000). Yale required all unmarried freshman and sophomore students under twenty-two years old to live in campus housing.

Four Orthodox Jewish undergraduate students requested exemptions from the housing requirement because all of Yale's residence halls were coeducational, and the students stated that their religion forbade them to live in a coeducational environment. When the university refused to exempt the students from the housing requirement, they filed a lawsuit claiming that the housing policy violated the U.S. Constitution by interfering with their free exercise of religion, that it also violated the Fair Housing Act (FHA) and the Sherman Antitrust Act, and that it constituted a breach of contract.

The court dismissed the students' constitutional claims, ruling that Yale was a private university and not subject to constitutional restrictions. The students had claimed that, because the governor and lieutenant governor of Connecticut were ex officio members of Yale's governing body, the university was a state actor. Citing *Lebron v. National Passenger R.R. Corp.*, 513 U.S. 374 (1995) (Section 1.5.2 of this book), the court ruled that having two public officials on a governing board of nineteen was insufficient under the test articulated in *Lebron* to constitute state action. The court then ruled that the plaintiffs did not have standing to sue under the Fair Housing Act because Yale had not refused to provide housing to the students on the basis of their religion; it had provided them housing that they had paid for, but in which they refused to live.

With respect to the antitrust claim, the court ruled that the students' complaint had not specifically stated whether the tying market that Yale was alleged to be attempting to monopolize was "a general university education or an Ivy League education" (16 F. Supp. 2d at 195). Furthermore, said the court, the plaintiffs had not identified the relevant market at issue; substitutes for Yale's campus housing could be obtained by attending a different university. Despite the plaintiffs' attempt to argue that the outcome in the Hamilton College antitrust case (Section 10.2.2) protected their claim against dismissal, the court responded that the Hamilton College case merely established that a private college affected interstate commerce, and that the plaintiffs' failure to define the relevant market alleged to be monopolized by Yale doomed their complaint to failure.

Federal civil rights regulations limit administrators' authority to treat students differently on grounds of race, sex, age, or disability. The Title VI regulations (see Section 11.5.2) apparently prohibit any and all different treatment of students by race (34 C.F.R. §§ 100.3(b)(1)–(b)(5), 100.4(d)). The Title IX regulations (see Section 11.5.3 of this book) require that the institution provide amounts of housing for female and male students proportionate to the number of housing applicants of each sex, that such housing be comparable in quality and in cost to the student, and that the institution not have different housing policies for each sex (34 C.F.R. §§ 106.32, 106.33). Furthermore, a provision of Title IX (20 U.S.C. § 1686) states that institutions may maintain single-sex living facilities.

Title IX's recognition that single-sex residence halls do not discriminate on the basis of sex was important to the outcome of a discrimination claim brought under the District of Columbia's Human Rights Act. In 2011, the president of Catholic University announced that the university would require first-year students to live in single-sex residence halls. The justification for this policy change was that the university administration believed the policy would reduce binge drinking and sexual promiscuity among first-year students. John Banzhaf, a professor at George Washington University Law School, filed a sex discrimination complaint with the District of Columbia's Office of Human Rights. That agency dismissed the complaint, ruling that single-sex residence halls do not violate the D.C. law's prohibition on sex discrimination because the university treated men and women the same. In *Banzhaf v. Garvey*, Docket No. 11-343-EI (D.C. Office of Human Rights, Nov. 29, 2011), the agency reasoned that if Banzhaf's interpretation of the law were credited, the university could not maintain single-sex restrooms, locker rooms, or athletic teams.

The regulations for Section 504 of the Rehabilitation Act on discrimination against people with disabilities (see Section 11.5.4 of this book) require institutions to provide "comparable, convenient, and accessible" housing for students with disabilities at the same cost as for nondisabled students (34 C.F.R. § 104.45). The regulations also require colleges to provide a variety of housing and that students with disabilities be given a choice among several types of housing (34 C.F.R. § 104.45(a)).

In *Fleming v. New York University*, 865 F.2d 478 (2d Cir. 1989), a graduate student who used a wheelchair claimed that the university overcharged him for his room, in violation of Section 504 of the Rehabilitation Act. The trial court dismissed his claim, and the appellate court affirmed. The student had requested single occupancy of a double room as an undergraduate; the university charged him twice the rate that a student sharing a double room paid. After intervention by the U.S. Office for Civil Rights, the university modified its room charge to 75 percent of the rate for two students in a room.

When the student decided to enroll in graduate school at the university, he asked to remain in the undergraduate residence hall. The university agreed and charged him the 75 percent fee. However, because of low occupancy levels in the graduate residence halls, graduate students occupying double rooms there were charged a single-room rate. When the student refused to pay his room bills, the university withheld his master's degree. The court ruled that the student's claim for his undergraduate years was time barred. The claim for disability discrimination based on the room charges during his graduate program was denied because the student had never applied for graduate housing; he had requested undergraduate housing. There was no discriminatory denial of cheaper graduate housing, the court said, because the student never requested it.

But in *Fialka-Feldman v. Oakland University Board of Trustees*, 678 F. Supp. 2d 576 (E.D. Mich. 2009), the plaintiff, a student with cognitive disabilities, was enrolled at the university in a non-credit continuing education program. He applied to live in on-campus housing, but his application was denied because he was not enrolled in a degree-granting program, which was required by the university's housing policy. The plaintiff sued under the Fair Housing Act, the Americans with Disabilities Act (ADA), and Section 504 of the Rehabilitation Act. The plaintiff later dropped his claim under the Fair Housing Act.

The university defended its policy, stating that the plaintiff was not a "qualified" student with a disability because he was not enrolled in a degree-granting program. The plaintiff argued that it was his cognitive disability that prevented him from pursuing a degree, and therefore the disability itself was the reason he was not permitted to live in campus housing. Although the university argued that allowing non-degree students to live in campus housing would defeat the academic purpose of such housing, the court characterized the plaintiff's request as a waiver of the housing policy for him alone rather than a change to the housing policy for all non-degree students. The court concluded that the university's refusal to engage in the interactive process required by the ADA and Section 504 violated these laws, and awarded summary judgment to the plaintiff. The court awarded summary judgment to the university on the plaintiff's disparate treatment claim, noting that he had been denied campus housing not because of his disability, but because of his enrollment status. The university appealed the summary judgment ruling; the appellate court ruled that since the student had completed the program and did not intend to return for more education, the appeal was moot. The appellate court vacated the judgment below (639 F.3d 711 (6th Cir. 2011)).

Students with disabilities may ask to bring service animals or comfort animals to campus and ask that they reside with them in their residence hall room (and perhaps accompany them to class). Under Titles II and III of the ADA, public colleges and private colleges that are "places of public accommodation" must modify their policies and practices to accommodate the use of a service animal by a person with a disability. The Department of Justice, which enforces Titles II and III of the ADA, defines a service animal as "any dog that is individually trained to do work or perform tasks for the benefit of an individual with a disability, including a physical, sensory, psychiatric, intellectual, or other mental disability" (28 C.F.R. §35.104). Comfort animals are not included within the definition of service animal. Section 504 also requires recipients of federal funds to permit "dog guides" in campus buildings (34 C.F.R § 104.44(b)).

The Fair Housing Act defines an "assistance animal" more broadly than the ADA's definition of a "service animal," and includes "emotional support" animals within its definition (73 Fed. Reg. 63836 (October 27, 2008)). The institution is allowed to require students requesting housing for an assistance animal to provide medical documentation that the animal "alleviates at least one of the identified symptoms or effects of the existing disability" (73 Fed. Reg. 63835). The Fair Housing Act regulations include college residence halls within their definition of "dwelling unit" (24 C.F.R. §100.201); although there have been few judicial rulings on the application of the Fair Housing Act to campus residence halls, the Department of Housing and Urban Development has indicated an intention to pursue enforcement actions in academe and initiated one action, which was settled, against Millikin University (*United States v. Millikin University*, FHEO No. 05-06-0829-8 (September 18, 2009)).

In late 2011, the U.S. Department of Justice filed a lawsuit against the University of Nebraska at Kearney, stating that the university's denial of the request of a student with a psychological disorder to keep a therapy dog in her apartment, owned by the university, violated the Fair Housing Act. In *United States of America v. University of Nebraska at Kearney*, 2013 U.S. Dist. LEXIS 56009 (D. Neb. Apr. 19, 2013), the trial court denied the university's motion for summary judgment, concluding that the antidiscrimination provisions of the Fair Housing Act apply to university housing. And in *Velzen v. Grand Valley State University*, 2012 U.S. Dist. LEXIS 145666 (W.D. Mich. October 10, 2012), a student was prescribed an "emotional support" animal to help control her depression. When Velzen asked that she be allowed to keep her guinea pig in her residence hall apartment, the request was denied because the animal did not meet the definition of "service animal" in that it was not trained to do work or perform tasks. The lawsuit sought injunctive relief and compensatory damages. Although the university asked the court to dismiss all of the claims, the plaintiffs' claims for injunctive relief under the Fair Housing Act and the compensatory damage claim for failure to accommodate under the Rehabilitation Act survived dismissal. The case was settled in 2013.

State laws may have broader definitions of "service animal" than the federal definition, so counsel should refer to state as well as federal law in this regard.

Another group protesting discrimination in housing policies are same-sex couples. These couples have claimed that because they are not allowed to marry, they are unfairly excluded from a benefit extended to married students. Furthermore, since many colleges and universities prohibit discrimination on the basis of sexual orientation, gay couples have argued that denying them housing violates the institution's nondiscrimination regulations. Several universities, including the University of Pennsylvania and Stanford University, have provided university housing to unmarried couples, including those of the same sex.

In *Levin v. Yeshiva University*, 691 N.Y.S.2d 280 (Sup. Ct. N.Y. 1999), *affirmed*, 709 N.Y.S.2d 392 (N.Y. App. Div. 2000), *affirmed in part and modified in part*, 96 N.Y.2d 484 (N.Y. 2001), a same-sex couple who were medical students at the university wished to live in university housing that was reserved for married students, their spouses, and dependent children. The medical school required proof of marriage in order for spouses to live with students in campus apartments. The plaintiffs had been offered student housing but were not permitted to live together. They argued that they were in a long-term committed relationship and that the medical school's housing regulations violated the New York State Roommate Law (N.Y. Real Prop. Law § 235-f) and the New York State and New York City Human Rights Laws (N.Y. Exec. Law §§ 296(2-a), 296(4), 296(5); N.Y.C. Admin. Code § 8-197(5)), because the regulations discriminated against the plaintiffs on the basis of their marital status. They also argued that the housing regulations had a discriminatory impact upon them because of their sexual orientation.

The trial court rejected all the plaintiffs' claims. Regarding marital status discrimination, the court cited New York case law that permitted landlords to "recogniz[e] the institution of marriage and distinguish between married and unmarried couples" (691 N.Y.S.2d at 282). The plaintiffs were not denied housing by the medical school, said the court; they were provided the same type of housing for which other single students were eligible. Furthermore, New York appellate courts had ruled that a domestic partnership was not a marriage for purposes of health benefits for public school teachers. Regarding the disparate impact claim, the court repeated that the plaintiffs had been given housing by the medical school and that Yeshiva University was not responsible for the fact that they could not marry.

Finally, the court rejected the claim under New York's Roommate Law that allows tenants to live with their spouses and children, or with friends of their own choosing. This law was not intended to cover college housing, according to the court, because college housing is short term, available only as long as the tenants are students, provided as a benefit and a convenience to students, and offered at below-market rates.

The students appealed, and although the appellate court affirmed the trial court's ruling in all respects, the students' subsequent appeal to New York's highest court was somewhat more successful. Although the high court affirmed the lower courts' rulings on marital status discrimination, the high court also reinstated the plaintiffs' cause of action claiming that the housing policy had a disproportionate impact on homosexuals, a potential violation of New York City's Human Rights Law. (Same-sex marriage is now legal in the state of New York, so the reasoning of this case will no longer apply to same-sex couples in those states that recognize same-sex marriages.)

Housing for transgender students has raised numerous practical issues on campus. Many colleges assign same-sex roommates, which may pose a problem for students in transition to a different gender. Locker rooms and restrooms are single-sex, which also may pose problems for students either in transition or who have completed the transition to the other gender. Particularly for those institutions that have added "gender identity or expression" as a category that is protected under their nondiscrimination policy (whether or not state law provides similar protection), housing and similar sex-related assignments may need to be rethought.

What is the responsibility—and potential legal liability—of an institution when a nonstudent who resides on campus engages in harassing or discriminatory behavior toward a student (or employee)? The New Jersey Supreme Court addressed that issue in *Godfrey v. Princeton Theological Seminary*, 952 A.2d 1034 (N.J. 2008). In *Godfrey*, two students at a private religiously affiliated institution sued the seminary under both Title IX and the New Jersey Law Against Discrimination, which forbids discrimination on the basis of sex in places of public accommodation. The students alleged that a tenant who lived in one of the seminary's housing units on campus, who was neither a student nor an employee, had stalked them, attempted to coerce them into a social relationship, and engaged in other behaviors that were annoying and bothersome. The students argued that the seminary had not responded appropriately to their complaints, first telling them that it was a police matter and not the seminary's responsibility, and later warning them that they could be liable for defamation if they persisted in complaining about the tenant's behavior to seminary authorities.

The court did not address whether the state nondiscrimination law's definition of "place of public accommodation" applied to a religiously affiliated entity, although the law specifically excludes any "educational facility operated or maintained by a bona fide religious or sectarian institution" (N.J. Stat. Ann. § 10:5–5(l)), because the trial and appellate courts had determined that the behavior complained of by the students did not meet the "severe or pervasive" requirement of the Court's earlier jurisprudence on sexual harassment. The trial and appellate courts had also found that the seminary's response to the students' complaints was not deliberately indifferent, and thus their Title IX claim failed as well. The New Jersey Supreme Court did, however, comment that had the behavior been more severe, or more pervasive, liability might have been found, and criticized the seminary for what the court perceived as an inadequate response to the students' concerns.

Counsel might consider reviewing their institution's policy against harassment to ensure that it applies to harassment of a student or employee by individuals who are not students or employees but who are on campus because of either a relationship with a student (for example, a student's spouse or partner living in on-campus housing) or because they are a vendor or independent contractor. Other types of individuals whose behavior might cause liability for institutions include individuals attending summer or winter break programs (such as programs for alumni) or guest lecturers who are housed on campus during their visit. The defendant seminary in *Godfrey* appeared reluctant to take action against the alleged harasser because he was neither a student nor an employee; under both Title IX and state nondiscrimination laws, this may not be an adequate defense to a claim of harassment.

Taken together, these cases indicate that the courts afford colleges some leeway in regulating on-campus student housing. An institution may require some students to live on campus; may regulate living conditions to fulfill legitimate health, safety, or educational goals; and may apply its housing policies differently to different student groups (as long as it does not violate the nondiscrimination laws). If students are treated differently, however, the basis for classifying them should be reasonable. The cases above suggest that classification based solely on financial considerations may not meet that test. Administrators should thus be prepared to offer sound nonfinancial justifications for classifications in their residence rules—such as the promotion of educational goals, the protection of the health and safety of students, or the protection of other students' privacy interests.

### 7.4.3. Searches and seizures.

The Fourth Amendment secures an individual's expectation of privacy against government encroachment by providing that

the right of the people to be secure in their persons, houses, papers, and effects, against unreasonable searches and seizures, shall not be violated, and no warrants shall issue, but upon probable cause, supported by oath or affirmation, and particularly describing the place to be searched, and the persons or things to be seized.

Searches or seizures conducted pursuant to a warrant meeting the requirements of this provision are deemed reasonable. Warrantless searches may also be found reasonable if they are conducted with the consent of the individual involved, if they are incidental to a lawful arrest, or if they come within a few narrow judicial exceptions, such as an emergency situation.

The applicability of these Fourth Amendment mandates to postsecondary institutions has not always been clear. In the past, when administrators' efforts to provide a "proper" educational atmosphere resulted in noncompliance with the Fourth Amendment, the deviations were defended by administrators and often upheld by courts under a variety of theories. While the previously common justification of *in loco parentis* is no longer appropriate (see Section 7.1.2), several remaining theories retain vitality. The leading case of *Piazzola v. Watkins*, 442 F.2d 284 (5th Cir. 1971), provides a good overview of these theories and their validity.

In *Piazzola*, the dean of men at a state university, at the request of the police, pledged the cooperation of university officials in searching the rooms of two students suspected of concealing marijuana there. At the time of the search, the university had the following regulation in effect: "The college reserves the right to enter rooms for inspection purposes. If the administration deems it necessary, the room may be searched and the occupant required to open his personal baggage and any other personal material which is sealed." The students' rooms were searched without their consent and without a warrant by police officers and university officials. When police found marijuana in each room, the students were arrested, tried, convicted, and sentenced to five years in prison. The U.S. Court of Appeals for the Fifth Circuit reversed the convictions, holding that "a student who occupies a college dormitory room enjoys the protection of the Fourth Amendment" and that the warrantless searches were unreasonable and therefore unconstitutional under that amendment.

*Piazzola* and similar cases establish that administrators of public institutions cannot avoid the Fourth Amendment simply by asserting that a student has no reasonable expectation of privacy in institution-sponsored housing. (Compare *State v. Dalton*, 716 P.2d 940 (Wash. Ct. App. 1986).) Similarly, administrators cannot avoid the Fourth Amendment by asserting its generalized interest in health or safety or by arguing that the institution's landlord status, standing alone, authorizes it to search to protect its property interests. Nor does the institution's landlord status, by itself, permit the institution to consent to a search by police, since it has been held that a landlord has no authority to consent to a police search of a tenant's premises (see, for example, *Chapman v. United States*, 365 U.S. 610 (1961)). Furthermore, one roommate may not consent to a search if another roommate who is present refuses to consent (*Georgia v. Randolph*, 547 U.S. 103 (2006)).

However, two limited bases remain on which administrators of public institutions or their delegates can enter a student's premises uninvited and without the authority of a warrant. Under the first approach, the institution can obtain the student's general consent to allow university officials to enter the room by including an authorization to enter in a written housing agreement or in housing regulations incorporated in the housing agreement. But, according to *Piazzola*, the institution cannot require the student to waive his or her Fourth Amendment protections as a condition of occupying a residence hall room. And according to *In re: People ex rel. Superior Court of Santa Clara County*, 2006 WL 2873256 (Cal. Ct. App. October 11, 2006), a provision in a housing contract allowing university officials entry does not provide consent for the police to enter; "such purported advance consent to warrantless police searches would be an illegal waiver of defendant's constitutional rights under the Fourth Amendment."

Thus, housing agreements or regulations must be narrowly construed to permit only such entry and search as is expressly provided, and in any case to permit only entries undertaken in pursuit of an educational purpose rather than a criminal enforcement function. *State v. Hunter*, 831 P.2d 1033 (Utah Ct. App. 1992), illustrates the type of search that may come within the *Piazzola* guidelines. The director of housing at Utah State University had instigated and conducted a room-to-room inspection to investigate reports of vandalism on the second floor of a dormitory. Upon challenge by a student in whose room the director discovered stolen university property in plain view, the court upheld the search because the housing regulations expressly authorized the room-to-room inspection and because the inspection served the university's interest in protecting university property and maintaining a sound educational environment.

Under the second approach to securing entry to a student's premises, the public institution can sometimes conduct searches (often called "administrative searches") whose purpose is to protect health and safety—for instance, to enforce health regulations or fire and safety codes. Although such searches, if conducted without a student's consent, usually require a warrant, it may be obtained under less stringent standards than those for obtaining a criminal search warrant. The leading case is *Camara v. Municipal Court*, 387 U.S. 523 (1967), in which the U.S. Supreme Court held that a person cannot be prosecuted for refusing to permit city officials to conduct a warrantless code-enforcement inspection of his residence. The Court held that such a search required a warrant, which could be obtained "if reasonable legislative or administrative standards for conducting an area inspection are satisfied"; such standards need "not necessarily depend upon specific knowledge of the condition of the particular dwelling."

In emergency situations when there is insufficient time to obtain a warrant, health and safety searches may be conducted without one. The U.S. Supreme Court emphasized in the *Camara* case (387 U.S. at 539) that "nothing we say today is intended to foreclose prompt inspections, even without a warrant, that the law has traditionally upheld in emergency situations."

Although a warrantless search based upon the possibility of a health or safety problem may be permissible under the Fourth Amendment, this exception is a narrow one. The Supreme Judicial Court of Massachusetts determined that a warrantless search of a residence hall room by campus police at Fitchburg State College violated the Fourth Amendment to the U.S. Constitution. In *Commonwealth v. Neilson*, 666 N.E.2d 984 (Mass. 1996), a student challenged his arrest for illegal possession of marijuana, asserting that the search of his room was unconstitutional. Neilson had signed a residence hall contract providing that student life staff members could enter student rooms to inspect for health or safety hazards. A maintenance worker believed he heard a cat inside a four-bedroom suite; one of the bedrooms was occupied by Neilson. The maintenance worker reported the sound to college officials, who visited the suite and informed the occupants that no cats were permitted in university housing. The official posted notices on the bedroom doors of the suite, stating that a "door-to-door check" would be held that night to ensure that no cat was present. When the officials returned, Neilson was not present. They searched his bedroom, and noticed that the closet light was on. Because they were concerned that there might be a fire hazard, they opened the door and discovered two 4-foot marijuana plants growing under the light. At that point, the campus police were called; they arrived, took pictures of the marijuana, and removed it from the room. No search warrant was obtained at any time.

The court stated that the initial search (to locate the cat) was reasonable, as was the decision to open the closet door, since it was based upon a concern for the students' safety. The constitutional violation occurred, according to the court, when the campus police arrived and seized the evidence without a warrant or the consent of Neilson. Neilson, in the residence hall contract, had consented to student life officials entering his room, but had not consented to campus police doing so. Furthermore, the "plain view" doctrine did not apply in this case because the campus police were not lawfully present in Neilson's room. The plain view doctrine allows a law enforcement officer to seize property that is clearly incriminating evidence or contraband when that property is in "plain view" in a place where the officer has a right to be. The court therefore concluded that all evidence seized by the campus police was properly suppressed by the trial judge.

Before entering a room pursuant to the housing agreement or an administrative (health and safety) search, administrators should usually seek to notify and obtain the specific consent of the affected students when it is feasible to do so. Such a policy not only evidences courtesy and respect for privacy but would also augment the validity of the entry in circumstances in which there might be some doubt about the scope of the administrator's authority under the housing agreement or the judicial precedents on administrative searches.

A state appellate court ruled that a "dormitory sweep policy" is prima facie unconstitutional. In *Devers v. Southern University*, 712 So. 2d 199 (La. Ct. App. 1998), the court addressed the legality of the university's policy, which stated: "The University reserves all rights in connection with assignments of rooms, inspection of rooms with police, and the termination of room occupancy." The plaintiff, Devers, was arrested when twelve bags of marijuana were discovered in his dormitory room. The drugs were found by university administrators and police officers during a "dormitory sweep" that the university stated was authorized by its housing policy. Devers was expelled from the university after a hearing in which the student judicial board found him guilty of violating the student code of conduct. Devers sued the university, claiming that the search violated the Fourth Amendment. Although the university reached a settlement with Devers with respect to his expulsion (it was reduced to a one-term suspension), his constitutional claim was not settled.

The trial court held that the housing regulation was prima facie unconstitutional, and the appellate court affirmed. The court distinguished *State v. Hunter* because the wording of the housing regulation in *Hunter* differed from the language adopted by Southern University. The regulation in *Hunter* authorized entry into students' dormitory rooms for maintaining students' health and safety, for maintaining university property, and for maintaining discipline. Southern's regulation was broader and would allow unauthorized entry into a student's room for any purpose. The court also distinguished *Piazzola v. Watkins* because its regulation did not authorize searches by police, as did Southern's. The court noted that Southern "has many ways to promote the safety interests of students, faculty and staff" without using warrantless police searches.

In addition to these two limited approaches (housing agreements and administrative searches) to securing entry, other even narrower exceptions to Fourth Amendment warrant requirements may be available to security officers of public institutions who have arrest powers. Such exceptions involve the intricacies of Fourth Amendment law on arrests and searches (see generally *Welsh v. Wisconsin*, 466 U.S. 740 (1984)). The case of *State of Washington v. Chrisman*, 455 U.S. 1 (1982), is illustrative. A campus security guard at Washington State University had arrested a student, Overdahl, for illegally possessing alcoholic beverages. The officer accompanied Overdahl to his dormitory room when Overdahl offered to retrieve his identification. Overdahl's roommate, Chrisman, was in the room. While waiting at the doorway for Overdahl to find his identification, the officer observed marijuana seeds and a pipe lying on a desk in the room. The officer then entered, confirmed the identity of the seeds, and seized them. Chrisman was later convicted of possession of marijuana and LSD, which security officers also found in the room.

By a 6-to-3 vote, the U.S. Supreme Court applied the "plain view" exception to the Fourth Amendment and upheld the conviction. The Court determined that, since an arresting officer has a right to maintain custody of a subject under arrest, this officer lawfully could have entered the room with Overdahl and remained at Overdahl's side for the entire time Overdahl was in the room. Thus, the officer not only had the right to be where he could observe the drugs; he also had the right to be where he could seize the drugs.

*Chrisman* thus recognizes that a security officer may enter a student's room "as an incident of a valid arrest" of either that student or his or her roommate. The case also indicates that an important exception to search warrant requirements—the plain view doctrine—retains its full vitality in the college dormitory setting. The Court accorded no greater or lesser constitutional protection from search and seizure to student dormitory residents than to the population at large. Clearly, under *Chrisman*, students do enjoy Fourth Amendment protections on campus; but, just as clearly, the Fourth Amendment does not accord residence hall students special status or subject campus security officials to additional restrictions that are not applicable to the nonacademic world.

A state appellate court ruled that students at public institutions have an expectation of privacy in the *hallways* of their residence halls and that police may not patrol the hallways without a search warrant unless one of the warrant exceptions exists (*State v. Houvener*, 186 P. 3d 370 (Wash. Ct. App. June 25, 2008)). The police had searched the hallways of a residence hall after a student reported the theft of items from his room. While searching the hallways, the police overheard the defendant, Houvener, discuss disposing of those items with other students in his room. The police entered the room and discovered the items, and Houvener was arrested. He sought to suppress the evidence of the theft, arguing that the police had no warrant and thus were not permitted to patrol the hallways. The court agreed, noting that the general public was not permitted in the hallways and that students engaged in "intimate activities" such as walking through the hallway clad in a towel on the way from the shower, which supported their expectation of privacy in the hallways.

Administrators at private institutions are generally not subject to Fourth Amendment restraints, since their actions are usually not state action (see Section 1.5.2 of this book). But if local, state, or federal law enforcement officials are in any way involved in a search at a private institution, such involvement may be sufficient to make the search state action and therefore subject to the Fourth Amendment. In *People v. Boettner*, 362 N.Y.S.2d 365 (N.Y. Sup. Ct. 1974), *affirmed*, 376 N.Y.S.2d 59 (N.Y. App. Div. 1975), for instance, the question was whether a dormitory room search by officials at the Rochester Institute of Technology, a private institution, was state action. The court answered in the negative only after establishing that the police had not expressly or implicitly requested the search; that the police were not aware of the search; and that there was no evidence of any implied participation of the police by virtue of a continuing cooperative relationship between university officials and the police. A similar analysis, and similar result, occurred in *State v. Nemser*, 807 A.2d 1289 (N.H. 2002), when the court refused to suppress evidence of drugs seized by a Dartmouth College security officer because the college's residence hall search policy had not been approved or suggested by the local police. A Virginia appellate court reached a similar conclusion in *Duarte v. Commonwealth*, 407 S.E.2d 41 (Va. Ct. App. 1991), because the dean of students at a private college had told college staff to search the plaintiff's room, and police were not involved in the search. And in *State v. Burroughs*, 926 S.W.2d 243 (Tenn. 1996), the Tennessee Supreme Court ruled that a warrantless search of a dormitory room by a director of residence life at Knoxville College, a private institution, did not involve state action, and thus his removal of drug paraphernalia and other evidence did not violate the student's Fourth Amendment rights. The court noted that the student handbook and housing contract both forbade the possession or use of alcohol and drugs, and gave the residence hall director authority to search student rooms. Moreover, noted the court, the search was conducted by a college official, not a police officer, to further the educational objectives of the college, not to enforce the criminal law.

In *Limpuangthip v. United States*, 932 A.2d 1137 (D.C. 2007), a university staff member at George Washington University (a private institution) who supervised three residence halls was informed by university police that they had received a tip that a room in one of those residence halls contained drugs. The search was an "administrative search," and all residential students had signed an occupancy agreement consenting to "administrative searches" whose purpose was to respond to health or safety concerns or to check for the presence of illegal substances. Although two university police were present, they did not participate in the search. The search yielded a sizable amount of marijuana and a large sum of cash. The student was convicted of possession of marijuana with intent to distribute and appealed his conviction on Fourth Amendment grounds. The court rejected the student's claim that the presence of the university policy constituted "state action" because the staff member made the decision to search the room, conducted the search by herself, and questioned the student who admitted possession of the drugs. The court characterized the participation of the university police as "peripheral and secondary" to the search.

If, however, the campus police conduct the search at a private institution, the Fourth Amendment may apply. In *Commonwealth v. Carr*, 918 N.E.2d 847 (Mass. App. Ct. 2009), *reversed*, 2010 Mass. LEXIS 871 (Mass. November 17, 2010), a case involving Boston College, a private institution, a resident advisor contacted campus police because two students told her that they had seen a student with a knife and believed that his roommate had a gun. Boston College's housing policy forbade weapons in the residence halls and also reserved the right to inspect students' rooms for safety reasons. The campus police went to the room, asked the student for the gun and other weapons, and were handed a plastic replica gun and two knives. The police then asked the students for permission to search the room, although neither student consented to the search in writing. The police found several types of unlawful drugs during the search.

Although a trial court ruled that the drug evidence must be suppressed because the students had not consented to the search, the appellate court disagreed. Because Boston College is private, said the court, the police officers' conduct did not violate the Fourth Amendment. The court characterized the officers' conduct as furthering the interests of their private employer in investigating to ascertain whether the housing policy was being violated by the students' possession of weapons.

But the Supreme Judicial Court of Massachusetts rejected that reasoning. It decided that the trial judge had ruled appropriately and did not address the appellate court's discussion of whether the Fourth Amendment should apply to a search by police of a private college residence hall room.

### Section 7.5. Campus Computer Networks

**7.5.1. Freedom of speech.**  Increasingly, free speech on campus is enhanced, and free speech issues are compounded, by the growth of technology. Cable and satellite transmission technologies, for instance, have had such effects on many campuses. But the clearest and most important example—now and for the foreseeable future—is computer communications technology. Computer labs, laptops, campus local area networks (LANs), servers, and Internet gateways have assumed a pervasive presence on most campuses, and are used increasingly by the campus community for e-mail communications, discussion groups, Web pages, research, access to information on campus programs and services, and entertainment. Students—the focus of this section—may be both senders (speakers) and receivers (readers); their purposes may be related to coursework or extracurricular activities, or may be purely personal; and their communications may be local (within the institution) or may extend around the world.

Further developments on the pervasiveness of computer communications have involved Facebook and other social networking sites that students commonly use to communicate with many other persons. Since the sites are not connected with the institutions that the students attend, these communicative activities are typically "off campus," and questions may be raised about the institution's authority to regulate them. Yet these communications may target other students at the institution, as well as faculty members and administrators or the institution itself, in ways that create actual or potential harm to the individuals involved or the institution.

Most of the cases thus far on students and social networking sites have involved elementary and secondary education. See, for example, *J.S. ex rel. Snyder v. Blue Mountain School District*, 650 F.3d 915 (3d Cir. 2011) (*en banc*); *Layshock* ex *rel. Layshock v. Hermitage School District*, 650 F.3d 205 (3d Cir. 2011) (*en banc*). The elementary and secondary education cases have raised issues concerning schools' authority to regulate "off-campus" speech, the application of the *Tinker* "material and substantial disruption" standard (see Section 9.4.1 of this book), and the application of the "true threats" doctrine (see discussion later in this section, under "question 2").

*Tatro v. University of Minnesota*, 800 N.W.2d 811 (Minn. App. Ct. 2011), *affirmed on other grounds*, 816 N.W.2d 509 (Minn. 2012), is an illustrative higher education case. A mortuary science student posted a statement on Facebook that she wanted "to stab a certain someone in the throat with a trocar," along with other statements that intimated a level of disrespect for the sanctity of the donor bodies used for student training. When the university disciplined the student, she claimed that her Facebook statements were protected free speech. The student emphasized that her statements were not made on a university computer network or on any online forum created by the university and that her statements did not constitute a "true threat." The intermediate appellate court determined, however, that if the student's speech had disrupted the mortuary science program, the university had an interest in disciplining the student and in doing so before the speech reached the level of a "true threat." The court noted that some professors believed the student's statements referred to them and that at least one professor was visibly shaken due to fear that resulted from the postings. Then, using the *Tinker* material and substantial disruption standard, the court held that the student's speech did substantially disrupt the operation of the mortuary science program at the University of Minnesota and therefore was not protected under the First Amendment.

The state supreme court affirmed the holding but not the reasoning of the lower court. In particular, the supreme court asserted that a different legal standard should apply: that the appropriate issue was that the student's Facebook posts "violated established program rules," not that the posts created a substantial disruption. The court then reasoned that the applicable standard required that the program rules "must be narrowly tailored and directly related to established professional conduct standards." Determining that the program rules and the university's application of them met these requirements, the supreme court held that the university had not violated the student's free speech rights.

As the amount, variety, and distance of computer communications have increased, so has the development of institutional computer use policies and other institutional responses to perceived problems. The problems may be of the "traffic cop" variety, occasioning a need for the institution to allocate its limited computer resources by directing traffic to prevent traffic jams. Or the problems may be more controversial, raising computer misuse issues such as defamation, harassment, threats, hate speech, copyright infringement, and academic dishonesty. The latter types of problems may present more difficult legal issues, since institutional regulations attempting to alleviate these problems may be viewed as content-based restrictions on speech.

Public institutions, therefore, must keep a watchful eye on the First Amendment when drafting and enforcing computer use policies. Just as federal and state legislation regulating computer communications may be invalidated under the free speech and press clauses, particular provisions of campus regulations can be struck down as well if they contravene these clauses. (Private institutions are not similarly bound by the First Amendment, as discussed below in this section.)

Under existing First Amendment principles (see generally Sections 9.4.1, 9.4.2, and 9.4.3), administrators should ask four main questions when devising new computer use policies, or when reviewing or applying existing policies:

1. Are we seeking to regulate, or do we regulate, the content of computer speech ("cyberspace speech")?

2. If any of our regulations are content based, do they fit into any First Amendment exceptions that permit content-based regulations—such as the exceptions for obscenity and "true threats"?

3. (a) Does our institution own or lease the computer hardware or software being used for the computer speech; and (b) if so, has our institution created "forums" for discussion on its computer servers and networks?

4. Are our regulations or proposed regulations clear, specific, and narrow?

For question 1, if a computer use policy regulates the content of speech—that is, the ideas, opinions, or viewpoints expressed—and does not fall into any of the exceptions set out under question 2, the courts will usually subject the regulation to a two-part standard of "strict scrutiny": (1) Does the content regulation further a "compelling" governmental interest, and (2) is the regulation "narrowly tailored" and "necessary" to achieve this interest? The need to act in cases of copyright infringement, bribery, fraud, blackmail, stalking, sexual harassment, or other violations of federal and state law may often be considered compelling interests, as may the need to protect the institution's academic integrity when computers are used for "cheating." Regulations furthering such interests may therefore meet the strict scrutiny standard if they are very carefully drawn. But otherwise this standard is extremely difficult to meet. In contrast, if a computer regulation serves "neutral" government interests not based on the content of speech (for example, routine "traffic cop" regulations), a less stringent standard that is easier to meet would apply.

In *American Civil Liberties Union of Georgia v. Miller*, 977 F. Supp 1228 (N.D. Ga. 1997), for instance, a federal district court in Georgia considered the validity of a state statute prohibiting data transmitters from falsely identifying themselves in Internet transmissions (Ga. Code Ann. § 16-9-93.1). In invalidating the Georgia statute, the court emphasized that a "prohibition of Internet transmissions which 'falsely identify' the sender constitutes a presumptively invalid content-based restriction" on First Amendment rights. Recognizing that there is a "right to communicate anonymously and pseudonymously over the Internet" (977 F. Supp. at 1230), the court held that the state may not in a blanket fashion prohibit all Internet transmissions in which speakers do not identify themselves or use some pseudonym in place of an accurate identification. The court in *Miller* also held, however, that "fraud prevention . . . is a compelling state interest." Thus, if speakers were to use anonymity or misidentification in order to defraud the receivers of their Internet messages, then prohibition of false identification would be appropriate so long as the regulation is narrowly tailored to meet the fraud prevention objective. The court suggested that, in order to be narrowly tailored, a regulation must, at a minimum, include a requirement that the speaker has intended to deceive or that deception has in fact occurred (977 F. Supp. at 1232). Thus, for instance, if a public institution were to promulgate narrowly tailored regulations that prohibit speakers from intentionally "misappropriat[ing] the identity of another specific entity or person" (977 F. Supp. at 1232), such regulations would apparently be a valid content-based restriction on speech.

Regarding question 2, if a restriction on computer speech is content based and thus presumptively invalid under the strict scrutiny standard of review, the restriction would still be able to survive if it falls into one of the exceptions to the First Amendment prohibition against content-based restrictions on expression. All these exceptions (often called "categorical exclusions") are technical and narrow, and collectively would cover only a portion of the computer speech institutions may wish to regulate, but in certain cases these exceptions can become very important.

In *State v. Drahota*, 788 N.W. 2d 796 (Neb. 2010), the Nebraska Supreme Court considered the applicability to e-mail communications of the "fighting words" exception established by *Chaplinski v. New Hampshire*, 315 U.S. 568 (1942). Drahota, a student, had sent the e-mail messages anonymously to a former professor of his, using the professor's university e-mail address. The e-mail messages were "laced with provocative and insulting rhetoric and—with the Iraq war as a background—suggested that [the professor] was a traitor and that he sympathized with Al Qaeda." After law enforcement authorities had identified Drahota as the author of the e-mail messages and charged him with breach of the peace, Drahota claimed that his e-mail messages were protected by the First Amendment.

The state argued that the e-mail messages were unprotected fighting words. Distinguishing *Chaplinsky*, the court disagreed. It held that a speaker cannot be punished "under the fighting words exception solely because [the speech] inflicts emotional injury, annoys, offends, or angers another person." It is, rather, "the tendency or likelihood of the words to provoke violent reaction that is the touchstone" of the exception (788 N.W. 2d at 636, quoting *Lemar v. Banks*, 684 F.2d at 718 (11th Cir. 1982)). Thus,

> [E]ven if a fact finder could conclude that in a face-to-face confrontation, Drahota's speech would have provoked an immediate retaliation, [the professor] could not have immediately retaliated. [He] did not know who sent the e-mails, let alone where to find the author [788 N.W. 2d at 638].[10]

Another pertinent example is obscenity, which is recognized in numerous cases, including computer cases, as a First Amendment exception (see Section 10.3.5). Another related exception is child pornography, which need not fall within the U.S. Supreme Court's definition of obscenity to be prohibited, but instead is subject to the requirements that the Court established in *New York v. Ferber*, 458 U.S. 747 (1982). The exception for false or deceptive commercial speech, and commercial speech that proposes unlawful activities, is also pertinent to computer speech (see *Central Hudson Gas and Electric Corp. v. Public Service Commission*, 447 U.S. 557, 563–64 (1980)), as is the exception for "true threats" that was established in *Watts v. United States*, 394 U.S. 705 (1969), and further developed in *Virginia v. Black* (see Section 9.5.2 of this book).

It is the exception for "true threats" that has received the greatest amount of attention in contemporary cyberspeech cases. In *United States v. Alkhabaz aka Jake Baker*, 104 F.3d 1492 (6th Cir. 1997) *affirming on other grounds*, 890 F. Supp. 1375 (E.D. Mich. 1995), for example, and again in *United States v. Morales*, 272 F.3d 284 (5th Cir. 2001), courts struggled with whether particular computer communications were threats for the purposes of 18 U.S.C. § 875(c). Ultimately, using a combination of statutory and constitutional analysis, the courts concluded that Baker's e-mail messages in the first case were not threats

---

[10] Even if the e-mail were not anonymous, and even if the receiver knew where to locate the sender, there would still be a viable argument that e-mail messages are not "face-to-face" communications and cannot provoke an immediate retaliation.

for purposes of the federal statute, but Morales's chat room postings in the second case were threats for purposes of the statute.

Another instructive example, providing more fully developed First Amendment analysis, is the case of *Planned Parenthood of Columbia/Willamette, Inc., et al. v. American Coalition of Life Advocates, et al.*, 290 F.3d 1058 (9th Cir. 2002). The defendants in this case were organizations and individuals engaged in antiabortion activities, and the plaintiffs included physicians claiming that they had been threatened and intimidated by these activities. On a Web site operated by a third party, the American Coalition of Life Advocates (ACLA) had posted the names and addresses of numerous doctors that the posting identified as abortionists. Those doctors on the list who had been murdered, allegedly by antiabortionists, were particularly noted, as were those doctors who had been wounded. These listings in the "scorecard" of murders and woundings were labeled as the "Nuremberg Files." Before posting these materials on the Web site, the ACLA had also circulated "wanted posters" containing similar information, and, in fact, three physicians were murdered after having been featured on a wanted poster. The court emphasized that the defendants' messages had to be understood in the context in which they were made, and that the relevant context included both the wanted posters and the Web site postings, as well as the pattern of murders of physicians whose names had been featured in these communications. Analyzing the speech in context, the court determined that the First Amendment's free speech clause did not protect the defendants because the speech could be considered to be a "death threat" message and therefore a "true threat" within the meaning of *Watts v. United States*. "If ACLA had merely endorsed or encouraged violent reactions of others, its speech would be protected. However, while advocating violence is protected, threatening a person with violence is not" (290 F.3d at 1072).

The court articulated this useful guideline for determining when speech constitutes a true threat and is therefore unprotected by the First Amendment: "Whether a particular statement may properly be considered to be a threat is governed by an objective standard—whether a reasonable person would foresee that the statement would be interpreted by those to whom the maker communicates the statement as a serious expression of intent to harm or assault" (290 F.3d at 1074, citing *United States v. Orozco-Santillan*, 903 F.2d 1262, 1265 (9th Cir. 1990)). Applying this test, the court emphasized that physicians on the lists of abortionists "wore bullet-proof vests and took other extraordinary security measures to protect themselves and their families." ACLA "had every reason to foresee that its expression of intent to harm" through the wanted posters and the Web site "would elicit this reaction." The physicians' fears "did not simply happen; ACLA intended to intimidate them from doing what they do. This . . . is conduct that we are satisfied lacks any protection under the First Amendment . . . ACLA was not staking out a position of debate but of threatened demise" (290 F.3d at 1086).

The case of *Murakowski v. University of Delaware*, 575 F. Supp. 2d 571 (D. Del. 2008), illustrates the application of the true threat exception to campus regulation of student cyberspeech. It also illustrates how the *Tinker* "material and substantial disruption" standard (Section 9.4.1) may be used in analyzing the validity of campus regulations of student cyberspeech. *Murakowski* concerned a student's free speech challenge to university discipline imposed for maintaining, on a university server, a personal Web site that university officials considered to be "graphic in nature, violent, derogatory, hostile, and disturbing." The court first applied the true threat doctrine, determining that the Web site's content did not constitute a true threat, and thus rejecting the university's first argument for upholding its disciplinary action even though it was based on the content of the student's speech. The court then applied the *Tinker* standard, determining that the university had not proven that the Web site's content created the disruption of campus life, and thus rejecting the university's second argument for upholding its disciplinary action. Regarding question 3, institutions may put themselves in a stronger regulatory position regarding student cyberspeech when they restrict communications on the institutions' own computers, servers, networks, or e-mail and other communication systems; and if they structure student use in a way that does not create a "public forum" (see generally Section 9.4.2 of this book). The First Amendment standards would be lower and would generally permit content-based restrictions on speech (regardless of whether they fall into one of the exceptions discussed above) other than those based on the particular viewpoint of the speaker. But if the institution, for policy reasons, chooses to use some portion of its computers, servers, or networks as an open "forum" for expression by students or by the campus community, then the normal First Amendment standards would apply, including the presumption that content-based restrictions on speech are unconstitutional. The public forum concept is no longer limited to physical spaces or locations and apparently extends to "virtual" locations as well. In *Rosenberger v. Rector and Visitors of University of Virginia* (Section 10.1.5), for instance, the U.S. Supreme Court declared a student activities fund to be a public forum, subject to the same legal principles as other public forums, even though it was "a forum more in a metaphysical than a spatial or geographic sense" (515 U.S. at 830).

*Loving v. Boren*, 956 F. Supp. 953 (W.D. Okla. 1997), provided the first illustration of public forum analysis being applied to a university computer system. The University of Oklahoma was concerned that some of the Internet news groups on the university news server were carrying obscene material. Consequently, the university adopted an access policy under which the university operated two news servers, A and B. The A server's content was limited to those news groups that had not been "blocked" or disapproved by the university; the B server's news group content was not limited. The A server was generally accessible to the university community for recreational as well as academic purposes; the B server could be used only for academic and research purposes, and then only by persons over age eighteen. Although the court rejected a challenge to this policy based on the free speech clause, the court did so on the basis of conclusory reasoning that reflects an incomplete understanding of the public forum doctrine. One conclusion the court reached, however, does appear to be valid and important: the restriction of the B server to academic and research purposes did not violate the First Amendment because "[a] university is by its nature dedicated to research and academic purposes" and "those purposes are the very ones for which the [computer] system was purchased" (956 F. Supp. at 955). The court apparently reached this conclusion because it did not view any part of the university's computer services as a public forum. The better view, however, is probably that the B server is a "limited forum" that the university has dedicated to academic use by restricting the purposes of use rather than the content as such. On this reasoning, the court should have proceeded to give separate consideration to the question of whether the A server was a public forum and, if so, whether its content could be limited as provided in the university's policy.

A later case, *Mainstream Loudoun v. Board of Trustees of Loudoun County Library*, 24 F. Supp. 2d 552 (E.D. Va. 1998), provides better guidelines for determining whether a computer system's server or network is a public forum. The defendant library system had installed site-blocking software on its computers to prevent patrons from using these computers to view sexually explicit material on the Internet. The issue was whether the library's restrictions were subject to the strict scrutiny standards applicable to a "limited public forum," or to the lesser standards applicable to a "non-public forum." The court indicated that there are three "crucial factors" to consider in making such a determination: (1) whether the government, by its words and actions, displayed an intent to create a forum; (2) whether the government has permitted broad use of the forum it has created and "significantly limited its own discretion to restrict access"; and (3) "whether the nature of the forum is compatible with the expressive activity at issue" (24 F. Supp. 2d at 562–63). Using these factors, the court determined that the public library system was a limited public forum, that is, a designated public forum "for the limited purposes of the expressive activities [it] provide[s], including the receipt and communication of information through the Internet." Because the library system was a public forum, the library system's restrictions on computer communications were subject to strict scrutiny analysis.

Under question 4 in the list above, the focus is on the actual wording of each regulatory provision in the computer use policy. Even if a particular provision has been devised in conformance with the First Amendment principles addressed in questions 1, 2, and 3, it must in addition be drafted with a precision sufficient to meet constitutional standards of narrowness and clarity. If it does not, it will be subject to invalidation under either the "overbreadth" doctrine or the "vagueness" doctrine (see generally Sections 9.4.1, 9.4.3, and 9.4.6 of this book).

In *American Civil Liberties Union v. Miller* (above), for instance, the court determined that the language of the Georgia statute presented both overbreadth problems and vagueness problems. Regarding overbreadth, the court remarked that "the statute was not drafted with the precision necessary for laws regulating speech" because it "prohibits . . . the use of false identification to avoid social ostracism, to prevent discrimination and harassment, and to protect privacy," all of which are protected speech activities. The statute was thus "overbroad because it operates unconstitutionally for a substantial category of the speakers it covers" (977 F. Supp. at 1233). Similarly, regarding vagueness, the court determined that the statute's language did not "give fair notice of proscribed conduct to computer network users," thus encouraging "self-censorship," and did not give adequate guidance to those enforcing the statute, thus allowing "substantial room for selective [enforcement against] persons who express minority viewpoints" (977 F. Supp. at 1234).

One may fairly ask whether all the preexisting First Amendment principles referenced in questions 1 through 4 should apply to the vast new world of cyberspace. Indeed, scholars and judges have been debating whether free speech and press law should apply in full to computer technology. Although courts are committed to taking account of the unique aspects of each new communications technology, and allowing First Amendment law to grow and adapt in the process, thus far none of the basic principles discussed above have been discarded or substantially transformed when applied to cyberspeech. In fact, in the leading case to date, *Reno v. American Civil Liberties Union*, 521 U.S. 844 (1997), the U.S. Supreme Court opinion relied explicitly on the principles referenced in the discussion above. Thus, although counsel and administrators will need to follow both legal and technological developments closely in this fast-moving area, they should work from the premise that established First Amendment principles remain their authoritative guides.

Unlike public colleges and universities, private institutions are not subject to First Amendment restrictions. See generally *CompuServe, Inc. v. Cyber Promotions, Inc.*, 962 F. Supp. 1015, 1025–27 (S.D. Ohio 1997); and see generally Section 1.5.2 of this book. In *Rollins v. Cardinal Stritch University*, 626 N.W.2d 464 (Minn. 2001), for example, First Amendment free speech was not an issue because the problem arose at a private institution. The university had removed the plaintiff student from his academic "cohort group" because he had sent unsolicited e-mail messages, over about a two-month period, to various members of the group. The university considered the student's conduct to be "unwelcome, persistent, and in some cases frightening." Challenging his removal, the student made two claims: that the university had violated a common law duty to avoid arbitrariness in decision making about student discipline; and that the university had violated student handbook provisions that constituted a contract between the student and the university (see generally Section 7.1.3 of this book). The appellate court rejected the first claim because "nothing in the record supports the suggestion that [the university] treated [the student] in any manner except fairly and in good faith." Also rejecting the second claim, the court determined that "the student handbook did not create a contract between [the university] and [the student]; even if it did, [the student] presented no evidence that any of [the university's] actions toward [the student] breached any contractual obligation."

Private institutions nevertheless may and do voluntarily protect student free expression through student codes or bills of rights, through computer use policies themselves, or through campus custom—and may occasionally be bound to protect free expression by state constitutions, statutes, or regulations. Thus administrators at private institutions will also want to be keenly aware of First Amendment developments regarding computer speech and to seek guidance from these developments.

**7.5.2. Right to privacy.** In addition to freedom of expression concerns, computer communications also present personal privacy concerns requiring the attention of colleges and universities. Unlike free expression rights (Section 7.5.1 above), which are usually constitutionally based, rights to privacy are commonly based on statutes as well; and the privacy statutes, unlike constitutional protections, often apply to both private and public institutions.

Most of the constitutional protections for privacy that bind public institutions derive from the U.S. Constitution's Fourth Amendment. In *United States v. Heckenkamp*, 482 F.3d 1142 (9th Cir. 2007), for example, the University of Wisconsin–Madison became entwined in events leading up to the prosecution, under the Computer Fraud and Abuse Act (18 U.S.C. § 1030, as amended), of a graduate student in computer science. The student defendant challenged the prosecution as violating the Fourth Amendment's search and seizure provisions. Although it was a government prosecution backed by the FBI, the primary issues concerned searches of the student's personal computer by university personnel. The student was suspected of using his personal computer, attached to the university network, to hack into (or gain unauthorized access to) the network of a private corporation. A computer system administrator for the corporation determined that the hacker had used a computer on the University of Wisconsin–Madison's network, and contacted the university's computer department. In response, a university network investigator examined the situation, finding evidence that a computer on the university network had hacked into the corporation's system and that the computer user had gained unauthorized access to the university's e-mail server. He traced the source of intrusion to a specific Internet protocol (IP) address located in university housing and determined that the student (Heckenkamp), and no one else, checked his e-mail from this IP address before the unauthorized access to the company's and the university's systems was established.

The university network investigator then took various steps to protect the university's e-mail server and network, and to gather further facts; he also contacted the FBI and university police. One of the actions he took—at night and working from home—came to be known in the later criminal prosecution as the "remote search." Checking the network, he determined that the student's personal computer was no longer connected to the network through the original IP address, but through a different IP address. To verify this conclusion, the investigator then "logged into the computer, using a name and password he had discovered in his earlier investigation . . . [He] used a series of commands to confirm that [that] computer was the same [one] and to determine whether the computer still posed a risk to the university server. After approximately 15 minutes of looking only in the temporary directory, without deleting, modifying, or destroying any files, [the investigator] logged off of the computer" (482 F.3d at 1145).

Regarding this "remote search," the court first held that the student "had a legitimate, objectively reasonable expectation of privacy in his personal computer." It then considered "whether the defendant's objectively reasonable expectation of privacy in his computer was eliminated when he attached it to the university network." It was not: "the mere act of accessing a network does not in itself extinguish privacy expectations, nor does the fact that others may have occasional access to the computer." "However, privacy expectations may be reduced if the user is advised that information transmitted through the network is not confidential and that the systems administrators may monitor communications transmitted by the user." And a "person's reasonable expectation of privacy may be diminished in 'transmissions over the Internet or e-mail that have already arrived at the recipient'" (482 F.3d at 1146–47, quoting *United States v. Lifshitz*, 369 F.3d 173, 190 (2d Cir. 2004)).

Applying these guidelines, the court determined that the university had "no announced monitoring policy on the network" and, to the contrary, provided substantial privacy protection to computer network users, except in narrow circumstances in which university access to private computers is "essential to . . . protect the integrity of the University and the rights and property of the state" (quoting the university's policy). Thus university computer policies did not eliminate the student's expectation of privacy in his computers; he retained an "objectively reasonable expectation of privacy in his personal computer, which was protected by a screensaver password, located in his dormitory room, and subject to no policy allowing the university actively to monitor or audit his computer usage" (482 F.3d at 1147).

This conclusion, however, did not mean that the student prevailed on his Fourth Amendment privacy claim. Instead, the court went on to consider whether there were any special circumstances that would justify the university network investigator's remote search of computer files on the student's hard drive, done without a warrant and without the student's consent. In particular, the court considered whether the search of the computer was justified under what is called the "special needs" exception to the warrant requirement—an exception that may apply if "special needs, beyond the normal need for law enforcement, make the warrant and probable-cause requirement impracticable" (482 F.3d at 1147).

In applying this exception, the court emphasized that the university investigator had acted to secure the university's e-mail server and not "to collect evidence for law enforcement purposes or at the request of law enforcement agents." Moreover, the "integrity and security of the campus e-mail system was in jeopardy," and the administrator "needed to act immediately to protect the system." The remote search, moreover, was "remarkably limited" in scope, such that the intrusion into the student's privacy was outweighed by the "university's interest in . . . determining the source" of the threat to the security of its network. The court thus concluded that, "although [the student] had a reasonable expectation of privacy in his personal computer, a [warrantless remote] search of the computer was justified under the special needs exception to the warrant requirement" (482 F.3d at 1149).

In addition to constitutional protections, federal and state privacy statutes may also protect students (or employees, or all members of the university community). Some privacy statutes may apply specifically and only to Internet communications; others may apply more generally but include the Internet and intranets in their coverage; and others may not apply to the Internet. It is therefore of key importance to study each privacy statute closely to ascertain the scope of its coverage.

One pertinent example of a federal privacy statute is the federal FERPA statute (see Section 7.8.1 of this book), which covers student records generally, including computerized records, and applies to both public and private institutions. In addition, the Electronic Communications Privacy Act (ECPA) specifically covers computer communications; protects computer users generally, including students; and applies to both public and private institutions as service providers. The Computer Fraud and Abuse Act (CFAA) covers unauthorized access to "protected computers," which has been broadly defined by the statute to include almost all computers. And the Privacy Protection Act (PPA) limits the search and seizure of work product and other documentary materials of someone who is a news disseminator or publisher. Although Congress originally passed the PPA with newspapers in mind, the court in *Steven Jackson Games, Inc., v. U.S. Secret Service*, 816 F. Supp. 432 (W.D. Tex 1993), *affirmed*, 36 F.3d 457 (5th Cir. 1994), held that the PPA covered the operator of an online bulletin board as well.

At the state level, there are numerous statutes, many of recent origin, that protect privacy of computer communications in various ways. (Some of these statutes apply to and protect students; others do not). Statutes protecting students are likely to protect them from their peers. For instance, a harassment statute in Alabama includes "any . . . form of . . . electronic communication" made "with the intent to harass or alarm another person" (Ala. Code § 13A-11-8(b) (2011)). In Pennsylvania, harassment may occur when a person, "with intent to harass, annoy or alarm another," by "electronic means" including the "Internet," communicates "to or about [another person] any lewd, lascivious, threatening or obscene words, language, drawings or caricatures," or "communicates repeatedly in an anonymous manner" (18 Pa. Cons. Stat. § 2709 (2012)). Pennsylvania's statute on stalking also prohibits a person from "repeatedly communicat[ing] to another person under circumstances which demonstrate an intent to place such other person in reasonable fear of bodily injury or to cause substantial emotional distress to such other person," via "electronic means" including the Internet (18 Pa. Cons. Stat. § 2709.1 (2012)). For a survey of such legislation by the National Conference of State Legislatures, see www .ncsl.org/issues-research/telecom/state-laws-related-to-internet-privacy.aspx.

In addition, at the state level, there are various common law privacy torts that were formulated well before the Internet but that could provide some protection for students in certain circumstances. In *Vurimindi v. Fuqua School of Business*, 435 F. App'x 129, 2011 WL 2601584 (3d Cir. 2011), for example, the court affirmed that Pennsylvania recognized the privacy tort of "intrusion upon seclusion" and considered whether the plaintiff student's allegations stated a claim covered by this tort. Citing, among other claims, the allegation that the defendant school had "monitored [the student's] computer activity with key logger software in order to obtain his bank information," the court reversed the district court's dismissal of the claim and remanded the case for further proceedings.

Some of the most difficult privacy issues arise in situations where interests in privacy conflict with interests in free expression. *Ostergren v. Cuccinelli*, 615 F.3d 263 (4th Cir. 2010), although not involving students, is an instructive example of a case pitting the value of personal privacy against the value of freedom of speech in the context of Internet speech. The federal appellate court in *Ostergren* upheld a federal district court's decision striking down a portion of the Virginia Personal Information Privacy Act (Va. Code Ann. §§ 59.1-442 through 59.1-444) on First Amendment free speech grounds. The relevant portion of the Virginia statute made it unlawful to publish the Social Security numbers of other individuals to the general public. Ostergren, an information privacy advocate, had used her Web site to post "publicly available Virginia land records containing unredacted Social Security numbers ('SSNs')."

In analyzing the statute under the First Amendment, the court used a strict scrutiny standard articulated in *Smith v. Daily Mail Publishing Co.*, 443 U.S. 97, 103 (1979): "if a newspaper lawfully obtains truthful information about a matter of public significance then state officials may not constitutionally punish publication of the information, absent a need to further a state interest of the highest order." The appellate court held that the statute, as applied to Ostergren, violated the First Amendment because it was not narrowly tailored to the state's interest in protecting citizens' privacy. In particular, the state's "failure to redact SSNs before placing land records online" undercut its argument "that barring Ostergren's protected speech [is] narrowly tailored to Virginia's interest in protecting individual privacy." Because the court found that the statute did not survive this prong of strict scrutiny analysis, it did not need to rule on whether the state's interest in protecting the privacy of social security numbers was an interest "of the highest order" (615 F.3d at 287).

**7.5.3. Liability issues.** Colleges and universities may become liable to students for violating students' legal rights regarding computer communications and computer files; and they may become liable to others for certain computer communications of their students effectuated through a campus network or Internet service. In addition, students may sometimes become liable to other students under state privacy statutes and common law. The following discussion surveys the major areas of liability concern.

To help minimize First Amendment liability arising from institutional regulation of campus computer speech, administrators at public institutions may follow the guidelines suggested by the four questions set out in Section 7.5.1. In addition, administrators might adopt an analogy to student newspapers to limit institutional liability for their students' uses of cyberspace. To adopt this analogy, the institution would consider students' own Web sites, blogs, discussion forums, or listservs to be like student newspapers (see generally Section 10.3) and would provide them a freedom from regulation and oversight sufficient to assure that the students are not viewed as agents of the institution (see Section 10.3.6). Institutions might also create alternatives to regulation that would either diminish the likelihood of computer abuse or enhance the likelihood that disputes that do arise can be resolved without litigation. For instance, institutions could encourage, formally and informally, the development of cyberspace ethics codes for their campus communities. To a large extent, the success of such codes would depend on widespread consensus about the norms established and the willingness to enforce them by peer pressure and cyberspace "counterspeech."

In two other leading areas of concern—tort law and copyright law—federal law now provides institutions some protection from liability for students' online statements and their unauthorized transmission of copyrighted materials. Regarding tort law, the Communications Decency Act (CDA) contains a section 509, codified at 47 U.S.C. § 230, that protects "interactive computer service" providers (which include colleges and universities) from defamation liability and other liability based on the content of information posted by others. Section 230(c)(1) applies when a third-party "information content provider" has posted or otherwise transmitted information through a provider's service, and protects the provider from the liabilities that a "publisher or speaker" might incur in such circumstances (47 U.S.C. §§ 230(c)(1), (f)(2)–(3)). As one court has explained:

> By its plain language, § 230 creates a federal immunity to any cause of action that would make service providers liable for information originating with a third-party user of the service. Specifically, § 230 precludes courts from entertaining claims that would place a computer service provider in a publisher's role. Thus, lawsuits seeking to hold a service provider liable with respect to a publisher's traditional editorial function—such as deciding whether or not to publish, withdraw, postpone, or alter content—are barred [*Zeran v. America Online, Inc.*, 129 F.3d 327, 330 (4th Cir. 1997)].

Section 230(c)(1) immunity apparently extends beyond state tort law claims to protect interactive computer service providers from other state and federal law claims that could be brought against publishers or speakers. For example, in *Noah v. AOL Time Warner, Inc.*, 261 F. Supp. 2d 532, 537–39 (E.D. Va. 2003), *affirmed per curiam*, 2004 WL 602711 (4th Cir.) (unpublished), the court held that Section 230(c)(1) protected an Internet service provider from liability under a federal civil rights statute, Title II of the Civil Rights Act of 1964 (42 U.S.C. § 2000a(b)). In addition, Section 230(c)(2) protects service providers from civil liability for actions that they take "in good faith to restrict access to or availability of material" that they consider "to be obscene, lewd, lascivious, filthy, excessively violent, harassing, or otherwise objectionable" (47 U.S.C. § 230(c)(2)(A); and see, for example, *Mainstream Loudoun v. Board of Trustees of Loudoun County Library*, 2 F. Supp. 2d 783, 789 (E.D. Va. 1998)). Section 230 does not provide any immunity, however, from prosecution under federal criminal laws or from claims under intellectual property laws (47 U.S.C. §§ 230(e)(1), (2)).

By its express language, Section 230 also protects "user(s)" of interactive computer services, such as persons operating Web sites or listservs on a provider's service. In *Batzel v. Smith*, 333 F.3d 1018 (9th Cir. 2003), for example, the court held that an operator of a listserv was a "user" who would be immune under Section 230(c)(1) from a defamation claim if another "information content provider" had provided the information to him and he reasonably believed that the material was provided for purposes of publication. Users apparently are protected under Section 230 to the same extent as providers. Litigation continues, however, on the scope of the user provisions and the extent of the immunity that Section 230 provides for users and providers. (In *Barrett v. Rosenthal*, 9 Cal. Rptr. 3d 142 (Cal. App. 2004), *opinion superseded and review granted*, 87 P. 3d 797 (Cal. 2004), *reversed*, 146 P.3d 510 (Cal. 2006), for example, the California Supreme Court held that, under the CDA, defamation plaintiffs may seek recovery only from the original source of the statement and not from "distributors" or "users" who republish material.)

Regarding copyright law, the Digital Millennium Copyright Act (DMCA) contains a provision, 17 U.S.C. § 512, that protects Internet "service provider(s)," including colleges and universities, from certain liability for copyright infringement. Specifically, the DMCA establishes "safe harbor" protections for Internet service providers against copyright infringement liability attributable to the postings of third-party users (including students and faculty members) in certain circumstances and under certain conditions (see 17 U.S.C. §§ 512(a)–(d)). The safe harbor provisions also provide some protection for Internet service providers against liability to alleged infringers (including faculty members and students) for erroneously removing material that did not infringe a copyright (17 U.S.C. § 512(g)), and some protection against persons who file false copyright infringement claims (17 U.S.C. § 512(f)). In addition, the DMCA contains a provision that, under certain circumstances, specifically protects colleges and universities, as Internet service providers, from vicarious liability for the acts of their faculty members and graduate students (17 U.S.C. § 512(e)).

In addition, provisions of the Higher Education Opportunity Act of 2008, specifically 20 U.S.C. §§ 1092(a)(1)(P) and 1094(a)(29), serve to channel institutions' efforts to curtail student copyright infringement. (These provisions, the implementing regulations, and a U.S. Department of Education "Dear Colleague" letter are discussed in Section 7.3.2 of this book.)

Individual students (and faculty members) also have some protections under the DMCA. If a student operates a Web site that is maintained on the institution's servers, he or she will have some protection against false copyright infringement claims (17 U.S.C. § 512(c)). In *Online Policy Group v. Diebold, Inc.*, 337 F. Supp. 2d 1195 (N.D. Cal. 2004), the plaintiff students sought monetary damages from the defendant, a copyright holder who claimed that the students' posting violated its copyright. The university removed the posting on the Web site after it had received the defendant's notice of an alleged copyright infringement. The court ruled in favor of the students and ordered the defendant to pay them money damages because "no reasonable copyright holder could have believed" that the postings in question "were protected by copyright."

Taken together, Section 230 of the CDA and Section 512 and related provisions of the DMCA provide some leeway for institutions to regulate and monitor their computer systems as their institutional missions and campus cultures may require, and also serve to encourage institutions to create alternatives to regulation as well as internal dispute-resolution processes.

One further emerging area of liability concern for institutions involves disabled students. Under Section 504 of the Rehabilitation Act (see Section 11.5.4 of this book) and Titles II and III of the Americans with Disabilities Act, institutions could become liable for discriminating against disabled students with respect to access to computer communications, or for failing to provide disabled students with computer-based auxiliary aids or services that would be considered reasonable accommodations. (See generally Sections 7.7.2 and 8.4 of this book.)

### Section 7.6. Campus Security

**7.6.1. Security officers.** Crime is an unfortunate fact of life on many college campuses. Consequently, campus security and the role of security officers have become high-visibility issues. Although contemporary jurisprudence rejects the concept that colleges are responsible for the safety of students (see Section 3.2.2), institutions of higher education have, in some cases, been found liable for injury to students when the injury was foreseeable or when there was a history of criminal activity on campus. Federal and state statutes, discussed in Section 7.6.3, also impose certain requirements on colleges and their staffs to notify students of danger and to work collaboratively with state and local law enforcement to prevent and respond to crime on campus.

The powers and responsibilities of campus security officers should be carefully delineated. Administrators must determine whether such officers should be permitted to carry weapons and under what conditions. They must determine the security officers' authority to investigate crime on campus or to investigate violations of student codes of conduct. Record-keeping practices also must be devised. The relationship that security officers will have with local and state police must be cooperatively worked out with local and state police forces. Because campus security officers may play dual roles, partly enforcing public criminal laws and partly enforcing the institution's codes of conduct, administrators should carefully delineate the officers' relative responsibilities in each role.

Administrators must also determine whether their campus security guards have, or should have, arrest powers under state or local law. For public institutions, state law may grant full arrest powers to certain campus security guards. In *People v. Wesley*, 365 N.Y.S.2d 593 (City Ct., Buffalo, N.Y. 1975), for instance, the court determined that security officers at a particular state campus were "peace officers" under the terms of section 355(2)(m) of the New

York Education Law. For public institutions not subject to such statutes, and for private institutions, deputization under city or county law (see *People of the State of Michigan v. VanTubbergen*, 642 N.W.2d 368 (Mich. Ct. App. 2002)) or the use of "citizen's arrest" powers may be options (see *Hall v. Virginia*, 389 S.E.2d 921 (Va. Ct. App. 1990)).

In *State v. Yencer*, 696 S.E.2d 875 (N.C. Ct. App. 2010), a state appellate court granted a motorist's motion to suppress evidence of driving while intoxicated because a campus police officer from Davidson College had performed the arrest near the campus. The state argued that a state law, the Campus Police Act, N.C. Gen. Stat. § 74G-2 (2009), had been enacted specifically to provide that private colleges "originally established by or affiliated with religious denominations" could have police protection, and thus the arrest was lawful. A state appellate court, however, ruled that the state law violated the First Amendment's establishment clause because Davidson College is affiliated with the Presbyterian Church.

The North Carolina Supreme Court reversed, 718 S.E.2d 615(N.C. 2011), stating that the law complied with the requirements of the *Lemon* test (see Section 1.6.3 of this book). The court ruled that the Campus Police Act had a secular purpose, that Davidson College was not a religious institution and its primary purpose of providing secular education was not religious in nature, and that the Presbyterian Church had a minimal influence over the management of the college. Therefore, the statute did not create excessive entanglement with religion.

If campus police have not specifically been granted arrest powers for off-campus law enforcement actions, the resulting arrests may not be lawful. Decisions from two state courts suggest that campus police authority may not extend beyond the borders of the campus if the alleged crime did not occur on campus. For example, in *Marshall v. State ex rel. Dept. of Transportation*, 941 P.2d 42 (Wyo. 1997), the Wyoming Supreme Court invalidated the suspension of the plaintiff's driver's license, stating that his arrest was unlawful and thus the license suspension was tainted as well. Marshall, the plaintiff, had been driving by (but not on) the campus, and a security officer employed by Sheridan College believed that Marshall was driving a stolen car. The security officer followed Marshall and pulled him over. Although Marshall was able to demonstrate that the car was not stolen, the security officer believed that Marshall was driving while intoxicated. Marshall refused to be tested for sobriety, and his license was suspended. Because this was not a situation where a campus police officer was pursuing a suspect, the court ruled that the campus police officer had no authority to stop or to arrest Marshall, and thus the license suspension was reversed.

And in *Commonwealth v. Hernandez*, 924 N.E.2d 709 (Mass. 2010), two Boston University police, acting as "special state police officers" under Massachusetts law, stopped an individual after running a check of the individual's car registration and learning that a warrant had been issued for a motor vehicle violation. The individual had not committed an offense on university property, nor did the officers stop him for any offense that they had observed. The officers arrested the individual, had him transported to the

Boston University police department, and searched his car; heroin and cocaine were found in the car. The court ruled that the evidence had to be suppressed because the university police did not have the authority to execute an arrest warrant, since the arrest did not occur on university property and the underlying crime for which the warrant had been issued had not occurred within the jurisdiction of the university.

But the Supreme Court of Montana ruled that an off-campus traffic stop made by a University of Montana security officer was a valid exercise of his authority and refused to suppress evidence that the person stopped was driving while intoxicated. In *State v. Howard*, 184 P.3d 344 (Mont. 2008), the court examined a memorandum of understanding entered by the University of Montana, the city police department, and the county sheriff's office. The memorandum gave university security officers authority within the boundaries of the campus, over an area within one mile of the exterior boundaries of the campus, and over other property owned, controlled, or administered by the university. Finding that the traffic stop occurred within the area covered by the memorandum, the court ruled that the security officer had the requisite authority and refused to suppress the evidence of the driver's intoxication. For a case using similar reasoning to reach the same outcome, see *State v. Hardgrove*, 225 P.3d 357 (Wash. Ct. App. 2010).

Campus police at private colleges and universities may be viewed by courts as "state actors" (see Section 1.5.2 of this book) if they have powers to arrest or other forms of authority derived from being commissioned by local government as police officers. For example, in *Maniaci v. Georgetown University*, 510 F. Supp. 2d 50 (D.D.C. 2007), campus police at Georgetown, a private university, removed a conference attendee from a building after he disrupted the proceedings, and he was injured in the process. He sued the university, claiming that his constitutional rights were violated by the Georgetown campus police. The court, noting that Georgetown's campus police are commissioned as "special police" by the Washington, D.C., police department and have the power of arrest, rejected the university's motion for summary judgment on the constitutional claim, stating that if the plaintiff could prove his allegations that the campus police had detained him and prevented him from leaving, such actions were incident to a potential arrest and could thus form the basis for a finding that the campus police had engaged in state action because their arrest power came from the city.

Some states have passed laws giving campus police at public colleges and universities powers similar to those of municipal police. See, for example, 71 Pa. Cons. Stat. § 646.1 (2003), which provides that campus police may "exercise the same powers as are now or may hereafter be exercised under authority of law or ordinance by the police of the municipalities wherein the college or university is located." This statute overrules two Pennsylvania cases, *Horton v. Commonwealth of Pennsylvania*, 694 A.2d 1 (Pa. Commw. Ct. 1997), and *Commonwealth of Pennsylvania v. Croushore*, 703 A.2d 546 (Pa. Super. Ct. 1997), in which state appellate courts had ruled that campus police had no authority to effect arrests beyond the borders of the campus. State laws vary considerably regarding the off-campus authority of campus police officers, and the particular facts of each incident may also have an effect on the court's determination. (For additional cases addressing this issue, see *People v. Smith*, 514 N.E.2d 1158 (Ill. App. Ct. 1987); and *Councill v. Commonwealth*, 560 S.E.2d 472 (Va. Ct. App. 2002).)

Police work is subject to a variety of constitutional restraints concerning such matters as investigations, arrests, and searches and seizures of persons or private property. Security officers for public institutions are subject to all these restraints. In private institutions, security officers who are operating in conjunction with local or state police forces (see Section 7.4.3) or who have arrest powers may also be subject to constitutional restraints under the state action doctrine (see Section 1.5.2). In devising the responsibilities of such officers, therefore, administrators should be sensitive to the constitutional requirements regarding police work.

Campus police or security guards responding to student protests and demonstrations must walk a fine line between protecting human and property interests and respecting students' constitutional rights of speech and assembly. In *Orin v. Barclay*, 272 F.3d 1207 (9th Cir. 2001), the federal appellate court rejected most of a student's constitutional challenges to limitations on a campus protest ordered by the dean and the campus security chief at a public community college, with the exception of the requirement that the protesters "not mention religion." The court ruled that the security officers had qualified immunity for their arrest of the plaintiff for trespassing, but that his claim of First Amendment violations for the prohibition of religious speech could proceed.

Administrators should also be sensitive to the tort law principles applicable to security work (see generally Sections 3.2.2 and 4.4.2). Like athletic activities (Section 10.4.9), campus security actions are likely to expose the institution to a substantial risk of tort liability. Using physical force or weapons, detaining or arresting persons, and entering or searching private property can all occasion tort liability if they are undertaken without justification or accomplished carelessly. *Jones v. Wittenberg University*, 534 F.2d 1203 (6th Cir. 1976), for example, dealt with a university security guard who had fired a warning shot at a fleeing student. The shot pierced the student's chest and killed him. The guard and the university were held liable for the student's death, even though the guard did not intend to hit the student and may have had justification for firing a shot to frighten a fleeing suspect. The appellate court reasoned that the shooting could nevertheless constitute negligence "if it was done so carelessly as to result in foreseeable injury."

Institutions may also incur liability for malicious prosecution if an arrest or search is made in bad faith. In *Wright v. Schreffler*, 618 A.2d 412 (Pa. Super. Ct. 1992), a former college student's conviction for possession and delivery of marijuana was reversed because the court found that the defendant had been entrapped by campus police at Pennsylvania State University. The former student then sued the arresting officer for malicious prosecution, stating that the officer had no probable cause to arrest him, since the arrest was a result of the entrapment. The court agreed, and denied the officer's motion for dismissal. See also *Penn v. Harris*, 296 F.3d 573 (7th Cir. 2002) (no liability for malicious prosecution because the police had probable cause to arrest him for disorderly conduct).

Campus police may also be held liable under tort law for their treatment of individuals suspected of criminal activity. In *Hickey v. Zezulka*, 443 N.W.2d 180 (Mich. Ct. App. 1989), a university public safety officer had placed a Michigan State University student in a holding cell at the university's department of public safety. The officer had stopped the student for erratic driving, and a Breathalyzer test had shown that the student had blood alcohol levels of between 0.15 and 0.16 percent. While in the holding cell, the student hanged himself by a noose made from his belt and socks that he connected to a bracket on a heating unit attached to the ceiling of the cell.

The student's estate brought separate negligence actions against the officer and the university, and both were found liable after trial. Although an intermediate appellate court upheld the trial verdict against both the university and the officer, the state supreme court, in *Hickey v. Zezulka*, 487 N.W.2d 106 (Mich. 1992), reversed the finding of liability against the university, applying Michigan's sovereign immunity law. The court upheld the negligence verdict against the officer, however, noting that the officer had violated university policies about removing harmful objects from persons before placing them in holding cells and about checking on them periodically. The court characterized the officer's actions as "ministerial" rather than discretionary, which, under Michigan law, eliminated her governmental immunity defense.

In light of *Hickey*, universities with local holding cells should make sure that campus police regulations are clear about the proper procedures to be used, particularly in handling individuals who are impaired by alcohol and drugs, and should ensure that the procedures are followed to reduce both the potential for harm to individuals and liability to the institution or its employees.

In *Baughman v. State*, 45 Cal. Rptr. 2d 82 (Cal. Ct. App. 1995), university police were sued for invasion of privacy, emotional distress, and conversion pursuant to the destruction of computer disks during a search undertaken in connection with a lawfully issued warrant. The court found that the officers had acted within their official capacity, that they were therefore immune from damages resulting from the investigation, and that the investigation justified an invasion of privacy.

Overlapping jurisdiction and responsibilities may complicate the relationship between campus and local police. California has attempted to address this potential for overlap in a law, section 67381 of the Education Code. This law, passed by the state legislature in 1998, requires the governing board of every public institution of higher education in the state to "adopt rules requiring each of their respective campuses to enter into written agreements with local law enforcement agencies that clarify operational responsibilities for investigations" of certain violent crimes that occur on campus (homicide, rape, robbery, and aggravated assault). These agreements are to designate which law enforcement agency will do the investigation of such crimes, and they must "delineate the specific geographical boundaries" of each agency's "operational responsibility."

### 7.6.2. *Protecting students against violent crime.* The extent of the institution's obligation to protect students from crime on campus—particularly, violent crimes committed by outsiders from the surrounding community—has become a sensitive issue for higher education. The number of such crimes reported, especially sexual attacks on women, has increased steadily over the years. As a result, postsecondary institutions now face substantial tactical and legal problems concerning the planning and operation of their campus security systems, as well as a federal law requiring them to report campus crime statistics.

Institutional liability may depend, in part, on where the attack took place and whether the assailant was a student or an intruder. When students have encountered violence in residence halls from intruders, the courts have found a duty to protect the students similar to that of a landlord. For example, in *Mullins v. Pine Manor College*, 449 N.E.2d 331 (Mass. 1983), the court approved several legal theories for establishing institutional liability in residence hall security cases. The student in *Mullins* was abducted from her residence hall room and raped on the campus of Pine Manor College, a women's college located in a suburban area. Although the college was located in a low-crime area and there was relatively little crime on campus, the court nevertheless held the college liable.

The court determined that residential colleges have a general legal duty to exercise due care in providing campus security. First, the court said that, because students living in campus residence halls cannot provide their own security, the college's duty is to take reasonable steps to ensure its students' safety. Second, the court determined "that a duty voluntarily assumed must be performed with due care," and held that when a college has taken responsibility for security, it is "subject to liability . . . for physical harm resulting from [the] failure to exercise reasonable care to perform [the] undertaking." An institution may be held liable under this theory, however, only if the plaintiff can establish that its "failure to exercise due care increased the risk of harm, or . . . the harm is suffered because of the student's reliance on the undertaking" (449 N.E.2d at 336).

Analyzing the facts of the case under these two broad theories, the appellate court affirmed the trial court's judgment in favor of the student. The facts relevant to establishing the college's liability included the ease of scaling or opening the gates that led to the residence halls, the small number of security guards on night shift, the lack of a system for supervising the guards' performance of their duties, and the lack of dead bolts or chains for residence hall room doors.

Courts have ruled in two cases that universities provided inadequate residence hall security and that lax security was the proximate cause of a rape in one case and a death in a second. In *Miller v. State*, 478 N.Y.S.2d 829 (N.Y. App. Div. 1984), a student was abducted from the laundry room of a residence hall and taken through two unlocked doors to another residence hall where she was raped. The court noted that the university was on notice that nonresidents frequented the residence hall, and it criticized the university for failing to take "the rather minimal security measure of keeping the dormitory doors locked when it had notice of the likelihood of criminal intrusions" (478 N.Y.S.2d at 833).

In the second case, *Nieswand v. Cornell University*, 692 F. Supp. 1464 (N.D.N.Y. 1988), a federal trial court refused to grant summary judgment to Cornell University when it denied that its residence hall security was inadequate and thus the proximate cause of a student's death. A rejected suitor (not a student) entered the residence hall without detection and shot the student and her roommate. The roommate's parents filed both tort and contract claims (see Sections 3.2 and 3.3 of this book) against the university. The court, citing *Miller*, ruled that whether or not the attack was foreseeable was a question of material fact, which would have to be determined by a jury. Furthermore, the representations made by Cornell in written documents, such as residence hall security policies and brochures, regarding the locking of doors and the presence of security personnel, could have constituted an implied contract to provide appropriate security. Whether a contract existed and, if so, whether it was breached was again a matter for the jury.

In another case involving Cornell, the university was found not liable for an assault in a residence hall by an intruder. The intruder scaled a two-story exterior metal grate and then kicked open the victim's door, which had been locked and dead-bolted. In *Vangeli v. Schneider*, 598 N.Y.S.2d 837 (N.Y. App. Div. 1993), the court ruled that Cornell had met its duty to provide "minimal security" as a landlord.

Even if a college provides residence hall security systems, courts have ruled that the institution has a duty to advise students living in the residence hall about the use of these systems and how to enhance their personal safety. In *Stanton v. University of Maine System*, 773 A.2d 1045 (Maine 2001), the Supreme Court of Maine vacated a lower court's award of summary judgment for the university, ruling that a sexual assault in a college residence hall room was foreseeable and that the college should have instructed the student, a seventeen-year-old girl attending a preseason soccer program, on how to protect herself from potential assault. Citing *Mullins*, discussed earlier in this section, the court ruled that the plaintiff's complaint raised sufficient issues of material fact to warrant a trial. The court rejected, however, the plaintiff's implied contract claim because no written or oral contract had been entered by the parties.

Institutions that take extra precautions with respect to instructing students about safety may limit their liability for assaults on students, as in *Murrell v. Mount St. Clare College*, 2001 U.S. Dist. LEXIS 21144 (S.D. Iowa, September 10, 2001). A second-year student was sexually assaulted by the guest of a fellow student whom she had allowed to spend the evening in her residence hall room. Earlier that day, the student asked the guests to leave, left her door unlocked, and prepared to take a shower. The guest entered the room and raped her. The court, in granting the college's motion for summary judgment, noted that the college had provided a working lock, which the plaintiff had not used; had provided the students with a security handbook with guidelines that, if ignored, could lead to fines; and had held a mandatory meeting at the beginning of the school year to discuss residence hall safety and to warn students against leaving doors unlocked or propped open.

And a state appellate court ruled that the University of Cincinnati was not liable for the rape of a student in a residence hall bathroom. In *Shivers v. University of Cincinnati*, 2006 Ohio App. LEXIS 5495 (Ohio Ct. App., October 24, 2006), a female student alleged that the university had provided insufficient security for the residence hall—in particular, that there were no locks on the bathroom doors. Although the trial court had found for the plaintiff, the appellate court reversed, ruling that the assault was not foreseeable. A previous rape that had occurred in a different building located at some distance from the residence and occurring two years earlier was not close enough in time or location to suggest that the assault in the bathroom was foreseeable, according to the appellate court.

An opinion of the Supreme Court of Nebraska linked a university's oversight of fraternal organizations with its duty as a landlord to find the institution liable for a student's injuries. Although *Knoll v. Board of Regents of the University of Nebraska*, 601 N.W.2d 757 (1999), ostensibly involves alleged institutional liability for fraternity hazing, the court rested its legal analysis, and its finding of duty, on the landowner's responsibility for foreseeable harm to invitees. The student, a nineteen-year-old fraternity pledge, was abducted from a building on university property and taken to the fraternity house, which was not owned by the university. University policy, however, considered fraternity houses to be student housing units subject to the university's student code of conduct, which prohibited the use of alcoholic beverages and conduct that was dangerous to others. Knoll was forced to consume a large quantity of alcohol and then was handcuffed to a toilet pipe. He broke free of the handcuffs and attempted to escape through a third floor window, from which he fell and sustained serious injuries.

Knoll argued that, because he was abducted on university property, the university had a duty to protect him because the abduction was foreseeable. Although the university argued that the actions were not criminal, but merely "horseplay," the court stated that the actions need not be criminal in nature in order to create a duty. And although the university did not own the fraternity house or the land upon which it was built, the court noted that the code of conduct appeared to apply with equal force to all student housing units, irrespective of whether they were located on university property. Therefore, the university's knowledge of prior code violations and criminal misconduct by fraternity members was relevant to the determination of whether the university owed the plaintiff a duty.

Unforeseeable "pranks" or more serious acts by students or nonstudents do not typically result in institutional liability. For example, in *Rabel v. Illinois Wesleyan University*, 514 N.E.2d 552 (Ill. App. Ct. 1987), the court ruled that the university had no duty to protect a student against a "prank" by fellow students that involved her abduction from a residence hall, despite the fact that the assailant had violated the college's policy against underage drinking. (See also *L.W. v. Western Golf Association*, 712 N.E.2d 983 (Ind. 1999).) A similar result was reached in *Tanja H. v. Regents of the University of California*, 278 Cal. Rptr. 918

(Cal. Ct. App. 1991); the court stated that the university had no duty to supervise student parties in residence halls or to prevent underage consumption of alcohol. And in *Eiseman v. State*, 518 N.Y.S.2d 608 (N.Y. 1987), the highest court of New York State refused to find that the university had a legal duty to screen applicants who were ex-convicts for violent tendencies before admitting them.

The difference in outcomes of these cases appears to rest on whether the particular harm that ensued was foreseeable. This was the rationale for the court's ruling in *Nero v. Kansas State University*, 861 P.2d 768 (Kan. 1993). In *Nero*, the Supreme Court of Kansas considered whether the university could be found negligent for permitting a student who had earlier been charged with sexual assault on campus to live in a coeducational residence hall, where he sexually assaulted the plaintiff, a fellow student. The court reversed a summary judgment for the university, declaring that a jury would have to determine whether the attack was foreseeable, given that, although the university knew that the student had been accused of the prior sexual assault, he had not yet been convicted. If the jury found that the second assault was foreseeable, then it would address the issue of whether the university had breached a duty to take reasonable steps to prevent the second attack.

State statutes may affect liability questions about campus security. In a later case, *Peterson v. San Francisco Community College District*, 205 Cal. Rptr. 842 (Cal. 1984), the court did rely on a statutory provision to impose liability on the defendant. The plaintiff was a student who had been assaulted while leaving the campus parking lot. Her assailant had concealed himself behind "unreasonably thick and untrimmed foliage and trees." Several other assaults had occurred at the same location and in the same manner. Community college officials had known of these assaults but did not publicize them. The court held that the plaintiff could recover damages under section 835 of the California Tort Claims Act (Cal. Govt. Code §§ 810 et seq.), which provides that "a public entity is liable for injury caused by a dangerous condition of its property" if the dangerous condition was caused by a public employee acting in the scope of his employment or if the entity "had actual or constructive notice of the dangerous condition" and failed to correct it. The court concluded that the failure to trim the foliage or to warn students of the earlier assaults constituted the creation of such a dangerous condition.

Altercations between roommates or fellow students may result in negligence claims against the college. In *Rhaney v. University of Maryland Eastern Shore*, 880 A.2d 357 (Md. 2005), the assailant had engaged in a previous physical altercation with other students and had been suspended from the college. Upon his return to the college, he was assigned to room with the plaintiff. The two had an altercation and the plaintiff was injured. He sued the university for negligence, arguing that the assault was foreseeable. The court rejected the negligence claim, ruling that the university, as a landlord, had no duty to protect the student from assault by a fellow student, and that one previous assault by the roommate did not create a "dangerous condition" nor make the assault foreseeable. The court also rejected Rhaney's assertion that he was a "business invitee," which would subject the university to a higher standard of care than that of a landlord.

If a crime victim has engaged in misconduct that could have contributed to the injury, at least in part, the institution may escape liability. In *Laura O. v. State*, 610 N.Y.S.2d 826 (N.Y. App. Div. 1994), the court held that a university in New York was not liable to a student who was raped in a campus music building after hours. She had been practicing the piano at a time when students were not allowed in the building. Although the student claimed that university officials knew that students used non-dormitory buildings after closing hours, the court stated that the university's security procedures were appropriate. Since the building was not a residence hall and the student was not a campus resident, the university did not owe the student a special duty of protection.

The question of whether or not to perform background checks on applicants for admission is troublesome, and a recent court ruling provides no reassurance on that matter. A federal trial court addressed the issue of protecting students from violence from their peers in *Estate of Levi Butler v. Maharishi University of Management*, 589 F. Supp. 2d 1150 (D. Iowa 2008). Butler was stabbed by a fellow student in a campus building and died of his wounds. Earlier on the day of the stabbing, the assailant had attacked another student, who was injured but who survived. Although university officials were aware of the attack, they did not call security or report the attack to the police. After the first attack, the dean of men assumed charge of the assailant, spent some time with him, and then returned him to campus where he mingled with other students and committed the second attack that resulted in Butler's death. Butler's father sued Maharishi University of Management (MUM) for premises liability, fraudulent misrepresentation, and negligence. MUM filed a motion for summary judgment on the second and third claims, which the court denied.

The plaintiff argued that recruiting materials from MUM stressed its peaceful environment and its focus on transcendental meditation, stating that the campus was safe and free from violence. The campus safety policy also stated that MUM officials worked closely with campus security and local police forces. The court found that the existence of these materials, and the potential that Butler relied on their representations, could support a claim of fraudulent misrepresentation, particularly because officials did not report the earlier assault to either security or the police. For similar reasons, the court rejected the defendant's motion for summary judgment on the negligent misrepresentation claim. And with respect to the plaintiff's claim of negligent admission of the assailant, the court referred to testimony that the assailant had told an admissions officer that he had been "arrested a few times," but that there was no investigation into the nature of the charges against the assailant, nor any attempt to ascertain whether he had mental health problems. At the time of the assaults, the assailant had stopped taking his medication for schizophrenia, and after he was admitted, he told a doctor at the university's student health center that he had previously suffered a "nervous breakdown." In light of its failure to investigate the nature of the assailant's criminal record and its failure to gather additional information about his mental status once it was aware of a previous problem, said the court, summary judgment on the negligent admission claim was inappropriate.

The cases in this section illustrate a variety of campus security problems and a variety of legal theories for analyzing them. Each court's choice of theories depended on the common and statutory law of the particular jurisdiction and the specific factual setting of the case. The theories used in *Nero*, where the security problem occurred in campus housing and the institution's role was comparable to a landlord's, differ from the theories used in *Stanton*, where the student was considered the institution's "invitee." Similarly, the first theory used in *Mullins*, establishing a standard of care specifically for postsecondary institutions, differs from theories in the other cases, which apply standards of care for landlords or landowners generally. Despite the differences, however, a common denominator can be extracted from these cases that can serve as a guideline for postsecondary administrators: when an institution has foreseen or ought to have foreseen that criminal activity will likely occur on campus, it must take reasonable, appropriate steps to safeguard its students and other persons whom it has expressly or implicitly invited onto its premises. In determining whether this duty has been met in a specific case, courts will consider the foreseeability of violent criminal activity on the particular campus, the student victim's own behavior, and the reasonableness and appropriateness of the institution's response to that particular threat.

### 7.6.3. *Federal statutes and campus security.*

Following what appeared to be an increase in violent crime on campus, the legislatures of several states and the U.S. Congress passed laws requiring colleges and universities to provide information on the numbers and types of crimes on and near campus. The federal legislation, known as the "Crime Awareness and Campus Security Act" (Title II of Pub. L. No. 101-542 (1990)), amends the Higher Education Act of 1965 (this book, Section 7.6.3) at 20 U.S.C. § 1092(f). The Campus Security Act, in turn, was amended by the Higher Education Amendments of 1992 (Pub. L. No. 102-325) and imposes requirements on colleges and universities for preventing, reporting, and investigating sex offenses that occur on campus. The Campus Security Act, passed in response to activism by parents of a student murdered in her college residence hall room and others with similar concerns, is also known as the "Clery Act," named after the young woman who was murdered. The Higher Education Opportunity Act of 2008 (Pub. L. No. 110-315) amended the Higher Education Act and the Clery Act, adding categories of crimes that must be reported and additional disclosure requirements.

The Campus Security Act requires colleges to[11]

1. Collect, classify, and count crime reports and crime statistics.
2. Issue campus alerts (called "timely warnings") for any Clery Act crime that represents an ongoing threat to the safety of students or employees,

---

[11] Portions of this section are adapted from *The Handbook for Campus Safety and Security Reporting* (2011), published by the Education Department, and available at http://www2.ed.gov/admins/lead/safety/handbook.pdf.

and provide an emergency notification and evacuation procedures upon the confirmation of a significant emergency or dangerous situation involving an immediate threat to the health or safety of students or employees occurring on the campus.

3. Publish an annual security report containing safety- and security-related policy statements and crime statistics and distribute it to all current students and employees. Schools also must inform prospective students and employees about the availability of the report.

4. Submit crime statistics to the Education Department.

5. If the institution maintains a campus police or security department, it must keep a daily crime log of alleged criminal incidents that is open to public inspection.

6. Disclose missing student notification procedures that pertain to students residing in campus residence halls.

7. Disclose fire safety information related to those facilities. The institution must keep a fire log that is open to public inspection, publish an annual fire safety report containing policy statements as well as fire statistics associated with each on-campus student housing facility, including number of fires, cause, injuries, deaths, and property damage. Colleges also must inform prospective students and employees about the availability of the report.

8. Submit fire statistics to the Education Department each fall.

The crime reporting provisions of the Campus Security Act require colleges to report statistics concerning the occurrence on campus, during the most recent calendar year, and during the two preceding calendar years for which data are available, of the following criminal offenses reported to campus security authorities or local police agencies:

(i) criminal homicide (including murder and non-negligent manslaughter, and negligent manslaughter);

(ii) sex offenses, forcible or nonforcible;

(iii) robbery;

(iv) aggravated assault;

(v) burglary;

(vi) motor vehicle theft;

(vii) arson;

(viii) hate crimes (any of the above-mentioned offenses, and any incidents of larceny-theft, simple assault, intimidation, or destruction/damage/vandalism of property that were motivated by bias);

(ix) arrests of persons referred for campus disciplinary action for liquor law violations, drug-related violations, and illegal weapons possession. [20 U.S.C. § 1092 f(1)(F)(i)]

The law also requires colleges to develop and distribute to students, prospective students and their parents, and the Secretary of Education

> (1) a statement of policy regarding—
>> (i) such institution's campus sexual assault programs, which shall be aimed at prevention of sex offenses; and
>> (ii) the procedures followed once a sex offense has occurred. [20 U.S.C. § 1092 (1)(J)(8)(A)(1)]

In addition, the law requires colleges to include in their policy (1) educational programs to promote the awareness of rape and acquaintance rape, (2) sanctions that will follow a disciplinary board's determination that a sexual offense has occurred, (3) procedures students should follow if a sex offense occurs, and (4) procedures for on-campus disciplinary action in cases of alleged sexual assault.

The Campus Security Act also requires colleges to provide information on their policies regarding the reporting of other criminal actions and regarding campus security and campus law enforcement. In addition, they must provide a description of the type and frequency of programs designed to inform students and employees about campus security.

In one of its most controversial provisions, the law defines "campus" as follows:

> (1) Any building or property owned or controlled by an institution within the same reasonably contiguous geographic area and used by the institution in direct support of, or in a manner related to, the institution's educational purposes, including residence halls; and
> (2) Any building or property that is within or reasonably contiguous to the area identified in paragraph (1) of this definition, that is owned by the institution but controlled by another person, is frequently used by students, and supports institutional purposes (such as a food or other retail vendor) [34 C.F.R. § 668.46]

The Education Department's *Handbook on Campus Safety and Security Reporting* (2011) explicitly includes fraternity and sorority houses as part of the "campus," even if they are not owned by the college and are not on land owned by the college. It also includes requirements for reporting crimes that occur overseas, including those that occur in homes and other private areas, even if the college does not own the property.

Regulations implementing the Campus Security Act appear at 34 C.F.R. § 668.46. The regulations provide that an institution is not required to report statistics concerning homicide or robbery if those crimes are reported to a "pastoral or professional counselor," but must report all other crimes reported to counselors and make timely reports to the campus community about crimes that could pose a threat to other students. The Violence Against Women Act, passed by Congress in 2013, adds several requirements to the Clery Act. For information on complying with the new requirements, see the Updates to this book at www.nacua.org/publications/lohe/index.asp.

Colleges must report on their security policies and crime statistics annually, and must distribute these reports to all enrolled students and current employees, to prospective students upon request, to prospective employees upon request, and to the U.S. Department of Education. Additional information about reporting requirements and other provisions of the Campus Security Act can be found at http://ifap.ed.gov. Another helpful Web site is http://www.securityoncampus.org.

The law gives the Education Department the authority to issue civil fines of up to $27,500 per violation for a "substantial misrepresentation of the number, location or nature of the crimes required to be reported or for a violation of any other provision of the safety- and security-related" regulations. The Department's Final Review Determination Reports are public records. In addition, the Higher Education Opportunity Act of 2008 added protections for whistleblowers, prohibiting retaliation against an individual who questions or complains about the implementation of Clery Act requirements. Since 1996, several colleges and universities have been sanctioned and fines have been levied for Clery Act violations.

Some states have promulgated laws requiring colleges and universities either to report campus crime statistics or to open their law enforcement logs to the public. See, for example, a Massachusetts law that requires the keeping of a crime log (Mass. Ann. Laws ch. 41, § 98F (1993)) and a Pennsylvania law that requires colleges to provide students and employees, as well as prospective students, with information about crime statistics and security measures on campus (18 Pa. Cons. Stat. § 20.303 (2011)).

These federal and state requirements to give "timely warning" may be interpreted as creating a legal duty for colleges to warn students, staff, and others about persons on campus who have been accused of criminal behavior. If the college does not provide such a warning, its failure to do so could result in successful negligence claims against it in the event that a student or staff member is injured by someone who one or more administrators know has engaged in allegedly criminal behavior in the past. (For analysis of institutional liability and potential defenses, see Section 3.2.2.1 of this book.)

A federal appellate court ruled that an institution's compliance with the requirements of the Clery Act does not expose it to liability for defamation. In *Havlik v. Johnson & Wales University*, 509 F.3d 25 (1st Cir. 2007), the plaintiff, Havlik, a student at the university, was alleged to have assaulted a fellow student, causing him to fracture his skull. Immediately following the attack, administrators at the university posted a "crime alert" in which they described the assault and named Havlik as the assailant. The crime alert also stated that the assault occurred because two fraternity members (of which Havlik was one) were angry that the victim had not joined the fraternity. Havlik stood trial for assault and was acquitted by a jury. He then sued the university for defamation and breach of contract. For the purposes of the litigation, the court assumed that the crime alert was defamatory, but ruled that the university had a qualified privilege to issue such alerts. The university had defended its actions by stating that it believed that the Clery Act required it to publish the crime alert. The court agreed, ruling that the incident occurred in an area contiguous to campus and that the law required the college to make "timely" reports to the campus community on a variety of crimes, of which the assault was one. The court awarded the university summary judgment on the defamation claim.

In 2000, Congress enacted the Campus Sex Crimes Prevention Act (CSCPA), Pub. L. No. 106-386, 114 Stat. 1464, which became effective on October 28, 2002. The CSCPA added subsection (j) to the Jacob Wetterling Crimes Against Children and Sexually Violent Offender Registration Act, 42 U.S.C. § 14071, which requires individuals who have been convicted of criminal sexually violent offenses against minors, and who have been determined by a court to be "sexually violent predators," to register with law enforcement agencies. The Wetterling Act was repealed in 2006 and replaced by the Sex Offender Registration and Notification Act (SORNA), codified at 42 U.S.C. §§16911 et seq., which also requires convicted sex offenders to register with law enforcement agencies.

The CSCPA requires individuals subject to the former Wetterling Act (and now the CSCPA) to provide the notice required in the statute if he or she is an employee, "carries on a vocation," or is a student at any institution of higher education in the state, as well as providing notice of any change in status. The law enforcement agency that receives the information then notifies the college or university. The CSCPA also amends the Campus Security Act at 20 U.S.C. § 1092(f)(1)(I), requiring colleges to include in their annual security report a statement as to where information about registered sex offenders who are employees or students may be found (see 34 C.F.R. § 668.46 (b)(12)). It also amends FERPA (Section 7.8.1 of this book) to provide that FERPA does not prohibit the release of information about registered sex offenders on campus. Guidelines implementing the CSCPA may be found at 67 Fed. Reg. 10758 (2002). The FERPA regulations have been revised several times since the passage of SORNA, and the language permitting the disclosure of information about registered sex offenders on campus, found at 34 C.F.R. §99.31(a)(16), remains.

Some colleges have banned any student who is a registered sex offender from enrolling or being present on campus. Such bans, if implemented unilaterally and without providing for individual consideration, could invite due process challenges for public colleges. A better strategy would be for institutions to permit students who are registered sex offenders or ex-offenders convicted of violent crimes to request a hearing to determine whether or not they pose a *present* threat to the safety and security of students and employees on campus.

## Section 7.7. Other Support Services

**7.7.1. Overview.** Institutions provide various other support services to students. Health services, services for students with disabilities, services for international students, child care services, and legal services are prominent examples that are discussed in this section. Other examples include academic and career counseling services, placement services, resident life programming, entertainment and recreational services, parking, food services, and various other student convenience services. An institution may provide many of these services directly through its own staff members; other services may be performed by outside third parties under contract with the institution or by student groups subsidized by the institution (see Section 10.1.3). Funding may come from the institution's regular budget, from mandatory student fees, from revenues generated by charging for the service, from government or private grants, or from donated and earmarked funds. In all of these contexts, the provision of support services may give rise to a variety of legal issues concerning institutional authority and students' rights, as well as legal liability (see generally Section 2.1), some of which are illustrated in Sections 7.7.2 and 7.7.3.

### 7.7.2. Services for students with disabilities. Both Section 504 of the Rehabilitation Act of 1973 (see Section 11.5.4 of this book) and the Americans with Disabilities Act (ADA) require colleges to provide both access and accommodations for students whose disabilities meet the laws' definitions. Academic and housing accommodations for specific student needs are discussed in Sections 8.4 and 7.4.2 of this book. This section discusses auxiliary aids and services for students with disabilities, such as interpreters, technology, special transportation services, and so forth.

Questions about who pays for services for students with disabilities have persisted for decades. A regulation promulgated under Section 504 (34 C.F.R. § 104.44(d)) obligates institutions to provide such services, and this obligation apparently is not negated by the student's ability to pay. One federal appellate court has ruled that the college must provide auxiliary aids, such as interpreters, free of charge to students, whether or not they are eligible for financial aid (*United States v. Board of Trustees of the University of Alabama*, 908 F.2d 740 (11th Cir. 1990)).

A related issue concerns the obligations of federally funded state vocational rehabilitation (VR) agencies to provide auxiliary services for eligible college students. Disputes have existed for decades as to whether the state VR agencies are legally obligated to provide auxiliary services to disabled college students and, if so, whether their obligation diminishes the obligation of universities to pay the costs. The Rehabilitation Act contains language requiring state vocational rehabilitation agencies to enter agreements with colleges for cost sharing for auxiliary services for students with disabilities.

In *Schornstein v. New Jersey Division of Vocational Rehabilitation Services*, 519 F. Supp. 773 (D.N.J. 1981), *affirmed*, 688 F.2d 824 (3d Cir. 1982), the court held that Title I of the Rehabilitation Act of 1973 (29 U.S.C. §§ 100 et seq.) requires state VR agencies to provide eligible college students with interpreter services they require to meet their vocational goals. In *Jones v. Illinois Department of Rehabilitation Services*, 504 F. Supp. 1244 (N.D. Ill. 1981), *affirmed*, 689 F.2d 724 (7th Cir. 1982), the court agreed that state VR agencies have this legal obligation. But it also held that colleges have a similar obligation under 34 C.F.R. § 104.44(d) and asked whose responsibility is primary. The court concluded that the state VR agencies have primary financial responsibility, thus diminishing universities' responsibility in situations in which the student is eligible for state VR services. There is a catch, however, in the application of these cases to students who do not provide evidence of financial need. As the district court in *Schornstein* noted, state VR agencies may consider the financial need of disabled individuals in determining the extent to which the agency will pay the costs of rehabilitation services (see 34 C.F.R. § 361.47). Thus, if a VR agency employs a financial need test and finds that a particular disabled student does not meet it, the primary obligation would again fall on the university.

Disputes have continued over whether state VR agencies must pay for support services, as well as tuition and books, for disabled students. New York courts resolved two cases in which student clients of the state Office of Vocational and Educational Services for Individuals with Disabilities demanded that the agency pay their tuition and fees for law school. In *Murphy v. Office of Vocational and Educational Services for Individuals with Disabilities*, 705 N.E.2d 1180 (N.Y. 1998), and in *Tourville v. Office of Vocational and Educational Services for Individuals with Disabilities*, 663 N.Y.S.2d 368 (N.Y. App. Div. 1997), the courts rejected the claims of students that, even though the agency had paid for their undergraduate education, it was legally bound to pay for their law school expenses as well. Although *Tourville* was decided on procedural grounds (the plaintiff had not entered an individualized written rehabilitation program (IWRP) plan with the agency), the *Murphy* court decided that the plaintiff had been prepared for the career that she agreed to in her IWRP, and the agency was not required to pay for additional education that was not contemplated by her plan.

These cases suggest that, although state vocational rehabilitation or similar agencies may have the primary responsibility to provide funding for their student clients, colleges and universities will be asked to provide additional support services or will be asked to provide more extensive services when a student's eligibility for state-funded services expires. State VR agencies are attempting to shift the funding responsibility for student support services to colleges and universities, a trend that, if it continues, may dissuade colleges from recruiting students with disabilities.

Students have had some success stating claims against institutions for denial of auxiliary services such as sign language interpreters and note-takers. In *Bennett-Nelson v. Louisiana Board of Regents*, 431 F.3d 448 (5th Cir. 2005), the court ruled that sovereign immunity did not protect the Board of Regents from a claim under Section 504 of the Rehabilitation Act because Louisiana Tech University was a recipient of federal funds.

**7.7.3. Services for international students.** International students, as noncitizens, have various needs that are typically not concerns for students who are U.S. citizens. Postsecondary institutions with significant numbers of international students face policy issues concerning the nature and extent of the services they will provide for international students, and the structures and staffing through which they will provide these services (for example, a network of international student advisors or an international services office). Simultaneously, institutions face issues concerning their legal obligations regarding international students enrolled in their academic programs. This section focuses primarily on the status of international students under federal immigration laws—a critical matter that institutions must consider both in determining how they will assist international students and prospective students with their immigration status and in fulfilling the reporting requirements and other legal requirements imposed on institutions by the applicable laws and regulations. Matters concerning admissions and in-state tuition, primarily of interest to state institutions, are addressed in Sections 7.2.4.4 and 7.3.5.

The immigration status of international students has been of increasing concern to higher education as the proportion of applicants and students from foreign countries has grown. In 1980 there were approximately 312,000 nonresident alien students on U.S. campuses. Over the decade this figure grew steadily, reaching 407,000 nonresident alien students in 1990 and 548,000 in 2000, at which time international students composed approximately 3.5 percent of all students enrolled in U.S. colleges (*Digest of Education Statistics* (National Center for Education Statistics, 2002), 483). In 2010, the number of international students reached nearly 691,000, a record high and a rebound after declines earlier in the decade attributable to the 9/11 tragedy. More than 18 percent of these international students in 2010 were from the People's Republic of China (Institute for International Education (IIE), *Open Doors 2010*, available at http://www.iie.org/Research-and-Publications/Open-Doors/Data.)

Foreign nationals may qualify for admission to the United States as students under one of three categories: bona fide academic students (8 U.S.C. § 1101(a)(15)(F)), students who plan to study at a vocational or "nonacademic" institution (8 U.S.C. § 1101(a)(15)(M)), or "exchange visitors" (8 U.S.C. § 1101(a)(15)(J)). In each category the statute provides that the "alien spouse and minor children" of the student may also qualify for admission "if accompanying him or following to join him."

The first of these three student categories is for aliens in the United States "temporarily and solely for the purpose of pursuing [a full] course of study . . . at an established college, university, seminary, conservatory, . . . or other academic institution or in a language training program" (8 U.S.C. § 1101(a)(15)(F)(i)). This category is called "F-1," a name that is also applied to the included students. There is also a more recently created "F-3" subcategory for citizens of Canada and Mexico who live near the U.S. border and wish to commute to a U.S. institution for part-time study. The second of the three student categories is for aliens in the United States "temporarily and solely for the purpose of pursuing a full course of study at an established vocational or other recognized nonacademic institution (other than a language training program)" (8 U.S.C. § 1101(a)(15)(M)(i)). This category is called "M-1," and the included students are "M-1s." The spouses and children of students in these first two categories are called "F-2s" and "M-2s," respectively. The third of the student categories, exchange visitor, is known as the "J" category. It includes, among others, any alien (and the family of any alien) "who is a bona fide student, scholar, [or] trainee, . . . who is coming temporarily to the United States as a participant in a program designated by the Director of the United States Information Agency, for the purpose of . . . studying, observing, conducting research . . . or receiving training" (8 U.S.C. § 1101(a)(15)(J)). Exchange visitors who will attend medical school, and the institutions they will attend, are subject to additional requirements under 8 U.S.C. § 1182(j).

Visa holders in other nonimmigrant categories not based on student status may also be able to attend higher educational institutions during their stay in the United States. G-4 visa holders are one such example; visa holders (temporary workers) are another. The rules for these visa holders who become students may be different from those described below with respect to students on F-1, M-1, and J-1 visas.

The Department of State's role in regulating international students is shaped by its power to grant or deny visas to persons applying to enter the United States. Consular officials verify whether an applicant alien has met the requirements under one of the pertinent statutory categories and the corresponding requirements established by State Department regulations. The State Department's regulations for academic student visas and nonacademic or vocational student visas are in 22 C.F.R. § 41.61. Requirements for exchange visitor status are also in 22 C.F.R. § 41.62.

The Department of Homeland Security's Bureau of Citizenship and Immigration Services (CIS) has authority to approve the schools that international students may attend and for which they may obtain visas from the State Department (8 C.F.R. § 214.3). The CIS is also responsible for ensuring that international students do not violate the conditions of their visas once they enter the United States. In particular, the CIS must determine that holders of F-1 and M-1 student visas are making satisfactory progress toward the degree or other academic objective they are pursuing. The regulations under which the CIS fulfills this responsibility are now located in 8 C.F.R. § 214.2(f) for academic students and 8 C.F.R. § 214.2(m) for vocational students.

The Department of Homeland Security's Bureau of Immigration and Custom Enforcement (ICE) operates the Student and Exchange Visitors Information System (SEVIS) that colleges must use to enter and update information on every student with a student or exchange visitor visa. The SEVIS regulations, 8 C.F.R. Parts 103 and 214, require each college or university to have a "Designated School Official" (DSO) who is responsible for maintaining and updating the information on F-1, F-3, and M-1 students (8 C.F.R. § 214.3) and a "Responsible Officer" for J-1 (exchange visitor) students (8 C.F.R. § 214.2).

In order to obtain an F-1 visa, the student must demonstrate that he or she has an "unabandoned" residence outside the United States and will be entering the United States in order to enroll in a full-time program of study. The student must present a SEVIS Form I-20 issued in his or her own name by a school approved by the CIS for attendance by F-1 international students. The student must have documentary evidence of financial support in the amount indicated on the SEVIS Form I-20. And, for students seeking initial admission only, the student must attend the school specified in the student's visa.

The regulations specify the periods of time for which international students may be admitted into the country and the circumstances that will constitute a "full course of study." In addition, the regulations establish the ground rules for on-campus employment of international students, off-campus employment (much more restricted than on-campus employment), transfers to another school, temporary absences from the country, and extensions of stay beyond the period of initial admission.

Given the complexity of the immigration legislation and regulations, and the substantial consequences of noncompliance (including the real possibility that international students may be required to return to their home countries before they have completed their studies), there is no substitute for experienced, informed staff and for expert legal advice. Training for new staff and professional development programming for established staff are also critically important, as is information technology support sufficient to implement the SEVIS requirements and other reporting and record-keeping requirements. Helpful guidance on legal requirements is available on the Citizenship and Information Services Web site (http://www.uscis.gov) and the Immigration and Customs Enforcement Web site (http://www.ice.gov). In addition, the Association of International Educators maintains a Web site (http://nafsa.org) with much useful information, including the Association of International Educators' publication *NAFSA Adviser's Manual of Federal Regulations Affecting Foreign Students and Scholars*, a comprehensive and frequently updated reference on federal requirements for students and visitors.

Due to SEVIS and the expanded reporting requirements for institutions, as well as the increased access of federal investigators to information concerning international students, their privacy has been a growing concern. While the Family Educational Rights and Privacy Act (FERPA) (Section 7.8.1 of this book) continues to protect the privacy of international students' student records, the federal government may now waive some FERPA requirements as needed to operate SEVIS (see Illegal Immigration Reform and Immigrant Responsibility Act (IIRIRA), section 641(c)(2), 8 U.S.C. § 1372(c)(2)), and to fight terrorism (see USA PATRIOT Act, section 507, 20 U.S.C. § 1232g(j)).

## *Section 7.8. Student Records*

### *7.8.1. Family Educational Rights and Privacy Act (FERPA).* The
Family Educational Rights and Privacy Act of 1974 (20 U.S.C. § 1232g), popularly known as FERPA (or sometimes as the Buckley Amendment, after its principal senatorial sponsor), places significant limitations on colleges' disclosure and handling of student records. The act and its implementing regulations, 34 C.F.R. Part 99, apply to all public and private educational agencies or institutions that receive federal funds from the U.S. Department of Education or whose students receive such funds and pay them to the agency or institution (34 C.F.R. § 99.1). While FERPA does not invalidate common law or state statutory law applicable to student records (see Section 8.8.2), the regulations are so extensive and detailed that they are the predominant legal consideration in dealing with student records.

FERPA establishes three basic rights for college students: the rights (1) to inspect their own education records; (2) to request that corrections to the records be made if the information in them was recorded inaccurately (and, if the school refuses, the right to a hearing by the school to determine whether the records should be corrected); and (3) to restrict the access of others (in some cases including even the students' own parents[12]) to personally identifiable records unless one of a number of enumerated exceptions is at issue. The regulations also require colleges to notify students annually of their rights under FERPA, and they provide a procedure for complaints to be filed with the Department of Education if a student believes that the college has not complied with FERPA.

The Family Policy Compliance Office (FPCO) of the Education Department is charged with the development, interpretation, and enforcement of FERPA regulations. The FPCO maintains a Web site that provides an overview of FERPA at http://www.ed.gov/policy/gen/guid/fpco/ferpa/index.html. The Web site also contains the FERPA regulations at http://www2.ed.gov/policy/gen/reg/ferpa/index.html.

The education records that are protected under FERPA's quite broad definition are all "those records that are (1) [d]irectly related to a student; and (2) [m]aintained by an educational agency or institution or by a party acting for the agency or institution" (20 U.S.C. § 1232g(a)(4)(A); 34 C.F.R. § 99.3).[13] This section of the regulations contains six exceptions to this definition, which exclude from coverage certain "sole possession" records of institutional personnel, certain campus law enforcement records, certain student employment records, certain records regarding health care, "records [such as certain alumni records] created or received . . . after an individual is no longer a student in attendance and that are not directly related to the individual's attendance as a student," and grades on certain peer-graded papers. There is also a partial exception for "directory information," which is exempt from the regulations' nondisclosure requirements under certain conditions (34 C.F.R. § 99.37).

Following a flurry of litigation concerning access by the press to campus law enforcement records involving students (considered, under FERPA's earlier definition, to be student education records and thus protected), Congress passed the Higher Education Amendments of 1992 (Pub. L. No. 102-325, codified at 20 U.S.C. § 1232g(a)(4)(B)(ii)), which amended FERPA to exclude from the definition of "education records" records that are both created and maintained by a law enforcement unit of an educational agency or institution at least in part for the purpose of law enforcement. This change enables institutions, under certain circumstances, to disclose information about campus crime contained in law

---

[12] If a student is a dependent for federal income tax purposes, the institution may, but is not required to, disclose the student's education records to the student's parents.

[13] It is important to recognize that the definition of "education record" is far broader than just a record of grades or other "educational" or "academic" information. For example, student course evaluation scores for courses taught by graduate students fall within the definition of "education record." Therefore, posting student course evaluation scores for these instructors, either physically or on a Web site, could be a violation of FERPA if the graduate student had not consented to the posting.

enforcement unit records to parents, the media, other students, and other law enforcement agencies. Regulations specifying institutional responsibilities with respect to law enforcement records under FERPA are codified at 34 C.F.R. § 99.8.

Although FERPA provides substantial protection for the privacy of student records, it has been amended numerous times to address public (and parental) concerns about campus safety and the shield that FERPA provided to alleged student perpetrators of violent crimes, as well as various other issues and concerns. FERPA regulations currently list sixteen exceptions to the requirement of prior consent before the release of a personally identifiable education record (34 C.F.R. § 99.31). Several of these exceptions are discussed below.

In one such instance, the Education Department revised the FERPA regulations to clarify the definition of a disciplinary record and to specify the conditions for its release. Disciplinary records generally are considered "education records" and are thus subject to FERPA's limitations on disclosure. However, the revised regulations permit the institution to disclose to the victim of an "alleged perpetrator of a crime of violence or non-forcible sex offense" the "final results" of a disciplinary proceeding involving the student accused of the crime (34 C.F.R. § 99.31(a)(13)). The regulations also allow the institution to disclose the "final results" of such a disciplinary proceeding to the general public if the institution determines that the student has violated one or more institutional rules and policies. (The victim may be informed regardless of the outcome.) Under either exception, the institution may not disclose the names of other witnesses, including the alleged victim, without the relevant student's or students' consent (34 C.F.R. § 99.31(a)(14)). Furthermore, the regulations prohibit institutions from requiring students to sign a nondisclosure or confidentiality agreement when the institution informs a student victim of an alleged act of violence or non-forcible sex offense of the outcome of a disciplinary proceeding (34 C.F.R. § 99.33(c)). Because of the specificity of these exceptions to the nondisclosure rule, most disciplinary records will still be protected by FERPA and may be disclosed only with permission of the student.

FERPA permits disclosure to teachers and other school officials at other institutions of information about a disciplinary action taken against a student for behavior that posed a significant risk to the student or to others (34 C.F.R. § 99.31(a)(2). FERPA also permits an institution to disclose information otherwise protected by FERPA in order to comply with a judicial order or a lawfully issued subpoena, as long as either the institution makes a "reasonable effort" to notify the student of the order or subpoena in advance or the subpoena is for law enforcement purposes and prohibits disclosure on its face (34 C.F.R. § 99.31(a)(9)(ii)).

The USA PATRIOT Act (Pub. L. No. 107-56; 115 Stat. 272, October 26, 2001) amended FERPA to permit an institution to disclose, without informing the student or seeking the student's consent, information about the student in response to an *ex parte* order issued by a court at the request of the U.S. Attorney General or his designee. To obtain such a court order, the Attorney General must demonstrate the need for this information in order to further the investigation or prosecution of terrorism crimes as specified in 18 U.S.C.

§§ 2332b(g)(5)(B), 2331. The USA PATRIOT Act also amends the recordkeeping provisions of FERPA (20 U.S.C. § 1232g(b)(4); 34 C.F.R. § 99.32); the institution is not required to record the disclosure of information in a student's education record in response to an *ex parte* order issued under the circumstances described above. (A more detailed explanation of the USA PATRIOT Act amendments and other exceptions to the requirement of student notice and consent is contained in a technical assistance letter of April 12, 2002, from the director of the Family Policy Compliance Office. It can be found at http://www.ed.gov/policy/gen/guid/fpco/pdf/htterrorism.pdf.)

Another FERPA exception delineates the circumstances under which institutions may notify parents, using information that otherwise would be protected by FERPA: (1) if the student is a dependent for federal income tax purposes (34 C.F.R. § 99.31(a)(8)); (2) if the disclosure is in connection with a health or safety emergency under the conditions specified in 34 C.F.R. § 99.36 (i.e., if knowledge of the information is necessary to protect the health or safety of the student or other individuals (34 C.F.R. § 99.31(a)(10))); and (3) if the student has violated any federal, state or local law, or any rule or policy of the institution, governing the use or possession of alcohol or a controlled substance, as long as the institution has determined that the student has committed a disciplinary violation regarding that use or possession and the student is under twenty-one at the time of the disclosure (34 C.F.R. § 99.31(a)(15)).

The tragic shootings at Virginia Tech in 2008 illuminated widespread misunderstanding among campus officials as to the breadth of FERPA protection. Much has been written since then about the interplay between FERPA and an institution's need to respond promptly and effectively to campus tragedies. The Education Department issued new guidance and regulations to clarify the degree to which faculty and administrators may communicate information concerning students who are believed to be a risk to themselves or to others. The regulations, found at 73 Fed. Reg. 74806 (December 9, 2008), reinforce the preexisting ability for institutions to disclose information to parents, law enforcement, and others if "there is an articulable and significant threat to the health or safety of the student or other individuals." The introduction to the regulations states that "the Department will not substitute its judgment for that of the agency or institution if, based on the information available at the time of the determination there is a rational basis for the agency's or institution's determination that a health or safety emergency exists." The regulations require the institution to record the "articulable and significant threat" to health and safety that motivated the disclosure. In addition, the regulations permit institutional representatives to share with each other and with representatives of other schools information about disciplinary actions taken against a student "for conduct that posed a significant risk to the safety or well-being of that student, other students, or other members of the school community."

The Campus Sex Crimes Prevention Act (section 1601 of the Victims of Trafficking and Violence Protection Act of 2000, Pub. L. No. 106-386) amends FERPA to permit the release of information provided to the college concerning sex offenders whom the law requires to register. This amendment to FERPA is codified at 20 U.S.C. § 1232g(b)(7). Interpretive guidance regarding this legislation and its implications for colleges may be found at http://www2.ed.gov/policy/gen/guid/fpco/hottopics/ht10-24-02.html.

The key to success in dealing with FERPA is a thorough understanding of the implementing regulations. Administrators should keep copies of the regulations at their fingertips and should not rely on secondary sources to resolve particular problems. Counsel should review the institution's record-keeping policies and practices, and every substantial change in them, to ensure compliance with the regulations. Administrators and counsel should work together to maintain appropriate legal forms to use in implementing the regulations, such as forms for a student's waiver of his or her rights under the act or regulations, forms for securing a student's consent to release personally identifiable information from his or her records (34 C.F.R. § 99.30), and forms for notifying parties to whom information is disclosed of the limits on the use of that information (34 C.F.R. § 99.34). Questions concerning the interpretation or application of the regulations may be directed to the Family Policy Compliance Office at the U.S. Department of Education.

In 2002, the U.S. Supreme Court ruled that there is no private right of action under FERPA, putting an end to more than two decades of litigation over that issue. In *Gonzaga University v. Doe*, 536 U.S. 273 (2002), the Court ruled 7 to 2 that Congress had not created a private right of action under FERPA and also ruled that the law created no personal rights enforceable under 42 U.S.C. § 1983. Doe, a former education student at Gonzaga University, a private institution in the state of Washington, had sued Gonzaga in state court, alleging violation of his FERPA rights for a communication between a university administrator and the state agency responsible for teacher certification. In that communication, the university administrator alleged that Doe had committed certain sex-based offenses against a fellow student, despite the fact that the alleged victim had not filed a complaint and no determination had been made as to the truth of the allegations, which the administrator had overheard from a third party. Doe also sued Gonzaga and the administrator under tort and contract theories. A jury found for Doe, awarding him more than $1 million in compensatory and punitive damages, including $450,000 in damages on the FERPA claim.

The Washington Court of Appeals reversed the outcome at the trial level, but, in *Doe v. Gonzaga University*, 24 P.3d 390 (Wash. 2001), the Washington Supreme Court reversed yet again, ruling that, although FERPA did not create a private cause of action, its nondisclosure provisions provided a right enforceable under 42 U.S.C. § 1983. Since the lower courts were divided as to the existence of FERPA's enforceability under Section 1983, the U.S. Supreme Court granted certiorari to resolve the conflict.

The Court compared the language of FERPA with that of Titles VI and IX (discussed in this book, Sections 11.5.2 and 11.5.3 respectively), which provide that "no person" shall be subject to discrimination. In FERPA, however, Congress focused on the obligation of the Secretary of Education to withhold federal funds from any institution that failed to comply with the law's nondisclosure provisions. This language, said the Court, did not confer the type of "individual entitlement" that can be enforced through Section 1983, citing *Cannon v. University of Chicago*, 441 U.S. 677 (1979), a case that found a private right of action under Title IX. Furthermore, said the Court, FERPA provides for penalties for institutions that have a "policy or practice" of permitting the release of education records, rather than penalties for a single act of noncompliance. In addition, the court noted, FERPA's creation of an administrative enforcement mechanism through the Secretary of Education demonstrates that Congress did not intend for the law to create an individual right, either under FERPA itself or through Section 1983. The Court reversed the Washington Supreme Court's ruling on the FERPA claim.

FERPA itself does not prohibit the practice of using Social Security numbers as identifiers, but it does regulate their disclosure. The Family Policy Compliance Office has taken the position that the use of even partial Social Security numbers to publicly post student grades is a FERPA violation (Family Policy Compliance Office, "Letter re: Hunter College" (May 29, 2001), available at http://www.ed.gov/policy/gen/guid/fpco/doc/hunter.doc). A New York law prohibits any public or private school or university from displaying a student's Social Security number for posting of grades, on class rosters, on student identification cards, in student directories, or for other purposes unless specifically authorized or required by law.

Although students do not have a private right of action under FERPA, they may, as in *Gonzaga*, still be able to state negligence claims for alleged FERPA violations. For example, in *Atria v. Vanderbilt University*, 142 F. App'x 246 (6th Cir. 2005) (unpublished), a professor distributed graded exams to students by leaving them stacked on a table outside the classroom. The exam sheets contained the students' names and Social Security numbers. The plaintiff, a pre-med student, obtained his graded exam several days later in class and asked that it be regraded because it appeared that some correct answers had been marked wrong. The professor had kept photocopies of the exam answer sheets, and noted that the version of the answer sheet that the student submitted differed from the photocopy. He accused the student of academic misconduct (changing some of the answers from wrong to correct), and the student was disciplined. The student argued that another student must have taken his answer sheet, changed some of the answers, and returned it to the pile outside the classroom. Although the trial court awarded summary judgment on the negligence claim and a breach of contract claim, the appellate court reversed, ruling that both must be tried to a jury because a jury could find that the professor's method of returning the exam answer sheets could have permitted tampering by other students.

***7.8.2. State law.*** In a majority of states, courts now recognize a common law tort of invasion of privacy, which, in some circumstances, protects individuals against the public disclosure of damaging private information about them and against intrusions into their private affairs. A few states have similarly protected privacy with a statute or constitutional provision. Although this body of law has seldom been applied to educational record-keeping practices, the basic legal principles appear applicable to record-keeping abuses by postsecondary institutions. This body of right-to-privacy law could protect students against abusive collection and retention practices where clearly intrusive methods are used to collect information concerning private affairs. In *White v. Davis*, 533 P.2d 222 (Cal. 1975) (see Section 11.1.3), for example, the court held that undercover police surveillance of university classes and meetings violated the right to privacy because "no professor or student can be confident that whatever he may express in class will not find its way into a police file." Similarly, right-to-privacy law could protect students against abusive dissemination practices that result in unwarranted public disclosure of damaging personal information.

In addition to this developing right-to-privacy law, many states also have statutes or administrative regulations dealing specifically with record keeping. These include subject access laws, open records or public records laws, and confidentiality laws. Such laws usually apply only to state agencies, and a state's postsecondary institutions may or may not be considered state agencies subject to record-keeping laws. Occasionally a state statute deals specifically with postsecondary education records. A Massachusetts statute, for instance, makes it an "unfair educational practice" for any "educational institution," including public and private postsecondary institutions, to request information or make or keep records concerning certain arrests or misdemeanor convictions of students or applicants (Mass. Gen. Laws Ann. ch. 151C, § 2(f)).

Since state laws on privacy and records vary greatly from state to state, administrators should check with counsel to determine the law in their particular state. And because state open records requirements may occasionally conflict with FERPA regulations, counsel must determine whether any such conflict exists. Although there have been several cases involving the conflict between FERPA's confidentiality requirements and the demands of state public records laws, there is little agreement as to how a public institution can comply with both laws.

A few state courts have ruled that public records laws trump the confidentiality provisions of FERPA. Although the changes to FERPA made by the 1998 Higher Education Amendments allow colleges to release limited information concerning the outcomes of student disciplinary hearings (Section 7.8.1), the law still does not provide for the complete release of transcripts, documentary evidence, or other records that meet FERPA's definition of "education records." Thus, the outcomes in the cases discussed below are still relevant to college administrators, who—until such time as FERPA is once again amended—may have to walk a tightrope in attempting to comply with conflicting state laws regarding public records and public meetings.

In a case whose rationale is similar to the *Red & Black* case (cited in Section 7.8.1), a Connecticut appellate court addressed a claim under Connecticut's Freedom of Information law that audiotapes of a student disciplinary hearing were public records and thus subject to disclosure. In *Eastern Connecticut State University v. Connecticut Freedom of Information Commission*, No. CV96-0556097, 1996 Conn. Super. LEXIS 2554 (Conn. Super. Ct. September 30, 1996), a faculty member who had filed disciplinary charges against a student enrolled in his class requested audiotapes of the hearing that had been held to adjudicate those charges. The college refused, citing FERPA's provision that protects records of disciplinary hearings from disclosure unless the student consents. Although the state Freedom of Information Commission (FOIC) found the hearings to fall squarely within FERPA's protection, it also found that the faculty member had a legitimate educational interest in the student's behavior and thus was entitled to the information under another FERPA provision (20 U.S.C. § 1232g(h); 34 C.F.R. § 99.3). The court held that FERPA did not prevent a state legislature from enacting a law providing for access to public records, and that FERPA does not prohibit disclosing the student records, but that nondisclosure is "merely a precondition for federal funds." Taken to its logical conclusion, this ruling would elevate the interest of the public in access to public records over the ability of the state institution to be eligible to receive federal funds.

A second state court differed sharply with the result in the *Eastern Connecticut State University* case. In *Shreveport Professional Chapter of the Society of Professional Journalists v. Louisiana State University*, No. 393, 334 (1st Judicial Dist. Ct. Caddo Parish, La., March 4, 1994) (unpublished opinion at 17), the court found that the results of a disciplinary hearing concerning theft of student government funds by student government members were education records (protected by FERPA) and not law enforcement records (not protected by FERPA). The court rejected the plaintiffs' claim that FERPA did not prohibit disclosure of disciplinary hearing records, stating: "[T]he intent of Congress to withhold millions of federal dollars from universities that violate [FERPA] is ample prohibition, regardless of how the word 'prohibit' is construed by the plaintiffs." Although the court determined that the disciplinary hearing records fell within the scope of the state's public records act, the court ruled that, given FERPA's requirements, the state constitution provided for an implied exception in the law for college disciplinary hearings. Distinguishing *Red & Black Publishing* on several grounds, the court held that the records should not be disclosed.

Despite the clarity of the FERPA regulations that include disciplinary records within the definition of education record, it took a lengthy legal battle pitting state courts against their federal counterparts to result, eventually, in a determination that FERPA privacy protections trumped state open records laws. In the state court litigation, the Supreme Court of Ohio held in *State ex rel Miami Student v. Miami University*, 680 N.E.2d 956 (Ohio 1997), that university disciplinary records are not education records under FERPA. The editor of the university's student newspaper had sought student disciplinary records, redacted of the students' names, Social Security numbers, student identification numbers, and any other information that would identify individual students. The university provided the information but, in addition to the redactions that the editor had agreed to, also deleted information on the sex and age of the accused individuals; the date, time, and location of the incidents; and memoranda, statements by students, and the disposition of some of the proceedings. The editor sought a writ of mandamus from the state supreme court requiring disclosure of those records. The majority opinion did not cite or analyze any of the implementing regulations. Instead, the opinion cited the *Red & Black* case and held that disciplinary records could be disclosed without violating FERPA because they were not related to "student academic performance, financial aid, or scholastic probation." Noting that the public records act was intended to be interpreted broadly, the court also noted that crime on campus was a serious problem and that the public should have access to the information requested by the student editor.

The U.S. Supreme Court denied certiorari in the *Miami Student* case (522 U.S. 1022 (1997)). The U.S. Education Department then brought a claim in a federal district court in Ohio, seeking to enjoin the colleges (Ohio State University was also affected by the state court decision) from complying with the state supreme court's ruling to release the disciplinary records. The federal court issued the requested injunction, stating that the disciplinary records at issue clearly met the FERPA definition of "education records" and that the Ohio Supreme Court's interpretation of FERPA as pertaining only to academic records was incorrect (*United States v. Miami University*, No. C2:98-0097 (February 12, 1998)).

The federal district court then permitted the addition of the *Chronicle of Higher Education* as a codefendant to argue that disciplinary records are law enforcement records, rather than education records, and that FERPA does not preempt the Ohio Public Records Act. The *Chronicle* asked the court to dismiss the Education Department's lawsuit for lack of subject matter jurisdiction, arguing that the department lacked standing to bring the action. The trial court ruled that FERPA expressly gave the Secretary of Education standing to enforce the law (20 U.S.C. § 1232g(f)), including enforcement by litigation (*United States of America v. The Miami University and The Ohio State University*, 91 F. Supp. 2d 1132 (S.D. Ohio 2000)). Additionally, said the court, the Secretary of Education had the authority to sue the recipients of federal funds to force them to comply with the terms of funding programs, one of which is compliance with FERPA. And, third, the court rejected the *Chronicle*'s argument that FERPA does not prohibit colleges from releasing education records, but rather merely authorizes the Department of Education to withdraw federal funding from an institution that does not comply with FERPA. The court stated that the inclusion in the statute of several enforcement mechanisms, in addition to termination of funds for FERPA violations, demonstrated that Congress intended that the law apply directly to colleges. The federal district court also made an explicit ruling that student disciplinary records are education records under FERPA. Denying the *Chronicle*'s motion to dismiss and awarding summary judgment to the Department of Education, the federal court issued a permanent injunction against Miami University and Ohio State University, forbidding the further release of student disciplinary records.

The intervening party, the *Chronicle of Higher Education*, appealed, and the U.S. Court of Appeals for the Sixth Circuit affirmed (294 F.3d 797 (6th Cir. 2002)). The *Chronicle* asserted that the Department of Education lacked standing to bring the action seeking to enjoin the release of the records, challenged the lower court's ruling as an implicit decision that FERPA preempts state open records laws, and asserted that the lower court was incorrect in ruling that disciplinary records were education records within the meaning of FERPA. The *Chronicle* also argued that FERPA violates the First Amendment because it limits access to otherwise publicly available records.

The appellate court ruled that the Department of Education had standing to seek the injunction on the same grounds that the trial court had relied upon. Furthermore, said the court, the Ohio Supreme Court's ruling that disciplinary records were not education records was incorrect; despite that ruling, the Ohio court had allowed Miami to redact all personally identifiable information from the records before disclosing them, an action that complied with FERPA's requirements. The federal appellate court relied on the specific, limited discipline-related exceptions to FERPA's prohibition against disclosure of education records to conclude that disciplinary records were, in fact, still included within the law's definition of education record, a result that supports the position of the FPCO. With respect to the First Amendment claim, the court explained that student disciplinary proceedings were not criminal trials, and therefore, jurisprudence related to the public's access to criminal trials was not applicable to disciplinary hearings in which students lacked the panoply of protections available to litigants in the courts. Student disciplinary hearings at both universities were closed to the public, and press or public access to such hearings would complicate, not aid, the educational purpose that the hearings were designed to further. The court rejected the *Chronicle*'s First Amendment claims. The court noted that the *Chronicle* could request student disciplinary records from which all individually identifying information had been redacted, as FERPA would not prohibit the release of such information.

Despite the first ruling of the federal trial court in the *Miami University* case (enjoining the release of the records prior to trial), the Court of Appeals of Maryland followed the lead of the Ohio Supreme Court. In *Kirwan v. The Diamondback*, 721 A.2d 196 (Md. 1998), the Maryland court ruled that Maryland's Public Information Act (Maryland Code § 10-611-28) authorizes the disclosure of information sought from the university by the student newspaper. The newspaper was seeking correspondence and parking violation records involving the basketball coach and several student players, which the university refused to provide. The university asserted that the parking violation records related to the coach were personnel records, which the law exempted from disclosure, and that the parking violation records related to the students were education records, protected from disclosure by FERPA. The court rejected both of the university's defenses.

The court held that the parking violation records of the student athletes were not education records because Congress had intended only that records related to a student's academic performance be covered by FERPA. The court held that a broad definition of "education record" would enable an educational institution to operate "in secrecy," thus "keeping very important information from other students, their parents, public officials, and the public" (721 A.2d at 204). The court upheld the ruling of the trial court that the university was required to release the information sought by the student newspaper.

But another state appellate court has ruled that, despite its finding that the "Undergraduate Court" at the University of North Carolina was a "public body" under North Carolina's Open Meetings Law (N.C. Gen. Stat. §§ 143–318.9 et seq.), that body was entitled to hold closed disciplinary hearings in order to comply with the dictates of FERPA. In *DTH Publishing Corp. v. The University of North Carolina at Chapel Hill*, 496 S.E.2d 8 (N.C. Ct. App. 1998), the court applied language in the Open Meetings Law that allowed a public body to hold a closed session, if it was necessary, to prevent the disclosure of information that is "privileged or confidential." The university had argued that FERPA's prohibition of the nonconsensual release of personally identifiable student records rendered the records of student disciplinary hearings "privileged and confidential" for the purposes of state law. The court distinguished the *Miami Student* state case, noting that the Ohio court had ordered only the release of "statistical data" from which student names had been deleted, and which included the location of the incident, age and sex of the student, nature of the offense, and the type of discipline imposed, but had not ordered the release of records from specific disciplinary hearings. The court also rejected arguments by the student newspaper that the state and federal constitutions required that judicial proceedings be open to the public, stating that the Undergraduate Court was not the type of court contemplated by these constitutions, and that there was no history at the university of open disciplinary hearings.

In *Caledonian-Record Publishing Company, Inc. v. Vermont State College*, 833 A.2d 1273 (Vt. 2003), Vermont's highest court was asked to decide whether the press could have access to the daily security logs, student disciplinary records, and student disciplinary hearings at Lyndon State College and the entire Vermont State College System under the state's Open Meeting Law and Public Records Act. The colleges provided the daily security logs compiled by their campus police departments, but refused to provide the requested student disciplinary records or to allow access to student disciplinary hearings.

The court found that Vermont's Public Records Act exempts "student records at educational institutions funded wholly or in part by state revenue" (1 Vt. Stat. Ann. § 317(c)(11)) from disclosure. Because the plaintiffs had stated that they did not want to attend the hearings, but only to have access to the minutes or other records of the hearings, the court did not reach the issue of whether the media should be allowed to attend student disciplinary hearings. It also found that minutes or other records documenting the proceedings and outcome of student disciplinary hearings also fit the definition of "student records" and thus were exempted from disclosure.

In 2011, two public universities defended against claims that state open records laws trump FERPA and require disclosure of education records. In *Chicago Tribune Co. v. University of Illinois Board of Trustees*, 781 F. Supp. 2d 672 (N.D. Ill. March 7, 2011), *vacated*, 680 F.3d 1001 (7th Cir. 2012), a newspaper claimed that the state's Freedom of Information Act required the University of Illinois to disclose a list of applicants and their test scores and grade point averages, the names of their parents, and the name of anyone who intervened on the applicants' behalf after a scandal involving a "clout list" of applicants who received favored treatment was discovered. The open records law exempts the release of information that is "specifically prohibited from disclosure by federal . . . law or rules and regulations implementing federal . . . law" (5 Ill. Comp. Stat 140/7(1)(a)). The newspaper argued, among other claims, that FERPA does not prohibit the release of education records. Because the university had asserted that FERPA did not allow such a release, the litigation was brought in federal court.

The trial court ruled for the newspaper. The judge noted that FERPA does not "forbid Illinois officials from taking any action," but "sets conditions on the receipt of federal funds" and "imposes requirements on the Secretary of Education to enforce the spending conditions by withholding funds in appropriate situations." Although the court nodded toward the "potential privacy interests implicated by the Tribune's request," it noted that it was construing the exemptions to the state's Freedom of Information Act narrowly, and awarded summary judgment to the newspaper. The university appealed this ruling, and the appellate court vacated the trial court's judgment, ruling that the case should have been brought in state court because interpretation of the state's freedom of information law was a state, not a federal, matter.

In Arizona, a state trial court ruled that Pima Community College had to turn over written communications regarding Jared Lee Loughner, a former student who shot and killed or wounded several people in Tucson, Arizona, including Representative Gabrielle Giffords. In *Phoenix Newspapers Inc. v. Pima Community College*, Case No. C20111954 (Ariz. Super. Ct., Pima County May 17, 2011), the court parsed the meaning of language in FERPA that defines education records as those "maintained by an educational agency or institution." The court ruled that e-mail messages sent and received by college staff members regarding Loughner were not "maintained" by the college because "documents are not 'maintained' by an educational institution under FERPA unless the institution has control over the access and retention of the record. Simply because emails exist on a central server and in inboxes at some point does not classify those documents as education records . . . If emails can be removed from the database in question simply by the account holder deleting the email from their inbox then emails that happen to remain on the server by no action of the educational institution are not maintained by the school" (sl. op. at 3). This ruling was not appealed, but has been criticized and is not consistent with FPCO guidance.

Federal and state courts have addressed the question of whether an education record that would otherwise be protected by FERPA loses that protection if identifying information about the student(s) is redacted. The courts have concluded that, if sufficient such redaction is done, FERPA does not apply because it no longer contains "information directly related to a student." See, for example, *United States v. Miami University*, 294 F.3d 797 (6th Cir. 2002); *Osborn v. Board of Regents of University of Wisconsin System*, 647 N.W.2d 158, 168 n.11 (Wis. 2002); *Unincorporated Operating Div. of Indiana Newspapers, Inc. v. Trustees of Indiana Univ.*, 787 N.E.2d 893 (Ind. Ct. App. 2003); and *Board of Trustees v. Cut Bank Pioneer Press*, 160 P.3d 482 (Mont. 2007). The FERPA regulations now expressly state this same principle (34 C.F.R. § 99.31(b)(1)).

Despite the outcome in the *Miami Student* case, it appears that the clash between open records laws and FERPA will continue, and outcomes may differ from state to state unless the U.S. Supreme Court resolves the conflict.

# 8

# Student Academic Issues

*Chapter 8 discusses issues that arise in the context of evaluating students. It examines the faculty's right—and obligation—to evaluate students and the institution's right to develop academic standards. It also discusses student challenges to these evaluations and standards. The chapter then addresses issues related to online programs, with particular emphasis on student legal claims involving online programs. The chapter then turns to academic accommodations for students with disabilities in domestic programs, study abroad programs, and online programs. The problem of sexual harassment of students by faculty members is examined, and finally, student challenges to academic dismissals, and the various legal theories they use to attempt to reverse these decisions, are addressed.*

## Section 8.1. Overview

Fewer legal restrictions pertain to an institution's application of academic standards to students than to its application of behavioral standards (see Chapter 9). Courts are more deferential to academia when evaluation of academic work is the issue, believing that such evaluation resides in the expertise of the faculty rather than the court.

This deference, however, does not discourage students from challenging decisions concerning their academic performance or issues that arise in the classroom. Section 8.2 discusses cases challenging grades and other academic judgments of students by faculty and academic administrators. Section 8.3 addresses the special (and in some cases, poorly understood) legal issues that arise in online courses. The conflict over academic accommodations for students with disabilities is reviewed in Section 8.4, and the seemingly perennial problem of sexual harassment of students by faculty members is addressed in Section 8.5. The various types of challenges to academic dismissals are reviewed in Section 8.6.

Despite the fact that judicial review of academic judgments is more deferential than judicial review of discipline for student misconduct, courts do require institutions to comply with their own rules, policies, and procedures, and to examine the foundations for academic decisions to determine whether they are based on genuine academic judgments. Faculty and administrators should ensure that they adhere to these requirements, and that they fully inform students of their procedural rights for challenging academic decisions.

## Section 8.2. Grading and Academic Standards

When a student alleges that a grade has been awarded improperly or that credits or a degree have been denied unfairly, the court must determine whether the defendant's action reflected the application of academic judgment or an arbitrary or unfair application of institutional policy. If the court is satisfied that the decision involved the evenhanded application of academic judgment, the court will typically defer to the institution's decision. But if the student can demonstrate arbitrary, discriminatory, or bad faith actions on the part of faculty or administrators, then the court will scrutinize the decision and may not defer to the institution's decision. Students challenging academic decisions at public institutions generally attempt to state constitutional due process claims, whereas students challenging decisions at private institutions usually allege breach of contract.

*Connelly v. University of Vermont*, 244 F. Supp. 156 (D. Vt. 1965), set the standard for judicial review of an academic decision. In *Connelly*, a medical student challenged his dismissal from medical school. He had failed the pediatrics-obstetrics course and was dismissed, under a College of Medicine rule, for having failed 25 percent or more of his major third-year courses. The court described its role and the institution's legal obligation in such cases as follows:

> Where a medical student has been dismissed for a failure to attain a proper standard of scholarship, two questions may be involved; the first is, was the student in fact delinquent in his studies or unfit for the practice of medicine? The second question is, were the school authorities motivated by malice or bad faith in dismissing the student, or did they act arbitrarily or capriciously? In general, the first question is not a matter for judicial review. However, a student dismissal motivated by bad faith, arbitrariness, or capriciousness may be actionable . . .
>
> This rule has been stated in a variety of ways by a number of courts. It has been said that courts do not interfere with the management of a school's internal affairs unless "there has been a manifest abuse of discretion or where [the school officials'] action has been arbitrary or unlawful" . . . or unless the school authorities have acted "arbitrarily or capriciously" . . . or unless they have abused their discretion . . . or acted in "bad faith" [citations omitted].
>
> The effect of these decisions is to give the school authorities absolute discretion in determining whether a student has been delinquent in his studies, and to place the burden on the student of showing that his dismissal was

motivated by arbitrariness, capriciousness, or bad faith. The reason for this rule is that, in matters of scholarship, the school authorities are uniquely qualified by training and experience to judge the qualifications of a student, and efficiency of instruction depends in no small degree upon the school's faculty's freedom from interference from other noneducational tribunals. It is only when the school authorities abuse this discretion that a court may interfere with their decision to dismiss a student [244 F. Supp. at 159–60].

The plaintiff alleged that his instructor had decided before completion of the course to fail the plaintiff regardless of the quality of his work. The court held that these allegations met its requirements for judicial review. The allegations therefore stated a cause of action, which if proven at trial would justify the entry of judgment against the college.

The U.S. Supreme Court has twice addressed the subject of the standard of review of academic judgments at public institutions. In the first case, *Board of Curators of the University of Missouri v. Horowitz*, 435 U.S. 78 (1978), a dismissed medical student claimed that the school applied stricter standards to her because of her sex, religion, and physical appearance. Referring particularly to *Gaspar v. Bruton*, 513 F.2d 843 (10th Cir. 1975), the Court rejected the claim in language inhospitable to substantive judicial review of academic decisions:

> A number of lower courts have implied in dictum that academic dismissals from state institutions can be enjoined if "shown to be clearly arbitrary or capricious." . . . Courts are particularly ill equipped to evaluate academic performance. The factors discussed . . . with respect to procedural due process [see Section 9.3.2] speak a fortiori here and warn against any such judicial intrusion into academic decision making [435 U.S. at 91–92].

In the second case, in which the Court relied heavily on *Horowitz*, a student filed a substantive due process challenge to his academic dismissal from medical school. The student, whose overall record of academic performance in medical school was mediocre, asserted that the school's refusal to allow him to retake the National Board of Medical Examiners examination violated his constitutional rights because other students had been allowed to retake the exam. In *Regents of the University of Michigan v. Ewing*, 474 U.S. 214 (1985) (discussed in Section 8.6.3), the Court assumed without deciding that Ewing had a property interest in continued enrollment in medical school. The Court noted that it was not the school's procedures that were under review—the question was "whether the record compels the conclusion that the University acted arbitrarily in dropping Ewing from the Inteflex program without permitting a reexamination" (474 U.S. at 225). The court then stated:

> Ewing's claim, therefore, must be that the University misjudged his fitness to remain a student in the Inteflex program. The record unmistakably demonstrates, however, that the faculty's decision was made conscientiously and with careful deliberation, based on an evaluation of the entirety of Ewing's academic career [474 U.S. at 225].

Citing *Horowitz*, the Court emphasized:

> When judges are asked to review the substance of a genuinely academic decision, such as this one, they should show great respect for the faculty's professional judgment. Plainly, they may not override it unless it is such a substantial departure from accepted academic norms as to demonstrate that the person or committee responsible did not actually exercise professional judgment [474 U.S. at 225].

Citing *Keyishian v. Board of Regents*, 385 U.S. 589 (1967) (discussed in Section 6.1.1), the Court also reminded the parties that concerns about institutional academic freedom limited the nature of judicial review of substantive academic judgments.

In addition to constitutional claims of lack of procedural or substantive due process, such as the claims in *Horowitz* and *Ewing*, courts may resolve legal questions concerning the award of grades, credits, or degrees by applying not only standards of arbitrariness or bad faith but also the terms of the student-institution contract (see Section 7.1.3 of this book). Statements in the catalog reserving the institution's right to make changes in programs, graduation requirements, or grading policy provide important protections in breach of contract claims (see, for example, *Bender v. Alderson-Broaddus College*, 575 S.E.2d 112 (W. Va. 2002), in which the court rejected a nursing student's claim that the college's decision to change its grading policy was arbitrary and capricious).

An example of a court's refusal to defer to a college's interpretation of its catalog or policy documents is *Russell v. Salve Regina College*, 890 F.2d 484 (1st Cir. 1989). Sharon Russell was asked to withdraw from the nursing program at the college because the administrators believed her obesity was unsatisfactory for a nursing student. Russell's academic performance in all but one course was satisfactory or better; the instructor in one clinical course gave her a failing grade, which the jury found was related to her weight, not to her performance. Although the nursing program's rules specified that failing a clinical course would result in expulsion, the college promised Russell that she could remain in the program if she would sign a contract promising to lose weight on a regular basis. She did so, and attended Weight Watchers during that year, but did not lose weight. At the end of her junior year, Russell was asked to withdraw from Salve Regina, and she transferred to a nursing program at another college, where she was required to repeat her junior year because of a two-year residency requirement. She completed her nursing degree, but in five years rather than four.

Although the trial judge dismissed her tort claims of intentional infliction of emotional distress and invasion of privacy (stemming from administrators' conduct regarding her obesity), the contract claim was submitted to the jury, which found for Russell and awarded her approximately $144,000. On appeal, the court discussed the terms of the contract:

> From the various catalogs, manuals, handbooks, etc., that form the contract between student and institution, the district court, in its jury charge, boiled the agreement between the parties down to one in which Russell on the one hand was required to abide by disciplinary rules, pay tuition, and maintain good academic standing, and the College on the other hand was required to provide

her with an education until graduation. The court informed the jury that the agreement was modified by the "contract" the parties signed during Russell's junior year. The jury was told that, if Russell "substantially performed" her side of the bargain, the College's actions constituted a breach [890 F.2d at 488].

The college had objected to the trial court's use of commercial contract principles of substantial performance rather than using a more deferential approach. But the appellate court disagreed, noting that the college's actions were based not on academic judgments but on a belief that the student's weight was inappropriate, despite the fact that the college knew of the student's obesity when it admitted her to both the college and the nursing program:

> Under the circumstances, the "unique" position of the College as educator becomes less compelling. As a result, the reasons against applying the substantial performance standard to this aspect of the student-college relationship also become less compelling. Thus, Salve Regina's contention that a court cannot use the substantial performance standard to compel an institution to graduate a student merely because the student has completed 124 out of 128 credits, while correct, is inapposite. The court may step in where, as here, full performance by the student has been hindered by some form of impermissible action [890 F.2d at 489].

Russell was not asking the court to award her a degree; she was asking for contract damages, which included one year of forgone income (while she attended the other college for the extra year). The appellate court found that this portion of the award, $25,000, was appropriate.

Courts appear increasingly willing to regard graduate program policies and rules as contracts (see, for example, the *Johnson v. Yale University* case discussed in Section 8.6.2). And in many states, a promise of good faith and fair dealing is an implied term in all contracts. In *Onawola v. Johns Hopkins University*, 412 F. Supp. 2d 529 (D. Md. 2006), *affirmed*, 221 F. App'x 211 (4th Cir. 2007), a doctoral student who had completed all of his requirements except his dissertation sued the university for breach of contract and race discrimination when it refused to extend the deadline for the completion of his dissertation. The university had already allowed the plaintiff fourteen years to complete his degree, but had not approved his dissertation because he had not included some elements, such as a survey, that his committee told him to include. The court distinguished the (few) cases in which courts had ordered the institution to award the degree because in those cases the students had completed all of their academic requirements. The court ruled that the university had made numerous accommodations for the plaintiff, "above and beyond any reasonably-imagined contractual requirement," including extending deadlines several times, and providing expertise and advice. The court noted that many of the issues of which the plaintiff complained

> are academic judgments, properly left to the faculty of the University, not [the plaintiff], and certainly not this court. No implied contract which might exist here could be understood to waive the University's right to maintain stringent academic standards; nothing in the record suggests that the faculty acted in an arbitrary or capricious manner toward [the plaintiff] [412 F. Supp. 2d at 533].

Although infrequent, challenges to grades or examination results have been brought by students. For example, in *Olsson v. Board of Higher Education of the City of New York*, 402 N.E.2d 1150 (N.Y. 1980), a student had not passed a comprehensive examination and therefore had not been awarded the master of arts degree for which he had been working. He claimed that his professor had misled him about the required passing grade on the examination. The professor had meant to say that a student must score three out of a possible five points on four of the five questions; instead, the professor had said that a student must pass three of five questions. The student invoked the "estoppel" doctrine—the doctrine that justifiable reliance on a statement or promise estops the other from contradicting it if the reliance led directly to a detriment or injustice to the promisee. He argued that (1) he had justifiably relied on the professor's statement in budgeting both his study and test time, (2) he had achieved the grade the professor had stated was necessary, and (3) injustice would result if the university was not estopped from denying the degree.

The trial court and the intermediate appellate court both accepted the student's argument. The state's highest appellate court, however, did not. Deferring to the academic judgment of the institution, and emphasizing that the institution had offered the student an opportunity to retake the exam, the court refused to grant a "degree by estoppel." Although conceding that principles of apparent authority and agency law would be relevant in a noneducational context, the court stated that

> such hornbook rules cannot be applied mechanically where the "principal" is an educational institution and the result would be to override a determination concerning a student's academic qualifications. Because such determinations rest in most cases upon the subjective professional judgment of trained educators, the courts have quite properly exercised the utmost restraint in applying traditional legal rules to disputes within the academic community . . .
>
> This judicial reluctance to intervene in controversies involving academic standards is founded upon sound considerations of public policy. When an educational institution issues a diploma to one of its students, it is, in effect, certifying to society that the student possesses all of the knowledge and skills that are required by his chosen discipline. In order for society to be able to have complete confidence in the credentials dispensed by academic institutions, however, it is essential that the decisions surrounding the issuance of these credentials be left to the sound judgment of the professional educators who monitor the progress of their students on a regular basis. Indeed, the value of these credentials from the point of view of society would be seriously undermined if the courts were to abandon their longstanding practice of restraint in this area and instead began to utilize traditional equitable estoppel principles as a basis for requiring institutions to confer diplomas upon those who have been deemed to be unqualified [402 N.E.2d at 1152–53].

Although the court refused to apply the estoppel doctrine to the particular facts of this case, it indicated that in other, more extreme, circumstances estoppel could apply to problems concerning grading and other academic judgments. The court compared Olsson's situation to that of the plaintiff in *Blank v. Board of Higher Education of the City of New York*, 273 N.Y.S.2d 7, in which the student had completed all academic requirements for his bachelor's degree but had not spent his final term "in residence." The student demonstrated reliance on the incorrect advice of several advisors and faculty members, and had failed to satisfy only a technical requirement, rather than an academic one. The court explained:

> The outstanding feature which differentiates *Blank* from the instant case is the unavoidable fact that in *Blank* the student unquestionably had fulfilled the academic requirements for the credential he sought. Unlike the student here, the student in *Blank* had demonstrated his competence in the subject matter to the satisfaction of his professors. Thus, there could be no public policy objection to [the court's] decision to award a "diploma by estoppel" [402 N.E.2d at 1154].

The *Olsson* case thus provides both an extensive justification of "academic deference"—that is, judicial deference to an educational institution's academic judgments—and an extensive analysis of the circumstances in which courts, rather than deferring, should invoke estoppel principles to protect students challenging academic decisions.

A college or university may decide not to award a degree, even if the student has completed all academic requirements satisfactorily, because the student has violated the institution's disciplinary code. In *Rosenthal v. New York University*, 2010 U.S. Dist. LEXIS 95080 (S.D.N.Y. November 13, 2010), *affirmed*, 2012 U.S. App. LEXIS 9817 (2d Cir. May 16, 2012)(unpublished), Rosenthal had completed all of his course work for the MBA degree from NYU. Unbeknownst to the business school faculty and dean, Rosenthal, who worked for Pricewaterhouse Coopers, had pleaded guilty to conspiracy to commit securities fraud by providing "insider information" about a publicly traded company to his brother. Rosenthal did not advise NYU that he was under investigation for securities fraud or that he pleaded guilty to conspiracy to commit securities fraud. NYU learned of Rosenthal's guilty plea, and charged him with a violation of the student code of conduct. A hearing was held (after Rosenthal was released from prison) and the business school's Judiciary Committee found that he had violated both the school's honor code and its code of conduct and recommended that he not be awarded the degree. The faculty concurred, and Rosenthal sued for breach of contract and a declaration that the degree had been awarded.

The court reviewed all of the steps taken by NYU to consider whether Rosenthal should be awarded the degree and found that the school had complied with its policies, that the process followed was fair to the plaintiff, and that the faculty had the authority to decide whether or not to award degrees. NYU, said the court, had no contractual obligation to award Rosenthal the MBA degree. (For additional cases rejecting students' challenges to the denial of their degrees on these grounds, see *Harwood v. Johns Hopkins University*, 747 A.2d

205 (Md. Ct. Spec. App. 2000), discussed in Section 7.1.3 of this book; *Dinu v. Harvard College*, 56 F. Supp. 2d 129 (D. Mass. 1999); and *Burch v. Moulton*, 980 So.2d 392 (Ala. 2008)).

Although rare, students occasionally challenge the grade given in one or more courses. Such a challenge to grades in two law school courses provided the New York courts with an opportunity to address another issue similar to that in *Olsson* (discussed above)—the standard of review to be used when students challenge particular grades. In *In the Matter of Susan M. v. New York Law School*, 544 N.Y.S.2d 829 (N.Y. App. Div. 1989), *reversed*, 556 N.E.2d 1104 (N.Y. 1990), a law student dismissed for inadequate academic performance sought judicial review of her grades in her constitutional law and corporations courses. The student claimed that she had received poor grades because of errors made by the professors in both courses. In the constitutional law course, she alleged, the professor gave incorrect instructions on whether the exam was open book; in the corporations course, the professor evaluated a correct answer as incorrect. The law school asserted that these allegations were beyond judicial review because they were a matter of professional discretion.

Although Susan M.'s claims were dismissed by the trial court, the intermediate appellate court disagreed with the law school's characterization of both grade disputes as beyond judicial review. It agreed that the dispute over the constitutional law examination was "precisely the type of professional, educational judgment the courts will not review" (544 N.Y.S.2d at 830); but the student's claim regarding her answer in the corporations exam, for which she received no credit, was a different matter. The court ruled that the student's allegation that the professor's decision had been arbitrary and capricious required the court to determine whether the professor's justification for giving the student no credit for one of her answers was "rational." The court remanded this issue to the law school for further consideration of petitioner's grade in the corporations course. The law school appealed, and the state's highest court unanimously reversed the appellate division's holding, reinstating the outcome in the trial court.

The court strongly endorsed the academic deference argument made by the law school, stating in the opinion's first paragraph: "Because [the plaintiff's] allegations are directed at the pedagogical evaluation of her test grades, a determination best left to educators rather than the courts, we conclude that her petition does not state a judicially cognizable claim" (556 N.E.2d at 1105). After reviewing the outcomes in earlier challenges to the academic determinations of colleges and universities, the state's highest court stated:

> As a general rule, judicial review of grading disputes would inappropriately
> involve the courts in the very core of academic and educational decision
> making. Moreover, to so involve the courts in assessing the propriety
> of particular grades would promote litigation by countless unsuccessful
> students and thus undermine the credibility of the academic determinations
> of educational institutions. We conclude, therefore, that, in the absence
> of demonstrated bad faith, arbitrariness, capriciousness, irrationality or a

constitutional or statutory violation, a student's challenge to a particular grade
or other academic determination relating to a genuine substantive evaluation of
the student's academic capabilities, is beyond the scope of judicial review
[556 N.E.2d at 1107].

Concluding that the plaintiff's claims concerned substantive evaluation of her
academic performance, the court refused to review them.

Student attempts to challenge a school's system of grading have met with
similar judicial skepticism. In *Keefe v. New York Law School*, 897 N.Y.S. 2d 94
(N.Y. App. Div. 2010), the student had transferred from another law school, and
claimed that he was disadvantaged because the law school refused to allow a
pass/fail grade to be given in his legal writing class. The student sought a court
order to require the law school to change its grading system. Not surprisingly,
the trial court dismissed his claim, saying that there was no implied contract to
grade him on a pass/fail basis and noting that the student handbook explicitly
stated that letter grades would be used. The court did not defer to the expertise of the faculty, but analyzed the student's allegations as a simple breach of
contract claim.

Students' attempts to challenge course requirements have also met with
judicial rejection. In *Altschuler v. University of Pennsylvania Law School*, 1997
U.S. Dist. LEXIS 3248 (S.D.N.Y. March 21, 1997), *affirmed without opinion*,
201 F.3d 430 (3d Cir. 1999), for example, a law student who had just graduated challenged a failing grade he received in his first year. The grade resulted
from the plaintiff's refusal to argue a "mock" case in a legal writing class on
the grounds of moral and ethical objections. The plaintiff claimed that the
professor "promised" him that he could argue and brief the opposite side but
later retracted her promise. When the plaintiff refused to argue the assigned
side, he received a failing grade in the course. The court dismissed all contract
and tort claims based on the failing grade, saying that the professor's "breach
of promise" was an academic decision, which had been reviewed by a faculty
committee and found to be appropriate.

And in *Disesa v. St. Louis Community College*, 79 F.3d 92 (8th Cir. 1996),
the court rejected a student's challenge to a particular grade based on alleged
"administrative deficiencies" in the testing process, including typographical
errors in the materials and test questions, testing on materials not covered in
class, an inability to review quizzes after they were graded, and arbitrary implementation of a class policy prohibiting erasure marks. Despite the plaintiff's
argument that these were not "academic" decisions per se, the court disagreed
and deferred to the college's actions. (For a contrasting example, in which a
student does successfully challenge a course requirement (on First Amendment
grounds), see the *Axson-Flynn* case, discussed in Section 7.1.4 of this book.)

Courts also have refused to review certain challenges to grades on the
basis that the claims were "frivolous." But in *Sylvester v. Texas Southern
University*, 957 F. Supp. 944 (S.D. Tex. 1997), a federal district court ordered
a law student's grade changed to a "Pass" from a D because the law school
had not followed its procedures for adjudicating a grade dispute. The law

school's rules provided that, if a student appealed a grade to the Academic Standing Committee, the committee was required to review the disputed grade. Neither the professor who gave the disputed grade nor the Academic Standing Committee complied with university regulations. The court criticized the institution and the professor for flouting the institution's own policies and procedures: "Between active manipulation and sullen intransigence, the faculty, embodying arbitrary government, have mistreated a student confided to their charge. This violates their duty to conduct the public's business in a rationally purposeful manner" (957 F. Supp. at 947).

Another type of claim sometimes alleged by students is a retaliation claim based on some kind of "bad faith" action by university personnel. In *Ross v. Saint Augustine's College*, 103 F.3d 338 (4th Cir. 1996), a federal appeals court upheld a jury award of $180,000 against a college for harassing an honors student who testified on behalf of a professor in a reverse discrimination suit against the institution. The court held that Leslie Ross "experienced a sudden reversal of fortune at Saint Augustine's College" when her grade point average fell from 3.69/4.0 to 2.2/4.0. The administration called a sudden student body meeting to impeach Ross as class president, and ultimately Ross was not able to graduate. Although the case involved only monetary damages, there is no indication that courts would afford deference to the academic decisions made under those circumstances had the student challenged the college's failure to award her a degree. (For additional cases in which students challenged specific course grades using retaliation theories, see *Davis v. Goode*, 995 F. Supp. 82 (E.D.N.Y. 1998) (court denied college's motion for summary judgment); and *Mostaghim v. Fashion Institute of Technology*, 2002 U.S. Dist. LEXIS 10968 (S.D.N.Y. 2002), *affirmed*, 57 F. App'x 497 (2d Cir. 2003) (court rejected student's claim that course requirement to design women's wear rather than men's wear constituted a Title IX violation, and that his subsequent grade of C and suspension from the institution were a form of retaliation under Title IX).)

### Section 8.3. Online Programs

**8.3.1. Overview.** Distance learning, or online education, programs have proliferated in the United States and around the world. Although the technology for transmitting information (and receiving student assignments) may differ from traditional face-to-face, time-bound instruction, many of the legal issues are the same, although they may arise in a different context. But new legal issues have also arisen that require institutions—and courts—to struggle to apply "old" law in new ways and to create new protections and requirements.

Issues that may have been settled for decades, such as who "owns" the course material for a faculty member's course taught in the traditional way, may differ when that course is offered in an online format. Students who enroll in an institution where they have never been physically present may still be required to follow the code of student conduct, but how should a disciplinary hearing be conducted when the student resides in a different state? How can the college ensure that students with disabilities—particularly visual impairments—can access the distance learning technology and participate fully in these programs? (Access by students with disabilities to course Web sites and other technology is discussed in Section 8.4.2.3). And the technology itself may also create legal problems for the college, particularly if it does not operate correctly or is subject to "hacking" by unauthorized individuals.

Faculty and administrators may need to adapt their policies and practices to respond to students' allegations of online sexual harassment (by faculty or by student peers) and to suspicions that someone other than the enrolled student is completing assignments and tests. Under what circumstances might an online discussion group be considered a limited public forum (see Section 9.4.2)? These and other issues will need to be addressed in light of the constraints, and opportunities, presented by the technology and process of online education.

There have been very few published court opinions on these matters, but the amount of federal regulation is increasing, and the sheer number of students and institutions that are involved in online learning makes it incumbent upon faculty and administrators to address these questions and respond in ways that limit liability—and prevent litigation in the first place.

### 8.3.2. Student legal claims about online programs. 

Many of the legal issues that arise in an online learning environment are the same as, or similar to, those that arise in traditional academic settings. Student academic dishonesty can be an issue in online education just as it is in traditional settings. Students' failure to follow online education protocols with respect to civil online discourse may lead to sanctions. Codes of student conduct should address the institution's expectations for honesty and civil behavior in online course settings as well as in traditional ones, and the institution's code of conduct may be applied to students who enroll in online courses. Conducting a "hearing" for a student who lives at a distance from the campus may be challenging, but the online student is entitled to the same due process or contractual protections as a student who is physically present on campus, unless the institution has created a different code of conduct for online students.

An example of the application of an institution's student code of conduct to a student enrolled in an online program is *Baird v. State University of New York*, 2011 U.S. Dist. LEXIS 5182 (N.D.N.Y. January 20, 2011). Baird, an online student at Empire State University (New York) living in Maryland, had engaged in two incidents of e-mail harassment addressed to faculty and to a dean, and was charged with a conduct code violation. A hearing required by the code of conduct was held before the Student Conduct Committee, in which Baird, the student, participated by telephone. The committee recommended expulsion, based upon Baird's misconduct. Baird exercised his right to appeal the committee's recommendation, but the provost agreed with the committee. Baird then sued, claiming race discrimination under Title VI (see Section 11.5.2) and due process violations. Finding no evidence of race discrimination and holding that Baird received appropriate due process, the court awarded summary judgment to the university.

Another example of the application of an institution's code of conduct to online communications occurred in *Harrell v. Southern Oregon University*, 2010 U.S. Dist. LEXIS 57162 (D. Or. March 20, 2010), *affirmed*, 381 F. App'x 731 (9th Cir. 2011). Harrell was a student in a traditional on-campus course, but the course required students to participate in online discussions about course material. Harrell made abusive, ad hominem attacks on some of the students in the online discussion forum. He was charged with violating a provision of the student code of conduct that prohibited

> [d]isruption, obstruction or interference with educational activities in classrooms, lecture halls, campus library, laboratories, computer laboratories, theatres, or any other place where education and teaching activities take place including, but not limited to, talking at inappropriate times, drawing unwarranted attention to self, engaging in loud or distracting behaviors, displaying defiance or disrespect of others, or threatening any University student or employee.

A student conduct hearing was held, which the plaintiff refused to attend, and he was found responsible for violating the code. After engaging in similar behavior in a second class, a second charge was made against the plaintiff, a hearing was held (again he did not attend), and he was placed on probation. The student then filed a lawsuit claiming that the university had denied his constitutional rights of free speech and due process, and demanding a preliminary injunction to require the university to cease enforcing the conduct code provision, which he alleged was unconstitutional.

The trial court rejected the student's constitutional claims and denied the motion for a preliminary injunction, explaining that the punishment was not for speech, but for behavior. The court explained that the university had not prohibited Harrell from communicating, but objected to his behavior. The court remarked, "Harrell remains free to express his thoughts. He has simply been asked to do so in a mature manner" (2010 U.S. Dist. LEXIS at *18–19). The court denied that Harrell had either a property or liberty interest, stating that he was not entitled to a public postsecondary education and that he was not subjected to embarrassment or ridicule, which could have given rise to a liberty interest. And finally, the process provided before and during the hearings on his conduct code violations satisfied the requirements of *Goss v. Lopez* (see Section 9.3.2.1 of this book), according to the court. The appellate court affirmed without comment on the merits.

Students attempting to state claims against institutions that host distance learning courses may have jurisdictional problems if they attempt to sue the college in the state in which the student resides, but where the college is not physically present. State laws differ on this matter, but generally examine whether the college was doing business in the state or merely gave students in that state access to its Web site. For cases denying jurisdiction, see *Kloth v. Southern Christian University*, 320 F. App'x 113 (3d Cir. 2008), and *Marten v. Godwin*, 499 F.3d 290 (3d Cir. 2007). And for a contrasting result, see

*Watiti v. Walden University*, 2008 U.S. Dist. LEXIS 43217 (D.N.J. May 20, 2008) (although the plaintiff did not prevail on the merits).

Occasionally faculty may allege that issues related to distance learning have legal consequences. For example, in *Hentea v. The Trustees of Purdue University*, 2006 U.S. Dist. LEXIS 25599 (N.D. Ind. May 1, 2006), a faculty member who was not reappointed sued the university for national origin, age, and sex discrimination, alleging, among other claims, that the department chair's requirement that she administer examinations for an online course online, rather than requiring students to come to campus, was a violation of her "academic freedom" and was sexual harassment. The court awarded summary judgment to the university on that and the remaining discrimination claims.

## Section 8.4. Academic Accommodations for Students with Disabilities

**8.4.1. Overview.** As noted in Section 11.5.4 of this book, Section 504 of the Rehabilitation Act and the Americans with Disabilities Act (ADA) of 1990 require colleges and universities to provide reasonable academic accommodations for qualified students with disabilities. Although the laws do not require institutions to change their academic criteria for disabled students, institutions may need to change the format of tests; to provide additional time, or readers or aides, to help students take examinations; or to change minor aspects of course requirements.

Lawsuits filed by students who assert that a college or university has not accommodated their disabilities have mushroomed. Although courts have addressed claims involving a wide range of disabilities, the largest proportion involve learning disabilities and academic accommodations, such as additional time on tests (or a different test format), waiver of required courses or prerequisites, and, in some cases, waiver of certain portions of the curriculum. Students in elementary and secondary education have been entitled to accommodations for physical, psychological, and learning disorders since the 1975 enactment of the Education for All Handicapped Children Act (Pub. L. No. 94-142), which was renamed the Individuals with Disabilities Education Act (IDEA) in 1990 and amended by the Individuals with Disabilities Education Improvement Act of 2004, Pub. L. No. 108-446. Many of the students who have received special services and other accommodations under this law are now enrolled in college and, due to their experiences with IDEA services, may have heightened expectations about receiving services at the postsecondary level as well.

Although the IDEA does not apply to a disabled student once he or she has completed high school or has reached the age of twenty-one (whichever occurs first), such students continue to be protected in higher education by Section 504 of the Rehabilitation Act of 1973 and by the Americans with Disabilities Act (ADA). As is the case with disputes over the admission of students with disabilities (see Section 7.2.4.3 of this book), issues related to classroom accommodations, testing issues, and accommodations for licensing examinations have multiplied in recent years, in part because of the expectations and aspirations of students who have grown up with IDEA.

In 2001, the U.S. Supreme Court ruled that the employment provisions of the ADA are subject to Eleventh Amendment immunity in *University of Alabama v. Garrett*, 531 U.S. 356 (2001) (discussed in Section 4.5.2.5). This means that public institutions cannot be sued for money damages under the ADA in federal court under Title I of the act. Federal appellate courts have applied the reasoning of *Garrett* to lawsuits brought against a university under Title II of the ADA, which forbids discrimination by public entities, including colleges and universities. For example, in *Robinson v. University of Akron School of Law*, 307 F.3d 409 (6th Cir. 2002), the student brought claims under both the ADA and the Rehabilitation Act, alleging that the law school had failed to provide accommodations to which the student was entitled as a result of his learning disability. The court ruled that the university had waived sovereign immunity against Rehabilitation Act claims, but that it was protected from ADA suits in federal court under the result in *Garrett*. In *United States v. Georgia*, 546 U.S. 151 (2006), however, the Supreme Court ruled that Congress had validly abrogated sovereign immunity for claims alleging conduct that would violate the Fourteenth Amendment, which suggests that students who claim that their due process or equal protection rights have been violated because of their disability may be able to state claims in federal court against public institutions under the ADA.

In order to receive the protections of either Section 504 or the ADA, a student must demonstrate that he or she has a disability that meets the statutory requirements. The ADA defines disability as "a physical or mental impairment that substantially limits one or more of the major life activities" of the individual, or "a record of such an impairment," or "being regarded as having such an impairment" (42 U.S.C. § 12102(2)). Whether or not an individual is disabled for ADA purposes is to be determined on an individualized basis (29 C.F.R. § 1630.21(j)). The definition of disability used in Section 504 is the same as the ADA definition (34 C.F.R. § 104.3(j)). Although most cases do not involve this issue (in contrast to employment litigation under the ADA, in which a common employer defense is that the individual's disorder does not meet the ADA definition; see Section 4.5.2.5 of this book), it is useful to remember that the institution is entitled to inquire into the nature of the disability, to require documentation of the disability, and to reach its own determination as to whether the disorder is a disability that requires accommodation under the ADA or Section 504.

The amendments to the ADA, discussed in Section 4.5.2.5 of this book, have broadened the definition of "disability" and made it easier for students to demonstrate that their disorder meets the law's definition. For that reason, cases decided prior to the effective date of the amendments on the ground that the student was not disabled provide limited guidance as to how courts may rule now that the amendments are in effect. The law did not, however, change the definition of a "qualified individual with a disability." And regulations implementing Section 504 of the Rehabilitation Act define a "qualified" individual with a disability as one who "meets the academic and technical standards requisite to admission or participation" (34 C.F.R. § 104.3(l)(3)). Students who cannot meet these standards, even with a reasonable accommodation, are not protected by either the ADA or Section 504.

*Zukle v. Regents of the University of California*, 166 F.3d 1041 (9th Cir. 1999), addresses this issue. Zukle, a medical student who had learning disabilities and who had received numerous accommodations but still could not meet the school's academic standards, was unable to convince the court that she could meet the eligibility requirements of the medical school, even with reasonable accommodations. The court ruled that the student's requested accommodation—lengthening the time during which she could complete her medical degree—would lower the school's academic standards, which is not required by either the ADA or the Rehabilitation Act.

At the time that this book went to press, few court opinions interpreting the amended ADA had been published. One example, however, suggests that courts will be less willing to award summary judgment to colleges, particularly if the claim is that the student's disorder does not meet the act's definition of a disability. In *Jenkins v. National Board of Medical Examiners*, 2009 U.S. App. LEXIS 2660 (6th Cir. February 11, 2009) (unpublished), a federal appellate court reversed the trial court's award of summary judgment to the National Board of Medical Examiners (NBME) on a student's claim that the board had not provided him with the accommodations he needed to take a standardized test. The lower court had followed previous Supreme Court rulings, overturned by the ADA amendments, that had required courts to consider mitigating measures in determining whether or not an individual had a disability that met the law's definition. The amendments to the ADA specifically prohibit considering mitigating measures in determining whether an individual's disorder meets the ADA's definition of disability. In *Jenkins*, the trial court had determined that the plaintiff was not disabled. The appellate court made no findings with respect to the merits, but remanded the case to the trial court to reconsider the plaintiff's claims in light of the new definition of "disability" contained in the amended ADA.

The amendments to the ADA, however, have not changed the requirement that a student must demonstrate that a disorder "substantially limits" a major life activity in order to meet the definition of "disabled." For example, a surgical resident's subsequent academic and professional success after being dismissed from a residency program by the University of Cincinnati persuaded a court that he was not disabled. In *Swanson v. University of Cincinnati*, 268 F.3d 307 (6th Cir. 2001), a federal appellate court rejected the former resident's ADA and Rehabilitation Act claims against the university, observing that the limitations posed by his depression were not the reason for his termination from the residency program, and his subsequent success at another university's residency program demonstrated that his depression did not substantially limit his ability to work. The reasoning of this case would appear to be unaffected by the changes in the ADA.

The ADA also protects students against discrimination when they are erroneously regarded as disabled. In *Lee v. Trustees of Dartmouth College*, 958 F.

Supp. 37 (D.N.H. 1997), a student contended that his professors and academic advisors regarded him as disabled and caused him to be dismissed from his medical residency. The plaintiff, a resident in neurosurgery, developed a disorder that mimicked the symptoms of multiple sclerosis (MS). Although the resident provided medical documentation that his condition was not MS, and also disputed the defendants' contention that he could not perform surgery, he was dismissed from the residency program. The court found that the medical school had not followed its own procedures, which included a meeting with the student to discuss his performance problems and a three-month probationary period. In addition, said the court, issues of material fact existed as to whether the defendants regarded the plaintiff as disabled and as to whether he could perform the physical demands of the neurosurgical residency. The summary judgment motion of the defendants was denied.

An important component of access for students with disabilities is access to instructional materials. The 2008 reauthorization of the Higher Education Act created an Advisory Commission on Accessible Instructional Materials in Postsecondary Education for Students with Disabilities. The commission released a report in 2011 that discusses the challenges posed by copyright law, in particular, to the creation of instructional materials in formats usable by students with certain disabilities. The report may be found at http://www2. ed.gov/about/bdscomm/list/aim/publications.html.

### 8.4.2. Requests for programmatic or other accommodations.

**8.4.2.1. Domestic programs.**  Courts have generally ruled that, unless an institution has knowledge of a student's disability, there is no duty to accommodate. For example, in *Goodwin v. Keuka College*, 929 F. Supp. 90 (W.D.N.Y. 1995), the plaintiff alleged that she had been improperly terminated from an occupational therapy program due to her mental disability. Under the school's policy, if a student failed to complete two field placements, he or she was automatically terminated from the program. The school policy also provided that a student would automatically fail a field placement if he or she left the assignment without prior permission. After failing one field assignment, passing another, and leaving a third incomplete, the plaintiff walked off her fourth field assignment after an argument with her supervisor. Nearly three weeks later, the plaintiff sent a letter to the college explaining that she was seeking an evaluation to determine if she had a learning disability and was eligible for accommodation. The college responded that she had been terminated from the program based on her actions, not on the basis of any disability. Although the plaintiff subsequently produced a psychiatric report that she did have a disability, the college refused to reinstate her. The court dismissed the plaintiff's suit, finding that she could not make out a prima facie case under either the Rehabilitation Act or the ADA because she could not allege she was dismissed on the basis of her disability. For a school to dismiss a student based on her disability, it must first be aware of that disability.

In addition to the institution having knowledge of the disability, courts have ruled that the ADA requires the student to demonstrate that the university has actually denied a specific request for an accommodation. In *Tips v. Regents of Texas Tech University*, 921 F. Supp. 1515 (N.D. Tex. 1996), the court dismissed the plaintiff's claim because it found that she had not requested the accommodation. After examining the relevant legislative history and regulations, the court held that the duty to accommodate is triggered only upon a request by (or on behalf of) the disabled student. Because the plaintiff did not make her request for accommodation until after her dismissal from the program, the court held that the plaintiff could not make out a case of disability discrimination. A similar result was reached in *Gill v. Franklin Pierce Law Center*, discussed in Section 7.2.6 of this book. And in *Scott v. Western State University College of Law*, 1997 U.S. App. LEXIS 9089 (9th Cir. 1997) (unpublished), the appellate court affirmed a trial court's summary judgment on behalf of a law school that had dismissed the plaintiff, Scott, for academic reasons after his first year. After he was dismissed, Scott asserted that he had a disability. The court ruled that the law school's action was unrelated to Scott's disability, since it had no notice of the alleged disability, and that, furthermore, Scott was not "otherwise qualified" for Rehabilitation Act purposes.

In *Di Lella v. University of District of Columbia David A. Clarke School of Law*, 570 F. Supp. 2d 1 (D.D.C. 2008), *dismissed*, 2009 U.S. Dist. LEXIS 90144 (D.D.C. Sept. 30, 2009), the student had been promised a variety of academic accommodations, including permission to tape classroom lectures. The law school had apparently agreed to transcribe the tapes for the student. The student alleged that the transcripts were provided late or not provided at all, which required her to reschedule examinations and disadvantaged her in other ways. She also alleged that the law school's finding that she had engaged in plagiarism was in retaliation for her complaint about a professor's public disclosure to the class that the plaintiff had learning disabilities. The trial court rejected the law school's motion to dismiss the failure to accommodate and retaliation claims.

Although the case was not decided on the merits and was later dismissed for lack of jurisdiction, the trial court's original refusal to dismiss the student's failure to accommodate claim is unusual, given that most students are unsuccessful when they challenge the sufficiency of the academic accommodations they have been given. The difference in this case appears to be that the student claimed that several accommodations she had been promised were not provided, rather than that the accommodations that the school agreed to provide, and did provide, were inadequate.

Institutions are entitled to require students who seek accommodation to provide recent documentation from a qualified health care provider or other appropriate diagnostician not only of the disability, but also of the restrictions or limitations placed on the student by the disability. This issue arose in a widely publicized case, *Guckenberger v. Boston University*, 957 F. Supp. 306 (D. Mass. 1997) (*Guckenberger I*), which ultimately resulted in three lengthy opinions by the district court. Students asserted that Boston University's new policy requiring students to present recent (no more than three years old) documentation of learning disabilities was in violation of state and federal nondiscrimination laws. They also challenged the evaluation and appeal procedure for requesting academic accommodations, as well as the university's "blanket prohibition" against course substitutions for mathematics and foreign language requirements. Furthermore, the students claimed that negative comments by the university's president about learning-disabled students had created a hostile learning environment for them.

The district court granted class action certification to the plaintiffs (all students with learning disabilities, attention deficit disorders, or both currently enrolled at Boston University), thus avoiding **mootness** concerns. In addition, the court examined the viability of a "hostile academic environment" claim based on disability, concluding that such a claim was possible but that the allegations of the plaintiffs' complaint fell short of such a claim. Although statements made by the university's president may have been offensive, the court considered the First Amendment concerns at hand and found that these remarks were not "sufficiently directed" toward the plaintiffs to constitute a hostile academic environment.

In a subsequent opinion, *Guckenberger v. Boston University*, 974 F. Supp. 106 (D. Mass. 1997) (*Guckenberger II*), the district court addressed the plaintiffs' claims that the university violated the ADA and Section 504 of the Rehabilitation Act by requiring students with learning disabilities to be retested every three years by a physician, a clinical psychologist, or a licensed psychologist, and by refusing to modify the requirement that students in the College of Arts and Sciences complete one semester of mathematics and four semesters of a foreign language. The court ruled that the university's previous policy and its application had, in several respects, violated the disability discrimination laws. But the university had changed its policy and some of its practices after the litigation began, and some of those changes had cured some of the violations.

The court ruled that requiring new documentation of a learning disability every three years, without regard to whether the updated information was medically necessary, violated the law because the requirements screened out or tended to screen out students with specific disabilities, and because the university did not demonstrate that the requirements were necessary to provide educational services or accommodations. The university's new policy permitted a waiver of the three-year retesting regulation when medically unnecessary; this change, said the court, cured the violation.

The court also ruled that the university's requirement that it would accept documentation only from professionals with certain types of doctorates violated the law because professionals with other degrees (doctorates in education and certain master's degrees) were also qualified to assess individuals for learning disabilities. The court did note, however, that for the assessment of attention deficit disorder, it was appropriate to require that the assessor have a doctorate.

The university's decision to implement the policy in the middle of the academic year, without advance notice to affected students, also violated the ADA and Section 504, according to the court. Furthermore, the court ruled that the president and his staff, who lacked "experience or expertise in diagnosing learning disabilities or in fashioning appropriate accommodations"

(974 F. Supp. at 118) had personally administered the policy on the basis of "uninformed stereotypes about the learning disabled." The university's new policy, which delegated the evaluation of accommodation requests to a licensed psychologist, cured that violation. (The third *Guckenberger* opinion is discussed later in this section.)

Although both Section 504 and the ADA require colleges and universities to provide reasonable accommodations to qualified disabled students, institutions need not do so if the accommodation will fundamentally alter the nature of the academic program (see *Southeastern Community College v. Davis*, Section 7.2.4.3). The question of how much change is required arose in *Wynne v. Tufts University School of Medicine*, 976 F.2d 791 (1st Cir. 1992). A medical student dismissed on academic grounds asserted that the medical school had refused to accommodate his learning disability when the school required him to take a multiple choice test rather than an alternative that would minimize the impact of his learning disability. Initially, the trial court granted summary judgment for Tufts, but the appellate court reversed on the grounds that the record was insufficient to enable the court to determine whether Tufts had attempted to accommodate Wynne and whether Tufts had evaluated the impact of the requested accommodation on its academic program (932 F.2d 19 (1st Cir. 1991) (*en banc*)).

On remand, the university provided extensive evidence to the trial court that it had permitted Wynne to repeat his first year of medical school, had paid for the neuropsychological testing of Wynne that identified his learning disabilities, and had provided him with tutors, note takers, and other assistance. The university had permitted him to take makeup examinations for courses he had failed, and the school had determined that there was not an appropriate alternative method of testing his knowledge in the biochemistry course.

On the strength of the school's evidence of serious consideration of alternatives to the multiple choice test, the district court again awarded summary judgment for Tufts, and the appellate court affirmed. In deferring to the school's judgment on the need for a certain testing format, the court said:

> [T]he point is not whether a medical school is "right" or "wrong" in making program-related decisions. Such absolutes rarely apply in the context of subjective decision-making, particularly in a scholastic setting. The point is that Tufts, after undertaking a diligent assessment of the available options, felt itself obliged to make "a professional, academic judgment that [a] reasonable accommodation [was] simply not available" [976 F.2d at 795].

Given the multiple forms of assistance that Tufts had provided Wynne, and its ability to demonstrate that it had evaluated alternative test forms and determined that none would be an appropriate substitute for the multiple choice format, the court was satisfied that the school had satisfied the requirements of the Rehabilitation Act.

In *Halasz v. University of New England*, 816 F. Supp. 37 (D. Me. 1993), a federal trial court relied on *Wynne* to review the challenge of a student that a school had failed to provide him with necessary accommodations and had discriminated against him on the basis of his disability. The school had a special program for students with learning disabilities who lacked the academic credentials necessary for regular admission to the university. The program provided a variety of support services for these students and gave them an opportunity for regular admission to the university after they completed the special one-year program. Despite the special services, such as tutoring, taped texts, untimed testing, and readers for some of his classes, the plaintiff was unable to attain an academic record sufficient for regular admission to the university. His performance in the courses and tests that he took during his year in the special program indicated, the university alleged, that he was not an "otherwise qualified" student with a disability and thus was not protected by the Rehabilitation Act. The university was able to demonstrate the academic rationale for its program requirements and to show that the plaintiff had been given the same amount and quality of assistance that had been given to other students who later were offered admission to the university's regular academic program.

The decisions in *Wynne* and *Halasz* demonstrate how important it is that institutions consider potential accommodations for students with disabilities. Given the tendency of courts to defer to academic judgments, but to hold colleges and universities to strict procedural standards, those institutions that can demonstrate, as could Tufts, that they gave careful consideration to the student's request and reached a decision on academic grounds that the accommodation was either unnecessary or unsuitable, should be able to prevail against challenges under either the Rehabilitation Act or the ADA.

The scope of the accommodation requirement was also addressed in the *Guckenberger* trilogy, and the case is particularly instructive because of the court's scrutiny of the process used by the university to make an academic determination concerning the requested accommodations. The students had challenged the university's refusal to waive the foreign language requirement in the College of Arts and Sciences, or to permit substitution of other courses taught in English, as a violation of the ADA. In *Guckenberger II*, the court agreed in principle that the university was not required to lower its academic standards or require substantial alteration of academic programs. The court found, however, that the university had not even considered the alternatives suggested by the students (or any other alternatives) that would have provided an appropriate accommodation while maintaining academic standards and programmatic integrity. Said the court: "[T]he University simply relied on the status quo as the rationale" (974 F. Supp. at 115). The court awarded damages for breach of contract and emotional distress to several of the students whose accommodations were delayed or denied because of the policy and its application by university officials. The court also ordered the university to develop a "deliberative procedure" for considering whether other courses could be substituted for the foreign language requirement of the liberal arts college without fundamentally altering the nature of its liberal arts degree program.

In response, the university turned to a faculty committee that advised the dean of arts and sciences on curricular and programmatic issues. That committee heard the views of some of the student plaintiffs during its deliberations; no administrators were committee members, nor did they attend the meetings. At the conclusion of its deliberations, the committee stated that the foreign language requirement was "fundamental to the nature of the liberal arts degree at Boston University" and recommended against permitting course substitutions as an alternative to the foreign language requirement. The president accepted the committee's recommendation. Then, in a third ruling, *Guckenberger v. Boston University*, 8 F. Supp. 2d 82 (D. Mass. 1998) (*Guckenberger III*), the court ruled that the university had complied with its order, approved the procedure that had been used, and dismissed the plaintiffs' challenge to the process and the outcome of the committee's work.

In determining whether the university used the appropriate process and standards to decide whether a requested accommodation was reasonable, the district court in *Guckenberger III* looked to the opinion of the U.S. Court of Appeals for the First Circuit in *Wynne v. Tufts University School of Medicine*, discussed earlier in this section.

> "If the institution submits undisputed facts demonstrating that the relevant officials within the institution considered alternative means, their feasibility, cost and effect on the academic program, and came to a rationally justifiable conclusion that the available alternatives would result either in lowering academic standards or requiring substantial program alteration, the court could rule as a matter of law that the institution had met its duty of seeking reasonable accommodation" [8 F. Supp. 2d at 87, quoting *Wynne I* at 26].

The *Guckenberger III* court first engaged in fact finding to determine whether Boston University had exercised "reasoned deliberation." It examined who the decision makers were, whether the deliberative group addressed why the foreign language requirement was unique, and whether it considered possible alternatives to the requirement. Although the committee had not kept minutes of its meetings in the past, it had been ordered by the court to do so; review of those minutes was an important factor in the court's determination. The minutes reflected that the committee had discussed why the foreign language requirement was important and why alternatives to the foreign language requirement would not meet the goals that the requirement was enacted to fulfill. The committee was insulated from those officials whose comments and decisions had been criticized by the court in earlier rulings, and the committee gave students an opportunity to provide information and their perspective on the issue. The court concluded that "the Committee's reliance on only its own academic judgment and the input of College students was reasonable and in keeping with the nature of the decision" (8 F. Supp. 2d at 87–88).

The court then evaluated "whether the facts add up to a professional, academic judgment that reasonable accommodation is simply not available" (8 F. Supp. 2d at 89, quoting *Wynne I* at 27–28). Despite the committee's decision not to consult external experts, and the fact that many elite universities, such as Harvard, Yale, and Columbia, have no similar foreign language requirement, the court ruled that the process used was appropriate and the outcome was rationally justifiable. As demonstrated in both *Wynne* and *Guckenberger*, determinations of whether accommodation requests would fall short of fundamental academic standards must be based on professional academic judgments.

Much of the litigation concerning conflicts between the accommodations sought by a student and the accommodations an institution is willing to grant occur with medical students or other students for whom a clinical experience is required. Most federal courts are deferential to a determination by faculty or academic administrators that a requested accommodation is either inappropriate for educational reasons or that the student cannot satisfactorily complete the required curriculum even with accommodation. For example, in *Zukle v. The Regents of the University of California*, 166 F.3d 1041 (9th Cir. 1999), the court treated as a matter of first impression the question of "judicial deference to an educational institution's academic decisions in ADA and Rehabilitation Act cases" (166 F.3d at 1047). Although the Tenth Circuit had rejected a deferential approach in *Pushkin v. Regents of the University of Colorado* (see Section 7.2.4.3 of this book), the Ninth Circuit determined that deference was appropriate, following the lead of the First, Second, and Fifth Circuits. In *Zukle*, a medical student with learning disorders that made reading slow and difficult, requested to be relieved of the requirement to complete several of her clinical rotations until after other academic requirements had been completed. The medical school refused. The court ruled that the medical school had offered the plaintiff "all of the accommodations that it normally offers learning disabled students," such as double time on exams, note-taking services, and textbooks on audiocassettes. But Zukle's request that she delay the completion of several clinical rotations and retake a portion of them at a later time was a "substantial alteration" of the curriculum, and thus the medical school was not required to acquiesce to her request. Because the student could not demonstrate that she could meet the academic requirements of the medical school, even with the accommodations it did provide, the court ruled that she was not qualified and thus had not established a prima facie case of disability discrimination.

Another Ninth Circuit case addressed the standard used by courts to review an institution's claim that it could not provide academic accommodations. In *Wong v. Regents of the University of California*, 192 F.3d 807 (9th Cir. 1999), a medical student with learning disabilities had been dismissed on academic grounds, primarily because he had difficulties completing his clinical rotations successfully. The trial court ruled that accommodations provided by the university were reasonable and that the plaintiff was not qualified to continue as a medical student. The appellate court disagreed.

Although the medical school dean had approved several accommodations for the student over a period of years, he had rejected the student's final accommodation requests. The court explained the standard of review appropriate to accommodation decisions of academic institutions:

> In the typical disability discrimination case in which a plaintiff appeals a district court's entry of summary judgment in favor of the defendant, we undertake this reasonable accommodation analysis ourselves as a matter of course, examining the record and deciding whether the record reveals questions of fact as to whether the requested modification substantially alters the performance

standards at issue or whether the accommodation would allow the individual to meet those requirements. In a case involving assessment of the standards of an academic institution, however, we abstain from an in-depth, de novo analysis of suggested accommodations that the school rejected if the institution demonstrates that it conducted such an inquiry itself and concluded that the accommodations were not feasible or would not be effective [192 F.3d at 818].

Because the university had not submitted evidence that the dean had made a reasoned determination that the accommodations requested by Wong were unreasonable, particularly since they were very similar to earlier accommodations that the dean had approved, and given the fact that the prior accommodations enabled Wong to perform very well (circumstances very different from those in *Zukle*), the court refused to defer to the university's determination "because it did not demonstrate that it conscientiously exercised professional judgment in considering the feasibility" of the requested accommodations. The court then addressed the issue of Wong's qualifications to continue as a medical student. Again the court rejected the deferential standard of review, because "the school's system for evaluating a learning disabled student's abilities and its own duty to make its program accessible to such individuals fell short of the standards we require to grant deference" (192 F.3d at 823). Because Wong had performed well when given additional time to prepare for each clinical rotation, the court ruled that he should be allowed to establish at trial that he was qualified.

The court concluded with some advice to institutions, and a warning:

> The deference to which academic institutions are entitled when it comes to the ADA is a double-edged sword. It allows them a significant amount of leeway in making decisions about their curricular requirements and their ability to structure their programs to accommodate disabled students. On the other hand, it places on an institution the weighty responsibility of carefully considering each disabled student's particular limitations and analyzing whether and how it might accommodate that student in a way that would allow the student to complete the school program without lowering academic standards or otherwise unduly burdening the institution . . . We will not sanction an academic institution's decision to refuse to accommodate a disabled student and subsequent dismissal of that student when the record contains facts from which a reasonable jury could conclude that the school made those decisions for arbitrary reasons unrelated to its academic standards [192 F.3d at 826].

On remand, the trial court determined that the student was not disabled (an issue that the earlier opinions had not addressed) because he had been able to achieve earlier academic success without accommodations; the appellate court affirmed that ruling (379 F.3d 1097 (1994)).

In another case, *Doe v. University of Maryland Medical System Corporation*, 50 F.3d 1261 (4th Cir. 1995), an HIV-infected neurosurgical resident had rejected the medical school's proposed accommodation and attempted to force the school to permit him to continue performing surgery. The third-year resident was stuck with a needle while treating an HIV-positive patient, and the resident later tested HIV-positive himself. The hospital permanently suspended Doe from surgical practice, offering him residencies in pathology and psychiatry. Doe rejected these alternatives and filed claims under the Rehabilitation Act and the ADA. The court ruled that he was not otherwise qualified because he posed a significant risk to patient safety that could not be eliminated by reasonable accommodation, and that the accommodations proposed by the medical school were reasonable.

As is the case with ADA claims by employees, students may ask to "telecommute" to college. In *Maczaczyj v. State of New York*, 956 F. Supp. 403 (W.D.N.Y. 1997), a federal trial court was asked to order Empire State College to permit the plaintiff to "attend" required weekend class sessions by telephone from his home, an accommodation that the college had refused to allow. The plaintiff, who suffered from panic attacks (a psychiatric disorder), had rejected the offer of the program faculty to modify certain program requirements, such as excusing him from social portions of the class sessions, providing an empty room for him to use when he became agitated, allowing him to bring along a friend of his choice, and allowing him to select the location on campus where the sessions would take place. The court credited the college's argument that attendance was required for pedagogical reasons and that the course was not designed to be delivered through distance learning or telecommunication technologies. Finding that telephone "attendance" would therefore not be the academic equivalent of the required class sessions, the court denied the plaintiff's request. For a similar case involving a student's request to complete a required social work practicum at her home, see *Klene v. Trustees of Indiana University*, 413 F. App'x 919 (7th Cir. 2011), in which the court rejected her request as unreasonable because it "ignores the necessity of observing and engaging the placement agency's professional staff and clients." The court concluded that the student was not qualified because she was either rejected or terminated by four practicum sites.

For students with cognitive or psychiatric disorders, internships, residencies, and other on-site learning experiences may pose special challenges. Students dismissed for misconduct unrelated to their disability cannot find relief from the courts; see *Herzog v. Loyola College in Maryland*, 2009 U.S. Dist. LEXIS 94454 (D. Md. October 9, 2009). Although some commentators have argued that behavior that is linked to a cognitive or psychiatric disorder should be accommodated, courts have not agreed, and tend to rule that a student who cannot meet the behavioral requirements of an internship or residency is not a qualified individual with a disability. See, for example, *Halpern v. Wake Forest University Health Sciences*, 2012 U.S. App. LEXIS 3996 (4th Cir. February 28, 2012).

Students may request permission to bring "comfort" or "therapy animals" to campus as an accommodation for certain psychiatric disorders. Although the ADA definition of a "service animal" is narrow, the U.S. Department of Justice has stated that the Fair Housing Act, which includes "therapy animals" as permitted accommodations, applies to college and university housing; these issues are discussed in Section 7.4.2 of this book.

As the court opinions (particularly *Guckenberger* and *Wong*) in this section illustrate, process considerations are of great importance in administering an institution's system for reviewing student requests for accommodation. The institution should consider such requests on an individualized, case-by-case basis. Documentation that is submitted by students or obtained by the institution should be prepared or evaluated by professionals with appropriate credentials. Determinations of whether accommodation requests would fall short of fundamental academic standards must be based on professional judgments of faculty and academic administrators. Once the institution can show that it has in effect and has relied upon a process meeting these requirements, however, it can expect to receive considerable deference from the courts if the institution's determination is challenged (see especially the *Zukle* case).

This area of the law continues to develop rapidly, but many other issues related to students with disabilities remain. How substantial must a requested change in an academic program be before it is considered an undue hardship for the institution? What should be the institution's response if a faculty member argues that a requested accommodation infringes his or her academic freedom rights? Can an institution require a student to receive counseling or to take medication as part of the accommodation agreement? These and other issues will challenge administrators, faculty, and university counsel as they seek to act within the ADA's requirements while maintaining the academic integrity of their programs.

### 8.4.2.2. Study abroad programs.

*8.4.2.2. Study abroad programs.* As study abroad programs become more popular, students with disabilities have sought to participate, and many institutions have worked to accommodate the individualized needs of students with mobility or other impairments. Although the Office for Civil Rights (OCR) of the U.S. Department of Education has ruled that Section 504 of the Rehabilitation Act and Title II of the ADA do not apply outside the United States, students have attempted to state both federal and state law claims challenging their institutions' alleged failure to accommodate them on study abroad trips.

But if a student can demonstrate that a college offered to provide accommodations in a study abroad program and then did not fulfill its promise, the student might be able to make a breach of contract or breach of fiduciary duty claim. In *Bird v. Lewis & Clark College*, 303 F.3d 1015 (9th Cir. 2002), *cert. denied*, 538 U.S. 923 (2003), a student who used a wheelchair participated in the college's study abroad program in Australia after college representatives assured her and her parents that she would be fully accommodated. Although the college made numerous accommodations for the student, she was unable to participate in several activities with her classmates, and she sued the college upon her return, claiming ADA violations and breach of the college's fiduciary duty to her, a state law claim. The college argued that neither Section 504 nor Title III of the ADA had extraterritorial application. Although the trial court ruled that both Title III and Section 504 applied to study abroad programs, the appellate court refused to rule on that issue because it determined that the college had reasonably accommodated the student. However, the court affirmed the jury's finding that the college breached its fiduciary duty to the student, based upon the assurances and representations that the college had made to the student and her parents, and affirmed the jury's award of $5,000 in damages.

***8.4.2.3. Online programs.*** As distance learning and online courses have become more prevalent, issues involving the access of students with disabilities to course Web sites and other technology have arisen. For example, students who are visually impaired may have difficulty using course Web sites if images or other graphics are not coded with text that can be interpreted by text readers for the visually impaired. Other disorders, such as color blindness, seizure disorders, dyslexia, and hearing impairments, may also limit or prevent students' participation in online courses.

As this book went to press, only a handful of cases had been reported. One such case, *Hartnett v. The Fielding Graduate Institute*, 198 F. App'x 89 (2d Cir. 2006), involved an online graduate program that included a required 300-hour residency program on campus. The student plaintiff had lupus and asked to be accommodated by "attending" required face-to-face "cluster group" meetings using videoconferencing, by being permitted to change to part-time status, and by being transferred to a different "cluster group" of students that met two miles closer to her home. The Institute argued that its accreditation depended on student-faculty face-to-face contact for the 300-hour residency. The student also claimed that the Institute had not engaged in the interactive process required by the ADA (see Section 8.4).

The trial court had awarded summary judgment to the Institute on all of the student's claims. The appellate court affirmed the award of summary judgment on the student's request for a cluster group transfer and part-time status (commenting that the program was already part-time), but reversed the trial court's rulings on the other claims. The appellate court was particularly concerned that there was little evidence that the required "interactive process" to determine whether accommodations were possible had occurred, since the meeting at which this process allegedly occurred was held after all of the plaintiff's accommodation requests had been denied.

Title III of the ADA requires a college or university to consider, as a potential accommodation, making reasonable modifications in policies, practices, or procedures "unless the [institution] can demonstrate that making such modifications would fundamentally alter the nature" of such policies, practices, or procedures (42 U.S.C. §12182(b)(2)(A)(ii)). In *Yount v. Regent University, Inc.*, 2009 U.S. Dist. LEXIS 32824 (D. Ariz. April 14, 2009), a student who lived in Arizona was enrolled in an online doctoral program at Regent University. The student had previously made satisfactory academic progress, but was disabled by back pain partway through the semester and had asked to receive a grade of "incomplete" in his courses, rather than having to withdraw and then reapply to the program because he could not complete the course on time. The associate dean refused his request because the university's policy was that a student had to have completed 75 percent of the coursework before a grade of incomplete would be permitted, although the university's written policies did not specify a percentage that had to have been completed. The student sent several e-mail messages to the university complaining about its refusal to give him a grade of incomplete and was denied several other requests related to his academic program.

The student claimed a failure to provide reasonable accommodation under Title III of the ADA, as well as retaliation because his additional requests had been denied. The trial court denied the university's motion for summary judgment on the accommodation claim, ruling that numerous issues of material fact required the case to be tried, but awarded summary judgment to the university on the retaliation claim.

Certain distance learning programs may require periodic attendance on campus for residency programs or to permit groups of students to interact in person. For an unsuccessful challenge to such a requirement of "in person" attendance, see *Maczaczyj v. State of New York*, 956 F.Supp. 404 (W.D.N.Y. 1997), discussed in Section 8.4.2.1 of this book.

In June 2010, the Civil Rights Division of the U.S. Department of Justice and the Office for Civil Rights of the U.S. Department of Education issued a joint letter to college and university presidents concerning access to electronic book readers by students with visual impairments. The letter explained that many of these readers, which are increasingly being required in some courses, "lack an accessible text-to-speech function" and thus are inaccessible to students with visual disorders. The letter discussed settlement agreements with some colleges and universities in which the colleges agreed not to require the use of electronic book readers unless they were accessible and also agreed to provide alternative methods of obtaining the information for these students. The letter may be found at http://www2.ed.gov/about/offices/list/ocr/letters/colleague-20100629.html.

In 2009, the National Federation for the Blind and several law school applicants sued the Law School Admission Council (LSAC), which operates a Web site used by numerous law schools to receive law school applications. Many of the law schools that use the LSAC's Web-based application process were also sued under California's laws against disability discrimination (Disabled Persons Act, California Civil Code §§ 54 et seq., and the Unruh Civil Rights Act, California Civil Code §§ 51 et seq.). A settlement was reached in 2011 in which the LSAC agreed to provide "full and equal access" to its Web site so that blind or visually impaired applicants "using screen-reader software may acquire the same information and engage in the same transactions as are available to sighted [applicants] with substantially equivalent ease of use." The settlement agreement may be found at http://www.ada.gov/LSAC.htm.

## Section 8.5. Sexual Harassment of Students by Faculty Members

Sexual harassment of students is prohibited by Title IX of the Education Amendments of 1972 (see Section 11.5.3 of this book), and if the student is an employee, Title VII (see Section 4.5.2.1 of this book) may be implicated as well. Whether one is addressing students' sexual harassment complaints against faculty members, as in this section, or students' sexual harassment complaints against other students (as in Section 7.1.5),[1] it is important to

---

[1] Other types of harassment may also create problems on campus and become the subject of internal complaints or litigation. The most important of these other types of harassment are discussed at the end of this section.

begin with a general understanding of what types of behavior constitute sexual harassment.[2] The following definitions and examples will provide a foundation for this understanding.

In guidelines issued by the U.S. Department of Education, sexual harassment is defined as "unwelcome [verbal, nonverbal, or physical] conduct of a sexual nature" ("Revised Sexual Harassment Guidance: Harassment of Students by School Employees, Other Students, or Third Parties," Part II (January 19, 2001), available at http://www2.ed.gov/about/offices/list/ocr/docs/shguide.pdf). In two studies by the American Association of University Women (AAUW), sexual harassment is defined as "unwanted and unwelcome sexual behavior [both physical and nonphysical] that interferes with the [victim's] life" *(Hostile Hallways: The AAUW Survey on Sexual Harassment in America's Schools* (AAUW Education Foundation, 1993), 6, 8; see also *Hostile Hallways: Bullying, Teasing, and Sexual Harassment in School* (AAUW Education Foundation, 2001), 9–11). And in a report by the National Coalition for Women and Girls in Education, sexual harassment is defined as "unwanted and unwelcome sexual behavior that creates a hostile environment, limiting full access to education" (*Title IX at 30: Report Card on Gender Equity* (June 2002), 40). Examples of sexual harassment from these sources include sexual advances; requests for sexual favors; sexual taunting; spreading sexual rumors; drawing graffiti of a sexual nature; making jokes, gestures, or comments of a sexual nature; showing sexually explicit photographs or illustrations; sending sexual notes or messages; pulling clothing down or off in a sexual way; forced kissing; touching, grabbing, or pinching in a sexual way; flashing; and intentionally brushing up against someone, blocking someone's path, or cornering someone in a sexual way. Consistent with the three general definitions, such behaviors must be "unwelcome" before they would be considered to be sexual harassment.

Harassment victims can be both male and female, just as perpetrators are both female and male. Moreover, sexual harassment can occur not only when the victim and perpetrator are of the opposite sex but also when they are of the same sex. Thus, as the Education Department's Sexual Harassment Guidance emphasizes, a female's harassment of another female or a male's harassment of another male is sexual harassment whenever the harasser's conduct is sexual in nature ("Revised Sexual Harassment Guidance," Part III).

Sexual harassment by faculty members (or other employees) may be divided into two categories: "*quid pro quo* harassment" and "hostile environment harassment." The Education Department's Sexual Harassment Guidance, for instance, distinguishes the categories as follows:

---

[2] When a student's sexual harassment complaint against a faculty member concerns the faculty member's classroom statements or classroom conduct, academic freedom arguments may also come into play. This problem is discussed in Section 6.2.2, most specifically with reference to the *Cohen, Silva,* and *Bonnell* cases.

*Quid pro quo* harassment occurs if a teacher or other employee conditions an educational decision or benefit on the student's submission to unwelcome sexual conduct, [regardless of whether] the student resists and suffers the threatened harm or submits and avoids the threatened harm . . .

By contrast, [hostile environment] harassment . . . does not explicitly or implicitly condition a decision or benefit on submission to sexual conduct [but does nevertheless] limit a student's ability to participate in or benefit from the school's program based on sex.

Teachers and other employees can engage in either type of harassment. Students . . . are not generally given responsibility over other students and, thus, generally can only engage in hostile environment harassment ["Revised Sexual Harassment Guidance," Part V.A].

Student complaints alleging harassment by a faculty member may implicate grades in two basic ways. In the first way, which is akin to quid pro quo harassment, a student may complain that she was denied a deserved grade because she refused the instructor's sexual advances, or that she was awarded a grade only after having submitted unwillingly to the instructor's advances. In *Crandell v. New York College of Osteopathic Medicine*, 87 F. Supp. 2d 304 (S.D.N.Y. 2000), for example, a female medical student claimed she was harassed by a medical resident who supervised her in a six-week rotation at a teaching hospital. She claimed she was subjected to numerous sexual comments, incidents of touching, and a threat to give her a failing grade for the rotation if she did not spend time with him on a regular basis. In context, the student interpreted this demand to be sexual in nature. The court determined that this conduct constituted quid pro quo harassment. (The *Alexander v. Yale University* case, discussed later in this section, is also this type of case.) In the second way, which is akin to hostile environment harassment, a student may complain that she received (or was in danger of receiving) a low grade because the instructor's sexual conduct had interfered with her ability to do her coursework. The case of *Hayut v. State University of New York*, 352 F.3d 733 (2d Cir. 2003), provides an excellent example of this second type of harassment claim.

In *Hayut*, the plaintiff student was in an undergraduate political science course in which the professor gave her the nickname "Monica," in light of "her supposed physical resemblance to Monica Lewinsky, a former White House intern who at that time was attaining notoriety for her involvement in a widely-covered sex scandal with then-President William Clinton." The professor's "use of this nickname persisted even after [the student] requested that he stop. Despite her protestations, [the professor] would occasionally, in dramatic fashion, attempt to locate [the student] in the classroom by sitting in front of his desk and screaming the name 'Monica.'" His comments "occurred at least once per class period throughout the rest of the semester." His conduct "was not limited to using the 'Monica' nickname, but included other comments as well. These added context to the nickname by associating [the student] with some of the more sordid details of the Clinton/Lewinsky scandal." The student claimed that the "Monica" comments "humiliat[ed] her in front of her peers, caus[ed] her to experience difficulty sleeping, and ma[de] it difficult for her to concentrate in school and at work." The court determined that, on these facts, a reasonable jury could conclude that the professor's actions constituted hostile environment sexual harassment. (See also *Kracunas and Pallett v. Iona College*, 119 F.3d 80 (2d Cir. 1997).)

This second type of claim may also arise in situations when a low grade precedes rather than follows the alleged harassment (see, for example, *Kadiki v. Virginia Commonwealth University*, 892 F. Supp. 746 (E.D. Va. 1995); *Kracunas and Pallett v. Iona College*, 119 F.3d 80 (2d Cir. 1997)); or when a student is allegedly harassed while being offered special course assignments (see *Kracunas and Pallett v. Iona College*); or when the alleged harasser is a patient or client in a clinical or internship setting, rather than the instructor (see, for example, *Murray v. New York University College of Dentistry*, 57 F.3d 243 (2d Cir. 1995)).

In situations such as those above, students may assert sex discrimination claims under Title IX or under a comparable state civil rights law. Section 1983 claims (see Sections 3.4 and 4.4.4 of this book) alleging a violation of the federal equal protection clause may also be brought in some circumstances. In addition, if a student works for the college or university and is harassed by a supervisor or coworker, the student may assert an employment discrimination claim under Title VII or the state's fair employment statute. (See, for example, *Karibian v. Columbia University*, 14 F.3d 773 (2d Cir. 1994), in which the university was held liable for the sexual harassment of a student employee by her supervisor; and see also *Lipsett v. University of Puerto Rico*, 864 F.2d 881 (1st Cir. 1988).) Depending on the source of law used, claims may be assertable against the college or university itself, against the alleged harasser or harassers, or against other institutional employees who have some role in supervising the alleged harasser or protecting against harassment on campus.

For all such claims, it is important, as a threshold matter, to focus on the claim's legal elements. The case of *Waters v. Metropolitan State University*, 91 F. Supp. 2d 1287 (D. Minn. 2000), provides a good shorthand description of these elements that would fit most statutes that cover hostile environment sexual harassment. According to that case, challenged conduct must have been "unwelcome," it must have been "based on sex," and it must have been "sufficiently severe as to alter the conditions of [the student's] education and create an abusive educational environment" (91 F. Supp. 2d at 1291). Further specificity on these elements is provided by the excellent analysis of Judge Calabresi in *Hayut v. State University of New York*, 352 F.3d 733 (2d Cir. 2003) (discussed earlier and later in this section), in which he carefully reviewed the severity requirement, a related pervasiveness requirement, the "on the basis of sex" or "because of sex" requirement, and the hostile or abusive educational environment requirement, as they applied to the student's claim in that case (352 F.3d at 746–49). The court in *Hayut* also reviewed the requirement that the educational environment be hostile not only from the victim's subjective perspective but also from the objective perspective of a reasonable person or reasonable fact finder (352 F.3d at 746). In addition, the court demonstrated how Title VII still provides important guidance for making hostile environment determinations under Title IX and 42 U.S.C. § 1983, even though Title IX's standards for determining institutional liability for an employee's acts are different from Title VII's (352 F.3d at 744).

First Amendment free speech law sometimes must also be taken into account in determining the parameters of sexual harassment,[3] since sexual harassment (whether of the quid pro quo or the hostile environment variety) is usually effectuated in large part through the spoken or written word or by symbolic gestures. Because much of the conduct alleged to be harassment is also expressive conduct, institutions and faculty members may seek to defend themselves against harassment claims by asserting that the challenged conduct is protected by the First Amendment. Pertinent background for such claims, as they may arise under Title IX or other civil rights spending statutes, is provided by a U.S. Department of Education, Office for Civil Rights (OCR) "Dear Colleague" letter issued in 2003 (http://www2.ed.gov/about/offices/list/ocr/firstamend.html). The letter affirms that all interpretations of OCR regulations and actions taken pursuant to these regulations must comport with First Amendment principles. This affirmation applies to both public and private institutions. The letter explains that "[b]ecause the First Amendment normally does not bind private institutions, some have erroneously assumed that OCR's regulations apply to private federal-funds recipients without the constitutional limitations imposed on public institutions." OCR rejects this position:

> OCR's regulations should not be interpreted in ways that would lead to the suppression of protected speech on public or private campuses. Any private post-secondary institution that chooses to limit free speech in ways that are more restrictive than at public educational institutions does so on its own accord and not based on requirements imposed by OCR.

The cases discussed in Section 6.2.2 of this book, especially the *Silva*, *Cohen*, and *Bonnell* cases, all present harassment issues in the context of First Amendment academic freedom claims in public institutions; and these cases, taken together, do provide some First Amendment protection for faculty members. This does not mean, however, that there is a viable free speech issue whenever a harasser uses expression as part of the harassment. In some cases, *Hayut v. State University of New York* (cited earlier in this section) being a major example, the faculty member's classroom comments are so far removed from any legitimate purpose that a free expression claim becomes marginalized or is not even addressed in the case (352 F.3d at 745–49).

The case of *Trejo v. Shoben*, 319 F.3d 878 (7th Cir. 2003), illustrates how courts may summarily dismiss free speech claims when they arise in contexts concerning a faculty member's conduct with respect to students. In this case, a professor had been denied reappointment, largely on the basis of various

---

[3] Free exercise and establishment issues may also become involved in sexual harassment cases when the defendant is a religious institution or a religious figure. For an example, see *Bollard v. California Providence of the Society of Jesus*, 196 F.3d 940 (9th Cir. 1999), in which a student priest alleged that his instructor, his superior priest, had sexually harassed him while he was attending the seminary. The defendant argued that the free exercise and establishment clauses compelled the court to dismiss the case; the appellate court disagreed, because religious reasons for the harassment and religious doctrine were not involved in the case, nor would a decision in the plaintiff's favor interfere with the defendant's freedom to select its ministers.

complaints and charges against him that suggested a "pattern of unwelcome, inappropriate, boorish behavior." The professor's oral statements were a major component of much of this behavior. For example, at an academic conference, while attending a private dinner party along with his graduate students, the professor made extended statements about "pregnancy, orgasms, and extra-marital affairs and went on to advocate sex outside marriage."

The professor had also accompanied his statements with "the use of hand gestures to demonstrate various parts of the female anatomy." At the same con-ference, he made various "sexually charged comments in the presence of male and female professors and students." In addition, on and around the campus, the professor had extended "unwelcome invitations" to his graduate students to meet with him to play cards or engage in other activities and had made various sexual comments about his female graduate students. The professor claimed that his various comments were protected speech under the First Amendment. The court rejected this contention. Regarding the academic conference, the court determined that the professor's "statements were simply parts of a calculated type of speech designed to further [his] private interest in attempting to solicit female companionship"; and that "the record is barren of any evidence besides Trejo's self-serving statements that [his] remarks were designed to serve any truly pedagogic purpose." Regarding other comments by the professor, on and off campus, the court determined that they were primarily "casual, idle, and flir-tatious chit-chat." The court concluded that these comments, and the comments at the academic conference, "were focused almost exclusively on matters of private concern" and did not merit protection either under the *Pickering-Connick* line of cases or under *Keyishian* (see Section 6.1.1 and 6.1.5 of this book).

Of the various types of harassment claims, Title IX claims have received the greatest attention from the courts. Title IX harassment claims are the primary focus of the rest of this section. Such claims are assertable only against institu-tions, and not against their individual officers or employees. In an early case, *Alexander v. Yale University*, 631 F.2d 178 (2d Cir. 1980), five female students alleged that Yale's practices and procedures for dealing with sexual harassment of students violated Title IX of the Education Amendments of 1972. One of the plaintiffs alleged that a faculty member had "offered to give her a grade of 'A' in the course in exchange for her compliance with his sexual demands" and that, when she refused, he gave her a C, which "was not the result of a fair evaluation of her academic work, but the result of her failure to accede to [the professor's] sexual demands." The remaining plaintiffs made other allegations concerning acts of harassment and the inadequacies of campus procedures to deal with them. The district court entered judgment for Yale, and the U.S. Court of Appeals affirmed. With the exception of the lowered-grade claim of one plaintiff, all the various claims and plaintiffs were dismissed for technical reasons: the plaintiffs had graduated and their claims were therefore "moot"; Yale had already adopted procedures for dealing with sexual harassment and thus, in effect, had already granted the primary remedy requested in the suit; other claims of harm were too "speculative" or "uncertain." The lowered-grade claim was dismissed because the plaintiff, at trial, did not prove the allegations.

Although all claims were rejected, the *Alexander* litigation by no means shut the door on Title IX actions alleging that the integrity of grading or other academic processes had been compromised by a faculty member's sexual harassment of students. Both the district and appellate courts made clear that the grade claim was a "justiciable claim for relief under Title IX." A denial or threatened denial of earned academic awards would be a deprivation of an educational benefit protected by Title IX; and when imposed for sexual reasons, that deprivation becomes sex discrimination prohibited by Title IX. As the district court held, and the appellate court quoted with apparent approval, "academic advancement conditioned upon submission to sexual demands constitutes sex discrimination in education" (459 F. Supp. at 4; 631 F.2d at 182).

Nevertheless, the lower courts in cases after *Alexander* expressed differing views on when, and the extent to which, Title IX would cover sexual harassment. It was not until 1992 that the U.S. Supreme Court resolved this matter in *Franklin v. Gwinnett County Public Schools*, 503 U.S. 60 (1992). The plaintiff, a high school student in Georgia, sued the school board under Title IX, seeking relief from both hostile environment and quid pro quo sexual harassment by a teacher. Her complaint alleged that the teacher, also a sports coach, had harassed her continually beginning in the fall of her sophomore year. The student accused the teacher of engaging her in sexually oriented conversations, forcibly kissing her on the mouth on school property, telephoning her at home, and asking her to see him socially. She also alleged that during her junior year, this teacher went to her class, asked the classroom teacher to excuse her, and then took her to a private office where he raped her. According to the student's complaint, school officials and teachers were aware of these occurrences, and although the school board eventually investigated them, it took no action to stop the harassment and agreed to let the teacher resign in return for dropping all harassment charges.

The student filed a complaint with the U.S. Department of Education's Office for Civil Rights (OCR), which investigated her charges. OCR determined that verbal and physical sexual harassment had occurred and that the school district had violated the student's Title IX rights. But OCR concluded that, because the teacher and the school principal had resigned and the school had implemented a grievance procedure, the district was in compliance with Title IX. The student then went to federal court, and ultimately the U.S. Supreme Court ruled in her favor. The teacher's actions were sexual harassment, and the district, in failing to intervene, had intentionally discriminated against her, in violation of Title IX.

The *Franklin* case clearly established that sexual harassment, including hostile environment harassment, may be the basis for a sex discrimination claim under Title IX, and that student victims of harassment by a teacher may sue their schools for money damages under Title IX. But other important issues remained unresolved by the Court's *Franklin* opinion—in particular the issue of when, and under what theories, courts would hold schools and colleges liable for money damages under Title IX for a faculty member's or other employee's sexual harassment of a student. In *Franklin*, the school administrators had actual knowledge of the teacher's misconduct. The Supreme Court did not address whether a school could be found liable only if it had such actual knowledge of the misconduct but failed to stop it, or whether a school could be liable even absent actual knowledge because an employee's intentional discrimination could be imputed to the school. (Under agency law, the employer may be held responsible for the unlawful conduct of its agent (called *respondeat superior*) even if the employer does not have actual knowledge of the conduct; see Section 2.1 of this book.)

The institutional liability questions left open by *Franklin* were extensively discussed in the lower courts in *Franklin*'s aftermath. No pattern emerged; different courts took different approaches in determining when liability would accrue to an educational institution for the actions of its teachers or other employees. Some courts determined that an educational institution could be vicariously liable on the basis of common law agency principles of *respondeat superior* (see, for example, *Kracunas and Pallett v. Iona College*, 119 F.3d 80 (2d Cir. 1997)). Other courts determined that an educational institution should be liable under a constructive notice, or "knew or should have known," standard (see, for example, *Doe v. Petaluma School District*, 949 F. Supp. 1415 (N.D. Cal. 1996)), or could be liable only in certain narrow circumstances where the institution had knowledge of the harassment and failed to respond (see, for example, *Rosa H. v. San Elizario Independent School District*, 106 F.3d 648 (5th Cir. 1997) (harassment)), or should not be liable at all, at least for hostile environment harassment (see *Bougher v. University of Pittsburgh*, 713 F. Supp. 139 (W.D. Pa. 1989), *affirmed on other grounds*, 882 F.2d 74 (3rd Cir. 1989)). The U.S. Department of Education also weighed in on these liability issues. The department's Office for Civil Rights published the first version of its sexual harassment guidelines in 1997, which provided that liability for harassment by teachers or other employees of a school or college should be governed by agency principles. This interpretation of Title IX was rejected, however, by the U.S. Supreme Court in a pair of cases, one involving harassment by a faculty member and a second involving harassment by a student peer.

In *Gebser v. Lago Vista Independent School District*, 524 U.S. 274 (1998), the issue was the extent to which "a school district may be held liable in damages in an implied right of action under Title IX . . . for the sexual harassment of a student by one of the district's teachers." In a 5-to-4 decision, the Court majority held that Title IX damages liability is based neither on common law agency principles of *respondeat superior* nor upon principles of constructive notice. Distinguishing Title IX from Title VII of the Civil Rights Act of 1964 (Section 4.5.2.1 of this book), which does utilize such principles, the Court insisted that "[i]t would 'frustrate the purposes' of Title IX to permit a damages recovery against a school district for a teacher's sexual harassment of a student based on [such] principles . . ., i.e., without actual notice to a school district official" (524 U.S. at 285). Thus, the Court held that students may not recover damages from a school district under Title IX for teacher-student sexual harassment "unless an official [of the school district], who at a minimum, has authority to address the alleged discrimination and to institute corrective measures on the [district's] behalf has actual knowledge of discrimination and fails adequately to respond" (524 U.S. at 276). Moreover, the official's response to the harassment

> must amount to deliberate indifference to discrimination. The administrative enforcement scheme presupposes that an official who is advised of a Title IX violation refuses to take action to bring the recipient into compliance. The premise, in other words, is an official decision by the recipient not to remedy the violation. That framework finds a rough parallel in the standard of deliberate indifference. Under a lower standard, there would be a risk that the recipient would be liable in damages not for its own official decision but instead for its employees' independent actions [524 U.S. at 290].

Putting aside the U.S. Department of Education's 1997 Sexual Harassment Guidance that had applied agency principles to teacher-student sexual harassment, the Court made clear that it would listen only to Congress (and not to the Department of Education) on these questions: "[U]ntil Congress speaks directly on the subject . . ., we will not hold a school district liable in damages under Title IX for a teacher's sexual harassment of a student absent actual notice and deliberate indifference" (524 U.S. at 292). In so doing, and in contrast with its methodology in other situations (see, for example, *Martin v. Occupational Safety and Health Review Commission*, 499 U.S. 144 (1991)), the Court refused to accord any deference to the decisions of the administrative agency authorized to implement the statute, as Justice Stevens emphasized in his dissent (524 U.S. at 300).

Applying these principles to the student's claim, the Court determined that the student had not met the standards and therefore affirmed the lower court's entry of summary judgment for the school district. In reaching this decision, the Court acknowledged that the school district had not implemented any sexual harassment policy or any grievance procedure for enforcing such a policy as required by the Department of Education's regulations (34 C.F.R. §§ 106.8(b), 106.9(a)). But the Court nevertheless held that the school district's failure in this regard was not evidence of "actual notice and deliberate indifference," nor did this failure "itself constitute 'discrimination' under Title IX" (524 U.S. at 292).

Four Justices vigorously dissented from the majority's holdings in *Gebser*. Point by point, the dissenting Justices refuted the majority's reasons for rejecting the application of agency principles under Title IX and for concluding that Title IX is based upon a different model of liability than Title VII. In addition, the dissenting Justices provided an extended argument to the effect that the refusal to provide meaningful protection for students subjected to harassment flies in the face of the purpose and meaning of Title IX. According to Justice Stevens:

> Congress included the prohibition against discrimination on the basis of sex in Title IX [in order] to induce school boards to adopt and enforce practices that will minimize the danger that vulnerable students will be exposed to such odious behavior. The rule that the Court has crafted creates the opposite incentive. As long as school boards can insulate themselves from knowledge

about this sort of conduct, they can claim immunity from damages liability. Indeed, the rule that the Court adopts would preclude a damages remedy even if every teacher at the school knew about the harassment but did not have "authority to institute corrective measures on the district's behalf." *Ante*, at 277.

\* \* \* \*

As a matter of policy, the Court ranks protection of the school district's purse above the protection of immature high school students . . . Because those students are members of the class for whose special benefit Congress enacted Title IX, that policy choice is not faithful to the intent of the policymaking branch of our Government [524 U.S. at 300–301, 306 (Stevens, J. dissenting); see generally 524 U.S. at 293–306 (Stevens, J., dissenting)].

The *Gebser* case thus establishes a two-part standard for determining institutional liability in damages for a faculty member's (or other employee's) sexual harassment of a student:[4]

1. An official of the school district (a) must have had "actual knowledge" of the harassment and (b) must have authority to "institute corrective measures" to resolve the harassment problem.

2. If such an official did have actual knowledge, then the official (a) must have "fail[ed] to adequately respond" to the harassment and (b) must have acted with "deliberate indifference."

In these respects, the *Gebser* test stands in stark contrast to the liability standards under Title VII. In two cases decided in the same court term as the *Gebser* case, the Supreme Court determined that liability under Title VII is based upon agency principles and a *respondeat superior* model of liability (*Faragher v. City of Boca Raton*, 524 U.S. 775 (1998); and *Burlington Industries v. Ellerth*, 524 U.S. 742 (1998)). Thus, under Title VII, but not under Title IX, an employer may be liable in damages for a supervisor's acts of harassment even though the employer did not have either actual knowledge or constructive notice of the harassment. It is therefore much more difficult for students to meet the Title IX liability standards than it is for employees to meet the Title VII standards, and consequently students have less protection against harassment under Title IX than employees have under Title VII. Although Title IX, as a spending statute, is structured differently from Title VII, a regulatory statute, and although courts interpreting and applying Title IX are not bound by Title VII judicial precedents and administrative guidelines, the result in *Gebser*

---

[4]*Gebser* standards may also be applicable to student-student harassment in certain narrow circumstances in which the institution has granted a student some kind of authority over other students. In *Morse v. Regents of the University of Colorado*, 154 F.3d 1124 (10th Cir. 1998), for instance, the court applied *Gebser* to a Title IX claim against the university brought by female Reserve Officer Training Corps (ROTC) cadets who were allegedly harassed by a higher-ranking male cadet. The university could be liable for the actions of the male cadet, said the court, if he was "acting with authority bestowed by" the university-sanctioned ROTC program.

nevertheless seems questionable. Students may be at a more vulnerable age than many employees and may be encouraged by the academic environment to have more trust in teachers than would usually be the case with supervisors in the work environment. It is thus not apparent, either as a matter of policy or of law, why students should receive less protection from harassment under Title IX than employees do under Title VII.

In practice, the *Gebser* two-part liability standard provides scant opportunity for student victims of harassment to succeed with Title IX damages actions against educational institutions. The difficulty of proving "actual knowledge" is compounded by the difficulty of proving "indifference" (see, for example, *Wills v. Brown University*, 184 F.3d 20 (1st Cir. 1999)). In addition, since "actual knowledge" must be possessed by an official with authority to take corrective action, there are difficulties in proving that the officials or employees whom the victim notified had such authority. In *Liu v. Striuli*, 36 F. Supp. 2d 452, 465–66 (D.R.I. 1999), for instance, a court applying *Gebser* rejected a graduate student's Title IX claim because neither the director of financial aid nor the director of the graduate history department, whom the student had notified, had "supervisory authority" over the alleged harasser. Therefore neither official had authority to correct the alleged harassment. Similarly, in *Delgado v. Stegall*, 367 F.3d 668 (7th Cir. 2004), a student confided to a professor that she had been harassed by another professor and had also discussed the matter with a counselor. But her Title IX harassment claim failed because neither the professor nor the counselor had authority to take corrective action, and neither they nor the student had reported the harassment to a university official who did have such authority.[5]

In *Hayut v. State University of New York*, 352 F.3d 733 (2d Cir. 2003), the court had no difficulty determining that a jury could conclude that a professor's classroom behavior was "hostile educational environment sexual harassment." But the university was not liable for the professor's misconduct because its authorized officials did not have knowledge of the harassment until after it had ceased. The student plaintiff also could not meet the deliberate indifference test. Although the court acknowledged that "deliberate indifference may be found . . . when remedial action only follows after a 'lengthy and unjustified delay,'" there was no such delay in this case. Once the student did report the alleged harassment to the dean, the dean's response thereafter was timely and adequate.

In *Oden v. Northern Marianas College*, 284 F.3d 1058 (9th Cir. N. Mar. I. 2002), the plaintiff student did have evidence of a lengthy delay, but her Title

---

[5]It is important that institutions do not overemphasize such technical questions concerning legal liability. In resolving students' harassment complaints through campus grievance mechanisms, for instance, the primary focus of attention should be on whether harassment occurred, not on whether the institution could be liable in court if it did occur. Moreover, much of the institution's policy and practice regarding sexual harassment may be driven more by educational and ethical concerns than by legal concerns, as discussed later in this section.

IX claim failed nevertheless. The student had complained to college officials that her music professor had sexually harassed her on various occasions with various inappropriate acts. Once the student had reported the harassment, college personnel helped the student draft a formal internal complaint, provided counseling for her, began an investigation, and took other actions, culminating in a hearing by the college's Committee on Sexual Harassment, which determined that the professor's actions constituted sexual harassment. The student, dissatisfied with various aspects of the college's response, filed her Title IX suit, claiming that the college had acted with deliberate indifference. Her primary contention was that almost ten months had passed between the date of her formal complaint and the date of her hearing. In the context of the various actions that the college had taken in responding to the student's harassment allegations, the court declined to consider the delay as deliberate indifference:

> Although there was a lengthy delay, there were also valid reasons for the delay: [the College] had a number of administrative hurdles to jump, including the formation of a sexual harassment hearing committee; [the student] had difficulty retaining an attorney; and . . . had relocated to the State of New Mexico. At most, [the College] is guilty of bureaucratic sluggishness. We decline to equate bureaucratic sluggishness with "deliberate indifference," especially where the school authorities began turning their bureaucratic wheels immediately after being notified of the alleged misconduct [284 F.3d at 1061].

In the *Delgado* case (cited earlier in this section), although the court rejected the student's claim, it did provide clarification of the actual notice standard that could prove helpful to student victims in subsequent cases. Specifically, the court explained that the university could have been liable under Title IX if university officials had foreknowledge that the alleged harasser (the professor) had harassed other students. It was not necessary, for purposes of the "actual knowledge" requirement, that officials knew of the professor's harassment of the plaintiff (the complaining student). "So if, for example, [the professor] had been known to be a serial harasser, [university officials] might well be found to have had a sufficient approximation to actual knowledge that [the plaintiff] would be harassed." This argument did not work for the student in this case because, even though the professor "had made advances to three other woman students, . . . they had never filed complaints" (367 F.3d at 670). The professor therefore "was not known by anyone in the university administration . . . to be harassing other students" (367 F.3d at 672).

Although the new *Gebser* standards are very difficult for plaintiffs to meet, these standards do not create an insurmountable barrier for students challenging a faculty member's harassment. For example, in *Chontos v. Rhea*, 29 F. Supp. 2d 931 (N.D. Ind. 1998), a student filed a Title IX claim against Indiana University, claiming that a professor of physical education had forcibly kissed and fondled her. The university had received three other complaints about this professor from three different women students over the prior seven years. After the first incident, he received a written reprimand and was warned that if he repeated the behavior he could be fired. After the second incident, the professor was sent for psychological counseling, but the university did not follow up to ascertain whether the counseling was successful. After the third incident (which, in contrast to the others, was limited to verbal harassment), the faculty member was told to "clean up his act." A sealed report was placed in his personnel file, but no disciplinary action was taken. After the fourth incident, which was the subject of this litigation, he was suspended and offered the choice of a dismissal proceeding or resignation. The professor resigned with full benefits. Ruling that a reasonable jury could find that the university was deliberately indifferent, the court rejected the university's motion for summary judgment. With respect to the university's defense that the students did not want to pursue formal complaints, which meant that, under university rules, they would not confront the professor in a formal termination hearing, the court replied that the university had other sanctions available short of dismissal, but chose "to do nothing."

A U.S. Court of Appeals has helpfully distinguished between sexual harassment cases such as *Gebser*, in which "the defendant did not learn about the alleged harasser's proclivities until the alleged harasser became a teacher . . . at the defendant's school," and cases in which the defendant had preexisting knowledge of the teacher's past sexual misconduct and hired the teacher despite this knowledge. In this case, *Williams v. Board of Regents of the University System of Georgia*, 477 F.3d 1282 (11th Cir. 2007) (discussed at greater length in Section 7.1.5 of this book), the court made clear that both types of situations may provide the basis for a valid Title IX sexual harassment claim. In other words, the defendant's "actual knowledge" and "deliberate indifference," required by *Gebser*, may come either before or after the harassment. For further recent support for this conclusion and the underlying concepts (although not in a context of harassment by faculty), see *Simpson v. University of Colorado Boulder*, 500 F.3d 1170 (10th Cir. 2007).

The *Gebser* court did not utilize the distinction between quid pro quo harassment and hostile environment harassment that previous courts had sometimes invoked. Although the *Gebser* liability standard clearly applies to hostile environment claims, it is not entirely clear whether it would apply in the same way to quid pro quo harassment—or, as courts increasingly put it, to harassment that involves a "tangible" adverse action against the victim. Thus, it is not entirely clear whether earlier cases applying a different liability standard (easier for plaintiffs to meet) to quid pro quo claims (see, for example, *Kadiki v. Virginia Commonwealth University*, cited earlier in this section) are still good law. So far, the answer is apparently no. The court in *Burtner v. Hiram College*, 9 F. Supp. 2d 852 (N.D. Ohio 1998), *affirmed without opinion*, 194 F.3d 1311 (6th Cir. 1999), applied the *Gebser* actual knowledge standard to both types of harassment; the court in *Liu v. Striuli*, 36 F. Supp. 2d 452 (D.R.I. 1999), applied the actual notice standard to quid pro quo harassment; and the court in *Klemencic v. Ohio State University*, 10 F. Supp. 2d 911 (S.D. Ohio 1998), *affirmed*, 263 F. 3d 504 (6th Cir. 2001), applied the actual notice and the deliberate indifference standards to quid pro quo harassment. Similarly, in the administrative realm, the Department of Education's Sexual Harassment Guidance "moves away from specific labels for types of sexual harassment," using the distinction between quid pro quo and hostile environment harassment only for explanatory purposes ("Revised Sexual Harassment Guidance," Part V.A and Preamble, under "Harassment by Teachers and Other School Personnel").

After *Gebser*, lawsuits against institutions for money damages are not the only way students may enforce their Title IX rights. There are two other ways: (1) suing the institution in court and seeking injunctive or declaratory relief rather than money damages; and (2) in lieu of or in addition to suit, filing an administrative complaint against the institution with the U.S. Department of Education and seeking administrative compliance. (See Figure 8.1.)

|  | Avenues of Enforcement | | |
|---|---|---|---|
| **Identities of Harassers** | Judicial Claims for Damages | Judicial Claims for Injunctive/ Declaratory Relief | Administrative Claims |
| Harassment by Teacher | Category 1 | Category 7 | Category 13 |
| Harassment by Staff Member | Category 2 | Category 8 | Category 14 |
| Harassment by Officer or Administrator | Category 3 | Category 9 | Category 15 |
| Harassment by Peer | Category 4 | Category 10 | Category 16 |
| Harassment by Peer with Authority | Category 5 | Category 11 | Category 17 |
| Harassment by Third Party | Category 6 | Category 12 | Category 18 |

Figure 8.1 A Typology of Title IX Claims

The first alternative, since it does not itself seek monetary damages, is apparently not directly governed by the *Gebser* case—whose factual context is limited to monetary liability and whose legal rationale seems dependent on the negative impact of monetary damage awards upon educational institutions. It is therefore not clear what the liability standard would be for a Title IX harassment claim seeking only injunctive or declaratory relief. Even if the actual knowledge standard did apply, it would likely be easily met, since the lawsuit itself would have provided such notice well before the court would order the institution to comply with Title IX.

The second alternative—the administrative complaint—is apparently not governed at all by *Gebser*. In the administrative process, the U.S. Department of Education is presumably free to use standards of institutional noncompliance that differ from the *Gebser* liability standards, as long as its standards are consistent with the nondiscrimination prohibitions in the Title IX statute and regulations. Since the institution would always receive notice of its noncompliance and the opportunity to make appropriate adjustments before any administrative penalty is imposed, and since an administrative proceeding would never result in a monetary damages remedy against the institution, it appears that the U.S. Department of Education may continue to apply its own Sexual Harassment Guidance (cited earlier in this section) to administrative complaints, compliance investigations, and fund cutoff hearings (see *Gebser* at 287, 292). Indeed, in the aftermath of *Gebser* and the successor *Davis* case on peer sexual harassment (see Section 7.1.5 of this book), the Education Department issued a revised guidance (66 Fed. Reg. 5512 (January 2001)) that reaffirms the department's own separate standards that it had first articulated in the 1997 guidance (above). (See "Revised Sexual Harassment Guidance: Harassment of Students by School Employees, Other Students, or Third Parties," 66 Fed. Reg. 5512 (January 19, 2001), available at http://www2.ed.gov/about/offices/list/ocr/docs/shguide.html.)

Colleges and universities have considerable leeway in fulfilling their legal obligations under the *Gebser* case (as well as the *Davis* case that deals with peer harassment; see Section 7.1.5). The monetary liability standards in these cases are not onerous and should be viewed as the minimum or floor—not the full extent—of the institution's responsibilities regarding sexual harassment. The standards for injunction and declaratory relief cases may be a bit stricter for institutions, but these cases are seldom pursued by students. The standards for compliance in the Department of Education's Sexual Harassment Guidance are stricter for institutions but nevertheless leave considerable discretion in the hands of institutions. Thus, as is true in other legal contexts as well, educational and ethical standards can be as important as Title IX legal standards in guiding institutional planning, and nonlegal solutions to campus problems can be as viable as legal solutions—or more so.

Since sexual harassment can do substantial harm to the victims and have substantial adverse consequences for the campus community, and since sexual harassment is such a sensitive matter to deal with, institutions will likely engage in considerable institutional planning and educational programming.

A highly pertinent perspective and useful starting point for doing so is contained in the "preamble" accompanying the Department of Education's Revised Sexual Harassment Guidance. The preamble emphasizes that a central concern of Title IX is whether schools can recognize when harassment has occurred and take "prompt and effective action calculated to end the harassment, prevent its recurrence, and, as appropriate, remedy its effects" ("Revised Sexual Harassment Guidance," under "Enduring Principles from the 1997 Guidance"). In this regard, the preamble makes two key points. First:

> If harassment has occurred, doing nothing is always the wrong response. However, depending on the circumstances, there may be more than one right way to respond. The important thing is for school employees or officials to pay attention to the school environment and not to hesitate to respond to sexual harassment in the same reasonable, commonsense manner as they would to other types of serious misconduct [id.].

Second, it is critically important

> [to have] well-publicized and effective grievance procedures in place to handle complaints of sex discrimination, including sexual harassment complaints . . . Strong policies and effective grievance procedures are essential to let students and employees know that sexual harassment will not be tolerated and to ensure that they know how to report it [id.; see also Parts V.D, X of Revised Sexual Harassment Guidance].

Following these two key points, there are numerous initiatives that colleges and universities might undertake. These include educational programs for students; workshops and other training programs for instructors, staff, and leaders of student organizations; counseling and support programs for victims; counseling programs for perpetrators; and alternative dispute resolution programs that provide mediation and other non-adversarial means for resolving some sexual harassment complaints (but not those involving sexual assault). Institutions should also make sure that sexual harassment is covered clearly and specifically in their student disciplinary codes and faculty ethics codes. It is equally important to ensure that retaliation against persons complaining of sexual harassment is clearly covered and prohibited in such codes. In addition, institutions should make sure that mechanisms are in place for protecting the confidentiality of students who report that they—or others—have been sexually harassed (see "Revised Sexual Harassment Guidance," Part VII.B); and for protecting the due process rights and free speech rights of anyone accused of harassment. Through such initiatives, colleges and universities can work out harassment problems in a multifaceted manner that lessens the likelihood of lawsuits against them in court. Effectuating such initiatives will require good teamwork between administrators and college counsel.

Another related decision institutions may face in drafting and enforcing sexual harassment policies is whether to prohibit all sexual relationships between students and faculty members, consensual or not. Proponents of a total ban argue that the unequal power relationships between student and faculty member mean that no relationship is truly consensual. Opponents of total bans, on the other hand, argue that students are usually beyond the legal age for consent and that institutions may infringe on constitutional rights of free association or risk invasion-of-privacy claims if they attempt to regulate the personal lives of faculty and students.

Sexual harassment claims may also be brought under 42 U.S.C. § 1983, which is used to enforce the Fourteenth Amendment equal protection clause against both institutions and individuals (see Section 3.4 of this book). Unlike Title IX claims, Section 1983 claims can be brought only against public institutions and individuals employed by public institutions. Moreover, claims against an institution can succeed only if the challenged actions were taken pursuant to an established institutional policy or custom (see Section 3.4 of this book). Claims against individuals can succeed only if the plaintiff can defeat the qualified immunity defense typically asserted by individuals who are Section 1983 defendants (see Section 4.4.4). In *Oona R.S. v. McCaffrey*, 143 F.3d 473 (9th Cir. 1998), for instance, a student who was allegedly harassed by a student teacher used Section 1983 to sue school officials who were allegedly responsible for permitting the harassment. The court held that the student had stated a valid equal protection claim for gender discrimination and rejected the officials' qualified immunity defense.

In *Hayut v. State University of New York*, 352 F.3d 733 (2d Cir. 2003), a student filed a Section 1983 claim against a professor whom she alleged had harassed her and against three administrators whom she claimed were supervisors of the professor at the time of the harassment. The court acknowledged that a hostile environment sexual harassment claim may also be an equal protection claim that can be brought under Section 1983 if the professor and the supervisors were acting "under color of law" (see Section 3.4 of this book). Since the student's evidence concerning the professor's classroom conduct was sufficient to sustain a Section 1983 claim, the appellate court reversed the district court's entry of summary judgment in the professor's favor. The student's failure to report the professor's harassment to a supervisor until after the course was over was not fatal to the student's claim. "Given the power disparity between teacher and student a factfinder could reasonably conclude that a student-victim's inaction, or counter-intuitive reaction does not reflect the true impact of objectionable conduct. . . 'What students will silently endure is not the measure of what a college must tolerate'" (*Hayut*, 352 F.3d at 749, quoting *Vega v. Miller* 273 F.3d 460, 468 (2d Cir. 2001)). Regarding the administrators, however, the appellate court affirmed summary judgment in their favor because the student had not introduced any evidence of their "personal involvement" in the harassment. To bring a Section 1983 claim against supervisory personnel for the actions of a subordinate, the plaintiff must have shown that the supervisors participated in the harassment, failed to take corrective action after being notified of the harassment, created "a policy or custom to foster the unlawful conduct," committed "gross negligence in supervising subordinates" who committed the harassment, or were deliberately indifferent "to the rights of others by failing to act on information regarding the [harassment]."

In *Lipsett v. University of Puerto Rico*, above, the plaintiff also sued university officials under 42 U.S.C. § 1983 in their individual capacities (see Section 4.4.4 of this book). The court held that individuals can be liable for a subordinate's actions (including harassment) in certain circumstances:

> A state official . . . can be held liable . . . if (1) the behavior of such subordinates results in a constitutional violation and (2) the official's action or inaction was "affirmative[ly] link[ed]," *Oklahoma City v. Tuttle*, 471 U.S. 808 . . . (1985), to that behavior in the sense that it could be characterized as "supervisory encouragement, condonation, or acquiescence" or "gross negligence amounting to deliberate indifference" [864 F.2d at 902].

Since the plaintiff had discussed the harassment numerous times with the dean, the director of surgery, and the director of the surgical residency program, the court concluded that "supervisory encouragement" could be found and that Section 1983 liability could attach.

Prior to the ruling of the U.S. Supreme Court in *Fitzgerald v. Barnstable School Committee*, 555 U.S. 246 (2009), it was unclear whether Title IX precluded lawsuits seeking damages for sexual harassment under 42 U.S.C. § 1983. In *Fitzgerald*, the U.S. Supreme Court ruled that such claims could be brought under Title IX, Section 1983, or both statutes. In a case decided prior to *Fitzgerald*, but consistent with its rationale, *Cox v. Sugg*, 484 F. 3d 1062 (8th Cir. 2007), the student plaintiff sued a professor (the alleged harasser), the university president, and the university chancellor individually; Title IX therefore could not apply, and the case proceeded as a Section 1983 suit asserting a violation of the equal protection clause. The court was concerned, however, about construing Section 1983 so broadly that it "would trump the Supreme Court's careful crafting of the implied statutory damage action under Title IX." To avoid such a result, the court applied the Title IX liability standards for *institutions* (under *Gebser*) to the equal protection claims against the president and chancellor as *individuals*. Finding that the student had not presented sufficient proof that the president or chancellor had actual notice or was deliberately indifferent, the court determined that these defendants were entitled to qualified immunity under 42 U.S.C. § 1983 and dismissed the case against them. Regarding the professor, however, the court determined that the Section 1983 claims "pending against [him] in the district court are analytically distinct" and therefore could still be heard by the district court. And in a case decided after *Fitzgerald*, the court applied the Title VII analysis to a sexual harassment claim brought by a student under Section 1983 (*Ray v. Bowers*, 767 F. Supp. 2d 575 (D.S.C. 2009) (awarding summary judgment to the professor and college because the student's conduct negated her claim that the professor's sexual conduct was unwelcome)). It appears that courts are still searching for appropriate standards by which to evaluate sexual harassment claims by students brought under Section 1983.

Another possibility for a student harassment victim is a claim brought under a state nondiscrimination law. In *Smith v. Hennepin County Technical Center*,

1988 U.S. Dist. LEXIS 4876 (D. Minn. 1988), two students brought suit under Minnesota's statute, charging their instructor in a dental laboratory with offensive touching and retaliation when they complained of his conduct. The court ruled that, under the state law, the, plaintiff must show that "she was subject to unwelcome harassment," that "the harassment was based on sex," and that "the harassment had the purpose or effect of unreasonably interfering with her education or created an intimidating, hostile, or offensive learning environment." In addition, using the federal Title VII law by analogy, the court determined that the educational institution would be liable for the acts of its employees if it "knew or should have known of the harassment and failed to take proper remedial action." Because the instructor was an employee of the institution, the court ruled that the institution would be directly liable for his acts of its employee if it should have known of them and could have prevented them through the exercise of reasonable care.

The case of *Godfrey v. Princeton Theological Seminary*, 952 A.2d 1034 (N.J. 2008), provides another example of how a student harassment victim may bring a claim under a state nondiscrimination law. The case, which is discussed in Section 7.4.2, also illustrates that students may bring claims involving alleged harassers who are neither other students nor faculty members.

State tort law claims challenging harassment can be brought against both institutions and individual employees, either public or private, but public institutions and their officials will sometimes be immune from suit (see Section 3.2.1). The types of tort claims that could cover harassment include intentional (or negligent) infliction of emotional distress, assault, battery, negligent hiring, negligent supervision, and negligent retention. In *Chontos v. Rhea*, 29 F. Supp. 2d 931 (N.D. Ind. 1998), for example, the court allowed a student to proceed with a negligent retention claim against a university based on the university's awareness of a professor's prior harassment of students. But in *Wills v. Brown University*, 184 F.3d 20 (1st Cir. 1999), the court determined that a student complaining of a professor's harassment had not established viable claims of intentional infliction or negligent hiring against the university. And in *Gonzales v. North Carolina State University*, 659 S.E.2d 9 (N.C. Ct. App. 2008), a state appellate court affirmed an Industrial Commission finding that the university's failure to respond to an *employee's* claim of harassment by a faculty member was the proximate cause of harassment of two *students* ten years later by the same faculty member. The students filed claims of negligent supervision (against the university) and negligent infliction of emotional distress (against the professor). The employee had not wished to file a formal complaint concerning the earlier harassment, so the university had not investigated, nor had administrators spoken with the alleged harasser. The court criticized the university, saying that "numerous members of the university's administration were aware of the allegations" by the employee, and that, with or without a formal complaint, an investigation should have been conducted.

Contract claims are also a possibility in harassment cases. In *George v. University of Idaho*, 822 P.2d 549 (Idaho Ct. App. 1991), a law student, who had ended a consensual relationship with a law professor, filed a breach of contract claim against the university, asserting that the professor's efforts to resume the relationship, and his retaliation in the form of actions disparaging her character within the law school and the legal community, constituted breach of an implied contract. The court denied summary judgment for the university, noting the existence of several questions of fact concerning the nature and scope of the university's responsibility to the student. First of all, the court noted, the university had an implied contract with the student—as evidenced by the university's sexual harassment policy and by its statement in the faculty handbook that it would "fulfill its responsibilities in pursuit of the academic goals and objectives of all members of the university community." Furthermore, when the student brought the professor's actions to the attention of the school, a written agreement had been executed, in which the professor promised to stop harassing the plaintiff if she would drop claims against him and the law school. The court found that the university had an obligation under that agreement independent of its implied contract with the plaintiff, an obligation that extended beyond her graduation, to take reasonable measures to enforce the agreement.

Another type of legal claim may be developing in the arena of sexual harassment law—breach of fiduciary duty. In *Schneider v. Plymouth State College*, 744 A.2d 101 (N.H. 1999), the court ruled that the relationship between students and professors is built on trust and that because students are subject to the power of the professor to award grades and provide reference letters, it is difficult for them to reject unwelcome sexual advances by a faculty member. Said the court:

> When the plaintiff enrolled at [the college], she became dependent on the defendants for her education, thereby requiring them 'to act in good faith and with due regard' for her interests . . . The relationship between students and those that teach them is built on a professional relationship of trust and deference, rarely seen outside the academic community. As a result, we conclude that this relationship gives rise to a fiduciary duty on behalf of the defendants to create an environment in which the plaintiff could pursue her education free from sexual harassment by faculty members [744 A.2d at 106, citations omitted].

Sexual harassment, of course, is not the only form of harassment that is a problem on college campuses or that may be actionable under the law. It is, however, the type of harassment most often associated with problems concerning grades and credits earned by students, and the type of harassment that is most often addressed in court opinions. Other forms of harassment, all of which would apparently fall within the scope of pertinent civil rights statutes, include racial harassment, harassment on the basis of national origin, harassment of students with disabilities, harassment on the basis of sexual orientation or gender identity, and harassment on the basis of age. The U.S. Department of Education has determined that racial harassment is within the scope of Title VI and has issued guidelines for dealing with racial harassment issues under that statute. See "Racial Incidents and Harassment Against Students at Educational Institutions: Investigative Guidance," 59 Fed.

Reg. 11448 (March 10, 1994), available at http://www2.ed.gov/about/offices/list/ocr/docs/race394.html. This guidance preceded the Sexual Harassment Guidance that was discussed earlier in this section and articulates liability standards in a slightly different way; but the policy is still comparable to the Sexual Harassment Guidance, and like that guidance, the standards are much tougher on institutions than the judicial standards for sexual harassment articulated in the *Gebser* case.

Another form of harassment that has created substantial problems for colleges and universities, as well as elementary and secondary schools, is harassment on the basis of sexual orientation. As indicated at the beginning of this section, same-sex harassment may sometimes be covered under Title IX as a form of sexual harassment. In other circumstances, it now seems clear that same-sex harassment is also covered by the equal protection clause of the Fourteenth Amendment, in which case victims of such harassment in public postsecondary institutions may use 42 U.S.C. § 1983 to sue individual instructors, administrators, staff persons, and other students who have participated in the harassment. And same-sex harassment may be prohibited by state law (see, for example, *L.W. v. Toms River Regional Schools Board of Education*, 886 A.2d 1090 (N.J. Super. Ct. App. Div. 2005)). In two public school cases concerning peer harassment, two federal courts of appeals have ruled that local school personnel may be held personally liable for failing to protect gay students from persistent patterns of peer harassment, including verbal and physical abuse (see *Nabozny v. Podlesny*, 92 F.3d 446 (7th Cir. 1996); and *Flores v. Morgan Hill Unified School District*, 324 F.3d 1130 (9th Cir. 2003)).

## Section 8.6. Academic Dismissals and Other Academic Sanctions

**8.6.1. Overview.** As noted in Section 8.1, judicial review of academic decisions is more deferential than judicial review of institutional decisions involving misconduct of some kind. Drawing the line between decisions that involve "academic" or professional judgment, on the one hand, and the application of the institution's student conduct rules and regulations, on the other, may be difficult.

This section reviews the legal issues that may be involved when a decision is made to dismiss or otherwise sanction a student on the basis of the student's academic performance. In some cases, however, inadequate academic performance may be combined with misconduct such as plagiarism, cheating, or breaches of professional codes of ethics. These cases are discussed in Section 9.3. In challenging academic dismissals and related sanctions, students may attempt to state breach of contract claims (Section 8.6.2), fiduciary duty claims (Section 8.6.2), constitutional claims (Section 8.6.3), or discrimination claims (Section 8.6.4). They may also claim that the procedures used to reach the decision were defective (Section 8.6.5).

An example of the difficulty in drawing the line between academic judgments and discipline for misconduct occurred in *Byrnes v. Johnson County Community College*, Civ. Act. No. 10-2690-EFM-DJW (D. Kan. 2010).

Four nursing students were suspended from their program for posting a picture of themselves with the placenta of a patient on a Facebook page—an apparent violation of patient privacy and professional ethics. No hearing was held, as the suspension was characterized as an academic judgment. One student sued, claiming constitutional due process violations. A trial judge ordered the student reinstated because "the college had not established that the students' action was a clear violation of professional conduct," and they believed that they had their instructor's permission to post the photo ("Judge Orders College to Reinstate Student Who Posted a Placenta Photo Online," *Chron. Higher Educ.*, January 6, 2011, available at http://chronicle.com/blogs/ticker/judge-orders-college-to-reinstate-student-who-posted-a-placenta-photo-online/29555).

***8.6.2. Contract issues and fiduciary duty issues.*** When students are either denied a degree or dismissed for academic reasons, they may claim a contract breach by the institution for failure to follow its policies. A case brought by a student against Yale University and his faculty advisors provides an interesting example of the use of contract law to challenge alleged professional misconduct by a graduate student's faculty mentors. In *Johnson v. Schmitz*, 119 F. Supp. 2d 90 (D. Conn. 2000), the student claimed that several professors had appropriated his ideas and used them in publications without his consent and without acknowledgment. The court refused to dismiss the student's breach of contract claims because the plaintiff stated that he had relied upon specific promises contained in university catalogs and documents, including "express and implied contractual duties to safeguard students from academic misconduct, to investigate and deal with charges of academic misconduct, and to address charges of academic misconduct in accordance with its own procedures" (119 F. Supp. 2d at 96). Although the university argued that judicial review of the student's claims involved inappropriate involvement in academic decisions, the court disagreed. Explaining that the student did not allege that he was provided a poor-quality education, but rather that the university breached express and implied contractual duties that it had assumed, the court said that its review would be limited to "whether or not Yale had a contractual duty to safeguard its students from faculty misconduct, and, if so, whether that duty was breached in Johnson's case" (119 F. Supp. 2d at 96).

The student also asserted a claim based upon the "fiduciary duty" theory. The concept of fiduciary duty, once applied primarily in the higher education context to members of an institution's board of trustees and senior administrators, is now being discussed as a potential duty assumed by academic advisors, particularly with respect to the relationship between a graduate student and his or her thesis advisor. *Black's Law Dictionary* defines "fiduciary" as a relationship "founded on trust or confidence reposed by one person in the integrity and fidelity of another." It does not arise from contract, and typically requires the trusted party to conform to a higher standard of conduct than the contractual concept of "good faith and fair dealing." Students have attempted to use this theory to argue that a graduate student is dependent upon the thesis advisor for assistance and support, and that the advisor must behave with complete integrity in carrying out his or her duties and always act in the best interest of the student.

Addressing the student's second claim, the trial court in *Johnson* said: "Given the collaborative nature of the relationship between a graduate student and a dissertation advisor who necessarily shares the same academic interests, the Court can envision a situation in which a graduate school, knowing the nature of this relationship, may assume a fiduciary duty to the student" (119 F. Supp. 2d at 97–98). The court also ruled that the student might be able to demonstrate that a fiduciary relationship existed between himself and his dissertation committee, and that the dissertation committee would need to demonstrate "fair dealing by clear and convincing evidence" because "the dissertation committee was created for no other purpose than to assist Johnson" (119 F. Supp. 2d at 98). The court in *Johnson* thus ruled that the case should proceed to trial on both of the student's claims. But another state court rejected a student's fiduciary duty claim; see *Swenson v. Bender*, 764 N.W.2d 596 (Minn. Ct. App. 2009), discussed in Section 7.1.3.

Students may also assert fiduciary duty claims in the context of sexual harassment. *Schneider v. Plymouth State College*, 744 A.2d 101 (N.H. 1999), is a case in which a state's highest court approved of this use of fiduciary duty theory. This case is discussed in Section 8.5.

Courts are increasingly holding institutions of higher education to their promises and representations in catalogs and policy documents, as suggested by the *Johnson* case above, but they have rejected students' attempts to claim that only the material in the written documents is binding on the student. For example, the Supreme Court of Alaska ruled in favor of a nursing professor at the University of Alaska who required a student who had failed a required course to take a course in "critical thinking." When the student complained to the dean of the School of Nursing and Health Sciences, the dean backed the professor, stating that because the requirement of this additional course was a condition of the student's remaining in the nursing program rather than removal from the program, the dean's decision was final and could not be appealed within the university. The student then filed a breach of contract claim in state court, asserting that the student handbook did not list the course in critical thinking as required for the nursing degree.

In *Bruner v. Petersen*, 944 P.2d 43 (Alaska 1997), the state's highest court affirmed a trial court's ruling that there was no breach of contract and also affirmed that court's award of attorney's fees to the university. Explicit language in the student handbook stated that it was not a contract and allowed for the possibility of establishing conditions for reenrollment in any required course that a student had failed. Furthermore, said the court, the student had received all of the appeal rights provided by the catalog.

In contrast, if an academic program applies unwritten criteria to a student who otherwise meets the published academic criteria for matriculation, a court may find a contract breach. In *McConnell v. LeMoyne College*, 808 N.Y.S. 2d 860 (N.Y. App. Div. 2006), a student applied to a master's program and was conditionally accepted. The department chair had indicated in a letter to the student that if he earned grades of B or better in his first four courses and completed all admission requirements, he would be accepted as a matriculated student. After spending one semester in the program, the student received a letter from the program director, stating that there was a "mismatch" between the student's "personal beliefs regarding teaching and learning and the [program's] goals," and that he was dismissed from the program. The student filed a C.P.L.R. 78 proceeding under New York law, a type of breach of contract claim. The court reviewed the letter and the stated criteria for admission in the program documents, concluding that the student had met all of the criteria and was matriculated at the time of his dismissal, which entitled him to "the due process procedures set forth in the College's rules and regulations" before he could be dismissed. The court ordered the student reinstated.

### 8.6.3. Constitutional issues.

As noted in Section 8.2, the Fourteenth Amendment's due process clause may apply to students facing suspension or dismissal from publicly supported schools for deficient academic performance. But even though academic dismissals may be even more damaging to students than disciplinary dismissals, due process affords substantially less protection to students in the former situation. Courts grant less protection because they recognize that they are less competent to review academic evaluative judgments than factually based determinations of misconduct and that hearings and the attendant formalities of witnesses and evidence are less meaningful in reviewing grading than in determining misconduct. Claims involving substantive due process are discussed in this section, as are First Amendment claims; claims involving procedural due process are discussed in Section 8.6.5.

Students attempting to state claims of substantive due process violations must demonstrate that they have been deprived of a liberty or property interest that is considered "fundamental," or (if the interest is not fundamental) that the action depriving them of a liberty or property interest was arbitrary and capricious. The U.S. Supreme Court reviewed the latter type of claim in *Regents of the University of Michigan v. Ewing*, 474 U.S. 214 (1985). In *Ewing* (discussed briefly in Section 8.1 earlier in this chapter), a medical student who had struggled academically failed a mandatory national examination. His request to retake the examination was denied by the medical school, despite the fact that other medical students had been permitted to retake the examination in the past. The Court assumed without deciding that Ewing had a property interest in remaining in medical school that is covered by the Fourteenth Amendment and then went on to consider whether Ewing had a right to be free of "arbitrary state action" depriving him of this interest. The Court explained that "any substantive constitutional protection against arbitrary dismissal would not necessarily give Ewing a right to retake the [examination]. The constitutionally protected interest alleged by Ewing in his complaint . . . and found by the courts below, derives from Ewing's implied contract right to continued enrollment free from arbitrary dismissal." But the trial court had ruled that there was no implied contract, nor any promise by the medical school, to allow Ewing to retake the examination. After citing cases cautioning courts to defer to "truly" academic judgments, the Court ruled for the university, saying "[t]his narrow avenue for judicial review precludes any conclusion that the decision to dismiss Ewing from the Inteflex program was such a substantial departure from accepted academic norms as to demonstrate that the faculty did not exercise professional judgment." Noting Ewing's "unenviable academic record," the Court concluded that the medical school's decision "rested on an academic judgment that is not beyond the pale of reasoned academic decision-making when viewed against the background of [Ewing's] entire career at the University of Michigan."

A federal appellate court further explained the very narrow protections of substantive due process in *Bell v. Ohio State University*, 351 F.3d 240 (6th Cir. 2003), noting that such protection extends only to liberty interests "protected by specific constitutional guarantees . . .," liberty interests that the Supreme Court "has found so rooted in the traditions and conscience of our people as to be fundamental," and liberty interests that the government has infringed by means that "shock the conscience." Noting that the Supreme Court has been reluctant to define substantive due process expansively, the court in *Bell* reminded the parties that the high court had never actually found that continued enrollment was a property interest protected by due process, but had only assumed this to be so in both *Horowitz* and *Ewing*. The *Bell* court rejected the plaintiff medical student's contention that dismissal from medical school could constitute a substantive due process violation. The court concluded that, even if it were to assume that the medical student was protected by substantive due process in this situation, the medical college had used "reasoned academic decision-making" to make the dismissal determination.

In *Rogers v. Tennessee Board of Regents*, 273 F. App'x 458 (6th Cir. 2008), another appellate panel from the same circuit, relying on *Bell*, rejected a nursing student's claim that her interest in continued enrollment in a public university's nursing program was protected by substantive due process. And in *Bissessur v. Indiana University Board of Trustees*, 581 F.3d 599 (7th Cir. 2009), the court stated flatly: "A graduate student does not have a federal constitutional right to a continued graduate education," citing *Williams v. Wendler*, 530 F.3d 584, 589 (7th Cir. 2008). To the same effect, see *Davis v. George Mason University*, 395 F. Supp. 2d 331 (E.D. Va. 2005), *affirmed*, 2006 U.S. App. LEXIS 19981 (4th Cir. August 3, 2006), holding that students have neither substantive nor procedural due process rights to continued enrollment. Thus, it appears that substantive due process claims brought by students challenging academic dismissals are unlikely to succeed, unless the student demonstrates that he or she was deprived of a liberty or property interest protected by the Fourteenth Amendment and also demonstrates a very clear case of arbitrary and capricious conduct on the part of the institution. Alternatively, the student could show that the dismissal implicates some interest, beyond continued enrollment, that a court could consider fundamental. With either type of attempted showing, it would have to be a very unusual case to result in a ruling for the student.

Students may be on stronger ground when they assert state constitutional claims involving free speech or free exercise of religion when challenging

academic dismissals or other negative decisions based upon academic requirements; the *Axson-Flynn* case discussed in Section 7.1.4 of this book is an excellent example of such a challenge. Two other instructive examples arise from
the rulings of two federal courts considering student claims that their constitutional rights of free speech, free exercise of religion, due process, and equal
protection were violated when master's programs in counseling required the
students to set aside their religious and moral beliefs when counseling clients. In *Ward v. Wilbanks*, 2010 U.S. Dist. LEXIS 127038 (E.D. Mich. July 26,
2010), *reversed and remanded sub nom Ward v. Polite*, 667 F.3d 727 (6th Cir.
2012), the plaintiff had been dismissed from a master's program in counseling
and sought summary judgment against the university. In *Keeton v. Anderson-
Wiley*, 733 F. Supp. 2d 1368 (S.D. Ga. 2010), *affirmed*, 664 F.3d 865 (11th Cir.
December 16, 2011), the plaintiff sought a preliminary injunction to keep a
graduate program in counseling from requiring her to meet certain academic
requirements. The appellate court in *Keeton* affirmed the trial court's rejection
of that plaintiff's request for a preliminary injunction. In contrast, the appellate
court in *Ward* remanded that case for trial, ruling that a jury would need to
determine whether, by dropping her from the program, the faculty was actually
punishing the student for her religious views or whether the faculty was only
enforcing the code of ethics. The parties settled *Ward* in late 2012. Both rulings
are reminders of how important it is that faculty and program administrators
have clear academic requirements based upon appropriate pedagogical goals
and ethical considerations, and also of how important it is that faculty members apply these requirements evenhandedly. The free speech and free exercise
claims in both of these cases are discussed in Section 7.1.4 of this book.

Constitutional claims by students disputing the evaluation of their performance in clinical settings, such as internships or hospital rotations, have
increased, but are rarely successful. For example, in *Heenan v. Rhodes*, 757
F. Supp. 2d 1229 (M.D. Ala. 2010), a nursing student alleged that her dismissal from the program was not for inadequate academic and clinical performance, as the school had maintained, but was in retaliation for her complaints
about faculty members and the way that she was evaluated. With respect to
her First Amendment claim, the court ruled that her speech was unprotected
because it was not a matter of public concern, citing *Tinker v. Des Moines* (see
Section 9.4.1), and that the school had ample pedagogical reasons to dismiss
her. In light of the fact that the speech at issue was not political, as was the
speech in *Tinker*, the court also analyzed her claims under *Brown v. Li* and
*Hazelwood* (see Section 7.1.4), and concluded that both cases supported the
school's authority to make academic judgments about student behavior and
performance, even if the content of the student's speech was at issue. Showing
some appreciation for the challenges faced by faculty, and deference to their
academic judgments, the court commented:

> How teachers grade, and, in particular, how they treat those students who
> attempt to use gripes about grades and the grading systems as excuses for
> poor performance, is one of those pedagogical concerns that are at the heart of

the teaching profession. These gripes, whether voiced privately or openly, are generally not constitutionally protected speech subject to court review [757 F. Supp. 2d at 1241].

*Snyder v. Millersville University*, 2008 U.S. Dist. LEXIS 97943 (E.D. Pa. December 3, 2008), addresses the interplay between student performance at an off-campus internship site and the university's decision not to award the student the degree she sought. In *Snyder*, the student was seeking the degree of bachelor of science in education (BSE), as well as certification as a teacher in Pennsylvania. In order to satisfy the degree requirements, she had to complete a term of student teaching with a satisfactory evaluation. Because of a number of problems with her performance, the school district evaluated her as unsatisfactory in several categories. Therefore, Millersville University refused to award her the degree in education, but awarded her a bachelor of arts degree in English instead. Because she had not fulfilled all of the requirements for certification, she could not receive a teaching certificate.

One of the reasons that the school district determined that Snyder's performance was unsatisfactory was that she did not maintain enough "professional distance" from her students. An example of that problem was that Snyder told her students that she had a Myspace Web page and that they should communicate with her through that Web page. Although her supervisor warned her not to discuss her Myspace account with her students, Snyder continued to do so and posted a picture of herself with a drink in her hand. The picture was captioned "drunken pirate." The school district decided that this posting, combined with other evidence of Snyder's substandard performance, meant that Snyder should not continue her student teaching assignment, and they informed her that she was not to return to the school.

Snyder sued the university and several faculty members and administrators individually for violating her First Amendment free speech rights and her Fifth and Fourteenth Amendment due process rights. Although the court dismissed the due process claims, ruling that Snyder had received sufficient process, it refused to dismiss her First Amendment claim. The court conducted a non-jury trial and concluded that Snyder was not entitled to judgment on her claims, or to an injunction ordering the university to award her the teaching degree.

The court rejected the student's claim that the university had violated her First Amendment free speech rights by denying her the BSE degree. In analyzing this claim, the court was first required to determine whether the student was acting as a "public employee" in her role as a student teacher, or whether she was in a student role. The court determined that she was acting in the capacity of a "public employee" when she created the MySpace posting. Therefore, she would be protected by the First Amendment only if the speech in the posting was a matter of public concern. Citing *Connick v. Myers* (discussed in Section 6.1.1), the court determined that the speech was not a matter of public concern because it raised only "personal matters." Had the court determined that the plaintiff was acting as a student, the court would have been required to apply the *Tinker* standard (discussed in Section 9.4.1), which would have required the university to demonstrate that the posting caused "material and substantial disruption."

The court explained that it was the school district's negative evaluation of Snyder that led the university to give her a failing grade in her student teaching assignment. The university lacked the authority to grant Snyder the BSE degree, according to the court, because Pennsylvania state law requires that an individual complete the student teaching assignment with a satisfactory grade in order to be entitled to receive the BSE degree. To Snyder's demand that the court order faculty at the university to change their evaluations of her student teaching so that she could seek certification as a teacher, the court repeated that not only did the university lack the authority to recommend her for certification (because she had not fulfilled the student teaching requirement), but also that she was asking them to deceive the Pennsylvania Department of Education as to her fitness to be a teacher.

This case poses a complex array of issues for faculty and administrators. Three organizations—the university, the school district, and the state agency that licenses teachers—have jurisdiction over various portions of the evaluation of the student. The case is instructive because it demonstrates the importance of close collaboration and communication between the faculty in the academic department and the supervisors of its students at the off-campus internship or student teaching site. In this particular case, it appears that the university and the school district were in agreement as to the outcome, but it is not unforeseeable that conflict could occur between a college or university and the sites it relies on for practical training for its students.

**8.6.4. Discrimination issues.** In addition to prohibiting discrimination in admission to college (see Section 7.2 of this book), Titles VI and IX, the Americans with Disabilities Act and Section 504 of the Rehabilitation Act, and the Age Discrimination Act also prohibit dismissal from college on the basis of race, sex, disability, or age. Students attempting to challenge academic dismissals on one of these grounds have been overwhelmingly unsuccessful.

In reviewing whether an academic dismissal was based upon race, gender, age, or disability, the courts have applied Title VII jurisprudence using the standard developed in *McDonnell Douglas Corp. v. Green* (see Section 4.5.2.1 of this book). Under that standard, a plaintiff must present a prima facie case of discrimination in order for the burden of producing evidence to shift to the institution, which then must present a "legitimate non-discriminatory reason" for the dismissal.

In *McConaughy v. University of Cincinnati*, 2010 U.S. Dist. LEXIS 142805 (S.D. Ohio, Sept. 28, 2010), the court explained the elements of a prima facie case when a student claims discrimination in challenging an academic dismissal:

> In the context of a claim involving discriminatory treatment . . ., the parties agree that plaintiff must first establish a *prima facie* case of discrimination by showing: (1) she was a member of a protected class; (2) she was performing the

academic requirements at a level well enough to meet her educator's legitimate expectations; (3) she suffered adverse treatment; and (4) the educational program continued to instruct and credit other students. *Darian v. University of Massachusetts Boston*, 980 F. Supp. 77, 91 (D. Mass. 1997)).

In *Manning v. Temple University*, 157 F. App'x 509 (3d Cir. 2005), the plaintiff, an African-American woman dismissed from medical school, argued that her dismissal was racially discriminatory. Her principal argument was that the medical school funneled all African-American medical students, irrespective of academic performance, into a special program that provided academic support for "socioeconomically disadvantaged" medical students. She argued that stereotyping, not her poor academic performance, was the reason for her dismissal. The court ruled that the plaintiff had not presented evidence sufficient to permit an inference that the dismissal was discriminatory and affirmed the lower court's award of summary judgment to the university.

Students claiming that an academic dismissal was a result of sex discrimination may bring Title IX claims (see Section 11.5.3). A doctoral student's claim that her inability to complete her doctoral degree was a result of retaliation for her complaints about sex discrimination persuaded a federal appeals court to allow her case to proceed. In *Emeldi v. University of Oregon*, 673 F.3d 1218 (9th Cir. 2012), a graduate student complained to university officials about alleged inequitable treatment of women students, including her, by her dissertation committee chair. The professor who was the subject of her complaint resigned as chair, and Emeldi could not find another faculty member to chair her dissertation committee. She filed a Title IX claim, asserting that the chair's resignation was in retaliation for her complaints about his behavior. The appellate court reversed a summary judgment award for the university and, in a 2-1 opinion, ordered that the case be tried. According to the court, although the university claimed that the chair resigned because the plaintiff would not listen to him or take his suggestions for improving her research, the close time proximity between the student's complaints and the professor's resignation suggested that the resignation was in retaliation for her complaints.

The student claimed that she had asked fifteen other faculty members to serve as her dissertation chair, but all of them had declined. The university argued that the other faculty members were either unable or unqualified to serve as Emeldi's dissertation chair. The majority suggested that the plaintiff's inability to identify a substitute chair was circumstantial evidence of "blackballing" by her former dissertation chair. One judge dissented vigorously from the majority's reversal of summary judgment, saying that the plaintiff's claims were speculative and unsupported by credible evidence.

The university requested a rehearing *en banc*, which was rejected, again over a vigorous dissent. The dissenting judge asserted that

> this decision will impair the open exchange of ideas in our schools and universities if applied, as the panel majority does, in the Title IX context . . .
> The relationship between professor and Ph.D. student requires both parties

to engage in candid, searing analysis of each other and each other's ideas. Methodology, philosophy and personality often lead to intractable disputes and, when they do, the professor must be free to walk away without fear of a frivolous discrimination suit [698 F.3d 715, 720].

The court's refusal to award summary judgment in this case suggests that faculty members may have less discretion to refuse to work with certain students, particularly if those students have filed complaints about the faculty member that could be linked to discrimination or whistleblower laws. Given the substantial investment of time that many faculty members make in mentoring graduate students, particularly at the dissertation stage, cases like *Emeldi* have the potential to alter the way that faculty members work with students.

Now that the U.S. Supreme Court has apparently resolved the issue of whether students can sue public institutions in federal court under Titles II and III of the ADA (see Section 8.4.1 earlier in this chapter), both public and private institutions may face challenges to academic dismissals under either the ADA or Section 504 of the Rehabilitation Act (or both). In reviewing student claims of failure to accommodate a disability, reviewing courts have examined the degree to which the institution attempted to accommodate the student's disabilities and the student's ensuing academic performance. For example, in *Kodatt v. Oklahoma City University*, 406 F. App'x 248 (10th Cir. 2010), the court reviewed the various accommodations provided to the student, including double time on exams and a quiet exam room. Although the student argued that the professor in one course knew that she had been given extra time to complete her exam and graded it "differently" than the exams of other students, the court ruled that it was the student's poor academic performance throughout her law school career, and not the alleged bias of one professor who gave her a D instead of a C–, that was the reason for her dismissal. Similarly, in *Falcone v. University of Minnesota*, 388 F.3d 656 (8th Cir. 2004), a student's allegation that he would have been able to remain in medical school if his professors had given him more or better feedback on his academic performance was rejected by the court. The court noted that, even in clinical rotations where the plaintiff received substantial feedback, he still failed the rotation, and that the medical school had provided numerous accommodations to the student. Despite these accommodations, the student was not able to meet the school's academic requirements.

Whether or not a student meets the definition of "disability" is a perennial issue in claims brought under the ADA or Section 504. As discussed in Section 8.4.2.1 earlier in this chapter, the student must demonstrate that the disability substantially interferes with a "major life activity." For example, in *Singh v. George Washington University School of Medicine and Health Sciences*, 508 F.3d 1097 (D.C. Cir. 2007), a medical student's inadequate performance on timed tests was deemed cause for dismissal. The student was diagnosed with learning disabilities just prior to her dismissal. She challenged the medical school's refusal to allow her to continue in the program with accommodations, and two trial and two federal appellate court rulings ensued. Ultimately, the appellate court determined that taking timed tests was not a "major life activity," and thus the student could not establish that she was disabled under the ADA. The court rejected her claim that the dismissal decision, made in 2003, should be reviewed under the broader definition of "disability" created by the ADA Amendments of 2008 (2011 U.S. App. LEXIS 24435 (D.C. Cir. December 9, 2011)).

As noted in Section 8.4.1, students must be judged "qualified" in order to be protected under either the ADA or Section 504. Students who cannot meet a program's academic and technical requirements, even if the students are provided "reasonable" accommodations, are not qualified and will not be able to state a claim under either the ADA or Section 504.

The civil rights laws do not provide for individual liability, and claims brought against individual faculty or administrators under Titles VI and IX, as well as under Section 504 and the ADA, will typically be dismissed. See, for example, *Machie v. Youssef*, 2011 U.S. Dist. LEXIS 129655 (D.D.C. November 9, 2011). Claims may, however, be brought against individuals employed by public institutions under 42 U.S.C. § 1983 (see Section 3.4 of this book).

### 8.6.5. Procedures for academic sanctions.

**8.6.5.1. Public institutions.** Although courts have not required public institutions to provide the type of procedural due process required for disciplinary sanctions to sanctions based upon academic performance, institutions must still provide reasons for their decisions and an opportunity for the student to respond (at least where a liberty or property interest is at stake). Although a few early cases began to suggest that Fourteenth Amendment procedural due process was required for academic as well as for disciplinary dismissals, the U.S. Supreme Court's ruling in *Horowitz* (discussed immediately below) halted that line of reasoning.

The leading case on the subject of judicial review of academic judgments is *Board of Curators of the University of Missouri v. Horowitz*, 435 U.S. 78 (1978). The university had dismissed the student, who had received excellent grades on written exams, for deficiencies in clinical performance, peer and patient relations, and personal hygiene. After several faculty members repeatedly expressed dissatisfaction with her clinical work, the school's council on evaluation recommended that Horowitz not be allowed to graduate on time and that, "absent radical improvement" in the remainder of the year, she be dropped from the program. She was then allowed to take a special set of oral and practical exams, administered by practicing physicians in the area, as a means of appealing the council's determination. After receiving the results of these exams, the council reaffirmed its recommendation. At the end of the year, after receiving further clinical reports on Horowitz, the council recommended that she be dropped from school. The school's coordinating committee, then the dean, and finally the provost for health sciences affirmed the decision.

Though there was no evidence that the reasons for the dismissal were conveyed to the liaison committee, the appellate court held that "Horowitz's dismissal from medical school will make it difficult or impossible for her to obtain employment in a medically related field or to enter another medical school." The court concluded that dismissal would so stigmatize the student as to deprive her of liberty under the Fourteenth Amendment and that, under the circumstances, the university could not dismiss the student without providing "a hearing before the decision-making body or bodies, at which she shall have an opportunity to rebut the evidence being relied upon for her dismissal and accorded all other procedural due process rights."

The Supreme Court found it unnecessary to decide whether Horowitz had been deprived of a liberty or property interest. Even assuming she had, Horowitz had no right to a hearing:

> Respondent has been awarded at least as much due process as the Fourteenth Amendment requires. The school fully informed respondent of the faculty's dissatisfaction with her clinical progress and the danger that this posed to timely graduation and continued enrollment. The ultimate decision to dismiss respondent was *careful and deliberate*. These procedures were sufficient under the due process clause of the Fourteenth Amendment. We agree with the district court that respondent was afforded full procedural due process by the [school]. In fact, the court is of the opinion, and so finds, that the school went beyond [constitutionally required] procedural due process by affording [respondent] the opportunity to be examined by seven independent physicians in order to be absolutely certain that their grading of the [respondent] in her medical skills was correct [435 U.S. at 85, emphasis added].

The Court relied on the distinction between academic and disciplinary cases that lower courts had developed in cases prior to *Horowitz*, finding that distinction to be consistent with its own due process pronouncements, especially in *Goss v. Lopez* (see Section 9.3.2 of this book):

> The Court of Appeals apparently read *Goss* as requiring some type of formal hearing at which respondent could defend her academic ability and performance . . . A school is an academic institution, not a courtroom or administrative hearing room. In *Goss*, this Court felt that suspensions of students for disciplinary reasons have a sufficient resemblance to traditional judicial and administrative fact finding to call for a "hearing" before the relevant school authority . . .
>
> Academic evaluations of a student, in contrast to disciplinary determinations, bear little resemblance to the judicial and administrative fact-finding proceedings to which we have traditionally attached a full hearing requirement. In *Goss*, the school's decision to suspend the students rested on factual conclusions that the individual students had participated in demonstrations that had disrupted classes, attacked a police officer, or caused physical damage to school property. The requirement of a hearing, where the student could present his side of the factual issue, could under such circumstances "provide a meaningful hedge against erroneous action." The decision to dismiss respondent, by comparison, rested on the academic judgment of school officials that she did not have the necessary clinical ability to perform adequately as a medical doctor and was making insufficient progress toward that goal. Such a judgment is by its nature more subjective and evaluative than the typical factual questions presented in

the average disciplinary decision. Like the decision of an individual professor as to the proper grade for a student in his course, the determination whether to dismiss a student for academic reasons requires an expert evaluation of cumulative information and is not readily adapted to the procedural tools of judicial or administrative decision making [435 U.S. at 85–90].

Seven years later, the U.S. Supreme Court again addressed the topic of the scope of judicial review in student challenges to academic dismissals. In *Regents of the University of Michigan v. Ewing*, 474 U.S. 214 (1985) (discussed in Section 8.6.3), the court elaborated on its decision in *Horowitz*, stating that courts would defer to the academic judgments of faculty and administrators unless "it is such a substantial departure from accepted academic norms as to demonstrate that the person or committee responsible did not actually exercise professional judgment." The combined effect of *Horowitz* and *Ewing* is to limit judicial scrutiny of "actual" academic judgments as long as the institution can demonstrate that the student was aware of the academic deficiencies and that the academic standards had been applied fairly. Thus, the due process required for "academic" decisions is not as formal as that required for disciplinary decisions.

Overall, two trends have emerged from the reported decisions in the wake of *Horowitz* and *Ewing*. First, litigation challenging academic dismissals on due process grounds has usually been decided in favor of the institutions. Second, courts have read *Horowitz* and *Ewing* as cases whose messages have meaning well beyond the context of constitutional due process and academic dismissal. Thus, *Horowitz* and *Ewing* also support the broader concept of "academic deference," or judicial deference to the full range of an academic institution's academic decisions. Both trends help insulate postsecondary institutions from judicial intrusion into their academic evaluations of students by members of the academic community. But just as surely, these trends emphasize the institution's own responsibilities to deal fairly with students and others and to provide appropriate internal means of accountability regarding institutional academic decision making.

*Horowitz* and *Ewing* signal the U.S. Supreme Court's lack of receptivity to procedural requirements for academic dismissals. Clearly, an adversary hearing is not required. Nor are all the procedures used by the university in *Horowitz* required, since the Court suggested that Horowitz received more due process than she was entitled to. But the Court's opinion does not say that *no* due process is required. Due process probably requires the institution to inform the student of the inadequacies in performance and their consequences on academic standing. Apparently, due process also generally requires that the institution's decision making be "careful and deliberate." See, for example, *Ceasar v. Holt*, 245 F. App'x 396 (5th Cir. 2007) (academic dismissal did not require a hearing if student had been given notice of his unsatisfactory academic progress and the decision to dismiss him was "careful and deliberate"). For the former requirements, courts are likely to be lenient on how much information or explanation the student must be given and also on how far in advance of formal dismissal the student must be notified. For the latter requirement, courts are likely to be very flexible, not demanding any particular procedure but rather accepting any decision-making process that, overall, supports reasoned judgments concerning academic quality. Even these minimal requirements would be imposed on institutions only when their academic judgments infringe on a student's "liberty" or "property" interest.

Since courts attach markedly different due process requirements to academic sanctions than to disciplinary sanctions, it is crucial to be able to place particular cases in one category or the other. The characterization required is not always easy. The *Horowitz* case is a good example. The student's dismissal was not a typical case of inadequate scholarship, such as poor grades on written exams; rather, she was dismissed at least partly for inadequate peer and patient relations and personal hygiene. It is arguable that such a decision involves "fact finding," as in a disciplinary case, more than an "evaluative," "academic judgment." Indeed, the Court split on this issue: five Justices applied the "academic" label to the case, two Justices applied the "disciplinary" label or argued that no labeling was appropriate, and two Justices refused to determine either which label to apply or "whether such a distinction is relevant."

So how does one distinguish between "academic" and "disciplinary"? Three federal appellate courts weighed in on the "academic" side in cases involving mixed issues of misconduct and poor academic performance. In *Mauriello v. University of Medicine and Dentistry of New Jersey*, 781 F.2d 46 (3d Cir. 1986), the court ruled that the dismissal of a medical student who repeatedly failed to produce thesis data was on academic rather than disciplinary grounds. In *Harris v. Blake*, 798 F.2d 419 (10th Cir. 1986), in reviewing a student's involuntary withdrawal for inadequate grades, the court held that a professor's letter to a student's file, charging the student with incompetent performance (including absence from class) and unethical behavior in a course, concerned academic rather than disciplinary matters. And in *Fenje v. Feld*, 398 F.3d 620 (7th Cir. 2005), the court characterized the dismissal of a medical resident for failing to disclose that he had been terminated from a previous residency as an academic rather than a disciplinary decision.

Although there is no bright line separating dismissals for the type of "academic" conduct to which a deferential standard of review should be applied from dismissals for academic misconduct (such as cheating), for which due process protections should be provided, the Supreme Court of Texas has provided some guidance. In *University of Texas Medical School at Houston v. Than*, 901 S.W.2d 926 (Tex. 1995), a medical student, Than, was dismissed for allegedly cheating on an examination. The University of Texas (UT) Medical School provided Than with the opportunity to challenge his dismissal before a hearing board. Than's hearing itself met due process requirements, but at the hearing's end, the hearing officer and the medical school official, who presented the case against Than, inspected the room in which the test had been administered. Than was not allowed to accompany them; he asserted that this decision was a denial of due process. The court agreed, characterizing the alleged cheating as conduct rather than a "failure to attain a standard of excellence in studies," and thus a disciplinary matter rather than an academic one. The court ruled that the exclusion of Than from the post-hearing inspection violated his procedural due process rights.

Also, a federal district court rejected the contentions of a defendant college that it was not required to follow its disciplinary procedures in cases of expulsion for "academic misconduct." In *Siblerud v. Colorado State Board of Agriculture*, 896 F. Supp. 1506 (D. Colo. 1995), Siblerud, a former student who was trying to complete his dissertation, was dismissed from the Ph.D. program in physiology after he twice submitted manuscripts to journals that included a footnote in which he represented himself as a current student. He was not given a hearing but was permitted to appeal his dismissal by using the graduate school's grievance process. Although the graduate school committee was divided, the provost affirmed the dismissal. Siblerud asserted that his dismissal was disciplinary, not academic, and the trial court agreed. Although the case was dismissed because the claim was time barred, the judge criticized the university's handling of the situation and characterized it as a disciplinary action, rather than one sounding in academic judgment.

These cases suggest that, when dismissal or other serious sanctions depend more on disputed factual issues concerning conduct than on expert evaluation of academic work, the student should be accorded procedural rights akin to those for disciplinary cases (see Section 9.3.2 of this book), rather than the lesser rights for academic deficiency cases. Of course, even when the academic label is clearly appropriate, administrators may choose to provide more procedural safeguards than the Constitution requires. Indeed, there may be good reason to provide some form of hearing prior to academic dismissal whenever the student has some basis for claiming that the academic judgment was arbitrary, in bad faith, or discriminatory (see Section 8.1). The question for the administrator, therefore, is not merely what procedures are constitutionally required but also what procedures would be the best policy choice for the particular institution.

**8.6.5.2. Private institutions.** Students challenging academic dismissals by private institutions are more limited in the legal theories they can select than students at public institutions. Students at private institutions may challenge a dismissal under a breach of contract theory, which would require a showing either that the institution did not follow its own policies and procedures or that the policies and procedures themselves were unfair. They may also claim some form of discrimination (discussed in Section 8.6.4).

In reviewing determinations of academic performance, rather than disciplinary misconduct, the courts have crafted lesser procedural requirements for private colleges. As is also true for public institutions, however, the line between academic and disciplinary cases may be difficult to draw. In *Napolitano v. Trustees of Princeton University*, 453 A.2d 263 (N.J. Super. Ct. App. Div. 1982), the court reviewed the university's withholding of a degree, for one year, from a student whom a campus committee had found guilty of plagiarizing a term paper. The student sued, claiming breach of contract, various constitutional issues, and several torts. In upholding the university's action, the court determined that the problem was one "involving academic standards and not a case of violation of rules of conduct." In so doing, the court distinguished "academic disciplinary actions" from disciplinary actions involving other types of "misconduct," according greater deference to the institution's decisions in the former context and suggesting that lesser "due process" protection was required. The resulting dichotomy differs from the dichotomy between academic and disciplinary decisions delineated in Section 8.6.5.1, suggesting the potential relevance of a third, middle category for "academic disciplinary" cases. Because such cases involve academic standards, courts should be sufficiently deferential to avoid interference with the institution's expert judgments on such matters; however, because such cases may also involve disputed factual issues concerning student conduct, courts should afford greater due process rights than they would in academic cases involving only the evaluation of student performance.

The Supreme Court of Iowa addressed the question of whether a medical student's dismissal for failure to successfully complete his clinical rotations was on academic or disciplinary grounds. In *Lekutis v. University of Osteopathic Medicine*, 524 N.W.2d 410 (Iowa 1994), the student had completed his coursework with the highest grades in his class and had scored in the 99th percentile in standardized tests. The student had serious psychological problems, however, and had been hospitalized several times while enrolled in medical school. During several clinical rotations, his instructors had found his behavior bizarre, inappropriate, and unprofessional and gave him failing grades. He was eventually dismissed from medical school.

The court applied the *Ewing* standard (see Section 8.6.1), reviewing the evidence to determine whether the medical school faculty "substantially departed from accepted academic norms [or] demonstrated an absence of professional judgment" (524 N.W.2d at 413). Although some evaluations had been delayed, the court found that the staff did not treat the student in an unfair or biased way and that there was considerable evidence of his inability to interact appropriately with patients and fellow medical staff.

New York courts addressing student challenges to academic dismissals rely on the language of *Susan M.*, discussed in Section 8.2 (involving a challenge to a law school grade), exhorting courts to limit judicial review of academic evaluations to "the question of whether the challenged determination was arbitrary and capricious, irrational, made in bad faith or contrary to Constitution or statute" (*In the Matter of Susan M. v. New York Law School*, 556 N.E.2d 1104, 1107 (N.Y. 1990)). In *Ochei v. Helene Fuld College of Nursing of North General Hosp.*, 802 N.Y.S. 2d 28 (N.Y. App. Div. 2005), the court rejected the breach of contract and human rights law claims of a student who was dismissed after failing a course twice. The court rejected the student's claim that the dismissal was arbitrary, capricious, and in bad faith.

Despite the judicial deference afforded academic dismissal decisions at private colleges and universities, good policy and good risk management suggest that students be given notice of their academic failings, provided with the opportunity to discuss these failings with a faculty member or academic administrator, and provided at least an informal appeal process before the dismissal is final. Such procedures will help ensure that the decision has been fairly reached and thoughtfully and thoroughly vetted.

# 9

# Student Disciplinary Issues

*Chapter 9 discusses a variety of issues related to student discipline. Legal guidelines for codes of student conduct, campus disciplinary systems, and student judicial hearings are examined, with particular attention to the constitutional due process requirements applicable to public colleges and universities. Student free speech and protest rights are also examined, and the "public forum doctrine" that undergirds and limits these rights is explained. The special problem of "hate speech" and the validity of hate speech codes is then addressed.*

## Section 9.1. Disciplinary and Grievance Systems

***9.1.1. Overview.*** Colleges and universities develop codes of student conduct (discussed in Section 9.2) and expect students to conform to those codes and standards. Sections 9.1 through 9.3 discuss student challenges to institutional attempts to discipline students for violations of these codes and standards. Section 9.1 presents the guidelines for disciplinary and grievance systems that afford students appropriate statutory and constitutional protections. Section 9.2 analyzes the courts' responses to student challenges to colleges' disciplinary rules, and Section 9.3 discusses a variety of legal limitations on institutions' authority to discipline students for social misconduct, with particular attention to the differences between public and private institutions. Sections 9.4 and 9.5 focus on the parameters of student free speech and expressive conduct, with special emphasis on student protests, free speech zones, and the phenomenon of "hate speech."

***9.1.2. Establishment of systems.*** Postsecondary institutions have extensive authority to regulate both the academic and the nonacademic activities and behavior of students. Within the confines of constitutional law, public institutions may create rules for student conduct, and develop systems to determine whether a student has violated one or more rules, and if so, what punishment should be meted out. Private institutions have somewhat more leeway than public institutions, but the rules of private colleges must comport with state law and any state constitutional protections that may exist.

It is not enough, however, for an administrator to understand the extent and limits of institutional authority. The administrator must also skillfully implement this authority through various systems for the resolution of disputes concerning students. Such systems should include procedures for processing and resolving disputes, substantive standards or rules to guide the judgment of the persons responsible for dispute resolution, and mechanisms and penalties with which decisions are enforced. The procedures, standards, and enforcement provisions should be written and made available to all students. Dispute resolution systems, in their totality, should create a two-way street; that is, they should provide for complaints by students against other members of the academic community as well as complaints against students by other members of the academic community.

The choice of structures for resolving disputes depends on policy decisions made by administrators, preferably in consultation with representatives of various interests within the institution. Should a single system cover both academic and nonacademic disputes, or should there be separate systems for different kinds of disputes? Should there be a separate disciplinary system for students, or should there be a broader system covering other members of the academic community as well? Will the systems use specific and detailed standards of student conduct, or will they operate on the basis of more general rules and policies? To what extent will students participate in establishing the rules governing their conduct? To what extent will students, rather than administrators or faculty members, be expected to assume responsibility for reporting or investigating violations of student conduct codes or honor codes? To what extent will students take part in adjudicating complaints by or against students? What kinds of sanctions can be levied against students found to have been engaged in misconduct? Can such students be fined, made to do volunteer work on campus, suspended or expelled from the institution, given a failing grade in a course or denied a degree, or required to make restitution? To what extent will the president, provost, or board of trustees retain final authority to review decisions concerning student misconduct?

Devices for creating dispute resolution systems may include honor codes or codes of academic ethics; codes of student conduct; bills of rights, or rights and responsibilities, for students or for the entire academic community; the use of various legislative bodies, such as a student or university senate; a formal judiciary system for resolving disputes concerning students; the establishment of grievance mechanisms for students, such as an ombudsperson or a grievance committee; and mediation processes that provide an alternative or supplement to judiciary and grievance mechanisms. On most campuses, security guards or some other campus law enforcement system may also be involved in the resolution of disputes and regulation of student behavior.

Occasionally, specific procedures or mechanisms will be required by law. Constitutional due process, for instance, requires the use of certain procedures before a student is suspended or dismissed from a public institution (see Section 9.3.2). The Title IX regulations (see Section 11.5.3 of this book) and the Family Educational Rights and Privacy Act (FERPA) regulations (see Section 7.8.1 of this book) require both public and private institutions to establish certain procedures for resolving disputes under those particular statutes. Even when specific mechanisms or procedures are not required by law, the procedures or standards adopted by an institution will sometimes be affected by existing law. A public institution's rules regarding student protest, for instance, must comply with First Amendment strictures protecting freedom of speech (see Section 9.4). And a public institution's rules regarding administrative access to or search of residence hall rooms, as well as the investigatory techniques of campus police at a public institution, must comply with Fourth Amendment strictures regarding search and seizure (Section 7.4.3). Although an understanding of the law is thus crucial to the establishment of disciplinary and grievance systems, the law by no means rigidly controls such systems' form and operation. To a large extent, the kind of system adopted will depend on the institution's history and campus culture.

Fair and accessible dispute resolution systems, besides being useful administrative tools in their own right, can also insulate institutions from lawsuits. Students who feel that their arguments or grievances will be fairly considered within the institution may forgo resort to the courts. If students ignore internal mechanisms in favor of immediate judicial action, the courts may refer the students to the institution. If students ignore internal mechanisms in favor of immediate judicial action, the courts may refuse to hear the case and refer the students back to the institution. In *Pfaff v. Columbia-Greene Community College*, 472 N.Y.S.2d 480 (N.Y. App. Div. 1984), for example, the New York courts dismissed the complaint of a student who had sued her college, contesting a C grade entered in a course, because the college had an internal appeal process and the student "failed to show that pursuit of the available administrative appeal would have been fruitless." See also *Brown v. State ex rel. State Board of Higher Education*, 711 N.W.2d 194 (N.D. 2006) (failure to exhaust internal remedies deprived the court of jurisdiction to review the revocation of a degree).

### 9.1.3. *Codes of student conduct.*
Three major issues are involved in the drafting or revision of codes of student conduct: the type of conduct the code will encompass, the procedures to be used when infractions of the code are alleged, and the sanctions for code violations.

Codes of student conduct typically proscribe both academic and social misconduct, whether or not the misconduct violates civil or criminal laws, and whether or not the misconduct occurs on campus. Academic misconduct may include plagiarism, cheating, forgery, or alteration of institutional records. In reviewing sanctions for academic misconduct and the degree of procedural protection required for students accused of such misconduct, courts have been relatively deferential (see Section 8.2 of this book).

Social misconduct may include disruption of an institutional function (including teaching and research) and abusive or hazing behavior (but limitations on speech may run afoul of free speech protections, as discussed in Section 9.5). Social misconduct may also encompass conduct that occurs off campus, particularly if the misconduct also violates criminal law and the institution can demonstrate that the restrictions are directly related to its educational mission or the campus community's welfare (*Krasnow v. Virginia Polytechnic Institute*, 551 F.2d 591 (4th Cir. 1977); *Wallace v. Florida A&M University*, 433 So. 2d 600 (Fla. Dist. Ct. App. 1983)).

Codes of student conduct should be sufficiently clear to inform students of the type of misconduct that may result in sanctions. This is particularly important at public institutions, where a code or rule that is vague or overbroad may result in claims of constitutional due process violations. For example, in *DeJohn v. Temple University*, 537 F.3d 301 (3d Cir. 2008), a federal appellate court agreed with a student's assertion that the university's code of conduct and, more specifically, its policy against sexual harassment, was overbroad and chilled his First Amendment right to free speech. *DeJohn* is discussed in Section 9.2.2 of this book.

Sanctions for code violations may range from a warning to expulsion, with various intermediate penalties, such as suspension or community service requirements. Students who are expelled may seek injunctive relief under the theory that they will be irreparably harmed; some courts have ruled that injunctive relief is not appropriate for sanctions short of expulsion (*Boehm v. University of Pennsylvania School of Veterinary Medicine*, 573 A.2d 575 (Pa. Super. Ct. 1990), but see *Jones v. Board of Governors*, 557 F. Supp. 263 (W.D.N.C.), *affirmed*, 704 F.2d 713 (4th Cir. 1983)). Students at public institutions may assert constitutional claims related to deprivation of a property or liberty interest (see Section 5.7.2.3 of this book), while students at both public and private institutions may file actions based on contract law.

If a code of conduct defines the offenses for which a student may be penalized by a public institution, that code must comply with constitutional due process requirements concerning vagueness. The requirement is a minimal one: the code must be clear enough for students to understand the standards with which their conduct must comply, and the code must not be susceptible to arbitrary enforcement. A public institution's code of conduct must also comply with the constitutional doctrine of overbreadth in any area where the code could affect First Amendment rights. Basically, this doctrine requires that the code not be drawn so broadly and vaguely as to include protected First Amendment activity along with behavior subject to legitimate regulation (see Sections 9.2.2 and 9.5 of this book). Finally, a public institution's student conduct code must comply with a general requirement of evenhandedness—that is, the code cannot arbitrarily discriminate in the range and types of penalties or in the procedural safeguards afforded various classes of offenders. *Paine v. Board of Regents of the University of Texas System*, 355 F. Supp. 199 (W.D. Tex. 1972), *affirmed per curiam*, 474 F.2d 1397 (5th Cir. 1973), concerned such discriminatory practices. The institution had given students convicted of drug offenses a harsher penalty and fewer safeguards than it gave to all other code offenders, including those charged with equally serious offenses. The court held that this differential treatment violated the equal protection and due process clauses.

The student codes of conduct at some institutions include an "honor code" that requires fellow students to report cheating or other misconduct that they observe. In *Vargo v. Hunt*, 581 A.2d 625 (Pa. Super. Ct. 1990), a state appellate court affirmed the ruling of a trial court that a student's report of cheating by a fellow student was subject to a conditional privilege. The Allegheny College honor code explicitly required students to report "what appears to be an act of dishonesty in academic work" to an instructor or a member of the honor committee. When Ms. Hunt reported her suspicions that Mr. Vargo was cheating, he was charged with, and later found guilty of, a violation of the disciplinary code, was suspended from the college for one semester, and received a failing grade in the course. Vargo then sued Hunt for defamation. The court ruled that Hunt had acted within the boundaries of the honor code and had not communicated the allegedly defamatory information beyond the appropriate individuals, and that the academic community had a common interest in the integrity of the academic process.

Sometimes a state law requires students to report wrongdoing on campus. A Texas anti-hazing law contains provisions requiring that anyone who has "firsthand knowledge of the planning of a specific hazing incident . . . or firsthand knowledge that a specific hazing incident has occurred," must report the incident to a college official (Tex. Educ. Code Ann. § 37.152). Failure to do so can result in a fine or imprisonment. Students charged with failure to report hazing, as well as with hazing and assault, challenged the law, arguing that compliance with the reporting provisions of the law required them to incriminate themselves in the alleged hazing incident, a violation of their Fifth Amendment rights. In *The State of Texas v. Boyd*, 2 S.W.3d 752 (Tex. App. 1999), a state appellate court affirmed the ruling of a trial court that held this provision of the law unconstitutional. The Court of Criminal Appeals of Texas reversed, however, noting that the anti-hazing law also provides for immunity from prosecution for anyone who testifies for the prosecution in such a case (38 S.W.3d 155 (Tex. Crim. App. 2001)).

As has been noted, codes of conduct can apply to students' off-campus actions as well as their on-campus activity. But the extension of a code to off-campus activity can pose significant legal and policy questions. The courts usually uphold the suspension or expulsion of students who were arrested and found guilty of a criminal offense, in particular, for drug possession or use. In *Woodis v. Westark Community College*, 160 F.3d 435 (8th Cir. 1998), the plaintiff, a nursing student expelled from the college after she pleaded nolo contendere to a charge of attempting to obtain a controlled substance with a forged prescription, asserted that the college's code of conduct was unconstitutionally vague. She also argued that the college's disciplinary procedure denied her procedural due process because the vice president of student affairs had too much discretion to determine the punishment for students who violated the code.

The college's code stated that students were expected to "conduct them-selves in an appropriate manner and conform to standards considered to be in good taste at all times" (160 F.3d at 436). The code also required students to "obey all federal, state, and local laws." The appellate court therefore rejected the student's vagueness claim, ruling that drug offenses are criminal violations and that she was on notice that criminal conduct was also a violation of college policy. With respect to the student due process claim, the court also rejected the student's claim and affirmed the ruling of the trial court that had used the principles developed in *Esteban v. Central Missouri State College* (Section 9.2.2): adequate notice, a clear indication of the charges against the student, and a hearing that provides an opportunity for the student to present her side of the case. Even if the vice president's discretion had been too broad (an issue that the court did not determine), the student had the right to appeal the vice president's decision to an independent disciplinary board and also to the president. The student had also been given a second hearing after her nolo contendere plea, at which she was permitted to consult with counsel, examine the evidence used against her, and participate in the hearing. These proce-dures provided the student with sufficient due process protections to meet the *Esteban* standard.

The degree to which the institution can articulate a relationship between the off-campus misconduct and the interests of the campus community is also an important consideration in these cases. In the *Woodis* case discussed above, the fact that it was a nursing student who had used a forged prescription very likely strengthened the institution's argument that her off-campus conduct was relevant to institutional interests. Particularly in cases in which the college or university links its attempt to regulate off-campus conduct to the health and safety of the campus community, courts have deferred to handbook language that includes off-campus misconduct within the ambit of the institution's disci-plinary rules and regulations. For example, in *Saliture v. Quinnipiac University*, 2006 U.S Dist. LEXIS 39326 (D. Ct. June 6, 2006), four students were dismissed from the university after hosting a party at their off-campus house at which underage students were provided alcohol. The student handbook expressly stated that it would "address issues with students who live off-campus and are involved in activities . . . off campus that may endanger the health, safety and welfare of Quinnipiac students . . . [The University] reserves the right to review and address incidents that occur off campus in which Quinnipiac students are involved." After a hearing, the students were dismissed from the university and sued for breach of contract and a preliminary injunction reinstating them to the university. The court pointed to the clear language of the handbook, said the university had followed the procedures for disciplinary hearings con-tained in the handbook, and ruled for the university.

Courts have generally upheld discipline meted out to students who have engaged in off-campus criminal misconduct. For example, in *Ali v. Stetson University*, 340 F. Supp. 2d 1320 (M.D. Fla. 2004), *affirmed*, 143 F. App'x 824 (11th Cir. 2005), the student, an individual of Iranian descent, had brandished a gun at individuals he encountered while vacationing with friends at a Florida beach. He was arrested for aggravated assault with a firearm several weeks later, and the police reported his arrest to administrators at Stetson. The university placed the student on interim suspension under the authority of a university policy that permits Stetson to take disciplinary action against a student for off-campus misconduct if the "student is charged with an off-campus conduct violation of federal, state, or local laws" or "when a student's behavior off-campus interferes with the rights of others [or] reflects adversely on the University." The student sued, claiming national origin discrimination. The court rejected that claim, ruling that the university had offered him the opportunity to return and required him only to agree to comply with the code of student conduct. (For another case involving off-campus criminal misconduct that persuaded a university to deny a student an MBA degree, despite his having completed all degree requirements, see *Rosenthal v. New York University*, 2012 U.S. App. LEXIS 9817 (2d Cir. May 16, 2012), discussed in Section 8.2 of this book.)

A new issue is whether a student may be disciplined for off-campus misconduct that occurred on a social network. In *Tatro v. University of Minnesota*, 800 N.W. 2d 811 (Minn. Ct. App. 2011), *affirmed*, 816 N.W.2d 509 (Minn. 2012), the student, who was enrolled in a mortuary science program, posted several comments on her Facebook page about her intent to "take out her aggression" on the cadaver with which she was working and her desire to "stab someone in the throat" with an embalming tool. The faculty filed a charge against her under the university's code of student conduct, accusing her of "threatening, harassing, or assaultive conduct," which is prohibited by the code. The panel found Tatro responsible for the violations and imposed several sanctions: a failing grade in the class, required enrollment in a clinical ethics course, composing a letter to department faculty addressing respect within the profession, and submission to a psychiatric examination. She was also placed on academic probation for the rest of her undergraduate career. Tatro appealed the panel's decision, and the provost upheld the decision and the sanctions. Tatro then filed a lawsuit and also released her Facebook postings to the media.

Tatro's lawsuit claimed that the university lacked the authority to sanction her for the off-campus misconduct and that its actions violated her right of free speech. (The free speech portion of this case is discussed in Section 7.5.) Reviewing the language of the code of conduct, the appellate court noted its provision that the code may apply "to off-campus student conduct when the conduct, as alleged, adversely affects a substantial University interest . . . or indicates that the student may present a danger or threat to the health or safety of the student or others." The court agreed with the university that Tatro's posts about taking out aggression and stabbing someone could have posed a danger to students or others. Thus, the court concluded that the university had the authority to charge Tatro with a code of conduct violation. The court also agreed that the university could include Tatro's violation of course rules as a code of conduct violation; a section of the code expressly included violation of "departmental regulations that have been posted or publicized" as a type of misconduct that the code addressed.

The Minnesota Supreme Court affirmed, but on different grounds. In a unanimous opinion, the high court confirmed that a university may not regulate "a student's personal expression at any time, at any place, for any claimed curriculum-based reason," but noted that the parties had agreed that "a university may regulate student speech on Facebook that violates established professional conduct standards." The court held that the program's requirement of ethical behavior, both on and off campus, was appropriate, and that the academic program's rules were "narrowly tailored and directly related to established professional conduct standards." The ruling is therefore most relevant to professional programs that are subject to ethical conduct standards, such as health science programs. (The free speech aspects of *Tatro*, and institutional reliance on ethical standards, are discussed in Section 7.1.4 of this book.)

Generally speaking, as long as the college can articulate a reasonable relationship between off-campus misconduct and the well-being of the college community, reviewing courts will not overturn a disciplinary action unless they find that the action was arbitrary, an abuse of discretion, or a violation of a student's constitutional rights. And if the college includes language in its student code of conduct specifying that off-campus conduct that affects the well-being of the college community is expressly covered by the code of conduct, the college will increase the likelihood that its defense of challenges to discipline for off-campus misconduct will be successful. Furthermore, to avoid problems in this area, administrators should ascertain that an off-campus act has a direct detrimental impact on the institution's educational functions before using that act as a basis for disciplining students.

Private institutions not subject to the state action doctrine (see Section 1.5.2 of this book) are not constitutionally required to follow these principles regarding student codes. Yet the principles reflect basic notions of fairness, which can be critical components of good administrative practice; thus, administrators of private institutions may wish to use them as policy guides in formulating their codes.

Another question that colleges and universities, irrespective of control, may wish to consider is whether the disciplinary code should apply to student organizations as well as to individual students. Should students be required to assume collective responsibility for the actions of an organization, and should the university impose sanctions, such as withdrawal of institutional recognition, on organizations that violate the disciplinary code?

**9.1.4. Judicial systems.** Judicial systems that adjudicate complaints of student misconduct must be very sensitive to procedural safeguards. The membership of judicial bodies, the procedures they use, the extent to which their proceedings are open to the academic community, the sanctions they may impose, the methods by which they may initiate proceedings against students, and provisions for appealing their decisions should be set out in writing and made generally available within the institution.

Whenever the charge could result in a punishment as serious as suspension, a public institution's judicial system must provide the procedures required by the due process clause (see Section 9.2.2). The focal point of these procedures is the hearing at which the accused student may present evidence and argument concerning the charge. The institution, however, may wish to include preliminary stages in its judicial process for more informal disposition of complaints against students. The system may provide for negotiations between the student and the complaining party, for instance, or for preliminary conferences before designated representatives of the judicial system. Full due process safeguards need not be provided at every such preliminary stage. *Andrews v. Knowlton*, 509 F.2d 898 (2d Cir. 1975), dealt with the procedures required at a stage preceding an honor code hearing. The court held that due process procedures were not required at that time because it was not a "critical stage" that could have a "prejudicial impact" on the final determination of whether the student violated the honor code. Thus, administrators have broad authority to construct informal preliminary proceedings—as long as a student's participation in such stages does not adversely affect his or her ability to defend the case in the final stage.

Although the due process requirements for student disciplinary systems are relatively modest (see Sections 9.1.2 and 9.1.3), public institutions that do not follow their own rules and regulations may face charges of constitutional due process violations. Depending on the severity of the deviation from the rules, the courts may side with the student. For example, in *University of Texas Medical School at Houston v. Than*, 901 S.W.2d 926 (Tex. 1995), discussed in Section 8.6.5.1, the Texas Supreme Court ruled that a medical student's procedural due process rights were violated when members of the hearing board that subsequently recommended his dismissal for academic dishonesty inspected the testing location without allowing Than to be present.

A question receiving increased attention is whether the judicial system will permit an accused student to have an attorney present. Several models are possible: (1) neither the college nor the student will have attorneys; (2) attorneys may be present to advise the student but may not participate by asking questions or making statements; or (3) attorneys may be present and participate fully in questioning and making opening and closing statements. A federal appellate court was asked to rule on whether a judicial system at Northern Illinois University that followed the second model—attorney present but a nonparticipant—violated a student's due process rights. In *Osteen v. Henley*, 13 F.3d 221 (7th Cir. 1993), the court wrote:

> Even if a student has a constitutional right to consult counsel . . . we don't think he is entitled to be represented in the sense of having a lawyer who is permitted to examine or cross-examine witnesses, to submit and object to documents, to address the tribunal, and otherwise to perform the traditional function of a trial lawyer. To recognize such a right would force student disciplinary proceedings into the mold of adversary litigation. The university would have to hire its own lawyer to prosecute these cases and no doubt lawyers would also be dragged in—from the law faculty or elsewhere—to serve as judges. The cost and complexity of such proceedings would be increased, to the detriment of discipline as well as of the university's fisc [13 F.3d at 225].

The court then balanced the cost of permitting lawyers to participate against the risk of harm to students if lawyers were excluded. Concluding that the risk of harm to students was "trivial," the court refused to rule that students have a constitutional right to the assistance of counsel.

Occasionally, a campus judicial proceeding may involve an incident that is also the subject of criminal court proceedings. The same student may thus be charged in both forums at the same time. In such circumstances, the post-secondary institution is not legally required to defer to the criminal courts by canceling or postponing its proceedings. As held in *Paine* (see Section 9.1.3) and other cases, even if an institution is public, such dual prosecution is not double jeopardy because the two proceedings impose different kinds of punishment to protect different kinds of state interests. The Constitution's double jeopardy clause applies only to successive criminal prosecutions for the same offense. Nor will the existence of two separate proceedings necessarily violate the student's privilege against self-incrimination.

The Supreme Court of Maine addressed the issue of double jeopardy in a situation in which a student was subject to criminal and college penalties for an offense he committed. *In State of Maine v. Sterling*, 685 A.2d 432 (Me. 1996), Sterling, a football team member and recipient of an athletic scholarship, had assaulted a teammate on campus. The university held a hearing under the student conduct code, determined Sterling had violated the code, and suspended him for the summer. In addition, the football coach withdrew the portion of Sterling's scholarship that covered room and board. Shortly thereafter, criminal charges were brought against Sterling. He pleaded not guilty and filed a motion to dismiss the criminal charges, stating that the prosecution of the criminal complaint constituted double jeopardy because he had already received a penalty through the revocation of his scholarship. A trial court agreed, and dismissed the criminal proceedings. The state appealed.

The Supreme Court of Maine reversed, determining that the withdrawal of the scholarship was not a punishment because it was done to further the purposes of the student disciplinary code and to protect the integrity of the public educational system. The court explained that protection from double jeopardy was available if each of three requirements was met:

1. the sanction in each forum was for the same conduct;
2. the non-criminal sanction and the criminal prosecution were imposed in separate proceedings; and
3. the non-criminal sanction constitutes punishment [685 A.2d at 434].

Although Sterling's situation satisfied elements 1 and 2, the court refused to characterize the withdrawal of the scholarship as "punishment," stating that the scholarship was a privilege that could be withdrawn for valid reasons.

A decision by the U.S. Supreme Court has clarified the double jeopardy standard. In *Hudson v. United States*, 522 U.S. 93 (1997), the Court held that bank officers who had been assessed civil monetary penalties by the Office of the Comptroller of the Currency could also be indicted for criminal violations based on the same transactions for which they had been assessed civil penalties. The majority stated that, despite the fact that civil monetary penalties had a deterrent effect, they could not be construed as so punitive that they had the effect of a criminal sanction because they were not disproportionate to the nature of the misconduct. *Hudson* suggests that it may now be more difficult for students to claim double jeopardy, particularly if the noncriminal proceeding occurs before the criminal proceeding (as is often the case in campus disciplinary actions). As always, those institutions that can demonstrate that their student codes of conduct and judicial systems are designed for educational purposes and to maintain order rather than to punish will be in the best position to defend against double jeopardy claims, whether they are used in the campus disciplinary case or a criminal matter.

While neither double jeopardy nor self-incrimination needs tie an administrator's hands, administrators may nevertheless choose, for policy reasons, to delay or dismiss particular campus proceedings when the same incident is in the criminal courts. It is possible that the criminal proceedings will adequately protect the institution's interests. Furthermore, student testimony at a campus proceeding could create evidentiary problems for the criminal court.

If a public institution proceeds with its campus action while the student is subject to charges still pending in criminal court, the institution may have to permit the student to have a lawyer with him or her during the campus proceedings. In *Gabrilowitz v. Newman*, 582 F.2d 100 (1st Cir. 1978), a student challenged a University of Rhode Island rule that prohibited the presence of legal counsel at campus disciplinary hearings. The student obtained an injunction prohibiting the university from conducting the hearing without permitting the student the advice of counsel. The appellate court, affirming the lower court's injunction order, held that when a criminal case based on the same conduct giving rise to the disciplinary proceeding is pending in the courts, "the denial to [the student] of the right to have a lawyer of his own choice to consult with and advise him during the disciplinary proceeding would deprive [him] of due process of law."

The court emphasized that the student was requesting the assistance of counsel to consult with and advise him during the hearing, not to conduct the hearing on the student's behalf. Such assistance was critical to the student because of the delicacy of the legal situation he faced:

> Were the appellee to testify in the disciplinary proceeding, his statement could be used as evidence in the criminal case, either to impeach or as an admission if he did not choose to testify. Appellee contends that he is, therefore, impaled on the horns of a legal dilemma: if he mounts a full defense at the disciplinary hearing without the assistance of counsel and testifies on his own behalf, he might jeopardize his defense in the criminal case; if he fails to fully defend himself or chooses not to testify at all, he risks loss of the college degree he is within weeks of receiving, and his reputation will be seriously blemished [582 F.2d at 103].

Similarly, a federal appellate court affirmed a trial court ruling that denying students facing both a campus disciplinary hearing and state criminal harassment charges the right to counsel violated their due process rights. In *Holmes v. Poskanzer*, 2008 U.S. Dist. LEXIS 13545 (N.D.N.Y. February 21, 2008), *affirmed*, 342 F. App'x 651 (2d Cir. 2009), two students who were disciplined for harassing a university administrator claimed that the discipline violated their due process rights and was in retaliation for their criticism of the university's administration. The trial court ruled that, although the denial of counsel violated due process, that right was not clearly established in the Second Circuit when the situation arose, and thus the defendants were protected by qualified immunity. After the rulings in *Holmes* and *Gabrilowitz*, a student's right to counsel in situations of simultaneous campus and criminal hearings is now established in the Second Circuit as well as the First Circuit.

If a public institution delays campus proceedings, and then uses a conviction in the criminal proceedings as the basis for its campus action, the institution must take care to protect the student's due process rights. A criminal conviction does not automatically provide the basis for suspension; administrators should still ascertain that the conviction has a detrimental impact on the campus, and the affected student should have the opportunity to make a contrary showing.

Given the deferential review by courts of the outcomes of student disciplinary proceedings (assuming that the student's constitutional or contractual rights have been protected), student challenges to these proceedings are usually unsuccessful. Even if the student is eventually exonerated, the institution that follows its rules and provides procedural protections will very likely prevail in subsequent litigation. For example, a state trial court rejected a student's attempt to state a negligence claim against a university for subjecting him to disciplinary proceedings for an infraction he did not commit. In *Weitz v. State of New York*, 696 N.Y.S.2d 656 (N.Y. Ct. Cl. 1999), the plaintiff was an innocent bystander during a brawl in his residence hall that involved individuals who did not live in the residence hall. In addition to claims of negligence with respect to the security of the residence hall, the student claimed that the university was negligent in prosecuting him for violating the institution's code of conduct when he had not done so. The court noted that there was no cause of action in New York for negligent prosecution and that it could find no public policy reason for creating such a cause of action simply because the student charged with a violation was ultimately found to be innocent.

## Section 9.2. Disciplinary Rules and Regulations

**9.2.1. Overview.** Postsecondary institutions customarily have rules of conduct or behavior that students are expected to follow. It has become increasingly common to commit these rules to writing and embody them in codes of conduct that are binding on all students (see Section 9.1.3). Although the trend toward written codes is a sound one, legally speaking, because it gives students fairer notice of what is expected from them and often results in a better-conceived and administered system, written rules also provide a specific target to aim at in a lawsuit.

Students have challenged institutional attempts to discipline them by attacking the validity of the rule they allegedly violated or by attacking the nature of the disciplinary proceeding that determined that the alleged violation occurred. This section discusses student challenges to the validity of institutional rules and regulations; Section 9.3 discusses challenges to the procedures used by colleges to determine whether, in fact, violations have occurred.

### 9.2.2. Public institutions.
In public institutions, students frequently contend that the rules of conduct violate some specific guarantee of the Bill of Rights, as made applicable to state institutions by the Fourteenth Amendment (see Section 1.5.2). These situations, the most numerous of which implicate the free speech and press clauses of the First Amendment, are discussed in Section 9.1 and various other sections of this chapter. In other situations, the contention is a more general one: that the rule is so vague that its enforcement violates due process; that is (as was noted in Section 9.1.3), the rule is unconstitutionally "vague" or "void for vagueness" or is overbroad and prohibits types of conduct or speech that are protected by the Constitution.

*Soglin v. Kauffman*, 418 F.2d 163 (7th Cir. 1969), is illustrative. The University of Wisconsin expelled students for attempting to block access to an off-campus recruiter as a protest against the Vietnam War. The university had charged the students under a rule prohibiting "misconduct" and argued in court that the university had inherent power to discipline, which need not be exercised through specific rules. Both the U.S. District Court and the U.S. Court of Appeals held that the misconduct policy was unconstitutionally vague. The appellate court reasoned:

> The [rule] . . . contains no clues which could assist a student, an administrator, or a reviewing judge in determining whether conduct not transgressing statutes is susceptible to punishment by the university as "misconduct."
> . . . [E]xpulsion and prolonged suspension may not be imposed on students by a university simply on the basis of allegations of "misconduct" without reference to any preexisting rule which supplies an adequate guide [418 F.2d at 167–68].

While similar language about vagueness is often found in other court opinions, the actual result in *Soglin* (the invalidation of the rule) is unusual. Most university rules subjected to judicial tests of vagueness have survived, sometimes because the rule at issue is less egregious than the "misconduct" rule in *Soglin*, sometimes because a court accepts the "inherent power to discipline" argument raised by the *Soglin* defendants and declines to undertake any real vagueness analysis, and sometimes because the student conduct at issue was so contrary to the judges' own standards of decency that they tended to ignore the defects in the rules in light of the obvious "defect" in behavior. *Esteban v. Central Missouri State College*, 415 F.2d 1077 (8th Cir. 1969), the case most often cited in opposition to *Soglin*, reveals all three of these distinctions. In this case, students contested their suspension under a regulation prohibiting "participation in mass gatherings which might be considered as unruly or unlawful."

In upholding the suspension, the court emphasized the need for "flexibility and reasonable breadth, rather than meticulous specificity, in college regulations relating to conduct" and recognized the institution's "latitude and discretion in its formulation of rules and regulations." The approach has often been followed in later cases—for instance, in *Jenkins v. Louisiana State Board of Education*, 506 F.2d 992 (5th Cir. 1975), where the court upheld a series of regulations dealing with disorderly assembly and disturbing the peace on campus.

Rules and policies may also be challenged on the basis of "overbreadth," a potential violation of the First Amendment. In *DeJohn v. Temple University*, 537 F.3d 301 (3d Cir. 2008), a graduate student challenged the university's code of student conduct, and in particular its sexual harassment policy, as unconstitutionally overbroad. The policy prohibited "expressive, visual or physical conduct of a sexual or gender-motivated nature and which has the purpose or effect of either unreasonably interfering with an individual's work, educational performance, or status, or creating an intimidating, hostile, or offensive environment." The court affirmed the trial court's conclusion that the policy was overbroad, saying "absent any requirement akin to a showing of severity or pervasiveness—that is, a requirement that the conduct objectively and subjectively creates a hostile environment or substantially interferes with an individual's work—the policy provides no shelter for core protected speech" (537 F.3d at 318). The appellate court also noted that colleges and universities have less leeway to regulate or punish harassing speech than administrators in K–12 schools, and that some speech that creates a hostile or offensive environment may nevertheless be protected by the First Amendment.

In addition to *procedural* due process and First Amendment challenges, institutional rules and their application may be challenged under *substantive* due process theories. Such challenges are possible when the institution may have violated fundamental privacy rights of a student or may have acted arbitrarily or irrationally. The latter argument, for instance, has been made in situations in which a college or school has enacted "zero tolerance" rules with respect to possession of controlled substances and weapons, a practice that requires punishment for possession despite the factual circumstances. In *Seal v. Morgan*, 229 F.3d 567 (6th Cir. 2000), a high school student was expelled after a knife was found in the glove compartment of his car. The student said that the knife belonged to a friend and that he was not aware that the knife was in the car. Under the school's zero tolerance rules, the student was expelled anyway. The trial and appellate courts rejected the school district's argument that the serious problem of weapons at school justified its summary action, stating that if the student had been unaware that he was "in possession" of a knife, then he could not have used it to harm anyone. Thus, said the court, the expulsion without an opportunity to determine whether the student had actual knowledge of his "possession" was a violation of substantive due process. The court remanded the case for trial on the issue of the student's credibility.

Although the judicial trend suggests that most rules and regulations will be upheld, administrators should not assume that they have a free hand in promulgating codes of conduct. *Soglin* signals the institution's vulnerability when it has no written rules at all or when the rule provides no standard to guide conduct. And even the *Esteban* court warned: "We do not hold that any college regulation, however loosely framed, is necessarily valid." To avoid such pitfalls, disciplinary rules should provide standards sufficient to guide both the students in their conduct and the disciplinarians in their decision making. A rule will likely pass judicial scrutiny if the standard "conveys sufficiently definite warning as to the proscribed conduct when measured by common understanding and practices" (*Sword v. Fox*, 446 F.2d 1091 (4th Cir. 1971), upholding a regulation that "demonstrations are forbidden in any areas of the health center, inside any buildings, and congregating in the locations of fire hydrants"). Regulations need not be drafted by a lawyer—in fact, student involvement in drafting may be valuable to ensure an expression of their "common understanding"—but it would usually be wise to have a lawyer play a general advisory role in the process.

Once the rules are promulgated, institutional officials have some latitude in interpreting and applying them, as long as the interpretation is reasonable. In *Board of Education of Rogers, Arkansas v. McCluskey*, 458 U.S. 966 (1982), a public school board's interpretation of one of its rules was challenged as unreasonable. The board had held that its rule against students being under the influence of "controlled substances" included alcoholic beverages. The U.S. Supreme Court, quoting *Wood v. Strickland* (see Section 4.4.4), asserted that "federal courts [are] not authorized to construe school regulations" unless the board's interpretation "is so extreme as to be a violation of due process" (458 U.S. at 969–70).

### 9.2.3. *Private institutions.*
Private institutions, not being subject to federal constitutional constraints (see Section 1.5.2 of this book), have even more latitude than public institutions do in promulgating disciplinary rules. Courts are likely to recognize that a broad right to make and enforce rules is inherent in the private student-institution relationship or to find such a right implied in some contractual relationship between student and school. Under this broad construction, private institutional rules will not be held to specificity standards such as those in *Soglin* (discussed in Section 9.2.2). Thus, in *Dehaan v. Brandeis University*, 150 F. Supp. 626 (D. Mass. 1957), the court upheld the plaintiff's suspension for misconduct under a policy in which the school "reserves the right to sever the connection of any student with the university for appropriate reason"; and in *Carr v. St. John's University, New York*, 231 N.Y.S.2d 410 (N.Y. App. Div. 1962), *affirmed*, 187 N.E.2d 18 (N.Y. 1962), the courts upheld the dismissal of four students for off-campus conduct under a regulation providing that "in conformity with the ideals of Christian education and conduct, the university reserves the right to dismiss a student at any time on whatever grounds the university judges advisable."

Despite the breadth of such cases, a private school administrator, like his or her public counterpart, should not assume a legally free hand in promulgating disciplinary rules. Courts can now be expected to protect private school students from clearly arbitrary disciplinary actions (see Section 1.5.3). When a school has disciplinary rules, courts may overturn administrators' actions taken in derogation of the rules. And when there is no rule, or the applicable rule provides no standard of behavior, courts may overturn suspensions for conduct that the student could not reasonably have known was wrong. Thus, in *Slaughter v. Brigham Young University*, 514 F.2d 622 (10th Cir. 1975), though the court upheld the expulsion of a graduate student for dishonesty under the student code of conduct, it first asked "whether the . . . [expulsion] was arbitrary" and indicated that the university's findings would be accorded a presumption of correctness only "if the regulations concerned are reasonable [and] if they are known to the student or should have been." To avoid such situations, private institutions may want to adhere to much the same guidelines for promulgating rules as are suggested for public institutions, despite the fact that private institutions are not required by law to do so.

### 9.2.4. Disciplining students with mental disorders.

Approximately one-third of college students have sought counseling or treatment for mental health disorders, according to a report issued in 2011 (Lauren Sieben, "Nearly a Third of College Students Have Had Mental-Health Counseling," *Chron. Higher Educ.*, March 14, 2011, available at http://chronicle.com/article/Nearly-a-Third -of-College/126726/). Students with mental or psychological disabilities are protected against discrimination by the Rehabilitation Act and the Americans with Disabilities Act (ADA) (see Sections 7.2.4.3. and 11.5.4 of this book; for student employees, see Section 4.5.2.5). Yet a student's misconduct may disrupt campus activities or the student may be dangerous to herself or to other students, faculty, or administrators. Opinion is divided among educators and mental health professionals on whether students suffering from mental disorders who violate the institution's code of student conduct should be subject to the regular disciplinary procedures or should be given a "medical withdrawal" if their presence on campus becomes disruptive or dangerous.

Several issues arise in connection with mentally ill students who are disruptive or dangerous. If campus counseling personnel have gained information from a student indicating that he or she is potentially dangerous, the teachings of *Tarasoff v. Regents of the University of California* (Section 4.4.2 of this book) and its progeny (as well as many state statutes codifying *Tarasoff*) may come into play and establish a duty to warn the potential target or targets of the violence. If administrators or faculty know that a student is potentially dangerous and that student subsequently injures someone, negligence claims based on the foreseeability of harm may arise (see Section 3.2.2). However, violations of the federal Family Educational Rights and Privacy Act (discussed in Section 7.8.1) and state privacy laws are possible if institutional officials routinely warn students' families or others of medical or psychological conditions.

Furthermore, college counseling staff may face tort claims for alleged negligence in treating or advising students with psychiatric disorders (see, for example, *Williamson v. Liptzin*, 539 S.E.2d 313 (N.C. 2000), in which the court rejected the claim by a student who shot two individuals that the negligence of the university psychiatrist who treated him was the proximate cause of his criminal acts and subsequent injuries). Or a student may claim that disclosure by a counselor of his psychiatric condition constitutes "malpractice" (see *Jarzynka v. St. Thomas University School of Law*, 310 F. Supp. 2d 1256 (S.D. Fla. 2004), in which the court rejected the plaintiff's malpractice claim because the counselor was not a mental health therapist).

Federal and state disability discrimination laws require colleges and universities, as places of public accommodation, to provide appropriate accommodations for otherwise qualified students with disabilities. But if a student's misconduct is related to the nature of the disability, and the conduct would otherwise violate the college's code of student conduct, administrators must face a difficult choice. This issue was addressed squarely in a case that has implications for higher education even though it involves a private elementary school. In *Bercovitch v. Baldwin School*, 133 F.3d 141 (1st Cir. 1998), a student with attention deficit disorder (ADD) performed acceptably in his studies, but consistently violated the school's code of conduct. The school made numerous attempts to accommodate his disruptive behavior even before it was aware of the diagnosis of ADD. After the diagnosis and medication, the student's disruptive behavior continued, and the school suspended the student. The parents brought a claim under Title III of the Americans with Disabilities Act. Although a trial court ruled that the school had to reinstate the student and make greater efforts to accommodate him, the appellate court disagreed. The student was not otherwise qualified for ADA purposes if he could not comply with the school's code of conduct, said the court. Furthermore, the student's disorder did not qualify for protection under the ADA because it did not substantially limit his ability to learn. (The court also explained that this private school was not subject to the Individuals with Disabilities Education Act (IDEA) (20 U.S.C. §§ 1400 et seq.), as are public schools, and had no obligation to provide an individualized educational plan or to provide accommodations that modified its disciplinary code or its academic programs.)

If a court determines that following the rules is an essential function of being a student, then the student may not be "otherwise qualified" and thus would be unprotected by disability discrimination law. A federal trial court rejected the claim of a graduate student that the university should have considered his learning disability when enforcing its code of conduct against him. In *Childress v. Clement*, 5 F. Supp. 2d 384 (E.D. Va. 1998), the plaintiff was charged with multiple violations of the honor code when he committed several acts of plagiarism. The honor board found him guilty of the violations and recommended his expulsion. The student appealed, but his appeal was denied and he was expelled from the university. He filed discrimination claims under the Americans with Disabilities Act and Section 504 of the Rehabilitation Act.

The court assumed without deciding that the plaintiff had a learning disability that qualified for protection under the ADA and Section 504. The court then turned to the issue of whether the plaintiff was a qualified individual with a disability—whether he could perform the essential functions of a graduate student. The court determined that complying with the honor code was an essential function of being a graduate student. Furthermore, said the court, the honor board had taken the plaintiff's disability into consideration when determining whether he had violated the honor code, thus complying with the ADA's requirement that an individualized determination be made as to whether an individual is qualified.

Students with disabilities who challenge disciplinary sanctions as discriminatory must establish that the college was aware of the student's disability and that the discipline resulted from that knowledge. In *Rosenthal v. Webster University*, 2000 U.S. App. LEXIS 23733 (8th Cir. 2000) (unpublished), a federal appellate court rejected a student's ADA and Rehabilitation Act claims that the university discriminated against him on the basis of his bipolar disorder by suspending him. The court found that the university was not aware of his disability before it suspended him, but took that action because the plaintiff had carried a gun onto campus and had threatened to use it.

In *Bhatt v. University of Vermont*, 958 A.2d 637 (Vt. 2008), a medical student was dismissed for falsifying evaluations from surgical rotations as well as his undergraduate academic record. The student sued the university under the Vermont Public Accommodations Act, 9 Vt. Stat. Ann. §§ 4500–4507 (the state's disability discrimination law), claiming that his Tourette's syndrome and obsessive compulsive disorder were the reason for his misconduct and for his dismissal. Because of his poor academic performance and his demonstrated misconduct, the court ruled that he was not a qualified person with a disability and therefore was not protected by the nondiscrimination law. And in *Ascani v. Hofstra University*, 1999 U.S. App. LEXIS 7654 (2d Cir. April 9, 1999), the court determined that a student whose behavior was determined to be a "direct threat" was not a qualified person with a disability.

If other courts rule that the ability to comply with reasonable code of conduct rules is an "essential function" of being a student, then students whose misconduct is linked to their disability will have considerable difficulty demonstrating that they should be exempt from that code of conduct under the ADA or Section 504.

Colleges and universities have struggled with how to respond to students who engage in behavior that may cause harm to themselves. Some institutions that have placed students with mental disorders on involuntary suspensions without due process or the interactive process required under the ADA and Section 504 have faced complaints to the Education Department's Office for Civil Rights (OCR) as well as lawsuits. (For a discussion of the enforcement mechanisms for Section 504, see Section 11.5.4 of this book).

Students challenging discipline or mandatory withdrawals for conduct related to a psychiatric disorder are more likely to file an OCR complaint than a lawsuit under either Section 504 or the ADA, given the length of time necessary for litigation. Until 2011, OCR required an institution seeking to discipline or exclude a student with a mental disorder to determine that the student is a "direct threat" to him- or herself or to others, and that the institution cannot provide a reasonable accommodation that will reduce or remove that threat. The institution must use an interactive process that will determine whether there is a "high probability of substantial harm and not just a slightly increased, speculative, or remote risk" (letter from OCR team leader to DeSales University, 2004, available at http://www.bcm.edu/ilru/dlrp/html/topical/FAPSI/OCR/ desales.html).

In 2010, the U.S. Department of Justice issued new final rules implementing Title II of the ADA (which applies to public colleges and universities) and narrowed the definition of "direct threat" to an individual who is a threat to others but not to him- or herself (75 Fed. Reg. 56180 (September 15, 2010)). This more limited definition of "direct threat," which the Office for Civil Rights has adopted for application to both public and private institutions, may limit an institution's ability to impose an involuntary withdrawal on a student whose risky behavior is potentially dangerous to the student him- or herself but not to others.

Given the potential for constitutional claims at public institutions and discrimination and contract claims at all institutions, administrators who are considering disciplinary action against a student with a mental or psychiatric disorder should provide due process protections (see Section 9.3.2). If the student has violated the institution's code of conduct and is competent to participate in the hearing, some experts recommend subjecting the student to the same disciplinary proceedings that a student without a mental or emotional impairment would receive (see, for example, Gary Pavela, *The Dismissal of Students with Mental Disorders* (College Administration Publications, 1985)). If the student is a danger to others, summary suspension may be appropriate, but post-suspension due process or contractual protections should be provided if possible.

## Section 9.3. Procedures for Suspension, Dismissal, and Other Sanctions

**9.3.1. Overview.** As Sections 9.1 and 8.6 indicate, both public and private postsecondary institutions have the clear right to dismiss, suspend, or impose lesser sanctions on students for behavioral misconduct or academic deficiency. But just as that right is limited by the principles set out in those sections, so it is also circumscribed by a body of procedural requirements that institutions must follow in effecting disciplinary or academic sanctions. These procedural requirements tend to be more specific and substantial than the requirements set out above, although they do vary depending on whether behavior or academics is involved and whether the institution is public or private (see Section 1.5.2).

At the threshold level, whenever an institution has established procedures that apply to the imposition of sanctions, the law will usually require that these procedures be followed. In *Woody v. Burns*, 188 So. 2d 56, 59 (Fla. 1966), for example, the court invalidated an expulsion from a public institution because a faculty committee had "circumvented . . . [the] duly authorized [disciplinary] committee and arrogated unto itself the authority of imposing its own penalty for appellant's misconduct." And in *Tedeschi v. Wagner College*, 49 N.Y.2d 652, 660 (N.Y. 1980), New York's highest court invalidated a suspension from a private institution, holding that "when a university has adopted a rule or guideline establishing the procedure to be followed in relation to suspension or expulsion, that procedure must be substantially observed."

There are three exceptions, however, to this "follow the rules" principle. First, an institution may be excused from following its own procedures if the student knowingly and freely waives his or her right to them, as in *Yench v. Stockmar*, 483 F.2d 820 (10th Cir. 1973), where the student neither requested that the published procedures be followed nor objected when they were not. Second, deviations from established procedures may be excused when they do not disadvantage the student, as in *Winnick v. Manning*, 460 F.2d 545 (2d Cir. 1972), where the student contested the school's use of a panel other than that required by the rules, but the court held that the "deviations were minor ones and did not affect the fundamental fairness of the hearing." And third, if an institution provides more elaborate protections than constitutionally required, failure to provide nonrequired protections may not imply constitutional violations (see Section 8.6.5).

Sections 9.3.2 and 9.3.3 focus on challenges to the fairness of the procedures that colleges use to determine whether a student has violated a campus rule or code of conduct, as well as the fairness of the sanction, if any, levied against the student. Because public colleges are subject to constitutional regulation as well as statutory and common law, disciplinary decisions at public colleges are discussed separately from those at private colleges.

### 9.3.2. Public institutions.

**9.3.2.1. Overview.** State institutions may be subject to state administrative procedure acts, state board of higher education rules, or other state statutes or administrative regulations specifying particular procedures for suspensions or expulsions. In *In re: Mary M. v. Clark*, 473 N.Y.S.2d 843 (N.Y. App. Div. 1984), the court refused to apply New York State's Administrative Procedure Act to a suspension proceeding at State University of New York–Cortland; but in *Mull v. Oregon Institute of Technology*, 538 P.2d 87 (Or. 1975), the court applied that state's administrative procedure statutes to a suspension for misconduct and remanded the case to the college with instructions to enter findings of fact and conclusions of law as required by one of the statutory provisions. And in *Morris v. Florida Agricultural and Mechanical University*, 23 So. 3d 167 (Fla. Dist. Ct. App. 2009), the court ruled that Florida's Administrative Procedure Act, Fla. Stat. §120.68(1) (2008), required a law school to provide a hearing for a student dismissed for falsifying his admission. The law provides that if a state agency takes a final action that adversely affects an individual without holding a hearing, and the validity of the agency's action depends on disputed facts, the district court must reverse the agency action. Because no hearing was held prior to the dismissal, the court ruled that the law school had to afford Morris a hearing.

The primary external source of procedural requirements for public institutions, however, is the due process clause of the federal Constitution, which prohibits the government from depriving an individual of life, liberty, or property without certain procedural protections. Since the early 1960s, the concept of procedural due process has been one of the primary legal forces shaping the administration of postsecondary education. For purposes of due process analysis, courts typically assume, without deciding, that a student has a property interest in continued enrollment at a public institution (see, for example, *Marin v. University of Puerto Rico*, 377 F. Supp. 613, 622 (D.P.R. 1974)). One court stopped short of finding a property interest, but said that the Fourteenth Amendment "gives rights to a student who faces expulsion for misconduct at a tax-supported college or university" (*Henderson State University v. Spadoni*, 848 S.W.2d 951 (Ark. Ct. App. 1993). Another court ruled explicitly that a student had a property interest in continued enrollment at a public community college (*Lankheim v. Florida Atlantic University*, 992 So. 2d 828 (Fla. Dist. Ct. App. 2008)). As did the court in *Marin*, the U.S. Supreme Court has assumed that a property interest exists in continued enrollment in a public institution (for example, in *Ewing* and *Horowitz*, discussed in Sections 8.6.3 and 8.6.5, respectively) but has not yet directly ruled on this point.

A landmark 1961 case on suspension procedures, *Dixon v. Alabama State Board of Education*, 294 F.2d 150 (5th Cir. 1961), is still very instructive. Several black students at Alabama State College had been expelled during a period of intense civil rights activity in Montgomery, Alabama. The students, supported by the National Association for the Advancement of Colored People (NAACP), sued the state board, and the court faced the question "whether [the] due process [clause of the Fourteenth Amendment] requires notice and some opportunity for hearing before students at a tax-supported college are expelled for misconduct." On appeal this question was answered in the affirmative, with the court establishing standards by which to measure the adequacy of a public institution's expulsion procedures:

> The notice should contain a statement of the specific charges and grounds which, if proven, would justify expulsion under the regulations of the board of education. The nature of the hearing should vary depending upon the circumstances of the particular case. The case before us requires something more than an informal interview with an administrative authority of the college. By its nature, a charge of misconduct, as opposed to a failure to meet the scholastic standards of the college, depends upon a collection of the facts concerning the charged misconduct, easily colored by the point of view of the witnesses. In such circumstances, a hearing which gives the board or the administrative authorities of the college an opportunity to hear both sides in considerable detail is best suited to protect the rights of all involved. This is not to imply that a full-dress judicial hearing, with the right to cross-examine witnesses, is required. Such a hearing, with the attending publicity and disturbance of college activities, might be detrimental to the college's educational atmosphere and impractical to carry out. Nevertheless, the rudiments of an adversary proceeding may be preserved without encroaching upon the interests of the college. In the instant case, the student should be given the names of the witnesses against him and an oral or written report on the facts to which each witness testifies. He should also be given the opportunity to present to the board, or at least to an administrative official of the college, his own defense against the charges and to produce either oral testimony or

written affidavits of witnesses in his behalf. If the hearing is not before the board directly, the results and findings of the hearing should be presented in a report open to the student's inspection. If these rudimentary elements of fair play are followed in a case of misconduct of this particular type, we feel that the requirements of due process of law will have been fulfilled [294 F.2d at 158–59].

Since the *Dixon* case, courts at all levels have continued to recognize and extend the due process safeguards available to students charged by college officials with misconduct. Such safeguards must now be provided for all students in publicly supported schools, not only before expulsion, as in *Dixon*, but before suspension and other serious disciplinary action as well (unless the student is a danger to the campus community and must be removed, in which case a post-removal hearing would be required). In 1975, the U.S. Supreme Court itself recognized the vitality and clear national applicability of such developments when it held that even a secondary school student faced with a suspension of less than ten days is entitled to "some kind of notice and . . . some kind of hearing" (*Goss v. Lopez*, 419 U.S. 565, 579 (1975)).

Although the Court in *Goss* was not willing to afford students the right to a full-blown adversary hearing (involving cross-examination, written transcripts, and representation by counsel), the Court did set out minimal requirements for compliance with the due process clause. The Court said:

We do not believe that school authorities must be totally free from notice and hearing requirements . . . [T]he student [must] be given oral or written notice of the charges against him and, if he denies them, an explanation of the evidence the authorities have and an opportunity to present his side of the story. The [Due Process] Clause requires at least these rudimentary precautions against unfair or mistaken findings of misconduct and arbitrary exclusion from school [419 U.S. at 581].

In cases subsequent to *Goss*, most courts have applied these "minimal" procedural standards and, for the most part, have ruled in favor of the college.

Probably the case that has set forth due process requirements in greatest detail and, consequently, at the highest level of protection, is *Esteban v. Central Missouri State College*, 277 F. Supp. 649 (W.D. Mo. 1967) (see also later litigation in this case, discussed in Section 9.2.2). The plaintiffs had been suspended for two semesters for engaging in protest demonstrations. The lower court held that the students had not been accorded procedural due process and ordered the school to provide the following protections for them:

1. A written statement of the charges, for each student, made available at least ten days before the hearing;
2. A hearing before the person(s) having power to expel or suspend;
3. The opportunity for advance inspection of any affidavits or exhibits the college intends to submit at the hearing;
4. The right to bring counsel to the hearing to advise them (but not to question witnesses);

5. The opportunity to present their own version of the facts, by personal statements as well as affidavits and witnesses;

6. The right to hear evidence against them and question (personally, not through counsel) adverse witnesses;

7. A determination of the facts of each case by the hearing officer, solely on the basis of the evidence presented at the hearing;

8. A written statement of the hearing officer's findings of fact; and

9. The right, at their own expense, to make a record of the hearing.

The judicial imposition of such specific due process requirements rankles many administrators. By and large, courts have been sufficiently sensitive to avoid such detail in favor of administrative flexibility (see, for example, *Moresco v. Clark*, 473 N.Y.S.2d 843 (N.Y. App. Div. 1984); *Henson v. Honor Committee of the University of Virginia*, 719 F.2d 69 (4th Cir. 1983)). Yet for the internal guidance of an administrator responsible for disciplinary procedures, the *Esteban* requirements provide a useful checklist. The listed items not only suggest the outer limits of what a court might require but also identify those procedures most often considered valuable for ascertaining facts where they are in dispute. Within this framework of concerns, the constitutional focus remains on *Dixon's* concept of notice and opportunity for hearing.

Although the federal courts have not required the type of protection provided at formal judicial hearings, deprivations of basic procedural rights can result in judicial rejection of an institution's disciplinary decision. In *Weidemann v. SUNY College at Cortland*, 592 N.Y.S.2d 99 (N.Y. App. Div. 1992), the court annulled the college's dismissal of a student who had been accused of cheating on an examination, and ordered a new hearing. Specifically, the court found these procedural defects:

1. Evidence was introduced at the hearing of which the student was unaware.

2. The student was not provided the five-day written notice required by the student handbook about evidence supporting the charges against him, and had no opportunity to defend against that evidence.

3. The hearing panel contacted a college witness after the hearing and obtained additional evidence without notifying the student.

4. The student was given insufficient notice of the date of the hearing and the appeal process.

5. The student was given insufficient notice (one day) of his right to appeal.

6. The student's attorney had advised college officials of these violations, but the letter had been ignored.

In *Phat Van Le v. University of Medicine & Dentistry of NJ*, 379 F. App'x 171 (3d Cir. 2010), however, a federal appellate court rejected the claims of a dental student who was expelled for cheating on an examination and asserted that the institution had violated due process by failing to follow the disciplinary process precisely. The court concluded that, despite the fact that the hearing committee was permitted to consider information that the student had not been provided, he was not denied due process because he was permitted to respond to those charges at a later time. The court explained that the student "was afforded extensive procedural protections: notice, a hearing before a panel of students and faculty, the right to present witnesses and evidence, the right to cross examine witnesses, a lay adviser in the room, an attorney outside the hearing room, two levels of appeal (during one of which he was represented by counsel), and the opportunity to submit further evidence after the hearing." Citing *Winnick* (discussed in Section 9.3.1), the court ruled that, as long as the procedural protections satisfy due process requirements, a school's failure to follow its own policies is not a per se violation of due process.

In addition to possible due process problems listed above, a long delay between the time a student is charged and the date of the hearing may disadvantage the student. Although a federal trial court rejected a student's claim that a nine-month delay in scheduling his disciplinary hearing was a denial of due process (*Cross v. Rector and Visitors of the University of Virginia*, 84 F. Supp. 2d 740 (W.D. Va. 2000), *affirmed without opinion*, 2000 U.S. App. LEXIS 22017 (August 28, 2000)), ensuring that hearings are held in a timely fashion should discourage such due process claims.

It appears that, in general, as long as the college provides notice of the charges, an opportunity to explain his or her side of the story, and a hearing before an unbiased body, due process requirements are met. See, for example, *Willis v. Texas Tech University Health Sciences Center*, 394 F. App'x 86 (5th Cir. 2010); see also *Esfeller v. O'Keefe*, 391 F. App'x 337 (5th Cir. 2010).

Students preparing for careers in professions subject to a code of ethics who have been charged with violations of the institution's code of student conduct may also be charged with ethical violations. In *Parker v. Duffey*, 251 F. App'x 879 (5th Cir. 2007), two students who were enrolled in a graduate program in professional counseling, marriage, and family therapy at Texas State University were charged with forging a faculty member's name on documents required for reimbursement for expenses incurred in traveling to a professional conference. The students had been told that the university could not fund their trip. The students waived their right to a disciplinary hearing, were given one year of disciplinary probation, and were required to pay back the funds they had obtained without permission.

Shortly thereafter, a faculty committee was convened to determine whether the students had "satisfied the requisite ethical standards needed to continue in the counseling graduate program." After meeting with each student individually, the faculty committee concluded that the students' conduct violated the ethical standards of the profession and ruled that they be suspended for two years and attend forty-five hours of ethical counseling. The students sued, claiming that they had the right to a full disciplinary hearing on the ethical issues.

A trial court rejected the students' claims, ruling that they had had notice of the charges against them and several opportunities to be heard because they had met with two administrators and with the faculty committee as well. The appellate court affirmed, saying: "While none of these meetings were formal, trial-type hearings, both Parker and Kauitzsch were able to fully discuss the charges against them and present evidence supporting their contentions. That is all the Due Process Clause requires in this situation" (251 F. App'x at 883). The court refused to characterize the issue as disciplinary or academic, ruling that the process the students had received was sufficient for either type of misconduct.

On occasion, a student complainant may claim that the disciplinary hearing provided to the alleged perpetrator violated the *complainant*'s due process rights. For example, in *Theriault v. University of Southern Maine*, 353 F. Supp. 2d 1 (D. Me. 2004), a campus hearing panel found a student charged with sexual assault not responsible for the violation. The complainant then sued the university for due process violations. The court ruled that the plaintiff had no property right at issue, since she had not been charged with a code of conduct violation.

Because of the potential for constitutional or other claims, administrators should ensure that the staff who handle disciplinary charges against students, and the members of the hearing panels who determine whether the campus code of conduct has been violated, are trained in the workings of the disciplinary system and the protections that must be afforded students. Judicial review of the outcomes of disciplinary hearings is typically favorable to the institution if it has followed its own procedures carefully, and if those procedures comport with basic constitutional requirements.

**9.3.2.2. Notice.** Notice should be given of both the conduct with which the student is charged and the rule or policy that allegedly proscribes the conduct. The charges need not be drawn with the specificity of a criminal indictment, but they should be "in sufficient detail to fairly enable . . . [the student] to present a defense" at the hearing (*Jenkins v. Louisiana State Board of Education*, 506 F.2d 992 (5th Cir. 1975), holding notice in a suspension case to be adequate, particularly in light of information provided by the defendant subsequent to the original notice). Factual allegations not enumerated in the notice may be developed at the hearing if the student could reasonably have expected them to be included.

There is no clear constitutional requirement concerning how much advance notice the student must have of the charges. As little as two days before the hearing has been held adequate (*Jones v. Tennessee State Board of Education*, 279 F. Supp. 190 (M.D. Tenn. 1968), *affirmed*, 407 F.2d 834 (6th Cir. 1969); see also *Nash v. Auburn University*, 812 F.2d 655 (11th Cir. 1987)). *Esteban* required ten days, however, and in most other cases the time has been longer than two days. In general, courts handle this issue case by case, asking whether the amount of time was fair under all the circumstances. And, of course, if the college's written procedures for student discipline provide for deadlines for notice to be given, or provide periods of time for the student to prepare for the hearing, those procedures should be followed in order to avoid potential breach of contract or constitutional claims.

***9.3.2.3. Hearing.*** The minimum requirement is that the hearing provide students with an opportunity to speak in their own defense and explain their side of the story. Since due process apparently does not require an open or a public hearing, the institution has the discretion to close or partially close the hearing or to leave the choice to the accused student. But courts usually will accord students the right to hear the evidence against them and to present oral testimony or, at minimum, written statements from witnesses. Formal rules of evidence need not be followed. Cross-examination, the right to counsel, the right to a transcript, and an appellate procedure have generally not been constitutional essentials, but where institutions have voluntarily provided these procedures, courts have often cited them approvingly as enhancers of the hearing's fairness.

When the conduct with which a student is charged in the disciplinary proceeding is also the subject of a criminal court proceeding, the due process obligations of the institution will likely increase. Since the student then faces additional risks and strategic problems, some of the procedures usually left to the institution's discretion may become constitutional essentials. In *Gabrilowitz v. Newman*, 582 F.2d 100 (1st Cir. 1978) (discussed in Section 9.1.4), for example, the court required that the institution allow the student to have a lawyer present to advise him during a disciplinary hearing.

The person or persons presiding over disciplinary proceedings and those with authority to make the final decision must decide each case on the basis of the evidence presented and must, of course, weigh the evidence impartially. Generally a student must show malice, bias, or conflict of interest on the part of the hearing officer or panel member before a court will make a finding of partiality. In *Blanton v. State University of New York*, 489 F.2d 377 (2d Cir. 1973), the court held that—at least where students had a right of appeal—due process was not violated when a dean who had witnessed the incident at issue also sat on the hearing committee. And in *Jones v. Tennessee State Board of Education*, 279 F. Supp. 190 (M.D. Tenn. 1968), *affirmed*, 407 F.2d 834 (6th Cir. 1969), the court even permitted a member of the hearing committee to give evidence against the accused student, in the absence of proof of malice or personal interest. But other courts may be less hospitable to such practices, and it would be wise to avoid them whenever possible.

A federal appellate court considered the question of the neutrality of participants in the hearing and discipline process. In *Gorman v. University of Rhode Island*, 837 F.2d 7 (1st Cir. 1988), a student suspended for a number of disciplinary infractions charged that the university's disciplinary proceedings were defective in several respects. He asserted that two students on the student-faculty University Board on Student Conduct were biased against him because of earlier encounters; that he had been denied the assistance of counsel at the hearing; that he had been denied a transcript of the hearing; and that the director of student life had served as advisor to the board and also had prepared a record of the hearing, thereby compromising the board's independence.

Finding no evidence that Gorman was denied a fair hearing, the court commented:

[T]he courts ought not to extol form over substance, and impose on educational institutions all the procedural requirements of a common law criminal trial. The question presented is not whether the hearing was ideal, or whether its procedure could have been better. In all cases the inquiry is whether, under the particular circumstances presented, the hearing was fair, and accorded the individual the essential elements of due process [837 F.2d at 16].

In some cases, an institution may determine that a student must be removed from campus immediately for his or her own safety or the safety of others. Even if the institution determines that a student is dangerous and that a summary suspension is needed, the student's due process rights must be addressed. Although case law on these points has been sparse, the U.S. Supreme Court's 1975 ruling in *Goss v. Lopez* explains:

As a general rule notice and hearing should precede removal of the student from school. We agree . . ., however, that there are recurring situations in which prior notice and hearing cannot be insisted upon. Students whose presence poses a continuing danger to persons or property or an ongoing threat of disrupting the academic process may be immediately removed from school . . . [and notice and hearing] should follow as soon as practicable [419 U.S. at 583 (1975)].

In *Ashiegbu v. Williams*, 1997 U.S. App. LEXIS 32345 (6th Cir. 1997) (unpublished), a student from Ohio State University (OSU) alleged that he had been called to the office of the vice president for student affairs, handed a letter stating that he was being suspended "because of a continuing pattern of threats and disruptions to the OSU community," and ordered not to return to campus until he had obtained both a psychiatric evaluation and OSU's consent to his return. Ruling that the indefinite suspension was the equivalent of a permanent expulsion, the court stated that the vice president should have provided Ashiegbu with notice, an explanation of the evidence against him, and an opportunity to present his side of the story. The court also ruled that Ashiegbu had the right to a pre-expulsion (but not necessarily a presuspension) hearing. Given these due process violations, the appellate court ruled that the trial court's dismissal of Ashiegbu's civil rights action was improper.

In contrast, a federal trial court rejected a student's claim that his suspension prior to a hearing violated due process guarantees. In *Hill v. Board of Trustees of Michigan State University*, 182 F. Supp. 2d 621 (W.D. Mich. 2001), Hill, a Michigan State University student, was caught on videotape participating in a riot after a basketball game and vandalizing property. Because Hill was already on probation for recent violations of the alcohol policy, an administrator suspended Hill and offered him a hearing before a student-faculty hearing panel the following week. The court ruled that the administrator was justified in using his emergency power of suspension prior to a hearing because of Hill's violent conduct, and that the subsequent hearing held a week later, at which Hill was represented by counsel who participated in the questioning, was timely and impartial.

A 2011 federal appellate court decision provides a good reminder of the importance of giving students who are disciplined for misconduct a meaningful hearing, as well as the importance of dealing with behavior problems promptly in order to avoid retaliation claims. In *Castle v. Appalachian Technical College*, 631 F.3d 1194 (11th Cir. 2011), a nursing student was suspended for "egregious misconduct," including allegedly threatening fellow students with physical harm and regularly disrupting classes. Just prior to her suspension, the student had informed administrators that one of her instructors was dismissing class after only an hour when the class was scheduled to run for several hours. The instructor was dismissed immediately, and the student was suspended for misconduct. The student claimed First Amendment retaliation because she had complained about the behavior of the instructor, and argued that her suspension without a hearing violated her right to procedural due process.

Although the college argued that it had given the student a hearing prior to her suspension, the court found that the "hearing" had actually been a meeting at which the college's decision to suspend her was presented to her, and that she had not been interviewed as part of the college's investigation into the complaints about her. She was, however, informed that she could appeal the dismissal decision, which she did. Although the jury concluded that Castle's due process rights had been violated, the trial court granted the individual defendants judgment as a matter of law, ruling that they were protected by qualified immunity (see Section 4.4.4.1 of this book) because it was not "clearly established at the time Castle was suspended that the immediate availability of an appeals process would not have adequately protected Castle's due process rights under the facts of this case." The appellate court agreed with the trial court that Castle's due process rights had been violated by the denial of a pre-termination hearing, but affirmed the trial court's ruling that the defendants were protected by qualified immunity.

Some victims of alleged violence by fellow students, or other witnesses, may be reluctant to actually "face" the accused at a hearing, and have requested that either they be allowed to sit behind screens, or the accused be required to do so, in order to shield the alleged victim (the complainant) and witnesses from view by the accused. The limited number of published court opinions that address this issue have rejected claims that such screening denies the accused procedural or substantive due process. *In Gomes v. University of Maine System*, 304 F. Supp. 2d 117 (D. Me. 2004), 365 F. Supp. 2d 6 (D. Me. 2005), the university had suspended two students for allegedly committing a sexual assault. The students and their attorneys had been required to sit behind screens so that the complainant did not have to face the students she had accused when she testified. The students and their attorneys could see the complainant in profile. The students challenged their suspensions on both substantive and procedural due process grounds. Although the trial court awarded summary judgment to the university on the students' substantive due process claims, finding that the university's decision was within the protections of the Fourteenth Amendment, it initially rejected the university's motion for summary judgment on the students' procedural due process claims. In a later proceeding, however, the trial court awarded summary judgment to the university on the procedural due process claim; the court noted that the students did not have a right to counsel at a disciplinary hearing under the university's rules. Even assuming that they had such a right, said the court, they were not denied the assistance of counsel because of the position of the screen. Nor were they denied the right to confront witnesses against them; they could see the complainant in profile when she testified, and their counsel was able to see her when he questioned her.

The court relied on an earlier case, *Cloud v. Trustees of Boston University*, 720 F.2d 721 (1st Cir. 1983), in which a federal appellate court rejected a similar claim by Cloud, the accused attacker, that screening a frightened complainant during a disciplinary hearing violated due process protections. Comparing the physical arrangement of the hearing rooms in *Cloud* and *Gomes*, the *Gomes* court commented:

> Here, the Plaintiffs were afforded an opportunity to see more of the Complainant than Cloud was. The Hearing Committee required all witnesses to be visible to the Plaintiffs while testifying. The Plaintiffs admit they could see the Complainant's profile during her testimony and were given an opportunity to cross-examine the Complainant and her witnesses. Under these circumstances, there is no due process violation [365 F. Supp. 2d at 27].

When students are accused of academic misconduct, such as plagiarism or cheating, conduct issues become mixed with academic evaluation issues (compare the *Napolitano* case in Section 8.6.5.2). Courts typically require some due process protections for students suspended or dismissed for academic misconduct, but not elaborate ones. For example, in *Easley v. University of Michigan Board of Regents*, 853 F.2d 1351 (6th Cir. 1988), the court found no constitutional deprivation in a law school's decision to suspend a student for one year after finding that he had plagiarized a course paper. The school had given the student an opportunity to respond to the charges against him, and the court also determined that the student had no property interest in his law degree because he had not completed the degree requirements.

And in *Matar v. Florida International University*, 944 So. 2d 1153 (Fla. Dist. Ct. App. 2006), a state appellate court rejected a student's claim that his expulsion for academic misconduct violated his due process rights. Although the student chose to have the matter adjudicated by an administrative hearing rather than a hearing before the university's academic conduct board, he later claimed that the hearing was defective because he was not given an opportunity to question the professor who accused him of academic misconduct. The court reviewed the conduct of the hearing and determined that the student had had ample opportunity to present his defense to the charges of academic misconduct. Matar had received timely notice of the charges against him, had been informed of the university's procedures in writing for the disposition of such charges, and had participated in the hearing that he himself selected from a list of options. The fact that the hearing officer would not allow Matar to cross-examine or argue with his accuser, but required Matar to speak through the hearing officer to the accuser, did not deprive him of his due process rights, according to the court.

### 9.3.3. Private institutions.

Federal constitutional guarantees of due process do not bind private institutions unless their imposition of sanctions falls under the state action doctrine explained in Section 1.5.2 of this book. But the inapplicability of constitutional protections, as Sections 9.1 and 9.2 suggest, does not necessarily mean that the student stands procedurally unprotected before the authority of the school.

Reviewing courts have held private institutions to a requirement of fairness. In *Carr v. St. John's University, New York* (see Section 9.2.3), a case limiting the impact of *Anthony* within New York State, the court indicated, even though it ruled for the university, that a private institution dismissing a student must act "not arbitrarily but in the exercise of an honest discretion based on facts within its knowledge that justify the exercise of discretion." In subsequently applying this standard to a discipline case, another New York court ruled that "the college or university's decision to discipline that student [must] be predicated on procedures which are fair and reasonable and which lend themselves to a reliable determination" (*Kwiatkowski v. Ithaca College*, 368 N.Y.S.2d 973, 977 (N.Y. Sup. Ct. 1975)).

As is true for public institutions, judges are more likely to require private institutions to provide procedural protections in the area of student misconduct than in the academic sphere. For example, in *Melvin v. Union College*, 600 N.Y.S.2d 141 (N.Y. App. Div. 1993), a breach of contract claim, a state appellate court enjoined the suspension of a student accused of cheating on an examination; the court took this action because the college had not followed all the elements of its written disciplinary procedure. But in *Ahlum v. Administrators of Tulane Educational Fund*, 617 So. 2d 96 (La. Ct. App. 1993), the appellate court of another state refused to enjoin Tulane University's suspension of a student found guilty of sexual assault. Noting that the proper standard of judicial review of a private college's disciplinary decisions was the "arbitrary and capricious" standard, the court upheld the procedures used and the sufficiency of the factual basis for the suspension. Since the court determined that Tulane's procedures exceeded even the due process protections required in *Goss v. Lopez*, the court did not attempt to determine the boundaries of procedural protections appropriate for the disciplinary actions of private colleges and universities. A similar result was reached in *In re Rensselaer Society of Engineers v. Rensselaer Polytechnic Institute*, 689 N.Y.S.2d 292 (N.Y. App. Div. 1999), in which the court ruled that "judicial scrutiny of the determination of disciplinary matters between a university and its students, or student organizations, is limited to determining whether the university substantially adhered to its own published rules and guidelines for disciplinary proceedings so as to ascertain whether its actions were arbitrary or capricious" (689 N.Y.S.2d at 295). See also *Quercia v. New York University*, 838 N.Y.S. 2d 538 (N.Y. App. Div. 2007), and *Matter of Ebert v. Yeshiva Univ.*, 813 N.Y.S. 2d 408 (2006), for application of the same degree of judicial scrutiny.

In an opinion extremely deferential to a private institution's disciplinary procedure, and allegedly selective administrative enforcement of the disciplinary code, a federal appellate court refused to rule that Dartmouth College's suspension of several white students violated federal nondiscrimination laws. In *Dartmouth Review v. Dartmouth College*, 889 F.2d 13 (1st Cir. 1989), *overruled on other grounds by Educadores Puertorriqueños en Accion et al. v. Hernandez*, 367 F.3d 61 (1st Cir. 2004), the students alleged that the college's decision to charge them with disciplinary code violations, and the dean's refusal to help them prepare for the hearing (which was promised in the student handbook), was based on their race. The court disagreed, stating that unfairness or inconsistency of administrative behavior did not equate to racial discrimination, and, since they could not demonstrate a causal link between their race and the administrators' conduct, the students' claims failed.

The apparent legal theory of choice for students challenging disciplinary or academic sanctions levied by private colleges is contract theory. In *Boehm v. University of Pennsylvania School of Veterinary Medicine*, 573 A.2d 575 (Pa. Super. Ct. 1990), the court, after reviewing case law, legal scholarship, and other sources, concluded that "where a private university or college establishes procedures for the suspension or expulsion of its students, substantial compliance with those established procedures must be had before a student can be suspended or expelled" [573 A.2d at 579].

In *Fellheimer v. Middlebury College*, 869 F. Supp. 238 (D. Vt. 1994), a student challenged his suspension for a violation of a "disrespect for persons" provision of the college's code of student conduct. The student had been charged with raping a fellow student. The hearing board found him not guilty of that charge, but guilty of the disrespect charge, a charge of which he had never received notice. The college accepted the hearing board's determination and suspended Fellheimer for a year, requiring him to receive counseling prior to applying for readmission. Fellheimer then filed a breach of contract claim (see Section 7.1.3), based upon his theory that the student handbook, which included the code of conduct, was a contract. The court agreed, ruling that the college was contractually bound to provide whatever procedural safeguards the college had promised to students.

Although the court rejected Fellheimer's argument that the college had promised to provide procedural protections "equivalent to those required under the Federal and State constitutions," the handbook's language did promise "due process . . . The procedures outlined [in the handbook] are designed, however, to assure fundamental fairness, and to protect students from arbitrary or capricious disciplinary action" (869 F. Supp. at 243–44). Fellheimer, thus, did not have constitutional due process rights, but he did have the contractual right to be notified of the charges against him. He had never been told that there were two charges against him, nor was he told what conduct would violate the "disrespect for persons" language of the handbook. Therefore, the court ruled, the hearing was "fundamentally unfair." The court refused to award Fellheimer damages until the college decided whether it would provide him with another hearing that cured the violation of the first hearing.

In contrast, the Massachusetts Supreme Court, while assuming that the student handbook was a contract, rejected a student's claim based on alleged violations of the handbook's provisions regarding student disciplinary hearings. In *Schaer v. Brandeis University*, 735 N.E.2d 373 (Mass. 2000), a student suspended after being found guilty of raping a fellow student challenged the discipline on the ground that the institution's failure to follow its own policies and procedures was a breach of contract. The student alleged that the university had failed to investigate the rape charge and that the disciplinary board had failed to make a record of the hearing, admitted irrelevant evidence and excluded relevant evidence, failed to apply the "clear and convincing evidence" standard set out in the student code, and failed to follow the institution's policies regarding instructing the hearing board on due process in a disciplinary hearing. The trial court dismissed his complaint, but the intermediate appellate court reversed and remanded, ruling that the university had made several procedural errors that had prejudiced Schaer and that could have constituted a breach of contract.

The university appealed, and the state's highest court, assuming without deciding that a contractual relationship existed between Schaer and the university, ruled in a 3-to-2 opinion that Schaer had not stated a claim for which relief could be granted. The majority took particular exception to the intermediate appellate court's criticism of the conduct of the hearing and the admission of certain evidence:

> It is not the business of lawyers and judges to tell universities what statements they may consider and what statements they must reject . . . A university is not required to adhere to the standards of due process guaranteed to criminal defendants or to abide by rules of evidence adopted by courts [735 N.E.2d at 380, 381].

Two of the five justices dissented vigorously, stating that "students should not be subject to disciplinary procedures that fail to comport with the rules promulgated by the school itself" (735 N.E.2d at 381) and that Schaer's allegations were sufficient to survive the motion to dismiss. The sharp differences of opinion in *Schaer* suggest that some courts will closely scrutinize colleges' compliance with their own disciplinary rules and regulations.

Thus, substantial departures from an institution's disciplinary policies may sometimes result in a student's victory. In *Morehouse College v. McGaha*, 627 S.E.2d 39 (Ga. Ct. App. 2005), for example, a student was expelled for allegedly "defrauding" another institution the student was attending under Morehouse's sponsorship. The student introduced evidence that the chair of the hearing board assumed that if a student came before the board, the student was guilty; that the chair did not inform the student of the charges against him; and that hearing board members laughed and walked around the room while the student was explaining his side of the situation. The jury found that the college had breached its contract with McGaha and awarded him nearly $700,000 in lost future wages. Although the appellate court reversed the damage award, ruling that a new trial was required on the amount of damages due McGaha, it upheld the jury's verdict on the breach of contract claim.

In *Doe v. University of the South*, 2011 U.S. Dist. LEXIS 35166 (E.D. Tenn. March 31, 2011), a trial court rejected the university's motion for summary judgment in a breach of contract and negligence lawsuit brought by a student whom a faculty disciplinary panel had found responsible for a sexual assault. The student claimed that the university did not follow the policies in its handbook with respect to student disciplinary processes. A jury later awarded him $26,500 to reimburse him for tuition, finding that the university had been negligent (Collin Eaton, "Jury Verdict in Sex-Assault Case at Sewanee Is Warning to Private Colleges," *Chron. Higher Educ.*, September 2, 2011, available at http://chronicle.com/article/Jury-Verdict-in-Sex-Assault/128884/).

Two trial court opinions on breach of contract claims by students challenging the outcomes of disciplinary hearings demonstrate the importance of careful drafting of procedural rules. In *Millien v. Colby College*, 2003 Maine Super. LEXIS 183 (Me. Super. Ct., Kennebec Co. August 15, 2003), the court rejected a student's breach of contract claim, in part because of a strong reservation of rights clause in the student handbook (see Section 7.1.3 of this book). The student complained that an additional appeal board, not mentioned in the student handbook, had reversed an earlier hearing panel decision in the student's favor. The court said that the handbook was not the only source of a potential contractual relationship between the college and the student, and ruled that the student was attempting to use a breach of contract claim to invite the court to review the merits of the appeal board's ruling, which the court refused to do.

But in *Ackerman v. President and Trustees of the College of Holy Cross*, 2003 Mass. Super. LEXIS 111 (Mass. Super. Ct., Worcester April 1, 2003), the court ordered a student reinstated pending a hearing before the campus hearing board. Citing *Schaer*, the court closely read the words of the student handbook. Because the handbook provided that disciplinary charges against a student that could result in suspension would "normally" be heard by the hearing board, failure to provide the student a hearing under such circumstances could be a breach of contract.

Given the tendency of courts to find a contractual relationship between the college and the student with respect to serious discipline (suspension, expulsion), it is very important that administrators and counsel review student codes of conduct and published procedures for disciplinary hearings. Terms such as "due process," "substantial evidence," and "just cause" should not be used unless the private college intends to provide a hearing that will meet each of these standards. Protocols should be developed for staff who interview students charged with campus code violations, especially if the charges have the potential to support criminal violations. Members of campus hearing boards should be trained and provided with guidelines for the admission of evidence, for the evaluation of potentially biased testimony, for assigning the burden of proof between the parties, for determining the evidentiary standard that the board should follow in making its decision, and for determining what information should be in the record of the proceeding or in the board's written ruling.

While the doctrinal bases for procedural rights in the public and private sectors are different, and while the law accords private institutions greater deference, the cases discussed in this section demonstrate that courts are struggling with the notion that students who attend private colleges are entitled to something less than the notice and opportunity to be heard that are central to the concept of due process that students at public colleges enjoy. Because many student affairs personnel view student conduct codes and the disciplinary process as part of the educational purpose of the institution (rather than as law enforcement or punishment for a "crime"), the language of the student handbook and other policy documents should reflect that purpose and make clear the rights of the accused student, the disciplinary board, and the institution itself.

## Section 9.4. Student Protests and Freedom of Speech

**9.4.1. Student free speech in general.** Student free speech issues arise in many contexts on the campus as well as in the local community. Issues regarding protests and demonstrations were among the first to receive extensive treatment from the courts, and these cases served to develop many of the basic general principles concerning student free speech. Issues regarding student protests and demonstrations also remain among the most difficult for administrators and counsel, both legally and strategically. Sections 9.4.3 through 9.4.5 and 9.4.7 below therefore focus on these First Amendment issues and the case law in which they have been developed and resolved. Other important free speech developments, of more recent origin, concern matters such as student communication via posters and leaflets (discussed in Section 9.4.5), hate speech (discussed in Section 9.5), student communication via campus computer networks (discussed in Section 7.5.1), students' freedom to refrain from supporting student organizations whose views they oppose (discussed in Sections 10.1.2 and 10.1.3), and student academic freedom (discussed in Section 7.1.4). The closely related topic of students' freedom of the press is discussed in Section 10.3.

Freedom of expression for students is protected mainly by the free speech and press provisions in the First Amendment of the U.S. Constitution, which applies only to "public" institutions (see *Coleman v. Gettysburg College*, 335 F. Supp. 2d 586 (M.D. Pa. 2004), and see generally Section 1.5.2 of this book). In some situations, student freedom of expression may also be protected by state constitutional provisions (see Section 1.4.2.1 and the *Schmid* case in Section 11.1.2) or by state statutes (see, for example, Cal. Educ. Code §§ 66301, 76120 (public institutions) and Cal. Educ. Code § 94367 (private institutions)). Regarding state constitutions, for example, the court in *Hagel v. Portland State University*, 203 P.3d 226 (Or. Ct. App. 2009), interpreted the free speech clause of the Oregon state constitution. The university had expelled a student for making statements that he wanted to harm or kill a staff member and his family. The student challenged his expulsion as violating article 1, section 8 of the

Oregon Constitution, the free speech clause. Although the Oregon Court of Appeals rejected the student's challenge, its discussion of the constitutional provision made clear that, in other types of circumstances, the provision would be a source of substantial protection for student free speech (see 203 P.3d at 229). And regarding state statutes, for example, a California appellate court in *Antebi v. Occidental College*, 47 Cal. Rptr. 3d 277 (Cal. App. 2006), interpreted section 94367 (the "Leonard Law") of the California Education Code. The court determined that a Leonard Law claim may be filed against a private institution only by a student currently enrolled in the institution; it therefore dismissed the plaintiff's claim because he filed it after he had graduated. The court also affirmed that current students may file Leonard Law claims in court without first seeking administrative relief but that students may obtain only injunctive and declaratory relief under the statute, not damages.

Student freedom of expression may also be protected by the institution's own bill of rights or other internal rules (see Section 1.4.2.3) in both public and private institutions. By this means, private institutions may consciously adopt First Amendment norms that have been developed in the courts and that bind public institutions, so that these norms sometimes become operative on private as well as public campuses. The following discussion focuses on these First Amendment norms and the case law in which they have been developed.

In a line of cases arising mainly from the campus unrest of the late 1960s and early 1970s, courts have affirmed that students have a right to protest and demonstrate peacefully—a right that public institutions may not infringe. This right stems from the free speech clause of the First Amendment as reinforced by that amendment's protection of "the right of the people peaceably to assemble, and to petition the Government for a redress of grievances." The keystone case is *Tinker v. Des Moines Independent Community School District*, 393 U.S. 503 (1969). Several high school students were suspended for wearing black armbands to school to protest the United States' Vietnam War policy. The U.S. Supreme Court ruled that the protest was a nondisruptive exercise of free speech and could not be punished by suspension from school. The Court made clear that "First Amendment rights, applied in light of the special characteristics of the school environment, are available to teachers and students" and that students "are possessed of fundamental rights which the state must respect, just as they themselves must respect their obligations to the State" (393 U.S. at 511).

Although *Tinker* involved secondary school students, the Supreme Court soon applied its principles to postsecondary education in *Healy v. James*, 408 U.S. 169 (1972).The *Healy* opinion carefully notes the First Amendment's important place on campus:

> State colleges and universities are not enclaves immune from the sweep of the First Amendment . . . [T]he precedents of this Court leave no room for the view that . . . First Amendment protections should apply with less force on college campuses than in the community at large. Quite to the contrary, "The vigilant protection of constitutional freedoms is nowhere more vital than in the community of American schools" (*Shelton v. Tucker*, 364 U.S. 479, 487

(1960)). The college classroom with its surrounding environs is peculiarly the "marketplace of ideas," and we break no new constitutional ground in reaffirming this Nation's dedication to safeguarding academic freedom [408 U.S. at 180–81].

In the *Tinker* case, the Court also made clear that the First Amendment protects more than just words; it also protects certain "symbolic acts" that are performed "for the purpose of expressing certain views." The Court has elucidated this concept of "symbolic speech" or "expressive conduct" in a number of subsequent cases; see, for example, *Virginia v. Black*, 538 U.S. 343, 358 (2003) (cross burning is symbolic speech); *Texas v. Johnson*, 491 U.S. 397, 404 (1989) (burning the American flag is symbolic speech). Lower courts have applied this concept to higher education and students' rights. In *Burnham v. Ianni*, 119 F.3d 668 (8th Cir. 1997) (*en banc*), for example, the dispute concerned two photographs that students had posted in a display case outside a departmental office (for further details, see Section 9.4.2). Citing *Tinker*, the court noted that the posting of the photographs was "expressive behavior" that "qualifies as constitutionally protected speech."

The free speech protections for students are at their peak when the speech takes place in a "public forum"—that is, an area of the campus that is, traditionally or by official policy, available to students, the entire campus community, or the general public for expressive activities. Since the early 1980s, the public forum concept has become increasingly important in student freedom of expression cases. The concept and its attendant "public forum doctrine" are discussed in Section 9.4.2.

Although *Tinker, Healy,* and *Widmar* apply the First Amendment to the campus just as fully as it applies to the general community, the cases also make clear that academic communities are "special environments," and that "First Amendment rights . . . [must be] applied in light of the special characteristics of the school environment" (*Tinker*, 393 U.S. at 506). In this regard, "[a] university differs in significant respects from public forums such as streets or parks or even municipal theaters. A university's mission is education, and decisions of this Court have never denied a university's authority to impose reasonable regulations compatible with that mission upon the use of its campus and facilities" (*Widmar v. Vincent*, 454 U.S. 263, 268 n.5 (1981)). The interests that academic institutions may protect and promote, and the nature of threats to these interests, may thus differ from the interests that may exist for other types of entities and in other contexts. Therefore, although First Amendment principles do apply with full force to the campus, their application may be affected by the unique interests of academic communities.

Moreover, colleges and universities may assert and protect their interests in ways that create limits on student freedom of speech. The *Tinker* opinion recognizes "the need for affirming the comprehensive authority of the States and of school officials, consistent with fundamental constitutional safeguards, to prescribe and control conduct in the schools" (393 U.S. at 507). That case also emphasizes that freedom to protest does not constitute freedom to disrupt:

"[C]onduct by the student, in class or out of it, which for any reason—whether it stems from time, place, or type of behavior—materially disrupts classwork or involves substantial disorder or invasion of the rights of others is . . . not immunized by the constitutional guarantee of freedom of speech" (393 U.S. at 513). *Healy* makes the same points.

### 9.4.2. The "public forum" concept.

As was indicated in Section 9.4.1, student expressive activities undertaken in a "public forum" receive more protection under the First Amendment than expressive activities undertaken in or on other types of government property. The public forum concept is therefore a key consideration in many disputes about freedom of speech on campus as well as in the local community.

Public forum issues arise, or may arise, when government seeks to regulate "private speech" activities that take place on its own property.[1] The public forum doctrine provides help in resolving these types of issues. The general questions addressed by the public forum doctrine are (1) whether a government's status as owner, proprietor, or manager of the property affords it additional legal rationales (beyond traditional rationales such as incitement, fighting words, obscenity, or defamation) for regulating speech that occurs on this property; and (2) whether the free speech rights of the speaker may vary depending on the character of the government property on which the speech occurs. In other words, can government regulate speech on its own property that it could not regulate elsewhere and, if so, does the constitutionality of such speech regulations depend on the character of the government property at issue? These questions are sometimes framed as access questions: to what extent do private individuals have a First Amendment right of access to government property for purposes of expressive activity?

Since the right of access is based in the First Amendment, and since the property involved must be government property, public forum issues generally arise only at public colleges and universities. Such issues could become pertinent to a private college or university, however, if its students were engaging, or planning to engage, in speech activities on public streets or sidewalks that cut through or are adjacent to the private institution's campus, or if students were using other government property in the vicinity of the campus for expressive purposes.

The basic question is whether the property is "forum" property; some, but not all, government property will fit this characterization. The U.S. Supreme

---

[1] "Private speech" is the speech of private individuals who are expressing their own ideas rather than those of the government. Private speech may be contrasted with "government speech," by which government conveys its own message through its own officials or employees, or through private entities that government subsidizes for the purpose of promoting the governmental message. See *Rosenberger v. Rectors and Visitors of University of Virginia*, 515 U.S. 819, 833 (1995); and see generally William Kaplin, *American Constitutional Law* (Carolina Academic Press, 2004), ch. 11, sec. F. Student speech is typically considered to be private speech, as it was in the *Rosenberger* case.

Court's cases reveal three categories of forum property: (1) the "traditional" public forum; (2) the "designated" public forum; and (3) the "nonpublic" forum. Government property that does not fall into any of these three categories is considered to be "nonforum" property, that is, "not a forum at all" (*Arkansas Educational Television Commission v. Forbes*, 523 U.S. 666, 678 (1998)). For such property, the government, in its capacity as owner, proprietor, or manager, may exclude all private speech activities from the property and preserve the property solely for its intended governmental purposes. These various categories of property are depicted graphically in Figure 9.1.

Courts have long considered public streets and parks, as well as sidewalks and town squares, to be traditional public forums. A traditional public forum is generally open to all persons to speak on any subjects of their choice. The government may impose restrictions regarding the "time, place, or manner" of the expressive activity in a public forum, so long as the restrictions are content neutral and otherwise meet the requirements for such regulations (see Section 9.4.3 of this chapter). But the government cannot exclude a speaker from the forum based on content or otherwise regulate the content of forum speech unless the exclusion or regulation "is necessary to serve a compelling state interest and . . . is narrowly drawn to achieve that interest" (*Arkansas Educational Television Commission*, 523 U.S. at 677, quoting *Cornelius*, 473 U.S. at 800). The traditional public forum category may also include a subcategory called "new forum" property or (ironically) "nontraditional forum" property that, according to some Justices, encompasses property that is the functional equivalent of, or a modern analogue to, traditional forum property.

A designated public forum, in contrast to a traditional public forum, is government property that the government has, by its own intentional action, designated to serve the purposes of a public forum. Designated forum property may be land or buildings that provide physical space for speech activities, but it also may include different forms of property, such as bulletin boards, space in print publications, or (as in *Rosenberger v. Rectors and Visitors of University*

Figure 9.1 The Public Forum Doctrine

*of Virginia*, 515 U.S. 819, 833 (1995)), even a student activities fund that a university uses to subsidize expressive activities of student groups. A designated forum may be just as open as a traditional forum, or access may be limited to certain classes of speakers (for example, students at a public university) or to certain classes of subject matter (for example, curriculum-related or course-related subjects). The latter type of designated forum is called a "limited public forum" or a "limited designated forum." (See *Widmar v. Vincent*, 454 U.S. 263 (1981) (discussed in Section 10.1.5 of this book).) Thus, unlike traditional public forums, which must remain open to all, governments retain the choice of whether to open or close a designated forum as well as the choice of whether to limit the classes of speakers or classes of topics for the forum. However, for speakers who fall within the classes of speakers and topics for which the forum is designated, the constitutional rules are the same as for a traditional forum. Government may impose content-neutral time, place, and manner requirements on the speaker but may not regulate the content of the speech (beyond the original designation of permissible topics) unless it meets the compelling interest standard set out above. In addition, if government does limit the forum by designating permissible classes of speakers and topics, its distinction between the classes must be "reasonable in light of the purpose served by the forum" (*Cornelius*, 473 U.S. at 806) and must also be viewpoint neutral (*Rosenberger*, 515 U.S. at 829–30; see generally *Good News Club v. Milford Central School*, 533 U.S. 98, 106–7 (2001)). As the Court explained in *Rosenberger*: "In determining whether the . . . exclusion of a class of speech is legitimate, we have observed a distinction between . . . content discrimination, which may be permissible . . . and viewpoint discrimination, which is presumed impermissible when directed against speech otherwise within the forum's limitations" (515 U.S. at 829–30).

A nonpublic forum, in contrast to a traditional or designated forum, is open neither to persons in general nor to particular classes of speakers. It is open only on a selective basis for individual speakers. In other words, "the government allows selective access for individual speakers rather than general access for a class of speakers" (*Arkansas Educational Television Commission v. Forbes*, 523 U.S. 666, 679 (1998)). Governments have more rationales for prohibiting or regulating speech activities in nonpublic forums, and governmental authority to exclude or regulate speakers is correspondingly greater, than is the case for traditional and designated forums. (See, for example, *International Society for Krishna Consciousness v. Lee*, 505 U.S. 672 (1992).) A reasonableness requirement and the viewpoint neutrality requirement, however, do limit government's discretion in selecting individual speakers and regulating their speech in a nonpublic forum. The constitutional requirements for a nonpublic forum, therefore, are similar to the requirements that apply to the government's designation of classes of speakers and topics for a limited designated forum. The nonpublic forum, however, is not subject to the additional strict requirements, noted above, that apply to a limited designated forum when government regulates the speech of persons who fall within classes designated for the forum.

When the public forum doctrine is applied to a public institution's campus, its application will vary depending on the type of property at issue. The entire grounds of a campus would not be considered to be public forum property, nor would all of the buildings and facilities. Even for a particular part of the grounds, or a particular building or facility, part of it may be a public forum while other parts are not. Thus, a public institution need not, and typically does not, open all of its grounds or facilities to expressive uses by students or others. In *State of Ohio v. Spingola*, 736 N.E.2d 48 (Ohio 1999), for example, the court considered Ohio University's uses of its College Green—"an open, square-shaped area surrounded on three sides by academic buildings." The court first held that "the green is not a traditional public forum" because "it does not possess the characteristics inherent in" such a forum, nor was there evidence that students or others had "traditionally used the green for public assembly and debate." As to the remaining two options for characterizing the green, the court held that part of the green was in the designated forum category and part (the part called "The Monument") was in the nonpublic forum category. The university "may designate portions of the green as a nontraditional public forum, but keep other areas of the green as nonpublic forums." Since the university had done so, it could exclude demonstrators or other speakers from using the nonpublic forum parts of the green (specifically, the Monument) for their expressive activities.

Public forum property is not limited to grounds, as in *Spingola*, or to rooms in buildings or comparable physical space. Public forum property may also be, for instance, a bulletin board (see Section 9.4.5 of this chapter), a table used for distribution of fliers, or a display case. In *Burnham v. Ianni*, 119 F.3d 668 (8th Cir. 1997) (*en banc*), for example, two students in the history department at the University of Minnesota at Duluth (UMD) had prepared a photographic display of the history faculty's professional interests. The display included a photograph of Burnham dressed in a coonskin cap and holding a .45-caliber military pistol, and a photograph of another professor wearing a cardboard laurel wreath and holding a Roman short sword. The display case was located in a public hallway outside the history department offices and classrooms. Asserting reasons relating to campus safety, the university's chancellor (Ianni) ordered the two photographs removed from the display case.

In the ensuing lawsuit, the two students, along with the two faculty members, claimed that the removal of the photographs violated their free speech rights. The chancellor argued that the display case was a "nonpublic forum" that the university could regulate subject only to a reasonableness test that the chancellor's actions had met. A seven-judge majority of the U.S. Court of Appeals, sitting *en banc*, rejected this argument; three judges dissented. According to the majority:

> In this case the nature of the forum makes little difference. Even if the display case was a nonpublic forum, . . . [the] Supreme Court has declared that "the State may reserve [a nonpublic] forum for its intended purposes, communicative or otherwise, as long as the regulation on speech is reasonable and not an effort to suppress expression merely because public officials oppose the speaker's

view." *Perry* [*Education Ass'n. v. Perry Local Educator's Ass'n.*, 460 U.S. 37, 46] ... Here we find that the suppression was unreasonable both in light of the purpose served by the forum and because of its viewpoint-based discrimination.

The display case was designated for precisely the type of activity for which the [plaintiff students and professors] were using it. It was intended to inform students, faculty and community members of events in and interests of the history department. The University was not obligated to create the display case, nor did it have to open the case for use by history department faculty and students. However, once it chose to open the case, it was prevented from unreasonably distinguishing among the types of speech it would allow within the forum. Since the purpose of the case was the dissemination of information about the history department, the suppression of exactly that type of information was simply not reasonable ...

The suppression of this particular speech was also viewpoint-based discrimination. As the Supreme Court has noted, in determining whether the government may legitimately exclude a class of speech to preserve the limits of a forum, we have observed a distinction between, on the one hand, content discrimination, which may be permissible if it preserves the purposes of that limited forum, and, on the other hand, viewpoint discrimination, which is presumed impermissible when directed against speech otherwise within the forum's limitations. *Rosenberger v. Rector & Visitors of Univ. of Virginia*, 515 U.S. 819, 830 (1995) (citing *Perry*, 460 U.S. at 46). As *Rosenberger* illustrates, what occurred here was impermissible. The photographs of [the professors] expressed the plaintiffs' view that the study of history necessarily involves a study of military history, including the use of military weapons. Because other persons on the UMD campus objected to this viewpoint, or, at least, to allowing this viewpoint to be expressed in this particular way, [the chancellor] suppressed the speech to placate the complainants. To put it simply, the photographs were removed because a handful of individuals apparently objected to the plaintiffs' views on the possession and the use of military-type weapons and especially to their exhibition on campus even in an historical context. Freedom of expression, even in a nonpublic forum, may be regulated only for a constitutionally valid reason; there was no such reason in this case [119 F.3d at 676 (internal citations omitted)].

*Bowman v. White*, 444 F.3d 967 (8th Cir. 2006), is another useful example of a court struggling to apply the public forum doctrine properly. The case concerned an outside speaker's challenge to university regulations that restricted his use of campus outdoor space (see the discussion of this case in Section 11.1.2 of this book). The primary public forum issue was whether the sidewalks, streets, and park-like areas (for example, malls, quads, plazas) of a public university campus are "traditional public forum" property, as they generally would be if they were the property of a city, town, or county government, or whether, because of the unique purposes of higher education, such property on a campus is instead more likely to be considered "designated public forum" property. The difference is substantial. A designated public forum may be redesignated for more restrictive expressive uses or even closed to speech activities; a traditional public forum may not. The court majority in *Bowman* took the position that the defendant university's sidewalks, streets, and park-like areas are designated public forums:

> A university's purpose, its traditional use, and the government's intent with respect to the property is quite different because a university's function is not to provide a forum for all persons to talk about all topics at all times. Rather, a university's mission is education and the search for knowledge . . .
>
> Thus, streets, sidewalks, and other open areas that might otherwise be traditional public fora may be treated differently when they fall within the boundaries of the University's vast campus [444 F.3d at 978].

One judge disagreed with this reasoning (although otherwise concurring with the majority's analysis of the case): "I cannot adopt the Court's view as to public areas on a public university campus not being traditional public fora but instead *designated* public fora which the University can redesignate to a non-public forum on a whim" (emphasis supplied) (444 F.3d at 984).

The public forum concept is complex, and there is considerable debate among judges and commentators concerning its particular applications—including its applications to the campus. Characterizing the property at issue, and assigning it to its appropriate category, requires careful analysis of institutional policies and practices against the backdrop of the case law. Administrators should therefore work closely with counsel whenever public forum issues may become pertinent to decision making concerning student expression on campus. And counsel should be cautious in working with lower court opinions on the public forum doctrine, since it is not unusual for the U.S. Supreme Court precedents to be misconstrued or the analysis to be otherwise garbled in these opinions.

**9.4.3. Regulation of student protest.** It is clear, under the U.S. Supreme Court's decisions in *Tinker* and *Healy* (see Section 9.4.1), that postsecondary institutions may promulgate and enforce rules that prohibit disruptive group or individual protests. Lower courts have upheld disruption regulations that meet the *Tinker-Healy* guidelines. In *Khademi v. South Orange Community College District*, 194 F. Supp. 2d 1011 (C.D. Cal. 2002), for example, the court cited *Tinker* in affirming the proposition that "the [college] has a compelling state interest in preventing 'the commission of unlawful acts on community college premises' and 'the substantial disruption of the orderly operation of the community college'" (194 F. Supp. 2d at 1027, quoting Cal. Educ. Code § 76120). Students may be suspended if they violate such rules by actively participating in a disruptive demonstration—for example, entering the stands during a college football game and "by abusive and disorderly acts and conduct" depriving the spectators "of the right to see and enjoy the game in peace and with safety to themselves" (*Barker v. Hardway*, 283 F. Supp. 228 (S.D. W. Va. 1968), *affirmed*, 399 F.2d 638 (4th Cir. 1968)), or physically blocking entrances to campus buildings and preventing personnel or other students from using the buildings (*Buttny v. Smiley*, 281 F. Supp. 280 (D. Colo. 1968)).

The critical problem in prohibiting or punishing disruptive protest activity is determining when the activity has become sufficiently disruptive to lose its protection under *Tinker* and *Healy*. In *Shamloo v. Mississippi State Board of*

*Trustees*, 620 F.2d 516 (5th Cir. 1980), for example, the plaintiffs, Iranian nationals who were students at Jackson State University, had participated in two on-campus demonstrations in support of the regime of Ayatollah Khomeini in Iran. The university disciplined the students for having violated campus regulations that required advance scheduling of demonstrations and other meetings or gatherings. When the students filed suit, claiming that the regulations and the disciplinary action violated their First Amendment rights, the defendant argued that the protests were sufficiently disruptive to lose any protection under the First Amendment. The appellate court asked whether the demonstration had "materially and substantially interfered with the requirements of appropriate discipline in the operation of the school"—the standard developed in an earlier Fifth Circuit case and adopted by the U.S. Supreme Court in *Tinker*. Applying this standard to the facts of the case, the court rejected the defendant's claim:

> There was no testimony by the students or teachers complaining that the demonstration was disrupting and distracting. Shamloo testified that he did not think any of the classes were disrupted. Dr. Johnson testified that the demonstration was quite noisy. Dr. Smith testified that he could hear the chanting from his office and that, in his opinion, classes were being disrupted. The only justification for his conclusion is that there are several buildings within a close proximity of the plaza that students may have been using for purposes of study or for classes. There is no evidence that he received complaints from the occupants of these buildings.
>
> The district court concluded that "the demonstration had a disruptive effect with respect to other students' rights." But this is not enough to conclude that the demonstration was not protected by the First Amendment. The court must also conclude (1) that the disruption was a material disruption of classwork or (2) that it involved substantial disorder or invasion of the rights of others. It must constitute a material and substantial interference with discipline. The district court did not make such a conclusion and we certainly cannot, especially in light of the conflicting evidence found in the record. We cannot say that the demonstration did not constitute activity protected under the First Amendment [620 F.2d at 522].

As *Shamloo* suggests, and *Tinker* states expressly, administrators seeking to regulate protest activity on grounds of disruption must base their action on something more substantial than mere suspicion or fear of possible disruption:

> Undifferentiated fear or apprehension of disturbance is not enough to overcome the right to freedom of expression. Any departure from absolute regimentation may cause trouble. Any variation from the majority's opinion may inspire fear. Any word spoken, in class, in the lunchroom, or on the campus, that deviates from the views of another person may start an argument or cause disturbance. But our Constitution says we must take this risk (*Terminiello v. Chicago*, 337 U.S. 1 (1949)); and our history says that it is this sort of hazardous freedom—this kind of openness—that is the basis of our national strength and of the independence and vigor of Americans who grow up and live in this relatively permissive, often disputatious, society [*Tinker*, 393 U.S. at 508–9].

Yet substantial disruption need not be a fait accompli before administrators can take action. It is sufficient that administrators have actual evidence on which they can "reasonably . . . forecast" that substantial disruption is imminent (*Tinker*, 393 U.S. at 514).

In addition to determining that a protest is or will become disruptive, it is also important to determine whether the disruption is or will be created by the protesters themselves or by onlookers who are reacting to the protestors' message or presence. "[T]he mere possibility of a violent reaction to . . . speech is . . . not a constitutional basis on which to restrict [the] right to speech . . . The First Amendment knows no heckler's veto" (*Lewis v. Wilson*, 253 F.3d 1077, 1081–82 (8th Cir. 2001)). In *Stacy v. Williams*, 306 F. Supp. 963 (N.D. Miss. 1969), for example, the court struck down a regulation limiting off-campus speakers at Mississippi state colleges because it allowed for such a "heckler's veto." The court emphasized that "one simply cannot be restrained from speaking, and his audience cannot be prevented from hearing him, unless the feared result is likely to be engendered by what the speaker himself says or does." Thus, either the protesters themselves must engage in conduct that is disruptive, as in *Barker* and *Buttny* (discussed earlier in this section), or their own words and acts must be "directed to inciting or producing imminent" disruption by others and "likely to produce" such disruption (*Brandenburg v. Ohio*, 395 U.S. 444 (1969)), before an administrator may stop the protest or discipline the protesters. Where the onlookers rather than the protesters create the disruption, the administrator's proper recourse is against the onlookers.

"Heckler's veto" problems may arise not only when protesters are being heckled or otherwise disrupted by onlookers, but also when a single speaker or panel of speakers (who may not be protesting anything) is disrupted by members of the audience—who in effect become the protesters. An invited outsider may deliver a speech on campus, for example, and students in the audience may seek to protest against the speaker's message or against a position that the speaker had previously taken on a public issue. To accomplish their objective, the students may use such tactics as calling out, questioning, chanting, booing, or rhythmic clapping. The case of *State of Vermont v. Colby*, 972 A.2d 197 (Vt. 2009), suggests that such situations may implicate the same free speech principles, and much the same analysis, as the situations where onlookers heckle protesters.

Audience members' rights to interrupt a speaker depend in the first instance on whether, in context, their actions would be considered expressive activities within the ambit of the free speech clause. If they are, as they usually would be in the type of situation described above, then the extent to which these activities are protected, according to the *Colby* case and an earlier California case that it relies on (*In re Kay*, 464 P.2d 142 (Cal. 1970)), depends on whether the activity "substantially impairs the effective conduct" of the meeting or the effective delivery of the speech. Since this is a First Amendment test, it is applicable in the first instance only to situations arising at public institutions. But the test (and the First Amendment) could also apply to situations arising in private institutions if (1) their administrators call in local police to handle the situation, or (2) the protesting audience members are subsequently charged under a state statute prohibiting disorderly conduct or other pertinent misconduct. The *Colby* case illustrates this circumstance, since it involves the validity of a disorderly conduct conviction of protesting audience members at a commencement ceremony of a private institution.

The "substantial impairment" test apparently parallels the "substantial disruption" test applicable to situations where onlookers heckle protesters. The impairment test requires an objective assessment of "the severity of the disruption" based on "the actual impact" of the audience members' activity "on the course of the meeting." The "timing, duration, [and] intensity" of the activity must all be considered. The assessment must also include consideration of "the nature and character of [that] particular kind of meeting, . . . the purpose for which it is held, and . . . the usage and practice governing such meetings."[2] The disruption must arise from the protesting audience members' own actions and not merely from the reactions of other audience members or the institution to the protesting audience members' expressive activity. Also pertinent is whether the protesting audience members were asked to cease their activity and whether they complied with the request. Rudeness, statements that offend other audience members, or a very brief interruption of the speech or meeting, without more, is usually not sufficient to constitute a "substantial impairment." Making "numerous and sustained efforts to disrupt a meeting [or speaker] after being asked to desist" usually will be sufficient to constitute "substantial disruption." (The quotes in this paragraph come from *State of Vermont v. Colby*, 972 A.2d 197, and from *In re Kay*, 464 P.2d 142, and other cases quoted in *Colby*.)

As is evident from the discussion above, the First Amendment rights of three groups are intertwined in these "heckler's veto" situations: the rights of the speaker to speak and be heard, the rights of objecting audience members to protest, and the other audience members' right to assemble and "right to hear" the speaker. All three sets of rights must be taken into account, and some kind of balance must be struck. As the court in *In re Kay* cautioned: "Freedom of everyone to talk at once can destroy the right of anyone effectively to talk at all. Free expression can expire as tragically in the tumult of license as in the silence of censorship" (464 P.2d at 149).

Besides adopting regulations prohibiting disruptive protest, public institutions may also promulgate "reasonable regulations with respect to the time, the place, and the manner in which student groups conduct their speech-related activities" (*Healy*, 408 U.S. at 192–93). Students who violate such regulations may be disciplined even if their violation did not create substantial disruption. As applied to speech in a public forum, however, such regulations may cover only those times, places, or manners of expression that are "basically incompatible with the normal activity of a particular place at a particular time" (*Grayned v. Rockford*, 408 U.S. 104, 116 (1972)). Incompatibility must be determined

---

[2]These considerations parallel those that courts may use under the public forum doctrine (Section 9.4.2). Some courts may therefore resort to the public forum doctrine as another source of legal principles that would sometimes be used in the type of situation that is the focus of this discussion.

by the physical impact of the speech-related activity on its surroundings and not by the content or viewpoint of the speech as such.

The *Shamloo* case (discussed earlier in this section) also illustrates the requirement that time, place, and manner regulations be "content neutral." The campus regulation at issue provided that "all events sponsored by student organizations, groups, or individual students must be registered with the director of student activities, who, in cooperation with the vice-president for student affairs, approves activities of a wholesome nature." Invalidating this regulation, the court reasoned that

> regulations must be reasonable as limitations on the time, place, and manner
> of the protected speech and its dissemination (*Papish v. Board of Curators of
> the University of Missouri*, 410 U.S. 667 . . . (1973); *Healy v. James*, 408 U.S. 169
> (1972)). Disciplinary action may not be based on the disapproved content of the
> protected speech (*Papish*, 410 U.S. at 670) . . .
>
> Limiting approval of activities only to those of a "wholesome" nature is a
> regulation of content as opposed to a regulation of time, place, and manner.
> Dr. Johnson testified that he would disapprove a student activity if, in his
> opinion, the activity was unwholesome. The presence of this language converts
> what might have otherwise been a reasonable regulation of time, place, and
> manner into a restriction on the content of speech. Therefore, the regulation
> appears to be unreasonable on its face [620 F.2d at 522–23].

Since *Shamloo*, various U.S. Supreme Court cases have elucidated the First Amendment requirements applicable to time, place, and manner regulations of speech in a public forum. *Clark v. Community for Creative Non-Violence*, 468 U.S. 288 (1984), and *Ward v. Rock Against Racism*, 491 U.S. 781 (1989), are particularly important precedents. In *Clark*, the Court upheld National Park Service regulations limiting protests in the parks. The Court noted that these regulations were "manner" regulations and upheld them because they conformed to this three-part judicial test: "[1] they are justified without reference to the content of the regulated speech . . ., [2] they are narrowly tailored to serve a significant governmental interest, and . . . [3] they leave open ample alternative channels for communication of the information" (468 U.S. at 293; numbering added). In *Ward*, the Court upheld a New York City regulation applicable to a bandstand area in Central Park. The Court affirmed that the city had a substantial interest in regulating noise levels in the bandstand area to prevent annoyance to persons in adjacent areas. The Court then refined the first two parts of the *Clark* test:

> [A] regulation of the time, place, or manner of protected speech must be
> narrowly tailored to serve the government's legitimate, content-neutral interests
> but . . . need not be the least restrictive or least intrusive means of doing so.
> Rather, the requirement of narrow tailoring is satisfied "so long as the . . .
> regulation promotes a substantial government interest that would be achieved
> less effectively absent the regulation" [quoting *United States v. Albertini*, 472
> U.S. 675, 689 (1985))(491 U.S. at 799)].

The overall effect of this *Ward* refinement is to create a more deferential standard, under which it is more likely that courts will uphold the constitutionality of time, place, and manner regulations of speech.

One particular type of time, place, and manner regulation that has been a focus of attention in recent years is the "free speech zone" or "student speech zone." An illustrative example is found in *Burbridge v. Sampson*, 74 F. Supp. 2d 940 (C.D. Cal. 1999), and *Khademi v. South Orange County Community College District*, 194 F. Supp. 2d 1011 (C.D. Cal. 2002)—twin cases involving student challenges to the free speech zones on the same community college campus. Under the district's free speech policies, three "preferred areas" were set aside for speech activities that involved twenty or more persons or would involve the use of amplification equipment. None of these three areas included the area in front of the student center, which was an "historically popular" place for speech activities and the "most strategic location on campus" (74 F. Supp. 2d at 951). In *Burbridge*, the court issued a preliminary injunction against enforcement of the preferred areas regulations because they were content-based prior restraints that did not meet a standard of strict scrutiny and were also overbroad (74 F. Supp. 2d at 949–52). Subsequently, the community college district amended its regulations, and students again challenged them. In *Khademi*, the court held that the new preferred areas regulations violated the students' free speech rights because they granted the college president "unlimited discretion" to determine what expressive activities would be permitted in the preferred areas (194 F. Supp. 2d at 1030).

Free speech zones sometimes have been implemented by requirements that students reserve the zone in advance, as in *Bayless, Auburn Alliance, Burbridge*, and *Khademi*, or that students obtain prior approval for any use outside the hours specified in the institutional policy, as in *Auburn Alliance*. Any such regulatory system would have to meet the prior approval requirements in the next section, Section 9.4.4. In addition, even if the institution does not employ any prior approval requirement, the free speech zone must meet the requirements of the U.S. Supreme Court's public forum cases (Section 9.4.2), including the three-part test for time, place, and manner regulations established in *Clark v. Community for Creative Non-Violence* (cited earlier in this section). Free speech zones will raise serious difficulties under these requirements in at least two circumstances. First, if the institution's regulations allow free speech only in the approved zone or zones, and if other parts of the campus that are unavailable for certain speech activities are considered traditional public forums, serious issues will arise because traditional public forum property cannot be entirely closed off to expressive uses. Second, if some but not all of the other campus areas that are public forums (besides the free speech zone or zones) are left open for some or all expressive activity, other serious issues may arise under the *Clark-Ward* three-part test (discussed earlier in this section). Specifically, there could be problems concerning (1) whether the institution selected other areas to be open and closed, or limited the expressive activity in the other open areas, on a content-neutral basis; (2) whether the closings of certain forum areas (or the limitations imposed on certain areas) were narrowly tailored to serve substantial interests of the institution; and (3) whether the areas that remain open are sufficient to provide "ample alternative channels for communication." In *Roberts v. Haragan*, 346 F. Supp. 2d

853(N.D. Tex. 2004), for example, the court invalidated provisions of a Texas Tech interim policy regulating speech in campus areas outside of six "forum areas" designated by the policy because these provisions of the policy were not "narrowly tailored."

Postsecondary administrators who are drafting or implementing protest regulations must be attentive not only to the various judicial requirements just discussed but also to the doctrines of "overbreadth" and "vagueness" (also discussed in Sections 5.6.1, 9.1.3, 9.2.2, and 9.5). The overbreadth doctrine provides that regulations of speech must be "narrowly tailored" to avoid sweeping within their coverage speech activities that would be constitutionally protected under the First Amendment. The vagueness doctrine provides that regulations of conduct must be sufficiently clear so that the persons to be regulated can understand what is required or prohibited and can conform their conduct accordingly. Vagueness principles apply more stringently when the regulations deal with speech-related activity: "'Stricter standards of permissible statutory vagueness may be applied to a statute having a potentially inhibiting effect on speech; a man may the less be required to act at his peril here, because the dissemination of ideas may be the loser'" (*Hynes v. Mayor and Council of Oradell*, 425 U.S. 610, 620 (1976), quoting *Smith v. California*, 361 U.S. 147, 151 (1959)). In the *Shamloo* case (cited earlier in this section), the court utilized both doctrines in invalidating campus regulations prohibiting demonstrations that are not "of a wholesome nature." Regarding the vagueness doctrine, the court reasoned:

> [t]he restriction on activities other than those of a "wholesome" nature raises the additional issue that the Jackson State regulation may be void for vagueness . . . An individual is entitled to fair notice or a warning of what constitutes prohibited activity by specifically enumerating the elements of the offense (*Smith v. Goguen*, 415 U.S. 566 . . . (1974)). The regulation must not be designed so that different officials could attach different meaning to the words in an arbitrary and discriminatory manner (*Smith v. Goguen*, supra). But, of course, we cannot expect "mathematical certainty" from our language (*Grayned v. City of Rockford*, 408 U.S. 104 . . . (1972)). The approach adopted by this court with respect to university regulations is to examine whether the college students would have any "difficulty in understanding what conduct the regulations allow and what conduct they prohibit" [quoting *Jenkins v. Louisiana State Board of Education*, 506 F.2d 992, 1004 (5th Cir. 1975)].
>
> The requirement that an activity be "wholesome" before it is subject to approval is unconstitutionally vague. The testimony revealed that the regulations are enforced or not enforced depending on the purpose of the gathering or demonstration. Dr. Johnson admitted that whether or not something was wholesome was subject to interpretation and that he, as the Vice-President of Student Affairs, and Dr. Jackson, Director of Student Activities, could come to different conclusions as to its meaning . . . The regulation's reference to wholesome activities is not specific enough to give fair notice and warning. A college student would have great difficulty determining whether or not his activities constitute prohibited unwholesome conduct. The regulation is void for vagueness [620 F.2d at 523–24].

The time, place, and manner tests and the overbreadth and vagueness doctrines, as well as principles concerning "symbolic" speech, all played an important role in another leading case, *Students Against Apartheid Coalition v. O'Neil*, 660 F. Supp. 333 (W.D. Va. 1987), and 671 F. Supp. 1105 (W.D. Va. 1987), *affirmed*, 838 F.2d 735 (4th Cir. 1988). At issue in this case was a University of Virginia (UVA) regulation prohibiting student demonstrations against university policies on investment in South Africa. In the first phase of the litigation, students challenged the university's policy prohibiting them from constructing shanties—flimsy structures used to protest apartheid conditions in South Africa—on the university's historic central grounds, "the Lawn." The federal district court held that the university's policy created an unconstitutional restriction on symbolic expression in a public forum. Specifically, the court declared that the "current lawn use regulations . . . are vague, are too broad to satisfy the University's legitimate interest in esthetics, and fail to provide the plaintiffs with a meaningful alternative channel for expression."

UVA subsequently revised its policy to tailor it narrowly to the achievement of the university's goals of historic preservation and aesthetic integrity. The students again brought suit to enjoin the enforcement of the new policy on the same constitutional grounds they had asserted in the first suit. The case was heard by the same judge, who this time held in favor of the defendant university and upheld the revised policy. The court determined that the amended policy applied only to "structures," as narrowly defined in the policy; that the policy restricted such structures from only a small section of the Lawn; and that the policy focused solely on concerns of architectural purity. Applying the *Clark* test, the court held:

> [UVA] may regulate the symbolic speech of its students to preserve and protect the Lawn area as an architectural landmark. To be constitutionally permissible, the regulation must be reasonable in time, place and manner. The revised Lawn Use Policy lies within the constitutional boundaries of the first amendment. The new policy is content-neutral, precisely aimed at protecting the University's esthetic concern in architecture, and permits students a wide array of additional modes of communication. The new policy is also sufficiently detailed to inform students as to the types of expression restricted on the Lawn [671 F. Supp. at 1108].

On appeal by the students, the U.S. Court of Appeals for the Fourth Circuit agreed with the reasoning of the district court and affirmed its decision.

The *O'Neil* case, together with the *Shamloo*, *Burbridge*, and *Khademi* cases discussed earlier, serves to illuminate pitfalls that administrators will wish to avoid in devising and enforcing their own campus's demonstration regulations. The *O'Neil* litigation also provides a good example of how to respond to and resolve problems concerning the validity of campus regulations.

**9.4.4. Prior approval of protest activities.** Sometimes institutions have attempted to avoid disruption and disorder on campus by requiring that protest activity be approved in advance and by approving only those activities that will not pose problems. Under this strategy, a protest would be halted, or its participants disciplined, not because the protest was in fact disruptive or violated reasonable time, place, and manner requirements but merely because it had not been approved in advance. Administrators at public institutions should be extremely leery of such a strategy. A prior approval system constitutes a "prior restraint" on free expression—that is, a temporary or permanent prohibition of expression imposed before the expression has occurred rather than a punishment imposed afterward. Prior restraints "are the most serious and the least tolerable infringement of First Amendment rights" (*Nebraska Press Association v. Stuart*, 427 U.S. 539, 559 (1976)).

*Khademi v. South Orange County Community College District*, 194 F. Supp. 2d 1011 (C.D. Cal. 2002), provides an example of prior restraint analysis. The court in *Khademi* invalidated four provisions of the community college district's regulations concerning student use of certain campus grounds and buildings for expressive purposes. Three of these provisions required students to obtain a reservation of the property in advance of any such use; and the other provision required an advance reservation for certain uses of amplification equipment. The decision of whether to grant a reservation was within the sole discretion of the college's president. The court held that these provisions were prior restraints because

> they condition expression in certain areas of the District's campuses upon approval of the administration . . . The four sections identified here delegate completely unfettered discretion to the campus president to permit or prohibit expression . . . Because these provisions provide the presidents with absolutely no standards to guide their decisions, they are unconstitutional and must be stricken [194 F. Supp. 2d at 1023].

The courts have not asserted, however, that all prior restraints on expression are invalid. In *Healy v. James* (see Sections 9.4.1 and 10.1), the U.S. Supreme Court stated the general rule this way: "While a college has a legitimate interest in preventing disruption on campus, which under circumstances requiring the safeguarding of that interest may justify . . . [a prior] restraint, a 'heavy burden' rests on the college to demonstrate the appropriateness of that action" (408 U.S. at 184). More recently, the Court has made clear that prior restraints that are "content neutral"—based only on the time, place, and manner of the protest activity and not on the message it is to convey—are subject to a lesser burden of justification and will usually be upheld. The key case is *Thomas v. Chicago Park District*, 534 U.S. 316 (2002), in which the Court upheld a requirement that groups of fifty or more persons, and persons using sound amplification equipment, must obtain a permit before using the public parks. This "licensing scheme . . . is not subject-matter censorship, but content-neutral time, place, and manner regulation," said the Court. "The Park District's ordinance does not authorize a licensor to pass judgment on the content of speech: None of the [thirteen] grounds for denying a permit has anything to do with what a speaker might say" (534 U.S. at 322). Although *Thomas* is not a higher education case, courts have applied the same principles to public colleges and universities. In *Auburn Alliance for Peace and Justice v. Martin*, 684 F. Supp. 1072 (M.D. Ala. 1988), *affirmed without opinion*, 853 F.2d 931 (11 Cir. 1988), for instance, the trial and appellate courts upheld the facial validity of Auburn's regulations for the "Open Air Forum," an area of the campus designated as a public forum for demonstrations; and also held that the university's denial of a student-faculty group's request for weeklong, round-the-clock use of this forum was an appropriate means of implementing time, place, and manner requirements.

If a prior restraint system would permit the decision maker to consider the message to be conveyed during a protest activity, however, the system will be considered to be "content based," and the "heavy burden" requirement of *Healy* clearly applies. To be justifiable under *Healy* and more recent cases, such a prior consideration of content must apparently be limited to factors that would likely create a substantial disruption on campus. It is therefore questionable whether a content-based prior approval mechanism could be applied to small-scale protests that have no reasonable potential for disruption. Also in either case, prior approval regulations would have to contain a clear definition of the protest activity to which they apply, precise standards to limit the administrator's discretion in making approval decisions, and procedures for ensuring an expeditious and fair decision-making process. Administrators must always assume the burden of proving that the protest activity would violate a reasonable time, place, or manner regulation or would cause substantial disruption. Given these complexities, prior approval requirements may invite substantial legal challenges. Administrators should carefully consider whether and when the prior approval strategy is worth the risk. There are always alternatives: disciplining students who violate regulations prohibiting disruptive protest; disciplining students who violate time, place, or manner requirements; or using injunctive or criminal processes.

### 9.4.5. Posters and leaflets.

Students routinely communicate by posters or fliers posted on campus and by leaflets or handbills distributed on campus. This means of communication is a classic exercise of free speech; "the distribution of leaflets, one of the 'historical weapons in the defense of liberty' is at the core of the activity protected by the First Amendment" (*Giebel v. Sylvester*, 244 F.3d 1182, 1189 (9th Cir. 2001), quoting *Schneider v. State of New Jersey*, 308 U.S. 147, 162 (1939)). The message need not be in the form of a protest, nor need it even express an opinion, to be protected. "[E]ven if [speech] is merely informative and does not actually convey a position on a subject matter," First Amendment principles apply (*Giebel*, 244 F.3d at 1187). Among the most pertinent of these principles are those concerning "public forums" (see Section 9.4.2 above). If posters appear on a bulletin board, wall, or other surface that is a public forum—usually meaning a designated public forum—these communications will receive strong First Amendment protection in public institutions. Similarly, if leaflets are distributed in an area that is a public forum, the communication will be strongly protected.

In *Khademi v. South Orange County Community College District*, 194 F. Supp. 2d 1011 (C.D. Cal. 2002), for example, the court considered the constitutionality of Board Policy 8000 ("BP 8000") under which the district regulated student expression on its two campuses. Some of the regulations included in BP 8000 applied specifically to the posting and distribution of written materials. BP 8000 was based upon, and served to implement, a California statute (Cal. Educ. Code § 76120, discussed in Section 9.4.1) that directed community college districts to implement regulations protecting student freedom of expression, including "the use of bulletin boards [and] the distribution of printed materials or petitions." The statute, however, also listed certain exceptions to First Amendment protection, such as expression that causes "substantial disruption of the orderly operation of the community college." One part of BP 8000 gave the district the absolute right to review writings after they were posted to determine whether they complied with section 76120 of the California Education Code. This part of BP 8000 also authorized the district to remove any writing that violated that statute and to order persons to stop distributing any material found to violate the statute. The court in *Khademi* found that these parts of BP 8000 were "content-based" restrictions on student speech in the public forum and thus permissible only if they "are necessary to further a compelling interest . . . and are narrowly drawn to achieve that end" (194 F. Supp. at 1026, quoting *Burbridge v. Sampson*, 74 F. Supp. 2d 940, 950 (C.D. Cal. 1999)). Applying this strict scrutiny standard, the court determined that the district had not demonstrated "a compelling interest justifying the examination of the content of student expression to root out all speech prohibited by § 76120," and that "the blanket enforcement of § 76120 is not narrowly tailored to those interests that the court finds compelling" (194 F. Supp. 2d at 1027, citing the *Tinker* case). The court therefore ruled that the regulations on student writings violated the First Amendment.

If the place of posting or distribution is a "nonpublic forum" rather than a public forum, the communication may be protected to a lesser degree—but it will usually be very difficult for students to prevail in such cases. In *Desyllas v. Bernstine*, 351 F.3d 934 (9th Cir. 2003), for example, a student at Portland State University challenged the university's alleged removal of his fliers announcing a press conference. The court determined that the campus areas that were approved for posting under the university's "Bulletin Board Posting Policy" are designated public forums; and that campus areas not approved for posting "are not designated public fora because the university did not intend to open them for expression, as manifested by the university's . . . Policy." The student's fliers were posted in unapproved areas, which the court considered to be nonpublic forums. The university could therefore remove them if the action was "reasonable," that is, "consistent with preserving the property" for its intended purposes, and was "not based on the speaker's viewpoint." The university's action met the second requirement because there was no proof that the defendants had selectively removed the student's fliers "while allowing others to remain" or that the university's action "was motivated by a desire to stifle [the student's] particular perspective or opinion."

Even if the place of posting or distribution is a public forum (traditional or designated), there is still some room for public colleges and universities to regulate these activities and to remove nonconforming posters and terminate nonconforming leafleting. To be valid, such regulations and enforcement actions must be not only "viewpoint neutral" (see *Desyllas*, cited earlier in this section, and see also *Giebel v. Sylvester*, 244 F.3d at 1188–89) but also "content neutral," meaning that they must be based only on the "time, place, and manner" of the posting or distribution and not on the subject matter or information expressed. The three-part test that the U.S. Supreme Court has crafted for time, place, and manner regulations of speech is discussed in Section 9.4.3 of this book with particular reference to *Clark v. Community for Creative Non-Violence* and *Ward v. Rock Against Racism*. Permissible types of time, place, and manner regulations may include prior institutional approvals for postings and leafleting on campus, so long as the approval process "does not authorize [the decision maker] to pass judgment on the content of the speech" (*Thomas v. Chicago Park District*, 534 U.S. 316 (2002)) and otherwise meets the three-part test (see Section 9.4.4 of this book).

In addition to such content-neutral regulations, the institution may also, in narrow circumstances, regulate the content of posters and handbills in a public forum. These types of regulations, called "content-based" regulations, must be very clear and specific, so that they meet constitutional requirements regarding "overbreadth" and "vagueness," as discussed in Section 9.4.3. Such regulations must also usually be implemented without using a prior approval process, since a prior approval process that takes the content of the speech into account will often be considered to be an unconstitutional prior restraint (see Section 9.4.4). The two content-based regulations most likely to be applied to posters and leaflets are regulations concerning obscenity and defamation (see generally Sections 10.3.5 and 10.3.6).

One problematic type of poster and handbill regulation is a requirement that posters and handbills identify the student or student organization that sponsors or that distributed the message. From one perspective, if such a requirement is applied across the board to all postings and distributions, the requirement is a content-neutral requirement that will be upheld if it meets the three-part test. From another perspective, however, such a requirement could "chill" the expression of controversial viewpoints and to that extent could be considered to be a "content-based" regulation. The U.S. Supreme Court took the latter approach in the classic case of *Talley v. California*, 362 U.S. 60 (1960), in which it invalidated a city ordinance requiring that all handbills include the name and address of the speaker. The Court reasoned that such an identification requirement could lead to "fear of reprisal" that would "deter perfectly peaceful discussions of public matters of importance." The Court thus, in effect, recognized a right to anonymous speech. At the same time, however, the Court left some room for carefully drafted identification requirements that can be shown to be necessary to the prevention of fraud, libel, or other similar harms. In *Spartacus Youth League v. Board of Trustees of Illinois Industrial University*, 502 F. Supp. 789 (N.D. Ill. 1980), the court relied on *Talley* in upholding some of the institution's identification requirements for handbills and postings while invalidating others (502 F. Supp. at 803–4).

A U.S. Court of Appeals considered the extent of protection for anonymous student speech in *Justice for All v. Faulkner*, 410 F.3d 760 (5th Cir. 2005), a case challenging the literature distribution policy of the University of Texas at Austin. The leaflets at issue were distributed by students in areas of the campus that were designated limited forums (Section 9.4.2). The university required that all such leaflets had to carry the identification of the student or student group responsible for the distribution. Such a requirement was necessary, the university claimed, because the forums were designated for student use, and university administrators who enforced the university's policy therefore needed "to know whether a given leaflet is or is not affiliated with the University."

The court agreed that, "within a forum that only certain persons may use," student leafleters could be required to identify themselves to the responsible university administrators, and that to this extent anonymity is lost. But there is a "residual anonymity"—a right of leafleters to remain anonymous in relation to other university staff, faculty members, and students—that is "critical to the expression of controversial ideas on university campuses." Since the university's literature policy required that student leafleters identify themselves, not only to university administrators, "but to every person who receives the literature being distributed," the court held that the policy violated the right of anonymity protected by the First Amendment's free speech clause. The policy, said the Court, "sacrifices far more anonymity than is necessary to effectively preserve the campus forum for its intended beneficiaries."

### 9.4.6. Protests in the classroom.

Student protest occasionally occurs in the classroom during class time. In such circumstances, general First Amendment principles will continue to apply. But an institution's interests in maintaining order and decorum are likely to be stronger than when a protest occurs in other areas of the campus, and student free speech interests are likely to be lessened because the classroom during class time is usually not considered a "public forum" (see *Bishop v. Aronov*, 926 F.2d 1066, 1071 (11th Cir. 1991); and see generally Section 9.4.2 earlier in this chapter). If the speech is by class members and is pertinent to the class discussion and subject matter of the course, the speech would usually be protected if it is not expressed in a disruptive manner. Moreover, if the classroom protest is by students enrolled in the course and is silent, passive, and nondisruptive—like the black armband protest in *Tinker v. Des Moines School District* (see Section 9.4.1)—it will usually be protected by the First Amendment even if it is not pertinent to the class. Otherwise, however, courts will not usually protect classroom protest.

In *Salehpour v. University of Tennessee*, 159 F.3d 199 (6th Cir. 1998), for instance, the court rejected the free speech claim of a first-year dental student, a native of Iran with American citizenship who was studying dentistry as a second career. The student disagreed with a "last row rule" imposed by two professors who prohibited first-year students from occupying the last row of seats in their classrooms. The student addressed his concerns about this rule to the professors and to the associate dean; he also protested the rule, on several occasions, by sitting in the last row in the professors' classes and remaining there after being asked to change seats. Ultimately the school took disciplinary action against the student, and he filed suit claiming that the school had retaliated against him for exercising his free speech rights. The court rejected this claim because

> [the student's] expression appears to have no intellectual content or even discernable purpose, and amounts to nothing more than expression of a personal proclivity designed to disrupt the educational process ... The rights afforded to students to freely express their ideas and views without fear of administrative reprisal, must be balanced against the compelling interest of the academicians to educate in an environment that is free of purposeless distractions and is conducive to teaching. Under the facts of this case, the balance clearly weighs in favor of the University [159 F.3d at 208].

The court relied on the *Tinker* case to support its reasoning, especially the passage in the opinion about "conduct by the student, in class or out of it, which ... materially disrupts classwork" (see Section 9.4.1).

As for students who are not class members, their rights to protest inside a classroom, or immediately outside, during class time are no greater than, and will often be less than, the rights of class members. Students who are not enrolled in the course would not likely have any right to be present in the classroom. Moreover, the presence of uninvited non–class members in the classroom during class time would be likely to create "a material disruption" of the class within the meaning of the *Tinker* case. And protest activity outside the classroom would often create noise that would be projected into the classroom, or would block ingress and egress to the classroom, thereby also creating a "material disruption" within the meaning of *Tinker*. In *Furumoto v. Lyman*, 362 F. Supp. 1267 (N.D. Cal. 1973), an example drawn from the civil rights era, students who were not class members had entered the classroom of Professor William Shockley at Stanford University. The uninvited students challenged the professor's views on eugenics, which the students claimed were racist views; the students did not leave the classroom when asked to do so; and the scheduled business for the class was not completed. After campus hearings, the students were indefinitely suspended. Citing the *Tinker* case, the court rejected the students' argument that the suspension violated their First Amendment free speech rights. The court also upheld the validity of the Stanford campus disruption policy (362 F. Supp. at 1280–84), which provided that "[i]t is a violation of University policy for a member of the ... student body to (1) prevent or disrupt the effective carrying out of a University function ..., such as lectures [or] meetings."

For further discussion of students' free speech rights in the classroom, see Section 7.1.4 of this book ("Student Academic Freedom").

## Section 9.5. Speech Codes and the Problem of Hate Speech[3]

**9.5.1. Hate speech and the campus.** Since the late 1980s, colleges and universities have frequently confronted the legal, policy, and political aspects of "hate speech" and its potential impacts on equal educational opportunity for targeted groups and individuals. Responding to racist, anti-Semitic, homophobic, and sexist incidents on campus, as well as to developments in the courts, institutions have enacted, revised, and sometimes revoked policies for dealing with these problems. (For state-by-state and institution-by-institution summaries of such policies, see http://thefire.org/spotlight, a Web site maintained by the Foundation for Individual Rights in Education (FIRE).) Typically, institutional policies have been directed at harassment, intimidation, or other abusive behavior targeting minority groups. When such harassment, intimidation, or abuse has been conveyed by the spoken, written, or digitalized word, or by symbolic conduct, difficult legal and policy issues have arisen concerning students' free speech and press rights.

Beginning in the mid-1990s, after the courts had decided a number of cases limiting postsecondary institutions' authority to regulate hate speech (see Section 9.5.2), and institutions had responded by developing more nuanced policies for dealing with hate speech, there was a period of relative quiet regarding these issues. In the aftermath of the terrorist attacks of September 11, 2001, however, and in light of continuing terrorist threats against the United States, the war in Iraq, and continuing violence associated with the Israeli-Palestinian conflict, the debate and controversy about hate speech and campus speech codes reemerged. Renewed concerns over "political correctness" on campus, and a push for an "Academic Bill of Rights" (see Section 7.1.4 of this book), also provided stimulus for the renewed debate about speech codes.

"Hate speech" is an imprecise catchall term that generally includes verbal and written words and symbolic acts that convey a grossly negative assessment of particular persons or groups based on their race, gender, ethnicity, religion, sexual orientation, or disability. Hate speech is thus highly derogatory and degrading, and the language is typically coarse. The purpose of the speech is more to humiliate or wound than it is to communicate ideas or information. Common vehicles for such speech include epithets, slurs, insults, taunts, and threats. Because the viewpoints underlying hate speech may be considered "politically incorrect," the debate over hate speech codes has sometimes become intertwined with the political correctness phenomenon on U.S. campuses (see, for example, the *Levin* case in Section 6.3 of this book).

---

[3]Some portions of this section were extracted and adapted (without further attribution) from William Kaplin, "A Proposed Process for Managing the First Amendment Aspects of Campus Hate Speech," 63 *J. Higher Education* 517 (1992), copyright © 1992 by the Ohio State University Press; and from William Kaplin, "Hate Speech on the College Campus: Freedom of Speech and Equality at the Crossroads," 27 *Land & Water Law Rev.* 243 (1992), copyright © 1992 by the University of Wyoming. All rights reserved.

Hate speech is not limited to a face-to-face confrontation or shouts from a crowd. Such speech takes many forms. It may appear on T-shirts, posters, classroom blackboards, bulletin boards (physical or virtual) or Web logs, or in fliers and leaflets, phone calls, letters, or e-mail messages. It may be a cartoon appearing in a student publication or a joke told on a campus radio station or at an after-dinner speech, a skit at a student event, an anonymous note slipped under a dormitory door, graffiti scribbled on a wall or sidewalk, or a posting in an electronic chat room. It may be conveyed through defacement of posters or displays; through symbols such as burning crosses, swastikas, Ku Klux Klan insignia, and Confederate flags; and even through themes for social functions, such as blackface Harlem parties or parties celebrating white history week.

When hate speech is directed at particular individuals, it may cause real psychic harm to those individuals and may also inflict pain on the broader class of persons who belong to the group denigrated by the hate speech. Moreover, the feelings of vulnerability, insecurity, and alienation that repeated incidents of hate speech can engender in the victimized groups may prevent them from taking full advantage of the educational, employment, and social opportunities on the campus and may undermine the conditions necessary for constructive dialogue with other persons or groups. Ultimately, hate speech may degrade the intellectual environment of the campus, thus harming the entire academic community.

Since hate speech regulations may prohibit and punish particular types of messages, they may raise pressing free expression issues not only for public institutions (see Section 1.5.2) but also for private institutions that are subject to state constitutional provisions or statutes employing First Amendment norms (see Section 9.4.1) or that voluntarily adhere to First Amendment norms. The free expression values that First Amendment norms protect may be in tension with the equality values that institutions seek to protect by prohibiting hate speech. The courts have decided a number of important cases implicating these values since 1989, as discussed in the next section.

**9.5.2. The case law on hate speech and speech codes.** Some of the hate speech cases have involved college or university speech codes; others have involved city ordinances or state statutes that covered hate speech activities or that enhanced the penalties for conduct undertaken with racist or other biased motivations. All of the college and university cases except one are against public institutions; the exception—the *Corry* case discussed below—provides an instructive illustration of how hate speech issues can arise in private institutions.

The U.S. Supreme Court's 1992 decision in *R.A.V. v. City of St. Paul*, 505 U.S. 377 (1992), addresses the validity of a city ordinance directed at hate crimes. This ordinance made it a misdemeanor to place on public or private property any symbol or graffiti that one reasonably knew would "arouse anger, alarm or resentment in others on the basis of race, color, creed, religion or gender." R.A.V., a juvenile who had set up and burned a cross in the yard of a black family, challenged the ordinance as overbroad (see Section 9.4.3 of this book). The lower courts upheld the validity of the statute by narrowly construing it to apply only to expression that would be considered fighting words or incitement. The U.S. Supreme Court disagreed and invalidated the ordinance, but the majority opinion by Justice Scalia did not use overbreadth analysis. Instead, it focused on the viewpoint discrimination evident in the ordinance and invalidated the ordinance because its restriction on speech content was too narrow rather than too broad:

> Although the phrase in the ordinance, "arouses anger, alarm or resentment in others," has been limited by the Minnesota Supreme Court's construction to reach only those symbols or displays that amount to "fighting words," the remaining, unmodified terms make clear that the ordinance applies only to "fighting words" that insult, or provoke violence, "on the basis of race, color, creed, religion or gender." Displays containing abusive invective, no matter how vicious or severe, are permissible unless they are addressed to one of the specified disfavored topics. Those who wish to use "fighting words" in connection with other ideas—to express hostility, for example, on the basis of political affiliation, union membership, or homosexuality—are not covered. The First Amendment does not permit St. Paul to impose special prohibitions on those speakers who express views on disfavored subjects [505 U.S. at 391].

The Court did note several narrow exceptions to this requirement of viewpoint neutrality but found that the St. Paul ordinance did not fall into any of these narrow exceptions (505 U.S. at 386–90). The Court also determined that the city could not justify its narrow viewpoint-based ordinance. The city did have a compelling interest in promoting the rights of those who have traditionally been subject to discrimination. But because a broader ordinance without the viewpoint-based restriction would equally serve this interest, the law was not "reasonably necessary" to the advancement of the interest and was thus invalid.

The Supreme Court visited the hate speech problem again in *Wisconsin v. Mitchell*, 508 U.S. 476 (1993). At issue was the constitutionality of a state law that enhanced the punishment for commission of a crime when the victim was intentionally selected because of his "race, religion, color, disability, sexual orientation, national origin or ancestry" (Wis. Stat. § 939.645(1)(b)). The state had applied the statute to a defendant who, with several other black males, had seen and discussed a movie that featured a racially motivated beating and thereupon had brutally assaulted a white male. Before the attack, the defendant had said, among other things, "There goes a white boy; go get him." A jury convicted the defendant of aggravated battery, and the court enhanced his sentence because his actions were racially motivated.

The Court unanimously upheld the statute because it focused on the defendant's motive, traditionally a major consideration in sentencing. Unlike the *R.A.V.* case, the actual crime was not the speech or thought itself, but the assault—"conduct unprotected by the First Amendment." Moreover, the statute did not permit enhancement of penalties because of "mere disagreement with offenders' beliefs or biases" but rather because "bias-inspired conduct . . . is thought to inflict greater individual and societal harm." The Court did caution, moreover, "that a defendant's abstract beliefs, however obnoxious to most people, may not be taken into consideration by a sentencing judge" (508 U.S. at 485). Thus, in order for a penalty-enhancing statute to be constitutionally applied, the prosecution must show more than the mere fact that a defendant is, for example, a racist. Such evidence alone would most likely be considered irrelevant and unduly prejudicial by a trial judge. Instead, the prosecution must prove that the defendant's racism motivated him to commit the particular crime; there must be a direct connection between the criminal act and a racial motive. This showing will generally be difficult to make and may necessitate direct evidence such as that in *Mitchell*, where the defendant's own contemporaneous statements indicated a clear and immediate intent to act on racial or other proscribed grounds.

In *Virginia v. Black*, 538 U.S. 343 (2003), the U.S. Supreme Court considered the constitutionality of a state statute prohibiting the use of a particular "symbol of hate": cross burnings (538 U.S. at 357). The Virginia statute at issue made it a crime to burn a cross in public with "an intent to intimidate a person or group of persons" (Va. Code Ann. § 18.2-423). In its opinion, the Court considered the First Amendment status of "true threats," a concept that arose from the earlier case of *Watts v. United States*, 394 U.S. 705 (1969), and was further developed in *R.A.V.* (505 U.S. at 388). Consistent with those cases, the Court in *Virginia v. Black* reaffirmed that "the First Amendment . . . permits a state to ban a 'true threat'" and defined a true threat as a statement "where the speaker means to communicate a serious expression of an intent to commit an act of unlawful violence to a particular individual or group of individuals" (538 U.S. at 359). The Court then determined that intimidation may be included within the category of true threats, so long as the intimidation is limited to statements in which "a speaker directs a threat to a person or a group of persons with the intent of placing the victim in fear of bodily harm or death" (538 U.S. at 360). According to the Court, such intentional statements, whether termed as threats or intimidation, are "constitutionally proscribable" and thus outside the scope of the First Amendment (538 U.S. at 365). Applying these principles to the cross burning, the Court determined that "the burning of a cross is symbolic expression," but it is also "a particularly virulent form of intimidation." The Court therefore upheld the constitutionality of the Virginia statute's prohibition of cross burning because a "ban on cross burning carried out with the intent to intimidate is fully consistent with our holding in *R.A.V.* and is proscribable under the First Amendment" (538 U.S. at 363).

Although no case involving campus hate speech has yet reached the U.S. Supreme Court, there have been several important cases in the lower courts. The first was *Doe v. University of Michigan*, 721 F. Supp. 852 (E.D. Mich. 1989). The plaintiff, a graduate student, challenged the university's hate speech policy, whose central provision prohibited "[a]ny behavior, verbal or physical, that stigmatizes or victimizes an individual on the basis of race, ethnicity, religion, sex, sexual orientation, creed, national origin, ancestry, age, marital status, handicap, or Vietnam-era veteran status." The policy prohibited such behavior if it "[i]nvolves an express or implied threat to" or "[h]as the purpose or reasonably foreseeable effect of interfering with" or "[c]reates an intimidating, hostile, or demeaning environment" for individual pursuits in academics, employment, or extracurricular activities. This prohibition applied to behavior in "educational and academic centers, such as classroom buildings, libraries, research laboratories, recreation and study centers." Focusing on the wording of the policy and the way in which the university interpreted and applied this language, the court held that the policy was unconstitutionally overbroad on its face because its wording swept up and sought to punish substantial amounts of constitutionally protected speech. In addition, the court held the policy to be unconstitutionally vague on its face. This fatal flaw arose primarily from the words "stigmatize" and "victimize" and the phrases "threat to" or "interfering with," as applied to an individual's academic pursuits—language that was so vague that students would not be able to discern what speech would be protected and what would be prohibited.

Similarly, in *UWM Post, Inc. v. Board of Regents of the University of Wisconsin System*, 774 F. Supp. 1163 (E.D. Wis. 1991), the court utilized both overbreadth and vagueness analysis to invalidate a campus hate speech regulation. The regulation applied to "racist or discriminatory comments, epithets, or other expressive behavior directed at an individual" and prohibited any such speech that "intentionally" (1) "demean[s]" the race, sex, or other specified characteristics of the individual, and (2) "create[s] an intimidating, hostile, or demeaning environment for education." The court held this language to be overbroad because it encompassed many types of speech that would not fall within any existing exceptions to the principle that government may not regulate the content of speech. Regarding vagueness, the court rejected the plaintiffs' argument that the phrase "discriminatory comments, epithets, or other expressive behavior" and the word "demean" were vague. But the court nevertheless held the regulation unconstitutionally vague because another of its provisions, juxtaposed against the language quoted here, created confusion as to whether the prohibited speech actually had to demean the individual and create a hostile educational environment, or whether the speaker only had to intend those results, which need not actually occur.

A third case, *Iota Xi Chapter of Sigma Chi Fraternity v. George Mason University*, 993 F.2d 386 (4th Cir. 1993), was decided (unlike *Doe* and *UWM Post*) after the U.S. Supreme Court's decision in *R.A.V. v. City of St. Paul*. In this case a fraternity had staged an "ugly woman contest" in which one member wore blackface, used padding and women's clothes, and presented an offensive caricature of a black woman. After receiving numerous complaints about the skit from other students, the university imposed heavy sanctions on the fraternity. The fraternity, relying on the First Amendment, sought an injunction that would force the school to lift the sanctions. The trial court granted summary judgment for the fraternity, and the appellate court affirmed the trial court's ruling.

Determining that the skit was "expressive entertainment" or "expressive conduct" protected by the First Amendment and that the sanctions constituted a content-based restriction on this speech, the court applied reasoning similar to that in *R.A.V.*:

The mischief was the University's punishment of those who scoffed at its goals of racial integration and gender neutrality, while permitting, even encouraging, conduct that would further the viewpoint expressed in the University's goals and probably embraced by a majority of society as well . . .

The University, however, urges us to weigh Sigma Chi's conduct against the substantial interests inherent in educational endeavors . . . The University certainly has a substantial interest in maintaining an environment free of discrimination and racism, and in providing gender-neutral education. Yet it seems equally apparent that it has available numerous alternatives to imposing punishment on students based on the viewpoints they express. We agree wholeheartedly that it is the University officials' responsibility, even their obligation, to achieve the goals they have set. On the other hand, a public university has many constitutionally permissible means to protect female and minority students. We must emphasize, as have other courts, that "the manner of [its action] cannot consist of selective limitations upon speech." [*R.A.V.*, 505 U.S. at 392] . . . The First Amendment forbids the government from "restrict[ing] expression because of its message [or] its ideas." *Police Department v. Mosley*, 408 U.S. 92, 95 (1972). The University should have accomplished its goals in some fashion other than silencing speech on the basis of its viewpoint [993 F.2d at 393].

In *Corry v. Stanford University*, No. 740309 (Cal. Super. Ct., Santa Clara Co. February 27, 1995), a state trial court judge invalidated Stanford's Policy on Free Expression and Discriminatory Harassment. Since Stanford is a private university, the First Amendment did not directly apply to the case, but it became applicable through a 1992 California law (the "Leonard Law," Cal. Educ. Code § 94367) that subjects private institutions' student disciplinary actions to the strictures of the First Amendment. Applying U.S. Supreme Court precedents such as *Chaplinsky v. New Hampshire*, 315 U.S. 568 (1942) (the "fighting words" case), and *R.A.V. v. City of St. Paul* (discussed earlier in this section), the court held that the Stanford policy did not fall within the scope of the "fighting words" exception to the First Amendment's application and also constituted impermissible "viewpoint discrimination" within the meaning of the *R.A.V.* case. Stanford did not appeal.

The more recent disputes about hate speech and speech codes, especially in the aftermath of 9/11 (see beginning of this section), have been more varied than the earlier disputes exemplified by the *Doe v. University of Michigan* case and the *UWM Post, Inc. v. Board of Regents* case discussed earlier. These newer disputes may not focus only on hate speech directed against minority groups as such, but instead may concern other types of speech considered hurtful to individuals or detrimental to the educational process. In *Bair v. Shippensburg University*, 280 F. Supp. 2d 357 (M.D. Pa. 2003), for example, the plaintiffs successfully challenged speech policies that not only prohibited "acts of intolerance directed at others for ethnic, racial, gender, sexual orientation, physical, lifestyle, religious, age, and/or political characteristics," but also prohibited communications that "provoke, harass, intimidate, or harm another" (regardless of that other's identity) and "acts of intolerance that demonstrate malicious intentions towards others" (regardless of the other's identity). The court ruled that such language made the university's speech policies unconstitutionally overbroad. Similarly, the institutional policies involved in these more recent disputes may not be hate speech codes as such, but instead may be speech policies covering a broader range of expression, or conduct codes focusing primarily on behavior and only secondarily on expression, or mission statements drawn from various institutional documents, or even unwritten policies and ad hoc decisions implicating expression. In the *Bair* case (cited earlier in this section), for example, the provisions being challenged were found in the preamble to and various sections of the code of conduct, and in the university's "Racism and Cultural Diversity Policy."[4] And the settings in which the more recent disputes arise may be more particularized than in the earlier disputes. The setting, for example, may be student speech in the classroom or student speech on the institution's computer network (see Section 7.5 of this book).

The case of *College Republicans at San Francisco State University v. Reed*, 523 F. Supp. 2d 1005 (N.D. Cal. 2007), provides another example of the newer, more varied controversies that have arisen after 9/11. After holding an "Anti-Terrorism" rally on campus, the College Republicans were charged by the university with violating several California State University system regulations, especially one stating:

> Students are expected to be good citizens and to engage in responsible behaviors that reflect well upon their university, to be *civil* to one another and to others in the campus community, and to contribute positively to student and university life [Cal. Code Regs. tit. 5, § 41301(a)].

The student organization claimed that the language requiring students to be "civil" would prevent them from engaging in many expressive activities and therefore was unconstitutionally overbroad. In granting the organization's motion for a preliminary injunction, the court held there was a strong likelihood that the organization would prevail on this claim, in particular because

> the requirement "to be civil to one another" and the directive to eschew behaviors that are not consistent with "good citizenship" reasonably can be understood as prohibiting the kind of communication that it is necessary to use to convey the full emotional power with which a speaker embraces her ideas or the intensity and richness of the feelings that attach her to her cause. Similarly, mandating civility could deprive speakers of the tools they most need to connect emotionally with their audience, to move their audience to share their passion [523 F. Supp. 2d at 1019].

As this quote suggests, the reasoning in the *College Republicans* case also relies on what may be called "the 'emotive content' principle" (see below in

---

[4]The court in the *Bair* case issued a preliminary injunction against the enforcement of the challenged speech provisions. Subsequently, the parties settled the case, with the university agreeing to rewrite portions of its conduct code and diversity policy. See Eric Hoover, "U. Agrees to Change Conduct Code in Settlement with Advocacy Group," *Chron. Higher Educ.*, March 5, 2004, A31.

this section) and uses it in conjunction with the concept of overbreadth. In determining that enforcement of the university's civility requirement would likely be at odds with the emotive content principle, the court gave this helpful explanation:

> There also is an emotional dimension to the effectiveness of communication. Speakers, especially speakers on significant or controversial issues, often want their audience to understand how passionately they feel about their subject or message. For many speakers on religious or political subjects, for example, having their audience perceive and understand their passion, their intensity of feeling, can be the single most important aspect of an expressive act. And for many people, what matters most about a particular instance of communication is whether it inspires emotions in the audience, i.e., whether it has the emotional power to move the audience to action or to a different level of interest in or commitment to an idea or cause. For such people, the effectiveness of communication is measured by its emotional impact, by the intensity of the resonance it creates [523 F. Supp. 2d at 1018–19].

For another example of the newer, more varied, type of disputes concerning hate speech and speech codes, see *De John v. Temple University*, 537 F.3d 301 (3d Cir. 2008), discussed in Section 7.1.4 of this book. The *De John* case involved sexual or "gender-motivated" speech rather than racist speech, a sexual harassment policy rather than a speech code as such, and student speech in the classroom rather than in extracurricular or non-curricular settings. The court in *De John*, like the court in *Bair v. Shippensburg University*, 280 F. Supp. 2d 357 (M.D. Pa. 2003), held the university policy to be unconstitutionally overbroad.

These lower court campus cases, combined with the U.S. Supreme Court's decisions in *R.A.V., Mitchell*, and *Virginia v. Black*, demonstrate the exceeding difficulty that any public institution would face if it attempted to promulgate hate speech regulations that would survive First Amendment scrutiny. Read against the backdrop of other Supreme Court cases on freedom of speech, both before and after *R.A.V.*, the hate speech cases reflect and confirm five major free speech principles that, together, severely constrain the authority of government to regulate hate speech.

Under the first free speech principle—the "content discrimination" principle—regulations of the content of speech (that is, regulations of the speaker's subject matter or message) are suspect. This principle applies with extra force whenever a government restricts a speaker's message because of its viewpoint rather than merely because of the subject matter being addressed. As the *R.A.V.* case makes clear, and as other cases such as *Rosenberger v. Rector and Visitors of University of Virginia* (see Section 10.1.5 of this book) have confirmed, "viewpoint discrimination" against private speakers is virtually always unconstitutional (see *R.A.V.*, 505 U.S. at 391–92). In addition to *R.A.V.*, the *Iota Xi Chapter* case and the *Corry* case discussed earlier in this section also rely on viewpoint discrimination analysis.

Under the second free speech principle—the "emotive content" principle—the emotional content as well as the cognitive content of speech is protected from government regulation. As the U.S. Supreme Court explained in *Cohen v. California*, 403 U.S. 15 (1971):

> [M]uch linguistic expression serves a dual communicative function: it conveys not only ideas capable of relatively precise, detached explication, but otherwise inexpressible emotions as well. In fact, words are often chosen as much for their emotive as their cognitive force. We cannot sanction the view that the Constitution, while solicitous of the cognitive content of individual speech, has little or no regard for that emotive function which, practically speaking, may often be the more important element of the overall message [403 U.S. at 26].

*The College Republicans* case, above in this section, illustrates how this emotive content principle may be applied in a speech code case and also illustrates how this principle may interact with the overbreadth and vagueness principle (below).

Under the third free speech principle—the "offensive speech" principle—speech may not be prohibited merely because persons who hear or view it are offended by the message. In a flag-burning case, *Texas v. Johnson*, 491 U.S. 397 (1989), the U.S. Supreme Court reaffirmed that "[i]f there is a bedrock principle underlying the First Amendment, it is that the government may not prohibit the expression of an idea simply because society finds the idea itself offensive or disagreeable" (491 U.S. at 414). The Court has often repeated this language and reaffirmed the underlying principle—most dramatically, perhaps, in *Snyder v. Phelps*, 131 S. Ct. 1207, 1219 (2011), extending First Amendment protection to persons picketing a Marine's military funeral, even though the speech was "particularly harmful" to many persons and added "anguish" to the "already incalculable grief" of the Marine's father.

Under the fourth free speech principle—the "overbreadth and vagueness" principle—government may not regulate speech activity with provisions whose language is either overbroad or vague and would thereby create a "chilling effect" on the exercise of free speech rights. As the U.S. Supreme Court has stated: "Because First Amendment freedoms need breathing space to survive, government may regulate in the area only with narrow specificity" (*NAACP v. Button*, 371 U.S. 415, 433 (1963)). The concurring opinion in *R.A.V.* provides an instructive example of how overbreadth analysis applies to hate speech regulations (505 U.S. at 397–415 (White, J., concurring)). The speech codes in the *Doe, UWM Post, Bair, College Republicans*, and *DeJohn* cases were all invalidated on overbreadth grounds, and the codes in the first three of these cases were invalidated on vagueness grounds as well. Another good example is *Dambrot v. Central Michigan University*, 55 F.3d 1177 (6th Cir. 1995), in which the appellate court invalidated the defendant university's "discriminatory harassment policy" on its face. Since the policy expressly applied to "verbal behavior," "written literature," and the use of "symbols, [epithets], or slogans," it clearly covered First Amendment speech. But the policy's language did not clearly specify when such speech would be considered "discriminatory harassment" and thus be prohibited. The policy was therefore unconstitutionally overbroad and unconstitutionally vague. (Although *Dambrot* concerned a basketball coach's speech rather than a student's speech, its overbreadth and vagueness analysis is equally applicable to student hate speech policies.)

Application of the overbreadth doctrine to speech codes may sometimes be combined with public forum analysis (see Section 9.4.2). Restrictions on student speech in a public forum are more likely to be found unconstitutional than restrictions on speech in a nonpublic forum; thus, the more public forum property a speech code covers, the more vulnerable it may be to an overbreadth challenge. In *Roberts v. Haragan*, 346 F. Supp. 2d 853 (N.D. Tex. 2004), for instance, the court determined that the "application of [Texas Tech University's] Speech Code to the public forum areas on campus would suppress [substantial amounts of] speech that, no matter how offensive," is protected by the First Amendment. The court therefore held the university's speech code to be "unconstitutional as to the public forum areas of the campus." In addition, since the policy covered only certain "racial or ethnic content" and left untouched other harassing speech, it constituted "impermissible viewpoint discrimination" (see discussion above of the first free speech principle).

And under the fifth free speech principle—the "underbreadth" principle—when government regulates what is considered an unprotected type, or proscribable category, of speech—for example, fighting words or obscenity—it generally may not restrict expression of certain topics or viewpoints in that unprotected area without also restricting expressions of other topics and viewpoints within that same area. For example, if government utilizes the "fighting words" rationale for regulation, it must generally regulate all fighting words or none; it cannot selectively regulate only fighting words that convey disfavored messages. This principle, sometimes called the "underbreadth" principle, is an addition to First Amendment jurisprudence derived from the *R.A.V.* case. There is an exception to this principle created by the *R.A.V.* case, however, that permits regulation of a portion or "subset" of the proscribable category if the regulation focuses on the most serious occurrences of this type of speech and does so in a way that does not involve viewpoint discrimination. The Court in *Virginia v. Black* (discussed earlier in this section) invoked this exception when using the "true threats" or intimidation category of proscribable speech to uphold the Virginia cross-burning statute. "[A] State [may] choose to prohibit only those forms of intimidation that are most likely to inspire fear of bodily harm," the Court reasoned; therefore, "[i]nstead of prohibiting all intimidating messages Virginia may choose to regulate this subset of intimidating messages in light of cross burning's long and pernicious history as a signal of impending violence" (538 U.S. at 344).

### 9.5.3. Guidelines for dealing with hate speech on campus.

In light of the imposing barriers to regulation erected by the five free speech principles in the preceding section, it is critical that institutions (public and private alike) emphasize *nonregulatory* approaches for dealing with hate speech. Such approaches do not rely on the prohibition of certain types of speech or the imposition of involuntary sanctions on transgressors, as do regulatory approaches. Moreover, nonregulatory initiatives may reach or engage a wider range of students than regulatory approaches can. Nonregulatory approaches also may have more influence on student attitudes and values and may be more effective in creating an institutional environment that is inhospitable to hate behavior. Thus, nonregulatory initiatives may have a broader and longer-range impact on the hate speech problem. Nonregulatory initiatives may also be more in harmony with higher education's mission to foster critical examination and dialogue in the search for truth. Nonregulatory initiatives, moreover, do not raise substantial First Amendment issues. For these reasons, institutions should move to regulatory options only if they are certain that nonregulatory initiatives cannot suitably alleviate existing or incipient hate speech problems.

In addition to nonregulatory initiatives, institutions may regulate hate *conduct* or *behavior* (as opposed to speech) on their campuses. Hateful impulses that manifest themselves in such behavior or conduct are not within the constitutional protections accorded speech (that is, the use of words or symbols to convey a message). Examples include kicking, shoving, spitting, throwing objects at persons, trashing rooms, and blocking pathways or entryways. Since such behaviors are not speech, they can be aggressively prohibited and punished in order to alleviate hate problems on campus.

If an institution also deems it necessary to regulate speech itself, either in formulating general policies or in responding to particular incidents, the institution should first consider the applicability or adaptability of regulations that are already in or could readily be inserted into its general code of student conduct. The question in each instance would be whether a particular type of disciplinary regulation can be applied to some particular type of hate speech without substantially intruding on free speech values and without substantial risk that a court would later find the regulation's application to hate speech unconstitutional. Under this selective incremental approach, much hate speech must remain unregulated because no type of regulation could constitutionally reach it. But some provisions in conduct codes might be applied to some hate speech. The following discussion considers five potential types of such regulations. Any such regulation must be drafted with language that would meet the overbreadth and vagueness requirements discussed under the fourth free speech principle in Section 9.5.2.

First, when hate speech is combined with nonspeech actions in the same course of behavior, institutions may regulate the nonspeech elements of behavior without violating the First Amendment. A campus building may be spray-painted with swastikas; homophobic graffiti may be chalked on a campus sidewalk; a KKK insignia may be carved into the door of a dormitory room; a student may be shoved or spit on in the course of enduring verbal abuse. All these behaviors convey a hate message and therefore involve speech; but all also have a nonspeech element characterizable as destruction of property or physical assault. While the institution cannot prohibit particular messages, it can prohibit harmful acts; such acts therefore may be covered under neutral regulations governing such nonspeech matters as destruction and defacement of property or physical assaults of persons.

Second, institutions may regulate the time or place at which hate speech is uttered or the manner in which it is uttered, as long as they use neutral regulations that do not focus on the content or viewpoint of the speech. For example, an institution could punish the shouting of racial epithets in a dormitory quadrangle in the middle of the night, as long as the applicable regulation would also cover (for example) the shouting of cheers for a local sports team at the same location and time.

Third, institutions may regulate the content of hate speech that falls within one of the various exceptions to the principle forbidding content-based restrictions on speech. Thus, institutions may punish hate speech (and other speech) that constitutes a "true threat" or intimidation, as provided in *Virginia v. Black* (see Section 9.5.2), and may prohibit hate speech (and other speech) that constitutes fighting words, obscenity, incitement, or private defamation. Any such regulation, however, must comply with the "underbreadth" principle, the fifth principle set out in Section 9.5.2. Under this principle, an institution could not have a specific hate speech code prohibiting (for example) "fighting words" directed at minority group members, but it could have a broader regulation that applies to hate speech constituting fighting words as well as to other types of fighting words.

In two more recent cases in 2010 and 2011, the U.S. Supreme Court considered attempts by government to expand the number of exceptions to the principle forbidding content-based restrictions on speech. The claim in each case was that certain "violent speech" or "depictions of violence" could be regulated because such expressions are exceptions from the principle. In the first case, *United States v. Stevens*, 130 S. Ct. 1577 (2010), the Court rejected this claim in the course of invalidating a federal statute prohibiting the sale or possession of depictions of animal cruelty. In the second case, *Brown v. Entertainment Merchants Association*, 131 S. Ct. 2729 (2011), the Court rejected the same claim in the course of invalidating a state statute regulating the sale of violent video games to minors. The lesson for public institutions is that, in their speech codes or codes of conduct, they may not prohibit speech merely because it depicts violence; instead they must meet the standard of "strict scrutiny" that applies to content-based restrictions on speech: that the institution has a "compelling interest" in regulating the particular type of violent speech it has targeted, and that the institution's regulation is "narrowly tailored" to further the particular compelling interest it has identified. The institution's authority to prohibit violent *conduct* is not affected by these two Supreme Court cases and remains in full force (see discussion of "hate conduct or behavior" earlier in this section).

In a 2007 case, however, *Morse v. Frederick*, 551 U.S. 393 (2007) (the "BONG HiTS 4 JESUS" case), the U.S. Supreme Court apparently did create another narrow exception to the content discrimination principle. By a 5 to 4 vote, the Court ruled that public high schools "may take steps to safeguard [students] entrusted to their care from speech that can reasonably be regarded as encouraging illegal drug use." This ruling thus identifies another type of speech that potentially could be prohibited by speech codes. But the case involved a public *high school*, and the ruling explicitly applies only to high schools. The Court did not suggest that this new exception for speech advocating drug use would extend to *colleges and universities*, and this exception therefore would apparently not be available to colleges and universities drafting or enforcing speech codes.

Fourth, institutions probably may regulate hate speech that occurs on or is projected onto private areas, such as dormitory rooms or library study carrels, and thereby infringes on substantial privacy interests of individuals who legitimately occupy these places. For First Amendment purposes, such private areas are not considered "public forums" open to public dialogue (see Section 9.4.2); and the persons occupying such places may be "captive audiences" who cannot guard their privacy by avoiding the hate speech (see *Frisby v. Schultz*, 487 U.S. 474 (1988)). For these two reasons, it is likely that hate speech of this type could be constitutionally reached under provisions dealing generally with unjustified invasions of students' personal privacy, so long as the regulation does not constitute viewpoint discrimination (see the first free speech principle discussed in Section 9.5.2).

Fifth, institutions probably may regulate hate speech that furthers a scheme of racial or other discrimination. If a fraternity places a sign in front of its house reading "No blacks allowed here," the speech is itself an act of discrimination, making it unlikely that black students would seek to become members of that fraternity. When such speech is an integral element of a pattern of discriminatory behavior, institutions should be able to cover it and related actions under a code provision prohibiting discrimination on the basis of identifiable group characteristics such as race, sex, or ethnicity. The *R.A.V.* majority opinion itself apparently supports such a rationale when it suggests that the nondiscrimination requirements of Title VII (the federal employment discrimination statute) could constitutionally be applied to sexual harassment accomplished in part through speech (505 U.S. at 409–10).

In addition to these five bases for regulating hate speech, institutions may also—as was suggested above—devise enhanced penalties under their conduct codes for hate behavior or conduct (such as the racially inspired physical attack in *Wisconsin v. Mitchell* discussed in section 9.5.2) that does not itself involve speech. An offense that would normally merit a semester of probation, for instance, might be punished by a one-semester suspension upon proof that the act was undertaken for racial reasons. Institutions must proceed most cautiously, however. The delicate inquiry into the perpetrator's motives that penalty enhancement requires is usually the domain of courts, lawyers, and expert witnesses, guided by formal procedures and rules of evidence as well as a body of precedent. An institution should not consider itself equipped to undertake this type of inquiry unless its disciplinary system has well-developed fact-finding processes and substantial assistance from legal counsel or a law-trained judicial officer. Institutions should also assure themselves that the system's "judges" can distinguish between the perpetrator's actual motivation for the offense (which is a permissible basis for the inquiry) and the perpetrator's thoughts or general disposition (which, under *Mitchell*, is an impermissible consideration).

# 10

# Rights and Responsibilities of Student Organizations and Their Members

*Chapter 10 discusses a variety of legal rights and responsibilities of student organizations and students as members of such organizations. The chapter first examines a variety of legal issues (especially freedom of association, freedom of speech, and nondiscrimination) related to the institution's recognition and funding of student organizations. It then addresses specific issues, including legal liability issues, related to particular types of student organizations: religious organizations, fraternal organizations, student publications, and athletics teams and clubs.*

## Section 10.1. Student Organizations

***10.1.1. The right to organize.*** Student organizations provide college students with the opportunity to learn leadership skills, to supplement students' formal education with extracurricular academic programming, and to pursue diverse nonacademic interests. While there are therefore many good reasons for institutions to support, and students to join, student organizations, it is also true—at least at public institutions—that students have a legal right to organize and join campus groups, and that administrators have a legal obligation to permit them to do so. Specifically, students in public postsecondary institutions have a general right to organize; to be recognized officially whenever the school has a policy of recognizing student groups; and to use meeting rooms, bulletin boards, computer terminals, and similar facilities open to campus groups. Occasionally a state statute will accord students specific organizational rights (see *Student Association of the University of Wisconsin–Milwaukee v. Baum*, 246 N.W.2d 622 (Wis. 1976)). More generally, organizational rights are protected by the freedom of expression and freedom of association guarantees of the First Amendment. Public institutions retain authority, however, to withhold or revoke recognition in certain instances and to regulate evenhandedly the organizational use of campus facilities. While students at private institutions do not have a constitutional right to organize (see *Jackson v. Strayer College*, at end of this section), many private institutions nevertheless provide organizational rights to students through institutional regulations; in such circumstances, the private institution's administrators may choose to be guided by First Amendment principles, as set out in this section, in their relations with student organizations.

The balance between the organization's rights and the institution's authority was struck in *Healy v. James*, 408 U.S. 169 (1972), the leading case in the field. *Healy* concerned a state college's denial of a student organization's request for recognition. The request for recognition as a local Students for a Democratic Society (SDS) organization had been approved by the student affairs committee at Central Connecticut State College, but the college's president denied recognition, asserting that the organization's philosophy was antithetical to the college's commitment to academic freedom and that the organization would be a disruptive influence on campus. The denial of recognition had the effect of prohibiting the student group from using campus meeting rooms and campus bulletin boards and placing announcements in the student newspaper. The U.S. Supreme Court found the president's reasons insufficient under the facts to justify the extreme effects of nonrecognition on the organization's ability to "remain a viable entity" on campus and "participate in the intellectual give and take of campus debate." The Court therefore overruled the president's decision and remanded the case to the lower court, ruling that the college had to recognize the student group if the lower court determined that the group was willing to abide by all reasonable campus rules.

The associational rights recognized in *Healy* are not limited to situations where recognition is the issue. In *Gay Students Organization of the University of New Hampshire v. Bonner*, 509 F.2d 652 (1st Cir. 1974), for instance, the plaintiff, Gay Students Organization (GSO), was an officially recognized campus organization. After it sponsored a dance on campus, the state governor criticized the university's policy regarding GSO; in reaction, the university announced that GSO could no longer hold social functions on campus. GSO filed suit, and the federal appeals court found that the university's new policy violated the students' freedom of association and expression. *Healy* was the controlling precedent, even though GSO had not been denied recognition:

> [T]he Court's analysis in *Healy* focused not on the technical point of recognition or nonrecognition, but on the practicalities of human interaction. While the Court concluded that the SDS members' right to further their personal beliefs had been impermissibly burdened by nonrecognition, this conclusion stemmed from a finding that the "primary impediment to free association flowing from nonrecognition is the denial of use of campus facilities for meetings and other appropriate purposes." The ultimate issue at which inquiry must be directed is

the effect which a regulation has on organizational and associational activity, not the isolated and for the most part irrelevant issue of recognition per se [509 F.2d at 658–59].

*Healy* and related cases reveal three broad bases on which public institutions may decline to recognize, or limit the recognition of, particular student organizations without violating associational rights. First, the institution may require that all recognized groups agree to comply with reasonable campus regulations concerning conduct. Such standards of conduct, of course, must not themselves violate the First Amendment or other constitutional safeguards, as the *Healy* court assumed when it stated that the comply-with-campus-rules requirement does not interfere with students' rights to "speak out, to assemble, or to petition for changes in school rules" (*Healy*, 408 U.S. at 193). Recognition, for instance, could not be conditioned on the organization's willingness to abide by a rule prohibiting all peaceful protest demonstrations on campus (see Section 9.4.3) or requiring all student-run newspaper articles to be approved in advance by the administration (see Section 10.3.3). But as long as campus rules avoid such pitfalls, student organizations must comply with them, just as individual students must. If an organization refuses to agree in advance to obey campus law, recognition may be denied until such time as the organization does agree. If a recognized organization violates campus law, its recognition may be suspended or withdrawn for a reasonable period of time.

Second, "[a]ssociational activities need not be tolerated where they . . . interrupt classes, or substantially interfere with the opportunity of other students to obtain an education" (*Healy*, 408 U.S. at 189). Thus, administrators may also deny recognition to a group that would create substantial disruption on campus, and they may revoke the recognition of a group that has created such disruption. In either case, the institution has the burden of demonstrating with reasonable certainty that substantial disruption will or did in fact result from the organization's actions—a burden that the college failed to meet in *Healy*. This burden is a heavy one, because "denial of recognition [is] a form of prior restraint" of First Amendment rights (*Healy*, 408 U.S. at 184).

Third, the institution may act to prevent organizational activity that is itself illegal under local, state, or federal laws, as well as activity that "is directed to inciting or producing imminent lawless action and is likely to incite or produce such action" (*Brandenburg v. Ohio*, 395 U.S. 444, 447 (1969), quoted in *Healy*, 408 U.S. at 188). Although the *GSO* case (cited earlier in this section) specifically supported this basis for regulation, the court found that the institution had not met its burden of demonstrating that the group's activities were illegal or inciting.

All rules and decisions regarding student organizations should be supportable on one or more of these three regulatory bases. Administrators should apply the rules evenhandedly, carefully avoiding selective applications to particular groups whose views or goals they find to be repugnant (see discussion that immediately follows). Decisions under the rules should be based on a sound factual assessment of the impact of the group's activity rather than on speculation or on what the U.S. Supreme Court has called "fear or apprehension" (*Tinker v. Des Moines Independent Community School District*, 393 U.S. 503, 508 (1969)). Decisions denying organizational privileges should be preceded by "some reasonable opportunity for the organization to meet the University's contentions" or "to eliminate the basis of the denial" (*Wood v. Davison*, 351 F. Supp. 543, 548 (N.D. Ga. 1972)). If a student committee makes decisions about recognizing student organizations, or the student government devises regulations for its operations or those of recognized student organizations, they are subject to the same First Amendment restrictions as the institution itself (see the *Southworth* litigation discussed in Section 10.1.3). Keeping these points in mind, administrators can retain substantial yet sensitive authority over the recognition of student groups.

One pitfall that public institutions will always want to avoid in applying the above regulatory approaches is the denial of funding to a student group because of the views its members espouse. That is a clear violation of constitutional free speech protections, even if a student government committee rather than an institutional official makes the decision. In *Gay and Lesbian Students Association v. Gohn*, 850 F.2d 361 (8th Cir. 1988), a committee of the student senate denied funds to an organization that provided education about homosexuality. The court, noting that the administration had upheld the committee's denial of funding, said: "The University need not supply funds to student organizations; but once having decided to do so, it is bound by the First Amendment to act without regard to the content of the ideas being expressed" (850 F.2d at 362). After *Rosenberger v. Rector and Visitors of the University of Virginia*, 515 U.S. 819 (1995), these same general rules apply to an institution's decisions regarding the funding of student religious organizations (see Section 10.1.5 of this book).

In a leading post-*Rosenberger* case, a federal appeals court invalidated the attempt of the Alabama legislature to deny funding to student organizations and other groups that advocate on behalf of homosexuality. In *Gay Lesbian Bisexual Alliance v. Pryor*, 110 F.3d 1543 (11th Cir. 1997), *affirming Gay Lesbian Bisexual Alliance v. Sessions*, 917 F. Supp. 1548 (M.D. Ala. 1996), the Alabama law at issue prohibited colleges and universities from using "public funds or public facilities . . . to, directly or indirectly, sanction, recognize, or support the activities or existence of any organization or group that fosters or promotes a lifestyle or actions prohibited by the sodomy and sexual misconduct laws" (Ala. Code § 16-1-28(a)). The law also declared that no student organization (or other campus group) that uses public funds or facilities "shall permit or encourage its members or encourage other persons to engage in any such unlawful acts or provide information or materials that explain how such acts may be engaged in or performed" (Ala. Code § 16-1-28(b)). Confronted with this law, the University of South Alabama denied funding for, and withheld recognition from, the Gay and Lesbian Bisexual Alliance (GLBA). GLBA then sued the university's president and dean of students as well as the state attorney general.

The federal district court held the entire law unconstitutional, despite subsection (c) of the law, which provided that the law "shall not apply to any organization or group whose activities are limited solely to the political advocacy of a change in the sodomy and sexual misconduct laws of this state." Relying almost exclusively on the U.S. Supreme Court's decision in *Rosenberger*, the court held the Alabama statute to be "naked viewpoint discrimination" that violated the free speech clause. The court emphasized that

> [a] viewpoint may include not only *what* a person says but *how* she says it. For example, as the defendants admitted at oral argument, the State does not seek to ban discussion about sexually transmitted diseases; rather, it only seeks to limit how such diseases may be discussed. In other words, the State seeks to impose its viewpoint on how the discussion may proceed [917 F. Supp. at 1554 (emphasis in the original)].

The district court was not persuaded by the state's argument that it was simply deterring crime—that is, homosexual acts. Quoting from *Healy v. James* (discussed earlier in this section), which in turn quoted from *Brandenberg v. Ohio* (also discussed earlier), the court ruled that the statute did not draw the required distinction between mere advocacy and incitement.

The U.S. Court of Appeals for the Eleventh Circuit affirmed the district court. Relying heavily on *Rosenberger*, the appellate court characterized the funding system for student organizations at the University of South Alabama (USA) as a limited public forum:

> [The law] as applied to GLBA clearly runs afoul of . . . *Rosenberger*. USA's limited public forum does not prohibit discussion of the sodomy or sexual misconduct laws in general. Rather, based on [the law], USA prohibited funding to GLBA based on the Attorney General's unsupported assumption that GLBA fosters or promotes a violation of the sodomy or sexual misconduct laws. The statute discriminates against one particular viewpoint because state funding of groups which foster or promote compliance with the sodomy or sexual misconduct laws remains permissible. This is blatant viewpoint discrimination [110 F.3d at 1549].

Given their detailed application of *Rosenberger*, the opinions in *Gay Lesbian Bisexual Alliance* provide extensive guidance for both administrators and student groups. In particular, the opinions illustrate how the *Rosenberger* case joins with the *Healy* case to enhance the constitutional protection of student organizations at public postsecondary institutions. In light of this impact of *Rosenberger*, there is now an even stronger basis for the decisions in earlier cases such as the *GSO* case and the *Gay Lib* case discussed earlier in this section.

The right to join campus organizations gives rise to additional complexities when the organization is a student government. Such organizations are generally composed of elected officers, both executive (for example, a student body president) and legislative (for example, senators). The institution generally exercises some regulatory authority over the student government and thus over elections for student government offices. The justifications for regulating elections, either through institutional rules or rules of the student government, are different from the justifications that apply to recognition decisions.

Occasionally students may challenge certain institutional or student government regulations of the election process that determine who may "join" the executive and legislative branches of the student government by being elected to office.

The case of *Flint v. Dennison*, 488 F.3d 816 (9th Cir. 2007), provides an illustrative example. The constitution and bylaws of the Association of Students of the University of Montana (ASUM), the university's student government, provided for the election of three student executive officers and twenty student senators, and also regulated the election process. One such regulation limited each candidate's campaign expenditures to $100. When the plaintiff, Flint, exceeded this limit (for the second time in two elections), he was denied the senate seat to which he had been elected. He brought suit claiming that the campaign expenditures limitation violated his First Amendment freedom of speech.

The appellate court agreed that "campaign expenditures implicate a student candidate's ability to convey his or her message to the University student body" and therefore "necessarily constitute 'speech' . . . qualif[ying] for First Amendment protection." The plaintiff argued that the U.S. Supreme Court had protected candidates for federal and state offices against limits on their campaign expenditures and that his campaign speech should be protected to the same extent. The court disagreed:

> [The] campaign expenditure limitations in this case involved election to *student government* and . . . the expenditures occurred mostly, if not exclusively, on
> a *university campus*. The educational context of a university, the specific
> educational purpose of ASUM student government, and the numerous other
> limits placed upon student campaigning distinguish the campaign expenditure
> limitations in this case from those in cases . . . which involve campaigns for
> national political office [488 F.3d at 827].

The court then considered the applicability of the "public forum" doctrine to its analysis. Applying public forum principles (see Section 9.4.2), the court concluded that "the relevant forum is the ASUM election itself"; that, "[a]lthough the ASUM election 'is a forum more in a metaphysical than in a spatial or geographic sense' [quoting the *Rosenberger* case], the forum analysis . . . is equally applicable"; and that "the ASUM student election constitutes a limited public forum," which 'is a sub-category of the designated public forum'" (quoting *Hopper v. City of Pasco*, 241 F.3d 1067, 1074 (9th Cir. 2001)).

Having characterized the elections as a limited public forum, the court applied the standard that the U.S. Supreme Court has devised for reviewing limitations on the classes of speakers that may use the forum: whether the limitation is (1) "viewpoint neutral" and (2) "reasonable given the purposes of the forum." (It is questionable whether this was the correct standard to apply; see Section 9.4.2.) The campaign spending limit met this standard because (1) there was no evidence "that the University's desire to limit student candidate spending results from a desire to suppress any student's viewpoint or that the limitation in any way suppresses a particular candidate's viewpoint"; and (2) the spending limit "reasonably serve[s] [the] pedagogical aim" of "providing student leaders an educational experience as they campaign for, and are elected to, student government." (For more on student governments, see section 10.1.2 below.)

Although students at public colleges typically have a constitutionally protected right to organize, such is not the case for students at private colleges. In *Jackson v. Strayer College*, 941 F. Supp. 192 (D.D.C. 1996), *affirmed*, 1997 WL 411656 (D.C. Cir. 1997), for example, the court dismissed a student's constitutional claims based on allegations that the college had obstructed his efforts to form a student government. The court held that federal constitutional protections do not extend to the formation of a private college student government; in the absence of "state action" (see Section 1.5.2), the alleged actions of the college could not constitute a First Amendment violation. Furthermore, the court held that the student's First Amendment "peaceful assemblage" claim failed because the college's campus was private property upon which students had no constitutional right to assemble that they could assert against the college.

Some private institutions, however, are subject to state or local civil rights laws that may serve to prohibit various forms of discrimination against students. In such circumstances, student organizations in private institutions, or their members, may have some statutory protection for their right to organize. The case of *Gay Rights Coalition of Georgetown University Law Center v. Georgetown University*, 536 A.2d 1 (D.C. 1987), illustrates such statutory protection and also examines the difficult issues concerning freedom of religion that may arise when these statutory protections are asserted against religiously affiliated institutions.

In the *Gay Rights Coalition* case, two student gay rights groups sought official recognition from the university. The university refused, citing Catholic doctrine that condemns homosexuality. Denial of recognition meant that the groups could not use the university's facilities or its mailing and labeling services, could not have a mailbox in the student activities office, and could not request university funds. The student group sued under a District of Columbia law (D.C. Code § 1-2520) that outlaws discrimination (in the form of denying access to facilities and services) on the basis of sexual orientation (among other characteristics). The university defended its actions on the ground of free exercise of religion. The appellate court issued seven separate opinions, which—although none attracted a majority of the judges—reached a collective result of not requiring the university to recognize the groups but requiring it to give the group access to facilities, services, and funding.

By severing the recognition process from the granting of access to university facilities and funding, the court avoided addressing the university's constitutional claim with regard to recognition. In interpreting the D.C. statute, the court found no requirement that "one private actor . . . 'endorse' another" (536 A.2d at 5). For that reason, Georgetown's denial of recognition to the student groups did not violate the statute. But the statute did require equal treatment, according to the court. And, the court concluded, the District of Columbia's compelling interest in eradicating discrimination based on sexual preference outweighed any burden on the university's freedom of religion that providing equal access would impose.

***10.1.2. The right not to join, or associate, or subsidize.*** The right-to-organize concept in Section 10.1.1 above has a flip side. Students often are organized into large associations representing all students, all undergraduate students, all graduate students, or the students of a particular school (for example, the law school). Typically these associations are recognized by the institution as student governments. Mandatory student activities fees are often collected by the institution and channeled to the student government association. The student government may then allocate (or the institution may allocate) portions of the mandatory fee collections to other recognized student organizations that do not represent the student body but serve special purposes—for example, minority and foreign student associations, gay and lesbian student alliances, social action groups, sports clubs, academic interest societies (pre-med society, French club, and so forth), religious organizations, and student publications. In public colleges and universities, such arrangements may raise various issues under the First Amendment. Regarding student government associations, the primary focus of concern has been whether institutions may require that students be members of the association or that they pay the activities fee that supports the association. Regarding recognized special purpose organizations, the primary focus of concern has been whether the institution may require students to have any relationship with student organizations that they would prefer to avoid, and especially whether institutions may require students to pay the portions of their activities fees that are allocated to particular organizations if the students object to the views that the organization espouses. The issues regarding mandatory fee allocations for student organizations are discussed in Sections 10.1.3 and 10.1.5, and issues regarding mandatory fee allocations for student publications are discussed in Section 10.3.2.

An early case, *Good v. Associated Students of the Univ. of Washington*, 542 P.2d 762 (Wash. 1975), distinguished between a university's requirement that students be members of the student government and a requirement that students pay a mandatory student activities fee that supports the student government. The student government in the *Good* case, the Associated Students of the University of Washington (ASUW), was a nonprofit organization representing all of the university's students. The university required all students to be members. The court held that this requirement violated the First Amendment freedom of association (see Section 10.1.1) because "[f]reedom to associate carries with it a corresponding right to not associate." According to the court, "[The ASUW] . . . espouses political, social and economic philosophies which the dissenters find repugnant to their own views. There is no room in the First Amendment for such absolute compulsory support, advocation and representation . . ." The mandatory fee requirement, however, was not unconstitutional; the university could collect, and the ASUW could use, the mandatory fees so long as the ASUW did not "become the vehicle for the promotion of one particular viewpoint, political, social, economic or religious" (542 P.2d at 769).

Since the *Good* case, it has been generally accepted that public institutions may not require students to be members of the student government association or any other student extracurricular organization (see, for example, *Carroll v. Blinken*, 957 F.2d 991, 1003 (2d Cir. 1992)). But for many years there were continuing disputes and uncertainties concerning mandatory student fee systems until the U.S. Supreme Court finally ruled on the matter in 2000, as discussed in the next section.

**10.1.3. Mandatory student activities fees.** Throughout the 1970s, 1980s, and 1990s, the state courts and lower federal courts decided numerous cases on mandatory student activities fees in public colleges and universities. These cases presented a variety of constitutional challenges to entire systems for funding student organizations (see, for example, *Smith v. Regents of the University of California*, 844 P.2d 500 (Cal. 1993)), to the use of mandatory fees by student governments (see, for example, *Smith v. Regents of the University of California*, 65 Cal. Rptr. 2d 813 (Cal. Ct. App. 1997)), and to the allocations of fees to particular student organizations (see, for example, *Rounds v. Oregon State Board of Higher Education*, 166 F.3d 1032 (9th Cir. 1999)). Other cases presented statutory challenges to public institutions' authority regarding particular aspects of student fee systems (see *Cortes v. State of Florida, Board of Regents*, 655 So. 2d 132 (Fla. Dist. Ct. App. 1995); *Smith v. Regents of the University of California*, 844 P.2d at 851). At least one case, *Associated Students of the University of California at Riverside v. Regents of the University of California*, 1999 WL 13711 (N.D. Cal 1999), turned the issues around, presenting a challenge by students who favored, rather than opposed, mandatory student fees, but who objected to a particular limitation on the use of the fees.

Finally, after such cases had bounced around the lower courts for many years, the constitutionality of mandatory student activities fees finally reached the U.S. Supreme Court in *Board of Regents of University of Wisconsin System v. Southworth*, 529 U.S. 217 (2000). The Court's ruling in *Southworth*, and a follow-up ruling by the U.S. Court of Appeals on remand (*Southworth v. Board of Regents of University of Wisconsin System*, 307 F.3d 566 (7th Cir. 2002)), serves to resolve most of the inconsistencies among lower court opinions and to establish a single analytical approach for freedom of speech and freedom of association issues concerning public institutions' imposition of mandatory student fees.

The *Southworth* case was brought by a group of students at the Madison campus who objected to the university's collection and allocation of mandatory fees, insofar as the fees were allocated to student organizations that expressed "political and ideological" views with which the objecting students disagreed. The student plaintiffs claimed that this use of the fees violated their First Amendment right to be free from governmental compulsion to support speech conflicting with their personal views and beliefs. When the case reached the U.S. Supreme Court, it upheld the university's authority to allocate the mandatory fees to student organizations for the "purpose of facilitating the free and open exchange of ideas by, and among, its students." At the same time, the Court recognized that objecting students have a right to "certain safeguards with respect to the expressive activities which they are required to support" (529 U.S. at 229). The primary requirement that a university must meet to assure that its fee system facilitates "free and open exchange of ideas," and the primary safeguard for objecting students, is "viewpoint neutrality"—a concept that the Court had relied on in its earlier *Rosenberger* ruling (see Section 10.1.5) and that it expanded upon in *Southworth*. Thus, the *Southworth* case establishes the principle of viewpoint neutrality as the primary criterion to use in evaluating the constitutionality of a public institution's mandatory fee system under the free speech clause.

Under the University of Wisconsin fee system challenged in *Southworth*, 20 percent of mandatory student fee collections went to registered student organizations (RSOs). The other 80 percent of student fees, not at issue in the case, were used for expenses such as student health services, intramural sports, and the maintenance and repair of student union facilities. Student fees were collected annually, and there was no opt-out provision by which students could decline to support certain RSOs and receive a pro rata refund of their fees. The collected fees were allocated to RSOs (of which there were more than six hundred at the time of the litigation) on the basis of applications from those RSOs requesting funding. Decisions on applications for funding were made by the student government, the Associated Students of Madison (ASM), through two of its committees, or by a student referendum in which the entire student body voted to fund or defund a particular RSO. Decisions to allocate funds were presented to the chancellor and the board of regents for final approval. RSOs generally received funding on a reimbursement basis, with reimbursement primarily paying for the organization's operating costs, the costs of sponsoring events, and travel expenses. According to university policy, reimbursements were not made for lobbying activities or for gifts or donations to other organizations, and RSOs with a primarily political mission could not be funded. The student plaintiffs in *Southworth* objected to the allocations to eighteen of the funded RSOs. These organizations included WISPIRG; the Lesbian, Gay Bisexual Campus Center; the UW Greens; Amnesty International; and La Colectiva Cultural de Aztlan.

Relying on *Abood v. Detroit Board of Education.*, 431 U.S. 209 (1977), and *Keller v. State Bar of California*, 496 U.S. 1 (1990), the U.S. District Court upheld the students' claim that the university's program violated their rights to free speech and association, and enjoined the board of regents from using its mandatory fee system to fund any RSO that engaged in ideological or political advocacy. The U.S. Court of Appeals for the Seventh Circuit affirmed in part, reversed in part, and vacated in part. Affirming the district court's reliance on *Abood* and *Keller*, the Seventh Circuit extended the analysis to include a three-part test articulated in *Lehnert v. Ferris Faculty Association*, 500 U.S. 507 (1991), a case concerning the expenditure of mandatory union dues in violation of the faculty members' First Amendment rights. Applying the *Lehnert* test, the appellate court determined that the educational benefits of the mandatory fee system did not justify the significant burden that the system placed on the free speech rights of the objecting students (*Southworth v. Grebe*, 151 F.3d 717, 732–33 (1998)). The U.S. Supreme Court then reversed the Seventh Circuit and remanded the case to the lower courts for further proceedings. Rather than applying the three-part test from the *Lehnert* case, the Court determined that the operation of the fee system was closely analogous to a public forum (see Section 9.4.2) and that the "standard of viewpoint neutrality found in the public forum cases provides the standard we find controlling."

Under the viewpoint neutrality standard, according to the U.S. Supreme Court, the university could allocate mandatory fee funds to RSOs via the student government and its committees so long as "viewpoint neutrality [is] the operational principle." But the university could not distribute these funds via a student referendum. "[I]t is unclear . . . what protection, if any, there is for viewpoint neutrality in [the referendum] process . . . The whole theory of viewpoint neutrality is that minority views are treated with the same respect as are majority views" (529 U.S. at 235). The student referendum aspect of the program for funding speech and expressive activities thus "appears to be inconsistent with the viewpoint neutrality requirement" (529 U.S. at 230).

The university could include an "opt-out" or refund mechanism in its fee system if it wished. But it was not constitutionally obligated to do so. "The restriction could be so disruptive and expensive that the program to support extracurricular speech would be ineffective. The First Amendment does not require the University to put the program at risk" (529 U.S. at 232).

Because the plaintiffs and the university had stipulated early in the litigation that the student government and its committees operated in a viewpoint-neutral manner when allocating funds to RSOs, the Court did not need to make its own determination on this key issue. But the Court did remand the case to the Seventh Circuit for "re-examin[ation] in light of the principles we have discussed," and the Seventh Circuit in turn remanded the case to the district court. After remand, the student plaintiffs moved to void their stipulation that the mandatory fee funds were allocated on a viewpoint-neutral basis, and the district court granted the motion. That court did not reexamine the referendum process, however, since the university had eliminated this method of funding RSOs, and the issue therefore was moot. The district court then reexamined the university's mandatory fee system to determine whether it was viewpoint neutral, concluding that it was not because "the absence of express objective standards vests unfettered and unbridled discretion in the program decisionmakers" (*Fry v. Board of Regents of University of Wisconsin System*, 132 F. Supp. 2d 744 (W.D. Wis. 2000)). To allow the university time to revise its allocation procedures and policies to create "express objective standards" for making fee allocations, the district court deferred its judgment for two months.

The university administration, in conjunction with student government committees, then established criteria and procedures for students' use in allocating funds and granting reimbursements in a viewpoint-neutral manner. The student government bylaws were amended to include a provision entitled "Viewpoint

Neutrality Compliance," which set procedures and guiding principles for student officers to follow and required student officers to take an oath to uphold the principle of viewpoint neutrality. An appellate process was also established by which an RSO could appeal a funding decision to the student judiciary, the chancellor and board of regents, or both. This appellate process included procedural safeguards such as adequate, public notice and hearings on the record. While these changes to the mandatory fee system were substantial, the district court, upon further review, decided that the student government still retained too much discretion in allocating fees and enjoined the university from collecting fees from objecting students to support RSO expressive activities to which the students objected.

On appeal to the Seventh Circuit, the parties did not contest the referendum provision, since the university had deleted that method of funding from its fee allocation system. The appellate court did note in passing, however, that the "student referendum mechanism" was "constitutionally deficient" (307 F.3d at 594). The primary issue on appeal was "whether the unbridled discretion standard" that the district court relied on "is part of the constitutional requirement of viewpoint neutrality" (307 F.3d at 578). The appellate court sought to untangle the relationship between the viewpoint neutrality principle that the U.S. Supreme Court had applied in its *Southworth* decision and the "no unbridled discretion" principle that the Court had applied in earlier cases challenging governmental denials of a license or permit to speak in a public forum. It determined that the two standards were linked:

> From the earliest unbridled discretion cases . . ., the Supreme Court has made clear that when a decisionmaker has unbridled discretion there are two risks: First, the risk of self-censorship, where the plaintiff may edit his own viewpoint or the content of his speech to avoid governmental censorship; and second, the risk that the decisionmaker will use its unduly broad discretion to favor or disfavor speech based on its viewpoint or content, and that without standards to guide the official's decision an as-applied challenge will be ineffective to ferret out viewpoint discrimination. Both of these risks threaten viewpoint neutrality [307 F.3d at 578–79].

The appellate court thus held that the unbridled discretion standard is a component of the viewpoint neutrality requirement.

Having established this framework for analysis, the appellate court then addressed the central issue in the case: "whether the University's mandatory fee system does in fact vest the student government with unbridled discretion" and thus whether it failed the viewpoint neutrality requirement. In resolving this issue, the appellate court reviewed every aspect of the university's mandatory student fee allocation system, especially the various provisions the university had added to its policies after the district court had ruled, after trial, that the policies then in effect did not meet the constitutional requirements. In its thorough and detailed review of the university's revised policies (307 F.3d at 581–88), the appellate court considered the university's financial and administrative policies, as amended after the trial; the student government's bylaws pertaining to mandatory student fee allocations for RSOs, as amended; and the rules of the student government's finance committee, as amended. The court considered the principles embodied in these various documents, the criteria for allocating funds set forth in the documents, and the various procedures that they established for applying for and challenging fund allocations. Grouping the various principles, criteria, and procedures together under the heading "Funding Standards," the court determined that they "greatly limit[ed] the discretion" of the student government and its committees in allocating the fees. The court took particular note of these features of the university's and student government's policies: (1) there were specific explicit statements requiring all persons involved in funding decisions to comply with the viewpoint neutrality requirement; (2) there was a requirement that every student involved in allocation decisions take an oath to support the viewpoint neutrality requirement, and there were provisions for removing from office any student who failed to do so; (3) there were "specific, narrowly drawn and clear criteria to guide the student government in their funding decisions"; (4) there were "detailed procedural requirements for the hearings" on funding applications; (5) there was a policy of full disclosure regarding all funding applications and the student government's decisions on these applications; and (6) there was a "comprehensive appeals process" by which any student organization that was denied funding, or any student who objected to a funding decision, could appeal the decision to the student council and then to the chancellor for the campus, whenever it was "alleged that the decision was based on an organization's extracurricular speech or expressive activities" (307 F.3d at 582). The court also highlighted "one particular aspect" of this appeal process:

> In reviewing funding decisions, the appeals procedures require the Student Council to compare the grant amounts [the student government committees] allocated to various RSOs to determine whether similar RSO's applications were treated equally. By comparing the funding decisions, the Student Council can determine whether the student government, while purporting to apply the Funding Standards in a viewpoint-neutral way, nonetheless treated similar RSOs with varying viewpoints differently. The Student Council can then rectify any differing treatment on appeal [307 F.3d at 588].

On the basis of this review, the court agreed with the university that the funding standards "provide narrowly drawn, detailed, and specific guidelines" for decision making that satisfy the constitutional requirements.

The court identified two exceptions, however, to this broad ruling supporting the university's funding standards and also issued two cautions about the scope of its ruling. The first exception concerned the criteria used by the ASM finance committee, which was responsible for awarding three types of grants to RSOs: events grants, operations grants, and travel grants. At the time of the trial, the university had provided the court with the criteria for awarding the events grants and the operations grants but had not provided any criteria for the travel grants. Absent any clear and specific criteria, such as those for the events and operations grants, the travel grant portion of the mandatory fee allocation system gave unbridled discretion to the ASM finance committee that awarded the grants. The student government therefore could not award the travel grants until such time as it had implemented constitutionally suitable criteria.

The second exception to the court's broad approval concerned two of the criteria that the student government committees used to allocate funds: a criterion providing for consideration of "the length of time that an RSO has been in existence" and a criterion providing for consideration of "the amount of funding the RSO received in prior years." These criteria were not viewpoint neutral, said the court, for two reasons (see 307 F.3d at 593–94). First, to the extent that current funding decisions were based on the length of time an RSO had been in existence, or the amount of funding that the RSO had received in the past, these current decisions could depend in part on "viewpoint-based decisions of the past." Second, considering the length of time in existence or the amount of prior funding served to favor "historically popular viewpoints" and to disadvantage nontraditional or minority viewpoints. Therefore, as to these two criteria, the court concluded that they were "related to the content or viewpoint of the applying RSO, as well as based on a prior system which lack[ed] the constitutional safeguard of viewpoint neutrality."

The first of the court's two cautions concerns another criterion for awarding mandatory fees: a criterion permitting the funding committees to consider the number of students participating in or benefiting from the speech activities for which funding was sought. Although the court acknowledged that there were various content-neutral reasons for considering such information, it cautioned that such information could also permit the committees to "use the popularity of the speech as a factor in determining funding," thus providing an advantage to majority viewpoints at the expense of minority viewpoints. Since this criterion could be applied in permissible content-neutral ways, it was not "facially invalid," but the court warned that "improper consideration of the popularity of the speech may justify an as-applied challenge" in some circumstances (307 F.3d at 595).

The court's second caution also concerned possible "as-applied" challenges to the university's funding standards. The court held that, on their face, the funding standards satisfied viewpoint neutrality and were thus "facially" constitutional. But such a ruling does not necessarily validate all applications of the funding standards to particular situations. Thus the court cautioned, at various points in its opinion, that the funding standards might be applied to particular circumstances in ways that would contravene the requirements of viewpoint neutrality and that, in such situations, the funding standards would be subject to "as-applied" challenges either through the university's own internal appeal process or through the courts.

When the Supreme Court's *Southworth* decision is put together with the Seventh Circuit's further elaboration, and these cases are viewed against the backdrop provided by the earlier *Rosenberger* case (see Section 10.1.5) and by the public forum cases (see Section 9.4.2), the result is a much clearer picture of this area of the law than has ever existed previously. This picture reveals the following guidelines that public institutions may use to help assure that their systems for allocating mandatory student activities fees to student organizations are constitutional under the First Amendment:

1. The fee allocation system should be designed and used to facilitate a wide range of student extracurricular speech and a free and open exchange of ideas by, and among, the institution's students.

2. The fee allocation system, on paper and in operation, must comply with the principle of viewpoint neutrality and the corollary principle prohibiting "unbridled discretion." These principles, at a minimum, require that the institution "may not prefer some [student] viewpoints over others" and must assure that "minority views are treated with the same respect as are majority views" (*Southworth*,529 U.S. at 233, 235). As a safeguard for this required neutrality, the institution should have narrowly drawn and clear criteria to guide the decision-makers in making funding decisions.

3. The institution should have an express written requirement that all mandatory student fee allocations to student organizations are subject to the viewpoint neutrality principle and that all student decision makers are bound to uphold this principle. In conjunction with this requirement, the institution should implement various procedures to assure that the viewpoint neutrality principles will be met in practice. One procedural safeguard meriting particular attention is a requirement that the decision makers who allocate the funds, or those who review their decisions, must compare the amounts allocated to particular student organizations.

4. Institutions should be wary of using funding criteria that require or permit consideration of the number of prior years in which a student organization has received fee allocations, the amounts of funds an organization has received in the past, the size of the organization's membership, or the number of nonmembers who have attended or are expected to attend the organization's speech-related activities. If any such criteria are used, they must be carefully limited to content-neutral considerations (for example, considering the size of the organization's membership or the size of the audience for an event in order to estimate the expenses of setting up and maintaining the type of room or facility needed for the organization's meetings or events). Any such criteria should also be used in ways that do not give an advantage to popular, traditional, or majoritarian viewpoints at the expense of controversial, nontraditional, or minority viewpoints.

5. A student referendum may not be used to make funding decisions regarding particular student groups.

6. An institution may choose to include in its fee allocation system an opt-out provision or refund mechanism to protect objecting students, but the Constitution does not require the inclusion of such a mechanism.

7. An institution may choose to distinguish between the on-campus and off-campus expressive activities of student organizations in its fee allocation system, but the institution may do so only if it implements the distinction through "viewpoint neutral rules." The Constitution, however, does not require that the institution adopt any "territorial boundaries" for student speech activities or impose any "geographic or spatial restrictions" on student organizations' "entitlement" to a fee allocation (529 U.S. at 234).

### 10.1.4. Principle of nondiscrimination.

While the law prohibits administrators from imposing certain restrictions on student organizations (as Sections 10.1.1–10.1.3 indicate), there are other restrictions that administrators may be required to impose. The primary example concerns discrimination, particularly on the basis of race or sex. Just as institutions are usually prohibited from discriminating on these grounds, their student organizations are usually prohibited from doing so as well. Thus, institutions generally have an obligation either to prohibit race and sex discrimination by student organizations or to withhold institutional support from those that do discriminate.

When an institution attempts to apply its nondiscrimination policies to student organizations, the institution may face challenges from organizations that wish to exclude students from their organizations' membership, leadership, or activities on the basis of religion, sexual orientation, race, or gender. These issues have been litigated over several decades, culminating in a 2010 U.S. Supreme Court opinion, the *Martinez* case, which is discussed in this section.

In public institutions, student organizations may be subject to constitutional equal protection principles under the federal Fourteenth Amendment or comparable state constitutional provisions if they act as agents of the institution or are otherwise controlled by or receive substantial encouragement from the institution (see generally Section 1.5.2). In *Joyner v. Whiting*, 477 F.2d 456 (4th Cir. 1973) (also discussed in Section 10.3.3), for example, a minority-oriented student newspaper allegedly had a segregationist editorial policy and had discriminated by race in staffing and in accepting advertising. Although the court prohibited the university president from permanently cutting off the paper's funds, because of the restraining effect of such a cutoff on freedom of the press, the court did hold that the president could and must prohibit the discrimination in staffing and advertising: "The equal protection clause forbids racial discrimination in extracurricular activities of a state-supported institution . . . and freedom of the press furnishes no shield for discrimination" (477 F.2d at 463).

*Uzzell v. Friday*, 625 F.2d 1117 (4th Cir. 1980) (*en banc*), presents a more complex illustration of the equal protection clause's application and a possible affirmative action justification for some racial classifications. The case concerned certain rules of student organizations at the University of North Carolina. The Campus Governing Council, the legislative branch of the student government, was required under its constitution to have at least two minority students, two males, and two females among its eighteen members. The student Honor Court, under its rules, permitted defendants to demand that a majority of the judges hearing a case be of the same race (or the same sex) as the defendant. Eschewing the need for any extended analysis, the appellate court at first invalidated each of the provisions as race discrimination. (The sex discrimination aspects of the provisions were not challenged by the plaintiff students or addressed by the court.) In *Friday v. Uzzell*, 438 U.S. 912 (1978), the U.S. Supreme Court, seeing possible affirmative action issues underlying this use of racial considerations, vacated the appellate court's judgment and remanded the case for further consideration in light of the *Bakke* decision (discussed in Section 7.2.5). The appeals court then reconsidered its earlier decision and, by a vote of 4 to 3, again invalidated the rules (*Uzzell v. Friday*, 591 F.2d 997 (4th Cir. 1979) (*en banc*)), saying that the classifications were an "affront" to *Bakke*.

The following year, the Fourth Circuit recalled its 1979 decision because the *en banc* court that had heard the appeal was improperly constituted: a senior judge sat as a member of the court—a violation of a federal statute (28 U.S.C. § 46) requiring that an *en banc* panel consist only of active circuit court judges. The new rehearing *en banc* placed the matter before the appeals court for the third time (*Uzzell v. Friday*, 625 F.2d 1117 (4th Cir. 1980) (*en banc*)). On this occasion the court voted 5 to 3 to remand the case to the district court for a full development of the record and reconsideration in light of *Bakke*. The majority indicated that race-conscious actions that impinge on one class of persons in order to ameliorate past discrimination against another class are not unlawful per se and that "the university should have the opportunity to justify its regulations so that the district court can apply the *Bakke* test: is the classification necessary to the accomplishment of a constitutionally permissible purpose?" On remand, the district court held that the university had not provided sufficient evidence to justify the racial classifications, and thus the classifications neither passed the strict scrutiny test nor were justified by *Bakke* (592 F. Supp. 1502 (M.D.N.C. 1984)). The university did not appeal.

The most contentious recent issues have concerned alleged religious discrimination. (See generally Burton Bollag, "Choosing Their Flock," *Chron. Higher Educ.*, January 28, 2005, A33.) The U.S. Supreme Court has now addressed the weighty and complex issues arising from public higher educational institutions' application of their nondiscrimination policies to religious student organizations that claim a constitutional right to exclude certain students from membership or from holding office. By a 5-to-4 vote in *Christian Legal Society v. Martinez*, 130 S. Ct. 2971 (2010), the Court affirmed the decision of the U.S. Court of Appeals for the Ninth Circuit in *Christian Legal Society Chapter of University of California, Hastings College of the Law v. Kane*, 319 F. App'x 645 (9th Cir. 2009), thus upholding Hastings's application of its nondiscrimination policy to registered student organizations. *Martinez* replaced *Christian Legal Society v. Walker*, 453 F.3d 853 (7th Cir. 2006), as the primary authority on these contentious issues.

At Hastings, registered student organizations (RSOs) receive various benefits, including "financial assistance" from mandatory student activity fee funds, use of law school "channels to communicate with students," use of law school "facilities for meetings and office space," and use of the Hastings "name and logo." In return, RSOs must comply with pertinent school policies, including the nondiscrimination policy stating that "Hastings College of Law shall not discriminate unlawfully on the basis of race, color, religion, national origin, ancestry, disability, age, sex, or sexual orientation." The local chapter of the Christian Legal Society (CLS) had applied for and was denied the status of an RSO because it did not comply with this policy. The chapter asserted that the national organization of the CLS requires its chapters to use a set of bylaws that includes a statement of faith to be signed by any student seeking to become a member or officer of the chapter. Hastings claimed that this statement of faith was not in compliance with the religion and sexual orientation provisions of Hastings's nondiscrimination policy. To become recognized, Hastings advised, the CLS chapter would have to open its membership to all students regardless of their religious beliefs or sexual orientation. The chapter declined to do so.

The CLS chapter brought suit, asserting that Hastings had violated the chapter's rights to free speech, freedom of expressive association, and free exercise of religion under the First Amendment. The parties agreed on a joint stipulation of facts that became important throughout the litigation. In an unpublished opinion, the federal district court rejected the chapter's claims and granted summary judgment in favor of Hastings. On appeal, the Ninth Circuit affirmed the decision of the district court but not its reasoning (*Christian Legal Society v. Kane*, 319 F. App'x 645(9 Cir. 2009)). In a one paragraph opinion, the appellate court reasoned: "The parties stipulate that Hastings imposes an open membership rule on all student groups—all groups must accept all comers as voting members even if those individuals disagree with the mission of the group. The conditions on recognition are therefore viewpoint neutral and reasonable" (319 F. App'x 645–646, citing *Truth v. Kent School District*, 542 F.3d 634, 649–50 (9th Cir. 2008)). Cryptic though it is, the appellate court's statement, read along with the cited pages from *Truth*, apparently accepts that the Hastings nondiscrimination policy restricted the CLS chapter's speech, not just its conduct; that free speech analysis of the restriction is therefore appropriate; that the requirements applicable to a limited public forum (Section 9.4.2) apply to the case; and that the nondiscrimination policy, being "viewpoint neutral" and "reasonable," complies with the requirements for restricting access to a limited public forum.

In affirming the Ninth Circuit, the Supreme Court took a similar approach to the case, emphasizing limited public forum analysis and relying on the parties' joint stipulation of facts. To understand the Court's opinion and its limits, it is critical to see exactly how the Court framed the issue. As stated by Justice Ginsburg, who wrote the majority opinion:

> This case concerns a novel question regarding student activities at public universities: May a public law school condition its official recognition of a student group—and the attendant use of school funds and facilities—on the organizations' agreement to open eligibility for membership and leadership to all students? [130 S. Ct. at 2978]

According to the facts stipulated by the parties, "Hastings requires that registered student organizations allow *any* student to participate, become a member, or seek leadership positions in the organization, regardless of [her] status or beliefs." This requirement was called an "all-comers" policy. Sticking to this stipulation, the Court majority "consider[ed] only whether conditioning access to a student-organization forum on compliance with an all-comers policy violates the Constitution" (130 S. Ct. at 2984). The issue addressed and answered by the Court, therefore, was both more limited and more general than it might have been. The Court did not resolve the constitutionality of the Hastings RSO policy "on its face," since it framed the issue in terms of the stipulation of facts rather than doing its own line-by-line review of Hastings's written non-discrimination policy or related RSO policies (as CLS and the Court's four dissenters had urged it to do). Nor did the Court resolve the constitutionality of the Hastings RSO policy "as applied" particularly to CLS or to religious student organizations, since the Court was constrained by the joint stipulation and thus explored neither the range of potential facts concerning the policy's application to CLS (or other religious organizations) nor the policy's specific impact on CLS. Thus, while the Court answered a highly important core question regarding the clash between free expression and nondiscrimination, at the same time the Court left for another day various other constitutional questions concerning the particular nondiscrimination policies of particular institutions and how they actually work in practice and as applied to particular student groups.

Equally important as the Court's framing of the issue is the Court's framing of the analysis. The Court focused primarily on CLS's free speech challenge, using public forum principles (Section 9.4.2) to reject the challenge. "Our decisions make clear, and the parties agree, that Hastings, through its RSO program, established a *limited* public forum" (citing *Rosenberger v. Rector and Visitors of the University of Virginia*, 515 U.S. 819, 829 (1995); emphasis added). "[W]e are persuaded that our limited-public-forum precedents adequately respect . . . CLS's speech . . . rights, and fairly balance those rights against Hastings's interests as property owner and education institution" (130 S. Ct. at 2986).

The two requirements for validly excluding a particular class of speakers or topics from a limited public forum are that the exclusion is (1) "viewpoint neutral" and (2) "reasonable" in light of the forum's purposes (see *Rosenberger*, 515 U.S. at 829–30; Section 9.4.2 of this book). The Court in *Martinez* held that the Hastings "all-comers" policy (as described in the parties' fact stipulation) met both requirements.

Regarding the first requirement, the Court emphasized the neutral, nondiscriminatory character of the all-comers policy. According to the majority:

> It is . . . hard to imagine a more viewpoint-neutral policy than one requiring *all* student groups to accept *all* comers . . . Hastings' all-comers requirement draws no distinction between groups based on their message or perspective. An all-comers condition on access to RSO status, in short, is textbook viewpoint neutral [130 S. Ct. at 2993].

In applying the second requirement, reasonableness, the majority focused on Hastings's statement of the purposes of the all-comers policy and on Hastings's educational policy judgments that supported the all-comers concept. Prefacing its determination on reasonableness, the majority made clear that it would accord a measure of deference to Hastings's policy judgments (see Section 2.2.2) because "judges lack the on-the-ground expertise and experience of school administrators," and courts should therefore "resist 'substitut[ing] their own notions of sound educational policy for those of the school authorities which they review'" (130 S. Ct. at 2988, quoting *Board of Education of Hendrick Hudson Central School District v. Rowley*, 458 U.S. at 206 (1982)). Reviewing the parties' arguments about reasonableness from this perspective, the majority concluded, inter alia, that Hastings "may decide, reasonably in our view, 'that the . . . educational experience is best promoted when all participants in the [student-organization] forum must provide equal access to all students'" (130 S. Ct. at 2989, quoting Brief for Hastings), and that Hastings "reasonably adheres to the view that an all-comers policy, to the extent it brings together individuals with diverse backgrounds and beliefs, 'encourages tolerance, cooperation, and learning among students'" (130 S. Ct. at 2990, quoting from the appendix in the record on appeal).

CLS's second challenge to the Hastings policy—the freedom of expressive association challenge (see generally Section 10.1.1)—was concisely dispatched by the Court. CLS had urged the Court to analyze this claim under a different line of cases using a somewhat stricter standard of review than the limited public forum cases. Declining the invitation, the Court determined that its public forum analysis "suppl[ies] the appropriate framework for assessing . . . CLS's . . . expressive-association claims" as well. The Court reasoned:

> First, . . . speech and expressive-association rights are closely linked . . .
> When these intertwined rights arise in exactly the same context, it would be anomalous for a restriction on speech to survive constitutional review under our limited-public-forum . . . test only to be invalidated as an impermissible infringement of expressive association.
>
> Second, and closely related, the strict scrutiny we have applied in some settings to laws that burden expressive association would, in practical effect, invalidate a defining characteristic of limited public forums—the State may "reserve[e] [them] for certain groups." *Rosenberger*, 515 U.S. at 829 . . .
>
> The same ground rules must govern both speech and association challenges in the limited-public-forum context, lest strict scrutiny trump a public university's ability to "confin[e] a [speech] forum to the limited and legitimate purposes for which it was created." *Rosenberger*, 515 U.S. at 829 . . .
>
> Third, this case fits comfortably within the limited-public-forum category, for CLS, in seeking what is effectively a state subsidy, faces only indirect pressure to modify its membership policies; CLS may exclude any person for any reason if it forgoes the benefits of official recognition. The expressive-association precedents on which CLS relies, in contrast, involved regulations that *compelled* a group to include unwanted members, with no choice to opt out. See, *e.g.*, *Boy Scouts of America v. Dale*, 530 U.S. at 648 (regulation "forc[ed] [the Boy Scouts] to accept members it [did] not desire" (internal quotation marks omitted)); *Roberts v. United States Jaycees*, 468 U.S. at 623 ("There can be no clearer example of

an intrusion into the internal structure or affairs of an association than" forced inclusion of unwelcomed participants.).

Application of the less-restrictive limited-public-forum analysis better accounts for the fact that Hastings, through its RSO program, is dangling the carrot of subsidy, not wielding the stick of prohibition [130 S. Ct. at 2985–86 (footnotes and some citations omitted)].

CLS's third challenge to the all-comers policy—the free exercise of religion challenge—was summarily rejected by the Court. It relied on *Employment Division v. Smith*, 494 U.S. 872 (1990) (see generally Section 1.6.2), a case holding that government regulations that burden religious practice are nevertheless valid if they are "generally applicable" and religiously "neutral." This case "forecloses" CLS's free exercise argument, the Court reasoned, because the Hastings "all-comers" policy, according to the parties' joint stipulation, was neutral toward religion and generally applicable to all recognized student groups.

Having disposed of CLS's three challenges (over a strenuous dissent by four Justices), the majority concluded:

In requiring CLS—in common with all other student organizations—to choose between welcoming all students and forgoing the benefits of official recognition, . . . Hastings did not transgress constitutional limitations. CLS, it bears emphasis, seeks not parity with other organizations, but a preferential exemption from Hastings' policy. The First Amendment shields CLS against state prohibition of the organization's expressive activity, however exclusionary that activity may be. But CLS enjoys no constitutional right to state subvention of its selectivity [130 S. Ct. at 2978].

As suggested above, the Court's limited and generalized ruling leaves various avenues open for future litigation. The following is an overview of the most likely constitutional developments to watch for at public institutions:

1. Issues may arise concerning the "facial" constitutionality (see above) of particular institutions' nondiscrimination or student organization policies. Such issues would require an analysis of the particular wording of particular institutions' written policies. It might be argued, for example, that a policy contains exceptions that prevent it from being a true "all-comers" policy, or that a policy's terms are so vague that one cannot determine whether the standards it sets for recognition are viewpoint neutral. The *Martinez* majority does not address the Hastings policy in this way (see above) but the dissent does illustrate how such arguments might arise (see generally 130 S. Ct. at 3016–20).

2. Issues may arise concerning the constitutionality "as applied" (see discussion earlier in this section) of particular institutions' RSO policies. Such issues would focus not only on the wording of particular policy provisions but also on the actual operation of the policy, as applied to a particular student

organization or type of student organization, a particular practice of a student organization, or some other particular factual circumstance. For example, CLS argued that Hastings "selectively enforces its all-comers policy" (130 S. Ct. at 2995) and that the policy provides a "pretext" for discrimination against religious student groups—an argument concerning the application of Hastings's policy and its actual effect in operation. The *Martinez* majority did not analyze the Hastings policy in this way, since the parties' joint stipulation of facts did not leave room for such an argument and neither of the lower courts had addressed the argument. (The majority did note, though, that the Ninth Circuit may consider this argument on remand "if, and to the extent, [the issue] is preserved" (130 S. Ct. at 2995).) Justice Kennedy in his concurrence, however, did provide examples of such arguments, in particular an argument based on a showing in a particular case "that the all-comers policy was either designed or used to infiltrate the group" or otherwise to "stifle [the group's ] speech or make it ineffective" (130 S. Ct. at 3000). The dissenters also provided other illustrations of how as-applied challenges might unfold under different sets of facts (see generally 130 S. Ct. at 3016–20).

3. Issues may arise concerning alleged "neutral" restrictions that student organizations impose on membership and office holding. While the Court in *Martinez* held that public institutions may not impose *viewpoint-based* or *viewpoint-discriminatory* restrictions on the membership policies of registered student organizations, it also makes clear that "RSO's . . ., in harmony with the all-comers policy, may condition eligibility for membership and leadership on attendance, the payment of dues, and other *neutral* requirements designed to ensure that students join because of their commitment to a group's vitality, not its demise" (130 S. Ct. at 2992 (emphasis added)). In the wake of *Martinez*, there may be challenges to such restrictions as imposed by particular student organizations, challenges to institutional policies that permit such restrictions, or challenges to institutional policies that prohibit RSOs from imposing such restrictions. The key issue often would be whether the restriction or policy in question, on its face or as applied, is genuinely "neutral" rather than viewpoint-based or otherwise discriminatory.

4. Issues may arise concerning institutional RSO policies that include exceptions to the "all-comers" policy—in particular an exception for religious student organizations that allows them to limit membership to adherents to the faith. This question was not before the Court in *Martinez*, and the majority specifically distinguished it:

> The question here . . . is not whether Hastings *could*, consistent with the Constitution, provide religious groups dispensation from the all-comers policy by permitting them to restrict membership to those who share their faith. It is instead whether Hastings *must* grant that exemption [130 S. Ct. at 2993 n.24].

The question left open—whether an institution may provide an exception for student religious groups—could present not only viewpoint neutrality issues but also establishment clause issues (see generally Section 1.6.2, and compare Section 4.7) and perhaps equal protection issues as well.

5. Issues may arise concerning the First Amendment rights of discriminatory student organizations that "commonly maintain a presence at universities without official school affiliation" (130 S. Ct. at 2991). Such organizations and their members retain First Amendment free speech rights as well as freedom of association—the right to join together, or associate with one another, to engage in expressive activities (see generally Sections 9.4.1 and 10.1.1). How, then, and to what extent, may institutions regulate these groups, compared to their regulation of recognized student groups? It seems clear from *Martinez* that unrecognized groups, like recognized groups, cannot be subjected to institutional regulations based on the group's or members' viewpoints; in either case, such regulations would constitute unlawful viewpoint discrimination. It also seems clear that institutions, in general, have less regulatory authority over the expressive activities of unrecognized groups that are not subsidized as recognized student groups are, since the institution can use the "carrot of subsidy" as justification for regulating the latter but not the former. Thus, while *Martinez* permits institutions to impose an all-comers requirement on recognized, subsidized student groups, it by no means follows that institutions could constitutionally impose the same requirement on unrecognized, unsubsidized groups.

Yet other questions may arise concerning institutional regulation of unrecognized student groups. Such questions may implicate both the extent of the institution's authority to limit the speech or association of unrecognized groups that discriminate, and the extent to which an institution may provide some subsidy (for example, use of campus meeting rooms and bulletin boards) to unrecognized groups that discriminate without running afoul of federal or state nondiscrimination requirements (see generally 130 S. Ct. at 2991–92).

Student affairs administrators, of course, will not be expected to master all the legal nuances of the issues left open by or decided by the Supreme Court in *Martinez*. In-depth involvement of legal counsel is a necessity. An administrator's first step should be to understand fully the concept of the "all-comers" policy as established by the majority in *Martinez*. The next step should be to review (along with counsel) the institution's policies on recognized student groups to determine whether, on their face, they establish a genuine all-comers policy. If so, the administrator should then review the experiences of the institutions' student groups in complying with the all-comers policy, and the experiences of responsible student affairs administrators in implementing and enforcing the all-comers policy. The goal would be to assure that the written all-comers policy remains a genuine all-comers policy in practice, such that the institution will be positioned to defend its policy as constitutional both "on its face" and "as applied."

If the institution's existing policy is not a genuine all-comers policy, the question becomes whether the institution chooses to revise the policy to come into compliance with *Martinez* or, alternatively, whether the institution wants to retain the existing policy. Either way, the administrator should call on counsel to determine whether or how to redraft the policy to come into compliance with *Martinez*.

In a leading post-*Martinez* case, *Alpha Delta Chi-Delta Chi Chapter v. Reed*, 648 F.3d 790 (9th Cir. 2011), San Diego State University (SDSU) had a policy providing that students could not be excluded from membership or leadership in a recognized student organization "on the basis of race, sex, color, age, religion, national origin, marital status, citizenship, sexual orientation, physical or mental handicap, ancestry, or medical condition." A Christian sorority and a Christian fraternity, having been denied recognition due to their religious requirements for membership, challenged the policy both on its face and as applied specifically to them, claiming that the policy violated their First Amendment rights to free speech, expressive association, and free exercise of religion.

The appellate court agreed that the case was not controlled by the U.S. Supreme Court's decision in *CLS v. Martinez* (discussed earlier in this section) because SDSU's nondiscrimination policy was materially different from the "all-comers" policy at issue in *Martinez*. The court did determine, however, that San Diego State's RSO program was a "limited public forum," and SDSU's membership policy was subject to the same "limited public forum" analysis that the Supreme Court had applied in *Martinez*. The viewpoint neutrality requirement that is central to the limited public forum analysis therefore became the focal point of the dispute.

The plaintiffs argued that the SDSU policy "prohibits only certain membership requirements, such as those based on race, gender, or religion, rather than prohibiting all membership requirements, as an all-comers policy does." This "more limited discrimination policy . . . discriminates on the basis of viewpoint because it allows secular belief-based discrimination while prohibiting religious belief-based discrimination." Under this policy, for instance, "a student Republican organization could permissibly exclude Democrats because the SDSU policy does not forbid discrimination on the basis of political belief, but a Christian group could not exclude a Muslim student because that would discriminate on the basis of religious belief." The court rejected this argument:

> Plaintiffs' argument, while seemingly compelling at first glance, does not survive closer scrutiny. We accept Plaintiffs' assertion that San Diego State's nondiscrimination policy incidentally burdens groups that wish to exclude others on the basis of religion, but does not burden groups that do not exclude or exclude on bases not prohibited by the policy. But this assertion is insufficient to prove viewpoint discrimination, because Plaintiffs have put forth no evidence that San Diego State implemented its nondiscrimination policy for the *purpose* of suppressing Plaintiffs' viewpoint, or indeed of restricting any sort of expression at all . . .
>
> As the Supreme Court has made clear, antidiscrimination laws intended to ensure equal access to the benefits of society serve goals "unrelated to the suppression of expression" and are neutral as to both content and viewpoint [citing Supreme Court cases] . . . San Diego State's nondiscrimination policy

does not "target speech or discriminate on the basis of its content," but instead serves to remove access barriers imposed against groups that have historically been excluded [citing Supreme Court cases] [648 F.3d at 801].

Having upheld the SDSU policy on its face, the appellate court then considered the plaintiffs' alternative argument: that the SDSU nondiscrimination policy, even if valid on its face, was nevertheless invalid as applied to the sorority and fraternity plaintiffs. This type of argument was not addressed by the majority in *Martinez*, but it became important in the SDSU case. The plaintiffs offered evidence that SDSU "has granted official recognition to some religious student groups even though those groups, like Plaintiffs, restrict membership or eligibility to hold office based on religious belief" and that "some non-religious but officially recognized groups appear to discriminate on prohibited grounds." This evidence, according to the court, created a triable issue of fact regarding possible "selective enforcement" of the SDSU policy that could violate the plaintiffs' free speech or expressive association rights. Moreover, the plaintiffs offered evidence suggesting that SDSU was "targeting them because of their religious beliefs." This evidence also created a triable issue of fact—this time an issue regarding possible violation of the plaintiffs' free exercise and equal protection rights. The court therefore remanded the case to the district court for further proceedings to resolve these issues.

Occasionally, student organizations at public institutions may also claim exemption from campus nondiscrimination requirements based on a "freedom of *intimate* association." Like the freedom of *expressive* association (see generally *Roberts v. U.S. Jaycees*, 468 U.S. 609 (1984)), freedom of intimate association may be invoked regardless of whether the student organization's discriminatory policies are based on religious belief. Unlike the First Amendment freedom of expressive association, however, freedom of intimate association is based on the concept of personal liberty in the Fourteenth Amendment's due process clause; it thus involves an analysis somewhat different than that for expressive association.

A 2007 case, *Chi Iota Colony v. City University of New York*, 502 F.3d 136 (2d Cir. 2007), provides an example. The plaintiff fraternity claimed that the university's refusal to recognize it because it discriminated on the basis of gender violated the fraternity's freedom of *intimate* association. Reversing the district court's decision in favor of the plaintiff (443 F. Supp. 2d 374), the appellate court determined that the university's interests in enforcing its nondiscrimination policy outweighed the fraternity's interests in associational freedom. (In the process, the court at some points mistakenly labeled the freedom of intimate association as a First Amendment freedom—a slip of the judicial pen that does not appear to have affected its reasoning.)

First, according to the appellate court, the fraternity had a "relatively weak" interest in intimate association. "Based on its size, level of selectivity, purpose, and inclusion of non-members [in fraternity activities], the Fraternity lacks the characteristics that typify groups with strong claims to intimate association" (502 F.3d at 147). Moreover, the university's refusal to recognize the fraternity or provide university meeting rooms only "interferes to a limited extent with the fraternity's associational rights": the fraternity could still exist, meet in other places, and carry on intimate associations. In contrast, the university's interests in enforcing its nondiscrimination policy were strong, in particular its interest in furthering its educational mission by promoting "diversity" and combating "bigotry." The appellate court therefore vacated the district court's preliminary injunction prohibiting the university from enforcing its gender non-discrimination policy against the fraternity.

Controversies such as those in the *Martinez* case and other cases discussed above can also arise in private institutions. Since First Amendment claims then would not be available to student organization members, the institution may have more leeway to use its discretion in resolving conflicts. This is especially the case if the institution is a religious institution with its own freedom of religion rights under the First Amendment. In *Romeo v. Seton Hall*, 875 A.2d 1043 (N.J. Super. Ct. 2005), for example, the court rejected a gay student's challenge to a Catholic-affiliated university's denial of an application for recognition of a group serving the needs of gay and lesbian students.

The student, on behalf of himself and other students, asserted two claims: (1) that the institution's refusal to recognize the group violated the New Jersey Law Against Discrimination (LAD); and (2) that the institution's denial of recognition was a breach of contract. These are the same two types of claims most likely to be available to students at private institutions in other nonrecognition cases. Regarding the first claim, the court acknowledged that the state LAD did cover sexual orientation and did apply to private sector entities (see, for example, the *Frank v. Ivy Club* case, discussed later in this section). But religious institutions such as Seton Hall, the court held, were exempted from the law.

Regarding the second claim, the court acknowledged that Seton Hall had its own nondiscrimination policy that covered sexual orientation discrimination. But neither the pertinent provisions of this policy, nor the student's application for recognition of the group, created a contract between the group and the university, particularly "where, as here, the [university] values and mission" at issue "address fundamental religious ideals" (875 A.2d at 1050). (For much the same reason, the court also held that the university nondiscrimination policy did not and could not constitute a waiver of the university's exemption from the New Jersey LAD.)

Federal civil rights laws (see Section 11.5 of this book) may also be pertinent to issues regarding discrimination by (or against) student organizations. These federal statutes and regulations, for example, may require private as well as public institutions to ensure, as a condition of receiving federal funds, that student organizations do not discriminate on specified grounds. (Sexual orientation and religion are not among the grounds covered by these statutes.) The Title VI regulations (see Section 11.5.2 of this book) contain several provisions broad enough to cover student organizations; in particular, 34 C.F.R. § 100.3(b)(1) prohibits institutions from discriminating by race, either "directly or through contractual or other arrangements," and 34 C.F.R. § 100.3(b)(4) prohibits institutions from discriminating by race in the provision of services or benefits that are offered "in or through a facility" constructed or operated in whole or part with federal funds. And the Title IX regulations (see Section

11.5.3 of this book) prohibit institutions from "providing significant assistance" to any organization "which discriminates on the basis of sex in providing any aid, benefit, or service to students" (34 C.F.R. § 106.31(b)(6); see also 34 C.F.R. § 106.6(c)). Title IX does not apply, however, to the membership practices of tax-exempt social fraternities and sororities (20 U.S.C. § 1681(a)6(A)). And more generally, under the Civil Rights Restoration Act, all "programs" and "activities" of an institution receiving federal funds are subject to the nondiscrimination requirements of the civil rights statutes.

State statutes and regulations may also provide some protection against discrimination by student organizations at both public and private institutions. In *Frank v. Ivy Club*, 576 A.2d 241 (N.J. 1990), for example, the court was asked to determine whether two private "eating clubs" affiliated with Princeton University, which at the time admitted only men to membership, were subject to a state law prohibiting nondiscrimination in places of public accommodation. The case began when Sally Frank, then an undergraduate at Princeton, filed a charge with the New Jersey Division on Civil Rights (the state's human rights agency), asserting that she was denied membership in the clubs on the basis of her gender and that this denial constituted unlawful discrimination by a place of public accommodation. She claimed that the university was responsible for supervising the clubs and therefore was partly responsible for their discriminatory activities. The university (and the clubs) contended that the clubs were private organizations not formally affiliated with the university. The Division on Civil Rights determined that the clubs were places of public accommodation and thus subject to the nondiscrimination requirements of state law. The Division on Civil Rights also ruled that the clubs enjoyed a "symbiotic relationship" with the university, since the university had assisted them in their business affairs, a majority of upper- division Princeton students took their meals at the clubs (relieving the university of the responsibility of providing meals for them), and the clubs would not have come into being without the existence of the university. From these findings, the Division on Civil Rights concluded that probable cause existed to believe that the clubs had unlawfully discriminated against Frank on the basis of her gender.

After several appeals to intermediate courts and other procedural wrangling, the New Jersey Supreme Court affirmed the Division on Civil Rights' jurisdiction over the case and accepted its findings and conclusions that the clubs had to cease their discriminatory membership practices. The court reasoned that

> [w]here a place of public accommodation [the university] and an organization that deems itself private [the clubs] share a symbiotic relationship, particularly where the allegedly "private" entity supplies an essential service which is not provided by the public accommodation, the servicing entity loses its private character and becomes subject to laws against discrimination [576 A. 2d at 257].

In light of such constitutional and regulatory requirements, it is clear that administrators cannot ignore alleged discrimination by student organizations. In some areas of concern, race and sex discrimination being the primary examples, institutions' obligations to prohibit such discrimination are relatively clear.

In other areas of concern, however, the law is either more sparse or less clear regarding the institution's obligations. The *Martinez* case, discussed above in this section, provides an excellent example of a case addressing issues concerning which the law had been relatively sparse and unclear.

***10.1.5. Religious activities.*** Numerous legal issues may arise concerning student organizations that engage in religious activities or have a religious purpose or a religious affiliation. The most significant issues usually arise under the free speech, free exercise, or establishment clauses of the First Amendment, or under parallel provisions of state constitutions, and are therefore of primary concern to public institutions. Section 10.1.4 addresses problems concerning student organizations' restrictive membership policies. This section, in contrast, is limited to religious student organizations and addresses other problems concerning their use of campus facilities and services, and their receipt of student activities fee allocations.

In *Widmar v. Vincent*, 454 U.S. 263 (1981), a case involving the University of Missouri–Kansas City (UMKC), the U.S. Supreme Court established important rights for student religious groups at public postsecondary institutions that seek to use the institution's facilities. In 1972, the Board of Curators of UMKC promulgated a regulation prohibiting the use of university buildings or grounds "for purposes of religious worship or religious teaching." In 1977, UMKC applied this regulation to a student religious group called Cornerstone. This group was "an organization of evangelical Christian students from various denominational backgrounds . . . [It] held its on-campus meetings in classrooms and in the student center. These meetings were open to the public and attracted up to 125 students. A typical Cornerstone meeting included prayer, hymns, Bible commentary, and discussion of religious views and experiences" (454 U.S. at 265 n.2). When UMKC denied Cornerstone permission to continue meeting in university facilities, eleven members of the organization sued the university, alleging that it had abridged their rights to free exercise of religion and freedom of speech under the First Amendment.

For the Supreme Court, as for the lower courts, the threshold question was whether the case would be treated as a free speech case. In considering this question, Justice Powell's opinion for the Court (with Justice White dissenting) characterized the students' activities as "religious speech," which, like other speech, is protected by the free speech clause. The university, by making its facilities generally available to student organizations, had created a "forum" open to speech activities, which the Court described both as a "limited public forum" and an "open forum." The free speech clause therefore applied to the situation. This clause did not require UMKC to establish a forum, but once UMKC had done so, the clause required it to justify any exclusion of a student group from this forum because of the content of its activities:

> In order to justify discriminatory exclusion from a public forum based on the religious content of a group's intended speech, the university must satisfy the standard of review appropriate to content-based exclusions. It must show that

its regulation is necessary to serve a compelling state interest and that it is narrowly drawn to achieve that end [454 U.S. at 269–70].

In attempting to justify its regulation under this standard, UMKC relied on the First Amendment's establishment clause and on the establishment clause in the Missouri state constitution. Its argument was that maintaining separation of church and state, as mandated by these clauses, was a "compelling state interest," which justified its no-religious-worship regulation under the free speech clause. Resorting to establishment clause jurisprudence, the Court rejected this argument. Although the Court agreed that maintaining separation of church and state was a compelling interest, it did not believe that an equal access policy violated the establishment clause. The Court relied on the three-part test of *Lemon v. Kurtzman*, 403 U.S. 602, 612–13 (1971): "First, the [governmental policy] must have a secular legislative purpose; second, its principal or primary effect must be one that neither advances nor inhibits religion . . .; finally, the [policy] must not foster an excessive government entanglement with religion." Applying the test, the Court rejected the university's contention that giving religious student groups access to university facilities would advance religion:

> We are satisfied that any religious benefits of an open forum at UMKC would be "incidental" within the meaning of our cases. Two factors are especially relevant.
>
> First, an open forum in a public university does not confer any imprimatur of state approval on religious sects or practices. As the court of appeals quite aptly stated, such a policy "would no more commit the University . . . to religious goals" than it is "now committed to the goals of the Students for a Democratic Society, the Young Socialist Alliance," or any other group eligible to use its facilities (*Chess v. Widmar*, 635 F.2d at 1317).
>
> Second, the forum is available to a broad class of nonreligious as well as religious speakers; there are over 100 recognized student groups at UMKC. The provision of benefits to so broad a spectrum of groups is an important index of secular effect [citations omitted]. If the Establishment Clause barred the extension of general benefits to religious groups, "a church could not be protected by the police and fire departments, or have its public sidewalk kept in repair" (*Roemer v. Maryland Public Works Board*, 426 U.S. 736, 747 . . . (1976) (plurality opinion)) . . . At least in the absence of empirical evidence that religious groups will dominate UMKC's open forum, we agree with the Court of Appeals that the advancement of religion would not be the forum's "primary effect" [454 U.S. at 271–75].

With regard to the university's argument that its interest in enforcing the Missouri constitution's prohibition against public support for religious activities outweighed the students' free speech claim, the Court stated that the university's interest in avoiding such public support "is limited by the Free Exercise Clause and in this case by the Free Speech Clause as well." In this constitutional context, the Court could not recognize the State's "interest . . . in achieving greater separation of church and State than is already ensured under the establishment clause of the Federal Constitution" as a "compelling" interest that would "justify content-based discrimination against [the students'] religious speech."

Since UMKC could not justify its content-based restriction on access to the forum it had created, the Court declared the university's regulation unconstitutional. The plaintiff students thereby obtained the right to have their religious group hold its meetings in campus facilities generally open to student groups. It follows that other student religious groups at other public postsecondary institutions have the same right to use campus facilities; institutions may not exclude them, whether by written policy or otherwise, on the basis of the religious content of their activities.

*Widmar* has substantial relevance for public institutions, most of which have created forums similar to the forum at UMKC. The opinion falls far short, however, of requiring institutions to relinquish all authority over student religious groups. There are substantial limits to the opinion's reach:

1. *Widmar* does not require (nor does it permit) institutions to create forums especially for religious groups or to give them any other preferential treatment.

2. Nor does *Widmar* require institutions to create a forum for student groups generally, or to continue to maintain one, if they choose not to do so. The case applies only to situations where the institution has created and voluntarily continues to maintain a forum for student groups.

3. *Widmar* requires access only to facilities that are part of a forum created by the institution, not to any other facilities. Similarly, *Widmar* requires access only for students.

4. *Widmar* does not prohibit all regulation of student organizations' use of forum facilities; it prohibits only content-based restrictions on access. Institutions can still impose reasonable regulations such as time, place, and manner regulations (see Section 9.5.3). Such regulations must be imposed on all student groups, however, not just student religious organizations, and must be imposed without regard to the content of the group's speech activities. If a student religious group or other student group "violate[s] [such] reasonable campus rules or substantially interfere[s] with the opportunity of other students to obtain an education" (454 U.S. at 277), the institution may prohibit the group from using campus facilities for its activities.

5. *Widmar* does not rule out every possible content-based restriction on access to a forum. A content-based regulation would be constitutional under the First Amendment if it were "necessary to serve a compelling state interest and . . . narrowly drawn to achieve that end." As *Widmar* and other First Amendment cases demonstrate, this standard is exceedingly difficult to meet. But the *Widmar* opinion suggests at least two possibilities, the contours of which are left for further development should the occasion arise. First, the Court hints that, if there is "empirical evidence that religious groups will

dominate . . . [the institution's] open forum" (454 U.S. at 275), the institution apparently may regulate access by these groups to the extent necessary to prevent domination. Second, if the student demand for use of forum facilities exceeds the supply, the institution may "make academic judgments as to how best to allocate scarce resources" (454 U.S. at 276). In making such academic judgments, the institution may apparently prefer the educational content of some group activities over others and allocate its facilities in accord with these academic preferences.

A subsequent Supreme Court case, *Rosenberger v. Rector and Visitors of the University of Virginia*, 515 U.S. 819 (1995), concerns religious student organizations' eligibility for funding from mandatory student fee assessments. A student group, Wide Awake Productions (WAP), had been recognized by the university and was entitled to use university facilities just as other organizations did. But the university's guidelines for allocating mandatory student fees excluded certain types of organizations, including fraternities and sororities, political and religious organizations, and organizations whose membership policies were exclusionary. The guidelines also prohibited the funding of, among others, religious and political activities. WAP published a journal containing articles written from a religious perspective, and its constitution stated that the organization's purpose included the expression of religious views. The student council, which had been delegated the authority to disburse the funds from student fees, had denied funding to WAP, characterizing its publication of the journal as "religious activity."

The student members of WAP sued the university, alleging that the denial of funding violated their rights to freedom of speech, press, association, religious exercise, and equal protection under both the federal and state constitutions. The district court rejected all of the plaintiffs' arguments and granted the university's motion for summary judgment on all claims. The appellate court, focusing particularly on the free speech and establishment clause issues, upheld the district court in all respects.

The U.S. Supreme Court then reversed the judgments of the district and appellate courts. By a 5-to-4 vote, the majority held that (1) the university's refusal to provide Student Activities Fund (SAF) funds to Wide Awake Productions violated the students' First Amendment free speech rights; and (2) university funding for WAP would not violate the First Amendment's establishment clause, and the university therefore could not justify its violation of the free speech clause by asserting a need to adhere to the establishment clause. Justice Kennedy wrote the opinion for the majority of five; Justice O'Connor wrote an important concurring opinion; and Justice Souter wrote the opinion for the four dissenters.

The tension between the free speech and establishment clauses of the First Amendment is clearly illuminated by the sharply divergent majority and dissenting opinions. The majority opinion addresses *Rosenberger* from a free speech standpoint and finds no establishment clause justification for infringing the rights of a student publication that reports the news from a religious perspective. In contrast, the dissent characterizes the students' publication as an evangelical magazine directly financed by the state and regards such funding to be a clear example of an establishment clause violation. Justice O'Connor's narrow concurring opinion, tailored specifically to the facts of the case, serves to limit the majority's holding and reduce the gulf between the majority and the dissent.

As the Court explained the situation, the university had established a mandatory student activities fee (SAF), the income from which supported a student activities fund used to subsidize a variety of student organizations. All recognized student groups had to achieve the status of a "Contracted Independent Organization" (CIO), after which some groups could then submit certain bills to the student council for payment from SAF funds. The eligible bills were those from "outside contractors" or "third-party contractors" that provided services or products to the student organization. Disbursement was made directly to the third party; no payments went directly to a student group. The university's SAF guidelines prohibited the use of SAF funds for, among other purposes, religious activity, defined by the guidelines as an activity that "primarily promotes or manifests a particular belief in or about a deity or an ultimate reality." Wide Awake Productions was a CIO established to publish a campus magazine that "'offers a Christian perspective on both personal and community issues'" (515 U.S. at 826, quoting from the magazine's first issue). WAP applied for SAF funding—funding already provided to fifteen student "media groups"—to be used to pay the printer that printed its magazine. The university rejected the request on grounds that WAP's activities were religious.

Explicating the majority's free speech analysis, Justice Kennedy described the SAF as a forum "more in a metaphysical sense than in a spatial or geographic sense," but nonetheless determined that the SAF, as established and operated by the university, is a "limited public forum" for First Amendment purposes. "Having opened the SAF to the university community, the university must respect the lawful boundaries it has itself set. [It] may not exclude speech where its distinction is not "reasonable in light of the purpose served by the forum", . . . nor may it discriminate against speech on the basis of its viewpoint (515 U.S. 827–28, citations omitted).

The majority then determined that the university had denied funding to WAP because of WAP's perspective or viewpoint, rather than because WAP dealt with the general subject matter of religion. Thus, although "it is something of an understatement to speak of religious thought and discussion as just a viewpoint," "viewpoint discrimination is the proper way to interpret the university's objection to Wide Awake":

> By the very terms of the SAF prohibition, the [u]niversity does not exclude religion as a subject matter but selects for disfavored treatment those student journalistic efforts with religious editorial viewpoints. Religion may be a vast area of inquiry, but it also provides, as it did here, a specific premise, a perspective, a standpoint from which a variety of subjects may be discussed and

considered. The prohibited perspective, not the general subject matter, resulted in the refusal to make the third-party payments [to the printer], for the subjects discussed were otherwise within the approved category of publications [515 U.S. at 831].

Furthermore, the majority rejected the university's contention that "no viewpoint discrimination occurs because the Guidelines discriminate against an entire class of viewpoints." Because of the "complex and multifaceted nature of public discourse . . . [i]t is as objectionable to exclude both a theistic and an atheistic perspective on the debate as it is to exclude one, the other, or yet another political, economic, or social viewpoint" (515 U.S. at 831).

Having determined that the university had violated the students' free speech rights, the majority considered whether providing SAF funds to WAP would nevertheless violate the establishment clause. In order for a government regulation to survive an establishment clause challenge, it must be neutral toward religion (see Section 1.6 of this book). Relying on past decisions upholding governmental programs when "the government, following neutral criteria and evenhanded policies, extends benefits to recipients whose ideologies and viewpoints, including religious ones, are broad and diverse" (515 U.S. at 839), the Court held that the SAF was neutral toward religion:

> The object of the SAF is to open a forum for speech and to support various student enterprises, including the publication of newspapers, in recognition of the diversity and creativity of student life . . . WAP did not seek a subsidy because of its Christian editorial viewpoint; it sought funding as a student journal, which it was [515 U.S. at 840].

Thus, the WAP application for funding depended not on the religious editorial viewpoint of the publication, nor on WAP being a religious organization, but rather on the neutral factor of its status as a student journal. "Any benefit to religion is incidental to the government's provision of secular services for secular purposes on a religion-neutral basis" (515 U.S. at 843–44).

In completing its establishment clause analysis, the majority distinguished another line of cases forbidding the use of tax funds to support religious activities and rejected the contention that the mandatory student activities fee was a tax levied for the support of a church or religion. Unlike a tax, which the majority described as an exaction to support the government and a revenue-raising device, the student activity fee was used for the limited purpose of funding student organizations consistent with the educational purposes of the university. No public funds would flow directly into WAP's coffers; instead, the university would pay printers (third-party contractors) to produce WAP's publications. This method of third-party payment, along with university-required disclaimers stating that the university was not responsible for or represented by the recipient organization, evidenced the attenuated relationship between the university and WAP.

Justice O'Connor's concurring opinion carefully limited her analysis to the facts of the case, emphasizing that "[t]he nature of the dispute does not admit of any categorical answers, nor should any be inferred from the Court's decision today." Justice O'Connor based her concurrence on four specific considerations that ameliorated the establishment clause concerns that otherwise would arise from government funding of religious messages. First, at the insistence of the university, student organizations such as WAP were separate and distinct from the university. All groups that wished to be considered for SAF funding were required to sign a contract stating that the organization existed and operated independently of the university. Moreover, all publications, contracts, letters, or other written materials distributed by the group had to bear a disclaimer acknowledging that, while members of the university faculty and student body might be associated with the group, the organization was independent of the "corporation which is the university and which is not responsible for the organizations' contracts, acts, or omissions." Second, no money was given directly to WAP. By paying a third-party vendor, in this case a printer that printed WAP's journal, the university was able to ensure that the funding that it had granted was being used to "further the University's purpose in maintaining a free and robust marketplace of ideas, from whatever perspective." This method of funding, according to the concurrence, was analogous to a school providing equal access to a generally available physical facility, like a printing press on campus. Third, because WAP did not exist "in a vacuum," it would not be mistakenly perceived to be university endorsed. This potential danger was greatly diminished by both the number and variety of other publications receiving SAF funding. O'Connor thus found it illogical to equate university funding of WAP with the endorsement of one particular viewpoint. And fourth, the "proceeds of the student fees in this case [may be distinguishable] from proceeds of the general assessments in support of religion that lie at the core of the prohibition against religious funding, . . . and from government funds generally," in that it was the students' money, not the government's, that made up the student activities fund. O'Connor suggested that "a fee of this sort appears conducive to granting individual students proportional refunds."[1]

Although the first three of Justice O'Connor's distinctions were also relied on by Justice Kennedy, Justice O'Connor stated her conclusions more narrowly than did Kennedy and limited her reasoning more tightly to the unique facts of the case. Justice O'Connor also added the fourth consideration regarding the character of the student fee proceeds. Since Justice O'Connor provided the critical fifth vote that formed the 5-to-4 majority, her opinion carries unusual significance. To the extent that her establishment clause analysis is narrower than Justice Kennedy's, it is her opinion rather than his that apparently provides the current baseline for understanding the establishment clause restrictions on public institutions' funding of student religious groups.

The four dissenting Justices disagreed with both the majority's free speech clause analysis and its establishment clause analysis. Regarding the former,

---

[1] The issue of proportional refunds for objecting students, or an "opt-out" system, was later addressed by the Court in *Board of Regents of the University of Wisconsin System v. Southworth,* 529 U.S. 217 (2000), discussed in Section 10.1.3 of this chapter.

Justice Souter insisted that the university's refusal to fund WAP was not viewpoint discrimination but rather a "subject-matter distinction," an educational judgment not to fund student dialogue on the particular subject of religion regardless of the viewpoints expressed. Regarding the establishment issue, which he termed the "central question in this case," Justice Souter argued that, because "there is no warrant for distinguishing among public funding sources for purposes of applying the First Amendment's prohibition of religious establishment, . . . the university's refusal to support petitioners' religious activities is compelled by the Establishment Clause." Emphasizing that WAP's publications call on Christians "'to live, in word and deed, according to the faith they proclaim . . . and to consider what a personal relationship with Jesus Christ means'" (551 U.S. at 868, quoting from WAP's first issue), Justice Souter likened the paper to an "evangelist's mission station and pulpit" (515 U.S. at 868). He thus argued that the use of public (SAF) funds for this activity was a "direct subsidization of preaching the word" and a "direct funding of core religious activities by an arm of the State" (515 U.S. at 863).

The majority's reasoning in *Rosenberger* generally paralleled the Court's earlier reasoning in *Widmar v. Vincent* (discussed earlier in this section) and generally affirmed the free speech and establishment principles articulated in that case. More important, both Justice Kennedy's and Justice O'Connor's opinions extended student organizations' First Amendment rights beyond access to facilities (the issue in *Widmar*) to include access to services. The Kennedy and O'Connor opinions also refined the *Widmar* free speech analysis by distinguishing between content-based restrictions on speech (the issue in *Widmar*) and viewpoint-based restrictions (the issue as the Court framed it in *Rosenberger*). The latter type of restriction, sometimes called "viewpoint discrimination," is the most suspect of all speech restrictions and the type least likely to be tolerated by the courts (see generally Sections 9.5.2 and 10.1.3). *Widmar* appears to reserve a range of discretion for a higher educational institution to make academic judgments based on the educational content of a student organization's activities; *Rosenberger* appears to prohibit any such discretion when the institution's academic judgment is based on consideration of the student group's viewpoints (see 515 U.S. at 845).

Some years after *Rosenberger*, the U.S. Supreme Court faced another type of problem regarding religious activities of student organizations: the clash between religious student organizations' interest in restricting membership or leadership to students who profess the organization's beliefs, and the public institution's interest in avoiding such restrictions. In the Supreme Court case, *Christian Legal Society v. Martinez*, 130 S. Ct. 2971 (2010) (discussed in Section 10.1.4), the focus was not on religious organizations' access to particular facilities (as in *Widmar*) or services (as in *Rosenberger*) but rather on eligibility for recognition as a student organization. Moreover, the issues did not center on the interrelationship between the free speech clause and the establishment clause, as in both *Widmar* and *Rosenberger*, but only on the application of the free speech and free exercise clauses. The *Martinez* case serves to limit the scope of free speech protections, expressive association protections implicit in the First Amendment, and free exercise of religion protections for student organizations that discriminate on the basis of religious belief but seek to become recognized organizations.

In a leading lower court case applying *Widmar* and *Rosenberger* (and also *Martinez*), *Badger Catholic v. Walsh*, 620 F.3d 775 (7th Cir. 2010), a Catholic religious organization that was an RSO at the University of Wisconsin was denied funding from the mandatory student fee fund for certain of its programs. One such program was a summer leadership training retreat that included daily masses and "communal prayer sessions." The university student fees policy permitted the use of funds for "dialog, discussion, or debate from a religious perspective." The university claimed, however, that the programs at issue fell within an exception to the university policy that prohibited subsidizing student programs dedicated to "worship, proselytizing, [or] religious instruction." The student organization sued, claiming that the university's denials of funding constituted viewpoint discrimination violating their free speech rights. The university responded that funding of any program falling within the exception would violate the establishment clause and that its denials of funding were therefore constitutional.

The Seventh Circuit, per Chief Judge Easterbrook, held in favor of the student organization. Relying on *Rosenberger* (cited earlier in this section) and *Southworth* (see Section 10.1.3), the court held that the University of Wisconsin had created a limited public forum for private speakers. In such a situation, a university may limit access to funding only if its criteria are viewpoint neutral and reasonable. The university's policy did not meet this requirement. Thus, still relying on *Rosenberger* and *Southworth*, and adding *Martinez* (the *Hastings* case discussed earlier in this section), the court determined that providing funding to all activities of RSOs except those whose purpose is religious is subject to strict scrutiny review because such a restriction is viewpoint discriminatory. "[T]he University's activities fee fund must cover Badger Catholic's six contested programs if similar programs that espouse a secular perspective are reimbursed" (620 F.3d at 781).

Regarding the university's establishment clause defense, the court rejected it on the authority of *Widmar* and *Rosenberger*: "The University would not violate the Establishment Clause by funding Badger Catholic's programs" (620 F.3d at 778). Funding student programs that promote religious activities does not violate the establishment clause so long as the funding is available to all RSOs based on viewpoint-neutral, reasonable criteria.

## Section 10.2. Fraternities and Sororities

**10.2.1. Overview.** Fraternal organizations have been part of campus life at many colleges and universities for more than a century. Some, such as Phi Beta Kappa, were founded to recognize academic achievement, whereas others have a predominantly social focus. Because of their strong ties to colleges and universities, whether because the houses occupied by members are on or near the college's property or because their members are students at the college, the consequences of the individual and group behavior of fraternity and sorority members can involve the college in legal problems.

The legal issues that affect nonfraternal student organizations (see Section 10.1) may also arise with respect to fraternities and sororities. But because fraternal organizations have their own unique histories and traditions, are related to national organizations that may influence their activities, and play a significant social role on many campuses, they may pose unique legal problems for the college with which they are affiliated.

Fraternities and sororities may be chapters of a national organization or may be independent organizations. The local chapters, whether or not they are tied to a national organization, may be either incorporated or unincorporated associations. If the fraternity or sorority provides a house for some of its members, it may be located on land owned by the colleges or it may be off campus. In either case, the college may own the fraternity house or an alumni organization (sometimes called a "house corporation") may own the house and assume responsibility for its upkeep.

Litigation concerning fraternal organizations has increased sharply in the past decade. Institutional attempts to regulate, discipline, or ban fraternal organizations have met with stiff resistance, both on campus and in the courts. Students or other individuals injured as a result of fraternal organizations' activities, or the activities of individual members of fraternal organizations, have sought to hold colleges legally responsible for those injuries. And fraternal organizations themselves are facing increasing **legal liability** as citizens and courts have grown less tolerant of the problems of hazing and other forms of misconduct that continue to trouble U.S. college campuses.

### 10.2.2. Institutional recognition and regulation of fraternal organizations. Recognition by a college is significant to fraternal organizations because many national fraternal organizations require such recognition as a condition of the local organization's continued affiliation with the national. The conditions under which recognition is awarded by the college are important because they may determine the college's power to regulate the conduct of the organization or its members.

Some colleges and universities require, as a condition of recognition of fraternal organizations, that each local fraternity sign a "relationship statement." These statements outline the college's regulations and elicit the organization's assurance that it will obtain insurance coverage, adhere to fire and building codes, and comply with the institution's policy on the serving of alcohol. Some of these statements also require members to participate in alcohol awareness programs or community service. Some statements include restrictions on parties and noise, and extend the jurisdiction of the college's student conduct code and disciplinary system to acts that take place where students live, even if they live off campus.

On some campuses, institutional regulation of fraternal organizations extends to their membership practices. Traditionally, fraternities and sororities have limited their membership to one gender, and in the past many of these organizations prohibited membership for nonwhite and non-Christian individuals.

In more recent years, however, several colleges and universities, including Middlebury, Bowdoin, and Trinity (Connecticut), have required fraternities and sororities to admit members of both sexes. Although private colleges may impose such requirements, it may be more difficult for public institutions to do so. A federal trial court, applying constitutional "freedom of association" concepts articulated by the U.S. Supreme Court in *Boy Scouts of America v. Dale* (see Section 10.1.4), granted a preliminary injunction to a fraternity denied recognition by a public college because its constitution limited its membership to males, but an appellate court reversed, concluding that the college's interest in discrimination and diversity outweighed the "relatively weak" associational interest of the fraternity members (*Chi Iota Colony v. City University of New York*, 502 F.3d 136 (2d Cir. 2007)).

Institutions may sanction fraternities and sororities whose members violate campus codes of student conduct or civil or criminal laws by revoking institutional recognition. Not surprisingly, such revocation decisions have spawned litigation. Two cases, one brought under state administrative law and a second claiming constitutional violations, are illustrative. When Washington State University revoked recognition of a fraternity following illegal drug use and policy violations by its members, the fraternity challenged that decision in state court under the state's Administrative Procedure Act (Wash. Rev. Code ch. 34.05). University policy required that any recognized student organization comply with university conduct policies. The university had received reports from local police that drug use and drug paraphernalia had been observed at the fraternity house; that the fraternity did not have a resident advisor, as required by university policy; that underage individuals had been served alcohol at fraternity social functions; and that hazing had occurred. Several police officers testified about drug buys and drug use on fraternity property and by current or former fraternity members and their guests. The conduct board found the fraternity and its members responsible for all of the policy violations and recommended a five-year suspension, followed by two years of probation. The university followed that recommendation.

In *Alpha Kappa Lambda Fraternity v. Washington State University*, 216 P.3d 451 (Wash. Ct. App., Div. 3 2009), the fraternity challenged the process and outcome of the student conduct board, which found that fraternity members had used illegal drugs and had otherwise violated institutional policy. The fraternity asserted that the conduct board's findings were not supported by substantial evidence and that the sanction of five years' suspension imposed by the university was arbitrary and capricious. The trial court upheld the sanction in all respects, and the appellate court affirmed. The appellate court noted that the university's policies and procedures permitted the admission of hearsay evidence in student conduct hearings, and thus the use of such evidence was not a violation. Nor was the use of evidence based upon confidential sources so unreliable as to be impermissible for the conduct board to consider; furthermore, said the court, there was sufficient evidence beyond that of confidential informants that many members of the fraternity were involved in illegal activities.

With respect to the sanction, the court explained that the conduct board had the discretion to impose a range of sanctions, and it had selected a five-year suspension to ensure that most, if not all, of the current fraternity members would no longer be at the university when the suspension was lifted. The court ruled that the conduct board's action was within its discretion.

In the second case, a federal appellate court rejected the claims of fraternity members that George Mason University's decision to sanction the fraternity and several of its members violated their First and Fourteenth Amendment rights. In *Iota XI Chapter of Sigma Chi Fraternity v. Patterson et al.*, 566 F.3d 138 (4th Cir. 2009), the university sanctioned the fraternity after five incidents in which other students were sexually assaulted or hazed and in which chapter members sang and danced in front of the university library. An interim sanction was imposed, which revoked the chapter's recognition, prohibiting it from participating in social events and recruitment. A disciplinary hearing was then held, and the student panel found the fraternity and its members responsible for several of the charges against it. The university revoked the chapter's charter for ten years, forbade its members from forming another fraternity, and published the outcome of the disciplinary hearing in the student newspaper. It also disciplined individual members for later wearing Sigma Chi clothing that identified them as chapter members at George Mason.

The trial court awarded summary judgment to the defendants, and the plaintiffs appealed. With respect to their Fourteenth Amendment due process claim for denial of their right to associate with fellow chapter members, the court ruled that the university had prohibited the plaintiffs, not from joining another fraternity, but from reconstituting their former chapter. Therefore, there was no deprivation of their right to associate with one another. With respect to the chapter's claim that publication of the university's sanctions impaired its property interest in its "good name," the court ruled that the plaintiffs had not identified any injury—"economic or otherwise"—occasioned by the publication of the sanctions. And with respect to the First Amendment claim, the court ruled that the sanctions were sufficiently justified by the misconduct of the chapter and its members, and, even if the members' speech had been abridged as a result of the sanctions, there were other lawful reasons to impose the sanctions. The court affirmed the award of summary judgment to the defendants.

In responding to misconduct by fraternity members, other colleges have banned fraternities altogether. For example, Colby College, a private liberal arts college, withdrew recognition of all its fraternities and sororities in 1984 because administrators believed that fraternal activities were incompatible with the college's goals for student residential life. When a group of students continued some of the activities of a banned fraternity, despite numerous attempts by the college's administration to halt them, the president and college dean imposed discipline on the "fraternity" members, ranging from disciplinary probation to one-semester suspensions.

In *Phelps v. President and Trustees of Colby College*, 595 A.2d 403 (Me. 1991), the students sought to enjoin the discipline and the ban on fraternities under Maine's Civil Rights Act, 5 Me. Rev. Stat. Ann. §§ 4681 et seq. (2003), and the state constitution's guarantees of free speech and the right to associate. Maine's Supreme Judicial Court rejected the students' claims. It held that the state law, directed against harassment and intimidation, did not apply to the actions of the college because the law "stopped short of authorizing Maine courts to mediate disputes between private parties exercising their respective rights of free expression and association" (595 A.2d at 407). The court also held that the actions of private entities, such as the college, were not subject to state constitutional restrictions.

Although private institutions are not subject to constitutional requirements, their attempts to discipline fraternal organizations and their members are still subject to challenge. In *In re Rensselaer Society of Engineers v. Rensselaer Polytechnic Institute*, 689 N.Y.S.2d 292 (N.Y. Ct. App. 1999), the Society of Engineers, a fraternity, brought a state administrative law claim against Rensselaer Polytechnic Institute (RPI), challenging the institution's decision to suspend the fraternity for several years for various violations of RPI's code of student conduct. The fraternity was already on disciplinary probation for earlier infractions of the code of conduct. Ruling that the institution's conduct was neither arbitrary nor capricious, the court said: "Judicial scrutiny of the determination of disciplinary matters between a university and its students, or student organizations, is limited to determining whether the university substantially adhered to its own published rules and guidelines for disciplinary proceedings" (689 N.Y.S.2d at 295). The institution's actions were eminently reasonable, said the court; it followed its "detailed" grievance procedure in both making and reviewing the challenged disciplinary decision, and afforded the fraternity three levels of administrative review.

But the decision of another private institution to suspend a fraternity was vacated by a state appellate court, and the university was ordered to provide additional procedural protections to the fraternity. In *Gamma Phi Chapter of Sigma Chi Fraternity v. University of Miami*, 718 So. 2d 910 (Fla. Dist. Ct. App. 1998), the fraternity had sought an injunction to prevent the university's enforcement of sanctions against it. The fraternity claimed that the procedure used by the university to impose sanctions, including the suspension of rushing, was based on an *ex parte* fact-finding process (a process that did not allow the fraternity an opportunity to participate or to speak in its own behalf). The appellate court enjoined the sanctions and ordered the university to provide a fair hearing. The vice president for student affairs then appointed a panel consisting of two students, two faculty members, and an attorney not employed by the university. The fraternity, however, sought a second injunction to prevent the panel from hearing the case, arguing that the Interfraternity Council had the responsibility to decide such matters. The court denied the second injunction, ruling that, until the university had acted and the fraternity had pursued all internal remedies, the court would not exercise jurisdiction.

Although some colleges have banned fraternities altogether, others have sought less drastic methods of controlling them. The attempt of Hamilton College to minimize the influence of fraternities on campus was stalled temporarily by an unusual use of the Sherman Act, which outlaws monopolies that are in restraint of trade. Hamilton College announced a policy, to become effective in the 1995–96 academic year, of requiring all students to live in college-owned facilities and to purchase college-sponsored meal plans. The college made this change, it said, to minimize the dominance of fraternities over the social life of the college and to encourage more women applicants. Four fraternities that owned their own fraternity houses, and that had previously received approximately $1 million in payment for housing and feeding their members, sought to enjoin the implementation of the new housing policy, arguing that it was an attempt by the college to exercise monopoly power over the market for student room and board. A trial court granted the college's motion to dismiss the lawsuit, stating that the provision of room and board to students was not "trade or commerce," and that there was no nexus between the college's conduct and interstate commerce. The trial court did not rule on the issue of whether the product market at issue was the market for room and board for Hamilton students (as the fraternities claimed), or the market for highly selective liberal arts colleges with which Hamilton competes for students (as the college had claimed).

The appellate court reversed the dismissal, stating that the fraternities had alleged sufficient facts that, if they could be proven, could constitute a Sherman Act violation (*Hamilton Chapter of Alpha Delta Phi v. Hamilton College*, 128 F.3d 59 (2d Cir. 1997)). The plaintiffs had claimed that the college's goal was to raise revenues by forcing students to purchase housing from the college, to raise its housing prices due to the lack of competition for housing, and to purchase the fraternity houses at below-market prices. Because Hamilton recruits students from throughout the United States, and because more than half of its room and board revenue was obtained from out-of-state students, there was clearly a nexus between Hamilton's housing policy and interstate commerce. Therefore, since antitrust jurisdiction was established, the appellate court reversed the lower court's judgment and remanded the case. On remand, the trial court ruled that the plaintiffs' characterization of the product market was incorrect and awarded summary judgment to the college (106 F. Supp. 2d 406 (N.D.N.Y. 2000)). For a more recent case with a similar ruling on the relevant product market, see *Delta Kappa Epsilon (DKE) Alumni Corporation v. Colgate University*, 492 F. Supp. 2d 106 (N.D.N.Y. 2007).

Dartmouth College's decision to eliminate fraternities and sororities drew litigation not from students, but from alumni who had contributed to the college's fund-raising campaign. Seven alumni sued the Dartmouth Trustees after the trustees used funds raised in a capital campaign to restructure the college's residential life program, eliminating Greek organizations in the process. In *Brzica v. Trustees of Dartmouth College*, 791 A.2d 990 (N.H. 2002), the New Hampshire Supreme Court rejected the plaintiffs' claim that the trustees had a fiduciary duty to the alumni and found that there was no evidence that the trustees had conspired to eliminate Greek organizations prior to the fund-raising campaign.

Public colleges and universities face possible constitutional obstacles to banning fraternities, including the First Amendment's guarantee of the right to associate (see Sections 9.4.1, 9.4.2, and 10.1). The U.S. Supreme Court, in *Roberts v. United States Jaycees*, 468 U.S. 609 (1983), and *Boy Scouts of America v. Dale*, 530 U.S. 640 (2000), established the parameters of constitutionally protected rights of association and provided the impetus for constitutional challenges to institutional attempts to suspend or eliminate fraternal organizations.

The U.S. Court of Appeals for the Third Circuit addressed the extent of a fraternity's constitutionally protected rights of association in *Pi Lambda Phi Fraternity v. University of Pittsburgh*, 229 F.3d 435 (3d Cir. 2000). The local and national fraternity challenged the university's decision to revoke the local chapter's status as a recognized student organization after a drug raid at the fraternity house yielded cocaine, heroin, opium, and Rohypnol (the "date rape" drug). Four chapter members were charged with possession of controlled substances. The university followed the recommendation of a student judiciary panel that determined that the chapter had violated the university's policy of holding fraternal organizations accountable "for actions of individual members and their guests." The local and national fraternities sued the university and several of its administrators under 42 U.S.C. § 1983 for violation of the chapter's First Amendment rights of intimate and expressive association. The trial court awarded summary judgment to the university, ruling that the fraternity's primary activities were social rather than either intimate or expressive, and thus unprotected by the First Amendment.

Although the appellate court affirmed the outcome, it performed a more extensive analysis of the fraternity's freedom of association claims. The local chapter did not meet the test of *Roberts* for intimate association, said the court, because of the large number of members (approximately eighty) and the fact that the chapter "is not particularly selective in whom it admits" (229 F.3d at 442). With respect to the expressive association claim, the court applied the three-step test created by the Supreme Court in *Dale*. First, the court ruled that the fraternity's purpose was not expressive because there was virtually no evidence that the chapter engaged in expressive activity (such as political advocacy or even extensive charitable activities). Second, the university's act to revoke the fraternity's charter had only an indirect or attenuated effect on its expressive activity. Furthermore, the reason for the university's "burden" on the fraternity's activities was punishing illegal drug activity, which was not a form of expression protected by the First Amendment. And third, the university's interest in enforcing its rules and regulations, and in preventing student use of drugs, outweighed any possible burden on the fraternity's expressive activity.

The court similarly rejected the fraternity's equal protection claim, ruling that the university's policy of holding fraternities accountable for the actions of their members and guests was virtually identical to a rule holding students living in residence halls responsible for the actions of their guests. And even if the university had treated fraternities differently from other student organizations, said the court, fraternities are not a suspect classification for constitutional purposes, and thus any differential treatment by a public university would be reviewed under the "rational basis" test, a relatively deferential standard for a public university to meet.

Although a clear articulation of the college's expectations regarding the behavior of fraternity members may provide a deterrent to misconduct, some courts have viewed institutional attempts to regulate the conduct of fraternity members as an assumption of a duty to control their behavior, with a correlative obligation to exercise appropriate restraint over members' conduct. For example, in *Furek v. University of Delaware*, 594 A.2d 506 (Del. 1991), the state's supreme court ruled that the university could be found liable for injuries a student received during fraternity hazing, since the university's strict rules against hazing demonstrated that it had assumed a duty to protect students against hazing injuries. (See Section 10.2.3 below for further discussion of these liability issues.)

Because of the potential for greater liability when regulation is extensive (because a student, parent, or injured third party may claim that the college assumed a duty to regulate the conduct of the fraternity and its members), some institutions have chosen to use "recognition" statements, such as those used to recognize other student organizations. Although this minimal approach may defeat a claim that the institution has assumed a duty to supervise the activities of fraternity members, it may limit the institution's authority to regulate the activities of the organization, although the institution can still discipline individual student members who violate its code of student conduct.

One area where institutional regulation of fraternal organizations is receiving judicial—and legislative—attention is the "ritual" of hazing, often included as part of pledging activities.[2] If an institution promulgates a policy against hazing, it may be held legally liable if it does not enforce that policy vigorously. A case not involving fraternal organizations is nevertheless instructive on the potential for liability when hazing occurs. In a case brought by a former student injured by hazing, the Supreme Court of Vermont affirmed a sizable jury verdict against Norwich University, a paramilitary college that entrusts to upper-class students the responsibility to "indoctrinate and orient" first-year students, called "rooks." Although Norwich had adopted policies against hazing and had included precautions against hazing in its training for the upperclass "cadre," who were entrusted with the "indoctrination and orientation" responsibility, the former student alleged that hazing was commonplace and tolerated by the university's administration, and that it caused him both physical and financial injury.

In *Brueckner v. Norwich University*, 730 A.2d 1086 (Vt. 1999), the student, who withdrew from Norwich after enduring physical and psychological harassment, filed claims for assault and battery, negligent infliction of emotional distress, intentional infliction of emotional distress, and negligent supervision. A jury found Norwich liable on all counts and awarded the student $488,600 in compensatory damages and $1.75 million in punitive damages. On appeal, the state supreme court affirmed the liability verdicts, holding that cadre members were authorized by Norwich to indoctrinate and orient rooks, and Norwich was

---

[2] Hazing may also be a violation of state law. More than thirty states have enacted laws prohibiting hazing.

thus vicariously liable for the tortious acts of the cadre because these actions were within the "scope of their employment" (despite the fact that Norwich forbade such behavior). The court affirmed the compensatory damage award but reversed the punitive damage award, stating that Norwich's behavior was negligent but did not rise to the standard of malice required by that state's case law on punitive damages. One justice dissented, arguing that Norwich's behavior had demonstrated indifference and its tolerance for hazing constituted reckless disregard for the safety of its students.

Although an institution may not wish explicitly to assume a duty to supervise the conduct of fraternity members, it does have the power to sanction fraternal organizations and their members if they violate institutional policies against hazing or other dangerous conduct. In *Psi Upsilon v. University of Pennsylvania*, 591 A.2d 755 (Pa. Super. Ct. 1991), a state appellate court refused to enjoin the university's imposition of sanctions against a fraternity whose members kidnapped and terrorized a nonmember as part of a hazing activity. The student filed criminal charges against the twenty students who participated in the "prank," and the university held a hearing before imposing sanctions on the fraternity. After the hearing, the university withdrew its recognition of the fraternity for three years, took possession of the fraternity house without compensating the fraternity, and prohibited anyone who took part in the kidnapping from participating in a future reapplication for recognition.

In evaluating the university's authority to impose these sanctions, the court first examined whether the disciplinary procedures met legal requirements. Noting that the university was privately controlled, the court ruled that the students were entitled only to whatever procedural protections university policies had given them. The court then turned to the relationship statement that the fraternity had entered into with the university.

Characterizing the relationship statement as contractual, the court ruled that it gave ample notice to the members that they must assume collective responsibility for the activities of individual members and that breaching the statement was sufficient grounds for sanctions. After reviewing several claims of unfairness in the conduct of the disciplinary proceeding, the court upheld the trial judge's denial of injunctive relief.

Although institutions may have the authority to sanction fraternities and their members for criminal conduct or violations of the campus conduct code, conduct that may be construed as antisocial but that is not unlawful may be difficult to sanction. For example, some public institutions have undertaken to prohibit such fraternity activities as theme parties with ethnic or gender overtones or offensive speech. These proscriptions, however, may run afoul of the First Amendment's free speech guarantees. For example, George Mason University sanctioned Sigma Chi fraternity for holding an "ugly woman contest," a fund-raising activity in which fraternity members dressed as caricatures of various types of women, including an offensive caricature of a black woman. (For a discussion of this case, see Section 9.5.2.) The fraternity sued the university under 42 U.S.C. § 1983 (see this book, Section 3.4), alleging a violation of its rights under the First and Fourteenth Amendments. In *Iota*

*Xi Chapter of Sigma Chi Fraternity v. George Mason University*, 993 F.2d 386 (4th Cir. 1993), a federal appellate court affirmed an award of summary judgment to the fraternity on the grounds that the skit was "expressive entertainment" and "expressive conduct," both protected under First Amendment jurisprudence.

Although colleges are limited in their ability to sanction fraternities for offensive speech (or expressive conduct), they can hold individual student members to the same code of conduct expected of all students, particularly with regard to social activities and the use of alcohol. The complexity of balancing the need for a college to regulate fraternal organizations with its potential liability for their unlawful acts is the subject of the next section.

### 10.2.3. Institutional liability for the acts of fraternal organizations.

*tions.* Despite the fact that fraternal organizations are separate legal entities, colleges and universities have faced legal liability from injured students, parents of students injured or killed as a result of fraternity activity, or victims of violence related to fraternity activities. Because most claims are brought under state tort law theories, the response of the courts has not been completely consistent. The various decisions suggest, however, that colleges and universities can limit their liability in these situations but that fraternities and their members face increased liability, particularly for actions that courts view as intentional or reckless.

As discussed in Section 3.2 of this book, liability may attach if a judge or jury finds that the college owed an individual a duty of care, then breached that duty, and that the breach was the proximate cause of the injury. Because colleges are legally separate entities from fraternal organizations, the college owes fraternities, their members, and others only the ordinary duty of care to avoid injuring others. But in some cases courts have found either that a special relationship exists between the college and the injured student or that the college has assumed a duty to protect the student.

In *Furek v. University of Delaware*, 594 A.2d 506 (Del. 1991), the Delaware Supreme Court reversed a directed verdict for the university and ordered a new trial on the issue of liability in a lawsuit by a student injured during a hazing incident. The court noted the following factors in determining that a jury could hold the institution at least partially responsible for the injuries: (1) The university owned the land on which the fraternity house was located, although it did not own the house. The injury occurred in the house. (2) The university prohibited hazing and was aware of earlier hazing incidents by this fraternity. The court said that the likelihood of hazing was foreseeable, as was the likelihood of injury as a result of hazing.

While *Furek* may be an anomaly among the cases in which colleges are sued for negligence (see Section 3.2.2.5), the opinion suggests some of the dangers of institutional attempts to regulate the conduct of fraternities or their members—for instance, by assuming duties of inspecting kitchens or houses, requiring that fraternities have faculty or staff advisors employed by the college, providing police or security services for off-campus houses, or assisting these organizations in dealing with local municipal authorities. Such actions may suggest to juries deliberating a student's negligence claim that the institution had assumed a duty of supervision.

Colleges and universities have been codefendants with fraternities in several cases. In most of these cases, the institution has escaped liability. For example, in *Estate of Hernandez v. Board of Regents*, 838 P.2d 1283 (Ariz. Ct. App. 1991), the personal representative of a man killed in an automobile accident caused by an intoxicated fraternity member sued the University of Arizona and the fraternity. The plaintiff asserted that the university was negligent in continuing to lease the fraternity house to the house corporation when it knew that the fraternity served alcohol to students who were under the legal drinking age of twenty-one.

The plaintiff cited the "Greek Relationship Statement," which required all fraternities to participate in an alcohol awareness educational program, as evidence of the university's assumption of a duty to supervise. The statement also required an upper-division student to be assigned to each fraternal organization to educate its members about responsible conduct relating to alcohol. Furthermore, the university employed a staff member who was responsible for administering its policies on the activities of fraternities and sororities. Despite these attempts to suggest that the university had assumed a duty to supervise the activities of fraternities, the court applied Arizona's social host law, which absolved both the fraternity and the university of liability and affirmed the trial court's award of summary judgment. (After two trips to the state supreme court, and various intermediate opinions, the national fraternity and the individual members who planned the party were found liable).

It may be difficult to hold either a university or a fraternity legally responsible for a death caused by an intoxicated individual who obtained alcohol at a fraternity party. In *Bland v. Scott*, 112 P.3d 941 (Kan. 2005), the state's highest court ruled that, absent a dram shop law, which the state did not have, the plaintiff, the personal representative of the motorist killed by the intoxicated driver, did not state a cause of action. And in *Pawlowski v. Delta Sigma Phi*, 2009 Conn. Super. LEXIS 170 (Conn. Super. Ct. January 23, 2009), a state court ruled that a university did not have a duty to ensure a student's safety, particularly when he had attended an off-campus private party and had become intoxicated at that location.

When the student's own behavior is a cause of the injury, the courts have typically refused to hold colleges or fraternities liable for damages. In *Whitlock v. University of Denver*, 744 P.2d 54 (Colo. 1987), the Colorado Supreme Court rejected a student's contention that the university had undertaken to regulate the use of a trampoline in the yard of a fraternity house, even though the university owned the land and had regulated other potentially dangerous activities in the past. Similarly, students injured in social events sponsored by fraternities have not prevailed when the injury was a result of the student's voluntary and intentional action. For example, in *Foster v. Purdue University*, 567 N.E.2d 865 (Ind. Ct. App. 1991), a student who became a quadriplegic after diving headfirst into a fraternity's "water slide" was unsuccessful in his suit against both the university and the fraternity of which he was a member. Similarly, in *Hughes v. Beta Upsilon Building Association*, 619 A.2d 525 (Maine 1993), a student who was paralyzed after diving into a muddy field on the fraternity's property at the University of Maine was unsuccessful because the court ruled that the Building Association, landlord for the local fraternity chapter, was not responsible for the chapter's activities.

When, however, the injury is a result of misconduct by other fraternity members, individual and organizational liability may attach. Particularly in cases where pledges have been forced to consume large amounts of alcohol as part of a hazing ritual, fraternities and their members have been held responsible for damages. For example, a Louisiana appellate court upheld a jury award of liability against Louisiana Tech on the grounds of negligence, stemming from an injury incurred by a student who encountered hazing during the pledging process. In *Morrison v. Kappa Alpha Psi Fraternity*, 738 So. 2d 1105 (La. Ct. App. 1999), *appeal denied*, 749 So. 2d 634 (La. 1999), a student at Louisiana Tech had been beaten by the president of the local chapter of Kappa Alpha Psi during pledging activities. The student sustained serious head and neck injuries, and reported the assault to the campus police. After an investigation, both the university and the national chapter of the fraternity suspended the local chapter. The injured student sued the university, the national fraternity, the local chapter, and the assailant. A jury found the university, the national fraternity, and the assailant equally liable, and awarded $312,000 in compensatory damages. (The charges against the local chapter were dismissed on procedural grounds.) The jury found that the university owed the student a duty to protect him against the tortious actions of fellow students. The university appealed.

The appellate court affirmed the jury verdict, ruling that the university's own actions and its knowledge of previous hazing incidents by the local chapter created a special relationship between the injured student and the institution. A university official had received written and oral complaints about hazing by the local chapter, and a local judge had called the official to express his concerns about hazing by chapter members that his son had experienced. The court found that the university's prior knowledge of hazing activity and the potential dangers of hazing justified the creation of a special relationship, which thus imposed a duty on the university to monitor the chapter's behavior and to prevent further hazing incidents.

This ruling is directly contrary to a ruling by the Supreme Court of Idaho, which rejected the "special relationship" standard in *Coghlan v. Beta Theta Pi et al.*, 987 P.2d 300 (Idaho 1999). In *Coghlan*, a student at the University of Idaho sued three national fraternities whose local chapter parties she had attended, her own sorority, and the university for injuries she sustained when, after becoming intoxicated at fraternity parties, she returned to her sorority house and fell off a third-floor fire escape. She sought to hold the university liable under the "special relationship" doctrine, arguing that such a relationship created a duty to protect her from the risks associated with her own intoxication. The court rejected that claim, citing *Beach* and *Bradshaw* (see Section 3.2.2). But the court was somewhat more sympathetic to the plaintiff's claim that the university had assumed a duty to the student because of the university's own behavior. The student argued that because two university employees were present at one of the fraternity parties and should have known that underage students were being served alcohol, the university had assumed a duty to protect her. Although the court declined to conclude as a matter of law that the university had assumed such a duty, it remanded the case for further litigation, overturning the trial court's dismissal of the action.

The majority rule, however, appears still to be that the college has no duty to protect an individual from injury resulting from a student's or fraternal organization's misconduct. For example, in *Lloyd v. Alpha Phi Alpha and Cornell University*, 1999 U.S. Dist. LEXIS 906 (N.D.N.Y., January 26, 1999), a student injured during hazing by a fraternity sued Cornell under three theories: negligent supervision and control, premises liability, and breach of implied contract. The court rejected all three claims. With respect to the negligent supervision claim, the court ruled that, despite the fact that Cornell published materials about the dangers of hazing and provided training to fraternities to help them improve the pledging process, it had not assumed a duty to supervise the student plaintiff and prevent him from participating in the pledging process because "this involvement does not rise to the level of encouraging and monitoring pledge participation." The court rejected the plaintiff's premises liability claim because it found that Cornell had no knowledge that recent hazing activities had taken place in the fraternity house (which Cornell owned). The local chapter had been forbidden by the national fraternity from taking in new members, so Cornell was entitled to presume that no pledging, and thus no hazing, was occurring. And although Cornell required fraternities to have an advisor, that did not transform the advisor into an agent of Cornell. The court rejected the breach of contract claim because the university had not promised to protect students from hazing. In fact, because hazing was a violation of Cornell's code of student conduct, it was the obligation of students, not the university, to refrain from hazing. Although Cornell argued that the plaintiff had assumed the risk of injury by participating in hazing activities, a theory that would bar a negligence claim, the court explicitly rejected this reasoning, which the Alabama Supreme Court had used in *Jones v. Kappa Alpha Order, Inc.*, 730 So.2d 203 (Ala. 1998), saying that New York law differed from Alabama law in this regard.

In *Rothbard v. Colgate University*, 652 N.Y.S.2d 146 (N.Y. App. Div. 1997), a New York intermediate appeals court rejected a fraternity member's claim that the university should be held liable for injuries resulting from his fall, while intoxicated, from the portico outside his window. University rules prohibited students both from underage drinking and from standing on roofs or porticos. The fraternity member claimed that the university should have been aware that both policies were routinely violated at the fraternity house and that the university's failure to enforce its own rules caused his injuries. The court held that the inclusion of rules in the student handbook did not impose a duty upon the university to supervise the plaintiff and take affirmative steps to prevent him from violating the rules. Quite succinctly, the court held that an institution has no duty to shield students from their own dangerous activities.

Although, for the most part, colleges appear to be shielded from a duty to supervise students and fraternal organizations, they may face liability under landlord-tenant law. A ruling by the Supreme Court of Nebraska held that the university has a duty to students to protect them from foreseeable risks when those students live in campus housing. In *Knoll v. Board of Regents of the University of Nebraska*, 601 N.W.2d 757 (1999), the state supreme court did not discuss the special relationship theory, but rather, the duty of a landowner to an invitee. In this case, which is discussed more fully in Section 7.6.2, a pledge was injured as the result of a fraternity's hazing activities. The court's analysis focused primarily on the fact that the student was abducted on university property, that the university considered fraternity houses to be student housing units that were subject to regulation by the university, and that university policy required that the plaintiff live in a university housing unit. The court ruled that the university had notice of earlier hazing activities by members of other fraternities and also had notice of several criminal incidents perpetrated by members of the fraternity that abducted the plaintiff. Therefore, said the court, the abduction and hazing of the plaintiff were foreseeable and created "a landowner-invitee duty to students to take reasonable steps to protect" them against such actions and the resultant harm. The court returned the case to the trial court for determination of whether the university breached its duty to act reasonably and whether the university's inaction was the proximate cause of the plaintiff's injury.

Given the volume of litigation by students and others who allege injuries as a result of the actions of local fraternities or their members, colleges and national fraternities—both of which have been found liable in several of these cases—should work to reduce the amount of underage drinking and to educate students about the dangers of hazing.

### Section 10.3. The Student Press

***10.3.1. General principles.*** In general, student newspapers and other student publications have the same rights and responsibilities as other student organizations on campus (see Section 10.1), and student journalists have the same rights and responsibilities as other students. The rights of student press organizations and their staffs (and contributors) vary considerably, however, depending on whether an institution is public or private. This is because the key federal constitutional rights of freedom of the press and freedom of association protect the student press in its relations with public institutions; in private institutions these constitutional rights do not apply (see Section 1.5.2), and the relationship of the student press with the institution is primarily a contractual relationship that may vary from institution to institution (see Section 7.1.3).[3]

Sections 10.3.2 through 10.3.6 focus primarily on the First Amendment free press rights of student publications at public institutions. Section 10.3.7 focuses on private institutions. Other First Amendment issues pertinent to student publications are discussed in Sections 7.1.4, 7.5.1, and 9.5.

Fourth Amendment rights regarding searches and seizures may also become implicated in a public institution's relationship with student publications. In *Desyllas v. Bernstine*, 351 F.3d 934 (9th Cir. 2003), for example, the editor of a student newspaper claimed that the institution's public safety director and a campus police officer violated his constitutional rights when they sought to recover some missing confidential student records that they believed were in the editor's possession. They had temporarily secured the newspaper office by locking the door with a "clamshell" lock; had allegedly detained the editor temporarily for questioning about the missing records; and had then convinced the editor to surrender the records. The court held that, under the circumstances (set out at length in the opinion), none of the actions—neither the locking of the office, nor the alleged detention of the editor, nor the recovery of the records—was an unlawful "seizure" under the Fourth Amendment. The court determined, moreover, that the First Amendment generally does not provide any additional protections from searches and seizures in such circumstances beyond what the Fourth Amendment already provides (see *Zurcher v. Stanford Daily*, 436 U.S. 547 (1978), discussed in Section 11.1.3) and that the student editor's position with the student newspaper did not accord him any greater rights under the Fourth Amendment than any other student would have in similar circumstances. (In circumstances in which a seizure directly "interfere[s] with the [newspaper's] publication of the news" (*Desyllas*, 351 F.3d at 942), however, the First Amendment would provide additional protections; see, for example, *Kincaid v. Gibson*, discussed in Section 10.3.3.)

Freedom of the press is perhaps the most staunchly guarded of all First Amendment rights. The right to a free press protects student publications from virtually all encroachments on their editorial prerogatives by public institutions. In a series of forceful cases, courts have implemented this student press freedom, using First Amendment principles akin to those that would protect a big-city daily from government interference.

The chief concern of the First Amendment's free press guarantee is censorship. Thus, whenever a public institution seeks to control or coercively influence the content of a student publication, it will have a legal problem on its hands. The problem will be exacerbated if the institution imposes a prior

---

[3] If a student publication at a private institution is restricted by an outside governmental entity, however, it is protected by federal constitutional rights in much the same way as a student publication at a public institution would be protected. Examples would include a libel suit in which a private institution's student newspaper is a defendant subject to a court's jurisdiction (see Section 10.3.6) and a search of the office of a private institution's student newspaper by local police officers (see Section 11.1.3).

restraint on publication—that is, a prohibition imposed in advance of publication rather than a sanction imposed subsequently (see generally Section 9.4.4). Conversely, the institution's legal problems will be alleviated if the institution's regulations do not affect the message, ideas, or subject matter of the publication and do not permit prior restraints on publication. Such "neutral" regulations might involve, for example, the allocation of office space, procedures for payment of printing costs, or limitations on the time, place, or manner of distribution.

According to the Student Press Law Center, eight states have laws protecting the free expression rights of college student journalists: Oregon, California, Colorado, Kansas, Iowa, Arkansas, Massachusetts, and Illinois. The Illinois law is the College Campus Press Act, 110 Ill. Comp. Stat. Ann. 13 et seq. (2007).

### 10.3.2. *Mandatory student fee allocations to student publications.* Objecting students have no more right to challenge the allocation of mandatory student fees to student newspapers that express a particular viewpoint than they have to challenge such allocations to other student organizations expressing particular viewpoints. These issues are now controlled, at least for public institutions and their recognized student organizations that produce publications, by the principles established by the U.S. Supreme Court in *Board of Regents, University of Wisconsin v. Southworth*, discussed in Section 10.1.3. Long before *Southworth*, however, lower federal courts had protected student newspapers from losing their student fee allocations because the newspapers had editorial viewpoints with which other students disagreed.

Shortly before its decision in the *Southworth* case, the U.S. Supreme Court decided *Rosenberger v. Rector and Visitors of University of Virginia*, 515 U.S. 819 (1995) (further discussed in Section 10.1.5), its first pronouncement on mandatory student fee allocations for student publications. The Court's reasoning in *Rosenberger* is consistent with the principles later developed in *Southworth*. But *Rosenberger* also went beyond the analysis in *Southworth*, and in the earlier lower court cases, in two important respects: (1) *Rosenberger* focuses specifically on viewpoint discrimination issues that may arise when a university or its student government decides to fund some student publications but not others; and (2) *Rosenberger* addresses the special situation that arises when a student publication has an editorial policy based on a religious perspective.

The plaintiffs in *Rosenberger* were students who published a magazine titled "Wide Awake: A Christian Perspective at the University of Virginia." The university's guidelines for student fee allocations ("Guidelines") permitted "student news, information, opinion, entertainment, or academic communications media groups," among other groups, to apply for allocations that the university would then use to pay each group's bills from outside contractors that printed its publication. The Guidelines provided, however, that student groups could not use fee allocations to support "religious activity," defined as activity that "primarily promotes or manifests a particular belief in or about a deity or an ultimate reality." Fifteen student publications received funding, but the Wide Awake publication did not because the student council determined that it was a religious activity. Wide Awake's members challenged this denial as a violation of their free speech and press rights under the First Amendment.

The U.S. Supreme Court upheld Wide Awake's claim because the university's action was a kind of censorship based on the publication's viewpoint. The Court then addressed the additional considerations that arose in the case because Wide Awake published religious viewpoints rather than secular viewpoints based on politics or culture. Since Wide Awake sought to use public (university) funds to subsidize religious viewpoints, the First Amendment establishment clause also became a focus of the analysis. The Court, however, rejected the argument that funding Wide Awake would violate the establishment clause (see the discussion in Section 10.1.5). Concluding that the university funding would be "neutral toward religion," the Court emphasized that this funding was part of a broad program that "support[ed] various student enterprises, including the publication of newspapers, in recognition of the diversity and creativity of student life;" and that WAP fit within the university's category of support for "'student news, information, opinion, entertainment, or academic communications media groups,'" seeking funding on that basis and not "because of its Christian editorial viewpoint."

### 10.3.3. Permissible scope of institutional regulation. Three classic 1970s cases—the *Joyner, Bazaar,* and *Schiff* cases, discussed in this section—illustrate the strength and scope of First Amendment protection accorded the student press in public institutions. These cases also illustrate the different techniques by which an institution may seek to regulate a student newspaper, and they explain when and why such techniques may be considered unconstitutional censorship.

In *Joyner v. Whiting*, 477 F.2d 456 (4th Cir. 1973), the president of North Carolina Central University had permanently terminated university financial support for the campus newspaper. The president asserted that the newspaper had printed articles urging segregation and had advocated the maintenance of an all-black university. The court held that the president's action violated the student staff's First Amendment rights:

> It may well be that a college need not establish a campus newspaper, or, if a paper has been established, the college may permanently discontinue publication for reasons wholly unrelated to the First Amendment. But if a college has a student newspaper, its publication cannot be suppressed because college officials dislike its editorial comment . . .
>
>   Censorship of constitutionally protected expression cannot be imposed by suspending the editors, suppressing circulation, requiring imprimatur of controversial articles, excising repugnant materials, withdrawing financial support, or asserting any other form of censorial oversight based on the institution's power of the purse [477 F.2d at 460].

The president also asserted, as grounds for terminating the paper's support, that the newspaper would employ only blacks and would not accept advertising from white-owned businesses. While such practices were not protected by the First Amendment and could be enjoined, the court held that the permanent cutoff of funds was an inappropriate remedy for such problems because of its broad effect on all future ability to publish.

In *Bazaar v. Fortune*, 476 F.2d 570, *rehearing*, 489 F.2d 225 (5th Cir. 1973), the University of Mississippi had halted publication of an issue of *Images*, a student literary magazine written and edited with the advice of a professor from the English department, because a university committee had found two stories objectionable on grounds of "taste." Although the stories concerned interracial marriage and black pride, the university disclaimed objection on this basis and relied solely on the stories' inclusion of "earthy" language. The university argued that the stories would stir an adverse public reaction, and, since the magazine had a faculty advisor, their publication would reflect badly on the university. The court held that the involvement of a faculty advisor did not enlarge the university's authority over the magazine's content. The university's action violated the First Amendment because

> speech cannot be stifled by the state merely because it would perhaps draw an adverse reaction from the majority of people, be they politicians or ordinary citizens, and newspapers. To come forth with such a rule would be to virtually read the First Amendment out of the Constitution and, thus, cost this nation one of its strongest tenets [476 F.2d at 579].

To similar effect, see *Stanley v. Magrath*, 719 F.2d 279 (8th Cir. 1983), another classic case invalidating a University of Minnesota decision to alter a student newspaper's funding, to the newspaper's detriment, after the newspaper had published a controversial issue. According to the court, the university failed to carry its burden of showing that its decision was not motivated by concern about the content of the issue.

*Schiff v. Williams*, 519 F.2d 257 (5th Cir. 1975), concerned the firing of the editors of the *Atlantic Sun*, the student newspaper of Florida Atlantic University. The university's president based his action on the poor quality of the newspaper and on the editors' failure to respect university guidelines regarding the publication of the paper. The court characterized the president's action as a form of direct control over the paper's content and held that such action violated the First Amendment. Poor quality, even though it "could embarrass, and perhaps bring some element of disrepute to the school," was not a permissible basis on which to limit free speech. The university president in *Schiff* attempted to bolster his case by arguing that the student editors were employees of the state. The court did not give the point the attention it deserved. Presumably, if a public institution chose to operate its own publication (such as an alumni magazine) and hired a student editor, the institution could fire that student if the technical quality of his or her work was inadequate. The situation in *Schiff* did not fit this model, however, because the newspaper was not set up as the university's own publication. Rather, it was recognized by the university as a publication primarily by and for the student body, and the student editors were paid from a special student activities fee fund under the general control of the student government association.

While arrangements such as those in *Schiff* may insulate a student newspaper from university control, it might nevertheless be argued that a newspaper's receipt of mandatory student fee allocations, and its use of university facilities and equipment, could constitute state action (see Section 1.5.2), thus subjecting the student editors themselves to First Amendment restraints when dealing with other students and with outsiders. In *Mississippi Gay Alliance v. Goudelock*, 536 F.2d 1073 (5th Cir. 1976), however, the court rejected a state action argument (over a strong dissent) and upheld a student newspaper's refusal to print an ad for a gay counseling service. And in *Sinn v. The Daily Nebraskan*, 829 F.2d 662 (8th Cir. 1987), the court held that a newspaper was not engaged in state action when it refused to print sexual preferences in classified ads. In *Gay and Lesbian Students Association v. Gohn*, 850 F.2d 361 (8th Cir. 1988), however, the court distinguished *Sinn* and found state action in a situation where the student organization's activity was "not free from university control." Later, in *Leeds v. Meltz*, 85 F.3d 51 (2d Cir. 1996) (discussed further in Section 1.5.2), the court—like the courts in *Goudelock* and *Sinn*—refused to find that a student newspaper was engaged in state action when it rejected an advertisement submitted to the paper.

In a more recent and highly important case, *Kincaid v. Gibson*, 236 F.3d 342 (6th Cir. 2001) (*en banc*), the court reaffirmed the strong protections of these earlier cases and also confirmed that a confiscation of the printed copies of a student publication will often be considered a classic First Amendment violation. In addition, moving beyond the reasoning in the earlier cases, the court emphasized the importance of "public forum" analysis (see generally Section 9.4.2) in First Amendment cases about student publications.

*Kincaid v. Gibson* concerned a student yearbook, *The Thorobred*, published by students at Kentucky State University (KSU). KSU administrators had confiscated the yearbook covering the 1992–93 and the 1993–94 academic years when the printer delivered it to the university for distribution. The vice president for student affairs (Gibson) claimed that the yearbook was of poor quality and "inappropriate," citing, in particular, the failure to use the school colors on the cover, the lack of captions for many photos, the inappropriateness of the "destination unknown" theme, and the inclusion of current events unrelated to the school. The yearbook's student editor and another student sued the vice president, the president, and members of the board of trustees, claiming that the confiscation violated their First Amendment rights.

Relying in part on *Hazelwood School District v. Kuhlmeier*, 484 U.S. 260 (1988), a case about a high school newspaper, the federal district court granted the defendants' motion for summary judgment, holding that the yearbook was a "nonpublic forum" and that the university's action was consistent with the principles applicable to nonpublic forums. A three-judge panel of the Sixth Circuit upheld the district court's decision (191 F.3d 719 (6th Cir. 1999)); but on further review the full appellate court, sitting *en banc*, disagreed with the panel, reversed the district court, and ordered it to enter summary judgment for the students.

The *en banc* court applied the leading U.S. Supreme Court public forum cases but, unlike the district court and the three-judge panel, it determined that the yearbook was a "limited public forum." Specifically, the court noted that KSU had a written policy placing the yearbook under the management of the Student Publications Board (SPB) but lodging responsibility for the yearbook's content with the student editors. Although the SPB was to appoint a school employee to act as advisor of the publication, the policy provided that "[i]n order to meet the responsible standards of journalism, an advisor may require changes in the form of materials submitted by students, but such changes must deal only with the form or the time and manner of expressions rather than alteration of content." The written policy thus indicated to the court that the university's "intent" was "to create a limited public forum rather than reserve to itself the right to edit or determine [the yearbook's] content."

Following the teachings of the *Rosenberger* case (see Section 10.3.2), the *en banc* court declined to follow the Court's decision in *Hazelwood*, the high school newspaper case. According to the court: "There can be no serious argument about the fact that, in its most basic form, the yearbook serves as a forum in which student editors present pictures, captions, and other written material, and that these materials constitute expression for purposes of the First Amendment." In particular, the yearbook was distinguishable from the newspaper in *Hazelwood* because it was not a "closely-monitored classroom activity in which an instructor assigns student editors a grade, or in which a university official edits content." Moreover, in a university setting, unlike a high school setting, the editors and readers of the yearbook "are likely to be young adults." Therefore, "there can be no justification for suppressing the yearbook on the grounds that it might be 'unsuitable for immature audiences'" (quoting *Hazelwood*, 484 U.S. at 271).

On the basis of these factors, the court concluded that the yearbook was a limited public forum open for student expression. In such a forum,

> the government may impose only reasonable time, place and manner regulations, and content-based regulations that are narrowly drawn to effectuate a compelling state interest . . . In addition, as with all manner of fora, the government may not suppress expression on the basis that state officials oppose a speaker's view [236 F.3d at 354].

The court then found that "KSU officials ran afoul of these restrictions" when they confiscated the copies of *The Thorobred* without notification or explanation and refused to distribute them. Such action "is not a reasonable time, place, or manner regulation of expressive activity. . . Nor is it a narrowly crafted regulation designed to preserve a compelling state interest" (236 F.3d at 354). Since Gibson had specifically named several content-related reasons for the confiscation, the *en banc* court determined that the university's action was based on the yearbook's content and emphasized that "[c]onfiscation ranks with forced government speech as amongst the purest forms of content alteration." The court also determined that, even if the yearbook were a nonpublic forum, rather than a limited public forum, the university's confiscation of the yearbooks would still have violated the First Amendment. This was because "suppression of the yearbook smacks of viewpoint discrimination as well," and "government may not regulate even a nonpublic forum based upon the speaker's viewpoint." According to the court, "an editor's choice of theme, selection of particular pictures, and expression of opinions are clear examples of the editor's viewpoint" (236 F.3d at 356).

Thus *Kincaid*, like the earlier cases of *Joyner, Bazaar*, and *Schiff*, clearly demonstrates the very substantial limits on administrators' authority to regulate the student press at public institutions. But these cases do not stand for the proposition that no regulation is permissible. To the contrary, each case suggests narrow grounds on which student publications can be subjected to some regulation. The *Joyner* case indicates that the student press can be prohibited from racial discrimination in its staffing and advertising policies. *Stanley* suggests that institutions may alter the funding mechanisms for student publications as long as it does not do so for reasons associated with a publication's content. *Bazaar* indicates that institutions may dissociate themselves from student publications to the extent of requiring or placing a disclaimer on the cover or format of the publication. *Schiff* suggests enigmatically that there may be "special circumstances" where administrators may regulate the press to prevent "significant disruption on the university campus or within its educational processes." And *Kincaid* indicates that institutions may impose content-neutral "time, place, and manner regulations" on the student press, and also suggests that institutions may regulate student publications that are part of a curricular activity or that are established to operate under the editorial control of the institution.

The latter points from *Kincaid* were further developed, and integrated with public forum analysis, in another highly important case decided by another U.S. Court of Appeals, also sitting *en banc*. *Hosty v. Carter*, 412 F.3d 731 (7th Cir. 2005 (*en banc*)), concerned the validity of a dean's alleged order to halt the printing of a subsidized student newspaper until she had reviewed and approved the issues. The *en banc* court used the U.S. Supreme Court's *Hazelwood* case as the "starting point" and the "framework" for its analysis. Following *Hazelwood*, the court held that, if a subsidized student newspaper falls within the category of a nonpublic forum, then it "may be open to reasonable regulation" by the institution, including content regulation imposed for "legitimate pedagogical reasons" (412 F.3d at 735, 737). The appellate court then remanded the case to the district court for further proceedings on the issue of whether the student newspaper was a nonpublic forum subject to such regulation or a public forum not subject to content regulation.

Subsequent to *Kincaid v. Gibson* and *Hosty v. Carter*, another U.S. Court of Appeals emphasized the developing distinction between the classic 1970s and 1980s student press cases and the more recent cases exemplified by *Kincaid* and *Hosty*. In *Husain v. Springer*, 494 F.3d 108 (2d Cir. 2007)), this court portrayed the classic cases as representing a "categorical" approach to student press rights, under which student media outlets are uniformly protected from institutional attempts to regulate the content of their publications. In contrast, the newer cases, according to this court, represent a "contextual" approach to student press rights. Under this approach, a student publication's protection from content regulation depends on whether the institution's recognition and support of the publication (the "context") indicates that the institution has created a limited public forum (greater protection for the publication) or a non-public forum (lesser protection for the publication). (Regarding public forum analysis, see Section 9.4.2.)

The specific problem in *Husain v. Springer* concerned a university president's nullification of a student government election because the student newspaper had published a special election issue in which it endorsed a slate of candidates, some of whom were newspaper staff members. The decision to publish the special issue and endorse the candidates was made by the members of the newspaper's editorial board, none of whom were candidates in the election. The student newspaper was funded largely through student activity fees. The university did not exercise "supervision or prior review" over the paper's content, and there was no rule prohibiting the paper from "endorsing candidates in student elections."

In a memo prepared after the elections, the university president found that the election issue "amounted to a thinly veiled student activity fee funded piece of campaign literature," and that "the electoral process was compromised beyond its ability to be fair to all candidates" in the election. During testimony explaining her decision to nullify the election results, the university president further asserted that the student newspaper's coverage of student government elections should provide a balanced view of all candidates and refrain from endorsing any particular candidate or slate of candidates.

Members of the newspaper staff (among other plaintiffs) brought suit, alleging that the university's action chilled their exercise of speech and press, thus violating the First Amendment. In resolving the case, the appellate court in *Husain* did not need to choose between the "categorical" and "contextual" approaches to analysis because, under either approach, the newspaper and its journalists would be protected. Because the university "had a policy in which it expressly placed no limits on the content of student publications," then even under "the less protective [contextual] approach," the student newspaper was clearly "a limited public forum in which there were no restrictions on the subjects that could be addressed." The court then articulated this basic principle for limiting colleges' and universities' regulatory control over student newspapers:

> [A]t a minimum, when a public university establishes a student media outlet and requires no initial restrictions on content, it may not censor, retaliate, or otherwise chill that outlet's speech, or the speech of the student journalists who produce it, on the basis of content or viewpoints expressed through that outlet [494 F.3d at 124].

Applying this principle, the court determined that the president's nullification of the student government elections was expressly predicated "on two types of viewpoint discrimination relating to the subject of student elections."

First, the university president had asserted that the only acceptable speech on student elections is speech that presents a balanced depiction of the candidates. Further, the president had expressed her belief that the endorsement of a slate of candidates is not a proper function of a student newspaper. This type of viewpoint discrimination, the court held, "is clearly impermissible in a limited public forum open to unrestricted speech on campaigns, candidates, and issues" affecting the university.

Lastly, the court held that, because the student newspaper had refrained from strongly endorsing candidates in subsequent elections, the president's nullification of the election had created a "chilling effect" on the student newspaper's publication decisions, thereby violating the First Amendment rights of the student newspaper's staff members.

Although the *Husain* court, in reaching its decision, did not rely on the differences between the "categorical" and "contextual" approaches, this distinction is an important one. Apparently the distinction has developed in part because of the U.S. Supreme Court's 1988 *Hazelwood* decision that restricted the press rights of high school student newspapers, and in part because of the Court's decision in *Rosenberger*, which enhanced the press rights of collegiate student newspapers. Both cases raised the visibility of, and *Rosenberger* expanded the applications of, the public forum doctrine, which is the basis for the newer, contextual approach to student press rights. As a result, public forum analysis is likely to be used more frequently in the future, with institutions sometimes seeking to characterize student publications as nonpublic forums in order to justify content regulations. A major caution is in order, however. Although the Court in *Hazelwood* determined that the student newspaper in that case was not a public forum, the standard it then used for permissible content regulation is not the same as the standard typically used for a nonpublic forum. The *Hazelwood* standard permits regulation of the content of "school-sponsored speech" if the regulation is "reasonably related to legitimate pedagogical concerns" (484 U.S. at 271–73). The nonpublic forum standard used in other cases permits reasonable regulation of the subject matter addressed by speakers in a nonpublic forum but prohibits regulation of the *viewpoints* expressed by the speakers. The *Hazelwood* standard is thus more lenient in permitting regulation of the content of speech than is the nonpublic forum standard. This difference lends urgency to the question whether *Hazelwood*, the high school case, may be extended to apply to college newspapers, thus affording institutions access to that case's more lenient regulatory standard.

Most of the federal appellate courts that have considered this issue have extended the *Hazelwood* analysis to higher education at least in part. But usually these courts have not resolved the more difficult questions that follow:

1. Should the regulatory judgments of higher education administrators receive the same degree of deference from the courts as do the judgments of high school administrators under *Hazelwood*?

2. Can the *Hazelwood* standard be stretched so far as to permit viewpoint-based regulation of collegiate student newspapers (that is, regulation that,

under public forum analysis, would not be permissible in any forum, including a nonpublic forum)?

3. Should student academic freedom, alive and well in higher education (see Section 7.1.4) but seldom recognized in K–12 education, add more weight to the press rights of collegiate student newspapers and thus afford them greater protection against content regulation than is enjoyed by high school student newspapers under *Hazelwood*?

4. Is a collegiate newspaper's receipt of support from student activity fees sufficient to convert its speech into "school-sponsored" speech within the meaning of *Hazelwood*, thus subjecting the newspaper to *Hazelwood*'s lenient regulatory standard that is more favorable to administrators?

The answers to the first three of these questions are uncertain under the precedents to date (although, if the choice is simply yes or no, the better-grounded answers appear to be (1) no, (2) no, and (3) yes). The answer to the fourth question is almost certainly no. This is because the U.S. Supreme Court's public forum precedents, particularly the *Rosenberger* case discussed earlier in this section, make clear that speech in a public forum remains the private speech of the speaker, even though the use of the public forum (the student activities fee fund in *Rosenberger*; a meeting room or outdoor campus space in other cases) provides tangible support for the speech. Moreover, the Court's decision in the *Southworth* case (see Section 10.1.3), involving a university's system for allocating student activity fees among student organizations, appears to strongly protect these organizations from the university's regulation of the content of their speech, even though all the organizations involved received student activity fee funds. In *Husain v. Springer*, discussed earlier in this section, the court acted consistently with these developments and explicitly answered no to the fourth question, by ruling that the student newspaper—which received "most of its funding through the allocation of student activity fees"—was a limited public forum.

The clear lesson of the student publication cases, then, is not so much "don't regulate" as it is "don't censor." So long as administrators avoid censorship, there will be some room for them to regulate student publications; and, in general, they may regulate publications by student organizations or individual students in much the same way that they may regulate other expressive activities of student organizations (see Section 10.1) or students generally (see Sections 9.2.2 and 9.4). Even content need not be totally beyond an administrator's concern. A disclaimer requirement can be imposed to avoid confusion about a publication's status within an institution. If a publication is a nonpublic forum, some content regulation for pedagogical purposes is permissible. Advertising content in a publication may also be controlled to some extent, as discussed in Section 10.3.4. Content that is obscene or libelous as defined by the U.S. Supreme Court may also be regulated, as Sections 10.3.5 and 10.3.6 suggest. And as the *Rosenberger* case discussed in Section 10.3.2 suggests, religious content may be regulated to an extent necessary to prevent establishment clause violations.

***10.3.4. Advertising in student publications.*** When issues arise concerning regulation of advertising in student newspapers at public institutions, the analysis tends to be somewhat different from that for issues concerning regulation of, say, news articles, editorials, or editorial policy. That is because advertising is generally considered to be "commercial speech" that receives a lower level of protection under the First Amendment. In many cases, nevertheless, courts have found the protection to be sufficiently strong to invalidate institutional or state agency regulations of advertising. See, for example, *The Pitt News v. Pappert*, 379 F.3d 96 (3d Cir. 2004), in which the court held that a state statute regulating alcoholic beverage advertising could not constitutionally be applied to a student newspaper.

In *Pittsburgh Press Co. v. Pittsburgh Commission on Human Relations*, 413 U.S. 376 (1973), the U.S. Supreme Court upheld a regulation prohibiting newspapers from publishing "help wanted" advertisements in sex-designated columns. And in *Virginia State Board of Pharmacy v. Virginia Citizens Consumer Council*, 425 U.S. 748 (1976), while invalidating a statutory ban on advertising prescription drug prices, the Court affirmed the state's authority to regulate false or misleading advertising and advertising that proposes illegal transactions. These foundational cases suggest that there is at least some narrow room within which public institutions may regulate advertising in student newspapers.

Issues regarding advertising in student newspapers are considered at length in *Lueth v. St. Clair County Community College*, 732 F. Supp. 1410 (E.D. Mich. 1990). The plaintiff, a former editor of the student newspaper, sued the college because it had prohibited the publication of ads for an off-campus nude-dancing club. Concluding that the advertising was "commercial speech" and that the student-run newspaper was a public forum (Section 9.4.2), the court applied the First Amendment standards for commercial speech set out in *Central Hudson Gas & Electric Corp. v. Public Service Commission*, 447 U.S. 557 (1980), as modified by *Board of Trustees of the State University of New York v. Fox*, 492 U.S. 469 (1989). Although the college had substantial interests in not fostering underage drinking or the degradation of women, the court held the advertising prohibition unconstitutional because the college had no advertising guidelines or other limits on its authority that would ensure that its regulation of advertising was "narrowly tailored" to achieve its interests. (To similar effect, see *The Pitt News v. Pappert*, 379 F.3d 96 (3d Cir. 2004), in which the court held a state statute regulating alcohol beverage advertising to be unconstitutional as applied to a student newspaper.)

As the *Lueth* and *Pitt News* cases suggest, advertising of alcoholic beverages has been a particular concern for colleges and universities for many years. Advertising of tobacco products, unlawful drugs, and firearms may raise similar concerns. The validity of regulations limiting such advertising has become more doubtful since the U.S. Supreme Court's decisions in *44 Liquormart v. Rhode Island*, 517 U.S. 484 (1996), invalidating certain state restrictions on advertising of alcoholic beverages, and *Lorillard Tobacco Co. v. Reilly*, 533 U.S. 525 (2001), invalidating certain state restrictions on advertising of tobacco products. Relying on *Lorillard*, the court in *Khademi v. South Orange County Community College District*, 194 F. Supp. 2d 1011, 1028–29 (C.D. Cal. 2002), invalidated campus regulations that prohibited advertising for alcoholic beverages, tobacco products, or firearms. The court, however, did uphold a campus regulation prohibiting advertising of "illegal substances as identified by the Federal Government, and/or by the State of California," because it was limited to products made illegal by criminal law. As to tobacco, alcohol, and firearms advertising regulations, they were content-based regulations of speech that did not meet the standard of justification required by the case law. It was not enough that some of the community college district's students were underage and, therefore, prohibited by state law from purchasing these products. According to the court, "sixty-eight percent of the District's students are legally of age to buy alcohol, tobacco, and firearms products," and a complete ban on advertising these products would therefore not be narrowly tailored to effectuate the community college's legitimate interests (194 F. Supp. 2d at 1029 n.13).

In a more recent case, however, *Educational Media Co. at Virginia Tech v. Swecker*, 602 F.3d 583 (4th Cir. 2010), the court reached the opposite result, upholding a state beverage control board's restriction on alcohol advertising in student newspapers. In this case, student newspapers at Virginia Tech and the University of Virginia challenged a board regulation (3 Va. Admin. Code § 5-20-40(B)(3)) that prohibits "various types of advertisements for alcohol in any 'college student publication,' which it defines as any college or university publication that is (1) prepared, edited, or published primarily by its students; (2) sanctioned as a curricular or extracurricular activity; and (3) 'distributed or intended to be distributed to persons under 21 years of age'" (paraphrasing by the court).

The appellate court acknowledged, as had the *Pitt News* court and other courts, that regulations of commercial speech are to be reviewed under the standards set forth in *Central Hudson Gas & Electric Corp. v. Public Service Commission of New York*, 447 U.S. 557 (1980):

> [1] For commercial speech to come within [the First Amendment], it at least must concern lawful activity and not be misleading. [2] Next, we ask whether the asserted governmental interest is substantial. [3] If both inquiries yield positive answers, we must determine whether the regulation directly advances the government interest asserted, and [4] whether it is not more extensive than is necessary to serve that interest [447 U.S. at 566; numbering added].

The parties agreed that the board's regulation met the second part of this test; issues arose, however, under the other three parts.

Regarding the first part of the *Central Hudson* test, the board argued that the advertising at issue concerned *unlawful* activity: drinking of alcoholic beverages by students under age twenty-one. The court rejected this argument since the audience for the advertising was not limited to underage students. Even if the newspapers intended the ads to be primarily for the underage students, the newspapers nevertheless were distributed to many students who were at least twenty-one and therefore could legally drink alcoholic beverages.

For the third part of the test, the court considered whether the regulation "directly advances" the government's interest, which the board asserted to be "combating the serious problem of underage drinking and abusive drinking by college students." The board contended that alcohol ads increase demand for alcohol, and ad bans consequently decrease the demand—a proposition that the board claimed was supported by "history, consensus, and common sense." In particular, the board claimed that, since vendors spend so much money on advertising, it must logically follow that alcohol ads increase demand, thus impinging on the government's interest in limiting underage drinking. The college newspapers responded that the board had not submitted any empirical evidence showing that the alcohol advertising ban decreased demand for alcohol among college students and that the ban was ineffective because college students still saw and heard alcohol ads in various other media.

The court sided with the board, agreeing that the relationship between the regulation and the government interest "need not be proven by empirical evidence" but instead "may be supported by 'history, consensus, and simple common sense.'" The court then determined that the board had established the link between advertising and student drinking, in particular because college newspapers play an influential role on campus and because advertisers must have concluded that advertising increases their sales or otherwise they would not invest so much money in it. (The *Pitt News* case reached the opposite conclusion in applying the third part of the *Central Hudson* test.)

Under the fourth part of the test, the government's regulation of commercial speech must be "narrowly drawn" to serve the government's interest. This does not mean that the regulation must be "the least restrictive means possible" for serving the government interest but only that it must have a "reasonable fit" to the government interest. The board's regulation met this requirement, the court reasoned, because

[it] is not a complete ban on alcohol advertising in college newspapers. First, it only prohibits certain types of alcohol advertisements. In fact, it allows restaurants to inform readers about the presence and type of alcohol they serve. Second, the restriction only applies to "college student publications"—campus publications targeted at students under twenty-one. It does not, on its face, affect all possible student publications on campus . . . Further, the Board not only considered non-speech related mechanisms to serve its interest; it actually implemented them through education and enforcement programs. [The Board's regulation] complements these non-speech alternatives. Within the Board's multi-pronged attack on underage and abusive drinking, [the regulation] constitutes an additional prevention mechanism. Without it, either education or enforcement efforts would have to be increased, and given the Board's limited resources, [the regulation] is a cost-effective prevention method that properly complements their non-speech related efforts [602 F.3d at 591].

(The court in *Pitt News* also reached the opposite conclusion in applying the fourth prong of the *Central Hudson* test.)

The *Educational Media Co.* case was a 2-to-1 decision. The dissenting judge, relying heavily on *Pitt News*, a case that the majority opinion did not discuss, specifically disagreed with the majority's reasoning under both the third prong and the fourth prong of the *Central Hudson* test. The contrast between the reasoning in the *Educational Media* case and that in the *Pitt News* case, as developed by the dissent in *Educational Media*, is striking. Resolving these differences will be a key to the future development of the law in this area.

**10.3.5. Obscenity.** It is clear that public institutions may discipline students or student organizations for having published obscene material. Public institutions may even halt the publication of such material if they do so under carefully constructed and conscientiously followed procedural safeguards. A leading case is *Antonelli v. Hammond*, 308 F. Supp. 1329 (D. Mass. 1970), which invalidated a system of prior review and approval by a faculty advisory board because the system did not place the burden of proving obscenity on the board, provide for a prompt review and internal appeal of the board's decisions, or provide for a prompt final judicial determination. *Baughman v. Freienmuth*, 478 F.2d 1345 (4th Cir. 1973), which sets out prior review requirements in the secondary school context, is also illustrative. Clearly, the constitutional requirements for prior review regarding obscenity are stringent, and the creation of a constitutionally acceptable system is a very difficult and delicate task.

Moreover, institutional authority extends only to material that is actually obscene, and the definition or identification of obscenity is, at best, an exceedingly difficult proposition. In a leading Supreme Court case, *Papish v. Board of Curators of the University of Missouri*, 410 U.S. 667 (1973), the plaintiff was a graduate student who had been expelled for violating a bylaw of the board of curators that prohibited distribution of newspapers "containing forms of indecent speech." The newspaper at issue had a political cartoon on its cover that "depicted policemen raping the Statue of Liberty and the Goddess of Justice. The caption under the cartoon read: 'With Liberty and Justice for All.'" The newspaper also "contained an article entitled 'MF Acquitted,' which discussed the trial and acquittal on an assault charge of a New York City youth who was a member of an organization known as 'Up Against the Wall, MF.'" After being expelled, the student sued the university, alleging a violation of her First Amendment rights. The Court, in a *per curiam* opinion, ruled in favor of the student:

> We think [*Healy v. James*, discussed in Section 10.1.1 of this chapter] makes it clear that the mere dissemination of ideas—no matter how offensive to good taste—on a state university campus may not be shut off in the name alone of "conventions of decency." Other recent precedents of this Court make it equally clear that neither the political cartoon nor the headline story involved in this case can be labeled as constitutionally obscene or otherwise unprotected [410 U.S. at 670].

Obscenity, then, is not definable in terms of an institution's or an administrator's own personal conceptions of taste, decency, or propriety. Obscenity can be defined only in terms of the guidelines that courts have constructed to prevent the concept from being used to choke off controversial social or political dialogue. As the U.S. Supreme Court stated in the leading case, *Miller v. California*, 413 U.S. 15 (1973):

> We now confine the permissible scope of . . . regulation [of obscenity] to works which depict or describe sexual conduct. That conduct must be specifically defined by the applicable state law, as written or authoritatively construed. A state offense must also be limited to works which, taken as a whole, appeal to the prurient interest in sex, which portray sexual conduct in a patently offensive way, and which, taken as a whole, do not have serious literary, artistic, political, or scientific value [413 U.S. at 24 (1973)].

Although these guidelines were devised for the general community, the Supreme Court made clear in *Papish* that "the First Amendment leaves no room for the operation of a dual standard in the academic community with respect to the content of speech." Administrators devising campus rules for public institutions are thus bound by the same obscenity guidelines that bind the legislators promulgating obscenity laws. Under these guidelines, the permissible scope of regulation is very narrow, and the drafting or application of rules is a technical exercise that administrators should undertake with the assistance of counsel, if at all.

As with the area of libel (Section 10.3.6), institutions that assert considerable control over a particular student publication could conceivably become liable for obscene statements contained in that publication. In addition, institutions could conceivably become liable for restraining publication of material that it deems obscene but does not actually fit the legal definition of obscenity. When the publication is an online publication, however, federal law (specifically 47 U.S.C. § 230(c)(2)) would provide some protection for institutions that take such action in good faith; see Section 7.5.3 of this book.

***10.3.6. Libel.*** As they may for obscenity, institutions may discipline students or organizations that publish libelous matter. Here again, however, the authority of public institutions extends only to matter that is libelous according to technical legal definitions. It is not sufficient that a particular statement be false or misleading. Common law and constitutional doctrines require that (1) the statement be false; (2) the publication serve to identify the particular person libeled; (3) the publication cause at least nominal injury to the person libeled, usually including but not limited to injury to reputation; and (4) the falsehood be attributable to some fault on the part of the person or organization publishing it. The degree of fault depends on the subject of the alleged libel. If the subject is a public official or what the courts call a "public figure," the statement must have been made with "actual malice"; that is, with knowledge of its falsity or with "reckless disregard" for its truth or falsity. In all other situations governed by the First Amendment, the statement need only have been made negligently. Courts make this distinction in order to give publishers extra breathing space when reporting on certain matters of high public interest.

A decision of the Virginia Supreme Court illustrates that a false statement of fact is at the heart of a defamation claim. The claim in *Yeagle v. Collegiate Times*, 497 S.E.2d 136 (Va. 1998), arose from the student newspaper's publication of an article about a program facilitated by the plaintiff, a university administrator. Although otherwise complimentary of the administrator, the article included a large-print block quotation attributed to her and identifying her as "Director of Butt Licking." The court rejected the defamation claim because the expression "cannot reasonably be understood as stating an actual fact about [the plaintiff's] job title or her conduct, or that she committed a crime of moral turpitude." Although the phrase "Director of Butt Licking" is "disgusting, offensive, and in extremely bad taste," in the circumstances of this case it was "no more than 'rhetorical hyperbole.'" The court further rejected the plaintiff's argument that "the phrase connotes a lack of integrity in the performance of her duties." Explaining that "inferences cannot extend the statements by innuendo, beyond what would be the ordinary and common acceptance of the statement," the court relied on the complimentary content of the article itself to find that there was no basis for the inference the plaintiff sought to draw.

An instructive illustration of the "public official" concept and the "actual malice" standard is provided by *Waterson v. Cleveland State University*, 639 N.E.2d 1236 (Ohio 1994). The plaintiff, then deputy chief of the campus police force at the defendant university, claimed that he had been defamed in an editorial published in the campus student newspaper and written by its then editor-in-chief, Quarles. The university claimed that the deputy chief was a "public official" within the meaning of the leading U.S. Supreme Court precedents and that he therefore could not prevail on a defamation claim unless he proved that Quarles or the university had acted with "actual malice" in publishing the editorial. The court accepted the university's argument, categorizing the plaintiff as a public official because he was second in command to the university chief of police and had major responsibilities and influence in a department in which the campus community had a substantial interest. The plaintiff then argued that, even if he was a public official, he had met his burden of proving "actual malice." Again, the court disagreed:

> [T]he focus of an actual-malice inquiry is on the conduct and state of mind of the defendant . . . To prevail, a plaintiff must show that the false statements were made with a "high degree of awareness of their probable falsity . . . The record in this case reveals that plaintiff presented no evidence of who Quarles' sources for the editorial were, and hence no evidence of the reliability of those sources. Nor did plaintiff present any evidence as to what, if any, investigations Quarles undertook prior to publishing her editorial. In fact, plaintiff presented no evidence whatsoever which would allow one to conclude that Quarles either knew that the allegations contained in her editorial were false or that she entertained serious doubts as to their veracity [639 N.E.2d at 1239–140].

The appellate court therefore affirmed the trial court's order dismissing the deputy chief's defamation claim.

Given the complexity of the libel concept, administrators should approach it most cautiously. Because of the need to assess both injury and fault, as well as identify the defamatory falsehood, libel may be even more difficult to combat than obscenity. Suppression in advance of publication is particularly perilous, since injury can only be speculated about at that point, and reliable facts concerning fault may not be attainable. Much of the material in campus publications, moreover, may involve public officials or public figures and thus be protected by the higher fault standard of actual malice.

Though these factors might reasonably lead administrators to forgo any regulation of libel, there is a countervailing consideration: institutions or administrators may occasionally be held liable in court for libelous statements in student publications. Such liability could exist where the institution sponsors a publication (such as a paper operated by the journalism department as a training ground for its students), employs the editors of the publication, establishes a formal committee to review the content of material in advance of publication, or otherwise exercises some control (constitutionally or unconstitutionally) over the publication's content. In any case, liability would exist only for statements deemed libelous under the criteria set out above. And when the student publication is an online publication, federal law provides institutions with some protection from liability for defamation and certain other legal claims; see Section 7.5.3 of this book.

Such potential liability, however, need not necessarily prompt increased surveillance of student publications. Increased surveillance would demand regulations that stay within constitutional limits yet are strong enough to weed out all libel—an unlikely combination. And since institutional control of the publication is the predicate to the institution's liability, increased regulation increases the likelihood of liability should a libel be published. Thus, administrators may choose to handle liability problems by lessening rather than enlarging control. The privately incorporated student newspaper operating independently of the institution would be the clearest example of a no-control, no-liability situation.

The decision of the New York State Court of Claims in *Mazart v. State,* 441 N.Y.S.2d 600 (N.Y. Ct. Cl. 1981), not only illustrates the basic steps for establishing libel but also affirms that institutional control over the newspaper, or lack thereof, is a key to establishing or avoiding institutional liability. The opinion also discusses the question of whether an institution can ever restrain in advance the planned publication of libelous material.

The plaintiffs (claimants) in *Mazart* were two students at the State University of New York–Binghamton who were the targets of an allegedly libelous letter to the editor published in the student newspaper, the *Pipe Dream.* The letter described a prank that it said had occurred in a male dormitory and characterized the act as prejudice against homosexuals. The plaintiffs' names appeared at the end of the letter, although they had not in fact written it, and the body of the letter identified them as "members of the gay community."

The court analyzed the case in three stages. First, applying accepted principles of libel law to the educational context in which the incident occurred, the court determined that this letter was libelous because it fostered "an unsavory opinion" of the plaintiffs and led to them being accosted by other students. Second, the court considered the state's argument that, even if the letter was libelous, its publication was protected by a qualified privilege because the subject matter was of public concern. Again using commonly accepted libel principles, the court concluded that a privilege did not apply because the editors had not verified that the purported signers of the letter were actually its authors.

Third, the court held that, although the letter was libelous and not privileged, the university (and thus the state) was not liable for the unlawful acts of the student newspaper. In its analysis the court considered and rejected two theories of liability:

> (1) [that] the state, through the University, may be vicariously liable for the torts of the *Pipe Dream* and its editors on the theory of *respondeat superior* (that is, the University, as principal, might be liable for the torts of its agents, the student paper and editors); and (2) [that] the state, through the University, may have been negligent in failing to provide guidelines to the *Pipe Dream* staff regarding libel generally, and specifically, regarding the need to review and verify letters to the editor [441 N.Y.S.2d at 600].

In rejecting the first theory, the court relied heavily on First Amendment principles that limited the institution's authority to control the content of a student newspaper (as discussed in Section 10.3.3). Due to these strong constitutional protections for student newspapers at public institutions, the defendant university had no authority "to prevent the publication of the letter." A "policy of prior approval of items to be published in a student newspaper, even if directed only to restraining the publication of potentially libelous material," would violate the First Amendment. The court therefore ruled that the university did not have a right of control over the *Pipe Dream* sufficient to sustain an agency theory.

The court then also rejected the plaintiffs' second liability theory. Focusing particularly on the tort law concept of duty (see generally Section 3.2.1), the court ruled that the university and state were not negligent "for failing to provide to the student editors guidelines and procedures designed to avoid the publication of libelous material." The issue, the court said, was "whether there was a duty on the part of the University administration" to furnish such guidelines; and the "constitutional limitations on the actual exercise of editorial control by the university," noted above, did "not necessarily preclude the existence of [such] a duty." But the courts, as well as the New York state legislature, regard college students as young adults and not children, and the *Pipe Dream* editors, as young adults, are therefore presumed to have "that degree of maturity and common sense necessary to comprehend the normal procedures for information gathering and dissemination."

The validity and importance of the *Mazart* case was reaffirmed in *McEvaddy v. City University of New York*, 633 N.Y.S.2d 4 (N.Y. App. Div. 1995). The *McEvaddy* court dismissed a defamation claim brought against City University of New York for an allegedly libelous article published in the student newspaper. Citing *Mazart*, the court held that "[t]he presence of a faculty advisor to the paper, whose advice is nonbinding, and the financing of the paper through student activity fees . . ., do not demonstrate such editorial control or influence over the paper by [the university] as to suggest an agency relationship"

(633 N.Y.S.2d at 4). The New York Court of Appeals, the state's highest court, denied the claimant's motion for leave to appeal (664 N.E.2d 1258 (N.Y. 1996)). (For another, more recent, affirmation of the principles in *Mazart* and *McEvaddy*, see *Lewis v. St. Cloud State University*, 693 N.W.2d 466 (Minn. Ct. App. 2005).)

*Mazart v. State* is an extensively reasoned precedent in an area where there had been little precedent. The court's opinion, together with the later opinions in *McEvaddy* and *Lewis*, provide much useful guidance for administrators of public institutions. The reasoning in these opinions depends, however, on the particular circumstances concerning the campus setting in which the newspaper operated and the degree of control the institution exercised over the newspaper and also, under *Mazart*, on the foreseeability of libelous actions by the student editors. Administrators will therefore want to consult with counsel before attempting to apply the principles of these cases to occurrences on their own campuses. Moreover, tort concepts of duty applicable to colleges and universities have been evolving since the *Mazart* case (see Robert Bickel & Peter Lake, *The Rights and Responsibilities of the Modern University: Who Assumes the Risk of College Life?* (Carolina Academic Press, 1999)).

**10.3.7. Obscenity and libel in private institutions.** Since the First Amendment does not apply to private institutions that are not engaged in state action (see Section 1.5.2), such institutions have a freer hand in regulating obscenity and libel. Yet private institutions should devise their regulatory role cautiously. Regulations broadly construing libel and obscenity based on lay concepts of those terms could stifle the flow of dialogue within the institution, whereas attempts to avoid this problem with narrow regulations may lead the institution into the same definitional complexities that public institutions face when seeking to comply with the First Amendment. Moreover, in devising their policies on obscenity and libel, private institutions will want to consider the potential impact of state law. Violation of state obscenity or libel law by student publications could subject the responsible students to damage actions, possibly to court injunctions, and even to criminal prosecutions, causing unwanted publicity for the institution. But if the institution regulates student publications to prevent such problems, the institution could be held liable along with the students if it exercises sufficient control over the publication (see generally Sections 2.1.3 and 3.2.4).

### Section 10.4. Athletics Teams and Clubs

**10.4.1. General principles.** Athletics, as a subsystem of the postsecondary institution, is governed by the general principles set forth elsewhere in this chapter and this book. These principles, however, must be applied in light of the particular characteristics and problems of curricular, extracurricular, and intercollegiate athletic programs. A student athlete's eligibility for financial aid, for instance, would be viewed under the general principles in Section 7.3, but aid conditions related to the student's eligibility for or performance in intercollegiate athletics create a special focus for the problem (see Section 10.4.5). The institution's tort liability for injuries to students would be subject to the general principles in Section 3.2, but the circumstances and risks of athletic participation provide a special focus for the problem (see Section 10.4.9). Similarly, the due process principles in Section 9.3 may apply when a student athlete is disciplined, and the First Amendment principles in Section 9.4 may apply when student athletes engage in protest activities. But in each case the problem may have a special focus (see Sections 10.4.2 and 10.4.3 below). Moreover, as in many other areas of the law, there are various statutes that have special applications to athletics (see Section 10.4.4 below).

Surrounding these special applications of the law to athletics, there are major legal and policy issues that pertain specifically to the status of "big-time" intercollegiate athletics within the higher education world. In addition to low graduation rates of athletes, the debate has focused on academic entrance requirements for student athletes; postsecondary institutions' recruiting practices; alleged doctoring or padding of high school and college transcripts to obtain or maintain athletic eligibility; academic fraud in the fulfillment of course and degree requirements; drug use among athletes and mandatory drug testing (see Section 10.4.8); other misconduct by student athletes, such as sexual assaults, and institutional responses to the alleged misconduct; alleged exploitation of minority athletes; improper financial incentives and rewards or improper academic assistance for student athletes; and the authority and practices of the National Collegiate Athletic Association (NCAA) and athletic conferences (see Section 12.1.3) regarding such matters. The overarching concern prompted by these issues is one of integrity: the integrity of individual institutions' athletic programs, the integrity of academic standards at institutions emphasizing major intercollegiate competition, and the integrity of higher education's mission in an era when athletics has assumed such a substantial role in the operation of the system. (For discussion of these issues see James L. Shulman & William G. Bowen, *The Game of Life: College Sports and Educational Values* (Princeton University Press, 2001), and for recommendations for reforming college athletics by two college presidents, see James J. Duderstadt, *Intercollegiate Athletics and the American University* (University of Michigan Press, 2000), and William G. Bowen & Sarah A. Levin, *Reclaiming the Game: College Sports and Educational Values* (Princeton University Press, 2003). For additional resources, see the Bibliography.

Occasionally a student athlete will turn to the courts to obtain compensation for the disappointment of being dismissed from a team or not given sufficient playing time. For an example of such an attempt, and its unsuccessful outcome, see *Giuliani v. Duke University*, 2009 U.S. Dist. LEXIS 44412 (M.D.N.C. May 19, 2009).

***10.4.2. Athletes' due process rights.*** If a student athlete is being disciplined for some infraction, the penalty may be suspension from the team. In such instances, the issue raised is whether the procedural protections accompanying suspension from school are also applicable to suspension from a team. For institutions engaging in state action (see Section 1.5.2), the constitutional issue is whether the student athlete has a "property interest" or "liberty interest" in continued intercollegiate competition sufficient to make suspension or some other form of disqualification a deprivation of "liberty or property" within the meaning of the due process clause. Several courts have addressed this question. (Parallel "liberty or property" issues also arise in the context of faculty dismissals (Section 5.6.2) as well as student suspensions and dismissals (Section 9.3.2).)

In *Behagen v. Intercollegiate Conference of Faculty Representatives*, 346 F. Supp. 602 (D. Minn. 1972), a suit brought by University of Minnesota basketball players suspended from the team for participating in an altercation during a game, the court reasoned that participation in intercollegiate athletics has "the potential to bring [student athletes] great economic rewards" and is thus as important as continuing in school. The court therefore held that the students' interests in intercollegiate participation were protected by procedural due process and granted the suspended athletes the protections established in the *Dixon* case (Section 9.3.2). In *Regents of the University of Minnesota v. NCAA*, 422 F. Supp. 1158 (D. Minn. 1976), the same district court reaffirmed and further explained its analysis of student athletes' due process rights. The court reasoned that the opportunity to participate in intercollegiate competition is a property interest entitled to due process protection, not only because of the possible remunerative careers that result but also because such participation is an important part of the student athlete's educational experience.[4] The same court later used much the same analysis in *Hall v. University of Minnesota*, 530 F. Supp. 104 (D. Minn. 1982).

In contrast, the court in *Colorado Seminary v. NCAA*, 417 F. Supp. 885 (D. Colo. 1976), relying on an appellate court's opinion in a case involving high school athletes (*Albach v. Odle*, 531 F.2d 983 (10th Cir. 1976)), held that college athletes have no property or liberty interests in participating in intercollegiate sports, participating in postseason competition, or appearing on television. The appellate court affirmed (570 F.2d 320 (10th Cir. 1978)). (The trial court did suggest, however, that revocation of an athletic scholarship would infringe a student's property or liberty interests and therefore would require due process safeguards (see Section 10.4.5).) And in *Hawkins v. NCAA*, 652 F. Supp. 602, 609–11 (C.D. Ill. 1987), the court held that student athletes have no property interest in participating in postseason competition. Given the intense interest and frequently high stakes for college athletes, administrators at both public and private colleges should provide at least a minimal form of due process when barring college athletes from playing in games or postseason tournaments, and should provide notice and an opportunity for the student to be heard if a scholarship is to be rescinded.

---

[4] Although the appellate court reversed this decision, 560 F.2d 352 (8th Cir. 1977), it did so on other grounds and did not question the district court's due process analysis.

Other forms of disqualification from competition may also implicate due process protections for students at public institutions of higher education. In *NCAA v. Yeo*, 114 S.W.3d 584 (Tex. App. 2003), *reversed*, 171 S.W.3d 863 (Tex. 2005), the Texas Supreme Court rejected a student athlete's claim that she possessed a "constitutionally protected interest" in participation in athletic events because she was an Olympic athlete. The due process claim arose from a dispute concerning the student-athlete's eligibility to complete after transferring to a new school. The athlete, Joscelin Yeo, argued that alleged errors made by the athletic director at her new school, the University of Texas (UT)–Austin, had resulted in ineligibility to compete in collegiate competition.

The Texas Court of Appeals, applying state rather than federal constitutional due process guarantees, had held that Yeo's athletic career was a protected interest requiring procedural due process protections because she already had an "established athletic reputation" prior to her college matriculation. After establishing that Yeo had a protected interest, the court then analyzed what process she was entitled to. The court found several procedural flaws in the UT athletic director's determination of Yeo's ineligibility. There was no record of the decision; Yeo was given no notice of the decision; and as a result, Yeo could not participate in the hearing. Even though UT was aware of the impact that an ineligibility determination would make on her career, it did not advise Yeo to retain counsel until well after the decision. According to the court, due process required that Yeo receive timely notice of the eligibility problem and be afforded an adequate opportunity to respond to the issues.

The Texas Supreme Court rejected the reasoning and outcome of the appellate court. The state's high court refused to distinguish between nationally ranked student athletes and nonranked students, and determined that Yeo's assertion that her future financial opportunities were substantial was "too speculative" to implicate constitutional protections. Furthermore, comparing Yeo's alleged liberty interest with that at issue in *University of Texas Medical School at Houston v. Than* (discussed in Section 8.6.5), the Texas Supreme Court "declined to equate an interest in intercollegiate athletics with an interest in graduate education" (171 S.W.3d at 870).

### 10.4.3. Athletes' freedom of speech.

When student athletes are participants in a protest or demonstration, their First Amendment rights must be viewed in light of the institution's particular interest in maintaining order and discipline in its athletic programs. An athlete's protest that disrupts an athletic program would no more be protected by the First Amendment than any other student protest that disrupts institutional functions. Although the case law regarding athletes' First Amendment rights is even more sparse than that regarding their due process rights, *Williams v. Eaton*, 468 F.2d 1079 (10th Cir. 1972), does specifically apply the *Tinker* case (see Section 9.4.1) to a protest by intercollegiate football players. Black football players had been suspended from the team for insisting on wearing black armbands during a game to protest the alleged racial discrimination of the opposing church-related school. The court held that the athletes' protest was unprotected by the First Amendment because it would interfere with the religious freedom rights of the opposing players and their church-related institution. The *Williams* opinion is unusual in that it mixes considerations of free speech and freedom of religion. The court's analysis would have little relevance to situations where religious freedom is not involved. Since the court did not find that the athletes' protest was disruptive, it relied solely on the seldom-used "interference with the rights of others" branch of the *Tinker* case.

In *Marcum v. Dahl*, 658 F.2d 731 (10th Cir. 1981), the court considered a First Amendment challenge to an institution's nonrenewal of the scholarships of several student athletes. The plaintiffs, basketball players on the University of Oklahoma's women's team, had been involved during the season in a dispute with other players over who should be the team's head coach. At the end of the season, they had announced to the press that they would not play the next year if the current coach was retained. The plaintiffs argued that the institution had refused to renew their scholarships because of this statement to the press and that the statement was constitutionally protected. The trial court and then the appellate court disagreed. Analogizing the scholarship athletes to public employees for First Amendment purposes, the appellate court held that (1) the dispute about the coach was not a matter of "general public concern" and the plaintiffs' press statement on this subject was therefore not protected by the First Amendment, and (2) the plaintiffs' participation in the dispute prior to the press statement, and the resultant disharmony, provided an independent basis for the scholarship nonrenewal.

Free speech issues may also arise when student athletes are the intended recipients of a message rather than the speakers. In such situations, the free speech rights at stake will be those of others—employees, other students, members of the general public—who wish to speak to athletes either individually or as a group. Sometimes the athlete's own First Amendment right to receive information could also be at issue.

In *Dambrot v. Central Michigan University*, 55 F.3d 1177 (6th Cir. 1995), the head basketball coach at Central Michigan University was terminated when it became widely publicized that he had used the word "nigger" in at least one instance when addressing basketball team members in the locker room. In terminating the coach, the university relied on the institution's discriminatory harassment policy. The coach and many of the team members sued the university, claiming that it had violated the coach's free speech rights. Dambrot argued that he was using the word in a positive manner, urging his players to be "fearless, mentally strong, and tough." Although the appellate court ruled that the university's discriminatory harassment policy was unconstitutionally overbroad and vague (see Section 9.5.2), it also held that the coach was not wrongfully terminated because his speech neither touched a matter of public concern nor implicated academic freedom.

In *Crue v. Aiken*, 370 F.3d 668 (7th Cir. 2004), the question was whether students and faculty members of the University of Illinois could speak with prospective student athletes being recruited for the university's athletic teams. The question arose because of a controversy concerning the university's athletic "mascot" or "symbol," called "Chief Illiniwek." To some, Chief Illiniwek was a respectful representation of the Illinois Nations of Native Americans, or the "fighting spirit," or "the strong, agile human body." To others, Chief Illiniwek was an offensive representation of the Illinois Nations, or a "mockery" or distortion of tribal customs, or the source of a "hostile environment" for Native American students (370 F.3d at 673–74). The plaintiffs wished to speak with prospective athletes about this controversy and the negative implications of competing for a university that uses the Chief Illiniwek symbol. The chancellor issued a directive prohibiting students and employees from contacting prospective student athletes without the express approval of the athletics director. The federal district court held that the university's directive violated the free speech rights of university employees and students, and the U.S. Court of Appeals affirmed by a 2-to-1 vote. Neither court directly addressed the free speech rights of students apart from those of employees who were restrained by the directive; nor did the courts address the potential free speech rights of the prospective student athletes to "receive" the message.[5]

Another issue has arisen that concerns speech directed to (rather than the speech of) student athletes. The issue usually involves the spectators at sporting events. The students in the student sections at intercollegiate basketball games, for instance, often have unique methods of communicating with the visiting team's athletes on the floor. In some situations, at some schools, the communicative activities of the student section have been considered by school officials, or by other spectators, to be profane or otherwise offensive.[6] The issue that then may arise is whether or not the university can limit the speech of students in the student section in ways that would not violate their First Amendment free speech rights. In Maryland, this issue was the subject of a memorandum from the State Attorney General's Office to the president of the University of Maryland (March 17, 2004), in which the attorney general's office concluded, without providing specific examples, that some regulation of student speech at university basketball games would be constitutionally permissible. In general, this delicate issue of student crowd speech at athletic events would be subject to the same five free speech principles, and the same suggestions for regulatory strategies, that are set out in Section 9.5.3 of this book concerning hate speech. There would likely be particular attention given to the problem of "captive audiences" that is mentioned in the fifth suggestion for regulating hate speech on campus.

---

[5]A related issue in the case was whether the employees' and students' contacts with the student athlete recruits would violate NCAA rules. See 370 F.3d at 679–80 (majority) and 686–87 (dissent).

[6]The opposite situation can also arise if student athletes seek to communicate with spectators at a game. In *State v. Hoshijo ex rel. White*, 76 P.3d 550 (Haw. 2003), for example, a student manager of the basketball team directed an offensive comment to a spectator during a game. A key question in the case that followed was whether the student manager's speech was protected by the First Amendment. The court concluded that the speech constituted "fighting words" (see Section 9.5.2) and was therefore not protected.

Because issues concerning the free speech rights of persons wishing to address student athletes arise in such varied contexts, as the examples just given indicate, and because there are substantial questions of strategy to consider along with the law, university administrators and counsel should be wary about drawing any fast and firm conclusions concerning problems that they may face. Instead, the analysis should depend on the specific context, including who the speaker is, where the speech takes place, the purpose of the speech, and its effect on others. If an institution chooses to regulate in this area, the cases make clear that the overbreadth and vagueness problem will be a major challenge for those drafting the regulations. In *Dambrot* (discussed earlier in this section), for example, even though the court upheld the termination of the coach, it invalidated the university's discriminatory harassment policy because it was overbroad and vague.

The advent of social media has prompted some athletics coaches either to monitor the social media postings of their players or to ban such postings altogether, at least during the sport's season. Policies that require athletes to remove social media postings that are deemed "offensive" or that may indicate a violation of NCAA rules are content-based restrictions on speech (see Section 9.4.1) and could face constitutional challenges.

Issues regarding student athletes' First Amendment rights may arise not only under the free speech clause but also under the establishment and free exercise clauses. A prime example is the issue of group prayer in the locker room or during a game, implicating both the right to engage in such prayer activities and the right to refrain from participation. See Kris Bryant, "Note, Take a Knee: Applying the First Amendment to Locker Room Prayers and Religion in College Sports," 36 *J. Coll. & Univ. Law* 329 (2009).

**10.4.4. Pertinent statutory law.** Similarly, state and federal statutory law has some special applications to an institution's athletes or athletic programs. Questions have arisen, for example, about the eligibility of injured intercollegiate athletes for workers' compensation. Laws in some states prohibit agents from entering representation agreements with student athletes (see, for example, Mich. Comp. Laws Ann. § 750.411e) or from entering into such an agreement without notifying the student's institution (see, for example, Fla. Stat. Ann. tit. 32, § 468.454 (2010)). State anti-hazing statutes may have applications to the activities of athletic teams and clubs (see, for example, 720 Ill. Comp. Stat. Ann. 120/5). An earlier version of this law was upheld in *People v. Anderson*, 591 N.E.2d 461 (Ill. 1992), a prosecution brought against members of a university lacrosse club. Regarding federal law, the antitrust statutes may have some application to the institution's relations with its student athletes when those relations are governed by athletic association and conference rules. And the Student Right-to-Know and Campus Security Act, discussed in this section, contains separate provisions dealing with low graduation rates of student athletes in certain sports.

The Student Right-to-Know Act (Title I of the Student Right-to-Know and Campus Security Act, 104 Stat. 2381-84 (1990)) ensures that potential student athletes will have access to data that will help them make informed choices when selecting an institution. Under the act, an institution of higher education that participates in federal student aid programs and that awards "athletically related student aid" must annually provide the U.S. Department of Education with certain information about its student athletes. Athletically related student aid is defined as "any scholarship, grant, or other form of financial assistance the terms of which require the recipient to participate in a program of intercollegiate athletics at an institution of higher education in order to be eligible to receive such assistance" (104 Stat. 2384, 20 U.S.C. § 1092(e)(8)).

Institutions must report the following information, broken down by race and gender: (1) the number of students receiving athletically related student aid in basketball, football, baseball, cross country/track, and all other sports combined (20 U.S.C. § 1092(e)(1)(A)); (2) the completion or graduation rates of those students (20 U.S.C. § 1092(e)(1)(C)); and (3) the average completion or graduation rate for the four most recent classes (20 U.S.C. § 1092(e)(1)(E)). The same types of information must be collected on students in general (20 U.S.C. § 1092(e)(1)(B, D, F)). In addition to reporting to the Department of Education, institutions must provide this information to potential student athletes and their parents, guidance counselors, and coaches (20 U.S.C. § 1092(e) (2)). Other students may receive the information upon request. The Secretary of Education may waive the annual reporting requirements if, in his or her opinion, an institution of higher education is a member of an athletic association or conference that publishes data "substantially comparable" to the information specified in the act (20 U.S.C. § 1092(e)(6)). Regulations implementing the act are published at 34 C.F.R. Part 668.

In addition to the Student Right-to-Know Act, Congress also passed the Equity in Athletics Disclosure Act, 108 Stat. 3518, 3970, codified at 20 U.S.C. § 1092(g). This act, like the earlier Student Right-to-Know Act, requires institutions annually to report certain data regarding their athletic programs to the U.S. Department of Education. Both acts are implemented by regulations codified in 34 C.F.R. Part 668 (the Student Assistance General Provisions) under subpart D (Student Consumer Information Services). Regulations particularly focused on the Equity in Athletics Disclosure Act are in 34 C.F.R. § 668.48, while those focused on the Student Right-to-Know Act are in 34 C.F.R §§ 668.46 and 668.49.

The Equity in Athletics Disclosure Act applies to "each co-educational institution that participates in any [Title IV, HEA student aid] program . . . and has an intercollegiate athletic program" (20 U.S.C. § 1092(g)(1)). Such institutions must make a variety of athletic program statistics available to prospective and current students, and the public upon request, including the number of male and female undergraduate students; the number of participants on each varsity athletic team; the operating expenses of each team; the gender of each team's head coach; the full- or part-time status of each head coach; the number and gender of assistant coaches and graduate assistants; statistics on "athletically-related student aid," reported separately for men's and women's teams and male and female athletes; recruiting expenditures for men's and for women's teams; revenues from athletics for men's and women's teams; and average salaries for male coaches and for female coaches.

**10.4.5. Athletic scholarships.** An athletic scholarship will usually be treated in the courts as a contract between an institution and a student. Typically the institution offers to pay the student's educational expenses in return for the student's promise to participate in a particular sport and maintain athletic eligibility by complying with university, conference, and NCAA regulations. Unlike other student-institutional contracts (see Section 7.1.3), the athletic scholarship contract may be a formal written agreement signed by the student and, if the student is underage, by a parent or guardian. Moreover, the terms of the athletic scholarship may be heavily influenced by athletic conference and NCAA rules regarding scholarships and athletic eligibility.

In NCAA member institutions, a letter of intent is provided to prospective student athletes. The student athlete's signature on this document functions as a promise that the student will attend the institution and participate in intercollegiate athletics in exchange for the institution's promise to provide a scholarship or other financial assistance. Courts have generally not addressed the issue of whether the letter of intent, standing alone, is an enforceable contract that binds the institution and the student athlete to their respective commitments. Instead, courts have viewed the signing of a letter of intent as one among many factors to consider in determining whether a contractual relationship exists. Thus, although the letter of intent serves as additional evidence of a contractual relationship, this document does not yet have independent legal status and, in effect, must be coupled with a financial aid offer in order to bind either party.

Although it is possible for either the institution or the student to breach a scholarship contract and for either party to sue, as a practical matter the cases generally involve students who file suit after an institution terminates or withdraws a scholarship. Such institutional action may occur if the student becomes ineligible for intercollegiate competition, has fraudulently misrepresented information regarding his or her academic credentials or athletic eligibility, has engaged in serious misconduct warranting substantial disciplinary action, or has declined to participate in the sport for personal reasons. The following three cases illustrate how such issues arise and how courts resolve them.

In *Begley v. Corp. of Mercer University*, 367 F. Supp. 908 (E.D. Tenn. 1973), the university withdrew from its agreement to provide an athletic scholarship for Begley after realizing that a university assistant coach had miscalculated Begley's high school grade point average (GPA) and that his true GPA did not meet the NCAA's minimum requirements. Begley filed suit, asking the court to award money damages for the university's breach of contract. The court dismissed the suit, holding that the university was justified in not performing its part of the agreement, since the agreement also required Begley to abide by all NCAA rules and regulations. Because Begley, from the outset, did not have the minimum GPA, he was unable to perform his part of the agreement. Thus, the court based its decision on the fundamental principle of contract law that "'where one party is unable to perform his part of the contract, he cannot be entitled to the performance of the contract by the other party'" (quoting 17 Am. Jur. 2d at 791–92, Contracts § 355). (For a more recent case involving issues of academic eligibility and the interpretation of NCAA rules, see *Williams v. University of Cincinnati*, 752 N.E.2d 367 (Ohio Ct. Cl. 2001).)

In *Taylor v. Wake Forest University*, 191 S.E.2d 379 (N.C. Ct. App. 1972), the university terminated a student's scholarship after he refused to participate in the football program. Originally, the student had withdrawn from the team to concentrate on academics when his grades fell below the minimum that the university required for athletic participation. Even after he raised his GPA above the minimum, however, the student continued his refusal to participate. The student alleged that the university's termination of his athletic scholarship was a breach and asked the court to award money damages equal to the costs incurred in completing his degree. He argued that, in case of conflict between his educational achievement and his athletic involvement, the scholarship terms allowed him to curtail his participation in the football program in order to "assure reasonable academic progress." He also argued that he was to be the judge of "reasonable academic progress." The court rejected the student's argument and granted summary judgment for the university. According to the court, permitting the student to be his own judge of his academic progress would be a "strained construction of the contract." Further, by accepting the scholarship, the student was obligated to "maintain his athletic eligibility . . . both physically and scholastically . . . When he refused to [participate] in the absence of any injury or excuse other than to devote more time to his studies, he was not complying with his contractual agreements" (191 S.E.2d at 121).

In *Conard v. University of Washington*, 814 P.2d 1242 (Wash. Ct. App. 1991), after three years of providing financial aid, the university declined to renew the scholarships of two student athletes for a fourth year because of the students' "serious misconduct." Although the scholarship agreement stipulated a one-year award of aid that would be considered for renewal under certain conditions, the students argued that it was their expectation, and the university's practice, that the scholarship would be automatically renewed for at least four years. The appellate court did not accept the students' evidence to this effect because the agreement, by its "clear terms," lasted only one academic year and provided only for the consideration of renewal (see generally Section 1.4.2.4). The university's withdrawal of aid, therefore, was not a breach of the contract. The appellate court, however, ruled that the informal hearing that the students had received violated their due process rights, and remanded the case to the university for an adversarial hearing.

Due process issues may also arise if an institution terminates or withdraws an athletic scholarship. The contract itself may specify certain procedural steps that the institution must take before withdrawal or termination. Conference or NCAA rules may contain other procedural requirements. And for public institutions, the federal Constitution's Fourteenth Amendment (or a comparable state constitutional provision) may sometimes superimpose other procedural obligations upon those contained in the contract and rules.

In the *Conard* case just cited, for example, the Washington Court of Appeals had held that the students had a "legitimate claim of entitlement" to the renewal of their scholarships because each scholarship was "issued under the representation that it would be renewed subject to certain conditions" and because it was the university's practice to renew athletic scholarships for at least four years. Declaring that this "entitlement" constituted a property interest under the Fourteenth Amendment, the court held that any deprivation of this entitlement "warrants the protection of due process" (see Section 10.4.2).

The Washington Supreme Court reversed the court of appeals on the due process issue (834 P.2d 17 (Wash. 1992)). The students' primary contention was that a "mutually explicit understanding" had been created by "the language of their contracts and the common understanding, based upon the surrounding circumstances and the conduct of the parties." The court rejected this argument, stating that "the language of the offers and the NCAA regulations are not sufficiently certain to support a mutually explicit understanding, [and] the fact that scholarships are, in fact, normally renewed does not create a 'common law' of renewal, absent other consistent and supportive [university] policies or rules." Consequently, the court held that the students had no legitimate claim of entitlement to renewal of the scholarships, and that the university thus had no obligation to extend them due process protections prior to nonrenewal.

Occasionally student athletes have sued their institutions even when the institution has not terminated or withdrawn the athlete's scholarship. Such cases are likely to involve alleged exploitation or abuse of the athlete, and may present not only breach of contract issues paralleling those in the cases above, but also more innovative tort law issues. The leading case, highly publicized in its day, is *Ross v. Creighton University*, 957 F.2d 410 (7th Cir. 1992). The plaintiff in this case had been awarded a basketball scholarship from Creighton even though his academic credentials were substantially below those of the average Creighton student. The plaintiff alleged that the university knew of his academic limitations but nevertheless lured him to Creighton with assurances that it would provide sufficient academic support so that he would "receive a meaningful education." While at Creighton, the plaintiff maintained a D average; and, on the advice of the athletic department, his curriculum consisted largely of courses such as Theory of Basketball. After four years, he "had the overall language skills of a fourth grader and the reading skills of a seventh grader."

The plaintiff based his suit on three tort theories and a breach of contract theory. The trial court originally dismissed all four claims. The appellate court agreed with the trial court on the tort claims but reversed the trial court and allowed the plaintiff to proceed to trial on the breach of contract claim. The plaintiff's first tort claim was a claim of "educational malpractice" based on Creighton's not providing him with "a meaningful education [or] preparing him for employment after college." The court refused to recognize educational malpractice as a cause of action, listing four policy concerns supporting its decision: (1) the inability of a court to fashion "a satisfactory standard of care by which to evaluate" instruction, (2) its inability to determine the cause and nature of damage to the student, (3) the potential flood of litigation that would divert institutions' attention from their primary mission, and (4) the threat of involving courts in the oversight of daily institutional operations. The plaintiff's second claim was that Creighton had committed "negligent admission" because it owed a duty to "recruit and enroll only those students reasonably qualified to and able to academically perform" at the school. The court rejected this novel theory because of similar problems in identifying a standard of care by which to judge the institution's admissions decisions. The court also noted that, if institutions were subjected to such claims, they would admit only exceptional students, thus severely limiting the opportunities for marginal students. The plaintiff's last tort claim was negligent infliction of emotional distress. The court quickly rejected this claim because its rejection of the first two claims left no basis for proving that the defendant had been negligent in undertaking the actions that may have distressed the plaintiff.

Although the court rejected all the plaintiff's negligence claims, it did embrace his breach of contract claim. In order to discourage "any attempt to repackage an educational malpractice claim as a contract claim," however, the court required the plaintiff to "do more than simply allege that the education was not good enough. Instead, he must point to an identifiable contractual promise that the defendant failed to honor." Judicial consideration of such a claim is therefore not an inquiry "into the nuances of educational processes and theories, but rather an objective assessment of whether the institution made a good faith effort to perform on its promise."

Following this approach, the court reviewed the plaintiff's allegations that the university failed (1) to provide adequate tutoring, (2) to require that the plaintiff attend tutoring sessions, (3) to allow the plaintiff to "red-shirt" for one year to concentrate on his studies, and (4) to afford the plaintiff a reasonable opportunity to take advantage of tutoring services. The court concluded that these allegations were sufficient to warrant further proceedings and therefore remanded the case to the trial court. (Soon thereafter, the parties settled the case.)

The court's disposition of the tort claims in *Ross* does not mean that student athletes can never succeed with such claims. In a similar case, *Jackson v. Drake University*, 778 F. Supp. 1490 (S.D. Iowa 1991), the court did recognize two tort claims—negligent misrepresentation and fraud—brought by a former student athlete. After rejecting an educational malpractice claim for reasons similar to those in *Ross*, the court allowed the plaintiff to proceed with his claims that "Drake did not exercise reasonable care in making representations [about its commitment to academic excellence] and had no intention of providing the support services it had promised." The court reasoned that the policy concerns "do not weigh as heavily in favor of precluding the claims for negligent misrepresentation and fraud as in the claim for [educational malpractice]."

But a student seeking to hold Clemson University responsible for the erroneous advice of an academic advisor, resulting in his ineligibility to play baseball under NCAA rules, was unsuccessful in his attempt to state claims of negligence, breach of fiduciary duty, and breach of contract. In *Hendricks v. Clemson University*, 578 S.E.2d 711 (S.C. 2003), a trial court had granted summary judgment to the university on the student's claims, but a state intermediate appellate court reversed, ruling that the case must proceed to trial. The state supreme court reinstated the summary judgment, ruling that no state law common law precedent could support the assumption by the university of a duty of care to advise the student accurately. Said the court: "We believe recognizing a duty flowing from advisors to students is not required by any precedent and would be unwise, considering the great potential for embroiling schools in litigation that such recognition would create" (578 S.E.2d at 715). Furthermore, said the court, "Historically, this Court has reserved imposition of fiduciary duties to legal or business settings, often in which one person entrusts money to another, such as with lawyers, brokers, corporate directors, and corporate promoters" (578 S.E. 2d at 716), and thus it would not recognize, as a matter of first impression, a fiduciary relationship between the student and the advisor. And finally, according to the court, citing *Ross v. Creighton*, it would not allow the breach of contract claim to go forward because the plaintiff's claim involved an evaluation of the adequacy of the university's services, a claim specifically rejected by the court in Ross. Here, said the court, the university had not made any written promise to ensure the athletic eligibility of the student.

Decisions to withdraw or not to renew an athletic scholarship may also involve alleged violations of the code of student conduct, thus requiring the institution to determinate whether the code has been violated prior to making the decision to withdraw or not renew the scholarship. A federal trial court addressed this issue in *Colli v. Southern Methodist University*, 2010 U.S. Dist. LEXIS 143582 (N.D. Tex. Aug. 17, 2010). The student, a former basketball player at the university, had made charges against the coach that the university determined were unsupported. The athletic director decided not to renew Colli's scholarship, in part because he determined that her actions violated the student code of conduct. The university's written policies and NCAA bylaws provided that scholarship nonrenewal notifications be made no later than July 1; Colli received notice in August that her scholarship would not be renewed. Furthermore, no disciplinary hearing had been held on the charges that she violated the student code of conduct; the student handbook guaranteed a hearing in all such cases. Reading the university's written policies and NCAA bylaws together, the court denied the university's motion for summary judgment, ruling that these documents required the university to provide the student with a hearing and to follow the notice provisions in their policies and the NCAA bylaws.

### 10.4.6. Sex discrimination.
The equitable treatment of male and female college athletes remains a major issue in athletic programs. Despite the fact that Title IX has been in existence for more than forty years, conflict remains as to whether it has provided appropriate standards for equalizing opportunities for men and women to participate in college sports. Litigation under Title IX has focused on two primary issues: providing equal access to resources for both men's and women's sports, and equal treatment of athletes of both genders. Equal access litigation involves allegedly inequitable resource allocation to

women's sports and the elimination of men's teams by some institutions in order to comply with Title IX's proportionality requirements. Equal treatment cases typically involve challenges to individual treatment of female athletes, including the availability of scholarships, the compensation of coaches, and related issues.

Before the passage of Title IX (20 U.S.C. §§ 1681 et seq.) (see Section 11.5.3 of this book), the legal aspects of this controversy centered on the Fourteenth Amendment's equal protection clause. As in earlier admissions cases (see Section 7.2.4.2), courts searched for an appropriate analysis by which to ascertain the constitutionality of sex-based classifications in athletics. Since the implementation in 1975 of the Title IX regulations (34 C.F.R. Part 106), the equal protection aspects of sex discrimination in high school and college athletics have played second fiddle to Title IX. Title IX applies to both public and private institutions receiving federal aid and thus has a broader reach than equal protection, which applies only to public institutions (see Section 1.5.2). Title IX also has several provisions on athletics that establish requirements more extensive than anything devised under the banner of equal protection. And Title IX is supported by enforcement mechanisms beyond those available for the equal protection clause.

In addition to Title IX, state law (including any state equal rights amendment) also has significant applications to college athletics. In *Blair v. Washington State University*, 740 P.2d 1379 (Wash. 1987), for example, women athletes and coaches at Washington State University used the state's equal rights amendment and the state nondiscrimination law to challenge the institution's funding for women's athletic programs. The trial court had ruled against the university, saying that funding for women's athletic programs should be based on the percentage of women enrolled as undergraduates. In calculating the formula, however, the trial court had excluded football revenues. The Washington Supreme Court reversed on that point, declaring that the state's equal rights amendment "contains no exception for football." It remanded the case to the trial court for revision of the funding formula.

Although the regulations interpreting Title IX with regard to athletics became effective in 1975, they were not appreciably enforced at the postsecondary level until the late 1980s—partly because the U.S. Supreme Court, in *Grove City College v. Bell*, 465 U.S. 555 (1984), had held that Title IX's nondiscrimination provisions applied only to those programs that were direct recipients of federal aid. Congress reversed the result in *Grove City* in the Civil Rights Restoration Act of 1987, making it clear that Title IX applies to all activities of colleges and universities that receive federal funds.

Section 106.41 of the Title IX regulations (34 C.F.R. § 106.41) is the primary provision on athletics; it establishes various equal opportunity requirements applicable to "interscholastic, intercollegiate, club, or intramural athletics." Section 106.37(c) establishes equal opportunity requirements regarding the availability of athletic scholarships. Physical education classes are covered by 34 C.F.R. § 106.34, and extracurricular activities related to athletics, such as cheerleading and booster clubs, are covered generally under 34 C.F.R. § 106.31.

The regulations impose nondiscrimination requirements on these activities whether or not they are directly subsidized by federal funds, and they do not exempt revenue-generating sports, such as men's football or basketball, from the calculation of funds available for the institution's athletic programs.

One of the controversies stirred by Title IX concerns the choice of sex-segregated versus unitary (integrated) athletic teams. The regulations develop a compromise approach to this issue, which roughly parallels the equal protection principles that emerged from the earlier court cases. Under 34 C.F.R. § 106.41(b):

> [An institution] may operate or sponsor separate teams for members of each sex where selection for such teams is based upon competitive skill or the activity involved is a contact sport. However, where [an institution] operates or sponsors a team in a particular sport for members of one sex but operates or sponsors no such team for members of the other sex, and athletic opportunities for members of that sex have previously been limited, members of the excluded sex must be allowed to try-out for the team offered unless the sport involved is a contact sport. For the purposes of this part, contact sports include boxing, wrestling, rugby, ice hockey, football, basketball, and other sports the purpose or major activity of which involves bodily contact.

This regulation requires institutions to operate unitary teams only for non-contact sports for which selection is not competitive. Otherwise, the institution may operate either unitary or separate teams and may even operate a team for one sex without having any team in the sport for the opposite sex, as long as the institution's overall athletic program "effectively accommodate[s] the interests and abilities of members of both sexes" (34 C.F.R. § 106.41(c)(1)). In a noncontact sport, however, if an institution operates only one competitively selected team, it must be open to both sexes whenever the "athletic opportunities" of the traditionally excluded sex "have previously been limited" (34 C.F.R. § 106.41(b)).

Regardless of whether its teams are separate or unitary, the institution must "provide equal athletic opportunity for members of both sexes" (34 C.F.R. § 106.41(c)). While equality of opportunity does not require either equality of "aggregate expenditures for members of each sex" or equality of "expenditures for male and female teams," an institution's "failure to provide necessary funds for teams for one sex" is a relevant factor in determining compliance (34 C.F.R. § 106.41(c)). Postsecondary administrators grappling with this slippery equal opportunity concept will be helped by 34 C.F.R. § 106.41(c)'s list of ten nonexclusive factors by which to measure overall equality:

1. Whether the selection of sports and levels of competition effectively accommodate the interests and abilities of members of both sexes

2. The provision of equipment and supplies

3. Scheduling of games and practice time

4. Travel and per diem allowance

5. Opportunity to receive coaching and academic tutoring
6. Assignment and compensation of coaches and tutors
7. Provision of locker rooms and practice and competitive facilities
8. Provision of medical and training facilities and services
9. Provision of housing and dining facilities and services
10. Publicity

The equal opportunity focus of the regulations also applies to athletic scholarships. Institutions must "provide reasonable opportunities for such awards for members of each sex in proportion to the number of each sex participating in . . . intercollegiate athletics" (34 C.F.R. § 106.37(c)(1)). If the institution operates separate teams for each sex (as permitted in 34 C.F.R. § 106.41), it may allocate athletic scholarships on the basis of sex to implement its separate-team philosophy, as long as the overall allocation achieves equal opportunity.

In 1979, after a period of substantial controversy, the U.S. Department of Health, Education and Welfare (now the Department of Education) issued a lengthy "Policy Interpretation" of its Title IX regulations as they apply to intercollegiate athletics (44 Fed. Reg. 71413 (December 11, 1979)). This Policy Interpretation, available on the Web site of the Office for Civil Rights (OCR) (http://www2.ed.gov/about/offices/list/ocr/docs/t9interp.html), is still considered authoritative and is currently used by federal courts reviewing allegations of Title IX violations. It addresses each of the ten factors listed in 34 C.F.R. § 106.41(c) of the regulations, providing examples of information the Department of Education will use to determine whether an institution has complied with Title IX. For example, "opportunity to receive coaching and academic tutoring" would include the availability of full-time and part-time coaches for male and female athletes, the relative availability of graduate assistants, and the availability of tutors for male and female athletes. "Compensation of coaches" includes attention to the rates of compensation, conditions relating to contract renewal, nature of coaching duties performed, and working conditions of coaches for male and female teams (44 Fed. Reg. at 71416). Also on the OCR Web site is a document entitled "Clarification of Intercollegiate Athletics Policy Guidance: The Three-Part Test" (available at http://www2.ed.gov/about/offices/list/ocr/docs/clarific.html). This clarification was issued in January 1996.

The debate over Title IX intensified during 2002–03 when a Commission on Opportunities in Athletics, appointed by then–U.S. Secretary of Education Rod Paige, deliberated about the possibility of changing the way that Title IX was enforced. The commission's final report made various recommendations about the operation and enforcement of the "three-prong test" and the Title IX athletics regulations (Secretary of Education's Commission on Opportunity in Athletics, *Open to All: Title IX at Thirty* (U.S. Department of Education, February 28, 2003). On July 11, 2003, the U.S. Department of Education issued a "Further Clarification of Intercollegiate Athletics Policy Guidance Regarding Title IX Compliance" (available at http://www2.ed.gov/about/offices/list/ocr/title9guidanceFinal.html). The ultimate outcome of the commission's work and the OCR's response to it was to ratify the "three-prong test" for determining whether an institution's athletic program is complying with Title IX, a result that disappointed critics of the "proportionality" requirement that had apparently stimulated some institutions to drop certain men's varsity sports in order to reallocate funding to women's sports. In March 2005, the OCR issued an "Additional Clarification of Intercollegiate Athletics: Three-Part Test— Part Three" that allowed institutions to use a survey to measure student athletic interest. The NCAA and proponents of gender equity in college sports criticized the new OCR policy, and it was withdrawn in 2010 by the Obama Administration ("Dear Colleague" letter, April 20, 2010, available at www2 .ed.gov/about/offices/list/ocr/letters/colleague-20100420.pdf). The 2010 Dear Colleague letter reaffirmed the applicability of the 1979 Policy Interpretation and the 1996 clarification, and elaborated on how an institution might determine the extent of the "interests and abilities" of the "underrepresented sex." The letter emphasizes that institutions may use multiple approaches to making this determination and provides guidance on how an institution might wish to develop a survey of interests, as well as how the OCR will evaluate the validity of the survey and other information used by the institution to determine its compliance with Title IX.

Most Title IX disputes have involved complaints to the Office for Civil Rights. In the past, the OCR has been criticized for its "lax" enforcement efforts and for permitting institutions to remain out of compliance with Title IX. Perhaps partly for this reason, women athletes in recent years have chosen to litigate their claims in the courts.

Although the first major court challenge to an institution's funding for intercollegiate athletics ended with a settlement rather than a court order (*Haffer v. Temple University*, 678 F. Supp. 517 (E.D. Pa. 1987)), this case set the tone for subsequent litigation. In *Haffer*, a federal trial judge certified a class of "all current women students at Temple University who participate, or who are or have been deterred from participating because of sex discrimination[,] in Temple's intercollegiate athletic program." Although the case was settled, with the university agreeing to various changes in scholarships and support for women athletes, it encouraged women students at other colleges and universities to challenge disparities in the resources allocated to women's and men's sports.

The leading case to date on Title IX's application to alleged inequality in funding for women's intercollegiate sports is *Cohen v. Brown University*, 991 F.2d 888 (1st Cir. 1993). In that case, a U.S. Court of Appeals upheld a district court's preliminary injunction ordering Brown University to reinstate its women's gymnastics and women's volleyball programs to full varsity status pending the trial of a Title IX claim. Until 1971, Brown had been an all-male university. At that time it merged with a women's college and, over the next six years, upgraded the women's athletic program. At the time of the litigation, Brown had fifteen women's varsity teams as compared to sixteen men's varsity teams; the women had 36.7 percent of all the varsity athletic opportunities available at the university, and the men had 63.3 percent. (Brown's student population at the time was approximately 48 percent women.) In 1991, however, the university cut four varsity teams: two men's teams (for a savings of $15,795) and two women's teams (for a savings of $62,028). These cuts disproportionately reduced the budgeted funds for women, but they did not significantly change the ratio of athletic opportunities, since women retained 36.6 percent of the available slots.

In upholding the district court's injunction, the appellate court first noted that an institution would not be found in violation of Title IX merely because there was a statistical disparity between the percentage of women and the percentage of men in its athletic programs. The court then focused on the ten factors listed in the Title IX regulations at 34 C.F.R. §106.41(c) (set out earlier in this section) and noted that the district court based its injunction on the first of these factors: "Brown's failure effectively to accommodate the interests and abilities of female students in the selection and level of sports." To be in compliance with this factor, a university must satisfy at least one of three tests set out in the Title IX Policy Interpretation:

(1) Whether intercollegiate level participation opportunities for male and female students are provided in numbers substantially proportionate to their respective enrollments; or

(2) Where the members of one sex have been and are underrepresented among intercollegiate athletes, whether the institution can show a history and continuing practice of program expansion which is demonstrably responsive to the developing interest and abilities of the members of that sex; or

(3) Where the members of one sex have been and are underrepresented among intercollegiate athletes, and the institution cannot show a continuing practice of program expansion such as that cited above, whether it can be demonstrated that the interests and abilities of the members of that sex have been fully and effectively accommodated by the present program [44 Fed. Reg. at 71418].

The appellate court agreed with the district court that Brown clearly did not fall within the first option. Further, the appellate court ruled that the district court did not abuse its discretion in deciding that, although the university had made a great amount of improvements between 1971 and 1977, the lack of continuing expansion efforts precluded the university from satisfying the second option. Thus, since the university could not comply with either of the first two options, "it must comply with the third benchmark. To do so, the school must fully and effectively accommodate the underrepresented gender's interests and abilities, even if that requires it to give the underrepresented gender . . . what amounts to a larger slice of a shrinking athletic-opportunity pie." The appellate court then focused on the word "fully" in the third option, interpreting it literally to the effect that the underrepresented sex must be "fully" accommodated, not merely proportionately accommodated as in the first option. Since Brown's cuts in the women's athletic programs had created a demand for athletics opportunities for women that was not filled, women were not "fully" accommodated. Thus, since Brown could meet none of the three options specified in the Policy Interpretation, the court concluded that the university had likely violated Title IX, and it therefore affirmed the district court's entry of the preliminary injunction.

Holding that the plaintiffs had made their required showing and that Brown had not, the court turned to the issue of remedy. Although the appellate court upheld the preliminary injunction, the court noted the need to balance the institution's academic freedom with the need for an effective remedy for the Title IX violation. The appellate court stated that, since the lower court had not yet held a trial on the merits, the lower court's order that Brown maintain women's varsity volleyball and gymnastics teams pending trial was within its discretion. The appellate court noted, however, that a more appropriate post-trial remedy, assuming that a Title IX violation was established, would be for Brown to propose a program for compliance. In balancing academic freedom against Title IX's regulatory scheme, the court noted:

> This litigation presents an array of complicated and important issues at a crossroads of the law that few courts have explored. The beacon by which we must steer is Congress's unmistakably clear mandate that educational institutions not use federal monies to perpetuate gender-based discrimination. At the same time, we must remain sensitive to the fact that suits of this genre implicate the discretion of universities to pursue their missions free from governmental interference and, in the bargain, to deploy increasingly scarce resources in the most advantageous way [991 F.2d at 907].

After the appellate court remanded the case to the district court, that court held a full trial on the merits, after which it ruled again in favor of the plaintiffs and ordered Brown to submit a plan for achieving full compliance with Title IX. When the district court found Brown's plan to be inadequate and entered its own order specifying that Brown must remedy its Title IX violation by elevating four women's teams to full varsity status, Brown appealed again. In late 1996, the First Circuit issued another ruling in what it called "*Cohen IV*" (*Cohen II* being its earlier 1993 ruling, and *Cohen I* and *Cohen III* being the district court rulings that preceded *Cohen II* and *Cohen IV*). By a 2-to-1 vote in *Cohen IV*, 101 F.3d 155 (1st Cir. 1996), the appellate court affirmed the district court's ruling that Brown was in violation of Title IX. The court explicitly relied upon, and refused to reconsider, its legal analysis from *Cohen II*. The *Cohen II* reasoning, as further explicated in *Cohen IV*, thus remains the law in the First Circuit and the leading example of how courts will apply Title IX to the claims of women athletes.

One of Brown's major arguments in *Cohen IV* was that women were less interested in participating in collegiate sports and that the trial court's ruling required Brown to provide opportunities for women that went beyond their interests and abilities. The court viewed this argument "with great suspicion" and rejected it:

> Thus, there exists the danger that, rather than providing a true measure of women's interest in sports, statistical evidence purporting to reflect women's interest instead provides only a measure of the very discrimination that is and

has been the basis for women's lack of opportunity to participate in sports . . .
[E]ven if it can be empirically demonstrated that, at a particular time, women
have less interest in sports than do men, such evidence, standing alone,
cannot justify providing fewer athletics opportunities for women than for men.
Furthermore, such evidence is completely irrelevant where, as here, viable and
successful women's varsity teams have been demoted or eliminated [101 F.3d at
179–80].

Regarding Brown's obligation to remedy its Title IX violation, however, the
*Cohen IV* court overruled the district court, because that court "erred in substi-
tuting its own specific relief in place of Brown's statutorily permissible proposal
to comply with Title IX by cutting men's teams until substantial proportionality was achieved." The appellate court "agree[d] with the district court that
Brown's proposed plan fell short of a good faith effort to meet the requirements
of Title IX as explicated by this court in *Cohen II* and as applied by the district
court on remand." Nevertheless, it determined that cutting men's teams "is a
permissible means of effectuating compliance with the statute" and that Brown
should have the opportunity to submit another plan to the district court. This
disposition, said the court, was driven by "our respect for academic freedom
and reluctance to interject ourselves into the conduct of university affairs."

In *Pederson v. Louisiana State University*, 213 F.3d 858 (5th Cir. 2000),
another federal appellate court ruled that the university had engaged in "systematic, intentional, differential treatment of women" and affirmed a trial
court's ruling that the university had violated Title IX. The plaintiffs, representing a class of all women students at Louisiana State University (LSU)
who wished to participate in varsity sports that were not provided by LSU,
alleged that the university had denied them equal opportunities to participate,
to receive athletic scholarships, and to receive benefits and services provided
to varsity athletes, as well as to have coaches who were compensated equally
with the coaches of men's teams. Because the record not only contained evidence of a lack of opportunities for women to play varsity soccer and fast-pitch
softball (the sports in question) and substantial differences in the financial
resources afforded women's sports compared with men's sports, but also
included a multitude of sexist comments to the women athletes by university
sports administrators and admissions that they would only add women's teams
"if forced to," the appellate court ruled that the discrimination was intentional
and "motivated by chauvinist notions" (213 F.3d at 882).

Both in *Cohen* and in *Pederson*, the courts appeared to serve warning on
institutions that do not provide equivalent athletic opportunities for men's and
women's sports. And *Cohen*, in particular, demonstrates that, for institutions
that have either a stringently limited athletic budget or one that must be cut,
compliance with Title IX can occur only if the institution reduces opportunities
for men's sports in order to be able to allocate additional resources to women's
sports. Both appellate opinions deferred to the institution's right to determine
for itself how it will structure its athletic programs, but once the institution was
out of Title IX compliance, these courts did not hesitate to order specific remedies. Financial problems do not exempt an institution from Title IX compliance.

Following the ruling in *Cohen*, many institutions determined that the only feasible method of achieving compliance with Title IX was to cut men's teams (and in some cases, women's teams as well). These decisions resulted in litigation from male students challenging these cuts and seeking reinstatement of the teams. The plaintiffs in these cases asserted that the Title IX regulations and Policy Interpretation violated both Title IX itself and the equal protection clause of the Constitution by requiring "affirmative action" or "quotas" for women student athletes. In every case, the federal courts have rejected these arguments. See, for example, *Equity in Athletics v. Department of Education*, 639 F.3d 91 (4th Cir. 2011), *National Wrestling Coaches Association v. U.S. Department of Education*, 366 F.3d 930 (D.C. Cir. 2004), and *Choike v. Slippery Rock University*, 2006 U.S. Dist. LEXIS 49886 (W.D. Pa. 2006).

An early example of such a case is *Kelley v. Board of Trustees of University of Illinois*, 35 F.3d 265 (7th Cir. 1994), in which a federal appellate court upheld the university's discontinuance of the men's swimming team. The appellate court deferred to the Title IX regulations and the Policy Interpretation on intercollegiate athletics. Because the university had done its cutting of teams in accordance with the regulations and the interpretation, seeking to achieve proportionality between men's and women's athletic teams, the court affirmed the district court's grant of summary judgment for the university.

The same appellate court (the Seventh Circuit) later expanded upon its *Kelley* ruling in *Boulahanis v. Board of Regents*, 198 F.3d 633 (7th Cir. 1999). That case involved Illinois State University's decision to cut the men's soccer and wrestling teams in order to achieve compliance with Title IX. Reiterating its ruling in *Kelley*, the court rejected the plaintiffs' attempt to distinguish their case from *Kelley* by arguing that the university in *Kelley* cut its men's athletic teams for budgetary reasons whereas the university here did so for the sole purpose of Title IX compliance. The court quickly recognized that financial considerations cannot be "neatly separated" from Title IX considerations and that decisions regarding which athletic programs to retain are "based on a combination of financial and sex-based concerns that are not easily distinguished."

Another leading case involving men's teams is *Neal v. California State University*, 198 F.3d 763 (9th Cir. 1999). In that case, California State University at Bakersfield (CSUB), in the face of shrinking budgetary resources, was working to achieve compliance with Title IX under a consent decree entered in a previous Title IX suit. CSUB decided to limit the size of several of its male athletic teams. After it required the men's wrestling team to reduce its roster, the wrestlers brought suit under Title IX, and the federal district court enjoined the reduction. On appeal, the Ninth Circuit vacated the injunction and upheld the university's actions.

The wrestlers argued that the "substantially proportionate" requirement in the Policy Interpretation could be met by providing opportunities in proportion to the interest levels of each gender, rather than in proportion to the actual enrollment figures. Rejecting this argument, the court determined that such an interest-based interpretation of the Policy Interpretation "'limit[s] required program expansion for the underrepresented sex to the status quo level of relative interests'" (198 F.3d at 768, quoting *Cohen IV* (cited earlier in this section), 101 F.3d at 174) and does so "'under circumstances where men's athletic teams have a considerable head start'" (198 F.3d at 768, quoting *Cohen II*, 991 F.2d at 900).

The appellate court also addressed the wrestlers' argument that Title IX does not permit cutting of men's teams as a means to remedy gender inequity in athletics, but provides only for increasing women's teams. In responding to this argument, the court relied on the decisions of other circuits, such as the Seventh Circuit's decision in *Kelley v. Board of Trustees* that had already approved of universities' cutting men's teams to comply with Title IX. The *Neal* court also asserted that the legislative history of Title IX indicates Congress was aware that compliance might sometimes be achieved only by cutting men's athletics.

Finally, the appellate court in *Neal* explained that the district court had erred in not deferring to the U.S. Department of Education's Policy Interpretation. Citing U.S. Supreme Court precedent, the court emphasized that "federal courts are to defer substantially to an agency's interpretation of its own regulations," unless that interpretation is plainly inconsistent with the statute or would raise "serious constitutional issues"—neither of which is the case with the Policy Interpretation.

Following *Boulahanis* and *Neal*, federal appellate courts rejected challenges to the elimination of varsity wrestling teams at the University of North Dakota (*Chalenor v. University of North Dakota*, 291 F.3d 1042 (8th Cir. 2002)), and Miami University (*Miami Wrestling Club v. Miami University*, 302 F.3d 608 (6th Cir. 2002)). In *Equity in Athletics, Inc. v. Department of Education*, 675 F. Supp. 2d 660 (W.D. Va. 2009), *affirmed*, 639 F.3d 91 (4th Cir. 2011), the plaintiff, a not-for-profit nonstock corporation, brought claims under Title IX and the equal protection clause against James Madison University and the U.S. Department of Education. The plaintiffs sought a preliminary injunction to prevent the university from eliminating ten varsity athletic teams in 2007—seven men's teams and three women's teams. The lawsuit also sought a ruling that the Education Department's interpretation of Title IX requirements with respect to the three-part test of the 1979 Policy Interpretation violated Title IX because it discriminated against men and denied them equal protection under the U.S. Constitution.

The trial court granted the defendants' motion to dismiss for failure to state a claim. The court reviewed decisions of other appellate courts with respect to the lawfulness of the three-prong test and concluded that reducing athletic opportunities for men violated neither Title IX nor the equal protection clause, saying that Title IX neither required nor prohibited such reductions and that Title IX's remedial purpose protected the university from liability under the equal protection clause because the university took gender into consideration only in a limited way when making team reduction decisions. The plaintiff had also claimed that the university's decision—and the 1979 Policy Interpretation—violated the players' associational rights under the First Amendment. The court disposed of that claim briskly, stating that playing on a sports team was neither expressive nor intimate association—the only types of association that courts have recognized as meriting protection under the Constitution. With regard to the plaintiff's contention that the 1979 Policy Interpretation was unreasonable because it examined athletic opportunities in relation to enrollment rather than in relation to expressed interest in participation, the court ruled that the Policy Interpretation was entitled to deference unless the plaintiffs could demonstrate that it was an arbitrary and capricious interpretation of the statute. And with respect to the plaintiff's claims that the university's decision to eliminate the ten sports teams denied those athletes procedural and substantive due process, the court declared that students do not have a property right in participating in intercollegiate athletics, citing a long line of state and federal appellate court rulings. Without a property right, there could be no procedural or substantive due process violation. The appellate court affirmed in all respects.

The National Wrestling Coaches Association brought a lawsuit against the U.S. Office for Civil Rights, challenging the 1996 "Clarification of Intercollegiate Athletics Policy Guidance: The Three Part Test" as well as the Policy Interpretation issued in 1979 (both of which are on the OCR's Web site, as cited earlier in this section). The district court dismissed the case on the grounds that the plaintiffs did not have standing to pursue that claim, and the appellate court affirmed (*National Wrestling Coaches Association v. U.S. Department of Education*, 263 F. Supp. 2d 82 (D.D.C. 2003), *affirmed*, 366 F.3d 930 (D.C. Cir. 2004)). According to the appellate court, even if the two documents challenged by the Coaches Association were revoked, the law would still permit an institution to eliminate the men's wrestling program in order to comply with Title IX's gender equity mandate.

The plaintiffs filed a motion for an *en banc* review by the appellate court. The panel, in a 2-to-1 decision, rejected the coaches' request for rehearing and the *en banc* court rejected the petition for a rehearing *en banc*, stating that the coaches' real dispute was with the institutions that had cut wrestling, not with the Department of Education (383 F.3d 1047 (D.C. Cir. 2004)). Rejecting the coaches' argument that the U.S. Department of Education had "forced" colleges and universities to adopt policies with respect to proportionality that are unlawful under Title IX, the majority noted that the department's policy statements are not regulations and that universities are not required to follow them. Because the plaintiffs had a "fully adequate" private cause of action against the institutions that dropped their wrestling teams, said the court, the coaches needed to look to the institutions for relief. As these cases suggest, male athletes are likely to have a much more difficult time contesting the cutting of men's teams than are female athletes in contesting the cutting of women's teams.

As noted earlier, individuals who believe that an institution is violating Title IX's requirements of equity in athletics have two choices: they may file a complaint with the Education Department's Office of Civil Rights, or they may file a lawsuit in federal court. The ruling of the U.S. Supreme Court in *Alexander v. Sandoval*, discussed in Section 11.5.5 of this book, may complicate litigation challenging the equity of athletics programs by gender. In *Alexander*, the Court ruled that there is no private right of action for disparate impact claims under Title VI (see Section 11.5.2 of this book). Because the language of Title IX is virtually identical to the language of Title VI, courts have applied Title VI jurisprudence to claims brought under Title IX. Thus, the outcome in *Alexander* suggests that courts might reject the attempts of plaintiffs to bring disparate impact claims under Title IX. A federal district court has confirmed this interpretation of *Alexander* in *Barrett v. West Chester University*, 2003 U.S. Dist. LEXIS 21095 (E.D. Pa. November 12, 2003), but found that the university had intentionally discriminated against women students by eliminating the women's gymnastics team, by failing to provide equal coaching resources to male and female teams, and by paying coaches of women's teams less than coaches of men's teams. The court granted the plaintiffs' motion for an injunction, requiring the reinstatement of the women's gymnastics team. Had the plaintiffs been limited to a claim of disparate impact, rather than intentional discrimination, the court would have dismissed their claim.

It is thus possible to interpret *Alexander v. Sandoval* as limiting plaintiffs to claims of intentional discrimination brought under section 901 of the Title IX statute, but not under the regulations or policy interpretations. Federal trial courts have rejected this argument, however (see *Equity in Athletics, Inc. v. Department of Education*, 675 F. Supp. 2d 660, 681 (W.D. Va. 2009), *affirmed*, 639 F.3d 91 (4th Cir. 2011) (ruling that the Policy Interpretation does not go beyond the plain language of the Title IX statute), and *Choike v. Slippery Rock University*, 2006 U.S. Dist. LEXIS 49886, at *33 (July 21, 2006) (finding that the regulations and policy interpretations "implement but do not expand the scope of Title IX"). However, should the Title IX regulations or Department of Education policy interpretations be interpreted as prohibiting discriminatory actions that are unintentional but that have a harsher impact on members of one gender, athletes with such disparate impact claims would be able to assert them only in the institution's Title IX grievance process or in the Department of Education's administrative complaint process. In addition, under *Alexander*, plaintiffs would not be able to bring private causes of action claiming intentional violations of the Title IX regulations or the Department of Education policy interpretations unless the plaintiffs can show that the cause of action is also grounded on the Title IX statute itself and not merely on the regulations or policy interpretations.

Although federal courts have analyzed cases involving equal access to athletic opportunities using one or more of the factors listed in the regulations just discussed, the appellate courts are divided as to whether the burden of proof created by the U.S. Supreme Court in 1998 for plaintiffs suing under Title IX for sexual harassment should also be applied to Title IX litigation concerning athletics. In *Gebser v. Lago Vista Independent School District*, discussed in Section 8.5, the U.S. Supreme Court ruled that a plaintiff must prove that (1) the school had actual notice of the alleged discrimination, and (2) the school demonstrated "deliberate indifference" in its response to the student's claim. The U.S. Court of Appeals for the Fifth Circuit in *Pederson v. Louisiana*

*State University*, discussed earlier in this section, rejected the defendant's argument that the *Gebser* test should apply in a lawsuit regarding equal access to athletic opportunities, using instead the traditional three-part test from the OCR's Policy Interpretation.

The *Pederson* court reasoned that the institution itself had intentionally discriminated against the women athletes, so the *Gebser* framework, which addressed whether the school was on notice of discriminatory conduct by an employee, was not relevant. The U.S. Supreme Court agreed in *Jackson v. Birmingham Board of Education*, 544 U.S. 167 (2005), stating that "[the notice] limitation on private damages actions is not a bar to liability where a funding recipient intentionally violates the statute" (544 U.S. at 182). And in *Mansourian v. Board of Regents of the University of California at Davis*, 602 F.3d 957 (9th Cir. 2010), the court rejected any requirement of prior notice as "inconsistent with funding recipients' affirmative obligations to provide non-discriminatory athletic participation opportunities and continually to assess and certify compliance with Title IX" (602 F.3d at 968). The court noted that a Title IX complaint about an "affirmative institutional decision" such as a change in policy with respect to a varsity sports team does not require prior notice to the institution. The court explained that "[d]ecisions to create or eliminate teams or to add or decrease roster slots for male or female athletes are official decisions, not practices by individual students or staff. Athletic programs that fail effectively to accommodate students of both sexes thus represent 'official policy of the recipient entity' and so are not covered by *Gebser*'s notice requirement." The case was settled for $1.35 million in 2012. "U. of California at Davis to Pay $1.35 Million to Settle Title IX Claim," *Chron. Higher Educ.* February 16, 2012, available at http://chronicle.com/blogs/ticker/u-of-california-at-davis-to-pay-1–35-million-to-settle-title-ix-claim/40592.

Another issue that has engendered litigation under Title IX is how a college or university determines whether a particular athletic activity is a "sport" for calculating the participation rates of male and female students. In *Biediger v. Quinnipiac University*, 728 F. Supp. 2d 62 (D. Conn. 2010), *affirmed*, 691 F.3d 85 (2d Cir. 2012), the university eliminated its women's volleyball team and stated that it would create a new women's "sport" of competitive cheerleading. Members of the women's volleyball team sued, alleging that the university's decision violated Title IX and that competitive cheerleading was not a sport. The trial court ruled that the university's practice of "roster manipulation" violated Title IX and that competitive cheerleading was "not yet" a sport because at that time it was "too underdeveloped and disorganized to be treated as offering genuine varsity athletic participation opportunities for students," and the appellate court agreed. The Education Department issued a "Dear Colleague" letter in 2008 on "Athletic Activities Counted for Title IX Compliance," which may be found at http://www2.ed.gov/about/offices/list/ocr/letters/colleague-20080917.html#skipnav2.

One of the factors used to determine gender equity under Title IX is the scheduling of games and practices. In 2012, a federal appellate court ruled that a lawsuit claiming Title IX and equal protection violations could go to trial.

A high school athlete's parents sued the school district, claiming that a larger percentage of girls' basketball games than boys' basketball games were scheduled on weeknights, leading to "disproportionate academic burdens resulting from a larger number of weeknight games, reduced school and community support, and psychological harms based on a feeling of inferiority" (*Parker v. Franklin County Community School Corporation*, 667 F.3d 910 (7th Cir. 2012)).

In addition to litigating the allocation of resources to men's and women's teams, individual athletes have occasionally used Title IX to gain a position on a varsity team. For example, in *Mercer v. Duke University*, 32 F. Supp. 2d 836 (M.D.N.C. 1998), *reversed*, 190 F.3d 643 (4th Cir. 1999), a student claimed that Duke University violated Title IX by excluding her from the university's intercollegiate football team. The student had been an all-state place kicker while in high school in New York State. During the first year of college, she sought to join the football team as a walk-on. Although she attended tryouts and practiced with the team for two seasons, the head coach ultimately excluded her from the team. The plaintiff alleged in the lawsuit that the university treated her differently from male walk-on place kickers of lesser ability and failed to give her full and fair consideration for team membership because of her gender. The district court held that, even if the student's allegations were true, the university would nevertheless prevail. Relying on the "contact sport" exception in applicable Title IX regulations prohibiting different treatment in athletics based on gender (34 C.F.R. § 106.41), the court granted the university's motion to dismiss.

On appeal, the U.S. Court of Appeals read the applicable regulation differently from the district court and reinstated the case for further proceedings. The appellate court determined that, contrary to providing a "blanket exemption for contact sports," subsection (b) of the regulation (34 C.F.R. § 106.41(b)) merely "excepts contact sports from the tryout requirement," that is, the requirement that members of the excluded sex be allowed to try out for a single-sex team. But "once an institution has allowed a member of one sex to try out for a team operated . . . for the other sex in a contact sport," the institution is subject to "the general anti-discrimination provision" in subsection (a) of the applicable regulation (34 C.F.R. § 106.41(a)). The appellate court therefore held that once a university has allowed tryouts, it is "subject to Title IX and therefore prohibited from discriminating against [the person trying out] on the basis of his or her sex" (190 F.3d at 647–648).

The Title IX controversy about dropping and adding men's and women's teams has extended to the area of athletic scholarships. The pertinent regulation is 34 C.F.R. § 106.37(c), as interpreted in 44 Fed. Reg. 71413, 71415–23. This regulation, somewhat like the regulation at issue in *Cohen* (34 C.F.R. § 106.41(c)), uses a proportionality test to determine whether benefits are equitably distributed between men and women. In 1998, the U.S. Department of Education's Office for Civil Rights issued a clarification of its requirements for scholarships. And litigation by male athletes whose teams (and scholarships) have been cut in order to comply with Title IX has been unavailing. (See, for example, *Harper v. Board of Regents, Illinois State University*, 35 F. Supp.

2d 1118 (C.D. Ill. 1999), *affirmed, Boulahanis et al. v. Board of Regents,* 198 F.3d 633 (7th Cir. 1999), in which the court awarded summary judgment to the university on the ground that elimination of men's teams and scholarships was not discriminatory; Title IX compliance was a legitimate nondiscriminatory reason for the action.)

As discussed in Section 8.5 of this book, students sexually harassed by faculty may file OCR complaints or lawsuits under Title IX. Some have claimed such harassment by coaches. In *Jennings v. University of North Carolina at Chapel Hill, et al.,* 482 F.3d 686 (4th Cir. 2007) (*en banc*), the trial court had granted the university's motion for summary judgment and an appellate panel had affirmed. The full appellate court agreed to consider the student's claim. She alleged that the soccer coach had engaged in sexually charged talk and touching with members of the women's soccer team and had created a hostile environment for her and other team members. She claimed that the coach asked the team members about their sexual activity, commented on their body parts, touched some of them inappropriately, and discussed his sexual fantasies, some of which included those students. She also claimed that she reported the alleged harassment to the university counsel and accused the counsel of not responding appropriately to her complaint.

In determining whether the plaintiff had demonstrated that sexual harassment had occurred so that the university could be found liable, the *en banc* court stated that the plaintiff had to establish four elements:

(1) she was a student at an educational institution receiving federal funds,
(2) she was subjected to harassment based on her sex, (3) the harassment was sufficiently severe or pervasive to create a hostile (or abusive) environment in an educational program or activity, and (4) there is a basis for imputing liability to the institution [482 F.3d at 695].

Because the university received federal funds, the first element was easily met. With respect to the second element, although the university argued that the coach's comments were teasing and joking, and were not severe enough to constitute harassment, the court ruled that his comments were "degrading and humiliating to his players because they were women" and constituted sexual harassment. In evaluating whether the plaintiff could meet the third element, the court examined the reasoning of cases involving sexual harassment claims brought under Title VII, and concluded that the frequency of the sexual remarks, the coach's power over the plaintiff and other members as their coach, and the age difference between the coach (who was forty-four) and the players (some as young as seventeen) meant that a jury could find that the coach's conduct was sufficiently severe and pervasive to create a hostile environment. And the court ruled that the plaintiff's evidence of emotional distress and poor academic achievement were sufficient to allow a jury to conclude that she had been denied access to educational opportunities or benefits.

The court then turned to the fourth element—examining whether there was a basis for imputing liability to the institution. The court used the two-part test created by the U.S. Supreme Court in *Gebser v. Lago Vista Independent School District* (discussed in Section 8.5): that an official had actual knowledge of the alleged harassment and that the institution either failed to respond or responded with deliberate indifference to the student's complaint. The court discussed the plaintiff's allegation that she had met with the university counsel and given her examples of the coach's behavior and statements, and that the counsel had told the student to work it out with the coach and had taken no action. The court ruled that this evidence could establish both actual notice to the university and "deliberate indifference" to the allegations.

Title IX or state civil rights laws may also be used by student athletes to challenge alleged harassment or discrimination on the basis of their sexual orientation or their transgender status. For a discussion of issues related to gender and sexuality in relation to college athletics, see the resources listed in the Bibliography.

### 10.4.7. Discrimination on the basis of disability.
Both Section 504 of the Rehabilitation Act of 1973 and the Americans with Disabilities Act (ADA) prohibit colleges from discriminating against students, including student athletes, with disabilities. Section 504's requirements are discussed in Section 11.5.4 of this book, and the ADA is discussed in Section 8.4.1.

Under Section 504 and its implementing regulations, institutions must afford disabled students an equal opportunity to participate in physical education, athletic, and recreational programs. Like Title IX, Section 504 applies to athletic activities even if they are not directly subsidized by federal funds. The Department of Education's regulations set forth the basic requirements at 34 C.F.R. § 104.47(a), requiring institutions to offer physical education courses and athletic activities on a nondiscriminatory basis to disabled students.

Under these regulations, a student in a wheelchair could be eligible to participate in a regular archery program, for instance, or a deaf student on a regular wrestling team (34 C.F.R. Part 104, Appendix A), because these students would retain full capacity to play those sports despite their disabilities. In these and other situations, however, questions may arise concerning whether a student's skill level would qualify the student to participate in a program or allow the student to succeed in the competition required for selection to intercollegiate teams.

Litigation involving challenges under Section 504 by disabled athletes has been infrequent, although there are several cases involving student challenges to NCAA eligibility rulings. In an early case, *Wright v. Columbia University*, 520 F. Supp. 789 (E.D. Pa. 1981), the court relied on Section 504 to protect a disabled student's right to participate in intercollegiate football. The student had been blind in one eye since infancy; because of the potential danger to his "good" eye, the institution had denied him permission to participate. In issuing a temporary restraining order against the university, the court accepted (pending trial) the student's argument that the institution's decision was discriminatory within the meaning of Section 504 because the student was qualified to play football despite his disability and was capable of making his own decisions about "his health and well-being."

But another federal trial court sided with the university in its determination that participation by a student was potentially dangerous. In *Pahulu v. University of Kansas*, 897 F. Supp. 1387 (D. Kan. 1995), the plaintiff was a football player who had sustained a blow to the head during a scrimmage and consequently experienced tingling and numbness in his arms and legs. After the team physician and a consulting neurosurgeon diagnosed the symptoms as transient quadriplegia caused by a congenitally narrow cervical cord, they recommended that the student be disqualified from play for his senior year— even though he obtained the opinions of three other specialists who concluded he was fit to play. The student then sought a preliminary injunction, claiming that the university's decision violated Section 504. The court disagreed, holding that the plaintiff (1) was not disabled within the meaning of Section 504 and (2) was not "otherwise qualified" to play football even if he was disabled. As to the first holding, the court reasoned that the plaintiff's physical impairment did not "substantially limit" the "major life activity" of learning, since he still retained his athletic scholarship, continued to have the same access to educational opportunities and academic resources, and could participate in the football program in some other capacity. As to the second holding, the court reasoned that the plaintiff did not meet the "technical standards" of the football program because he had failed to obtain medical clearance and that the university's position was reasonable and rational, albeit conservative.

*Knapp v. Northwestern University*, 101 F.3d 473 (7th Cir. 1996), used reasoning similar to—but more fully developed than—that in *Pahulu* to deny relief to a basketball player who had been declared ineligible due to a heart problem. Applying the Section 504 definition of disability, the court ruled that (1) playing intercollegiate basketball was not itself a "major life activit[y]," nor was it an integral part of "learning," which the Section 504 regulations do acknowledge to be a major life activity; (2) the plaintiff's heart problem only precluded him from performing "a particular function" and did not otherwise "substantially limit" his major life activity of learning at the university; and (3) consequently, the plaintiff was not disabled within the meaning of Section 504 and could not claim its protections. The court also ruled that the plaintiff could not claim Section 504 protection because he was not "otherwise qualified," since he could not meet the physical standards. In reaching this conclusion, the court deferred to the university's judgment regarding the substantiality of risk and the severity of harm to the plaintiff, stating that, as long as the university and its medical advisors used reasonable criteria to make the decisions, the court should not second-guess those judgments.

A student who lost his scholarship and was dismissed from the golf team could not demonstrate that his psychiatric disorder "substantially interfered" with participating on the team. In *Costello v. University of North Carolina at Greensboro*, 2006 U.S. Dist. LEXIS 90519 (M.D.N.C. December 14, 2006), the student missed several practices and other required activities because he had scheduled appointments with his therapist. He was dismissed for violating team rules and missing too many practices. Although the student claimed that the nonrenewal of his scholarship was the result of discrimination, and that the coach and athletic administrators regarded him as disabled, the court disagreed. Noting that playing golf was not a "major life activity," the court ruled that it was the student's scheduling problems, not his disorder, that was the reason for the loss of his scholarship, and awarded summary judgment to the university.

In addition to Section 504, the Americans with Disabilities Act (see Section 8.4.1) may also provide protections for student athletes subjected to discrimination on the basis of a disability in institutional athletic programs. Title II of the act (public services) (42 U.S.C. §§ 12131–34) would apply to students in public institutions, and Title III (public accommodations) (42 U.S.C. §§ 12181–89) would apply to students in private institutions.

In addition to the right of disabled students to participate in a particular sport, an emerging issue concerns whether academic eligibility requirements for student athletes may discriminate against learning-disabled athletes. The cases thus far have arisen primarily under the Americans with Disabilities Act rather than under Section 504. Although these cases have focused on eligibility requirements of the NCAA (especially the "core course requirement") rather than separate requirements of individual institutions, many of the same legal issues would arise if a learning-disabled athlete were to challenge his or her school's own eligibility requirements or were to challenge the school for following NCAA requirements. These issues would include whether the learning disability is a "disability" within the meaning of the ADA; whether the institution's academic eligibility requirements are discriminatory because, for instance, they "screen out or tend to screen out" learning-disabled students under Title III of the ADA, section 12182(b)(2)(A)(i); whether the student's requested modifications to the eligibility requirements are "reasonable" or, to the contrary, would fundamentally alter the intercollegiate athletic program or the institution's academic mission as it interfaces with athletics; and whether the institution has conducted a suitable individualized assessment of the student's need for modifications.

**10.4.8. Drug testing.** Drug testing of athletes has become a focus of controversy in both amateur and professional sports. Intercollegiate athletics is no exception. Legal issues may arise under the federal Constitution's Fourth Amendment search and seizure clause and its Fourteenth Amendment due process clause; under search and seizure, due process, or right-to-privacy clauses of state constitutions; under various state civil rights statutes; under state tort law (see generally Section 3.2.2); or under an institution's own regulations, including statements of students' rights. Public institutions may be subject to challenges based on any of these sources; private institutions generally are subject only to challenges based on tort law, their own regulations, civil rights statutes applicable to private action, and (in some states) state constitutional provisions limiting private as well as public action (see generally Section 1.5).

For public institutions, the primary concern is the Fourth Amendment of the federal Constitution, which protects individuals against unreasonable searches and seizures, and parallel state constitutional provisions that may provide similar (and sometimes greater) protections. In *Skinner v. Railway Labor Executives Association*, 489 U.S. 602, 619 (1989), the U.S. Supreme Court held that the collection of urine or blood for drug testing constitutes a search within the meaning of the Fourth Amendment and that the validity of such a search is determined by balancing the legitimacy of the government's interest against the degree of intrusion upon the individual's privacy interest.

Drug testing policies may provide for testing if there is a reasonable suspicion that a student either may have used drugs recently or may be currently impaired; or such policies may provide for random testing, so that a reasonable suspicion of drug use is not an issue. The courts have examined both types of policies. Although policies that require a reasonable suspicion are more likely to be upheld than those involving random testing, the former are still subject to the standards set forth in *Skinner*. And policies that require either random testing or testing of all students may run afoul of the Fourth Amendment. See, for example, Jim Salter, "ACLU Files Suit over Linn State Technical College's Drug Testing" (September 15, 2011), available at http://www.huffingtonpost.com/2011/09/15/aclu-files-suit-over-linn_n_963848.html.

*Derdeyn v. University of Colorado*, 832 P.2d 1031 (Colo. App. 1991), *affirmed*, 863 P.2d 929 (Colo. 1993), provides an example of a university drug testing program held to be unreasonable under the *Skinner* standard. The university initiated a program for testing its student athletes when it had a "reasonable suspicion" that they were using drugs. As a condition to participation in intercollegiate athletics, all athletes were asked to sign a form consenting to such tests. The university initiated the program "because of a desire to prepare its athletes for drug testing in NCAA sanctioned sporting events, a concern for athletes' health, an interest in promoting its image, and a desire to ensure fair competition" (832 P.2d at 1032). In a class action suit, student athletes challenged this program on several grounds. The Supreme Court of Colorado held that the program violated both the federal Constitution's Fourth Amendment and a similar provision of the Colorado constitution. Applying the *Skinner* test, the court determined that the drug testing program was unconstitutional. In addition, the court held that the university's consent form was not sufficient to waive the athletes' constitutional rights. The university bore the burden of proof in showing that the waiver was signed voluntarily. Relying on the trial testimony of several athletes, which "revealed that, because of economic or other commitments the students had made to the University, [the students] were not faced with an unfettered choice in regard to signing the consent" (832 P.2d at 1035), the Colorado Supreme Court invalidated the university's program and prohibited its continuation.

The U.S. Supreme Court addressed the lawfulness of testing student athletes in K–12 settings twice since its *Skinner* ruling, and in both cases the Court upheld the testing program. *Vernonia School District 47J v. Acton*, 515 U.S. 646 (1995), involved a constitutional challenge to a public school district's random drug testing of student athletes. Seventh-grader James Acton and his parents sued the school district after James had been barred from the school football team because he and his parents refused to sign a form consenting to random urinalysis drug testing. In an attempt to control a "sharp increase" in drug use among students, the district had implemented a policy requiring that all student athletes be tested at the beginning of each season for their sport, and that thereafter 10 percent of the athletes be chosen at random for testing each week of the season. In a 6-to-3 decision, the U.S. Supreme Court reversed the U.S. Court of Appeals for the Ninth Circuit (23 F. 3d 1514 (9th Cir. 1994)) and upheld the policy.

The majority opinion by Justice Scalia relied on *Skinner v. Railway Labor Executives Association* to conclude that the collection of urine samples from students is a search that must be analyzed under the reasonableness test. The majority then examined three factors to determine the reasonableness of the search: (1) "the nature of the privacy interest upon which the search . . . intrudes"; (2) "the character of the intrusion that is complained of"; and (3) "the nature and immediacy of the governmental concern at issue . . ., and the efficacy of [the drug test in] meeting it." Regarding the first factor, the Court emphasized that "particularly with regard to medical examinations and procedures," student athletes have even less of an expectation of privacy than students in general due to the "communal" nature of locker rooms and the additional regulations to which student athletes are subject on matters such as preseason physicals, insurance coverage, and training rules.

Regarding the second factor, the Court stated that urinalysis drug testing is not a significant invasion of the student's privacy because the process for collecting urine samples is "nearly identical to those [conditions] typically encountered in restrooms"; the information revealed by the urinalysis (what drugs, if any, are present in the student's urine) is negligible; the test results are confidential and available only to specific personnel; and the results are not turned over to law enforcement officials. And regarding the third factor, the Court determined that the school district had an "important, indeed perhaps compelling," interest in deterring schoolchildren from drug use as well as a more particular interest in protecting athletes from physical harm that could result from competing in events under the influence of drugs; that there was evidence of a crisis of disciplinary actions and "rebellion . . . being fueled by alcohol and drug abuse," which underscored the immediacy of the district's concerns; and that the drug testing policy "effectively addressed" these concerns. The plaintiffs had argued that the district could fulfill its interests by testing when it had reason to suspect a particular athlete of drug use and that this would be a less intrusive means of effectuating the district's interests. The Court rejected this proposal, explaining that it could be abused by teachers singling out misbehaving students, and it would stimulate litigation challenging such testing.

Although *Vernonia* is an elementary/secondary school case, its reasonableness test and the three factors for applying it will also likely guide analysis of Fourth Amendment challenges to drug testing of student athletes at colleges and universities. Some of the considerations relevant to application of the three factors would differ for higher education, however, so it is unclear whether the balance would tip in favor of drug testing plans, as it did in *Vernonia*. The

Court itself took pains to limit its holding to public elementary/secondary education, warning that its analysis might not "pass constitutional muster in other contexts." (On remand in *Vernonia*, the Ninth Circuit ruled on the merits that the defendant's drug testing program did not violate the Fourth Amendment or the Oregon constitution (66 F.3d 217 (9th Cir. 1995)).)

The Supreme Court issued another ruling in 2002, this time upholding a random drug testing policy that covered any student who participated in extracurricular school activities, whether or not the activities involved athletics. In *Board of Education of Independent School District No. 92 v. Earls*, 536 U.S. 822 (2002), a 5-to-4 decision with a vigorous dissent, the Court, following the three-part test it had established in *Vernonia*, found the random drug testing policy reasonable. First, said the Court, the students had a limited expectation of privacy, even though most nonathletic activities did not involve disrobing or regular physical examinations. The limited expectation of privacy, according to the Court, did not depend upon communal undress, but on the custodial responsibilities of the school for the children in its care. Second, the Court found the invasion of the students' privacy to be minimally intrusive and virtually identical to that found lawful in *Vernonia*. And third, the Court found that the policy had a close relationship to the school district's interest in protecting the students' health and safety. There was evidence of some drug use by students who participated in extracurricular activities, although the Court stated that "a demonstrated problem of drug abuse . . . is not always necessary to the validity of a testing regime" (536 U.S. at 835). The dissenting justices found the school district's testing program to be unreasonable because it targeted students "least likely to be at risk from illicit drugs and their damaging effects" (536 U.S. at 843).

Although most of the litigation involving drug testing policies has involved federal constitutional claims, two cases decided prior to the Supreme Court's *Vernonia* opinion illustrate that state constitutions or civil rights laws provide avenues to challenge these policies. In *Hill v. NCAA*, 273 Cal. Rptr. 402 (Cal. Ct. App. 1990), *reversed*, 865 P.2d 633 (Cal. 1994), Stanford University student athletes challenged the university's implementation of the NCAA's required drug testing program. The constitutional clause at issue was not a search and seizure clause as such but rather a right-to-privacy guarantee (Cal. Const. art. I, § 1). Both the intermediate appellate court and the Supreme Court of California determined that this guarantee covered drug testing, an activity designed to gather and preserve private information about individuals. Further, both courts determined that the privacy clause limited the information-gathering activities of private as well as public entities, since the language revealed that privacy was an "inalienable right" that no one may violate. Although the private entity designated as the defendant in the *Hill* case was an athletic conference (the NCAA) rather than a private university, the courts' reasoning would apply to the latter as well.

In *Hill*, the intermediate appellate court's privacy analysis differed from the Fourth Amendment balancing test of *Skinner* because the court required the NCAA "to show a compelling interest before it can invade a fundamental privacy right"—a test that places a heavier burden of justification on the alleged violator than does the Fourth Amendment balancing test. The Supreme Court of California disagreed on this point, holding that the correct approach "requires that privacy interests be specifically identified and carefully compared with competing or countervailing privacy and nonprivacy interests in a 'balancing test'" (865 P.2d at 655). Under this approach, "[i]nvasion of a privacy interest is not a violation of the state constitutional right to privacy if the invasion is justified by a legitimate and important competing interest" (865 P.2d at 655–56), rather than a compelling interest, as the lower court had specified. Using this balancing test, the California Supreme Court concluded that "the NCAA's decision to enforce a ban on the use of drugs by means of a drug testing program is reasonably calculated to further its legitimate interest in maintaining the integrity of intercollegiate athletic competition" and therefore did not violate the California constitution's privacy guarantee (865 P.2d at 669).

In addition to its illustration of state privacy concepts, the *Hill* case also demonstrates the precarious position of institutions that are subject to NCAA or conference drug testing requirements. As the intermediate appellate court indicated, Stanford, the institution that the *Hill* plaintiffs attended, was in a dilemma: "as an NCAA member institution, if it refused to enforce the consent provision, it could be sanctioned, but if it did enforce the program, either by requiring students to sign or withholding them from competition, it could be sued." To help resolve the dilemma, Stanford intervened in the litigation and sought its own declaratory and injunctive relief. These are the same issues and choices that other institutions will continue to face until the various legal issues concerning drug testing have finally been resolved.

In *Bally v. Northeastern University*, 532 N.E.2d 49 (Mass. 1989), a state civil rights law provided the basis for a challenge to a private institution's drug testing program. The defendant, Northeastern University, required all students participating in intercollegiate athletics to sign an NCAA student athlete statement that includes a drug testing consent form. The institution's program called for testing of each athlete once a year as well as other random testing throughout the school year. When a member of the cross-country and track teams refused to sign the consent form, the institution declared him ineligible. The student claimed that this action breached his contract with the institution and violated his rights under both the Massachusetts Civil Rights Act and a state right-to-privacy statute. A lower court granted summary judgment for the university on the contract claim and for the student on the civil rights and privacy claims.

The Massachusetts Supreme Court reversed the lower court's judgment for the student. To prevail on the civil rights claim, according to the statute, the student had to prove that the institution had interfered with rights secured by the Constitution or laws of the United States or the Commonwealth of Massachusetts and that such interference was by "threats, intimidation, or coercion." Although the court assumed *arguendo* that the drug testing program interfered with the student's rights to be free from unreasonable searches and seizures and from invasions of reasonable expectations of privacy, the court nevertheless denied his claim because he had made no showing of "threats, intimidation, or coercion." Similarly, the court denied the student's claim under the privacy statute because "[t]he majority of our opinions involving a claim of an invasion of privacy concern the public dissemination of information," and the student had made no showing of any public dissemination of the drug testing results. In addition, because the student was not an employee, state case law precedents regarding employee privacy, on which the student had relied, did not apply.

Given the outcomes in *Vernonia* and *Earls*, students challenging random or for-cause drug testing policies in K–12 school districts have sought relief under state constitutions rather than the Fourth Amendment. The results have been mixed. For example, although the New Jersey Supreme Court upheld, under the state constitution, a random drug and alcohol testing program that covered all students participating in extracurricular activities in *Joye v. Hunterdon Central Regional High School Board of Education*, 826 A.2d 624 (N.J. 2003), the Pennsylvania Supreme Court struck down a similar policy. In *Theodore v. Delaware Valley School District*, 836 A.2d 76 (Pa. 2003), the state's high court pointed out that the state constitution's privacy protections went beyond those of the U.S. Constitution's Fourth Amendment. While the challenged random drug and alcohol screening policy of the Pennsylvania school district might have been permissible under the Fourth Amendment, said the court, the school district had not provided evidence of a drug problem at the high school sufficient to outweigh the students' privacy rights under the Pennsylvania constitution. The court also rejected the school district's explanation that the policy had been extended to the plaintiffs, honor students whose extracurricular activities were only academic, because they were "role models" for other students, stating that this rationale did not justify the invasion of their privacy.

As this book went to press, a federal trial court granted a preliminary injunction sought by students at Linn State Technical College, a public two-year college in Missouri offering programs in mechanical, electrical, civil, and computer engineering. In *Barrett v. Claycomb*, 2013 WL 1397822 (W.D. Mo. March 22, 2013), the students objected to an institution-wide requirement that all students submit to urine testing as a condition of admission. Although the college insisted that drug testing was required because many students were enrolled in programs in which they used mechanical equipment (such as a welding course), the court rejected that defense, ruling that the students had a "fair chance" of prevailing on the merits. The court noted that many students were enrolled in courses that involved no safety risk at all and that the potential risk of harm was insufficient to outweigh the students' Fourth Amendment interests.

Since the courts have not spoken definitively with respect to higher education, it is not clear what drug testing programs and procedures will be valid. In the meantime, institutions (and athletic conferences) that wish to engage in drug testing of student athletes may follow these minimum suggestions, which are likely to enhance their program's capacity to survive challenge under the various sources of law listed at the beginning of this section:

1. Articulate and document both the strong institutional interests that would be compromised by student athletes' drug use and the institution's basis for believing that such drug use is occurring in one or more of its athletic programs.

2. Limit drug testing to those athletic programs where drug use is occurring and is interfering with institutional interests.

3. Develop evenhanded and objective criteria for determining who will be tested and in what circumstances.

4. Specify the substances whose use is banned and for which athletes will be tested, limiting the named substances to those whose use would compromise important institutional interests.

5. Develop detailed and specific protocols for testing of individuals and lab analysis of specimens, limiting the monitoring of specimen collection to that which is necessary to ensure the integrity of the collection process, and limiting the lab analyses to those necessary to detect the banned substances (rather than to discover other personal information about the athlete).

6. Develop procedures for protecting the confidentiality and accuracy of the testing process and the laboratory results.

7. Embody all the considerations listed here into a clear written policy that is made available to student athletes before they accept athletic scholarships or join a team.

**10.4.9. Tort liability for athletic injuries.** Tort law (see Sections 3.2 and 4.4.2) poses special problems for athletic programs and departments. Because of the physical nature of athletics and because athletic activities often require travel to other locations, the danger of injury to students and the possibilities for institutional liability are greater than those resulting from other institutional functions. In *Scott v. State*, 158 N.Y.S.2d 617 (N.Y. Ct. Cl. 1956), for instance, a student collided with a flagpole while chasing a fly ball during an intercollegiate baseball game; the student was awarded $12,000 in damages because the school had negligently maintained the playing field in a dangerous condition and the student had not assumed the risk of such danger. But an experienced baseball player injured when hit by a ball was judged to have assumed the risk of injury (*Bukowski v. Clarkson University*, 2012 N.Y. LEXIS 1283 (N.Y. June 5, 2012)).

Although most of the litigation involving injuries to student athletes has involved injuries sustained during either practice or competition, students have also attempted to hold their institution responsible for injuries resulting from assaults by students or fans from competing teams, or from hazing activities. Although students have not been uniformly successful in these lawsuits, the courts appear to be growing more sympathetic to their claims.

In considering whether student athletes may hold their institutions liable for injuries sustained in practice, competition, or hazing, courts have addressed whether the institution has a duty to protect the student from the type of harm that was encountered. The specific harm that occurred must have been reasonably foreseeable to the institution in order for a duty to arise. On the other hand, institutions have argued that the athlete assumes the risk of injury because sports, particularly contact sports, involve occasional injuries that are not unusual. The courts have traced a path between these two concepts.

One area of litigation focuses on whether a university can be held liable for its failure to prepare adequately for emergency medical situations. In *Kleinknecht v. Gettysburg College*, 989 F.2d 1360 (3d Cir. 1993), parents of a student athlete sued the college for the wrongful death of their son, who had died from a heart attack suffered during a practice session of the intercollegiate lacrosse team. The student had no medical history that would indicate any danger of such an occurrence. No trainers were present when he was stricken, and no plan prescribing steps to take in medical emergencies was in effect. Students and coaches reacted as quickly as they could to reach the nearest phone, more than two hundred yards away, and call an ambulance. The parents sued the college for negligence (see generally Section 3.2.2), alleging that the college owed a duty to its student athletes to have measures in place to provide prompt medical attention in emergencies. They contended that the delay in securing an ambulance, caused by the college's failure to have an emergency plan in effect, resulted in their son's death. The federal district court, applying Pennsylvania law, granted summary judgment for the college, holding that the college owed no duty to the plaintiffs' son in the circumstances of this case and that, even if a duty were owed, the actions of the college's employees were reasonable and did not breach the duty.

The appellate court reversed the district court's judgment and remanded the case for a jury trial, ruling that a special relationship existed between the student and the college because he was participating in a scheduled athletic practice supervised by college employees. Thus, the college had a duty of reasonable care. The court then delineated the specific demands that that duty placed on the college in the circumstances of this case. Since it was generally foreseeable that a life-threatening injury could occur during sports activities such as lacrosse, and given the magnitude of such a risk and its consequences, "the College owed a duty to Drew to have measures in place at the lacrosse team's practice . . . to provide prompt treatment in the event that he or any other members of the lacrosse team suffered a life-threatening injury." However, "the determination whether the College has breached this duty at all is a question of fact for the jury" (989 F.2d at 1370, 1372).

Similarly, a North Carolina appellate court found that a special relationship might have existed between the University of North Carolina and members of its junior varsity cheerleading squad sufficient to hold the university liable for negligence when a cheerleader was injured during practice. In *Davidson v. University of North Carolina at Chapel Hill*, 543 S.E.2d 920 (N.C. Ct. App. 2001), a cheerleader was injured while practicing a stunt without mats or other safety equipment. The university did not provide a coach for the junior varsity squad and had provided no safety training for the students. It provided uniforms, transportation to away games, and access to university facilities and equipment. Although certain university administrators had expressed reservations about the safety of some of the cheerleaders' stunts, including the pyramid stunt in which the plaintiff was injured, no action had been taken to supervise the junior varsity squad or to limit its discretion in selecting stunts.

The appellate court ruled that the degree of control that the university exercised over the cheerleading squad created a special relationship that, in turn, created a duty of care on the part of the university. Relying on *Kleinknecht*, the court limited its ruling to the facts of the case, refusing to create a broader duty of care that would extend to the general activities of college students.

Student athletes seeking remedies for injuries sustained during practice or games face challenges if their institution is public and their employees are protected by sovereign immunity. In *Sellers v. Rudert*, 918 N.E. 2d 586 (Ill. App. Ct. 2009), for example, a student athlete injured during a football game attempted to sue his coaches and athletic trainers for negligence. Although the court ruled that the coaches were protected by sovereign immunity, it rejected that defense for the athletic trainers, explaining that a state law, the Athletic Trainers Practice Act (225 Ill. Comp. Stat. 5/3 (2008)), established a standard of care for trainers that was independent of their responsibilities as employees of the state.

Coaches and other athletics staff at private institutions are not protected by sovereign immunity and may face negligence claims if a student athlete is injured. For example, in *Zides v. Quinnipiac University*, 2006 Conn. Super. LEXIS 473 (Conn. Super. Ct. February 7, 2006), a baseball player suffered a head injury because a screen intended to protect him from a pitched ball was defective. The student and his parents sued the assistant coach, the athletics director, the university, and its president. The court dismissed the claims against the president and the athletics director, but let the allegations against the assistant coach and the university stand so that it could be determined whether the assistant coach was aware that the screen was not maintained properly. The court also rejected the university's claim that a release signed by the student protected it from liability for any negligence that its employees might have committed.

Even when an institution does or may owe a duty to a student athlete in a particular case, the student athlete will have no cause of action against the institution if its breach of duty was not the cause of the harm suffered. In *Hanson v. Kynast*, 494 N.E.2d 1091 (Ohio 1986), for example, the court avoided the issue of whether the defendant university owed a duty to a student athlete to provide for a proper emergency plan, because the delay in treating the athlete, allegedly caused by the university's negligent failure to have such a plan, caused the athlete no further harm. The athlete had suffered a broken neck in a lacrosse game and was rendered a quadriplegic; the evidence made it clear that, even if medical help had arrived sooner, nothing could have been done to lessen the injuries. In other words, the full extent of these injuries had occurred before any alleged negligence by the university could have come into play. For a similar result in a case concerning a student athlete's death, see *Ashburn v. Bowling Green State University*, 2011 Ohio App. LEXIS 1297 (Ohio Ct. App. March 29, 2011).

As the *Kleinknecht* court's reasoning suggests, the scope of an institution's duty to protect student athletes in emergencies and otherwise may depend on a number of factors, including whether the activity is intercollegiate (versus a club team) or an extracurricular activity, whether the particular activity was officially scheduled or sponsored, and perhaps whether the athlete was recruited or not. The institution's duty will also differ if the student athlete is a member of a visiting team rather than the institution's own team. In general, there is no special relationship such as that in *Kleinknecht* between the institution and a visiting athlete; there is only the relationship arising from the visiting student's status as an invitee of the institution (see generally Section 3.2.2.2). In *Fox v. Board of Supervisors of Louisiana State University and Agricultural and Mechanical College*, 576 So. 2d 978 (La. 1991), for example, a visiting rugby player from St. Olaf's club team was severely injured when he missed a tackle during a tournament held at Louisiana State University (LSU). The court determined that the injured player had no cause of action against LSU based on the institution's own actions or omissions. The only possible direct liability claim he could have had would have been based on a theory that the playing field onto which he had been invited was unsafe for play, a contention completely unsupported by the evidence.

In addition to the institution's liability for its own negligent acts, there are also issues concerning the institution's possible vicarious liability for the acts of its student athletes or its athletic clubs. In the *Fox* case above, the visiting athlete also claimed that the university was vicariously liable for negligent actions of its rugby club in holding a cocktail party the night before the tournament, in scheduling teams to play more than one game per day (the athlete was injured in his second match of the day), and in failing to ensure that visiting clubs were properly trained and coached. His theory was that these actions had resulted in fatigued athletes playing when they should not have, thus becoming more susceptible to injury. The appellate court held that LSU could not be vicariously liable for the actions of its rugby club. Although LSU provided its rugby team with some offices, finances, and supervision, as well as a playing field for the tournament, LSU offered such support to its rugby club (and other student clubs) only to enrich students' overall educational experience by providing increased opportunities for personal growth. The university did not recruit students for the club, and the university did not control the club's activities. The club therefore was not an agent of the university and could not bind LSU by its actions.

In *Regan v. State*, 654 N.Y.S.2d 488 (N.Y. App. Div. 1997), the court addressed whether a student at a state college who suffered a broken neck while playing rugby and was rendered a quadriplegic had assumed the risk of such injury and was therefore barred from recovery against the state. The student had played and practiced with the college's rugby club for three years at the time of the incident. During those three years, the student had regularly practiced with student coaches on the same field where the injury occurred and had witnessed prior rugby injuries. Relying on these factors, the court affirmed summary judgment in favor of the state, finding unpersuasive the plaintiff's contention that he was unaware of the inherent risk in playing rugby. See also *Bukowski v. Clarkson University*, 928 N.Y.S. 2d 369 (N.Y. App. Div. 2011), in which the court affirmed the dismissal of a negligence claim brought by a baseball player hit by a baseball during practice. The court ruled that the student, a pitcher, was aware of the risks and additional protective equipment was not "standard" in the sport.

In *Sicard v. University of Dayton*, 660 N.E.2d 1241, 1244 (Ohio Ct. App. 1995), the court noted that a player assumes the ordinary risks of playing a contact sport but does not assume the risk of injuries that occur when rules are violated. Because of these assumed risks, according to the court in *Sicard*, injured athletes suing in tort must make a stronger showing of misconduct than persons injured in nonathletic contexts. The defendant's misconduct must amount to more than ordinary negligence and must rise to the level of "intentional" or "reckless" wrongdoing.

Using these principles, the court in *Sicard* reversed the trial court's summary judgment for the defendants—the university and an employee who was a "spotter" in the weight room and allegedly failed to perform this function for the athlete, which could have prevented his injury. The court remanded the case for trial because "[a] reasonable mind could . . . conclude that . . . [the spotter's] acts and omissions were reckless because they created an unreasonable risk of physical harm to Sicard, one substantially greater than that necessary to make his conduct merely negligent" (660 N.E.2d at 1244).

The same conclusion was reached in *Hanson v. Kynast* (cited earlier in this section), which concerned a university's vicarious liability for a student's actions. During an intercollegiate lacrosse game, Kynast body-checked and taunted a player on the opposing team. When Hanson (another opposing team player) grabbed Kynast, Kynast threw Hanson to the ground, breaking his neck. Hanson sued Kynast and Ashland University, the team for which Kynast was playing when the incident occurred. The court held that Ashland University, which Kynast attended, was not liable for his actions because he received no scholarship, joined the team voluntarily, used his own playing equipment, and was guided but not controlled by the coach. In essence, the court held that Kynast was operating as an individual, voluntarily playing on the team, not as an agent of the university. (See also *Townsend v. State*, 237 Cal. Rptr. 146 (Cal. Ct. App. 1987), in which the court, relying on state statutes, similarly refused to hold a university vicariously liable for a nonscholarship varsity basketball player's assault on another team's player.)

A similar result would also likely obtain when a student is injured in an informal recreational sports activity. In *Swanson v. Wabash College*, 504 N.E.2d 327 (Ind. Ct. App. 1987), for example, a student injured in a recreational basketball game sued the college for negligence. The court ruled that the college had no legal duty to supervise a recreational activity among adult students and that the student who had organized the game was neither an agent nor an employee of the college, so *respondeat superior* liability did not attach.

An Arkansas case warns that institutions may incur tort liability not only due to athletic injuries, but also due to the administration of painkillers and other prescription drugs used for athletic injuries. In *Wallace v. Broyles*, 961 S.W.2d 712 (Ark. 1998), a varsity football player at the University of Arkansas shot and killed himself. His mother sued the university's director of athletics, the head athletic trainer, the football team physician, and various doctors, alleging that, after her son had sustained a severe shoulder injury during a football game, university personnel had supplied him with heavy doses of Darvocet, a "mind-altering drug" with "potentially dangerous side effects." The Darvocet allegedly caused the state of mind that precipitated the football player's suicide. The player's mother claimed that the defendants had been negligent in the way they stored and dispensed prescription drugs and in failing to keep adequate records of inventory or of athletes' use of prescription drugs; and that the athletic department's practices were inconsistent both with federal drug laws and with guidelines that the NCAA had issued to the university.

The Supreme Court of Arkansas reversed the trial court's grant of summary judgment for the defendants and let the case proceed to trial. The court emphasized that "to be negligent, the defendants here need not be shown to have foreseen the particular injury which occurred, but only that they reasonably could be said to have foreseen an appreciable risk of harm to others." On that basis, the court concluded that "the pleadings and evidentiary documents raise a fact issue concerning whether the defendants' acts or omissions were negligence in the circumstances described" (961 S.W.2d at 716).

In contrast to their potential liability for injuries to their student athletes during practice or competition, institutions have been more successful in persuading courts that they should not be liable for assaults on their students by students or fans from visiting teams, or for assaults on visitors by their students. An example of the first category is *Blake v. University of Rochester*, 758 N.Y.S.2d 323 (N.Y. App. Div. 2003), in which a student playing in an intramural basketball game was assaulted by a player on the opposing team. Because no one on either team knew the player who assaulted Blake, Blake argued that the university's security was lax in that it allowed an intruder to gain access to the gymnasium where the game took place. The court rejected Blake's theory as speculative and dismissed the case.

Similarly, a player for a visiting team who was punched by a Boston University basketball player during a game was unable to persuade the Massachusetts Supreme Court to hold the university vicariously liable for his injury. In *Kavanagh v. Trustees of Boston University*, 795 N.E.2d 1170 (Mass. 2003), the court refused to recognize a special relationship between the university and a student from another institution. Furthermore, according to the court, the assault was not foreseeable, and therefore there was no duty to protect the visiting student.

Hazing in college athletics is a common practice that is only recently receiving the type of attention that hazing by members of fraternal organizations has attracted. Hazing of college athletes has attracted some recent litigation, but there have been no published court opinions. Kathleen Peay sued the University of Oklahoma for "physical and mental abuse" resulting from hazing activities required by the soccer team and its coach. The case was settled (see

Joshua A. Sussberg, Note, "Shattered Dreams: Hazing in College Athletics," 24 *Cardozo Law Rev.* 1421 (2003)). The University of Vermont was sued by a student hockey team member, Corey LaTulippe, who was required to endure a hazing ritual at the hands of his teammates. The university settled the lawsuit (see R. Brian Crow & Scott R. Rosner, "Institutional and Organizational Liability for Hazing in Intercollegiate and Professional Team Sports," 76 *St. John's Law Rev.* 87 (2002)). Given the existence of state laws against hazing, and the lack of any rational relationship between hazing that exposes a student to danger and the educational mission of the institution, it is likely that courts will expect institutions to prevent hazing, to make hazing a violation of the student code of conduct, and to hold students who engage in hazing activities strictly accountable for their actions, whether or not they result in physical or mental injury to students.

# PART FIVE

# THE COLLEGE AND THE OUTSIDE WORLD

# The College and Government

*Chapter 11 focuses on the external governance of higher education by local and state governments and the federal government. Consideration is given to governmental authority to regulate, to fund, and to establish and operate colleges and universities, and to how this authority differs from one level of government to another. Regarding local governments, the chapter addresses a variety of regulatory initiatives by local governments, with particular attention to the enforcement of trespass statutes and regulations. Regarding state governments, the chapter addresses both the creation and oversight of public colleges and universities and the chartering and licensing of private colleges and universities. Regarding the federal government, the chapter briefly reviews the broad range of federal regulation of higher education and focuses on one key area of concern: copyright regulations and the "fair use" doctrine; it then reviews the legal structure of federal spending programs and the variety of conditions placed on federal fund recipients and focuses on another key area of concern: the nondiscrimination requirements of the civil rights spending statutes (Title VI, Title IX, and Section 504).*

## Section 11.1. Local Government Regulation

**11.1.1. Overview of local government regulation.** Postsecondary institutions are typically subject to the regulatory authority of one or more local government entities, such as cities, towns, and counties. Some local government regulations, such as fire and safety codes, are relatively uncontroversial. Other regulations or proposed regulations may be highly controversial. Controversies have arisen, for instance, over local governments' attempts to regulate or prohibit genetic experimentation, nuclear weapons research or production, storage of radioactive materials, laboratory experiments using animals, stem cell or cloning research, and bioterrorism research involving biological agents.

Other, more common examples of local government actions whose effects on postsecondary institutions can become controversial include ordinances requiring permits for large-group gatherings at which alcohol will be served, ordinances restricting smoking in the workplace, rent control ordinances, building permit ordinances, ordinances prohibiting discrimination on the basis of sexual orientation, and ordinances requiring the provision of health insurance benefits for domestic partners. (For an example of the latter, see *University of Pittsburgh v. City of Pittsburgh, Commission on Human Relations*, No. G.D. 99-21287 (Pa. Ct. of Common Pleas, Allegheny County, April 20, 2000)).

Local land use regulations and zoning board rulings are also frequently controversial. In addition, local governments' exertion of taxing powers may become controversial either when a postsecondary institution is taxed on the basis of activities it considers educational and charitable or when it is exempted and thus subject to criticism that the institution does not contribute its fair share to the local government's coffers.

In dealing with local government agencies and officials, postsecondary administrators should be aware of the scope of, and limits on, each local government's regulatory and taxing authority. A local government has only the authority delegated to it by state law. When a city or county has been delegated "home rule" powers, its authority will usually be broadly interpreted; otherwise, its authority will usually be narrowly construed. In determining whether a local government's action is within the scope of its authority, the first step is to determine whether the local government's action is within the scope of the authority delegated to it by the state. In addition to construing the terms of the delegation, the court must also determine whether the scope of the particular local government's authority is to be broadly or narrowly construed. If the local government action at issue falls outside the delegation of authority, it will be found to be **ultra vires**—that is, beyond the scope of authority and thus invalid.

In *Lexington-Fayette Urban County Board of Health v. Board of Trustees of the University of Kentucky*, 879 S.W.2d 485 (Ky. 1994), for example, a local board of health had sought to apply local health code regulations to the university's construction of a "spa pool" in a university sports facility. The parties agreed that the board of health had authority to enforce *state* regulations against the university; the issue was whether the state legislature had also delegated authority to the board to enforce *local* regulations. The Supreme Court of Kentucky distinguished between these two levels of regulation:

> We agree, and the University concedes, that the Board of Health is the enforcement agent for the Cabinet for Human Resources and has the authority to inspect and enforce state health laws and state health regulations against the University. However, we do not believe that when the legislature designated the Board of Health as the enforcement agent of the Cabinet for Human Resources that the legislature intended to grant the Board of Health authority to enforce local health laws or enact local regulations against state agencies [879 S.W.2d at 485–86].

In the key part of its reasoning, the court interpreted the terms of the statute delegating authority to the board, using the following rule of construction:

"Statutes in derogation of sovereignty should be strictly construed in favor of the state, so that its sovereignty may be upheld and not narrowed or destroyed, and should not be permitted to divest the state or its government of any of its prerogatives, rights, or remedies, unless the intention of the legislature to effect this object is clearly expressed" [879 S.W.2d at 486, quoting *City of Bowling Green v. T. & E. Electrical Contractors*, 602 S.W.2d 434 (1980)].

Applying this rule, the court held that "the legislature has not made clear its intention to grant authority" and "has [not] granted specific authority" to the board to enforce local health regulations against state agencies. The board's application of such regulations to the university's construction of the spa pool was therefore invalid.

Where a local body is acting within the scope of its state-delegated authority, but the action arguably violates state interests or some other state law, the courts may use other methods to determine whether local or state laws will govern. For instance, courts have held that (1) a local government may not regulate matters that the state has otherwise "preempted" by its own regulation of the field; (2) a local government may not regulate matters that are protected by the state's sovereign immunity; and (3) a local government may not regulate state institutions when such regulations would intrude upon the state's "plenary powers" granted by the state constitution. Usually the state will win such contests.

Although these principles apply to regulation (and sometimes taxation) of both public and private institutions, public institutions are more likely than private institutions to escape a local government's net. For instance, since public institutions are more closely tied to the state and are usually "arms" of the state (see Section 11.2.2), they are more likely in particular cases to have **preemption** defenses. Public institutions may also defend against local regulation by asserting sovereign immunity, a defense not available to private institutions.

When the public institution being regulated is a local community college, however, rather than a state college or university, somewhat different issues may arise. The community college may be considered a local political subdivision (community college district) rather than a state entity, and the question may be whether the community college is subject to the local laws of some other local government whose territory overlaps its own (see, for example, *Stearns v. Mariani*, 741 N.Y.S.2d 357 (N.Y. App. Div. 2002)). Or the community college may be established by a county government (pursuant to state law), and the question may be whether the college is an arm of the county government and whether county law or state law governs the college on some particular matter. *Atlantic Community College v. Civil Service Commission*, 279 A.2d 820 (N.J. 1971), illustrates some of these issues, as do *Appeal of Community College of Delaware County*, 254 A.2d 641 (Pa. 1969) (Section 11.2.2), and *People ex rel. Cooper v. Rancho Santiago College*, 277 Cal. Rptr. 69 (Cal. Ct. App. 1990).

The preemption doctrine governs situations in which the state government's regulatory activities overlap with those of a local government. For example, in the University of Pittsburgh dispute about domestic partner benefits cited earlier in this section, the Pittsburgh City Council enacted an ordinance prohibiting discrimination in employment on the basis of sexual orientation, and the city's Commission on Human Relations agreed to hear a case on whether the ordinance prohibited employers from denying health insurance benefits to same-sex domestic partners. While the case was pending, the state legislature passed a statute exempting state colleges and universities from any municipal ordinance that required employers to provide health care benefits (53 Pa. Stat. Ann. § 2181). The university could then claim (in addition to any other arguments it had) that the new state law preempted the city council's nondiscrimination ordinance.

If a local government ordinance regulates the same kind of activity as a state law (as in the Pittsburgh situation), the institution being regulated may be bound only by the state law (as the University of Pittsburgh claimed). Courts will resolve any apparent overlapping of state law and local ordinances by determining, on a case-by-case basis, whether state law has preempted the field and precluded local regulation.

The state preemption doctrine also has a counterpart in federal law. Under the federal preemption doctrine, courts may sometimes invalidate local government regulations because the federal government has preempted that particular subject of regulation. In *United States v. City of Philadelphia*, 798 F.2d 81 (3d Cir. 1986), for example, the court invalidated an order of Philadelphia's Human Relations Commission that required Temple University's law school to bar military recruiters from its placement facilities because the military discriminated against homosexuals. By statute, Congress had prohibited the expenditure of defense funds at colleges or universities that did not permit military personnel to recruit on campus. The court held that the city commission's order conflicted with the congressional policy embodied in this legislation and was therefore preempted.

The sovereign immunity doctrine holds that a state institution, as an arm of state government, cannot be regulated by a lesser governmental entity that has only the powers delegated to it by the state. In order to claim sovereign immunity, the public institution must be performing state "governmental" functions, not acting in a merely "proprietary" capacity. A sovereign immunity defense was successful in *Board of Regents of Universities and State College v. City of Tempe*, 356 P.2d 399 (Ariz. 1960). The board sought an injunction to prohibit the city from applying its local construction codes to the board. In granting the board's request, the court reasoned:

> The essential point is that the powers, duties, and responsibilities assigned and delegated to a state agency performing a governmental function must be exercised free of control and supervision by a municipality within whose corporate limits the state agency must act . . . The legislature has empowered the Board of Regents to fulfill that responsibility subject only to the supervision of the legislature and the governor . . . A central, unified agency, responsible to State officials rather than to the officials of each municipality in which a university or college is located, is essential to the efficient and orderly

administration of a system of higher education responsive to the needs of all the people of the State [356 P.2d at 406–7].

A similar result was reached in *Inspector of Buildings of Salem v. Salem State College*, 546 N.E.2d 388 (Mass. App. Ct. 1989). The inspector of buildings for a city issued a stop-work order interrupting the construction of six dormitories at the defendant college because they did not adhere to local zoning requirements regarding height and other dimensional criteria. The question for the court was whether the local zoning ordinance could apply to the college, and to the state college building authority, when they were engaged in governmental functions. In answering no to this question, the court noted that generally "the State and State instrumentalities are immune from municipal zoning regulations, unless a statute otherwise expressly provides the contrary." Analyzing the state statute that delegated zoning powers to municipalities, as it applied to state building projects for state educational institutions, the court concluded that the statute's language did not constitute an "express and unmistakable suspension of the usual State supremacy." The court therefore held that the college could continue the project without complying with the local zoning laws. The court noted, however, that the college did not have free rein to construct buildings without regard to air pollution, noise, growth, traffic, and other considerations, since the college still had to comply with state environmental requirements imposed on state instrumentalities.

Under the plenary powers doctrine, a state's laws creating and authorizing a state postsecondary institution may be considered so all-inclusive that they prevail even over a local government's home rule powers. In two separate decisions, an appellate court in Illinois held that the state constitution delegated "plenary powers" to the board of trustees of a state university and that a city's constitutionally granted local home rule powers did not enable the city to enforce local ordinances against the state university without specific authorization by state statute. In *City of Chicago v. Board of Trustees of the University of Illinois*, 689 N.E.2d 125 (Ill. App. Ct. 1997), the court rejected the city's argument that its home rule powers authorized it to require the board to collect certain local taxes from university students and customers and remit these taxes to the city. In a later case concerning the same parties, *Board of Trustees of the University of Illinois v. City of Chicago*, 740 N.E.2d 515 (Ill. App. Ct. 2000), the court rejected the city's argument that its home rule powers authorized it to inspect university buildings, to cite the university for violations, and to collect fees for proven violations of the city's building, fire safety, and health ordinances. The court held that the state legislature, acting under the Illinois constitution, had granted full "plenary powers" to the board to operate a statewide educational system. "The state has 'plenary power' over state-operated educational institutions, and any attempt by a home rule municipality to impose burdens on those institutions, in the absence of state approval, is unauthorized" (740 N.E.2d at 518, quoting *City of Chicago*, 689 N.E.2d at 130). Consequently, the court refused to recognize any city authority to enforce tax collections or to monitor and cite the state university for violations of the city's fire, safety, and health ordinances.

College counsel and administrators will want to carefully consider all of these principles concerning authority in determining whether particular local government regulations can be construed to apply to the college or university, and whether the college or university will be bound by such regulations.

### 11.1.2. Trespass statutes and ordinances, and related campus regulations. 
States and local governments often have trespass or unlawful entry laws that limit the use of a postsecondary institution's grounds and facilities by outsiders. Such statutes or ordinances typically provide that offenders are subject to ejection from the property and that violating an order to leave made by an authorized person is punishable as a criminal misdemeanor, subject to damage awards and injunctive relief in a civil suit, or both. Enforcement of such laws by local police forces and courts provides a major example of local governments' involvement in higher education, as well as a major example of potential clashes between the local community and the campus.

Some trespass laws may cover all types of property; others may cover only educational institutions. Some laws may cover all postsecondary institutions, public or private; others may apply only to public or only to private institutions. Some laws may be broad enough to restrict members of the campus community under some circumstances; others may be applicable only to outsiders. There may also be technical differences among statutes and ordinances in their standards for determining what acts will be considered a trespass or when an institution's actions will constitute implied consent to entry.

There may also be differences concerning when the alleged trespasser has a "privilege" to be on the institution's property. The issue of "privilege" is often shaped by consideration of the public forum doctrine (see Section 9.4.2). If the alleged trespasser sought access to the campus property for expressive purposes, and if the property were considered to be a traditional public forum or a designated forum open to outsiders, the speaker will generally be considered to have a "privilege" to be on the property, and the trespass law cannot lawfully be used to exclude or eject the speaker from the forum property (see *State of Ohio v. Spingola*, 736 N.E.2d 48 (Ohio 1999)).

When a trespass law is invoked, there may also be questions of whether or when local police or campus security officers have probable cause to arrest the alleged trespasser. The presence of such probable cause may be a defense to claims of false arrest, false imprisonment, or other torts that the alleged trespasser may later assert against the institution or the arresting officer.

An Ohio case provides an example of how probable cause issues may arise in situations where campus or local police are enforcing criminal trespass laws on campus. In *Harper v. Amweg*, 2006 WL 745394 (S.D. Ohio 2006), *affirmed*, 231 Fed.Appx. 405 (6th Cir. 2007), Ohio State University had decided to prohibit individuals from selling handmade buckeye necklaces on the university's campus. To implement this decision, the university appointed law enforcement officers and other officials to serve as a "Vendor Detail" that was instructed to order individuals selling the necklaces to leave the campus.

Harper, the plaintiff, was a vendor who had been selling handmade buckeye necklaces on campus. At the start of the 2003 football season, a member of the vendor detail, Officer Amweg, approached Harper while she was selling the necklaces on university property and asked her to leave. Harper asked where she could sell the necklaces and Amweg replied, "Lane Avenue." At the next game, following Amweg's advice, Harper sold buckeye necklaces in the area of Lane Avenue. Amweg again approached her and asked her to leave the property, stating that his previous advice was mistaken.

As Harper was leaving the property to return to her car, some persons stopped her and asked to buy necklaces. Harper sold them the necklaces and continued on to her car; but before she got there, Amweg and another detail member, Deputy Hamburger, detained her, searched her belongings, and then arrested her. Campus police charged her with criminal trespass under Ohio Rev. Code § 2911.21, but the charges were later dismissed.

Harper then brought a suit under 42 U.S.C. § 1983 against Officer Amweg and Deputy Hamburger, alleging that they had violated her Fourth Amendment rights. Harper claimed that she had been arrested without probable cause, subjected to an illegal search and seizure of her person and belongings, and detained through the use of excessive force.

Regarding probable cause to arrest, the court rejected Harper's claim: "Plaintiff continued to sell buckeye necklaces on Ohio State property despite direct orders not to do so. Based on Plaintiff's disregard for the law, Defendants had probable cause to arrest her for criminal trespass and therefore did not violate Plaintiff's constitutional rights." Similarly, the court rejected Harper's claim that no probable cause existed to search her belongings: "[B]ecause the officers made a lawful arrest, they were justified in conducting a warrantless search of Plaintiff's person and her belongings."

Third, the court considered Harper's claim of excessive force, that is, a claim that the officers had "physically held, moved, and handcuffed her," rejecting this claim as well. The court noted that under *Graham v. Connor*, 490 U.S. 386, 396 (1989),

> [t]he fourth amendment requires that an officer's use of force be objectively reasonable, and courts must balance the consequences to the individual against the government's interest in effecting the seizure . . . In this case, there is no evidence that Plaintiff complained to the officers, nor that she suffered any injury as a result of being handcuffed . . . The officers were justified in handcuffing Plaintiff as a result of the lawful arrest and . . . conduct[ing] a lawful search of her person and her belongings [2006 WL 745394, at *7].

The district court thus agreed with the defendants and granted summary judgment for Officer Amweg and Deputy Hamburger, concluding that they had not violated Mrs. Harper's Fourth Amendment rights. On appeal, the U.S. Court of Appeals affirmed the decision based on the reasoning of the district court. A dissenting judge, although agreeing with most of the majority's opinion, argued that the excessive force claim should be returned to the district court and presented to a jury, since fact questions existed as to the reasonableness of the force used by the arresting officers.

A number of reported cases have dealt with the federal and state constitutional limitations on a state or local government's authority to apply trespass laws or related regulations to the campus setting. *Braxton v. Municipal Court*, 514 P.2d 697 (Cal. 1973), is an early, instructive example. Several individuals had demonstrated on the San Francisco State campus against the publication of campus newspaper articles that they considered "racist and chauvinistic." A college employee notified the protestors that they were temporarily barred from campus. When they disobeyed this order, they were arrested and charged under section 626.4 of the California Penal Code. This statute authorized "the chief administrative officer of a campus or other facility of a community college, state college, or state university or his designate" to temporarily bar a person from the campus if there was "reasonable cause to believe that such person has willfully disrupted the orderly operation of such campus or facility." The protestors argued that the state trespass statute was unconstitutional for reasons of overbreadth and vagueness (see Sections 9.2.2, 9.4.3, and 9.5.2 of this book).

The California Supreme Court rejected the protestors' argument, but did so only after narrowly construing the statute to avoid constitutional problems. Regarding overbreadth, the court reasoned:

> Without a narrowing construction, section 626.4 would suffer First Amendment overbreadth ... [because], on its face fails to distinguish between protected activity such as peaceful picketing or assembly and unprotected conduct that is violent, physically obstructive, or otherwise coercive ...
>
> In order to avoid the constitutional overbreadth that a literal construction of section 626.4 would entail, we interpret the statute to prohibit only incitement to violence or conduct physically incompatible with the peaceful functioning of the campus ... The disruption must also constitute "a substantial and material threat" to the orderly operation of the campus or facility (*Tinker v. Des Moines School District*, 393 U.S. 503, 514 (1969)). The words "substantial and material" appear in the portion of the statute which authorizes reinstatement of permission to come onto the campus (Penal Code § 626.4(c)). Accordingly, we read those words as expressing the legislature's intent as to the whole function of the statute; we thus construe section 626.4 to permit exclusion from the campus only of one whose conduct or words are such as to constitute, or incite to, a substantial and material physical disruption incompatible with the peaceful functioning of the academic institution and of those upon its campus. Such a substantial and material disruption creates an emergency situation justifying the statute's provision for summary, but temporary, exclusion [514 P.2d at 701, 703–5].

The court then also rejected the vagueness claim:

> Our examination of the legislative history and purposes of section 626.4 reveals, however, that the Legislature intended to authorize the extraordinary remedy of summary banishment only when the person excluded has committed acts illegal under other statutes; since these statutes provide ascertainable standards for persons seeking to avoid the embrace of section 626.4, the instant enactment is not void for vagueness [514 P.2d at 705].

In comparison with *Braxton*, the court in *Grody v. State*, 278 N.E.2d 280 (Ind. 1972), did invalidate a state trespass law because of its overbreadth. The law provided that "[i]t shall be a misdemeanor for any person to refuse to leave the premises of any institution established for the purpose of the education of students enrolled therein when so requested, regardless of the reason, by the duly constituted officials of any such institution" (Ind. Code Ann. § 10-4533). As the court read the law:

> This statute attempts to grant to some undefined school "official" the power to order cessation of any kind of activity whatsoever, by any person whatsoever, and the official does not need to have any special reason for the order. The official's power extends to teachers, employees, students, and visitors and is in no way confined to suppressing activities that are interfering with the orderly use of the premises. This statute empowers the official to order any person off the premises because he does not approve of his looks, his opinions, his behavior, no matter how peaceful, or *for no reason at all*. Since there are no limitations on the reason for such an order, the official can request a person to leave the premises solely because the person is engaging in expressive conduct even though that conduct may be clearly protected by the First Amendment. If the person chooses to continue the First Amendment activity, he can be prosecuted for a crime under § 10-4533. This statute is clearly overbroad [278 N.E.2d at 282–83].

The court therefore held the trespass law to be facially invalid under the free speech clause.

Even if a trespass statute or ordinance does not contain the First Amendment flaws identified in *Braxton* and *Grody*, it may be challenged as a violation of Fourteenth Amendment procedural due process. The court in *Braxton* ruled in favor of the plaintiffs' due process arguments (514 P.2d at 700). This does not mean, however, that an outsider's procedural rights should be equated with those of students. If a student is ejected from the campus, the ejection will usually infringe a property or liberty interest of the student (see generally Section 9.4.2); that is not necessarily the case, however, if a nonstudent is ejected. In *Souders v. Lucero*, 196 F.3d 1040 (9th Cir. 1999), for example, the court rejected an outsider's claim to procedural due process protections because he had no constitutional liberty or property interest in access to the campus.

Postsecondary institutions may also have their own regulations that prohibit entry of outsiders into campus buildings or certain outside areas of the campus, or that provide for ejecting or banning outsiders from the campus in certain circumstances. For public institutions, such regulations are subject to the same federal constitutional restrictions as the state trespass statutes discussed above. In addition, if the institution's regulation were facially unconstitutional, or if the institution were to apply its regulation in an unconstitutional manner in a particular case, it would be impermissible for the institution to invoke a state trespass law or local ordinance to enforce its regulation. *Orin v. Barclay*, 272 F.3d 1207 (9th Cir. 2001), illustrates these principles.

In *Orin v. Barclay*, the court considered the constitutionality of a speech regulation prohibiting protestors from engaging in religious worship or instruction. The issue arose when members of the antiabortion group Positively Pro-Life approached the interim dean of Olympic Community College (OCC), Richard Barclay, and asked for a permit to stage an event on the school's main quad. Barclay declined to grant the protestors a permit but gave them permission to hold a demonstration provided they did not (1) breach the peace or cause a disturbance; (2) interfere with campus activities or access to school buildings; or (3) engage in religious worship or instruction. With the dean's permission, the protestors began their antiabortion demonstration. After "four factious hours," the protestors were asked to leave the campus. They refused, and at least one protestor, Benjamin Orin, was arrested for criminal trespass and failure to disperse. Orin subsequently sued Barclay, among others, under 42 U.S.C. § 1983 for violating his First Amendment rights.

Reversing the district court's grant of summary judgment for the defendants, the appellate court focused on the conditions that Barclay had imposed on the antiabortion group's protest. The first two conditions—that the protestors not breach the peace or interfere with campus activities or access to school buildings—were permissible content-neutral regulations. However, the third condition, that the protestors refrain from religious worship or instruction, violated the First Amendment. Relying on *Widmar v. Vincent* (discussed in Section 10.1.5), the court held that Barclay had created a public forum by granting the protestors permission to demonstrate. Consequently, he could not constitutionally limit the content of the protestors' speech by permitting secular speech but prohibiting religious speech.

Other access cases concerning institutional regulations suggest, as *Orin v. Barclay* does, that the most contentious issues are likely to be First Amendment issues, especially free speech issues, and that the analysis will often turn on public forum considerations (see Section 9.4.2) and on the distinction between content-based and content-neutral regulations of speech. The public forum analysis applicable to outsiders' rights may differ from that for students' or faculty members' rights because institutions may establish limited forums (designated limited forums) that provide access for the campus community but not for outsiders. Overbreadth and vagueness analysis (as in the *Braxton* and *Grady* cases discussed earlier in this section) may also be pertinent in cases challenging institutional regulations.

In *Giebel v. Sylvester*, 244 F.3d 1182 (9th Cir. 2001), the court used forum analysis and viewpoint discrimination analysis in protecting an outsider who had posted notices on university bulletin boards. In *Mason v. Wolf*, 356 F. Supp. 2d 1147 (D. Colo. 2005), the court used forum analysis and time, place, and manner analysis in protecting an outside group seeking to have a demonstration on campus. In contrast, in *State of Ohio v. Spingola*, 736 N.E.2d 48 (Ohio 1999), the court used public forum analysis, content-neutral analysis, and vagueness analysis in rejecting the free speech claim of an outside preacher. The court in *Bourgault v. Yudof*, 316 F. Supp. 2d 411 (N.D. Tex. 2004), *affirmed without opinion*, 2005 WL 3332907 (December 8, 2005), used forum analysis and viewpoint discrimination analysis in rejecting a traveling evangelist's free speech challenge to University of Texas System rules that provided no access to outsiders. And in *American Civil Liberties Union v. Mote*, 423 F.3d 438 (4th Cir. 2005), the court used public forum analysis to uphold a University of Maryland policy that prohibited outsiders from speaking in outdoor areas of the campus unless they had been invited by a department of the university or by a registered student organization.

In *Bowman v. White*, 444 F.3d 967 (8th Cir. 2006), a Christian street preacher challenged several provisions of a University of Arkansas policy on use of its grounds by "Non-University Entities." Bowman, who used outdoor spaces on the campus for preaching, claimed that several requirements in the policy violated the First Amendment by restricting his freedom to speak on public property. At issue in *Bowman* were these requirements: (1) a requirement that a permit be obtained in advance for each use of space "for one eight-hour day"; (2) a "three-business-day advance notice" requirement for when the user must apply for the permit; (3) a prohibition on using space during "dead days," that is, final exam periods, days of commencement activities, and "one quiet study day per semester"; and (4) a "five-day cap per semester" on the number of times a particular outsider could use the university grounds. The court determined that each of these requirements was content-neutral and that, in Bowman's case, these requirements were applied to speech in a designated public forum (see Section 9.4.2). The court therefore subjected each requirement to the accepted U.S. Supreme Court test applicable to these circumstances: whether the restriction on speech is "narrowly tailored to serve a significant governmental interest" and "leaves open ample alternative channels of communication."

Using this test, the court held that the first three of the university's requirements were constitutional but the fourth (the five-day cap) was not. Regarding the five-day cap on permits, the university did have significant interests in "fostering a diversity of viewpoints and avoiding the monopolization of space." But the cap was not "narrowly tailored" to these interests:

> The Policy as written does not by itself foster more viewpoints; it merely limits Bowman's speech. If no one else wants to use the space after Bowman has used his five permits, the space will go unused even if Bowman still wants to use the space. A more narrowly tailored policy might grant Bowman more than just five days per semester to speak if the space is not being used, but give preference to other speakers who have not already obtained five permits [444 F.3d at 982].

In another U.S. Court of Appeals case, *Gilles v. Blanchard*, 477 F.3d 466 (7th Cir. 2007), the court relied on the *Mote* case and distinguished *Bowman* (also questioning "the soundness of the decision") in rejecting the free speech claim of a "traveling evangelist" who sought to preach on the library lawn at Vincennes University. The university had a written policy that restricted "solicitations" by uninvited outsiders to a walkway in front of the student union. The court cautioned that this policy, as applied to the plaintiff's preaching activities, "is hopelessly vague and thus a supple weapon for excluding from the university lawn those outsiders whose message the university disapproves of." But the university nevertheless prevailed because, besides the written policy, it had an established unwritten "policy against use of the lawn by uninvited speakers." This policy "has long been a norm, and not just a practice," and the plaintiff could not demonstrate that the university had failed to comply with this policy in the past or had used it to "discriminate[e] against disfavored points of view." The university therefore could rely on this unwritten policy or "norm" as the basis for prohibiting the plaintiff from preaching on the library lawn.

In its opinion, the court in *Gilles v. Blanchard* did not rely on the public forum doctrine to the same extent as the earlier cases had. The plaintiff appeared to argue that the library lawn was a traditional public forum; and the university argued that it was a "limited designated public forum." The court did not adopt either characterization. Instead, it cautioned against "turning the search for sensible results into a classification game." The sensible results sought by the court required consideration of viewpoint neutrality, the fostering of a "reasonable diversity of viewpoints," and the university's rights as a property owner.

Most of the litigation concerning trespass laws and campus access regulations, such as the cases just discussed, has involved public institutions and has probed federal constitutional limits on states and public postsecondary institutions. The debate was extended to private institutions, however, by the litigation in *State v. Schmid*, 423 A.2d 615 (N.J. 1980), sometimes known as the Princeton University case.

In this case, a nonstudent and member of the United States Labor Party, Chris Schmid, was arrested and convicted of trespass for attempting to distribute political materials on the campus of Princeton University. Princeton's regulations required nonstudents and non-university-affiliated organizations to obtain permission to distribute materials on campus. No such requirement applied to students or campus organizations. The regulations did not include any provisions indicating when permission would be granted or what time, manner, or place of expression would be appropriate. Schmid claimed that the regulations violated his rights to freedom of expression under both the federal Constitution and the New Jersey state constitution.

First addressing the federal constitutional claim under the First Amendment, the court held that Princeton's exclusion of Schmid did not constitute state action under any of the theories.

Although the federal First Amendment could not apply to Schmid's claim, the court determined that the state constitutional provisions protecting freedom of expression (even though similar to the First Amendment provision) could be construed more expansively than the First Amendment so as to reach Princeton's actions. The court reaffirmed that state constitutions are independent sources of individual rights; that state constitutional protections may surpass the protections of the federal Constitution; and that this greater expansiveness could exist even if the state provision is identical to the federal provision, since state constitutional rights are not intended to be merely mirror images of federal rights (see Section 1.4.2.1).

In determining whether the more expansive state constitutional provision protected Schmid against the trespass claim, the court balanced the "legitimate interests in private property with individual freedoms of speech and assembly." To strike the required balance, the court announced a "test":

> This standard must take into account (1) the nature, purposes, and primary use of such private property, generally, its "normal" use, (2) the extent and nature of the public's invitation to use that property, and (3) the purpose of the expressional activity undertaken upon such property in relation to both the private and public use of the property. This is a multifaceted test which must be applied to ascertain whether in a given case owners of private property may be required to permit, subject to suitable restrictions, the reasonable exercise by individuals of the constitutional freedoms of speech and assembly.
>
> Even when an owner of private property is constitutionally obligated under such a standard to honor speech and assembly rights of others, private property rights themselves must nonetheless be protected. The owner of such private property, therefore, is entitled to fashion reasonable rules to control the mode, opportunity, and site for the individual exercise of expressional rights upon his property. It is at this level of analysis—assessing the reasonableness of such restrictions—that weight may be given to whether there exist convenient and feasible alternative means to individuals to engage in substantially the same expressional activity. While the presence of such alternatives will not eliminate the constitutional duty, it may lighten the obligations upon the private property owner to accommodate the expressional rights of others and may also serve to condition the content of any regulations governing the time, place, and manner for the exercise of such expressional rights [423 A.2d at 630].

Applying each of the three elements in its test to the particular facts concerning Princeton's campus and Schmid's activity on it, the court concluded that Schmid did have state constitutional speech and assembly rights that Princeton was obligated to honor:

> The central purposes of a university are the pursuit of truth, the discovery of new knowledge through scholarship and research, the teaching and general development of students, and the transmission of knowledge and learning to society at large . . . Free speech and peaceable assembly are basic requirements of the university as a center for free inquiry and the search for knowledge and insight.

The court next examined "the extent and nature of a public invitation to use [the University's] property," determining that "a public presence within Princeton University is entirely consonant with the university's expressed educational mission." And finally, the court examined "the expressional activities undertaken by the defendant in this case are discordant in any sense with both the private and public uses of the campus and facilities of the university." The court found no evidence that Schmid had been evicted because his distribution of literature "offended the university's educational policies" or disrupted the university's operations.

Princeton, however, invoked the other considerations included in the court's test. It argued that, to protect its private property rights as an owner and its academic freedom as a higher education institution, it had to require that out-siders have permission to enter its campus and that its regulations reasonably implemented this necessary requirement. The court did not disagree with the first premise of Princeton's argument, but it did disagree that Princeton's regulations were a reasonable means of protecting its interests:

> [P]rivate colleges and universities must be accorded a generous measure of autonomy and self-governance if they are to fulfill their paramount role as vehicles of education and enlightenment.
>
> In this case, however, the university regulations that were applied to Schmid . . . contained no standards, aside from the requirement for invitation and permission, for governing the actual exercise of expressional freedom. Indeed, there were no standards extant regulating the granting or withholding of such authorization, nor did the regulations deal adequately with the time, place, or manner for individuals to exercise their rights of speech and assembly. Regulations thus devoid of reasonable standards designed to protect both the legitimate interests of the university as an institution of higher education and the individual exercise of expressional freedom cannot constitutionally be invoked to prohibit the otherwise noninjurious and reasonable exercise of such freedoms . . . [423 A.2d at 632–33].

The court thus reversed Schmid's conviction for trespass.

Princeton sought U.S. Supreme Court review of the New Jersey court's decision. The university argued that the court's interpretation of state constitutional law violated its rights under *federal* law. Specifically, it claimed a First Amendment right to institutional academic freedom (see Section 6.1.7) and a Fifth Amendment right to protect its property from infringement by government (here the New Jersey court). In a *per curiam* opinion, the Supreme Court declined to address the merits of Princeton's arguments, declaring the appeal moot because Princeton had changed its regulations since the time of Schmid's conviction (*Princeton University and State of New Jersey v. Schmid*, 455 U.S. 100 (1982)). Although the Supreme Court therefore dismissed the appeal, the dismissal had no negative effect on the New Jersey court's opinion, which stands as authoritative law for that state.

The New Jersey Supreme Court's reasoning was subsequently approved and followed by the Pennsylvania Supreme Court in *Pennsylvania v. Tate*, 432 A.2d 1382 (Pa. 1981), in which the defendants had been arrested for trespassing at Muhlenberg College, a private institution, when they distributed leaflets on campus announcing a community-sponsored lecture by the then FBI director. In a later case, however, *Western Pennsylvania Socialist Workers 1982 Campaign v. Connecticut General Life Insurance Co.*, 515 A.2d 1331 (1986), the Pennsylvania Supreme Court apparently limited its *Tate* ruling to situations in which a private institution has opened up the contested portion of its property for a use comparable to that of a public forum (515 A.2d at 1338). A few other states also have case law suggesting that their state constitution includes some narrow protections for certain speakers seeking to use private property.

The *Schmid* precedent does not create the same access rights to all private campuses in New Jersey; as the court emphasized, the degree of access required depends on the primary use for which the institution dedicates its campus property and the scope of the public invitation to use that particular property. Nor does *Schmid* prohibit private institutions from regulating the activity of outsiders to whom they must permit entry. Indeed, the new regulations adopted by Princeton after Schmid's arrest were cited favorably by the New Jersey court, which noted that "these current amended regulations exemplify the approaches open to private educational entities seeking to protect their institutional integrity while at the same time recognizing individual rights of speech and assembly and accommodating the public whose presence nurtures academic inquiry and growth" (423 A.2d at 633). The revised Princeton regulations, which are set out in full in the court's opinion (423 A.2d at 617–18 n.2), thus provide substantial guidance for private institutions that may be subject to state law such as New Jersey's or that as a matter of educational policy desire to open their campus to outsiders in some circumstances.

**11.1.3. Relations with local police.**  Since the academic community is part of the surrounding community, it will generally be within the geographical jurisdiction of one or more local (town, village, city, county) police forces. The circumstances under which local police may and will come onto the campus, and their authority once on campus, are thus of concern to every administrator. The role of local police on campus depends on a mixture of considerations: the state and local law of the jurisdiction, federal constitutional limitations on police powers, the adequacy of the institution's own security services, and the terms of any explicit or implicit understanding between local police and campus authorities.

If the institution has its own uniformed security officers, administrators must decide what working relationships these officers will have with local police. This decision will depend partly on the extent of the security officers' authority, especially regarding arrests, searches, and seizures—authority that should also be carefully delineated (see generally Section 7.6.1). Similarly, administrators must understand the relationship between arrest and prosecution in local courts, on the one hand, and campus disciplinary proceedings on the other (see Section 9.1). Although administrators cannot make crime an internal affair by hiding evidence of crime from local police, they may be able to assist local law enforcement officials in determining prosecution priorities. Campus and local officials may also be able to cooperate in determining whether a campus proceeding should be stayed pending the outcome of a court proceeding, or vice versa.

The powers of local police are circumscribed by various federal constitutional provisions, particularly the Fourth Amendment strictures on arrests, searches, and seizures. These provisions limit local police authority on both public and private campuses. Under the Fourth Amendment, local police usually must obtain a warrant before arresting or searching a member of the academic community or searching or seizing any private property on the campus (see Section 7.4.3). On a private institution's campus, nearly all the property may be private, and local police may need a warrant or the consent of whoever effectively controls the property before entering most areas of the campus. On a public institution's campus, it is more difficult to determine which property would be considered public and which private, and thus more difficult to determine when local police must have a warrant or consent prior to entry. In general, for both public and private institutions, police need a warrant or consent before entering any area in which members of the academic community have a "reasonable expectation of privacy" (see generally *Katz v. United States*, 389 U.S. 347 (1967)). The constitutional rules and concepts are especially complex in this area, however, and administrators should consult counsel whenever questions arise concerning the authority of local police on campus.

In *People v. Dickson*, 154 Cal. Rptr. 116 (Cal. Ct. App. 1979), the court considered the validity of a warrantless search of a chemistry laboratory conducted by local police and campus security officers at the Bakersfield campus of California State University. The search uncovered samples of an illegal drug and materials used in its manufacture—evidence that led to the arrest and conviction of the defendant, a chemistry professor who used the laboratory. The court upheld the search and the conviction because, under the facts of the case (particularly facts indicating ready access to the laboratory by many persons, including campus police), the professor had no "objectively reasonable expectation of privacy" in his laboratory.

Under a similar rationale, the court in *Commonwealth v. Tau Kappa Epsilon*, 560 A.2d 786 (Pa. Super. Ct. 1989), *vacated on other grounds*, 609 A.2d 791 (Pa. 1992), rejected the argument that undercover police were required to obtain a search warrant before they entered a fraternity party. Two undercover officers, recent graduates of Pennsylvania State University, had entered parties at eleven fraternities and observed the serving of beer to minors. When fraternities were convicted of serving beer to minors, they appealed the convictions, arguing that the police officers' warrantless entry violated the Fourth Amendment. The court disagreed:

> Security was so lax as to be virtually nonexistent; a person could enter and be furnished beverages almost at will. Under these circumstances, the fraternities could be found to have consented to the entry of [the police] and to have surrendered any reasonable expectation of privacy with respect to the events occurring in their houses [560 A.2d at 791].

That these particular searches were upheld even though the officers did not procure a warrant, however, does not mean that local police forces may routinely dispense with the practice of obtaining warrants. In circumstances where a person has a reasonable expectation of privacy that would be invaded by a search, procuring a warrant or the consent of the person to be searched is generally required.

In 1980, Congress enacted legislation that limits police search and seizure activities on college campuses. The legislation, the Privacy Protection

Act of 1980 (42 U.S.C. §§ 2000aa et seq.), was passed in part to counter the U.S. Supreme Court's decision in *Zurcher v. Stanford Daily*, 436 U.S. 547 (1978). In *Zurcher*, the Palo Alto, California, Police Department had obtained a warrant to search the files of the *Stanford Daily*, a student newspaper, for photographs of participants in a demonstration during which several police officers had been assaulted. The lower court found probable cause to believe that the *Stanford Daily*'s files did contain such photographs, but no probable cause to believe that the newspaper itself was engaged in any wrongdoing. The U.S. Supreme Court held that the *Stanford Daily*, even though an innocent third party and even though engaged in publication activities, had no First or Fourth Amendment rights to assert against the search warrant.

The Privacy Protection Act's coverage is not confined to newspapers, the subject of the *Zurcher* case. As its legislative history makes clear, the act also protects scholars and other persons engaged in "public communication"—that is, the "flow of information to the public" (see S. Rep. No. 874, 96th Cong., 2d Sess., *reprinted in* 4 U.S. Code Cong. & Admin. News 3950, 3956 (1980)).

The act's language and legislative history clearly indicate that the act applies to local and state, as well as federal, government officers and employees. It thus limits the authority of city, town, and county police officers both on campus and in off-campus investigations of campus scholars or journalists. The act limits police officers and other government officials, however, only when they are investigating criminal, as opposed to civil, offenses. Scholars and journalists thus are not protected, for example, from the seizure of property to satisfy outstanding tax debts or from the regulatory inspections or compliance reviews conducted by government agencies administering civil laws. Moreover, the act's legislative history makes clear that traditional subpoena powers and limitations are untouched by the act (see S. Rep. No. 874, 96th Cong., 2d Sess., *reprinted in* 4 U.S. Code Cong. & Admin. News 3950, 3956–60 (1980)).

Different problems arise when local police enter a campus not to make an arrest or conduct a search but to engage in surveillance of members of the campus community. In *White v. Davis*, 533 P.2d 222 (Cal. 1975), a history professor at UCLA sued the Los Angeles police chief to enjoin the use of undercover police agents for generalized surveillance in the university. Unidentified police agents had registered at the university and compiled dossiers on students and professors based on information obtained during classes and public meetings. The California Supreme Court held that the surveillance was a prima facie violation of students' and faculty members' First Amendment freedoms of speech, assembly, and association, as well as a violation of the right-to-privacy provision of the California constitution. Such police actions could be justifiable only if they were necessary to accomplish a compelling state interest. The court returned the case to the trial court to determine whether the police could prove such a justification.

The principles of *White v. Davis* would apply equally to local police surveillance at private institutions. As government agents, the police are prohibited from violating any person's freedom of expression or right to privacy under the federal and state constitutions, whether on a public campus or a private one.

## Section 11.2. State Government Regulation

***11.2.1. Overview.*** Unlike the federal government (see Section 11.3) and local governments (Section 11.1), state governments have general rather than limited powers and can claim all power that is not denied them by the federal Constitution or their own state constitutions, or that has not been preempted by federal law. Thus, the states have the greatest reservoir of legal authority over postsecondary education, although the extent to which this source is tapped varies substantially from state to state.

In states that do assert substantial authority over postsecondary education, questions may arise about the division of authority between the legislative and the executive branches. In *Inter-Faculty Organization v. Carlson*, 478 N.W.2d 192 (Minn. 1991), for example, the Minnesota Supreme Court invalidated a governor's line item vetoes of certain expenditure estimates in the legislature's higher education funding bill because the action went beyond the governor's veto authority, which extended only to identifiable amounts dedicated to specific purposes. Similar questions may concern the division of authority among other state boards or officials that have functions regarding higher education.

Questions may also be raised about the legal authority of the state in relation to that of the federal government under federal spending or regulatory programs. In *Shapp v. Sloan*, 391 A.2d 595 (Pa. 1978), for instance, the specific questions were (1) whether, under Pennsylvania state law, the state legislature or the governor was legally entrusted with control over federal funds made available to the state; and (2) whether, under federal law, state legislative control of federal funds was consistent with the supremacy clause of the U.S. Constitution and the provisions of the funding statutes. In a lengthy opinion addressing an array of legal complexities, the Pennsylvania Supreme Court held that the legislature had control of the federal funds under state law and that such control had not been exercised inconsistently with federal law.

The states' functions in matters concerning postsecondary education include operating public systems, regulating and funding private institutions and programs, statewide planning and coordinating, supporting assessment and accountability initiatives, and providing scholarships and other financial aid for students (see, for example, Section 1.6.3). These functions are performed through myriad agencies, such as boards of regents; departments of education or higher education; statewide planning or coordinating boards; institutional licensure boards or commissions; construction financing authorities; and state approval agencies (SAAs) that operate under contract to the federal Veterans Administration to approve courses for which veterans' benefits may be expended. In addition, various professional and occupational licensure boards indirectly regulate postsecondary education by evaluating programs of study and establishing educational prerequisites for taking licensure examinations.[1]

---

[1]Under federal law (20 U.S.C. § 1099a(a)), each state, acting through one or more of the agencies and boards listed in this paragraph, must assist the U.S. Secretary of Education with a program to ensure the "integrity" of the federal student aid program.

Various other state agencies whose primary function is not education—such as workers' compensation boards, labor relations boards, ethics boards, civil rights enforcement agencies, environmental quality agencies, and licensing departments—may also regulate postsecondary education as part of a broader class of covered institutions, corporations, or government agencies. And in some circumstances, states may regulate some particular aspect of postsecondary education through the processes of the criminal law rather than through state regulatory agencies.

In addition, states exert authority or influence over postsecondary institutions' own borrowing and financing activities. For instance, states may facilitate institutions' borrowing for capital development projects by issuing tax-exempt government bonds. In Virginia, for example, under the Education Facilities Authority Act (Va. Code §§ 23–30.39 et seq.; see also Va. Const. art. VIII, § 11), the Virginia College Building Authority issues revenue bonds to finance construction projects for nonprofit higher education institutions in the state. States may also influence institutional financing by regulating charitable solicitations by institutions and their fund-raising firms. Moreover, a state can either encourage or deter various financial activities (and affect institutions' after-tax bottom line) through its system of taxation. Private institutions, or institutional property and activities within the state, usually are presumed subject to taxation under the state's various tax statutes unless a specific statutory or constitutional provision grants an exemption. *In re Middlebury College Sales and Use Tax*, 400 A.2d 965 (Vt. 1979), is illustrative. Although the Vermont statute granted general tax-exempt status to private institutions meeting federal standards for tax exemption under the Internal Revenue Code, the statute contained an exception for institutional "activities which are mainly commercial enterprises." Middlebury College operated a golf course and a skiing complex, the facilities of which were used for its physical education program and other college purposes. The facilities were also open to the public upon payment of rates comparable to those charged by commercial establishments. When the state sought to tax the college's purchases of equipment and supplies for the facilities, the college claimed that its purchases were tax exempt under the Vermont statute. The court rejected Middlebury's claim, holding that the college had failed to meet its burden of proving that the golfing and skiing activities were not "mainly commercial enterprises."

In addition to performing these planning, regulatory, and fiscal functions through their agencies and boards, the states are also the source of eminent domain (condemnation) powers by which private property may be taken for public use. The scope of these powers, and the extent of compensation required for particular takings, may be at issue either when the state seeks to take land owned by a private postsecondary institution or when a state postsecondary institution or board seeks to take land owned by a private party.

In *In the Matter of Parminder Kaur v. New York State Development Corporation*, 933 N.E.2d 721 (N.Y. 2010), owners of private property in Harlem challenged the determination of a state agency, the New York State Development Corporation, that the property was blighted and that the agency should use its power of eminent domain to purchase the property in conjunction with the proposed use for a new campus for Columbia University. The project would include both academic and retail space as well as open space and faculty and student housing. The state's highest court, applying the state's law of eminent domain, determined both that the property at issue was blighted and that development would be in the civic interest of the city and its inhabitants.

In contrast, in *Regents of University of Minnesota v. Chicago and North Western Transportation Co.*, 552 N.W.2d 578 (Minn. App. 1996), the university was not successful in a condemnation action. The regents challenged the trial court's dismissal of its petition to acquire a thirty-acre tract of land, owned by the defendant railway company, located near the university's East Bank campus. The appellate court affirmed the trial court's ruling that the university had not shown the requisite necessity for taking the property by means of eminent domain. According to the appellate court:

> First, the record indicates that the University has not included this property on its master plan for its anticipated development of the Twin Cities campus. Second, although the University claims to have at least three potential uses for the land, the uses are mutually exclusive, and the Board of Regents has not yet approved a single project for the property. Finally, because of soil contamination problems, it is undisputed that the University could not currently use the property for any of its proposed uses. The parties have not yet agreed on a remediation plan; decontamination of the property will require from approximately two to seven years to complete [552 N.W.2d at 580].

Thus, the university's plans for using the land were too speculative to justify approving the condemnation.

But in *Gyrodyne Company of America, Inc. v. State University of New York at Stony Brook*, 794 N.Y.S. 2d 87 (N.Y. App. Div. 2005), a New York state appellate court ruled that the use of condemnation and eminent domain by SUNY Stony Brook in order to build a research and development campus was an appropriate "educational purpose" under state law. And in *Mt. San Jacinto Community College District v. Superior Court of Riverside County (Azusa Pacific University)*, 151 P.3d 1166 (Cal. 2007), the California Supreme Court affirmed the right of a public community college to acquire by eminent domain property owned by a private university, and established that the valuation of the land was to be determined as of the date the court approved the taking by eminent domain.

Finally, the states, through their court systems, are the source of the common law (see Section 1.4.2.4) that provides the basis for the legal relationships between institutions and their students, faculties, and staff and also provides general legal context for many of the transactions and disputes in which institutions may become involved. Common law contract principles, for example, may constrain an institution's freedom to terminate the employment of its personnel (see Section 4.2); tort law principles may shape the institution's responsibilities for its students' safety and well-being (see Sections 3.2.2.1–3.2.2.7); and contract law, tort law, and property law principles may guide the institution's business relationships with outside parties.

Given the considerable, and growing, state involvement in the affairs of higher educational institutions that is suggested by this discussion and is illustrated by the topics covered in the rest of this section, administrators and counsel should stay abreast of pertinent state agency processes, state programs, and state legal requirements affecting the operations of their institutions, as well as the oversight activities and legislative initiatives of the state legislature's education committees. In addition, presidents, key administrators, and legal counsel (especially for public institutions) should follow and be prepared to participate in the vigorous and wide-ranging debates on higher education policy that are now occurring in various states. Prime topics concern structural changes in state governance of higher education (see generally Section 1.3.3), state financing of higher education, and strategies for serving underserved population groups.

**11.2.2. State provision of public postsecondary education.** Public postsecondary education systems vary in type and organization from state to state. Such systems may be established by the state constitution, by legislative acts, or by a combination of the two, and may encompass a variety of institutions—from the large state university to smaller state colleges or teachers colleges, to community colleges, technical schools, and vocational schools.

Every state has at least one designated body that bears statewide responsibility for at least some aspects of its public postsecondary system.[2] These bodies are known by such titles as board of higher education, commission on higher education, board of regents, regents, board of educational finance, or board of governors. Most such boards are involved in some phase of planning, program review and approval, and budget development for the institutions under their control or within their sphere of influence. Other responsibilities—such as the development of databases and management information systems or the establishment of new degree-granting institutions—might also be imposed. Depending on their functions, boards are classifiable into two groups: governing and coordinating. Governing boards are legally responsible for the management and operation of the institutions under their control. Coordinating boards have the lesser responsibilities that their name implies. Most governing boards work directly with the institutions for which they are responsible. Coordinating boards may or may not do so. Although community colleges are closely tied to their locales, most come within the jurisdiction of some state board or agency.

The legal status of the institutions in the public postsecondary system varies from state to state and may vary as well from institution to institution within the same state. Typically, institutions established directly by a state constitution have more authority than institutions established by statute and, correspondingly, have more autonomy from the state governing board and the state legislature. In dealing with problems of legal authority, therefore, one must

---

[2] The information in this paragraph is drawn heavily from Richard M. Millard, *State Boards of Higher Education*, ERIC Higher Education Research Report no. 4 (American Association for Higher Education, 1976).

distinguish between "statutory" and "constitutional" institutions and, within these basic categories, carefully examine the terms of the provisions granting authority to each particular institution.

State constitutional and statutory provisions may also grant certain authority over institutions to the state governing board or some other state agency or official. It is thus also important to examine the terms of any such provisions that are part of the law of the particular state. The relevant statutes and constitutional clauses do not always project clear answers, however, to the questions that may arise concerning the division of authority among the individual institution, the statewide governing or coordinating body, the legislature, the governor, and other state agencies (such as a civil service commission or a budget office) or officials (such as a commissioner of education). Because of the uncertainties, courts often have had to determine who holds the ultimate authority to make various critical decisions regarding public postsecondary education.

Disputes over the division of authority among some combination of the state, a statewide governing or coordinating body, the legislature, and other entities typically arise in one of two contexts: the creation or dissolution of an institution, and the management and control of the affairs of a public institution. Although public institutions created by a state constitution, such as the flagship universities of California and Michigan, can be dissolved only by an amendment to the state constitution and are insulated from legislative control because of their constitutional status, public institutions created by legislative action (a statute) can also be dissolved by the legislature and are subject to legislative control. In some states, however, the allocation of authority is less clear. For example, in South Dakota, the state constitution created the statewide governing board for public colleges and universities (the board of regents), but the state colleges and universities were created by statute. In *Kanaly v. State of South Dakota*, 368 N.W.2d 819 (S.D. 1985), taxpayers challenged the state legislature's decision to close the University of South Dakota–Springfield and transfer its campus and facilities to the state prison system. The state's supreme court ruled that the decision to change the use of these assets was clearly within the legislature's power. However, under the terms of a perpetual trust the legislature had established to fund state universities, the prison system had to reimburse the trust for the value of the land and buildings.

The court distinguished between the power to manage and control a state college (given by the state constitution to the board of regents) and the "power of the purse" (a legislative power). The state constitution, said the court, did not create the board of regents as "a fourth branch of government independent of any legislative policies." Previous decisions by the South Dakota Supreme Court had established that the board of regents did not have the power to change the character of an institution, to determine state educational policy, or to appropriate funding for the institutions (368 N.W.2d at 825). "The legislature has the power to create schools, to fund them as it has the power of the purse, and to establish state educational policy and this necessarily includes the power to close a school if efficiency and economy so direct" (368 N.W.2d at 825). Transferring the property upon which the university was located to the state prison system was not the same, said the court, as transferring control of the institution itself from the regents to the prison system.

In situations where a state governing or coordinating board has the authority to establish or dissolve a college, a court's powers to review the criteria by which such a decision is made are limited. For example, a group of citizens formed a nonprofit corporation and asked the State of Missouri to approve the corporation's application to form a community college. In *State ex rel. Lake of the Ozarks Community College Steering Committee v. Coordinating Board for Higher Education*, 802 S.W.2d 533 (Mo. Ct. App. 1991), the steering committee of the corporation sued the state coordinating board for rejecting its application. The court dismissed the lawsuit as moot because the board had considered the petition and had acted within the board's authority in rejecting the petition. The court noted that it was not proper in this instance for a court to define the standards by which the board evaluated the application.

Litigated issues related to the management and control of colleges and universities are numerous. They include academic matters, such as the registration of doctoral programs, as well as resource allocation matters, such as the approval of budget amendments and appropriation of funds for the university.

### 11.2.3. State chartering and licensure of private postsecondary institutions. 
The authority of states to regulate private postsecondary education is not as broad as their authority over their own public institutions (see Section 1.5.1). Nevertheless, under their police powers, states do have extensive regulatory authority that they have implemented through statutes and administrative regulations. This authority has generally been upheld by the courts. In the leading case of *Shelton College v. State Board of Education*, 226 A.2d 612 (N.J. 1967), for instance, the court reviewed the authority of New Jersey to license degree-granting institutions and approve the basis and conditions on which they grant degrees. The State Board of Education had refused to approve the granting of degrees by the plaintiff college, and the college challenged the board's authority on a variety of grounds. In an informative opinion, the New Jersey Supreme Court rejected all the challenges and broadly upheld the board's decision and the validity of the statute under which the board had acted.

Similarly, in *Warder v. Board of Regents of the University of the State of New York*, 423 N.E.2d 352 (N.Y. 1981), the court rejected state administrative law and constitutional due process challenges to New York's authority to charter postsecondary institutions. The Unification Theological Seminary, a subdivision of the Unification Church (the church of Reverend Sun Myung Moon), sought to incorporate in New York and offer a master's degree in religious education. It applied for a provisional charter. In reviewing the application, the state education department subjected the seminary to an unprecedented lengthy and intensive investigation. The department had been concerned about charges of brainwashing and deceptive practices directed against the Unification Church. The department's investigation did not substantiate these charges but did uncover evidence suggesting other deficiencies. Ultimately, the department determined that the seminary had misrepresented itself as having degree-granting status, had refused to provide financial statements, and had not enforced its admissions policies.

The New York Court of Appeals held that, despite the singular treatment the seminary had received, the education department had a legitimate basis for conducting its investigation and had a rational basis for its decision to deny the charter. The seminary also charged that the legislature's grant of authority to the education department was vague and overbroad and that the department had reviewed the seminary in a discriminatory and biased manner. Rejecting the latter argument, the court found that the record did not contain evidence of discrimination or bias. Also rejecting the former argument, the court held that the New York statutes constituted a lawful delegation of authority to the state's board of regents:

> Authority over private postsecondary institutions is exercised, in varying degrees depending on the state, in two basic ways. The first is incorporation or chartering, a function performed by all states. In some states, postsecondary institutions are subject to the nonprofit corporation laws applicable to all nonprofit corporations; in others, postsecondary institutions come under corporation statutes designed particularly for charitable institutions; and in a few states, there are special statutes for incorporating educational institutions. Proprietary (profit-making) schools often fall under general business corporation laws. The states also have laws applicable to "foreign" corporations (that is, those chartered in another state), under which states may "register" or "qualify" out-of-state institutions that seek to do business in their jurisdiction.

The second method for regulating private postsecondary institutions is licensure. Imposed as a condition to offering education programs in the state or to granting degrees or using a collegiate name, licensure is a more substantial form of regulation than chartering.

There are three different approaches to licensure:

> First, a state can license on the basis of *minimum standards*. The state may choose to specify, for example, that all degree-granting institutions have a board, administration, and faculty of certain characteristics, an organized curriculum with stipulated features, a library of given size, and facilities defined as adequate to the instruction offered. Among states pursuing this approach, the debate centers on what and in what detail the state should prescribe—some want higher levels of prescription to assure "quality," others want to allow room for "innovation."
>
> A second approach follows models developed [for classical] regional accreditation and stresses *realization of objectives*. Here the focus is less on a set of standards applicable to all than on encouragement for institutions to set their own goals and realize them as fully as possible. The role of the visiting team is not to inspect on the basis of predetermined criteria but to analyze the institution on its own terms and suggest new paths to improvement. This help-oriented model is especially strong in the eastern states with large numbers of well-established institutions; in some cases, a combined state-regional team will be formed to make a single visit and joint recommendation.

A third model would take an *honest practice* approach. The essence of it is that one inspects to verify that an institution is run with integrity and fulfills basic claims made to the public. The honesty and probity of institutional officers, integrity of the faculty, solvency of the balance sheet, accuracy of the catalogue, adequacy of student records, equity of refund policies—these and related matters would be the subject of investigation. If an institution had an occupation-related program, employment records of graduates would be examined. It is unclear whether any state follows this model in its pure form, though it is increasingly advocated, and aspects of it do appear in state criteria. A claimed advantage is that, since it does not specify curricular components or assess their strengths and weaknesses (as the other two models might), an "honest practice" approach avoids undue state "control" of education [*Approaches to State Licensing of Private Degree-Granting Institutions* (Postsecondary Education Convening Authority, George Washington University, 1975), 17–19].

Almost all states have some form of licensing laws applicable to proprietary institutions, and the trend is toward increasingly stringent regulation of the proprietary sector. Some states apply special requirements to non-degree-granting proprietary schools that are more extensive than the requirements for degree-granting institutions. In *New York Association of Career Schools v. State Education Department*, 749 F. Supp. 1264 (S.D.N.Y. 1990), the court upheld the New York regulations on non-degree-granting schools against an attack under the equal protection clause.

Regarding licensure of nonprofit institutions, in contrast, there is considerable variance among the states in the application and strength of state laws and in their enforcement. Often, by statutory mandate or the administrative practice of the licensing agency, institutions accredited by a recognized accrediting agency (see Section 12.1.2 of this book) are exempted from all or most licensing requirements for nonprofit schools.

In addition to chartering and licensure, some states also have a third way of exerting authority over private postsecondary institutions: through the award of financial aid to such institutions or their students. By establishing criteria for institutional eligibility and reviewing institutions that choose to apply, states may impose additional requirements, beyond those in corporation or licensure laws, on institutions that are willing and able to come into compliance and thus receive the aid.

State corporation laws ordinarily do not pose significant problems for postsecondary institutions, since their requirements can usually be met easily and routinely. Although licensing laws contain more substantial requirements, even in the more rigorous states these laws present few problems for established institutions, either because the institutions are exempted by accreditation or because their established character makes compliance easy. For these institutions, problems with licensing laws are more likely to arise if they establish new programs in other states and must therefore comply with the various licensing laws of those other states. The story is quite different for new institutions, especially if they have innovative (nontraditional) structures, programs, or delivery systems, or if they operate across state lines. For these institutions, licensing laws can be quite burdensome because they may not be adapted to the particular characteristics of nontraditional education or receptive to out-of-state institutions.

When an institution does encounter problems with state licensing laws, administrators may have several possible legal arguments to raise, which generally stem from state administrative law or the due process clauses of state constitutions or the federal Constitution. Administrators should insist that the licensing agency proceed according to written standards and procedures, that it make them available to the institution, and that the agency scrupulously follow its own standards and procedures. If any standard or procedure appears to be outside the authority delegated to the licensing agency by state statute, that standard or procedure may be questioned before the licensing agency and challenged in court. Occasionally, even if standards and procedures are within the agency's delegated authority, the authorizing statute itself may be challenged as an unlawful delegation of legislative power. In *Packer Collegiate Institute v. University of the State of New York*, 81 N.E.2d 80 (N.Y. 1948), the court invalidated New York's licensing legislation because "the legislature has not only failed to set out standards or tests by which the qualifications of the schools might be measured, but has not specified, even in most general terms, what the subject matter of the regulations is to be." In *State v. Williams*, 117 S.E.2d 444 (N.C. 1960), the court used similar reasoning to invalidate a North Carolina law. However, a much more hospitable approach to legislative delegations of authority is found in more recent cases, such as *Shelton College* and *Warder*, both discussed earlier in this section, in which the courts upheld state laws against charges that they were unlawful delegations of authority.

The case of *Ramos v. California Committee of Bar Examiners*, 857 F. Supp. 702 (N.D. Cal. 1994), is an illustrative procedural due process case. It was a challenge to a government decision to deny recognition to a law school. The court addressed a threshold due process issue that may present difficulties in denial cases, but generally not in withdrawal or termination cases: whether the government action deprived the institution of a "property interest" or "liberty interest" (see generally Section 5.7.2). The plaintiff in *Ramos* had been denied registration as a law school in the state of California. Focusing on property interests, the court considered whether "the statutory and regulatory provisions pertaining to the availability of registration" created any "right or entitlement" for applicants for state registration. Because the answer was no, the plaintiff had no property interest at stake and therefore no basis for a due process claim.

The *Ramos* opinion also indicates that, even if the plaintiff did have a property interest at stake, the due process claim would still fail because the committee of bar examiners had provided all the procedure the Fourteenth Amendment would then require. In particular, the committee had provided the plaintiff with registration forms, had provided the opportunity for a hearing, and had notified the plaintiff of the hearing date. Moreover, the committee's findings apparently were supported by "substantial evidence," and its conclusions were not "arbitrary" (or at least the plaintiff did not contend that they were).

Although state incorporation and licensing laws are often sleeping dogs, they can bite hard when awakened. Institutional administrators and counsel—especially in new, expanding, or innovating institutions—should remain aware of the potential impact of these laws and of the legal arguments available to the institution if problems do arise.

### 11.2.4. Other state regulatory laws affecting postsecondary education programs.

***11.2.4.1. Laws on gun possession on campus.*** Legislative developments concerning guns on campuses have expanded in the wake of various campus shootings, such as occurred at Virginia Tech in 2007, and in the wake of the U.S. Supreme Court's 2008 and 2010 decisions recognizing the right of individuals, under the Second Amendment, to "keep and bear" arms. In *District of Columbia v. Heller*, 554 U.S. 570 (2008), the Court held that the Second Amendment created an individual right that is not limited to arming militias and that various gun control regulations of the District of Columbia violated this individual right. In *McDonald v. City of Chicago*, 130 S. Ct. 3020 (2010), the Court concluded that the Second Amendment applied not only to the federal government but also to the states, and invalidated city ordinances prohibiting the possession of handguns by private citizens. These cases and the various state laws that expand or contract gun possession rights are proving to be of great importance in determining whether and how institutions may regulate guns on campus.

There are often two contending, and frequently incompatible, forces at work in disputes concerning gun control. Viewing events from one perspective, some members of a campus community may push for state legislation banning guns from campuses (for community safety). Viewing events from another perspective, other members may push for state legislation permitting guns on campus (for personal protection). Analysis of such legislation, and of campus regulations that may be inconsistent with such legislation, may implicate not only the *Heller* and *McDonald* cases (and the numerous questions about their scope), but also provisions of the state constitution that (1) grant to particular public universities a range of autonomy from state legislative enactments or (2) establish a state constitutional right to keep and bear arms.

Public institutions in several states have attempted to avoid the application of state legislation that permits students and employees to possess or carry guns on campus if they are licensed. For example, the University of Utah has wrestled with Utah Code § 63-98-102, which prohibits state or local entities from promulgating a statute, policy, or rule that in "any way inhibits or restricts the possession or use of firearms on either public or private property." There is no exception for colleges and universities. The university, to the contrary, had had a policy that prohibited faculty, staff, and students from possessing firearms on campus. The state attorney general issued an opinion stating that the university's policy violated state law, and the university then sued the attorney general in state court. The Utah Supreme Court ruled against the university in *University of Utah v. Shurtleff*, 144 P.3d 1109 (Utah 2006). Although the university did enjoy a form of autonomy under the state constitution, the court said, that constitution also guaranteed the citizens of Utah the right to keep and bear arms. Furthermore, the constitutional autonomy of the university did not limit the legislature's power to exercise "general control and supervision" over the university. Specifically, the court said, "the Utah Constitution does not grant the University authority to promulgate firearms policies in contravention of legislative enactments, and it is not our place to do so" (144 P.3d at 1121). And, in response to the university's claim that the firearms law violated its academic freedom, the court responded that, although the university enjoyed "broad powers," it was not free from legislative oversight. The chief justice dissented, arguing that the state constitution gave the university the authority to forbid the possession and use of firearms on campus.

Subsequently, in March 2007, the Utah legislature passed S.B. 251, which amended section 53B-3-103 of the Laws of Utah. The amendment specifically requires the boards of trustees of universities and colleges in Utah to acknowledge "that the Legislature has the authority to regulate, by law, firearms at higher education institutions." After such acknowledgment is made, the law authorizes the board of trustees to allow the colleges and universities under its purview to "make a rule that allows a resident of a dormitory located at the institution to request only roommates who are not licensed to carry a concealed firearm" under the relevant state laws.

Similarly, in Oregon, a foundation representing gun owners challenged an administrative regulation of the Oregon State Board of Higher Education that sanctioned individuals who possessed or used firearms on the campuses of state universities. In *Oregon Firearms Educational Foundation v. Board of Higher Education*, 2011 Or. App. LEXIS 1340 (Or. Ct. App. 2011), the plaintiff argued that the regulation was preempted by state law and also violated the Second Amendment to the U.S. Constitution. The court acknowledged that the state board had broad authority to make rules concerning the conduct of individuals while on state university property, but ruled that state law, which vested exclusive authority to regulate firearms in the state legislature, preempted the rule in question. The court did not reach the issue of the effect of the Second Amendment. Although the board did not appeal that ruling, it issued a policy prohibiting individuals who wish to do business on university property from carrying guns; individuals with concealed weapon permits may walk across campus but may not enter any building or arena. Police officers and participants in military programs are exempt from the rule.

In *Students for Concealed Carry on Campus v. Regents of the University of Colorado*, 2010 Colo. App. LEXIS 541 (Colo. App. April 15, 2010), a state trial court had rejected a student group's challenge to a University of Colorado prohibition on the possession of "firearms or other weapons" anywhere on a campus of the university by any individual except certified law enforcement personnel. The group claimed that the regulation violated the state constitution as well as the Colorado Concealed Carry Act (CCA). Noting that the regents constituted a "statewide authority with its own legislative powers over distinct geographical areas" and that state legislation can supplant the authority of the regents "only when a legislative enactment expressly so provides," the trial court ruled that the regents' regulation was an appropriate exercise of the state's police power.

The state appellate court reversed the trial court, ruling that the Colorado law authorizing concealed carrying of handguns did not contain an exemption for colleges and universities. Furthermore, said the court, the students had stated a valid claim that prohibition of concealed weapons on campus violated the state constitution's provision concerning the right to bear firearms for self-defense. The court remanded the students' constitutional claim to the trial court for further proceedings.

The state's supreme court affirmed, ruling that "the CCA's comprehensive statewide purpose, broad language, and narrow exclusions show that the General Assembly intended to divest the Board of Regents of its authority to regulate concealed handgun possession on campus." Because the court reached its conclusion on statutory grounds, it declined to rule on the students' constitutional claim (*Regents of the University of Colorado v. Students for Concealed Carry on Campus*, 271 P.3d 496 (Colo. 2012)).

But in *DiGiacinto v. The Rector and Visitors of George Mason University*, 704 S.E.2d 365 (Va. 2011), the plaintiff challenged a regulation promulgated by George Mason University, a public university in Virginia, that stated:

> Possession or carrying of any weapon by any person, except a police officer, is prohibited on university property in academic buildings, administrative office buildings, student residence buildings, dining facilities, or while attending sporting, entertainment or educational events. Entry upon the aforementioned university property in violation of this prohibition is expressly forbidden [704 S.E.2d at 367].

The plaintiff argued that the regulation violated his Second Amendment right to bear arms and that the university did not have the delegated authority to regulate handguns on campus.

The court cited the sentence in *Heller* (cited at the beginning of this subsection) that cautioned that "nothing in our opinion should be taken to cast doubt on . . . laws forbidding the carrying of firearms in sensitive places such as schools and government buildings" (554 U.S. at 625–626). Characterizing George Mason University as a "sensitive place," the state court explained that *Heller* had recognized that Second Amendment protections were not absolute and that prohibitions on guns in "sensitive places such as government buildings and schools" continued to be lawful. The court noted that the regulation regarding firearms did not prohibit weapons from all campus property:

> The regulation does not impose a total ban of weapons on campus. Rather, the regulation is tailored, restricting weapons only in those places where people congregate and are most vulnerable—inside campus buildings and at campus events. Individuals may still carry or possess weapons on the open grounds of GMU, and in other places on campus not enumerated in the regulation [704 S.E. 2d at 136–137].

Noting that the legislature had authorized the university's governing board to develop policies that "promote safety" on its campus, the court upheld the regulation. The court rejected the university's claim that sovereign immunity protected it from the plaintiff's constitutional challenges, because the university was not "a separate government," but ruled that no constitutional violation had been committed.

Subsequent to the ruling in *DiGiacinto*, the University of Virginia requested an opinion by the state attorney general on the validity of the university's policy prohibiting the possession of firearms and ammunition by visitors on university property or inside university facilities. The opinion concluded that the policy regarding gun possession inside university buildings was valid after *DiGiacinto* but that the aspects of the policy that were broader than those discussed in *DiGiacinto*, such as a ban on weapons in the university's "controlled outdoor area," did not comport with the reasoning of *DiGiacinto*. And the university's ban on concealed weapons, even for those individuals authorized to carry concealed weapons, did not comport with state law, which authorized banning concealed weapons if "such possession is otherwise prohibited by law." The opinion noted that regulations have the force of law, but policies do not. Since the university's ban was a policy rather than a regulation, it did not have the force of law and could not be used to ban individuals from carrying concealed weapons inside university buildings.

In December of 2011, a state trial court rejected a student's challenge to the University of Idaho's policy prohibiting firearms in campus housing. The student argued that the ban violated Idaho's law prohibiting local regulation of firearms; violated the Second Amendment; and also violated article 1, section 11 of the Idaho Constitution, which guarantees the right to bear and possess arms. In *Tribble v. State Board of Education and Nellis*, Case No. CV-2011-0069 (Idaho Dist. Ct., 2d Jud. Dist. December 7, 2011), the trial court rejected all of the plaintiff's claims. First, the court ruled that by signing the housing agreement, which explicitly banned the possession of weapons both on campus generally and in campus housing, the student had waived his constitutional right to keep and bear arms. With respect to the constitutional claims, the court ruled that the university's policy was "substantially related to the Regents' important interesting in ensuring that the University campus is a safe and violence-free learning environment." Furthermore, said the court, the Idaho Constitution recognized the independence of the Regents, as did a decision of the state's supreme court (*State ex rel. Black v. State Board of Education*, 196 P.201, 205 (Idaho 1921)), which stated that the Regents were not subject to control by other branches of state government, "including the legislature." With respect to the U.S. Constitutional claim, the court cited *Heller*'s acknowledgment that some regulation of gun possession could be permissible in "sensitive places" such as schools and government buildings. Since the plaintiff was residing in a campus apartment owned by a public university, the court said, the "residence" was more like a government building than a private home, and the proximity of children, playgrounds, and large numbers of people to the campus apartment justified, under an intermediate scrutiny test, the gun prohibition.

And in *Mitchell v. University of Kentucky*, 2012 Ky. LEXIS 47 (Ky. April 26, 2012), the Kentucky Supreme Court reversed summary judgment for a university in a case involving an employee dismissed for having a loaded gun in the glove compartment of his car. Kentucky law (Ky. Rev. Stat. Ann. § 237.115(1)) permitted institutions of higher education to prohibit guns on university property, but another Kentucky law (Ky. Rev. Stat. Ann. § 527.020) permitted individuals with concealed carry permits to store guns in their vehicle. The court resolved the apparent conflict between the laws by determining that the constitutional right to bear arms was superior and that Mitchell, an at-will employee, had been dismissed in violation of public policy.

The issue of guns on campus is active and the outcome in many states is uncertain. The results in Virginia, which appear to allow at least some restrictions on gun possession in certain parts of campus, may not be consistent with laws or constitutions in other states. The constitutions of most states guarantee their citizens the right to bear arms. Administrators and counsel should follow this issue closely, as it is high on the political agenda.

### Section 11.3. Federal Government Regulation

**11.3.1. Overview of federal constitutional powers over education.** The federal government is a government of limited powers; it has only those powers that are expressly conferred by the U.S. Constitution or that can reasonably be implied from those conferred. The remaining powers are, under the Tenth Amendment, "reserved to the states respectively, or to the People." Although the Constitution does not mention education, let alone delegate power over it to the federal government, it does not follow that the Tenth Amendment reserves all authority over education to the states or the people (see *Case v. Bowles*, 327 U.S. 92 (1946)). Many federal constitutional powers— particularly the spending power (U.S. Const. Art. I, Sec. 8, ¶ 1), the taxing power (Art. I, Sec. 8, ¶ 1), the commerce power (Art. I, Sec. 8, ¶), and the civil rights enforcement powers (Amend. 14, Sec. 5)—are broad enough to extend to many matters concerning education. Whenever an education activity falls within the scope of one of these federal powers, the federal government has authority over it.

When Congress passes a law pursuant to its federal constitutional powers, and the law is within the scope of these powers, the federal law will "preempt" or supersede any state or local laws that impinge on the effectuation of the federal law. The application of this federal "preemption doctrine" to postsecondary education is illustrated by *United States v. City of Philadelphia*, 798 F.2d 81 (3d Cir. 1986), 798 F.2d 81 (3d Cir. 1986), discussed briefly in Section 11.1 of this book. Noting that the federal military recruiting laws and policies at issue in that case were within the scope of Congress's constitutional powers to raise and support armies, the court held that the federal laws and policies preempted a local civil rights ordinance prohibiting discrimination against homosexuals. In addition, when Congress passes a federal law pursuant to Congress's constitutional powers, it sometimes may abrogate the states' Eleventh Amendment immunity from suit and permit private individuals to enforce the law by suing the states for money damages.

In a number of cases since the early 1990s, the U.S. Supreme Court has emphasized principles of federalism and the limits that they place on federal power. In so doing, the Court has created new protections against federal authority for the states and state agencies. In *Printz v. United States*, 521 U.S. 898 (1997), for example, the Court relied on a principle of state sovereignty. The question was whether Congress could compel state officers (in this case sheriffs) "to execute Federal Laws." The Court answered this question in the negative, thus invalidating provisions of the federal Brady Handgun Violence Prevention Act that commanded state and local law enforcement officers to conduct background checks on prospective handgun purchasers. According to the Court, these provisions of the federal Brady law violated state sovereignty protections:

> [I]t is the whole *object* of the law to direct the functioning of the state executive, and hence to compromise the structural framework of dual sovereignty . . . It is the very *principle* of separate state sovereignty that such a law offends . . . The Federal Government may neither issue directives requiring the States to address particular problems, nor command the States' officers, or those of their political subdivisions, to administer or enforce a Federal regulatory program [521 U.S. at 944].

Similarly, in *Seminole Tribe v. Florida* (1996), in several successor cases relying on *Seminole Tribe*, in *Alden v. Maine* (1999), and in *Federal Maritime Commission v. South Carolina Ports Authority* (2002), the Court again cited state sovereignty principles in providing states a broad immunity from private plaintiffs' suits raising federal claims in federal and state courts and before federal administrative agencies. In 1997 in *City of Boerne v. Flores*, in several successor cases relying on *Boerne*, and in 2000 in *United States v. Morrison*, the Court narrowed Congress's authority to regulate the states under its civil rights enforcement powers. And in 1995 in *United States v. Lopez*, and in 2000 in *United States v. Morrison*, the Court limited Congress's commerce power not only over the states but, more particularly, over private individuals and institutions. All of these cases were controversial. The extent of the controversy, and the contested nature of the law in this arena, is illustrated by the Court's voting patterns in these cases: *Printz, Seminole Tribe, Alden, South Carolina Ports Authority, City of Boerne, Morrison*, and *Lopez* were all decided by 5-to-4 votes, as were most of the cases following them.

### 11.3.2. Federal regulation of postsecondary education

**11.3.2.1. Overview.** Despite the attempts of institutions and their national associations to limit the impact of federal regulations and federal funding conditions on postsecondary education, the federal presence on campus has continued to expand. Although higher education has experienced some successes in asserting its autonomy, particularly with respect to "who may teach, what may be taught, how it shall be taught, and who may be admitted to study" (*Sweezy v. New Hampshire*; see Section 6.1.5 of this book), federal regulation affects even the academic core of a college or university. Although mandated self-regulation is still used in some areas of federal regulation, such as restrictions on the use of human subjects or research on animals, self-regulatory actions by institutions have been criticized as insufficient or self-serving. And while the federal government has relied on the private accrediting agencies to help ensure the integrity of certain federal aid programs, these agencies' standards and practices have been periodically criticized by federal officials, and federal regulation of the accrediting process has increased over time (see Section 12.1.2).

Federal laws of particular importance to institutions of higher education include laws regulating research, which require Institutional Review Boards for research involving human or animal subjects. The USA PATRIOT Act (Pub. L. No. 107-56, 115 Stat. 272) places limitations on the sharing of research results and, in some cases, who may participate in a research project. It also regulates the record-keeping policies of academic libraries, the monitoring of international students' immigration status, the release of information about students, and the operation of the campus's computer systems, among other requirements. Copyright laws (17 U.S.C. § 101 et seq.) and patent laws (Title 35 of the *United States Code*) pose a myriad of challenges for institutions of higher education and, in particular, their faculties, as they provide protections for faculty work under some circumstances but limit faculty and students' ability to use information in other ways (see Section 11.3.3). In addition, trademark law (15 U.S.C. § 1051 et seq.) is important to the protection of institutions' symbols and logos, and antitrust law (15 U.S.C. § 1 et seq; 15 U.S.C. § 12 et seq.) has been used to challenge the sharing of student financial aid information and on-campus housing regulations. Environmental laws (in particular, the Resource Conservation and Recovery Act of 1976 (RCRA), 42 U.S.C. § 6901 et seq., and the Comprehensive Environmental Response, Compensation, and Liability Act of 1980 (CERCLA, also known as the Superfund Law, 42 U.S.C. §9601 et seq.)) regulate the operation of science laboratories, heating plants, and a multitude of other institutional activities. Other federal laws regulate the immigration status of international students and staff, campus computer network communications (such as the Computer Fraud and Abuse Act of 1986, 18 U.S.C. § 1030), and the delivery of health care (for example, the Medicare and HIPAA laws). Other federal laws, such as Title VII (see Section 4.5.2.1) and the Americans with Disabilities Act (see Section 4.5.2.5) prohibit discrimination in employment.

In addition, other federal statutes and regulations may also become important to colleges and universities in particular circumstances. The federal bankruptcy law (11 U.S.C. § 101 et seq.), for instance, is important when a student loan recipient declares bankruptcy and when an institution encounters severe financial distress. The Military Selective Service Act (50 U.S.C. § 451 et seq.) is important when the federal government seeks to prohibit individuals who have not registered from receiving federal student aid (see Section 7.3.2). And the Lobbying Disclosure Act of 1995 (2 U.S.C. §§ 1601 et seq.) requires the disclosure of efforts by paid lobbyists to affect decisions by the executive and legislative branches of the federal government.

The National Voter Registration Act, 42 U.S.C. § 1973gg5(a)(2)(B), commonly known as the "motor voter" law, requires states to designate as voter registration agencies all offices that are primarily engaged in providing services to persons with disabilities. A federal appellate court has ruled that the offices at two public universities in Virginia that provide services to disabled students are subject to this law. *National Coalition for Students with Disabilities Education and Legal Defense Fund v. Gilmore*, 153 F.3d 283 (4th Cir. 1998). A second lawsuit involving this law, *United States of America v. State of New York*, 700 F. Supp. 2d 186 (N.D. N.Y. 2010), resulted in summary judgment for the U.S. Department of Justice and a consent order requiring the CUNY and SUNY systems to designate their disabled student services offices as mandatory voter registration offices.

Corporate accounting scandals of the early twenty-first century prompted Congress to enact the Sarbanes-Oxley Act (15 U.S.C. §§ 7201 et seq.), which applies to publicly traded organizations. Although most of its provisions do not apply directly to colleges and universities, the law nevertheless raises significant issues concerning governance of organizations, transparency in accounting for financial matters, and the responsibilities of top executives. As such, the law has importance as guidance for trustees and senior administrators of colleges and universities.

The CAN-SPAM Act of 2003 ("Controlling the Assault of Non-Solicited Pornography and Marketing Act of 2003"), 15 U.S.C. §§ 7701 et seq., is important for institutions that use broadcast e-mail to contact alumni, potential students, or other audiences. Regulations implementing the law are found at 16 C.F.R. Part 316. The law imposes limitations on the use of unsolicited e-mail that is sent for a commercial purpose and provides for penalties for violations.

The laws mentioned briefly here have important consequences for postsecondary institutions' ability to manage their affairs efficiently and to exchange information. The arena of federal regulation has expanded even more in areas related to terrorism and technology. The subsections that follow can only hint at the scope and complexity of regulation in these and other areas. The assistance of expert counsel is recommended when issues arise for institutions in these areas.

*11.3.2.2. Regulation of research.* Federal agencies that fund academic research have developed a complex system for overseeing this research on campus, assuring that there are appropriate financial controls on spending under research grants and contracts, and reviewing research proposals to ensure the safety of the research subjects, whether they are human or animal. Federal regulations also prescribe the manner in which research misconduct must be investigated and the timing and content of reports that investigatory committees make to the funding agency. Other regulations prescribe conflict of interest. In addition, statutes and regulations cover various aspects of scientific research that may have national security implications.

The regulations of several federal agencies that fund research require that each institution that receives federal research funding establish an Institutional Review Board (IRB) to approve research that involves humans as subjects. A similar committee, the Institutional Animal Care and Use Committee (IACUC), must be established at institutions that receive federal funding for research involving animals. Although not all academic research is funded by the federal government, most colleges and universities use the federally mandated system for reviewing research proposals and investigating research misconduct for all human subject and animal research conducted by faculty, staff, or students. And some federal regulatory schemes, such as the Food and Drug Administration's regulation of "clinical investigations" and the U.S. Department of Agriculture's Animal Welfare Act regulations, apply regardless of funding source.

### 11.3.2.3. *Regulation of intellectual property.*[3] Federal regulation (and protection) of "intellectual property" involves copyright law, trademark law, and patent law. These three concepts are similar in that they provide certain protections for the owners of intellectual property, allowing them to control who uses the property and how it is used. This section focuses on copyright law, in particular the principles of "fair use." A fuller discussion of copyright law appears in *LHE 5th* in Section 14.2.5. Patent and trademark law are discussed in *LHE 5th* Sections 14.2.6 and 14.2.7, respectively.

Article I, section 8, clause 8 of the U.S. Constitution authorizes Congress to create the Copyright Act "to promote the Progress of Science and useful Arts, by securing for limited Times to Authors and Inventors the exclusive Right to their respective Writings and Discoveries." This purpose, simply stated, is to increase knowledge. The Supreme Court has explained that the copyright clause "motivate[s] the creative activity of authors and inventors by the provision of a special reward, and . . . allow[s] the public access to the products of their genius after the limited period of exclusive control has expired" (*Sony Corp. of America v. Universal City Studios, Inc.*, 464 U.S. 417, 429 (1984)).

In 1790 Congress protected only maps, charts, and books. See Copyright Act of 1790, ch. 15, § 4, 1 Stat. 124, 125 (1790). Over time, more and more works have been given copyright protection, often to address new forms of expression made possible by new technology. The Copyright Act now protects a wide array of content including dance and musical scores, film, audio and video, recordings, architectural works, and software. The history of U.S. copyright legislation reveals an unmistakable expansion of copyright owners' rights and a diminution of their administrative responsibilities. Formalities once necessary to acquire the bundle of copyright rights have been discarded. For example, before the passage of the 1976 Copyright Act, authors were required to adhere to a number of formalities such as depositing the work in the Copyright Office and affixing notice on published works in order to receive copyright protection (Copyright Act of 1909, ch. 320, §§ 12, 19, 35 Stat. 1075, 1078–1079 (1909)).

---

[3]This section was updated and revised by Madelyn Wessel, associate general counsel, University of Virginia, who also prepared the section on copyright for *LHE 5th*.

These formalities are no longer required in order to secure copyright protection (see 17 U.S.C. §§ 401–412 (2006)).

Congress has enacted many changes to the copyright regime in recent decades. In the late 1980s and 1990s Congress passed amendments affecting state sovereign immunity, artists' moral rights, the fair use of unpublished manuscripts, penalties (including criminal sanctions for significant infringements), digital archiving in university libraries, special procedures to protect works on the Internet, and the legal status for technological protections of copyrighted works, among other things. Courts tried many cases involving classroom materials, personal research copies, Internet service provider liability limitations, authorship and ownership of creative works, and states' sovereign immunity for claims for damages in federal courts. By 2000, most legislative and court battles were pitched around digital themes.

In the second decade of the twenty-first century, copyright litigation encompasses both challenges to conventional reuse and remix of print or artistic materials as well as titanic struggles between content industries and entities (including higher education) engaged in digital distribution activities. Certain core issues remain central to higher education: fair use, performance rights, ownership, vicarious liability, the implications of the shift from acquiring books and journals to licensing digital databases of information, and anti-circumvention. As institutions of higher education and major research sponsors (including the federal government) have begun to grapple with questions of mass digitization, open access to scholarly research, and the management of digital needs, a lagging copyright statutory framework has ensured that both legislative and judicial battles are ever more complex.

Section 106 of the Copyright Act affords copyright owners the exclusive rights in copyrighted works to do and to authorize any of the following: (1) to *reproduce* the copyrighted work in copies or phonorecords; (2) to *prepare derivative works* based upon the copyrighted work; (3) to *distribute copies* or phonorecords of the copyrighted work to the public by sale or other transfer of ownership, or by rental, lease, or lending; (4) in the case of literary, musical, dramatic, and choreographic works, pantomimes, and motion pictures and other audiovisual works, to *perform the copyrighted work publicly*; (5) in the case of literary, musical, dramatic, and choreographic works, pantomimes, and pictorial, graphic, or sculptural works, including the individual images of a motion picture or other audiovisual work, to *display the copyrighted work publicly*; and (6) in the case of sound recordings, to *perform the copyrighted work publicly by means of a digital audio transmission*. It is important to understand that these copyrights are distinct and that each can be licensed differently. An author can decide to license one or all of his or her copyrights, or can assign or transfer certain rights for a specific period of time only. Publishers traditionally attempt to obtain all of the rights of an author in agreeing to publish and distribute a work. A transfer of all the effective copyrights can be accomplished even though an author may retain the formal "copyright" registration in his or her name. Exclusive transfers of all of an author's copyrights (which remains the norm in scholarly publishing) create contractual issues for faculty who later wish to share scholarly works with students or colleagues.

Critically, the rights of a copyright holder are subject to important statutory limitations in sections 107 through 122 of the Copyright Act. Many of these exclusions provide significant "safe harbors" and otherwise enable uses and activities that are centrally important to higher education. Whether these statutory limitations should be understood to limit rights otherwise afforded to copyright holders under section 106, or instead constitute affirmative defenses that can be asserted against a claim of copyright infringement, is a topic of considerable interest as some rights holders seek to impose contractual restrictions through licensing on uses authorized under these exceptions.

The most critical of all the copyright exceptions is found in section 107 of the Copyright Act. While other exceptions are laden with detailed and sometimes confounding technical requirements, section 107 offers a powerful and seductively simple vision, with its clear preamble stating that "the fair use of a copyrighted work, including such use by reproduction in copies or phonorecords or by any other means specified by that section, for purposes such as criticism, comment, news reporting, teaching (including multiple copies for classroom use), scholarship, or research, is not an infringement of copyright." Nevertheless, fair use involves a case-by-case inquiry that requires balancing of the following four statutory factors:

1. *Purpose and character* of the use, including whether the use is for educational versus commercial purposes

2. The *nature of the copyrighted work*—is it a factual or creative work?

3. The *amount and substantiality* of the portion to be used in relation to the work as a whole

4. The *effect or impact* of the use upon the potential market for or value of the work

The Supreme Court has made it clear that this statutory balancing takes place in the context of the central purpose of copyright law, to promote knowledge and learning (*Campbell v. Acuff-Rose Music, Inc.*, 510 U.S. 569, 577–78 (1994)). No single section 107 factor is dispositive; all must be considered. Educational and scholarly uses are clearly at the heart of the examples set forth in the preamble to section 107, and when a use matches one of those examples, *Campbell* makes clear that fact will tend to weigh in favor of fair use when analyzing the first fair use factor. Indeed, even if a use is commercial in the sense that the author may profit from it, the first factor may weigh in favor of fair use if the context matches one of the categories listed in the preamble.

Unfortunately, despite the seemingly clear language of section 107, cases involving fact patterns taken directly from the preamble such as "multiple copies for classroom use" and "news reporting" have generated outcomes in which courts have found some uses to be fair and others to be infringing. Decades of judicial interpretation of these provisions have not created the clarity that one would hope might have evolved from the text. As the U.S. Supreme Court itself made clear in *Campbell*: "The task is not to be simplified with bright-line rules, for the statute, like the doctrine it recognizes, calls for case-by-case analysis" (510 U.S. 569, 576 (1994) (citing *Harper & Row, Publishers, Inc. v. Nation Enterprises*, 471 U.S. 539, 560 (1985)). Notwithstanding the unpredictable path of fair use law, however, new cases provide a robust basis on which to revisit old assumptions about fair use and to feel more confident asserting educational fair use rights. These new cases and theories about fair use will be instrumental as higher education grapples with today's challenges arising in the context of video streaming, course reserves, scholarly communications, publishing, digitization of rare materials, and more.

Fair use law has evolved considerably in evaluation of three of the four fair use factors: the impact of the fourth factor's market analysis, which was at one time considered to be the most important and even the decisive factor in evaluating a fair use case; the impact of a finding that a use was transformative under the first factor; and the impact on the third factor when use of an entire work is considered necessary and noncompeting.

In 1985, the Supreme Court identified the fourth fair use factor (market impact) as the most significant, influencing many subsequent lower court decisions. See *Harper & Row Publishers, Inc. v. Nation Enterprises*, 471 U.S. 539, 566 (1985) ("This last factor is undoubtedly the single most important element of fair use"). Nine years after issuing this pronouncement, however, the Supreme Court revised its thinking on the fair use test. In *Campbell*, 510 U.S. at 584, the Court found the Sixth Circuit Court of Appeals committed reversible error in "giving virtually dispositive weight" to the fourth factor. Instead, the Court instructed that all four section 107 factors "are to be explored, and the results weighed together, *in light of the purposes of copyright*" (*id.* at 578 (emphasis added)). The *Campbell* Court found even a commercial use to be fair where 2 Live Crew sought a license, in a well-established music market, to create a rap version of "Oh, Pretty Woman" and then ignored the copyright holder's refusal to grant the requested rights.

Numerous subsequent lower federal court decisions show that the impact of *Campbell* has been significant, causing courts to affirm the use of works as fair even if a licensing market exists. For example, the Ninth Circuit Court of Appeals held that transformative use of thumbnail images by Google's image search engine was fair use notwithstanding the existence of an emerging cellular phone download market for the thumbnail images. See *Perfect 10, Inc. v. Amazon.com, Inc.*, 487 F.3d 701, 724–25, *as amended and superseded by* 508 F.3d 1146 (9th Cir. 2007). Similarly in *Bill Graham Archives v Dorling Kindersley Ltd.*, 448 F.3d 605 (2d Cir. 2006), the Court of Appeals for the Second Circuit found the unauthorized reproduction of seven images of Grateful Dead posters to be protected by fair use. This decision is notable for its emphasis on the format (which was small but not quite as small as a thumbnail) of the images used, which the court found critical to its findings of transformative use; the immateriality of the commercial interest of the fair use proponent; and the almost total disregard paid to the copyright owner's complaint that the defendant ignored its "established market for licensing its images" (*id.* at 614–15). The parties had negotiated for use of these images but were unable to agree on a price. The court found that the use of the images was "transformatively different from their original expressive purpose," and ruled that the fair use tests had been met.

In summary, although market harm will weigh against a finding of fair use, a thoughtful fair use analysis should not use this factor as a shortcut. Especially when the use is transformative, the use of the work may be considered fair even if market harm may be present.

The new fair use cases illustrate the increasing importance of considering whether a particular use is "transformative" in evaluating the first factor, which requires examination of the purpose and character of the defendant's use of the copyrighted work. The first factor instructs the courts to examine "whether such use is of a commercial nature or is for nonprofit educational purposes," with "nonprofit educational" uses weighing in favor of fair use and "commercial" uses weighing against such a finding (see *Campbell*, 510 U.S. at 577–80). However, two recent technology cases involving Web functionality illustrate the impact of the focus on transformative uses, per se, even without a finding of "nonprofit educational" use. Those who use thumbnail images as indices in the online environment received guidance in the Ninth Circuit's opinion in *Kelly v. Arriba Soft Corporation*, 280 F. 3d 934 (9th Cir. 2002), *amended by* 336 F.3d 811 (9th Cir. 2003). Kelly is a well-known photographer who publishes images on his Web site. Arriba Soft, which has since changed its name to Ditto.com, is a search engine that searches for images, rather than text, and displays search results in the form of a "list" of thumbnail copies of the original images that meet the search criteria. Kelly complained that this use, and the subsequent displays of the images in full size outside the original Web site environment where they were located, was an infringement. Although the trial court found both uses to be fair use, the Ninth Circuit agreed only with respect to the thumbnails. The Ninth Circuit found that Arriba's use of the images served a different function than Kelly's use did—improving access to information on the Internet versus artistic expression. Furthermore, the court noted that it was unlikely that anyone would use Arriba's thumbnails for illustrative or esthetic purposes because enlarging the thumbnails sacrifices their clarity.

In *Perfect 10, Inc. v. Amazon.com, Inc.*, 487 F.3d 701, *as amended and superseded by* 508 F.3d 1146 (9th Cir. 2007), Google was sued for infringing copyrighted photographs of nude models. The plaintiff alleged that Google's search engine provided access to full-sized images by directing users to third party sites that hosted them and provided access to thumbnail images of the photographs through Google's image search feature. The court affirmed the lower court's ruling that in-line linking is not copyright infringement because Google did not display or distribute the image. The court held that the plaintiff had, however, made out a prima facie case that Google violated Perfect 10's display right by creating, storing, and displaying thumbnail images of Perfect 10's photographs. Google could avoid liability only if the court found that its use of the thumbnail images was fair. Instead of focusing on the fourth factor, the Ninth Circuit proceeded to focus on the first, specifically the "purpose and character of the use." In examining whether Google's use of the work was transformative, the court looked not just at guidance from *Campbell* on whether the use added a new "expression, meaning or message," but also to whether a defendant used the plaintiff's copyrighted work *"in a new context to serve a different purpose"* (508 F.3d at 1165 (emphasis added)). Applying this principle to the facts before it, the Ninth Circuit held that a search engine, because it incorporates "an original work into a new work, namely, an electronic reference tool," was transformative and thus met the fair use test.

A strong finding of transformative use was also instrumental in a Second Circuit decision in which that court emphatically affirmed that the use of copyrighted images by the artist Jeff Koons was fair use (*Blanch v. Koons*, 467 F.3d 244 (2d Cir. 2006)). Koons had used a portion of a copyrighted commercial image in a painting, only to be sued by the photographer. In ruling for Koons, the court found that Koons was using the plaintiff's image as "fodder" for his commentary on the social and aesthetic consequences of mass media, not to merely repackage the plaintiff's work, but to create "new information, new aesthetics, new insights and understandings" (*id.* at 253 (citations omitted)). The same court had earlier dismissed such arguments by the artist in *Rogers v. Koons*, 960 F.2d 301 (2d Cir. 1992), decided before the Supreme Court's decision in *Campbell*.

The third fair use factor requires weighing "the amount and substantiality of the portion used in relation to the copyrighted work as a whole." One must ask whether the use is "reasonable in relation to the purpose of the copying" (*Campbell*, 510 U.S. at 586). The evaluation of this factor is highly contextual. The Supreme Court has indicated that "substantial quotations might qualify as a fair use in a review of a published work or a news account of a speech" (*Harper & Row Publishers, Inc. v. Nation Enterprises*, 471 U.S. 539, 601 (1985)), but not if the work was an unpublished presidential memoir that was stolen so one publisher could "scoop" a competitor. In some situations, such as the unauthorized downloading of a copyrighted song readily available at a reasonable price, copying the entire copyrighted work may weigh strongly against a finding of fair use. Cases like the Ninth Circuit's decision in *Perfect 10*, however, make clear that uses of whole works may be fair, especially if the use does not interfere with the copyright owner's market or potential market. Courts are also more likely to conclude that an entire work may be copied if the use is transformative—for example, the use may be for illustrative purposes or for comment and criticism. Similarly, in *Bill Graham Archives v. Dorling Kindersley Ltd.*, 448 F.3d 605 (2d Cir. 2006), the use of reduced sized images of Grateful Dead posters in a retrospective "coffee-table" book was found to be fair. In *Nunez v. Caribbean International News Corp.*, 235 F.3d 18 (1st Cir. 2000), the reprinting of modeling photographs in their entirety was found to be a fair use because the images were an indispensable element needed to assess the critique that they were pornographic. For this reason, the third factor was deemed "of little consequence." In *Perfect 10*, although entire images were copied, the court held that because of the transformative context, the third factor "favored neither party." In the case of short works, it may be necessary to copy the whole work in order to give one's audience a sufficient quantity for evaluation or to undertake a serious scholarly analysis. Therefore, for cases involving short works, the third factor may not be weighed as heavily. In *Hustler Magazine, Inc. v. Moral Majority, Inc.*, 796 F.2d 1148 (9th Cir. 1986), the copying and distribution of thousands of copies of an entire parody was found to be fair use because the intent was to criticize the advertisement. The work at issue included three hundred words of text. Use of an entire long work may weigh against a finding of fair use with respect to the third fair use factor. But, in contrast to earlier understandings that use of an entire work would virtually never be considered fair, these new cases involving technologies undreamed of a generation before, or those involving artistic and scholarly analyses in which an entire work is needed for purposes seemingly protected by the very core of fair use, show that the doctrine is evolving.

Certainly not all the new fair use cases involve findings for allegedly infringing defendants. In a closely watched case from the New York City art world, *Cariou v. Prince*, 784 F. Supp. 2d 337 (S.D.N.Y. 2011), a federal court rejected fair use claims made by the collage artist Richard Prince, who took dozens of published art images by photographer Patrick Cariou and converted them into highly profitable new works. Prince had attempted to justify his unauthorized use of Cariou's images by arguing that the use of copyrighted materials as "raw ingredients" in the creation of new works was a fair use, per se. The court disagreed.

In *Gaylord v. United States*, 595 F.3d 1364 (Fed. Cir. 2010), Frank Gaylord, the sculptor who had created the soldier sculptures in the Korean War memorial in Washington, D.C., brought a copyright infringement action against the United States after the U.S. Postal Service issued a stamp containing a much-modified image of some of the sculptures. The government argued that it had an unlimited license as a joint author since the original sculptures had in fact been commissioned and paid for by the government itself; that the stamp fell under the exclusion from liability for copyright infringement for architectural works under the Architectural Works Copyright Protection Act (AWCPA); and that the government's use was a fair use. The Court of Federal Claims determined that Mr. Gaylord was the sole copyright owner and that the sculpture did not qualify as an architectural work under the AWCPA (*Gaylord v. United States*, 85 Fed. Cl. 59 (2008)). However, the Court of Federal Claims also determined that the government was not liable for copyright infringement because the government's use of the sculpture was fair use. The Federal Circuit upheld the Court of Claims' first two findings and reversed the third, finding that the Postal Service's use of the images to create its stamp was not a fair use and that the Postal Service had infringed Mr. Gaylord's copyrights. The Federal Circuit's finding essentially ignored the question found so important in other post-*Campbell* cases, whether the stamp was transformative. The Court's sole interest under the first factor was to focus on the purpose and character of the stamp. Because the Court found that the stamp and sculpture shared "a common purpose: to honor veterans of the Korean War," the government's fair use claims were doomed.

These decisions highlight the significant role of judicial judgment involved in these case-specific fair use challenges. The doctrine of transformative uses thus invites courts to examine closely the specific artistic (or scholarly, or other) motivations of the fair use actor, inviting potentially mercurial and qualitative discernments to play a central role in fair use determinations.

Repeated attempts have been made to develop guidelines for application and interpretation of fair use, but none has been formally adopted so as to have the force of law. Probably the most influential such document is part of the legislative history of the revised Copyright Act itself, the *Agreement on Guidelines for Classroom Copying in Not-for-Profit Educational Institutions* (in H.R. Rep. No. 94-1476, 94th Cong., 2d Sess. (1976), available at http://www.copyright.gov/circs/circ21.pdf). A second document in the legislative history, the *Guidelines for the Provision of Subsection 108(g)(2)* (the *"Contu Guidelines"*) (Conf. Rep. No. 94-1733, 94th Cong., 2d Sess. (1976), also available at http://www.copyright.gov/circs/circ21.pdf), provides comparable guidance on the provision in section 108 of the Copyright Act dealing with copying for purposes of interlibrary lending. Although the *Guidelines for Classroom Copying* were adopted by thirty-eight educational organizations and the publishing industry to set minimum standards of educational fair use under section 107 of the act, the Association of American Law Schools and the American Association of University Professors (AAUP) did not endorse the provisions and described them as too restrictive in the university setting (H.R. Rep. No. 94-1476, at 65–74). The *Guidelines* establish limits for "Single Copying for Teaching" (for example, a chapter from a book may be copied for the individual teacher's use in scholarly research, class preparation, or teaching) as well as for "Multiple Copies for Classroom Use" (for example, one copy per pupil per course may be made, provided that the copying meets several tests; these tests, set out in the House Report, concern the brevity of the excerpt to be copied, the spontaneity of the use, and the cumulative effect of multiple copying in classes within the institution). During the mid-1990s, the Conference on Fair Use produced additional guidelines covering synchronous distance education, image archives, and multimedia works; however, there was insufficient consensus on these documents to confer upon them the status enjoyed by the *Guidelines for Classroom Copying* and the *Contu Guidelines* for copying for interlibrary lending by libraries.

The *Guidelines for Classroom Copying* were cited by a federal district court in the first higher education copyright case resulting in a judicial opinion, *Basic Books v. Kinko's Graphics Corp.*, 758 F. Supp. 1522 (S.D.N.Y. 1991). A group of publishers brought a copyright infringement action against a chain of copying shops for copying excerpts from their books without permission, compiling those excerpts into coursepacks and selling them to college students. Kinko's argued that its actions fit within the fair use doctrine of section 107 of the Copyright Act. The trial judge wrote: "The search for a coherent, predictable interpretation applicable to all cases remains elusive. This is so particularly because any common law interpretation proceeds on a case-by-case basis" (758 F. Supp. at 1530). Using the four factors in the statute, as well as the *Guidelines for Classroom Copying*, the court ruled that (1) Kinko's was merely repackaging the material for its own commercial purposes; (2) the material in the books was factual (which would suggest a broader scope of fair use); (3) Kinko's had copied a substantial proportion of each work; and (4) Kinko's copying reduced the market for textbooks. Furthermore, the court ruled that for an entire compilation to avoid violating the act, each item in the compilation must pass the fair use test. The judge awarded the plaintiffs $510,000 in statutory damages plus legal fees. Kinko's decided not to appeal the decision and settled the case in October 1991 for $1.875 million in combined damages and legal fees. Significantly, however, the court left open whether the outcome would have been different in a "pure" educational setting, specifically noting: "The decision of this court does not consider copying performed by students, libraries, nor on-campus copyshops, whether conducted for-profit or not" (758 F. Supp. at 1537 n.13).

A subsequent appellate ruling of the Sixth Circuit further undercut activities of commercial copy shops, limiting the reach of fair use. Michigan Document Services (MDS) was a commercial copying service that created coursepacks and sold them to students at the University of Michigan. Although other copy shops near the university paid copyright fees and royalties, MDS did not and stated this policy in its advertising. Despite the earlier holding in *Basic Books v. Kinko's Graphics Corp.*, the owner of MDS had been advised by his attorney that the opinion was "flawed"; he believed that production of coursepacks was protected under the fair use doctrine. Although the trial court found that the copying was not protected under the fair use doctrine, the original three-judge appellate panel of the Sixth Circuit reversed; however, after rehearing, an *en banc* panel sided with the trial court in most respects (*Princeton University Press v. Michigan Document Services, Inc.*, 99 F.3d 1381 (6th Cir. 1996)). The full court analyzed the copying under the four elements of the fair use test and found that because MDS profited from the sale of coursepacks, the purpose of the copying was commercial; furthermore, the loss of copyright permission fees diminished the value of the books to their copyright owners. In response to the defendant's argument that under the fourth factor the court should look only at the effect on actual sales of the books, rather than the diminished revenue from copyright fees, the court stated that there was a strong market for copyright permission fees and that the reduction in such fees should be considered in an analysis of the market impact of the alleged infringement. With respect to the remaining factors, the court ruled that the copied material was creative and that the excerpts were lengthy (8,000 words and longer), given the 1,000-word "safe harbor" established in the *Guidelines for Classroom Copying*. Although the trial court had ruled that MDS's behavior was a willful violation of the Copyright Act and thus supported enhanced statutory damages, the full appellate court stated that the fair use doctrine was "one of the most unsettled areas of the law," and thus the defendant's belief that his interpretation of the fair use doctrine was correct was not so unreasonable that the violation could be termed willful. The court also made clear that it was not deciding a case involving copying by students or faculty: "[a]s to the proposition that it would be fair use for the students or professors to make their own copies, the issue is by no means free from doubt. We need not decide this question, however, for the fact is that the copying complained of here was performed on a profit-making basis by a commercial enterprise" (99 F.3d at 1389).

In *Blackwell Publishing, Inc. v. Excel Research Group*, 661 F. Supp. 2d 786 (E.D. Mich. 2009), a federal district court in Michigan ruled that an attempt to evade the outcomes in *Kinko's* and *Michigan Document Services* by requiring students themselves to "push the button" at a commercial copy shop ran afoul of the decisions in both cases. Unless these issues are revisited by other appellate courts, these cases make clear that the involvement of commercial entities in the copying or distribution of course materials will be considered a violation of the distribution right protected under section 106 if done without permission and the payment of fees. Today, most colleges and universities obtain permission to make and sell coursepacks, even in their own internal copy shops, especially for repeated use of the same article by the same faculty member for the same course. Permission for many materials can be efficiently handled through the Copyright Clearance Center (CCC). The CCC "manages rights relating to over 1.75 million works and represents more than 9,600 publishers and hundreds of thousands of authors and other creators, directly or through their representatives." For additional information, see http://www.copyright.com.

Electronic course reserves ("e-reserves") do not involve distribution of print materials via coursepacks or other means and such systems (whether via home-grown software or platforms licensed from companies such as Blackboard) have transformed the way educational materials are delivered to students at many institutions. Unlike coursepacks, e-reserves systems are handled by libraries or information technology units within the university, and fees are not charged for access. Often faculty themselves control the deposit of content to individual access-restricted online course environments created for students enrolled in particular classes. E-reserves have generated the latest legal confrontation over course materials in *Cambridge University Press v. Becker*, filed in 2008. The plaintiffs in *Becker* sued the board of regents, the president, and various other high-ranking university officials, including the dean of libraries at Georgia State University, seeking declaratory and injunctive relief on multiple claims. This case has the potential to decide the very issue left open in *Kinko's*, *Blackwell Publishing*, and *Michigan Document Services*—namely, whether faculty, students, and librarians in purely academic settings have fair use rights that are broader and more protective than those of the commercial entities involved in those cases. The complaint in *Becker* asserts that various officials and administrators facilitated unauthorized distribution of copyrighted materials (such as individual book chapters or journal articles) to students through e-reserves and other campus online sites. The complaint specifically notes the university's alleged failure to take advantage of the "campus license" or other revenue-generating licensing mechanisms provided by such entities as the CCC. It is difficult to read the complaint in *Becker* as anything other than a full-scale attack on any "unlicensed" reproduction of materials for students through e-reserves, at least to the extent that any of the content in question is available for purchase. The selection of several (nonprofit) academic presses to serve as plaintiffs appears to have been designed to affect the fair use playing field and thereby influence the court's assessment of the first and fourth fair use factors. The court dismissed most of the plaintiffs' claims prior to or during the trial, leaving a sole remaining claim of direct infringement based on the creation and implementation of the university's new course reserves and fair use policy. As this book went to press, the trial court ruled for the defendants; an appeal is expected.

The existence of the Copyright Clearance Center also undercut a fair use argument in a corporate case involving the kinds of materials it licenses. In *American Geophysical Union v. Texaco, Inc.*, 802 F. Supp. 1 (S.D.N.Y. 1992), a federal trial judge found that Texaco had infringed the copyrights of several scientific journals by making multiple copies of scientific articles for its scientists and researchers to keep in their files. The judge noted that Texaco could have obtained a license that permitted copying of the journals licensed by the CCC and found that Texaco's failure to take advantage of that license weighed against fair use in consideration of the fourth factor. The court also acknowledged, however, that to avoid using circular reasoning in the analysis of the fourth factor (that is, assuming the use is unfair and would therefore result in lost permission fees in the process of trying to determine whether the use is fair), the availability of a license might not have weighed against fair use had the analysis of the first three factors favored fair use. In this case, however, the court found that two of the first three factors also weighed in favor of getting permission, so the court took the lost revenues into account.

The result in *American Geophysical Union v. Texaco* was affirmed by the Court of Appeals for the Second Circuit (37 F.3d 881 (2d Cir. 1994)), but the Second Circuit subsequently amended its earlier opinion to distinguish between institutional researchers, such as Texaco, and individual scientists or professors (60 F.3d 913, 916 (2d Cir. 1994)). The court also limited its ruling to "systematic" copying that advanced the commercial goals of a business organization like Texaco. Although *American Geophysical Union* illuminates the unpredictability of fair use litigation, the concept that individual scholars at colleges and universities are allowed to make personal research copies of library materials as a matter of fair use is now very well established. Indeed, most major publishers have specifically acknowledged such rights in campus library licensing agreements.

The copyright laws cover unpublished as well as published material. Although the unauthorized use of unpublished material would ordinarily result in liability for the researcher, a college or university could also face vicarious liability if the research was funded by an external grant made to the institution or if the faculty member was otherwise performing the research within the scope of his or her employment.

A pair of cases in the late 1980s interpreted the scope of fair use in publishing unpublished materials so narrowly as to nearly bar any use of such materials. See *New Era Publications International v. Henry Holt and Co.*, 873 F.2d 576 (2d Cir. 1989); *Salinger v. Random House*, 811 F.2d 90 (2d Cir. 1987). Legal scholars so criticized this pair of decisions that Congress reacted by passing the Copyright Amendments Act in late 1992 (Pub. L. No. 102-492, 106 Stat. 3145).

The law amends the fair use doctrine by adding the following sentence: "The fact that a work is unpublished shall not itself bar a finding of fair use if such finding is made upon consideration of all the above factors." This restored the balance inherent within the fair use statute as it applies to unpublished works.

The gaps between what technology makes possible and what the copyright exceptions explicitly address have increased interest in and pressures on the doctrine of fair use. In evaluating the viability of a fair use claim regarding an activity for which there appears to be no other clear copyright enablement, there is no substitute for a careful review of relevant case law, a hard-headed assessment of specific facts, and a weighing of all four statutory factors. For those interested in asserting or defending fair use claims through such a process, the courts have provided significant doctrinal advances. Much of the received doctrine of fair use law (for example the dispositive significance of market impact or the inability to copy whole works) has been changed as courts have grappled with new technology and dug deeply into ways of thinking about transformative uses. For institutions of higher education and their students, faculty, and staff, fair use empowers critically important activities that advance teaching, research, and scholarship. The specific breadth of the protections afforded under fair use to institutional activities, ranging from digitization to access, will be shown as some of the cases outlined in this section are decided in coming years.

As practices change and as new case law develops, postsecondary institutions should thoroughly review their policies and practices on photocopying and digitizing supplementary reading materials, the use of others' works in the creation of online courses and multimedia works, and preservation, repository, and publication standards. Institutions are now required to provide faculty and staff with accurate information on the use of copyrighted material, including text, unpublished material, computer software, images, and music, in order to take advantage of certain limits on their liability. An institution's policy and educational materials should be published online for staff and students as well as faculty members, and a notice apprising users of the policy's existence and location should be posted at campus photocopying and computer facilities.

## Section 11.4. Federal Aid-to-Education Programs

### 11.4.1. Functions and history.

The federal government's major function regarding postsecondary education is to establish national priorities and objectives for federal spending on education and to provide funds in accordance with those decisions. To implement its priorities and objectives, the federal government attaches a wide and varied range of conditions to the funds it makes available under its spending power and enforces these conditions against postsecondary institutions and against faculty members, students, and other individual recipients of federal aid. Some of these conditions are specific to the program for which funds are given. Other "cross-cutting" conditions apply across a range of programs; examples include the Drug-Free Workplace Act of 1988 (41 U.S.C. § 701 et seq.), the Drug-Free Schools and Communities

Act Amendments (20 U.S.C. § 7101), and the Student Right-to-Know Act (104 Stat. 2381–2384 (1990), codified in 20 U.S.C. § 1092). The nondiscrimination requirements discussed in Section 11.5 are also major examples of cross-cutting conditions. Cumulatively, such conditions have exerted a substantial influence on postsecondary institutions and have sometimes resulted in institutional cries of economic coercion and federal control. There have periodically also been charges that the federal government provides insufficient funds for higher education or that its priorities are misguided. In light of such criticisms, the federal role in funding postsecondary education has for many years been a major political and policy issue. The particular national goals to be achieved through funding and fund conditions, the adjustment of priorities, and the delivery and compliance mechanisms best suited to achieving these goals will likely remain subjects of debate for the foreseeable future.

Federal spending for postsecondary education has a long history. Shortly after the founding of the United States, the federal government began endowing public higher education institutions with public lands. In 1862, Congress passed the first Morrill Act, providing grants of land or land scrip to the states for the support of agricultural and mechanical colleges, for which Congress later provided continuing appropriations. The second Morrill Act, providing money grants for instruction in various branches of higher education, was passed in 1890. In 1944, Congress enacted the first GI Bill, which was followed in later years by successive programs providing funds to veterans to further their education. The National Defense Education Act, passed in 1958 after Congress was spurred by Russia's launching of Sputnik, included a large-scale program of low-interest loans for students in institutions of higher education. The Higher Education Facilities Act of 1963 authorized grants and low-interest loans to public and private nonprofit institutions of higher education for constructing and improving various educational facilities. Then, in 1965, Congress finally jumped broadly into supporting higher education with the passage of the Higher Education Act of 1965 (20 U.S.C. §§ 1001 et seq.). The act's various titles authorized federal support for a range of postsecondary education activities, including community educational services; resources, training, and research for college libraries and personnel; strengthening of developing institutions; and student financial aid programs (see Section 7.3.2 of this book). The act has been frequently amended since 1965 and continues to be the primary authorizing legislation for federal higher education spending.

### 11.4.2. Legal structure of federal aid programs.

Federal aid for postsecondary education is disbursed by a number of federal agencies. The five most important are the U.S. Department of Education, the U.S. Department of Health and Human Services, the National Foundation on the Arts and Humanities (comprising the National Endowment for the Humanities, the National Endowment for the Arts, and the Institute of Museum Services), the National Science Foundation, and (at least with respect to student aid) the Department of Veterans Affairs.

Federal aid to postsecondary education is dispensed in a variety of ways. Depending on the program involved, federal agencies may award grants or make loans directly to individual students; guarantee loans made to individual students by third parties; award grants directly to faculty members; make grants or loans to postsecondary institutions; enter "cooperative agreements" (as opposed to procurement contracts) with postsecondary institutions; or award grants, make loans, or enter agreements with state agencies, which in turn provide aid to institutions or their students or faculty. Whether an institution is eligible to receive federal aid, either directly from the federal agency or a state agency or indirectly through the institution's student recipients, depends on the requirements of the particular aid program. Typically, however, the institution must be accredited by a recognized accrediting agency or demonstrate compliance with one of the few statutorily prescribed substitutes for accreditation.

The "rules of the game" regarding eligibility, application procedures, the selection of recipients, allowable expenditures, conditions on spending, records and reports requirements, compliance reviews, and other federal aid requirements are set out in a variety of sources. The starting point is the statute that authorizes a particular federal aid program, along with the statute's legislative history. Occasionally, the appropriations legislation funding the program for a particular fiscal year will also contain requirements applicable to the expenditure of the appropriated funds. The next source, adding specificity to the statutory base, is the regulations for the program. These regulations, which are published in the *Federal Register* (Fed. Reg.) and then codified in *the Code of Federal Regulations* (C.F.R.), are the primary source of the administering agency's program requirements. Title 34 of the *Code of Federal Regulations* is the location of the U.S. Department of Education's regulations.

Published regulations have the force of law and bind the government, the aid recipients, and all the outside parties. In addition, agencies may supplement their regulations with program manuals, program guidelines, policy guidance or memoranda, agency interpretations, and "Dear Colleague" letters. These materials generally do not have the status of law; although they may sometimes be binding on recipients who had actual notice of them before receiving federal funds, more often supplemental materials are treated as agency suggestions that do not bind anyone. Additional requirements or suggestions may be found in the grant award documents or agreements under which the agency dispenses the aid, or in agency grant and contract manuals that establish general agency policy.

Yet other rules of the game are in executive branch directives or congressional legislation applicable to a range of federal agencies or their contractors or grantees. The circulars of the executive branch's Office of Management and Budget (OMB), for instance, set government-wide policy on matters such as allowable costs, indirect cost rates, and audit requirements. These circulars are available from OMB's home page at http://www.whitehouse.gov/omb/circulars. One of the most important of these circulars is OMB Circular A-21, titled "Cost Principles for Educational Institutions"; and OMB Circular A-110, "Uniform Administration Requirements for Grants and Agreements with Institutions of Higher Education, Hospitals, and Other Non-Profit Organizations."

A federal statute, the General Education Provisions Act (GEPA) (20 U.S.C. §§ 1221 et seq.), applies specifically and only to the U.S. Department of Education. The act establishes numerous organizational, administrative, and other requirements applicable to Department of Education spending programs. For instance, the act establishes procedures that the Department of Education must follow when proposing program regulations (20 U.S.C. § 1232). The GEPA provisions on enforcement of conditions attached to federal funds do not apply, however, to Higher Education Act programs (20 U.S.C. § 1234i(2)). To supplement GEPA, the Department of Education has promulgated extensive general regulations published at 34 C.F.R. Parts 74–86 and 97–99. These Education Department General Administrative Regulations (EDGAR) establish uniform policies for all Department of Education grant programs. The applicability of Part 74 of these regulations to higher education institutions is specified at 34 C.F.R. §§ 74.1(a) and 81.2. Running to well over one hundred pages in the Code of Federal Regulations, EDGAR tells you almost everything you wanted to know but were afraid to ask about the legal requirements for obtaining and administering Department of Education grants.

Other funding agencies also have general regulations that set certain conditions applicable to a range of their aid programs. Several agencies, for example, have promulgated regulations on research misconduct. Similarly, some agencies have promulgated "rules of the game" on financial conflicts of interest.

### Section 11.5. Civil Rights Compliance[4]

**11.5.1. General considerations.** Postsecondary institutions receiving assistance under federal aid programs are obligated to follow not only the programmatic and technical requirements of each program under which aid is received (see Section 11.4 earlier in this chapter) but also various civil rights requirements that apply generally to federal aid programs. These requirements are a major focus of federal spending policy, importing substantial social goals into education policy and making equality of educational opportunity a clear national priority in education. As conditions on spending, the civil rights requirements represent an exercise of Congress's spending power, implemented by delegating authority to the various federal departments and agencies that administer federal aid programs. There has often been controversy, however, concerning the specifics of implementing and enforcing such civil rights requirements. Some argue that the federal role is too great, and others say that it is too small; some argue that the federal government proceeds too quickly, and others insist that it is too slow; some argue that the compliance process is too cumbersome and costly for the affected institutions; others argue that such effects are inevitable for any system that is to be genuinely effective. Despite the controversy, it is clear that these federal civil rights efforts, over time, have provided a major force for social change in the United States.

---

[4]This section was revised and updated by Jonathan R. Alger, former senior vice president and general counsel at Rutgers University and currently president of James Madison University.

Four different federal statutes prohibit discrimination in educational programs receiving federal financial assistance. Title VI of the Civil Rights Act of 1964 prohibits discrimination on the basis of race, color, or national origin. Title IX of the Education Amendments of 1972 prohibits discrimination on the basis of sex. Section 504 of the Rehabilitation Act of 1973, as amended in 1974, prohibits discrimination against individuals with disabilities. The Age Discrimination Act of 1975 prohibits discrimination on the basis of age. Title IX is specifically limited to educational programs receiving federal financial assistance, while Title VI, Section 504, and the Age Discrimination Act apply to all programs receiving such assistance.

Each statute delegates enforcement responsibilities to each of the federal agencies disbursing federal financial assistance. Postsecondary institutions may thus be subject to the civil rights regulations of several federal agencies, the most important one being the Department of Education, created in 1979. At that time, the Department of Education assumed the functions of the former Department of Health, Education, and Welfare's (HEW) Office for Civil Rights with respect to all educational programs transferred from the U.S. Office of Education, which had been a constituent part of HEW. The Department of Education has its own Office for Civil Rights (OCR) under an assistant secretary for civil rights. The HEW civil rights regulations, formerly published in volume 45 of the Code of Federal Regulations (C.F.R.), were redesignated as Department of Education regulations and republished in 34 C.F.R. Parts 100–106. These administrative regulations, as amended over time, have considerably fleshed out the meaning of the statutes. The Department of Education's Office for Civil Rights has also published "policy interpretations" and "guidance" regarding the statutes and regulations in the Federal Register, and has circulated "Dear Colleague" letters that are posted on its Web site. Judicial decisions contribute additional interpretive gloss on major points and resolve major controversies, but the administrative regulations and OCR interpretations remain the initial, and usually the primary, source for understanding the civil rights requirements.

Although the nondiscrimination language of the four statutes is similar, each statute protects a different group of beneficiaries, and an act that constitutes discrimination against one group does not necessarily constitute discrimination if directed against another group. "Separate but equal" treatment of the sexes is sometimes permissible under Title IX, for instance, but such treatment of the races is never permissible under Title VI. Similarly, the enforcement mechanisms for the four statutes are similar, but they are not identical. There may be private causes of action for damages under Title VI, Title IX, and Section 504, for instance, but under the Age Discrimination Act only equitable relief is available.

Over the years, various issues have arisen concerning the scope and coverage of the civil rights statutes. During their time in the limelight, these issues have become the focus of various U.S. Supreme Court cases. As the volume of the litigation has increased, it has become apparent that the similarities of statutory language among the four civil rights statutes give rise to similar scope and coverage issues. Answers to an issue under one statute will thus provide guidance in answering comparable issues under another statute, and the answers will often be the same from one statute to another. There are some critical differences, however, in the statutory language and implementing regulations for each statute. For example, Title VI and the Age Discrimination Act have provisions placing limits on their applicability to employment discrimination, whereas Title IX and Section 504 do not. Each statute also has its own unique legislative history, which sometimes affects interpretation of the statute in a way that may have no parallel for the other statutes. Title IX's legislative history on coverage of athletics is an example. Therefore, to gain a fine-tuned view of particular developments, administrators and counsel should approach each statute and each scope and coverage issue separately, taking account of both similarities to and differences from the other statutes.

**11.5.2. Title VI.** Title VI of the Civil Rights Act of 1964 (42 U.S.C. § 2000d) declares: "No person in the United States shall, on the ground of race, color, or national origin, be excluded from participation in, be denied the benefits of, or be subjected to discrimination under any program or activity receiving federal financial assistance."

Courts have generally held that Title VI incorporates the same standards for identifying unlawful racial discrimination as have been developed under the Fourteenth Amendment's equal protection clause (see the discussion of the *Bakke* case in Section 7.2.5 of this book, and see generally Section 7.2.4.1). But courts have also held that the Department of Education and other federal agencies implementing Title VI may impose nondiscrimination requirements on recipients beyond those developed under the equal protection clause (see *Guardians Association v. Civil Service Commission of the City of New York*, 463 U.S. 582 (1983), discussed in Section 11.5.5).

The Education Department's regulations, found at 34 C.F.R. § 100.3(b), provide the basic and most specific reference point for determining what actions are unlawful under Title VI. The regulations prohibit a recipient of federal funds from denying or providing a different quality of service, financial aid, or other benefit of the institution's programs on the basis of race, color, or national origin. The regulations also prohibit institutions from treating individuals differently with respect to satisfying admission, enrollment, eligibility, membership, or other requirements, as well as denying individuals the opportunity to participate in programs or on planning or advisory committees on the basis of race, color, or national origin.

The dismantling of the formerly *de jure* segregated systems of higher education has given rise to considerable litigation over more than seven decades. Although most of the litigation has attacked continued segregation in the higher education system of one state, the lengthiest lawsuit involved the alleged failure of the federal government to enforce Title VI in ten states. This litigation, begun in 1970 as *Adams v. Richardson*, continuing with various Education Department secretaries as defendant until it became *Adams v. Bell* in the 1980s, and culminating in *Women's Equity Action League v. Cavazos* in 1990, 906

F.2d 742 (D.C. Cir. 1990), focused on the responsibilities of the Department of Health, Education and Welfare (HEW), and later the Education Department, to enforce Title VI, rather than examining the standards applicable to state higher education officials. HEW had approved the desegregation plans of several states; a district court judge ordered HEW to revoke its acceptance of desegregation plans submitted by those states and to devise criteria for reviewing new desegregation plans to be submitted by the states affected by the case (see *Adams v. Califano*, 430 F. Supp. 118 (D.D.C. 1977)). Finally, in 1990, the U.S. Court of Appeals for the D.C. Circuit ruled that no private right of action against government enforcement agencies existed under Title VI, and dismissed the case for lack of jurisdiction (*Women's Equity Action League v. Cavazos*, 906 F.2d 742 (D.C. Cir. 1990)).

After developing the criteria (42 Fed. Reg. 40780 (August 11, 1977)), HEW revised and republished them (43 Fed. Reg. 6658 (February 15, 1978)) as the "Revised Criteria Specifying the Ingredients of Acceptable Plans to Desegregate State Systems of Public Higher Education." The criteria required affected states to take various affirmative steps, such as enhancing the quality of black state-supported colleges and universities, placing new "high-demand" programs on traditionally black campuses, eliminating unnecessary program duplication between black and white institutions, increasing the percentage of black academic employees in the system, and increasing the enrollment of blacks at traditionally white public colleges.

Litigation alleging continued *de jure* segregation resulted in federal appellate court opinions in four states, including a U.S. Supreme Court ruling. Despite years of varied litigation, settlements, and conciliation attempts, the standards imposed by the equal protection clause of the Fourteenth Amendment and by Title VI are still unclear. Most cases were brought under both the equal protection clause (by private plaintiffs and the United States) and Title VI (by the United States), though judicial analysis generally relied upon the equal protection clause standard. Although the U.S. Supreme Court's opinion in *United States v. Fordice*, 505 U.S. 717 (1992), is controlling, the history of appellate court rulings leading up to it demonstrates the complexities of this issue and the remaining disputes over the state's responsibilities.

*Fordice* and other related federal court opinions must be read in the context of Supreme Court precedent in cases related to desegregating public elementary and secondary schools. It is clear under the Fourteenth Amendment's equal protection clause that, in the absence of a "compelling" state interest (see Section 7.2.5 of this book), no public institution may treat students differently on the basis of race. The leading case, of course, is *Brown v. Board of Education*, 347 U.S. 483 (1954). Though *Brown* concerned elementary and secondary schools, the precedent clearly applies to postsecondary education as well.

The crux of the legal debate in the higher education desegregation cases has been whether the equal protection clause and Title VI require the state simply to enact race-neutral policies (the "effort" test), or whether the state must go beyond racial neutrality to ensure that any trace of the formerly segregated system is removed. Unlike elementary and secondary students, college students select their institutions of choice, and therefore the remedies used to desegregate elementary and secondary schools, such as busing and race-conscious assignment practices, are not available to colleges and universities.

In *Geier v. University of Tennessee*, 597 F.2d 1056 (6th Cir. 1979), *cert. denied*, 444 U.S. 886 (1979), the court ordered the merger of two Tennessee universities, a predominantly black and a predominantly white institution in Nashville. Despite the state's claim that the racial imbalances at the schools were created by the students' exercise of free choice, the court ruled that the state's adoption of an "open admissions" policy had not effectively dismantled the state's dual system of higher education, ordering state officials to submit a plan for desegregating public higher education in Tennessee (later approved in *Richardson v. Blanton*, 597 F.2d 1078 (6th Cir. 1979)). The court required "affirmative action to remove these vestiges" of segregation (597 F.2d at 1065). Furthermore, the Sixth Circuit rejected the state's argument that elementary and secondary school desegregation precedent, most specifically *Green v. County School Board*, 391 U.S. 430 (1968), did not apply to higher education.[5]

Next in the line of desegregation cases, *Fordice* originated in 1975 as a case where Jake Ayers and other private plaintiffs sued the governor of Mississippi and other state officials, alleging that the state system retained vestiges of a *de jure* segregated system. Although HEW had begun Title VI enforcement proceedings against Mississippi in 1969, it had rejected both desegregation plans submitted by the state. The United States intervened, and the parties attempted to resolve the dispute for twelve years prior to going to trial in 1987.

Mississippi had designated three categories of public higher education institutions: comprehensive universities (three historically white, none historically black); one urban institution (black); and four regional institutions (two white, two black). Admission standards differed both within and among the various institutions, with the lowest admission standards at the historically black regional institutions. The plaintiffs argued, among other things, that the state's admissions standard, institutional classification and mission designations, duplication of programs, faculty and staff hiring and assignments, and funding perpetuated the prior segregated system of higher education. Among other data, they cited the concentration of black students at black institutions, where more than 95 percent of the students at each of the three black institutions were black, whereas blacks comprised fewer than 10 percent of the students at the three white universities and 13 percent at both white regional institutions. The state asserted that the existence of racially identifiable universities was permissible, since students self-selected their institutions of choice, and the admissions policies and practices were racially neutral in intent.

Although the district court acknowledged that the state had an affirmative duty to desegregate its higher education system, the court rejected the *Green* precedent as inapplicable to higher education and followed the U.S. Supreme

---

[5] For a fuller discussion of this case and the cases upon which the court relied, see *LHE 5th*, Section 14.5.2.

Court's ruling in *Bazemore*, finding the proper inquiry was whether state higher education policies and practices were racially neutral, not whether there was racial balance in the various sectors of public higher education. Applying this standard to the state's actions, and relying on the freedom of student choice under *Bazemore*, the court found no violation of law.

The U.S. Court of Appeals for the Fifth Circuit reversed the district court finding, holding *Bazemore* inapplicable because it applied to de facto segregation, not *de jure* as in the instant case. Citing *Geier v. Alexander*, the court cited the lower admission standards for predominantly black institutions, the small number of black faculty at white colleges, program duplication at nearby black and white institutions, and continued underfunding of black institutions as evidence of an illegal dual system (*Ayers v. Allain*, 893 F.2d 732 (5th Cir. 1990)).

Upon review *en banc*, the court relied upon *Alabama State Teachers Assn. v. Alabama Public School and College Authority*, 289 F. Supp. 784 (M.D. Ala. 1968), *affirmed per curiam*, 393 U.S. 400 (1969), which held that the scope of the state's duty to dismantle a racially dual system of higher education was different from, and less strict than, its duty to public elementary and secondary schools. The court said that *Green* did not apply to the desegregation of higher education and that *Bazemore* should have been applied in this case. Furthermore, the appellate court saw no conflict between *Green* and *Bazemore*, stating that *Green* had not outlawed all "freedom-of-choice" desegregation plans outside elementary and secondary education. Despite its conclusion that the state's conduct did not violate the equal protection clause (and, in turn, Title VI), the court did find some remnants of *de jure* segregation. The majority concluded that the inequalities in racial composition were a result of the different historical missions of the three sectors of public higher education, but that current state policies provided equal educational opportunity irrespective of race. The *en banc* majority interpreted the legal standard to require affirmative efforts, but not to mandate equivalent funding, admission standards, enrollment patterns, or program allocation. The plaintiffs appealed to the U.S. Supreme Court.

At the same time, similar litigation was in progress in Louisiana. In 1974, the U.S. Department of Justice sued the state of Louisiana under both the equal protection clause and Title VI, asserting that the state had established and maintained a racially segregated higher education system as evidenced by duplicate programs at contiguous black and white institutions and the existence of three systems of public higher education. Despite a consent decree negotiated in 1981, six years later the United States alleged that almost all of the state's institutions of higher education were still racially identifiable.

In *United States v. Louisiana*, 692 F. Supp. 642 (E.D. La. 1988), a federal district judge granted summary judgment for the United States, agreeing that the state's actions had been insufficient to dismantle the segregated system, later requiring Louisiana to merge its three systems of public higher education, create a community college system, and reduce unwarranted duplicate programs, especially in legal education (718 F. Supp. 499 (E.D. La. 1989), 718 F. Supp. 525 (E.D. La. 1989)). Appeals to the Supreme Court followed from all parties but were denied for want of jurisdiction (*Louisiana, ex rel. Guste v. United States,* 493 U.S. 1013 (1990)).

Despite the flurry of appeals, the district court continued to seek a remedy in this case. It adopted the report of a special master, which recommended creating a single governing board, classifying each institution by mission, and evaluating graduate programs for possible termination. The court also required new admissions criteria that considered high school grades, rank, courses, recommendations, extracurricular activities, and essays in addition to test scores (751 F. Supp. 621 (E.D. La. 1990)). After the Fifth Circuit's *en banc* opinion in *Ayers v. Allain* was issued, however, the district court judge vacated his earlier summary judgment, stating that although he disagreed with the Fifth Circuit's ruling, he had no choice but to follow it (*United States v. Louisiana,* 751 F. Supp. 606 (E.D. La. 1990)). The governor of Louisiana appealed this ruling, but the judge stayed both the appeal and the remedies he had ordered, pending the Supreme Court's opinion in *Ayers v. Allain,* now titled *United States v. Fordice.*

The U.S. Supreme Court was faced with the issue addressed in *Geier:* which Supreme Court precedent controlled equal protection and Title VI jurisprudence in higher education desegregation—*Bazemore* or *Green*? In *United States v. Fordice,* 505 U.S. 717 (1992), the Court reversed the decision of the Fifth Circuit's *en banc* majority, sharply criticizing the court's reasoning and the legal standard it had applied. First, the Court refused to choose between the two precedents. Justice White, writing for the eight-Justice majority, rejected the Fifth Circuit's argument that *Bazemore* limited *Green* to segregation in elementary and secondary education. He rejected the lower courts' assertion that a state's adoption of race-neutral policies was sufficient to cure the constitutional wrongs of a dual system.

> In a system based on choice, student attendance is determined not simply by admission policies, but also by many other factors. Although some of these factors clearly cannot be attributed to State policies, many can be. Thus, even after a State dismantles its segregative *admissions* policy, there may still be state action that is traceable to the State's prior *de jure* segregation and that continues to foster segregation . . . If policies traceable to the *de jure* system are still in force and have discriminatory effects, those policies too must be reformed to the extent practicable and consistent with sound educational practices [505 U.S. at 729, emphasis in original].

The Court discussed four policies that appeared to perpetuate the effects of prior *de jure* discrimination: admission policies (for discussion of this portion of the case, see Section 7.2.4.1 of this book), the duplication of programs at nearby white and black colleges, the state's "mission classification," and the fact that Mississippi operated eight public institutions. For each category, the court noted the foundations of state policy in previous *de jure* segregation and a failure to alter that policy when *de jure* segregation officially ended.

The Court emphasized that it was not calling for racial quotas; in its view, the fact "that an institution is predominantly white or black does not in itself make out a constitutional violation" (at 743). The Court also refused the plaintiffs'

invitation to order the state to provide equal funding for the three traditionally black institutions. The Court remanded the case to determine whether the
state "met its affirmative obligation to dismantle its prior dual system." Justice
O'Connor's concurrence reminded the Court that only in the most "narrow"
of circumstances should a state be permitted to "maintain a policy or practice
traceable to *de jure* segregation that has segregative effects" (at 744). Justice
Thomas stressed that the *Fordice* ruling focused on the policies themselves, not
the resulting imbalances. Thomas wrote:

> [This holding] does not compel the elimination of all observed racial imbalance, it
> portends neither the destruction of historically black colleges nor the severing of
> those institutions from their distinctive histories and traditions [505 U.S. at 745].

Thomas emphasized the majority opinion's use of "sound educational practices" as a touchstone for determining whether a state's actions are justifiable:

> In particular, we do not foreclose the possibility that there exists "sound
> educational justification" for maintaining historically black colleges . . . I think
> it indisputable that these institutions have succeeded in part because of their
> distinctive histories and traditions . . . Obviously, a State cannot maintain such
> traditions by closing particular institutions, historically white or historically
> black, to particular racial groups . . . Although I agree that a State is not
> constitutionally *required* to maintain its historically black institutions . . . I do
> not understand our opinion to hold that a State is *forbidden* from doing so. It
> would be ironic, to say the least, if the institutions that sustained blacks during
> segregation were themselves destroyed in an effort to combat its vestiges [505
> U.S. at 747–49; emphasis in original].

Justice Scalia wrote a blistering dissent, criticizing the "effectively unsus-
tainable burden the Court imposes on Mississippi, and all States that formerly
operated segregated universities" and arguing that the *Bazemore* standard was
controlling and that *Green*, having "no proper application in the context of
higher education, provides no genuine guidance to States and lower courts, and
is as likely to subvert as to promote the interests of those citizens on whose
behalf the present suit was brought" (505 U.S. at 750–51).

On remand, the district court (879 F. Supp. 1419 (N.D. Miss. 1995)) considered a wide range of issues including admission standards, collegiate missions and the duplication of academic programs, racial identifiability of the
campuses, campus climate, and the impact of institution and state policies and
practices on the perpetuation of segregation. The court found that the admissions standards proposed by the state were discriminatory. In particular, the use
of American College Test (ACT) scores as the only admission criterion was discriminatory, whereas the use of ACT scores for awarding scholarships was not.
The court approved the defendants' proposal for uniform admission standards
for all Mississippi colleges and universities, rejecting the plaintiffs' argument
that some of the colleges should have open admissions policies until greater
racial balance was achieved. The court ordered a study of program duplication,

as not all duplication necessarily resulted in segregation, and insisted that funding should not be completely tied to institutional mission, given that mission assignments were made during the period of segregation.

On appeal of the district court's holding, the U.S. Court of Appeals for the Fifth Circuit upheld part of the district court's findings, reversed another part, and remanded for further proceedings (111 F.3d 1183 (5th Cir. 1997)). The appellate court held that the financial aid policies of the historically white colleges perpetuated prior discrimination on the basis of race and that the uniform admissions standards proposed by the state were appropriate. The court remanded the remedial decree requiring the state to submit proposals for increasing the enrollment of white students at historically black institutions. The U.S. Supreme Court denied review (522 U.S. 1084).

The *Fordice* opinion has been criticized by individuals of all races and political affiliations as insufficiently clear to provide appropriate guidance to states as they attempt to apply its outcome to desegregation of the still racially identifiable public institutions in many states.

In addition to providing an avenue for desegregation of higher education, Title VI has also been used to prevent harassment of students based on race, ethnicity, and even religion (see "Dear Colleague" Letter on Bullying and Discriminatory Harassment, October 2010 (stating where religious group shares a common ancestry or ethnic characteristic, Title VI may offer protection)). A finding of harassment under Title VI requires the university to have notice of severe and pervasive harassment based on an individual's race or ethnicity. *Maislin v. Tennessee State University*, 665 F. Supp. 2d 922 (M.D. Tenn. 2009).

As the history of the past three decades of Title VI litigation makes clear, the desegregation of higher education is very much an unfinished business. Its completion poses knotty legal, policy, and administrative enforcement problems and requires a sensitive appreciation of the different missions and traditions of historically black and white institutions. The challenge is for lawyers, administrators, government officials, and the judiciary to work together to fashion solutions that will be consonant with the law's requirement to desegregate but will increase rather than limit the opportunities available to minority students and faculty.

### 11.5.3. Title IX.[6]

The central provision of Title IX of the Education Amendments of 1972 (20 U.S.C. §§ 1681 et seq.) declares: "No person in the United States shall, on the basis of sex, be excluded from participation in, be denied the benefits of, or be subjected to discrimination under any education program or activity receiving federal financial assistance."

Unlike Title VI, Title IX has various exceptions to its prohibition on sex discrimination. Title IX does "not apply to an educational institution which is controlled by a religious organization if the application of this subsection would not be consistent with the religious tenets of such organization" (20 U.S.C. § 1681 (a)(3)). Title IX does "not apply to an educational institution

---

[6]The application of Title IX to athletics is discussed in Section 10.4.6.

whose primary purpose is the training of individuals for the military services of the United States, or the merchant marine" (20 U.S.C. § 1681(a)(4)). There are also several exceptions concerning admissions (20 U.S.C. §§ 1681(a)(1), (2), (5)). In addition, Title IX excludes from its coverage the membership practices of tax-exempt social fraternities and sororities (20 U.S.C. § 1681(a)(6)(A)); the membership practices of the YMCA, YWCA, Girl Scouts, Boy Scouts, Campfire Girls, and other tax-exempt, traditionally single-sex "youth service organizations" (20 U.S.C. § 1681(a)(6)(B)); American Legion, Boys State, Boys Nation, Girls State, and Girls Nation activities (20 U.S.C. § 1681(a)(7)); and father-son and mother-daughter activities if provided on a reasonably comparable basis for students of both sexes (20 U.S.C. § 1681(a)(8)).

The Department of Education's regulations implementing Title IX (34 C.F.R. Part 106) specify in much greater detail the types of acts that are considered to be prohibited sex discrimination. Educational institutions may not discriminate on the basis of sex in admissions and recruitment, with exceptions for certain institutions as noted above (see Section 7.2.4.2 of this book). Institutions may not discriminate in awarding financial assistance (see Section 7.3.3 of this book), in athletic programs (see Section 10.4.6), or in the employment of faculty and staff members (see Section 4.5.2.3). Section 106.32 of the Title IX regulations prohibits sex discrimination in housing accommodations with respect to fees, services, or benefits, but does not prohibit separate housing by sex (see Section 7.4.2 of this book). Section 106.33 of the regulations requires that separate facilities for toilets, locker rooms, and shower rooms be comparable. Section 106.34 prohibits sex discrimination in student access to course offerings. Sections 106.36 and 106.38 require that counseling services and employment placement services be offered to students in such a way that there is no discrimination on the basis of sex. Section 106.39 prohibits sex discrimination in health and insurance benefits and services. Section 106.40 prohibits certain discrimination on the basis of "parental, family, or marital status" or on the basis of pregnancy or childbirth. In addition to these regulations, the Department of Education has published guidelines and interpretive advice on certain, particularly difficult, applications of Title IX. Among the most important of these documents are *Sexual Harassment Guidance: Harassment of Students by School Employees, Other Students, or Third Parties*, which is discussed in Sections 7.1.5 and 8.5 of this book, and the Policy Interpretation on intercollegiate athletics, which is discussed in Section 10.4.6.

Litigation brought under Title IX has primarily addressed alleged sex discrimination in the funding and support of women's athletics (see Section 10.4.6 of this book), the employment of women faculty and athletics coaches (male or female), and sexual harassment of students by faculty members (see Section 8.5) or by other students (see Section 7.1.5). In *Franklin v. Gwinnett County Public Schools*, 503 U.S. 60 (1992) (discussed in Section 8.5), the U.S. Supreme Court ruled unanimously that private parties who are victims of sex discrimination may bring "private causes of action" for money damages to enforce their nondiscrimination rights under Title IX. As a result of this 1992 ruling, which resolved a long-standing split among the lower courts, an increasing number of both students and faculty have used Title IX to sue postsecondary institutions. The availability of a money damages remedy under Title IX is particularly important to students, for whom typical equitable remedies, such as back pay and orders requiring the institution to refrain from future discriminatory conduct, are of little use because students are usually due no pay and are likely to have graduated or left school before the litigation has been completed. The Court's ruling in *Franklin* thus has great significance for colleges and universities because it increases the incentives for students, faculty members, and staff members to challenge sex discrimination in court. The ruling also may persuade individuals considering litigation over alleged employment discrimination to use Title IX instead of Title VII, since Title IX has no caps on damage awards and no detailed procedural prerequisites, as Title VII does (see Section 4.5.2.1 of this book). Courts are split, however, on whether the availability of express private causes of actions for employment discrimination under Title VII precludes the use of Title IX for the same purpose (see Section 4.5.2.3 of this book).

In addition to being used to equalize educational opportunities in athletics, Title IX has also traditionally been used to protect students from sexual harassment by teachers (*Mennone v. Gordon*, 889 F. Supp. 53, 58 (D. Conn. 1995)). A shift has been made recently, however, from protecting students from harassment by teachers to protecting against harassment by other students. In 2011, the Office for Civil Rights issued a Dear Colleague letter on sexual violence, particularly identifying the issue of student on student harassment (available at http://www2.ed.gov/about/offices/list/ocr/letters/colleague-201104.html). The letter provides additional guidance to universities as to their obligations to provide notice of the nondiscrimination policy to students, parents, and employees; to designate a Title IX coordinator; and to improve the response to and resolution of sexual harassment cases by training the campus community on reporting procedures, taking immediate steps to eliminate a hostile environment, responding to reports of sexual violence more quickly, and requiring the use of a preponderance of the evidence standard to be used in all accusations of sexual violence (which complies with other OCR standards of review). The OCR also broadened the scope of sexual violence to incorporate cyber-harassment. In a similar fashion, a Dear Colleague letter was issued by the OCR in October 2010 regarding the prohibition against bullying and discriminatory harassment (available at http://www2.ed.gov/about/offices/list/ocr/letters/colleague-201010.html). The Office for Civil Rights has focused higher education's attention on the issue of student-on-student harassment and has reminded colleges and universities of their obligations to respond efficiently and effectively under Title IX.

As litigation has progressed, courts have emphasized the distinction between institutional liability and individual (or personal) liability under Title IX. Title IX imposes liability only on the institution (the college, university, or college or university system as an entity) and not on its officers, administrators, faculty members, or staff members as individuals. This distinction is made because individual officers and employees are not themselves "education programs or activities" within the meaning of Title IX and usually are not themselves the recipients of the "federal financial assistance."

Courts have seldom addressed whether institutional employees can be sued in their official, rather than individual, capacities under Title IX. In *Doe v. Lance*, 1996 WL 663159, 1996 U.S. Dist. LEXIS 16836 (N.D. Ind. 1996), the court seemed willing to permit a Title IX suit against a school superintendent in her official capacity but held that such a suit against the superintendent was the same as a suit against the school district itself. Because the school district was already a party to the lawsuit, the court dismissed the claim against the superintendent in her official capacity because it afforded the plaintiff "no additional avenue of relief."

Sex discrimination that is actionable under Title IX may also be actionable under the federal civil rights statute 42 U.S.C. § 1983 (see Sections 3.4 and 4.4.4 of this book) if the discrimination amounts to a "deprivation" of rights "secured by the [federal] Constitution." The Fourteenth Amendment's equal protection clause would be the basis for this type of claim. The advantage for victims of discrimination is that they may sue the individuals responsible for the discrimination under 42 U.S.C. § 1983, which they cannot do under Title IX. Section 1983 claims, however, may be brought only against individuals who are acting "under color of law," such as faculty and staff members at public institutions.

Although defendants have sometimes asserted that Title IX "subsumes" or "precludes" Section 1983 claims covering the same discriminatory acts, it is clear that courts will reject such arguments, at least when the Section 1983 equal protection claim is asserted against individuals rather than the institution itself. In *Crawford v. Davis*, 109 F.3d 1281 (8th Cir. 1997), for instance, the court emphatically recognized that Title IX "in no way restricts a plaintiff's ability to seek redress under § 1983 for the violation of independently existing constitutional rights," such as equal protection rights. And in *Delgado v. Stegall*, 367 F.3d 668 (7th Cir. 2004), the court reached the same result as to a student's Section 1983 claim against the alleged harasser (a professor), while adding nuance to the analysis.

***11.5.4. Section 504 of the Rehabilitation Act.*** Section 504 of the Rehabilitation Act of 1973, as amended (29 U.S.C. § 794), states: "No otherwise qualified individual with a disability in the United States . . . shall, solely by reason of his disability, be excluded from the participation in, be denied the benefits of, or be subjected to discrimination under any program or activity receiving federal financial assistance."

The Department of Education's regulations on Section 504 (34 C.F.R. Part 104) contain specific provisions that establish standards for postsecondary institutions to follow in their dealings with "qualified" students and applicants with disabilities, "qualified" employees and applicants for employment, and members of the public with disabilities who are seeking to take advantage of institutional programs and activities open to the public. A "qualified individual with a disability" is "any person who (i) has a physical or mental impairment which substantially limits one or more major life activities, (ii) has a record of such an impairment, or (iii) is regarded as having such an impairment" (34 C.F.R. § 104.3(j)). In the context of postsecondary and vocational education services, a "qualified" person with a disability is someone who "meets the academic and technical standards requisite to admission or participation in the recipient's education program or activity" (34 C.F.R. § 104.3(l)(3)). Whether an individual with a disability is "qualified" in other situations depends on different criteria. In the context of employment, a qualified individual with a disability is one who, "with reasonable accommodation, can perform the essential functions of the job in question" (34 C.F.R. § 104.3(l)(1)). With regard to other services, a qualified individual with a disability is someone who "meets the essential eligibility requirements for the receipt of such services" (34 C.F.R. § 104.3(l)(4)).

Although the Section 504 regulations resemble those for Title VI and Title IX in the types of programs and activities considered, they differ in some of the means used for achieving nondiscrimination. The reason for these differences is that "different or special treatment of handicapped persons, because of their handicaps, may be necessary in a number of contexts in order to ensure equal opportunity" (42 Fed. Reg. 22676 (May 4, 1977)). Institutions receiving federal funds may not discriminate on the basis of disability in admission and recruitment of students (see this book, Section 7.2.4.3); in providing financial assistance (Section 7.3.3); in athletic programs (Section 10.4.7); in housing accommodations (Section 7.4.2); or in the employment of faculty and staff members (Section 4.5.2.5) or students (see 34 C.F.R. § 104.46(c)). The regulations also prohibit discrimination on the basis of disability in a number of other programs and activities of postsecondary institutions.

Section 104.43 of the regulations requires nondiscriminatory "treatment" of students in general. Besides prohibiting discrimination in the institution's own programs and activities, this section requires that, when an institution places students in an educational program or activity not wholly under its control, the institution "shall assure itself that the other education program or activity, as a whole, provides an equal opportunity for the participation of qualified handicapped persons." In a student teaching program, for example, the "as a whole" concept allows the institution to make use of a particular external activity even though it discriminates, provided that the institution's entire student teaching program, taken as a whole, offers student teachers with disabilities "the same range and quality of choice in student-teaching assignments afforded nonhandicapped students" (42 Fed. Reg. at 22692 (comment 30)). Furthermore, the institution must operate its programs and activities in "the most integrated setting appropriate"; that is, by integrating disabled persons with nondisabled persons to the maximum extent appropriate (34 C.F.R. § 104.43(d)).

The Education Department's regulations recognize that certain academic adjustment may be necessary to protect against discrimination on the basis of disability. However, those academic requirements that the institution "can demonstrate are essential to the program of instruction being pursued by such student or to any directly related licensing requirement" need not be adjusted.

Adjustments that do not affect the academic integrity of a program, such as changes in the length of time to earn a degree or the modification of certain course requirements, are examples of adjustments that may be required by the regulations. The regulations also limit the institution's right to prohibit tape recorders or service animals if a disabled student needs these accommodations to participate in the educational program. The regulations also discuss the modification of examination formats and the provision of "auxiliary aids" such as taped texts or readers (34 C.F.R. § 104.44).

Section 104.47(b) of the regulations provides that counseling and placement services be offered on the same basis to disabled and nondisabled students. The institution is specifically charged with ensuring that job counseling is not more restrictive for disabled students. Under 34 C.F.R. § 104.47(c), an institution that supplies significant assistance to student social organizations must determine that these organizations do not discriminate against disabled students in their membership practices.

The institution's programs or activities—"when viewed in their entirety"—must be physically accessible to students with disabilities, and the institution's facilities must be usable by them. The regulations applicable to existing facilities differ from those applied to new construction; existing facilities need not be modified in their entirety if other methods of accessibility can be used (34 C.F.R. § 104.22). All new construction must be readily accessible when it is completed.

As advancements in adaptive technology improve, it has become clear that auxiliary aids specifically referenced in the regulations do not present an exhaustive list, but evolve as technology does. While just outside the scope of higher education, several licensing boards have been challenged on their failure to provide the most current adaptive technology, and the courts developed a heightened standard for the accommodation, requiring one that would "best ensure" an accurate reflection of the student's ability, rather than a limitation of speech, sight, or hearing. In contrast, institutions must also be cautious in the use of new technologies in the curricula. While convenient and economical, the use of e-readers has been criticized at many institutions and challenged by the Office for Civil Rights because of e-readers' inaccessibility to students with limitations in seeing. While e-readers have not been banned on campus, the OCR reminded many institutions that use of e-readers must be implemented in a way that is accessible.

Following the implementation of the Post 9/11 GI Bill (2008 H.R. 2642 (Title V)) in 2009, colleges and universities are seeing more student veterans coming to campus. Although the bill imposes admissions obligations, many veterans are also coming to campus with increased reports of physical and psychological disabilities, at a rate far exceeding their nonveteran peers. In addition to providing accommodations in accordance with the Americans with Disabilities Act and Section 504 of the Rehabilitation Act, the courts have begun to find a delay in mental health treatment for veterans a violation of their due process rights.

In *Southeastern Community College v. Davis*, 442 U.S. 397 (1979), discussed in Section 7.2.4.3 of this book, the U.S. Supreme Court added some important interpretive gloss to the regulation on academic adjustments and assistance for disabled students (34 C.F.R. § 104.44). The Court quoted but did not question the validity of the regulation's requirement that an institution provide "aux-iliary aids"—such as interpreters, taped texts, and Braille materials—for students with sensory impairments. The Court made very clear, however, that the law does not require "major" or "substantial" modifications in an institution's curriculum or academic standards to accommodate disabled students. To require such modifications, the Court said, would be to read into Section 504 an "affirmative action obligation" not warranted by its "language, purpose, [or] history." Moreover, if the regulations were to be interpreted to impose such obligation, they would to that extent be invalid. (Academic accommodations for students with disabilities are discussed in Section 8.4 of this book).

The Court acknowledged, however, that the line between discrimination and a lawful refusal to take affirmative action is not always clear. Thus, in some instances programmatic changes may be required where they would not fundamentally alter the program itself. In determining where this line is to be drawn, the Court would apparently extend considerable deference to postsecondary institutions' legitimate educational judgments respecting academic standards and course requirements. Although *Davis* thus limits postsecondary institutions' legal obligation to modify their academic programs to accommodate disabled students, the opinion does not limit an institution's obligation to make its facilities physically accessible to qualified students with disabilities, as required by the regulations (34 C.F.R. § 104.22)—even when doing so involves major expense. In *Davis*, the Court found that, because of the plaintiff's hearing disability, the plaintiff was not "otherwise qualified" for admission to the nursing program. When a person with a disability is qualified and has been admitted, however, 34 C.F.R. § 104.22 requires that facilities as a whole be "readily accessible" to that person.

The use and application of *Davis* may be limited for an additional reason, in that the Americans with Disabilities Act affords broader rights of access and accommodation to students, employees, and, in some cases, the general public than is contemplated by *Davis*. The employment provisions of the ADA are discussed in Section 4.5.2.5 of this book, while its public accommodations and other provisions are discussed generally in Section 8.4. Remedies under the ADA are broader than those provided for by Section 504 and apply to all colleges and universities, whether or not they receive federal funds.

The U.S. Supreme Court spoke a second time on the significance of Section 504—this time with regard to whether individuals with contagious diseases are protected by Section 504 of the Rehabilitation Act. In *School Board of Nassau County v. Arline*, 480 U.S. 273 (1987), the Court held that a teacher with tuberculosis was protected by Section 504 and that her employer was required to determine whether a reasonable accommodation could be made for her. Subsequent to *Arline*, Congress, in amendments to Section 504 (42 U.S.C. § 706 (8)(D)), and the Equal Employment Opportunity Commission (EEOC), in regulations interpreting the employment provisions of the Americans with Disabilities Act (ADA) (29 C.F.R. § 1630.2(r)), provided other statutory protections for students and staff with contagious diseases.

The availability of compensatory damages under Section 504 was addressed in *Tanberg v. Weld County Sheriff*, 787 F. Supp. 970 (D. Colo. 1992). Citing *Franklin v. Gwinnett County Public Schools* (Section 8.5), the federal trial judge ruled that a plaintiff who proves intentional discrimination under Section 504 can be entitled to compensatory damages.

The U.S. Supreme Court has ruled that the federal government may not be sued for damages for violating Section 504 of the Rehabilitation Act because Congress did not explicitly waive the federal government's sovereign immunity from such suits. In *Lane v. Pena*, 518 U.S. 187 (1996), a student at the U.S. Merchant Marine Academy was dismissed after he was diagnosed with diabetes during his first year at the academy. The Merchant Marine Academy is administered by a unit of the U.S. Department of Transportation. Although the trial court initially ordered him reinstated and awarded him damages, it vacated the damages award when a higher court stated, in a different case, that plaintiffs could not be awarded damages against the federal government for claims under Section 504. The appellate court affirmed summarily, and Lane appealed to the U.S. Supreme Court. In a 7-to-2 decision written by Justice O'Connor, the Court ruled that Congress had not "unequivocally expressed" its intent to waive federal sovereign immunity. Examining both the language of the statute and its legislative history, the Court declined to read into the statute a waiver that had not been clearly articulated by Congress.

Like Title IX (see Section 11.5.3 of this book), Section 504 apparently imposes liability only on institutions as such and not on individual officers or employees of the institution. In *Coddington v. Adelphi University*, 45 F. Supp. 2d 211 (E.D.N.Y. 1999), a suit by a former nursing student alleging discrimination based on learning disabilities, the district court dismissed four individual defendants—the former university president, the current president, the nursing school dean, and an associate professor of law—and let the case proceed only against the university itself. In an earlier case, however, the court in *Lee v. Trustees of Dartmouth College*, 958 F. Supp. 37 (D.N.H. 1997), did indicate that a "person who discriminates in violation of [Section 504] may be personally liable if he or she is in a position to accept or reject federal funds" (958 F. Supp. at 45).

Despite the broader reach of the ADA, Section 504 remains an important source of rights for students, employees, and visitors to the campus. For public institutions that now cannot be sued in federal court under the ADA, Section 504 may become a more significant source of remedies for plaintiffs who seek damages from these institutions.

**11.5.5. Coverage of unintentional discrimination.** None of the four civil rights statutes explicitly states whether it prohibits actions whose effects are discriminatory (that is, actions that have a disproportionate or disparate impact on the class of persons protected) or whether such actions are prohibited only if taken with a discriminatory intent or motive. The regulations for Title VI and the Age Discrimination Act, however, contain provisions that apparently prohibit actions with discriminatory effects, even if those actions are not intentionally discriminatory (34 C.F.R. § 100.3(b)(2); 45 C.F.R. § 90.12); and the Section 504 regulations prohibit actions that have the effect of subjecting a qualified individual to discrimination on the basis of disability (34 C.F.R. § 104.4(b) (4), (5)). Title IX's regulations prohibit testing or evaluation of skill that has a discriminatory effect on the basis of sex (34 C.F.R. §§ 106.21(b)(2), 106.34), and prohibit the use of "any rule concerning a student's actual or potential parental, family, or marital status" that would have the effect of discriminating on the basis of sex (34 C.F.R. § 106.40). The Title IX regulations also prohibit certain employment practices with discriminatory effects (34 C.F.R. § 106.51(a)(3)). In addition, some of the Title IX regulations on intercollegiate athletics programs could be construed to cover unintentional actions with discriminatory effects, especially as those regulations are interpreted in the 1979 Policy Interpretation (see Section 10.4.6 of this book).

In a leading U.S. Supreme Court case, *Guardians Association v. Civil Service Commission of the City of New York*, 463 U.S. 582 (1983), the Court could not agree on the legal status of disparate impact cases under Title VI. The Justices issued six opinions in the case, none of which commanded a majority and which, according to Justice Powell, "further confuse rather than guide." The Court's basic difficulty was reconciling *Lau v. Nichols*, 414 U.S. 563 (1974), which held that the Title VI regulations issued by the Department of Health, Education and Welfare (now the Department of Education) validly prohibited actions with discriminatory effects, with Regents of the *University of California v. Bakke*, 438 U.S. 265 (1978), which indicated that Title VI reaches no further than the Fourteenth Amendment's equal protection clause, prohibiting only intentional discrimination.

Although the Court could not agree on the import of these two cases, or on the analysis to adopt in the case before it, one can extract some meaning from *Guardians* by pooling the views expressed in the various opinions. A majority of the Justices did hold that the discriminatory intent requirement is a necessary component of the Title VI statute. A different majority, however, held that, even though the statute embodies an intent test, the Department of Education regulations that adopt an effects test are nevertheless valid. In his opinion, Justice White tallied the differing views of the Justices on these points (463 U.S. at 584 n.2, 607 n.27). He then rationalized these seemingly contradictory conclusions by explaining that "the language of Title VI on its face is ambiguous; the word 'discrimination' is inherently so." The statute should therefore be amenable to a broader construction by the Department of Education, "at least to the extent of permitting, if not requiring, regulations that reach" discriminatory effects (463 U.S. at 592; see also 463 U.S. at 643–45 (opinion of Justice Stevens)).

The result of this confusing mélange of opinions is to validate the Education Department's regulations extending Title VI coverage to actions with discriminatory effects. At the same time, however, the *Guardians* opinions suggest that, if the department were to change its regulations so as to require proof of discriminatory intent, such a change would also be valid. Any such change, though, would in turn be subject to invalidation by Congress, which could amend the Title VI statute (or other statutes under which the issue arose) to replace its intent standard with an effects test.

In *Alexander v. Choate*, 469 U.S. 287 (1985), the Court also considered the discriminatory intent issue under Section 504 of the Rehabilitation Act. After reviewing the various opinions in the *Guardians* case on Title VI, the Court determined that that case does not control the intent issue under Section 504 because Section 504 raises considerations different from those raised by Title VI. In particular:

> Discrimination against the handicapped was perceived by Congress to be most often the product, not of invidious animus, but rather of thoughtlessness and indifference—of benign neglect . . . Federal agencies and commentators on the plight of the handicapped similarly have found that discrimination against the handicapped is primarily the result of apathetic attitudes rather than affirmative animus.
>
> In addition, much of the conduct that Congress sought to alter in passing the Rehabilitation Act would be difficult if not impossible to reach were the Act construed to proscribe only conduct fueled by a discriminatory intent. For example, elimination of architectural barriers was one of the central aims of the Act (see, for example, S. Rep. No. 93-318, p. 4 (1973), U.S. Code Cong. & Admin. News 1973, pp. 2076, 2080), yet such barriers were clearly not erected with the aim or intent of excluding the handicapped [469 U.S. at 295–97].

Although these considerations suggest that discriminatory intent is not a requirement under Section 504, the Court also noted some countervailing considerations:

> At the same time, the position urged by respondents—that we interpret Section 504 to reach all action disparately affecting the handicapped—is also troubling. Because the handicapped typically are not similarly situated to the nonhandicapped, respondents' position would in essence require each recipient of federal funds first to evaluate the effect on the handicapped of every proposed action that might touch the interests of the handicapped, and then to consider alternatives for achieving the same objectives with less severe disadvantage to the handicapped. The formalization and policing of this process could lead to a wholly unwieldy administrative and adjudicative burden [469 U.S. at 298].

Faced with these difficulties, the Court declined to hold that one group of considerations would always have priority over the other: "While we reject the boundless notion that all disparate-impact showings constitute prima facie cases under Section 504, we assume without deciding that Section 504 reaches at least some conduct that has an unjustifiable disparate impact upon the handicapped." Thus "splitting the difference," the Court left for another day the specification of what types of Section 504 claims will not require evidence of a discriminatory intent.

A related, but different, issue is whether private plaintiffs (those claiming discrimination) may bring private causes of action in court to enforce the

Department of Education's (or other agencies') disparate impact regulations, rather than relying solely on the administrative complaint process. If disparate impact regulations are valid under the four civil rights statutes, it necessarily follows that they may be enforced through the administrative processes of the agencies that promulgate the regulations. It does not automatically follow, however, that disparate impact regulations may be enforced through the implied private cause of action that, under *Cannon* and *Franklin*, may be used to enforce the statues themselves. The Court's *Lau v. Nichols* ruling in 1974 did permit a private cause of action to enforce Title VI impact regulations, but the status of *Lau* became unclear after *Bakke*. *Guardians* then validated the Title VI impact regulations, and a bare majority of the Justices seemed willing to permit their enforcement by private causes of action. Most lower courts took this position as well. But in *Alexander v. Sandoval*, 532 U.S. 275 (2001), in an opinion by Justice Scalia, the Court reconsidered these cases and ruled directly on the issue of private causes of action to enforce Title VI's impact regulations. The Court majority assumed, for purposes of the case, that the Title VI impact regulations were valid, and it acknowledged that five Justices in *Guardians* had taken that position. But in a hotly contested 5-to-4 decision, the Court prohibited private causes of action to enforce these regulations. Since there is no private cause of action to enforce the disparate impact regulations, and since private causes of action to enforce the Title VI statute itself require a showing of discriminatory intent, it follows from *Sandoval* that individuals claiming race discrimination may not sue fund recipients under Title VI for actions that have discriminatory effects but are not intentionally discriminatory. The same conclusion apparently applies to Title IX, since the courts have treated the two statutes in much the same way, and probably also to the Age Discrimination Act. Section 504 is different, however, since the Section 504 statute does not require proof of discriminatory intent for all claims of statutory violations (see *Alexander v. Choate*, above).

# The College and External Private Entities

*Chapter 12 addresses external governance issues and other issues that arise from colleges' and universities' relationships with private (nongovernmental) organizations and entities. The chapter first reviews the education associations and their roles, giving particular emphasis to legal issues involving colleges' and universities' relationships with accrediting associations and with athletics associations and conferences. It then examines a variety of issues related to colleges' and universities' relationships with commercial entities, especially with respect to collaborative research and sponsored research.*

## Section 12.1. The Education Associations

***12.1.1. Overview of the education associations.*** The myriad of associations related, either wholly or in part, to postsecondary education exemplifies the diversity of missions, structure, and program mix of U.S. colleges and universities. From the American Council on Education (ACE), which monitors and informs college presidents about a variety of issues affecting colleges and universities generally, to the League for Innovation in the Community Colleges, an organization devoted to "improving community colleges through innovation, experimentation, and institutional transformation," these associations perform numerous functions, whether on behalf of all colleges and universities, or only some institutions, or just a few specialized institutions. The Web site of the U.S. Department of Education contains a searchable Education Resources Information Directory listing thousands of organizations, related to either K–12 or postsecondary education and updated at least annually (available at wdcrobcolp01.ed.gov/Programs/EROD/directory_benefits.cfm). Although many education associations are in Washington, D.C., others are located in various cities throughout the United States. Education associations, particularly those whose members are institutions or boards of trustees, exist at the state level as well.

Various education associations, with institutions as members, focus on monitoring and lobbying for (or against) federal legislation and regulatory changes that affect postsecondary education. Those institutional-membership organizations include the American Council on Education (www.acenet.org), the American Association of Community Colleges (www.aacc.nche.edu), the American Association of State Colleges and Universities (www.aascu.org), the Association of American Universities (www.aau.edu), the Association of Public and Land Grant Universities (www.aplu.org), and the National Association of Independent Colleges and Universities (www.naicu.edu).

Other education associations, such as the American Association of University Professors (AAUP) (www.aaup.org), NASPA (National Association of Student Personnel Administrators)–Student Affairs Administrators in Higher Education (www.naspa.org), and ACPA (American College Personnel Association) (www2 .myacpa.org), have individuals as members, and focus, at least in part, on the professional development of their members and the advancement of the profession. The "National Academies," consisting of the National Academy of Sciences (www.nasonline.org), the National Research Council (www.nationalacademies. org/nrc), the National Academy of Engineering (www.nae.edu), and the Institute of Medicine (www.iom.edu), are private, nonprofit institutions that "provide science, technology and health policy advice under a congressional charter," according to their Web sites. Membership in the National Academies is by election by current members. The American Council of Learned Societies (www.acls.org) provides funding for research in the humanities and social sciences, and the American Association for the Advancement of Science (www.aaas.org) advances the interests of science and publishes a journal, books, newsletters, and reports.

Regardless of whether their members are institutions or individuals, most of these organizations fulfill multiple purposes. Many, particularly those located in the nation's capital, engage in lobbying activities, attempting to influence congressional action or the regulatory activities of executive branch agencies. Representatives of education associations may advise congressional staff in drafting legislation and ascertaining its impact on postsecondary education; they may also appear before congressional committees or assist congressional staff in inviting others to appear. They may attend agency meetings and hearings on draft regulations, to make drafting suggestions and to explain the implications of these regulations for postsecondary education. The state-level equivalents of the education associations perform similar activities with regard to state legislation and regulations. Many associations develop statements of policy on good professional practice and other matters for their constituencies. The statements promulgated by the American Association of University Professors, for instance, have had a substantial impact on the status of faculty on many campuses and on the judicial interpretation of "national custom and usage" in faculty employment relations.

Education and training, and information sharing, are significant activities of the education associations as well. Most have annual conferences, and many produce publications to inform and update their constituencies. Many serve an important monitoring function for their members, particularly with regard to new legislative, administrative, and judicial developments. In addition, most agencies have Web sites on which they post recent developments in the law and regulatory activities, standards of good practice, publications, and other important materials.

Many associations have special interests or expertise regarding the legal issues in this book and are excellent sources of legal information and law-related conferences and workshops. The American Council on Education, for example, prepares important analyses and alerts on current legal issues, especially those concerning congressional legislation and legislative proposals. NASPA–Student Affairs Administrators in Higher Education sends periodic legal updates to members. The Association for Student Conduct Administration (www.theasca.org) has an annual national conference, regional gatherings, and summer institutes at which legal issues of interest to personnel responsible for campus judicial affairs are discussed. And the National Association of College and University Attorneys (NACUA) (www.nacua.org) provides a comprehensive array of services for member institutions and the attorneys who represent them, as well as for other "associate" members.

Some of the associations also act as *amici curiae*, or "friends of the court," in litigation affecting the interests of their members. When ongoing litigation affects the interests of postsecondary education generally, or a large group of institutions, many of the education organizations often will band together to submit an amicus brief, particularly if the case is before the U.S. Supreme Court. The associations have, on occasion, also provided expert witnesses to explain academic custom and practice, or to interpret the academic community's "general understanding" of important concepts such as tenure and academic freedom.

In addition, some associations perform the critical function of accrediting institutions or particular academic programs within institutions. The U.S. Department of Education relies on these private, nonprofit accrediting actions as a basis for certifying an institution's eligibility to participate in federal aid programs (see Section 12.1.2). The accrediting associations also play a significant role in the higher education community's self-regulation.

In their roles as monitors, quasi-regulators, or accreditors of higher education institutions, the education associations may make decisions that precipitate litigation against them by a college or university. For example, on many occasions a college or university has sued the National Collegiate Athletic Association (NCAA; www.ncaa.org) over its regulation of college athletics (see Section 12.1.3). Institutions have also sued accrediting associations to challenge a withdrawal, threatened withdrawal, or denial of accreditation (see Section 12.1.2).

The education associations are a source of information, assistance, and practical advice for colleges and universities and for members of the academic community, particularly with regard to federal regulation and professional and ethical practices. The associations provide services and expertise that few institutions have the resources to provide for themselves, as well as a network of colleagues with similar interests and concerns.

There are various "advocacy organizations" that engage in litigation, lobbying, education, and training activities focusing on particular sets of issues of concern to higher education. These organizations often represent interests—of students and of other members of the academic community—that are in opposition to interests staked out by particular institutions or by higher education associations such as those discussed in this section. Selected examples of such advocacy organizations include the Foundation for Individual Rights in Education (FIRE) (www.thefire.org); Students for Academic Freedom (www.studentsforacademicfreedom.org); the Center for Law and Religious Freedom, a project of the Christian Legal Society (www.clsnet.org); the Alliance Defending Freedom and its Center for Academic Freedom (www.alliancedefendingfreedom.org), a Christian legal alliance that focuses on religious freedom; the Student Press Law Center (www.splc.org); and the Center for Individual Rights (www.cir-usa.org), which has been particularly active in the cases on affirmative action in admissions. More traditional examples of advocacy groups that address education issues include the American Civil Liberties Union (ACLU) (www.aclu.org) and the NAACP Legal Defense and Educational Fund, Inc. (www.naacpldf.org). In addition, national higher education associations such as those discussed in the first part of this section also sometimes assume the role of advocacy organizations and engage in advocacy, in court or in legislative or administrative agency forums, on behalf of their members.[1]

### 12.1.2. Accrediting agencies.

**12.1.2. Accrediting agencies.** Among the associations with which postsecondary administrators must deal, the ones most concerned with the educational missions of institutions and programs are the educational accrediting agencies. Educational accreditation, conducted by private associations rather than by a ministry of education or other government agency, is a development unique to the United States. As the system has evolved, the private accrediting agencies have assumed an important role in the development and maintenance of standards for postsecondary education and have gained considerable influence over individual institutions and programs seeking to obtain or preserve the accreditation that only these agencies may bestow.

There are two types of accreditation: institutional (or "regional") accreditation and program (or "specialized") accreditation. Institutional accreditation

---

[1] A partial listing of education associations and their Web sites, in addition to those mentioned in the text of this section, includes American Association of Collegiate Registrars and Admissions Officers, www.aacrao.org; American College Counseling Association, www.collegecounseling.org; Association of American Colleges and Universities, www.aacu-edu.org; Association of American Medical Colleges, www.aamc.org; Association of Catholic Colleges and Universities, www.accunet.org; Association of College and University Housing Officers—International, www.acuho-i.org; Association of Community College Trustees, www.acct.org; University Risk Management and Insurance Association, www.urmia.org; Association of Governing Boards of Universities and Colleges, www.agb.org; Association of Jesuit Colleges and Universities, www.ajcunet.edu; College and University Professional Association for Human Resources, www.cupahr.org; Council for Opportunity in Education, www.coenet.us.

applies to the entire institution and all its programs, departments, and schools; program accreditation applies to a particular school, department, or program within the institution, such as a school of medicine or law, a department of chemistry, or a program in medical technology. Program accreditation may also apply to an entire institution if it is a freestanding, specialized institution, such as a business school or technical school, whose curriculum is all in the same program area.

Institutional accreditation is granted by six regional agencies—membership associations composed of the accredited institutions in each region. Since each regional agency covers a separate, defined part of the country, each institution is subject to the jurisdiction of only one such agency. Program accreditation is granted by a multitude of proliferating "specialized" (or "professional" or "occupational") accrediting agencies, which may or may not be membership associations and are often sponsored by the particular profession or occupation whose educational programs are being accredited. The jurisdiction of these specialized agencies is nationwide.

From 1975 until 1993, a private organization, the Council on Postsecondary Accreditation (COPA), operated a nongovernmental recognition process for both regional and specialized agencies and served as their representative at the national level. The organization disbanded effective December 31, 1993. A successor organization to COPA, the Council for Higher Education Accreditation (CHEA), began operations in 1996 through the initiative of a group of college presidents. See generally Harland Bloland (ed.), *Creating the Council for Higher Education Accreditation* (Greenwood, 2001). CHEA oversees both institutional (regional) and program (specialized) accreditation.

Being private, accrediting agencies owe their existence and legal status to state corporation law and to the common law of "voluntary" (or private) associations. Their powers are enforced through private sanctions embodied in their articles, bylaws, and rules, the primary sanctions being the withdrawal and denial of accreditation. The force of these private sanctions is greatly enhanced, however, by the extensive public and private reliance on accrediting agencies' decisions.

The federal government relies in part on these agencies to identify the institutions and programs eligible for a wide range of aid-to-education programs, particularly those administered by the U.S. Department of Education. The states demonstrate their reliance on the agencies' assessments when they exempt accredited institutions or programs from various licensing or other regulatory requirements (see Section 11.2.3). Some states also use accreditation to determine students' or institutions' eligibility under their own state funding programs; and the state approving agencies operating under contract with the Department of Veterans Affairs depend on accreditation in approving courses for veterans' programs. State professional and occupational licensing boards rely on the accrediting agencies by making graduation from an accredited school or program a prerequisite to obtaining a license to practice in the state. Some states also rely on an institution's accredited status in granting tax exemptions.

Private professional societies may use professional accreditation in determining who is eligible for membership. Students, parents, and guidance counselors may employ accreditation as one criterion in choosing a school. And post-secondary institutions themselves often rely on accreditation in determining the acceptability of transfer credits and in deciding what academic credentials will qualify persons to apply for particular academic positions. In *Merwine v. Board of Trustees for State Institutions of Higher Learning*, 754 F.2d 631 (5th Cir. 1985), for example, the court upheld the defendant's requirement that applicants for certain faculty librarian positions must hold a master's degree from a program accredited by the American Library Association.

Despite the clear importance of accreditation and the long-term continuing existence of accrediting agencies, the role of accrediting agencies over the years has been sometimes controversial and often misunderstood. There have been frequent, sometimes intense debates about accreditation among college presidents, federal and state evaluation officials, Congress, accreditation agency officials, and officials of other higher education associations. Much of this debate since the early 1990s has concerned accrediting agencies' relationships with the federal government—especially the agencies' role in monitoring institutional integrity regarding federal student aid programs.

Debate in modern times has also sometimes focused on particular existing or proposed functions of accrediting agencies—for example, monitoring academic abuses on the part of student athletes, overseeing programs that accredited institutions sponsor in foreign countries or on branch campuses in the United States, and monitoring nondiscrimination and academic freedom in religiously affiliated institutions and other institutions. The need for, and the composition and functions of, private umbrella groups to oversee the accreditation systems (such as the former Council on Postsecondary Accreditation) have also periodically been debated. Other issues continuing into the twenty-first century include the accreditation of new "virtual" or "online" institutions, the evaluation of distance education courses and other technological teaching innovations within established institutions, accreditation standards concerning use of part-time faculty members, the accreditation of teacher education programs, accreditation of medical residency training programs, especially with respect to duty hour rules for residents, accrediting standards to promote racial, ethnic, and cultural diversity at accredited institutions, and the role (if any) of Congress and the Secretary of Education in requiring that accrediting agencies use specific, concrete measures of the quality of student learning, in particular "output" rather than "input" measures.

Another major accreditation issue that has been prominent since the beginning of the twenty-first century concerns accountability. The focus has been on accrediting agencies' accountability to students, parents, and the general public, particularly with respect to student achievement, as well as on the role of the U.S. Department of Education in overseeing an enhancement of accrediting agencies' accountability. In the Higher Education Opportunity Act of 2008 (HEOA), P.L. No. 110-315, 122 Stat. 3078, Congress addressed various aspects of accrediting agency accountability, as well as other issues concerning accreditation. The overall result, it appears, is to expand the federal government's role in accreditation and particularly in accrediting agency accountability. Critics have argued that the new accreditation provisions in HEOA, and the Department of Education's regulations and guidelines that implement these provisions, will result in federal government involvement in certain academic judgments of institutions, thus eroding institutional autonomy, and will push accreditation away from its traditional role as a voluntary process of peer and professional review toward a new role of monitoring institutional compliance with federal government priorities.

### 12.1.3. Athletic associations and conferences.[2] Various associations and conferences have a hand in regulating intercollegiate athletics. Most institutions with intercollegiate programs are members of both a national association (for example, the National Collegiate Athletic Association (NCAA)) and a conference (for example, the Atlantic Coast Conference (ACC)).

The NCAA (http://www.ncaa.org) is the largest and most influential of the athletic associations. It is an unincorporated association with a membership of more than one thousand public and private colleges and universities, which are grouped into three divisions. The association has a constitution that sets forth its fundamental law and has enacted extensive bylaws that govern the NCAA's operations. (Information on the NCAA bylaws and enforcement is available on the NCAA's Web site; click on "Enforcement" and also on "Resources.") To preserve the amateur nature of college athletics and the fairness of competition, the NCAA includes in its bylaws complex rules regarding recruiting, academic eligibility, other eligibility requirements, and the like. There are different rules for each of the three divisions, compiled into an NCAA manual for each division, which is updated periodically. Regarding eligibility, for instance, the NCAA Manual for Division I has requirements on minimum grade point average (GPA) and Scholastic Aptitude Test (SAT) or American College Testing (ACT) scores for incoming freshman student athletes; requirements regarding satisfactory academic progress for student athletes; restrictions on transfers from one school to another; rules on "redshirting" and longevity as a player; limitations on financial aid, compensation, and employment; and limitations regarding professional contracts and players' agents. To enforce its rules, the NCAA has an enforcement program that includes compliance audits, self-reporting, investigations, and official inquiries, culminating in a range of penalties that the NCAA can impose against its member institutions but not directly against the institutions' employees. The various conferences affiliated with the NCAA may also have their own rules and enforcement processes, so long as they meet the minimum requirements of the NCAA.

Legal issues often arise as a result of the rule-making and enforcement activities of the various athletic associations and conferences. Individual institutions

---

[2]This section was revised and updated by Jonathan R. Alger, former senior vice president and general counsel at Rutgers University and currently president of James Madison University.

have become involved in such legal issues in two ways. First, coaches and student athletes penalized for violating conference or association rules have sued their institutions as well as the conference or association to contest the enforcement of these rules. Second, institutions themselves have sued conferences or associations over their rules, policies, or decisions. The majority of such disputes have involved the NCAA, since it is the primary regulator of intercollegiate athletics in the United States. The resulting litigation frequently presents a difficult threshold problem of determining what legal principles should apply to resolution of the dispute.

The cases indicate that institutions of higher education do have legal weapons to use in disputes with the NCAA and other athletic associations or conferences. State common law clearly applies to such disputes.(See, for example, *Trustees of State Colleges and Universities v. NCAA*, 147 Cal. Rptr. 187 (Cal. Ct. App. 1978).) Antitrust law also has some applicability, as does federal civil rights law. Federal constitutional rights may still have some application in a narrow range of cases. And some role may still be found for state statutes regulating athletic associations' enforcement activities. These weapons are two-edged: student athletes may also use them against the institution when the institution and the athletic association are jointly engaged in enforcing athletic rules against the student.

## Section 12.2. Business Partners

### 12.2.1. Research collaboration.
It has become increasingly common for higher education institutions to align themselves with one another or with other outside entities in the pursuit of common entrepreneurial objectives. The primary area of growth and concern is research collaboration involving institutions, individual faculty members, corporate sponsors, and government. The resulting structural arrangements, such as research consortia, joint ventures, and partnerships, are more complex and more cooperative than those for purchasing and selling transactions.

Universities and faculty members undertake various types of research in collaboration with industry, but the primary focus is on biomedical and biotechnological research. The concerns escalate when such research moves from the realm of pure science to the realm of technology transfer and product development, thus potentially placing entrepreneurial considerations in tension with academic considerations. In this applied research context, questions about compliance with the federal government's environmental requirements and workplace safety requirements will often arise. Government also may become involved as a partial sponsor of university research done in affiliation with outside entities, thus raising legal questions about various government grant and contract requirements, such as the scientific misconduct prohibitions attached to research funding. Moreover, since biomedical and biotechnological research sometimes is conducted with human subjects, researchers will be expected to comply with federal requirements for such research (Section 11.3.2.2). When animals are used, other federal requirements concerning animal research (Section 11.3.2.2) must be followed. States also may place restrictions on medical research under both common law and statute. Research collaborations with industry will also frequently involve the university in complex legal problems concerning contract and corporation law, patent ownership and patent licenses, antitrust laws, copyright and trademark laws, federal and state taxes, federal technology transfer incentives, and conflict-of-interest regulations, all of which are discussed below. There may also be academic freedom issues when sponsors of research require confidentiality or prior approval of publication as a condition of receiving funding.

There are many reasons why universities seek to collaborate with business and industry. The financial benefits of such arrangements may be a major motivating factor, as institutions have sought to enhance research budgets that are shrinking because of reductions in federal and state research funding and institutional budgeting pressures. Clearly, however, research relationships can produce benefits other than the purely financial. An institution may seek to broaden the dialogue in which its researchers are engaged, especially to blend theory with practice; to open new avenues and perspectives to the institution's students; to improve placement opportunities for graduate students, thereby improving the institution's competitive position in recruiting applicants to graduate programs; to enhance the institution's ability to recruit new faculty members; or simply to gain access to new equipment and new or improved facilities for research. Institutions may also be motivated by a good-faith commitment to benefit society by putting academic research discoveries to practical use through the transfer of technology.

Various competitive and budgetary pressures also may encourage individual faculty members or their research groups to form their own relationships with industry. Faculty salaries that do not keep pace with salaries in industry or with inflation may be one factor. Pressures to produce research results in order to meet the demands of promotion and tenure may also encourage faculty members to seek the funds, resources, and technical information available from industrial liaisons in order to boost their productivity. Some researchers may also need particular types of equipment or facilities, or access to particular technology, that cannot be made available within the institution for reasons of cost or scarcity. Faculty members also face pressures to place their graduate students in desirable industrial positions and to have placement prospects that will help in recruiting new graduate students.

In addition, federal and state governments have themselves encouraged university-industry collaboration. By placing new emphasis on economic vitality and technological competitiveness, federal and state governments have created an increasingly hospitable governmental climate within which such collaborations can expand and flourish.

Universities or their faculties may engage in entrepreneurial research activities using various structural and organizational arrangements. The most traditional relationship is the grantor-grantee relationship, under which an industrial entity—the commercial sponsor—makes a grant to a particular university for the use of particular faculty members or departments in return for certain rights to use the research produced. Another traditional form is the purchase-of-services contract, under which the university provides training, consultant services, or equipment or facilities to an industrial entity for a fee. The most basic form, which is of great current importance, is the research agreement, especially the agreement for contracted research. Another basic form is the patent-licensing agreement. A different type of arrangement is the industrial affiliation, an ongoing, usually long-term relationship between a particular university and a particular industrial entity, in which mutual benefits (such as access to each other's research facilities and experts) flow between the parties.

More complicated structural arrangements include partnerships, limited partnerships, joint ventures (a business arrangement undertaken for a limited period of time or for a single purpose, thus differing from a partnership), and the creation (by the institution) of subsidiary corporations to engage in entrepreneurial research functions or to hold and license patent rights. The particular arrangements that may emerge from such structures or a combination of them include the research consortium, the research park, the specialized laboratory, and the patent-holding company. More than one university and more than one business corporation may be involved in such arrangements, and government funding and sponsorship may also play an important role. The legal and policy issues that may arise in such research relationships will depend, in part, on the particular structural arrangement that is used.

Individual faculty members or research groups may form their own independent research relationships with industry. Faculty members may become part-time consultants or employees of a private research corporation, receive grants from industry and undertake particular research obligations under these grants, or enter contract research agreements of their own with industry. On another level, faculty members may become officers or directors of a private research corporation; they may become stockholders with an equity position in such a corporation; or they may establish their own private research corporations, in which they become partners or sole proprietors.

Virtually all such arrangements, involving either institutional or faculty relationships with industry, have the potential for creating complex combinations of legal, policy, and managerial issues. Perhaps most difficult are the potential issues of conflict of interest arising from arrangements that precipitate split loyalties, which could detract attention and drain resources from the academic enterprise. Research priorities might be subtly reshaped, for instance, to focus on areas where money is available from industry rather than on areas of greatest academic challenge or need. Split loyalties may also encourage faculty to give more attention to research than to instruction or to favor graduate education over undergraduate education. In addition, the university's traditional emphasis on open dialogue and the free flow of academic information may be undercut by university-industry arrangements that promote secrecy in order to serve industrial profit motives. Disputes may also arise over the ownership and use of inventions and other products of research, as well as of equipment and facilities purchased for research purposes. The institution and its faculty may engage in contractual disputes over the faculty's obligations to the institution or freedom to engage in outside activities; the university and its research sponsors or partners may have similar disputes over interpretations of their research agreements. Product liability issues may arise if any persons are injured by products that are moved to the market. And various other legal, financial, and political risks may be associated with university-industry relationships.

In addition, the scope and complexity of this array of law, policy, and managerial considerations are being expanded by the growth of global digital communication. This development has made collaboration across national borders easier and faster. Federal regulation has expanded in the arena of cross-border research collaboration, and significant penalties have been levied for violations.

**12.2.2. The research agreement.** The research agreement is typically the heart of the university-industry research relationship. It is a type of contract, interpreted and enforced in accordance with the contract law of the state whose law governs the transaction. This agreement may be the entire legal arrangement between the parties, as in contracted research, or it may be part of a broader collaboration that involves other legal documents or other agreements on activities besides research. One or more universities or university research foundations, and one or more industrial sponsors, are typically the parties to the contract. Particular faculty members (or departments or research groups) may be named in the agreement as principal investigators or may occasionally themselves be parties to the agreement. When the research will involve human subjects, there will also usually be subsidiary agreements with these persons, as discussed later in this section. The research agreement may be either a short-term or a long-term agreement; the agreement may be for a specific single project or a combination of projects. Depending on the type of project contemplated and the purposes of the arrangement, threshold questions may arise concerning the institution's authority to enter the agreement.

The complex process of negotiating and drafting a research agreement requires scientific and technical expertise as well as legal and administrative expertise. In addition, there are numerous special concerns that will require the insertion of special provisions into the agreement. Examples may include provisions regarding: (1) inventions discovered during the project (who will own the patents, and who will have rights to license and royalty payments); (2) the university's obligations to disclose research results to the industrial sponsor; (3) researchers' rights to publish their research results—and whether the sponsor may require a delay in publication for a period of time necessary to apply for patent protection; (4) the university's obligations to protect any trade secrets and proprietary information that the sponsor may release to university researchers or that may result from the project research; (5) rights of the sponsor to use the university's name, marks, and logos, or prohibitions on their use by the sponsor; (6) indemnification, hold-harmless, or insurance requirements regarding special matters, such as environmental hazards and products liability; and (7) the parties' obligations to protect university and faculty academic freedom and to protect against university or faculty conflicts of interest.[3]

---

[3] Adapted from Donald Fowler, "University-Industry Research Relationships: The Research Agreement," 9 *J. Coll. & Univ. Law* 515 (1982–83).

If an industrial sponsor or university located in a foreign country is to be a party to the research agreement, the U.S. university will require additional expertise in U.S. laws governing foreign relations—for instance, the export control laws—and in international and foreign law (see Section 1.4.2.5). The university also will need to understand and protect against its potential liabilities (including antitrust liability; product liability; and liability for patent, copyright, or trademark infringement) under the law of any foreign country in which project activities will take place or to which research products will be shipped. Equally, the university will need to understand and be ready to assert its rights under foreign law—for instance, rights to protection against patent, copyright, trademark, and trade secret infringement by others. Taxation and tariff questions may also arise. The applicable law may be found not only in the codes and regulations of particular foreign countries but also in the provisions of treaties and conventions that may apply, such as the Berne Convention for the Protection of Literary and Artistic Works, the Paris Convention for the Protection of Industrial Property, the European Patent Convention, the Patent Cooperation Treaty, the Universal Copyright Convention, or the Beirut Agreement (the Agreement for Facilitating the International Circulation of Visual and Auditory Materials of an Educational, Scientific, and Cultural Character).

These concerns, among others, should be anticipated in the negotiation and drafting of international research agreements, and may lead to the inclusion of special provisions such as the following: (1) a choice-of-law clause specifying what role (if any) foreign law will have in the interpretation and application of the research agreement; (2) special indemnification, hold-harmless, or insurance clauses dealing with liabilities that arise under foreign or international law; (3) a special arbitration clause, or other dispute resolution clause, adapted to the international context of the agreement; (4) clauses regarding the parties' obligations to secure patent, trademark, or copyright protection under foreign or international law; (5) a clause establishing responsibilities for payment of taxes and tariffs imposed by foreign governments; (6) a clause providing for instruction for project staff in the language, culture, and business practices of foreign countries where project activities will be conducted; and (7) a clause allocating responsibility for paying particular foreign travel and shipping costs.

Whether the research agreement is domestic or international, problems of performance may arise that could result in contract interpretation disputes, claims of breach, or attempts to terminate the agreement. In the latter case, the terminating party may argue that it has terminated the agreement because of the breach of the other party. The other party may argue that the terminating party has breached the agreement. In either situation, questions will arise concerning the rights and obligations of the parties upon termination. In general, the answers will depend on interpretation of the agreement's terms in accordance with the contract law of the state whose law governs the transactions. If the termination constitutes or was occasioned by a breach, the answers will also depend on the state law concerning money damages and other remedies for breach of contract.

The case of *Regents of the University of Colorado v. K.D.I. Precision Products, Inc.*, 488 F.2d 261 (10th Cir. 1973), illustrates the types of performance problems that can arise under a research agreement and, by implication, underscores the importance of a comprehensive and clear contract. The case addresses three questions that are likely to be asked when a research agreement is terminated: (1) What constitutes substantial performance under the contract? (2) Which party, or who besides the parties, has the rights to inventions developed or patents obtained under the contract? (3) Which party owns the equipment used in the project? The court looked to the express provisions of the agreement to resolve each of these issues.

The University of Colorado, the plaintiff, had entered into a three-year research and development contract with K.D.I., the defendant, under which the university, for remuneration, was to help K.D.I. develop certain scientific devices. After the first year, K.D.I. terminated the contract. The university sued to recover payment for the work that the university had performed up to the date of termination. K.D.I. defended on two grounds: first, that the university had failed to substantially perform its contract obligations and therefore was not entitled to recovery; second, that even if the university did substantially perform the contract, the university's recovery was subject to a set-off for the value of project equipment the university had allegedly "converted" to its use.

Regarding its first defense, K.D.I. made three arguments. First, it alleged that the university had failed to give it "exclusive" rights to the technical data developed under the research contract, including rights to all the original plans and designs. The court found that the university had specifically agreed to give K.D.I. "unlimited" (rather than "exclusive") rights to use, duplicate, or disclose the technical data and that the university had performed its obligations to extend such "unlimited" rights to K.D.I. Second, K.D.I. alleged that the university did not substantially perform because it failed to complete a prior research contract whose work was continued in the current research contract. The court rejected this argument as well, because the current contract was "complete in itself as to the duties and obligations of the parties thereto. It comprises a separate research contract, and there is no intimation therein of the **incorporation by reference** to prior contracts." Third, K.D.I. argued that the university did not substantially perform the research contract because it failed to disclose its development of a device called the Optical Communication Link (OCL). The court also rejected this argument, finding that the OCL was not developed under the research contract with K.D.I. Rather, it was developed by two of the university's professors, with the university's money and for use by the university; it was used for the university's own purposes; and it was not necessary to K.D.I.'s purposes. The university therefore had no obligation to disclose the development of the OCL.

Regarding its second defense, K.D.I. argued that certain equipment used by the university for the research project, and retained by the university at termination, was actually the property of K.D.I. The court found that, although K.D.I. had contributed a small amount toward the purchase of one piece of equipment and had made some attempts under the contract to correct problems with another piece, K.D.I. had no legal claim to the equipment. K.D.I. had not loaned or assigned the contested equipment to the university; the equipment had been donated to the project by the university itself and other corporate donors. Moreover, "in the operative and dispositive portions of the contract, as it describes the research to be undertaken, there is no suggestion that title to the equipment was either in K.D.I. or was to vest therein" (488 F.2d 266–67). Since K.D.I. did not have legal rights to the equipment, the university could not have converted it; thus, there was no basis for set-off.

In rejecting K.D.I.'s second defense, the court compared the contract's treatment of equipment ownership (as to which the contract was silent) to the contract's treatment of patent rights—as to which the contract contained detailed clauses assigning patent rights to K.D.I. and requiring written disclosure by the university of each invention. K.D.I., therefore, did have patent rights under the contract, but not rights to equipment. No issue concerning patent rights arose in the case, however, because the university conceded K.D.I.'s rights in this realm, and K.D.I. did not allege that the university had attempted to assert patent rights belonging to K.D.I.

If the research project is to involve human subjects, the research agreement should contain supplementary provisions covering the special legal and ethical issues that arise in this context. If the parties contemplate using federal funds for some or all of the human subject research, or if the human subject research is to involve drugs within the jurisdiction of the Food and Drug Administration, the research agreement's provisions must satisfy all requirements in the applicable federal regulations (see Section 11.3.2.2 of this book). In addition, whether or not federal regulations apply, the parties should arrange for separate agreements with each of the human subjects that are recruited for the project. These subsidiary agreements may be brief documents whose primary purpose is to document the participants' informed consent, or these agreements may cover in more detail the research subject's duties and the prospective benefits and risks of the research for the subject and for others. (If federal regulations apply, these subsidiary agreements will, of course, need to comply with the federal requirements on informed consent and other matters.)

In a case the court termed one "of first impression," *Grimes v. Kennedy Krieger Institute, Inc.*, 782 A.2d 807 (Md. 2001), Maryland's highest court analyzed many of the legal aspects (and some ethical aspects) of informed consent agreements with human research subjects. The defendant, Kennedy Krieger Institute (KKI), "a prestigious research institute, associated with Johns Hopkins University" (782 A.2d at 811), conducted a research project in cooperation with the university, the federal Environmental Protection Agency (EPA) (which awarded a contract for the project), and the Maryland Department of Housing and Community Development. The research project's purpose was to determine the relative effectiveness of "varying degrees of lead paint abatement procedures" performed on Baltimore low-income housing units, as measured "over a two-year period of time." The plaintiffs were two children who were human subjects in the project; they had lived in two different housing units included in the study and had had their blood tested periodically for evidence of lead contamination. A parent for each of the children had signed a consent form. Subsequently, however, after tests had revealed elevated levels of lead in dust collected from the housing units and in the children's blood samples, each parent, on behalf of her child, sued KKI for negligence. The primary thrust of the claims was that KKI had failed in its duty to fully inform the parents of the study's risks when the consent form was signed and later when the researchers' tests revealed a hazard to the children.

The trial court in each case granted KKI's motion for summary judgment, holding that the consent form was not a contract and that the families had no special relationship with KKI that would give rise to a duty of care. On appeal, the Court of Appeals of Maryland reversed the trial courts' summary judgments for KKI. The appellate court determined that the signed consent form created a "bilateral contract" between the parties: "Researcher/subject consent in non-therapeutical research can, and in this case did, create a contract." The parents' consent was not "fully informed," however, "because full material information was not furnished to the subjects or their parents." The "consent" in the contract was therefore not valid and could not be used by KKI as a defense. The appellate court also determined that the researcher-subject relationship under the contract should, in this circumstance, be considered a "special relationship":

> [T]rial courts appear to have held that special relationships out of which duties arise cannot be created by the relationship between researchers and subjects of the research. While in some rare cases that may be correct, it is not correct when researchers recruit people, especially children whose consent is furnished indirectly, to participate in nontherapeutic procedures that are potentially hazardous, dangerous or deleterious to their health . . . [T]he creation of study conditions or protocols or participation in the recruitment of otherwise healthy subjects to interact with already existing, or potentially existing, hazardous conditions, or both, for the purpose of creating statistics from which the scientific hypotheses can be supported, would normally warrant or create such special relationships as a matter of law [782 A.2d at 845–46].

In addition, the appellate court determined that the research project was subject to "standards of care that attach to federally funded or sponsored research projects that use human subjects." These standards, found in the federal HHS regulations, imposed a duty of care on KKI. According to the court:

> In this case, a special relationship out of which duties might arise might be created by reason of the federally imposed regulations. The question becomes whether this duty of informed consent created by federal regulation, as a matter of state law, translates into a duty of care arising out of the unique relationships that is researcher-subject, as opposed to doctor-patient. We answer that question

in the affirmative. In this state, it may, depending on the facts, create such a duty [782 A.2d at 849].

An analysis of state tort law principles provided the appellate court yet another basis for determining that KKI owed a duty of care to the children. Focusing primarily on the foreseeability of personal harm, the court concluded that

> [t]he relationship that existed between KKI and both sets of appellants in the case at bar was that of medical researcher and research study subject. Though not expressly recognized in the Maryland Code or in our prior cases as a type of relationship which creates a duty of care, evidence in the record suggests that such a relationship involving a duty or duties would ordinarily exist, and certainly could exist, based on the facts and circumstances of each of these individual cases ... [T]he facts and circumstances of both of these cases are susceptible to inferences that a special relationship imposing a duty or duties was created in the arrangements [at issue] and, ordinarily, could be created in similar research programs involving human subjects [782 A.2d at 842–43].

Based on all these reasons, the Court of Appeals of Maryland stated its conclusion as follows:

> We hold that informed consent agreements in nontherapeutic research projects,[4] under certain circumstances can constitute contracts; and that, under certain circumstances, such research agreements can, as a matter of law, constitute "special relationships" giving rise to duties, out of the breach of which negligence actions may arise. We also hold that, normally, such special relationships are created between researchers and the human subjects used by the researchers. Additionally, we hold that governmental regulations can create duties on the part of researchers towards human subjects out of which "special relationships" can arise ...
>     We hold that there was ample evidence in the cases at bar to support a fact finder's determination of the existence of duties arising out of contract, or out of a special relationship, or out of regulations and codes, or out of all of them, in each of the cases [782 A.2d at 858].

The court therefore remanded the case to the two trial courts for further proceedings consistent with its rulings.

---

[4] *Author's footnote:* The distinction between "nontherapeutic" and "therapeutic" research projects was important to the court and is also important in the ethics of medical research on human subjects. The former projects, unlike the latter, are not designed to directly benefit the human subjects participating in the project (782 A.2d at 812). This distinction appears to be important primarily for projects in which minors are the human subjects. The court in *Grimes* was unwilling to allow a parent to consent to his or her child's participation in a nontherapeutic research project that involves more than minimal risk to the child (782 A.2d at 858, 862); but the court would apparently be more lenient if the research were therapeutic.

# Appendix A:
# Constitution of the United States of America: Provisions of Particular Interest to Postsecondary Education

Article I

Section 1. All legislative Powers herein granted shall be vested in a Congress of the United States, which shall consist of a Senate and House of Representatives.

* * * *

Section 7. All bills for raising Revenue shall originate in the House of Representatives; but the Senate may propose or concur with Amendments as on other Bills.

Every Bill which shall have passed the House of Representatives and the Senate, shall, before it becomes a Law, be presented to the President of the United States; If he approves he shall sign it, but if not he shall return it, with his Objections to that House in which it shall have originated, who shall enter the Objections at large on their journal, and proceed to reconsider it. If after such Reconsideration two thirds of that House shall agree to pass the Bill, it shall be sent, together with the Objections, to the other House, by which it shall likewise be reconsidered, and if approved by two thirds of that House, it shall become a Law.

* * * *

Section 8. The Congress shall have Power to lay and collect Taxes, Duties, Imposts and Excises, to pay the Debts and provide for the common Defence and general Welfare of the United States;

\* \* \* \*

To regulate Commerce with foreign Nations, and among the several states, and with the Indian Tribes;

To establish a uniform Rule of Naturalization, and uniform Laws on the subject of Bankruptcies throughout the United States;

\* \* \* \*

To promote the Progress of Science and useful Arts, by securing for limited Times to Authors and Inventors the exclusive Right to their respective Writings and Discoveries;

\* \* \* \*

To provide for calling forth the Militia to execute the Laws of the Union, suppress Insurrections and repel Invasions;

To provide for organizing, arming, and disciplining, the Militia, and for governing such Part of them as may be employed in the Service of the United States, reserving to the States respectively, the Appointment of the Officers, and the Authority of training the Militia according to the discipline prescribed by Congress;

\* \* \* \*

To make all Laws which shall be necessary and proper for carrying into Execution the foregoing Powers, and all other Powers vested by this Constitution in the Government of the United States, or in any Department or Officer thereof.

\* \* \* \*

Section 10. No State shall . . . pass any Bill of Attainder, ex post facto Law, or Law impairing the Obligation of Contracts.

Article II

Section 1. The executive Power shall be vested in a President of the United States of America.

\* \* \* \*

Section 3. He shall from time to time give to the Congress Information of the State of the Union, and recommend to their Consideration such Measures as he shall judge necessary and expedient; . . . he shall take Care that the Laws be faithfully executed. . .

\* \* \* \*

Article III

Section 1. The judicial Power of the United States, shall be vested in one supreme Court, and in such inferior Courts as the Congress may from time to time ordain and establish.

\* \* \* \*

Section 2. The judicial Power shall extend to all Cases, in Law and Equity, arising under this Constitution, the Laws of the United States, and Treaties made, or which shall be made, under their Authority; . . . to Controversies to which the United States shall be a party; to Controversies between two or more States; between a State and Citizens of another State; between Citizens of different States, . . . and between a State, or the Citizens thereof, and foreign States, Citizens or Subjects.

\* \* \* \*

Article IV

Section 1. Full Faith and Credit shall be given in each State to the Public Acts, Records, and judicial Proceedings of every other State.

\* \* \* \*

Section 2. The Citizens of each State shall be entitled to all Privileges and Immunities of Citizens in the several States.

\* \* \* \*

Article VI

\* \* \* \*

This Constitution, and the laws of the United States which shall be made in Pursuance thereof; and all Treaties made, or which shall be made, under the Authority of the United States, shall be the supreme Law of the Land; and the judges in every State shall be bound thereby, any Thing in the Constitution or Laws of any State to the Contrary notwithstanding.

\* \* \* \*

Amendment I

Congress shall make no law respecting an establishment of religion, or prohibiting the free exercise thereof; or abridging the freedom of speech, or of the press; or the right of the people peaceably to assemble, and to petition the Government for a redress of grievances.

\* \* \* \*

Amendment IV

The right of the people to be secure in their persons, houses, papers, and effects, against unreasonable searches and seizures, shall not be violated, and no warrants shall issue, but upon probable cause, supported by oath or affirmation, and particularly describing the place to be searched, and the persons or things to be seized.

## Amendment V

No person shall be held to answer for a capital, or otherwise infamous crime, unless on a presentment or indictment of a Grand jury . . .; nor shall any person be subject for the same offence to be twice put in jeopardy of life or limb; nor shall be compelled in any criminal case to be a witness against himself, nor be deprived of life, liberty, or property, without due process of law; nor shall private property be taken for public use, without just compensation.

## Amendment VI

In all criminal prosecutions, the accused shall enjoy the right to a speedy and public trial, by an impartial jury of the State and district wherein the crime shall have been committed, which district shall have been previously ascertained by law, and to be informed of the nature and cause of the accusation; to be confronted with the witnesses against him; to have compulsory process for obtaining witnesses in his favor, and to have the assistance of counsel for his defence.

* * * *

## Amendment X

The powers not delegated to the United States by the Constitution, nor prohibited by it to the States, are reserved to the States respectively, or to the people.

## Amendment XI

The judicial Power of the United States shall not be construed to extend to any suit in law or equity, commenced or prosecuted against one of the United States by Citizens of another State, or by Citizens or Subjects of any Foreign State.

* * * *

## Amendment XIII

Section 1. Neither slavery nor involuntary servitude, except as a punishment for crime whereof the party shall have been duly convicted, shall exist within the United States, or any place subject to their jurisdiction.

Section 2. Congress shall have power to enforce this article by appropriate legislation.

## Amendment XIV

Section 1. All persons born or naturalized in the United States, and subject to the jurisdiction thereof, are citizens of the United States and of the State wherein they reside. No State shall make or enforce any law which shall abridge the privileges or immunities of citizens of the United States; nor shall any State deprive any person of life, liberty, or property, without due process of law; nor deny to any person within its jurisdiction the equal protection of the laws.

* * * *

Section 5. The Congress shall have power to enforce, by appropriate legislation, the provisions of this article.

\* \* \* \*

Amendment XXVI

Section 1. The right of citizens of the United States, who are eighteen years of age or older, to vote shall not be denied or abridged by the United States or by any State on account of age.

Section 2. The Congress shall have power to enforce this article by appropriate legislation.

\* \* \* \*

# Appendix B:
# The American Court System

The role and functions of courts are outlined in Section 1.4.4 of this *Student Version* of *The Law of Higher Education*. The litigation process as it takes place in cases involving colleges and universities is addressed in Section 2.2. This appendix provides more detailed, basic information on the structure of the American judicial system and the jurisdiction of the various types of courts.

The American system of courts is based on principles of federalism. The system is actually two interrelated systems: the federal court system and the state court system. The judicial power (the power to hear and decide cases) is divided between these two systems. The federal courts are primarily responsible for interpreting and enforcing federal law, although they occasionally may also interpret and enforce state law. The state courts are primarily responsible for interpreting and enforcing state law, although they also may interpret and enforce federal law. Under the U.S. Constitution's supremacy clause (Art. VI, ¶ 2), federal law and federal court interpretations of federal law are "supreme" over state law and state court interpretations of federal law. Thus, when state courts interpret state law, they must assure that their interpretations do not create a conflict between state and federal law; in case of such conflict, federal law will prevail. Similarly, when state courts interpret federal law, they must adhere to any applicable precedents of the U.S. Supreme Court and of the lower federal courts whose jurisdiction includes the state whose court is hearing the case.

The federal court system is comprised of: (1) the federal district courts; (2) the U.S. Courts of Appeal; and (3) the U.S. Supreme Court. The district courts are the trial courts, or entry-level courts. There are now ninety-four such courts, each of which has jurisdiction over one of the ninety-four geographical districts into which the United States is divided.[1] The courts of appeal are the first level of appellate courts, each of which hears appeals from decisions of the district courts within its jurisdiction. There are now twelve such courts, each of which has jurisdiction over one of the twelve geographical "circuits" into which the United States is divided (the First through the Eleventh Circuit, plus the District of Columbia Circuit).[2] The Supreme Court is the court of last resort, the "highest court in the land." It covers the entire United States, of course, and has discretion to determine which cases it will review from among those decided by the federal courts of appeal *and* the highest courts of the states (see below). Litigants apply for such review by filing a "writ of certiorari" with the Supreme Court; the Court grants only a small percentage of these writs each year.

The system of state courts is really fifty separate systems, one for each state. Although there is variation among the states, most states have a three-level court structure somewhat like that for the federal system. The first level is the state trial courts, or entry-level courts, each of which has jurisdiction over one of the districts (which are often counties and sometimes cities) into which the state is divided. The second level is the intermediate appellate court or courts, which hear appeals from the state trial courts. Some states have several intermediate appellate courts, each of which has jurisdiction over part of the state; other states have a single intermediate court that covers the entire state; and a few states have no intermediate appellate court. The third level is the state supreme court (or, in a few states, the state court of appeals), which exercises discretionary review of selected cases from the intermediate appellate court(s). This court is the highest judicial authority within the state, but it is not always the *final* authority. This is because rulings of the highest state courts that resolve *federal* law questions or otherwise implicate federal law issues may be reviewed by the U.S. Supreme Court by writ of certiorari.

In both federal and state court systems, a single judge presides over proceedings in the trial courts. Some cases are tried before a jury; others are tried only before the judge. In both federal and state appellate courts, multiple judges hear the appeals, and the outcome is determined by a majority vote. In the federal courts of appeals, the courts sit in panels of three judges, selected randomly from among the total number of judges on the court. The losing party may move for reconsideration *en banc*, meaning before the entire court rather than a three-judge panel; courts only occasionally grant such requests. In the state's intermediate appellate courts, the entire court may hear each case, or in some states panels may be used. In the U.S. Supreme Court and the highest state courts, all the judges (or justices) hear each case, unless one of the

---

[1] There are also various specialized federal trial courts that hear particular kinds of cases, for example, federal bankruptcy courts and the federal tax court.

[2] There is also a U.S. Court of Appeals for the Federal Circuit that hears certain specialized cases, for example, patent cases.

members has "recused" himself or herself due to a conflict of interest involving the lawsuit.

Federal courts are courts of *limited* jurisdiction—meaning they have jurisdiction only over the types of cases assigned to them by Article III of the federal Constitution and Congress's implementing statutes. The most common and important category of such cases is the "federal question" category—cases that involve federal law issues and arise under the "federal question jurisdiction" of the federal courts. The state courts, in contrast, are courts of *general* jurisdiction, meaning that they have jurisdiction over all cases other than those for which a specific exception is made by state or federal law.[3] Or, put another way, state courts may generally hear the full range of cases that do not fall within the federal courts' limited jurisdiction, as well as many of the types of cases that do fall within federal court jurisdiction.

In both the federal and state court systems, there is a well-established distinction between the functions of trial courts and appellate courts. Trial courts are courts of "original jurisdiction," because cases originate there. Appellate courts are courts of "appellate jurisdiction," because cases arrive there by appeal from trial courts or lower-level appellate courts. The trial courts' functions include receiving evidence and making findings of fact, as well as reviewing and applying the law. The appellate courts' functions, in contrast, focus on reviewing the legal rulings of trial courts (and lower appellate courts), correcting errors of law, and otherwise clarifying and developing the law of the jurisdiction in which the court sits. Appellate courts do not receive any new evidence; they must instead work from the evidence and the fact findings (if any) in the official record of the trial court proceedings. An appellate court may agree or disagree with a trial court's (or lower appellate court's) view of the law and its legal rulings and may affirm, reverse, or vacate the lower court's judgment based on the law as the appellate court articulates it. But the appellate court may not change or supplement the facts, or ignore relevant facts, or set aside the trial court's factual determinations unless they are "clearly erroneous" or meet some other similar standard that may vary somewhat with the type of case and with the court system whose court is hearing the case. If an appellate court does determine that there are factual disputes left unresolved, or that necessary facts are missing from the record, or that the trial court's fact findings are clearly erroneous, its only options are to decide the case against the party having the "burden of proof" on the issues for which necessary facts are missing or disputed, or to remand the case to the trial court for further evidentiary proceedings.

For guidance on reading and analyzing the opinions of federal and state courts, see Appendix C to this book, which follows.

---

[3]This does not mean that every state court may hear every kind of case. Some states allocate the general jurisdiction among various trial courts that may hear only certain kinds of cases; in addition to civil courts, for example, there may be criminal courts, family courts, or small claims courts.

# Appendix C:
# Reading and Analyzing Court Opinions

Section 1.4.4 of this *Student Version* reviews the concepts of "case law" and "precedent" and outlines the role and functions of judicial opinions in the American legal system. Section 1.4.5 explains how to find case law. This appendix provides additional guidance on reading and analyzing court opinions.

A judicial opinion is a particular kind of legal document, drafted by a judge and issued by a court in order to resolve a lawsuit or to dispose of particular issues arising in ongoing litigation. In appellate courts, there may be "majority" opinions as well as "concurring" and "dissenting" opinions that express agreements and disagreements with the majority. Published opinions become authoritative precedents binding on the court that issued the opinion and (for appellate courts) on other lower courts subject to that court's jurisdiction. The published majority opinions of the U.S. Supreme Court become authoritative precedent binding on all federal and state courts in the United States.

Court opinions serve many purposes in legal analysis. For instance, they provide case "holdings" that may be invoked by advocates and applied by courts in later cases; they articulate particular standards and tests to use in analyzing and resolving particular types of legal issues; they provide information on what types of facts are relevant to the analysis of particular legal issues; and they provide assistance in determining what sources of law apply to particular types of problems.

For the reader of a judicial opinion, as for the reader of other legal documents, the starting point is the express language of the document. The reader's first task in analyzing a court opinion is thus to read it carefully, being attentive to each word, to *determine what the opinion says*. This task may be termed "descriptive" analysis and includes descriptions of the relevant facts, legal issue(s), and holding(s) in the case; and of the legal standards or rules that the court applies in resolving the issues—and that may be used in resolving similar future issues in that jurisdiction.

The reader's second, more complex, task in analyzing a court opinion is to *evaluate* the opinion. This task may be called "normative" analysis. The goal, simply put, is to determine whether the opinion is "good law." The necessary predicate to this *normative analysis* is a careful *descriptive analysis* of the opinion to determine what it says. In light of the understanding gained from descriptive analysis, one can then consider the opinion's consistency with legal norms by weighing factors such as: (1) whether the opinion's reasoning and result are supported by applicable precedent; (2) whether the opinion's reasoning and result are supported by the facts in the record; and (3) whether the result or decision the court reaches is consistent with relevant policy analysis and social science or other research regarding postsecondary education. The goal of this normative analysis is to determine whether the opinion serves to legitimate or "justify" the result reached by the court.

The legal opinions of the courts are the building blocks with which lawyers and judges work and the typical diet of students in many law courses, including education law courses. The following ten steps provide detailed practical guidance for education law students on reading and analyzing judicial opinions. Steps 1 and 2 set the stage for analyzing the opinion; steps 3 through 9 guide descriptive analysis; and step 10 shifts to normative analysis.

1. Think of the opinion as a legal document, with a judge or court as the drafter. As with other legal documents, the *words* themselves are of critical importance; read them as scrupulously as possible.

2. Identify: (a) the court that is deciding the case and, if the opinion is an appellate court opinion, the lower court whose ruling is being appealed (see Appendix B regarding the American court system); (b) the parties whose interests are in conflict and the type of legal relationship between them (see the General Introduction, Section D); (c) the sector of the education law universe into which the case falls (see the General Introduction, Section A); and (d) the source or sources of law (see Section 1.4 of this book) that the parties have invoked. When the dispute before the court was previously addressed in an internal campus dispute resolution process, or in a government administrative agency process, it will also be helpful to identify this process and any decision it made (see the General Introduction, Section B).

3. Identify the legal issue(s) in the case, as framed by the court; the facts that are relevant to each legal issue; and the legal principle, standard, or rule that applies to each issue. (A helpful way to begin this part of the analysis is to identify the legal claim(s) asserted by the plaintiff (or, in a criminal case, by the state) and the defense(s) asserted by the defendant.)

4. Determine the court's "holding" for each legal issue (that is, determine what the court's ruling or resolution is for each issue in the case).

5. Determine the rationale, or reasoning, that the court uses to support its holding on each issue. In particular, check to see how the court uses precedent (opinions in other previously decided cases) to support its rationale, how the court uses the facts, and what other considerations (if any) the court takes into account. Also check to see if you can discern any "analytical pathway," or step-by-step progression of reasoning, that the court sets out to organize or elucidate its rationale.

6. Thinking of the opinion as a document controlling the future (as other legal documents do), ask: How and to what extent does this opinion affect the actions of the parties to the case, *or other persons or institutions*, in the future? In particular, what legal standard(s) does this opinion establish by which similar future actions may be judged?

7. When an opinion is an appellate court opinion, check to see if it commands a majority of the court. In some cases, especially in the U.S. Supreme Court, there is no majority opinion; instead there is only a *plurality* opinion, or an opinion "announcing the judgment of the Court," neither of which has the status of an authoritative precedent that controls the future. In other cases, the main opinion will command a majority for some of its parts but not for others, and it becomes important to distinguish the parts that constitute a majority opinion from those that do not.

8. When the opinion is an appellate court opinion, check to see if there is any concurring or dissenting opinion. For concurrences, distinguish between an opinion that concurs with the majority opinion's reasoning and its result and an opinion that concurs "in the result" only. Read any concurring or dissenting opinions carefully for any additional light they may shed on the rationale or reasoning in the majority opinion.

9. Identify the final result in the case, that is: (a) who wins (if anyone); (b) what remedy the court orders (if any); and (c) if the opinion is an appellate opinion, whether the court remands the case to the lower court for further proceedings. Regarding (a), the court may either enter judgment for one of the parties or order further proceedings in the case. Regarding (b), if the plaintiff wins in a civil (noncriminal) case, the court may order that the defendant pay monetary damages, or may issue an injunction ordering the defendant to do or refrain from doing certain things, or may enter a "declaratory judgment" stating that a statute or administrative regulation that the plaintiff had challenged is invalid. Regarding (c), an appellate court may affirm the lower court's judgment for one of the parties, reverse the lower court's judgment and order judgment for the other party, or identify errors or omissions in the lower court proceedings and remand the case to that court for further proceedings.

10. On the basis of the understanding gained by working through points 1–9, consider whether the court's opinion is "good law," and, in particular, whether the case serves to legitimate or "justify" the result the court reaches. The guidelines above for normative analysis will assist you in this task.

# Appendix D:
# Glossary of Legal Terms

Terms appearing in this glossary appear in **boldface** in the text.

**Academic deference:** See **Judicial deference** below.

**Academic freedom:** The prerogatives of faculty members and students to pursue research, teaching, and learning without interference from their institution or the government. These prerogatives may be protected by law or by custom and usage. The phrase also sometimes refers to the prerogatives of higher educational institutions ("institutional academic freedom;" see Section 6.1.3.7 of this book).

**Administrative procedure acts:** The federal law, the Administrative Procedure Act or APA, and similar state laws that govern practice and proceedings before federal, or state, administrative agencies.

**Administrative regulations:** Rules promulgated by an administrative agency, federal, state, or local, to implement a particular law or body of laws enacted by a legislative body.

**Affirmative action:** The consideration of race, gender, national origin, or some other characteristic protected under federal or state nondiscrimination laws to provide a preference or other advantage for an underrepresented or disadvantaged group. The phrase is usually used in the context of admissions decisions or employment decisions (see Sections 4.6 & 7.2.5).

**Agency fee:** A payment in lieu of union dues by an individual who is not a member of a union but who, as a member of the bargaining unit, is represented by that union.

**Arbitration:** A dispute resolution process in which a neutral individual, acting as a "private judge," conducts a hearing, receives evidence, and issues an opinion, called an "award." The arbitrator is typically selected by the parties to the dispute.

**Authority:** The legally recognized power of a board of trustees, and of officers and other personnel to whom the board delegates power, to make decisions that bind the institution. May also refer to the powers of branches of government (for example, Congress) or administrative agencies (for example, the U.S. Department of Education).

**Captive organization:** An organization that, although a legally independent entity, is wholly controlled by a college or university.

**Cause of action:** A set of facts or allegations that will allow an individual to bring a lawsuit against another individual or organization. For example, an allegation of employment discrimination on the basis of race could create a cause of action against the employer for discrimination under state and/or federal law.

**Charitable immunity:** A common law (or statutory) doctrine that immunizes nonprofit organizations whose purpose is educational or charitable from liability for common law negligence. Most states have abrogated or limited this form of immunity.

**Collective bargaining:** A process whereby a group of employees votes to authorize an organization (called a union or an association) to negotiate with the employer over their terms and conditions of employment. All employees in the "bargaining unit" are represented by the union or association, whether or not the employees are actually dues-paying members of the organization. See **Agency fee** above.

**Common law:** A body of law that does not derive from a constitution, statutes, or administrative regulations, and instead derives from the cumulative decisions over time of the courts of the jurisdiction. See Section 1.4.2.4.

**Concurring opinion:** An appellate court opinion in which one or more judges or justices in the minority agrees with the reasoning and result of the majority but adds additional reasoning, or agrees only with the majority's result and states alternative reasoning to support it.

**Constitution:** Refers to the U.S. Constitution or to the constitution of a state. These constitutions are the fundamental law of the United States and the states, respectively. Each constitution organizes the government, provides for the distribution and exercise of governmental powers, and limits the powers of government. See Section 1.4.2.1 of this book.

**Contract:** An agreement between two or more parties that creates mutual obligations to take or not take a particular action or actions. The obligations are usually enforceable in court.

**Contract, express:** An agreement between the parties, the terms of which are stated in explicit language, either orally or in writing.

**Contract, implied:** When no explicit contract exists, a court may rule that, as a result of the parties' behavior, an "implied-in-fact" contract exists in order that the mutual understandings and expectations of both parties will be upheld. For example, if a college makes certain promises or statements in student handbooks or other policy documents and the students rely on those promises or statements, a court may rule that the promises or statements have created an "implied-in-fact" contract.

**Discovery:** A process prior to trial by which the parties attempt to obtain facts and information about the case from each other in order to prepare for trial. Includes depositions, written interrogatories, production of documents or things, physical and mental examinations, and requests for admission of facts.

**De facto tenure:** A claim that a faculty member has tenure by the elapsing of the contractual probationary period without the institution making any negative employment decision about that faculty member.

**De novo:** A phrase typically used when a reviewing court examines a matter independently, without relying on the fact finding of, or according deference to, previous decision makers who have examined the same matter (called *review de novo* or *trial de novo*).

**Due process clause:** A provision of the federal Constitution or a state constitution that prohibits the government from depriving an individual of life, liberty, or property without providing that individual certain protections (especially procedural protections such as notice and a hearing). The federal Constitution has two due process clauses, one in the Fifth Amendment (binding the federal government) and the other in the Fourteenth Amendment (binding the state governments).

**Establishment clause:** A provision of the federal Constitution or a state constitution that prohibits the government from sponsoring or supporting any particular religion or religion in general. The establishment clause of the federal constitution is in the First Amendment.

**Estoppel:** A common law doctrine providing that one person's (the promisee's) justifiable reliance on a statement or promise of another person (the promisor) estops the promisor from contradicting the statement of promise if the promisee's reliance on it led directly to a detriment or injustice to the promisee.

**Faculty:** Usually refers to the faculty of a department, school, or institution as a collective body. May also refer to an individual faculty member or a group of faculty members as individuals. Faculty members generally are assigned a rank at hiring (instructor, assistant professor, associate professor, professor, or perhaps a chaired professor or "distinguished professor"). Those appointed to lower ranks may be promoted to a higher rank (for example, from assistant professor to associate professor) after a process of evaluation that typically includes several levels of review by faculty peers, other faculty groups, academic administrators, and the board of trustees. Faculty members are either "tenure-track" faculty (meaning that they are either eligible to apply for tenure after meeting any time-in-rank requirements, or have been awarded tenure) or "non-tenure-track" (meaning they have no right to apply for or receive tenure).

**Federalism:** The basic concept upon which the American governmental system is based. Deriving from the U.S. Constitution, federalism provides for the division of power between the federal government and the states. See Section 11.3.1.

**Fiduciary duty:** The requirement that a person must act primarily for another's benefit. The concept applies in certain circumstances in which the individual for whom the fiduciary acts has placed great reliance and trust in the fiduciary.

**Foreign commerce clause:** A sub-clause of the commerce clause of the U.S. Constitution (Art. I, sec. 8, ¶ 3) that authorizes Congress to regulate commerce with foreign nations.

**Free exercise clause:** A provision of the federal constitution or a state constitution that prohibits government from infringing upon the religious practice of individuals or religious bodies. The federal constitution's free exercise clause is in the First Amendment.

**Governance:** Refers to the structures and processes by which higher education institutions and systems are managed in their day-to-day operations as well as their longer-range policy making. See Section 1.3.1.

**Governmental immunity:** A set of doctrines that in various ways protect government bodies from certain types of lawsuits and legal claims, for example, tort claims. Sometimes also called "sovereign immunity." A government usually may, and sometimes does, "waive," or relinquish, part of its immunity from suit (called a "waiver of immunity").

**Holding (as in the "holding" of the court):** A part of a judicial opinion that constitutes the court's ruling on, or resolution of, each particular legal issue in the case.

**Implied private cause of action:** A cause of action that private individuals may bring in court to enforce rights granted by a particular statute (or regulation implementing a statute) even though the statute does not expressly authorize such suits. Whether or not courts will authorize such suits depends on the particular statute involved. These issues have most frequently arisen under laws passed under the federal spending power (such as Title IX and Section 504 of the Rehabilitation Act).

**Incorporation by reference:** The inclusion of one document into another by specifically naming the former in the text of the latter. When a document (for example, a faculty handbook or an AAUP statement) is thus "incorporated" into an institutional contract or policy, the terms of the incorporated document become part of the terms of the contract or policy and are enforceable in court to the same extent as the contract or policy is enforceable.

**Indemnification:** An agreement to reimburse, or the process of reimbursing, an agent of the institution for any money damages the agent is liable for on a legal claim against the agent involving actions taken on behalf of the institution. Indemnification may also cover the costs and expenses an agent incurs in defending against such a legal claim or provide for legal representation for the agent. Indemnification may also refer to another party's contractual obligation to reimburse the institution for damages or expenses the institution has incurred in performing the contract.

**In loco parentis:** Latin, meaning "in the role (or place) of the parents." This concept, no longer used by the courts, gave colleges the authority to control students' conduct to a similar extent as parents could do so (as, for instance, by implementing safety measures and disciplining misbehavior) and exempted the college from most legal liability for taking such actions.

**Judicial deference:** A concept encompassing the circumstance in which a court applies a relaxed or lenient approach to reviewing a challenged academic decision or policy of a college or university, and does so because it is deferring to the academic or scholarly expertise of the institution or of its faculty and academic administrators. Also sometimes called "academic deference." See Section 2.2.2. There is also a related concept of judicial deference that encompasses circumstances in which a court defers to the expertise of an administrative agency of government.

**Legal liability:** The responsibility that one party has for a wrong done to another, when a court or administrative agency has found that the wrong constitutes a violation of law. See Section 2.1.1.

**Mediation:** A dispute resolution process in which a neutral third party is engaged to assist the parties to a dispute to resolve the conflict. The mediator has no authority to resolve the dispute but instead works with the parties so that they may reach their own voluntary resolution.

**Mootness:** A doctrine under which a court refuses to assert or continue jurisdiction over a case, or an issue in a case, because the controversy is no longer "live" or viable.

**Negligence:** A legal claim or cause of action that arises when a person or entity: (a) owes a "duty of care" to another person or entity; (b) fails to exercise reasonable care with respect to that person or entity; and (c) thereby causes injury to that person or entity. Negligence is a subcategory of the broader category of tort law, which is based on state common law.

**Official immunity:** A state law doctrine that protects higher level government officials from liability for certain torts, such as negligence and defamation. Usually the official's act must have been within the scope of his or her authority and must have been a discretionary act involving policy judgment.

**Overbreadth (or Overbreadth doctrine):** A First Amendment doctrine requiring that governmental regulations of speech be "narrowly tailored" to avoid sweeping within their coverage speech activities that would be constitutionally protected. Regulations that fail to meet this requirement are "overbroad," or suffer from "overbreadth."

**Plaintiff:** The individual who initiates a lawsuit.

**Plurality opinion:** A judicial opinion that gains the most votes among the judges or justices ruling on the case, but an insufficient number of votes to constitute a majority of the court. A plurality opinion, unlike a majority opinion, is therefore not a binding precedent.

**Precedent:** A ruling by a court in a prior case with similar facts or applying similar principles of law as a current case under consideration. May also refer to the entire body of case law (judicial opinions) of a particular jurisdiction. Precedents are binding only in the jurisdiction in which the case is decided, and only upon courts of the same or lower status in that jurisdiction (see Appendix B).

**Preclusive effect (or Preclusion):** Refers to the effect that a court ruling in a particular case may have on the capacity of the parties to raise similar issues or arguments in a later case. When there is preclusion (or preclusive effect), the court in the later case will prohibit one of the parties from proceeding with certain issues or arguments.

**Preemption:** A legal doctrine applicable to situations in which a statute or administrative regulation of one government potentially conflicts with or intrudes upon a statute or regulation of another government. Under the preemption doctrine, the enactment of the superior government will prevail if the statute or regulation is within that government's scope of authority. For example, a federal statute may supersede or "preempt" a similar state statute, and a state statute may supersede or "preempt" a similar county or city ordinance.

**Private institution (or college, or university):** An institution that is not created or operated by a federal, state, or local government entity. Usually, a private institution is created by and operated under a corporate charter. Compare **Public institution** below.

**Private right of action:** A cause of action that private individuals may bring in court to enforce rights granted by a particular statute (or regulation implementing a statute). A private right of action may be either *express* (expressly authorized by statute) or *implied*. See **Implied private cause of action** above.

**Property interest:** A term that refers to legal interests in property that may be less than property rights as such. The term has special meaning under the Fourteenth Amendment and Fifth Amendment due process clauses of the federal Constitution and some due process clauses of state constitutions. See Section 5.7.2.1.

**Property right:** A legal right to specific real or personal property, whether tangible or intangible. Property rights are often based on state common law but may also be created by state or federal statutes (for example, the federal copyright statute), which may also provide for the enforcement of property rights.

**Public forum:** In First Amendment law, government property (usually land or portions of buildings) that is traditionally, or by official policy or practice, available to persons for expressive activities. The "public forum doctrine" limits the extent to which government may regulate the use of such property for expressive purposes. For application of the public forum concept to higher education, see Section 9.4.2.

**Public institution (or college, or university):** An institution that is created or operated by a state government or, sometimes, by the federal government or a local government. Usually a public institution is created by, and operated pursuant to, state statutes or provisions of the state constitution. Compare **Private institution** above.

**Qualified immunity:** A set of doctrines that in various ways protect government officers and employees from certain types of lawsuits and legal claims. In particular, qualified immunity is a defense to damages claims brought against government officers or employees under the federal civil rights statute known as "Section 1983"; see Section 4.4.4.1 of this book. In state law, qualified immunity may sometimes be called official immunity (see **Official immunity** above) or qualified privilege (a term used particularly in defamation law).

**Religious institution:** A private educational institution that is operated by a church or other sectarian organization (a "sectarian institution"), or is otherwise formally affiliated with a church or sectarian organization (a "religiously affiliated institution"), as well as an institution that has no affiliation with an outside religious organization but nevertheless proclaims a religious mission and is guided by religious values.

**Remand:** An order by an appellate court that returns a case to the lower court from which the case came and directs that court to receive new evidence, proceed to trial, or otherwise reconsider its previous ruling, being guided by the principles articulated by the appellate court.

**Respondeat superior:** A legal doctrine under which an employer may sometimes be held liable for the torts or other unlawful conduct of its employees even though the employer did authorize the conduct or have actual knowledge of it.

**Section 1983:** A federal civil rights statute, originally enacted in the Reconstruction era, that provides for suits against state and local government agencies and employees to enforce federal constitutional rights. See Section 3.4 of this book.

**Sovereign immunity:** A doctrine that precludes litigants from suing "the sovereign"—usually meaning a state government or the federal government—unless the sovereign has waived its immunity and consented to suit. Sometimes also called governmental immunity (see **Governmental immunity** above). State law concepts of sovereign immunity are particularly important with respect to tort litigation; and federal law concepts of sovereign immunity are particularly important in federal civil rights litigation.

**Standing:** A technical legal doctrine referring to the capacity of a party to bring a lawsuit on a particular matter or to raise a particular issue in litigation. In general, a party will have "standing" whenever that party has a sufficient "personal stake" in the controversy that is before the court.

**State action:** In constitutional law, a decision or action that is made or taken by government, or is otherwise attributable to government (federal, state, or local), and may therefore be challenged as violating federal constitutional rights. The "state action doctrine" provides that certain decisions or actions of ostensibly private entities may be considered state action when they have a sufficiently close relationship to government; see Section 1.5.2.

**Statute:** An official act of a legislature enacted pursuant to the constitutional requirements for law making.

**Strict scrutiny:** A strong or maximal form of judicial review that courts use for certain types of constitutional claims and that places a heavy burden on the governmental defendant to justify its actions. Strict scrutiny is most commonly used in equal protection cases where government has discriminated on grounds of race or national origin and in freedom of expression cases where government has restricted expression due to its content or viewpoint. Courts applying strict scrutiny usually require the governmental defendant to prove that the action being challenged was in furtherance of a "compelling state (or government) interest" and was "narrowly tailored" to achieve that interest.

**Substantive due process:** A body of constitutional law, derived from the Fourteenth Amendment's due process clause or comparable state constitutional clauses, that focuses on the validity of certain governmental decisions (the "substance"), rather than on the procedures government used to reach the decisions. (The latter is called *procedural* due process). Usually a substantive due process claim is based on government action that deprives an individual of some liberty that is alleged to be "fundamental," for instance, the liberty of parents to raise their children.

**Summary judgment:** A judgment on the merits issued by a trial court prior to and in lieu of a trial. The judgment may resolve the entire case or only certain issues in the case. The court must determine that there are no disputed "material facts" and that, even when the court accepts the version of the facts articulated by the party opposing the motion for summary judgment, that party cannot meet the requirements for the claim(s) or defense(s) at issue. Summary judgments may be appealed, since they are final rulings on the merits.

**Supremacy clause [of the U.S. Constitution]:** The clause in Article VI, Section 2 of the U.S. Constitution, which makes federal law "the supreme law of the land" and gives federal law precedence over all inconsistent state law. Federal law includes not only the federal Constitution, but also federal statutes, administrative regulations, treaties, and executive orders, so long as they are within the scope of the federal government's powers under the Constitution.

**Suspect class:** A term used under the Fourteenth Amendment's equal protection clause to signify a class of persons that is defined by race, national origin, or other characteristic that courts consider to be an impermissible basis for governmental decision making. When government relies on such a characteristic to disadvantage a class of persons, courts will be "suspicious" of the government's action and will uphold it only if the government can meet the standards of "strict scrutiny" (see above).

**Tenure:** An employment status that institutions award to faculty members who meet certain predefined standards. Tenure entitles the faculty member to a set of protections, established by statute or contract, that precludes the institution from dismissing the faculty member unless it can demonstrate a substantial cause for doing so, such as incompetence, neglect of duty, moral turpitude, or financial exigency; and unless it first provides the faculty member with a formal due process hearing.

**Tort:** A civil wrong, other than a breach of contract, for which the common law will allow a remedy through the courts. Negligence is the most frequently asserted type of tort claim; see **Negligence** above.

**Ultra vires:** An action that is beyond the scope of authority of a government agency, an organization, or a person (such as an employee), and is thus invalid.

**Vagueness (or Vagueness doctrine):** A due process doctrine that prohibits government from enforcing regulations of conduct that are sufficiently unclear that the persons being regulated cannot understand what is required or prohibited and conform their conduct accordingly. There is also a First Amendment version of the vagueness doctrine that requires an even higher standard of clarity when government is regulating speech.

# Bibliography

This bibliography lists books, monographs, articles, reports, and Web sites that may be useful for research on and independent study of topics covered in each chapter of the *Student Version* of *The Law of Higher Education*, as well as other related issues and topics.

## Chapter 1

Bakken, Gordon M. "Campus Common Law," 5 *J. Law & Educ.* 201 (1976).

Bok, Derek. "Universities: Their Temptations and Tensions," 18 *J. Coll. & Univ. Law* 1 (1991).

Campus Legal Information Clearinghouse (CLIC), http://counsel.cua.edu, a joint project of The Catholic University of America and the American Council on Education.

*The Chronicle of Higher Education*, "Academe Today," http://www.chronicle.com.

Clark, Burton R. *The Academic Life: Small Worlds, Different Worlds* (Carnegie Foundation for the Advancement of Teaching, 1987).

Farrington, Dennis J., & Palfreyman, David. *The Law of Higher Education* (3d ed., Oxford University Press, 2012), a presentation of higher education law in the United Kingdom.

Finkelstein, Martin J., Seal, Robert K., & Schuster, Jack H. *The New Academic Generation: A Profession in Transformation* (Johns Hopkins University Press, 1998).

Hobbs, Walter C. "The Courts," in Philip G. Altbach, Robert O. Berdahl, & Patricia J. Gumport (eds.), *Higher Education in American Society* (3d ed., Prometheus Books, 1994).

Kaplin, William A. *American Constitutional Law: An Overview, Analysis, and Integration* (Carolina Academic Press, 2004) (Chap. 9, sec. D & Chap.13).

Kaplin, William A. *The Importance of Process in Campus Administrative Decision-Making*, IHELG Monograph 91–10 (Institute for Higher Education Law and Governance, University of Houston, 1992).

Kerr, Clark. *The Great Transformation in Higher Education, 1960–1980* (State University of New York Press, 1991).

Matasor, Richard. "Private Publics, Public Privates: An Essay on Convergence in Higher Education," 10 *J. of Law & Pub. Policy* 5 (1998).

McGuinness, Aims C. (ed.). *State Postsecondary Education Structures Sourcebook* (National Center for Higher Education Management Systems, 1997 and periodic Web site updates).

McMahon, Walter W. *Higher Learning, Greater Good: The Private and Social Benefits of Higher Education* (Johns Hopkins University Press, 2009).

Metzger, Walter, et al. *Dimensions of Academic Freedom* (University of Illinois Press, 1969).

Moots, Philip R., & Gaffney, Edward M. *Church and Campus: Legal Issues in Religiously Affiliated Higher Education* (University of Notre Dame Press, 1979).

Morphew, Christopher C., & Eckel, Peter D. (eds.). *Privatizing the Public University: Perspectives from Across the Academy* (Johns Hopkins University Press, 2009).

O'Neil, Robert. *Free Speech in the College Community* (Indiana University Press, 1997).

Sorenson, Gail, & LaManque, Andrew S. "The Application of *Hazelwood v. Kuhlmeier* in College Litigation," 22 *J. Coll. & Univ. Law* 971 (1996).

Russo, Charles (ed.). *Encyclopedia of Law and Higher Education* (Sage, 2010).

Schrecker, Ellen. *The Lost Soul of Higher Education: Corporatization, the Assault on Academic Freedom, and the End of the American University* (New Press, 2010).

Terrell, Melvin C. (ed.). *Diversity, Disunity, and Campus Community* (National Association of Student Personnel Administrators, 1992).

See the Bickel and Lake entry for Chapter 3.

# Chapter 2

Aiken, Ray, Adams, John F., & Hall, John W. *Legal Liabilities in Higher Education: Their Scope and Management* (Association of American Colleges, 1976), printed simultaneously in 3 *J. Coll. & Univ. Law* 127 (1976).

Bales, Richard A. *Compulsory Arbitration: The Grand Experiment in Employment* (Cornell University Press, 1997).

Bickel, Robert. "A Revisitation of the Role of College and University Legal Counsel," 85 *West's Educ. Law Rptr.* 989 (1993), updating the author's earlier article published at 3 *J. Law & Educ.* 73 (1974).

Brand, Norman (ed.). *How ADR Works* (Bureau of National Affairs, 2002).

Burgoyne, Robert, McNabb, Stephen, & Robinson, Frederick. *Understanding Attorney-Client Privilege Issues in the College and University Setting* (National Association of College and University Attorneys, 1998).

Connell, Mary Ann, & Savage, Frederick G. "Releases: Is There Still a Place for Their Use by Colleges and Universities?" 29 *J. Coll. & Univ. Law* 525 (2003).

Long, Nicholas Trott, & Weeks, Kent. *Strategic Legal Planning: The College and University Legal Audit* (College Legal Information, 1998).

Menkel-Meadow, Carrie. "What Will We Do When Adjudication Ends? A Brief Intellectual History of ADR," 44 *UCLA L. Rev.* 1613 (1997).

Moss, Scott A. "Against 'Academic Deference': How Recent Developments in Employment Discrimination Law Undercut an Already Dubious Doctrine," 27 *Berkeley Journal Employment & Labor Law* 1 (2006).

O'Neil, Robert M. "Judicial Deference to Academic Decisions: An Outmoded Concept?" 36 *J. Coll. & Univ. Law* 729 (2010).

Ruger, Peter H. "The Practice and Profession of Higher Education Law," 27 *Stetson L. Rev.* 175 (1997).

Symposium, "Focus on Ethics and the University Attorney," 19 *J. Coll. & Univ. Law* 305 (1993).

# Chapter 3

Association of Governing Boards. *Statement on Board Accountability* (2007) (available at http://www.agb.org).

Bazluke, Francine T., & Clother, Robert C. *Defamation Issues in Higher Education* (National Association of College and University Attorneys, 2004).

Bess, James L. *Collegiality and Bureaucracy in the Modern University* (Teachers College Press, 1988).

Bickel, Robert D., & Lake, Peter F. *The Rights and Responsibilities of the Modern University: Who Assumes the Risk of College Life?* (Carolina Academic, 1999).

Bowman, Cynthia Grant, & Lipp, MaryBeth. "Legal Limbo of the Student Intern: The Responsibility of Colleges and Universities to Protect Student Interns Against Sexual Harassment," 23 *Harv. Women's L.J.* 95 (2000).

Burling, Philip. *Crime on Campus: Analyzing and Managing the Increasing Risk of Institutional Liability* (National Association of College and University Attorneys, 1990).

Evans, Eileen M., & Evans, William D., Jr. "'No Good Deed Goes Unpunished': Personal Liability of Trustees and Administrators of Private Colleges and Universities," 33 *Tort & Insurance L.J.* 1107 (1998).

Gehring, Donald D., & Geraci, Christy P. *Alcohol on Campus: A Compendium of the Law and a Guide to Campus Policy* (College Administration Publications, 1989).

Harpool, David. "The *Sibley Hospital* Case: Trustees and Their Loyalty to the Institution," 23 *J. Coll. & Univ. Law* 255 (1996); supplemented by Harpool, "Minimum Compliance with Minimum Standards: Managing Trustee Conflicts of Interest," 24 *J. Coll. & Univ. Law* 465 (1998).

Hornby, D. Brock. "Delegating Authority to the Community of Scholars," 1975 *Duke L.J.* 279 (1975).

Houle, Cyril O. *Governing Boards* (Jossey-Bass, 1997).

Hoye, William P. "An Ounce of Prevention Is Worth . . . The Life of a Student: Reducing Risk in International Programs," 27 *J. Coll. & Univ. Law* 151 (2000).

Lake, Peter F. "The Rise of Duty and the Fall of *In Loco Parentis* and Other Protective Tort Doctrines in Higher Education Law," 64 *Mo. L. Rev.* 1 (1999).

Lake, Peter F. "The Special Relationship(s) Between a College and a Student: Law and Policy Ramifications for the Post In Loco Parentis College," 37 *Idaho L. Rev.* 531 (2001).

Pavela, Gary. *Questions and Answers on College Student Suicide* (College Administration Publications, 2006).

# Chapter 4

Anderson, Terry H. *The Pursuit of Fairness: A History of Affirmative Action* (Oxford University Press, 2004).

Angell, George W., Kelly, Edward P., Jr., & Associates. *Handbook of Faculty Bargaining* (Jossey-Bass, 1977).

Brown, Deborah C. (ed.). *Employment Issues in Higher Education: A Legal Compendium* (3d ed., National Association of College and University Attorneys, 2008).

Cole, Elsa (ed.). *Sexual Harassment on Campus: A Legal Compendium* (4th ed., National Association of College and University Attorneys, 2003).

DelPo, Amy, & Guerin, Lisa. *Dealing With Problem Employees: A Legal Guide* (Nolo Press, 2001).

Euben, Donna R., & Thornton, Saranna R. *The Family and Medical Leave Act: Questions and Answers for Faculty* (American Association of University Professors, 2002).

Jewett, Cynthia L., & Rutherford, Lisa H. *What to Do When the U.S. Department of Education, Office for Civil Rights Comes to Campus* (National Association of College and University Attorneys, 2005).

Lee, Barbara A. "Faculty Role in Academic Governance and the Managerial Exclusion: Impact of the *Yeshiva University* Decision," 7 *J. Coll. & Univ. Law* 222 (1980–81).

Perritt, Henry H., Jr. *Americans with Disabilities Act Handbook* (3d ed., Wiley, 1997, and periodic supp.).

Rabban, David. "Is Unionization Compatible with Professionalism?" 45 *Indust. & Labor Rel. Rev.* 97 (1991).

Traynor, Michael. "Defamation Law: Shock Absorbers for Its Ride into the Groves of Academe," 16 *J. Coll. & Univ. Law* 373 (1990).

# Chapter 5

American Association of University Professors. *AAUP Policy Documents and Reports* (the "Redbook") (Johns Hopkins Press, 2006).

American Association of University Professors. *Post-Tenure Review: An AAUP Response* (AAUP, 1999). Available at http://www.aaup.org/postten.htm.

American Federation of Teachers (AFT). *Promoting Gender Diversity in the Faculty: What Higher Education Unions Can Do* (AFT, 2011, available at www.aft.org/pdfs/highered/genderdiversity0511.pdf).

American Federation of Teachers (AFT). *Promoting Racial and Ethnic Diversity in the Faculty: What Higher Education Unions Can Do* (AFT, 2010, available at www.aft.org/pdfs/highered/facultydiversity0210.pdf).

Babbitt, Ellen M. (ed.). *Academic Program Closures: A Legal Compendium* (2d ed., National Association of College and University Attorneys, 2002).

Benjamin, Ernst, & Mauer, Michael (eds.). *Academic Collective Bargaining* (New York: Modern Language Association, 2006).

Brown, Ralph S., & Kurland, Jordan E. "Academic Tenure and Academic Freedom," 53 *Law & Contemp. Probs.* 325 (1990).

Cole, Elsa, & Hustoles, Thomas P. *How to Conduct a Sexual Harassment Investigation* (rev. ed., National Association of College and University Attorneys, 2006).

Euben, Donna R., & Lee, Barbara A. "Faculty Discipline: Legal and Policy Issues in Dealing with Faculty Misconduct," 32 *J. Coll. & Univ. Law* 241 (2006).

Finkin, Matthew W. (ed.). *The Case for Tenure* (Cornell University Press, 1996).

Franke, Ann. *Supporting the Culminating Stages of Faculty Careers: Legal Issues* (American Council on Education, 2011), available at http://www.acenet.edu/AM/Template.cfm?Section = Faculty_Career_Flexibility&Template = /CM/ContentDisplay.cfm&ContentID = 41776.

Hensel, Wendy F. "Rights Resurgence: The Impact of the ADA Amendments Act on Schools and Universities," 25 *Georgia State Univ. Law Rev.* 641 (2009).

Hustoles, Thomas P., & DiGiovanni, Nicholas, Jr. "Negotiating a Faculty Collective Bargaining Agreement" (National Association of College and University Attorneys, 2005).

LaNoue, George, & Lee, Barbara A. *Academics in Court: The Consequences of Faculty Discrimination Litigation* (University of Michigan Press, 1987).

Lee, Barbara A. "Balancing Confidentiality and Disclosure in Faculty Peer Review: Impact of Title VII Litigation," 9 *J. Coll. & Univ. Law* 279 (1982–83).

McKee, Patrick W. "Tenure by Default: The Non-Formal Acquisition of Academic Tenure," 7 *J. Coll. & Univ. Law* 31 (1980–81).

Olswang, Steven G. "Planning the Unthinkable: Issues in Institutional Reorganization and Faculty Reductions," 9 *J. Coll. & Univ. Law* 431 (1982–83).

Olswang, Steven G., & Fantel, Jane I. "Tenure and Periodic Performance Review: Compatible Legal and Administrative Principles," 7 *J. Coll. & Univ. Law* 1 (1980–81).

Sandler, Bernice R., & Shoop, Robert J. (eds.). *Sexual Harassment on Campus: A Guide for Administrators, Faculty, and Students* (Allyn & Bacon, 1997).

Weber, Mark C. "Disability Discrimination Litigation and Institutions of Higher Education," 25 *J. Coll. & Univ. Law* 53 (1998).

# Chapter 6

"Academic Freedom Symposium," 22 *Wm. Mitchell L. Rev.* 333–576 (1996).

Byrne, J. Peter. "Academic Freedom: A 'Special Concern of the First Amendment,'" 99 *Yale L.J.* 251 (1989).

Byrne, J. Peter. *Academic Freedom Without Tenure?* (American Association for Higher Education, 1997).

Byrne, J. Peter, "The Threat to Constitutional Academic Freedom," 31 *J. Coll. & Univ. Law* 79 (2004).

Cecil, Joe S., & Wetherington, Gerald T. (eds.). "Court-Ordered Disclosure of Academic Research: A Clash of Values of Science and Law," 59 *Law & Contemp. Probs.* 1 (1996).

DeChiara, Peter. "The Need for Universities to Have Rules on Consensual Sexual Relationships Between Faculty Members and Students," 21 *Columbia J. Law & Social Probs* 137 (1988).

Doumani, Beshara (ed). *Academic Freedom After September 11* (MIT Press/Zone Books, 2006).

Finkin, Matthew, & Post, Robert. *For the Common Good: Principles of American Academic Freedom* (Yale University Press, 2009).

Laycock, Douglas. "The Rights of Religious Academic Communities," 20 *J. Coll. & Univ. Law* 15 (1993).

McConnell, Michael W. "Academic Freedom in Religious Colleges and Universities," 53 *Law & Contemp. Probs.* 303 (1990; also reprinted in William W. Van Alstyne (ed.), *Freedom and Tenure in the Academy* (Duke University Press, 1993).

Menand, Louis (ed.). *The Future of Academic Freedom* (University of Chicago Press, 1996).

O'Neil, Robert. *Academic Freedom in the Wired World: Political Extremism, Corporate Power and the University* (Harvard University Press, 2008).

O'Neil, Robert M. "Artistic Freedom and Academic Freedom," 53 *Law and Contemp. Probs.*, issue no. 3 (1990).

O'Neil, Robert M. *Free Speech in the College Community* (Indiana University Press, 1997).

"Symposium on Academic Freedom," 66 *Tex. L. Rev.*, issue no. 7 (1988).

Van Alstyne, William W. (special ed.). "Freedom and Tenure in the Academy: The Fiftieth Anniversary of the 1940 Statement of Principles," 53 *Law & Contemp. Probs.*, issue no. 3 (1990); also published as a separate book, *Freedom and Tenure in the Academy* (Duke University Press, 1993).

White, Lawrence. "Fifty Years of Academic Freedom Jurisprudence," 36 *J. Coll. & Univ. Law* 791 (2010).

# Chapter 7

Alger, Jonathan R. "From Desegregation to Diversity and Beyond: Our Evolving Legal Conversation on Race and Higher Education," 36 *J. Coll. & Univ. Law* 983 (2010).

American Association of Collegiate Registrars and Admissions Officers. *The AACRO 2010 FERPA Guide* (AACRAO, 2010).

Bowen, William, Kurzweil, Martin, & Tobin, Eugene. *Equity and Excellence in American Higher Education* (University of Virginia, 2005).

Cherry, Robert L., Jr. "The College Catalog as a Contract," 21 *J. Law & Educ.* 1 (1992).

Coleman, Arthur, & Palmer, Scott. *Diversity in Higher Education: A Strategic Planning and Policy Manual Regarding Federal Law in Admission, Financial Aid, and Outreach* (2d ed., College Entrance Examination Board, 2004).

Connell, Mary Ann. "Race and Higher Education: The Tortuous Journey Toward Desegregation," 36 *J. Coll. & Univ. Law* 945 (2010).

EDUCAUSE/Cornell Institute for Computer Policy and Law Web site, http://www.educause.edu/icpl/.

Fossey, Richard, & Bateman, Mark (eds.). *Condemning Students to Debt* (Teachers College Press, 1998).

Gehring, Donald D. (ed.). *Administering College and University Housing: A Legal Perspective* (rev. ed., College Administration Publications, 1992).

Geller, Randolph. *Criminal Conduct of Students: The Institution's Response* (National Association of College and University Attorneys, 2007).

"Joint Statement on Rights and Freedoms for Students," 52 *AAUP Bulletin* 365 (1967), reprinted in *AAUP Policy Documents and Reports* (the "Redbook"), pp. 261–267.

Loewe, Eugene Y. (ed.). *Promise and Dilemma: Perspectives on Racial Diversity and Higher Education* (Princeton University Press, 1999).

McDonald, Steven J. (ed.). *The Family Educational Rights and Privacy Act (FERPA): A Legal Compendium* (2d ed., National Association of College and University Attorneys, 2002).

Meers, Elizabeth, & Thro, William. *Race-Conscious Admissions and Financial Aid Programs* (National Association of College and University Attorneys, 2004).

Melear, K. B., & Beckham, Joseph C. *Collegiate Consumerism: Contract Law and the Student-University Relationship* (College Administration Publications, 2003).

Office of Information Technology, University of Maryland. "NEThics," http://www.inform.umd.edu/CompRes/NEThics/.

Olivas, Michael A. "Administering Intentions: Law, Theory, and Practice of Postsecondary Residency Requirements," 59 *J. Higher Educ.* 263 (1988).

O'Neil, Robert M. "The Internet in the College Community," 17 *N. Ill. L. Rev.* 191 (1997).

St. John, Edward P. *Refinancing the College Dream: Access, Equal Opportunity, and Justice for Taxpayers* (Johns Hopkins University Press, 2003).

Sermersheim, Michael. *Computer Access: Selected Legal Issues Affecting Colleges and Universities* (2d ed., National Association of College and University Attorneys, 2003).

Sullivan, Kathleen M. "After Affirmative Action," 59 *Ohio St. L.J.* 1039 (1998).

Weeks, Kent M. *Managing Campus Cyberspace and the Law* (College Legal Information, 2007).

Williams, Wendy M. (ed.). "Special Theme: Ranking Ourselves: Perspectives on Intelligence Testing, Affirmative Action, and Educational Policy," 6 *Psychol. Public Policy & Law* 5 (2000).

Tribbensee, Nancy. *The Family Educational Rights and Privacy Act: A General Overview* (National Association of College and University Attorneys, 2002).

# Chapter 8

Babbitt, Ellen M. (ed.). *Accommodating Students with Learning and Emotional Disabilities* (National Association of College and University Attorneys, 2005).

Berger, Curtis J., & Berger, Vivian. "Academic Discipline: A Guide to Fair Process for the University Student," 99 *Colum. L. Rev.* 289 (1999).

Center for Academic Integrity. *The Fundamental Values of Academic Integrity* (Center for Academic Integrity, 1999).

Francis, Leslie Pickering. *Sexual Harassment as an Ethical Issue in Academic Life* (Rowman & Littlefield, 2001).

Jones, Nancy Lee. *The Americans with Disabilities Act: Application to the Internet.* Congressional Research Service Report No. 7-5700 (July 22, 2010).

Kibler, William L., Nuss, Elizabeth M., Peterson, Brent G., & Pavela, Gary. *Academic Integrity and Student Development* (College Administration Publications, 1988).

Lee, Barbara A. "Judicial Review of Student Challenges to Academic Misconduct Sanctions," 39 *J. Coll. & Univ. Law* 511 (2013).

Neiger, Jan Alan. "Actual Knowledge Under *Gebser v. Lago Vista*: Evidence of the Court's Deliberate Indifference or an Appropriate Response for Finding Institutional Liability?" 26 *J. Coll. & Univ. Law* 1 (1999).

Pavela, Gary. "Applying the Power of Association on Campus: A Model Code of Academic Integrity," 24 *J. Coll. & Univ. Law* 97 (1997).

Schweitzer, Thomas A. "'Academic Challenge' Cases: Should Judicial Review Extend to Academic Evaluations of Students?" 41 *American Univ. Law Rev.* 267 (1992).

Wilhelm, Suzanne. "Accommodating Mental Disabilities in Higher Education: A Practical Guide to ADA Requirements," 32 *J. Law & Education* 217 (2003).

# Chapter 9

Beckstrom, Darryn Cathryn. Comment: "Who's Looking at Your Facebook Profile? The Use of Student Conduct Codes to Censor College Students' Online Speech," 45 *Willamette Law Rev.* 261 (2008).

Byrne, J. Peter. "Racial Insults and Free Speech Within the University," 79 *Georgetown L.J.* 399 (1991).

Coleman, Arthur L., & Alger, Jonathan R. "Beyond Speech Codes: Harmonizing Rights of Free Speech and Freedom from Discrimination on University Campuses," 23 *J. Coll. & Univ. Law* 91 (1996).

Dannels, Michael. *From Discipline to Development: Rethinking Student Conduct in Higher Education*. ASHE-ERIC Higher Education Report, Vol. 25, no. 2 (ERIC Clearinghouse on Higher Education, 1997).

Faulkner, Janet E., & Tribbensee, Nancy E. *Student Disciplinary Issues: A Legal Compendium* (National Association of College and University Attorneys, 2004).

Grey, Thomas C. "How to Write a Speech Code Without Really Trying: Reflections on the Stanford Experience," 29 *U. Cal. Davis L. Rev.* 891 (1996).

Kaplin, William A. *American Constitutional Law: An Overview, Analysis, and Integration* (Carolina Academic Press, 2004, with 2012 Update, Chaps. 11, 12, and 14.

Kaplin, William A. "A Proposed Process for Managing the Free Speech Aspects of Campus Hate Speech," 63 *J. Higher Educ.* 517 (1992).

Lake, Peter F. *Beyond Discipline* (Hierophant Enterprises, 2009).

Massaro, Toni M. "Equality and Freedom of Expression: The Hate Speech Dilemma," 32 *Wm. & Mary L. Rev.* 211 (1991).

Munsch, Martha Hartle, & Schupansky, Susan P. *The Dismissal of Students with Mental Disabilities* (National Association of College and University Attorneys, 2003).

Paterson, Brent G., & Kibler, William L. (eds.). *The Administration of Campus Discipline: Student, Organization and Community Issues* (College Administration Publications, 1998).

Pavela, Gary. *The Dismissal of Students with Mental Disorders: Legal Issues, Policy Considerations, and Alternative Responses* (College Administration Publications, 1985).

Pavela, Gary. "Limiting the Pursuit of Perfect Justice on Campus: A Proposed Code of Student Conduct," 6 *J. Coll. & Univ. Law* 137 (1980).

Stoner, Edward N., & Lowery, John Wesley. "Navigating Past the 'Spirit of Insubordination': A 21st Century Model for a Student Conduct Code with a Model Hearing Script," 31 *J. Coll. & Univ. Law* 1 (2004).

Weberman, Melissa. "University Hate Speech Policies and the Captive Audience Doctrine," 36 *Ohio Northern U. L. Rev.* 553 (2010).

# Chapter 10

Aronofsky, David. "Higher Education Student Elections and Other First Amendment Student Speech Issues: What *Flint v. Dennison* Portends," 34 *J. Coll. & Univ. Law* 637 (2008).

Brake, Deborah. *Getting in the Game: Title IX and the Women's Sports Revolution* (New York University Press, 2010).

Brake, Deborah. "The Struggle for Sex Equality in Sport and the Theory Behind Title IX," 34 *U. Mich. J.L. Reform* 13 (2000–2001).

Burns, Beverly H. (ed.). *A Practical Guide to Title IX in Athletics: Law, Principles, and Practices* (2d ed., National Association of College and University Attorneys, 2000).

Clotfelter, Charles T. *Big Time Sports in American Universities* (Cambridge University Press, 2011).

Davis, Timothy. "College Athletics: Testing the Boundaries of Contract and Tort," 29 *U.C. Davis L. Rev.* 971 (1996).

Freitas, Mark. "Applying the Rehabilitation Act and the Americans with Disabilities Act to Student-Athletes," 5 *Sports Law. J.* 139 (1998).

Gregory, Dennis E., et al. *The Administration of Fraternal Organizations on North American Campuses: A Pattern for a New Millennium* (College Administration Publications, 2003).

Hauser, Gregory F. "Intimate Associations Under the Law: The Rights of Social Fraternities to Exist and to Be Free from Undue Interference by Host Institutions," 24 *J. Coll. & Univ. Law* 59 (1997).

Ingelhart, Louis E. *Student Publications: Legalities, Governance, and Operation* (Iowa State University Press, 1993).

Lakowski, Terri. "Athletes with Disabilities in School Sports: A Critical Assessment of the State of Sports Opportunities for Students with Disabilities," 27 *Boston University International Law Journal* 283 (2009).

MacLachlan, Jenna. "Dangerous Traditions: Hazing Rituals on Campus and University Liability," 26 *J. Coll. & Univ. Law* 511 (2000).

National Collegiate Athletic Association. *NCAA Inclusion of Transgender Student Athletes* (available at http://ncaa.org/wps/wcm/connect/ fd9a78804841ff93953f9fbf5e8bc9cc/Transgender_Handbook_2011_Final.pdf?MOD = AJPERES&CACHEID = fd9a78804841ff93953f9fbf5e8bc9cc).

Nuwer, Hank. *Wrongs of Passage: Fraternities, Sororities, Hazing, and Binge Drinking* (Indiana University Press, 1999).

Pieronek, Catherine. "Title IX and Intercollegiate Athletics in the Federal Appellate Courts: Myth vs. Reality," 27 *J. Coll. & Univ. Law* 447 (2000).

Pieronek, Catherine. "Title IX Beyond Thirty: A Review of Recent Developments," 30 *J. Coll. & Univ. Law* 75 (2003).

Symposium, "Gender & Sports: Setting a Course for College Athletics," 3 *Duke J. Gender L. & Pol'y* 1–264 (1996).

Symposium, "Race and Sports," 6 *Marquette Sports L.J.* 199–421 (1996).

Williams, Claire. "Sexual Orientation Harassment and Discrimination: Legal Protection for Student Athletes," 18 *J. Legal Aspects of Sports* 253 (2007).

# Chapter 11

Byman, Abigail, & Geller, Randolph (eds.). *Intellectual Property Issues in Higher Education: A Legal Compendium* (National Association of College and University Attorneys (NACUA), 2001).

Crews, Kenneth D. "Distance Education and Copyright Law: The Limits and Meaning of Copyright Policy," 27 *J. Coll. & Univ. Law* 15 (2000).

Dunham, Stephen S. "Government Regulation of Higher Education: The Elephant in the Middle of the Room," 36 *J. Coll. & Univ. Law* 749 (2010).

Dutile, Fernand, & Gaffney, Edward. *State and Campus: State Regulation of Religiously Affiliated Higher Education* (University of Notre Dame Press, 1984).

Finkin, Matthew. "On 'Institutional' Academic Freedom," 61 *Tex. L. Rev.* 817 (1983).

Gasaway, Laura N. "Impasse: Distance Learning and Copyright Law," 62 *Ohio St. L.J.* 783 (2001).

Harper, Georgia K. *Copyright Issues in Higher Education, 2005 Edition* (National Association of College and University Attorneys, 2005).

Harper, Georgia. "Developing a Comprehensive Copyright Policy to Facilitate Online Learning," 27 *J. Coll. & Univ. Law* 5 (2000).

Kaplin, William A. *American Constitutional Law: An Overview, Analysis, and Integration* (Carolina Academic Press, 2004, with 2012 Update), Chap. 5, Sec. E; Chap. 6, Secs. C–E and G; Chap. 14, Secs. C and D.

McGuinness, Aimes, & Paulson, Christine. *State Postsecondary Education Structures Handbook* (Education Commission of the States, 1991).

McSherry, Corynne. *Who Owns Academic Work?* (Harvard University Press, 2001).

Ugland, Erik. "Hawkers, Thieves and Lonely Pamphleteers: Distributing Publications in the University Marketplace," 20 *J. Coll. & Univ. Law* 935 (1996).

Wallick, Robert D., & Chamblee, Daryl A. "Bridling the Trojan Horse: Rights and Remedies of Colleges and Universities Under Federal Grant-Type Assistance Programs," 4 *J. Coll. & Univ. Law* 241 (1977).

Ware, Leland. "The Most Visible Vestige: Black Colleges After *Fordice*," 35 *B.C. L. Rev.* 633 (1994).

# Chapter 12

Bloland, Harland. *Associations in Action: The Washington, D.C. Higher Education Community.* ASHE-ERIC Higher Education Report no. 2 (Association for the Study of Higher Education, 1985).

Bok, Derek. *Universities in the Marketplace: The Commercialization of Higher Education* (Princeton University Press, 2003).

Cook, Constance Ewing. *Lobbying for Higher Education: How Colleges and Universities Influence Federal Policy* (Vanderbilt University Press, 1998).

Eisenberg, Rebecca S. "Academic Freedom and Academic Values in Sponsored Research," 66 *Tex. L. Rev.* 1363 (1988).

Fairweather, James S. *Entrepreneurship and Higher Education: Lessons for Colleges, Universities, and Industry.* ERIC/Higher Education Research Report no. 6 (Association for the Study of Higher Education, 1988).

Harrington, Peter J. "Faculty Conflicts of Interest in an Age of Academic Entrepreneurialism: An Analysis of the Problem, the Law and Selected University Policies," 27 *J. Coll. & Univ. Law* 775 (2001).

Hutcheson, Philo A. *A Professional Professoriate: Unionization, Bureaucratization, and the AAUP* (Vanderbilt University Press, 2000).

Lyall, Katharine, & Sell, Kathleen. *The True Genius of America at Risk: Are We Losing Our Public Universities to De Facto Privatization?* (Praeger, 2005).

Melear, Kerry, & Leas, Terrence. *Community College Governance: A Compendium of State Organizational Structures* (College Administration Publications, 2006).

Symposium, "NCAA Institutional Controls and Mechanisms and the Student-Athlete," 1995 *Wis. L. Rev.* 545 (1995).

Young, Kenneth E., Chambers, Charles M., Kells, H. R., & Associates. *Understanding Accreditation: Contemporary Perspectives on Issues and Practices in Evaluating Educational Quality* (Jossey-Bass, 1983).

# Statute Index

865

# Case Index

# Subject Index

Page references followed by *fig* indicate an illustrated figure.

pay discrimination prohibited by, 172; reasonable accommodations required by Section 504 and, 175–176, 348–349, 453, 519–533, 810–811; school code of conduct discipline and the, 585–586; student housing discrimination claims under, 451–453; Title I, Section 503 of the, 172, 180; Title II prohibiting discrimination by public entity, 177–178; Title II rules by the U.S. Department of Justice, 587; Title III on athletic eligibility requirements, 733. *See also* Civil right law; Disabilities; Students with disabilities

*Amici curiae* ("friends of the court"), 818

Animal Welfare Act, 783

Antidiscrimination laws. *See* Civil rights law

Apparent Authority: agency law on, 68; definition of, 94

Arbitrariness standard of admissions, 377–379

Architectural Works Copyright Protection Act (AWCPA), 789

Association for Student Conduct Administration, 818

Association of American Medical Colleges (AAMC), 393–394

Association of American Universities, 817

Association of Governing Boards of Universities and Colleges (AGB), 89

Association of International Educators, 495

Association of Public and Land Grant Universities, 817

At-will doctrine, 139–140

Athletic associations and conferences: Americans with Disabilities Act application to, 731–733; common law governing, 823; due process requirement of, 705–707; overview of, 822–823; Title IX application to, 716–731, 806

Athletic scholarships: challenge of property interests in renewal of, 427; contract law governing, 712–716

Athletic teams and clubs: athletes' due process rights, 705–707; controversy over Chief Illiniwek mascot, 708–709; discrimination on the basis of disability, 731–733; drug testing of athletes, 733–739; freedom of speech by, 707–710; general principles applying to, 704–705; hazing activities by, 744–745; NCAA Division I requirements, 822–823; pertinent statutory law, 710–712; sex discrimination related to, 138, 716–731; tort liability for athletic injuries, 739–745

Athletic Trainers Practice Act, 741

Atlantic Coast Conference (ACC), 822

*Atlantic Reporter*, 32

Attention deficit disorder (ADD), 585

Attorneys, comparing administrators' roles in policy making to, 63–64

Authority: of administrative agencies to adjudication, 26–27; apparent, 68, 94; central to a determination of liability for harm to third parties, 96–97; contract law limiting institutional authority over faculty, 287; express, 94; external legal relationships in higher education institutions, 6*fig*; implied, 94; *in loco parentis* doctrine on institutional, 17, 344, 456; internal legal relationships in higher education institutions, 5*fig*–6; overview, types, and sources of, 93–97; trustee, 97

**B**

B visa (nonimmigrant visa), 302

*Bakke* test, 653

Balancing test (Fourth Amendment), 736–737

Beirut Agreement, 827

Berne Convention for the Protection of Literary and Artistic Works, 827

"BFOQ" (religion, sex, or national origin) exception, 161–162

Bickel, R. D., 704

Bill of Rights, RFRA enforcement of the, 48–49

Blackmun, H., 299

Bloland, H., 920

Board of trustees (or regents): external legal relationships of, 6*fig*; internal governance role of, 20–21; internal legal relationships of, 5*fig*–6

Board Policy 8000 ("BP 8000"), 620

Bollag, B., 653

Bombardieri, M., 117

Bowen, W. G., 705

Breach of contract: ADR disallow argument on preclusive effect in a, 81; discipline perceived as, 599–601; educational malpractice doctrine and claim of, 119–121, 714–715; institutional liability for, 125–129; student housing and, 447. *See also* Contracts

Brennan, W. J., 194, 196, 200

Bryant, K., 710

Bullying: "Dear Colleague" letter, 375–376, 805, 807; of religious groups sharing ethnic characteristic, 805

Burton, S., 8

Business partnerships: with foreign or international companies, 827–828; by individual faculty members, 825; research agreements between institutions and, 826–831; research collaboration between institutions and, 6*fig*, 823–826

**C**

*California Reporter*, 32

Campus: access to, 754–763; gun possession on, 775–779; security of, 476–490

Campus access: "limited designated public forum" and, 760–763; trespass statutes and ordinance and campus regulations, 754–763

Campus computer networks: child pornography and, 465; First Amendment principles that apply to, 463–470; freedom of speech and, 461–470; liability issues related to, 473–476; right to privacy and, 470–473; Strict scrutiny standard applied to, 464. *See also* E-mail; Electronic documents

Campus security: federal statutes governing, 486–490; protecting students against violent crime, 481–486; security officers role in, 476–486; state regulation on gun possession on campus, 775–779

Campus Security Act ("Clery Act"), 138, 486–490, 710–711

Campus security personnel: Campus Security Act issues related to, 138; claim under the Equal Pay Act by female, 171; Family Educational Rights and Privacy Act (FERPA) issues for, 138; legal liability of, 137–138; privacy issues of student judicial officer records, 138. *See also* Police authority

Campus Sex Crimes Prevention Act (CSCPA), 490, 498–499

CAN-SPAM Act (2003), 782

Canadian Association of University Teachers, 299

Captive organizations, 94

Case law: researching, 32; role in higher education law, 31–32

Censorship of student publications, 688–695

Center for Academic Freedom, 819

Center for Individual Rights, 12